Second Edition

Cases
in
Strategic
Marketing

Linda E. Swayne

Peter M. Ginter

PRENTICE HALL, Englewood Cliffs, New Jersey 07632

To our children—
Lisa, Heather, and Maru,
Robert and Karen
Unique and challenging case studies themselves

Contents

Preface

Strategic marketing is the central activity of modern enterprise. Strategic marketing articulates the organization's vision, mission, objectives, and culture. More than any other organizational activity, strategic marketing establishes and maintains the desired relationship between the organization and its environment. In fitting the organization to the needs of the environment, strategic marketing molds the organization, determining production specifications, indicating financial requirements, and dictating needed human skills. Strategic marketing ignites and fuels organizational action. Strategic marketing creates competitive advantage.

Fitting the organization to the needs of the environment has never been more critical. Today the rate of change in the world has accelerated. At no previous time have organizations faced a more turbulent, confusing, and threatening environment. Inpetus for significant change will come from many sources, including government, international and domestic economic and market forces, demographic shifts and lifestyle changes, and the structural evolution of many industries. Marketers will have to anticipate and understand these changes if they are to develop effective marketing strategies to ensure the organization's survival.

College education must be directed toward preparing students to enter this complex decision-making environment. For today's students, there will be few situations to which they can apply "classic" solutions developed in college classrooms. Rather, students will have to apply an independent critical intelligence and make judgments in a complex world of different and competing points of view.

The case approach has proven to be useful in allowing students to practice their decision-making skills without financial risk to an employer. Realizing the importance of developing decision-making skills, marketing strategy and market-ing management instructors have adopted the case approach to provide situations in which students may integrate and apply their marketing knowledge to gain experience. Students must apply this knowledge to many different types of situations using a systematic and well-thought-out approach. Therefore, this edition of *Cases in Strategic Marketing* includes case studies that provide a variety of strategic marketing situations and appendices that concern case analy-sis, financial analysis, and oral presentations.

THE CASE APPROACH

In order to effectively use cases it is essential that both students and instructors understand the nature of case studies and the teaching objectives of cases. A case typically is a record of a business situation that actually has been faced by business executives, together with surrounding facts, opinions, and prejudices on which executive decisions have to depend.

A case study attempts to vicariously place students into a managerial posi-tion in which they will have to "size up" the situation and suggest some action for the organization. The action is typically a plan (set of decisions) that addresses the key issues of the case. Therefore, the case most often provides some degree of focus for the student, as well as some discussion of the environment, in order to develop the decision-making situation.

The objective of the case approach is not for students to develop "right" solutions, or rote knowledge, that he or she will be able to apply to a future situation. Rather, the case approach provides the student with a perspective concerning the complexity of the issues that organizations face, practice in dis-cerning the critical issues, application of theory, an understanding of the interre-latedness of business functions, and discussion concerning important issues faced by modern enterprise. Case studies provide the student an in-depth learning experience in a given business situation that is difficult to obtain elsewhere.

THE CASEBOOK

This casebook is designed to be used in upper-level marketing strategy and marketing management courses. Marketing strategy or marketing management is usually the capstone course in marketing and is typically required for all market-ing majors and minors. The general objective of the capstone course is to pull together marketing theory and practice into a broad understanding of marketing and its application. Other courses in marketing provide an overview of marketing, as in the principles of marketing course, or an in-depth study of the various functional areas such as sales management, advertising, pricing, channels, and so on. The marketing strategy or marketing management course asks students to solve problems and develop comprehensive marketing strategies in situations that are not clearly predetermined as promotional, segmentation, or channels of distribution. Utilizing a top-management perspective, students must consider all of an organization's systems and their interrelationships in developing marketing recommendations.

The Cases

The marketing case studies developed and chosen for this casebook offer students a broad exposure to a cross section of strategic marketing situations. We think you will find this collection of 40 cases to be pedagogically sound, appealing to students, stimulating to teach, and on target with respect to the leading problems and issues in strategic marketing.

All of the cases included in this book are concerned with real companies, although a few are disguised at the company's request. They are supported with extensive industry information to provide the background material necessary to understand and assess an organization's markets. In addition, the book contains many new cases that have not previously appeared in marketing casebooks or texts: 58 percent (23) are new in the second edition. Of the remaining 17, 7 have been revised and updated. As with the first edition, the cases are not listed under predetermined categories that may indicate the nature of the problem or opportunity facing the organization. It is our philosophy that it is important *not* to cue or prejudice students as to the type of issues or problems.

Among the 40 cases, 20 deal with well-known national organizations, 7 with moderately sized regional companies, 5 are small businesses, and 15 are concerned with international firms. These companies' products are in various stages of the product life cycle. Of these companies, 7 have products in the introductory stage of the product life cycle, 8 in the growth stage, 20 in maturity, and 3 in the decline stage. The book also has excellent balance with regard to market position: 13 organizations are considered market leaders, 8 are market challengers, 11 are currently nichers, and 6 are product/market followers. The cases are multidimensional and comprehensive in that all of the marketing functional areas, as well as the target market, must be considered in the analysis of the case.

The Appendices

Another significant change from the first edition is the inclusion of three appendices. The first two appendices provide an orientation to case analysis through a practical analytical framework for addressing strategic marketing issues (Appendix A—Analyzing Strategic Marketing Cases) and fundamentals for financial analysis (Appendix B—Financial Analysis for Marketing Strategists). The third appendix (Presenting Marketing Cases Orally) assists the student in developing and making oral presentations. These appendices are designed for the student's benefit when initially approaching case analysis and to lend some structure to the process of marketing analysis. Because some instructors prefer a different format for case analysis, these sections have been placed after the cases. Therefore, the instructor can assign those appendices considered appropriate to his or her personal teaching style. In addition, with this approach, instructors have the flexibility of using the case-only approach or supplementing the casebook with their own materials, a collection of strategic marketing readings, or a traditional textbook.

ACKNOWLEDGMENTS

We are deeply indebted to many individuals for their assistance and encouragement in the preparation of this casebook. First, we would like to thank the appendix contributors—W. Jack Duncan (Appendix A), Bennie H. Nunnally, Jr. (Appendix B), Gary F. Kohut and Carol M. Baxter (Appendix C). Their work provides structure and pedagogical guidance. Also, a special thanks to Dean M. Gene Newport of the School of Business at the University of Alabama at Birmingham and Dean Richard E. Neel of the College of Business Administration at the University of North Carolina at Charlotte, both of whom have always been supportive of our efforts. An additional thanks to all the fine people at Prentice Hall for their constant help and guidance, especially Jennifer Young and Sandra Steiner, who provided encouragement, enthusiasm, and ideas. Thanks to Edie Pullman, production editor, for her professionalism in all areas, particularly her willingness to put in extra hours to ensure timely publication. Thanks also to Kay Webb, who tirelessly typed the cases so that we could submit the manuscript in a electronic format and reduce production time (ensuring up-to-date cases). We would also like to thank the Prentice Hall reviewers. These colleagues were particularly helpful in balancing the types of cases and identifying "teachable" cases.

Finally, this book would not have been possible without the case writers and the organizations about which they have written. Typically, the organizations have given a great deal of time to contribute to the education of tomorrow's business leaders. Case writing is a difficult art requiring many hours of library research, personal interviews, and detailed analysis. The case contributors listed in this text represent some of the finest case researchers anywhere. We think you will appreciate and enjoy their craft.

Linda E. Swayne
Peter M. Ginter

CASE CONTRIBUTORS

Moustafa Abdelsaman
Southeastern Massachusetts
  University

Sexton Adams
University of North Texas

M. Edgar Barrett
American Graduate School
  of International Business

Tanya Bisch
University of Alabama at Birmingham

Charles W. Boyd
Southwest Missouri State University

Lew G. Brown
University of North Carolina at
  Greensboro

James W. Camerius
Northern Michigan University

Stuart A. Capper
University of Alabama at Birmingham

David B. Croll
University of Virginia

Bernard A. Deitzer
University of Akron

W. Jack Duncan
University of Alabama at Birmingham

Paul Farris
University of Virginia

Philip C. Fisher
University of South Dakota

Peter M. Ginter
University of Alabama at Birmingham

Kent N. Gourdin
University of North Carolina at
  Charlotte

Walter E. Greene
University of Texas-Pan American

Adelaide Griffin
Texas Woman's College

H. Michael Hays
University of Colorado at Denver

Diane Hoadley
University of South Dakota

Charles Hoffheiser
University of Tulsa

H. Donald Hopkins
Temple University

William C. House
University of Arkansas

Sheekant G. Joag
St. John's University

Daniel Kopp
Southwest Missouri State University

Alan G. Krigline
University of Akron

Robert O. Lewis
Apple Computer

Michael Martin
HEALTHSOUTH Corporation

Eleanor G. May
University of Virginia

John H. Murphy II
University of Texas

Lester A. Neidell
University of Tulsa

James E. Nelson
University of Colorado at Boulder

James Olver
University of Virginia

Steven K. Paulson
University of North Florida

Thomas C. Peterson
University of Akron

Lynne D. Richardson
University of Alabama at Birmingham

Woodrow D. Richardson
University of Alabama at Birmingham

Earl Sage
University of North Carolina at
  Charlotte

Lois Schufeldt
Southwest Missouri State University

JoAnn K. L. Schwinghammer
Mankato State University

Ram Subramanian
Grand Valley State University
Linda E. Swayne
University of North Carolina at
   Charlotte
Jeffrey W. Totten
University of Wisconsin at Oshkosh

Chris M. Tucker
University of North Carolina at
   Charlotte
Charles R. Wagner
Mankato State University
Thomas L. Wheelen
University of South Florida

Case Abstracts

1 **Gatorade Defends Its No. 1 Position**

Gatorade, a subsidiary of the Quaker Oats Company, dominated the sports drink market. Gatorade was originally developed in the 1960s at the University of Florida by a team of researchers studying heat exhaustion. The research team, headed by Dr. Robert Cade, developed a formula that would help prevent severe dehydration brought about by fluid and mineral loss during physical exercise. Although Gatorade commanded 90 percent of market share in 1991, aggressive efforts by soft drink manufacturers and other companies to enter this profitable (35 percent margins) and growing (30 percent growth) market represented significant challenges for Quaker Oats. Products that had recently entered the market included 10-K, PowerBurst, Mountain Dew Sport, and several regional offerings. Quaker Oats executives knew that other companies would continue to challenge Gatorade's enviable market share. Gatorade was a brand worth protecting.

2 **Kodak versus Fuji: A Case of Japanese-American Strategic Interaction**

Kodak planned the introduction of an innovative new product and pondered over what Fuji would do in response. In the past, Kodak and Fuji had a fierce rivalry that included competition in film innovations, the "battle of the MBAs," the "battle of the blimps," Kodak's "me-too" tactics, the "battle of the throwaways," and the attack and counterattack of each other's domestic markets. Information on the U.S. photographic market based on government statistics and business reference sources profiled both Kodak and Fuji. What would happen next? Would Fuji imitate Kodak, could it leapfrog Kodak, or would it stay away from this product segment? Could Kodak predict Fuji's response and plan what it would do in turn? Could Kodak do anything to block or minimize Fuji's reaction?

3 Golden Flake Snack Foods: Competing in an Increasingly Hostile Environment

Golden Flake was a full-line manufacturer of snack food products including potato chips, corn and tortilla chips, popcorn, cheese curls, pork skins, roasted peanuts, and cheese or peanut butter-filled crackers. Golden Flake products were manufactured in Alabama, Tennessee, and Florida, and were distributed in 13 southeastern states. Revenues in 1990 were over $134 million. Golden Flake had been able to double sales every five years until the mid-1980s. However, as Golden Flake moved further from its home market, the company was finding this objective increasingly more difficult to accomplish. Expansion into the Florida and North Carolina markets brought more aggressive head-to-head competition with the industry giant, Frito-Lay, and additional smaller, but no less formidable competitors such as Borden, Charles Chips, Lance, Keebler, and Anheuser-Busch. Such intense competition spurred management into renewed efforts to develop a marketing strategy that would enable the company to continue to grow in an increasingly competitive market.

4 Gillette and the Men's Wet-Shaving Market

Executives of Gillette's North Atlantic Group gathered at its headquarters in the Prudential Center in Boston to discuss Gillette's situation in the U.S. wet-shaving market. Despite the market's maturity, there were a number of significant forces and trends at work in the industry. Two major trends that dominated the industry were the rise of disposable razors threatening the system razor market (permanent handles with replacement blade cartridges) and the steady, although slow, growth of electric razors. Competition in the wet shaving market was aggressive, and a variety of products were available. For years Gillette had attempted to understand competing products through extensive testing and sophisticated research, in order to gain a clear understanding of the consumer behavior aspects of the wet-shaving market. Extensive market and competitive information, product information, and knowledge of consumers' behavior had to be synthesized by Gillette executives to develop a new marketing strategy for the company to pursue.

5 Chemical Additives Corporation—Specialty Products Group

Specialty Products Group (SPG) was an organization struggling to meet changing competitive conditions. A division of Chemical Additives Corporation, SPG was a medium-sized company ($294 million in sales) faced with maturing and declining primary markets, severe price competition, a changing set of competitors, and a need and desire to develop new products and markets. The executive group of SPG had to make positioning and pricing decisions for three new products. Some executives advocated a low-price, commodity-type approach, but others preferred a segmentation and value-based pricing approach. The general manager, Nick Williamson, had to come to terms with the positioning and pricing decisions as well as a range of related issues.

6   J. M. Smucker Company: With a Name Like Smucker's, It Has to Be Good

Smucker was an internationally respected family-managed company whose basic beliefs still underscored its premier jam and jelly business. Beginning with a colorful history of early entrepreneurship, Smucker had met modern marketing challenges and opportunities through a consciously developed corporate marketing program with supportive plans, objectives, and implementing strategies. A skilled leadership team consisting of a perceptive father and two spirited sons developed well-conceived strategies of market growth through acquisitions and product innovations while fostering brand loyalty through intensive advertising and promotions. Its product and advertising messages were among the most recognized in the marketplace. Management had a distinctive consumer orientation based on high-quality products, upscale manufacturing technology, and solid distributor relationships. The challenges that faced Smucker were how to increase market share in a mature market and how to enhance its international position in a dynamic foreign environment.

7   Pan Am Attempts Survival in the 1990s

Pan American Airways was formed in 1927 by Juan Trippe. Trippe led the company until 1968, guiding the firm's development into the world-spanning airline it eventually became. The carrier developed as an overseas airline but had virtually no domestic route structure in the United States. Lack of integration between domestic and overseas flights, combined with increased competition resulting from airline deregulation and various environmental factors, forced the company into bankruptcy in 1991. Delta Airlines agreed to purchase most of Pan Am's routes, with the exception of those connecting the United States with Central and South America, which a much smaller, "new" Pan Am would continue to serve. Pan Am's management knew that the company's existence hinged on its ability to succeed in this extremely competitive environment.

8   The Chevrolet Corvette

After not producing a 1983 model, Chevrolet introduced the "fifth-generation" Corvette in 1984. The new model showcased General Motors' latest developments in suspension, braking, and electronic engine control. The "new" Corvette also targeted a different market segment. Along with the product changes, Chevrolet started an aggressive comparative advertising campaign against Porsche, Ferrari, and Lamborghini. Independent testing supported Corvette superiority claims, but reactions to the comparative ads were mixed. Executives were concerned with Chevrolet's branding strategy and the strategic role of the Corvette for Chevrolet and General Motors.

9   Wal-Mart Stores: Strategies for Market Dominance

In 1991, Wal-Mart Stores, with corporate headquarters in Bentonville, Arkansas, was not only the nation's largest discount department store chain, but it had recently surpassed Sears Roebuck, & Company as the largest retail organization in sales volume in the United States. The firm operated stores under a variety of names and retail formats including Wal-Mart Stores, Sam's Wholesale Clubs, and Wal-Mart Supercenters. In addition, it had experimented with hypermarkets through Hypermart*USA. The firm was perceived to be in the accelerated development or growth stage of the institutional life cycle in which sales increase rapidly, profits are high, new stores are opened, existing stores are refurbished, the product line is reevaluated, services are upgraded. automation is introduced to store operations, and better management controls are developed. Although Wal-Mart was considered in the accelerated growth stage, the industry was viewed as being in maturity. The industry was faced with increased competition, leveling of sales, moderate profits, overstored markets, and more complex operational problems. Could Wal-Mart sustain such growth without Mr. Sam at the helm?

10   JJ's Women's Clothing Store: On the Move Again?

After struggling for the first four years in a retail location off the main street, JJ's moved to leased retail space on the main business thoroughfare of St. Peter, Minnesota. That change resulted in increased sales and profitability for the women's clothing store. Although the cash flow situation could be improved by more timely collection of accounts receivable, a more pressing issue for the store owners revolved around another impending move. A proposed mall for downtown St. Peter might oust JJ's from its current location. The store owners had to consider the viability of accepting reduced floor space and increased rent to be included in the new mall, relocating into the only available, but more remote, space in the downtown area, or going out of business.

11   Kraft

The objective of Kraft was to become recognized as the leading food company in the world. In order to accomplish this objective, the company's management team had to contend with a decline in the U.S. population growth rate, changing dietary habits, and a worldwide restructuring of major food-processing companies. Kraft's top managers were coping with these changes through the product mix, including retrenchment in fluid milk products, and growth in frozen desserts, such as the acquisition of Frusen Gladje, a premium ice cream. In 1986, Dart and Kraft was separated into Kraft, and Premark International, which controlled Tupperware, West Bend, Hobart, and Wilsonart. As a result, Kraft was composed of the food lines and the Duracell Battery Division. In order to gain the top position in the world food-processing industry, Kraft had to develop outstanding marketing strategies.

12   Humana Strategic Directions for the 1990s

Humana, an international company, provided an integrated system of for-profit health services that included hospital care, prepaid health care, and indemnity insurance plans. At the end of fiscal 1990, company operations included 85 hospitals and over 1 million members insured by Humana health care plans. Prior to 1986, Humana enjoyed financial success. This performance was a direct result of acquiring or building new hospitals and selling unprofitable ones. However, the company stumbled in 1986 by misreading the numbers and overexpanding into walk-in clinics and health insurance without a proper understanding of the market. The company also had some problems with its marketing strategy. Since the mid-1980s, Humana recovered from its blunders and had a better understanding of the health care market. Still, Humana faced an ever-changing industry and new challenges.

13 The Environment for Health Care Marketing: A Health Care Industry Note

As health care costs approached 12 percent of gross national product (GNP), the second largest component behind real estate, health care costs became an extremely important factor in the U.S. economy. This industry note provides an overview of the health services sector. In addition to describing the most significant organizational and professional participants and suggesting a brief conceptual framework for the "products" of health care, this note attempts to provide an understanding of the health services environment. The environment is described in terms of recent history, selected key historical events, and major current characteristics. Finally, descriptions of selected macroenvironmental trends relevant to the future of the health care environment are presented.

14 Ito-Yokado Company

The Ito-Yokado Company consisted of three business segments: Superstores and other Retail Operations (Ito-Yokado superstores, Daikum discount stores, York Mart, York Benimaru, Robinson's Department Stores, and Oshman's Sporting Goods); Restaurant Operations (Denny's and Family Restaurants); and Convenience Store Operations (7-Eleven Japan). Ito-Yokado had just acquired the struggling Southland Corporation. Transitional and long-term strategies for Southland would have to be developed. Although diversified, Southland's largest business segment was its Stores Group, responsible for operating and franchising of over 7,500 7-Eleven convenience stores. Masanori Takahashi, a senior strategy analyst for Ito-Yokado, was considering whether long-term strategies that had been successful in Japan could be successful in the United States as well. He realized that the convenience store industry in the United States was vastly different from that of Japan. Nevertheless, he was confident that, through careful and thorough planning, Southland could become profitable.

15 AT&T and the Residential Long-Distance Market (A)

In early 1984 AT&T prepared to implement the "equal access" provisions of Judge Harold Greene's order deregulating the telecommunications industry. Monica Barnes, a mid-level manager in AT&T's southern region marketing division, had to prepare a marketing strategy for the residential customers to induce them to select AT&T as their long-distance provider. AT&T found itself in the position of having all its customers specifically asked to choose a long-distance provider. This unique situation provided a real marketing challenge in an industry not previously known for marketing prowess.

16 AT&T and the Residential Long-Distance Market (B)

One year later AT&T had implemented a strategy based on the rules and regulations established by Judge Greene. However, in mid-1985, the FCC published new rules that changed the "default" provisions of the earlier procedure. Whereas previously customers who failed to select a long-distance carrier had been "defaulted" to AT&T, the FCC decided that defaulters would be allocated based on the percentages of customers actually selecting each carrier in the first round. Further, customers already defaulted would be given another opportunity to decide. Monica Barnes had to rethink the established strategy in light of these significant and unexpected changes.

17 Apple Computer Targets Desktop Engineering

Matthew Robertson, previously a member of the highly successful development team for desktop publishing, had a new assignment. The engineering workstation market had been identified as having considerable potential for Apple's Macintosh II microcomputer. In terms of features and price, the Mac II was ideal for low-end workstation applications. Yet engineers were going to be hard to convince that the Mac II was more than a toy and could handle sophisticated engineering software. Because the engineering workstation market was already established and included several formidable competitors, Matthew knew this new assignment was going to be more challenging than desktop publishing, a market that Apple established.

18 Shades of Black

Shades of Black's mission was to produce greeting cards and social awareness items for black consumers in the United States. It was a very small company in the greeting card and social expression industry with sales of $42,396 after its first year of incorporation. The founder, Alex Corbbrey, was primarily an artist, although he had retail training and experience at I. Magnin's in Los Angeles. Shades of Black, located in Tulsa, Oklahoma, was considering four product/market expansion opportunities including expansion of distribution to selected drugstores, supermarkets, and specialty card shops; attempts to sell through the Army and Air Force Exchange Service; distribution to predominantly black colleges' student and alumni organizations; and development of condolence packages aimed at black-owned funeral homes.

19 TenderCare Disposable Diapers

TenderCare diapers were different, offering a superior product that did indeed keep babies drier. Just under its liner was a wicking fabric that drew moisture from the surface around a soft, waterproof shield to an absorbent reservoir of filler. Pampers and all other disposable diapers on the market kept moisture nearer to the liner and, consequently, the baby's skin. It was important for the Rocky Mountain Medical Corporation (developer of TenderCare brand diapers) that the product reach the market as soon as possible. Every month of delay meant deferred revenue, postponed benefits that would derive from a successful introduction, and the chance that an existing competitor might develop its own drier diaper and effectively block the company from reaping the fruits of its development efforts.

20 Burroughs Wellcome and AZT

Burroughs Wellcome Company marketed the drug azidothymidine (AZT), which was proven to be effective in combating AIDS. However, the price of the drug per patient per year was an astronomical $10,000. The well-orchestrated AIDS lobby protested the company's pricing policy on the grounds that it effectively put the drug out of the reach of a vast majority of patients. In addition, the protesters claimed that since the company did not discover the drug (the drug was originally snythesized by government researchers), it could not claim enormous developmental costs in defending its pricing policy. The often novel and audacious forms of protest snowballed into a large-scale effort by the AIDS lobby. The company defended its pricing policy by saying that government restrictions limited the market for the drug and that the developmental costs had to be spread over a much smaller volume than what the lobbyists claimed. As the charges flew back and forth, the government initially took a back seat. In response to the lobby, the government began investigating. The company reduced the drug's price to $6,400 per patient per year; however, Burroughs Wellcome claimed that the price reductions were because of improvements in the production process and not the result of government action.

21 Verbatim Challenges 3M for Market Leadership

In 1990, in an effort to enter the floppy disk market with instant brand awareness, Mitsubishi Kasei, the chemical division of the $9 billion Japanese conglomerate, acquired Verbatim from Eastman Kodak. By 1992, Verbatim was challenging 3M Corporation for market share leadership in the floppy disk market. Verbatim produced a wide variety of data storage media including magnetic storage media (floppy disks) and advanced mass storage devices (tape storage products and optical disks). From its beginning in 1969, Verbatim had been a leader in innovation and had developed a quality image. Verbatim's DataLife and DataLifePlus brands competed directly with 3M, Sony, and Maxwell brands in the premium segment of the market and its successful Bonus brand competed against TDK and Highland brands in the economy segment. Over the years, the computer media market had changed and product differentiation had become more difficult. Increasingly, particularly in the mass market, floppy disks were viewed as a commodity product. In addition, the life cycle for new computer media technologies had become compressed. Developing a strategy to challenge the market leader would be difficult.

22 Anheuser-Busch Dominates in the 1990s

The Anheuser-Busch Company was founded in 1852. Since 1860, members of the Busch family led the corporation in developing and maintaining its position of leadership in the beer industry. Vertical integration to control the total production process (including raw materials, packaging, and so on) and diversification into food products (including Eagle-brand snacks) was undertaken. Diversified operations included theme parks, the St. Louis Cardinals baseball team, railroads, and others. August A. Busch III, chief executive officer, expected 50 percent of the beer market by the mid-1990s. Because of the anticipated decline in the number of 20- to 39-year-olds, growth in the consumption of beer was projected to be flat. In addition, Congress was again investigating the elimination of beer and wine advertising in the broadcast media.

23 HEALTHSOUTH Rehabilitation Corporation

Richard M. Scrushy, the chairman, chief executive officer, and president of HEALTHSOUTH Rehabilitation Corporation (HRC) recognized that the implementation of Medicare's prospective payment system would create the need for outpatient rehabilitation services. Unable to convince either LifeMark Corporation or American Medical International of the potential benefits of forming a comprehensive outpatient rehabilitation facility, in 1983 Scrushy and his colleagues decided to form one of their own. As of 1991, HRC had experienced 19 consecutive quarters of growth. The company was publicly traded and operated 43 outpatient and 11 inpatient facilities in 24 states. In December 1989, HRC acquired the marginally profitable South Highlands Hospital (an acute-care facility specializing in sports injuries and orthopedic surgery). Top management believed the marginal profitability of the hospital was because of its limited ability to obtain financing to provide the state-of-the-art facilities needed. South Highland's world-famous physicians provided orthopedic services for celebrities such as Bo Jackson, Jack Nicklaus, Charles Barkley, Jane Fonda, and the prince of Saudi Arabia. HRC faced the challenge of sustaining additional continuous growth.

24 Circuit City Stores

Circuit City, a very successful regional retailer of appliances, and audio, video, and consumer electronics, had grown to 93 stores with $519 million in sales and $20 million in profit. The Circuit City strategy had shifted from small stores with various names and various merchandise selections to 30,000- to 40,000-square-foot stores with a vast selection of popular brand-name merchandise. The stores typically obtained a large share of the retail market. Growth had been accomplished by high levels of customer service, including repair services, along with guaranteed low prices on all merchandise. Circuit City had to develop a strategy to maintain growth and market position. One opportunity would be to reintroduce sales by mail-order catalog.

25 Harley-Davidson

Harley-Davidson had been quite successful during the 1950s and 1960s; however, the company lost its dominant position in the United States and most of its world market share to Japanese companies (Honda, Yamaha, Suzuki, and Kawasaki) in the 1970s. Harley's meager 3 percent share of total motorcycle sales led experts to speculate that Harley-Davidson would not last into the 1980s. Tariff protection and a management-led leveraged buyout from parent company AMF helped Harley-Davidson improve quality and recover market share. In addition, Harley-Davidson diversified by purchasing Holiday Rambler Corporation, a manufacturer of recreational and commercial vehicles. Despite improving the Harley image (away from beer-drinking leather-clad bikers), emphasis on "made in America," and the development of a new customer base (Rubbies—rich urban bikers), Harley remained subject to seasonal fluctuations and the performance of the U.S. economy. The weak economy of the early 1990s and increasingly aggressive competition portended more problems for Harley-Davidson.

26 Carolco Pictures

Carolco Pictures was formed in the early 1980s as an international movie distribution company that later ventured into film production. The original purpose of the partnership was to obtain better terms by buying rights to movies for both the Far East and Middle East. Carolco Pictures was quite successful by making *First Blood* and later *Rambo: First Blood Part II* starring Sylvester Stallone. Rather than limiting risks by making numerous small-budget productions, Carolco's strategy was to make four or five "event" pictures a year with budgets of $20 million and up and sell distribution rights in advance to help cover costs. The production of *Terminator 2: Judgment Day* left Carolco in an ominous financial position. The company had a negative cash flow from operations from 1988 to 1991 and a $6.3 million loss. *Terminator 2* opened to massive crowds exceeding all expectations, but would this be enough to save Carolco?

27 Baldor Electric Company: Positioning for the 21st Century

Baldor Electric manufactured electric motors for the industrial market. Company growth exceeded industry growth dramatically. Baldor ranked third in the industry, with sales of $200 million. After 22 years of progressive growth, and despite an increasing market share, dollar and unit sales declined from 1982 to 1986. By 1988, the company appeared to be back on target. The company's product line included electric motors sold through distributors and to original equipment manufacturers. Its primary comparative advantage was energy-efficient motors at competitive prices. Recent diversifications into motor starters and motor drivers had broadened the company's opportunity for growth.

28 The Electric Motor Industry

The electric motor industry was extremely concentrated, with the top 11 (of 340 nationally) companies accounting for over 80 percent of industry sales. The various kinds of motors, motor applications, major competitors, major markets, and market niches, as well as industry forecasts, are included as background material for the student.

29 Rubbermaid

The spectacular success of Rubbermaid in the marketplace for more than two decades was largely due to its unique marketing strategy. Paramount to the strategy was the company's dedication to quality. Although competitive products were seldom identified by the manufacturer, the top-of-the-line products manufactured by Rubbermaid carried the logo prominently. Rubbermaid was so convinced of its superior quality and the satisfaction of consumers that it made identification easy in order to build brand loyalty. Rubbermaid's sales showed growth and unusual stability due to the relatively low cost of the everyday household type of products that were the mainstay of its market niche. The product line was continuously being upgraded. About 200 new products were added yearly. Although some products were added by acquisition of compatible manufacturing firms, most were developed through in-house research and development. Rubbermaid had to develop a strategy to maintain growth in a saturated market for household goods and find the answer to the question "What happens to Rubbermaid when the brilliant strategic Stanley Gault retires?"

30 Dakotah

In 1971, George Whyte started a cooperative of farmwives to alleviate some of the financial stress in the depressed agricultural region of northeastern South Dakota. The co-op manufactured bedcoverings and associated textile home furnishings enjoying record sales of over $13 million in 1986 and record profits of almost $400,000. Its products were marketed by department stores as top-of-the-line textile home furnishings. In May 1987, Dakotah appeared to be on the brink of a new era of growth and profitability. Taking advantage of marketing opportunities might require abandoning policies that were once the company's reason for existence.

31 Pirates Cove Inn

Pirates Cove Inn was a "rustic resort" located off of the main roads in northern Belize, Central America. Carole Hartman, a Canadian entrepreneur, was the developer and manager of the inn, which catered to archaeologists, amateur explorers, and others who appreciated the integration of the inn with the natural beauty of the Yucatan jungle and Caribbean Sea. A continuing struggle existed between the desire to maintain the inn in a rustic condition and to develop the business. Carole was considering three attractive courses of action, but they presented very different marketing and management consequences.

32 Lance Takes on New Challenges

Lance was a publicly owned, although family-dominated, regional producer of snack foods. The founder invented the peanut butter and cracker sandwich in an individual package. The company made extensive use of vending machine sales, primarily along the East Coast. Little advertising was done aside from vending machines and sides of trucks, and the company was hesitant to compete against the giant, Frito-Lay, in grocery stores or supermarkets. The conservative management team emphasized stability over growth. Further, the company had no debt. Although the company had an excellent history of performance, growth in vending was projected to be flat.

33 Sun Microsystems: Competing in a High-Tech Industry

Sun Microsystems was created by four young entrepreneurs enamored with the idea of developing and marketing a low-end computer workstation for scientists and engineers using the UNIX operating system. Until recently, Sun operated on the philosophy that it had to obtain market share, no matter what the cost, in anticipation of the likelihood that large companies such as IBM, DEC, and Hewlett-Packard would aggressively move into the workstation market. The company expanded rapidly, developed a large number of product prototypes, and created numerous autonomous divisions. The market share/sales growth emphasis contributed to sales and production bottlenecks, inventory shortages, activity duplication, and information inadequacies. At the same time, Sun announced plans to move into the high-end workstation market where processing power and sophisticated capabilities were essential. A key question was whether Sun could continue to meet its announced goals of significant increases in sales revenue, new product acceptance, improved profit margins, and book value increases with a narrow product focus, loose organization structure, a weak distribution system, and increasing competition from mid-range computer marketers, as well as personal computer manufacturers.

34 American Greetings Faces New Challenges in the 1990s

American Greetings (AG) was the world's largest publicly owned manufacturer of greeting cards and related social-expression merchandise. In 1990, AG reached sales of $1.286 billion; however, profit margins had slipped from a 1984 high. Chief Executive Officer Morry Weiss realized that AG's increase in sales had come at a high price with an escalated and intensified battle for market share dominance among the industry leaders, Hallmark, Gibson, and AG. Even with the raging battle, market shares had not really changed that much among the big three and now each was determined to defend its respective market share. AG's growth strategy to attack the industry leader and its niche, as well as Gibson's growth strategy, and Hallmark's defensive moves, changed the once-placid industry. As Weiss thought about the future, he wondered what changes AG should make in its competitive strategies.

35 Supportive HomeCare: Positioning for the 1990s

Supportive HomeCare was a privately owned, independent, state-licensed home care agency in small, urban areas along the Fox River Valley in central Wisconsin. Five hospitals were located in the general area with a total of 1,157 beds. Terri Hansen, a nurse/entrepreneur, started the company in 1983 along with a silent partner who was employed full time in insurance. Their small business was a quality-oriented health care service provider in the patient's home. The primary customers of Supportive HomeCare were patients recovering from accidents and outpatient surgery, handicapped and disabled individuals, single and working parents of sick children, and children/parents/friends providing individualized care for a gravely ill loved one. The early years were characterized by rapid growth, but more recently competition, changes in reimbursement practices, and a tight labor market made the operation of the home health care provider more challenging. Two competitors controlled the discharge planning of the two largest hospitals in the area.

36 Grasse Fragrances SA

Grasse Fragrances was a major supplier of chemically produced fragrances, sold to manufacturers of perfumes, toiletries, detergents, and other household products. Buying patterns in these industries had changed substantially. Approximately 50 percent of sales came from international accounts, and this was predicted to grow to 80 percent. Smaller, single-country customers were still important and could be very profitable, even in the future when they were expected to represent only 20 percent of sales. Jean-Pierre Volet, the marketing director, had reorganized the headquarters marketing organization to reflect changes in its served markets. He had established product managers and international client coordinators (ICCs). Their efforts were increasing the coordination in developing briefs (the industry term for a fragrance specification and request for quotation) and selling efforts to the larger international accounts.

37 LOTUS Development Corporation: Maintaining Leadership in the Electronic Spreadsheet Industry

LOTUS, developer of 1-2-3 microcomputer spreadsheet software, was faced with a serious marketing challenge. At one time, the company had 70 to 80 percent of the market of IBM PC and PC-compatible spreadsheet programs. However, numerous competitors established spreadsheet entries in the current market and were continually providing updated versions. LOTUS's updated version 3.0 for 1-2-3 did not debut until 1989. Meanwhile, its competitors introduced 1-2-3-compatible products with advanced features not available in current versions of 1-2-3 at the same price or at lower prices. Market share was eroding. LOTUS had to decide how to maintain its competitive position without sacrificing the simplicity and familiar interface provided to existing users in an environment featuring slower growth rates for spreadsheet sales and more intense price and product competition.

38 The Army and Air Force Exchange Service: A New Era

In 1986, the Army and Air Force Exchange Service (AAFES), a worldwide retail, food, and service organization, was one of the largest retailers in the United States with sales of over $4.5 billion. The primary mission of AAFES was to provide authorized patrons (military personnel and their dependents) with merchandise and services of necessity and convenience at low prices. However, the 1980s had brought increased competition in retailing both in the United States and worldwide. General Long, commander of AAFES, believed that some fundamental change in the exchange system was required if it was to continue to be successful into the 1990s.

39 Schweppes Raspberry Ginger Ale

The Schweppes division of Cadbury Beverages North America (CBNA) was a leading marketer of adult soft drinks in the United States. Its primary competitor was another division of CBNA—Canada Dry. The mixer image of the adult soft drinks and specifically of the Schweppes Ginger Ale (SGA) had, on one hand, insulated them from the intense competition from the mainstream general soft drinks. However, on the other hand, it had isolated them from exploiting their full sales and profit potential as a legitimate general-purpose soft drink. The company recently developed a new product, Schweppes Raspberry Ginger Ale (SRGA). Management believed that the product had the potential to break away from the conventional image of the "adult soft drinks as mixers" and present itself as a legitimate mainstream general soft drink. The major challenges for the company were first to assess the marketing feasibility of the new product for the company and its channel members and second to interpret the performance of the product during the first six months of its introduction to determine future marketing strategies.

40 The *Dallas Morning News*

The *Dallas Morning News* (MN) and the *Dallas Times Herald* (TH) had been battling for years, but in the first half of 1985, the MN had gained a significant circulation advantage in Dallas County—long the TH's strongest market. Some industry analysts suggested the battle in Dallas for newspaper supremacy was over, won by the MN. But late in 1986, MediaNews Group purchased the TH and immediately filed a circulation fraud suit against the MN. MediaNews Corporation assembled an experienced and aggressive management team to lead the TH. With a countersuit filed by the MN, it appeared that rather than the battle being over, a new skirmish was under way.

Gatorade Defends Its No. 1 Position

Gatorade, a subsidiary of the Quaker Oats Company, had an important objective for 1991: defend its dominant position in the sports drink market. Although Gatorade had achieved more than 90 percent market share, aggressive efforts by soft drink manufacturers and other companies to enter this profitable and growing market had generated a strong reaction from Quaker Oats. The company expected as many as four strong competitors by 1995. Its objective was to keep Gatorade synonymous with sports drinks well into the 21st century.

With current margins in the industry as high as 35 percent, projections of growth ranging to 30 percent for the next several years, and Gatorade sales estimated to be approximately $600 million, it was not surprising that established beverage producers as well as newcomers were eager to enter the sports drink market. However, Quaker Oats clearly recognized the marketing muscle of some of its challengers and had mounted defensive campaigns to specifically halt the erosion of its maket share.

In 1989, Quaker designed a marketing strategy to counter the expansion of 10-K. The campaign concentrated on protecting distribution and shelf space, communicating Gatorade's product superiority, eliminating any sports market segment voids, and eclipsing the visibility of 10-K in its home market of New Orleans. Gatorade sponsored the Louisiana High School football playoffs and ran an aggressive public relations campaign that included an effort to get Gatorade back on the sidelines of the New Orleans Saints.

Similarly, when Pepsi introduced Mountain Dew Sport (MDS) in test markets in 1989, Quaker again mobilized its forces to promote product superiority and to portray MDS as another "soda pop." Part of the strategy was to convince stores to shelve MDS with soft drinks where it would compete with other Pepsi products rather than with Gatorade. Ultimately, MDS was not well received and was withdrawn. Pepsi immediately followed MDS with another entry—AllSport, which was an indication of the appeal of the sports drink market. Quaker Oats executives knew that other companies would continue to challenge Gatorade's enviable market share. Gatorade was a brand worth protecting.

This case was prepared by Linda E. Swayne and Peter M. Ginter as a basis for class discussion rather than to illustrate either effective or ineffective handling of an administrative situation. Used with permission from Linda E. Swayne.

HISTORY

Gatorade was developed in the 1960s by Dr. Robert Cade (a kidney expert at the University of Florida) and a team of researchers studying heat exhaustion among the players on the University of Florida football team. By analyzing the content of the football players' perspiration, they devised a formula that would prevent severe dehydration brought about by fluid and mineral loss during physical exertion in high temperatures. In 1965, they tested the rehydration product on 10 players from the football team—the Florida Gators. The beverage became known, and was later trademarked, as Gatorade. During the 1966 season, the Gators used Gatorade on the sidelines of every game. That season they became known as the "second-half team" by consistently outplaying the competition in the final half of the game. Florida's coach noted the advantages of Gatorade as the players enjoyed increased efficiency and greater endurance. That year the Florida Gators won the Orange Bowl over Georgia Tech, after which Tech coach Bobby Dodd said, "We didn't have Gatorade. That made the difference." That statement was carried by *Sports Illustrated* and marked the beginning of Gatorade becoming the best-selling sports drink in the United States.

Stokely-Van Camp Grows the Brand

In May 1967, Stokely-Van Camp, a leading processor and marketer of fruits and vegetables, purchased the rights to Gatorade from Dr. Cade and began marketing it in the summer of 1968. Stokely's original objective was to promote Gatorade as not only a sports drink, but as a health food product. It was determined that it could be used as an electrolyte replacement for colds and flu, diarrhea and vomiting, and (although not publicized) as a cure for hangovers.

By May 1969, Gatorade was available throughout most of the United States (some areas of the Northeast did not have distribution). By September 1969, it was selling in every state except Alaska. Throughout the 1970s, as Americans became more interested in fitness, Gatorade sales increased accordingly.

Many competing products were introduced once it became apparent that Stokely had a very successful product. Most were unsuccessful; however, a few were able to compete in the institutional team sales market. Due to strong brand loyalty, no other sports drink could compete with Gatorade in the retail market in those early years. In addition, sports trainers continued to select Gatorade over all other thirst quenchers.

One very successful promotion used by Stokely was to provide participating National Basketball Association (NBA) and National Football League (NFL) teams with free coolers, squeeze bottles, and cups. When the team competed, the Gatorade coolers were visible to spectators and television audiences.

Quaker Oats Ownership

In the summer of 1983, Quaker Oats bought Stokely-Van Camp. Quaker Oats was a worldwide marketer of consumer grocery products. Acquiring

Gatorade proved to be a win/win situation by boosting Quaker Oats' sales and providing the product with needed financial backing. Quaker saw an opportunity to use its marketing prowess to widen distribution and to further increase penetration throughout the country. Marketing expenditures for Gatorade were doubled, and national promotion was stressed. The expected synergies have been realized, as Gatorade has posted an average compound growth rate of 28 percent since the 1983 acquisition. Sales have grown more than sixfold from approximately $100 million in 1983 to $600 million for fiscal 1990.

Quaker Oats Legacy.   The Quaker Mill Company was founded in 1877 in Ravenna, Ohio; however, its legacy as a marketing organization began under Henry Parson Crowell, who purchased the company in 1881. During his long tenure at Quaker, he continuously broke new ground in advertising and marketing. Quaker oatmeal was the first food product to be packaged in a cardboard container. It was the first to print recipes on the package, and it was the first to advertise nationally and then globally. Crowell put the Quaker name on billboards, buildings, trucks, and manufacturing plants to a greater extent than any one had previously attempted. He also made extensive use of the print media experimenting with emotional appeals including humor, sex, and love. All of this was done without the aid of advertising agencies because they did not yet exist. Crowell, however, was pragmatic and quickly turned the burden of advertising over to agencies after they came into existence in the early 1900s.

Crowell managed daily operations in conjunction with Robert Stuart, another major shareholder. Stuart was a perceptive businessman with an interest in diversification and expansion and an appreciation for Crowell's marketing genius. He instituted a strategy of acquiring promising products and using Quaker's marketing strengths to build the product's market share. Even today, this strategy continues and has built Quaker into a giant that offers dozens of food products globally and produced sales of $5 billion in 1990 (see Exhibit 1.1 for financial statements). Throughout the 20th century, Stuart's son and grandson maintained the company's marketing culture as presidents of Quaker. The grandson, Robert D. Stuart, Jr., stressed in 1964 that "marketing was the ultimate goal, which could be accomplished only as the end effort in a complex process of production and distribution. Costs were to be controlled. Quality was to be maintained without fail. Every job was important as a step forward to that payoff in the marketplace."[1]

The Stuart family no longer manages Quaker, but the corporate commitment to the marketplace still exists. William D. Smithburg, the chief executive officer since 1983, was promoted through the ranks at Quaker. True to his corporate heritage, Smithburg acquired the Gatorade brand with the intent to grow the product through marketing.

---

[1] Arthur F. Marquette, *Brands, Trademarks, and Goodwill* (New York: McGraw-Hill, 1967), p. 258.

EXHIBIT 1.1   The Quaker Oats Company Financial Statement
(In millions except per share data)

Consolidated Statements of Income Year Ended June 30

	1988	1989	1990
Net Sales	$4,508.0	$4,879.4	$5,030.6
Cost of Goods Sold	2,397.0	2,655.3	2,685.9
Gross Profit	2,111.0	2,224.1	2,344.7
Selling, General, and Administrative Expenses	1,697.8	1,799.0	1,844.1
Interest Expense—Net of $11.0, $12.4, and $15.1 Interest Income	41.0	56.4	101.8
Other Expense—Net	57.6	149.6	16.4
Income from Continuing Operations before Income Taxes	314.6	239.1	382.4
Provision for Income Taxes	118.1	90.2	153.5
Income from Continuing Operations	196.5	148.9	228.9
Income (loss) from Discontinued Operations—Net of Tax	59.2	54.1	(59.9)
Net Income	255.7	203.0	169.0
Preferred Dividends—Net of Tax	—	—	4.5
Net Income Available for Common	$ 255.7	$ 203.0	$ 164.5
Per Common Share			
Income from Continuing Operations	$ 2.46	$ 1.88	$ 2.93
Income (Loss) from Discontinued Operations	.74	.68	(.78)
Net Income	3.20	2.56	2.15
Dividends Declared	$ 1.00	$ 1.20	$ 1.40
Average Number of Common Shares Outstanding (In thousands)	79,835	79,307	76,537

Consolidated Balance Sheets

	1988	1989	1990
Assets			
Current Assets			
Cash and Cash Equivalents	$ 47.4	$ 21.0	$ 17.7
Short-Term Investments, at Cost which Approximates Market	35.6	2.7	.6
Receivables—Net of Allowances	555.0	594.4	629.9
Inventories			
Finished Goods	281.5	326.0	324.1
Grain and Raw Materials	95.3	114.1	110.7
Packaging Materials and Supplies	37.0	39.0	39.1
Total inventories	413.8	479.1	473.9
Other Current Assets	29.8	94.2	107.0
Net Current Assets of Discontinued Operations	342.4	328.5	252.2
Total Current Assets	1,424.0	1,519.9	1,481.3
Other Receivables and Investments	20.7	26.4	63.5
Property, Plant, and Equipment	1,403.1	1,456.9	1,745.6
Less Accumulated Depreciation	480.6	497.3	591.5
Properties—Net	922.5	959.6	1,154.1
Intangible Assets, Net of Amortization	414.3	484.7	466.7
Net Noncurrent Assets of Discontinued Operations	104.6	135.3	160.5
Total Assets	$2,886.1	$3,125.9	$3,326.1

Exhibit 1.1   (Cont.)

	1988	1989	1990
Liabilities and Common Shareholders' Equity			
Current Liabilities			
Short-Term Debt	$ 310.3	$ 102.2	$ 343.2
Current Portion of Long-Term Debt	29.2	30.0	32.3
Trade Accounts Payable	262.2	333.8	354.0
Accrued Payrolls, Pensions, and Bonuses	107.3	118.1	106.3
Accrued Advertising and Merchandising	70.6	67.1	92.6
Income Taxes Payable	41.5	8.0	36.3
Other Accrued Liabilities	185.4	164.9	173.8
Total Current Liabilities	1,006.5	824.1	1,138.5
Long-Term Debt	299.1	766.8	740.3
Other Liabilities	101.0	89.5	100.3
Deferred Income Taxes	228.4	308.4	327.7
Preferred Stock, No Par Value, Authorized 1,750,000 shares; Issued 1,282,051 of $5.46 Cumulative Convertible Shares in 1989 (liquidating preference $78 per share)	—	100.0	100.0
Deferred Compensation	—	(100.0)	(98.2)
Common Shareholders' Equity			
Common Stock, $5 Par Value, Authorized 200,000,000 Shares; Issued 83,989,396 Shares	420.0	420.0	420.0
Additional Paid-in Capital	19.5	18.1	12.9
Reinvested Earnings	998.4	1,106.2	1,164.7
Cumulative Exchange Adjustment	(36.5)	(56.6)	(29.3)
Deferred Compensation	(17.4)	(165.8)	(164.1)
Treasury Common Stock, at Cost, 8,402,871 Shares; 5,221,981 Shares and 4,593,664 Shares, respectively	(132.9)	(184.8)	(386.7)
Total Common Shareholders' Equity	1,251.1	1,137.1	1,017.5
Total Liabilities and Common Shareholders' Equity	$2,886.1	$3,125.9	$3,326.1

Source: Quaker Oats, *Annual Report,* 1990.

Quaker Oats Organization.   Quaker is a decentralized company organized by product groups or categories. Quaker's grocery products divisions include breakfast foods, frozen foods, grocery specialties, pet foods, Golden Grain, and food service. Exhibit 1.2 lists the major brands included in each of Quaker's divisions. Gatorade was included in the grocery specialties division, which also contained Van Camp's Beans and Wolf Brand Chili. Gatorade constituted 65 percent of the sales of the division, and the grocery specialties division accounted for 20 percent of Quaker's total sales. Thus, Gatorade contributed approximately 13 percent to Quaker's overall sales. The president of the Grocery Specialties Division, Peter J. Vituli, was a 13-year veteran with Quaker. He had been responsible for introducing Quaker Oat Squares cereal and two products for pets, plus the relaunch of Cap'n Crunch cereal. He also spent two years marketing products in the United

EXHIBIT 1.2   Quaker Oats Divisions and Brands

North American Foods **$1,583.2 million**	**Food Service** **$460.2 million**

North American Foods
$1,583.2 million

Old Fashioned Quaker Oats
Old Fashioned Quick Quaker Oats
Instant Quaker Oatmeal
Cap'n Crunch
Quaker Oat Squares
Life
Oh!s
Quaker 100% Natural
Aunt Jemima Syrup
Aunt Jemima Pancake Mix
Aunt Jemima frozen waffles, pancakes,
    French toast, etc.
Quaker Chewy Granola Bars
Dipps
Quaker Rice Cakes
Celeste Frozen Pizza

Pet Foods
$517.7 million

Kibbles 'n Bits 'n Bits 'n Bits
Cycle
Gravy Train
Ken-L Ration
Gaines
Puss'n Boots
Ken-L Ration Sausages
PupPeroni
Puss'n Boots Pounce

Food Service
$460.2 million

Quaker Breakfast Products
Grocery Specialty Products
plus:
    Ardmore Farms
    Liqui-Dri Foods
    Richardson/Snyder Foods
    Continental Coffee

Golden Grain
$275 million

Rice-A-Roni
Noodle Roni
Savory Classics
Golden Grain
Mission
Ghirardelli (chocolate)

Grocery Specialities
$764.9 million

Gatorade
Wolf Brand Chili
Van Camp's Beans

International Grocery Products
$1,420.6 million

Various Quaker brands in Europe
    and South America

Kingdom. The sales structure under Mr. Vituli's control began with a vice president for broker sales and included individual territory managers who provided the company's contact with food brokerage companies. The food brokers represented Quaker's direct point of distribution to the retailer.

THE MARKET

Gatorade competes in the isotonic beverage category, typically referred to as the sports drink market. These thirst quenchers are designed to replace the fluids and minerals lost during physical activity. Competition centers on rehydration performance, taste, health, and calories. According to research done for Gatorade, the effectiveness of fluid replacement beverages depends on several factors:

Fluid absorption—A sports beverage should promote rapid fluid absorption; glucose/sucrose and sodium must be present in proper concentrations to help stimulate fluid absorption. Research shows that exercising people can absorb fluids containing 2 to 8 percent carbohydrate at rates similar to water. Above 10 percent carbohydrate has been shown to slow absorption rate.

Carbohydrate percentage/type—A sports beverage should provide enough carbohydrates for use as a fuel by working muscles, yet avoid slowing fluid absorption. Research indicates formulations containing 6 to 8 percent carbohydrates are optimal for achieving a balance between energy and fluid delivery. Formulations below 6 percent provide less energy; there is no added performance advantage at levels above 6 percent. Glucose and sucrose, working in combination, deliver the most effective energy; fructose, as a sole source of carbohydrate, has been shown to be less effective.

Electrolytes—To help the body maintain physiological homeostasis, electrolytes, particularly sodium, are needed in fluid replacement beverages for strenuous and lengthy exercise. Research indicates that 55 milligrams to 275 milligrams of sodium per serving enhance fluid absorption. (Gatorade contains less sodium than one cup of 2 percent milk.) An amount less than that found in Gatorade may not be effective in promoting optimal fluid electrolyte balance during exercise.

Taste—Research shows that noncarbonated beverages with a mild, slightly sweet flavor are preferred by most people when they are hot and sweaty. If a sports drink tastes good, it is more likely to be consumed in the quantities necessary for proper rehydration.

Gatorade contained no vitamins, as there is no scientifically substantiated evidence to indicate that vitamins are advantageous in a rehydration product. An eight-ounce serving of Gatorade contained 50 calories (from the glucose and sucrose), which is about half the calories found in fruit drinks and nondiet soft drinks.

Each competitor in the isotonic category claims that it has the superior product for thirst quenching. With the exception of the carbonated drinks, most formulations could be argued to be adequate for fluid and mineral replacement. Therefore, flavor or taste is going to be the key competitive issue in the category.

The market is highly seasonal; the majority of sales occur during the hot summer months. Thus, it is no surprise that the majority of the sports drinks are distributed in the South, Southeast, and Southwest, where warm weather is prevalent. In Gatorade's case, 38 percent of total volume is sold in the states of Florida, Texas, and California, the very states being targeted by competition. Although most of the new brands are regional in scope, their concentration is in Gatorade's prime markets.

Competition

Gatorade management expected the sports drink category to continue to grow at a forecasted rate of about 15 percent per year during the 1990s. This meant continued growth for Gatorade, but its success had not gone unnoticed by potential competitors. Each one considered Gatorade to be its main competition, and each one was trying to capture a portion of Gatorade's 91 percent share in this $700 million sports drink market. This forced Gatorade to defend its position and placed a drain on funds previously set aside for growth. The major competing brands in the industry are summarized in Exhibit 1.3.

The international market offered the greatest growth potential. Gatorade was successfully introduced in Italy, Germany, and Brazil. Giulio Malgara, president of Quaker, Europe, predicted that Gatorade would be sold throughout the continent within five years. In Italy, Gatorade captured 93 percent of the sports drink market and induced two competing products—Isotar (4 percent share) and Acqusport (2 percent share). The next major area targeted for expansion was the Far East. In 1992, Gatorade was only marketed under license in Japan, where it competed with Coca-Cola's Aquarius drink. Quaker's international experience and expertise made global growth very appealing, plus the competition outside the United States was minimal at this time.

10-K

10-K, Gatorade's top competitor, was a subsidiary of the Japanese beverage giant, Suntory. The company had the financial strength to aggressively market its product and had achieved impressive results in key areas. Introduced in 1985, 10-K was a noncarbonated drink made from salt-free spring water that featured 100 percent of the USRDA of vitamin C, all-natural flavors and sweeteners (fructose), 60 calories per serving, and half the sodium of other thirst quenchers. 10-K contained no caffeine, Nutrasweet, or saccharin. Flavors offered were fruit punch, lemonade, orange, lemon-lime, and tea. Sizes available were 16-, 32-, 46-, and 64-ounce plastic containers. In 1991, distribution was in 28 states in the Southeast, Southwest, and Northeast. The brand captured almost 20 percent of the New Orleans market, 12 percent of the San Francisco market, and was doing 37 percent of its total volume in Florida and the Carolinas. 10-K was channeled to grocery stores and team sports' dealers. In 1989, the product market share increased from 1.9 percent to 4.5 percent of the total U.S. market and from 4.5 percent to 9 percent in 10-K's market areas. In a head-to-head taste test with Gatorade, 10-K was rated a better-tasting drink. 10-K's thirst satisfaction was rated equal to Gatorade's. Test results from respondents who used both Gatorade and 10-K over a three-month period indicated a higher repurchase rate for 10-K over Gatorade.[2]

---

[2] Tracey L. Walker, "Sports Drinks, Suddenly Everyone Wants to Play," *Beverage Industry*, February 1991, pp. 3–4.

EXHIBIT 1.3   Sports Drink Competitors

Brand and Introduction	Manufacturer	Distribution	Flavors/Sizes
Gatorade 1966	Stokely Van Camp, subsidiary of Quaker Oats Company	National	5 flavors; 3 sizes in glass bottles; 64-oz plastic bottles; 11.6-oz cans; powder pouches; aseptic packages (3-pack, 8.45-oz)
Gatorade Light April 1990	Stokely Van Camp, subsidiary of Quaker Oats Company	Southeast, Southwest, California	3 flavors; 2 sizes in glass bottles
Freestyle July 1990	Stokely Van Camp, subisidary of Quaker Oats Company	California and Arizona	3 flavors; 4-pack bottles in 2 sizes
10-K 1986	Beverage Products, division of Suntory Water Group, Atlanta; subsidiary of Suntory International	28 states in the Southeast, Southwest, and Northeast	5 flavors; 4 sizes in glass bottles
PowerBurst January 1989	PowerBurst Corporation Fresno, California	Los Angeles to New Orleans; Alaska and Hawaii; 21 states	4 flavors; 4 sizes in cans; aseptic packs; 3 sizes powdered
Workout, Workout Light, April 1989	White Rock Products Corporation, White Stone, New York	Illinois, Michigan, Ohio, North Carolina, South Carolina, New York, California, Florida	5 flavors; 16-oz
Pro-formance July 1990	Pro-formance Charlotte, NC	North Carolina, South Carolina, Tennessee, Atlanta, North Florida	4 flavors; 3 sizes
Pro Motion developed 1985 tested 1988	Sports Beverage Plano, Texas	Texas, Louisiana, Arkansas, Oklahoma, Minnesota, North Dakota, New Mexico, Colorado, Illinois, Indiana, Yuma, Arizona	4 flavors; 3 sizes in bottles, 2 sizes in cans
Mountain Dew Sport regular/diet 1990	Pepsi-Cola Company Somers, New York	Philadelphia, Minneapolis, San Diego, Eau Claire, Charlotte	12-oz cans; 2 sizes in bottles
PowerAde March 1990	Coca-Cola USA Houston, Texas	Exclusively through fountains in convenience stores, nationwide	3 flavors

Source: Pat Natschke Lenius, "New Sports Drinks Heating Up Competition," *Supermarket News,* October 1, 1990, p. 20, and promotional literature from PowerBurst Corporation and Pro-formance.

Suntory planned to spend $9 million on advertising in 1991. 10-K's promotional strategy targets men aged 18–34 and women aged 25–54. The company used television, radio, free-standing inserts (FSIs), coupons, print media, direct mail, sports marketing, local events, outdoor, and point-of-purchase merchandising to reach 90 percent of its targeted customers. The brand's advertising message focused on claims that consumers prefer 10-K because it:

- Tasted better than the leading competitor
- Was lower in sodium—no salty aftertaste
- Was enriched with Vitamin C
- Contained fructose for prolonged energy
- Was available in three popular sizes and five popular flavors

The pitch to retailers was that 10-K helped the thirst quencher category grow and that this growth meant faster turnover. The company reminded retailers that competition builds category profits and incremental sales.

PowerBurst

Introduced in December 1988 by PowerBurst Corporation and designed as an "advanced performance beverage," PowerBurst claimed nutritional superiority to existing products because it was lower in sodium and less salty in taste; had no artificial color, flavor, or preservatives; and had more sports vitamins and minerals.

Edward Debartolo, Jr., owner of the San Francisco 49ers and the Pittsburgh Penguins, had controlling interest in this privately held company that was headquartered in Fresno, California. His team ownership enabled PowerBurst to enlist quarterback Joe Montana and running back Roger Craig as endorsers. The product was promoted with full-scale television, radio, and outdoor exposure in 1990. Its goal was to capture a 15 percent share in its distribution markets. Currently, the company holds the third position in the category (nationally) at a little less than 2 percent share.

PowerBurst strayed from the traditional market of males between ages 14 and 34, claiming that its better flavor would attract younger consumers. Marketing was also directed toward sports-minded females. PowerBurst's marketing focused around its alleged superiority to Gatorade in a comparison of seven product points. Advertisements generally included a comparison scoreboard similar to the one in Exhibit 1.4.

PowerBurst sports drink was noncarbonated and offered four flavors: orange, berry punch, lemon-lime, and lemonade. Packaging provided seven different sizes ranging from 16-ounce glass bottles to 120-ounce plastic bottles and 11.5-ounce powder canisters. In 1991, distribution was in 17 states as far west as

EXHIBIT 1.4   PowerBurst "Scoreboard"

Points	Powerburst	Gatorade
Better tasting	1	0
Easier to Drink	1	0
Less Salty Taste	1	0
No Brominated Oils	1	0
No Artificial Color	1	0
Lower in Sodium	1	0
Essential Sports Vitamins and Minerals	1	0
Score	7	0

Montana and into the southern states of Arkansas, Louisiana, and Oklahoma. PowerBurst was available in large supermarket chains, convenience stores, and athletic and sports clubs.[3]

Mountain Dew Sport/AllSport

Pepsi-Cola Corporation introduced Mountain Dew Sport (MDS) in 1989 as its entry to the sports drink market. It was a lightly carbonated, caffeine-free beverage that came in regular and two-calorie formulas. Similar to other competitors, MDS asserted that it was better tasting than Gatorade. However, too much carbonation in this isotonic drink reduced its appeal to consumers and, as indicated earlier, Gatorade encouraged positioning on the shelf with other "soda pops." Subsequently Pepsi replaced MDS with AllSport. Unlike Mountain Dew, AllSport was offered in four flavors: orange, fruit punch, lemon-lime, and diet lemon-lime. This more lightly carbonated drink was available in 16- and 32-ounce glass containers and 12-ounce cans. Distributed in Philadelphia, Minneapolis, San Diego, Eau Claire (Wisconsin), and Charlotte, AllSport was channeled to grocery and convenience stores.[4] PepsiCo had the financial and promotional strength to provide extensive marketing support. Pepsi used its own distribution network instead of food brokers. This allowed Pepsi to move into stores quickly and to maintain optimal shelf conditions—all at a lower cost because of enormous volume. (When Pepsi test-marketed MDS in Eau Claire, 100 percent distribution was achieved in five days.) Additionally, a global distribution system was already in place in 1991, should the company decide to go international with a sports drink brand.

[3] Ibid.
[4] Ibid.

PowerAde

After a four-month test in Bakersfield, California, Coca-Cola went national with its second attempt at developing a successful thirst quencher drink. The first entry, Maxx, was a failure. PowerAde was "designed to rapidly replace body fluids lost through perspiration during physical exertion." Caffeine free and noncarbonated, PowerAde came in lemon, orange, and fruit punch flavors and was sold only at fountains. Its advertising in print and radio featured the slogan, "When you're sweating bullets . . . reach for PowerAde."

Snap-Up

Snapple Natural Beverage Company introduced Snap-Up in 1990 as a noncarbonated, mineral and fluid-replacing sports drink. Snap-Up contained maltodextrin and fructose, which reportedly enters the blood stream at a more gradual rate for a more sustained energy boost. Flavors offered were orange, lemon, lemon-lime, and fruit punch. Snap-Up was available in 16- and 32-ounce sizes and powder in 11.5-ounce cans. It was distributed on the East Coast, in the Midwest and the South, and California through health clubs, retail outlets, and convenience stores.

Pro Motion

Introduced by Sports Beverage in 1989, Pro Motion was a low-sodium, high-potassium, noncarbonated drink. It offered 100 percent recommended daily allowance for vitamin C and reportedly satisfied thirst with no salty or sweet aftertaste. Pro Motion flavors included lemon-lime, fruit punch, citrus cooler, and orange. Available in several sizes of plastic containers, Pro Motion was marketed in 20 states around the country. It was channeled through convenience stores, grocery store chains, independent stores, and institutions such as hospitals, hotels, and vending machines.

Workout

White Rock Products Corporation introduced Workout in April 1989 as an all-natural, complex carbohydrate, low-sodium, no-caffeine thirst reliever. This noncarbonated sports drink was also available in a diet formulation that contained Nutrasweet. Flavors included lemonade, lemon-lime, orange, punch, and Workout Light Iced Tea. It was packaged in a 16-ounce glass bottle and was marketed in 30 states around the country. Shelf space was sought at convenience and small independent stores.

Nautilus

Test marketed by Dr Pepper in October 1990 in Mobile, Alabama, Nautilus combined the attributes of soft drink refreshments with the benefits of a sports drink. This lightly carbonated thirst quencher offered low calories, vitamin C,

60 milligrams of sodium per 6-ounce serving, and two flavors: lemon-lime and orange. It was packaged in 2-liter plastic bottles and 12-ounce cans. It was available in grocery and convenience stores, and vending machines.

Pro-formance

Pro-formance was introduced by a Charlotte sports drink company of the same name. Joey Caldwell, North Carolina State karate champion in 1976 and 1977, developed a sports drink to help competitors "carb up" for training and competition. Pro-formance was noncarbonated and had 165 calories per 8-ounces (70 percent more than the same amount of Coca-Cola Classic and the equivalent of nine teaspoons of sugar).[5] Positioned as an energy drink, it was made from mountain water and all-natural fruit flavors and contained no sodium. Its real benefit was that it was made from a powder containing complex carbohydrates, which burn more slowly than sugar or corn syrup. It offered 12-ounce, 0.5-liter, and 1-liter servings. Pro-formance was marketed in five states and was shelved at supermarkets, convenience stores, and Wal-Mart.

GATORADE

When Quaker Oats purchased Gatorade in 1983, it was the only isotonic sports drink on the national market. Positioned as *the* sports drink, its name was almost generic. When competitors claimed their product tasted better, the Gatorade stance was that "when you're hot and sweaty Gatorade was the taste you reached for, the fluid your body craved, and ordinary taste tests were irrelevant. It was the quintessential sports drink, not a soda pop."

As the market has matured, Gatorade expanded its product line to stave off competition in various segments of the sports drink market and to reach secondary markets that would extend the franchise and build volume and profit. Although Gatorade was targeted toward "hard-core" athletes, Gatorade Light and Freestyle were introduced to compete in the low-calorie and flavor segments of the sports drink market.

Product Line Extensions

Introduced in 1990, Gatorade Light is aimed at the calorie-conscious aerobic exercisers, women, and joggers. They exercise for short or moderate lengths of time at low or moderate intensity. Gatorade Light contained 25 calories in an 8-ounce serving—about half the number of calories of regular Gatorade—and it had less sodium (80 milligrams). It was offered in three flavors and three package

[5] "Will Pro-formance Be a Pop Star?" *Business North Carolina*, March 1991, p. 10.

sizes. Gatorade Light sought and generally received placement on the juice aisle near regular Gatorade, thereby extending the family of products and shelf space.

Freestyle, a new, more flavorful product made with fruit juice, was aimed at people more interested in taste than the rehydration aspects of the product. Light exercisers and moderate exercisers of short to moderate duration were in the target market for this brand. Freestyle generally scored higher on taste tests than other sports drinks that did not contain fruit juice. It contained only 10 milligrams of sodium.

In 1991, Gatorade was available in six flavors. New tropical fruit flavor Gatorade was introduced to appeal to male and female teens and female adults and to broaden the product line. Each flavor had a unique appeal as indicated in Exhibit 1.5.

Packaging Options

The Gator Gallon was targeted to mothers, who purchase approximately 35 percent of Gatorade. Available in lemon-lime and orange, the plastic container was shatterproof and recyclable and had built-in handles. It was thought to be appropriate for warehouse-type (club) stores. Actually the most economical form of Gatorade was the powdered drink packaged to make four or eight quarts. Powdered Gatorade was promoted heavily at the beginning of the warm weather season and targeted to team mothers and heavy users. In 1991, eight different packages were available (Exhibit 1.6 contains the percentage of sales for each).

Newly available in convenience stores, the 23.5-ounce aluminum can was dubbed "the Slammer" and was heavily advertised in connection with Michael Jordan. Appearing in May 1991, the large can played directly on the popularity of wide-mouthed, slammable containers.[6] Also, test marketing included a 32-ounce recyclable plastic bottle and a 12-pack of 12-ounce cans. Consumers are felt to have strong preferences for their favorite flavors and packages.

In 1989, Quaker tested a fountain drink system and brought it to food service and convenience stores in 1990. The company saw this system as a source for future growth.

Distribution

In 1991, Gatorade was marketed in all states except Alaska. It was distributed primarily through food brokers who called on grocery stores and convenience stores, and institutional purchases by professional and college sports programs. Plans were under way to market Gatorade in Europe (France, Germany, Italy, and Spain) and South America (Brazil). Expansion to Europe and South America was another opportunity. Quaker viewed Gatorade as a worldwide trademark with significant opportunity for profitable growth.

[6] "Gatorade Bites Back with the 'Slammer,' " *Beverage Industry*, June 1991, pp. 4, 36.

EXHIBIT 1.5   Gatorade Flavors by Percent of Sales and Appeal

Flavor	Percent of Sales	Appeal
Lemon-Lime	38	Original flavor, loyal users
Orange	21	Improved taste, popular with ethnics
Fruit Punch	16	Improved taste, popular with kids
Citrus Cooler	13	Attracts new, light users
Lemonade	12	Popular summertime flavor
Tropical Fruit	new	Family appeal

Similar to other consumer packaged goods companies, Gatorade had to first sell its product to the trade. The retailers would then serve as the distribution mechanism to get the products into the hands of the ultimate consumers. In the case of retailers, demand is dependent on the profits the product generates. That profit can come in the form of increased sales volume, or in increased profit margins due to discounts or other promotional incentives.

A part of Gatorade's strategy was to point out that large shelf space and inventory were required to prevent consumers from going to another store for their purchases. Sales reps sold retail store managers on the idea that the sports beverage category should have as much shelf space on the juice aisle as the Nielsen share. For example, if a juice aisle were 64 feet long, 10 feet should be devoted to sports beverages (64-foot juice aisle × 15.3 percent sports beverage share = 10 feet). With a margin of 35 plus percent, the argument carried clout. Out-of-stocks can be costly to a given retailer. A Gatorade study found that 42 percent of consumers would not buy Gatorade if their favorite item was not available and that 18 percent would continue to shop for Gatorade at another store. Not wanting to miss a single detail in regard to visibility, the lid on Gatorade containers were changed in 1991 to heighten shelf awareness.

EXHIBIT 1.6   Gatorade Package Sizes as a Contribution to Sales

Package	Percent of Sales
64-ounce	36
32-ounce	21
46-ounce	13
Powder	11
16-ounce	9
Aseptic	8
Gallon	1
Cans	1

Gatorade distributed its products through two separate retailing industries—retail grocery stores and convenience stores. In retail sales, grocery stores represented about 55 percent of Gatorade's distribution and convenience stores accounted for the other 45 percent. Gatorade pushed for further development in convenience stores. The rationale underlying this strategy was that bottles and canned drinks were the fourth most popular item sold in convenience stores and they were a logical distribution point for Gatorade. The number of convenience stores grew 15 percent between 1988 and 1990.

The use of food brokers may prove to be a serious disadvantage for Gatorade if Pepsi or Coke develop viable products. They both offered direct store delivery (DSD), which provided greater control over shelf facings and reduced costs to retailers because DSD personnel stock the shelf, rotate product, attend to and set up displays, and monitor facings (a facing is one product width on the shelf regardless of the package's size) on a regular basis. This approach translated into fewer out-of-stocks and as a result fewer lost sales. Initial distribution was also accomplished faster through DSD. Direct sales personnel were in a store about three times a week; a food broker might be in the store only once a month and was responsible for a large number of products. Thus, interest and attention to a given product line may wane if a greater incentive is offered on another of their products. However, this problem can be circumvented by supplying enough business to the broker to make its very existence dependent on the manufacturer's business. Gatorade pursued this strategy whenever possible.

Because Gatorade had such a limited line of products and limited volume, management believed that it did not make economic sense to offer DSD. Gatorade sold approximately $600 million in product. Pepsi, on the other hand, sold syrup and licensed the name to bottlers that collectively did approximately $25 billion in business in a year. Management thought it would be difficult for Gatorade to be distributed along with other Quaker products, such as Ken-L Ration pet foods, because that would spread the Quaker personnel too thin. "They would have so many products that they would only be able to get finished with about two stores a day," commented Chris Nowokunski, Gatorade brand manager.

The shift in the balance of power from manufacturers to retailers in the food industry resulted in greater difficulty in introducing new products. "Slotting allowances" are fees charged by retailers for their shelf space. In effect, retailers are leasing shelf space to manufacturers for new products. Existing products are having to prove their value, resulting in almost continuous trade incentives (such as reduced price deals, display building contests and Gatorade cooler give-aways for store managers, and others) to maintain shelf space.

Pricing

In 1991, Gatorade pricing tended to be higher than 10-K, the only serious competitor, but with heavy in-store couponing, it was often less expensive. Gatorade's pricing strategy was in part designed to maintain a perception of quality. The use of in-store coupons promoted value because they brought Gatorade's cost below 10-K's but maintained a higher price. Although Gatorade set its price to be the quality brand, the company had no control over the price set by the retailer. Sometimes retailers set Gatorade's price low to act as a loss leader (low price on a product to induce shopping at that store). Exhibit 1.7 provides a price comparison of Gatorade and some of its competitors in various markets.

Promotion

Gatorade used a variety of promotional activities. The primary selling season was March through October; however, the heaviest promotion occurred from May to August. Advertising was designed to further strengthen Gatorade's posi-

EXHIBIT 1.7   Gatorade Price Comparisons in Selected Markets, February 1992

Brand/Package	Birmingham	Charlotte	Dallas	New Orleans	Tampa
Gatorade 32-oz	Hi $1.09 Lo .89 Avg .978	Hi $ .89 Lo .89 Avg .89	Hi $1.09 Lo .89 Avg .99	Hi $1.19 Lo .75 Avg .975	Hi $1.19 Lo .89 Avg 1.064
Gatorade 64-oz	Hi $2.25 Lo 1.89 Avg 1.99	Hi $1.89 Lo 1.89 Avg 1.89	Hi $2.35 Lo 2.09 Avg 2.22	Hi $2.49 Lo 1.79 Avg 2.055	Hi $1.98 Lo 1.75 Avg 1.87
10-K 32-oz	Hi $ .99 Lo .99 Avg .99[a]	Hi $ .99 Lo .99 Avg .99[a]	Hi $ .99 Lo .99 Avg .99[a]	Hi $ .99 Lo .72 Avg. .918	Hi $ .85 Lo .85 Avg .85[a]
10-K 64-oz	Hi $1.75 Lo 1.75 Avg 1.75[a]	Hi $1.97 Lo 1.59 Avg 1.78	n/a	Hi $2.39 Lo 1.74 Avg 1.93	Hi $1.77 Lo 1.77 Avg 1.77[a]
PowerBurst 32-oz	Hi $ .89 Lo .89 Avg .89[a]	Hi $ .95 Lo .95 Avg .95[a]	n/a[b]	n/a	Hi $1.08 Lo .69 Avg .93
Workout 16-oz	n/a	n/a	n/a	n/a	n/a
Pro-formance 1-liter	n/a	Hi $1.49 Lo 1.29 Avg 1.39	n/a	n/a	n/a
Pro Motion 32-oz	n/a	n/a	n/a	n/a	n/a
AllSport 32-oz	n/a	n/a	n/a	n/a	n/a
PowerAde 16-oz cup	n/a	n/a	n/a	n/a	n/a

Miscellaneous brands:

Enduro .5 liter	$ .75	Tampa
Daily's 1-qt	.59	Tampa, 2/$.89 Charlotte
Sports Shot 64-oz	1.50	Dallas
Quick Kick 2-liter	1.59	Dallas

[a] Only one store that was visited carried the package size and brand.

[b] The 64-oz size was available for $2.25.

n/a = not available in February 1992.

tion as the undisputed sports beverage leader. In 1989, commercials were aired during NBA games, major league baseball games, Atlantic Coast Conference (ACC) games, South Eastern Conference (SEC) games, and South West Conference (SWC) games. Prime-time television included *The Cosby Show, Wiseguy, The Wonder Years, thirtysomething*, and *Moonlighting*. Late night included David Letterman and Johnny Carson. In 1991, print ads ran in *Sports Illustrated, Inside Sports, Sporting News, Rolling Stone, GQ, Family Circle, Good Housekeeping, Better Homes & Gardens*, and *Parents* magazines. Free-standing inserts (FSIs) were often used in newspapers for coupon delivery.

Michael Jordan, basketball superstar, was featured in TV and print ads (see Exhibit 1.8). Gatorade was advertised during major collegiate and professional sporting events and on prime-time and late-night shows on network TV from April to August. During March and September, additional spots were purchased for the Sunbelt areas. Ads focused on product benefits and strong sports imagery. The TV plan reached over 95 percent of all households. Spots were primarily cast with men who were dressed in the clothing attributed to a particular sport. Models were attractive and athletic looking. The product appeared cold and refreshing—something to be gulped down, not sipped.

Print and billboards primarily reinforced these images. Because women do much of the buying, ads were placed on daytime TV and in women's magazines. The Gatorade Light campaign was targeted slightly more to female athletes than the traditional Gatorade ads. Full-season coverage targeted a growing Hispanic market and radio programming reached teens. In 1991, the advertising budget was approximately $31 million. The next closest competitor was 10-K, with $9 million in advertising.

Gatorade planned to increase its in-store presence and maintain shelf space with trade incentives and promotions in an effort to keep the competition out. Gatorade took advantage of its entrenched position and cost advantages while its competitors had to battle high costs of entry, such as slotting allowances (both 10-K and PowerBurst had to pay $1,500 in slotting allowances to each store for each item).

During the 1991 season, Gatorade was the official sports beverage of all major sports. Exhibit 1.9 summarizes the sponsorship activities.

Other promotional efforts were aimed at very aggressively maintaining outstanding retail conditions. The objective of the flurry of display activity was to increase shelf space within the juice aisle by adding a new section for Gatorade Light and reducing space devoted to competitors' beverages. Because 46 percent of Gatorade's sales were considered to be impulse purchases, displays were a critical part of the retail strategy. Regular displays were further enhanced by point-of-purchase (POP) signs, cards, and posters. Stores were encouraged to place coolers of iced units near doors or in heavily trafficked areas.

EXHIBIT 1.8 Gatorade Print Advertisement

After leading the league in scoring.

After taking the Bulls to the
Eastern Conference Championship.

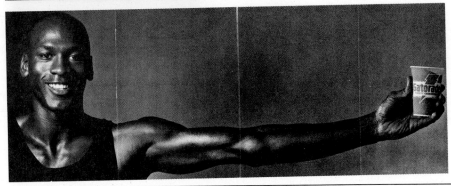

And after winning the NBA title,
what is there left to reach for?

EXHIBIT 1.9   Gatorade Sponsorships in 1991

National Football League

Sideline presence at all play-off, Super Bowl, and Pro Bowl games.
Sideline presence with 27 of 28 teams.

National Basketball Association

Continued sponsorship of the Gatorade Slam Dunk Championship.
Sideline presence with all teams.

Major League Baseball

Dugout presence at League Championship Series, World Series, and All-Star games.
Sponsorship of Home Run Derby on Gatorade All Star Day Workout Day.
Dugout presence with all teams.

PGA Tour/LPGA

Golf course presence at over 100 tournament events.
Junior golf clinics with PGA tour.

NASCAR

New sponsor of Daytona 500 qualifiers—Gatorade Twin 125s.
Continued sponsorship of Gatorade 200 and Gatorade Circle of Champions.

National Hockey League

Sideline presence at Stanley Cup.
Sideline presence with all clubs.

NCAA

Corporate partner of NCAA.
Individual sponsorships with many leading colleges and universities.

National Federation of High School Associations

Title sponsor of "High School Games of the Week" on Sports Channel America.
Official sports beverage of the federation.
First participant in the "National Sponsor of High School Sports" program.

Divisional Objectives

Each division of Quaker Oats was subject to company-wide goals and objectives. As one of Quaker's high-growth products (others were ready-to-eat and hot cereals, microwave meals, food service, and international operations), Gatorade played a major role in the company's effort to reach inflation-adjusted earnings growth of 7 percent per year, and a return on equity of 25 percent or more. Gatorade's goal, however, was to continue its growth of about 28 percent annually and to maintain its 91 percent market share. President Vituli stated, "The division intends to take a very aggressive approach and try things we've never done before. . . . Specifically that means increasing the frequency with which customers use the product, improving convenience, leading segmentation of the sports beverage category and increasing distribution of Gatorade to everywhere people get hot and thirsty."[7] Plans for 1991 called for $150 million in advertising plus merchandising expenditures, with the majority being spent on sports promotions and tie-ins.

Gatorade's strategic objectives included achieving high visibility and presence in order to establish Gatorade as the undisputed sports beverage leader, dominating sports beverage merchandising, and controling the sports beverage shelf sets (position on the shelf).

THE FUTURE PRESENTS CHALLENGES AND OPPORTUNITIES

The fitness trend that has driven growth in the isotonic category is expected to continue. The category is expected to reach $2 billion by the year 2000. Demographically, however, the isotonic market faces a decline in its traditional target ages of 12 to 34. The aging of the population will force reassessment of the targeted age group in order to continue growth. Opportunities may exist if aging Americans actively pursue better health through exercise and more active lives. The aging population is expected to fuel the growth of the sunbelt region, a factor that must be considered in Gatorade's marketing strategy. In addition, growing minority groups represent a highly concentrated market that should not be ignored. Estimates are that blacks and Hispanics will constitute nearly 25 percent of the U.S. population by the year 2000.

Timothy Ramey, analyst at County NatWest Securities USA, commented, "It's going to be a David vs. Goliath-type battle for Coke and Pepsi, but it's hard to see how over time Gatorade can avoid giving away a lot of this market." Michael Bellas, president of Beverage Marketing Corporation, made a similar comment: "The market is gearing up for a substantial battle. These are some big players looking at the category in a substantial way."[8]

[7] *Quaker Quarterly*, first quarter, 1991, p. 12.
[8] Julie Liesse and Patricia Winters, "Gatorade Set to Bench New Rivals," *Advertising Age*, March 19, 1990, p. 4.

CASE 2

Kodak Versus Fuji:
A Case of Japanese-American Strategic Interaction

"I wonder how Fuji will react," mused Frank Harris, analyst for Morris Stinson Brokers and a specialist on Kodak stock. He was referring to the planned introduction of Kodak's Photo CD, that came out in March 1992. Kodak's Photo CD was a system of electronic photography that allowed prints to be stored on a compact disk, later to be shown on a television or a computer.

For several years, Fuji and Kodak were very sensitive to each other's competitive moves, and particularly since Fuji started to gain headway in the United States with its bright green boxes of film. Harris noted, "After the 'Battle of the Blimps' anything is possible between these two firms."

MILESTONES IN THE KODAK-FUJI RIVALRY

When Fuji first began selling film in the United States Kodak did not take the competitor seriously. Kodak felt Fuji's film colors were unrealistically bright. But Fuji gained significant market share, reaping 10 percent of the U.S. market by 1990. The two most fascinating episodes of rivalry between these arch competitors could be labeled the "Battle of the MBAs" and the "Battle of the Blimps."

Battle of the MBAs

The University of Rochester is located in Kodak's hometown of Rochester, New York. The university received a significant portion of its endowment from George Eastman, Kodak's founder, before he committed suicide. In the 1980s and early 1990s, Kodak pledged $5 million to the university, the majority of which was targeted for the William E. Simon School of Business. In addition, Kodak sent scores of employees to the Simon School's MBA program.

To the shock and dismay of Kodak, Tsuneo Sakai was accepted in the Simon School's MBA program for the September 1987 semester. It happened that Mr.

This case was prepared by H. Donald Hopkins as a basis for class discussion rather than to illustrate either effective or ineffective handling of an administrative situation. Used with permission from H. Donald Hopkins.

Sakai was an employee of the Fuji Photo Film Company. His position was that of planner of new imaging products.

It was later reported that Kodak officials persuaded the university to rescind its acceptance of Mr. Sakai. Instead, the university arranged for him to attend the Massachusetts Institute of Technology's business school. Apparently, Kodak feared that confidential information might be conveyed to him during classroom discussions. The university, on the other hand, feared that Kodak would withdraw "a significant number of students" from the MBA program if Mr. Sakai did attend.

Reacting to criticism of this decision, the university decided to readmit Mr. Sakai. Kodak's chairman at the time, Colby Chandler, commented, "Our actions are seen by some as an infringement upon academic integrity which was certainly not our intent."[1]

A final chapter in this academic war happened in 1988 when Fuji announced a scholarship at the Rochester Institute of Technology (RIT) for photography students. Kodak is a large contributor to RIT, having given between $4 million and $8 million over the past 10 years. The Fuji scholarship was to be devoted solely to photography and thus would be the first of its kind at the school. A Fuji spokeswoman said they picked RIT "because of its reputation, not because it was in Rochester [home of Kodak]."

Battle of the Blimps

In the 1980s, a strange air war occurred in the skies over Tokyo. Two large blimps, one bright green, the other yellow, fought for air supremacy. This battleground was a new theater for an undeclared war pitting the two largest film companies against each other.

Kodak, after observing the green Fuji blimp keeping watch over sporting events in the United States and Europe, decided to imitate it and use that same tactic in Japan. What ensued could be characterized as blimp "dogfights." Kodak apparently escalated the rivalry by flying their yellow blimp in sight of Fuji's Tokyo headquarters. Fuji executives were amazed to be able to look out the window and observe their arch rival's name overhead.

Several months later, in November, the Fuji and Kodak blimps had a "dogfight" over nearby sporting events. Fuji was sponsoring a baseball series between American and Japanese all-stars, while Kodak was sponsoring a judo tournament a short distance away. The manager of Fuji's advertising department, Hidenobu Miyata, complained that the Kodak blimp was perilously near Fuji's blimp. He claimed that the yellow aircraft refused to comply with requests to retreat. Mr. Miyata said, "I think they were being a little too aggressive not to back off. We felt like Kodak was up for a fight."[2]

[1] "Fuji Employee Is Accepted as University Shifts Stance," *Wall Street Journal*, September 14, 1987, p. 16.
[2] Karl Schoenberger, "In Skies over Tokyo, Kodak and Fuji Fight Battle of the Blimps," *Wall Street Journal*, December 30, 1986, p. A1.

Kodak, on the other hand, accused Fuji of intentionally scheduling its blimp's flight over the baseball series to compete with Kodak's blimp. Toshio Nakano, manager of public relations for Kodak Japan, said, "So why did they wait until now? I don't call it a gentleman's act. It's nasty. It seems to me this is a hit-and-run operation on their part."[3]

Still later, in January 1987, Kodak tweaked Fuji's nose further by sending out its customary Japanese New Year's greeting cards showing the Kodak blimp with Mt. Fuji in the background. The blimp battle apparently had its opening salvo when Fuji outbid Kodak and spent $7 million to become the official film of the 1984 Los Angeles Olympics. The Fuji blimp was flown over the Olympic grounds. Kodak responded by buying immense periods of commercial time on the network that carried the games.

"If you watched the Olympics on American TV, you never saw the Fuji blimp," said William Reyea, a securities analyst in Tokyo. "It was part of the contract when they bought 102 ads."[4] A Kodak spokesman denied this. Kodak was the official film for the 1988 Olympics in Seoul and stationed its blimp overhead.

Me-Too Tactics

Regardless of the origin of the Battle of the Blimps, the Fuji surprise at the 1984 Olympics led Kodak from complacency to obsession. Fuji increased its market share in the United States from 2 percent to 10 percent in photographic film and paper. Much of that increase had not come at the expense of Kodak, but from weaker firms, such as 3M and Agfa-Gavaert, which Fuji specifically targeted to avoid making Kodak feel threatened.

Kodak has kept a constant eye on Fuji's moves and countermoves. Researchers in Rochester painstakingly analyzed Fuji films to understand their attributes. "It's me-too technology," said one researcher with apparent disdain. "We do what Fuji does. We're obsessed with Fuji."[5]

Supersaturated colors were one attribute of Fuji film for years. Kodak thought the colors were unrealistically bright. However, to their dismay they found that customers liked Fuji's film. In 1986, Kodak introduced its VR-G film series that offered colors just as bright.

Battle of the Throwaways

Kodak and Fuji announced at almost the same time, during February 1987, plans to introduce throwaway cameras in the United States later that year. Kodak, however, beat Fuji to the punch when it announced its camera one day before Fuji had scheduled a news conference for the same purpose. Kodak's

---

[3] Ibid.
[4] Ibid., p. A12.
[5] Leslie Helm and Barbara Buell, "Kodak Fights Fuji with 'Me-Too' Tactics," *Business Week*, February 23, 1987, p. 138.

camera was called the "Fling," while Fuji's was called the "Fujicolor Quick Snap." For both versions, the camera was sent in its entirety to a photofinisher instead of just the film.

Kodak apparently learned the importance of timing at the hand of Fuji. In a previous episode of one-upmanship or "being quicker on the draw" in 1983, Fuji stole Kodak's thunder by introducing a new series of films immediately before Kodak did likewise.

Thrust and Parry

After Fuji's thrust into the United States, Kodak decided in 1984 to make a strategic parry into the $1.5 billion Japanese market for film and paper. Actually Kodak had been in Japan for many years, but the company just had never given it much attention. From 1984 to 1990, Kodak spent an estimated $500 million on the Japanese photographic film and papers markets. The company created a new subsidiary for Japan and increased employment from 12 to 4,500. Yet some argued that Kodak was too late in emphasizing the Japanese market.

In Japan, Kodak had to contend with Fuji's entrenched position and dominant technical prowess. Fuji matched Kodak on quality, and surpassed it in high-speed color films. In addition, Fuji had a dominant position in major Japanese film processing labs, where it controlled about 250 labs to Kodak's fewer than 150 in 1985. These labs are the main end-users of photographic paper.

Kodak's drive into Japan was partly an attempt to keep up with Japanese R&D activities by developing joint ventures with Japanese partners, as well as with its own R&D center and technical assistance center for helping customers. For example, Kodak bought 10 percent of a 35-mm Japanese camera maker, and its Verbatim floppy disk subsidiary operated a joint venture with Mitsubishi Chemical Industries.

A second element of Kodak's strategy in Japan was to try to gain greater control over the distribution of its own products. Kodak purchased Kusuda Business Machines, a company that had been marketing Kodak's micrographic and business imaging systems in Japan. Film sales in Japan were handled by a Japanese firm, Nagase & Co. In 1986, Kodak increased its control over distribution and marketing by forming a new joint venture company called Kodak-Nagase.

Kodak was successful in getting space in the 30,000 to 60,000 camera stores that sell most of Japan's film. However, it was unsuccessful in getting into the mom-and-pop stores that can afford to carry only one brand of film. That one brand was usually in a green box.

The Japanese rail network (which had thousands of small kiosks that typically carry only Fuji film) was especially hard for Kodak to crack. To get into these kiosks, Kodak would have to work with up to four agents including the kiosk operator, real estate agent, and wholesaler. Usually, regardless of Kodak's pitch, Fuji was given a chance to match or beat the offer.

One of Kodak's new products introduced in Japan to combat Fuji's lead in film processing and paper sales was the mini-lab. These were targeted to chip away at Fuji's 100-plus advantage in large labs. Fuji fought back by offering bigger enlargement sizes than the mini-labs. Recently Fuji introduced its own mini-labs.

The only two times Kodak was able to directly take shelf space away from Fuji was when they had products which were unmatched by their arch rival. These products were the waterproof disposable camera and panoramic disposable camera. Kodak apparently had the technology for the panoramic camera for years but did not see a market for it. Kodak-Japan pushed the product, since the Japanese are known to take a lot of pictures of large groups. William Jack, vice president of Kodak-Japan, noted, "When the Japanese have golf outings, they often want everyone lined up for a group picture, and getting everyone in with a conventional camera is quite difficult."[6] The waterproof disposable was a hit with Japanese youth who love to snorkel. The disposable cameras have been the central thrust of Kodak's youth-oriented advertising in Japan.

On the promotional front, besides the battle of the blimps, Kodak beat Fuji in the "battle of the neon signs." Its victory came with the construction of a gigantic yellow sign that took years to finish. It is located at the Japanese equivalent of Times Square. In terms of price, Kodak was more willing to cut prices in Japan than in the United States, where it generally sold at a premium.

Kodak claimed its market share has gone up in the amateur color film market in Japan. According to *Japan Economic Journal (JEJ)*, however, Kodak had 10 percent of the color film market in 1989 versus 13 percent in 1987. *JEJ* also reported that Fuji had gone from 71 percent to 73 percent and Konica from 16 percent to 17 percent during the same period. However, Kodak's sales of all products in Japan increased 600 percent, to about $1.3 billion during the same period.

THE U.S. PHOTOGRAPHIC MARKET

Overall market growth in the United States was sluggish and was expected to remain slow for the foreseeable future. Information about the industry is hard to obtain because it is so concentrated. Growth rates are provided in Exhibit 2.1. Additional information is given in Appendix 2.A.

Slow growth rates and significant overcapacity put pressure on prices. Fuji added film production lines to its large paper factory in Tilburg, the Netherlands, and built its first manufacturing plant in the United States in South Carolina in 1990 (although this plant initially was scheduled to produce sensitized plates for offset printing, not film or paper, it was expected to add these if Fuji's sales in the United States warranted expansion). Fuji was not the first Japanese photographic

---

[6] Clare Ansberry and Masayoshi Kanabayashi, "Kodak Bid to Sell More Color Film to Japanese Remains Out of Focus," *Wall Street Journal*, December 7, 1990, p. B7.

EXHIBIT 2.1   Profile of the Photography Industry (In millions)

	1984	1985	1986	1987	1988
Still Camera Sales (Units)	17.0	17.8	16.4	18.7	17.8
Film Sales (Rolls)	610	667	694	781	811
Photofinishing in Dollars	$3,500	$3,700	$4,000	$4,400	$4,800

Source: *Wall Street Journal,* December 7, 1990, p. B-7.

firm to build a plant in the United States. Konica built a U.S. manufacturing plant for photographic paper in Greensboro, North Carolina, in 1988. In addition, Polaroid increased the competition for shelf space with its entry in 1989 into conventional photography with a film called "One-Film." This film was designed to be an all-purpose film that would eliminate the need for consumers to choose among the vast array of film types available. Although it was well received by large U.S. retail chains, neither Kodak nor Fuji has responded.

Other film competitors in the United States include Fotomat (Konishiroko), 3M's Scotch brand, Agfa-Gevaert AG of West Germany, and several private label brands. GAF withdrew several years ago due to declining margins. Kodak held about 80 percent of the film market and Fuji about 10 percent.

KODAK: THE GREAT YELLOW FATHER

Kodak was described as large, lumbering, elephantine, and bureaucratic. For its traditionally paternalistic employment practices, it was sometimes referred to as the "Great Yellow Father." Kodak, along with Xerox, dominated the upstate New York town of Rochester, where its headquarters and plants spread over a 3,000-acre area.

George Eastman, Kodak's founder, sold his first camera in 1883. Kodak was the first fully integrated photographic company in the world. Its motto was, "You press the button and we do the rest." Although Kodak's share of the film market was about 80 percent in 1990, its share of film processing was only about 15 percent because of a 1954 U.S. Justice Department consent decree that required the company to unbundle the sale of film and film development. Previously, when a customer bought Kodak film the price of development was part of the price of the film. When a roll of film was completed it would be sent by the customer to a Kodak processing lab at no extra cost. After the 1954 consent decree, independent processing labs developed rapidly to account for 85 percent of film processing. However, if the paper, processing equipment, and chemicals that Kodak sold to independent developers were included, Kodak's share was close to 50 percent.

Kodak's control of the industry as a whole grew from its leadership in film technology. Of all its photographic products, film was its premier profit maker. It was only recently that a broad scope competitor such as Fuji had been able to challenge it in this area. Previously, Kodak had almost total mastery of the photographic industry and kept ahead of every other competitor in virtually every dimension of photography. In part it was due to the tied-in nature of film and processing prior to the 1954 consent decree that eliminated the motivation of other companies to pursue innovations in color film technology.

Following the consent decree, other film manufacturers have had more incentive but still had trouble making inroads, as Kodak was an aggressive competitor. It would hold new innovations in reserve until a competitor would come to the market with a product it had spent vast sums to develop. Kodak would then introduce what it had been saving in reserve and wipe out the competitor's product and sunk investment. For example, in the early 1960s a joint venture between DuPont and Bell & Howell to develop a color film research program totally failed. In every instance where the partnership was able to improve its film, Kodak's film would miraculously incorporate the same improvements. In 1961, when the venture decided to introduce a new film based on tens of millions of dollars in research, Kodak retaliated with Kodachrome II, a far better quality film. The joint venture film was withdrawn before it reached the market.

For some time, competitors tried to compete with Kodak by charging lower prices. However, this tactic largely failed because consumers seemed unwilling to accept film that might be of lower quality. Fuji was able to overcome this perception somewhat by stressing a quality brand image charging slightly lower prices. Other competitors were mostly niche players that focused on a small group of consumers who wished to avoid supersaturated colors, a very high resolution, or the nonexotic image of Kodak. Polaroid's niche was instant photography, and Fotomat's niche was speedy film processing.

Systems Approach

Kodak's emphasis in the photographic market utilized a "systems approach" beginning with the highly successful Instamatic camera to the disc camera. A system was a unique film format packaged in a cartridge or magazine compatible with only cameras designed specifically for that film format.

Some of these Kodak systems were major successes. The Instamatic sold 10 million cameras in the first 26 months after its introduction in 1963. In 1972, Kodak introduced a smaller version of the Instamatic called the Pocket Instamatic. It has been estimated that by 1975 Kodak sold 60 million Instamatics, while competitors sold just 10 million clones. The company reinforced its dominance in the industry by surprising competitors with radical changes in camera design and film requirements. Others were required, often on short notice, to invest heavily in complex production equipment to remain competitive. For this reason Kodak rarely announced product developments ahead of time. They preferred to surprise their competitors and retain a monopoly on a new system until competitors caught up. Apparently, this was the concern when the Fuji employee was accepted at the University of Rochester.

To deflect criticism and possible antitrust action, Kodak began licensing its systems. Realistically, however, the main motive for licensing was that it increased the number of cameras that could use Kodak's highly profitable films.

Not all of Kodak's systems have been successful. Kodak's disc camera, introduced in 1982, was a disappointment. The graininess of the photographs it produced apparently left consumers dissatisfied. The disc camera sold poorly in Europe and Japan, where photographers were used to the high resolution of 35-mm photos. It seemed unlikely that the disc system would provide the 8- to 10-year life cycle of healthy sales that other products, such as the Instamatic, had. It was unlikely that Kodak would recover its development costs, estimated at $300 million. In fact, Kodak announced in 1988 it was suspending production of the disc camera.

Kodak's run at the camcorder video market was also a disappointment. In 1984, Kodak teamed up with Matsushita Electric Industrial Company to market its 8-mm video camera. It was billed as the "world's finest commercial 8-mm camcorder." It was lighter and more compact than camcorders already on the market but required narrower tape. Thus, it was considered a pioneering effort. However, the product ultimately failed; some analysts blamed outdated camera designs supplied by Matsushita.

Then there was Kodak's instant camera system, announced on April 20, 1976. Kodak explained that its camera would go on sale in Canada in May and in the United States in July. Kodak's system was billed as "completely new" compared to Polaroid's offering. It required many more components to manufacture than Polaroid's cameras. Polaroid filed a patent infringement suit at 4:59 P.M. on April 26, 1976. Polaroid ultimately prevailed in this suit, and Kodak was required to pay a large fine ($873.2 million) and withdraw from the instant photography business. They were also required to give the purchasers of the Kodak instant camera a refund, as film would no longer be available.

Prior to the judgment, however, Kodak had been disappointed with the instant photography sales. It was a much smaller market than management anticipated. What appeared to possibly be a replacement for conventional photography turned out to be a novelty or niche product.

Kodak's intention was to be the "world's best in both conventional and electronic imaging. . . . We now have in place the strategic architecture for managing the alliance of chemical-based and electronic imaging, technology centers for development of core product platforms, and an international organization providing a fully global reach."[7] Kodak is in four business segments—photography, copiers, drugs, and chemicals. The size of each segment can be assessed in Exhibit 2.2. International sales in 1990 were 46 percent of total sales. In an independent survey that ranked the best-known brands, Kodak ranked fifth in the United States, Japan, and Europe, and fourth overall.

[7] Kodak *Annual Report*, 1990, pp. 3, 10.

EXHIBIT 2.2   Industry Statistics for SIC code 3861ᵃ—Photographic Equipment and Supplies

Year/Source	Number of Firms	Value Added	Materials	Shipments
1988/ASM	n/a	14,223.2	6,638.0	20,545.8
1987/Census	719	12,908.0	6,233.5	19,240.5
1986/ASM	n/a	12,335.9	6,110.5	18,580.4
1985/ASM	n/a	12,257.4	5,890.1	18,114.4
1984/ASM	n/a	12,960.9	5,682.4	18,701.9
1983/ASM	n/a	11,654.7	5,887.0	17,366.3
1982/Census	723	10,859.5	5,859.7	17,037.5
1981/ASM	n/a	11,199.2	5,902.3	16,927.3
1980/ASM	n/a	9,930.8	6,199.8	15,867.0
1979/ASM	n/a	8,812.6	4,698.5	13,410.2
1978/ASM	n/a	7,837.8	3,747.5	11,535.9
1977/Census	700	6,728.8	3,236.0	9,933.2
1976/ASM	n/a	6,077.4	2,914.7	8,844.5
1975/ASM	n/a	5,177.0	2,443.4	7,627.0
1974/ASM	n/a	5,075.0	2,565.5	7,493.4
1973/ASM	n/a	4,735.6	1,821.3	6,435.0
1972/Census	554	4,087.9	1,487.9	5,623.9

Legend

ASM = *Annual Survey of Manufactures*
Census = *Census of Manufactures*
Number of Firms = number of firms operating during year
n/a = not available
Value Added = shipments minus material and payroll in millions of dollars
Materials = cost of materials consumed in millions of dollars
Shipments = total value of shipments in millions of dollars

ᵃ Figures on SIC industry 3861—photographic equipment and supplies—are given in Exhibit 2.2. This category is defined and described as follows by the Department of Commerce:

> This industry is made up of establishments primarily engaged in manufacturing: (1) photographic apparatus, equipment, parts, attachments, and accessories, such as still and motion projection apparatus; photocopy and microfilm equipment; blueprinting and diazotype (white printing) apparatus and equipment; and other photographic equipment; and (2) sensitized film, paper, cloth and plates, and prepared photographic chemicals for use therein. . . .

> Establishments in virtually all industries ship secondary products as well as products primary to the industry to which they are classified and have some miscellaneous receipts, such as resales and contract receipts. Industry 3861 shipped $15.0 billion of photographic equipment and supplies products considered primary to the industry [in 1987], $1.2 billion of secondary products, and had $3.0 billion of miscellaneous receipts, resales, and contract work. Thus, the ratio of primary products to the total of both secondary and primary products shipped by establishments in the industry was 93 percent (specialization ratio).

Kodak's strengths were described in its 1990 *Annual Report* as follows: "Organic chemistry, imaging, and color form the basis of the company's leadership in photography. These technologies have led to new initiatives in other fields of endeavor such as pharmaceuticals. As diverse as Kodak may appear on the surface, each of its businesses is a natural outgrowth of these core strengths."[8]

One recent initiative was the new plant built by Eastman Chemical Company in Kingsport, Tennessee, which would supply 100 percent of the company's need for acetic anhydride, a petroleum-based chemical that is a primary ingredient for the base material for photographic film.

Partly because of the problems previously discussed, profits at Kodak started sagging in the early 1980s. Financial data are provided in Exhibit 2.3. As a result, Kodak tried to cut costs and increase productivity. Employment was

EXHIBIT 2.3   Kodak Financials (In millions of dollars)

	1986	1987	1988	1989	1990
Income Statement Data					
Sales	$11,550	$13,305	$17,034	$18,398	$18,908
Earnings	724	2,078	2,812	1,591	2,844
Earnings before Income Taxes	598	1,984	2,236	925	1,257
Net Earnings	374	1,178	1,397	529	703
Return on Sales	3.2%	8.9%	8.2%	2.9%	3.7%
Balance Sheet Data					
Current Assets	$ 5,857	$ 6,791	$ 8,684	$ 8,591	$ 8,608
Properties at Cost	12,919	13,789	15,667	16,774	17,648
Accumulated Depreciation	6,643	7,126	7,654	8,146	8,670
Total Assets	12,994	14,698	22,964	23,652	24,125
Current Liabilities	3,811	4,140	5,850	6,573	7,163
Long-Term Borrowings	981	2,382	7,779	7,376	6,989
Shareholders' Equity	6,388	6,013	6,780	6,642	6,737
Supplemental Information					
Sales—Imaging	$ 8,352	$ 6,206	$ 6,642	$ 6,998	$ 7,128
Information		3,494	3,937	4,200	4,140
Chemicals	2,378	2,635	3,123	3,522	3,588
Health	1,056	1,206	3,597	4,009	4,349
R&D Expenditures	$ 1,059	$ 992	$ 1,147	$ 1,253	$ 1,329
Employees in United States	83,600	81,800	87,900	82,850	80,350
Employees Worldwide	121,450	124,400	145,300	137,750	134,450

Notes: 1990 earnings before income taxes reflect $888 million for litigation judgment, which reduced net earnings by $564 million.

1989 earnings reflect restructuring costs of $875 million, which reduced net earnings by $549 million.

Source: Kodak *Annual Report,* 1990.

[8] Ibid., p. 4.

reduced to 121,500 in 1986 from about 146,500 in 1983. This happened despite Kodak's virtually guaranteed lifetime employment policies that led to its being called the Great Yellow Father. Kodak profit margins had declined from 15.7 percent in 1972 to 10.7 percent in 1982. Some of this was the result of Japanese price competition; however, the advent of video and Kodak's own failure in video contributed to the decline.

Walter Fallon retired as chairman in June 1983. He was heralded as the man who made the elephant dance, but of the four major product lines introduced while Fallon was calling the shots, only the copier business has done well. Ektaprint copiers have done well at the top of the copier market, where Xerox is dominant. These high-speed, volume copiers typically sold for $75,000 to $125,000. The company's Ektaplus 7016 copier/printer was the only small-volume copier manufactured in the United States. Fallon's failures included the Kodamatic Instant camera, the disc camera, and the Ektachem 400, a blood analysis machine that proved to be unreliable.

Fallon was reported to have pounded his desk when he heard that Fuji had won sponsorship of the 1984 Olympics. Later, to become more cost competitive, he centralized some manufacturing in Rochester just as the strong dollar wiped out the resulting productivity gains.

Fallon was succeeded by Colby Chandler, who initiated corporatewide strategic planning. In addition, he created a marketing intelligence group and gave the marketing area a stronger voice in what has traditionally been a technically dominated company.

Kodak moved into electronics in a big way. To help in this effort, it acquired a small California company called Spin Physics in 1972. Spin specialized in recording heads for high-density data storage.

In 1982, Kodak was surprised when Sony introduced its Mavica camera, a "filmless" video still camera that displayed pictures immediately on TV. However, the pictures produced were fuzzy because of the small number of pixels (280,000 versus 4 million in the Instamatic), and it was a failure. However, Kodak was shocked by the prospect of photos that could be displayed on a screen and printed out on hard copies followed by erasing and reusing the tape. This led Kodak to do what it almost never does. The following October, Kodak demonstrated a product in development—a video display unit permitting film negatives to appear in color on TV. The film had to be developed and could not be erased. This was an inferior product to Sony's but in effect said to others: Think twice before marketing filmless still photography products.

With its move into electronics, Kodak was competing in areas where it was not the leader, did not have the technical advantage, and did not have cost leadership. And in some of these areas it bumped heads with arch rival Fuji. Fuji sold copiers, videotapes, and computer floppy disks. Kodak, through its Verbatim floppy disk subsidiary, competed against Fuji. In fact, in 1988 Kodak lodged an unfair trading claim against Fuji and others with the International Trade Commission. Kodak charged that Fuji, Sony, and Hitachi charged 40 percent to 60 percent less for floppy disks in the United States than they did in Japan.

Kodak moved into a totally different area when it acquired the Sterling Drug Company for $5.1 billion in 1988. Previously the company had established its own drug R&D lab in Philadelphia; however, prior to the acquisition no products had been readied for the market. The potential fit between chemical-based drug research and film research seemed to be one argument for the move. Yet this large acquisition had the danger of diverting too much attention and too many resources away from photography.

Sterling's best-selling product was Omnipaque. According to Kodak, it was the number one pharmaceutical product purchased by hospitals in the United States. The product allowed for the contrasting of body organs and blood vessels for X-rays and CAT scanning. Sterling had joined with a French company, Sanofi, in a joint venture to improve its global reach. Also, Sterling broke ground in 1990 for a new $300 million R&D center in Upper Providence Township, Pennsylvania, that employed 1,200.

In the past Kodak had problems accepting non-Kodak corporate cultures. According to Al Edwards, a former vice president of Atex (a manufacturer of electronic publishing systems acquired by Kodak in 1981), "The people at Kodak are hard working but bureaucratic. They do not understand the competitive nature of computer technology. You sometimes have to react to the marketplace on a weekly basis. At Kodak, if you came up with an idea, it would be five years before you saw the product."[9] And, of course, Kodak was the company that passed up an invention called xerography, which was then developed by a small Rochester company called Haloid (now Xerox).

Gerald Zornow, Kodak chairman from 1972 to 1976, did not believe that outsiders could adjust to the Kodak culture. "They tried some people from the outside before and it never worked out," he said. "Kodak is like an old family that grows up together, and it is tough for outsiders to fit in."[10]

A critical concern affecting the development of electronic products, such as the photo CD, was the ability of glacial, slow, elephantine, stodgy, stuffy, conservative Kodak in cold, gray, unhip Rochester to attract "notoriously disloyal electronic cowboys who thrive best in Silicon Valley."[11] Kodak had trouble holding onto managers with a background in electronics.

Kay Whitmore, who was promoted to chairman on June 1, 1990, was enthusiastic about the prospects for Kodak's Photo CD. Photo CD was a product developed in reaction to Sony's Mavica (Canon, Toshiba, and Fuji came out with a similar product, though Toshiba and Fuji used a "memory card" rather than a floppy disk). Kodak's initial response was, "Holy cow, let's circle the wagons,"

[9] Thomas Moore, "Embattled Kodak Enters the Electronic Age," *Fortune*, August 22, 1983, p. 128.
[10] Ibid.
[11] Ibid.

noted William Fowbie, vice president and general manager for consumer imaging projects. The second reaction was Photo CD. To avoid the bureaucracy of Kodak, Photo CD functions as an independent business. With Photo CD, introduced in March 1992, photographers snapped pictures using *film* as they always have, but when the film was sent to the lab they would have the option of storing their photos on CD. Viewing what is on the CD would require a TV and a special player made by NV Philips. Photographers could then enlarge or crop their photos and return edited photos to the lab to obtain prints.

In uncharacteristic style, Kodak announced Photo CD long before its actual introduction date. The early announcement was intended to give warning to any firms developing electronic photographic products. That warning was, in effect, that Kodak, which frequently sets the standard in photographic products, was developing an electronic camera with high resolution that used film. The fact that this product used film, while the first venture into electronic photography, Sony's Mavica, did not, was obviously important to Kodak, the king of film. But the early announcement also had another effect. It gave Fuji, another company sensitive to filmless substitutes, plenty of warning.

Many analysts expressed concern about Kodak's obsession with Fuji: "Kodak is so focused on Fuji it may ignore other important current or potential rivals." New competition from Japanese consumer electronics firms and Polaroid might be a concern in the future.

FUJI PHOTO FILM COMPANY: A PROFILE

Fuji was moving in the same direction as Kodak by emphasizing electronics. It was aware that electronic, filmless photography was potentially the next era in photography. Fuji learned that where Kodak goes, it must follow. But sometimes, when it knew where Kodak was headed, it moved faster and beat them to the punch.

In 1967, Fuji spent millions of dollars designing a new 8-mm home movie system. Fuji was set to announce its new system when Kodak "knocked them out of the water." Kodak released its Super 8, a camera with a larger film format that could not use Fuji film. Fuji junked its product.

It was at this point that Fuji decided it would be a follower to Kodak's lead. A prime consideration in its move into the United States was to avoid gaining the attention or retaliation of Kodak. Instead, it wanted to focus on taking market share away from weaker competitors such as 3M.

Fuji knew it had a problem in the United States. Kodak was too entrenched to be beat in the way the Japanese later beat U.S. firms in TVs, stereos, radios, and autos. But similar to many other Japanese companies, Fuji could subsidize the attack on the U.S. market through its dominance of the Japanese market. The latest estimate showed Fuji to have 73 percent market share in Japan. Fuji decided to target a 15 percent share in the United States, but the company made a critical miscalculation. Kodak not only noticed Fuji, they became obsessed with Fuji.

The elevation of Minoru Ohnishi over many more senior managers marked the beginning of the reign of the youngest president in the history of Fuji. With his promotion the company sought new avenues of growth given the highly saturated, slow-growth Japanese photographic market. Ohnishi moved Fuji into the United States in 1964. Under his leadership the conservative company began to move faster in the marketplace. For example, Fuji was first to market a film compatible with Kodak's disc system. Fuji engineers produced it in just eight months.

Fuji, founded in 1936, was in a variety of businesses including cameras, medical equipment, copiers, bicycles, and videotape. Film was its main business, however; 50.5 percent of its sales came from film in 1990, 10.2 percent from magnetic products (videotape, audio tape, memory tape, and floppy disks), and 39.4 percent from commercial products (printing, medical, office, and motion picture equipment and supplies). Overseas sales represented 38.3 percent of net sales in 1990. Part of Fuji's overseas strategy is what it called "globalization through localization," which meant to compete globally but produce locally.

Despite the various battles in the aerial and academic arenas, Fuji never went looking for a fight. "Fuji is gun-shy; they've found they can live happily under the Kodak umbrella," said analyst Reginald Duquesnoy of Merrill Lynch. "Both Fuji and Kodak [traditionally] make fat margins, and they're not in the business of destroying that profitability."[12]

The goal of 15 percent in the United States was, according to Ohnishi, a long-term goal to be reached in a gradual, nonthreatening way. This gun-shyness was because almost every time the challenger (Fuji) attacked the leader, the challenger had its nose bloodied. One example occurred in 1977—Fuji reduced the price of its print paper to undercut Kodak. Kodak matched it on price and then mounted an aggressive marketing program. As another example, in 1983, Fuji brought out a new high-resolution film in two speeds. Kodak introduced a similar product without missing a beat, but one-upped Fuji by offering a high-resolution film in four speeds.

Fuji pursued a growth strategy with two elements: product diversification and increased emphasis on foreign sales. By 1991, the company had gained a 50 percent share of the photographic market in Asia and 15 percent in Europe. On a worldwide basis, Fuji had about a 15 percent market share. Diversification for Fuji mostly meant a search for niche products in electronics. Ohnishi said that he will "only enter areas where Fuji can modify and improve on products [and] develop hybrids that combine electronics and photography. We want a small part of the large pies."[13]

---

[12] Johnathon Greenberg, "If Everyone Else Makes Videotape, Why Doesn't Kodak?" *Forbes*, November 22, 1982, p. 56.

[13] "Fuji Photo: Sharpening Its Image in the U.S. as It Develops New Products," *Business Week*, October 24, 1983, pp. 88, 92.

Fuji was recognized for its expertise and quality in the "imaging industry." For example, in a joint venture with Xerox it had about 40 percent of the copier market in Japan as of 1981.

Fuji was a heavy spender on R&D, which resulted in many new products. These products included office and medical equipment, semiconductors, and home computers, all areas that are growing faster than the photographic market. Fuji had a highly flexible work force. Its employees were able to move between plants making different products as demand required. It operated one of the lowest-cost videotape plants in the world in Odawara, Japan. Its first videotape plant in the United States started production in 1991. Companywide, Fuji's sales per employee almost doubled to $157,000 per worker from 1978 to 1982. Fuji, with traditional profit margins around 10 percent, is one of the most profitable firms in Japan. Fuji's financial statements are given in Exhibit 2.4.

When it started in the United States in 1964, Fuji began as a private label film supplier. In 1972, it began selling under its own name but was marketed as a promotional item free with the purchase of Japanese cameras.

In 1978, given the highly saturated photographic market in Japan, Fuji decided to be a little more aggressive in the United States. It expanded distribution beyond camera stores and emphasized food stores, drug stores, and discount stores.

EXHIBIT 2.4   Fuji Photo Film Company Financial (In millions of U.S. dollars)

	1986	1987	1988	1989	1990
Income Statement Data					
Net sales: Domestic	$2,905.0	$3,633.4	$4,459.1	$4,416.2	$ 4,528.5
Overseas	1,602.5	2,002.2	2,379.3	2,312.3	2,815.7
Total	4,507.5	5,635.6	6838.4	6,728.5	7,344.3
Cost of Sales	2,530.7	3,067.8	3,740.0	3,577.5	3,862.6
Operating Expenses					
Selling, General, and Administrative	937.7	1,232.0	1,531.2	1,615.1	1,845.8
R&D	263.3	346.8	429.4	411.5	410.6
Interest and Dividend Income	121.1	144.4	176.0	198.5	268.4
Interest Expense	58.0	63.6	75.7	89.4	136.9
Earnings before Interest and Taxes	803.1	1,030.9	1,219.9	1,212.7	1,351.2
Net Income	$ 369.3	$ 497.8	$ 640.0	$ 603.6	$ 622.6
Balance Sheet Data					
Total Assets	$5,631.9	$7,234.0	$9,140.1	$9,683.7	$10,547.8
Long-Term Debt	205.2	192.9	357.4	503.1	691.5
Total Liabilities	2,328.4	2,872.5	3,529.2	3,749.7	4,244.2
Shareholders' Equity	$3,303.5	$4,361.5	$5,610.9	$5,934.0	$ 6,303.7
Supplemental Information					
Number of Employees	17,180	17,703	18,195	19,677	21,946
Exchange Rate (yen/dollar)	168	145	128	138	145

Source: Fuji Photo Film, Co. *Annual Report, 1990.*

Fuji has tried to change its image by going after the professional market. It introduced a line of professional films and advertised to this market in photo trade books. The professional market is about as large as the amateur market, since professionals are "heavy users"—shooting perhaps 30 to 50 rolls per assignment.

Despite the desire for growth, Fuji emphasized the desire to avoid threatening Kodak. It targeted weaker firms such as 3M, Europe's Agfa-Gevaert, and Japan's Konishiroko. "We are a piquant but small Japanese pepper," says President Ohnishi. "If I were Kodak, I wouldn't worry about us at all."[14]

APPENDIX 2.A THE PHOTOGRAPHIC INDUSTRY

About 17.8 million cameras were sold to U.S. dealers in 1988 (latest available), down 4.8 percent from the year before. Demand continued to be strong for lens-shutter 35-mm cameras, which accounted for more than half of industry dollar volume. . . . Gains for lens-shutter cameras have come largely at the expense of higher-end 35-mm single-lens reflex (SLRs) and lower and disc cameras. Unit sales of the sophisticated and expensive SLRs fell about 6 percent in 1988, to approximately 1.5 million, accounting for only 8.4 percent of industry unit volume, versus 14.7 percent of that volume four years earlier. However, SLRs represented 23.6 percent of the dollar value of industry camera sales in 1988, reflecting their higher price. The rate of decline in SLR unit sales slowed in 1988, after a 16 percent drop in 1987.

The market share, in units, of disc cameras plunged to just 5.6 percent in 1988 from 27.1 percent in 1984, when 1.0 million of the pocket-size cameras were sold to dealers. Due to their lower price, these cameras accounted for only 1.9 percent of the dollar value of cameras sold. Weak prospects for disc cameras were indicated by Eastman Kodak's announcement in early 1988 that it was suspending production of this type of camera.

Sales of instant cameras have also been fading. In 1988, according to PMA (Photo Marketing Association International), about 2.1 million instant cameras were sold to U.S. dealers, down from 2.7 million the year before. Instant cameras represented 11.8 percent of industry unit volume and 7.8 percent of dollar value. As recently as 1983, about 4 million instant cameras were sold, at a time when Eastman Kodak and Polaroid were both in the market. Eastman Kodak withdrew from this segment in early 1986 following a court ruling that the company had infringed upon Polaroid patents. . . .

Meanwhile, cartridge camera sales totaled about 5.6 million units, down about 7 percent from the year before. Cartridge cameras accounted for 31 percent of industry unit volume, but only about 4.8 percent of dollar volume.

According to PMA, 811 million rolls of film were purchased in the United States during 1988, up about 4 percent from the year before. Film for 35-mm cameras was the most popular format (61 percent), followed by cartridge (16 percent), instant (11 percent), and disc (11 percent). Not surprisingly, 35-mm film also provided the bulk of the industry's processing volume, accounting for 75 percent of the 15.43 billion conventional exposures processed in 1988. In comparison, prior to the

[14] Lee Smith, "The Little Pepper That's Got Kodak Hot," *Fortune*, August 22, 1983, p. 122.

fast sales of "point and shoot" cameras, 35-mm film represented just 34 percent of processing volume in 1980 and 12.4 percent in 1975, according to PMA. Cartridge film represented 15 percent of processing volume in 1987 followed by disc film at 7 percent. PMA estimated that color print developing accounted for 93 percent of the 15.4 billion conventional exposures processed in 1988, followed by slide (4.5 percent) and black and white print developing (2.6 percent). (Note: Some of PMA's numbers may be only for the amateur photography market, excluding professional activity.)

Stand-alone mini-labs accounted for an estimated 28.9 percent of the retail dollars spent on photoprocessing in 1988, down slightly from 1987's 29.4 percent. Another 22.6 percent of photoprocessing sales were made through drugstores, followed by discounter/mass merchandisers (15.4 percent), camera stores (13.5 percent), and a variety of others (19.6 percent), according to PMA.

Source: *Standard & Poor's Industry Surveys*, March 15, 1990, p. 49.

CASE 3

Golden Flake Snack Foods: Competing in an Increasingly Hostile Environment

----

As Julie Strauss, director of marketing for Golden Flake, drove toward her office located adjacent to the Golden Flake Snack Food plant, her thoughts wandered back to a recent board meeting at which many important questions were raised. Although geographic expansion was progressing as planned, competition had intensified and the company's market share had slipped, particularly in the home market of Alabama. In addition, the increased competition had caused earnings per share and the stock price to decline. Was it time for a new strategy? Over the years the company had done quite well with its conservative manage-

This case was prepared by Peter M. Ginter, Linda E. Swayne, Lynne D. Richardson, and Woodrow D. Richardson as a basis for class discussion rather than to illustrate either effective or ineffective handling of an administrative situation. Used with permission from Woodrow D. Richardson.

ment approach, but would this approach continue to serve it well in the 1990s? Was head-to-head competition with the industry giants, even in a regional market, going to pay off in the long run? Was there a marketing approach that would improve the situation? As she turned her car into the parking lot, she knew there were no easy answers to these questions. She also knew that if the declines in market share, earnings per share, and stock price were to be reversed, she must come to terms with these questions.

COMPANY ORGANIZATION

Golden Flake Snack Foods became a wholly owned subsidiary of Golden Enterprises in 1977. A full line of snack foods was manufactured, including potato chips, corn and tortilla chips, cheese curls, popcorn, and pork skins. Other products marketed under the Golden Flake name included roasted peanuts, onion rings, and cheese or peanut butter-filled crackers. Golden Flake snack products were manufactured in Alabama, Tennessee, and Florida and sold in 13 states.

COMPANY HISTORY

Magic City Food Products was founded in 1923 in Birmingham, Alabama. Mose Lischkoff and Frank Mosher started the company in the basement of a Hills Grocery store in North Birmingham. Introduced as a new item, their fresh, kettle-cooked potato chips caught on quickly.

Helen Friedman was one of the first employees hired. Deemed the "Golden Flake Girl," she was the driving force in Magic City's rapid expansion. In fact, Helen and her mother financed the buy-out of Mr. Mosher's partner, Mose Lischkoff. Miss Friedman married Mr. Mosher in 1928, but later divorced him and received the company in settlement.

Under Helen Friedman's leadership, Magic City Food Products reached sales of almost $1 million by 1946. That year the company was incorporated and sold to the Bashinsky family. One of the first moves of the new owners was to officially change the name of the company to be more descriptive: Golden Flake.

Sloan Bashinsky, the chairman of the board in 1992, had purchased the company from his father in 1956. Although he was one of the charter members of the board of directors and secretary-treasurer, Sloan Bashinsky worked his way up through both route sales and production. He initiated the construction of Golden Flake's current Birmingham plant and later two additional plants in Nashville, Tennessee, and Ocala, Florida.

In 1968, the company became a public corporation. Over the years the company engaged in diversification into insurance and real estate and fasteners (Steel City), although the insurance/real estate operation was divested in 1977.

EXHIBIT 3.1   Golden Flake Snack Food Sales and Income History
(In thousands except per share data)

	1984	1985	1986	1987	1988	1989	1990	1991
Total Revenues	$95,991	$112,289	$115,064	$118,810	$124,710	$121,658	$129,732	$125,284
Operating Profit	15,664	14,495	11,608	14,228	10,094	7,612	6,786	6,714
Earnings Per Share	$.67	$.73	$.53	$.61	$.60	$.42	$.35	$.35

The company had steady sales growth. From 1946 to the early 1980s, Golden Flake Snack Foods doubled sales every five years. Golden Enterprises reported total revenues of over $130 million in 1991. Golden Flake Snack Foods accounted for 96 percent of the holding company's total revenue and 97 percent of the profit (see Exhibit 3.1).

THE SALTED SNACK FOOD MARKET: INDUSTRY PROFILE

Snack foods have been around for over two centuries. "Snack" is actually a Dutch word that means "to bite." Thus, snacks are bite-sized foods perfect for quick meals or quick energy. Sales of salted snack foods steadily increased, and in fact, tripled over the past decade. Sales for 1990 were $12.67 billion, which was an increase of 6.2 percent over 1989.

In terms of dollars, over 32 percent of the salted snack food market was attributed to potato chip sales. Corn/tortilla chips represented 17.7 percent of industry sales. The remainder of the market consisted of popcorn, cheese curls, pork rinds, pretzels, and salted nut sales (see Exhibit 3.2).

EXHIBIT 3.2   Salted Snack Food Sales (In millions)

	1988 Sales		1989 Sales		1990 Sales	
Product Category	$	lbs.	$	lbs.	$	lbs
Potato Chips	$ 3,596	1,409	$ 3,917	1,469	$ 4,124	1,522
Tortilla Chips	1,843	827	2,104	912	2,238	968
Snack Nuts	1,530	494	1,527	483	1,258	403
Extruded Snacks	649	250	658	244	1,090	355
Microwavable Popcorn	783	282	822	300	898	321
Pretzels	470	293	558	331	622	350
Corn Chips	521	226	636	245	601	234
Meat Snacks	471	61	484	68	491	64
Ready-to-Eat Popcorn	302	94	368	111	428	125
Variety Packs	182	45	213	51	321	73
Pork Rinds	171	32	195	37	205	40
Unpopped Popcorn	183	237	185	230	157	198
Party Mix	123	44	157	52	120	33
Other Snacks	84	24	111	30	110	29
Total	$10,905	4,393	$11,930	4,560	$12,663	4,715

Source: Snack Food Association, June 1990 and 1991.

Potato Chips

Potato chip sales totaled $4.124 billion in 1990, an increase of 5.3 percent over 1989. Sales volume increased 3.6 percent from the previous year as well to 1.522 billion pounds. Barbecue was the most popular flavor of potato chip, but low-salt potato chips shot up 266.7 percent, reflecting consumer taste for this relatively new product. It accounted for only 1 percent of chip sales in 1990 but will likely grow rapidly in the next few years. Ridged potato chips lost market share in 1990, and kettle-style chips increased in popularity (see Exhibit 3.3).

To make potato chips, a potato is washed, peeled, sliced, and fried for about two minutes in vegetable oil. Approximately 100 pounds of raw potatoes yield 25 pounds of potato chips. Although many might consider potato chips to be junk food or "empty" calories, potato chips do have some nutritional value. Fresh potatoes are approximately 80 percent water. In the quick frying of chips, most of the water is boiled away, leaving a dehydrated potato much as a raisin is a dehydrated grape. A one-ounce bag of chips has most of the nutrient value of 3.5 ounces of fresh peeled potato. Specific nutrition information is included in Exhibit 3.4.

EXHIBIT 3.3   Industry Averages: Potato Chip Sales by Flavor and Type (In millions of pounds)

	Sales Volume		
Flavors	*1988*	*1989*	*1990*
Salted Unflavored	1,059	1,029	1,015
Barbecue Flavored	140	161	178
Sour Cream and Onion	135	130	124
Cheddar Cheese Flavored	52	48	54
Unsalted	37	35	28
Low Salt	n/a	6[a]	16
Salt and Vinegar	n/a	9[a]	12
Jalapeno	9	11	11
Hot and Spicy	23	14	5
Onion	n/a	7[a]	5
Cajun	n/a	n/a	5[a]
Others	26	19	69
Total	1,522	1,469	1,481
Types			
Regular	699	678	752
Rippled/Ridged	512	504	455
Kettle-Style	99	108	104
Fabricated	171	179	211
Total	1,481	1,469	1,522

[a] First-year data.
na = not available.
Source: Snack Food Association, June 1990 and 1991.

EXHIBIT 3.4   Potato Chip Nutrition Information

Nutrition Information per Serving		Percentage of U.S. Recommended Daily Allowances (USRDA)			
Serving Size	1 ounce	Protein	2	Calcium	*
Calories	150	Vitamin A	*	Iron	2
Protein	2 grams	Vitamin C	10	Vitamin B	4
Carbohydrate	14 grams	Thiamine	2	Phosphorus	4
Fat	10 grams	Riboflavin	*	Magnesium	4
		Niacin	6		

* Less than 2 percent of the U.S. recommended daily amount of this nutrient.

Corn/Tortilla Chips

Corn chip sales were up 8.5 percent in 1989 over 1988, but dropped 5.4 percent in 1990. Tortilla chip sales showed increases of 10.3 and 5.4 percent in 1989 and 1990, respectively. Approximately 100 pounds of corn yield approximately 110 pounds of corn products, making corn products highly profitable for producers.

The total sales for the category were considered to be $2.8 billion in 1990, with tortilla chips accounting for three-fourths of that amount. As recently as 1986, tortilla sales only accounted for two-thirds of this category, but corn chip sales have not been keeping up with the tortilla growth over the past several years. The introduction of new flavors helped spur the growth of tortilla chips, now a $2.104 billion category, up from $1.170 billion in 1986 (see Exhibit 3.5).

EXHIBIT 3.5   Corn/Tortilla Chip Sales by Flavor
(In millions of pounds)

Flavors	Corn Chips			Tortilla Chips		
	1988	1989	1990	1988	1989	1990
Regular	188.9	182.9	179.0	457.0	401.0	418.1
Unsalted	—	2.6[a]	.6	—	25.0[a]	40.0
Low Salt	—	.8[a]	.6	—	34.0[a]	38.0
Hot and Spicy	1.0	.4	10.9	10.0	12.0	27.0
Cheese	—	—	8.2[a]	282.0	314.0	297.1
Ranch	—	—	16.0[a]	—	98.0[a]	88.0
Barbecue	17.0	16.9	18.2	no	no	no
Salsa	no	no	no	—	20.0[a]	28.0
Jalapeno	no	no	no	—	7.0[a]	6.0
Other	19.0	41.5	41.5	—	1.0[a]	19.0

[a] First-year data.

no = no flavor produced.

Source: Snack Food Association, June 1990 and 1991.

Extruded Snacks

Extruded snacks are products that have the shape defined as the product is pushed (extruded) through machinery. Extruded snack pound volume fell 2.2 percent in 1989, about the same as in 1988, but grew 5.6 percent in 1990 to 355.3 million pounds. Almost 70 percent of this category was made up of cheese-flavored extruded snacks. The "other" extruded snacks included all pellet-based snacks.

Salted Meat Snacks (Including Pork Rinds)

Sales of salted meats increased 1.5 percent to $491.0 million in 1990. Higher prices for raw materials forced meat snack producers to raise prices in 1990, which resulted in this slight rise in dollar sales but a 5 percent drop in pound volume. Sales volume of pork rind products increased over 14 percent in 1989 and 6.4 percent in 1990, with a substantial portion of the increase attributed to President George Bush's love of the product. Although the regular flavor showed an increase in sales, greater increases were shown for the barbecue and hot and spicy flavors, indicating that consumers are following the president's lead, since he says he prefers the hot varieties of pork rinds (see Exhibit 3.6).

Popped Corn, Pretzels, and Nuts

Ready-to-eat popcorn is a salted snack product that has had phenomenal growth during the past several years. Dollar sales shot up 16.2 percent in 1990, following over 20 percent increases for both 1988 and 1989. The introduction of white cheddar cheese popcorn has had the biggest impact in this category. Although while microwavable and unpopped popcorns showed modest increases in dollar sales, they were no match for the ready-to-eat segment. Pretzels were lauded by health professionals and dietary experts as healthful snacks because they are baked products that are low in fat and add bulk to a diet without a lot of calories. Following a 2.4 percent increase in dollar sales in 1988, pretzels rebounded in 1989 with an 18.6 percent increase in dollar sales to $557.7 million. In 1990, this number increased an additional 11.6 percent to $622.4 million.

EXHIBIT 3.6   Pork Rind Sales by Flavors (In millions of pounds)

Flavors	1988	1989	1990
Regular	20.1	22.4	22.3
Hot and Spicy	7.1	8.1	8.2
Barbecue	4.8	5.9	6.0
Other	0.6	0.9	3.2

Source: Snack Food Association, June 1990 and 1991.

Snack nuts suffered consecutive drops in pound volume during 1988, 1989, and 1990, falling 9.4, 2.2, and 4.3 percent, respectively. Dollar sales, however, showed less decline, falling 6.7 percent in 1988, 0.2 percent in 1989, and 3.8 percent in 1990.

Salted Snack Food Industry Averages

Companies in the salted snack food industry reported gross margins before taxes of 10.5 percent in 1990, up from margins of 4.5 percent for 1989. The increase is largely attributed to the lower prices of commodities and ingredients in 1990.

Companies in the industry reported the following average expenses as percentages of sales for 1990: commodities and other ingredients—28.5 percent; salaries—10.3 percent; packaging materials—13.5 percent; transportation and delivery—10.2 percent; general and administrative—9.2 percent; direct labor—10.0 percent; and advertising and promotion—7.8 percent.

For 1990, 54 percent of snack companies reported spending more money on advertising and promotion, the highest percentage in three years. Only 12 percent said they spent less. The majority of promotional funds was spent for price reductions and point-of-purchase displays, with only 34 percent spent for various forms of advertising in the media (see Exhibit 3.7).

Most new product development in the industry was left up to Frito-Lay and other large, national manufacturers. Regional manufacturers introduced new products; however, it was usually after the larger manufacturers introduced them. Frito-Lay debuted Sun Chips in 1989, a multigrain snack made from whole wheat

EXHIBIT 3.7   1990 Snack Company
Advertising and Promotion Expenditures

Promotional Activity	Percent of Promotional Budget
Price Reductions	41.0
Point-of-Purchase Displays	14.5
Co-Op Advertising	8.0
Trade Shows and Trade Events	6.8
Radio Advertising	5.7
In-Store Demonstrations/Samples	4.3
Television Advertising	4.2
Print Advertising	4.0
In-Store Features	3.3
On-Pack or In-Pack Promotions	3.0
Outdoor Advertising	—
Community Event Sponsorships	1.0
Other Methods	3.2

Source: Snack Food Association, June 1991.

and corn. Its black-and-green packaging was designed to convey a premium image. Frito-Lay spent $150 million to introduce its "light" line products that were lower in fat and calories. Most of the new products introduced by regional manufacturers in 1989 were kettle-cooked potato chips, although white cheddar cheese popcorn was successful.

The salted snack food market grew at a rate of 9.4 percent in 1989 and 6.2 percent in 1990, reaching $12.67 billion in total sales in 1990. The major products, such as potato chips and corn chips, reached the maturity stage of the product life cycle.

In 1992, the snack chip market was about 1.32 percent of the total food industry and was expected to keep growing. Snack chips were projected to make up 1.66 percent of food industry sales by 1995 (according to statistics from the U.S. Department of Agriculture) as a result of rising per capita income and increasing snack food purchases. Among consumers, health concerns and more meals eaten away from home will reduce the purchases of salted snack food products, as most meals eaten away from home are in fast food restaurants that do not serve snack foods.

Snack company executives were worried about other issues as well. One of their major concerns was over slotting allowances (the cost of shelf space charged by retailers to manufacturers). Some companies reported that it cost them up to $1,000 per section-foot in certain stores for a year-long contract, but others indicated that $200 to $250 per section-foot was more common. Half of the snack food companies reported paying slotting allowances in 1990 to gain additional space, and 37 percent reported paying fees to retain existing space. Competition, especially from the large companies, such as Frito-Lay, Borden, and Eagle, was expected to be strong in the future. Consolidation occurred in the industry and was expected to continue.

THE COMPETITION

Frito-Lay, a subsidiary of Pepsico, was Golden Flake's major competition throughout the Southeast. Such familiar brands as Fritos, Lay's, Ruffles, Cheetos, Doritos, and Tostitos were all Frito-Lay products. This formidable competitor held a four-to-one advantage in domestic sales over its nearest competitor, Borden, and cracked the $3 billion domestic sales barrier in 1989. The company had "state-of-the-art" manufacturing facilities in North Carolina, Connecticut, and Indiana and had an extensive direct retail store delivery distribution system using company-owned, tractor-trailer trucks. In 1991, Frito announced lay-offs of over 1,600 workers in an effort to streamline operations.

Borden became the second largest snack food maker by acquiring a series of regional snack brands. During the 1980s, Borden acquired Wise Foods in the East, Guy's Foods in the Midwest, Clover Club in the Mountain states, and Moore's Quality Snack Foods in the Southeast. The company was attempting to build these regional brands into a national identity. In 1989, Borden's snack group tallied $762 million in domestic sales. Borden converted 4 of its 17 plants into hyperplants.

Eagle Snacks was a division of the brewing giant Anheuser-Busch. Eagle Snacks attempted to buy its way into the market with lower prices. This pricing strategy coupled with insufficient volumes led to substantial losses. The company stated that it did not expect to turn a profit until sometime in 1993. The company's efforts to obtain market share triggered an on-going price war. Eagle's willingness and ability to absorb large losses placed a strain on the smaller producers in the industry.

The other national competitors are Keebler and Procter & Gamble (P&G). Keebler priced competitively but focused on innovative niche products. Long famous for its cookies and cracker products, Keebler gained prominence in salted snacks with the introduction of its fabricated potato snack chips (O'Boise's and Ripplin's). Procter & Gamble added to the success of its Pringles potato chips with the successful introduction of Corn Crisps in 1989. The company became a strong contender in the nut segment by purchasing Fisher Nut Company from Beatrice/Hunt Wesson in 1989. Despite its limited product line, Procter & Gamble was a formidable competitor because of its advertising prowess. In 1989, P&G spent $1.66 billion on advertising (for all company products), which ranked second only to Philip Morris.

Other competitors had spikes of excellence, producing some very competitive brands. Some were national in market coverage, and others, such as Golden Flake, were regionally oriented. A summary of Golden Flake's salted snack food competitors is presented in Exhibit 3.8.

GOLDEN FLAKE SNACK FOODS

Corporate Goals and Management Philosophy

Golden Flake's corporate objective was to be the market share leader in Alabama and a very strong number two in its other markets. The company realized that Frito-Lay's resources made it unrealistic for Golden Flake to be the market share leader in other states.

Golden Flake's number one goal was quality. The company believed the quality goal could be achieved by setting the standard for the industry in production, taste, freshness, and productivity. Another goal was to provide exceptional service and to deliver the freshest products. Despite its high cost, the direct-delivery distribution system was considered to be the best way to continue to accomplish this goal.

Further, Golden Flake had the objective of doubling sales dollars every five years. This has been a goal of the company since it was acquired by the Bashinsky family in 1946. The goal was met until recent years.

Finally, Golden Flake wanted to attract and retain the best employees in the

EXHIBIT 3.8   Competitive Summary

Competitor	Snack Brands	Market
American Brands New York	Sunshine, Bell, Bluebell Compadres, Squiggles, Humpty-Dumpty	United States, Canada
Anheuser-Busch St. Louis	Eagle Snacks, Cape Cod	United States
Borden New York	Cheez Doodles, Cottage Fries, New York Deli, Wise, Granny Goose, Moore's	United States
Charles Chips Pennsylvania	Charles Chips	38 states and international
Frito-Lay Texas	Fritos, Lay's, Ruffles, Munchos, Cheetos, Doritos, Tostitos, Funyuns, Santitas, Sun Chips, Light, Rold Gold	United States
G. Heileman Brewing Wisconsin	Barrel O'Fun, Red Seal	Southwestern states Minnesota, Maryland
Keebler Company Illinois	Krunch Twists, Tato Skins, O'Boisies, Ripplin's	United States
Lance North Carolina	Lance, Gold-n-Cheese, Lanchos	35 eastern states
Mike-Sell's Tennessee	Mike-Sell's	Tennessee, Ohio
Nabisco Brands New Jersey	Planters	United States
Procter & Gamble Ohio	Pringles, Corn Crisps, Fisher Nuts	United States
Ralston-Purina Co. St. Louis	Chex Snack Mix	United States
Southland Corp. Texas	Pate, El-Ge, private labels	Northwestern, midwestern states
Tom's Georgia	Tom's	United States
Zapp's Louisiana	Zapp's	Southwestern states

industry. Although over 1,700 people were employed by Golden Flake, the company continued to emphasize a family atmosphere by including employees in stock purchase plans and quarterly small-group meetings. In fact, every month the president and vice presidents of the company met with employees whose birthdays fell within that month; they celebrated together, and employees were able to ask any questions that were on their minds (supervisors were not present). The leadership in the company did this for every shift; some of these meetings lasted several hours. This resulted in a strong employee loyalty to the company. Twice in the past decade the employees voted down union certification. Golden Flake's organizational chart is illustrated in Exhibit 3.9.

EXHIBIT 3.9   Golden Flake Snack Food Organization Chart

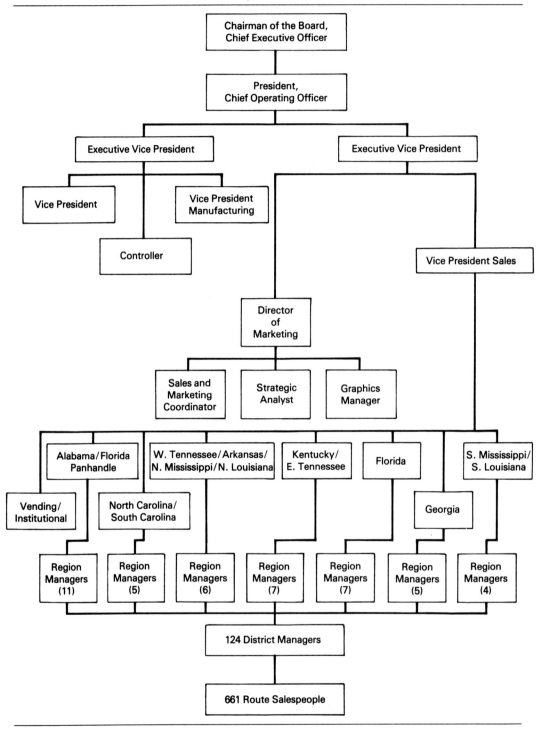

Operating Results

Earnings for 1991 were almost equal to the previous year's despite a decline in sales. Deep discounting continued in 1991 as typical competitive behavior. For part of the year Golden Flake reduced its discounting resulting in lower but more profitable sales. Fortunately in 1991, prices for potatoes and other ingredients were lower than in 1990.

No major new products were introduced in 1990 (although mesquite-flavored dip-style potato chips, white cheddar cheese-flavored popcorn, and cheddar-bits cheese crackers were included as line extensions). The primary company strategy was market penetration—increased sales in existing markets with existing products. The company did begin an expansion into North Carolina and South Carolina in fiscal 1990 and, although current earnings are being penalized, long-term growth in sales and profits was expected.

Productivity

The primary reason for increased productivity in 1990 and 1991 came from the installation of a Norand computerized route management system. The implementation of this system allowed route personnel to be more efficient and professional. Sales and inventory data were generated and transmitted daily to the Birmingham headquarters from the entire marketing area. Routes were consolidated (approximately 40 in 1991), resulting in improved route averages and lowered cost of sales.

Golden Flake had state-of-the-art processing and packaging equipment that allowed for efficient use of raw materials. The newest plant in Ocala, Florida, utilized the latest technologies. These modern facilities enabled Golden Flake to compete with Frito-Lay in quality, taste, and freshness.

By establishing manufacturing plants in Ocala, Florida, and Nashville, Tennessee, Golden Flake was able to provide quick delivery to customers in these areas. The Ocala plant could produce 2,100 pounds per hour of potato chips plus either 1,400 pounds of tortilla chips or 1,000 pounds of corn chips per hour.

The potato warehouse in Birmingham had the capacity to store 20 million pounds of potatoes in an atmosphere that was controlled for temperature and humidity by a computer. The warehouse utilized hydraulic lifts, conveyer systems, and water flumes for unloading trucks and moving the potatoes to cleaning or storage. Potato warehouses helped to ensure that temporary fluctuations in potato supply did not have a significant impact on company operations. The warehouses were also important to supply the company's needs during the break in the growing season from late November to February. By March, the Florida crop of potatoes is harvested and used in potato chip production. The company obtains its potatoes from different farms in various states as the growing season progresses. In October, the thicker-skinned potatoes of North and South Dakota are harvested and stored for use in the winter months.

As capacity increased, expansion into new markets was sought. Originally selling only in the Birmingham area, Golden Flake marketed snack products in 13 states in the Southeast in 1991.

Marketing Strategy

Golden Flake did not purport to be a leader in the snack food market. Similar to others in the industry, Golden Flake had been using a follow-the-leader strategy (57 percent of responding snack food companies reported they received new product ideas from other companies). In 1990, Frito-Lay spent $150 million in developing a new light line of products that contained one-third less fat and calories. Originally introduced with approximately 5 feet of retail shelf space, Frito-Lay cut the space allocated to the light line to approximately 2 feet a short time later. Consumers say they want healthy snacks, but they bought the products that taste good. Golden Flake took a wait-and-see stance to assess how well the new line was selling before pursuing a light line of its own.

The company felt that its distribution system would be useful for future growth. Company-owned trucks, driven by company employees, were important in providing outstanding service to customers and controlling distribution costs. In 1990, Golden Flake spent over $1 million on new trucks and operated a maintenance and rebuild shop in Birmingham to maintain the fleet's appearance and safety. Rebuilt route trucks were returned to service for a fraction of the cost of a new one.

Moreover, the direct distribution system allowed for expansion into new territories by what the company called the ink blot method. Golden Flake expanded its market territory gradually outward in every direction from Alabama. Management was unwilling to skip or jump over a large area of rural population to target a city despite industry figures that indicated on average suburban routes produced $4,700 per week, while rural routes brought in $3,700 per week. Despite these industry figures, the company maintained that rural coverage afforded good profit potential due to the reduced competition in these areas. Exhibit 3.10 indicates the geography served by Golden Flake.

Market Share

Golden Flake represented only a small part of the total snack food market both in terms of geographic markets and sales volume. Nationally, Frito-Lay was the market leader with a 40 percent share. However, Golden Flake had the largest market share in Alabama until 1987. Subsequently, Frito-Lay became the market share leader in Alabama. In the new expansion states of Arkansas, Kentucky, Louisiana, Ohio, South Carolina, and North Carolina, the company's products were increasing in market share (see Exhibit 3.11).

EXHIBIT 3.10   Golden Flake Market Area

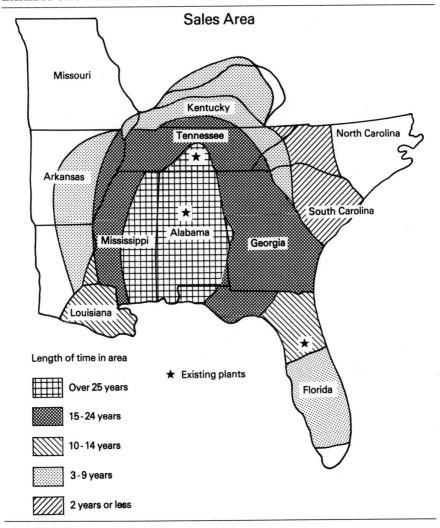

Positioning.   Research on consumer perceptions developed a competitive price-quality positioning map (Exhibit 3.12) that was different from the map that the company believed reflected the actual positions in the marketplace (Exhibit 3.13). Although Golden Flake's positioning was similar to its competitors, its target market was different. Moore's, recently acquired by Borden, is the only brand with a similar target market, but it appeared to be a significant competitor only in Tennessee.

EXHIBIT 3.11   Golden Flake Market Share by State (Established market)

	Percent in 1989	Percent in 1990
Alabama		
Frito-Lay	38.2	41.6
Golden Flake	35.3	32.1
Eagle	5.4	5.8
Keebler	5.4	4.8
Charles	2.5	2.1
Tom's	0.7	0.4
Others	12.5	13.2
Florida		
Frito-Lay	48.9	48.3
Keebler	5.1	5.3
Golden Flake	5.6	4.7
Eagle	3.2	3.2
Tom's	3.2	3.2
Charles	4.1	2.4
Others	18.1	20.5
Georgia		
Frito-Lay	51.7	49.9
Eagle	6.8	9.3
Golden Flake	8.4	5.8
Keebler	5.1	5.6
Wise	2.9	4.1
Charles	4.8	3.4
Tom's	0.6	0.4
Others	19.7	21.5
Kentucky		
Frito-Lay	47.5	46.8
Golden Flake	11.3	9.8
Charles	8.2	7.9
Keebler	6.1	6.9
Eagle	5.2	5.3
Tom's	0.2	0.1
Others	21.5	23.2
Tennessee		
Frito-Lay	53.3	49.8
Golden Flake	10.5	11.2
Keebler	6.1	6.9
Eagle	3.8	5.1
Charles	3.6	4.3
Tom's	4.3	3.8
Wise	0.2	0.4
Others	18.2	18.5

Source: Nielsen market research data.

EXHIBIT 3.12   Competitive Positioning Price/Quality—Customer Perception

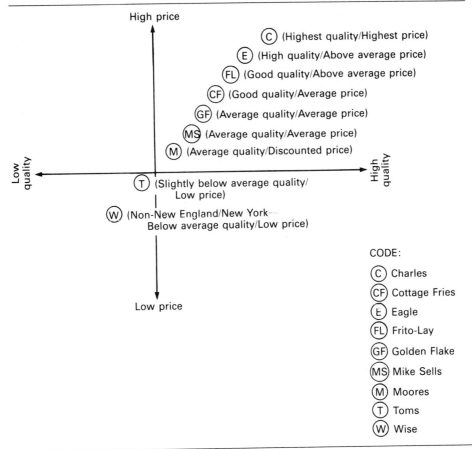

Target Market.   Demographically Golden Flake defined its target market as follows:

- Women aged 20–44
- Families with two or more children
- Upper-lower to middle income
- Blue and gray collar (homemakers, sales, clerical, craftpersons, farmers, manufacturing, service, and others)
- High school graduate or college graduate
- Rural roots, nontransient

EXHIBIT 3.13   Positions in the Market—Company Perception

		High	Medium	Low
PRODUCT QUALITY	High	Premium strategy 1. Charles #1 2. Eagle 3. O'Gradys 4. Delta Gold	Penetration strategy 1. Golden Flake 2. Lays/Ruffles 3. Moores 4. Mike Sells	Super Bargain Strategy 1. Tops Brand
	Medium	Overpricing strategy	Average quality strategy 1. Toms 2. Cottage Fries 3. Wise	Bargain strategy 1. Private Label
	Low	Hit and run strategy	Shoddy goods strategy	Cheap goods strategy 1. Generic Chips
		High	Medium	Low
			PRICE	

The psychographic characteristics were very traditional:

- Two incomes, hard working
- Strong work ethic; traditional values such as God, country, family, and home
- Belongers, conformers

Purchases were for regular-use occasion, and the dominant buying motive was value. Company research showed the primary product attributes to be quality, freshness, and fun. Loyalty had been strong, but that was no longer necessarily true, as higher discounting made consumers more price sensitive. Approximately 75 percent of the buyers purchased the same brand consistently. Children were purchase influencers. Over 75 percent of purchases were made in grocery stores, supermarkets, and convenience stores. The market potential for this segment was considered to be 35 to 42 percent of the salted snack food market.

Product.   Golden Flake's product line was characterized as mature products with low-involvement purchasing. Nearly 85 percent of snack products were impulse purchases.

Potato chips of various types made up over 51 percent of Golden Flake's product line. Golden Flake was considered to be an exceptional name by the company because it represented two very desirable attributes of a potato chip—golden in color and flaky in texture. The next major contributor to sales volume

**EXHIBIT 3.14   Golden Flake
Sales by Product, May 30, 1990**

Product	Percent
Potato Chips	51.8
Tortilla Chips	10.8
Cheese Products	9.1
Pork Skins	6.7
Corn Chips	4.8
Popcorn	3.5
Sandwiches	3.5
Pretzels	1.6
Peanuts	1.2
Onion Rings	1.0
Other Snacks	6.0

was tortilla chips, with approximately 10.8 percent of sales. Corn chips, cheese products, pork skins, popcorn, and others contributed lesser percentages to sales volume (Exhibit 3.14). In addition, the company distributed a line of cake and cookie items, pretzels, and nuts manufactured by others.

In April 1991, Golden Flake began distributing Pace salsa in the "squatty" jar. Golden Flake displayed this item with its Tostados. Golden Flake's own research indicated that Pace salsa tasted better than the other leading brands, and the product was performing well. Pace's top seven markets for this product were distributed by Golden Flake.

Product quality was a major criterion for Golden Flake. Quality testing was continuous. Golden Flake tested chips for color, size, amount of salt, oil absorption, and the number of defective chips—those with brown spots or holes. Product testing was done in a very modern quality control lab and through live taste tests using consumers.

Many consumers perceived Golden Flake to be of high quality and freshness; however, Frito-Lay was generally perceived to have higher quality. To illustrate, a study in Tennessee indicated that Golden Flake had 97 percent aided awareness but only 20 percent market share. Exhibit 3.15 contains detailed results of the study. Using machine-controlled, scientific testing, Golden Flake's product met higher standards for color, size, amount of salt, oil absorption, and defective chips than Frito-lay's brand, yet these factors were not perceived by the consumer.

New product development was based on customer requests, competitive moves, and sales force suggestions. Acknowledging that Golden Flake could not and did not expect to make the kind of research and development commitment that was made by the market leader, Frito-Lay, the company was comfortable with its follower strategy.

Golden Flake used a metallized-plastic bag or a foil bag that was heat sealed to provide product freshness for up to eight weeks. Freshness dating was stamped

EXHIBIT 3.15   Average-Respondent Profile Comparisons of Golden Flake, Lay's, and Moores—Knoxville, Tennessee, 1985

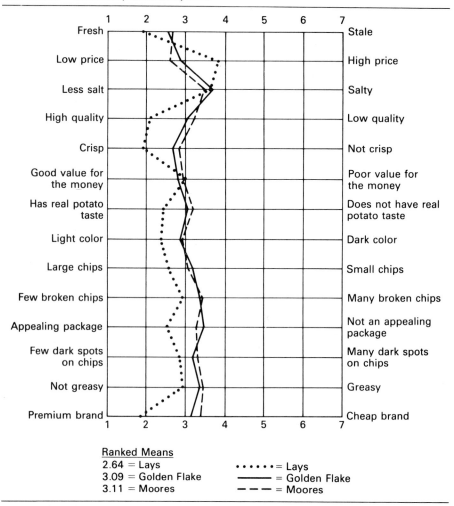

Ranked Means
2.64 = Lays   • • • • • • = Lays
3.09 = Golden Flake ———— = Golden Flake
3.11 = Moores   — — — = Moores

on the bag as a guarantee and to generate customer awareness of the freshness of the product. Packaging costs averaged approximately 11 percent of manufacturing costs at Golden Flake versus approximately 14 percent for the industry.

Several colors were used to differentiate the various flavors of chips and other snacks. The logo common to all packages was a "cloud" (originally a potato chip) containing the Golden Flake name in block letters (see Exhibit 3.16). The typeface (style of type or font) differed for each product category. Results from consumer focus groups have caused management to rethink its logo and packaging. In fact, Golden Flake tested several new package designs; however, the original package proved to be most appealing to its target market.

EXHIBIT 3.16   Golden Flake package design

Pricing.   Golden Flake priced its products to be competitive. Prices and package sizes were very similar to Frito-Lay and others in the industry. An audit of retail prices in Birmingham for several products indicated that Golden Flake's prices, at least at retail, were in line with the competition. The great variety in package size—3½ ounces versus 3⅛ ounces, for example—complicated direct price comparisons by consumers.

Setting prices for snack foods was hampered by the drastic fluctuation of supply and price for the commodity products (potatoes and corn) used as ingredients. Golden Flake purchased raw materials used in manufacturing on the open market under contract through brokers and directly from growers. Potato shortages caused by the weather in 1989 and 1990 caused prices to rise dramatically, cutting into Golden Flake's (and other snack food manufacturers') profits.

The company traded in farm commodity futures to reduce risk and control costs. Golden Flake's costs and expenses rose in part due to inflation, but efficient purchasing, increased volume, improvements in production, distribution, administration, and increased sales prices enabled the company to maintain a profit margin above the industry average.

Distribution.   Distribution was concentrated in grocery stores and convenience stores with a minimal effort directed to mass merchandisers, membership stores, and vending machines. Membership stores such as Sam's Wholesale Club generally negotiated with producers with national coverage. Because of this, Golden Flake had entered the membership stores in its region on a store-by-store basis. Vending machines played a key role in testing new products, but did not constitute a major distribution outlet.

As snack products are perishable with a shelf life of approximately six to eight weeks, Golden Flake used direct-to-retail-store delivery. The direct-store-delivery system allowed quicker delivery, which maintained freshness, and less handling, which reduced damage to the product. In addition, the fact that company salespeople stocked the racks in the store ensured that the rack had an attractive appearance, the stock was rotated for freshness, and the display was prepared in a way most conducive to impulse buying by the customer.

Because any grocer's primary expense is the cost of labor, the direct delivery system provided the store substantial savings in labor as well as warehousing costs. In order to provide this service to retailers, the company had a chain of 29 company-owned sales warehouses with several others in various phases of development from planning to construction. The company warehouses ranged in size from 2,400 to 8,000 square feet. They were constructed in locations within a marketing area where there was a large enough concentration of routes to make ownership feasible (Exhibit 3.17). The leased warehouses in small areas were unattended and each salesperson was assigned his or her own secured area. The salesperson was responsible for ordering and inventory control. The larger warehouses had a clerk to handle this function for the sales representatives assigned to the facility.

A fleet of over 1,000 company-owned and maintained vehicles provided service directly to the retail stores. The direct-store-delivery system was considered to be one of the major strengths of the company because it ensured maximum service for the accounts and maximum control for the company.

Promotion.   Each salesperson/driver had an assigned territory and operated from the nearest company warehouse. Sales aids included price sheets, plan-o-grams for effective store settings (design for the retail shelf layout), trade promotions (discounts), at least quarterly price "deals" for specific time periods, storyboards to illustrate company TV advertising, and occasionally special "incentives" (gifts) for store managers.

EXHIBIT 3.17   Location of Golden Flake Warehouses

Alabama	Georgia
Anniston/Oxford	Atlanta/Decatur
Birmingham	Macon
Demopolis	Marietta
Dothan	
Forest Park	**Kentucky**
Fort Payne	
Huntsville	Louisville
Mobile	
Montgomery	**Louisiana**
Muscle Shoals	
Phenix City	Baton Rouge
Tuscaloosa	New Orleans
	Mississippi
Florida	
	Gulfport
Jacksonville	Jackson
Orlando	
Pensacola	**Tennessee**
St. Petersburg	
Tallahassee	Chattanooga
Tampa	Knoxville
	Memphis

Salespeople were formally trained in-house by the regional manager. Following training, a newly hired salesperson/driver rode with an experienced route salesperson until the end of the 12-week training program. Then a territory was assigned.

In Alabama, Golden Flake had high brand awareness due primarily to its past sponsorship with Coca-Cola of the Bear Bryant football program. Golden Flake has continued its sponsorship of the University of Alabama football show since Coach Bryant's retirement in 1983. With the expansion of Golden Flake to other markets, advertising needed to build awareness and develop the desired image. During the 1991 college football season, Golden Flake cosponsored all Southeastern Conference (SEC) coaches' TV programs, as well as football coaches' shows at Florida State University, Southern Mississippi, Clemson, and the University of South Carolina. It sponsored University of Alabama at Birmingham (UAB), Louisville, and Kentucky basketball TV programs. Golden Flake was also a corporate sponsor of the Southeastern Conference and "The Favorite Snack of the SEC."

In 1990, advertising and promotion expenditures were approximately $16 million. In 1987, Babbitt & Reiman Advertising in Atlanta was hired. As a result a new campaign "One Taste and You're Stuck—On Golden Flake" began in May 1987, and was still being used in 1991. The ads featured researchers discovering that Napoleon's hand was in his jacket in a bag of Golden Flake potato chips. Another ad in the series depicted that the arms of the Venus De Milo were missing because they "were stuck on Golden Flake."

Nearly all products were sold under the family brand of Golden Flake. Due to the regional nature and small advertising budget, the company did not attempt to fully develop individual brands as Frito-Lay had done with Ruffles, Cheetos, Tostitos, Doritos, and others. In June 1986, the first attempt at individual branding with "Southern Farms" brand kettle-fried potato chips resulted in Southern Farms generating 1.2 percent of total company sales in 1987.

The company offered two-for-one deals to customers in new markets. The customers paid for one bag of Golden Flake chips and received the second similar-sized bag for no additional charge. On-pack cents-off deals were also offered to consumers.

Golden Flake participated in the adopt-a-school program and provided plant tours for school-aged children who had the opportunity to sample many types of snacks. The company participated in three to eight trade shows each month.

Financial Condition

Golden Flake's conservative management kept the company in very good financial condition. In 1991, the stock price fluctuated from a low of 6⅞ to a high of 11½. The 1990 earnings per share dropped slightly for the fourth consecutive year to 35 cents per share and remained at that level during 1991.

The consolidated income statements and balance sheets for Golden Flake for 1986 to 1990 are provided in Exhibits 3.18 and 3.19. Exhibits 3.20 and 3.21 summarize business segment information.

EXHIBIT 3.18   Consolidated Statements of Income Golden Enterprises, Inc. (Years ended May 31)

	1989	1990	1991
Revenues			
Net Sales	$125,703,032	$133,114,758	$128,945,082
Other Income, Including Gain on Sale of Equipment of $278,999 in 1991, $300,947 in 1990, $280,418 in 1989	769,201	994,936	668,662
Net Investment Income	1,038,414	762,343	810,245
Total revenues	127,510,647	134,872,037	130,423,989
Costs and Expenses			
Cost of Sales	58,610,441	60,601,718	55,940,893
Selling, General, and Administrative Expenses	59,515,682	66,849,008	66,791,411
Contributions to Employee Profit-Sharing and Employee Stock Ownership Plans	1,118,880	655,618	643,559
Interest	34,379	22,799	14,431
Total Costs and Expenses	119,279,382	128,129,143	123,390,294
Income before Income Taxes	8,321,265	6,742,894	7,033,695
Provision for Income Taxes			
Currently Payable			
Federal	2,171,000	2,527,000	2,578,000
State	317,000	257,000	359,000
Deferred	352,000	(480,000)	(304,000)
Total Provision for Income Taxes	2,840,000	2,304,000	2,633,000
Net Income	$ 5,391,265	$ 4,438,894	$ 4,400,695
Per Share of Common Stock	$0.42	$0.35	$0.35

EXHIBIT 3.19   Consolidated Balance Sheets Golden Enterprises, Inc. (As of May 31)

	1989	1990	1991
Assets			
Current Assets			
Cash and Cash Equivalents	$ 2,679,618	$ 2,309,100	$ 1,495,167
Marketable Securities	16,518,636	9,315,843	13,817,194
Receivables			
Trade Notes and Accounts	9,441,038	9,428,846	8,787,587
Other	458,114	178,727	504,709
	9,899,152	9,607,573	9,292,296
Less: Allowance for Doubtful Accounts	20,000	20,000	20,000
	9,879,152	9,587,573	9,272,296

EXHIBIT 3.19   (continued)

	1989	1990	1991
Inventories			
Raw Materials	2,510,466	2,747,807	2,053,100
Finished Goods	3,397,398	3,221,554	4,119,122
	5,907,864	5,969,361	6,172,222
Prepaid Expenses	1,710,402	2,283,773	1,730,132
Total Current Assets	36,695,672	29,465,650	32,487,011
Property, Plant, and Equipment			
Land	4,913,157	4,913,157	4,913,157
Buildings	19,645,096	19,721,670	19,721,620
Machinery and Equipment	25,789,094	28,784,075	29,335,042
Transportation Equipment	16,458,305	17,460,978	17,582,931
	66,805,652	70,879,880	71,552,800
Less: Accumulated Depreciation	35,405,006	40,070,159	44,645,993
	31,400,646	30,809,721	26,906,807
Other Assets	431,454	735,984	857,595
Total	$68,257,772	$61,011,355	$60,251,413
Liabilities and Stockholders' Equity			
Current Liabilities			
Checks Outstanding in Excess of Bank			
Balances	$ 1,419,873	$ 2,202,494	$ 2,892,300
Accounts Payable	2,947,279	1,718,150	1,783,856
Accrued Income Taxes	—	258,658	263,163
Other Accrued Expenses	1,480,100	1,054,854	1,115,556
Deferred Income Taxes	367,932	729,526	720,130
Current Installments of			
Long-Term Debt	63,808	63,808	147,538
Total Current Liabilities	6,278,992	6,027,490	6,922,543
Long-term Liabilities	126,664	243,694	88,098
Deferred Income Taxes	3,639,108	2,927,632	2,626,868
Stockholders' Equity			
Common stock—$.66 2/3 par value.			
Authorized 35,000,000 Shares; Issued			
13,828,793 Shares	9,219,195	9,219,195	9,219,195
Additional Paid-in Capital	5,939,261	6,376,261	6,242,511
Retained Earnings	47,525,496	41,091,261	40,535,447
	62,683,952	56,686,717	55,997,153
Less: Cost of Shares in Treasury			
(1,160,366 Shares in 1991,			
1,073,666 Shares in 1990, and			
1,026,993 Shares in 1989)	4,200,944	4,618,016	5,252,779
Deferred Compensation	—	256,162	130,470
Total Stockholders' Equity	58,483,008	51,812,539	50,613,904
Total	$68,527,772	$61,011,355	$60,251,413

EXHIBIT 3.20   Golden Enterprises, Inc., and Subsidiaries Summary of Business Segment Information (In thousands)

	Year Ended May 31				
	1987	*1988*	*1989*	*1990*	*1991*
Total Revenues					
Snack Food Products	$118,810	$124,710	$121,658	$129,732	$125,284
Bolts and Other Fasteners	4,514	5,373	5,853	5,132	5,112
	123,324	130,083	127,511	134,864	130,396
Operating Profit					
Snack Food Products	14,228	10,094	7,612	6,786	$ 6,714
Bolts and Other Fasteners	21	521	528	193	222
	14,249	10,615	8,140	6,979	6,936
Elimination of Intercompany Items	(2)	(5)	(4)	—	—
Investment Income of Parent	18	8	3	8	28
Interest Expense	(88)	(57)	(34)	(23)	(14)
Parent Company Expense Less Than (in Excess of) Management Fees from Subsidiaries	182	104	126	(221)	84
Income Before Income Taxes[a]	$ 14,359	$ 10,665	$ 8,231	$ 6,743	$ 7,034
Assets					
Snack Food Products	$ 62,201	$ 65,176	$ 64,794	$ 57,316	$ 56,053
Bolts and Other Fasteners	2,409	2,821	3,083	2,722	2,849
Elimination of Intercompany Items	—	(88)	—	—	—
Corporate Assets	841	449	651	973	1,349
Total Assets at May 31	65,451	68,358	68,528	61,011	60,251
Depreciation and Amortization					
Snack Food Products	7,490	7,292	6,359	5,550	4,955
Bolts and Other Fasteners	92	100	105	115	107
Consolidated	7,586	7,397	6,467	5,667	5,069
Additions to Property, Plant, and Equipment					
Snack Food Products	3,462	5,192	3,347	5,020	1,082
Bolts and Other Fasteners	71	123	161	56	31
Consolidated	$ 3,546	$ 5,315	$ 3,508	$ 5,076	$ 1,166

[a] Before cumulative effect of a change in accounting principle in 1988.

EXHIBIT 3.21   Golden Enterprises, Inc., and Subsidiaries—Financial Review (In thousands except per share data)

	Year Ended May 31				
	1987	1988	1989	1990	1991
Operations					
Net Sales and Other Operating Income	$122,871	$129,269	$126,472	$134,110	$129,614
Investment Income	469	817	1,038	762	810
Total Revenues	123,340	130,086	127,510	134,872	130,424
Cost of Sales	53,059	58,528	58,610	60,602	55,941
Selling, General, and Administrative Expenses	55,834	60,836	60,635	67,504	67,435
Interest	88	57	34	23	14
Income before Income Taxes and Cumulative Effect of a Change in Accounting Principle	14,359	10,665	8,231	6,743	7,034
Federal and State Income Taxes	6,406	3,927	2,840	2,304	2,633
Income before Cumulative Effect of a Change in Accounting Principle	7,953	6,738	5,391	4,439	4,401
Cumulative Effect on Prior Years of a Change in Accounting for Income Taxes	—	1,025	—	—	—
Net Income	$ 7,953	$ 7,763	$ 5,391	$ 4,439	$ 4,401
Financial Data					
Depreciation and Amortization	$ 7,586	$ 7,397	$ 6,467	$ 5,667	$ 5,069
Cash Flow (Net Income Plus Depreciation and Amortization)	15,539	15,160	11,858	10,106	9,470
Capital Expenditures, Net of Disposals	3,867	5,315	3,508	5,076	1,166
Working Capital	23,495	26,892	30,417	23,438	25,564
Long-term Debt	254	190	127	244	88
Stockholders' Equity	55,646	58,010	58,483	51,813	50,614
Total Assets	$ 65,451	$ 68,358	$ 68,528	$ 61,011	$ 60,251

EXHIBIT 3.21   (continued)

	1987	1988	1989	1990	1991
			Year Ended May 31		
Common Stock Data					
Net Income before Cumulative Effect of a Change in Accounting Principle	$0.61	$0.52	$0.42	$0.35	$0.35
Cumulative Effect on Prior Years of a Change in Accounting for Income Taxes	—	.08	—	—	—
Net Income	.61	.60	.42	.35	.35
Dividends	.23	.27	.31	.85	.39
Book Value	$4.26	$4.50	$4.57	$4.06	$4.00
Price Range (High and Low Bid)	$15.5–11.75	$16.5–9.0	$9.25–11.375	$11.375–7.75	$11.5–6.875
Financial Statistics					
Current Ratio	5.42	4.94	5.84	4.89	4.69
Net Income as Percent of Total Revenues	6.4%	6.0%	4.2%	3.3%	3.4%
Net Income as Percent of Stockholders' Equity	15.0%	13.7%	9.3%	8.0%	8.6%
Other Data					
Weighted Average Common Shares Outstanding	13,066,054	12,991,842	12,815,219	12,781,105	12,707,477
Common Shares Outstanding at Year-End	13,071,212	12,894,800	12,801,800	12,755,127	12,668,427
Approximate Number of Stockholders	2,100	2,100	2,000	1,900	1,900

a Average amounts at beginning and end of fiscal year.

LOOKING TO THE FUTURE

It had been a long day. Julie Strauss and Wayne Pate, Golden Flake's president, had spent the day reviewing the situation—Golden Flake's strengths and weaknesses, present markets and potential markets for growth, the competition, sales and promotional plans, and industry trends. The president wanted Julie to analyze the information and make some specific recommendations to the executive staff on Friday. What would she recommend? It was a challenging situation, but it was time to make some decisions regarding the future of Golden Flake.

————————— CASE 4 —————————

Gillette and the Men's Wet-Shaving Market

SAN FRANCISCO

Michael Johnson dried himself and stepped from the shower in his Marina district condominium. He moved to the sink and started to slide open his drawer in the cabinet beneath the sink. Then he remembered that he had thrown away his last Atra blade yesterday. He heard his wife, Susan, walk past the bathroom.

"Hey, Susan, did you remember to pick up some blades for me yesterday?"

"Yes, I think I put them in your drawer."

"Oh, okay, here they are." Michael saw the bottom of the blade package and pulled the drawer open.

"Oh, no! These are Trac II blades, Susan, I use an Atra."

"I'm sorry. I looked at all the packages at the drug store, but I couldn't remember which type of razor you have. Can't you use the Trac II blades on your razor?"

"No. They don't fit."

"Well, I bought some disposable razors. Just use one of those."

"Well, where are they?"

"Look below the sink. They're in a big bag."

"I see them. Wow, ten razors for $1.97. Must have been on sale."

"I guess so. I usually look for the best deal. Seems to me that all those razors are the same, and the drug store usually has one brand or another on sale."

"Why don't you buy some of those shavers made for women?"

"I've tried those, but it seems that they're just like the ones made for men, only they've dyed the plastic pink or some pastel color. Why should I pay more for color? Why don't you just use disposables?" Susan asked. "They are simpler to buy, and you just throw them away. And you can't beat the price."

"Well, the few times I've tried them they didn't seem to shave as well as a regular razor. Perhaps they've improved. Do they work for you?"

"Yes, they work fine. And they sure are better than the heavy razors if you drop one on your foot while you're in the shower!"

"Never thought about that. I see your point. Well, I'll give the disposable a try."

This case was prepared by Lew G. Brown and Jennifer M. Hart as a basis for class discussion rather than to illustrate either effective or ineffective handling of an administrative situation. Used with permission from Lew G. Brown.

HISTORY OF SHAVING

Anthropologists do not know exactly when or even why men began to shave. Researchers do know that prehistoric cave drawings clearly present men who were beardless. Apparently these men shaved with clamshells or sharpened animal teeth. As society developed, primitive men learned to sharpen flint implements. Members of the early Egyptian dynasties as far back as 7,000 years ago shaved their faces and heads, probably to deny their enemies anything to grab during hand-to-hand combat. Egyptians later fashioned copper razors and, in time, bronze blades. Craftsmen formed these early razors as crescent-shaped knife blades, like hatchets or meat cleavers, or even as circular blades with a handle extending from the center. By the iron age, craftsmen were able to fashion blades that were considerably more efficient than the early flint, copper, and bronze versions.

Before the introduction of the safety razor, men used a straight-edged, hook-type razor and found shaving a tedious, difficult, and time-consuming task. The typical man struggled through shaving twice a week at most. The shaver had to sharpen the blade (a process called stropping) before each use and had to have an expert cutler hone the blade each month. As a result, men often cut themselves while shaving; few men had the patience and acquired the necessary skill to become good shavers. Most men in the 1800s agreed with the old Russian proverb: "It is easier to bear a child once a year than to shave every day." Only the rich could afford a daily barber shave, which also often had its disadvantages because many barbers were unclean. Further, another proverb observed that "barbers learn to shave by shaving fools."

Before King C. Gillette of Boston invented the safety razor in 1895, he tinkered with other inventions in pursuit of a product that could be thrown away after being used. The customer would have to buy more, and the business would build a long-term stream of sales and profits with each new customer.

"On one particular morning when I started to shave," wrote Gillette about the dawn of his invention, "I found my razor dull, and it was not only dull but beyond the point of successful stropping and it needed honing, for which it must be taken to a barber or cutler. As I stood there with the razor in my hand, my eyes resting on it as lightly as a bird settling down on its nest, the Gillette razor was born." Gillette immediately wrote to his wife who was visiting relatives, "I've got it; our fortune is made."

Gillette had envisioned a "permanent" razor handle onto which the shaver placed a thin, razor "blade" with two sharpened edges. The shaver would place a top over the blade and attach it to the handle so that only the sharpened edges of the blade were exposed, thus producing a "safe" shave. A man would shave with the blade until it became dull, and he would then simply throw the used blade away and replace it. Gillette knew his concept would revolutionize the process of shaving; however, he had no idea that his creation would permanently change men's shaving habits.

SHAVING IN THE 1980s

Following the invention of the safety razor, the U.S. men's shaving industry grew slowly but surely through World War I. A period of rapid growth followed, and the industry saw many product innovations. By 1989, U.S. domestic razor and blade sales (the wet-shave market) had grown to a $770 million industry. A man could use three types of wet shavers to remove facial hair. Most men used the disposable razor—a cheap, plastic-handled razor that lasted for 8 to 10 shaves on average. Permanent razors, called blade-and-razor systems, were also popular. These razors required new blades every 11 to 14 shaves. Customers could purchase razor handles and blade cartridges together, or they could purchase packages of blade cartridges as refills. The third category of wet shavers included injector and double-edge razors and accounted for a small share of the razor market. Between 1980 and 1988, disposable razors had risen from a 22 percent to a 41.5 percent market share of dollar sales, while cartridge systems had fallen from 50 percent to 45.8 percent and injector and others had fallen from 28 percent to 12.7 percent. In addition, the development of the electric razor spawned the dry-shave market, which accounted for about $250 million in sales by 1988.

Despite the popularity of disposable razors, manufacturers found that the razors were expensive to make and generated very little profit. Some industry analysts estimated that, by 1988, manufacturers earned three times more on a razor-and-blade system than on a disposable razor. Also, retailers preferred to sell razor systems because they took up less room on display racks and the retailers made more money on refill sales. However, retailers liked to promote disposable razors to generate traffic. As a result, U.S. retailers allocated 55 percent of their blade and razor stock to disposable razors, 40 percent to systems, and 5 percent to double-edged razors.

Electric razors also posed a threat to razor-and-blade systems. Unit sales of electric razors jumped from 6.2 million in 1981 to 8.8 million in 1987. Low-priced imports from the Far East drove demand for electric razors up and prices down during this period. However, less than 30 percent of men used electric razors, and most of these men also used wet-shaving systems.

Industry analysts predicted that the sales of personal care products would continue to grow, but the slowing of the overall U.S. economy in the late 1980s meant that sales increases resulting from an expanding market would be minimal and companies would have to fight for market share to continue to increase sales.

THE U.S. WET-SHAVE MARKET

In 1988, the Gillette Company dominated the wet-shave market with a 60 percent share of the worldwide razor market and a 61.9 percent share of the U.S. market. Gillette also had a stake in the dry-shave business through its Braun subsidiary. The other players in the wet-shave market were Schick with 16.2 percent of the market, BIC with 9.3 percent, and others, including Wilkinson Sword, made up the remaining 12.6 percent.

The Gillette Company

King Gillette took eight years to perfect his safety razor. In 1903, the first year of marketing, the American Safety Razor Company sold 51 razors and 168 blades. Gillette promoted the safety razor as a saver of both time and money. Early ads proclaimed that the razor would save $52 and 15 days' shaving time each year and that the blades required no stropping or honing. During its second year, Gillette sold 90,884 razors and 123,648 blades. By its third year, razor sales were rising at a rate of 400 percent per year, and blade sales were booming at an annual rate of 1,000 percent. In that year, the company opened its first overseas branch in London.

Such success attracted much attention, and competition quickly developed. By 1906, consumers had at least a dozen safety razors from which to choose. Some, like the Zinn razor made by the Gem Cutlery Company, sold for $5, as did the Gillette razor. Others, such as the Ever Ready, Gem Junior, and Enders, sold for as little as $1.

With the benefit of a 17-year patent, Gillette found himself in a very advantageous position. However, it was not until World War I that the safety razor gained wide consumer acceptance. One day in 1917, King Gillette had a visionary idea: present a Gillette razor to every soldier, sailor, and marine. In this way, millions of men just entering the shaving age would adopt the self-shaving habit. By March 1918, Gillette had booked orders from the U.S. military for 519,750 razors, more than it had sold in any single *year* in its history. During World War I, the government bought 4,180,000 Gillette razors as well as smaller quantities of competitive models.

Although King Gillette believed in the quality of his product, he realized that marketing, especially distribution and advertising, would be the key to success. From the beginning, Gillette set aside 25 cents per razor for advertising and by 1905 had increased the amount to 50 cents. Over the years, Gillette used cartoon ads, radio shows, musical slogans and theme songs, prizes, contests, and cross promotions to push its products. Perhaps, however, consumers best remember Gillette for its Cavalcade of Sports programs that began in 1939 with the company's sponsorship of the World Series. Millions of men soon came to know Sharpie the parrot and the tag line "Look Sharp, Feel Sharp, Be Sharp!"

Because company founder King Gillette invented the first safety razor, Gillette had always been an industry innovator. In 1932, Gillette introduced the Gillette Blue Blade, which was the premier men's razor for many years. In 1938, the company introduced the Gillette Thin Blade; in 1946, it introduced the first blade dispenser that eliminated the need to unwrap individual blades; in 1959, it introduced the first silicone-coated blade, the Super Blue Blade. The success of the Super Blue Blade caused Gillette to close 1961 with a commanding 70 percent share of the overall razor-and-blade market and a 90 percent share of the double-edged market, the only market in which it competed.

In 1948, Gillette began to diversify into new markets through acquisition. The company purchased the Toni Company to extend its reach into the women's grooming-aid market. In 1954, the company bought Paper Mate, a leading maker of writing instruments. In 1962, Gillette acquired the Sterilon Corporation, which manufactured disposable hospital supplies. As a result of these moves, a marketing survey found that the public associated Gillette with personal grooming as much as, or more than, with blades and razors.

In 1989, the Gillette Company held the position of a leading producer of men's and women's grooming aids. Exhibit 4.1 lists the company's major divisions. Exhibit 4.2 shows the percentages and dollar volumes of net sales and profits from operations for each of the company's major business segments from 1984 to 1988. Exhibits 4.3 and 4.4 present income statements and balance sheets for 1986 to 1988.

Despite its diversification, Gillette continued to realize the importance of blade and razor sales to the company's overall health. Gillette had a strong foothold in the razor and blade market, and it intended to use this dominance to help it achieve the company's goal—sustained profitable growth. To reach this goal, Gillette's mission statement indicated that the company should pursue "strong technical and marketing efforts to assure vitality in major existing product lines; selective diversification, both internally and through acquisition; the elimination of product and business areas with low growth or limited profit potential; and strict control over product costs, overhead expenses, and working capital."

EXHIBIT   4.1   Gillette 1988 Product Lines by Company Division

Safety Razor	Stationery Products
Trac II	Paper Mate
Atra	Liquid Paper
Good News	Flair
	Waterman
Toiletries and Cosmetics	Write Bros.
Adorn	**Oral Care**
Toni	
Right Guard	Oral B Toothbrushes
Silkience	
Soft and Dri	**Braun Products**
Foamy	
Dry Look	Electric Razors
Dry Idea	Lady Elegance
White Rain	Clocks
Lustrasilk	Coffee Grinders and Makers
Aapri Skin Care Products	

EXHIBIT 4.2 Gillette's Sales and Operating Profits by Product Line (In millions)

	1986		1987		1988	
	Sales	Profit	Sales	Profit	Sales	Profit
Blades and Razors	$903	$274	$1,031	$334	$1,147	$406
Toiletries and Cosmetics	854	69	926	99	1,019	79
Writing Instruments and Office Products	298	11	320	34	385	56
Braun Products	657	63	703	72	824	85
Oral-B	148	8	183	7	202	18
Other	48	(1)	4	2	5	(0.1)
Total	$2,908	$424	$3,167	$548	$3,582	$643

Gillette's Net Sales and Profit by Product Line as a Percent of the Business

	Blades and Razors		Toiletries and Cosmetics		Stationery Products		Braun Products		Oral B Products	
Year	Sales	Profit	Sales	Profit	Sales	Profit	Sales	Profit	Sales	Profit
1988	32%	61%	28%	14%	11%	9%	23%	13%	6%	3%
1987	33	61	29	18	10	6	22	13	6	2
1986	32	64	30	16	11	3	20	15	5	2
1985	33	68	31	15	11	2	17	13	6	3
1984	34	69	30	15	12	3	17	12	3	2

EXHIBIT 4.3 Gillette Income Statements (In millions)

	1986	1987	1988
Net Sales	$2,818.3	$3,166.8	$3,581.2
Cost of Sales	1,183.8	1,342.3	1,487.4
Other Expenses	1,412.0	1,301.3	1,479.8
Operating Income	222.5	523.2	614.0
Other Income	38.2	30.9	37.2
Earnings before Interest and Taxes	260.7	554.1	651.2
Interest Expense	85.2	112.5	138.3
Nonoperating Expense	124.0	50.1	64.3
Earnings before Tax	51.5	391.5	448.6
Tax	35.7	161.6	180.1
Earnings after Tax	$15.8	$229.9	$268.5
Retained Earnings	$944.3	$1,083.8	$1,261.6
Earnings per Share	$.12	$2.00	$2.45
Average Number of Common Shares, Outstanding (000)	127,344	115,072	109,559
Dividends Paid/Share	$0.68	$0.785	$0.86
Stock Price Range			
High	$34 1/2	$45 7/8	$49
Low	$17 1/8	$17 5/8	$29 1/8

Source: Gillette Company *Annual Reports*, 1985–1988.

EXHIBIT   4.4   Gillette Balance Sheets (In millions)

	1986	*1987*	*1988*
Assets			
Cash	$94.8	$119.1	$156.4
Receivables	608.8	680.1	729.1
Inventories	603.1	594.5	653.4
Other Current Assets	183.0	184.5	200.8
Total Current Assets	1,489.7	1,578.2	1,739.7
Fixed Assets, Net	637.3	664.4	683.1
Other Assets	412.5	448.6	445.1
Total Assets	$2,539.5	$2,731.2	$2,867.9
Liabilities and equity			
Current Liabilities[a]	$900.7	$960.5	$965.4
Current Portion Long-Term Debt	7.6	41.0	9.6
Long-Term Debt	915.2	839.6	1,675.2
Equity	$460.8	$599.4	$(84.6)

[a] Includes current portion of long-term debt.
Source: Gillette Company *Annual Reports*, 1986–1988.

Gillette introduced a number of innovative shaving systems in the 1970s and 1980s as part of its strategy to sustain growth. Gillette claimed that Trac II, the first twin-blade shaver, represented the most revolutionary shaving advance ever. The development of the twin-blade razor derived from shaving researchers' discovery of the hysteresis process—the phenomenon of whiskers being lifted up out of the follicle during shaving and, after a time, receding. Gillette invented the twin-blade system so that the first blade would cut the whisker and the second blade would cut it again before it receded. This system produced a closer shave than a traditional one-blade system. Gillette also developed a clog-free, dual-blade cartridge for the Trac II system.

Because consumer test data showed a nine-to-one preference for Trac II over panelists' current razors, Gillette raced to get the product to market. Gillette supported Trac II's 1971 introduction, which was the largest new product introduction in shaving history, with a $10 million advertising and promotion budget. Gillette cut its advertising budgets for its other brands drastically to support Trac II. The double-edged portion of the advertising budget decreased from 47 percent in 1971 to 11 percent in 1972. Gillette reasoned that growth must come at the expense of other brands. Thus, it concentrated its advertising and promotion on its newest shaving product and reduced support for its established lines.

Gillette launched Trac II during a World Series promotion and made it the most frequently advertised shaving system in the United States during its introductory period. Trac II users turned out to be predominantly young, college-educated men who lived in metropolitan and suburban areas and earned higher incomes. As the fastest-growing shaving product on the market for five years, Trac II drove the switch to twin blades. The brand reached its peak in 1976 when consumers purchased 485 million blades and 7 million razors.

Late in 1976, Gillette, apparently in response to BIC's pending entrance into the U.S. market, launched Good News!, the first disposable razor for men sold in the United States. In 1975, BIC had introduced the first disposable shaver in Europe; and by 1976 BIC began to sell disposable razors in Canada. Gillette realized that BIC would move its disposable razor into the United States after its Canadian introduction, so it promptly brought out a new, blue plastic disposable shaver with a twin-blade head. By year's end, Gillette also made Good News! available in Austria, Canada, France, Italy, Switzerland, Belgium, Greece, Germany, and Spain.

Unfortunately for Gillette, Good News! was really bad news. The disposable shaver delivered lower profit margins than razor and blade systems, and it undercut sales of other Gillette products. Good News! sold for much less than the retail price of a Trac II cartridge. Gillette marketed Good News! on price and convenience, not performance; but the company envisioned the product as a step-up item leading to its traditional high-quality shaving systems.

This contain-and-switch strategy did not succeed. Consumers liked the price and the convenience of disposable razors, and millions of Trac II razors began to gather dust in medicine chests across the country. Many Trac II users figured out that for as little as 25 cents, they could get the same cartridge mounted on a plastic handle that they had been buying for 56 cents to put on their Trac II handle. Further, disposable razors created an opening for competitors in a category that Gillette had long dominated.

Gillette felt certain that disposable razors would never gain more than a 7 percent share of the market. However, the disposable razor market share soon soared past 10 percent, forcing Gillette into continual upward revisions of its estimates. In terms of units sold, disposable razors reached a 22 percent market share by 1980 and a 50 percent share by 1988.

BIC and Gillette's successful introduction of the disposable razor represented a watershed event in commoditization. Status, quality, and perceived value had always played primary roles in marketing of personal care products. But consumers were now showing that they would forgo performance and prestige in a shaving product—about as close and personal as one can get.

In 1977, Gillette introduced a new blade-and-razor system at the expense of Trac II. It launched Atra with a $7 million advertising campaign and over 50 million $2 rebate coupons. Atra (which stands for automatic tracking razor action) was the first twin-blade shaving cartridge with a pivoting head. Engineers had designed the head to follow a man's facial contours for a closer shave. Researchers began developing the product in Gillette's British research and development lab in 1970. They had established a goal of improving the high performance standards of twin-blade shaving and specifically enhancing the Trac II effect. The company's scientists discovered that instead of moving the hand and face to produce the best blade shaving angle, the razor head itself could produce a better shave if it could pivot to maintain the most effective shaving angle. Marketers selected the name "Atra" after two years of extensive consumer testing.

After Atra's first year, consumers had purchased it at a faster rate than they had purchased Trac II during its first year; Atra quickly achieved a 7 percent share of the blade market and about one-third of the razor market. The company introduced Atra in Europe a year later under the brand name Contour. Although Atra increased Gillette's share of the razor market, 40 percent of Trac II users switched to Atra in the first year.

In the early 1980s, Gillette introduced more new disposable razors and product enhancements. Both Swivel (launched in 1980) and Good News! Pivot (1984) were disposable razors featuring movable heads. Gillette announced Atra Plus (the first razor with the patented Lubra-smooth lubricating strip) in 1985 just as BIC began to move into the United States from Canada with the BIC shaver for sensitive skin. A few months later, Gillette ushered in MicroTrac—the first disposable razor with an ultra-slim head. Gillette priced the MicroTrac lower than any other Gillette disposable razor. The company claimed to have designed a state-of-the-art manufacturing process for MicroTrac. The process required less plastic, thus minimizing bulk and reducing manufacturing costs. Analysts claimed that Gillette was trying to bracket the market with Atra Plus (with a retail price of $3.99 to $4.95) and MicroTrac ($.99), and protect its market share with products on both ends of the price and usage scale. Gillette also teased Wall Street with hints that, by the end of 1986, it would be introducing a state-of-the-art shaving system that could revolutionize the shaving business.

Despite these product innovations and introductions in the early 1980s, Gillette primarily focused its energies on its global markets and strategies. By 1985, Gillette marketed 800 products in more than 200 countries. The company felt a need at this time to coordinate its marketing efforts regionally, and then globally. Unfortunately for Gillette's management team, others noticed its strong international capabilities. Ronald Perelman, chairman of the Revlon Group, attempted an unfriendly takeover in November 1986. To fend off the takeover, Gillette bought back 9.2 million shares of its stock from Perelman and saddled itself with additional long-term debt to finance the stock repurchase. Gillette's payment to Perelman increased the company's debt load from $827 million to $1.1 billion, and put its debt-to-equity ratio at 70 percent. Gillette and Perelman signed an agreement preventing Perelman from attempting another takeover until 1996.

In 1988, just as Gillette returned its attention to new product development and global marketing, Coniston Partners, after obtaining 6 percent of Gillette's stock, engaged the company in a proxy battle for four seats on its 12-person board. Coniston's interest had been piqued by the Gillette–Perelman $549 million stock buy-back and its payment of $9 million in expenses to Perelman. Coniston and some shareholders felt Gillette's board and management had repeatedly taken actions that prohibited its stockholders from realizing their shares' full value. When the balloting concluded, Gillette's management won by a narrow margin— 52 to 48 percent. Coniston made $13 million in the stock buy-back program that Gillette offered to all shareholders, but Coniston agreed not to make another run at Gillette until 1991. This second takeover attempt forced Gillette to increase its debt load to $2 billion and pushed its total equity negative to $−84.6 million.

More importantly, both takeover battles forced Gillette to "wake up." Gillette closed or sold its Jafra Cosmetics operations in 11 countries and jettisoned weak operations such as Misco (a computer supply business), and S.T. Dupont (a luxury lighter, clock, and watch maker). The company also thinned its work force in many divisions, such as its 15 percent staff reduction at the Paper Mate pen unit. Despite this pruning, Gillette's sales for 1988 grew 13 percent to $3.6 billion, and profits soared 17 percent to $268 million.

Although Gillette concentrated on fending off these takeover attempts, it continued to enhance its razor and blade products. In 1986, Gillette introduced the Contour Plus in its first pan-European razor launch. The company marketed Contour Plus with one identity and one strategy. In 1988, the company introduced Trac II Plus, Good News! Pivot Plus, and Daisy Plus—versions of its existing products with the Lubra-smooth lubricating strip.

Schick

Warner-Lambert's Schick served as the second major competitor in the wet-shaving business. Warner-Lambert, incorporated in 1920 under the name William R. Warner & Company, manufactured chemicals and pharmaceuticals. Numerous mergers and acquisitions over the past 70 years resulted in Warner-Lambert's involvement in developing, manufacturing, and marketing a widely diversified line of beauty, health, and well-being products. The company also became a major producer of mints and chewing gums, such as Dentyne, Sticklets, and Trident. Exhibit 4.5 presents a list of Warner-Lambert's products by division as of 1988.

Warner-Lambert entered the wet-shave business through a merger with Eversharp in 1970. Eversharp, a long-time competitor in the wet-shave industry, owned the Schick trademark and had owned the Paper Mate Pen Company prior to selling it to Gillette in 1955. Schick's razors and blades produced $180 million in revenue in 1987, or 5.2 percent of the Warner-Lambert's worldwide sales. (Refer to Exhibit 4.6 for operating results by division and Exhibits 4.7 and 4.8 for income statement and balance sheet data.)

In 1989, Schick held approximately a 16.2 percent U.S. market share, down from its 1980 share of 23.8 percent. Schick's 16.2 percent share of the razor market was broken down as follows: blade systems, 8.8 percent; disposable razors, 4.1 percent; and double-edged and injectors, 3.3 percent.

Schick's loss of market share in the 1980s occurred for two reasons. First, although Schick pioneered the injector razor system (it controlled 80 percent of this market by 1979), it did not market a disposable razor until mid-1984—eight years after the first disposable razors appeared. Second, for years Warner-Lambert had been channeling Schick's cash flow to its research and development in drugs.

In 1986, the company changed its philosophy; it allocated $70 million to Schick for a three-year period and granted Schick its own sales force. Despite

EXHIBIT 4.5   Warner-Lambert 1988 Product Lines by Company Division

Ethical Pharmaceuticals	Gums and Mints
Parke-Davis drug	Dentyne
	Sticklets
Nonprescription Products	Trident
	Beemans
Benadryl	Chiclets
Caladryl	Freshen-up
Rolaids	Bubblicious
Sinutab	Charleston Chew
Listerex	Clorets
Lubraderm	Certs
Anusol	Dynamints
Tucks	Junior Mints
Halls	Sugar Daddy
Benylin	Sugar Babies
Listerine	Rascals
Listermint	
Efferdent	**Other Products**
Effergrip	
	Schick razors
	Ultrex razors
	Personal Touch
	Tetra Aquarium

EXHIBIT 4.6   Warner-Lambert's Net Sales and Operating Profit by Division
(In millions)

	Net Sales				Operating Profit (Loss)			
	1985	1986	1987	1988	1985	1986	1987	1988
Health Care Division								
Ethical Products	$880	$964	$1,093	$1,213	$224	$246	$351	$420
Nonprescription Products	992	1,077	1,195	1,296	177	176	256	305
Total Health Care	1,872	2,041	2,288	2,509	401	422	607	725
Gums and Mints	626	678	777	918	138	122	173	187
Other Products[a]	334	384	420	481	72	61	86	92
Divested Businesses					(464)			
R&D					(208)	(202)	(232)	(259)
Net Sales and Operating Profit	$3,200	$3,103	$3,485	$3,908	$(61)	$599	$634	$745

[a] Other products include Schick razors which accounted for $180 million in revenue in 1987.
Source: Warner-Lambert Company *Annual Report*, 1987 and *Moody's Industrial Manual*.

EXHIBIT 4.7   **Warner-Lambert Income Statements (In thousands)**

	1986	1987	1988
Net Sales	$3,102,918	$3,484,700	$3,908,400
Cost of Sales	1,052,781	1,169,700	1,351,700
Other Expenses	1,616,323	1,819,800	2,012,100
Operating Income	433,814	495,200	544,600
Other Income	69,611	58,500	61,900
Earnings before Income Taxes	503,425	553,700	606,500
Interest Expense	66,544	60,900	68,200
Earnings before Tax	436,881	492,800	538,300
Tax	136,297	197,000	198,000
Nonrecurring Item	8,400	—	—
Earnings after Tax	$308,984	$295,800	$340,000
Retained Earnings	$1,023,218	$1,384,100	$1,577,400
Earnings per Share	$4.18	$4.15	$5.00
Average Common Shares Outstanding (000)	73,985	71,355	68,035
Dividends Paid/Share	$1.59	$1.77	$2.16
Stock Price Range			
High	$63 1/8	$87 1/2	$79 1/2
Low	$45	$48 1/4	$59 7/8

Source: *Moody's Industrial Manual.*

EXHIBIT 4.8   **Warner-Lambert Balance Sheets (In thousands)**

	1986	1987	1988
Assets			
Cash	$26,791	$24,100	$176,000
Receivables	445,743	469,900	525,200
Inventories	317,212	379,000	381,400
Other Current Assets	720,322	379,600	181,300
Total Current Assets	1,510,068	1,252,600	1,264,500
Fixed Assets, Net	819,291	959,800	1,053,000
Other Assets	186,564	263,500	385,300
Total Assets	$2,515,923	$2,475,900	$2,702,800
Liabilities and equity			
Current Liabilities[a]	$969,806	$974,300	$1,025,200
Current Portion Long-Term Debt	143,259	4,200	7,100
Long-Term Debt	342,112	293,800	318,200
Equity	$907,322	$874,400	$998,600

[a] Includes current portion of long-term debt.
Source: *Moody's Industrial Manual.*

Schick's loss of market share, company executives felt they had "room to play catch up, especially by exploiting new technologies." In late 1988, Schick revealed that it planned to conduct "guerrilla warfare" by throwing its marketing resources and efforts into new technological advances in disposable razors. As a result, Warner-Lambert planned to allocate the bulk of its $8 million razor advertising budget to marketing its narrow-headed disposable razor, Slim Twin, which it introduced in August 1988.

Schick believed that the U.S. unit demand for disposable razors would increase to 55 percent of the market by the early 1990s from its 50 percent share in 1988. Schick executives based this belief on their feeling that men would rather pay 30 cents for a disposable razor than 75 cents for a refill blade. In 1988, Schick held an estimated 9.9 percent share of dollar sales in the disposable razor market.

Schick generated approximately 67 percent of its revenues overseas. Also, Schick earned higher profit margins on its nondomestic sales—20 percent versus its 15 percent domestic margin. Europe and Japan represented the bulk of Schick's international business, accounting for 38 percent and 52 percent, respectively, of 1988's overseas sales. Schick's European business consisted of 70 percent systems and 29 percent disposable razors, but Gillette's systems and disposable razor sales were 4.5 and 6 times larger than Schick's respective European sales.

However, Schick dominated in Japan. Warner-Lambert held over 60 percent of Japan's wet-shave market. Although Japan had typically been an electric shaver market (55 percent of Japanese shavers use electric razors), Schick achieved an excellent record and reputation in Japan. Both Schick and Gillette entered the Japanese market in 1962; their vigorous competition eventually drove Japanese competitors from the industry, which by 1988 generated $190 million in sales. Gillette's attempt to crack the market flopped because it tried to sell razors using its own salespeople, a strategy that failed because Gillette did not have the distribution network available to Japanese companies. Schick, meanwhile, chose to leave the distribution to Seiko Corporation. Seiko imported razors from the United States and then sold them to wholesalers nationwide. By 1988, Schick generated roughly 40 percent of its sales and 35 percent of its profits in Japan. Disposable razors accounted for almost 80 percent of those figures.

BIC Corporation

Marcel Bich founded the BIC Corporation in the United States in 1958, but its roots grew from France. In 1945, Bich, who had been the production manager for a French ink manufacturer, bought a factory outside Paris to produce parts for fountain pens and mechanical lead pencils. In his new business, Bich became one of the first manufacturers to purchase presses to work with plastics. With his knowledge of inks and experience with plastics and molding machines, Bich set himself up to become the largest pen manufacturer in the world. In 1949, Bich introduced his version of the modern ball-point pen, originally invented in 1939, which he called "BIC," a shortened, easy-to-remember version of his own name. He supported the pen with memorable, effective advertising; its sales surpassed even his own expectations.

Realizing that a mass-produced, disposable ball-point pen had universal appeal, Bich turned his attention to the U.S. market. In 1958, he purchased the Waterman-Pen Company of Connecticut and then incorporated as Waterman-BIC Pen Corporation. The company changed its name to BIC Pen in 1971 and finally adopted the name BIC Corporation in 1982.

After establishing itself as the country's largest pen maker, BIC attacked another market—the disposable lighter market. When BIC introduced its lighter in 1973, the total disposable lighter market stood at only 50 million units. By 1984, BIC had become so successful at manufacturing and marketing its disposable lighters that Gillette, its primary competitor, abandoned the lighter market. Gillette sold its Cricket division to Swedish Match, Stockholm, the manufacturer of Wilkinson razors. By 1989, the disposable lighter market had grown to nearly 500 million units, and BIC lighters accounted for 60 percent of the market.

Not just content to compete in the writing and lighting markets, BIC decided to enter the U.S. shaving market in 1976. A year earlier, the company had launched the BIC Shaver in Europe and Canada. BIC's entrance into the U.S. razor market started an intense rivalry with Gillette. Admittedly, the companies were not strangers to each other—for years they had competed for market share in the pen and lighter industries. However, razors were Gillette's primary business and an area where the company had no intention of relinquishing market share. However BIC established a niche in the U.S. disposable-razor market.

BIC, similar to Gillette, frequently introduced new razor products and product enhancements. In January 1985, following a successful Canadian test in 1984, BIC announced the BIC Shaver for Sensitive Skin. BIC claimed that 42 percent of the men surveyed reported that they had sensitive skin, while 51 percent of those who had heavy beards reported that they had sensitive skin. Thus, BIC felt there was a clear need for a shaver that addressed this special shaving problem. The $10 million ad campaign for the BIC Shaver for Sensitive Skin featured John McEnroe, a highly ranked and well-known tennis professional, discussing good and bad backhands and normal and sensitive skin. BIC repositioned the original BIC white shaver as the shaver men with normal skin should use, while it promoted the new BIC Orange as the razor for sensitive skin.

BIC also tried its commodity strategy on sailboards, car-top carriers, and perfume. In 1982, BIC introduced a sailboard model at about half the price of existing products. The product generated nothing but red ink. In April 1989, the company launched BIC perfumes with $15 million in advertising support. BIC's foray into fragrances was as disappointing as its sailboard commoditization attempt. Throughout the year, Parfum BIC lost money, forcing management to concentrate its efforts on reformulating its selling theme, advertising, packaging, and price points. Many retailers rejected the product, sticking BIC with expensive manufacturing facilities in Europe. BIC found that consumers' perceptions of commodities did not translate equally into every category. For example, many women cut corners elsewhere just to spend lavishly on their perfume. The last thing they wanted to see was their favorite scent being hawked to the masses.

Despite these failures, BIC Corporation was the undisputed king of the commoditizers. BIC's success with pens and razors demonstrated the upside potential of commoditization, while its failures with sailboards and perfumes illustrated the limitations. BIC concentrated its efforts on designing, manufacturing, and delivering the best-quality products at the lowest possible prices. And although the company produced large quantities of disposable products (i.e., over 1 million pens a day), it claimed that each product was invested with the BIC philosophy: "Maximum service, minimum price."

One of BIC's greatest assets was its distribution and its strength in retail. The high profile the company enjoyed at supermarkets and drugstores enabled it to win locations in the aisles and display space at the checkout—the best positioning.

Although BIC controlled only the number three spot in the wet-shaving market by 1989, it had exerted quite an influence since its razors first entered the U.S. market in 1976. In 1988, BIC's razors generated $52 million in sales with a net income of $9.4 million and held a 22.4 percent share of the disposable razor market. Exhibits 4.9 through 4.11 present operating data by product line and income statement and balance sheet data.

The introduction of the disposable razor revolutionized the industry and cut into system razor profits. However, despite the low profit margins in disposable razors and the fact that the industry leader, Gillette, emphasized razor-and-blade systems, BIC remained bullish on the disposable razor market. In 1988, BIC held a 22.4 percent share of the dollar sales in the disposable razor market. In 1989, a

EXHIBIT 4.9   BIC'S Net Sales and Income before Taxes (In millions)

	1986	1987	1988
Net Sales			
Writing Instruments	$91.7	$106.7	$118.5
Lighters	115.0	120.0	113.9
Shavers	49.6	47.1	51.9
Sport	11.3	16.8	10.6
Total	$267.6	$290.6	$294.9
Income (Loss) before Taxes			
Writing Instruments	$15.0	$17.5	$16.7
Lighters	28.5	28.2	22.9
Shavers	8.0	8.5	9.4
Sport	(3.6)	(3.5)	(4.)
Total	$47.9	$50.7	$44.3

Source: BIC *Annual Report,* 1988 and 1989.

EXHIBIT 4.10   BIC Corporation Consolidated Income Statements (In thousands)

	1986	1987	1988
Net Sales	$267,624	$290,616	$294,878
Cost of Sales	147,602	165,705	172,542
Other Expenses	67,697	73,785	81,023
Operating Income	52,325	51,126	41,313
Other Income	7,534	1,836	4,119
Earnings before Income Taxes	59,859	52,962	45,432
Interest Expense	11,982	2,301	1,097
Earnings before Tax	47,877	50,661	44,335
Tax	24,170	21,944	17,573
Extraordinary Credit	2,486a	—	—
Utilization of Operating Loss Carryforward	—	—	2,800
Earnings after Tax	$26,193	$28,717	$29,562
Retained Earnings	$121,784	$142,501	$159,942
Earnings per Share	$2.16	$2.37	$2.44
Average Number of Common Shares Outstanding (000)	12,121	12,121	12,121
Dividends Paid/Share	$0.48	$0.66	$0.75
Stock Price Range			
High	$35	$34 7/8	$30 3/8
Low	$23 1/4	$16 1/2	$24 3/8

a Gain from elimination of debt.
Source: *Moody's Industrial Manual* and BIC *Annual Report*.

EXHIBIT 4.11   BIC Corporation Balance Sheets (In thousands)

	1986	1987	1988
Assets			
Cash	$5,047	$4,673	$5,314
Certificates of Deposit	6,401	803	3,117
Receivables, Net	32,960	41,704	43,629
Inventories	50,058	59,779	70,930
Other Current Assets	34,898	47,385	37,603
Deferred Income Taxes	5,622	6,691	7,939
Total Current Assets	134,986	161,035	168,532
Fixed Assets, Net	58,385	62,797	74,973
Total Assets	$193,371	$223,832	$243,505
Liabilities and equity			
Current Liabilities	$45,104	$54,034	$55,031
Current Portion Long-Term Debt	287	247	157
Long-Term Debt	1,789	1,511	1,521
Equity	$142,848	$164,068	$181,194

Source: *Moody's Industrial Manual.*

spokesperson for BIC claimed that BIC "was going to stick to what consumers liked." The company planned to continue marketing only single-blade, disposable shavers. BIC also stated that it planned to maintain its strategy of underpricing competitors, but it would also introduce improvements such as the patented metal guard in its BIC Metal Shaver. Research revealed that the BIC Metal Shaver provided some incremental, rather than substitute, sales for its shaver product line. BIC executives believed that the BIC Metal Shaver would reach a 5 to 8 percent market share by 1990.

Wilkinson Sword

Swedish Match Holding Incorporated's subsidiary, Wilkinson Sword, came in as the fourth player in the U.S. market. Swedish Match Holding was a wholly owned subsidiary of Swedish Match AB, Stockholm, Sweden. The parent company owned subsidiaries in the United States that imported and sold doors, produced resilient and wood flooring, and manufactured branded razors, blades, self-sharpening scissors, and gourmet kitchen knives. (Exhibits 4.12 and 4.13 present income statement and balance sheet data on Swedish Match AB.)

A group of sword smiths founded Wilkinson in 1772, and soldiers used the company's swords at Waterloo, the charge of the Light Brigade, and in the Boer War. However, as the sword declined as a combat weapon, Wilkinson retreated to producing presentation and ceremonial swords. By 1890, Wilkinson's cutlers had begun to produce straight razors, and by 1898 it was producing safety razors similar to King Gillette's. When Gillette's blades became popular in England, Wilkinson made stroppers to resharpen used blades. Wilkinson failed in the razor market, however, and dropped out during World War II.

EXHIBIT 4.12 Swedish Match AB Income Statements (In thousands)

	1986	1987	1988
Net Sales	$1,529,704	$2,505,047	$2,814,662
Cost of Sales	n/a	n/a	n/a
Operating Expenses	1,387,360	2,291,023	2,541,128
Other Expenses	48,711	95,420	108,206
Earnings before Income Taxes	93,633	118,604	165,328
Interest Expense	21,618	19,084	5,386
Earnings before Tax	72,015	99,520	159,942
Tax	39,165	29,996	57,612
Earnings after Tax	$32,850	$69,554	$102,330
Dividends Paid/Share	$1.75	$0.51	$0.53
Stock Price Range			
High	$66.75	$19.65	$22.53
Low	$22.00	$11.06	$15.00

n/a = not available.
Source: *Moody's International Manual.*

EXHIBIT   4.13   Swedish Match AB Balance Sheets (In thousands of U.S. dollars)

	1986	1987	1988
Assets			
Cash and Securities	$323,993	$117,027	$159,616
Receivables	297,321	561,479	611,372
Inventories	258,858	415,116	421,563
Total Current Assets	880,172	1,093,622	1,192,551
Fixed Assets, Net	397,411	671,409	707,664
Other Assets	93,211	132,799	161,085
Total Assets	$1,370,794	$1,897,830	$2,061,300
Liabilities and Equity			
Current Liabilities	$576,534	$905,778	$996,214
Current Portion Long-Term Debt	n/a	n/a	n/a
Long-Term Debt	244,118	316,542	298,505
Equity	n/a	n/a	n/a

n/a = not available.
Source: *Moody's International Manual.*

By 1954, Wilkinson decided to look again at the shaving market. Manufacturers used carbon steel to make most razor blades at that time, and such blades lost their serviceability rapidly due to mechanical and chemical damage. Gillette and other firms had experimented with stainless steel blades; but they had found that despite their longer-lasting nature, the blades did not sharpen well. But some men liked the durability, and a few small companies produced stainless steel blades.

Wilkinson purchased one such small German company and put Wilkinson Sword blades on the market in 1956. Wilkinson developed a coating for the stainless blades (in the same fashion that Gillette had coated the Super Blue Blade) that masked their rough edges, allowing the blades to give a comfortable shave and to last two to five times longer than conventional blades. Wilkinson called the new blade the Super Sword-Edge. Wilkinson introduced the blades in England in 1961 and in the United States in 1962, and they became a phenomenon. Schick and American Safety Razor followed a year later with their own stainless steel blades, the Krona-Plus and Personna. Gillette finally responded by late 1963 with its own stainless steel blade. By early 1964 Gillette's blades were outselling Wilkinson, Schick, and Personna combined. Wilkinson, however, had forever changed the nature of the razor blade.

In 1988, Wilkinson Sword claimed to have a 4 percent share of the U.S. wet-shave market; it was predicting a 6 percent share by mid-1990. Industry analysts, however, did not confirm even the 4 percent share; they projected Wilkinson's share to be closer to 1 percent. Wilkinson introduced many new products over the years, but they generally proved to be short-lived. The company never really developed its U.S. franchise.

However, in late 1988, Wilkinson boasted that it was going to challenge the wet-shave category leader by introducing Ultra-Glide, its first lubricating shaving system. Wilkinson designed Ultra-Glide to go head-to-head with Gillette's Atra Plus and Schick's Super II Plus and Ultrex Plus. Wilkinson claimed that Ultra-Glide represented a breakthrough in shaving technology because of an ingredient, hydromer, in its patented lubricating strip. According to Wilkinson, the Ultra-Glide strip left less residue on the face and provided a smoother, more comfortable shave by creating a cushion of moisture between the razor and the skin.

Wilkinson introduced Ultra-Glide in March 1989 and supported it with a $5 million advertising and promotional campaign (versus Atra Plus' $80 million multimedia investment). Wilkinson priced Ultra-Glide 5 to 8 percent less than Atra Plus. Wilkinson was undaunted by Gillette's heavier advertising investment, and it expected to cash in on its rival's strong marketing muscle. Wilkinson did not expect to overtake Gillette but felt its drive should help it capture a double-digit U.S. market share within two to three years.

Many were skeptical about Wilkinson's self-predicted market share growth. One industry analyst stated, "Gillette dominates this business. Some upstart won't do anything." One Gillette official claimed his company was unfazed by Wilkinson. In fact, he was quoted as saying in late 1988, "They [Wilkinson] don't have a business in the United States; they don't exist."

Nonetheless, Gillette became enraged and filed legal challenges when Wilkinson's television ads for Ultra Glide broke in May 1989. The ads stated that Ultra Glide's lubricating strip was six times smoother than Gillette's strip and that men preferred it to the industry leader's. All three major networks had reservations about continuing to air the comparison commercials. CBS and NBC stated that they were going to delay airing the company's ads until Wilkinson responded to questions they had about its ad claims. In an 11th-hour counterattack, Wilkinson accused Gillette of false advertising and of trying to monopolize the wet-shave market.

GILLETTE'S SOUTH BOSTON PLANT

Robert Squires left his work station in the facilities engineering section of Gillette's South Boston manufacturing facility and headed for the shave test lab. He entered the lab area and walked down a narrow hall. On his right were a series of small cubicles Gillette had designed to resemble the sink area of a typical bathroom. Robert opened the door of his assigned cubicle precisely at his scheduled 10 A.M. time. He removed his dress shirt and tie, hanging them on a hook beside the sink. Sliding the mirror up as one would a window, Robert looked into the lab area. Rose McCluskey, a lab assistant, greeted him.

"Morning, Robert. See you're right on time as usual. I've got your things all ready for you." Rose reached into a recessed area on her side of the cubicle's wall and handed Robert his razor, shave cream, after-shave lotion, and a clean towel.

"Thanks, Rose. Hope you're having a good day. Anything new you've got me trying today?"

"You know I can't tell you that. It might spoil your objectivity. Here's your card." Rose handed Robert a shaving evaluation card (Exhibit 4.14).

EXHIBIT 4.14   Evaluation Form Used by Gillette Employees

GILLETTE SHAVING EVALUATION CARD

NUMB	CODE	STATION	TEST #	NAME	EMP #	DATE

INPLANT SHAVE TEST SCORECARD

INSTRUCTIONS: Please check one box in each column.

OVERALL EVALUATION OF SHAVE	FREEDOM FROM NICKS AND CUTS	CAUTION	CLOSENESS	SMOOTHNESS	COMFORT
☐ Excellent	☐ Excellent	☐ Exceptionally Safe	☐ Exceptionally Close	☐ Exceptionally Smooth	☐ Exceptionally Comfortable
☐ Very Good	☐ Very Good	☐ Unusually Safe	☐ Very Close	☐ Very Smooth	☐ Very Comfortable
☐ Good	☐ Good	☐ Average	☐ Average	☐ Average Smoothness	☐ Average Comfort
☐ Fair	☐ Fair	☐ Slight Caution Needed	☐ Fair	☐ Slight Pull	☐ Slight Irritation
☐ Poor	☐ Poor	☐ Excessive Caution Needed	☐ Poor	☐ Excessive Pull	☐ Excessive Irritation

Source: Gillette Company.

Robert had been shaving at the South Boston Plant off and on for all of his 25 years with Gillette. He was one of 200 men who shaved every work day at the plant. Gillette used these shavers to compare its products' effectiveness with competitors' products. The shavers also conducted R&D testing of new products and quality control testing for manufacturing. An additional seven to eight panels of 250 men each shaved every day in their homes around the country, primarily conducting R&D shave testing.

Like Robert, each shaver completed a shave evaluation card following every shave. Lab assistants like Rose entered data from the evaluations to allow Gillette researchers to analyze the performance of each shaving device. If a product passed R&D hurdles, it became the responsibility of the marketing research staff to conduct consumer-use testing. Such consumer testing employed 2,000 to 3,000 men who tested products in their homes.

From its research, Gillette had learned that the average man has 30,000 whiskers on his face that grow at the rate of 1/2 inch per month. He shaved 5.8 times a week and spent three to four minutes shaving each time. A man with a life span of 70 years would shave more than 20,000 times, spending 3,350 hours (130 days) removing 27 1/2 feet of facial hair. Yet, despite all the time and effort involved in shaving, surveys found that if a cream were available that would eliminate facial hair and shaving, most men would not use it.

Robert finished shaving and rinsed his face and shaver. He glanced at the shaving head. A pretty good shave, he thought. The cartridge had two blades, but it seemed different. Robert marked his evaluation card and slid it across the counter to Rose. William Mazeroski, manager of the South Boston shave test lab, walked into the lab area carrying computer printouts with the statistical analysis of last week's shave test data.

Noticing Robert, William stopped. "Morning, Robert. How was your shave?"

"Pretty good. What am I using?"

"Robert, you are always trying to get me to tell you what we're testing! We have control groups and experimental groups. I can't tell you which you are in, but I was just looking at last week's results, and I can tell you that it looks like we are making progress. We've been testing versions of a new product since 1979, and I think we're about to get it right. Of course, I don't know if we'll introduce it or even if we can make it in large quantities, but it looks good."

"Well, that's interesting. At least I know I'm involved in progress. And, if we do decide to produce a new shaver, we'll have to design and build the machines to make it ourselves because there is nowhere to go to purchase blade-making machinery. Well, I've got to get back now; see you tomorrow."

THE PRUDENTIAL CENTER, 37th FLOOR

Paul Hankins leaned over the credenza in his 37th floor office in Boston's Prudential Center office building and admired the beauty of the scene that spread before him. Paul felt as though he were watching an impressionistic painting in motion. Beyond the green treetops and red brick buildings of Boston's fashionable Back Bay area, the Charles River wound its way toward Boston Harbor. Paul could see the buildings on the campuses of Harvard, MIT, and Boston University scattered along both sides of the river. Soon the crew teams would be out practicing. Paul loved to watch the precision with which the well-coordinated teams propelled the boats up and down the river. If only, he thought, we could be as coordinated as those crew teams.

Paul had returned to Boston in early 1988 when Gillette had created the North Atlantic Group by combining what had been the North American and the European operations. Originally from Boston, he had attended Columbia University and earned an MBA at Dartmouth's Tuck School. He had been with Gillette for 19 years. Prior to 1988, he had served as marketing director for Gillette Europe from 1983 to 1984, as the country manager for Holland from 1985 to 1986, and finally as manager of Holland and the Scandinavian countries.

During this 1983 to 87 period, Paul had worked for Jim Pear, vice president of Gillette Europe, to implement a pan-European strategy. Prior to 1983, Gillette had organized and managed Europe as a classic decentralized market. The company had treated each country as a separate market to meet the perceived nuances within each cultural area. For example, Gillette offered the same products under a variety of sub-brand names. The company sold its Good News! disposable razors under the name Blue II in the United Kingdom, Parat in Germany, Gillette in France and Spain, Radi e Getta (shave and throw) in Italy, and Economy in other European markets.

Jim Pear believed that in the future Gillette would have to organize across country lines, and he had developed the pan-European idea. He felt that shaving was a universal act and that Gillette's razors were a perfect archetype for a "global" product.

Gillette had launched Contour Plus, the European version of Atra Plus, in 1985–86 and had experienced greater success than the U.S. launch, which took place at the same time. The pan-European strategy seemed to be both more efficient and more effective. Colman Mockler, Gillette's chairman, noticed the European success and asked Pear to come to Boston to head the new North Atlantic Group. Paul had come with him as vice president of marketing for the Shaving and Personal Care Group.

Paul turned from the window as he heard people approaching. Sarah Kale, director of marketing research; Brian Mullins, vice president of marketing for the Shaving and Personal Care Group; and Scott Friedman, business director of Blades and Razors Group, were at his door.

"Ready for our meeting?" Scott asked.

"Sure, come on in. I was just admiring the view."

"The purpose of this meeting," Paul started, "is to begin formulating a new strategy for Gillette North Atlantic, specifically our shaving products. I'm interested in your general thoughts and analysis. I want to begin to identify options and to select a strategy that we want to pursue. What have you found out?"

"Well, here are the market share numbers you asked me to develop," Scott observed as he handed each person copies of tables he had produced (see Exhibits 4.15 and 4.16). Like Paul, Scott had earned an MBA from the Tuck School and had been with Gillette for 17 years.

"These are our U.S. share numbers through 1988. As you can see, Atra blades seem to have leveled off and Trac II blades are declining. Disposable razors now account for over 41 percent of the market, in dollars, and for over 50 percent of the market in terms of units. In fact, our projections would indicate that disposable razors will approach 100 percent of the market by the mid to late 1990s given current trends. Although we have 56 percent of the blade market and 58 percent of the disposable razor market, our share of the disposable razor

EXHIBIT 4.15 **Gillette Market Share of Dollar Sales (Percent)**

Product or Category	1981	1982	1983	1984	1985	1986	1987	1988
ATRA Blades	15.4%	17.3%	19.4%	18.7%	20.2%	20.9%	20.0%	20.5%
TRAC II Blades	17.5	16.4	15.2	14.6	14.1	13.5	11.8	11.4
Gillette Blades	47.3	48.9	52.1	54.2	55.8	57.1	54.1	56.0
Gillette Disposables	14.3	15.4	17.4	20.0	21.1	22.7	22.2	24.0
All Disposables	23.0	23.2	27.0	30.6	32.7	34.9	38.5	41.1
Gillette Disposables/ All Disposables	67.9	66.9	64.7	65.7	64.6	64.2	57.6	58.4
Gillette Razors	50.3	52.5	54.9	58.8	62.2	67.6	64.1	61.0

Source: Prudential-Bache Securities.

market has fallen. Further, you are aware that every 1 percent switch from our system razors to our disposable razors represents a loss of $10 million on the bottom line."

"I don't think any of this should surprise us," Sarah Kale interjected. Sarah had joined Gillette after graduating from Simmons College in Boston and had been with the firm for 14 years. "If you look back over the 1980s, you'll see that we helped cause this problem."

EXHIBIT 4.16 **Gillette System Cartridges Dollar Share of the U.S. Blade Market**

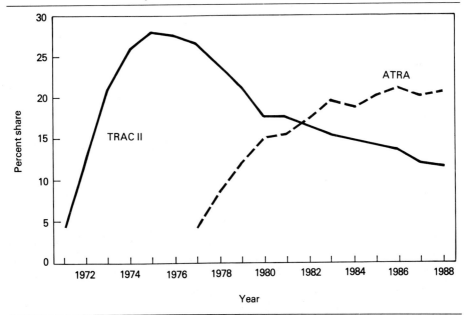

Source: Gillette Company and Prudential-Bache Securities.

"What do you mean by that?" asked Paul.

"Well, as market leader, we never believed that the use of disposable razors would grow as it has. We went along with the trend, but we kept prices low on our disposable razors, which made profitability worse for us as well as the competition. Then, at the same time we realized the impact on our profitability from the growth of the disposable razor market, we were raising the prices on our system razors. This made disposable razors even more attractive for the more price-sensitive users and further fueled the growth of disposable razors. This has occurred despite the fact that our market research shows that men rate system shavers significantly better than disposable razors. We find that the weight and balance contributed by the permanent handle used with the cartridge contributes to a better shave."

"Yes, but every time I tell someone that," Paul added, "they just look at me as if they wonder if I really believe that or if it is just Gillette's party line."

"There's one other thing we've done," Scott added. "Look at this graph of our advertising expenditures in the United States over the 1980s (see Exhibit 4.17). In fact, in constant 1987 dollars, our advertising spending has fallen from $61 million in 1975 to about $15 million in 1987. We seem to have just spent what was left over on advertising. We are now spending about 50 percent of our advertising on Atra and 50 percent on Good News!. Tentative plans call for us to increase the share going to Good News!. Our media budget for 1988 was about

EXHIBIT 4.17   Blade and Razor U.S. Media Spending

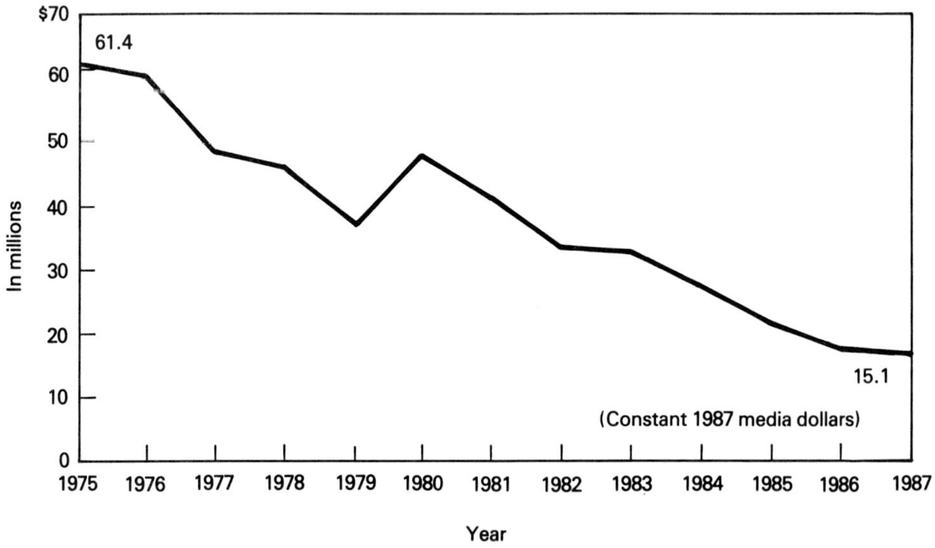

Source: Gillette Company.

$43 million. Further, we've tried three or four themes, but we haven't stuck with any one for very long. We're using the current theme, 'The Essence of Shaving' for both system and disposable products. Our advertising has been about 90 percent product based and 10 percent image based.''

"Well, Scott's right,'' Sarah noted, "but although share of voice is important, share of mind is what counts. Our most recent research shows a significant difference in how we are perceived by male consumers based on their age. Despite our reduced advertising, men over 40 still remember Gillette, from their youth. They remember Gillette's sponsorship of athletic events, like the Saturday baseball Game of the Week and the Cavalcade of Sports. They remember 'Look Sharp! Feel Sharp! Be Sharp!' and Sharpie the parrot. They remember their fathers loaning them their Gillette razors when they started shaving. There is still a strong connection with Gillette and the male image of shaving.''

"How about with younger men?'' asked Brian. Brian had joined Gillette in 1975 after graduating from Washington and Lee University and earning a masters in administration from George Washington University.

"Younger men's views can be summed up simply—twin blade, blue, and plastic,'' Sarah reported.

"Just like our disposable razors!'' Paul exclaimed.

"Precisely,'' Sarah answered. "Like I said, we've done this to ourselves. We have a 'steel' man and a 'plastic' man. In fact, for males between 15 and 19, BIC is better known than Gillette with respect to shaving. Younger men in general, those under 30, these 'plastic' men, feel all shavers are the same. Older men and system users feel there is a difference.''

"Yes,'' Paul interjected, "and I've noticed something else interesting. Look at our logo. We use the Gillette brand name as our corporate name. And the brand name is done in thin, block letters. I'm not sure it has the impact and masculine image we want. And to top that, look at these razor packages. We have become so product focused and brand-manager driven that we've lost focus on the brand name. Our brands look tired; there's nothing special about our retail packaging and display.''

"Speaking of the male image of shaving, Sarah, what does your research show about our image with women?'' asked Brian.

"Well, we've always had a male focus and women identify the Gillette name with men and shaving, even those who use our products marketed to women. You know that there are more women wet shavers than men in the North Atlantic market, about 62 million versus 55 million. However, due to seasonality and lower frequency of women's shaving, the unit volume used by women is only about one-third that of the volume used by men. Women use about 8 to 12 blades a year versus 25 to 30 for men. It is still very consistent for us to focus on men.''

"Well, we've got plenty of problems on the marketing side, but we also have to remember that we are part of a larger corporation with its own set of problems,'' Brian suggested. "We're only 30 percent or so of sales but we are 60 percent of profits. And, given the takeover battles, there is going to be increased pressure on the company to maintain and improve profitability. That pressure has always been on us, but now it will be more intense. If we want to develop some bold, new strategy, we are going to have to figure out where to get the money to finance it. I'm sure the rest of the corporation will continue to look to us to throw off cash to support diversification."

"This can get depressing," Paul muttered as he looked back at the window. "I can sense the low morale inside the company. People sense the inevitability of disposability. We see BIC as the enemy even though it is so much smaller than Gillette. We've got to come up with a new strategy. What do you think our options are, Scott?"

"Well, I think we're agreed that the 'do-nothing' option is out. If we simply continue to do business as usual, we will see the erosion of the shaving market's profitability as disposable razors take more and more share."

Scott continued, "We could accept the transition to disposable razors and begin to try to segment the disposable-razor market based on performance. You might call this the 'give up' strategy. We would be admitting that disposable razors are the wave of the future. There will obviously continue to be shavers who buy only based on price, but there will also be shavers who will pay more for disposable razors with additional benefits, such as lubricating strips or movable heads. In Italy, for example, we have done a lot of image building and focused on quality. Now, Italian men seem to perceive that our disposable razors have value despite their price. In other words, we could try to protect the category's profitability by segmenting the market and offering value to those segments willing to pay for it. We would de-emphasize system razors."

"Or we could try to turn the whole thing around. We could develop a strategy to slow the growth of disposable razors and to reinvigorate the system razor market," Scott concluded.

"How does the new razor system fit into all this?" Paul asked.

"I'm pleased that we have continued to invest in R&D despite our problems and the takeover battles," Brian answered. "Reports from R&D indicate that the new shaver is doing well in tests. But it will be expensive to take to market and to support with advertising. Further, it doesn't make any sense to launch it unless it fits in with the broader strategy. For example, if we decide to focus on disposable razors, it makes no sense to launch a new system razor and devote resources to that."

"What's the consumer testing indicating?" asked Scott.

"We're still conducting tests," Sarah answered, "but so far the results are very positive. Men rate the shave superior to either Atra or Trac II and superior to our competition. In fact, I think we'll see that consumers rate the new shaver as much as 25 percent better on average. The independently spring-mounted twin blades deliver a better shave, but you know we've never introduced a product until it was clearly superior in consumer testing on every dimension."

"Okay, here's what I'd like to do," Paul concluded. "I'd like for each of us to devote some time developing a broad outline of a strategy to present at our next meeting. We'll try to identify and shape a broad strategy then that we can begin to develop in detail over the next several months. Let's get together in a week, same time. Thanks for your thoughts."

_____ CASE 5 _____

Chemical Additives Corporation—Specialty Products Group

Nick Williamson, general manager of the Specialty Products Group within Chemical Additives Corporation (CAC), looked out his window and sighed. It was August 1990 and the atmosphere inside his office was as unpleasant as the 100-degree-plus weather of the Ft. Smith, Arkansas, headquarters of Specialty Products Group (SPG). He swiveled back to face his management team, and said, "Okay, I've heard your arguments about positioning and pricing for R&D #601, #602, and #603. I wish there were some way to get a consensus from you guys. I'll consider our options over the weekend."

After his subordinates left his office, Nick looked at the spreadsheets and memoranda covering his desk, and made a mental note that next weekend would definitely be reserved for fishing.

The marketing decisions facing Nick would have substantial impact on the future of SPG. A strategy of moving away from large volume, commodity wax markets toward becoming a premier supplier of specialty chemical additives to niche markets was not going as smoothly as anticipated. This set of newly developed products might well be the catalyst to hasten that shift. The three new products, known by their experimental designations R&D #601, #602, and #603, were corrosion inhibitors used during the transportation and storage of liquid urea ammonium nitrate (UAN) fertilizer.

This case was prepared by Lester A. Neidell and Charles Hoffheiser as a basis for class discussion rather than to illustrate either effective or ineffective handling of an administrative situation. Used with permission from Lester A. Neidell.

Products and Markets

These liquid fertilizers had numerous advantages over the traditional solid fertilizers principally used in U.S. agriculture: (1) excellent performance under a variety of weather conditions; (2) reduced toxicity; (3) ability to be easily blended with other nutrients, insecticides, and herbicides; and (4) milder environmental impact (but not benign—a spill or leak of undiluted UAN could still kill wildlife and vegetation).

Unfortunately UAN liquids corroded the steel tanks, pipelines, rail cars, and barges used for transport, resulting in repair costs that could exceed $1 million per incident for the typical UAN producer. The industry had tried a variety of corrosion inhibitors (chemicals that were added in small dosages to UAN after production) to reduce the rate at which the UAN ate away the metal surface with which it came in contact. (Inhibitors did not prevent corrosion; they slowed the chemical reaction of metal dissolving into UAN.) An excellent inhibitor might increase the average life of a typical $20 million storage system from as little as 3 years to longer than 20 years.

Leaks and spills also created liabilities for Environmental Protection Agency (EPA) fines. If a tank failure resulted in massive environmental damage, federal lawsuits potentially could bankrupt a producer. Corrosion inhibitor suppliers might also be liable for leaks and environmental damages.

UAN fertilizer was produced in continuous process facilities with typical minimum capacities of 10,000 tons per year. After production, UAN was stored in tanks to await shipment. Corrosion inhibitors were added just prior to storage. Upon shipment UAN traveled through a distributor/dealer network that delivered the product to the right farmer, at the right time, and with the appropriate other agricultural chemicals added as necessary. Some larger dealers provided custom application services to apply UAN blends to fields and crops. The same distribution system also handled the solid fertilizers that UAN was slowly replacing.

The three experimental products were designed to replace SPG's earlier entries into this market, as well as to regain business previously lost to a widely used, foreign-sourced material, Corblok 105-B. Contrary tactical marketing positions were held by the sales and marketing managers. Vice president of sales, Ron White, argued that despite any performance advantages of the new SPG products, market conditions in the U.S. fertilizer industry required that the products be priced as low as possible using only the mandatory minimum corporate mark-up over standard cost. Ron had always operated under the objective that CAC/SPG plants had to be kept operating close to capacity to minimize standard costs. Price leadership and volume were, in his eyes, the key to SPG's success. Jim Walker, newly hired as director of marketing (a new position at SPG), was just as vehement in his recommendation that a value-based pricing approach, recognizing both product performance and competitive conditions, be applied to the new products. The technical director regularly reminded these two managers that the three products performed differently in different producer's UANs, and added,

"You guys better start selling some of this stuff soon to pay off our investment of over four man-years of technical effort!"

CHEMICAL ADDITIVES CORPORATION

SPG was one of four divisions of the Chemical Additives Corporation, a multinational company providing solutions to production problems in oil fields, refineries, chemical plants, and other industrial applications. CAC's mission statement read as follows: "To produce and market specialty chemical products and the technical services and equipment necessary to utilize CAC's products effectively."

Its principal strategy was to develop customized equipment and chemical treatment programs to add value to customers' operations through optimization of operating efficiency or increased reliability. CAC's strengths included expertise in organic phosphate ester chemistry (the key to advanced technology corrosion inhibitors) and in the mixing of incompatible fluids (e.g., oil and water). It considered itself to be the worldwide leader in oil industry corrosion control. It developed and patented much of the technology historically used in these applications, but over the past 10 years competitors found it increasingly easy to design products outside patent coverage, particularly as advanced computer modeling techniques were introduced into the R&D departments. Many recent advances in chemical industry technology were created by applying computer modeling to the design of new chemical species. CAC was organized into four operating groups, Oil Field Chemicals, Refinery Chemicals, Instruments, and Specialty Products. Each group maintained its own sales, marketing, and product development functions. A central research department conducted long-range, basic chemical research for all divisions.

The Oil Field Chemicals Group was the world's largest supplier of oil field production chemicals, including corrosion inhibitors and drilling aids. Because its products went "down the hole," appearance, odor, and handling characteristics, such as foaming, were not often of concern to customers. Product development was driven by the sales force's requests for customer-specific products. This division had over 4,000 products in its line. Justification of this product line breadth was twofold: (1) no two oil deposits were identical in chemical make-up; and (2) as wells aged, increasing amounts of exotic chemicals were needed to enhance oil production.

The Refinery Chemicals Group marketed process efficiency aids for the production side of refineries. They also sold fuel additives such as fuel injector cleaners to refiners and to wholesalers of gasoline and truck diesel fuel.

The Instrument Group designed and marketed filtration and purification systems that solved a variety of water and oil-related process problems in refineries. This equipment was often used in conjunction with CAC's chemical treatment programs. In addition, this group sold a complete line of premium-quality corrosion-monitoring instruments.

The Specialty Products Group's product line consisted of two major groups: (1) about 100 types of commodity petroleum waxes (similar but not identical to the types used in candles) that were separated from crude oil and (2) synthetic polymers based on a chemical called propylene. Common examples of polymers are plastic food wrap film or vinyl siding for houses. SPG's synthetics, however, were not the type used in plastic film, cups, or containers. In fact, its customers often called them "synthetic waxes" because they had properties similar to commodity petroleum waxes. Williamson tried to alter this perception by extensive trade advertising and by instructing division personnel to refer to all division products as "specialty polymers." SPG's products were used in hundreds of applications, ranging from shoe polish to chewing gum to cardboard box sealing adhesives. Various SPG products had found modest use as antidust and anticaking additives for solid fertilizers, and as a result, SPG was responsible for all of CAC's business in the worldwide fertilizer industry.

Exhibit 5.1 contains selected CAC and divisional financial data; Exhibit 5.2 shows the distribution of SPG revenue and profit by end-use market.

SPG's Competitors

Each division had its own set of specialized competitors as well as competition from various divisions of large chemical companies such as DuPont, Dow, Witco, and Shell. A key competitive characteristic of the chemical industry in the 1980s was the onset of worldwide competition. Corblok, principal competitor to SPG's UAN anticorrosion additives, was an example of this. Foreign suppliers directly impacted other SPG markets. These included Mitsui, BASF, Hoechst, and Dead Sea Works (an Israeli government-owned coal gasification plant that produced waxes as byproducts of gasoline production). Except for Dead Sea, all of these competitors were much larger than SPG (and CAC), and were reputed to be among the most efficient chemical companies in the world. A key disadvantage SPG had compared to major chemical firms was that SPG's synthetic process required liquid polypropylene, a product form supplied by only one company. The majors often had captive supply and used much larger volumes of less expensive gaseous polypropylene, available from many suppliers.

SPG Marketing

Prior to 1980, SPG sold its products only through distributors. The U.S. market was served by Galaxy Wax and Schmidt Associates, both of which maintained regional warehouses. Sales to Europe, Africa, and the Middle East were the responsibility of the Leveque Group, headquartered in Brussels, Belgium. This company was also principal distributor of wax products manufactured by BASF and Hoechst, both headquartered in West Germany, as well as SPG products. Far East sales were the domain of a joint venture between CAC and Nissan Trading Company of Japan.

EXHIBIT 5.1 **CAC Financial Data, 1985–1989 (In thousands except per share data)**

	1985	1986	1987	1988	1989
Income Statement					
Net Sales	$253,841	$297,208	$302,567	$287,931	$294,068
Cost of Goods Sold	160,268	189,498	181,531	174,919	171,769
Gross Profit	93,573	107,710	121,036	113,012	122,299
Selling Expense	33,623	41,532	49,746	53,235	56,292
R&D Expense	6,370	7,520	9,487	11,537	12,065
General/Administrative Expense	10,860	12,470	14,107	14,614	15,455
Operating Profit	42,720	46,188	47,696	33,626	38,487
Investment Income	774	2,500	2,139	2,533	3,722
Interest Expense	(2,089)	(1,893)	(1,552)	(1,384)	(1,191)
Other Net	623	1,136	203	585	1,782
Earnings before Income Tax	42,028	47,931	48,486	35,360	42,800
Income Tax	17,143	20,174	19,190	13,310	17,000
Net Earnings	$ 24,885	$ 27,757	$ 29,296	$ 22,050	$ 25,800
Balance Sheet					
Cash	$ 16,581	$ 12,478	$ 3,018	$ 37,201	$ 43,461
Accounts Receivable	45,127	61,981	55,836	51,055	56,896
Inventory	39,639	43,751	39,785	39,976	41,296
Other Current Assets	64,466	77,768	77,711	91,869	104,175
Total Current Assets	104,105	121,519	117,496	130,845	145,471
Total Assets	$175,544	$197,782	$200,318	$209,105	$221,514
Current Liabilities	$ 44,468	$ 48,579	$ 39,957	$ 39,808	$ 45,675
Long-Term Debt	12,500	11,250	10,000	8,750	7,500
Stockholders' Equity	112,999	132,989	145,159	153,042	164,148
Other Information					
Shares (000)	5,972	11,864	11,864	11,865	11,715
Dividends Per Share	$1.20	$0.76	$0.95	$1.00	$1.03
Revenue by Division					
Oil Field Chemicals	$158,048	$181,614	$201,378	$199,498	$211,804
Refinery Chemicals	33,069	32,524	32,117	30,342	32,499
Specialty Products	41,554	46,410	41,483	36,969	40,041
Instruments	21,170	36,660	27,589	21,122	9,724
	$153,841	$297,208	$302,567	$287,931	$294,068

EXHIBIT 5.2 **SPG End-Use Segments in 1989**

End-Use Market	Percent of Total SPG Sales	Percent of Total Pretax Profits	Stage in Product Life Cycle
Plastics	5	12	Late growth, maturity
Coatings	10	18	Late growth, maturity
Sealants	25	25	Mature
Food Additives	5	3	Mature
Laminating Wax	25	15	Decline
Others	30	27	Mostly mature

In 1979 in an attempt to capture the distributor margin for SPG, Nick Williamson hired Ron White as vice president of sales to establish a direct sales force. By 1990, SPG had two regional managers and nine sales reps active in the United States:

Philadelphia - East Regional Sales Office
              2 sales representatives
Atlanta   - 1 sales representative
Cleveland   - 1 sales representative
Chicago   - 2 sales representatives
Ft. Smith   - 1 sales representative
Houston   - 1 sales representative
Los Angeles   - West Regional Sales Office
              1 sales representative

After 11 years of direct selling there were still situations in which SPG was beaten by wax distributors on price, delivery, and in some cases, technical service.

Annual salary and benefit costs for each sales rep averaged $80,000; the two regional managers were paid about 20 percent more. The salary/benefit figure included a company car, but not travel and other selling expenses, which averaged about 10 percent of sales revenue. Nor did these numbers include the profit bonus plan, which typically added 2 percent of sales revenue to selling costs. An annual "sales rep of the year" award, usually based on exceeding forecasted poundage figures, provided a further bonus of 5 percent of $50,000 base to one sales person. Salespeople were responsible for annual territorial sales forecasts, which provided important input to plan production runs and to order raw materials. Very little sales effort was devoted to "prospecting" because White kept a "sales efficiency" log for each representative. He calculated this as follows:

$$\frac{\text{sales calls that yielded an order}}{\text{total sales calls}} = \text{sales efficiency}$$

The UAN Corrosion Inhibitor Opportunity

In February 1985, Nick Williamson received a memo from the general manager of the Refinery Chemical Group suggesting that certain of CAC's products might be useful in solving corrosion problems encountered by the Jackson Pipeline Company (JPL) of Ft. Smith. One of the Refinery Group's (and CAC's) largest customers, JPL was a major U.S. pipeline company, active in the transport of crude oil, gasoline, diesel and jet fuels, chemicals, and natural gas. The memo noted that as a result of the oil bust of 1980 to 1983 JPL attempted to build its transportation volume of other products, and began shipping UAN produced by JPL's wholly owned fertilizer company, Fertex Chemicals (also with its main plant in Ft. Smith). UAN was distributed throughout JPL's pipeline system, which extended to Texas, Arkansas, Oklahoma, Missouri, Kansas, Iowa, the Dakotas, Illinois, and Indiana. The maturing of the U.S. petrochemical industry further drove JPL to pursue and obtain UAN shipping business from Farm

Products (Kansas City, Missouri) and Agriproducts (Sioux Falls, South Dakota). Historically UAN was shipped by (in order of increasing cost) barge, rail tank car, and tank truck. To use JPL's pipeline system UAN producers were required to incorporate a corrosion inhibitor approved by JPL. However, unexpected corrosion problems with UAN were severely impacting profitability of the fertilizer shipping business.

This memo was timely; SPG, also, had suffered from the petrochemical industry recession. In addition, Nick was being pushed by CAC's executive committee to move away from commodity wax products into chemical specialties that could provide some protection against the price wars impacting chemical commodity markets.

Initial Entry into the Corrosion Control Market

Assuming that corrosion control was the same regardless of end-use environment, SPG, late in 1986, introduced Stealth 3660, an oil field corrosion inhibitor, for use in transporting liquid UAN. After testing, JPL recommended 3660 to Fertex, Farm Products, and Agriproducts. Because Stealth 3660 cost 50 percent less to use than previously approved Corblok 105-B inhibitor, all three UAN manufacturers were soon buying the product.

However, Fertex detected toxic fumes exceeding OSHA-defined lethal concentrations at the top hatch of trucks used to deliver the product from CAC's Chicago plant. In 1987, Fertex reverted to using Corblok. Unwilling to lose this market, Williamson instructed R&D to select another product from the oil field corrosion inhibitor line. Consequently, Stealth 3662 was introduced to JPL and its three customers in mid-1987. The toxicity problem appeared to be solved, and the usage cost was the same as for 3660. By late 1987, all three fertilizer companies were buying 3662 in tank truck quantities. As mid-1988 approached, word of mouth in the fertilizer industry convinced firms such as Iowa Fertilizer, Ferticon, Nitrogen Industries, Marathon Chemical, and others to use SPG's Stealth 3662.

Both Stealth 3660 and 3662 were priced at 100 percent mark-up over standard cost. Tank truck (40,000-pound) quantities sold for 80 cents per pound and 55 gallon drums for 83 cents per pound, with costs of 40 cents per pound and 41½ cents per pound, respectively. According to CAC policy, if a product was not priced at least 100 percent above cost, it was not defined as a "specialty" and did not qualify for recognition of supporting the corporate mission of becoming a specialty chemical firm. SPG's goal was to derive at least 30 percent of its gross sales revenue from specialties by 1990.

In late 1988, Fertex reported to SPG that their UAN was causing severe foaming problems when mixed with other fertilizer components such as pesticides and herbicides, a practice that was typical at the fertilizer dealer level. By spring 1989, Fertex switched back to Corblok. From the foaming incidents, SPG became aware that UAN passed through a dealer/distributor network before it was ultimately applied to fields and crops. SPG sales people typically called on fertilizer producers and not other channel members. Exhibit 5.3 contains the 1989 capacities of all North American UAN producers and brand of inhibitor used in mid-1988 and mid-1989.

EXHIBIT 5.3 UAN Corrosion Inhibitor Market 1989 Capacities (0.25 pound/ton dosage)

Company[a]	City[a]	State	Country	Capacity 000 Tons	Potential SPC Volume 000 Lbs	Mid-1988 Inhib	Mid-1989 Inhib	Needs Easy Mix Product	SPG Advantage
Farm Products	Kansas City	KS	USA	250	63	3662	3662	No	—
Nitron, Inc.	St. Petersburg	FL	USA	10	3	3662	3662	Yes	—
Can-Am Corp.	Edmonton	AS	Canada	15	4	3662	3662	Yes	—
Can-Am Corp.	Lincoln	NE	USA	80	20	3662	3662	Yes	—
Agriproducts	Sioux Falls	SD	USA	238	60	3662	3662	No	—
Iowa Fertilizer	Dubuque	IA	USA	230	58	3662	Corblok	No	SVC/Cost
Marathon	Toledo	OH	USA	180	45	3662	Corblok	No	SVC/Cost
Ferticon	New Orleans	LA	USA	510	128	3662	Corblok	No	SVC/Cost
Iowa Fertilizer	Santa Fe	NM	USA	10	3	3662	Corblok	No	—
Fertex	Ft. Smith	AR	USA	1400	350	3662	Corblok	No	SVC/Cost
Nitrogen Inds.	Spokane	WA	USA	160	40	3662	Corblok	No	SVC/Cost
Iowa Fertilizer	Miami	OK	USA	51	13	3662	RG-2064	Yes	?
Nitro Products	Pensacola	FL	USA	65	16	Ammonia	Ammonia	No	Perform.
RJS Inc	Idaho Falls	ID	USA	230	58	Ammonia	Ammonia	No	Perform.
Georgia Chemical	Savannah	GA	USA	680	170	Ammonia	Ammonia	No	Perform.
Jackson Chemical	Jackson	MS	USA	500	125	Ammonia	Ammonia	No	Perform.
Illini Fertilizer	Marietta	GA	USA	329	82	Ammonia	Ammonia	No	Perform.
NC Fertilizer	Jacksonville	NC	USA	230	58	Borax	Borax	No	SVC/Pits
RJS Inc	Fresno	CA	USA	129	32	Chromate	Chromate	No	Cost/Safe
Novatec	Windsor	MN	Canada	175	44	Corblok	Corblok	No	SVC/Cost

Company	City	State	Country						
Eagle Industries	Bettendorf	IA	USA	175	44	Corblok	Corblok	No	SVC/Cost
RJS Inc	Winnipeg	MN	Canada	210	53	Corblok	Corblok	No	SVC/Cost
Edsel Chemical	Sacramento	CA	USA	90	23	Corblok	Corblok	No	SVC/Cost
Edsel Chemical	Portland	OR	USA	55	14	Corblok	Corblok	Yes	SVC/Cost
Edsel Chemical	Spokane	WA	USA	200	50	Corblok	Corblok	No	SVC/Cost
Comanche Powder	Tucson	AZ	USA	20	5	Corblok	Corblok	No	SVC/Cost
Illini Fertilizer	Cincinnati	OH	USA	150	38	DAP	DAP	No	SVC/Pits
Nutricorp	Council Bluffs	IA	USA	500	125	DAP	DAP	No	SVC/Pits
Ferticon	Evansville	IN	USA	80	20	DAP	DAP	No	SVC/Pits
US Industries	Cherokee	AL	USA	65	16	DAP	DAP	Yes	SVC/Pits
Illini Fertilizer	Dalton	GA	USA	100	25	DAP	DAP	No	SVC/Pits
Illini Fertilizer	LaSalle	IL	USA	300	75	DAP	DAP	No	SVC/Pits
Farm Product	Hays	KS	USA	250	63	DAP	DAP	No	SVC/Pits
Nitrotech	Kingston	ON	Canada	25	6	DAP	DAP	Yes	SVC/Pits
Cherokee Nitrogen	Enid	OK	USA	270	68	DAP	DAP	No	SVC/Pits
Nutricorp	Baton Rouge	LA	USA	1000	250	DAP	DAP	No	SVC/Pits
Nitrogen Inds.	Lincoln	NE	USA	158	40	DAP	DAP	Yes	SVC/Pits
Canadian Nitrogen	Niagara Falls	ON	Canada	120	30	OA-5	OA-5	No	SVC/Foam
Fertilex	Stockton	CA	USA	200	50	OA-5	OA-5	No	SVC/Foam
Fertilex	Compton	CA	USA	100	25	OA-5	OA-5	No	SVC/Foam
Edsel Chemical	Burlington	IA	USA	200	50	OA-5	OA-5	No	SVC/Foam

[a] Names and locations changed to protect confidentiality.

Worried about SPG's ability to compete effectively in the UAN corrosion control market, Williamson directed Ron White to hire a sales engineer or product manager to get the UAN corrosion inhibitor program on track. In August 1989, Bob Brown joined SPG in this capacity.

Williamson also hired a director of marketing, Jim Walker, in October 1989. Walker was charged with changing the culture of SPG from a sales/manufacturing/technology-driven business to a market-driven business. SPG's 1989 organizational chart is shown in Exhibit 5.4; Exhibit 5.5 contains background information on SPG's key personnel.

Corrosion Inhibitor Technology

Corrosion is a complex chemical reaction, changing steel to useless iron oxide. Two basic types of corrosion inhibitors were available: passivators and film-formers. Passivators formed a protective "coating" by chemically reacting with the steel surfaces they were supposed to protect. Although some people believed them to be effective, evidence was mounting that corrosive materials could penetrate the coating, resulting in rapid formation of deeply corroded pits. Typical repair costs for a storage tank exceeded $1 million, and there had even been one or two complete tank failures. Film-formers left a microscopic layer of inhibitor on the steel surface by incompletely dissolving in the corrosive liquid UAN. This new technology was considered by the National Association of Corrosion Engineers (NACE) to be a sound alternative to designing tanks and piping with expensive, exotic steel alloys or with plastics.

EXHIBIT 5.4   Organizational Chart—Specialty Products Group, Chemical Additives Corporation

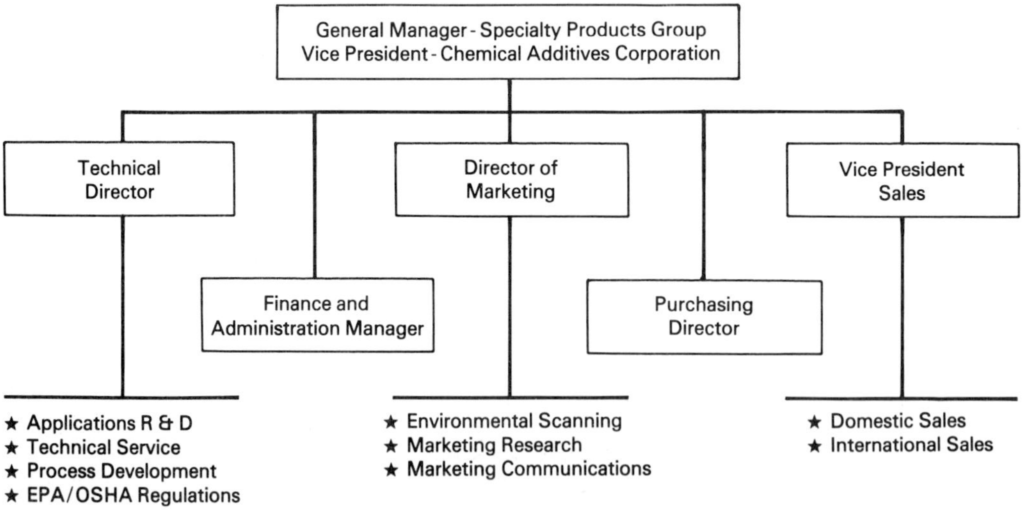

EXHIBIT 5.5   Key SPG Personnel

Nick Williamson—Executive Vice President and General Manager

With a degree in chemical engineering, Williamson joined SPG in 1966 as a process engineer and worked his way through the production and process engineering ranks to his current position in 1982. He had no sales, marketing, or finance experience. Along the way, he completed his masters in chemical engineering and developed a process to make synthetic wax. He convinced corporate management to invest $10 million in 1975 to build a plant for these products, and it came on stream in 1976. First commercial sale of any significance occurred in 1979 to a hot melt adhesive manufacturer, a mature industry at the time. His management philosophy is to be involved in every detail of the SPG operation.

Ron White—Vice President of Sales

A personal friend of Williamson's, he was hired in 1980. A former Air Force KC-135 tanker pilot, he had for years been a member of the leading country club in Ft. Smith, and was a 3 handicap golfer. Before his employment at SPG, he was the sole U.S. distributor of potassium permanganate, a commodity reagent widely used as a catalyst in research laboratories. His college degree was in chemistry.

Jim Walker—Director of Marketing

With a chemical engineering degree, he joined American Cyanamid in 1970 as a process engineer. He moved to sales and marketing in 1974, responsible for contract sales of sulfuric acid and alum. He became marketing manager for specialty urethane catalysts at Dow in 1978. By this time, he had earned his MBA in chemical marketing from Fairleigh Dickinson University. He was appointed director of marketing for Corn Products Corporation in 1984. He joined SPG in 1989.

Bob Brown—Sales Engineer

The newest member of the management team, Bob graduated from Carnegie Mellon University with a chemistry degree in 1978. First employed by Firestone's Chemical division, he concentrated in specialty urethane adhesives sales. Three years later he became a water management chemicals and services specialist at Western Corporation. He was a highly successful salesman, with a specific training in consultative needs, satisfaction selling, and technical service.

All products SPG introduced to the UAN industry were of the film-forming variety. This, as well as control of solubility, was a basic and very strong technology for CAC, and the source of numerous patents.

The UAN Corrosion Inhibitor Market

For most of the 1980s, the U.S. agricultural industry was depressed. By 1988, the fertilizer industry (including UAN producers) experienced a shake-out that saw a 20 percent reduction in industry capacity. One UAN plant with book assets of more than $40 million netted just $3.5 million on the auction block. Although the prospects for U.S. farmers were looking better by the end of 1988, fertilizer producers were facing stiff, low-cost foreign competition on their largest-volume solid products, sometimes losing money on every ton sold. Although the cost of ocean shipment of liquid UAN prohibited imports attacking the North American market, domestic producers, in a competitive frenzy, had cut UAN prices such that they sometimes made only $1 per ton pretax. The shake-out led many to believe that this would soon return to the more "normal" $30 per ton.

UAN liquids were produced as 28 percent and 32 percent blends in water. They had to be diluted with more water at the dealer level before being suitable for application to crops. As a rule, the more dilute the UAN, the more corrosive it was to steel. Once a corrosion inhibitor such as Corblok 105-B or Stealth 3662 was successfully added in the proper dosage at the producer's plant, corrosion control was effective through the entire distribution network.

Corrosion control was necessary once UAN entered the distribution system. A number of different products had been used over the years to reduce corrosion. Some UAN producers tried (unsuccessfully) to differentiate based on the presence of a corrosion inhibitor. Dealers and farmers were more concerned with the cost per acre of fertilized land and on-time, fast delivery, especially during the hectic schedules of spring planting and fall harvest. Processing problems, such as incompatibility with other agricultural chemicals and foaming, could not be tolerated. There was little dealer loyalty among farmers when they needed to plant or harvest.

Competitive Products

A variety of inhibitors were available in January 1989 as SPG began its program to develop a replacement for Stealth 3662 (Exhibit 5.6 outlines the typical products used). Except for borax, all were liquid materials.

EXHIBIT 5.6   Competitive Inhibitors, 1990

Product	Supplier	Type[a]	Price/Pound	Treatment Cost/Ton[b]
Ammonia	Many	P	$ 0	$ 0
Borax	Many	P	.14–.17	.28–.35
Chromate	Many	F	.47	.28
Corblok	IWC	F	1.87	.47
DAP	Many	P	.082	.20–.25
OA-5	Tennessee	F	.375	.30
RG 2064	Western	F	1.90	.19–.38
Stealth 3662	SPG	F	.80	.24

[a] P = Passivating; F = Film Former.
[b] Treatment cost is per ton of UAN.

Ammonia.   A toxic gas used as a fertilizer, ammonia was the cheapest source of nitrogen—the same nutrient provided by UAN. Some producers believed that corrosion could be eliminated simply by neutralizing acids from the production process by adding ammonia. It was one of the raw materials in the manufacture of UAN. During the 1970s, instances of rapid pitting corrosion led many producers to try other inhibitors. Ammonia's principal advantage was that it was virtually free.

Borax.   Although classified as "acceptable" by the Tennessee Valley Authority (TVA), only one manufacturer used it. Several other UAN manufacturers had found it to be unacceptable.

Sodium Chromate.   The fact that a material considered by the Environmental Protection Agency (EPA) to be a primary pollutant was allowed in fertilizer points out the strange regulatory environment typically faced by the chemical industry. This product was an excellent corrosion inhibitor but was toxic to fish and wildlife. Only one plant used sodium chromate. It was a film-former.

Corblok.   A phosphate ester film-former produced in Germany by Servo, a well-respected chemical firm, Corblok was supplied to North American markets by IWC, a Dutch company, and sold through M. Joseph & Company of Philadelphia. Corblok was shipped to Houston via ocean freight. Storage facilities were leased at the port of Houston. Although this product did not foam, it was difficult to dissolve in UAN, but provided excellent corrosion protection. Technical service was the responsibility of a corrosion engineer based in Holland. The Leveque Group confirmed claims of many European customers for this product.

DAP.   Also a fertilizer (at 100 percent strength), DAP was made by several UAN producers. Tested "effective" by the TVA, Jackson Pipeline had tried it, but found that it left deposits that interfered with pipeline pumps and that there was pitting corrosion beneath the deposits. Still, DAP enjoyed a 30 percent market share and was sold by direct sales reps or distributors depending on the location. The nutrient content that it imparted to UAN was negligible, but it enjoyed a psychological benefit of "providing crop nutrients."

Stealth 3662.   Similar in chemistry to Corblok, Stealth 3662 was easily soluble in UAN. It was an excellent inhibitor, but as noted previously, there were some foaming problems. It was produced in Chicago and Galveston, Texas, using the same process equipment as many other CAC products.

OA-5.   Tennessee Chemical produced this material in Knoxville and sold it through a direct sales force. SPG's own tests proved OA-5 to be effective, but it was extremely difficult to dissolve in UAN. Sometimes it merely floated to the surface of the UAN storage tank, even after plant operators were sure that they had mixed it properly. Several plants reported foaming problems when attempting to mix OA-5 with their UAN. This foaming was of a different type than that reported for Stealth 3662. This film-former was completely different in composition from Corblok or Stealth 3662.

RG-2064 and Equivalents.   Although neither Consolidated nor Western had promoted any products specifically for UAN transport and storage, both were strong in organic phosphate ester chemistry, and they had applied it to water treatment applications, a market much larger than UAN. Both companies employed many more sales reps than SPG and CAC and were already selling water treatment chemicals to UAN plants for boiler, cooling, and waste water treatment applications. These operations were run by the same people who ran the UAN process equipment. These companies were attacking CAC's oil field business and achieving significant success, despite the fact that their products were more expensive to use than CAC's. Consolidated's revenue was equal to CAC's, but its profit rate was 20 percent higher than CAC. Western had sales and profits double those of CAC.

Product Development

After the foaming problems with Stealth 3662, SPG began to develop a product specifically designed for UAN corrosion control. In 1988, SPG's technical director estimated that four man-years of technical effort over two years were required. The typical cost per man-year was $100,000, including salary and benefits, the use of all group and corporate laboratory facilities, and the cost to build corrosion test apparatus. Jim Walker believed that a one man-year marketing effort at $80,000 per year was required to adequately understand market needs and to develop literature and marketing communications programs. Additional annual marketing expenses of $5,000 incurred by hosting a hospitality suite at the annual meeting of the Ammonium Nitrate Producers Study Group (ANPSG). White was confident that his department could sell any product, given a good price; the technical director was confident in the success of the development effort. Selling could be done one of two ways: (1) 100 percent of Brown's time at $80,000 per year (salary, benefits, car) plus 2 percent of revenue for travel and entertainment costs (T&E), or (2) 5 percent of the entire sales force's time (including regional managers) plus the same T&E.

Williamson considered these cost and success estimates and reviewed the following data:

1. Tax rate 33 percent.
2. Corporate cost of capital 8 percent.
3. Corporate mandate for 30 percent value after tax return on investment.
4. SPG requirement that new businesses generate at least $2,000,000 in sales or $800,000 gross profit within three years of market entry.

He then instructed his technical director to develop a direct replacement for Corblok.

Early in 1989, Brown arranged a trip with a Fertex sales representative to several fertilizer dealers. He obtained extensive information about how UAN was used at the dealer level—other nutrients added, mixing techniques, blending with pesticides and herbicides, and so forth. Brown was quite surprised when dealers responded to his questions about foaming. Despite using Fertex UAN containing Stealth 3662, they had not experienced this condition. Brown began to wonder if only certain blends and ingredients foamed, and if these blends were used only in certain regions of the country.

He also learned that a considerable amount of UAN "trading" occurred in the industry. For example, if Fertex had a customer in North Dakota, they would receive the sales revenue, but Agriproducts' Sioux Falls plant would actually supply the UAN. Fertex would return the favor if Agriproducts had a customer in Arkansas. Computerized accounting systems kept track of the trades, and accounts were settled quarterly.

In addition to these market factors, the technical director's staff, after running hundreds of corrosion and foaming tests with several producers' UANs, discovered three factors that influenced the interaction between UAN and steel surfaces: (1) higher temperature; (2) higher UAN velocity, especially in a pipeline environment; and (3) presence of impurities. The technical department also found that different producers' UANs, though identical in nutrient content, required different dosages of any corrosion inhibitor for effective corrosion control. Other inhibitor suppliers (including IWC/Corblok) recommended the same dosage throughout the industry. SPG's technical director suggested using an industry-wide inhibitor dosage rate of 1.5 to 2.0 pounds per ton of UAN, so that even the most drastic conditions would not cause corrosion problems.

Although the three newly developed products were similar, each had slightly different performance characteristics. R&D #601 worked well in Fertex UAN but would not function in several others. It was easier to disperse than #602, but #602 was effective in all UAN brands. Most UAN plants used high-speed pumps to move the UAN through their systems. For this reason it was believed that there would be few problems dispersing SPG's R&D #601 and #602 products into the UAN. Once dispersed, no separation occurred. R&D #603 was easiest to disperse (although not quite as easy as the existing 3662 product), but it exhibited a slight foaming tendency (not believed to be as severe as that of 3662). R&D #603 was effective in all UANs.

All three products could be delivered in tank truck (40,000 pound) quantities. Also, in response to increased state and local regulations on the disposal of empty drums, SPG planned to offer all three products in 300-gallon returnable and reusable tote tanks, each costing $1,200. The tank supplier estimated 30 to 40 round trips could be obtained before the tanks had to be refurbished at a cost of $300 each. Exhibit 5.7 shows the cost structure of SPG's products.

Sales (White) and marketing (Walker) continually debated the UAN corrosion inhibitor marketing program as fall 1990 approached. The planned October 1990 roll-out would give SPG a "strategic window" of approximately three months as UAN producers went to high production rates to prepare for spring

EXHIBIT 5.7   SPG Inhibitor Costs, October 1989
(Per pound in
tank car lots)

Product	Fixed	Variable	Total
Stealth 3662	$0.100	$0.300	$0.400
R&D #601	0.160	0.480	0.640
R&D #602	0.160	0.480	0.640
R&D #603	0.160	0.480	0.640

Notes:
(1) R&D #601 for "easy to treat" UAN such as Fertex.
(2) R&D #602 for "hard to treat" UAN such as Agriproducts.
(3) R&D #603 for easy dispersion all UANs, but very slight foam.
(4) Add $0.015 to variable costs for 55 gallon drums, net weight: 473 lbs (215 Kg).
(5) Add $0.06 to variable cost for 300 gallon returnable tote tanks: net weight 2580 lbs (1173 Kg).
(6) Billing terms net 30, freight collect, FOB CAC plant.

fertilizer consumption. Failure to obtain business by February would effectively close the window until July, when another production push would occur for fall fertilizer consumption.

DECISIONS, DECISIONS, DECISIONS

As Nick Williamson shuffled the papers on his desk, he thought about the decisions he had to make. The discussion earlier in the afternoon focused on pricing issues of the new products, but Nick realized that pricing was only one of many factors that had to be resolved. The R&D #601, #602, #603 nomenclature was the standard in-house descriptor for developmental products. White wanted to continue to use the Stealth name to provide continuity to salespeople and customers. Walker desired a new name to convey the technological newness of these products.

White lobbied long and hard with Williamson to price at $1.04 per pound and then to "turn my salespeople loose." Walker was just as adamant that selective pricing to different market segments was desirable. R&D had concluded that all inhibitors (UANs) are not the same in terms of corrosion control and a single dosage of one inhibitor may not be effective in all UANs under all conditions.

As he packed his briefcase, Nick knew that he had to have some decisions by Monday morning.

_____ CASE 6 _____

J.M. Smucker Company:
With a Name Like Smucker's, It Has to Be Good

There are two reasons the J.M. Smucker Company is so successful. First, they have very high quality product lines and as they expand, they keep high quality related food products as their number one goal. Secondly, they have very good employees. The Smucker family are honorable people who are good businessmen that can be trusted. That same business and moral standard is evident in all employees of the J.M. Smucker Company.[1]

Vice President for Sales, Grocery Company Chain

The Early Years

As the 19th century gave way to the 20th, business in rural America consisted mainly of the entrepreneur as a sole proprietorship. Products were most likely manufactured on site or purchased locally. Mass transit was by waterway or railroad. Smaller loads could be carried by horse and wagon over dirt roads for short distances or even longer distances if enough time was available.

The country dweller was largely individualistic and highly self-sufficient, raising his own food and making do with what was at hand. Jerome Monroe Smucker of quiet Orrville, Ohio, was one of the more entrepreneurial of these self-reliant people. He owned four farms and gradually expanded into the then new creamery business. His two creameries turned out butter, swiss cheese, and occasionally ice cream. Using the newly laid railroad, he marketed his homemade products as far away as Cleveland and New York.[2]

The adventuresome Jerome Smucker did not limit himself to the farms and creamery business. For two years he attended a business course at the nearby academy in Smithville, Ohio. In between tutoring penmanship, he built two creameries for others in Pennsylvania. His small business reflected the influence of Jerome's strong Mennonite religious beliefs, beliefs that today are still a part of the Smucker tradition. In his early years he traveled in three states helping to

[1] Memo to B. A. Deitzer, unpublished, July 11, 1989.
[2] W. D. Ellis, "With a Name Like . . ." J.M. Smucker Company, Orrville, Ohio, 1987. This reference is the primary source for all historical data.

This case was prepared by Bernard A. Deitzer, Alan G. Krigline, and Thomas C. Peterson as a basis for class discussion rather than to illustrate either effective or ineffective handling of an administrative situation. Used with permission from Bernard A. Deitzer.

establish libraries in Mennonite Sunday schools. He was also involved with the Mennonite Aid Plan, a mutual insurance program, and eventually became its president.

The J.M. Smucker Company

One of the many businesses that forward-minded Jerome Smucker tried was the cider mill business. In 1897, he purchased a power-driven mill to press apple cider for neighboring farmers at a nominal 1 cent per gallon. From this modest beginning was to evolve the company that would bear his name. The first year's apple crop was so good that he repurchased cider from his neighbors for use in making apple butter from a down-on-the-farm family recipe. The apple butter was dispensed in stone crocks and was personally guaranteed. Each crock had a tied paper top covering with the signature of J.M. Smucker on it attesting to its quality. The Smucker horse-drawn wagon with Jerome at the reins went throughout Wayne and neighboring counties in a 25-mile radius selling to grocers and farmers. It was solidly established from the outset that only the highest-quality product would be sold. There is neither recollection nor record that Jerome's apple butter guarantee ever evoked a claim against it.

Another hallmark of the company soon emerged. Jerome Smucker found that heating the cider by passing steam through copper coils immersed in the liquid not only improved the quality by controlling the heat but also speeded up the evaporation process. Thus, the avowed principle of selling only the highest-quality product was further joined by continuous technological innovation. A fact the company would witness many times in its future was that the improvement in the product quality almost always resulted in improved productivity.

Growth of Smucker

As the cider and apple butter business grew and prospered, the company sold off the creamery business to a Salem, Ohio, dairy firm. The output of apple butter in 1906 reached 350 gallons per day. Sales for the year 1915 were $59,803 with profits of $2,859. A good hourly wage at that time, incidentally, was 30 cents. Sales continued to grow and reached $159,000 in 1918. However, sales in 1921 were off and dropped to $147,084. In this same year on September 19, the company earlier established in 1897 was incorporated as J.M. Smucker Company, with 1,000 shares of capital stock at $100 per share.

Sales resumed their upward trend and reached $318,845 in 1931. The increased sales were partly due to the introduction in 1922 of jams and jellies to the original product line of cider and apple butter. The familiar stone crock was replaced by a new clear glass jar in 1939 as sales reached nearly $1 million. Sales topped the $1 million mark for the first time in 1941, reaching $1,087,000. From founding to World War I and the Great Depression, there were only two loss years, 1932 and 1933. Smucker had learned that even in hard times people still enjoyed apple butter.

Growth by Acquisition

The Smucker Company's first venture outside Orrville was mostly un-planned and largely dictated by circumstance. Increasing demand for the company's products had outgrown the local supply of apples. Looking for new markets in which to buy apples, Smucker discovered there was a quality and cost advantage on the West Coast. The state of Washington would allow only the highest quality of apples for shipment out of state and the abundant supply consequently kept the price low. Accordingly, a plant was built in 1935 at Wenatchee, Washington, to transship apples to Orrville.

The next plant addition was leased and then eventually purchased in Salem, Ohio. This plant, originally acquired to produce applesauce, was used mainly to dehydrate potatoes for the nation's armed forces. The dried potatoes were ground into flour at a Salem mill, and some of this potato flour was flown into Berlin by way of the Berlin Airlift to allow the blockaded German people to bake bread.

By 1952, sales were over $6 million and nearly $10 million in 1955 when the Wenatchee plant was sold. The Salem plant, sold earlier in 1953, and the Wenatchee plant had now become unprofitable operations. Meanwhile, since 1948 a new plant to process and freeze fruit for Orrville was being phased into opera-tions in Oregon City, Oregon. The Oregon City plant situated in a rich fruit belt, could supply the kind of apples used for jelly.

Growth by Product Line Extension

By 1958, the Orrville plant employed 225 people including 20 drivers and a sales force of 11. The plant produced 47 million packages that year. Products that were being sold on the West Coast had a cost disadvantage when compared with competing local products. Smucker was shipping fruit east to make their jams, jellies, and preserves and then shipping it west as finished products. The competitive market on the West Coast would not support the double shipping costs indefinitely. A West Coast manufacturing plant would be needed for Smucker to remain competitive.

Strategic Planning at Smucker

Strategic planning at Smucker had four major goals: (1) there was to be vertical integration from field to final package, (2) company operations would be national as opposed to regional, (3) growth would be by product line extensions and by compatible acquisitions, and (4) the company would be a public corpora-tion and yet still seek to be an independent family-type operation.

The Salinas, California, manufacturing plant was built in 1960. The plant, costing over $1 million, would support sales of $5 million per year. West Coast sales at that time were about $1 million, and total company sales for 1961 were $14.3 million. Salinas was a continuation of the company's small-town flavor and was very similar in character to both Orrville and Wenatchee. The Salinas plant was Smucker's first commitment to national operations.

The change from a private to a public corporation was dictated by the possibility of senior family members needing to pay estate taxes in the event of death. Life in rural Orrville with its conservative Amish-Mennonite heritage did not require large sums of money; therefore, for over 60 years the money generated from selling jams and jellies was reinvested in the company. Moreover, the Smucker family's wealth in assets was not reflected by wealth in cash. Consequently, it might be necessary to sell important assets of the company to settle estate tax claims.

Smucker's Public Offering

The transition to a public corporation started on October 12, 1959, when Smucker filed with the Securities and Exchange Commission for a public offering of 165,000 common shares at $20 per share (on December 31, 1989, the value of that $20 share was $927.84). This represented one-third of the 495,000 shares that had been issued from the 600,000 shares authorized. The shares for the offering came from the holdings of company directors and did not represent new financing.

The new public corporation, with 350 employees producing 50 million packages of product for some 2,000 customers, had sales in 1959 of $11.1 million and income of $812,000. The product mix by dollar volume was 35 percent preserves and jams in 24 flavors, 20 percent ice cream toppings, 18 percent fruit jellies, 11 percent apple butter, 9 percent apple-based jellies, and 7 percent dietetic jams and jellies. Just three years later, in 1962, with sales at $15.8 million, Smucker became the largest domestic independent producer of jellies, jams, preserves, and fruit butters with 11 percent of the total U.S. market.

West Coast Growth

Company growth accelerated after the transition to a public corporation. Mary Ellen's, with a volume of $4 million, was acquired in 1963. Since the Mary Ellen brand of jams and jellies was well-known on the West Coast, the brand was maintained as a separate product line. Production, however, was moved from Mary Ellen's Berkeley, California, plant to Smucker's Salinas plant in order to utilize the latter's unused production capacity. Mary Ellen's Woodburn, Oregon, fruit-processing plant was retained as a source of supply for the Salinas operations.

Acquisitions continued in quick succession. In 1961, H.B. DeViney Company of New Bethlehem, Pennsylvania, a peanut butter manufacturer with sales of $300,000, was purchased. This acquisition was followed by Wooster Preserving Company in 1965, a producer of pickles that had sales of about $300,000. Two other packers acquired were the H.W. Madison Company with facilities in Cleveland, Delta, and Medina, Ohio, and the Albro Packing Company in Springboro, Pennsylvania.

In order to ensure that its processing plants had an adequate fruit supply, Smucker contracted for its fruit over a year in advance. They were one of a few manufacturers that did not rely on the open market and its attendant uncertainties for its fruit supply. To further improve fruit supplies in California, California Farm Products of Watsonville was acquired; a processing plant was built in Oxnard and another plant was leased in Vista.

As Smucker's market share increased to 17 percent, a longer lead time was needed for fruit acquisition in order to anticipate price increases, droughts, or crop failures. In 1971, the A.F. Murch Company of Paw Paw, Michigan, was acquired, providing vineyards in Michigan and Washington as well as processing plants in Paw Paw and Grandview, Washington.

Divested Acquisitions

Not all acquisitions were found to be compatible. Smucker, for example, had entered the frozen pie business by purchasing McMillan & Company of North East, Pennsylvania. Frozen pies were the only product requiring refrigeration, which resulted in costly and inefficient marketing. Another acquisition, Houston Foods of Chicago, a company that sold gourmet food gift packs through 7,000 department and gift stores, did not fit the corporation well. The gourmet gift packs were replaced by gift boxes filled with products carrying Smucker's brand name. The two companies were divested, followed eventually by the entire pickle business. The purchasing public apparently did not perceive either taste or quality differences in pickles as they had in jams and jellies.

Continued Growth through Acquisitions

Acquisitions continued in 1979 when Smucker purchased the Dickinson Family brands of Portland, Oregon. Dickinson had a reputation for selling premium-quality preserves, and the brand name was retained by Smucker as was done with the previously acquired Mary Ellen brand. In addition to the premium lines, Dickinson also enjoyed strong institutional sales, selling to better-class hotels and restaurants. By 1980, Smucker had a 25.8 percent share of the jam and jelly market.

Market share and sales continued to climb and reached 29.5 percent and $200 million in 1983. In the next year Knudsen & Sons of Chico, California, was acquired, giving Smucker a prestige entry into the growing pure fruit juice segment of the market. Again, the established brand names of Nice & Natural and R.W. Knudsen Family were retained. In 1984, Smucker introduced 100 percent fruit juices under its own name.

In keeping with its strategy of growth through related business acquisitions and line and brand extensions, Smucker acquired all outstanding shares of R-Line Foods of Ripon, Wisconsin, for $7 million in cash in September 1987. The R-Line products enhanced Smucker's food service portion-control capability, primarily fruit spreads and condiments packaged in popular small-sized containers. The over 150 flavors of jams, jellies, and preserves in more than 30 sizes and styles of packages were marketed under R-Line's private label "Lost Acres."

Smucker had then achieved its goal for expansion from regional to national operations first with its Salinas, California, manufacturing plant in 1960 serving the West Coast and then with its Memphis, Tennessee, manufacturing plant in 1969 serving 11 southern states. The next move was into international operations.

International Expansion

To position itself for opportunities in the international market, Smucker acquired the Canadian-based Good Morning brand of marmalades and the Shirriff line of preserves and ice cream toppings in April 1988. In May 1988, all of the outstanding shares of Elsenham Quality Foods of Elsenham, England, were purchased for $9.25 million in cash. Elsenham manufactured gourmet preserves, spreads, condiments, and other food products in Great Britain.

Continuing in 1989, the most recent international acquisition was Henry Jones Foods, a subsidiary of Goodman Fielder Wattie of Sydney, Australia. Purchased for an undisclosed amount, Henry Jones, with a sales volume of $20 million, was one of Australia's leading manufacturers of preserves, jams, and honey and was also a supplier of fruit-related products to food service operators and industrial customers in Australia.[3] International sales were 5 percent of Smucker's total sales; the addition of Henry Jones doubled that percentage in 1990.

Thus, Smucker had strategically established footholds in both the European Community and the Pacific Rim. Another acquisition with international ties was the purchase of the Vitari line of frozen whipped fruit desserts made with 99.2 percent fruit. The purchase from Olympus Industries of Spokane, Washington, included trademarks, patents, technology, and worldwide rights. Smucker then licensed brand and trademark rights for the Vitari line of products (similar to soft-serve yogurt or ice cream) back to Olympus for distribution in Australia, New Zealand, and Japan.[4]

The deliberate strategy by Smucker's management for either in-house or acquired products was developed early in the company's history. Over the ensuing years, each additional acquisition to the growing list of products in the Smucker line was destined to be food or beverage products or services—products, like Smucker's current lines, of the highest quality, with well-respected brand names, and perceived to be better than the competition's. The potential acquisitions would provide higher penetration of current geographic markets, the particular market segments, or customer segments served. New geographic markets and market segments not served were sought where there was a need for Smucker's products. Tim Smucker, chairman, summarized the policy by saying, "We want to do it right the first time. We want what we think are high quality companies. We want the number 1 or number 2 businesses in their market and we generally have been able to accomplish that."[5]

[3] "Smucker to Acquire Aussie Manufacturer," *Akron Beacon Journal*, May 23, 1989, p. B5.
[4] "Washington Juice Maker Bought by Smucker," *Akron Beacon Journal*, July 7, 1989, p. C9.
[5] Jackie Mitchell, "Smucker Spreads Itself Around," *Akron Beacon Journal*, August 7, 1989, p. B4.

A Changing Company and a Changing Product Line

With the increase in the size of the military during World War II, Smucker's sales to the government increased so that by 1947 the majority of its output, 52 percent, went to the military. Management realized at that time that a new market must be found to replace the military market as the economy readjusted to peacetime conditions. Although government and military sales were still an important segment of Smucker's sales, a new market was found in private brands or processed foods under the buyer's labels. By the early 1950s, 50 percent of Smucker's sales went to private brands.

The development of this new market and its large contribution to sales revenue was viewed unfavorably by management. Smucker was gradually losing its identity as a nationally recognized and accepted premier brand. Historically, planning horizons were long for this family-owned firm. Consequently, it planned for future generations rather than for the short term. Smucker's management accordingly decided to surrender half its business in favor of promoting its own labeled brands.

Changes in consumer tastes were followed closely by Smucker's management in order to match products offered to those demanded by customers. For example, Smucker's franchised line of Slenderella jams, jellies, and marmalades provided artificially sweetened products for diabetics and weight-conscious customers. In more recent times, as consumers became concerned about sugar consumption and about the consumption of artificial sweeteners (the products contained no artificial flavors, colors, or preservatives), new products were introduced while keeping the old line for diabetics. The new products for the weight- and health-conscious consumer were Low Sugar Spreads and Simply Fruit; the first had one-half the usual amount of sugar found in jams and jellies, and the second was sweetened with fruit juice.

Smucker carefully watched the development of the take-out or away-from-home dining market. At $170 billion, it was the third largest industry in the United States. Smucker's primary market, groceries, was second largest at $271 billion. The industry had some 123,000 grocery stores and 38,000 convenience food stores. The typical supermarket stocked 15,000 items and had sales of $100,000 to $150,000 per week. For the away-from-home dining market, it was estimated that 50 percent of meals in cities, where the two-career family predominated, were eaten out. Moreover, the hotels, restaurants, and fast food outlets in this market segment purchased single-serving containers of various products.

Technology and Product Quality Control

From the very first, when steam heating was applied to the cooking process through copper coils, the company was a leader in the development of automated process technology in the food industry. The first laboratory was opened in 1932. In 1946, constant in-plant inspection was initiated. Smucker reimbursed the U.S. Department of Agriculture for the services of a full-time inspector. The continuous federal inspection for color, flavor, and consistency permitted the company to use the official designation "U.S. Grade A Fancy" on its labels. Later the word "fancy" was deleted from the labels and the words "packed under continuous inspection of the U.S. Department of Agriculture" were added.

Food Processing at Orrville

The decade of the 1950s saw many advances in manufacturing and industry-leading technology. In 1947 for the first time, the company used $1 million of sugar. Standard industry practice had been to purchase sugar in 100-pound bags. In order to cut handling time as well as costs, Smucker began bulk sugar purchasing, a practice that was soon adopted by the industry. Another packaging innovation for Smucker's raw materials was the switch from the then traditional wooden barrel for shipments to the use of steel drums. This permitted better space utilization in railroad box cars and resulted in savings of $66,000 per year. Again the industry followed suit.

Product Innovations

Innovations continued regularly at the Orrville plant. Prior to 1953, there was an ever-present strawberry-like aroma in the plant's atmosphere. Production workers, sensing its value, often discussed how to bottle it. Equipment was eventually designed to capture the escaping essence, which was then returned to the product itself. This resulted in such a marked improvement in flavor that some thought the company was using artificial flavoring. Assuredly it was not. In 1992, the plant, with essence recovery and the use of totally enclosed vacuum cookers (another Smucker first) had no hint of the product being processed. The vacuum cooker, with rotating steam coils for heating, allowed the product to be prepared at lower temperatures with improved quality through prevention of heat damage.

Ever mindful of its consumers, Smucker pioneered the development of the easy twist-off cap replacing the pry-off type. This allowed both easier removal and resealing of the jams and jellies. In response to consumer's awareness for better health and more information, a second label with content and calorie count information was added. The following year, content labeling by the industry was required by law. Other packaging improvements followed in the portion control or single-serving-size packages. Furthermore, Smucker's innovative packaging technology, with its state-of-the-art machinery, was considered the ultimate in the industry in single-service items.

In the early days, Smucker's policy was to add just a little more to each jar so that it contained more than the label indicated. In 1992 when statistical process control was used to control container filling, the aim was to make sure consumers received what they paid for. As in the case for improved product information labeling, statistical process control was introduced as a matter of company policy rather than in response to laws relating to fill weights.

The Processing Plant

Directly across the street from its headquarters building stood Smucker's red brick processing plant. Any visitor was immediately impressed by the overall cleanliness of the surrounding grounds. The well-scrubbed plant interior could only be described as immaculate. Even the steel lattice and brick work of the floors were spotless. The complex of sparkling stainless steel cookers, piping, processing lines, and quality control instruments (manual as well as electronic) were operated by surprisingly few people. The fruit being processed was only exposed for visual inspection. All employees and visitors wore white elastic band gauze caps completely covering their hair. Watches or jewelry that might harbor a speck of dirt were prohibited. Employees were constantly being reminded of the "message" by ever-present signs reading "Safety, quality, and pride is *our* secret ingredient at Smucker's" and "At Smucker's safety and quality go hand in hand."

Long-Range Strategic Planning

Strategic planning at Smucker evolved as the company grew over the years. Planning had never been for the short term. The first plans called for improving the business for future generations of the Smucker family. It was only when the company went public in 1959 that some shorter-range planning was introduced as the newly acquired stockholders inquired about the company's one-year and five-year plans.

Corporate planning was grounded in the firm's basic principles, time-honored beliefs from which its corporate objectives flowed naturally (Exhibit 6.1). From this starting point, managerial planning was focused on six key areas: financial performance, key business indicators, improvement opportunities, production planning, inventory control, and customer order services. Shorter-range operational planning, for day-to-day operations, was derived from managerial guidelines.

CEO Paul Smucker decidedly believed that Smucker's overall strategy for growth was consistent with the firm's objectives (Exhibit 6.2). "We have a definite idea of products which are keys to the future markets we serve. We also think we know how to meet the needs of those markets. Smucker's will continue to produce and deliver products similar to those we have. And new products will have qualities similar to those of our current line. Furthermore, we will focus on higher penetration of existing markets and customer groups where there is a need for Smucker's products."[6]

Included in the strategic planning process were new product additions. Managers from marketing, research, and manufacturing met to evaluate new

---

[6] Paul H. Smucker, interview, August 30, 1989.

EXHIBIT 6.1   The J.M. Smucker Company Basic Beliefs

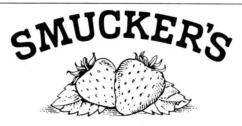

THE J.M. SMUCKER COMPANY

Basic Beliefs

Basic Beliefs are an expression of the Company's values and principles that guide strategic behavior and direction. The Basic Beliefs are deeply rooted in the philosophy and heritage of the founder, Jerome Smucker.

In 1897, the Smucker Company was formed by a dedicated, honest, forward-looking businessman, J.M. Smucker. Because he made a quality product, sold it at fair prices, and ran the Company with sound policies, this Company prospered. Today, we who inherit the Smucker name and the Smucker tradition of successful business operations, base present policies on these time-honored principles. We interpret them, in terms of modern corporate thinking, to be the guideposts of our operations; and they are as follows:

Quality

Quality is the key word and shall apply to our people, our products, our manufacturing methods, and our marketing efforts. We will market the highest quality products offered in our respective markets.

- Consistent high quality is required.
- The Company's growth and success has been built on quality.
- Quality comes first; earnings and sales growth will follow.

We will only produce and sell products that enhance the quality of life and well-being.

Ethics

Just as this Company was founded and has developed based on strong ethical values, these same values are ingrained in our management team today. This style of management is the standard by which we conduct our business, as well as ourselves, no less of which is acceptable under any circumstances. Therefore, we will maintain the highest standards of business ethics with customers, suppliers, employees, and communities where we work.

Independence

Because of our strong commitment to stewardship of the Smucker name and heritage, our desire to control our own direction, and our motivation to succeed on our own, we will remain an independent company. We seek to serve as an example of the success of a company which operates by these principles within the free enterprise system.

EXHIBIT 6.1   (Continued)

Growth

As we are concerned with day-to-day operations, we are also concerned with the potential of our Company. Growing is reaching for that potential whether it be in the development of new products and new markets, the discovery of new manufacturing or management techniques, or the personal growth and development of our people and their ideas.

We are committed to a strong balanced growth that will protect or enhance our consumer franchise within prudent financial parameters. We want to provide a fair return for our stockholders on their investment in us.

People

We will be fair with our employees and expect fair effort in return. We will seek employees who are committed to preserving and enhancing these values and principles through their own actions.

- Highest quality products and service require the highest quality people.
- Highest business ethics require the highest personal ethics.

These Basic Beliefs regarding quality, ethics, independence, growth, and people have served as a strong foundation in our history, and will be the basis for future strategy, plans, and achievements.

EXHIBIT 6.2   The Company Objectives

The Company Objectives

1. Make and market quality products. Quality shall be the key word in our operations and shall apply to ingredients, recipes, and manufacturing processes. In marketing these products, we shall price them all at the lowest possible price that will still assure a fair profit.
2. Provide for business growth. As we are concerned with day-to-day operation, so shall we be concerned with the potential of our company. We will be ready to grow in every area . . . in our search for quality in ingredients, recipes, processes of manufacture, new products, and marketing methods.
3. Deal fairly with everyone. We want to provide a satisfying work atmosphere for our employees with ample opportunity for growth. We want to provide a fair return for our stockholders. We want to provide good service and fair treatment for our suppliers and the trade. We want to provide quality for the public and an understanding of what we try to do to achieve quality standards and a superior product.

Source: W. D. Ellis, "With A Name Like . . ." J.M. Smucker Company, Orrville, Ohio, 1987, p. 117.

product ideas using the following guidelines: market need, competition, projected volume potential, profitability, marketing expense, pay-out period, R&D costs, raw material availability, seasonality, and stability of product category versus faddish product ideas.[7]

Paul Smucker described the development of strategic planning as evolving from a turning point. "As with most family manufacturing businesses, our orientation was plant output. We judged the business by what was going out the shipping door. But some of us were saying we should look at the business from the marketing end first. We are in several businesses which require different types of marketing, but we're looking upon it as one business."[8] The several business segments alluded to were grocery, food service, industrial, general merchandise, gifts and incentives, government, export, health food, convenience, and gourmet.

Strategic Business Areas

From the 10 business segments, the Smucker Company formulated its five strategic business areas: Consumer, Foodservice, Industrial, Specialty, and International.

The Consumer Strategic Business Area was comprised of the following market centers: Grocery, General Merchandise, Natural Foods, Government/ Military, and Gifts and Incentives. Products offered were mainstream grocery/ health foods in retail packages. They were marketed under the "Smucker's," "Mary Ellen," "Knudsen's," and "Nice N' Natural" brands and sold either as individual units or as gift packages. The Foodservice Strategic Business Area was comprised of numerous segments dispersed within the commercial and noncommercial sectors. Products offered were a range of portion control and bulk items. They were marketed under the "Smucker's," "Dickinson's," "Knudsen's," "Lost Acres," and "Elsenham" brands.

The Industrial Strategic Business Area was comprised of two segments: frozen fruit and formulated items. Products offered ranged from various forms of frozen fruit, purees, and concentrates to various formulated aseptic and ambient temperature items. In virtually all instances, industrial products were combined with the customers' own ingredients to form the customers' proprietary consumer products (as, for example, the fruit in Kellogg's Pop Tarts and the fruit in Dannon Yogurt).

The Specialty Strategic Business Area was comprised of the following segments: specialty food stores, department stores, upscale supermarkets, and conventional supermarkets. Products offered were gourmet retail packages. They were marketed under the "Dickinson's," "Elsenham," and "Lost Acres" brands and sold either as individual units or as gift packages.

The International Strategic Business Area was comprised of the following segments: JMS Canada, JMS Export, Elsenham Quality Foods, and IXL/Henry

[7] Ellis, "With a Name Like . . . ," p. 120.
[8] Ibid., p. 134.

Jones Foods. Markets served by JMS Export were all countries worldwide with the exclusion of the United States and Canada. Markets served by Elsenham Quality Foods and IXL/Henry Jones Foods were all countries worldwide with the exclusion of the United States. Products offered included all corporate product forms and all corporate brands.[9]

Marketing at Smucker

> The Smucker Company. . . . Top down and company wide, a people company focused on the customer. They hire people sensitive to the needs of their customers and, in my experience, always a cut above other manufacturers. . . . What you would expect from a company with an address on Strawberry Lane.[10]
>
> Supermarket Corporation President

The first venture into national advertising cost Smucker $30,000 in the 1950s. The results were considered poor and advertising was abruptly discontinued. In 1960, the company decided to advertise for the first time on the West Coast. This modest level of advertising, at about $75 per week, was attempted in order to generate sales for the opening of the new Salinas, California, plant which would have excess capacity. The agency selected for the task was Wyse Advertising of Cleveland, Ohio. The agency's president earlier made a presentation to Smucker management, who were most impressed by his sincere interest in the Smucker Company. Subsequently, sales on the West Coast were better than sales on the East Coast, and management attributed this to the results of advertising.

As a result, advertising was further expanded, although still on a modest scale. In 1962, with a $50,000 budget, the Wyse Agency hit upon what became one of the most recognized phrases in American advertising—"With a name like Smucker's, it has to be good." The slogan emerged as the main theme for all company advertising and was adopted as the company's motto.

The company's sales were strongest in the midwest, followed by the West Coast and then by sales in major cities on the East Coast. Advertising expenditures were less than 2½ percent of total sales (1987—$6.6 million on $288 million of sales, 1988—$6.5 million on $314 million of sales, and 1989—$8.8 million on $367 million of sales). Some of Smucker's major competitors spent more on advertising than the total of Smucker's sales revenues. Kraft, for example, had an astounding advertising budget of $400 million for 1987.[11] However, Kraft's large advertising budget was not totally spent on products competing directly with Smucker products. Large competitors had divisions that competed with Smucker's, and these divisions had operating budgets approximating those of

[9] Courtesy of Timothy P. Smucker in a September 5, 1989, communication to B. A. Deitzer, unpublished.
[10] Memo to B. A. Deitzer, July 5, 1989, unpublished.
[11] *Advertising Age*, September 28, 1988, p. 1.

Smucker's. Smucker had to, nonetheless, directly compete with Kraft's national image and highly recognized brand name.

Financial Performance

The company had been able to use ample cash flows (Exhibit 6.3) to purchase its acquisitions. In 1989, the firm's cash position was $36.7 million in cash and cash equivalents on total assets of $198.5 million (18½ percent). Typically the cash equivalents were held as follows (for 1988): commercial paper, $7.5 million; municipal notes, $2.5 million; bankers' acceptance, $5 million; certificates of deposit, $8 million; and Eurodollar time deposits, $2.9 million. Smucker's long-term debt was among the lowest in its industry (Exhibit 6.4).

Smucker's policy was to pay cash for its acquisitions. President Richard Smucker stated, "We're in a business that has a very good cash flow . . . and we do spend that cash when we have a key investment to make. We'd rather acquire it with cash than stock. Our cash flow is more than sufficient." The positive cash flow enabled the company to maintain a debt-to-equity ratio of about 3 to 5 percent. Richard Smucker further explained that "we could easily go higher. We could go to a 50 percent debt-to-equity ratio and feel comfortable with it. And we would if we wanted to make a large acquisition."[12]

EXHIBIT 6.3   Statements of Consolidated Income (In thousands except per share data)

| | Year Ended April 30, | | |
	1987	1988	1989
Net Sales	$288,263	$314,245	$366,855
Cost of Products Sold	192,169	206,144	240,227
	96,094	108,101	126,628
Selling, Distribution, and Administrative Expenses	62,032	70,529	83,907
	34,062	37,572	42,721
Interest Income	993	1,360	2,048
Other Income, Net	273	85	234
	35,328	39,017	45,003
Interest Expense	598	425	421
Income before Income Taxes	34,730	38,592	44,582
Income Taxes			
Federal			
Currently Payable	14,520	14,332	14,265
Deferred (credit)	608	(918)	708
State and Local	1,923	2,308	2,054
Total Income Taxes	17,051	15,722	17,027
Net Income	$17,679	$22,870	$27,555
Net Income Per Common Share	$2.41	$3.12	$3.75

[12] Mitchell, "Smucker Spreads Itself Around," p. B-4.

EXHIBIT 6.4   Consolidated Balance Sheets (In thousands)

	April 30,	
	1988	*1989*
Assets		
Current Assets		
Cash and Cash Equivalents	$ 27,111	$ 36,652
Trade Receivables	24,799	29,640
Inventories		
Finished Products	17,885	19,856
Raw Materials, Containers, and Supplies	29,115	27,324
	47,000	47,180
Other Current Assets	2,937	4,657
Total Current Assets	101,847	118,129
Goodwill	8,129	10,581
Intangible Assets	3,465	3,430
Other Assets	2,601	4,403
Property, Plant, and Equipment		
Land and Land Improvement	5,190	7,095
Buildings and Fixtures	32,157	34,960
Machinery and Equipment	47,670	58,039
Construction in Progress	3,019	2,390
	88,036	102,484
Accumulated Depreciation	(34,053)	(40,570)
Total Property, Plant, and Equipment	53,983	61,914
Total Assets	$170,025	$198,457
Liabilities and Shareholders' Equity		
Current Liabilities		
–Accounts Payable	$ 23,517	$ 30,651
–Salaries, Wages, and Additional Compensation	5,239	5,922
–Taxes Other Than Federal Income Taxes	2,678	2,120
–Federal Income Taxes	1,903	573
–Dividends Payable	1,620	1,913
Current Portion of Long-Term Debt	667	677
Total Current Liabilities	35,624	41,856
Long-Term Liabilities		
–Long-Term Debt	3,081	4,954
–Deferred Federal Income Taxes	4,254	5,641
–Other Liabilities	1,744	1,470
Total Long-Term Liabilities	9,079	12,065
Shareholders' Equity		
Serial Preferred Shares—No Par Value:		
Authorized—1,000 Shares; Outstanding—none	—	—
Common shares—No Par Value:		
Authorized—15,000,000 Shares		
Outstanding, at Stated Capital Amount:		
1989—7,356,852 Shares, after Deducting 749.292 Shares		

(*continued*)

EXHIBIT 6.4   (Continued)

	April 30,	
	1988	*1989*
Held in Treasury		
1988—7,362,685 Shares, after Deducting 743,459 Shares		
Held in Treasury	3,681	3,678
Additional Capital	5,746	7,733
Retained Income	122,797	143,383
Less		
Deferred Compensation	(1,980)	(1,017)
Amount Due from ESOP Trust	(4,922)	(8,807)
Currency Translation Adjustment	—	(434)
Total Shareholders' Equity	125,322	144,536
Total Liabilities and Shareholders' Equity	$170,025	$198,457

SMUCKER'S MANAGEMENT

Founder Jerome Smucker had the business acumen legendary among American farmers in addition to two years of formal business courses at the academy in Smithville, near Orrville. Jerome Smucker was succeeded by his son Willard, who learned from close association with his father and long years with the company. Willard Smucker led the company as chairman from 1947 to 1970.

CEO Paul H. Smucker

Willard's son Paul H. Smucker, 72, trained in business at Miami University of Oxford, Ohio, assumed the leadership of the company in 1970, and became its chief executive officer and chairman of the executive committee. In 1992, Paul Smucker's son Timothy, 45, was the chairman and son Richard, 41, was president of the company. The responsibilities of the two brothers are illustrated in the firm's organization charts (Exhibits 6.5 and 6.6).

The Smucker Brothers

The next generation of leadership represented by the younger Smuckers reflected the firm's transition to modern corporate practices. Tim Smucker started with the company in marketing after graduating from the Wharton School of Finance in 1969. He became manager of advertising and product development and in 1973 was appointed vice president for planning. A strong believer in strategic planning, he developed an extensive program covering the areas of finance, key business indicators, improvement opportunities, production planning and inventory control, and customer order services. He progressed to president and

EXHIBIT 6.5   Organization Chart

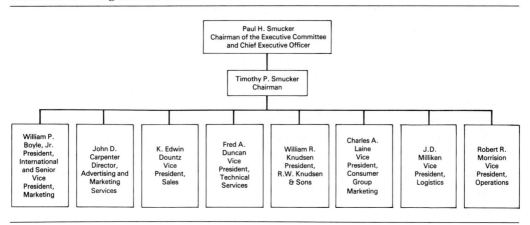

chief operating officer in 1981 and became chairman in 1986 when Paul Smucker became chairman of the executive committee.

Richard Smucker started as a systems analyst with the company after graduating with a master's degree from the Wharton School of Business. In this position he installed the company's first West Coast computer system in 1972. Working as an administrative and financial officer, he became executive vice president and chief administrative officer in 1981 and was appointed president in 1986.

EXHIBIT 6.6   Organization Chart

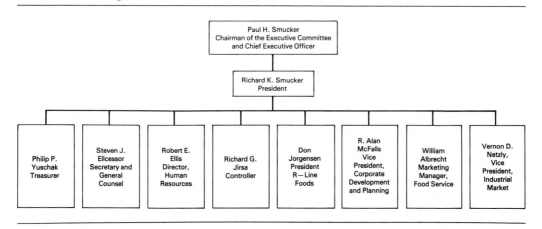

From an operational standpoint, Tim Smucker, chairman, was responsible for the Consumer and International Strategic Business Areas as well as all sales and marketing activities, logistics, operations, and technical services, which included product development, process and technical development, quality assurance, and management information systems. Richard Smucker, on the other hand, as president was primarily responsible for the Specialty, Foodservice, and Industrial Strategic Areas. He was also responsible for corporate development, legal, human resource, treasury, and controller functions.

The three Smuckers, Paul and his sons Timothy and Richard, began their association with the family business long before their official entry positions—Paul as a low-level cost accountant, Tim in the marketing department, and Richard as a systems analyst. As teenagers they began working in various parts of the plant as cook's helper or in salvage as a bottle washer or even in helping to pick crops processed at the plant. During those years they became acquainted personally with many of their employees, following the style of founder J. M. Smucker, who made it a practice to personally speak with each of his employees. The practice not only boosted employee morale but also allowed processing workers to voice operational improvements.

This tradition of employee involvement has continued to 1992 in the form of group meetings held twice yearly at each facility worldwide. As *Fortune* magazine stated, "The Smuckers take an old-fashioned approach to management. Richard, Tim, and Paul describe themselves as hands-on executives frequently visiting plants and meeting employees. Says Tim: 'Our five basic beliefs are quality, ethics, independence, growth and people. Maybe that sounds like motherhood and apple pie.'"[13] At Smucker the combination seemed to work.

The Corporate Complex

Opposite Paul Smucker's office, in the corner office on the other side of the upstairs lobby, Tim Smucker carried on the day-to-day business of guiding not the largest company in its field but the one having the largest market share (37 percent) in jams, jellies, and preserves. On the wall facing Tim Smucker's desk was a series of shelves holding at least 100 assorted jars of competitor's jams, jellies, and preserves acquired while traveling—visual reminders of the ever-challenging competition. The good-natured Smuckers not only knew the competitions' products but were also personally acquainted with many of their competitors.

Although the styles of the two men and their offices were different, they both nonetheless accomplished their tasks rooted in identical basic beliefs and mission statements. Both men genuinely conveyed to visitors the impression that Smucker's corporate principles were warmly exemplified in the owners' daily lives.

A small plastic laminated card stating the company's basic beliefs was given to each new employee. Tim Smucker added, "You have to live what you're

[13] Julianne Slovak, "Companies to Watch," *Fortune*, January 16, 1989, p. 80.

talking about on an every day basis. We go to great lengths to hire people that understand our basic beliefs. You can always find a financial person or an engineer but you can't find people that understand the values of the company. Sometimes we'll go two years before we find a person that puts these values first. You have to have those kinds of values personally."[14]

In the 92 years of operation, the company has had only three generations of Smuckers at the helm with the fourth generation making itself ready to take over. Paul Smucker, who has 50 years with the company, perhaps best summed up the reasons why the Smuckers work so long "The business is a fun business. You meet nice people, customers are nice. You feel like you're contributing something to society."[15]

[14] Timothy P. Smucker, interview, August 30, 1989.
[15] Paul H. Smucker, interview, August 30, 1989.

―――――――――――――― CASE 7 ――――――――――――――

PAN AM ATTEMPTS SURVIVAL IN THE 1990s

INTRODUCTION

In September 1991, the new president of Pan Am sat in his office, contemplating the lights of New York City as he attempted to calm himself before heading home. Delta and Pan Am had finally reached an accord that would allow Pan Am to survive, something few industry analysts had predicted. Delta agreed to purchase all of Pan Am's European routes, the East Coast shuttle, and related equipment, leaving Pan Am with a much smaller route structure confined to Central and South America. The president knew that many critics viewed this as merely postponing the inevitable; Pan Am, they said, could no longer compete. Better to let it go quietly rather than prolong the agony. The president could not accept that. "Pan Am's long and glorious history must count for something," he

This case was prepared by Kent N. Gourdin as a basis for class discussion rather than to illustrate either effective or ineffective handling of an administrative situation. Used with permission from Kent N. Gourdin.

thought. "The challenge will be to bring Pan Am back to profitability—to survive this brutally competitive industry."

A HISTORY OF PAN AM

Pan American Airways was formed by Juan Trippe in 1927 to carry mail between Florida and Cuba utilizing three Fokker trimotor aircraft. Trippe led the company until 1968, and it was his vision that guided the firm's development into the world-spanning airline it eventually became. Pan Am was a company of firsts: first to fly across the Pacific, first across the Atlantic, and first to successfully fly commercial jets. Furthermore, Pan Am was the only carrier to ever offer around-the-world service, with one daily flight traveling eastbound from New York while another flew west.

The magnitude of Trippe's accomplishments cannot be overemphasized. Prior to World War II, airlines were responsible for building their own infrastructure. Thus, Pan Am's Pacific expansion began with the arrival of ships carrying equipment and construction workers at places such as Honolulu, Midway Island, Wake Island, and Guam. The company's resources were then utilized to build and staff the airports, communications systems, and passenger support facilities that today are provided by the government. Pan Am repeated this pattern in Latin America, Alaska, and across the Atlantic. In addition, Trippe traveled around the world negotiating his own air rights with foreign countries.

Following World War II, Pan Am continued its domination of international commercial aviation, and came to symbolize U.S. supremacy in that area. Though other U.S. carriers began flying overseas as well, none enjoyed the comprehensive route network or long-standing reputation of Pan Am. Its world-spanning coverage reached its zenith in 1984 and is shown in Exhibit 7.1.

Management historically placed a great deal of emphasis on the physical aspects of the business. Pan Am pioneered in-flight dining and entertainment in the 1930s. It was the first customer for both the Boeing 707 in the late 1950s and the Boeing 747 10 years later. Trippe placed large initial orders for these revolutionary wide-body aircraft before they were even off the drawing board, thus ensuring that Pan Am would be the first airline to operate them. Indeed, the airline's commitment to technical excellence combined with its extensive international route structure made it the only choice for travel to or from the United States. In other words, you flew Pan Am or you did not go.

The second by-product of the company's international domination was that it had virtually no domestic route structure to feed traffic into its overseas routes. Congress had historically been supportive of Pan Am's worldwide growth, viewing the carrier as an instrument of national policy. This support took the form of subsidies and lucrative international route awards with little or no U.S. competi-

EXHIBIT 7.1   Pan Am Points Served, 1984

United States

Austin
Boston
Charlotte
Chicago
Cincinnati
Cleveland
Dallas/Fort Worth
Detroit
Honolulu
Houston
Indianapolis
Kansas City
Los Angeles
Miami
Minneapolis/St. Paul
Nashville
New Orleans
New York
Orlando
Philadelphia
Pittsburgh
Raleigh/Durham
St. Louis
San Antonio
Seattle/Tacoma
Tampa/St. Petersburg
Washington, D.C.

Atlantic/Caribbean Islands

Antigua
Bahamas: Freeport
  Nassau
Barbados
Bermuda
Guadeloupe
Martinique
St. Kitts
St. Lucia
St. Maarten
Trinidad
U.S. Virgin Islands
  St. Croix
  St. Thomas

Mexico and Central America

Guatemala City
Mexico City

South America

Buenos Aires
Caracas
Maracaibo
Montevideo
Rio de Janeiro
Santiago
Sao Paulo

Europe

Amsterdam
Athens
Belgrade
Bucharest
Budapest
Dubrovnik
Frankfurt
Geneva
Hamburg
Istanbul
London
Munich
Nice
Nuremberg
Paris
Rome
Stuttgart
Vienna
Warsaw
Zagreb
Zurich

Middle East

Dhahran
Dubai

Africa

Dakar
Johannesburg
Lagos
Monrovia
Nairobi

Orient/Asia

Bangkok
Beijing
Bombay
Delhi
Hong Kong
Karachi
Manila
Osaka
Seoul
Shanghai
Singapore
Taipei
Tokyo

South Pacific

Auckland
Melbourne
Sydney

Source: Pan Am Corporation, *Annual Report,* 1984, p. 2.

tion. However, that attitude changed dramatically in the late 1940s, when Congress began awarding overseas routes to other U.S. airlines such as TWA, Braniff, and Northwest. Indeed, this signaled the beginning of an "anti–Pan Am" sentiment in the government that would haunt the future development of the carrier. The government became so concerned about the size of Pan Am that Congress consistently refused to allow the airline to expand domestically for fear that it would become an overpowering competitor for other U.S. carriers. Thus, as other airlines grew and gradually expanded overseas, Pan Am was precluded from responding in kind domestically.[1]

As was the case with most other U.S. airlines, Pan Am was highly profitable during the 1960s, but its fortunes changed in the 1970s. Just after it introduced the first 747 jumbo jets in 1969, international travel promptly declined, the value of the dollar fell, and the price of oil skyrocketed. (Another by-product of the airline's international route structure was that Pan Am bought the majority of its fuel at overseas locations, where the cost was much greater than in the United States.) After turning a profit in 1977 and 1978, Pan Am again attempted to resolve its lack of a domestic route structure. Two months prior to the passing of the Airline Deregulation Act in 1978, Pan Am applied to merge with National Airlines.

The merger proved unexpectedly challenging for several reasons. First, the company got into a bidding war with Eastern Airlines and Texas International that resulted in Pan Am paying $50 per share for National's stock ($430 million total) versus the $30 per share initially offered.[2] Second, after finally taking over in January 1980, Pan Am raised the pay of National employees to Pan Am's higher wage scales almost immediately. Third, Pan Am failed to integrate the two operations smoothly. Finally, they failed to build the domestic network they were seeking.[3] The most distressing part of all, though, was that the deregulation of the U.S. airline industry just two months later permitted Pan Am to expand at its discretion; the company need not have put itself through the National agony at all.

The explosive growth of airline competition resulting from deregulation, together with Pan Am's on-going trouble, combined with various other environmental factors to produce ever-growing losses. Draconian actions were taken (1980—sale of the headquarters building in midtown Manhattan for $400 million; 1981—sale of the Intercontinental Hotel chain for $500 million; 1985—sale of Pan Am's entire Pacific division to United Airlines for $750 million), but to no avail. A terrorist bomb destroyed one of the airline's 747s over Lockerbie, Scotland, in December 1988, killing all aboard and costing the carrier $350 million in lost revenue and increased expenses. With the outbreak of war in the Middle East in 1990, Pan Am's fate was sealed. Foreign travel virtually stopped, and passengers that *did* fly avoided Pan Am studiously, concerned that it was a tempting terrorist

---

[1] Richard L. Stern, "The End of an Empire," *Forbes*, February 4, 1991, p. 76.
[2] "Pan Am's Flight to a New Hangar," *Newsweek*, August 6, 1979, p. 63.
[3] *Wall Street Journal*, July 12, 1991, p. A5.

target. In a final effort to survive, the airline sold most of its London routes along with its highly prized Heathrow hub, to United for $400 million. However, on January 8, 1991, Pan Am filed for protection from its creditors under Chapter 11 of the Federal Bankruptcy Code, which permits a company to continue operating while it attempts to reorganize. Financial data on Pan Am and its three largest U.S. competitors are presented in Exhibits 7.2 and 7.3.

EXHIBIT 7.2   Selected Financial Data, 1981–1990

	American	Delta	Pan Am	United
Operating Revenues (Millions of Dollars)				
1990	$10,639	$8,673	$3,969	$10,501
1989	9,961	8,648	3,612	9,742
1988	8,551	7,393	3,592	8,796
1987	7,124	6,094	3,121	7,863
1986	5,856	4,497	2,733	6,688
1985	5,860	4,738	3,156	4,920
1984	5,088	4,497	3,382	6,097
1983	4,532	3,905	3,529	5,287
1982	3,978	3,632	3,471	4,614
1981	3,911	3,644	3,586	4,470
Operating Expenses (Millions of Dollars)				
1990	10,249	8,518	4,250	10,284
1989	9,230	7,972	3,930	9,185
1988	7,749	6,868	3,698	8,129
1987	6,651	5,659	3,292	7,712
1986	5,465	4,271	3,106	6,698
1985	5,353	4,507	3,364	5,248
1984	4,748	4,209	3,517	5,547
1983	4,282	3,962	3,516	5,134
1982	3,996	3,718	3,844	4,682
1981	3,868	3,558	3,963	4,617
Operating Margin (Operating Revenue/Expenses)				
1990	103.8	101.8	.934	102.1
1989	107.9	108.5	.919	106.1
1988	110.3	107.6	.971	108.3
1987	107.1	107.7	.948	102.0
1986	107.2	105.3	.880	.999
1985	109.5	105.1	.938	.938
1984	107.2	106.8	.970	110.0
1983	106.8	.986	100.0	103.0
1982	.995	.977	.900	.985
1981	101.1	102.4	.900	.968

Source: *Standard and Poors Industry Surveys:* January 6, 1986, pp. A31, A32; April 28, 1988, pp. A33, A34; June 20, 1991, pp. A37, A38.

EXHIBIT 7.3   Net Operating Income and Net Income Figures (In thousands)

	American	Delta	Pan Am	United
Net Operating Income				
1990	$8,082	$ − 31,525	$ − 8,231	$112,051
1989	22,967	− 87	− 201,266	154,983
1988	7,528	84,110	75,832	206,367
1987	− 9,198	51,637	88,891	54,800
1986	14,025	12,774	− 89,526	− 61,021
1985	506,484	231,207	− 207,577	− 328,004
1984	339,065	287,344	− 135,216	550,006
1983	249,517	− 57,207	13,131	152,362
1982	− 18,247	− 85,948	− 372,736	− 68,549
1981	43,356	86,505	− 377,431	− 146,729
Net Income				
1990	$3,255	$ − 15,423	$ − 166,868	$101,823
1989	9,135	18,571	− 165,535	100,752
1988	− 416	58,972	70,411	163,739
1987	− 10,686	32,229	112,854	11,737
1986	6,893	8,571	− 157,461	− 36,884
1985	322,640	156,775	37,474	− 88,223
1984	208,606	258,641	64,080	235,856
1983	217,874	37,892	356,915	119,716
1982	− 14,476	− 17,058	−5,331	− 17,358
1981	47,440	91,640	− 18,875	− 104,893

Source: *Standard and Poors Industry Surveys,* January 6, 1986, pp. A31, A32; April 28, 1988, pp. A33, A34; June 20, 1991, pp. A37, A38.

AIRLINE DEREGULATION

In 1938, the U.S. government began regulating the domestic airline industry. For the next 40 years, the Civil Aeronautics Board (CAB), which was created for the express purpose of monitoring the economic aspects of commercial aviation, had the final authority regarding rates, routes, and services provided by the airlines. Economic regulation occurred for several reasons. First, Congress was concerned that uncontrolled competition would weaken the airlines and negatively impact the U.S. air transportation system. Second, transportation was, at the time, viewed as a service that should be made available to everyone. Since carriers would, if left alone, provide transportation only over profitable routes, Congress utilized the regulatory process to "force" them to serve unprofitable routes as well.

This was accomplished by limiting the number of airlines permitted to serve profitable routes. In exchange for this quasi monopoly, carriers were required to serve nonprofitable routes as a public service. Fares were, to a large degree, fixed, so that price competition was virtually unknown. Seeking CAB permission to fly a new route or alter fares was a difficult and time-consuming process for a carrier that, as often as not, ended in failure for the applicant, so the whole system was extremely stable. In essence, consumers chose their airline based upon which one flew to the destination of choice, and they paid the published fare.

This equilibrium was destroyed in October 1978 when Congress passed the Airline Deregulation Act, which freed the airlines from economic regulation, a move that signified the government's willingness to let market forces guide the allocation of transportation resources. If a route was not profitable, the carrier could stop service; generally new routes could be added at will. Carriers were given more freedom in setting rates; price became a function of demand and could be actively utilized as a marketing tool. Deregulation put the business of air transportation back into the hands of the managers, who became free to decide which routes they would serve and what fares they would charge. Managers had to bear the burden of their mistakes as deregulation also implied the freedom to fail, something that had been quite difficult under the sheltering umbrella of economic regulation.

Impact of Deregulation on the U.S. Airline Industry

In the late 1970s and early 1980s, there were numerous new airlines challenging the established carriers. Some (People Express, New York Air) offered low prices and minimal services; others (Presidential Air, Air One) adopted a high-service/high-price strategy. In fact, the number of scheduled carriers grew from 36 just prior to deregulation to a peak of 229 in 1984.[4] Although this number included companies of all sizes, this discussion focuses only on the larger, more well known airlines. In 1984, there were approximately 24 of these. By 1991, this number dwindled to roughly 13 as a result of mergers, acquisitions, and outright failures.[5] As shown in Exhibit 7.4, six of the survivors were operating under conditions of bankruptcy or default. Of great concern, however, was the fact that the five strongest airlines controlled approximately 75 percent of the market,[6] with American, Delta, and United accounting for 14.6, 13.1, and 11.5 percent, respectively.[7]

Despite this consolidation, however, opportunities continued to attract new entrants. By mid-1991, 17 requests for new operating certificates had been received by the Department of Transportation, despite a recession and a general downturn in air travel. Companies such as Air Reno, U.S.–Africa Airways, and Miami Air all hoped to succeed by exploiting niche markets of little interest to the major airlines.[8]

---

[4] Robert M. Kane and Allan D. Vose, *Air Transportation* (Dubuque, IA: Kendall/Hunt, 1987), pp. 11–24.

[5] Michael Oneal, Wendy Zellner, and Seth Payne, "Fly the Lucrative Skies of United American Delta," *Business Week*, October 14, 1991, p. 91.

[6] Ibid., p. 90.

[7] "Few Carriers Win Battle for Survival," *USA Today*, August 5, 1991, p. 1B.

[8] Edward L. McKenna, "More Entrant Airlines Seeking U.S. Approval, Defying Tight Market," *Aviation Week and Space Technology*, November 18, 1991, pp. 24–25.

EXHIBIT 7.4   Major Scheduled Airlines, 1984 and 1991

1984	1991
Air Cal[a]	Alaskan
Air Florida[b]	American
Alaskan	America West[j]
American	Continental[j]
America West	Delta
Continental	Midway[j]
Delta	Northwest
Eastern[c]	Pan Am[j]
Empire[d]	Southwest
Frontier[e]	Trump Shuttle[j]
Midway	TWA[j]
New York Air[c]	United
Northwest	USAir
Ozark[f]	
Pacific Southwest[g]	
Pan Am	
People Express[c]	
Piedmont[g]	
Republic[h]	
Southwest	
TWA	
United	
USAir	
Western[i]	

[a] Merged with American.
[b] Merged with Midway.
[c] Merged with, or absorbed by Continental.
[d] Merged with Piedmont.
[e] Merged with Delta.
[f] Merged with People Express.
[g] Merged with TWA.
[h] Merged with USAir.
[i] Merged with Delta

[j] Operating in bankruptcy or default.

Source: "Fly the Lucrative Skies of United American Delta," *Business Week,* October 14, 1991, p. 91.

Hub-and-Spoke Systems

Airlines adopted hub-and-spoke systems in an attempt to increase service and decrease costs. Passengers were brought from outlying cities (spokes) into the hub (large central airports), where they changed planes and proceeded to their destinations. For example, travelers flying from Knoxville, Tennessee, to Los

Angeles on USAir, would board a plane in Knoxville, fly to USAir's Charlotte hub, change planes, and complete their trip to the West Coast. This system allowed the carrier to offer more frequent service utilizing smaller aircraft. Unfortunately, it also meant that nonstop flights became less common, unless passengers were originating or terminating their trip at a hub.

One result of this route structure was that carriers were able to completely dominate the traffic into or out of their respective hubs, effectively limiting competition from new carriers. This occurred because the dominant airline (or airlines) leased all of the airport's gate space, thereby denying access to other carriers. Furthermore, the sheer number of flights operated at the hub by the dominant carrier made utilizing another airline simply less attractive to the passenger, since doing so meant making a stop at *their* hub versus going nonstop. USAir, for example, operated about 470 daily flights to or from Charlotte, North Carolina, accounting for approximately 94 percent of the total scheduled traffic at that airport in 1991. Exhibit 7.5 depicts the hubs maintained by U.S. air carriers as of late 1991.

EXHIBIT 7.5   Major U.S. Airlines and Hub Locations

Airline	Location of Hub Airports		
American	Dallas-Fort Worth Raleigh-Durham San Juan	San Jose, Calif. Miami	Chicago (O'Hare) Nashville
United	Chicago (O'Hare) Washington, D.C. (Dulles)	Denver Tokyo	San Francisco London
Delta	Atlanta Salt Lake City New York (JFK)	Cincinnati Los Angeles Frankfurt	Dallas-Fort Worth Orlando
Northwest	Detroit Washington, D.C. (National)	Memphis	Minneapolis
USAir	Pittsburgh Philadelphia	Charlotte	Baltimore
Continental	Denver Newark	Cleveland	Houston
TWA	New York	St. Louis	Paris (deGaulle)
Pan Am	Miami		
America West	Phoenix	Honolulu	Las Vegas
Southwest	Dallas	Houston	Phoenix
Alaska	Anchorage	Portland	Seattle
Midway	Chicago (Midway)		

Source: "Dogfight in the Skies," *USA Today,* August 5, 1991, pp. 2B, 3B.

Productivity

Deregulation forced airline companies to become more productive, both from the standpoint of increasing their output (moving more people) and lowering their input (controlling their costs). The computerized reservation system (CRS) emerged as a powerful tool for doing both. Many of the large carriers developed these highly sophisticated programs, which allowed travel agents and other service agencies to immediately present prospective travelers with all of the flight options available for their desired routing. American's SABRE system and United's APOLLO accounted for about 68 percent of the market, while SYSTEM ONE (Continental), WORLDSPAN (Delta/Northwest/TWA), and several foreign networks (GALILEO and AMADEUS in Europe, ABACUS in Asia, GEMINI in Canada) competed for the rest.[9] Typically, the host airline's flights were presented first, so that the agent might have to scroll through multiple screens in order to examine flights offered by competing carriers. Airlines that did not maintain their own CRS paid a fee to be listed on those belonging to other carriers.

A CRS could provide a significant competitive advantage to an airline. First, they were extremely costly to develop; second, in addition to air travel, the CRS could also be used to book hotel, rental car, and transportation services via other modes (i.e., rail); third, travel agents tended to subscribe only to one CRS; and, finally, with the multitude of ticket prices available, they provided travel agents and users virtually the only means of quoting reliable fare information. In short, computer reservation systems became such a powerful competitive weapon that the U.S. government was considering action that would force those airlines, such as American, United, and Delta, that owned large CRSs to either divest themselves of those assets or render them unbiased in their treatment of other carriers.

Airlines also adopted a very sophisticated pricing system. Commonly referred to as yield management, carriers were able to price based on the passengers' demand elasticity for air transportation. On any given plane, people may have paid any one of 12 to 15 different fares for the same basic service: movement from point A to point B. For example, passengers who were willing to book, and pay for, a flight far in advance and incur restrictions on their travel (no changes, cancellations, and so on) could often obtain a low fare. On the other hand, a person who needed to fly immediately, and who could not live with travel limitations, paid a much higher price. What made this pricing system work was the tremendous analytical capacity of the CRS, which provided management the utilization history on each flight so that fares could be tailored to extract the maximum revenue based on demand patterns. Obviously, what these efforts were intended to do was to fill the airplane, as an empty seat represented revenue that was lost forever. To that same end, management also became skilled at getting more people into each plane. Knee room was gradually reduced, as was the extent to which each seat could recline. Seats themselves were thinner and aisles

---

[9] *Standard and Poors Industrial Surveys 1991* (New York: Standard and Poors, 1991), p. A36.

narrower, all for the purpose of increasing the passenger-carrying capability of the aircraft.

Management also became adept at cutting costs (reducing input). As was mentioned previously, the hub-and-spoke system was initially devised as a way to lower costs and improve passenger loads. Airlines were utilizing aircraft that were extremely reliable, that were fuel efficient, and that in many cases only required the use of two cockpit crew members. Lower labor rates in general were negotiated, surplus jobs eliminated, and passenger services brought more into line with customer needs.

In light of the above discussion, one key point emerged with respect to deregulation's impact on the airline industry: Bigger seemed to be better. Rightly or wrongly, the key to success, at least in the United States, were computer reservations systems, hub domination, yield management, and cost control. This was not to say, however, that there were no longer opportunities available to smaller carriers. The entrepreneurial spirit still seemed to live in the airline industry, be it in the form of geographic markets that were underserved, or customer segments whose needs could not be met by the large carriers.

THE DELTA DEAL

The situation at Pan Am continued to worsen during 1991. By late summer, the carrier's continued viability was seriously in doubt. Several potential buyers began negotiations to purchase pieces of the ailing company, and in August Delta Airlines presented the bid that was ultimately accepted by Pan Am's management. They agreed to pay $416 million for Pan Am's New York–based transatlantic operations, the Pan Am Shuttle, and related aircraft, spares, and fixed assets. In addition, Pan Am would remain as an operating airline. The "new" Pan Am would be owned jointly by Delta (45 percent) and Pan Am's creditors (55 percent) including its major employee groups.[10] Delta would spend approximately $455 million more to turn Pan Am into a smaller Miami-based carrier primarily serving Latin America, the Caribbean, and one route each connecting Frankfurt and Paris with Miami.[11] The points served by the smaller Pan Am are shown in Exhibit 7.6.

There was little doubt that Pan Am would be a radically different company. Historically the Latin American division had been the firm's most lucrative, generating an operating profit of $46.9 million in the first quarter of 1991.[12] These routes supported a higher-than-usual percentage of first-class and business travelers, resulting in larger revenues per passenger-mile. In addition, many Latin

[10] James T. McKenna, "Delta Wins Pan Am Bidding, Gains on Larger Competitors," *Aviation Week and Space Technology*, August 19, 1991, p. 19.

[11] Ibid., p. 18.

[12] Alison Leigh Cowan, "The New Pan Am Rumbas Ahead," *New York Times*, August 19, 1991, p. C2.

EXHIBIT 7.6   Points Served by Pan Am, November 1, 1991

United States	Caribbean
Atlanta	Hamilton
Boston	Barbados
Chicago	Grand Cayman
Dallas/Fort Worth	Grand Turk
Detroit	Kingston
Houston	Montego Bay
Los Angeles	Nassau
Miami	Port-au-Prince
Newark	Port-of-Spain
New Orleans	Providenciales
New York	Puerto Plata
Orlando	San Juan
San Francisco	Santo Domingo
Tampa/St. Petersburg/Clearwater	St. Croix
Washington, D.C.	St. Maarten
	St. Thomas

Western Europe

London
Paris

Mexico

Cancun
Mexico City

Central America

Guatemala City
Panama City
San Jose

South America

Buenos Aires
Caracas
Maracaibo
Montevideo
Recife
Rio de Janeiro
Santiago
Sao Paulo

Source: *Wall Street Journal,* October 18, 1991, pp. A8–A9.

American countries had erected protectionist barriers intended to shield their respective airlines from rigorous competition. Thus, in contrast to the 30 or 40 carriers competing over the North Atlantic, only 3 dominated in Latin America: Pan Am, Varig Brazilian Airlines, and American. However, Pan Am had only 7,000 U.S. employees versus the 26,000 it had at the start of 1991. In addition, its aircraft fleet dropped from 152 to approximately 50. Finally, massive organizational changes were required to cope with the new situation.[13]

[13] McKenna, "Delta Wins Pan Am Bidding," p. 21.

INTERNATIONAL COMMERCIAL AVIATION

The world of commercial air travel was extremely complex. Although the United States had an air transport system made up of privately held airlines, the rest of the world did not. In fact, most other international air carriers were either owned or controlled to some degree by their governments, which often adopted extremely protectionist policies designed to favor those companies vis à vis competing airlines. In addition, foreign airlines were often willing to operate at a loss just to "show the flag" for their home country, something U.S. firms were not able to do.

International aviation rights were negotiated between governments and were, for all practical purposes, treaties between the nations involved. Known as bilateral agreements, these accords were very specific regarding (among other things) service frequency and destinations, carriers providing that service, and occasionally even the equipment each airline could operate. If circumstances relative to the bilateral agreement changed (i.e., a new carrier wanted to provide service, or additional destinations were desired), the countries involved had to accede to the new conditions before they could take effect. Thus, Delta, despite having purchased Pan Am's right to fly to Germany from New York, could not start service until the Germans agreed. In some instances, the entire bilateral agreement had to be renegotiated, a time-consuming and often heated process conducted by the State Department.

When the United States deregulated its airline industry, the rest of the world did not. At the heart of that move was the encouragement of competition, which the United States did in the international arena by adopting very liberal bilateral agreements that encouraged foreign airlines to begin, or increase, their service to the United States. Of course, by definition, there were always a minimum of two carriers serving each route: one from each country. Unfortunately, the U.S. market was often much more lucrative for the foreign carrier than the foreign market was for the U.S. airline. Although there were signs that other countries (Canada, Australia, Brazil, members of the European Community) were slowly moving toward an "open skies" policy similar to that found in the United States, the facts were that air rights were closely guarded national assets that were awarded only after laborious diplomatic procedures wherein each nation negotiated to achieve the maximum benefit for itself.

Unfortunately, 1990 and 1991 were disastrous years for the airline industry in general. The combined effects of the Persian Gulf War (high fuel costs, fears of terrorism, and so forth), a worldwide economic slowdown, and low fares resulted in U.S. carriers losing over $3 billion in 1990, with similar results anticipated in 1991.[14] In fact, world airline traffic declined 4.1 percent in 1991, the first drop

---

[14] James Ott, "Airline Officials Fear Forecasts of Recovery Were Too Upbeat," *Aviation Week and Space Technology*, September 30, 1991, p. 30.

since the 1940s.[15] The result was a much smaller industry dominated by three major airlines.

There were signs, however, that the worst might be over. Fuel prices declined and stabilized after soaring to a high of $1.40 per gallon in late 1990.[16] (An increase of 1 cent per gallon cost U.S. carriers an extra $160 million annually.)[17] Certain markets showed significant growth in 1990 as well. Demand for travel over Pacific routes increased more than 20 percent over 1989, while Latin American services grew by 9.5 percent. Even traffic on the North Atlantic, the world's most heavily traveled air corridor, expanded 7.2 percent. In addition, the weak value of the dollar made travel to the United States a bargain for many foreign tourists, thus increasing the demand for air travel to, from, and within the United States.[18]

It was clear, however, that the industry was continuing to change dramatically. Worldwide passenger traffic was generally expected to expand on average by 5.2 percent over the next 15 years, although the strongest growth was anticipated for Europe-Asia (12.6 percent), Intra-Asia (9.0 percent), and Transpacific (8.5 percent) routes.[19] Assuming foreign governments continued to move toward airline deregulation, international competition between carriers would increase as more destinations opened to both U.S. and overseas airlines. In addition, if the U.S. experience was any indication, consolidations could be expected among the world's airlines as weaker carriers were taken over by stronger ones or simply failed.

Several companies, perhaps in anticipation of more competition, were attempting to establish nonowner partnerships with other carriers in order to form multinational groups of independent firms that would coordinate activities such as scheduling, marketing, and training. British Airways, KLM Royal Dutch Airlines, and Northwest Airlines were discussing just such an arrangement, as were Lufthansa and USAir.[20] Furthermore, the U.S. Department of Transportation had recently decided that foreign airlines could own as much as 49 percent of the shares of a U.S. carrier, further encouraging the development of global air transport systems.[21] Scandinavian Airline System (SAS) already owned 17 percent of Continental, while Ansett Airlines of Australia owned 20 percent of America West and KLM owned 49 percent of Northwest.[22]

Companies attempting to survive and prosper in an increasingly competitive global airline industry found that they would also have to become more adept at

---

[15] "World Airline Traffic Declined 4.1% in 1991," *Wall Street Journal*, January 2, 1991, p. A6.

[16] *Standard and Poors Industrial Survey*, p. A33.

[17] *1991 U.S. Industrial Outlook* (Washington, D.C.: U.S. Department of Commerce), pp. 41–43.

[18] Ibid.

[19] *Standard and Poors, Industry Survey*, p. A-27.

[20] James Ott, "European Airlines Eye Mergers to Match Global Competition," *Aviation Week and Space Technology*, November 25, 1991, p. 39.

[21] *Standard and Poors, Industry Survey*, p. A.33.

[22] Asra Q. Nomani and Laurie McGinley, "Airlines of the World Scramble for Routes in Industry Shakeout," *Wall Street Journal*, July 23, 1991, p. A8.

meeting customer needs as well as controlling costs. The temptation was to price for market share rather than profit; that is, to utilize low fares that did not cover costs. Fare increases were difficult to sustain when a competitor was offering lower prices, especially when passengers had become so price sensitive. The other difficulty was that many of an international carrier's revenues and costs could be impacted by events beyond management's control. The negative effects of the worldwide recession and the Persian Gulf War have already been discussed, as has the volatility of fuel prices. Similarly, governmental influences continued to impact managerial decision making even in a deregulated environment. Such issues as ticket taxes, noise requirements, and air traffic control could directly affect both the airline's costs and the quality of its service, yet managers had no direct control over these events. The competitive (some would say impossible) challenge, then, was to meet the passenger's price and service expectations and at the same time keep costs as low as possible.

MARKETING AIRLINE SERVICES

Historically, airlines were extremely "product" oriented; that is, they did not pay too much attention to their customers' needs and wants. Rather, managers relied on reputation and technological superiority (i.e., flying the newest airplanes) to draw passengers. In many cases, because of regulations, passengers had little choice among carriers depending on where they wanted to go. This was especially true for international travel on a U.S. airline. All of that changed dramatically in 1978 when Congress ushered in the era of deregulation. Competition from new and established domestic and foreign carriers offered alternatives for airline passengers dissatisfied with air service. Managers had to satisfy passengers or risk losing them. In short, for the first time airlines were faced with having to market their services.

Service

The airlines were challenged with the difficult task of differentiating what is, in many cases, a generic service: movement from point A to point B at a certain time. As a result of deregulation, any number of competitors could (at least theoretically) provide that service, so a carrier had to seek other ways of distinguishing itself from another airline. This might take the form of something tangible like operating the newest aircraft, offering roomier seating, better in-flight meals and entertainment, or a unique interior decor. These tended to be expensive (which raised costs) and could, in the case of seating options, lower the aircraft's revenue potential. Alternatively, intangible attributes could be stressed. Prompt baggage handling, responsiveness to customer complaints or suggestions, and attentiveness to passenger needs both on the ground and in the air were examples of service traits that could be turned into significant competitive advantages.

Price

Initially following deregulation, price was the key marketing variable, at least domestically. During the late 1970s and early 1980s, fares dropped dramatically as carriers sought to fill up airplanes with first-time air travelers. Airlines like Midway, which started service in 1979, and People Express, which followed in 1981, entered the industry as no-frills alternatives to the established carriers. These new entrants offered extremely low fares, although passengers had to accept fewer, or pay additional charges for, amenities such as meals and baggage checking. The success of this low-price approach was phenomenal: People Express became the success story of deregulation. It quickly became clear, however, that pricing strategies were easily imitated and offered little long-term competitive advantage. Strong carriers were able to match the low fares *and* provide services passengers had come to expect. But the fundamental truth that emerged from the initial use of low fares was that, even with a full airplane, the company was often losing money. People Express failed in the mid-1980s, while several other no-frills carriers were bought out by full-service airlines. Thus, while pricing was still a key part of an airline's marketing mix, it became less attractive as a means of differentiating one company from another.

Price was less useful in the marketing strategy of international carriers. Often, fare levels were established in the bilateral agreement specifying how the air service between two countries would be conducted. Any deviation from that agreement had to be agreed to by the governments involved, thus allowing managers little control over the prices they could charge.

Promotion

Airlines adopted several unique promotional activities to attract and keep customers. Frequent-flier programs rewarded continued patronage with premiums, free tickets, and other benefits based on the accumulation of miles on a specific airline. Often, airlines had reciprocal agreements with other carriers that allowed passengers from one frequent-traveler program to accumulate miles on the other airline. Typically, it cost nothing to join a frequent-flier club; the whole idea was to tie passengers to one airline by making it worth their while to fly that carrier all the time. Indeed, some passengers were willing to go out of their way (figuratively and literally) to stay on a particular airline just to accumulate the frequent-flier mileage. Foreign carriers were slower to adopt frequent-flier programs as a marketing tool on a wide scale, although mileage accrued through a U.S. carrier's plan could often be redeemed for flights on a foreign airline.

Carriers often maintained executive clubs at various airports that offered members a quiet alternative to the noisy, congested terminal area. Work space might be provided, along with complimentary beverages, food, and other services. Passengers paid a yearly fee and, in addition to the amenities mentioned earlier, also received a fair degree of exclusivity for their money.

Management also had to come up with an appropriate promotional mix to present their service offering to prospective customers. Here again, international carriers faced unique challenges, since media and message decisions were different for each country the carrier served. Indeed, promotional opportunities could be extremely limited in those markets that lacked commercial media such as television, radio, and newspapers.

Place

Airlines distributed their services in two ways. First, they sold directly to the passenger; that is, the customer arrived at the airport, bought a ticket, and departed. Alternatively, an intermediary in the form of a travel agent could be used. Many airlines spent enormous sums of money to develop their own computerized reservation systems, which were then utilized by travel agencies. Airlines other than the host, although their flights could be listed on the system, often felt they were at a disadvantage by virtue of their placement in the data base. In fact, foreign carriers had been known to use their reservation systems as a means of discriminating against their U.S. competitors.

THE COMPETITION

Whereas Pan Am once competed with many airlines, the smaller Pan Am had to compete with just two major carriers for South American traffic.

Varig Brazilian Airlines

Varig began operations on February 3, 1928, utilizing a single Dornier Wal aircraft over the Porto Alegre–Rio Grande route. In 1961, Varig became the largest airline in South America and in 1965 significantly expanded its international coverage when it was awarded the European routes of Panair do Brazil. Privately owned, the carrier offered extensive domestic and regional services as well as long-haul international routes to Europe, South Africa, Japan, Mexico, and the United States from its primary hub in Rio de Janeiro.[23] Varig's international destinations are presented in Exhibit 7.7.

American Airlines

American was organized on May 13, 1934, as a successor to American Airways, which was formed on January 25, 1930, to consolidate the services of numerous predecessor companies dating back to 1926.[24] Over the years, the carrier introduced innovations such as supersaver fares, frequent-flier programs, and lower wage scales to increase revenue and hold down costs.[25] Based on 1990 fiscal year revenues, American was the largest airline in the world.[26] Headquar-

---

[23] Gunter G. Endres, *World Airline Fleets 1987–1988* (London: Browcom, 1988), p. 246.
[24] Ibid., p. 133.
[25] Doug Carroll, "Few Carriers Win Battle for Survival," *USA Today*, August 5, 1991, p. 2B.
[26] James Ott, "Future of Global Environment Dictates Airlines' Agenda," *Aviation Week and Space Technology*, November 25, 1991, p. 49.

EXHIBIT 7.7   **Varig Brazilian Airlines Points Served on International Routes, 1991[a]**

South America	Africa	Europe
Asuncion	Capetown	Amsterdam
Belem	Johannesburg	Barcelona
Boa Vista	Lagos	Copenhagen
Bogota	Luanda	Frankfurt
Buenos Aires		Lisbon
Caracas	**North America**	London
Cayenne		Madrid
Florianopolis	Chicago	Milano
Foz Do Iguacu	Los Angeles	Oporto
Georgetown	Miami	Paris
Guayaquil	New York	Rome
Iquitos	San Francisco	Zurich
La Paz	Toronto	
Lima		
Macapa	**Asia**	
Manaus		
Montevideo	Tokyo	
Paramaribo		
Porto Alegre	**Central America**	
Quito		
Recife	Mexico City	
Rio de Janeiro	Panama City	
Salvador	San Jose	
Santa Cruz de La Sierra		
Santiago		
Sao Paulo		
Tabatinga		
Tefe		

[a] International routes are supported by an extensive domestic network connecting approximately 50 cities and towns within Brazil.

Source: Varig Brazilian Airlines Timetable, August 19, 1991.

tered in Fort Worth, Texas, the carrier operated seven major hubs in the United States, and provided services to 33 countries and the Caribbean. American's international destinations are depicted in Exhibit 7.8.

In comparing the three carriers over competitive routes, there were several similarities as well as a few notable differences. First, all offered essentially the same basic service between the United States and South America. All flew daily nonstop flights, and all operated wide-body aircraft such as the Boeing 747, DC10/MD11, Boeing 767, and Airbus A300. Two or three class services (first and economy; or first, executive or business, and economy) were provided, with first-

EXHIBIT 7.8   American Airlines Points Served on International Routes, 1991[a]

North America	South America	Asia
Anchorage	Asuncion	Hong Kong
Bermuda	Barranquilla	Tokyo
Boston	Bogota	
Calgary	Buenos Aires	**South Pacific**
Chicago	Cali	
Dallas/Fort Worth	Caracas	Auckland
Edmonton	Guayaquil	Sydney
Fairbanks	La Paz	
Honolulu	Lima	**Caribbean**
Kahului	Quito	
Los Angeles	Rio de Janeiro	Anguilla
Miami	Santa Cruz	Antigua
Montreal	Santiago	Aquadilla
Nashville	Sao Paulo	Aruba
New York		Barbados
Newark	**Europe**	Casa de Campo/La Romana
Raleigh/Durham		Fort-de-France
San Francisco	Brussels	Freeport
San Jose	Budapest	Governor's Harbour
Seattle/Tacoma	Duesseldorf	Grand Cayman
Toronto	Frankfurt	Grenada
Vancouver	Glasgow	Kingston
	London	Marsh Harbour
	Madrid	Mayaguez
Central America	Manchester	Montego Bay
	Milan	Nassau
Acapulco	Munich	Pointe-a-Pitre
Belize City	Paris	Ponce
Cancun	Stockholm	Port-au-Prince
Guadalajara	Zurich	Port-of-Spain
Guatemala City		Puerto Plata
Managua		St. Croix
Mexico City		St. Thomas
Monterrey		St. Kitts/Nevis
Panama City		St. Maarten
Puerto Vallarta		St. Lucia
San Jose		San Juan
San Pedro Sula		Santo Domingo
San Salvador		Tortola
Tegucigalpa		Treasure Cay
		Virgin Gorda

[a] International routes are supported by a domestic route network connecting over 200 points within the United States.

Source: American Airlines Passenger Schedule and Cargo Service Guide, World Edition, October 1, 1991.

class passengers enjoying sleeperette-type (lounger) seating on all three airlines. Fares were determined as a part of the agreement between respective countries establishing air service and thus were largely uncontrollable by management. Finally, promotional activities for all three included various forms of media advertising and tended to differ little in content across companies. Local and national newspaper ads tended to predominate, together with selected use of popular magazines and television.

On the other hand, Pan Am's aircraft fleet was significantly older than that operated by American and Varig (Exhibit 7.9 compares the aircraft fleet of Pan Am, American, and Varig). Indeed, Pan Am still operated some of the oldest B747s in commercial service. Both American and Pan Am offered passengers the opportunity to participate in frequent-flier programs. In addition, both maintained exclusive clubs at many of the airports they served, which passengers could utilize for an annual membership fee. Varig offered neither of these services. However, an airline survey conducted in 1990 found that U.S. travelers overwhelmingly preferred foreign air carriers. In fact, out of 27 airlines identified, not one based in the U.S. made the top 10. Asian and European carriers filled those

EXHIBIT 7.9   Passenger Jets in Service as of November 1, 1991 (By airline and type)

Aircraft Type	Pan Am	American	Delta	Varig
Boeing				
727	29	164	153	9
737	—	12	72	36
747[a]	8	2	—	8
757	—	37	69	—
767[a]	—	45	46	10
McDonnell-Douglas				
DC-9	—	—	30	—
DC-10[a]	—	59	—	10
MD-11[a]	—	3	2	—
MD-80/88	—	234	85	—
Lockheed				
L1011[a]	—	—	49	—
Airbus				
A300/310[a]	13	26	21	—
Fokker				
F100	—	—	—	—
Total	50	582	527	73

[a] Wide-body aircraft.

Source: Compiled from Alison Leigh Cowan, "The New Pan Am Rumbas Ahead," *New York Times,* August 19, 1991, p. C2; Report of Annual Meeting of AMR's Stockholders, 1991, p. 14; James Ott, "D-Day Due for Delta Takeover of Most Pan Am Operations," *Aviation Week and Space Technology,* October 14, 1991, p. 44; and Varig System Timetable, August 15, 1991, p. 8.

top spots with one exception: Varig. American was the highest ranked U.S. airline at number 11, while Pan Am was far down the list.[27]

THE CHALLENGE

As the Pan Am president slipped on his coat and headed for the elevator, he wondered how best to take advantage of this new beginning. Being the pragmatist that he was, he knew that Pan Am was still skating on extremely thin ice. "Our fleet is old, our reputation is tarnished, and our employees dispirited. If we fail this time, there will be no reprieve," he thought. "If we've learned one thing, it's that we can build on past glories, but we cannot rest on them. We have to figure out a way to entice the return of our old customers and capture new ones despite the bad press. We *will* succeed in the highly competitive and turbulent international aviation industry of the 1990s."

[27] Asra Q. Nomani, "U.S. Airlines Come up Short in Survey," *Wall Street Journal*, September 7, 1990, p. B6.

——————————————— CASE 8 ———————————————

The Chevrolet Corvette

In mid-1983 Chevrolet introduced a new, redesigned version of the Corvette. Simultaneously the price was increased and an advertising campaign comparing Corvette to imported sports cars, primarily Porsche, was begun. Initial sales were strong, but by early 1986 sales were down 25 percent from the same period in

This case was written from public sources by Frank Conley and Nancy Trap under the supervision of Paul Farris, as a basis for class discussion rather than to illustrate either effective or ineffective handling of an administrative situation. Copyright © 1986 by the Darden Graduate Business School Foundation, Charlottesville, Virginia. Used with permission.

1985. The April 14, 1986, issue of *Autoweek* (p. 3) reported, "Corvette and Fiero production will be cut significantly this month to stem a stockpile of sports cars, which are selling slower than predicted according to General Motors. Second-shift production at the Bowling Green, Kentucky, Corvette plant will be eliminated. . . . " The Corvette's advertising support appeared to have been reduced from 1983–84 levels, but special lease rates and financing plans were offered in late 1985 and early 1986.

The time was appropriate for addressing several important questions: What was the proper strategic role for Corvette within GM and Chevrolet? How important was advertising in fulfilling that role? What kind of advertising and promotion program would be appropriate? How useful would price promotions be? Finally, what kind of advertising program should be used?

GENERAL MOTORS AND THE AUTOMOTIVE INDUSTRY

In 1985, it was estimated that 16 percent of private, nonagricultural workers in the United States were employed in the manufacture, distribution, maintenance, and commercial use of motor vehicles.[1] Some 52.8 percent of all households owned two or more cars. In households with incomes of $40,000 or more, 87 percent owned two or more cars and 43 percent owned three or more cars.[2] The net sales of GM, Ford, Chrysler, and American Motors accounted for 3.9 percent of the 1983 gross national product.[3] Of the U.S. auto manufacturers, GM was by far the largest, dominating the 1985 new-car market with 6 of the top 10 selling cars in the country.

In recent years the U.S. auto industry had faced major market competition from foreign manufacturers. "Voluntary" quotas slowed import penetration in 1984, but imports still accounted for 23.5 percent of total U.S.-market automobile sales.

Recent Developments at GM

In response to an increasingly competitive environment, GM had recently reorganized five former autonomous car divisions into two groups, the Oldsmobile-Buick-Cadillac group and the Chevrolet-Pontiac-GM group. This reorganization reflected a concern by GM that historic divisional distinctions between Chevrolet, Pontiac, Oldsmobile, Buick, and Cadillac had become blurred. The problem was compounded by the fact that many of GM's cars looked alike.

Two acquisitions, Hughes Aircraft Company and Electronic Data Systems (EDS), provided access to leading-edge technologies as GM began to design its auto lines for the 21st century. The hope was that the aerospace technology would be adapted in automotive areas ranging from computer-integrated manufacturing

---

[1] Motor Vehicle Manufacturers' Association of the United States, Public Affairs Division, *Facts and Figures '85.*
[2] U.S. Department of Transportation, Federal Highway Administration, *Highway Statistics 1984.*
[3] Harry A. Stark, ed., *Ward's Automotive Yearbook*, 46th ed. (1984).

EXHIBIT 8.1   Chevrolet Model Line Sales

Model	1984 Units	1985 Units
Cavalier	377,446	431,031
Chevette	164,917	129,927
Camaro	202,172	199,985
Celebrity	322,198	363,619
Citation	92,174	43,667
Corvette	34,024	37,956
Monte Carlo	159,301	12,585
Other Chevrolet	258,902	280,800
Total Chevrolet	1,565,143	1,600,200
Total GM Sales	4,587,508	4,607,458

to futuristic car dashboard displays. In 1986, GM also bought Group Lotus Cars, a British automobile engineering and production firm known for state-of-the-art automotive technology in racing cars.

New ventures included a GM-Toyota joint venture that produced the new Chevrolet Nova, and the Saturn project that would produce GM's first new make since the 1930s. Additionally, GM imported and marketed cars from three foreign companies.

Chevrolet

Chevrolet sold several different models of passenger cars (Exhibit 8.1) and a line of trucks. Each model came in a variety of options and prices. In 1985, the Cavalier was the number one selling car in the United States, and the Celebrity and Caprice were third and seventh, respectively. (See Appendix 8.A for a brief description of these models.) Exhibit 8.2 summarizes Corvette and Chevrolet production.

EXHIBIT 8.2   Corvette Production Data for Selected Years[a]

	Total Corvette Production (In thousands)	Total Chevrolet Production (In thousands)	Corvette Percent of Chevrolet	Chevrolet as Percent of Domestic Production
1953	0.315	1,447	.02	24
1958	9.300	2,367	.39	40
1963	21.500	2,303	.93	30
1968	28.300	2,148	1.31	24
1973	34.500	2,334	1.47	24
1978	46.800	2,347	1.99	26
1982	25.400	1,004	2.52	20
1984	28.200	1,294	2.18	19
1985	46.300	1,626	2.85	19

[a] No 1983 model was produced.
Source: Harry A. Stark, ed. *Ward's Automotive Yearbook,* 46th ed. (1984).

Chevrolet sales were especially subject to swings in the economy, perhaps because the cars were priced lower than other GM cars in the same body type. In 1983, Chevrolet Motor Division General Manager Robert Stempel commented, "The last people who stop buying new cars are rich people, and the last people out of work are rich people. That 10 percent unemployment is a helluva lot more important to me at Chevrolet than it is at a lot of upscale car companies."[4]

SEGMENTATION OF THE SPORTS CAR MARKET

Segmentation of the automobile market was complex. Individuals considered economic, status/image, comfort, and performance factors in making a purchase decision, and segments often overlapped. Product features and price varied considerably (Exhibit 8.3). See Exhibit 8.4 for an example of a market map depicting the position of various models. Even the sports market could be further segmented.

Economy sports cars were mass produced and generally constructed from subassemblies taken from the manufacturer's parts bin and then modified and assembled to increase the overall performance of the final product. The *grand turismo* (GT) class of sports cars seated four people and had superior performance and handling characteristics. The *high-performance* sports cars were usually produced in relatively small numbers and often had a racing heritage. These cars generally had much higher resale values than others and were looked at by some as investments.[5] (Peter Shutz, CEO of Porsche, paid $8,500 for a 1976 Corvette,

EXHIBIT 8.3   Product and Price Data for Selected Sports Car Models

Model	Wheel Base	Length	Weight	Horse-power	Price	U.S. Sales (In units)	U.S. Sales (Percent of production)	Number of U.S. Dealers
Corvette	96.2	176.5	3280	230	$24,891	37,956	81.0	5,050
Ferraro 308 GTBi	92.1	174.2	3250	230	54,300	n/a	n/a	42
Jaguar XJ SC	102.0	187.6	4025	295	32,250	3,784	n/a	167
Mazda RX7 Turbo	95.7	168.9	2850	182	14,145	53,810	n/a	767
Nissan 300ZX Turbo	99.2	178.7	3255	228	17,699	67,409	n/a	1,101
Porsche 944	94.5	168.9	2900	147	21,440	16,705	n/a	317
Porsche 911	89.5	168.9	2750	200	31,950	5,882	n/a	317
Porsche 928S	98.4	175.7	3540	288	50,000	2,586	n/a	317

n/a = not applicable.

Source: *Road & Track* and *Motor Trend Magazines,* 1986 issues and *Automotive News Market Data Book,* 1985, 1986.

[4] Daniel F. McCosh, "Marketing the 83s," *Wards Auto World,* October 1982.
[5] David E. Gumpert, "Porsche on Nichemanship," *Harvard Business Review,* March/April 1986.

EXHIBIT 8.4 Sports Car Segmentation Map

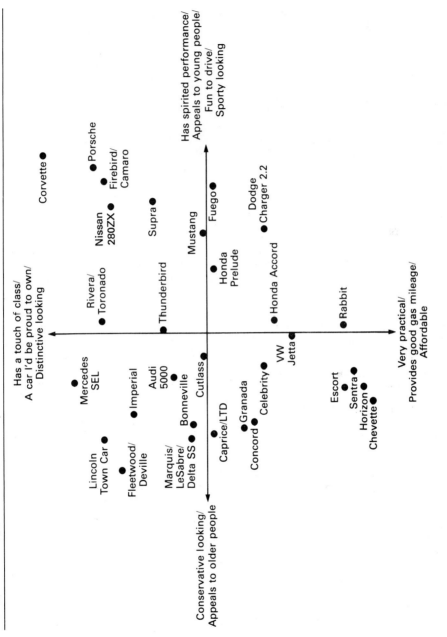

EXHIBIT 8.5   New-Car Buyer Demographics, 1984

Car Make	Percent Male	Median Age (Years)	Percent Married	Medium Household Income	Median Price Paid[a]
BMW	65	35	58	$ 61,000	$17,800
Chevrolet	56	41	65	33,400	10,466
Corvette[b]	85	38	59	59,200	26,000
Jaguar	64	44	80	100,000+	33,520
Mercedes-Benz	68	46	70	87,500	28,904
Porsche	78	36	62	81,200	26,118

[a] Price could vary on a Corvette depending on the time of year the car was purchased, whether the car was bought off the lot or ordered, and purchaser's negotiating skill. Other car prices were believed to be *relatively* firm.

[b] In 1981, "median age" and "income" for Corvette owners were 33 years and $33,000, respectively.

Source: *Automotive News,* "New Car Buyer Demographics," April 1984.

and three years later sold it for the same price when he moved to Europe.) High-performance sports cars also could be viewed as a subset of the *luxury-car* market. (Exhibit 8.5 gives demographics for buyers of selected models.)

GM was expected to launch its ultra-luxury two-seat convertible, the Cadillac Allante, in the beginning of 1987. The Allante, designed by Pininfarina, the Italian firm responsible for many Ferrari models, was scheduled for low-volume production and a price tag of $50,000. Industry analysts believed that GM was hoping the Allante would provide a "halo" effect for Cadillac, helping to update and differentiate its product image. The car had been premiered on the television series *Dallas* in fall 1986, replacing a Mercedes-Benz 450SEL that had been driven by J. R. Ewing the previous season.

HISTORY OF THE CORVETTE MODELS

1953–1955

Years ago this land knew cars that were fabricated out of sheer excitement. Magnificent cars that uttered flame and rolling thunder from exhaust pipes as big around as your forearm, and came towering down through the white summer dust of American roads like the Day of Judgement . . . today, they have an inheritor—the Chevrolet Corvette.

1955 Corvette ad copy

The Corvette dream car was introduced to the public at the 1952 Motorama show, and the fiberglass-bodied, two-seat convertible was the hit of the show. Chevrolet began regular production of the car in 1953 and limited the production run to 300 cars that were sold to people who qualified as VIPs—political figures, movie stars, business executives, and preferred customers. Unfortunately, the

VIPs were not impressed by a sports car that had pop-in plastic windows and leaked in rainstorms, had an anemic six-cylinder engine with an uncivilized two-speed powerglide automatic transmission, and was slower than a well-tuned Cadillac or Oldsmobile.[6]

The production run in 1954 of 3,640 cars ended with a surplus of 1,500 new Corvettes. Rumors circulated that the car would be scrapped, but the Corvette's salvation occurred in two forms: First, Ford, Chevrolet's major competition, came out with the Thunderbird, a two-seat "personal" car that brought out GM's competitive spirit. Second, a 45-year-old German-trained enthusiast, race driver, and designer named Zora Arkus-Duntov began his 20-year association with the Corvette as its head of engineering. For 1955, the production run was 674 cars with a new V-8 engine that improved the Corvette's performance.

1956–1962

Even in Turin (Italy) no one has fuel injection? Si, e'vero'. But the really fantastic item about the new Corvette is not the fuel injection engine, the new four-speed gearbox, the slingshot acceleration or the pasted-to-the-road stability. It is the fact that the Corvette, above all other high performance sports cars in the world, is a true dual-natured vehicle. It is a genuine luxury car and a sports car, both wrapped in one sleek skin . . . .

1957 Corvette ad copy

The second generation of Corvettes received a major body change, but Chevrolet had to determine if the Corvette was to remain a sports car or forge into Ford Thunderbird territory as a personal luxury car. The 1956–57 Corvettes seemed to appeal to both markets. In 1956, Corvettes took the Sports Car Club of America (SCCA) "C" Production Championship, and in 1960 four Corvettes were entered in the international Le Mans Twenty-Four-Hour Endurance Race. The car was continually refined both mechanically and stylistically. By 1962, *Motor Trend* was saying, "This is an exciting high-performance automobile with real hair on its chest—the type of car that only true enthusiasts will appreciate."

1963–1967

Corvette is America's one true sports car—has been for years. But Corvette is also two body styles. Five engines and three transmissions available. Plus enough other equipment you can order to make any kind of sports car you want. For aficionados, there's the snarly Corvette. Ordered with a 375 horsepower Ramjet, fuel injected V-8. . . . For boulevardiers, there's the plush Corvette, ordered with power brakes, steering, and windows, tinted glass . . . .

1965 Corvette ad copy

[6] Auto Editors of Consumers Guide, *Corvette, America's Sports Car* (New York: Beekman House, 1984).

The third-generation Corvette was derived from a GM styling exercise and was dubbed the Corvette Stingray. It came in convertible and fastback coupe configurations and had many optional features. The car was available with a variety of engines, the most powerful approaching 500 HP. Lasting only five years, this model was the most short-lived of the Corvette body styles, but its timeless styling made it the most popular model with car collectors and enthusiasts.

1968–1979

> Here it is. It's not really a whole lot different looking. But in 17 years we've never changed it just to change it. . . . It's still a car that's built for the person who drives for the sheer excitement of it. . . . No, it isn't a hard-core sports car. There are too many nice things about it. No, it isn't the smoothest riding car you'll find. But then again it won't rattle your bones. What it is is a new Corvette. It's refined for 1970.
>
> 1970 Corvette ad copy

The fourth-generation Corvette was introduced in 1968, and the "Vette" had gone through some drastic changes. Corvette production was reduced to 21,801 units in 1971 from the 1969 high of 38,762, which allowed Chevrolet Division General Manager John DeLorean to place emphasis on improving the car's slipping quality control. The 1970s ushered in the era of government regulation. Corvette's performance steadily declined with the addition of catalytic converters and the unleaded-gasoline mandate. Its horsepower reached a low of 165 in 1975. A T-Top removable roof was introduced in 1968, offering "top-down" motoring without the hassles. Subsequently, Corvette convertible models waned in popularity and were discontinued. In spite of these changes and the oil shortages and economic downturns of the 1970s, Corvette sold well. The entire 1975 Corvette production of 38,465 cars was sold out by March, and 1976 production jumped to 46,558. Because 1978 was the Corvette's 25th anniversary, it was chosen as the pace car for the Indy 500; 6,502 replicas of the pace car were made and sold at a handsome premium over the base list price of $13,653.

1980–1982

> In this ever-changing world some things endure. A fine red wine, soft smoke on an autumn evening. A walk along the seashore. And Chevrolet Corvette. Now 26 years young. And still America's only true production sports car. . . . But beyond the machinery, there is the dream—Corvette and the open road.
>
> 1980 Corvette ad copy

In 1980, Chevrolet sent the Corvette to the fat farm so it wouldn't suffer an Environmental Protection Agency (EPA) "gas guzzler" tax. The car lost 280 pounds, and aerodynamic styling changes were added to improve fuel economy. The only engine available was a 305-cubic-inch V-8, and the option of manual transmission was discontinued. All models sold were automatics. One industry observer commented that the Corvette had become a car for upwardly mobile secretaries. Even though the Corvette had lost much of its performance, it remained popular with the public and the motoring press. *Road & Track* pointed out in its November 1982 issue that the Corvette remained a car whose function was on par with its form: "No matter how much luxury, electric seats, remote mirrors, or teddy bear hide velour interior you pack into a Corvette, the basic honesty of the car rises above its own image."

THE "NEW" CORVETTE

> Now that the skeptics have been silenced, we can get down to business. The most important piece of business concerning the new Corvette. Performance. And in tests on GM's proving grounds, conducted by professional drivers, the new Corvette performs beautifully.
>
> 1984 introductory Corvette ad copy

There was no 1983 Corvette, as manufacturing was shifted to a plant built specifically for producing the new Corvette model (it had 50 percent more production capacity than the old plant). The fifth-generation Corvette was a radical change and showcased GM's latest developments in suspension, braking, and electronic engine control while still remaining true to the basic Corvette layout: front engine/rear-wheel drive and fiberglass body, a two-seat, high-performance sports car.

The new Corvette had a pop-off targa roof and a 350-cubic-inch V-8 engine. It featured new technology in the use of fiberglass springs and alloy castings in the suspension system, digital and LED display instrumentation, and electronically controlled fuel injection and overdrive. For 1985, improvements to the fuel-injection system increased power, and in 1986 an antilock braking system (ABS) and an improved antitheft system were added. The ride was substantially softened through adjustments to the shock absorbers, and torsional steering shake was reduced with the addition of restrictors in the power steering lines. The convertible model was reintroduced in 1986, at a $4,518 premium over the base sticker price of $27,502. (See Exhibits 8.6 and 8.7 for prices and estimates of maintenance costs, respectively, for selected models.) A *New York Times* article of July 26,

EXHIBIT 8.6   1986 Dealer's Sticker Price Information (In thousands)

	Corvette	*Porsche 944*	*Porsche 944 Turbo*	*Porsche 928S*	*Datsun 300ZX Turbo*
Base car	$27.5	$24.5	$29.8	$52.0	$20.8
Average price paid	23.4	24.1	n/a	n/a	n/a

n/a = not available.

Source: Casewriter's survey of Charlottesville, Virginia, car dealers, April 1986 and NADA Official Used Car Guide.

EXHIBIT 8.7   Maintenance and Repair Cost Comparison

Maintenance Parts	Average Replacement Time[a]	Corvette	Porsche 944T	Nissan 300ZX	Mazda RX7
Exhaust system	70,000	$ 413	$ 425	$ 164	$ 180
Engine tuneup cost		90	160	160	100
Clutch	n/a	270	892	117	160
Sport shocks	60,000	360	517	685	344
Factory engine	100,000	3,900[b] (New)	5,246 (New)	5,153 (New)	1,000 (New)
Car Warranty Months/ Miles	—	36/ 36,000	24/ unlimited	12/ 12,000	12/ 12,000

[a] Longevity of parts depends greatly on driver use and maintenance.
   The average vehicle was driven 10,300 miles per year.
[b] With multiport fuel injection.
Source: Casewriters' survey of dealers.

1983, wondered "whether the new Corvette has not been priced out of its traditional strength, the youth-oriented market, and into one of older professionals. . . ." The article went on to say, "For GM, the Corvette represents only a small part of the company's auto output . . . but the Corvette's real value, analysts say, is its ability to lure curious customers into showrooms."

Corvette Advertising

The advertising campaign that introduced the 1984 Corvette was lavish and technically oriented. Chevrolet ran multipage spreads in magazines touting the advanced technology and engineering that were incorporated in the newest generation of Corvettes and stressing its high-performance characteristics. The advertising budget was the highest in the car's history. Chevrolet spent $7,778,900 on the 1984 Corvette—compared to a previous high of $285,300 in 1977. (See Exhibits 8.8 and 8.9 for data on advertising budgets and magazine media respectively.)

EXHIBIT 8.8   Advertising Dollars Spent by Corvette and Competition (In millions)

Car make	1981	1982	1983	1984
Corvette	—	—	$ 7.8	$ 2.2
Jaguar XJS	—	$ 1.3	3.9	2.0
Mazda RX7	$ 3.1	9.7	6.1	13.1
Nissan 280/300ZX	6.7	7.0	11.9	15.5
Nissan Total	36.3	48.9	54.7	60.1
Porsche (Total)	6.0	8.0	6.4	2.8

Source: Leading national advertisers, 1985.

The comparison campaign was launched with TV and print ads (see Exhibits 8.10 and 8.11). The cars compared to the 1985 Corvette ($26,703 price as tested) were the Lamborghini Countach, Porsche 944, Porsche 928S, Ferrari 308 GTSi, and Lotus Turbo Esprit. They ranged in price from $26,121 to $103,700 and were tested on 0–60 mph acceleration, braking from 60–0 mph, time through a slalom course, and lateral acceleration on a skid pad. The United States Automobile Club (USAC) certified the testing, and the Corvette scored first in two of the tests and second and third in the remaining two tests. The scoring system that was used allotted six points for first place, five for second, and so on. The Corvette was declared the overall winner in the comparison with a score of 21 points. The $103,700 Lamborghini placed second with 18 points.

> . . . Corvette, Ferrari, Porsche, Lotus, Lamborghini. They're Europe's exotic few. And they don't let just anyone into their club. But in the case of the Chevrolet Corvette, they really didn't have a choice. In independent tests conducted by the United States Automobile Club, Corvette was the overall winner.
>
> 1985 Corvette comparison ad copy

The comparison campaign was continued in 1986, when Corvette made the Bosch ABS II antibraking system a standard feature on the car and then compared the braking characteristics of the Lamborghini Countach, Ferrari 308 GTSi, Porsche 944, Lotus Turbo Esprit, and Corvette on a rain-slick curve. The Corvette was the only car to demonstrate the ability simultaneously to stop and steer the curve under maximum braking conditions. Once again it was proclaimed "Corvette, A World Class Champion" against a collection of European exotic cars.

Promotion and Racing Activities

The Chevrolet Division of GM published *Corvette News* quarterly and sent it free of charge to purchasers of new Corvettes for three years (thereafter $18 for three years). The 30-page, full-color, glossy magazine kept Corvette owners informed of new Corvette model developments, news of Corvettes on the race track, and do-it-yourself repairs. *Vette Magazine, Vette Vues, Corvette Fever,* and *Keep'in Track* were the titles of four independently published monthly magazines devoted exclusively to Corvette enthusiasts.

There were over 700 organized Corvette clubs in the United States and Canada and a few in Europe. These clubs were federated under the National Council of Corvette Clubs. Club activities included car shows, rallies, slalom races, drag races, and social gatherings. A separate Corvette organization was the National Corvette Restorers Society, organized for people dedicated to restoring older Corvettes to "original" condition.

John Pierce, a member of Chevrolet's Special Products Group, explained in the summer 1985 issue of *Corvette News*, "Our policy is to develop the hardware and technology necessary to win and make sure it's properly represented in

EXHIBIT 8.9 Selected Sports Car Magazine Advertising, 1983[a]

	Corvette (In thousands)	Nissan 280ZX (In thousands)	Porsche 911 (In thousands)	Porsche 928S (In thousands)	Porsche 944 (In thousands)	Readership: Median Age	Readership: Percent Median Income	Readership: Percent College Graduates
Architect's Digest	$133.5			$ 56.8		n/a	n/a	n/a
Business Week	350.0	$162.6	$156.1	117.1	$ 78.1	39.4	25.2	46.9
Car & Driver	31.4	115.6	57.3	111.5	26.7	29.6	18.3	19.9
Duns Business				25.6	22.5	n/a	n/a	n/a
Esquire		86.4	83.4	90.1	64.6	35.2	17.6	39.1
Food & Wine	62.3			129.3	71.4	39.4	16.3	32.2
Forbes			64.6	142.8		42.1	27.8	57.7
Fortune	300.9		207.7			37.7	28.8	55.2
Golf		32.5				42.6	22.3	37.4
Gourmet			46.9			n/a	n/a	n/a
Inc.			40.1	85.3	42.6	36.4	25.2	58.4
Los Angeles	19.6					n/a	n/a	n/a
Money	69.0		67.0			37.3	22.8	41.9
New Yorker		69.9	40.6	40.6	40.6	41.7	23.2	51.7
Newsweek	925.8	55.8	151.1	226.7	151.1	36.4	18.3	34.0
Penthouse				37.0	34.0	29.4	17.6	15.6
Playboy		118.6	118.6	118.6		31.1	17.9	19.6

Publication								
Road & Track	67.2	95.6	47.8	95.6	75.0	29.4	19.9	29.8
Science Digest	79.2					36.4	17.6	31.0
Science 83	110.0		22.5			36.2	17.7	44.5
Signature						n/a	n/a	n/a
Smithsonian	265.5			64.7		43.4	20.1	45.3
Sports Illustrated	913.6	60.2	60.2			32.8	18.6	24.8
Sports News	32.7					33.7	18.9	27.5
Sunset			54.3			44.2	20.3	34.5
Tennis				32.7		29.7	16.5	32.4
Texas Monthly				47.4	11.3	n/a	n/a	n/a
Time	382.2		451.4	334.3	255.7	36.0	18.3	31.8
Town & Country	41.7					40.2	17.5	34.7
Travel & Leisure	142.1					45.7	25.1	36.8
TV Cable	3.6					n/a	n/a	n/a
U.S. News & World Report	103.8		103.8	196.1	103.8	42.1	21.2	32.6
Venture	43.4		43.4	24.6				
Total[b]	$4,084.6	$944.1	$1,605.3	$2,298.9	$1,031.6			

n/a = not available.

[a] Higher dollars per ad usually indicate multipage layouts were used.

[b] Not all magazines are listed; therefore, totals and individual entries may not agree.

Source: The PIB/LNA Magazine Advertising Analysis for 1983 and Simmons 1983 Study of Media and Markets in Home Audiences.

EXHIBIT 8.10   Ad Campaign for the 1985 Corvette

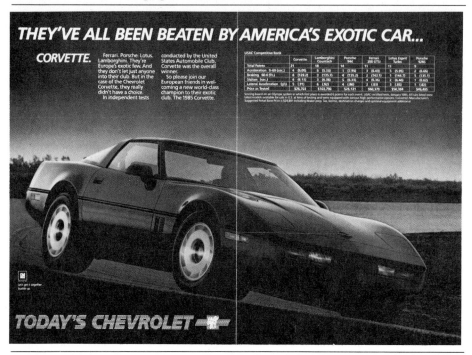

competition. We [Chevrolet] figure if we can put together a winner, then there'll be a demand for a better mousetrap.'' The group's efforts resulted in privately owned Corvette GTPs (Grand Touring Prototypes) participating in the IMSA (International Motor Sports Association) GT's circuit that visited 17 U.S. cities in the 1985 racing season.

For the second race of the 1986 season, the Corvette GTP car qualified but retired early due to mechanical failure. At the fourth race, Road Atlanta, the Corvette's second appearance was greeted with skepticism: "if they last. . . ." (from the Ford folk); "if they live. . . ." (the Porsche persons); "They can't run that fast in the race . . ." (Jaguarists).[7] The Corvette's first victory in the Road Atlanta race broke Porsche's string of 16 consecutive IMSA wins.

In another race series, Showroom Stock, Corvettes dominated. These races pitted stock production cars against machines of similar performance capability. The Chevrolet Camaro was also promoted in a series of races in which professional drivers competed in modified Camaros capable of 200 mph speeds.

In 1986, the new Corvette roadster was chosen to be the Indianapolis 500 Pace Car. Chevrolet also developed a futuristic car, the Corvette Indy, that was shown on the 1986 automobile show circuit. Built by Lotus, the Indy was a

---

[7] Sylvia Wilkinson, "Hand Grenades One and Two," *Autoweek*, April 14, 1986.

EXHIBIT 8.11   Corvette Comparative Advertisement

You're driving 55 MPH on a rain-slick curve. Suddenly the unexpected: You stand on the brake pedal and steer to stay in your lane. You might expect Europe's most exotic cars to handle such a crisis effortlessly. Yet for all its awesome straight-line braking ability, Ferrari 308 GTSi failed to negotiate a 150-foot radius curve at maximum braking in USAC-certified testing. Lamborghini Countach failed. Lotus Esprit Turbo failed. Porsche 944 failed. Only the 1986 Corvette demonstrated the ability to steer and stop in these conditions at the same time. Only Corvette made the turn while coming to a controlled stop. When conditions turn foul, Corvette's new computerized Bosch ABS II anti-lock braking system is designed to help improve a driver's ability to simultaneously brake and steer out of trouble. Why does the Corvette feature the world's most advanced braking technology? Because a world-class champion should give you the edge in an emergency. **Corvette. A world-class champion.**

showcase of technology to be used in the next generation Corvette—mid-engine, four-wheel drive, and four-wheel steering.[8]

The value of racing to an automobile's image was difficult to assess. Many sports cars, including Corvette, were featured in ads for tires, auto stereo systems, other accessories, and unrelated products. For example, a Corvette was the

[8] George Damon Levy, "Corvette Indy," *Autoweek*, January 20, 1986.

grand prize in a toothpaste coupon sweepstakes and in numerous other promotions and contests.

Distribution

The Corvette was sold by the Chevrolet network of over 5,000 Chevrolet dealers in the United States. (Porsche, for example, had only 330 authorized dealers.) Some dealers, especially those near large population centers, were known for selling many Corvettes. However, most small dealers rarely stocked Corvettes and sold only through special orders. To help those dealers with less experience learn to sell the "new" Corvette, Chevrolet implemented a special dealer-training program for 1986. Corvette mechanics also received special training.

Often the Corvette occupied a prominent place on the showroom floor and "Register-to-win a Corvette" campaigns were used by Chevrolet to increase dealer traffic.

THE COMPETITION

Porsche

Porsche was a family-owned European company known for its product quality. In recent years Porsche introduced new models aimed at new segments. Notable successes were the 944 and 928. Standard company policy was to keep production levels just below the demand level.[9] From 1980 to 1985, Porsche sales grew 56 percent.

Shutz, CEO of Porsche, stated in the 1986 March/April issue of the *Harvard Business Review*, "Our customers are people who place high expectations on themselves. And they expect no less from the companies and people with whom they associate. . . . As a result, in positioning our company we have to strive to be what these people are as individuals. That means, among car companies, we have very high goals. And we have to pursue those goals virtually without compromise." He considered Porsche competition to come from two sectors: luxury discretionary items, such as sailboats and airplanes, and other automobile manufacturers. He believed the Porsche 944's competition included Corvette, Pontiac Fiero, and certain Japanese cars; the 928's competition came from Jaguars, Ferraris, Mercedes-Benz large coupes, and the Cadillac Allante; and that the 911 had no competition: "It drives like no other car and sounds like no other car."

In its advertising, Porsche concentrated on the thoroughness and competence of its cars. The ads appeared to be aimed at people who were not familiar with Porsche and told a story about the company's engineers, the cars they had designed, and the constant development of Porsche cars being done on the world's most demanding race tracks. Early in 1986, Porsche began a series of lavish magazine spreads, some as many as 12 pages each (see example in Exhibit 8.12). Magazines in the campaign included *Business Week*, *Time*, and *Newsweek*.

---

[9] op. cit.

Shutz said Porsche supported cars in international sports car racing for three reasons: "First, it is probably the single most effective way to do our advertising and public relations. It gets us free space in the auto enthusiasts' magazines. The second factor is the contribution that it makes to our technical development . . . the most important . . . is the contribution that racing makes to our corporate culture. The racing activity is highly visible, and it has a couple of characteristics that I find extremely valuable in achieving the kind of quality we want." He added, "Racing is an opportunity for us to demonstrate our competence, to demonstrate the state of technology with which we're building their [the public's] automobile."[10]

Porsche's bimonthly magazine, *Christophorus*, continued articles on Porsche race activities and recent developments, art, travel, and books. The "They Drive Porsche" section read like a "Who's Who" and carried pictures of world-class athletes, royalty, VIPs, and race car drivers with their Porsches. Among those featured in the August 1985 issue were Olympic swimming champion Michael Gross, King Carl Gustaf XVI of Sweden, and a prominent West German physician. Typical advertisers in the magazine were high-quality clothing and accessory manufacturers, jewelers, and European airlines.

In August 1984, as Porsche's distribution contract with Volkswagen of America was about to expire, Shutz created a new distribution plan to abolish dealers and replace them with agents who would order the cars as they were sold. Instead of keeping inventories, the agents would be supplied by 40 company centers. Two Porsche warehouses would operate in the United States—one in Reno, Nevada, and one on the East Coast. Three weeks after the announcement of the new distribution system, Shutz abandoned it; he stayed committed only to severing Porsche's U.S. link to Volkswagen.[11]

Nissan

In the 1980s, Nissan's (originally Datsun) 240Z model had increased in size, weight, and price. During this time it had evolved from an "economy" sports car to something more like a GT car. A change in image resulted.

> Those in marketing who ply their trade with demographics describe the 300ZX purchaser as one who is not as concerned with ultimate performance as with the "image" of performance. To the Nissan engineers this means a suspension system whose main priority is ride comfort, not cornering power or balance. Under the hood it means a priority on smooth, docile power characteristics rather than serious horses—which might require too much driver attention, detracting from image-enhancement time. To paraphrase Nissan television advertising: "You may never need this kind of performance, but knowing it's there is awesome."
>
> *Motor Trend*, January 1986

Nissan advertising for the 300ZX stressed that it was the best Z car ever, technically advanced with a plethora of functional electronic wizardry. The ads

[10] Gumpert, "Porsche on Nichemanship."
[11] David B. Tinnin, "Porsche's Civil War with Its Dealers," *Fortune*, April 16, 1984.

EXHIBIT 8.12   Porsche Magazine Spread—1986 Campaign

It took us five years to get from here...

At Porsche, we're in the business of building high-performance sports cars.

It's what our customers expect.

It's what we expect of ourselves.

And, after 39 years, it's still one thing that very clearly sets Porsches apart from the majority of cars in this world.

But not the only thing.

Just as 0-60 times and top-end speeds are important, so too is the slow and measured pace at which, year after year,

we take every new Porsche another step closer to perfection.

Consider the Porsche 944. A car which, in its first year of existence, was declared one of the Ten Best in America by Car and Driver magazine.

The average engineer might well have viewed such praise as an invitation to kick back and relax for awhile. Our engineers saw it as a challenge. To make a great car even better.

to here.

Which may serve to explain why the 944 has appeared on the Ten Best list every year since.

To the casual eye, the '83 944 and '87 944S pictured below could be two photographs of the same car.

But, beneath the familiar countenance, the new 16-valve 944S—like this year's standard 944—reflects five years of meticulous refinements that have improved everything from performance,

handling and mileage to seating position and music appreciation.

Thanks to the new four-valve head design, horsepower is up considerably. As is top speed. And 0-60 time is a significant 6/10ths of a second faster.

All the natural result of a process that began when the very first Porsche emerged from a converted sawmill in Gmünd, Austria, in 1948.

A process that will end only when the very last Porsche is built.

EXHIBIT 8.12 (continued)

What it takes to turbocharge a Porsche, including the turbocharger.

The theory that a whole is greater than the sum of its parts did not originate with Professor Porsche.

But he, for one, wholeheartedly subscribes to it.

Because if he's learned anything in four decades of building cars, it's that a change in one component can profoundly affect the performance of the others. And ultimately, the performance of the whole car.

Nowhere is this truth more evident than in the area of turbocharging.

Porsche pioneered this technology for production cars back in 1975. And realized right from the start that simply bolting on a turbocharger, tweaking the engine a little and re-naming the car was the wrong way to go about it.

The right way is revealed below.

Every component shown here was deemed necessary to transform a normally aspirated 944 into a turbocharged 944.

Major engine components, more than 30 in all, to compensate for increased internal loads and heat.

Chassis components, from shock absorbers and brakes to wheels and tires, to meet higher performance demands.

Front and rear body components, to improve wind resistance at higher speeds, while controlling lift and drag.

To say nothing of the turbocharger itself which, among other innovative bits of technology, includes two water cooling systems to protect turbine bearings, even after the engine is turned off.

Of course, if we hadn't gone to such lengths with the 944, we could still have built a turbo.

We just couldn't have built a Porsche.

How fast it gets from one place to another has always been an important measure of a Porsche.

If you were so inclined, you could go out right now and buy yourself a new Porsche 944 or 944 Turbo, roll it out of the showroom, gas it up, enter it in a certified Showroom Stock event and do with it exactly what nature intended.

Race it.

Of course, you'd have to go to racing school and get your license first.

You'd have to add the necessary safety equipment and number decals to the car.

And you'd have to have a certain amount of talent.

But you could race it.

Fresh off the showroom floor.

Depending on the event, you might be required to run your Porsche completely stock, including the equipment normally sold with the car—things like air conditioning and a stereo. And you could win. As our 944's do.

Or you might opt for an event that allows minor wheel and suspension modifications. And you'd be out there holding your own against cars with engines more than twice as big as yours. As our 944 Turbos do.

The point being that Porsche's reputation for performance isn't built solely on the exotic, highly modified, one-of-a-kind cars we produce for the likes of Monte Carlo, Nürburgring, Daytona and LeMans.

It's built just as much on the cars we've been selling to people like you for almost 40 years.

People for whom driving a car is much more than simply a means of getting to a destination.

People who may never take their Porsche to its limits.

But who take joy in the knowledge that they could.

PORSCHE

944 Turbo 4-cylinder, in-line, single overhead camshaft, liquid-cooled, front engine with turbocharger and intercooler. 247bhp. 217 hp, transaxle design. Weight: 2998 lbs. Top speed: 152 mph.

did not mention any performance statistics or measurements for the car (see Exhibit 8.13).

Mazda

With the second generation of the very successful RX-7 introduced in 1986, Mazda continued to emphasize the advanced technology and engineering of its sports car model. The ads were dominated by written copy and had technical drawings of components as well as a cut-away view of the car's mechanics. Mazda also ran ads in car-enthusiast magazines concerning the RX-7's successful racing career. Mazda's evolution was somewhat similar to that of the Nissan Z series. It was initially built and priced to compete in the economy sports car segment, but successive generations became heavier and more expensive with more standard

EXHIBIT 8.13   Nissan Advertisement, 1986

options. Recent models were thought by some to resemble the Porsche 944 in appearance.

PRESS REACTIONS TO THE NEW CORVETTE

May 1983—Motor Trend tested the Ferrari 308 GTBi, Porsche 928S, Jaguar XJS, and the 1984 Corvette on a race track to determine the best-handling production car available in the United States. The Corvette was "markedly superior in every handling category and stands alone at the top of the heap . . . the Vette is now something it has never been; a world class performer." *Motor Trend* also voted the Ferrari the most sexually appealing car and the Jaguar "one to live with day in and day out." (See Exhibit 8.14 for a Jaguar ad.) Corvette's appeal as a "daily runner" was diluted by its harsh riding characteristics (the ride was substantially softened in subsequent model years), but it was the choice for "the hardest-charging backroad burner money can buy." The Porsche 928S "by any clear-headed standard, maybe the best car in the world."

August 1983—Road & Track did a "comparison test" of the Corvette, Ferrari 308GTBi Quattrovalve, Porsche 944, and Porsche 928S. They saw the new Corvette as GM's effort "to build sophistication and high technology into a package that still embodies traditional Corvette values . . . the car is still the bargain leader in its high-roller performance class." In performance tests the Corvette was on par with the competition and best in the lateral acceleration and slalom course speed tests. In "Cumulative Ratings—Subjective Evaluations" (points awarded for performance, comfort/controls, and design/styling), the Corvette scored 420 points; Ferrari, 451 points; Porsche 928, 428 points; and Porsche 944, 482 points. The staff's price-independent choice was Ferrari, and the price-dependent choice was the Porsche 944.

November 1985—Motor Trend compared the improved 1986 Corvette to the just-released Porsche 944 Turbo. The Corvette was fastest for 0–70 mph; the Porsche was faster for 70–90 mph in covering the quarter-mile and in top speed. The Corvette won the braking, skidpad, slalom, and road course portions of the testing. In conclusion, the testers stated, "Pressed to make a choice between these two exceptional GT's, we'd probably opt for the Corvette. But the final choice lies in individual tastes and driving habits. There's a lot of hot rod in the Vette. A lot of flash and American brashness. The turbo Porsche is understated elegance. Quiet, confident, and subtle. Whichever approach reflects your individual driving habits and ego is the one you'll swear is the hands-down winner and the only logical choice. Just make sure you bring plenty of green stuff."

April 1986—Road & Track's latest testing of the Corvette involved taking it to Italy and running it over a 1,000-mile course of autostradas, city streets, and country roads that once made up the famous Mille Miglia Race, competed on in 1927 to 1957. Other cars included in the test were European versions of the Alfa Romeo GTV 6/2.5, Jaguar XJS Cabriolet, Nissan 300ZX Turbo, and the Porsche

EXHIBIT 8.14   Jaguar Advertisement, 1986

THE BEST JAGUAR EVER BUILT
An exhilarating 4.2 double overhead cam six
with electronic ignition and fuel injection.
Perfected year after year, it is probably the most
thoroughly proven luxury car engine in the world.

On the Jaguar family tree can be found some of the most famous high performance engines that ever powered a car across a finish line. The engine that moves Jaguar's 1984 XJ6 sedan is a sophisticated descendant of this proud heritage. It is 4.2 liters of purebred Jaguar and you have only to turn the key to discover what that means.

Ignition is almost instantaneous, even in very cold weather, for the car is equipped with an electronic cold start fuel enrichment system as well as advanced electronic ignition and fuel injection. The engine is very strong. Its crankshaft is supported by seven bearings. It is an in-line six with the simplicity of twin overhead camshafts designed to enhance the precision of valve timing and eliminate the wear of push rods and rocker arms. The aluminum cylinder head contains hemispherical combustion chambers to speed the flow of the fuel/air mixture and the exhaust. The result is a smooth, unflagging and unflappable power plant that has proven its capabilities in literally millions of miles of testing, racing and pleasure driving.

The XJ6 engine is backed up by equally strong and well proven handling and suspension technology. Precise power rack and pinion steering guides the car. Four wheel independent suspension and front antidive geometry insure that the car is surefooted and balanced in turns, level in braking. The car's brakes are power assisted discs on all four wheels, for Jaguars must stop as confidently as they go.

Outstanding performance, ride and handling are only a part of the many pleasures available to Jaguar owners. While writing its name in many a track record book, Jaguar has also set standards for automotive luxury. The leather is supple. The walnut is hand matched for graining. Conveniences pamper you: power sunroof; cruise control; trip computer; power windows and doorlocks; four speaker stereo radio and cassette player are all standard.

The best Jaguar ever built might just be the best car you've ever driven. Discover that for yourself. Call this toll-free number for the Jaguar dealer nearest you: (800) 447-4700. JAGUAR CARS INC., LEONIA, NJ 07605.

JAGUAR
A BLENDING OF ART AND MACHINE

EXHIBIT 8.15   Performance Comparison of Selected Sports Cars, 1986

Manufacturer and Model	0–60 mph (sec)	¼ mile (sec)	Top Speed (mph)	Braking 80 mph (ft)	Slalom (mph)	Skidpad (G's)	Interior Noise at 70 mph (DBA)	MPG
Alfa Romeo Spider	10.4	17.6	103	288	58.4	.77	93	23.8
Corvette Coupe	5.8	14.4	154	243	58.9	.91	77	19.0
Ferrari 308 GTBi	6.8	15.2	142	262	58.0	.81	80	16.0
Jaguar XJS HE	7.8	15.6	148	276	56.6	.73	72	13.5
Mercedes-Benz 380SL	10.9	18.4	110	277	54.2	.70	74	19.0
Mazda RX7 GXL	8.5	16.5	119	267	62.0	.83	n/a	n/a
Nissan 300ZX Turbo	7.4	15.7	133	249	62.8	.80	73	17.0
Porsche 911 Cabriolet	5.7	14.3	130	266	59.8	.80	79	18.6
Porsche 928S	6.3	14.5	162	247	57.9	.83	71	16.3
Porsche 944	8.9	16.6	123	256	62.5	.86	72	22.1
Porsche 944 Turbo	6.0	14.6	155	255	62.8	.90	72	19.4

Source: *Motor Trend's* performance summary, 1986 issue.

944 Turbo. In this test of cars driven by a group of famous former race car drivers, the questions posed were: "If the Mille Miglia were held today, in what order would the cars finish?" and "Which car would you choose for a vacation tour of the Mille Miglia route?" The drivers scored the first question: Corvette 23, Porsche 22, Alfa 13, Nissan 12, and Jaguar 5. They scored the second question: Porsche 25, Corvette 17, Alfa 13, Nissan 11, Jaguar 9.

A summary of *Motor Trend* performance data is contained in Exhibit 8.15. See Appendix 8.B for definitions of technical terms used in the industry.

APPENDIX 8.A

The 1986 Chevrolet Line

Chevette: An inexpensive subcompact with standard four-speed manual transmission, rack-and-pinion steering, fully reclining bucket seats, and rear hatch with fold-down rear seat. Available in two models: two-door coupe and four-door sedan. Price: $5,280.

Cavalier: America's best selling compact for three years running. Standard features included front-wheel drive with rack-and-pinion steering, four-speed manual transmission, and V-6 engine. Options included sunroof, choice of Delco Bose music systems, and rear luggage carrier. Thirteen models available including convertible sedan and wagon. Price: $7,600.

Celebrity: America's best selling mid-size car. Standard features were front-wheel drive with rack-and-pinion steering, V-6 engine with electronic fuel injection, and cloth interior. Models included coupe, sedan, and wagon body types. Wide variety of options allowed for personally "customized" car. Price: $15,000.

Camaro: America's best selling 2 + 2 sports coupe came standard with V-6 multiport fuel-injection engine, five-speed manual transmission, power steering, sports suspension, rally wheels, and rear hatch. Available options included: Delco Bose wrap-around music system, electric rearview mirror controls, and rear window louvers. Camaro had long received "hand-me-down" Corvette technology, and the Iroc Z28 was available with a Corvette engine option. Camaro races were becoming increasingly popular. Four models to choose from. Price: $10,400.

Caprice: Full-size car that offered standard V-6 engine with electronic fuel injection and three-speed automatic transmission, rear-drive power steering, and 20.9 cubic feet of luggage space. Model selection included Brougham and Classic series in sedan and wagon body types. Many options available for personalized customizing. Price: $11,400.

Monte Carlo: Full-size rear-drive automobile with full coil suspension, power steering, and brakes. Standard features included three-speed automatic transmission, electronically fuel-injected V-6 engine, and cloth bench seat with center arm rest. Available in luxury sport and super sport models. Price: $11,700.

Corvette: Performance sports car with standard features including a V-8 engine with tuned-port fuel injection in a choice of four-speed manual with overdrive or four-speed automatic transmissions, vehicle antitheft system, Bosch ABS II antilock brake system, corrosion-resistant fiberglass body, targa roof, air conditioning, and electronic instrument cluster. Options available included leather seats. Delco Bose stereo system, and performance handling package. Also available in convertible model. Price: $28,500.

APPENDIX 8.B Technical Terms

Tests Used in Performance Comparisons

Skidpad Test—Measured the cornering ability of a car in a steady state. Cars that generated numbers of greater than 0.8 grams of force had a stiff suspension and harsh riding characteristics on surfaces rougher than a smooth race track.

Slalom Test—Measured a car's cornering ability in transient maneuvers as it wove through a course of eight pylons spaced at 100-foot intervals.

Braking Test—Measured the minimal distance required to come to a full stop from a stated speed. Typically tested from 60 to 80 mph.

Innovations in Automobile Technology
Braking

Antilock Braking System (ABS)—Disc brake calipers had an electronic sensor that prevent brake lock up in panic stops. This innovation resulted in better stopping power and eliminated loss of control (skidding).

Suspension

Dynamic Suspensions—Being developed so that electronic sensors can detect road conditions, allowing a car's suspension components to react.

Active Suspensions—Sensors monitoring load-induced flex in the rear suspension to adjust the rear wheel suspension automatically.

Driver Adjustable Suspensions—Allowed the driver to alter the stiffness of a car's shock absorber to increase a car's handling performance or ride characteristics.

Engine

Turbocharging—A method of increasing a car's horsepower output by increasing the air flow into the engine's combustion chambers.

Intercooling—Creating a denser charge and increasing the horsepower of a turbo-charged engine by cooling the air charge of a turbo-charger.

Fuel Injection—A system, usually electronic, that controlled and injected fuel directly into the combustion chamber.

—————————————— CASE 9 ——————————————

Wal-Mart Stores:
Strategies for Market Dominance

It was dusk in the foothills of the Ozark mountains in north central Arkansas. A battered red 1980 Ford pickup, minus two hubcaps with a hunting dog named Buck seated inside the cab, was headed down the rural road for some coffee and conversation with friends at Fred's Hickory Inn in Bentonville. Inside the truck, driving, was one of the most successful retailing entrepreneurs in modern history, who continues to be down-to-earth and old fashioned in his views of the past, the present, and the future. "I didn't sit down one day and decide that I was going to put a bunch of discount stores in small towns and set a goal to have a billion-dollar company some day," Sam Walton said. "I started out with one store and it did well, so it was a challenge to see if I could do well with a few more. We're still going and we'll keep going as long as we're successful." From these humble beginnings, Wal-Mart emerged as a modern retail success story.

AN EMERGING ORGANIZATION

Wal-Mart Stores, with corporate offices in Bentonville, Arkansas, had completed its 28th consecutive year of growth in both sales and earnings in 1991. The firm operated stores under a variety of names and retail formats including Wal-Mart stores, which existed as discount department stores; Sam's Wholesale Clubs, which were wholesale/retail membership warehouses; Hypermart*USA, which were combination grocery and general merchandise stores in excess of 200,000 square feet; Wal-Mart Supercenters, scaled-down versions of hypermarkets; Dot Discount Drugstores, a super discount drug chain; and Bud's, off-price outlet stores. In sales volume, it was not only the nation's largest discount department store chain, but it had recently surpassed Sears, Roebuck, & Co. as the largest retail organization in the United States.

The Sam Walton Spirit

Much of the initial and continuing success of Wal-Mart was attributed to the entrepreneurial spirit of its founder and chairman of the board, Samuel Moore Walton. Sam Walton, or "Mr. Sam" as some referred to him, traced his down-to-earth, old-fashioned, home-spun, evangelical ways to growing up in rural Oklahoma, Missouri, and Arkansas. Although he was remarkably blasé about his roots, some suggested that it was a simple belief in hard work and ambition that had "unlocked countless doors and showered upon him, his customers, and his employees . . . the fruits of . . . years of labor in building [this] highly successful company."

"Our goal has always been in our business to be the very best," he said in an interview, "and, along with that, we believe that in order to do that, you've got to make a good situation and put the interests of your associates first. If we really do that consistently, they in turn will cause . . . our business to be successful, which is what we've talked about and espoused and practiced.

"The reasons for our success," Sam Walton said, "is our people and the way that they're treated and the way they feel about their company." Many have suggested it is this people-first philosophy that guided the company through the challenges and setbacks of its early years and allowed the company to maintain its consistent record of growth and expansion in later years.

There was little about Walton's background that reflected his amazing success. He was born in Kingfisher, Oklahoma, on March 29, 1918, to Thomas and Nancy Walton. Thomas Walton was a banker at the time and later entered the farm mortgage business and moved to Missouri. Sam Walton, growing up in rural Missouri in the depths of the Great Depression, discovered early that he "had a fair amount of ambition and enjoyed working," as he suggested in a company interview. He completed high school in Columbia, Missouri, and received a Bachelor of Arts in Economics from the University of Missouri in 1940. "I really had no idea what I would be," he said. He added as an afterthought, "At one point in time, I thought I wanted to become President of the United States."

A unique, enthusiastic, and positive individual, Sam Walton was called "just your basic home-spun billionaire" by *Business Week* magazine. One source suggested that "Mr. Sam is a life-long small-town resident who didn't change much as he got richer than his neighbors." Walton drove an old Ford pickup truck, would grab a bite to eat at Fred's Hickory Inn in Bentonville, and as a matter of practice would get his hair cut at the local barbershop. He had tremendous energy, enjoyed bird hunting with his dogs, and flew a corporate plane. When the company was much smaller, he could boast that he personally visited every Wal-Mart store at least once a year. A store visit usually included Walton leading Wal-Mart cheers that began "Give me a W, give me an A. . . ." To many employees, he had the air of a fiery Baptist preacher. Paul R. Carter, a Wal-Mart executive vice president, said: "Mr. Walton has a calling." He became the richest man in the United States, and by 1991 he had created a personal fortune for his family in excess of $21 billion.

For all that Walton's success has been widely chronicled, its magnitude is hard to comprehend. Sam Walton was selected by the investment publication *Financial World* in 1989 as the "CEO of the Decade." He had honorary degrees from the University of the Ozarks, the University of Arkansas, and the University of Missouri. He received many of the most distinguished professional awards from the industry such as "Man of the Year," "Discounter of the Year," and "Chief Executive Officer of the Year" and was the second retailer to be inducted into the Discounting Hall of Fame. He was the recipient of an Horatio Alger Award in 1984 and acknowledged by *Discount Stores News* as "Retailer of the Decade" in December of 1989. "Walton does a remarkable job of instilling near-religious fervor in his people," said analyst Robert Buchanan of A. G. Edwards. "I think that speaks to the heart of his success." In late 1989 Sam Walton was diagnosed as having multiple myeloma, or cancer of the bone marrow. Although he curtailed some activities, he planned to continue in the firm as chairman of the board.

THE MARKETING CONCEPT

Genesis of An Idea

Sam Walton started his retail career in 1940 as a management trainee with the J.C. Penney Company in Des Moines, Iowa. He was impressed with the Penney method of doing business and later modeled the Wal-Mart chain on "The Penney Idea" as reviewed in Exhibit 9.1. The Penney Company had found strength in calling employees "associates" rather than clerks. Founded in Kemerer, Wyoming, in 1902, Penney stores were located on the main streets of small towns and cities.

Following service in the U.S. Army during World War II, Sam Walton acquired a Ben Franklin variety-store franchise in Newport, Arkanas, which he operated successfully until losing the lease in 1950. He opened another store

EXHIBIT 9.1   The Penney Idea—1913

1. To serve the public, as nearly as we can, to its complete satisfaction.
2. To expect for the service we render a fair remuneration and not all the profit the traffic will bear.
3. To do all in our power to pack the customer's dollar full of value, quality, and satisfaction.
4. To continue to train ourselves and our associates so that the service we give will be more and more intelligently performed.
5. To improve constantly the human factor in our business.
6. To reward men and women in our organization through participation in what the business produces.
7. To test our every policy, method, and act in this wise: "Does it square with what is right and just?"

Source: Vance H. Trimble, *Sam Walton: The Inside Story of America's Richest Man* (New York: Dutton, 1990).

under the name of Walton's 5 and 10 in Bentonville, Arkansas, the following year. By 1962, he was operating a chain of 15 stores.

The early retail stores owned by Sam Walton in Newport and Bentonville, Arkansas, and later in other small towns in adjoining southern states, were variety-store operations. They were relatively small stores of 6,000 square feet, located on "main street," and displayed merchandise on plain wooden tables and counters. Operated under the Ben Franklin name and supplied by Butler Brothers of Chicago and St. Louis, they were characterized by a limited price line, low gross margins, high merchandise turnover, and concentration on return on investment. The firm, operating under the Walton 5 and 10 name, was the largest Ben Franklin franchise in the country in 1962. The variety stores were phased out by 1976 to allow the company to concentrate on the growth of Wal-Mart stores.

Foundation of Growth

The original Wal-Mart discount concept was not a unique idea. Sam Walton became convinced in the late 1950s that discounting would transform retailing. He traveled extensively in New England, the cradle of off-pricing. "He visited just about every discounter in the United States," suggested William F. Kenney, the retired president of the now-defunct Kings Department Stores. He tried to sell the discount store concept to Butler Brothers executives in Chicago. The first Kmart, as a "conveniently located one-stop shopping unit where customers could buy a wide variety of quality merchandise at discount prices," had opened in 1962 in Garden City, Michigan. Walton's theory was to operate a discount store in a small community where he would offer name-brand merchandise at low prices and would add friendly service. Butler Brothers executives rejected the idea. Undaunted, he opened the first Wal-Mart Discount City in late 1962 in Rogers, Arkansas.

Wal-Mart stores would sell nationally advertised, well-known brand merchandise at low prices in austere surroundings. As corporate policy, they would cheerfully give refunds, credits, and rain checks. Management conceived the firm as a "discount department store chain offering a wide variety of general merchandise to the customer." Early emphasis was placed upon opportunistic purchases of merchandise from whatever sources were available. Heavy emphasis was placed upon health and beauty aids (H&BA) in the product line and "stacking it high" in a manner of merchandise presentation. By the end of 1979, there were 276 Wal-Mart stores located in 11 states.

The firm developed an aggressive expansion strategy as it grew from its first 16,000-square-foot discount store in Rogers. New stores were located primarily in towns of 5,000 to 25,000 in population. The stores' sizes ranged from 30,000 to 60,000 square feet with 45,000 being the average. The firm also expanded by locating stores in contiguous areas, town by town, state by state. When its discount operations came to dominate a market area, it moved to an adjoining area. Although other retailers built warehouses to serve existing outlets, Wal-Mart built the distribution center first and then spotted stores all around it, pooling advertising and distribution overhead. Most stores were less than a six-hour drive from one of the company's warehouses. The first major distribution center, a 390,000-square-foot facility opened in Search, Arkansas, outside Bentonville in 1978.

National Perspectives

At the beginning of 1991, the firm had 1,573 Wal-Mart stores in 35 states with expansion planned for adjacent states. Wal-Mart became the largest retailer and the largest discount department store by continuing to follow the unique place strategy of first locating discount stores in small-town America and later in suburban markets. As a national discount department store chain, Wal-Mart Stores offered a wide variety of general merchandise to the customer. The stores were designed to offer one-stop shopping in 36 departments that included family apparel, health and beauty aids, household needs, electronics, toys, fabric and crafts, automotive supplies, lawn and patio, jewelry, and shoes. In addition, at certain store locations, a pharmacy, automotive supply and service center, garden center, or snack bar was included. The firm operated its stores with an "everyday low price" as opposed to putting heavy emphasis on special promotions, which called for multiple newspaper advertising circulars. Stores were expected to "provide the customer with a clean, pleasant, and friendly shopping experience."

Although Wal-Mart carried much the same merchandise, offered similar prices, and operated stores that looked much like the competition, there were many differences. In the typical Wal-Mart store, employees wore blue vests for easy identification, aisles were wide, apparel departments were carpeted in warm colors, a store employee followed customers to their car to pick up their shopping carts, and the customer was welcomed at the door by a "people greeter," who gave directions and struck up conversations. In some cases, merchandise was bagged in brown paper sacks rather than plastic bags because customers seemed to prefer them. A simple Wal-Mart logo in white letters on a brown background on the front of the store served to identify the firm. In consumer studies it was determined that the chain was particularly adept at striking the delicate balance needed to convince customers its prices were low without making people feel that its stores were too cheap. In many ways, competitors such as Kmart, sought to emulate Wal-Mart by introducing people greeters, by upgrading interiors, by developing new logos and signage, and by introducing new inventory response systems. In 1989, sales per square foot of retail space at Wal-Mart were $227. Kmart, in contrast, sold only $139 per square foot worth of goods annually.

A satisfaction guaranteed refund and exchange policy was introduced to inspire customer confidence in Wal-Mart's merchandise and quality. Technological advancements like scanner cash registers, hand-held computers for ordering merchandise, and computer linkages of stores with the general office and distribution centers improved communications and merchandise replenishment. Each store was encouraged to initiate programs that would make it an integral part of the community in which it operated. Associates were encouraged to "maintain the highest standards of honesty, morality, and business ethics in dealing with the public."

The External Environment

Industry analysts had labeled the 1980s as an era of economic uncertainty for retailers. Some firms faced difficulty with merger or acquisition. After acquiring U.S.-based Allied Department Stores in 1986 and Federated Department Stores in 1988, Canadian developer Robert Campeau declared bankruptcy with over $6 billion in debt. Upon reevaluation, several divisions and units of this organization were either sold or closed. Rich's flagship downtown Atlanta store, a division of Federated, was closed after completing a multi-million-dollar remodeling program. Specific merchandise programs in divisions such as Bloomingdale's were reevaluated to lower inventory and to raise cash. The notion of servicing existing debt became a significant factor in the success or failure of a retailing organization in the latter half of the decade. Selected acquisitions of U.S. retailers by foreign firms over the past decade are summarized in Exhibit 9.2

Other retailers experienced change in ownership. The British B.A.T. Industries PLC sold the Chicago-based Marshall Field department store division to the Dayton-Hudson Corporation. L. J. Hooker Corporation, the U.S. arm of Australia's Hooker Corporation, sold its Bonwit Teller and Sakowitz stores; it liquidated its B. Altman chain after fruitless sales efforts. The R.H. Macy Company saddled itself with $4.5 billion in debt as a result of acquiring Bullock's and I. Magnin specialty department stores. Chicago-based Carson, Pirie, Scott & Company was sold to the P. A. Bergner & Company, operator of the Milwaukee Boston Store and Bergner Department Stores. Bergner declared Chapter 11 bankruptcy in 1991.

EXHIBIT 9.2   **Selected Acquisitions of U.S. Retailers by Foreign Firms, 1980–1990**

U.S. Retailer	Foreign Acquirer	Country of Acquirer
Allied Stores (General Merchandise)	Campeau	Canada
Alterman Foods (Supermarkets)	Delhaie-Le Leon	Belgium
Bonwit Teller (General Merchandise)	Hooker Corp.	Australia
Brooks Brothers (Apparel)	Marks & Spencer	Great Britain
Federated Department Stores (Diversified)	Campeau	Canada
Great Atlantic & Pacific (Supermarkets)	Tengelmann	West Germany
Herman's (Sporting Goods)	Dee Corp.	Great Britain
International House of Pancakes (Restaurants)	Wienerwald	Switzerland
Talbots (Apparel)	Jusco	Japan
Zale (Jewelry)	PS Associates	Netherlands

Source: Barry Berman and Joel R. Evans, *Retail Management: A Strategic Approach,* 4th ed. (New York: Macmillan, 1989).

Many retail enterprises confronted heavy competitive pressure by lowering prices or changing merchandise strategies. Sears, Roebuck & Company, in an effort to reverse sagging sales and less than defensible earnings, unsuccessfully introduced a new policy of "everyday low pricing" in 1989. It later introduced name-brand items alongside its traditional private-label merchandise and introduced the store-within-a-store concept to feature the name-brand goods. For example, Whirlpool appliances were sold next to Kenmore (Sears brand) appliances. Montgomery Ward, and to a lesser extent Kmart and Ames Department Stores, followed similar strategies. The J.C. Penney Company, despite repositioning as a more upscale retailer, felt that an impending recession plus concerns about the Persian Gulf War had combined to erode consumer confidence. "As a result," the company noted in its 1990 annual report, "sales and profits within the industry were more negatively impacted than at any time since the last major recession of 1980 to 1982."

The discount department store industry by the early 1990s had changed in a number of ways and was thought to have reached maturity by many analysts. Several formerly successful firms like E.J. Korvette, W.T. Grant, Atlantic Mills, Arlans, Federals, Zayre, Heck's, and Ames had declared bankruptcy and as a result either liquidated or reorganized. Regional firms like Target Stores and Shopko Stores began carrying more fashionable merchandise in more attractive facilities and shifted their emphasis to more national markets. Specialty retailers such as Toys 'R' Us, Pier 1 Imports, and Oshmans were making big inroads in toys, home furnishings, and sporting goods. The superstores of drug and food chains were rapidly discounting increasing amounts of general merchandise. Other firms such as May Department Stores Company (Caldor and Venture) and the F.W. Woolworth Co. (Woolco) had withdrawn from the field by either selling their discount divisions or closing them down entirely.

Several new retail formats had emerged in the market place to challenge the traditional discount department store format. The superstore, a 100,000- to

300,000-square-foot operation, combined a large supermarket with a discount general-merchandise store. Originally a European retailing concept, these outlets were known as "malls without walls." Super Kmart and American Fare owned by Kmart and Supercenter stores and Hypermart*USA owned by Wal-Mart were examples of this trend toward large operations. Warehouse retailing, which involved some combination of warehouses and showroom facilities, used warehouse principles to reduce operating expenses and thereby offer discount prices as a primary customer appeal. Home Depot combined the traditional hardware store and lumber yard with a self-service home improvement center to become the largest home center operation in the nation.

Some retailers responded to changes in the marketplace by selling goods at price levels 20 to 60 percent below regular retail prices. These off-price operations appeared as two general types: (1) factory outlet stores like Burlington Coat Factory Warehouse, Bass Shoes, and Manhattan's Brand Name Fashion Outlet, and (2) independents like Loehmann's, T.J. Maxx, Marshall's, and Clothesline, which bought seconds, overages, closeouts, or leftover goods from manufacturers and other retailers. Others chose to dominate a product classification. Some superspecialists such as Sock Appeal, Little Piggie, and Sock Market, offered a single narrowly defined classification of merchandise with an extensive assortment of brands, colors, and sizes. Others, as niche specialists, such as Kids Mart, a division of F.W. Woolworth, and McKids, a division of Sears, targeted an identified market with carefully selected merchandise and appropriately designed stores. Some retailers such as Silk Greenhouse (silk plants and flowers), Office Club (office supplies and equipment), and Toys 'R' Us (toys) were called "category killers" because they had achieved merchandise dominance in their respective product categories. Firms such as The Limited, Victoria's Secret, and the Banana Republic became mini-department specialists by showcasing new lines and accessories alongside traditional merchandise.

Wal-Mart became the nation's largest retail and discount department store chain in sales volume in 1991. Kmart Corporation, now the industry's second largest retailer and discount department store chain, with over 2,300 stores and $32,070,000 in sales in 1990, was perceived by many industry analysts and consumers in several independent studies as a laggard, even though it had been the industry sales leader for a number of years. In the same studies, Wal-Mart was perceived as the industry leader even though according to the *Wall Street Journal*: "They carry much the same merchandise, offer prices that are pennies apart, and operate stores that look almost exactly alike." "Even their names are similar," noted the newspaper. The original Kmart concept of a "conveniently located, one stop shopping unit where customers could buy a wide variety of quality merchandise at discount prices," had lost its competitive edge in a changing market. As one analyst noted in an industry newsletter: "They had done so well for the past 20 years without paying attention to market changes. Now they have to." Wal-Mart and Kmart sales growth over the past 10 years is reviewed in Exhibit 9.3. A competitive analysis is shown of four major retail firms in Exhibit 9.4.

EXHIBIT 9.3   Competitive Sales and Store Comparison

| | Kmart | | Wal-Mart[a] | |
Year	Sales (In thousands)	Number of Stores	Sales (In thousands)	Number of Stores
1990	$32,070,000	2,350	$32,601,594	1,573
1989	29,533,000	2,361	25,810,656	1,402
1988	27,301,000	2,307	20,649,001	1,259
1987	25,627,000	2,273	15,959,255	1,114
1986	23,035,000	2,342	11,909,076	980
1985	22,035,000	2,332	8,451,489	859
1984	20,762,000	2,173	6,400,861	745
1983	18,597,000	2,160	4,666,909	642
1982	16,772,166	2,117	3,376,252	551
1981	16,527,012	2,055	2,444,997	491
1980	14,204,381	1,772	1,643,199	330

[a] Wal-Mart fiscal year ends January 31. Figures are assigned to previous year.

Some retailers like Kmart had initially focused on appealing to professional, middle-class consumers who lived in suburban areas and were likely to be price sensitive. Other firms like Target, which had adopted the discount concept early, generally attempted to go after an upscale consumer who had an annual household income of $25,000 to $44,000. Fleet Farm and Menard's served the rural consumer, and some firms such as Chicago's Goldblatt's Department Stores returned to their immigrant heritage to serve blacks and Hispanics in the inner city.

In rural communities Wal-Mart success often came at the expense of established local merchants and units of regional discount store chains. Hardware stores, family department stores, building supply outlets, and stores featuring fabrics, sporting goods, and shoes were among the first to either close or relocate elsewhere. Regional discount retailers in the Sunbelt states, including Roses, Howard's, T.G.& Y, and Duckwall-ALCO, that once enjoyed solid sales and earnings, were forced to reposition by renovating stores, opening bigger and more modern units, remerchandising assortments, and offering lower prices. In many cases, stores such as Coast-to-Coast, Pamida, and Ben Franklin closed upon a Wal-Mart announcement to build in a specific community. "Just the word that Wal-Mart was coming made some stores close up," indicated a local newspaper editor.

Corporate Strategies

The corporate and marketing strategies that emerged at Wal-Mart to challenge a turbulent and volatile external environment were based upon a set of two main objectives that had guided the firm through its growth years in the 1980s. In the first objective the customer was featured: "Customers would be provided

EXHIBIT 9.4   An Industry Competitive Analysis, 1991

	Wal-Mart	Sears, Roebuck	Kmart	J.C. Penney
Sales (Thousands)	$32,601,584	$55,972,000	$32,070,000	$17,410,000
Net Income (Thousands)	1,291,024	902,000	756,000	577,000
Net Income per Share	1.14	2.63	3.78	4.33
Dividends per Share	.14	2.00	1.72	2.64
Number of Stores (see Note)	1,724	1,765	4,180	3,889
Percent Sales Change	26.0%	1.2%	.6%	2.1%

Note: Wal-Mart and Subsidiaries (Number of Outlets)
       Wal-Mart Stores—1,573
       Sam's Wholesale Club—148
       Hypermart*USA—3

   Sears, Roebuck & Company
       Sears Merchandise Group (Number of Outlets)
           Department Stores—863
           Paint and Hardware Stores—98
           Catalog Outlet Stores—101
           Western Auto—504
           Eye Care Centers of America—94
           Business Systems Centers—65
           Pinstripes Petites—40

       Allstate Insurance Group
       Dean Witter Financial Services Group
       Coldwell Banker Real Estate Group

   Kmart Corporation (Number of Outlets)
       General Merchandise—2,350
       Specialty Retail Stores—1,830
         PACE Membership Warehouse
         Builders Square
         Payless Drug Stores
         Waldenbooks
         The Sports Authority

   J.C. Penney Company (Number of Outlets)
       Stores—1,312
         Metropolitan Market Stores—697
         Geographic Market Stores—615
       Catalog Units—2,090
         J.C. Penney Stores—1,312
         Free-Standing Sales Centers—626
         Drug Stores—136
         Other, Principally Outlet Stores—16
       Drug Stores (Thrift Drug or Treasury Drug)—487

what they want, when they want it, all at a value." In the second objective the team spirit was emphasized: "Treating each other as we would hope to be treated, acknowledging our total dependency on our Associate-partners to sustain our success." The approach included aggressive plans for new store openings; expansion to additional states; upgrading, relocation, refurbishing, and remodeling of existing stores; and opening new distribution centers. The plan was to avoid having a single operating unit that had not been updated in the past seven years. In the 1991 annual report to stockholders, the 1990s were described as "A new era for Wal-Mart; an era in which we plan to grow to a truly nationwide retailer, and should we continue to perform, our sales and earnings will also grow beyond where most could have envisioned at the dawn of the 80s." Appendix 9.A contains a 10-year financial summary for Wal-Mart.

In the 1980s, Wal-Mart developed a number of new retail formats. The first Sam's Wholesale Club opened in Oklahoma City in 1983. The wholesale club was an idea that had been developed earlier by other firms but that found its greatest success and growth in acceptability at Wal-Mart. Sam's Wholesale Club featured a vast array of product categories with limited selection of brand and model, cash-and-carry business with limited hours, large (100,000-square-foot) bare-bones facilities, rock-bottom wholesale prices, and minimal promotion. The limited membership plan permitted wholesale members who bought a membership and others who usually paid a percentage above the ticket price of the merchandise. At the beginning of 1991, there were 148 Sam's Wholesale Clubs open in 28 states. Effective February 2, 1991, Sam's Clubs merged the 28 units of the Wholesale Club of Indianapolis, Indiana, into the organization.

The first Hypermart*USA was a 222,000-square-foot superstore that combined a discount store with a large grocery store and contained a food court of restaurants and a variety of other service businesses such as banks or videotape rental stores. It opened in 1988 in the Dallas suburb of Garland. A scaled-down version of Hypermart*USA was called the Wal-Mart SuperCenter. It had similar merchandise offerings, but with about half the square footage of hypermarkets. These expanded store concepts also included convenience stores and gasoline distribution outlets to "enhance shopping convenience." The company proceeded slowly with these plans and later suspended its plans for building any more hypermarkets in favor of the supercenter concept.

The McLane Company, a provider of retail and grocery distribution services for retail stores, was acquired in 1991. In October 1991, management announced that it was starting a chain of stores called Bud's, which would sell damaged, outdated, and overstocked goods at discounts even deeper than regular Wal-Mart stores.

Several programs were launched to "highlight" popular social causes. The "Buy American" theme was a Wal-Mart retail program initiated in 1985. Additionally, "Bring It Home to the USA" was selected to communicate the company's support for U.S. manufacturing. In the program, Wal-Mart encouraged manufacturers to produce goods in the United States rather than import them from other countries. Vendors were attracted into the program by encouraging manufacturers to initiate the process of contracting the company directly with proposals to sell goods that were made in the United States. Buyers also targeted specific import items in their assortments on a state-by-state basis to encourage domestic manufacturing. According to Haim Dabah, president of Gitano Group, a maker of fashion discount clothing that at one time imported 95 percent of its clothing and now makes about 20 percent of its products in the United States, "Wal-Mart let it be known loud and clear that if you're going to grow with them, you sure better have some products made in the U.S.A." Farris Fashion (flannel shirts); Roadmaster Corporation (exercise bicycles); Flanders Industries (lawn chairs); and Magic Chef (microwave ovens) were examples of vendors that chose to participate in the program.

From the Wal-Mart perspective, the "Buy American" program centered on value—producing and selling quality merchandise at a competitive price. The promotion included television advertisements featuring factory workers, a soaring American eagle, and the slogan "We buy American whenever we can, so you can, too." Prominent in-store signage and store circulars were also included. One store poster read "Success Stories—These items formerly imported, are now being purchased by Wal-Mart in the U.S.A."

Wal-Mart was one of the first retailers to embrace the concept of "green" marketing. The program offered shoppers the option of purchasing products that were better for the environment in three respects: manufacturing, use, and disposal. Introduced through full-page advertisements in the *Wall Street Journal* and *USA Today,* in-store signage identified the environmentally safe products. As Wal-Mart executives saw it, "Customers are concerned about the quality of land, air, and water, and would like the opportunity to do something positive." To initiate the program, 7,000 vendors were notified that Wal-Mart had a corporate concern for the environment and to ask for their support in a variety of ways. Wal-Mart television advertising showed children on swings, fields of grain blowing in the wind, and roses. Green and white store signs printed on recycled paper marketed products or packaging that had been developed or redesigned to be more environmentally sound.

Wal-Mart was the channel commander in the distribution of many brand name items. As the nation's largest retailer and in many geographic areas the dominant distributor, it exerted considerable influence in negotiations for the best price, delivery terms, promotion allowances, and continuity of supply. Many of these benefits could be passed on to consumers in the form of quality name-brand items available at lower-than-competitive prices. As a matter of corporate policy, management often insisted on doing business only with a producer's top sales executives rather than going through a manufacturer's representative. Wal-Mart had been accused of threatening to buy from other producers if firms refused to sell directly to it. In the ensuing power struggle, Wal-Mart executives refused to talk about the controversial policy or admit that it existed. As suggested by a representative of an industry association, "In the Southwest, Wal-Mart's the only show in town." Added an industry analyst, "They're extremely aggressive. Their approach has always been to give the customer the benefit of any corporate savings. That builds customer loyalty and market share."

Another key factor in the mix was an inventory control system that was recognized as the most sophisticated in retailing. A high-speed computer system linked virtually all the stores to headquarters and the company's distribution centers. It electronically logged every item sold at the checkout counter, automatically kept the warehouses informed of merchandise to be ordered, and directed the flow of goods to the stores and even to the proper shelves. Most important for management, it helped detect sales trends quickly and speeded up market reaction time substantially.

Decision Making in a Market-Oriented Firm

One factor that distinguished Wal-Mart from other companies was the unusual depth of employee involvement in company affairs. Corporate strategies put emphasis on human resources management. Employees of Wal-Mart became "associates," a name borrowed from Sam Walton's early association with the J.C. Penney Company. Input was encouraged at meetings at the store and corporate level. The firm hired employees locally, provided training programs, encouraged employees to ask questions through a "Letter to the President" program, and made words like "we," "us," and "our" a part of the corporate language. A number of special award programs recognized individual, department, and division achievement. Stock ownership and profit-sharing programs were introduced as part of a "partnership concept."

The corporate culture was acknowledged by the editors of the trade publication *Mass Market Retailers* when it recognized all 275,000 associates collectively as the 1989 "Mass Market Retailers of the Year." The editors noted, "In this decade that term [Wal-Mart associate] has come to symbolize all that is right with the American worker, particularly in the retailing environment and most particularly at Wal-Mart." The store-within-a-store concept, as a Wal-Mart corporate policy, trained individuals to be merchants by being responsible for the performance of their own departments as if they were running their own businesses. Seminars and training programs afforded them opportunities to grow within the company. "People development, not just a good 'program' for any growing company but a must to secure our future," was how Suzanne Allford, vice president of the Wal-Mart People Division, explained the firm's decentralized approach to retail management development.

"The Wal-Mart Way" was a phrase that was used by management to summarize the firm's unconventional approach to business and the development of the corporate culture. Referring to a recent development program, the 1991 annual report noted, "We stepped outside our retailing world to examine the best managed companies in the United States in an effort to determine the fundamentals of their success and to 'benchmark' our own performances." The term "total quality management" (TQM) was used to identify this "vehicle for proliferating the very best things we do while incorporating the new ideas our people have that will assure our future.''

The Growth Challenge

David Glass, 53 years old, had assumed the role of president and chief executive officer at Wal-Mart, the position previously held by Sam Walton, founder of the company. Known for his hard-driving managerial style, Glass gained his experience in retailing at a small supermarket chain in Springfield, Missouri. He joined Wal-Mart as executive vice president for finance in 1976. He was named president and chief operating officer in 1984.

And what of Wal-Mart without Mr. Sam? "There's no transition to make," said Glass, "because the principles and the basic values he used in founding this company were so sound and so universally accepted." "As for the future," he suggested, spinning around in his chair at his desk in his relatively spartan office at corporate headquarters in Bentonville, "there's more opportunity ahead of us than behind us. We're good students of retailing and we've studied the mistakes that others have made. We'll make our own mistakes, but we don't repeat theirs. The only thing constant at Wal-Mart is change. We'll be fine as long as we never lose our responsiveness to the customer."

For over 25 years Wal-Mart Stores experienced tremendous growth and as one analyst suggested was "consistently on the cutting edge of low-markup mass merchandising." Much of the forward momentum came from the entrepreneurial spirit of Samuel Moore Walton. Mr. Sam remained chairman of the board of directors and corporate representative for the immediate future. A new management team was in place. As the largest retailer in the country, the firm had positioned itself to meet the challenges of the next decade as an industry leader. The question now was: Could the firm maintain its blistering growth pace—outmaneuvering the competition with the innovative retailing concepts that it has continued to develop better than anyone else?

REFERENCES

"A Supercenter Comes to Town," *Chain Store Age Executive,* December 1989, pp. 23–30+.

ABEND, JULES, "Wal-Mart's Hypermart: Impetus for U.S. Chains?" *Stores,* March 1988, pp. 59–61.

The Almanac of American Employers (Chicago: Contemporary Books, 1985), p. 280.

"Another Record Year at Wal-Mart," *Chain Store Age,* General Merchandise Edition, June 1987, p. 70.

BARD, RAY, and SUSAN K. ELLIOGG, *The National Director of Corporate Training Programs* (New York: Doubleday, 1988), pp. 351–352.

BARRIER, MICHAEL, "Walton's Mountain," *Nation's Business,* April 1988, pp. 18–20+.

BEAMER, WAYNE, "Discount King Invades Marketer Territory," *National Petroleum,* April 1988, pp. 15–16.

BERGMAN, JOAN, "Saga of Sam Walton," *Stores,* January 1988, pp. 129–130+.

BLUMENTHAL, KAREN, "Marketing with Emotion: Wal-Mart Shows the Way," *Wall Street Journal,* November 20, 1989, p. B3.

BRADFORD, MICHAEL, "Receiver Sues to Recoup Com Payments," *Business Insurance,* September 11, 1989, p. 68.

BRAGG, ARTHUR, "Wal-Mart's War on Reps," *Sales & Marketing Management,* March 1987, pp. 41–43.

BRAUER, MOLLY, "Sam's: Setting a Fast Pace," *Chain Store Age Executive,* August 1983, pp. 20–21.

BROOKMAN, FAYE, "Will Patriotic Purchasing Pay Off?" *Chain Store Age,* General Merchandise Edition, June 1985, p. 95.

CAMINITI, SUSAN, "What Ails Retailing," *Fortune,* January 30, 1989, pp. 63–64.

COCHRAN, THOMAS N., "Chain Reaction," *Barron's,* October 16, 1989, p. 46.

CORWIN, PAT, JAY L. JOHNSON, and RENEE M. ROULAND, "Made in U.S.A.," *Discount Merchandiser,* November 1989, pp. 48–52.

"David Glass's Biggest Job Is Filling Sam's Shoes," *Business Month,* December 1988, p. 42.

"Discounters Commit to Bar-code Scanning," *Chain Store Age Executive,* September 1985, pp. 49–50.

"The Early Days: Walton Kept Adding 'a Few More' Stores," *Discount Store News,* December 9, 1985, p. 61.

EDGERTON, JERRY, and JORDAN E. GOODMAN, "Wal-Mart for Hypergrowth," *Money,* March 1988, p. 12.

ENDICOTT, R. CRAIG, " '86 Ad Spending Soars," *Advertising Age,* November 23, 1987, pp. S-2+.

ENDICOTT, R. CRAIG, "Leading National Advertisers (Companies Ranked 101–200)," *Advertising Age,* November 21, 1988, pp. S-1+.

"Explosive Decade," *Financial World,* April 4–17, 1984, p. 92.

"Facts about Wal-Mart Stores, Inc.," Press Release, Corporate and Public Affairs, Wal-Mart Stores.

FISHER, CHRISTY, and JUDITH GRAHAM, "Wal-Mart Throws 'Green' Gauntlet," *Advertising Age,* August 21, 1989, pp. 1+.

FISHER, CHRISTY, and PATRICIA STRAND, "Wal-Mart Pulls Back on Hypermart Plans," *Advertising Age,* February 19, 1990, p. 49.

"The Five Best-Managed Companies," *Dun's Business Month,* December 1982, p. 47.

GILLIAM, MARGARET A., "Wal-Mart and the Investment Community," *Discount Merchandiser,* November 1989, pp. 64+.

"Glass Is CEO at Wal-Mart," *Discount Merchandiser,* March 1988, pp. 6+.

"Great News: A Recession," *Forbes,* January 8, 1990, p. 194.

GRUBER, CHRISTINA, "Will Competition Wilt Rose's," *Chain Store Age,* General Merchandise Edition, May 1984, p. 40.

HARTNETT, MICHAEL, "Resurgence in the Sunbelt," *Chain Store Age,* General Merchandise Edition, October 1985, pp. 13–15.

HELLIKER, KEVIN, "Wal-Mart's Store of the Future Blends Discount Prices, Department-Store Feel," *Wall Street Journal,* May 17, 1991, pp. B1, B8.

HIGGINS, KEVIN T., "Wal-Mart: A Pillar in a Thousand Communities," *Building Supply Home Centers,* February 1988, pp. 100–102.

HUEY, JOHN, "America's Most Successful Merchant," *Fortune,* September 23, 1991, pp. 46–48+.

HUEY, JOHN, "Wal-Mart, Will It Take over the World?" *Fortune,* January 30, 1989, pp. 52–56 + .

"Hypermart*USA Makes a Few Adjustments," *Chain Store Age Executive,* May 1988, p. 278.

"In Retail, Bigger Can Be Better," *Business Week,* March 27, 1989, p. 90.

"Jack Shewmaker, Vice Chairman, Wal-Mart Stores, Inc.," *Discount Merchandiser,* November 1987, pp. 26 + .

JACOBER, STEVE, "Wal-Mart: A Boon to U.S. Vendors," *Discount Merchandiser,* November 1989, pp. 41–46.

JACOBER, STEVE, "Wal- Mart: A Retailing Catalyst," *Discount Merchandiser,* November 1989, pp. 54–58.

JOHNSON, JAY L., "Are We Ready for Big Changes?" *Discount Merchandiser,* August 1989, pp. 48, 53–54.

JOHNSON, JAY L., "The Future of Retailing," *Discount Merchandiser,* January 1990, pp. 70 + .

JOHNSON, JAY L., "Hypermart*USA Does a Repeat Performance," *Discount Merchandiser,* March 1988, pp. 52 + .

JOHNSON, JAY L., "Hypermarkets and Supercenters—Where Are They Heading?" *Discount Merchandiser,* November 1989, pp. 60 + .

JOHNSON, JAY L., "Internal Communication: A Key to Wal-Mart's Success," *Discount Merchandiser,* November 1989, pp. 68 + .

JOHNSON, JAY L., "The Supercenter Challenge," *Discount Merchandiser,* August 1989, pp. 70 + .

JOHNSON, JAY L., "Supercenters: Wal-Mart's Future?" Discount Merchandiser, May 1988, pp. 26 + .

JOHNSON, JAY L., "Walton Honored by Harvard Business School Club," *Discount Merchandiser,* June 1990, pp. 30, 34.

KEITH, BILL, "Wal-Mart Places Special Emphasis on Pharmacy," *Drug Topics,* July 17, 1989, pp. 16–17.

KELLY, KEVIN, "Sam Walton Chooses a Chip off the Old CEO," *Business Week,* February 15, 1988, p. 29.

KELLY, KEVIN, "Wal-Mart Gets Lost in the Vegetable Isle," *Business Week,* May 28, 1990, p. 48.

KERR, DICK, "Wal-Mart Steps up 'Buy American,'" *Housewares,* March 7–13, 1986, pp. 1 + .

KLAPPER, MARVIN, "Wal-Mart Chairman Says His Buy American Program Working," *Women's Wear Daily,* December 3, 1985, p. 8.

"Leader in New Construction," *Chain Store Age Executive,* November 1985, p. 46.

LLOYD, BRUCE A., "Wal-Mart to Build Major Distribution Center in Loveland, Colorado," *Site Selection,* June 1989, pp. 634–635.

"Management Style: Sam Moore Walton," *Business Month,* May 1989, p. 38.

MARSCH, BARBARA, "The Challenge: Merchants Mobilize to Battle Wal-Mart in a Small Community," *Wall Street Journal,* June 5, 1991, pp. A1, A4.

MASON, TODD, "Sam Walton of Wal-Mart: Just Your Basic Homespun Billionaire," *Business Insurance,* October 14, 1985, pp. 142–143 + .

MCLEOD, DOUGLAS, "Micro Exceeded Authority on Wal-Mart Cover: Judge," *Business Insurance,* July 20, 1987, p. 28.

"$90 Million Expansion Bill at Wal-Mart," *Chain Store Age Executive,* November 1982, p. 73.

"Number of Units Set to Climb by 62%," *Chain Store Age Executive,* November 1983, p. 34.

"Our People Make the Difference: The History of Wal-Mart," Video Cassette (Bentonville, Arkansas: Wal-Mart Video Productions, 1991).

PADGETT, TIM, "Just Saying No to Wal-Mart," *Newsweek,* November 13, 1989, p. 65.

"Perspectives on Discount Retailing," *Discount Merchandiser,* April 1987, pp. 44+.

RAWN, CYNTHIA DUNN, "Wal-Mart vs. Main Street," *American Demographics,* June 1990, pp. 58–59.

REED, SUSAN, "Talk About a Local Boy Making Good: Sam Walton, the King of Wal-Mart, Is America's Second-Richest Man," *People,* December 19, 1983, pp. 133+.

REIER, SHARON, "CEO of the Decade: Sam M. Walton," *Financial World,* April 4, 1989, pp. 56–57.

"Rex Chase—Pure Wal-Mart Lore," *Chain Store Age,* General Merchandise Edition, March 1983, p. 35.

RUDNITSKY, HOWARD, "How Sam Walton Does It," *Forbes,* August 16, 1982, pp. 42–44.

RUDNITSKY, HOWARD, "Play It Again Sam," *Forbes,* August 10, 1987, p. 48.

"Sam Moore Walton," *Business Month,* May 1989, p. 38.

"Sam Walton, the Retail Giant: Where Does He Go from Here?" *Drug Topics,* July 17, 1989, p. 6.

"Sam's Wholesale Club Racks up $1.6 Billion in Sales in 1986," *Discount Merchandiser,* February 1987, p. 26.

SAPORITO, BILL, "The Mad Rush to Join the Warehouse Club," *Fortune,* January 6, 1986, pp. 59+.

SCHACHNER, MICHAEL, "Wal-Mart Chief Fined $11.5 Million for Court Absence," *Business Insurance,* January 9, 1989, pp. 1+.

SCHWADEL, FRANCINE, "Little Touches Spur Wal-Mart's Rise," *Wall Street Journal,* September 22, 1989, p. B1.

SHEETS, KENNETH R., "How Wal-Mart Hits Main Street," *U.S. News & World Report,* March 13, 1989, pp. 53–55.

"Small Stores Showcase Big Ideas," *Chain Store Age,* General Merchandise Edition, September 1985, pp. 19–20.

"Small Town Hit," *Time,* May 23, 1983, p. 43.

SMITH, SARAH, "America's Most Admired Corporations," *Fortune,* January 29, 1990, pp. 56+.

SPROUT, ALISON L., "America's Most Admired Corporations," *Fortune,* February 11, 1991, pp. 52+.

TAUB, STEPHEN, "Gold Winner: Sam M. Walton of Wal-Mart Stores Takes the Top Prize," *Financial World,* April 15, 1986, pp. 28+.

TAYLOR, MARIANNE, "Wal-Mart Prices Itself in the Market," *Chicago Tribune,* April 28, 1991, Section 7, pp. 1+.

"Tending Wal-Mart's Green Policy," *Advertising Age,* January 29, 1991, pp. 20+.

THURMOND, SHANNON, "Sam Speaks Volumes about New Formats," *Advertising Age,* May 9, 1988, p. S-26.

TRIMBLE, VANCE H., *Sam Walton: The Inside Story of America's Richest Man* (New York: Dutton, 1990).

"Wal-Mart Associates Generate over $5.5 Million for United Way," January 2, 1990, Corporate and Public Affairs, Wal-Mart Stores.

"Wal-Mart Beats the Devil," *Chain Store Age,* August 1986, p. 9.

"Wal-Mart Expands: Tests New 'Wholesale' Concept," *Chain Store Age,* General Merchandise Edition, June 1983, p. 98.

"Wal-Mart Has No Quarrel with 1984," *Chain Store Age,* General Merchandise Edition, June 1985, p. 36.

"Wal-Mart on the Move," *Progressive Grocer,* August 1987, p. 9.

"Wal-Mart Policy Asks for Supplier Commitment," *Textile World,* May 1985, pp. 27–28.

"Wal-Mart Raises over $3 Million for Children's Hospital," Press Release, June 1989, Corporate and Public Affairs, Wal-Mart Stores.

"Wal-Mart Rolls out Its Supercenters," *Chain Store Age Executive,* December 1988, pp. 18–19.

"Wal-Mart Stores Penny Wise," *Business Month,* December 1988, p. 42.

"Wal-Mart: The Model Discounter," *Dun's Business Month,* December 1982, pp. 60–61.

"Wal-Mart to Acquire McLane, Distributor to Retail Industry," *Wall Street Journal,* October 2, 1990, p. A8.

"Wal-Mart's Glass to Reps: 'That's a Bunch of Baloney!'" *Discount Merchandiser,* September 1987, p. 12.

"Wal-Mart's Goals," *Discount Merchandiser,* January 1988, pp. 48–50.

"Wal-Mart Goes on Its Own," *Progressive Grocer,* June 1987, p. 9.

"Wal-Mart's 'Green' Campaign to Emphasize Recycling Next," *Adweek's Marketing Week,* February 12, 1990, pp. 60–61.

"Wal-Mart's 1990 Look," *Discount Merchandiser,* July 1989, p. 12.

WEINER, STEVE, "Golf Balls, Motor Oil, and Tomatoes," *Forbes,* October 30, 1989, pp. 130–131+.

WEINER, STEVE, "Pssst! Wanna buy a Watch? A Suit? How about a Whole Department Store?" *Forbes,* January 8, 1990, pp. 192+.

"Wholesale Clubs," *Discount Merchandiser,* November 1987, pp. 26+.

"Why Wal-Mart Is Recession Proof," *Business Week,* February 22, 1988, p. 146.

"Work, Ambition—Sam Walton," Press Release, June 1990, Corporate and Public Affairs, Wal-Mart Stores.

ZWEIG, JASON, "Expand It Again, Sam," *Forbes,* July 9, 1990, p. 106.

APPENDIX 9.A Wal-Mart Stores, Inc.—Financial Performance (In thousands except per share data)[a]

10-Year Financial Summary	1982	1983	1984	1985	1986	1987	1988	1989	1990	1991
Earnings										
Net Sales	$2,444,997	$3,376,252	$4,666,909	$6,400,861	$8,451,489	$11,900,076	$15,959,255	$20,649,001	$25,810,656	$32,601,594
Licensed Department Rentals and Other Income—Net	17,650	22,435	36,031	52,167	55,127	84,623	104,783	136,867	174,644	261,814
Cost of Sales	1,787,496	2,458,235	3,418,025	4,722,440	6,361,271	9,053,219	12,281,744	16,056,856	20,070,034	25,499,834
Operating, Selling, and General and Administrative Expenses	495,010	677,020	892,887	1,181,455	1,485,210	2,007,645	2,599,367	3,267,864	4,069,695	5,152,178
Interest Costs										
Debt	16,053	20,297	4,935	5,207	1,903	10,422	25,262	36,286	20,346	42,716
Capital Leases	15,351	18,570	29,946	42,506	54,640	76,367	88,995	99,395	117,725	125,920
Taxes on Income	65,943	100,416	160,903	230,653	276,119	395,940	441,027	488,246	631,600	751,736
Net Income	$ 82,794	$ 124,140	$ 196,244	$ 270,767	$ 327,473	$ 2,353,271	$ 627,743	$ 837,221	$ 1,075,900	$ 1,291,024
Financial Position										
Current Assets	589,161	720,537	1,005,567	1,303,254	1,784,275	2,353,271	2,905,145	3,630,987	4,712,616	6,414,775
Net Property, Plant, Equipment, and Capital Leases	333,026	457,509	628,151	870,309	1,303,450	1,676,282	2,144,852	2,661,954	3,430,059	4,712,039
Total Assets	937,513	1,187,448	1,652,254	2,205,229	3,103,645	4,049,092	5,131,809	6,359,668	8,198,484	11,388,915
Current Liabilities	339,961	347,318	502,763	688,968	992,683	1,340,291	1,743,763	2,065,909	2,845,315	3,990,414
Long-Term Debt	104,581	106,465	40,866	41,237	180,682	179,234	185,672	184,439	185,152	740,254
Long-Term Obligations under Capital Leases	154,196	222,610	339,930	449,886	595,205	764,128	866,972	1,009,046	1,087,403	1,158,621
Preferred Stock with Mandatory Redemption Provisions	7,438	6,861	6,411	5,874	4,902					
Shareholders' Equity	$ 323,942	$ 488,109	$ 737,503	$ 984,672	$1,277,659	$1,690,493	$ 2,257,267	$ 3,007,909	$ 3,965,561	$ 5,365,524
Stores in Operation at the End of this Period										
Wal-Mart Stores	491	551	642	745	859	980	1,114	1,259	1,402	1,573
Sam's Wholesale Clubs	—	—	3	11	23	49	84	105	123	148

Source: Wal-Mart Annual Report, January 31, 1991

[a] On beginning year balance.

CASE 10

JJ's Women's Clothing Store: On the Move Again?

On April 1, 1990, Beth and Ann celebrated their fifth anniversary as partners in the women's retail clothing business. "Our efforts last year were very successful, don't you agree?" Ann commented as she and Beth reminisced. The business had been moved from a back-street location to one on Minnesota Avenue, the main street of St. Peter, Minnesota. The new location opened for business on April 1, 1989, and had become well known to its customers and the general public. The move had permitted a much better lighted and more appealing layout of the merchandise; selling space had increased nearly three times. In addition, their initial equity investment of $5,000 each had tripled.

"You're right, Ann," Beth returned. "Even with our success, we still have some things to work out. It's especially disheartening to think that we're possibly facing another move."

A proposal for a downtown mall in St. Peter had been under consideration since 1985—ironically, about the time the partners started in business. In 1991, the mall plans were progressing. The mall's development meant that JJ's would be faced with another move or at least a reduction in store size to about two-thirds of its present floor space.

BACKGROUND OF THE STORE

JJ's was owned by Ann Winters, a resident of St. Peter for all of her 20-some years, and Beth Sommers, in her mid-40's. They had learned the clothing business while working together at another St. Peter women's clothing store whose owner was somewhat of a matriarch of women's clothiers in town, having been in retailing for 54 years. Their dream had been to have a store of their own, and when they learned that JJ's was being sold, they decided to take advantage of the opportunity. JJ's had been in existence for three years when Beth and Ann purchased it. The previous owner, Jane Johnson, had done most of the work of

This case was prepared by JoAnn K. L. Schwinghammer and Charles Wagner as a basis for class discussion rather than to illustrate either effective or ineffective handling of an administrative situation. The data in this case are disguised but based on actual data. Used with permission from JoAnn K. L. Schwinghammer.

running the store herself and was tired of the demands it placed on her. The sale was "sealed with a hug" on April 1, and Beth and Ann energetically set about operating their own store.

For four years Beth and Ann tried to improve their sales by creative advertising, cooperating in retail community events, and carrying lines of clothing they believed would be appealing. They realized, however, that their location out of the mainstream retail activity was a hindrance, and they ultimately rented and moved to their current site on the west side of Minnesota Avenue.

THE STORE TODAY

Merchandise

When Ann and Beth purchased JJ's in 1985, the lines of clothing carried by the store were appropriate for young women aged 12 to 18. Believing that those ages represented a limited market for long-term business, they chose to keep three vendors' lines and changed the others. Since then, they made additional changes for a variety of reasons: Some of the clothing was not the quality the owners were seeking, and some sales representatives were difficult.

Beth characterized the lines of clothing that JJ's carried as "young career," appealing to young to middle-aged women of moderate means. In the early days of their business, they carried lines for which a mother would probably shop with or for her daughter; after the lines changed, items were usually selected by the intended wearer. This change in focus was appropriate, the owners believed, because the young college women, and particularly the young career women (women who would be working in or near St. Peter), had the need and the ability to buy.

Although JJ's did not carry the more expensive brands of Guess? or Esprit, each of which required a minimum order of $5,000, they did carry other popular brands: D. D. Sloane, Zena, White Stag, and Catalina, for example. The types of merchandise varied rather broadly, including slacks, skirts, blouses and tops, casual dresses, and a few semidressy dresses. They carried several lines of accessories, as well.

Considered to be a moderately priced line by Ann and Beth, the Zena brand sold between $45 and $50 at retail. Available in missy (8–18) and junior (5–13) sizes, Zena products could only be ordered in even dozens. In addition, Ann and Beth had no choice regarding the sizes or sometimes even the colors that were included in each dozen they would receive from Zena. This sometimes created a problem as the larger sizes were often the first to sell, with little demand for the very small sizes. Zena used a "factor," a representative (often a bank) through which to handle payments from store owners and managers. Dealing with this channel facilitator sometimes added complexity to their communications with Zena, even to the point of delaying orders if there were misunderstandings on payments.

Under the D. D. Sloane label, JJ's stocked sweaters, knit dresses, sports-wear, jackets, pants, and shorts, usually retail priced at $50 to $70, somewhat higher than most of JJ's other merchandise. In this more expensive line, the owners were able to buy pieces in lots of four. Garland was another moderately priced line carried by JJ's that Beth and Ann considered to be good quality. Well known for many years as a sweater manufacturer, Garland also manufactured print skirts. Priced between $35 and $45, JJ's could purchase Garland in minimum quantities of six items.

White Stag was a widely distributed brand of good-quality knit separates, with tops cut a little fuller, and pants, skirts, and shorts with elastic waistbands. Available in missy sizes, White Stag was a popular brand for JJ's. Usually purchased by women over age 25, this line was moderately priced. Catalina knitwear was also sized for the missy figure and included moderately priced swimwear and sportswear. JJ's could order any amount and size from this manu-facturer.

Either Ann or Beth would go to market five or six times a year, usually in Minneapolis, where they could visit several vendors at a time. It was necessary to order merchandise at least four months prior to the selling season. On occasion, Beth and Ann would be able to special-order items if they needed a special size or color, although most vendors did not make this service available to small retailers.

Although the two owners employed one other person on a part-time basis, they were responsible for all the duties necessary to keep the store operating—ordering, selling, planning and preparing displays and advertisements, pressing and marking clothing, making payments to vendors, handling customer service, and doing any other tasks that needed to be done. They shared responsibilities flexibly, adapting to each other's personal schedules as the need arose, which was infrequent. They did not have a formal partnership agreement; however, they had discussed the benefits of having one.

Service

Ann and Beth offered many services to their customers that would not be found in larger stores. Perhaps their most important service was the personal attention they were able to provide. For many women shopping for clothing, having assistance in selecting correct sizes and colors was desirable. In addition to accepting Visa and Mastercard (for a $15 minimum purchase), Beth and Ann offered a store charge account with monthly payments and no interest on the unpaid balance. Lay-away was available, with a 30 percent initial payment and additional payments arranged according to the customer's needs. Customers could take home an item of clothing for trial, with next-day payment or return. The owners stressed that because St. Peter was a small town, they knew people and had a good idea of who could and who could not be trusted.

JJ's also offered to take back unacceptable merchandise. In fact, the owners sometimes felt that this service was too good, since occasionally customers would take advantage of it. They also offered free gift wrapping, and Beth would do alterations, such as hemming, if it was not too involved.

Pricing

The owners set their margins slightly lower, by a dollar or two, than most other area stores. Some items, however, such as White Stag, came preticketed. For accessories, they generally used the standard 100 percent mark-up.

The fee paid for Visa and Mastercard sales was 4 percent, but they had more cash sales than credit sales. They had but an occasional bad debt. For their lay-away customers, when a payment was received, that amount was rung up as a sale for that day.

Promotions

Ann and Beth made their own advertising decisions and understood the value of advertising in generating customer traffic and sales. They developed their own message but had an artist friend do the layout and design. They appreciated her help, even though she was sometimes hard to motivate, resulting in insufficient lead time to prepare good ads. Although more advertising was being done than during the previous owner's management, they were uncertain if they were doing enough, or if what they were doing was effective.

There were several activities that the Retail Council organized for St. Peter retailers. The events were chosen by a subcommittee of the council, and voted on by the full membership. Ann and Beth had participated actively in these events. In addition, they carried out a number of other promotional events, not all of which resulted in increased business. For example, a hospital auxiliary style show, with attendance of over 350 people, and a style show for students of Gustavus Adolphus College successfully brought in customers with coupons and gift certificates. On the other hand, a Welcome Wagon promotion that cost $90 reached 850 new and transfer students at Gustavus Adolphus but resulted in no coupon redemptions.

For their numerous special events and regular awareness builders, Beth and Ann used newspaper advertisements in the *St. Peter Herald,* the *Valley,* the *Mankato Free Press,* and radio advertisements on KRBI, and KEEZ. The *Herald* was used for specials, perhaps twice a month; ads were placed in the *Valley* and *Free Press* about once a month. KRBI, the only local St. Peter radio station, was used for ads with the Retail Council about once a month, while KEEZ (Mankato) was used periodically on a "saturation" basis, when ads were aired at regular intervals over a week's time. Area residents typically had access to several Minneapolis-St. Paul television and radio stations, as well as the St. Peter and Mankato media.

In addition to their anniversary sale each April, the owners typically held end-of-season sales and a year-end clearance sale during which merchandise was marked down by as much as 50 percent to reduce the level of old inventory. They believed shrinkage due to shoplifting was at a minimum, since they kept careful track of items taken to and from changing booths and of shoppers as they left the store.

JJ's was open Mondays through Thursdays from 9:00 A.M. to 5:30 P.M., despite the typical closing time of 5:00 P.M. for retail businesses in St. Peter. In addition, JJ's was open until 9:00 P.M. on Fridays, and 5:00 P.M. on Saturdays. No retail clothing stores were open on Sundays in St. Peter.

The owners believed Fridays and Saturdays to be their busiest days, although sometimes Mondays were busy. Sales fluctuated by season; weather also had an effect on sales. In mild winters, for example, little fluctuation in sales was apparent, but in severely cold or snowy winters, shoppers stayed home more. The owners believed that about 50 percent of the people who entered the store were "just looking." These people were important, however, because they were likely to be future customers. If people came into the store once, the owners felt they were likely to come back. However, St. Peter was a small enough town that people would look elsewhere to find something different.

Trade Area and Composition

Although Ann and Beth did not know exactly what their trade area was, they believed it to be St. Peter, towns to the north such as Le Sueur where store selection was extremely limited, Henderson, and perhaps even as far as Belle Plaine, which was 25 miles away. They were quite sure they drew from other small towns nearby. JJ's also drew some people from Mankato, on their way to Minneapolis. The owners even had some business from people who lived in towns such as Madelia, 20 miles south of Mankato. Occasionally, they would be visited by Minneapolis residents who preferred small-town retail shopping areas because of the services offered.

Of the other women's clothing stores in St. Peter, none carried clothing especially appropriate for the young career woman. One well-established store appealed to older people who were willing to pay higher prices; another store that catered to women with children had gone out of business in January 1990. Exhibit 10.1 summarizes JJ's competition. A clothing store that was located on the river (east) side of Minnesota Avenue and catered to the college/career woman had closed its doors the previous year. With most of the town of St. Peter lying to the west of Minnesota Avenue, business located on the east side of the busy street seemed to have a harder time. Some observers believed that the recent closings were indicative of retailing trends in general and questioned the continued viability of specialty retail activity in small towns such as St. Peter.

Accounting Practices and Financial Condition

Limited financial records were maintained at the store. Essentially, these consisted of cash register tapes, a checkbook, vendor files for unpaid and paid invoices, and a spreadsheet journal form on which daily entries were made for the

EXHIBIT 10.1   Retail Competition—Women's Clothing

Store	Types	Merchandise Styles	Sizes	Customers' Ages	Quality	Prices
St. Peter						
Bonnie's[a]	Casual/ Business	Traditional	6–20 Half Sizes	30+	m	m
Bundie's	Casual/ Dressy	Traditional	6–16 Petite	25+	m-h	m
JJ's	Casual	Contemporary	6–18	18–30	m	m
Mankato						
Mankato Mall, Downtown:						
Brett's	Department Store		Various		m-h	m-h
J.C. Penney	Department Store		Various		m	m
Benneton	Casual	Trendy	3–13	13–40	h	m-h
County Seat	Casual/ Jeans/Tops	Trendy	1–16	13–24	m	m
Creeger Coat Co.	Casual/ Coats/ Dresses	Contemporary	4–20	25+	m	l-m
Dahl House[b]	Casual/ Business	Traditional	Petite to 16	13+	m-h	m-h
Ehler's	Casual/ Business	Traditional	3–24+	14–80	m-h	m
Just Girls	Sports/ Dresses	Traditional/ Trendy	Infant to 14	Moms Grandmas	h	m
Kristine	Casual/ Business/ Formal	Traditional	4–14	15+	h	h
Lancers[b]	Casual/ Business	Traditional	6–18	20–60	m	m
Lorraine Shop	Casual/ Bridal	Traditional	6–20 4–42	40–70 18–35	m-h m-h	m-h m-h
Lindberg's	Casual/ Sports	Traditional	8–20	30+	m-h	m
Maurices[b]	Casual/ Formal[c]	Traditional/ Trendy	3–14	13–60	m	m
Nina B	Casual	Trendy	3–13	17–30	m	m
Stevenson's[b]	Casual/ Formal	Contemporary	3–28	13+	m	m
Vanity	Casual	Contemporary/ Trendy	3–13	12–40	m	m
Madison East Mall, East Side of Mankato						
Sears	Department Store		Various		m	m

(Cont.)

EXHIBIT 10.1   **(Cont.)**

Store	Types	Merchandise Styles	Sizes	Customers' Ages	Quality	Prices
F.W. Woolworth	Discount Store		Various		l-m	m
Brann's	Casual	Traditional	3–16	20–30	m	m
The Closet	Casual/ Formal[c]	Traditional/ Trendy	3–14	13–25	m	m
Jean Nicole	Casual	Trendy	3–13	13–25	m	m
LaPetite	Casual/ Business/ Formal	Traditional	4–16 Petites	16–40	m	m
M.E. Robinson[d]	Casual/ Business/ Formal[c]	Traditional Contemporary	4–18	30+	h	h
Peck & Peck	Casual/ Business	Traditional	4–16	30+	m-h	m-h
Free-Standing Stores						
Kmart	Discount Store		Various		l-m	l
Lewis Eastgate	Discount Store		Various		l-m	l
Shopko	Discount Store		Various		l-m	l

Note: Merchandise is described by the types of lines carried, from casual to business to formal; unless specified, refers to a mix of dresses, skirts, slacks, tops, coats, and accessories. Styles refer to how fashionable, from traditional styles to contemporary to trendy (faddish). Women's sizes are usually given in even numbers if misses sizes; junior sizes are given in odd numbers and are usually cut for a younger figure.

[a] Closed January 1990.
[b] Also has store at Madison East Mall.
[c] Formal wear is seasonal only.
[d] Closed fall 1989.
Codes: h = high, m = medium, l = low.

operations. The spreadsheet journal was given periodically to a licensed public accounting firm, for statement compilation. The CPA firm offered no additional analysis.

The owners paid rent on a monthly basis, based on a flat fee; there was no per-square-foot charge or percent-of-sales charge. They were committed to a one-year lease. In the early years, in some months when sales were particularly low, the owners did not take a salary at all. Now, Ann took her payment on the 15th of the month, Beth on the 30th.

By 1989, the partners' initial equity investment of $10,000 had grown to more than $30,000. In addition, each of the women had been able to take a salary (withdrawal) of more than $15,000. Using 1986 and 1989 data, the partners noted that net sales improved from $83,000 in 1986 to $236,000 in 1989 and net profit had increased from $14,000 to $28,000 (Exhibits 10.2 and 10.3 contain financial statements). Both women were pleased with the 88.4 percent return on 1989 beginning equity.

Although the 1989 financial statements revealed that sales had nearly tripled and net profit had doubled since 1986, there were some troublesome areas. The gross profit ratio declined from 32.7 percent to 27.6 percent, and the net profit ratio decreased from 16.5 percent to 12.2 percent. The owners were bothered by the cash outflow for inventory purchases and for the bank loan. Another concern was collection of the accounts receivable that were being carried "off the books." (JJ's used a cash-basis for its accounting records; sales on store credit were not recorded in the formal accounting records.)

Charge customers carried directly by the store had built up a total accounts receivable balance of $3,865. The store accepted Mastercard and Visa charge cards; however, the partners allowed a considerable number of the customers that they knew well to run in-store charge accounts. Some were slow in paying these bills, yet no interest or finance/carrying charges were added to accounts not paid within a month. No accounting entries were made to record these sales as they occurred. The accountant had to make a number of adjusting entries for the 1989 year-end to properly account for the $3,865 unpaid customer purchases and for certain other accounts (refer to Exhibit 10.2). The partners had discussed the problem of collecting the in-store charge balances and reducing or eliminating such future transactions, but as yet they had not implemented a solution.

Initially, Beth and Ann had been ultraconservative in spending money. As their experience, skills, and knowledge concerning fashions grew, they were generally able to maintain what they considered to be a reasonable dollar amount in inventory for the old store. Anticipating the larger selling floor space in the new location and hopefully increased sales, the partners added $15,000 in inventory for the new store's opening. Then, starting in September 1989, the inventory was increased each month until it reached $58,649 at the end of December 1989.

The cash flow from operations was impacted by the $3,865 in-store charge balances. Cash flow from operations and working capital were affected by the increased investment in inventory from $26,309 to $58,649 (about 2.23 times) from January to December 1989. Beth and Ann had to borrow money from the bank in eight of the months during 1989 for a total of $60,756, and made payments in only three months of that year for a total of $28,256. As a consequence, JJ's ended 1989 with a bank loan balance of $32,500. Early in 1990, the bank asked for projected monthly income statements, cash flow statements, and balance sheets for 1990. The bank wanted JJ's to utilize a regular monthly payment schedule for the bank loan and to establish a credit line for future loans.

Beth and Ann had some trepidation about the financial aspects of their women's clothing store operation. However, they were determined to learn and do whatever was needed to ensure a conservative yet successful business. Their goals included maintaining continued growth, if possible, or, at the very least, achieving stability at their present level of performance—preferably at the current location.

EXHIBIT 10.2 Monthly Trend Statement and Adjustments for the 12 Months Ending December 31, 1989

	January	February	March	April	May	June
Income						
Sales	$14,824	$10,744	$13,048	$19,489	$22,829	$19,856
Taxable Sales[a]	725	559	412	1,396	1,270	772
Sales Returns/Allowances	(230)	(73)	(141)	(177)	(248)	(279)
Total Sales	15,319	11,230	13,319	20,707	23,851	10,349
Cost of Goods Sold						
Purchases	10,574	7,686	9,153	14,201	16,387	14,027
Freight	0	54	7	0	6	41
Store Supplies	104	264	205	438	58	204
Laundry/Alterations	0	0	0	45	0	6
Total COGS	10,678	8,004	9,365	14,684	16,451	14,278
Gross Profit	4,641	3,227	3,954	6,024	7,400	6,071
General Operating Expenses						
Wages	0	0	0	0	0	0
Payroll Tax Expense	0	0	0	0	0	0
Advertising	722	640	297	1,042	1,532	441
Accounting and Legal	0	0	0	0	0	0
Credit Card Charge	102	27	81	107	85	111
Contributions	10	10	20	13	10	0
Business Association Dues	0	75	0	0	0	125
Insurance	0	0	626	0	0	162
Interest	0	0	234	0	0	632
Rent	395	395	395	500	500	1,000
Utilities and Telephone	128	134	170	128	431	628
Office Supplies	27	25	0	73	26	28
Travel and Market	140	0	21	177	41	130
Repairs and Maintenance	0	11	0	25	88	0
Miscellaneous	0	0	0	56	0	0
Depreciation Expense	0	0	0	0	0	0
Amortization Expense	0	0	0	0	0	0
Total Operating Expense	1,524	1,317	1,844	2,120	2,714	3,257
Net Operating Profit	3,118	1,909	2,110	3,904	4,685	2,813
Less: Partners' Salaries						
Beth	1,568	950	900	1,690	900	2,990
Ann	900	950	4,400	900	900	1,250
Profit (Loss)	$ 650	$ 9	$(3,190)	$ 1,314	$ 2,885	$(1,427)

Notes: Repairs and maintenance adjustment writes off incorrect charge to store furniture and fixtures. Contributions adjustment reflects clothing donated to charitable organizations. Taxable sales adjustment represents error in calculating unremitted sales tax.

[a] In Minnesota, necessary clothing is not taxed; however, most accessories are.

July	August	September	October	November	December	Adjustments	Year to Date
$29,211	$15,724	$17,717	$16,224	$16,126	$29,254	$ 3,865	$228,910
872	920	1,039	988	660	1,674	(14)	11,272
(283)	(146)	(177)	(106)	(40)	(519)	(1,228)	(3,647)
29,800	16,498	18,579	17,106	16,745	30,049	2,624	236,536
20,456	11,318	12,754	11,093	11,414	21,031	7,181	167,275
13	2	29	22	18	34	–	227
348	427	169	200	546	546	–	3,535
58	0	0	0	0	0	–	109
20,875	11,747	12,979	11,315	11,978	21,611	7,181	171,146
8,925	4,751	5,600	5,791	4,767	8,797	(4,557)	65,390
248	283	334	324	74	144	–	1,407
0	0	0	65	0	0	52	117
322	1,130	994	677	761	1,356	–	9,914
0	0	150	0	150	0	–	300
129	112	96	89	117	212	–	1,270
5	20	52	40	0	0	348	528
100	0	0	0	0	125	–	425
0	0	386	0	0	0	–	1,174
0	0	440	0	0	0	244	1,550
0	500	500	500	500	500	–	5,685
324	465	651	519	440	410	311	4,740
203	82	31	80	50	201	–	826
71	100	45	254	0	0	–	979
0	0	0	0	11	45	1	180
0	55	0	0	0	0	–	111
0	0	0	0	0	0	6,956	6,956
0	0	0	0	0	0	400	400
1,402	2,747	3,680	2,549	2,103	2,992	8,312	36,562
7,523	2,004	1,920	3,242	2,664	5,805	(12,870)	28,828
175	1,150	1,740	1,000	1,000	1,200	–	15,263
1,125	1,150	950	1,000	1,000	1,200	–	15,725
$ 6,223	$ (296)	$ (770)	$ 1,242	$ 664	$ 3,405	$(12,870)	$ (2,160)

EXHIBIT 10.3   JJ's Women's Clothing Store Condensed Income, Cash Flow, and Balance Sheet Statements

1989 Monthly Actual	January	February	March	April	May
Income Statement					
Net Sales	$15,319	$11,230	$13,319	$20,707	$23,851
Cost of Sales	10,678	8,004	9,365	15,684	16,451
Gross Profit	4,641	3,226	3,954	6,023	7,400
Expenses					
Advertising	722	640	297	1,042	1,532
Rent	395	395	395	500	500
Depreciation	0	0	0	0	0
Amortization	0	0	0	0	0
All Other	406	282	1,152	577	683
Total Expenses	1,523	1,317	1,844	2,119	2,715
Net Profit	$ 3,118	$ 1,909	$ 2,110	$ 3,904	$ 4,685
Cash Flow Statement					
Plus Noncash					
Depreciation Expense	$ 0	$ 0	$ 0	$ 0	$ 0
Amortization Expense	0	0	0	0	0
Cash from Operations	3,118	1,909	2,110	3,904	4,685
CA (Increase) Decrease	(3,029)	(8,155)	(6,776)	(5,237)	1,677
CA (Decrease) Increase	(115)	33	25	(18)	76
Cash Operations and Working Capital	(26)	(6,213)	(4,641)	(1,351)	6,438
Increase in Bank Loan	7,000	0	10,250	2,500	750
Total Cash In	6,974	(6,213)	5,609	1,149	7,188
Uses-Cash Out					
Store Equipment	0	306	492	841	1,162
On Bank Loan	0	0	0	0	0
Salary, Beth	1,568	950	900	1,690	900
Salary, Ann	900	950	4,400	900	900
Total Uses	2,468	2,206	5,792	3,431	2,962
Net Cash (Negative)	4,506	(8,419)	(183)	(2,282)	5,226
Beginning Cash	$ 6,070	$10,576	$ 2,157	$ 1,974	$ (308)
Balance Sheet					
Assets					
Ending Cash	$10,576	$ 2,157	$ 1,974	$ (308)	$ 3,918
Noncash CA	26,309	34,464	41,240	46,477	44,800
Fixed Assets	10,157	10,463	10,955	11,796	12,958
(−) Depreciation/Amortization	(6,636)	(6,636)	(6,636)	(6,636)	(6,636)
Total Assets	$40,406	$40,448	$47,533	$51,329	$55,040
Current Liabilities	$ 161	$ 194	$ 219	$ 201	$ 277
Note Payable	7,000	7,000	17,250	19,750	20,500
Equity-Beth (+NP)	16,215	16,220	16,375	16,637	18,079
Equity-Ann (−Sal)	17,030	17,035	13,690	14,742	16,184
Total Liability and Equity	$40,406	$40,448	$47,533	$51,329	$55,040

Notes: Underlying spreadsheet calculations and rounding to nearest dollar causes some minor errors in some totals. December 1989 net income data reflect year-end adjusting entries made by the accountant.

	June	July	August	September	October	November	December	1989 12 Months
	$20,349	$29,800	$16,498	$18,579	$17,106	$16,745	$33,033	$236,536
	14,278	20,875	11,747	12,979	11,315	11,978	28,792	171,146
	6,071	8,925	4,751	5,600	5,791	4,767	4,241	65,390
	441	322	1,130	994	677	761	1,356	9,914
	1,000		500	500	500	500	500	5,685
	0	0	0	0	0	0	6,956	6,956
	0	0	0	0	0	0	400	400
	1,817	1,080	1,117	2,196	1,372	842	2,093	13,607
	3,258	1,402	2,747	3,680	2,549	2,103	11,305	36,562
	$ 2,813	$ 7,523	$ 2,004	$ 1,920	$ 3,242	$ 2,664	$ 292	$ 36,184
	$ 0	$ 0	$ 0	$ 0	$ 0	$ 0	$ 6,956	$ 6,956
	0	0	0	0	0	0	400	400
	2,813	7,523	2,004	1,920	3,242	2,664	292	36,184
	4,130	12,485	(9,793)	(10,191)	(10,132)	(6,193)	5,845	(35,369)
	46	(160)	76	88	(145)	46	488	440
	6,989	19,848	(7,713)	(8,183)	(7,035)	(3,483)	6,625	1,255
	0	0	8,000	7,500	7,900	16,856	0	60,756
	6,989	19,848	287	(683)	865	13,373	6,625	62,011
	1,284	300	666	517	0	0	370	5,938
	2,000	14,000	0	0	0	0	12,256	28,256
	2,990	175	1,150	950	1,000	1,000	1,200	15,725
	1,250	1,125	1,150	950	1,000	1,000	1,200	15,725
	7,524	15,600	2,966	3,207	2,000	2,000	15,026	65,182
	(535)	4,248	(2,679)	(3,890)	(1,135)	(11,373)	(8,401)	(3,171)
	$ 3,918	$ 3,383	$ 7,361	$ 4,952	$ 1,062	$ (73)	$11,300	$ 6,070
	$ 3,383	$ 7,631	$ 4,952	$ 1,062	$ (73)	$11,300	$ 2,899	$ 6,070
	40,670	28,185	37,978	48,169	58,301	64,494	58,649	58,649
	14,242	15,208	15,725	15,725	15,725	15,725	16,095	16,095
	(6,636)	(6,636)	(6,636)	(6,636)	(6,636)	(6,636)	(13,992)	(13,992)
	$51,659	$43,722	$51,502	$58,320	$67,317	$84,883	$63,651	$63,651
	$ 323	$ 163	$ 239	$ 327	$ 182	$ 228	$ 716	$ 716
	18,500	4,500	12,500	20,000	27,900	44,756	32,500	32,500
	16,496	20,082	19,934	19,514	19,775	20,107	15,375	15,375
	16,341	18,977	18,829	18,839	19,460	19,792	15,060	15,060
	$51,659	$43,722	$51,502	$58,320	$67,317	$84,883	$63,651	$63,651

ST. PETER

St. Peter, Minnesota, a city of approximately 9,200 residents, was located on the Minnesota River 65 miles southwest of Minneapolis-St. Paul, and 12 miles northeast of Mankato. The city enjoyed some recognition in the state, since it was one of the oldest cities in Minnesota, founded in 1853, and had 13 sites on the National Registry. St. Peter had produced five governors, and may itself have been the state capital, had the bill declaring it as such not been stolen while awaiting the governor's signature.

Minnesota Avenue (U.S. Highway 169), running the length of the city, was lined with most of St. Peter's retail trade. The central business district could be defined as an area approximately one and one-half blocks on either side of Minnesota Avenue from Walnut Street to midway between Broadway Avenue and Chestnut Street (see Exhibit 10.4). Industries in St. Peter were varied, ranging from a regional treatment center with extensive mental health facilities, education, and electronics, each employing several hundred persons, to a woolen mill and a small organ factory employing eight persons. St. Peter was also the home of Gustavus Adolphus College, a private, four-year, liberal arts school with a sound reputation. Since tuition at Gustavus Adolphus was higher than Minnesota state schools and several other regional private schools, students were likely to be from relatively wealthy families or were likely to work to partially support their college educations. A St. Peter community profile prepared in 1987 is included in Exhibit 10.5.

The partners recognized that St. Peter was growing—but more slowly than estimated in the profile. In 1984, the population count was 9,049; in 1987, 9,144; and in 1988, 9,257. The population increase had been averaging about 1 percent per year, with 1989 and 1990 not expected to change much from that rate. Counter to the population growth had been the decline in retail establishments. According to a November 9, 1989, *St. Peter Herald* article, "In 1982, there were 84 retail establishments. By 1987, that had dropped to 67, [a decrease of] over 20 percent. During the same period, total sales had risen from $42,105,000 to $45,764,000." Other data available from a May 1990 article in the *Herald* indicated that the total number of Nicollet County unemployed workers rose from 438 in October 1989 to 607 in March 1990; the March unemployment rate statewide matched the national rate of 5.4 percent.

Discussions of downtown renovation had been going on for several years. At city meetings, residents and community leaders expressed overwhelming support for keeping retail and entertainment activities downtown, rather than on some outlying acreage yet to be determined. Of the factors considered in developing a retail area, those most important to the residents included retaining downtown retailing, stopping shopping center competition, and improving the retail mix. The Retail Council, a committee of the St. Peter Chamber of Commerce, had undertaken numerous planned activities to encourage and support St. Peter's retail establishments. The retailers believed consumers in the region were quite typical, though sometimes they seemed more prone to bargain hunting.

EXHIBIT 10.4   Map of St. Peter, Minnesota

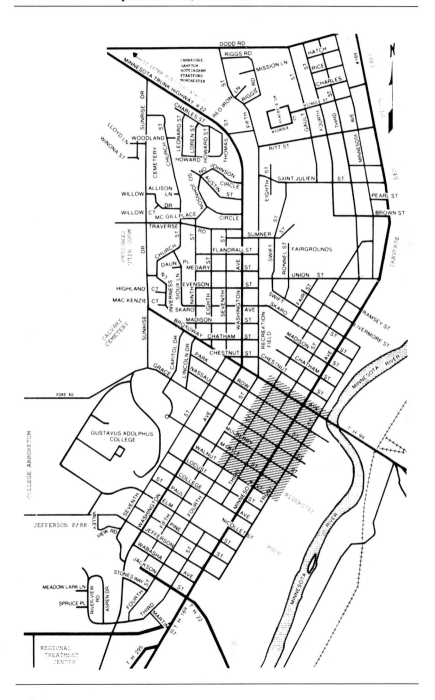

EXHIBIT 10.5   St. Peter Community Profile

Population	1960	1970	1980	1985
St. Peter	8,484	8,339	9.056	9.082
Nicollet County	23,196	24,518	26,920	28,190

Industry	Number of Employees
Health Care	1,025
Education	630
Electronics	245
Total Manufacturing	2,900
Total Nonmanufacturing	4,960 (Mostly Farming)
Total Labor Force	13,601 (County)
Unemployment	4.2% Annual Average

Transportation

Rail: 2 lines daily, no passenger service
Truck Lines: 4
Bus: 1 intercity line
Air: 1 airport; nearest commercial airport: Mankato
Highways: 35 miles to I35; 60 miles to I90
    federal: #169 through city; state: #99, 22, 295, 333

Community Services

Motels: 3 units, 50 rooms
Hospital Beds: 46; Nursing Home Beds: 150
Doctors: 10; Dentists: 8
Churches: 12
Banks: 2; Deposits; $120 million
Sports: College
News Media: Newspaper, 1 weekly; Radio Stations, 2 AM, 2 FM
Television: 0
Retail Sales: County, $70.9 million (1985)
    St. Peter, $41.9 million (1985)
Per Capita Income: County $11,123 (1984)

Education	Number	Enrollment	Grades
Elementary Schools	2	860	K–6
Senior High Schools	1	805	7–12
Parochial Schools	1	141	K–6
Colleges	1	2,230 (1,252 women)	Gustavus Adolphus

Source: *Minnesota Department of Energy and Economic Development, 1987,* St. Paul, Minn.

Much of the concern that retailers and residents had for downtown improvement stemmed from growing recognition of the impact of competing market areas. A St. Peter resident could drive to Minneapolis in just over an hour. Large malls built in the south and east suburbs of Minneapolis enticed shoppers from outlying areas. In addition, St. Peter shoppers were attracted to Mankato, which, together with North Mankato, offered many nationally known chain stores, services, and recreational opportunities (refer to Exhibit 10.1). Although the population of Mankato and North Mankato was around 50,000 people, several educational institutions added to this population base: Mankato State University, Bethany Lutheran College, Mankato Technical College, and Rasmussen Business College. Many of the students, particularly those attending Mankato State University, lived in the twin cities of Minneapolis-St. Paul and suburbs and commuted there to work on the weekends.

BACKGROUND FOR THE PROPOSED MALL

Concern about the future of St. Peter's business climate led to the formation in 1985 of St. Peter Revitalization, Inc. (SPRI), a group composed of representatives from several sectors in the community. After raising over $50,000 from private sources, SPRI hired a consulting firm to conduct a feasibility study and to make recommendations for a mall. The consulting firm began the marketing study with an intensive data collection process. The original consulting firm then hired another specialty firm to conduct a separate analysis of the downtown retail market. All of these studies were completed in May 1987. The studies concluded that a shopping mall and redevelopment for downtown St. Peter were endorsed by retailers, other community groups, and individuals.

SPRI then went in search of a developer and found the Small Town New Mall Development Company, which had built several malls in towns approximately the size of St. Peter. The City Council accepted SPRI's recommendation to hire Small Town; the council subsequently visited three cities within the region where Small Town had built malls.

The most successful of these three Small Town malls had opened about four or five years earlier and contained approximately 50 businesses. After the initial leases expired, about 60 percent of the spaces were occupied. This particular mall experienced difficulty in attracting anchor stores and long-term lessees. Franchise units of three different national chain stores, one branch unit of a national chain store, and a local hairstyling salon had been the only tenants to remain throughout the entire period of the mall's operation. During the 1989 Christmas season, the mall tried attracting long-term tenants by renting stores on a one-, two-, or three-month basis. This strategy was not successful, as none of the short-term renters signed over to long-term leases. In March 1990, the mall was sold to a local owner for $1.1 million; its original cost was over $6 million. The newest of the three Small Town malls, located in a town about 30 miles west of St. Peter, opened in October 1989. The 75,000-square-foot retail center contained 23 business spaces; 19 were rented at the time of the opening. At its peak, it was expected that the mall would provide employment for about 200 people.

THE PROPOSED MALL

The St. Peter mall was planned to encompass at least one full block in the central business district (on both the north and south sides of that block), plus another half-block was expected to be included (see Exhibit 10.6). The full block currently included a discount food store, a small car lot, and a large vacant lot. The half-block to the north included two buildings: an empty building on the corner and the building that currently housed JJ's. The retailers to the north and in the same block as JJ's included a men's clothing store, a women's clothing store, a florist, and an office housing an insurance company and a travel business. All of these tenants were in buildings owned by the same landlord, who declined to sell the buildings or pay the mall access fee. Consequently, JJ's would be the north-ernmost store in the mall and the only presently existing clothing store to be included. The half-block on the south side contained a gas station and a food store.

The completed mall was planned to house approximately 20 businesses, including a two-screen theater and a restaurant. Although the developer was hoping to attract national and regional chain stores, none had yet committed to leasing space. The developer had also tried to attract a large regional food store as the anchor. After lengthy negotiations, the store did not sign a lease.

Partly owing to the length of time the St. Peter mall project had been "studied," businesspeople and citizens alike wondered about its eventual con-struction. In February 1990, the city administrator commented, "Rumors that the [mall] project is derailed are false." In a presentation to SPRI, he pointed out, "This is an SPRI project. The shopping center is only about one-half of the project. The other half of the $7.2 million is for public improvements that the downtown area would need with, or without, a shopping center." Other city officials, in the same SPRI briefing, noted that the first batch of appraisals should be completed by March 1, site plans were to be in by June 30, and vacating of properties was to begin in July. As of April, however, Small Town had apparently completed its appraisals but had not been able to secure adequate financing from banking or other lending institutions. As a consequence, no one really knew at that time whether construction would actually begin in September, or later, or even anytime in the future.

OTHER NEARBY MALLS

In Mankato, approximately 12 miles southwest of St. Peter, the General Growth Companies from Des Moines was developing a regional mall planned to encompass about 740,000 square feet. This was supposed to include space for 130 retail tenants with five anchor stores. In addition, plans included a multiscreen movie theater and a food court seating 550 customers to be serviced by a dozen food tenants.

EXHIBIT 10.6   St. Peter Downtown and Proposed Mall

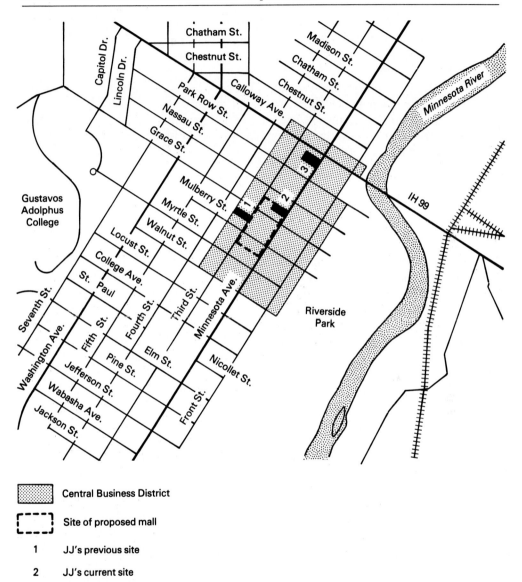

Central Business District

Site of proposed mall

1   JJ's previous site

2   JJ's current site

3   Alternative site

Within a half-mile of that regional mall, a Wal-Mart store, with 110,000 square feet, was scheduled to be constructed for an October 1990 opening. A strip-type shopping center adjacent to Wal-Mart was also planned. Close to both of the above Mankato malls, JoAnn Fabrics was planning to construct a 10,000-square-foot superstore. The fabric store was expected to be open in late May or early June 1990.

Mankato already had two malls in operation—one on the east side and one in the downtown area. There had been much discussion, if not controversy, among city officials, businesspeople, and other interested parties in Mankato about the need for both the existing and proposed Mankato malls to service that market area.

JJ'S CHOICES

Beth and Ann, like many others in St. Peter, were very uncertain about the actions that should be taken, especially because the space that they rented for their store was in one of the buildings likely to be included in the new mall. The grapevine news was that the rear 41 feet would be chopped off their building plus the building immediately adjacent to the south for mall excess. Both buildings would then be converted into a restaurant with access from both the mall and Minnesota Avenue. The landlords would bear the cost of enclosing the buildings at the rear and any interior renovations or remodeling plus an estimated cost, again according to the grapevine, of $20,000 for mall access.

The loss of the 861 square feet (41' x 21') of floor space for mall access would eliminate the present store operation's work and storage areas (see Exhibit 10.7). This could be offset by using the basement; however, major clean-up and renovation of the basement, at additional cost to the landlord, would be necessary. The only use presently made of the basement was to house the restroom. The mall access construction, if the basement was to be used, would require the landlord to expend funds to relocate the furnace, thoroughly clean and seal the walls, and build adequate shelving, racks, and office work space.

JJ's partners had not heard from their landlord—he was still "wintering" in Florida. They believed, however, that there was a 50–50 chance that he would prefer to keep their women's clothing store rather than change to the restaurant tenant, even if he accepted the mall access construction. They also expected, if the store remained at its present location but with the mall access, that the rent would increase dramatically, even though the store operation would lose 861 square feet of space. Beth and Ann estimated the store's new rent would be double the 1990 figure.

"If the mall is finally built and we're unable to arrange a satisfactory new lease for this location, the alternatives for our store are not very appealing, Ann. Remember the vacant store two blocks north of here that we looked at before moving here?" questioned Beth.

EXHIBIT 10.7   JJ's Women's Clothing Store Layout

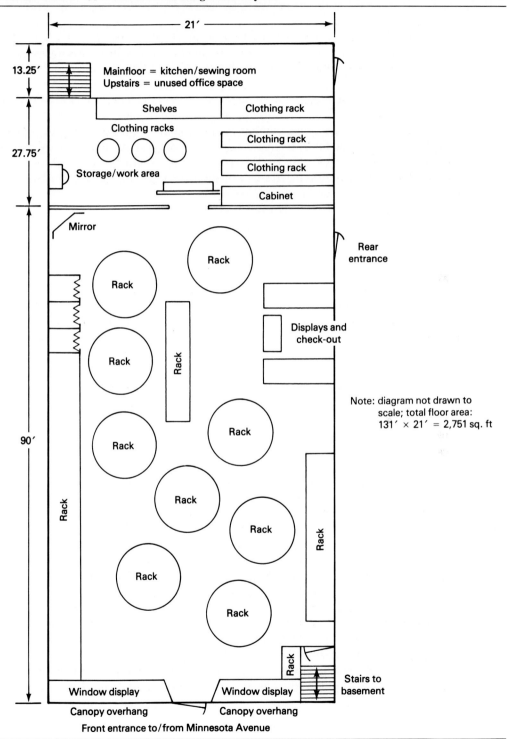

21′

13.25′

Mainfloor = kitchen/sewing room
Upstairs = unused office space

Shelves   Clothing rack

Clothing racks

Clothing rack

27.75′

Clothing rack

Storage/work area

Cabinet

Mirror

Rack

Rack

Rear
entrance

Rack

Rack

Rack

Displays and
check-out

Note: diagram not drawn to
scale; total floor area:
131′ × 21′ = 2,751 sq. ft

90′

Rack

Rack

Rack

Rack

Rack

Rack

Rack

Rack

Rack

Window display   Window display

Canopy overhang   Canopy overhang

Front entrance to/from Minnesota Avenue

Stairs to
basement

"Yes, I do. That store is still the only vacant store available on this side of the street, and it's about the same size as this store. But being even one block away from the clothing store area in this town could be too much," Ann cautioned.

Near to that location were an electronics store, a hardware and appliance store, a laundromat, a cable TV office, an insurance/finance office, a savings and loan institution, and a dry cleaning establishment. The partners had serious doubts about putting their store in a location not surrounded by compatible clothing retailers. Their recent experiences with the Third Street and Minnesota Avenue locations had convinced them of the marketing appeal that clustering of clothing retailers had for the female customer.

"And getting that store ready for our use would mean spending $6,000 to $8,000 for clean-up, carpeting, lighting, dressing rooms, painting and other repairs, to say nothing of spending $800 to $1,000 for rent," Ann continued.

"If all else fails, we could have a 'going-out-of-business' sale just before they chop off the back of this store!" Beth remarked, with a half-laugh.

"I suppose we do need to think about that, Beth, but I really hope it doesn't come to that," Ann replied.

Although quitting business was an alternative to be considered, it was not a desirable one for either of the owners. They had enjoyed the hard work and success that the store operation had achieved. And they found satisfaction in being two independent individuals who had been able to combine their skills and knowledge into a thriving, viable business.

──────────────────────── CASE 11 ────────────────────────

Kraft

Some of America's best-known brand names in food products were produced by Kraft. These included Kraft, Velveeta, Parkay, Miracle Whip, Philadelphia, Cracker Barrel, Sealtest, Light n' Lively, Breyers, and Breakstone's. The company's products were sold to stores and restaurants in 130 countries by

This case was prepared by Charles W. Boyd as a basis for class discussion rather than to illustrate either effective or ineffective handling of an administrative situation. Copyright © 1987 by Charles W. Boyd. Used with permission from Charles W. Boyd.

over 5,000 salespeople. Kraft ranked second only to General Foods in the food-processing industry. The company was truly an industry giant that grew from very humble beginnings.

Even as Kraft changed, so had the food-processing industry. In the 1980s, Kraft and its competitors realized that the recent and projected slow population growth in the United States meant that most future gains in market share must come at the expense of one another. As a result, the industry was being restructured through mergers and acquisitions as the major firms sought to strengthen their competitive positions. In order to remain at the top of the industry, Kraft's top managers had to make correct strategic decisions regarding the company's product mix and the manner in which to structure the organization in order to best compete in the changing environment.

HISTORY OF THE COMPANY

James L. Kraft came to Chicago from Canada in 1903 and began wholesaling cheese from a rented, horse-drawn wagon. His four brothers—Fred, Charles, Norman, and John—joined the prospering business. By 1914, they were selling 31 varieties of cheese under the brand names Kraft and Elkhorn.

Kraft merged with a rival company, Phenix Cheese, in 1928. Kraft-Phenix accounted for 40 percent of U.S. cheese production and also had operations in Canada, Australia, Great Britain, and Germany. The company was acquired in 1930 by National Dairy. The new company ranked as one of the largest in the United States, with annual sales of $375 million. For the next four decades, Kraft functioned as a separate entity in Chicago, while National Dairy functioned primarily as a holding company from its headquarters in New York City.

James L. Kraft died in 1953 at age 78. In 1969, the National Dairy Company name was changed to Kraftco, and in 1972 the corporate headquarters was moved from New York City to the Chicago suburb of Glenview. In 1976, the company name was changed to Kraft, Incorporated.

Kraft merged with Dart Industries in 1980 to form Dart & Kraft, Incorporated. Dart Industries had gone through significant restructuring of its business units during the few years preceding the merger with Kraft. In 1985, Dart & Kraft operated in four major business segments, as seen in Exhibit 11.1. Results for 1985 were marked by strong growth for Kraft, Hobart commercial equipment, and the Wilsonart decorative laminate businesses. Success in these segments offset profit declines at Tupperware, Duracell, West Bend, and KitchenAid. Dart & Kraft ranked 34th among the 1985 *Fortune* 500 with annual sales of $9.9 billion and net income of $446 million.

Dart & Kraft acquired nine businesses at a cost of $300 million during 1985. These included Frusen Gladje superpremium ice cream; Invernizzi S.P.A., an Italian cheese company; and the Westman Commission Company, a full-line foodservice distributor. Top management expected these and the other 1985 acquisitions to be compatible with their strategy of maintaining a mix of high-quality, primarily consumer-oriented businesses. John Richman, chairman and

EXHIBIT 11.1   Dart & Kraft, 1985

Business Segments	Strategic Business Units
Food Products	Kraft
Direct Selling	Tupperware (plastic storage, preparation, and serving ware for food)
Consumer Products	Duracell (batteries)
	Kitchen Aid (home appliances)
	West Bend (small appliances and physical fitness equipment)
	Health care businesses
Commercial Products	Hobart (food service cooking equipment, cookware washers, refrigeration products, and supermarket weighing and wrapping equipment)
	Wilsonart (decorative laminates and disposable plastic and rubber items)

chief executive officer, stated in the company's 1985 annual report that such acquisitions were likely to continue in 1986. In early 1986, the company signed an agreement to acquire Vulcan-Hart Corporation, a leading producer of gas cooking equipment, which was expected to add further competitive strength to Dart & Kraft's food equipment business.

Dart & Kraft took actions directed toward divesting most of the company's small health care operations, and on January 31, 1986, the sale of KitchenAid to Whirlpool Corporation was consummated. Mr. Richman stated in his annual letter to the stockholders that this sale was opportunistic, rather than the result of strategic reappraisal. The sale resulted in an after-tax gain of $41 million to be recorded in the first quarter of 1986.[1]

Dart & Kraft's strategy in early 1986 was summarized by Chairman Richman and President Warren L. Batts as follows:

> As to the longer term, our strategy will not be dramatically different. Contrary to the current industry trend, we continue to believe that there are benefits to be derived from our particular type of controlled and related diversification. For example, our ability to balance the cash-generating capacity of our retail food business and Tupperware with higher-growth, cash-using businesses like Duracell is an important benefit.[2]

OPERATIONS AT KRAFT

Michael A. Miles was president and chief operating officer of Kraft in 1985. Kraft's mission statement from that year is presented in Exhibit 11.2. Mr. Miles had publicly identified five strengths and three weaknesses of Kraft. The five strengths and supporting reasons for them were as follows:

1. Huge mass and resources—Kraft was one of the four largest food businesses in the world, and second only to General Foods in the United States.

[1] Dart & Kraft, 1985 *Annual Report,* p. 31.
[2] Ibid., p. 4.

EXHIBIT 11.2 Kraft Mission Statement

Mission Summary

Kraft's mission is to become the leading food company in the world, based on achieving superiority versus competition in a balance of these factors:

- Outstanding overall quality of people, products, and business plans.
- Return on management investment (ROMI).
- Rate of growth in unit sales and operating income.
- Innovation.

Customers

Kraft's businesses will be built on the fundamental concept of achieving superiority versus competition in:

- Identifying the wants and needs of customers, both end-customers and trade.
- Providing high-quality products and/or services to meet those needs in unique or advantageous ways.
- Marketing those products/services to reinforce their appeal and achieve superior acceptance.

Industries/Markets—Channels

Kraft will compete in any segment of the food business, in any geographic market, and in any channel of distribution, where:

- Participation can make a material long-term contribution to sales and income, while generating returns at or above corporate targets.
- The combination of product quality, management quality, and innovation provides us with a sustainable competitive advantage—or the prospect of same in a reasonable time.

Competition

Kraft has mass resources that enable it to compete with any company in the world, and will utilize these resources to the fullest legal, ethical, and moral extent.

Kraft will engage any competitor in any geographical market, category, or channel of distribution of interest, where the combination of product quality, management quality, and innovation provides us with a sustainable competitive advantage.

Kraft will defend its established businesses ferociously.

People/Organization

Kraft recognizes that the quality of its people is the critical element in achieving the success of its mission.

Kraft's human resource policies and practices will be built on a standard of excellence and a total commitment to equal opportunity and fair treatment.

Kraft will promote based on merit and from within wherever possible.

Business Style

Kraft's business style will be characterized by:

- Overreaching commitment to quality
- Openness, honesty
- Initiative
- Innovation
- Aggressiveness
- Action orientation
- Competitiveness
- Efficiency
- Risk acceptance
- Superior analysis and planning
- A standard of excellence in people

What we say we do, we *do* do.

James L. Kraft

2. Growth markets and growth categories—from 1979 to 1983, per capita consumption of cheese in the United States increased 23 percent, pourable dressings 14 percent, and premium ice cream 18 percent.

3. Extremely strong brand names and market share positions—Kraft was either the leader or a strong contender in virtually all of the major categories in which it competed.

4. Excellent customer relations—research indicated Kraft had the best reputation for quality in the food industry and that only Procter & Gamble compared with Kraft in sales-force skill and effectiveness.

5. Worldwide infrastructure—the human and financial resources were in place to support new business initiatives anywhere in the world.

Mr. Miles also reported the following weaknesses:

1. No recent track record of success in developing significant new products
2. Too conservative; need more challenges
3. Increasing competition

In addition, Mr. Miles outlined five broad strategies Kraft was currently pursuing:

1. To protect and build the existing businesses:—for branded products increased spending on advertising, competitive pricing, and more emphasis on advertisable product improvement:—for commodity products being the lowest-cost producer.

2. To gradually weight the business mix toward branded, value-added products and away from commodities.

3. To augment the growth of existing branded positions by a more active new business development effort.

4. To continue to pursue expense and asset minimization in all areas.

5. To increase organizational vitality.[3]

President Miles believed that these strategies would best capitalize on Kraft's major strength—a quality reputation in producing and promoting branded food products. As these branded products were expanded, the company planned to continue the retreat from fluid milk and certain private-label items, and from its bulk cheese and edible-oil businesses in Europe.

The fifth strategy—increasing organizational vitality—involved many actions that included increasing employee communications, eliminating some excess layers of middle management, and a large-scale test of doubling the size of the U.S. retail sales force. The intent of these actions was to increase the sense of urgency and the timeliness of decision making. Some employees in Kraft's Retail Food Group dubbed this the M/B/F program, meaning more/better/faster.

---

[3] Warren L. Batts, president and chief operating officer, Dart & Kraft, presentation to the Consumer Analyst Group of New York, St. Petersburg, Florida, February 21, 1984.

KRAFT PRODUCT LINES

The key performers during 1985–1986 were the Retail Food, Food Service, and Dairy Groups. These and Kraft's other operating units and their principal products are identified in Exhibit 11.3.

Refrigerated Product's Division.   Kraft began the national distribution of Light Philadelphia Brand process cream cheese, another of several new products aimed at calorie-conscious consumers. The expansion of this product continued during 1986.

Grocery Products Division.   Kraft experienced success with reduced-calorie versions of Miracle Whip Salad Dressing and Kraft Real Mayonnaise. Both products became the leading share brands in their categories. Velveeta Shells and Cheese Packaged Dinner, introduced in 1984, also experienced significant sales increases. Presto, a new Italian salad dressing, was introduced nationally in 1985. Even as volume declined, profitability on Parkay Margarine increased due to lower edible-oil costs.

Venture Division.   This division completed two acquisitions during 1984—Lender's Bagel Bakery and Celestial Seasonings. Both did well in 1985. The bagel business was geographically expanded beyond the Northeast during the year, necessitating the building of additional capacity that was completed in 1986. Profit declined slightly in the Celestial Seasonings herb tea business because of costs incurred in creating new marketing programs and strengthening channels of dis-

EXHIBIT 11.3   Key Performers, 1985–1986

Group and Division	*Principal Products*
Retail Food Groups	
Refrigerated Products Division	Process, natural, and cream cheese
Grocery Products Division	Salad dressings, mayonnaise, dry packaged dinners, and barbecue sauce
Venture Division	Bagels and herb teas
International Group	
Primary Operations in Canada, West Germany, Italy, Australia, the Philippines, Latin America, and Mexico	Wide variety of products representing all Kraft divisions
Dairy Group	Ice cream, ice milk, lowfat yogurt, cottage cheese, and sour cream
Food Service Group	Distributes products from the retail food group to restaurants
Industrial Foods Group	Supplies food manufacturers with edible oils and edible-oil-based products, cheese items, snack seasonings, imitation cheese, flavorings, confections, dairy and nondairy proteins, and other ingredients

tribution. In addition, four new tea flavors were added in 1985—Lemon Zinger, Raspberry Patch, Island Orange, and Cranberry Cove.

The venture division entered an agreement with DNA Plant Technology for the development and marketing of Vegisnax raw vegetables bred for superior taste and texture. The division also entered an agreement in 1986 with San Francisco French Bread Company to market a line of sourdough products.

Foodservice Group.   This group attempted to capitalize on the almost 50 percent of the U.S. food dollar that is spent on meals away from home. The group accounted for 13 percent of Kraft's total sales, and experienced a 12 percent growth of tonnage sales during 1985. Many products, such as the familiar individual-serving packets of Kraft's jams and jellies, were distributed by the Foodservice Group. The group engaged in extensive research and development activity. Because the company manufactured nearly 50 percent of what the Foodservice Group sold, profit was captured from both production and distribution. This group also added value to Retail Food Group acquisitions by broadening distribution of products such as Lender's Bagels and Celestial Seasonings herb teas.

Two acquisitions were completed by the Foodservice Group in 1985—the Westman Commission Company, a full-line distributor serving seven Rocky Mountain states, and Seaboard Foods, a broadline distributor in North Carolina. Letters of intent were signed in 1986 to acquire distribution businesses in Kansas City, Chicago, Phoenix, and the New York areas.

The Foodservice Group developed innovations to add efficiency in 1985. A portable entry terminal for sales representatives shortened order processing time and supported next-day delivery service. A computerized restaurant management system called Kraft Link connected customers with the nearest Kraft food service location and assisted them with menu, food-cost and sales analysis, as well as order entry and inventory control. This system also provided customers with automatic price updating, on-line order verification, and other helpful services.

Dairy Group.   This group accounted for 9 percent of total company sales. With an overall 10 percent sales increase, the group experienced market share and profit gains in almost every product line in 1985.

The group's excellent year in ice cream was enhanced by the acquisition of Frusen Gladje, a superpremium ice cream line. This line's sales tripled following the acquisition as a result of a quick move to expand its sales territory and the creation of new television and print advertising.

Kraft's all-natural premium ice cream line, Breyers, expanded into nine western states in 1985. Sealtest ice cream celebrated its 50th anniversary with a 16 percent volume increase, aided by its new Cubic Scoops flavors. Double-digit sales gains were also registered by Polar B'ar ice cream squares and Light n' Lively ice milk. Sales increases were also achieved by Light n' Lively lowfat yogurt, Breakstone's, Sealtest, and Light n' Lively lowfat cottage cheese; and Breakstone's and Sealtest sour cream.

The only Dairy Group product to show a sales decline during 1985 was Breyers yogurt. This product was improved in late summer by adding larger chunks of fruit and more graphically appealing packaging.

International Group.   This group, which accounted for 24 percent of company sales, reported lower 1985 profits. This was primarily due to poor results in West Germany, Kraft's largest European market. Other European operations did well, especially Kraft S.P.A. in Italy, where the company acquired a major interest in Invernizzi S.P.A., a Milan-based producer and distributor of natural cheeses.

Kraft Australia acquired the Everest Group, a small, regional producer of pasta, ice cream, and frozen dinners. This acquisition was designed as a base from which Kraft could diversify from its dependence on cheese in the Australian market.

Anticipating that the poor economic conditions in Venezuela were going to persist, Kraft was in the process of introducing a new line of lower-cost products there. The company sold the small business interest it had in Brazil.

Industrial Foods Group.   This group accounted for 7 percent of Kraft's sales. Price declines in the edible-oil market during 1985 caused a significant decrease in group profits even though sales volume increased. The industrial ingredients business, however, achieved higher sales and profits.

Two important actions were taken in the Industrial Foods Group during 1985. The industrial emulsifier business was sold because it was not achieving satisfactory return, and the decision was made to phase out the California oil-refining operations by September 1986. This latter action was designed to remove Kraft from the low-return bulk oils market. The company planned to continue supplying the West Coast with higher-margin speciality oil products from its two refineries located in Tennessee and Illinois.

All of these activities in Kraft's five groups were designed to move the company toward the major goal expressed in its mission statement to become the leading food company in the world. As Kraft's top management directed efforts toward this goal, the U.S. food industry was changing. The dairy industry in which Kraft competed had witnessed changes in consumer preferences and consumption patterns during recent years. In addition, the larger food processing industry of which Kraft was a part was undergoing major restructuring.

THE U.S. DAIRY INDUSTRY

Three significant developments affected the dairy industry in 1985:

1. Cheese made a major comeback after three low-growth years.
2. The dairy farmers' advertising and promotional campaign completed its first year of operation.

3. Concern within the dairy industry intensified as Congress debated the dairy provisions of the 1985 farm bill.[4]

Four firms that operated in several segments of the dairy industry accounted for 18.3 percent of total 1985 sales, down 1 percent from 1984: Dart & Kraft, 6.8 percent; Beatrice, 4.6 percent; Borden, 3.7 percent; and Nestle, 3.2 percent.

Fluid Milk

Per capita consumption of two major fluid items—whole milk and cottage cheese—declined consistently during recent years. Many consumers perceived that lowfat and skim milk are more healthful than whole milk. Lowfat and skim milk were also less expensive than whole milk. As a result, milk consumption patterns have changed. From 1980 to 1984, consumption of whole milk declined 3.4 percent annually, and it declined another 4 percent during 1985. Skim milk consumption grew by 8.8 percent during 1985, while lowfat milk use increased 3.9 percent. From 1980 to 1984, total per capita consumption of all milk declined 0.9 percent, and then remained unchanged in 1985.

Estimated per capita consumption of cottage cheese decreased 1.4 percent in 1985, while per capita consumption of lowfat cottage cheese (a yogurt rival) rose 5.0 percent. Per capita yogurt consumption increased 12.6 percent.

The four leading processors of fluid milk achieved 19.3 percent of total sales, as follows: Southland, 6.8 percent; Beatrice, 4.6 percent; Borden, 4.3 percent; and Dairymen, a cooperative, 3.6 percent.

Cheese

Per capita consumption of all cheese declined an estimated 1.6 percent in 1985, but some product categories gained as others lost (see Exhibit 11.4). For example, per capita consumption of American cheese declined 2.4 percent, although that of Italian-type varieties increased 2.9 percent. One-half of cheese production is of American cheese; Italian varieties account for one-fourth of production.

Cheese substitutes fortified by the milk protein casein appeared on the market in recent years. For example, many brands of frozen pizza contained these less costly substitutes.

Producer prices for all natural cheese dropped 1.1 percent in 1985, yet those for all processed cheeses declined 1.7 percent. Four producers of natural and processed cheeses accounted for 33 percent of total sales: Dart & Kraft, 21 percent; Schrieber Food, 5 percent; Land O' Lakes, 4 percent; and Beatrice, 3 percent.

---

[4] Facts relating to 1985 events and forecasts for the dairy industry are drawn from *1986 U.S. Industrial Outlook.* (Washington D.C., U.S. Department of Commerce, International Trade Administration), pp. 40-13–40-19.

EXHIBIT 11.4   U.S. per Capita Consumption of Cheeses (In pounds)

Types of Cheese	1983	1984	1985[a]
American	11.62	12.02	11.77
Cheddar	9.13	9.73	9.53
Other American[b]	2.49	2.29	2.24
Italian	5.73	5.82	5.99
Mozzarella	3.71	4.06	4.20
Ricotta	.54	.58	.61
Provolone	.90	.55	.57
Other Italian varieties	.58	.63	.61
All other cheese	5.85	5.46	5.15
All cheese	23.20	23.30	22.91

[a] Estimated by International Trade Administration.
[b] Includes washed curd, stirred curd, and Monterey Jack.
Source: U.S. Department of Commerce: Bureau of the Census and International Trade
      Administration; U.S. Department of Agriculture.

Frozen Desserts

Consumption of ice cream and other frozen desserts had been quite steady in recent years. In 1985, estimated per capita consumption of ice cream melted 2.3 percent, while sherbet declined 3.9 percent. At the same time, per capita consumption of ice milk increased 2 percent and mellorine climbed 62.4 percent. Mellorine contains soy-based products such as frozen tofu, that many consumers considered to be more healthful than ice cream.

Along with mellorine, gelatin bars and frozen fruit bars gained popularity among adults as well as children. Among the major food processors, Castle and Cooke manufactured fruit bars and General Foods produced gelatin bars.

A few years ago, several small companies began to achieve success in the premium ice cream market. Premium ice cream has a higher butterfat content than standard ice cream, and is often produced with only natural ingredients, such as milk, sugar, and real fruit flavorings. Major food processors have not recognized the potential of this market segment. In 1983, Pillsbury acquired Haagen-Dazs, a popular regional producer of premium ice cream. In April 1985, Dart & Kraft acquired Frusen Gladje, a privately held manufacturer of premium ice cream.

In 1985, the average retail price for a half-gallon of ice cream reached $2.31, as producer prices edged up an estimated 2 percent. Four ice cream makers garnered 31 percent of the market for ice cream and frozen desserts: Southland, 11 percent; Dart & Kraft, 8 percent; Borden, 8 percent; and Beatrice, 4 percent.

Outlook for the U.S. Dairy Industry

Exhibit 11.5 summarizes the estimated and forecasted values of industry shipments of various dairy products from 1982 to 1986. The aggregate value of shipments for 1986 was expected to increase 0.7 percent, although total per capita

EXHIBIT 11.5   Recent Performance and Forecast: Dairy Products (In millions)

	1982	1983	1984a	1985b	1986c	Percent Change			
						1982–83	1983–84	1984–85	1985–86
Value of Shipmentsd	$39,063	$40,219	$40,832	$42,689	$43,879	3.0	1.5	4.5	2.8
Creamery Butter	1,687	1,737	1,778	1,835	1,853	3.0	2.4	3.2	1.0
Cheese	10,763	10,907	11,064	12,332	12,785	1.3	1.4	11.5	3.7
Condensed and									
Evaporated Milk	4,731	5,746	5,673	5,603	5,631	21.5	−1.3	−1.2	0.5
Ice Cream	2,855	2,963	3,126	3,244	3,302	3.8	5.5	3.8	1.8
Fluid Milk	19,028	18,865	19,191	19,675	20,308	−0.9	1.7	2.5	3.2

a Estimated by International Trade Administration (ITA) except for exports and imports.
b Estimated by ITA.
c Forecast by ITA.
d Value of all products and services sold by the dairy products industry.
Source: U.S. Department of Commerce: Bureau of the Census, Bureau of Economic Analysis, and International Trade Administration.

consumption was expected to increase 0.8 percent, less than the predicted rate of population increase. Predictions for the real (inflation-adjusted) growth of specific products ranged from a 1.7 percent gain for cheese to a 1.6 percent decline for ice cream and frozen desserts.

Per capita consumption of all cheese may remain static, but consumption of Italian types was expected to increase 3 percent. Consumption of most types of cheese was predicted to be static or to decline.

Shipments of premium ice cream were expected to increase, thus preventing further decline in the real growth of frozen desserts. Novelty items and frozen tofu would continue to serve market niches. Demand for lowfat milk, skim milk, and yogurt were expected to continue to rise, while demand for whole milk would continue its decline. The volume of dairy shipments was expected to rise 0.2 percent annually from 1985 to 1990, while the population increased 0.9 percent a year. This slow expansion would be spread unevenly among the industry's product segments.

Ice cream and frozen desserts were expected to register slight declines. Shipments of fluid milk were likely to remain unchanged because the population of the prime consuming group, children aged 15 and under, would expand only 0.2 percent annually. Expansion of the butter market would prove difficult, as an increasing number of people reach maturity would have used very little of it.

RECENT EVENTS IN THE FOOD-PROCESSING INDUSTRY

The U.S. food market tends to grow in line with population increases. The population has been growing less than 1 percent annually, and per capita food consumption trends have been relatively flat. As a result, there was low overall growth in the U.S. food market in recent years. U.S. food expenditures rose 3.2 percent in real terms in 1985, compared to 2.1 percent in 1984.

The increasing number of two-wage-earner households in the United States resulted in higher disposable incomes and a growing need for convenience. Although Americans wanted more healthful meals, they had less time to prepare them, but more money to ·spend for them. As a result, spending for food away from home increased much faster than spending for food prepared at home. Although real food-at-home spending rose faster than real foodservice sales during 1985 (+2.6 percent versus +1.2 percent), the reverse was true for the 1983–85 period (+11.3 percent for food away from home versus +6.6 percent for food at home.)[5]

These two trends—slow growth in the food industry and increased food consumption away from home—indicated that it would be difficult for competitors in the food-processing industry to make continued large gains in the market simply through internal growth of existing products. For this reason, several large food processors began to reposition themselves into propitious product and geographic markets and to capitalize on the trend toward eating away from home. The slow-growing market meant that the majority of future market-share gains would result from taking existing market share away from competitors. Thus, the market became, and was expected to remain, fiercely competitive. Food processors were second only to department stores in advertising expenditures during 1984 with outlays of $4.2 billion (see Exhibit 11.6).[6]

Repositioning efforts also resulted in 315 mergers and acquisitions involving 260 firms in the food sector during the first six months of 1985. This was only a slight increase from the number of similar mergers during the same period in 1984.

Three 1985 mergers with a combined transaction cost approaching $14 billion achieved the most notoriety during 1985; R.J. Reynolds acquired Nabisco Brands for $5 billion; Phillip Morris spent $5.6 billion for General Foods Corporation; and Nestle S.A. purchased Carnation Company for $3 billion. In addition, Beatrice Foods agreed to a leveraged buyout that would take the company private. Food and beverage industry shipments accounted for about 60 percent of these four firms' annual sales, and together these companies sold 15 percent of total food and beverage industry shipments.[7] The slow growth of demand and the rapid change in consumer tastes may portend continued mergers in the food industry. In addition, food companies have been repurchasing their own stock at an unprecedented rate, partly to prevent becoming takeover targets. Stock held by the largest food processors as a percentage of their total shares outstanding increased from about 2 percent in 1981 to 15 percent by the end of 1985. These

[5] "Food, Beverages, and Tobacco: Current Analysis," *Standard & Poor's Industry Surveys,* Vol. 54, No. 9, Sec. 1, February 27, 1986, p. 1.

[6] "Advertising: Special Report," *Standard & Poor's Industry Surveys,* Vol. 153, No. 40, Sec. 1, October 3, 1985, p. 1.

[7] "Food and Kindred Products," *1986 U.S. Industrial Outlook* (Washington, D.C., U.S. Department of Commerce, International Trade Administration), pp. 40–1.

EXHIBIT 11.6   Top 20 Spenders on Advertising, 1984 (In millions)

Company	1983	1984
Procter & Gamble	$915.0	$976.0
Sears	898.0	925.1
General Motors	823.5	892.3
Phillip Morris	810.6	892.0
Ford	787.2	808.5
Reynolds (RJR)	633.0	702.0
Beatrice	288.0	680.0
Warner-Lambert	592.0	607.0
PepsiCo	488.3	595.9
Coca-Cola	463.2	535.8
Sara Lee	456.0	513.0
Anheuser Busch	403.9	490.0
American Express	384.0	480.2
J.C. Penney	381.0	465.0
General Foods	395.9	431.8
Eastman Kodak	390.0	430.0
Ralston Purina	438.0	429.6
Dart & Kraft	339.6	418.6
American Home Products	409.9	412.0
General Electric	363.0	356.0

Source: Compustat Services, Inc.

buybacks have added strength to the market price of these stocks. Moreover, financiers discovered the value of strong, established brand names in the food industry. The combination of realized market strength from good brand names and the stock buybacks caused food industry stock prices to jump 60 percent during 1985, despite a 2 percent decline in industry profits.[8]

Several indicators pointed to a good year for food processors during 1986:

1. Cost savings resulting from lower oil prices.
2. Stable prices for food commodities were predicted.
3. The average company's bottom line could be increased by 10 percent if Congress passed proposed tax legislation.
4. Despite recent merger activity, there was no sign that the Justice Department was concerned about concentration in the industry.[9]
5. Operating efficiencies and economies of size resulting from the recent mergers and acquisitions.[10]

[8] Kenneth Dreyfack, "The Stage Is Set for More Megadeals," *Business Week,* January 13, 1986, p. 67.
[9] Ibid.
[10] "Food and Kindred Products," pp. 40–1.

The following statement regarding the food-processing industry appeared in a January 1986 *Business Week* article: "As recently as five years ago, when high tech was king, the packaged-food industry drew nothing but yawns. Food companies themselves were weary of low margins and slow growth. But now a new ethic has taken hold, and the industry is alive and thriving. Boring had become beautiful."[11]

The cost savings from lower commodity prices and possible tax legislation mentioned above would help companies finance the advertising costs that would continue to be necessary in this highly competitive market. It appeared that those firms that could most successfully identify and satisfy the rapidly changing customer needs with strong, high-value-added brands would be the winners in this slow-growth market during coming years.

DART & KRAFT BECOMES DART AND KRAFT

In July 1986, Dart & Kraft Chairman John M. Richman surprised the investment community by announcing that he would divide the corporation into two parts: a new Kraft, consisting of Kraft's food operations and the Duracell battery business, to be headed by Richman; and a corporation (later named Premark International) composed of Tupperware, West Bend, Hobart, and Wilsonart, that would be spun off to shareholders and headed by Dart & Kraft President Warren L. Batts. Richman felt that the Kraft-Duracell combination would be more attractive on Wall Street. He was quoted as saying in reference to the former Dart & Kraft, "Over time we feel Kraft would not be recognized for the power it is in the food industry."[12]

From 1980 to 1985, Dart & Kraft's overall operating profit grew at a compound annual rate of 4 percent, while Kraft's rate was 10.3 percent, and Duracell's was 15 percent. During the same period, Tupperware's contribution to Dart & Kraft's earnings fell from 30 percent in 1980 to about 10 percent in 1985. Premark's management had to contend with Tupperware's problems, the slow growth of its other units, and the loss of cash flow from the food business.[13]

When the announced spinoff raised questions about the wisdom of the 1980 merger, Richman pointed out that a $1 investment in Dart & Kraft at the time of the 1980 merger would have appreciated to $5.34 by mid-June 1986. "The numbers tell it all," said Richman.[14]

[11] Dreyfack, "The Stage Is Set for More Megadeals."

[12] James E. Ellis, "Dart & Kraft: Why It'll Be Dart and Kraft," *Business Week,* July 7, 1986, p. 33.

[13] Ibid.

[14] Ibid.

FINANCIAL DATA

Exhibits 11.7 to 11.12 present a summary of Kraft's financial performance during recent years as presented in the firm's 1986 annual report. Inventories were valued at the lower of cost or market. In 1985, costing for virtually all domestic inventories was changed from FIFO (first in first out) to the LIFO (last in first out) method. The FIFO method was used for other inventories, which represented approximately 43 percent of all inventories. Inventory cost included cost of raw materials, labor, and overhead. Due to the nature of the business, management considered it impractical to segregate inventories into raw materials, work in progress, and finished goods.

EXHIBIT 11.7   Summary of Selected Financial Data (In millions, except per share data)

	1982	1983	1984	1985	1986
Summary of Operations					
Net Sales	$7,618	$7,425	$7,628	$7,920	$8,742
Cost and Expenses					
Cost of Products	5,754	5,395	5,442	$5,478	5,970
Delivery, Sales and					
Administrative Expenses	1,399	1,475	1,550	1,727	2,055
Interest Expense	87	68	94	79	71
Interest Income	(58)	(63)	(70)	(50)	(39)
Other Income, Net	(33)	(19)	(37)	(34)	(25)
Total Costs and Expenses	7,149	6,856	6,979	7,200	8,032
Income from Operations	469	569	649	720	710
Nonoperating Items	(91)	—	—	—	—
Income from Continuing Operations					
before Income Taxes	378	569	649	720	710
Provision for Income Taxes	168	252	295	312	320
Net Income from Continuing Operations	210	317	354	408	390
Net Income from Discontinued					
Operations	140	118	102	58	23
Net Income	$ 350	$ 435	$ 456	$ 466	$ 413

EXHIBIT 11.7   (continued)

Net Income per Share					
From Continuing Operations	$ 1.27	$ 1.92	$ 2.33	$ 2.82	$ 2.77
From Discontinued Operations	.86	.72	.68	.40	.16
Total	$ 2.13	$ 2.64	$ 3.01	$ 3.22	$ 2.93
Dividends	$ 197	$ 210	$ 209	$ 219	$ 234
Per Share	1.20	1.28	1.38	1.52⅓	1.68
Financial Position					
Current Assets	$2,286	$2,476	$2,339	$2,326	$2,475
Current Liabilities	1,134	1,256	1,479	1,415	2,283
Working Capital	1,152	1,220	860	911	192
Property, Plant, and Equipment, Net	901	900	948	1,075	1,350
Total Assets	4,709	4,998	4,882	5,091	4,749
Long-Term Debt	574	549	508	439	232
Shareholders' Equity	2,774	2,923	2,598	2,880	1,798[a]
Per Share	$16.89	$17.77	$18.09	$19.95	$13.29
Statistical Information					
Return on Equity[b]	12.8%	17.7%	22.7%	22.3%	21.7%
Return on Total Capital[b]	11.0%	14.2%	17.0%	18.4%	15.4%
Long-Term Debt to Equity[b]	34.9%	30.6%	32.6%	23.9%	12.9%
Total Debt to Total Capital[b]	28.9%	27.2%	34.0%	24.5%	34.9%
Capital Expenditures	$ 257	$ 137	$ 164	$ 181	$ 209
Depreciation	$ 116	$ 96	$ 104	$ 99	$ 113
Payroll and Employee Benefits	$1,104	$1,118	$1,114	$1,208	$1,386
Average Number of Employees	50,500	49,500	47,400	50,100	51,300
Number of Shareholders, Year-End	78,808	74,443	70,807	72,249	70,190
Number of Shares of Common Stock Outstanding at Year-End (in thousands)	164,237	164,483	143,627	144,334	135,279
Average Number of Common and Common Equivalent Shares (In thousands)	164,265	164,887	151,589	144,898	140,970

Note: Amounts have been restated to reflect the results from continuing operations, where appropriate. In 1986, Kraft adopted the new pension accounting standards issued by the Financial Accounting Standards Board. In 1985, Kraft adopted the LIFO inventory method of accounting for substantially all domestic inventories. Number of shares and per share data reflect a three-for-one stock split in 1985.

[a] Shareholders' equity for 1986 reflects the spinoff of Premark International and the repurchase of shares.
[b] Equity and total capital are year-end balances reduced by the net assets of discontinued operations for these ratios.

EXHIBIT 11.8   Segments of Business by Classes of Products—Five-Year Summary

		1982	1983	1984	1985	1986
Net Sales	Food Products					
	Retail Food	$3,259.2	$3,016.2	$3,182.3	$3,289.9	$3,365.0
	Dairy Group	821.2	701.8	591.8	621.4	651.1
	Food Service Group	625.3	686.4	773.3	889.7	1,314.3
	Industrial Foods Group	437.9	486.3	576.0	531.3	441.6
	International Group	1,897.5	1,769.7	1,707.2	1,733.0	2,007.7
	Total	7,041.1	6,668.4	6,830.6	7,065.3	7,779.7
	Consumer Products	576.9	764.4	797.8	854.2	962.5
	Net Sales	$7,618.0	$7,424.8	$7,628.4	$7,919.5	$8,742.2
Operating Profit	Food Products					
	Domestic	$ 365.4	$ 413.2	$ 467.7	$ 579.9	$ 613.9
	International	137.4	165.0	168.5	150.4	190.0
	Total	502.8	578.2	636.2	730.3	803.9
	Consumer Products	46.4	65.0	93.9	82.6	29.9[a]
	Total Operating Profit	$ 549.2	$ 642.2	$ 730.1	$ 812.9	$ 833.8
Identifiable Assets	Food Products					
	Domestic	$1,480.0	$1,430.3	$1,604.5	$1,607.8	$2,378.0
	International	772.7	680.9	701.1	786.4	849.6
	Total	2,252.7	2,111.2	2,305.6	2,394.2	3,227.6
	Consumer Products	493.0	576.1	661.3	757.7	849.6
	Corporate	833.8	1,182.3	875.3	891.3	672.1
	Total Identifiable Assets of Continuing Operations	$3,579.5	$3,869.6	$3,842.2	$4,043.2	$4,749.3

[a] After restructuring charges of $37.0 million.

224

EXHIBIT 11.9   Common Stock Prices and Dividends

	1985			1986		
	High	*Low*	*Dividend*	*High*	*Low*	*Dividend*
First Quarter	$31-1/2	$27-7/8	$.35-1/3	$53-1/2	$38-7/8	$.39
Second Quarter	36-5/8	29-3/4	.39	65-7/8	47-1/2	.43
Third Quarter	38-3/8	33-5/8	.39	65	51-3/4	.43
Fourth Quarter	44-7/8	36	.39	58-1/2[a]	47-1/8[a]	.43

[a] On October 31, 1986, Kraft spun off the businesses that make up Premark International.

EXHIBIT 11.10   Consolidated Statement of Changes in Financial Position (In millions)

	Year Ending December 29, 1984	Year Ending December 28, 1985	Year Ending December 27, 1986
Cash Provided from Continuing Operations			
Net Income from Continuing Operations	$ 353.6	$ 408.0	$ 390.1
Items Not Resulting in Cash Flow			
Depreciation and Amortization	111.3	112.2	135.5
Deferred Income Taxes	49.9	39.5	60.8
(Increase) Decrease in Working Capital Used in Continuing Operations (Except Cash, Temporary Investments, and Borrowings)			
Adjusted for Translation	(73.1)	46.5	65.2
Cash Provided from Continuing Operations	$ 441.7	$ 606.2	$ 651.6
Investments			
Capital Expenditures	$(164.3)	$(180.6)	$(209.0)
Book Value of Properties Sold	33.6	15.0	12.5
Business Acquistions and Divesture, Net	(153.4)	(64.8)	(562.3)
(Increase) Decrease in Investments and Long-term Receivables	28.5	(62.2)	45.8
Other, Net	9.9	5.7	11.3
Cash Used for Investments	$(245.7)	$(286.9)	$(701.7)
Financing			
Dividends Paid	$(208.5)	$(219.3)	$ 234.0
Purchase of Treasury Stock	(531.7)	0.0	(597.7)
Decrease in Long-term Debt	(33.9)	(72.3)	(114.9)
Increase (decrease) in Short-term Borrowings	$ 164.6	$(135.0)	$ 485.9
Cash Used for Financing	$(609.5)	$(426.6)	$ 460.7
Cash Provided from Discontinued Operations	167.9	65.6	356.0
Decrease in Cash and Temporary Investments	$(245.6)	$ (41.7)	$(154.8)

EXHIBIT 11.11   Consolidated Balance Sheet (In millions except par value)

	December 28, 1985	December 27, 1986
Assets		
Cash, Time Deposits, and Certificates of Deposit	$ 160.9	$ 194.1
Temporary Investments, at Cost That Approximates Market	3.6	127.6
Total Cash and Temporary Investments	476.5	321.7
Accounts and Notes Receivable, Less Allowance of $27.4 in 1986 and $19.1 in 1985	734.4	941.7
Inventories	1,115.3	1,211.3
Total Current Assets	2,326.2	2,474.7
Investments and Long-term Receivables	284.4	246.5
Prepaid and Deferred Items	115.7	139.6
Property, Plant and Equipment	32.6	45.1
Buildings and Improvement	495.6	584.6
Machinery and Equipment	1,249.5	1,504.7
Construction in Progress	90.9	87.8
Total Cost	1,868.6	2,222.2
Less—Accumulated Depreciation	(794.1)	(872.1)
Property, Plant and Equipment, Net	1,074.5	1,350.1
Intangibles, Net of Accumulated Amortization of $55.9 in 1986 and $35.5 in 1985	242.4	538.4
Net Assets of Discontinued Operations	1,047.4	—
Total Assets	5,090.6	4,749.3
Liabilities and Shareholders' Equity		
Accounts Payable	$ 434.3	$ 551.4
Short-Term Borrowings	130.0	615.9
Accrued Compensation	169.4	193.7
Other Accrued Liabilities	333.5	447.7
Accrued Income Taxes	321.4	356.0
Current Portion of Long-Term Debt	26.0	118.3
Total Current Liabilities	1,414.6	2,283.0
Long-Term Debt	438.7	231.5
Deferred Income Taxes	228.6	284.8
Other Liabilities	128.5	152.0
Shareholders' Equity		
Preferred Stock, $5.00 Par Value; Authorized 150,000 Shares; Issued—None	—	—
Common Stock, $1.00 Par Value; Authorized 600,000,000 Shares; Issued 164,735,955 Shares	164.7	164.7
Capital Surplus	317.5	33.2
Retained Earnings	3,191.8	2,810.9
Treasury Stock, 29,457,022 Shares in 1986 and 20,402,106 Shares in 1985, at Cost	(503.3)	(1,074.9)
Unearned Portion of Restricted Stock Issued for Future Services	(1.0)	(.9)
Cumulative Foreign Current Adjustments	(289.5)	(135.0)
Total Shareholders' Equity	2,880.2	1,798.0
Total Liabilities and Shareholders' Equity	$5,090.6	$4,749.3

**EXHIBIT 11.12   Segments of Business by Geographical Area—
Three-Year Summary (In millions)**

	1984	1985	1986
Net Sales			
United States	$5,581.1	$5,819.3	$6,278.3
Canada	673.1	638.6	628.6
Latin America	131.6	132.7	106.2
Europe and Africa	929.4	1,060.9	1,445.1
Pacific Area	313.2	268.0	284.0
Total Net Sales	$7,628.4	$7,919.5	$8,742.2
Operating Profit			
United States	$ 522.6	$ 623.7	$ 644.7
Canada	81.9	70.1	67.7
Latin America	16.9	18.1	15.2
Europe and Africa	76.8	67.9	69.7
Pacific Area	31.9	33.1	36.5
Total Operating Profit	$ 730.1	$ 812.9	$ 833.8
Identifiable Assets			
United States	$2,017.1	$2,060.7	$2,864.9
Canada	217.2	227.2	218.1
Latin America	90.9	75.2	65.5
Europe and Africa	411.8	594.2	710.3
Pacific Area	229.9	194.6	218.4
Corporate	875.3	891.3	672.1
Total Identifiable Assets of Continuing Operations	$3,842.2	$4,043.2	$4,749.3

_____ CASE 12 _____

Humana: Strategic Directions for the 1990s

Humana was an international company that provided an integrated system of health care services including hospital care, prepaid health care, and indemnity insurance plans. Humana's hospitals provided general medical and surgical care and had programs for clinical research and medical training. At the end of fiscal 1989, the company's operations included 83 hospitals (a total of 17,421 beds) and 979,000 members insured by Humana Health Care Plans. As of March 31, 1990, Humana operated 85 hospitals (a total of 17,850 beds) and insured 1,070,000 members. As of January 31, 1990, the company had 56,163 employees. The corporation was headquartered in Louisville, Kentucky, and its hospitals were primarily situated in the Sunbelt states of Florida, Kentucky, Louisiana, and Texas (Exhibit 12.1).

Humana was founded in 1961 by David A. Jones and Wendell Cherry, two young attorneys in Louisville. In the company's infancy, the legal name was Extendicare, which was derived from the words "extended care" and clearly identified the company's original business—nursing homes. In 1968, the company constructed its first hospital in Huntsville, Alabama. During the next decade, the company embarked on major projects to build and acquire hospitals, and it owned more than 40 by 1977. The nursing homes were sold so that the company's attention and energy could be focused on managing hospitals. The name was changed to Humana in 1974 to reflect the company philosophy in terms of its dedication to humankind's health needs. In 1978, Humana acquired American Medicorp, a multihospital system, which doubled the size of the company and made it the largest chain of proprietary hospitals.

Up until 1986, Humana enjoyed financial success as a direct result of acquiring or building new hospitals and selling unprofitable ones (Exhibit 12.2). Humana was listed on the New York Stock Exchange in 1971. From 1972 to 1982, Humana outperformed *Fortune* magazine's top 100 largest diversified service companies. Earnings per share increased 34.6 percent, gaining the company a position in the top four. Humana was number one on the list for total return to

This case was prepared by Jeffrey W. Totten as a basis for class discussion rather than to illustrate either effective or ineffective handling of an administrative situation. Used with permission from Jeffrey W. Totten.

EXHIBIT 12.1   Location of Humana Facilities

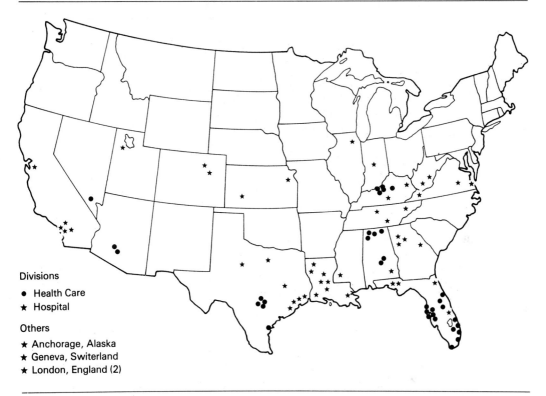

Divisions
- Health Care
★ Hospital

Others
★ Anchorage, Alaska
★ Geneva, Switerland
★ London, England (2)

Source: Humana *Annual Reports* and company documents.

investors with an annual average of 36.7 percent. This performance greatly added to the company's ability to acquire outside capital in an industry where vast amounts of investment capital are needed to finance health care advances. Michael M. LeComey of Merrill Lynch, Pierce, Fenner & Smith stated in the *Wall Street Journal*, "With Humana, investors are dealing with what I believe may be the most aggressive and smartest major company in the United States. That's a lot to say about any company, but Humana's success and the absolutely uncanny accuracy of its corporate strategy make it a supportable statement."[1]

Humana stumbled in 1986. One company goal was to integrate or gather all of its products (hospitals, MedFirst clinics, and Humana Care Plus insurance) under the Humana brand name. A key component of the company's growth plans was Humana Care Plus, its group health insurance division. This division was expected to provide the company with maximum exposure and earnings. It was

[1] *Humana, Inc. 1984 Annual Report.*

EXHIBIT 12.2   Performance Charts

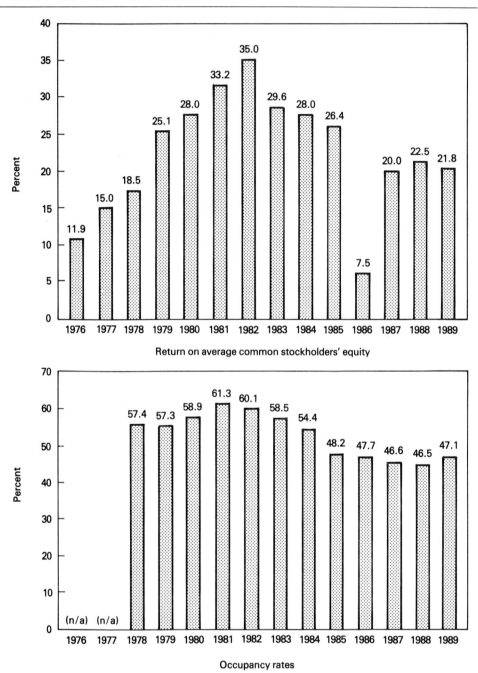

Return on average common stockholders' equity

Occupancy rates

Source: Humana Inc. *Annual Reports* and company documents.

formed in 1982 in anticipation of government and business initiatives to halt increasing health care costs. The theme of Humana Care Plus was, "The health care plans from the health care professionals." This insurance program for growing companies was to provide a solution to rising health care costs, a two-year rate guarantee, a choice of plans to meet the employees' needs, freedom to choose the physician, quality hospital care, comprehensive quality and cost management, personal service, and simplified claims processing.

In 1985, the insurance program already had 359,200 members enrolled, a dramatic increase from 40,900 the previous year. Humana Care Plus revenues reached $89.1 million last year, and it accounted for about 4 percent of Humana hospital admissions. Members of Humana Care Plus are automatically covered if they go to Humana hospitals. If admitted to non-Humana hospitals, members are still covered, although they pay a $500 penalty per visit. For Humana, that incentive to go to Humana hospitals means more inpatient days in an environment of declining admissions and more activity for its newly developed outpatient programs. Humana Care Plus hospital admissions last year grew to 9,300, compared to 700 in 1984.[2]

Humana also planned to invest more in its MedFirst clinics. Humana Med-First was the company's health services division. The clinics worked with the basic building block of the health care system: the doctor's office. These clinics, totaling 148 at the end of fiscal 1985, were the nation's largest network of primary medical care centers. They offered high-quality, affordable care at convenient locations and hours. The private physicians who practiced in the offices remained independent owners of the medical practices. Humana supplied the office space, administration, and support services on a contractual basis. Humana hoped to have by "year-end 1986, as many as 350 clinics . . . in operation nationwide, compared to 68 two years ago, and corporate will continue to feed its local markets campaigns to be used in appropriate media. At Humana hospitals, the emphasis will be on outpatient care programs, the current trend for hospitals across the country."[3]

Unfortunately, Humana misread the numbers. "From $216 million [in 1985], earnings plunged last August [1986] to $54.4 million."[4] The company branched out into walk-in clinics and diversified into health insurance without adequately studying the markets. There were several problems with the insurance packages: First, without restrictions, members tended *not* to go to Humana hospitals (e.g., the company expected 70 percent of patients to use its hospitals; actually 46 percent on average did in 1985–1986), and doctors did not refer patients to Humana's hospitals. Second, the company mispriced its policies. Premiums failed to cover costs by at least 20 percent. Third, hospitalization rates were high, discouraging admissions. Meanwhile, Humana also encountered financial losses

[2] Deborah Silver, "Healthy Competition: The Human Touch," *Marketing & Media Decisions*, April 1986, p. 101.

[3] Ibid.

[4] Laura Sachar, "At the Threshold of Pain," *Financial World*, February 24, 1987, p. 20.

with its MedFirst units, losing $23.3 million in 1986 and $5 million to $10 million in 1987. One medical company president attributed the losses to Humana's size, its inflexible approach to localized ambulatory care, too many clinics opening at one time, and lack of aggressive promotion.[5]

Jones, the chief executive officer, acted quickly, bringing in new management for Humana Care Plus (HCP) and slashing the number of markets covered by the program from 51 to 16. Premium rates were increased, new policies were not written for 10 months, and physicians were required to sign contracts in which they agreed to use Humana hospitals. Screening procedures were tightened and claims processing was streamlined through automation, software changes, and incentives for billing department personnel. HCP referral rates improved from 46.9 percent in May 1986 to 55.2 percent in February 1987, to 63 percent for 1989.[6] Since then, "the division has come a long way. It cut its losses to $37 million in the fiscal year ended August 1, 1988, from $66.8 million in fiscal 1986. And in the second quarter ended February 28, 1989, it achieved a milestone by posting its first operating profit, earning $1.9 million on revenues of $267 million."[7]

Humana moved quickly on its walk-in clinics, selling 85 of 150 MedFirst units by May 1987. The biggest buyers were Primedical Corporation (68 units) and Ohio State University Hospital (9 units).[8] Another 34 units located in the Chicago area were finally sold in June 1987 to Health Stop Medical Management. The remaining units were absorbed into nearby Humana hospitals.

MANAGEMENT PHILOSOPHY

Humana's 29-year success record is largely attributed to its management philosophy. In 1981, top-level management recognized the need to explore alternatives in health care delivery at a time when the hospital business was thriving. In the company's 1981 annual report, CEO Jones said, "The world is turning, the system is evolving, and those who do tomorrow what they did yesterday are likely to be caught short." That foresight in 1981—the early recognition of the need to change—has given Humana an unparalleled opportunity for market leadership. Management's philosophy is to pay constant and close attention to the way the environment is changing so that the company can anticipate the changing needs of customers. Environmental monitoring is evidenced by management's concern about the U.S. health care delivery system, as expressed in Humana's 1989 annual report: "We're convinced that, as a nation, we must let each American citizen make his or her own health care choice, and we must remove the obstacles

[5] Leigh Page, "Despite Humana Sell-off, Future Is Still Bright for Walk-in Centers," *American Medical News*, May 15, 1987, pp. 11, 14.

[6] M. R. Traska, "Humana: Where Will Its Strategic Plan Lead It?" *Hospitals*, July 5, 1987, p. 30; Howard Larkin, "HMO Ownership Pays off for Systems That Stick with It," *Hospitals*, February 5, 1990, p. 57.

[7] Howard Kim, "Growth through Coordination," *Modern Healthcare*, April 21, 1989, p. 37.

[8] Page, "Despite Humana Sell-off."

that limit the freedom to do so. The consequence necessarily will be the kind of improvement in quality and affordability that we have seen in so many aspects of American life."[9]

MISSION STATEMENT

It is no longer business as usual in the health care industry: Public policy continues to change; advances in medicine and technology are proliferating; the number of elderly people is multiplying; consumers are demanding increasingly higher-quality, lower-cost services; competition within the industry is maturing and changing; employers are aggressively managing their health care benefits; and the impetus of overall cost containment and government regulation has thrown added weight behind the continued push for change.

This convergence of powerful forces created enormous opportunity for a company that respected the best in traditional health care and was committed to responsive, effective innovation. Within this dynamic environment, Humana's commitment remained clear: The mission of Humana is to achieve an unequaled level of measurable quality and productivity in the delivery of health services that are responsive to the needs and values of patients, physicians, employers, and consumers.[10] The company's strategy was threefold: to insist on excellence and productivity, to create an integrated health care system, and to explore new services that address the needs and values of customers.

HUMANA OPERATIONS

In September 1989, Jones reorganized the company in order to speed up the vertical integration process. Humana was divided into two divisions: the hospital division and the health care division. In addition, considerable emphasis was placed on maintaining centers of excellence and research efforts. Exhibit 12.3 lists Humana's key staff and operating management.

Hospital Division

As of March 31, 1990, Humana's 51 hospitals in the hospital division were located in the United States, London, and Geneva. The focus was on providing high-quality hospital care at an affordable price. When the company's fiscal year began on September 1, 1984, it was known primarily as a hospital company. But by the end of the year (August 31, 1985), the company had achieved recognition as a provider of an integrated system of health care services.

[9] "Building on Success: A Statement on American Health Policy," *Humana Inc. 1989 Annual Report*, p. 12.
[10] Ibid., p. 1.

EXHIBIT 12.3   Officers of Humana

Chairman of the Board and Chief Executive Officer: David A. Jones
President and Chief Operating Officer: Wendell Cherry
Staff Management:
  Executive Vice Presidents:
    William C. Ballard, Jr., Finance and Administration
    Thomas J. Flynn, General Counsel
  Senior Vice Presidents:
    W. Roger Drury, Finance
    H. Linden McLellan, Facility Management
    H. Herbert Phillips, Administration
    Fred Pirman, Jr., Information Systems
  Vice Presidents: 25 officers in 19 areas
Operating Management:
  Senior Executive Vice President: Carl F. Pollard
  Executive Vice Presidents and Division Presidents:
    Paul A. Gross, Hospital Division
    Wayne T. Smith, Health Care Division
  Hospital Division: Regions 4, 5, and 6, six areas
  Health Care Division: Regions 1, 2, and 3, six areas, and marketing operations officers in
  six geographic markets.

Note: According to Tim Moody, Investor Relations Department, Humana Inc., there is no formal
organizational chart for the company (July 23, 1990, telephone interview).
Source: *Humana 1989 Annual Report,* Officers, pp. 30–31.

Health Care Division

This division represented Humana's success at vertical integration, as well
as the company's tenacity and faith. After three or four years of struggling and
financial losses, Humana's insurance plans finally showed a profit for four consecutive quarters. According to Jones and Cherry:

> We believe that the vertical-integration strategy we adopted to win a larger
> share of this declining market is largely responsible for the improvement in our
> hospital admissions. . . . To build on the success of this integration, our hospital and
> health plan operations were brought closer together on September 1 with a new
> organizational alignment based on markets. The former Group Health Division and
> Hospital Division were based on lines of business. The new structure places the nine
> markets where we have concentrations of health plan members and the 32 hospitals
> serving them into one division, the Health Care Division. . . . In the nine markets
> that comprise [this division] and contain 92 percent of our plans' members, hospital
> admissions were 4.6 percent ahead of the previous year's level [while] in all other
> markets [i.e., Hospital Division], admissions declined 1.2 percent.[11]

Two more hospitals were recently added to the integrated network, one in
Pembroke Pines, Florida, and the other in San Antonio, Texas.

[11] Ibid., p. 3.

Humana Health Care Plans offer employers and consumers a wide range of coverage options including modified indemnity plans, preferred provider organizations (PPOs), health maintenance organizations (HMOs), Medicare HMO and Medicare supplement plans.[12]

Centers of Excellence

A Center of Excellence is Humana's concept of the highest ideals of medicine; that is, excellence in patient care, medical education, and the search for new knowledge. This concept was introduced in 1982 as a way to encourage and support physicians who were interested in clinical research and medical education in Humana hospitals. The centers were established as referral and consultation centers with state-of-the-art technology, supporting services, and education and research programs that sustained the physicians' and the hospital's reputation for excellence. After a Center of Excellence was designated in a certain specialty, the Humana Institute received a grant from the Humana Foundation to support research and educational activities. Continued funding was based on the performance of these programs. This major commitment to fund medical education and clinical research for practicing physicians was a pioneering effort for the investor-owned hospital industry.

These centers "help build physician loyalty to the hospital, increase the hospital's and physicians' referral base, enhance the hospital's reputation, and possibly attract more private-pay patients."[13] Currently, the program includes 28 centers at 19 hospitals, representing 12 specialties: pulmonary, diabetes, cardiovascular, orthopedics, ophthalmology, spinal injuries, burn treatment, digestive treatment, urology, craniofacial surgery, neurosciences, and women's medicine (Exhibit 12.4).

Research

The recent decline in federal spending on medical research created a financial dilemma for scientists, research-oriented doctors, and the nation's academic medical centers. The federal cuts clearly signaled the government's unwillingness to shoulder its accustomed medical research burden. This reluctance opened the way for support from successful private health care firms with financial resources and medical facilities sufficient to share the load. Clinical investigation requiring high-quality hospital care was a research area in which these firms were beginning to have an impact. Humana's support for clinical investigation of the artificial heart and Dr. William DeVries' heart implant operations in the early to mid-1980s were notable examples of this trend.

Humana's commitment to research extended beyond artificial heart research to such areas as the use of laser technology to open clogged arteries (at

[12] Humana Fact Sheet, 1990.
[13] Cynthia Wallace, "Centers for Excellence," *Modern Healthcare*, May 20, 1988, p. 30.

EXHIBIT 12.4 **Locations of Centers of Excellence**

Humana Hospital	—Phoenix (AZ): Cardiovascular, diabetes, orthopedics —Aurora (CO): (n/a) —Lucerne (Orlando, FL): Spinal injury
Humana Women's Hospital	—Tampa (FL): Women's medicine
Humana Hospital	—Palm Beaches (FL): Adolescent psychiatry —Augusta (GA): Burn treatment —Lexington (KY): Diabetes, ophthalmology —Suburban (Louisville, KY): Orthopedics —Audubon (Louisville, KY): Cardiovascular, neuroscience —New Orleans (LA): Women's medicine —East Ridge (TN): Diabetes, women's medicine —Medical City Dallas (TX): Cardiovascular, neuroscience
Humana Women's Hospital	—South Texas (San Antonio): Women's medicine
Humana Hospital	—San Antonio, (TX): Diabetes, gastroenterology, urology —Clear Lake (TX): Pulmonary —St. Lukes/Bluefield (WV): Ophthalomology —Wellington I (England): Cardiovascular

Note: Two hospitals and four centers are not identified and are not known to the authors. Two centers are in development.
Source: *Centers of Excellence Status Report,* July 2, 1990, Humana, Public Relations Department.

Humana Hospital, Phoenix), trauma and birth defect surgery (at Humana Hospital, Medical City Dallas), cancer treatment via bone marrow transplants (at Humana Hospital, University of Louisville), and various technologies such as hip implants and implantable insulin pumps.[14]

Other Programs

Humana had one of the oldest corporate training programs in the health care industry. More than 500 current managers and executives have been trained by this in-service program. Training actually consisted of two courses, a specialist course and an internship course. Both employed on-the-job exposure that lasted 18 months to 2 years, in addition to classroom work. Trainees for the specialist course were recruited from graduate university programs, as well as from among current Humana employees. The internship course took recent college graduates and exposed them to a variety of health care administration experiences.

Humana launched a new program for senior citizens in 1987. Membership in the Humana Seniors Association was expected to reach 200,000 as of fiscal year

[14] Humana Fact Sheet, 1990.

1989. Members received a number of benefits for their $12 annual fee, including such services at Humana hospitals as the help of a registered nurse, health screenings, field trips, help with insurance forms, and discounted medical and recreational rates.

Humana created a central electronic data base at its headquarters. The data base consisted of clinical measures, including patient outcome data, gathered each evening. The objective was to provide the company with an effective way to track and monitor the quality of care that each hospital provided. Humana added mortality data, published by the Health Care Financing Administration, to its data-base collection. Reports were generated every three months and sent to each hospital. The reports were useful in monitoring costs and identifying problem areas. The process used was considered to be similar to statistical process control (pioneered by Edward Deming).[15]

HUMANA MARKETING

In the past, marketing in the health care industry was basically in the form of public relations. It was not product-specific; rather, it was aimed at general positioning and image building and included such activities as sponsorship of community events, educational programs, newsletters, hospital tours, exhibits, and health fairs.

Humana began its marketing efforts (other than public relations) with the inception of its customer relations department in 1981. Initially, the purpose of this department was to collect market research in the form of patient satisfaction questionnaires. All patients who were discharged from Humana hospitals received a questionnaire that asked specific questions regarding nursing care, ancillary services, dietary, housekeeping, business office performance, and that *all-important* question: "Would you return to this hospital should you need hospital services in the future? If not, please explain."

The results of a six-month study revealed that 96 percent of Humana patients were very satisfied with the services, but the company's executives looked very closely at that 4 percent who said they would not return. The patients indicated that the facilities, equipment, and medical care were good, but that employees needed to work on caring, understanding, smiling, communicating, and having a positive attitude. They said the employees needed to respond to patients' fears and apprehension. This research showed that caring is an integral part of excellent health care service. With this valuable information, the top executives gave the company's education department the project of developing a human relations training program for all employees. The program was developed

[15] Compiled from Howard Kim, "Humana Builds for Future on History of Quality Care," *Modern Healthcare*, April 21, 1989, p. 40; "Humana Seniors Association," *Humana 1988 Annual Report*, pp. 8–10; and Mary T. Koska, "It's Systematic, Automatic Quality at Humana," *Hospitals*, February 20, 1989, p. 28.

and began in 1982. Named Humana Care, it became a companywide employee education and sensitivity training program that focused on excellence in the human aspects of providing good health services. Stated simply, Humana Care meant that each employee treated patients as if they were members of the employee's own family.

Marketing strategies for Humana have tended to be product oriented. Some of the programs that were available for the facilities to utilize included, but were not limited to, day surgery, cardiovascular, obstetrics, physicians' practice building, burn treatment, cancer (oncology), chemical dependency/substance abuse, diabetes, emergency, industrial medicine, ENT, gastroenterology, home health, infertility, neurology/neurosurgery, ophthalmology, orthopedics, pediatrics, psychiatry, pulmonary, rehabilitation, research, senior citizens, spinal injuries, urology, wellness, and women's programs. An example of the research and other marketing activities for one product, breast diagnostics, is seen in Exhibit 12.5.

Another Humana marketing strategy was aimed at name recognition. All Humana facilities were given the company name with the location rather than individual names as they had in the past. The hospital name changes were gradual and were associated with special events; for example, construction, replacement hospitals, or anniversaries. In 1985, the health services division's MedFirst was changed to Humana MedFirst. The insurance product name became Humana Care Plus. This added to Humana's overall name recognition and the integration of its businesses. Humana became a national brand name.

In moving toward branded medicine, Humana hired Neal Westermeyer as its new marketing vice president in late 1985 and centralized all marketing activities under a reorganized corporate marketing department. Objectives at that time included improved strategic focus, enhanced strategic linkage of marketing efforts within the company, increased ability to respond to change, and identification of new business opportunities.

Grey Advertising was selected in December 1985 to prepare Humana's first-ever brand image advertising campaign. The ads premiered in mid-May 1986, with definite unifying themes: "Quality care at affordable prices" and "Bringing the human being in need into the hands of a doctor."[16]

Marketing expenditures in health care soared in 1986. An American Hospital Association study indicated that the average marketing budget for hospitals in 1986 was $266,100, of which $140,240 was spent on advertising. Advertising spending had increased 147 percent since 1984.[17]

Humana continued using "integrated marketing" in 1986 to 1987, building a brand image. The company even filed a trademark abuse claim against NBC's *St. Elsewhere* for using the fake name Ecumena for its fictional hospital chain in the show. NBC agreed to a name change in an out-of-court settlement.[18] Humana's

[16] Ronald Alsop, "New Ad Campaign Prescribes Humana's Brand of Medicine," *Wall Street Journal*, May 15, 1986, p. B1.

[17] "A Tale of 3 Cities' Marketing Battles," *Modern Healthcare*, April 10, 1987, p. 47.

[18] Kari Super Palm, "Humana Claims Trademark Abuse on 'St. Elsewhere,'" *Modern Healthcare*, October 23, 1987, p. 76.

EXHIBIT 12.5   Breast Diagnostic Center (BDC) Research Highlights

Consumer Research

Points of Difference (Versus Outpatient Mammography)

> "Someone is responding to our needs, and this is a need. Someone is concerned about us."
> "Experts" due to specialization.
> Perceived as state-of-the-art and committed to remain so in the future.
> Benefits of separate facility:

- More convenient, time savings
- Hospital is for sick people, center is for education and testing
- Perceived as less expensive than hospital
- Less red tape and bureaucracy

Current education is perceived as inadequate—few women believe they are competent to perform their breast self-exam.

Physician Reaction

> High degree of sensitivity in some locations.
> Overall perception of the service offered is very favorable.
> A strong education program tends to legitimize the center.

Product Definition

Multimodality	Mammography: gold standard, highest use for screening and diagnostic.
Technology	Ultrasound: screening for young or pregnant, diagnostic for symptomatic.
	Other: procedures of local interest or innovations Humana may wish to investigate.
Education	Education important to consumers and essential for physician acceptance.
	MammaCare preferred due to its exclusivity and perceived superiority over other education packages currently available.
Physicians	Radiologists dedicated to the concept and willing to commit necessary time and interest.
	Primary-care referral base, that must be worked with and through design and implementation phase with emphasis on potential referrals from program.
Staffing	All-woman staff with strong technical and people skills. "Primary care" technologists that follow patient through screening modalities and education.
Facility	A wellness, noninstitutional, homelike environment.
	Sufficient floor space to accommodate basic model and with expansion capabilities when volumes dictate.
Pricing	Below market, presuming volume. (Test for price elasticity is planned.)
Positioning	"A special place for women."
	"Not a cancer clinic."
	"Specializing in early detection and education of breast disease."
	The *most* important phrases consistently identified in consumer research.
	If we are to achieve screening volumes, we must avoid strong consumer promotion of the treatment side (cancer clinic), even though expertise in this area is a natural spin-off.

Criteria for Successful Breast Diagnostic Center

1. A population base large enough to support a center.

- 30,000–50,000 females ages 35–64
- 180,000–300,000 total population base

This is a general guideline based on U.S. age distribution studies. Because of variables, calculations should be made on a market-to-market basis.

(Cont.)

EXHIBIT 12.5 (Cont.)

2. A radiologist who is committed to building volumes. Many excellent radiologists are not widely experienced in mammography and prefer not to do large volumes. Because the radiologist is so important to the success of the Center, it is essential that he or she be interested in the Center and willing to help promote it. Indications of commitment would include special training in mammography or ultrasound.

3. Approximately 2,000 square feet of space. The center should be located in an area easily accessible for outpatients and the radiologists. The ground floor of a medical office building or an area of the hospital with a separate entrance is most desirable. Outside signage should be easily identifiable from the parking lot.

4. Purchase of the newest low radiation dose mammography and dedicated breast ultrasound equipment.

5. Wellness-oriented feminine decor that will set Humana Breast Diagnostic Centers apart from the competition. The special decor and amenities that go with it will help business to the facility by word of mouth.

6. A base of primary-care physicians to support the center. OB/GYNs, internal medicine, and family practitioners with offices located on the hospital campus are an important source for patients. Hospitals that have or plan to establish a number of services oriented to women are prime candidates for Breast Diagnostic Centers.

7. A public relations director, agency, or individual responsible for initiating news media coverage and building understanding and support among local women's groups.

8. A commitment to an extensive marketing campaign to educate women and physicians about the service and promote its use.

Overview

Concept		A *dedicated unit* for the education and early detection of breast disease. Environment: wellness-oriented, feminine decor. Technologies: mammography and ultrasound.
Need		Breast cancer is the leading cause of cancer deaths among women. Early detection increases five-year survival rate from less than 50 percent to 90 percent. The American Cancer Society (ACS) has established guidelines for routine mammography: all women 35 and older. Less than 5 percent currently comply with mammography screening guidelines.
Target		To attract women with no known breast disease (asymptomatic) to screen for early detection based primarily on ACS mammography guidelines (46 percent of all females), versus past breast diagnostics, which was dedicated almost solely to diagnosing symptomatic patients (after lump was found) resulting in a survival rate of less than 50 percent (2 percent of all females).
Strategy	Consumer	Educate, motivate and build awareness/preference for BDC.
	Physician	"Pull" through education and detailing, "push" through consumer pressure.
Objective	Primary	Leadership position among area physicians, consumers, and media (especially important in women's programs).
	Secondary	Financial viability from center operation and spin-off business (related and unrelated).

Source: Company documents.

hopes for creating a national brand name image were put on hold in late 1987 when the company ended its relationship with Grey. The company shifted the control back to individual hospitals, allowing them to choose local agencies and develop local campaigns and strategies. Financial problems contributed to the breakup, as did discouragement over the lack of an immediate payoff from all the heavy promotional spending. Humana spent $8.3 million in measured advertising in 1985, but only $3.5 million in 1986. Hospital Corporation of America, a major national competitor, also ceased national advertising at the same time.[19]

Since then, Humana followed a product-line approach, as shown by its recent corporate reorganization into two divisions, which was intended to further its vertical integration strategy. In June 1990, Humana launched another attempt to build a long-term brand image for itself. The campaign consisted of two 30-second and two 60-second commercials, set to Willie Nelson's hit song, "On the Road Again." A series of vignettes illustrated the theme in the commercials, which aired through stations in Louisville, Lexington, and Las Vegas. Humana expected to use these commercials in 25 markets by the fall of 1990. Westermeyer hoped that this campaign would last 10 years, since the company felt it had advanced sufficiently in its vertical integration to attempt the new image campaign. Advertising experts estimated that Humana would have to spend $100,000 to $300,000 per market just to get its message across to the public. In keeping with the commercials' theme, the company would redesign the product-specific material to complement and reinforce the image.[20]

HEALTH CARE INDUSTRY PROBLEMS AND TRENDS

The health care industry has had to deal with several major problems and was facing serious obstacles in the 1990s and beyond, including a continued decline in inpatient business, rising health care costs, high technology, changes in Medicare reimbursement, an aging population, and a debate over the values of for-profit (investor-owned) hospitals with respect to indigent care. In sum, our nation was faced with major decisions with respect to health care delivery.

Declining Inpatient Business for Hospitals

During the past few years, there was a nationwide and industry-wide decline in the number of people using hospitals as inpatients. People used outpatient services, if possible, in lieu of being admitted to the hospital. The result of this trend was a dramatic increase in hospitals' acuity levels because those who did become inpatients needed more services and care. Therefore, the problem was twofold: fewer patient days to produce revenue and a higher acuity level that

[19] Julie Leisse Erickson, "Healthcare Giants Pull Plug on Big Ad Plans," *Advertising Age*, November 16, 1987, p. 3 et seq.; Linda Perry, "Humana Launches Multimillion-Dollar Image Campaign," *Modern Healthcare*, June 18, 1990, p. 66.
[20] Perry, "Humana Launches Multimillion-Dollar Image Campaign," p. 41.

required more sophisticated equipment, increased technology, and highly trained staff members. Many experts felt that hospital usage peaked in 1975. In 1982, admissions and total inpatients dropped for the first time, despite an aging, highly susceptible population. Since 1982, admissions continued to decline.

The average occupancy rates for approximately 2,000 community hospitals rose slightly from 64.5 percent in 1988 to 64.9 percent in 1989. The American Hospital Association also reported that, for both years, admissions fell at an annual rate of 0.7 percent. Admissions for 1989 totaled 33.18 million patients. The drop in admissions was attributed to a decline in admissions of people under the age of 65. On the other hand, outpatient admissions grew, reaching 308 million in 1989, a 4.3 percent increase over 1988 figures. The average length of stay for 1989 was about 6.6 days per admission. For Humana, the average length of stay in May 1990 was 5.9 days per admission.[21] Recently, it was reported that, despite the closings of some 500 hospitals in the 1980s, occupancy rates fell in six years from 59.3 percent to approximately 48.5 percent.[22]

Rising Health Care Costs

Health care costs spiraled upward over the past two decades and were expected to continue that direction in the 1990s. Health care costs were rising annually at an average annual rate of 8 to 11 percent; without a solution, this rate was expected to continue in the 1990s.[23] A recent American Hospital Association report indicated fluctuating rates for cost increases for the 1980s: 19 percent in 1981, 4.6 percent in 1984, 9.9 percent in 1988, and 10.2 percent in 1989.[24] At present, the United States spends 12 percent of its GNP on health care, more than any other nation.[25]

The growth of health care expenditures has become an issue of national concern. The media, both popular and professional, have devoted expanded coverage to the situation. Although the increasing cost of health care contributed to the financial success of Humana, the burdens that this staggering growth placed on individuals, the government, and employers (who were primarily responsible for paying the nation's health care bills) were widely recognized. Many employers increased the deductible and copayment amounts their employees had to pay for health care, causing inpatient utilization to shrink. Some started charging penalties for employees who smoked or were overweight, while others provided incentives for those employees who stayed healthy.[26] A recent Conference Board

---

[21] Figures taken from "AHA: Utilization Declines; Financial Pressures Moderate," *Hospitals*, May 5, 1990, pp. 42, 44; Jay Greene and Judith Nemes, "Multi-Unit Providers Survey," *Modern Healthcare*, May 21, 1990, p. 22; Jerry Holt, Public Relations Department, Humana, faxed information, July 23, 1990.

[22] "Hospital, Heal Thyself," *Business Week*, August 27, 1990, p. 67.

[23] Vincent W. K. Wong, "Cost to Remain Driving Force of Health Care in the 1990s," *Marketing News*, January 22, 1990, p. 8.

[24] "AHA: Utilization Declines," p. 42.

[25] "Hospital, Heal Thyself," p. 68.

[26] Aaron Bernstein, "Making It Pay to Stay Healthy," *Business Week*, May 21, 1990, pp. 46–47.

survey on perceived value of goods and services received by consumers reported that hospitals received the lowest rating of all goods and services covered in the study. "Hospital charges are considered to be overpriced by three out of five consumers."[27] Answers to the health care cost problem will not come easily. Focus has turned to evaluating the success of nationalized health care systems in Canada and Great Britain, among other countries. Humana's management basically opposed "socialized medicine." Managed health care was seen to be one possible solution.[28]

Technology

Advances in technology, with its appropriate use and assessment of clinical applications, were extremely important. Replacing obsolete equipment would be a major financial undertaking. Technology was evolving at an intense pace, which made it almost impossible for health care administrators and physicians to remain current with the equipment and methods that provide the most cost-effective diagnosis, treatment, and management of patients. Moreover, the general public was not aware of the high cost of equipment—a CAT scanner alone was priced at approximately $1 million.

One author identified emerging streams of technology for this decade. These streams include artificial intelligence, diagnostic imaging, genetic engineering, home health services, new-wave surgery (lasers), office automation, and super drugs.[29] As technology advances, the health care industry is having to face ethical issues that are a by-product of these streams, such as genetics.

Medicare Reimbursement

Health care subsidies were diminishing. That was a hard fact for the American public, which for years had received well-intended subsidies that disguised the true cost of health care, encouraged excessive use, and resulted in a staggering national medical bill. The government paid hospitals to treat Medicare patients on the basis of diagnoses that had predetermined prices; if the treatment cost less, the hospitals kept the difference, but if it cost more, the hospitals absorbed the additional cost. For example, Medicare would only pay up to $7,600, excluding surgeons' fees, for a hip replacement. The procedure usually costs a hospital $10,000 to $12,000.[30] The hospital could not bill the patient for the difference, so it tried to reduce costs by cutting back on hospital recuperation time.

---

[27] "The Consumer's View of Value Received," *Special Consumer Survey Report*, the Conference Board, New York, February 1990, p. 4.

[28] See Wong, "Cost to Remain Driving Force"; Jeff Goldsmith, "A Radical Prescription for Hospitals," *Harvard Business Review*, May–June 1989, pp. 104–111; and Russell C. Coile, Jr., "The Megatrends—and the Backlash," *Healthcare Forum Journal*, March–April 1990, pp. 37–40. Also see an opinion by columnist Joan Beck, "It May Sound Good, but National Health Has Many Pitfalls," *Chicago Tribune*, July 23, 1990, Sec. 1., p. 11.

[29] Coile, "The Megatrends," pp. 38–39.

[30] "Hospital, Heal Thyself," p. 67.

This "diagnosis related group" method of reimbursement began to affect hospitals treating Medicare patients in October 1983. It created incentives for efficiency, since high-cost hospitals would receive basically the same payment as low-cost hospitals. Thus, efficiency and cost effectiveness became important to hospitals. There are some serious questions being raised by this reimbursement method. The concern is that patients were being "hustled out of hospitals sicker and quicker." For example, in Milwaukee, Wisconsin area hospitals, the average length of stay for Medicare patients dropped dramatically from 1982 to 1985. The following statistics show several examples:[31]

Diagnosis	1982	1985
Heart Failure	12 days	9 days
Cataract Surgery	3–4 days	0 days (outpatient)
Stroke	19.2 days	11 days

Reimbursement from Medicaid, which financed health care for 24 million low-income people, had also changed to a fixed rate per diagnostic group. State and federal legislatures have not been funding either program adequately, in response to taxpayers' demands for lower taxes. In fact, in 1988 the Illinois Medicaid program ran out of money and almost stopped all payments before the state legislature intervened. A recent Supreme Court ruling allowed hospitals and nursing homes to sue states for higher Medicaid reimbursement rates. Such lawsuits had been filed in several states including Pennsylvania, Virginia, and Wisconsin.[32]

Medicare's contribution to Humana's revenues fell from 31 percent for 1985 to 1986 to 28 percent for 1987 to 1989. Medicaid's contribution held steadily at around 2 to 3 percent over the five years from 1985 to 1989. Humana's health plans' contribution grew from 1 percent in 1986 to 5 percent in 1989. Blue Cross (cost-basis) accounted for 1 percent in 1989. All other payers, including private insurance companies, accounted for 63 percent of revenues in 1989, down from a high of 66 percent in 1987.[33]

An Aging Population

Americans are growing older. "The aging of America is the single most dominant factor in the future of the health industry in the Nineties."[34] Business people, politicians, and health administrators realized that the "gray market" is not one big market. In reality, there are several segments in this population group. The fastest-growing segment of our population today is those Americans age 85 or

[31] Neil D. Rosenberg, "Some Say Hospital Patients Released 'Sicker and Quicker,'" *Milwaukee Journal*, August 11, 1986, p. 4A.
[32] "States Face Higher Costs for Health Care," *Milwaukee Journal*, July 6, 1990, p. A3.
[33] Humana Inc., Form 10-K, August 31, 1989, p. 4.
[34] Coile, "The Megatrends," p. 37.

older. "Young elders," another segment of people between the ages of 55 and 70, are still very active, mobile, and healthy. Each segment's needs differ greatly, and the health care industry must realize this and address its needs appropriately. The over-85 group will need greater levels of health and support services to maintain their independence, which has ramifications for nursing homes, home health care agencies, hospitals, and adult day health programs, among others.

For-Profit Hospitals and Indigent Care

An investor-owned or for-profit hospital is owned by private investors. It obtains capital from investors and pays taxes. A not-for-profit hospital, in contrast, may be privately owned (by a religious group) or publicly owned (by the government) and pays no taxes, yet produces the same revenues. Not-for-profit really refers to its tax status.

A big issue for all hospitals, regardless of tax status, is that of indigent care: providing health care for those individuals who cannot pay for the services. Indigent care continues to be a substantial financial burden for everyone—hospitals, taxpayers, communities, and so on.

For-profit hospitals tend to have a negative image in the minds of the public with respect to indigent care. For example, in a 1987 survey by National Research Corporation, consumers indicated that religious-affiliated and independent, not-for-profit hospitals provided the best care (23 percent each). For-profit hospitals (12 percent) did come in ahead of city/county hospitals (9 percent).[35] There was some criticism of nonprofit hospitals,[36] but for the most part, for-profits received the brunt of the criticism for performing "wallet biopsies" (seeing if people can pay before providing care).[37] Recently, a federal emergency room law was strengthened to "dissuade private hospitals from 'dumping' indigent patients onto public facilities. The law now requires that hospitals examine and treat—before asking whether they can pay—all people who show up at their emergency rooms."[38]

To its credit, Humana responded to the indigent care issue in its headquarters city, Louisville. In May 1983, Humana leased the University of Louisville hospital and agreed to provide necessary hospital care to indigent residents of Jefferson County, Kentucky, in return for the government's payment of an annual fixed sum guaranteed by Humana to increase no faster than tax receipts. In addition to arranging for Humana to lease the hospital and establishing a trust to fund the hospital care of the county's poor people, the agreements set up an affiliation between Humana and the University of Louisville School of Medicine, which benefited both financially and academically through improved programs.

[35] "Hospital Care" (chart), *Wall Street Journal*, February 24, 1987, p. 31.
[36] See Regina E. Herzlinger, "Nonprofit Hospitals Seldom Profit the Needy," *Wall Street Journal*, March 23, 1987, p. 18.
[37] For a scathing critique, see Peter Downs, "Your Money or Your Life," *The Progressive*, January 1987, pp. 24–28.
[38] Steven Morris, "Emergency-Room Law Strengthened," *Chicago Tribune*, July 2, 1990, Sec. 4, p. 1 et seq.

Since 1984, the "payment, by contract, has increased annually by either the percentage increase in the consumer price index, or the percentage increase in government tax revenues, whichever is less. For six years this contractual arrangement has capped governments' indigent care expenditures at an annual compound rate of increase of just 1 percent, while providing a highly acceptable level of service and beneficiary satisfaction. An ombudsperson . . . has never had to rule, as all persons claiming indigency, and all pre-admission transfers . . . have been accepted without question."[39]

Humana made a bold move in 1987, when it bought an insolvent HMO in Florida. "In exchange for a fixed monthly payment equal to 95 percent of the scheduled Medicare payment per member from the federal government, Humana covers all mandated Medicare benefits, as well as the $560 hospital co-payment, the 20 percent physician copayment, eye care, and prescriptions, which are not covered by Medicare's traditional program."[40] Its managed care plan included Medicare beneficiaries and was the largest such plan in the nation. Humana was able to turn the insolvent HMO around in two years and made it a success story for the company and for the people and the state of Florida.

HUMANA FINANCES

Humana enjoyed a high level of financial success and growth until 1986. Mistakes that were made in plans for its MedFirst clinics and its group health insurance program showed up on the company's bottom line in 1986 and 1987. Since then, Humana recovered financially, but not to the level of performance it previously enjoyed. As with all hospital corporations, Humana was struggling with the problems discussed. Income statements and balance sheets are provided in Exhibit 12.6.

COMPETITION

In addition to the various religious and other private nonprofit hospitals and local public hospitals that provided localized competition to individual Humana hospitals, there were several major investor-owned hospital chains that competed as well. The four major chains were American Medical International, Hospital Corporation of America, Humana, and National Medical Enterprises. A brief overview of Humana's three chief competitors in this category is provided.

American Medical International (AMI)

AMI, headquartered in Beverly Hills, California, "owns, manages, and operates hospitals, provides health care services and is involved in the develop-

---

[39] *Humana Inc. 1989 Annual Report*, p. 8.
[40] Ibid.

EXHIBIT 12.6   Humana Financial Data, 1987–1989

Humana Inc.
Louisville, Kentucky

	Fiscal Year Ending (In thousands except share data)		
	August 31, 1987	*August 31, 1988*	*August 31, 1989*
Income Statement			
Sales	$ 2,973,643	$ 3,435,397	4,087,994
Gross Profit	2,973,643	3,435,397	4,087,994
General Selling & Administrative Expense	(2,340,178)	(2,786,230)	(3,401,884)
Income Before Depreciation and Amortization	633,465	649,167	686,100
Depreciation and Amortization	(180,197)	(195,651)	(209,469)
Nonoperating Income	n/a	46,064	60,570
Interest Expense	(123,233)	(145,938)	(138,477)
Income Before Taxes	330,035	353,642	398,734
Provision for Income Taxes	(147,196)	(126,602)	(142,747)
Net Income before Extraordinary Items	182,839	227,040	255,987
Extraordinary Items and Discontinued Operations	n/a	81	n/a
Net Income	$ 182,830	$ 227,121	$ 255,987
Outstanding Shares	97,660,445	97,886,147	98,438,852
Balance Sheet			
Assets			
Cash	$ 73,745	$ 140,202	$ 105,340
Market Securities	137,812	106,490	79,104
Receivables	494,029	507,141	616,210
Inventories	58,698	69,786	80,632
Other Current Assets	92,268	104,788	133,615
Total Current Assets	856,552	928,407	1,014,901
Property, Plant and Equipment	2,819,846	2,975,549	3,206,354
Accumulated Depreciation	(852,480)	(987,790)	(1,154,868)
Net Property and Equipment	1,967,366	1,987,759	2,051,486
Investment and Advertising to Subsidiaries	266,410	315,875	462,541
Deposits and Other Assets	118,437	189,921	167,646
Total Assets	$ 3,208,765	$ 3,421,962	$ 3,696,574
Liabilities and Shareholders' Equity			
Accounts Payable	$ 82,342	$ 107,666	$ 115,338
Current Long-Term Debt	55,626	32,680	35,045
Accrued Expenses	222,900	256,140	324,961
Income Taxes	82,426	95,475	106,241
Other Current Liabilities	141,457	141,773	194,925
Total Current Liabilities	584,751	633,734	776,510
Deferred Charges/Income	374,506	422,993	452,722
Long-Term Debt	1,237,466	1,210,618	1,140,366
Total Liabilities	2,196,723	2,267,345	2,369,598

(Cont.)

EXHIBIT 12.6   (continued)

	August 31, 1987	August 31, 1988	August 31, 1989
Common Stock, Net	16,277	16,314	16,406
Capital Surplus	229,737	233,898	243,398
Retained Earnings	769,446	915,452	1,078,201
Other Liabilities	(3,418)	(11,047)	(11,029)
Shareholders' Equity	1,012,042	1,154,617	1,326,976
Total Liabilities and Shareholders' Equity	$ 3,208,765	$ 3,421,962	$ 3,696,574

Five-Year Summary (In thousands)

Date	Sales	Net Income	Earnings per share
1989	$4,087,994	$255,987	$2.56
1988	3,435,397	227,121	2.30
1987	2,973,643	182,839	1.86
1986	2,710,592	54,452	0.56
1985	2,283,513	216,220	2.19

Cash Flow (In thousands)

	August 31, 1987	August 31, 1988	August 31, 1989
Cash Flow Provided by Operating Activity			
Net Income (Loss)	$ 182,839	$ 227,121	$ 255,987
Depreciation/Amortization	180,197	195,651	209,469
Net Increase (Decrease), Assets/Liabilities	(132,545)	(82,252)	(77,896)
Cash Provided (Used), Discontinued Operations	n/a	25,730	n/a
Other Adjustments, Net	196,623	145,146	144,998
Net Cash From Operations	$ 427,114	$ 511,396	$ 532,558
Cash Flow Provided by Investing Activity			
Increase (Decrease), Property & Plant	$ (125,370)	$ (185,230)	$ (288,422)
(Acquisition) Disposal of Subsidiaries	(18,706)	(42,952)	n/a
Increase (Decrease), Securities Investment	(140,754)	(59,477)	(129,797)
Other Cash Inflow (Outflow)	(24,917)	(1,906)	n/a
Net Cash Provided (Used), Investment	$ (309,747)	$ (289,565)	$ (418,219)
Cash Flow Provided by Financing Activity			
Issue (Purchase), Equity Share	$ 1,899	$ 1,848	$ 8,036
Increase (Decrease) in Borrowing	(15,536)	(77,843)	(63,980)
Dividends/Other Distribution	(75,075)	(81,115)	(93,238)
Other Cash Inflow (Outflow)	(1,162)	1,736	(19)
Net Cash Provided (Used), Financing	$ (89,874)	$ (155,374)	$ (149,201)
Net Change in Cash or Equivalent	$ 27,493	$ 66,457	$ (34,862)
Cash or Equivalent at Year Start	46,252	73,745	140,202
Cash or Equivalent at Year End	$ 73,745	$ 140,202	$ 105,340

n/a = not applicable.

ment of additional health care centers and implementation of allied support services worldwide."[41] As of fiscal 1989, AMI had 43,700 employees and 81 hospitals (14,617 beds) worldwide. Financial data are presented in Exhibit 12.7. The company reported a $12.76 million loss in 1989, compared to a profit of $115.3 million in 1988.[42]

Similar to Humana, AMI developed an insurance plan (Amicare) in the mid-1980s. By 1987, the company contributed more than its share to the $200 million loss experienced by all four chains on insurance plans, and bailed out of the insurance business. The company sold off some of its hospitals that year, and rejected a takeover bid. The company continued to sell off hospitals, office buildings, and other related medical services throughout 1988 and 1989. A private group bought control through a tender offer of $1.927 billion in 1989.[43] The company was ranked 967th out of 1,000 in terms of stock market value by *Business Week* in April 1990 (as compared to Humana's ranking of 162nd out of 1,000).

Hospital Corporation of America (HCA)

HCA, headquartered in Nashville, Tennessee, "provides health care services through ownership and operation of medical/surgical and psychiatric hospitals."[44] As of fiscal 1989, HCA had 68,000 employees and 148 hospitals (27,070 beds) worldwide.

HCA's financial information is included in Exhibit 12.8. The company posted pretax profits of $428 million in fiscal 1988 and lost $13 million in 1989.[45]

In 1985, the company derived 75 percent of its revenues from inpatient hospitals. Most of its facilities were in the south, much like Humana. Similar to Humana, HCA began labeling its hospitals that year. By 1986, HCA was the nation's largest investor-owned company, with 458 hospitals in 44 states and 8 foreign countries. The company put together an insurance plan package and started purchasing insurance companies. A three-tiered marketing effort for the plans began in 1984, based on direct mail and seminars, aimed at women, the elderly, and employers. There was no marketing department before 1984.

Financial problems developed in 1986. The company moved away from acquiring and building new hospitals to retrofitting existing facilities in an attempt to cut back on high-cost, acute-care services. HCA sold 104 hospitals in September 1987, which left it with 393 hospitals in 45 states. The company took a fourth-quarter 1986 loss of $42 million and rejected a takeover bid in 1987. HCA dropped national advertising plans in late 1987 and focused instead on locally

---

[41] American Medical International, Complete Company Records, Compact Disclosure, UWO, July 3, 1990.
[42] Greene and Nemes, "Multiunit Providers Survey," p. 37.
[43] "The Top 200 Deals," *Business Week*, April 13, 1990, p. 38.
[44] Hospital Corporation of America, Complete Company Records, Compact Disclosure, UWO, July 3, 1990.
[45] Greene and Nemes, "Multiunit Providers Survey," p. 37.

EXHIBIT 12.7 AMI Financial Data, 1987–1989

American Medical International, Inc.
Beverly Hills, California

	Fiscal Year Ending (In thousands except share data)		
	August 31, 1987	August 31, 1988	August 31, 1989
Income Statement			
Sales	$ 2,882,440	$ 3,111,542	$ 2,750,202
Gross Profit	2,882,440	3,111,542	2,750,202
General Selling and Administrative Expense	(2,303,507)	(2,569,610)	(2,354,816)
Income Before Depreciation and Amortization	578,933	541,932	404,386
Depreciation and Amortization	(195,299)	(208,703)	(191,309)
Nonoperating Income	n/a	400	(87,600)
Interest Expense	(203,228)	(179,728)	(146,037)
Income Before Taxes	180,406	153,901	(20,560)
Provision for Income Taxes	(69,100)	(55,400)	7,800
Net Income before Extraordinary Items	111,306	98,501	(12,760)
Extraordinary Items and Discontinued Operations	(5,897)	16,800	n/a
Net Income	$ 105,409	$ 115,301	$ (12,760)
Outstanding Shares	87,778,000	78,107,000	69,930,000
Balance Sheet			
Assets			
Cash	$ 71,966	$ 28,092	$ 153,733
Receivables	373,012	260,540	242,577
Inventories	89,764	69,707	71,581
Other Current Assets	13,093	474,084	13,398
Total Current Assets	547,835	832,423	481,559
Property, Plant and Equipment	3,235,306	2,727,066	2,918,291
Accumulated Depreciation	(694,825)	(655,648)	(784,938)
Net Property and Equipment	2,540,481	2,071,418	2,133,357
Investment and Advertising to Subsidiaries	85,571	78,937	174,369
Other Noncurrent Assets	204,540	140,231	150,226
Deferred Charges	111,569	74,409	70,824
Intangibles	222,312	212,208	204,211
Deposits and Other Assets	n/a	122,612	n/a
Total Assets	$ 3,712,308	$ 3,532,238	$ 3,214,546
Liabilities and Shareholders' Equity			
Accounts Payable	$ 119,054	$ 122,247	$ 143,386
Current Long-Term Debt	9,225	106,008	5,760
Accrued Expenses	264,219	287,187	299,005
Income Taxes	22,932	95,320	42,102
Total Current Liabilities	415,430	609,762	490,253
Deferred Charges/Income	439,107	319,169	290,409
Convertible Debt	175,559	141,032	92,735
Long-Term Debt	1,646,230	1,422,411	1,460,102
Other Long-Term Liabilities	63,946	81,905	94,905
Total Liabilities	2,740,272	2,574,279	2,428,404

EXHIBIT 12.7   (continued)

	August 31, 1987	August 31, 1988	August 31, 1989
Minority Interest (Liability)	12,684	69,239	72,947
Common Stock, Net	87,778	78,107	69,930
Capital Surplus	448,062	327,822	208,445
Retained Earnings	421,663	480,167	443,486
Other Liabilities	1,849	2,624	(8,666)
Shareholders' Equity	959,352	888,720	713,195
Total Liabilities and Shareholders' Equity	$ 3,712,308	$ 3,532,238	$ 3,214,546

Five-Year Summary (In thousands)

Date	Sales	Net Income	Earnings per share
1989	$2,750,202	$(12,760)	$(0.18)
1988	3,111,542	115,301	1.41
1987	2,882,440	105,409	1.20
1986	2,685,889	(97,279)	(1.12)
1985	2,251,333	163,792	1.94

Cash Flow (In thousands)

	August 31, 1987	August 31, 1988	August 31, 1989
Cash Flow Provided by Operating Activity			
Net Income (Loss)	$ 111,306	$ 98,501	$ (12,760)
Depreciation/Amortization	195,299	208,703	191,309
Net Increase (Decrease), Assets/Liabilities	41,784	105,920	202,105
Other Adjustments, Net	81,212	55,736	(119,444)
Net Cash Provided (Used) by Operations	$ 429,601	$ 468,860	$ 261,210
Cash Flow Provided by Investing Activity			
Increase (Decrease), Property and Plant	$ n/a	$ (181,847)	$ n/a
Increase (Decrease), Securities Investment	n/a	108,472	n/a
Other Cash Inflow (Outflow)	(36,606)	(76,875)	142,742
Net Cash Provided (Used), Investment	$ (36,606)	$ (150,250)	$ 142,742
Cash Flow Provided by Financing Activity			
Issue (Purchase), Equity Share	$ 14,431	$ (129,911)	$ 19,157
Increase (Decrease) in Borrowing	(384,188)	(172,177)	(90,926)
Dividends/Other Distribution	n/a	(56,797)	(37,185)
Other Cash Inflow (Outflow)	n/a	n/a	(175,536)
Net Cash Provided (Used), Financing	(369,757)	(358,885)	(284,490)
Effect of Exchange Rate on Cash	$ 6,581	$ (3,599)	$ 6,179
Net Change in Cash or Equivalent	$ 29,819	$ (43,874)	$ 125,641
Cash or Equivalent at Year Start	42,147	71,966	28,092
Cash or Equivalent at Year End	$ 71,966	$ 28,092	$ 153,733

n/a = not applicable.

EXHIBIT 12.8 HCA Financial Data, 1987–1989

Hospital Corporation of America
Nashville, Tennessee

	Fiscal Year Ending (In thousands except share data)		
	December 31, 1987	*December 31, 1988*	*December 31, 1989*
Income Statement			
Sales	$ 4,675,879	$ 4,111,169	$ 3,147,750
Gross Profit	4,675,879	4,111,169	3,147,750
General Selling and			
Administrative Expense	(3,892,734)	(3,326,106)	(2,525,657)
Income Before Depreciation and			
Amortization	783,145	785,063	622,093
Depreciation and Amortization	(285,018)	(234,930)	(209,275)
Nonoperating Income	(91,031)	76,761	46,141
Interest Expense	(268,890)	(198,064)	(472,149)
Income Before Taxes	138,206	428,830	(13,190)
Provision for Income Taxes	(196,600)	(170,000)	(1,000)
Net Income	$ (58,394)	$ 258,830	$ (14,190)
Outstanding Shares	82,443,041	71,084,158	70,803,657
Balance Sheet			
Assets			
Cash	$ 933,898	$ 13,133	$ 3,238
Receivables	726,521	708,408	733,919
Inventories	86,900	90,877	82,175
Other Current Assets	68,105	90,919	149,784
Total Current Assets	1,815,424	903,337	969,116
Property, Plant and Equipment	3,734,197	4,083,903	3,216,475
Accumulated Depreciation	(891,189)	(1,078,453)	(179,374)
Net Property and Equipment	2,843,008	3,005,450	3,037,101
Investment and Advertising to			
Subsidiaries	1,198,212	1,173,850	1,296,899
Deferred Charges	20,593	19,653	147,394
Intangibles	305,360	286,018	1,429,178
Total Assets	$ 6,182,597	$ 5,388,308	$ 6,879,688
Liabilities and Shareholders' Equity			
Accounts Payable	$ 162,119	$ 148,992	$ 174,651
Current Long-Term Debt	371,343	32,493	409,302
Accrued Expenses	294,350	297,475	355,463
Income Taxes	24,082	3,201	4,285
Total Current Liabilities	851,894	482,161	943,701
Deferred Charges/Income	718,417	719,921	503,483
Long-Term Debt	2,222,938	2,062,235	4,373,582
Other Long-Term Liabilities	443,687	506,501	494,650
Total Liabilities	4,236,936	3,770,818	6,315,416
Common Stock, Net	82,443	71,084	708
Capital Surplus	605,146	533,580	577,754
Retained Earnings	1,272,713	1,013,648	(14,190)
Other Liabilities	(14,641)	(822)	n/a
Shareholders' Equity	1,945,661	1,617,490	564,272
Total Liabilities and			
Shareholders' Equity	$ 6,182,597	$ 5,388,308	$ 6,879,688

EXHIBIT 12.8   (continued)

Five-Year Summary (In thousands)

Date	Sales	Net Income	Earnings per share
1989	$3,147,750	$(14,190)	n/a
1988	4,111,169	258,830	3.62
1987	4,675,879	(58,394)	(.71)
1986	4,930,652	174,644	2.08
1985	4,352,306	338,613	3.75

Cash Flow (In thousands)

	December 31, 1987	December 31, 1988	December 31, 1989
Cash Flow Provided by Operating Activity			
Net Income (Loss)	$ (58,394)	$ 258,830	$ (14,190)
Depreciation/Amortization	285,018	234,930	209,275
Net Increase (Decrease), Assets/Liabilities	(303,423)	(162,210)	(62,373)
Other Adjustments, Net	474,816	166,128	223,659
Cash Provided (Used) by Operations	$ 398,017	$ 497,678	$ 356,371
Cash Flow Provided by Investing Activity			
Increase (Decrease), Property and Plant	$ 1,187,022	$ (262,521)	$ (172,439)
(Acquisitions) Disposal of Subsidiaries	(47,098)	(14,694)	n/a
Increase (Decrease), Securities Investment	(99,017)	(39,854)	20,441
Other Cash Inflow (Outflow)	8,098	373	171,583
Net Cash Provided (Used), Investment	$ 1,049,005	$ (316,696)	$ 19,585
Cash Flow (In thousands)			
Cash Flow Provided by Financing Activity			
Issue (Purchase), Equity Share	$ 20,927	$ (549,710)	$ n/a
Increase (Decrease) in Borrowing	(620,147)	(499,553)	(465,665)
Dividends/Other Distribution	(56,945)	(51,110)	n/a
Other Cash Inflow (Outflow)	(7,222)	(1,374)	26
Net Cash Provided (Used), Financing	(663,387)	(1,101,747)	(465,639)
Net Change in Cash or Equivalent	$ 783,635	$ (920,765)	$ (89,683)
Cash or Equivalent at Year Start	150,263	933,898	92,921
Cash or Equivalent at Year End	$ 933,898	$ 13,133	$ 3,238

n/a = not applicable.

253

oriented campaigns. Psychiatric hospitals accounted for 33 percent of HCA's business in fiscal 1987.

In March 1989, the company concluded a $4.9 billion leveraged buyout (LBO), that took the company private. There were debt problems and financial worries after the LBO. The company was obligated to repay a $1.3 billion bridge loan in March 1991 after having lost $14.2 million in the last three quarters of 1989. In May 1989, the company spun off a contract-management group, HCA Management Company (changed to Quorum Health Group), and an attempt to sell off its 54 psychiatric hospitals to a group of employees failed. Recently, the company made substantial cuts in capital spending, from over $600 million in 1986 to under $300 million in 1989–1990. On a positive note, HCA's occupancy rate was running around 52 percent.[46]

National Medical Enterprises (NME)

NME, headquartered in Santa Monica, California, "provides a broad range of health care services through the ownership and management of acute care hospitals, long-term-care facilities, psychiatric hospitals, and other related businesses."[47] As of fiscal 1989, NME had 74,600 employees and 140 hospitals (12,800 beds) worldwide. Financial data on NME are included in Exhibit 12.9. Profits continued to grow in 1988 due to continued expansion in the area of specialty hospitals; however, profits fell off slightly in 1989.[48]

In 1985, NME received half of its revenues from nonhospital sources. NME offered HealthPace through a major insurance broker and had 130,000 members. But, as did the other chains, the company ran into problems, underestimating the amount of work involved in gaining doctors' acceptance. Insurance-related operations were scaled back during the period from 1985 to 1987, and several hospitals were sold off in 1987. NME's marketing focus during this time was on launching individually developed campaigns for each of its hospitals, as part of an overall focus on individual marketing strategies.[49]

The company spun off its nursing home group, Hillhaven Corporation, in January 1990, and sold five more nursing homes to Hillhaven in June 1990 in order to focus more on developing specialty psychiatric hospitals. This focus was indicated by CEO Richard Eamer's letter to the shareholders, in which he stated:

> The primary engine driving our growth is the Specialty Hospital Group, including Psychiatric Institutes of America (PIA), Rehab Hospital Services Corporation (RHSC) and Recovery Centers of America (RCA), which concentrates on substance abuse treatment.[50]

[46] Chuck Hawkins, "Hospital Corp. May Be a Little Too Quick with the Scalpel," *Business Week,* April 16, 1990, pp. 29–30.

[47] National Medical Enterprises, Complete Company Records, Compact Disclosure, UWO, July 3, 1990.

[48] Greene and Nemes, "Multiunit Providers Survey," p. 37.

[49] Linda Perry, "Hospital Chains Adopting Local Market Approach," *Modern Healthcare,* December 18, 1987, p. 66.

[50] "President's Letter," National Medical Enterprises, Compact Disclosure.

EXHIBIT 12.9   NME Financial Data, 1987–1989

National Medical Enterprises, Inc.
Santa Monica, California

Income Statement

Fiscal Year Ending (In thousands except share data)

	May 31, 1987	May 31, 1988	May 31, 1989
Sales	$ 2,881,000	$ 3,202,000	$ 3,676,000
Gross Profit	2,881,000	3,202,000	3,676,000
General Selling and Administrative Expense	(2,496,000)	(2,680,000)	(3,094,000)
Income before Depreciation and Amortization	385,000	522,000	582,000
Depreciation and Amortization	(129,000)	(139,000)	(156,000)
Nonoperating Income	23,000	26,000	27,000
Interest Expense	n/a	(125,000)	(137,000)
Income before Taxes	279,000	284,000	316,000
Provision for Income Taxes	(139,000)	(114,000)	(124,000)
Net Income before Extraordinary Items	140,000	170,000	192,000
Extraordinary Items and Discontinued Operations	(77,000)	(22,000)	(49,000)
Net Income	$ 63,000	$ 148,000	$ 143,000
Outstanding Shares	74,188,110	73,380,474	74,367,983
Balance Sheet			
Assets			
Cash	$ 74,000	$ 32,000	$ 49,000
Marketable Securities	n/a	63,000	60,000
Receivables	669,000	670,000	726,000
Inventories	68,000	56,000	61,000
Other Current Assets	73,000	50,000	102,000
Total Current Assets	884,000	871,000	998,000
Property, Plant and Equipment	2,361,000	2,558,000	2,894,000
Accumulated Depreciation	(427,000)	(467,000)	(576,000)
Net Property and Equipment	1,934,000	2,091,000	2,318,000
Investment and Advertising to Subsidiaries	n/a	166,000	178,000
Other Noncurrent Assets	347,000	159,000	165,000
Intangibles	269,000	220.000	218,000
Total Assets	$ 3,434,000	$ 3,507,000	$ 3,877,000
Liabilities and Shareholders' Equity			
Notes Payable	81,000	57,000	25,000
Accounts Payable	131,000	147,000	142,000
Current Long-Term Debt	73,000	38,000	25,000
Accrued Expenses	247,000	240,000	291,000
Income Taxes	35,000	25,000	26,000
Other Current Liabilities	12,000	47,000	43,000
Total Current Liabilities	579,000	554,000	552,000
Deferred Charges/Income	248,000	321,000	355,000
Convertible Debt	530,000	549,000	860,000
Long-Term Debt	970,000	968,000	811,000
Other Long-Term Liabilities	195,000	153,000	198,000
Total Liabilities	2,509,000	2,545,000	2,776,000

(Cont.)

EXHIBIT 12.9   (continued)

	May 31, 1987	May 31, 1988	May 31, 1989
Common Stock, Net	12,000	12,000	12,000
Capital Surplus	538,000	477,000	497,000
Retained Earnings	492,000	593,000	686,000
Treasury Stock	(111,000)	(115,000)	(92,000)
Other Liabilities	6,000)	(5,000)	(2,000)
Shareholders' Equity	925,000	962,000	1,101,000
Total Liabilities and Shareholders' Equity	$ 3,434,000	$ 3,507,000	$ 3,877,000

Five-Year Summary (In thousands)

Date	Sales	Net Income	Earnings per share
1989	$3,676,000	$143,000	$1.93
1988	3,202,000	148,000	1.99
1987	2,881,000	63,000	0.83
1986	2,577,000	116,000	1.48
1985	2,191,000	144,000	1.88

Cash Flow (In thousands)

	May 31, 1987	May 31, 1988	May 31, 1989
Cash Flow Provided by Operating Activity			
Net Income (Loss)	$ 63,000	$ 148,000	$ 143,000
Depreciation/Amortization	144,000	141,000	157,000
Net Increase (Decrease), Assets/Liabilities	(253,000)	(82,000)	(157,000)
Cash Provided (Used), Discontinued Operations	91,000	(39,000)	22,000
Other Adjustments, Net	195,000	217,000	200,000
Net Cash Provided (Used) by Operations	$ 240,000	$ 385,000	$ 365,000
Cash Flow Provided by Investing Activity			
Increase (Decrease), Property and Plant	$ (188,000)	$ (294,000)	$ (342,000)
(Acquistition) Disposal of Subsidiaries	(20,000)	147,000	(20,000)
Increase (Decrease), Securities Investment	(13,000)	(25,000)	(15,000)
Other Cash Inflow (Outflow)	11,000	(15,000)	(14,000)
Net Cash Provided (Used), Investment	$ (210,000)	$ (187,000)	$ (391,000)
Cash Flow Provided by Financing Activity			
Issue (Purchase), Equity Share	$ (113,000)	$ (82,000)	$ 20,000
Increase (Decrease) in Borrowing	116,000	(64,000)	(220,000)
Dividends/Other Distribution	(44,000)	(46,000)	(49,000)
Other Cash Inflow (Outflow)	n/a	n/a	292,000
Net Cash Provided (Used), Financing	$ (41,000)	$ (192,000)	$ 43,000
Net Change in Cash or Equivalent	$ (11,000)	$6,000	$ 17,000
Cash or Equivalent at Year Start	37,000	26,000	32,000
Cash or Equivalent at Year End	$ 26,000	$ 32,000	$ 49,000

n/a = not available.

Business Week recently ranked NME 241st out of 1,000 corporations in terms of stock market value.[51]

HUMANA STRATEGIES FOR THE 1990s

Humana was obviously a leader in health care and performed well in its 29 years of operation. It survived a major blunder in the mid-1980s and was entering the last decade of the 20th century with a better understanding of the health care market. The industry, however, continues to be in a frightening period of change. Major challenges still lie ahead for health care and individual hospitals/chains. Decisions made today will have far-reaching implications.

[51] "The Business Week 1000," *Business Week*, April 13, 1990, p. 176.

CASE 13

The Environment for Health Care Marketing: A Health Care Industry Note

---

The purpose of this industry note is to provide an overview of the health services sector to serve as background for the health care marketing cases presented. In addition to describing the most significant organizational and professional participants in this market and suggesting a brief conceptual framework for the products, this note attempts to provide an understanding of health care purchasers and the health services environment. Descriptions of selected macroenvironmental trends relevant to the future of the health care environment are presented.

This case was prepared by Stuart A. Capper, W. Jack Duncan, Peter M. Ginter, and Linda E. Swayne as a basis for class discussion rather than to illustrate either effective or ineffective handling of an administrative situation. Used with permission from Stuart A. Capper.

HISTORY OF THE HEALTH SERVICES ENVIRONMENT

The recent history of the health services sector has been characterized by two basic trends—growth and change. Since 1960, the percentage of the U.S. gross national product (GNP) devoted to health expenditures has more than doubled. This has occurred during a period when the GNP itself increased nine-fold from $515 billion to $4.88 trillion.[1] Hence, health services have been acquiring an increasingly significant proportion of a rapidly growing domestic resource pie. The growth in health expenditures per capita has been dramatic. Per capita health care expenditures between 1960 and 1988 increased 15-fold. In 1991, the United States spent more than $2,124 per person annually on health care, significantly more than other industrialized nations.

Concurrent with the rapid growth in resources committed to the health services sector has been accelerated change for health services providers and organizations. Prior to World War II, there was little government involvement in the health services industries and a relatively simple and stable market. Two fundamental factors have altered the environment. First, the pace of government experimentation with resource allocation for health care has quickened, and the public policy debate concerning these experiments has involved an increasing number of constituency groups. Second, the pace of technological advances in science and medicine has accelerated. Rapidly advancing technology and unstable public policy have combined to create an environment that is complex and dynamic for the producers of health care services and products.

CHARACTERISTICS OF THE HEALTH SECTOR

As previously indicated the two most prominent characteristics of the health services sector have been growth and change. Although numerous statistics that illustrate the growth of various subcomponents of the health services sector will be presented, it is useful to consider how the health services sector as a whole has performed in relation to other sectors of the economy.

The overall size of the nation's economy is often gauged by the use of GNP statistics. GNP measures the value of all goods and services produced by all sectors of the economy. The relationship of the health services component of GNP to other components can be illustrated by considering the sector breakdown in 1960 versus the most recent comparable figures for 1987. In 1960, the health services sector was $11.5 billion of a total GNP of $515.3 billion. There were numerous sectors of the economy that were larger in dollar terms than health services (Exhibit 13.1).

[1] National Center for Health Statistics, *Health United States 1990* (Hyattsville, MD: Public Health Service, 1991), Table 103, p. 184.

EXHIBIT 13.1   Selected Sector Breakdown of GNP, 1960 and 1987 (In billions)

	1960	*1987*
Total Gross National Product	**$515.3**	**$4,526.7**
Real Estate	54.1	519.3
Health Services	11.5	223.7
Federal Government	24.8	181.3
Transportation	23.4	150.8
Gas, Electric, and Sanitary Services	13.3	136.4
Agriculture, Forestry, and Fisheries	21.7	94.9
Mining	12.8	85.4
Machinery Manufacturing	13.2	81.2
Food Products	16.4	74.0
Primary Metals Manufacturing	12.1	36.4

Source: U.S. Bureau of Economic Analysis, *National Income and Product Accounts of the United States, 1929–1982,* Table 6, p. 252; U.S. Bureau of the Census, *Statistical Abstract of the United States, 1990,* Table 641, p. 426.

By 1987, the situation had significantly changed; health services made up $223.7 billion of a $4.5 trillion GNP. The only sector of the economy that remained larger than health services was real estate. Health services expenditures became larger than the entire federal government's. Even real estate, which had been five times the size of the health services sector in 1960, was only slightly over twice as large as the health services sector in 1987. The relationship of the health services industries to other sectors of the U.S. economy has been significantly altered by the extraordinarily rapid growth in expenditures for health care.

Change in the health services sector can be illustrated in several ways. One of the most important changes has taken place in the sources of payment for health care services and products. In 1960, almost 55 percent of all payments for personal health care services and goods were made directly by households. By 1987, this had dropped to 27.8 percent. In 1990, direct payments by individuals amounted to about one-fourth of all payment for health care. In contrast, the federal government in 1960 provided less than 10 percent of the payments for personal health care, but by 1987 this had more than tripled to nearly 30 percent. Over the past 25 years, there has been a significant change in the mix of payer categories in the health services sector (Exhibit 13.2).

Other dramatic changes can be illustrated in the distribution of physicians. In 1970, there were 255,000 nonfederal patient care physicians in active practice in the United States. Of that number, almost 20 percent (50,000) considered themselves to be in general or family practice. By 1987, the number of nonfederal patient care physicians in active practice had nearly doubled to 453,000. However, the absolute number that considered themselves in general and family practice had not changed, with the result that general and family practitioners accounted for only 12 percent of active, nonfederal physicians.

EXHIBIT 13.2   **Health Services and Supplies**

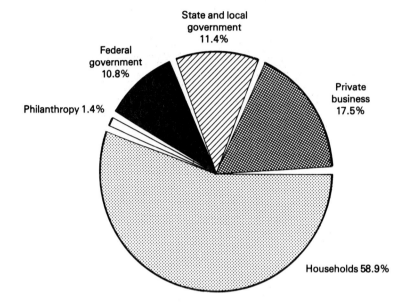

Payer mix — 1965

State and local government 11.4%

Federal government 10.8%

Philanthropy 1.4%

Private business 17.5%

Households 58.9%

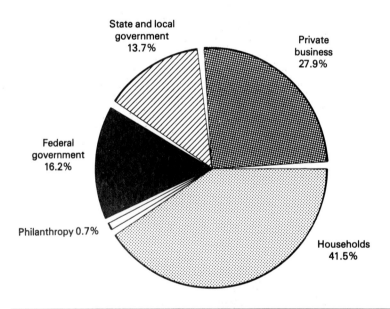

Payer mix — 1987

State and local government 13.7%

Private business 27.9%

Federal government 16.2%

Philanthropy 0.7%

Households 41.5%

Source: K. R. Levit, M. S. Freeland, and D. R. Waldo, ''Health Spending and Ability to Pay: Business, Individuals, and Government,'' *Health Care Financing Review*, Vol. 10, No. 3 (Spring 1989), p. 6.

Physicians in other specialties and subspecialties had shown significant, and in some cases dramatic, increases. Specialists in pulmonary medicine had increased more than fourfold, the number of plastic surgeons had tripled, and the number of orthopedic surgeons had more than doubled. One of the most dramatic increases was in diagnostic radiology. The number of physicians in this specialty increased nearly 10-fold from 1970 to 1987, from 896 physicians to over 8,500 physicians.[2] The number of physicians in active practice has grown much faster than the general population. Hence, there are now fewer people for the practice of each physician (Exhibit 13.3).

Although the decreasing number of patients per physician may suggest increased competition among physicians and hence a decrease in physician income, the income effect is not evident. As shown in Exhibit 13.4, the trend in physician before-tax income continues to be positive.

A final example of rapid change in the health services sector can be seen in the utilization rates for hospitals. Although the hospital sector has accounted for

EXHIBIT 13.3   Population per Active Physician, 1970–1990 (Projected)

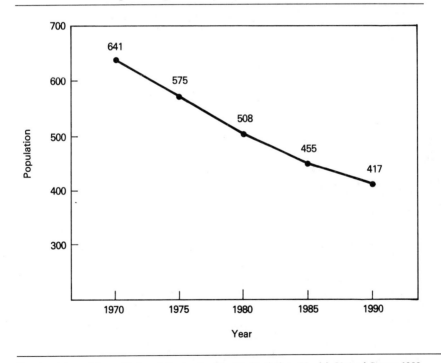

Source: Adapted from National Center for Health Statistics, *Health United States 1989* (Hyattsville, MD: United States Public Health Service, 1990), Table 85, p. 206.

[2] Ibid., Table 86, p. 207.

EXHIBIT 13.4   Trends in Physicians' Incomes, Before-Tax Net Income 1977–1988

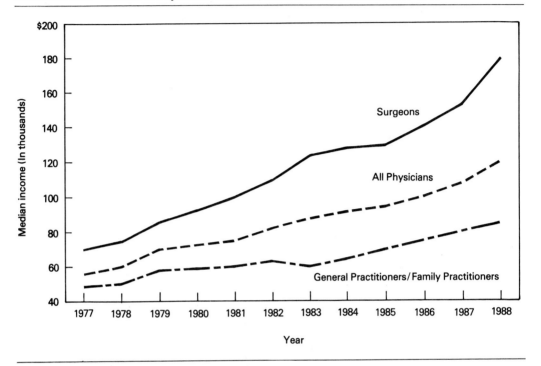

Source: Center for Health Policy Research, *Socioeconomic Characteristics of Medical Practice*, M. L. Gonzales and D. W. Emons, eds. (Chicago: American Medical Association, 1989), Table 48, p. 130.

approximately 40 percent of total expenditures for over a decade, the actual use of the inpatient component of the hospital sector has been declining. Discharges from nonfederal short-stay hospitals per 1,000 population have decreased significantly. In 1981, there were 160.2 discharges per 1,000 population. By 1989, this number had decreased to 115.5 discharges per 1,000. During the same period, the actual hospital days of care provided per 1,000 population declined from 1,134 to 732.[3] As inpatient utilization of hospitals declined, outpatient utilization increased. Between 1970 and 1988, the number of visits to hospital outpatient departments nearly doubled. Total outpatient visits in hospitals increased from 173 million in 1970 to over 326 million in 1988.[4]

Growth and change will continue to be the dominant characteristic of the health care sector for the foreseeable future (Exhibit 13.5). Already, trends in the environment are clearly discernible that will maintain these two fundamental health sector characteristics.

[3] Ibid., Table 73, p. 143. (See Appendix 1 of this source for cautions concerning estimates of change from these numbers.)
[4] Ibid., Table 79, p. 153.

EXHIBIT 13.5   National Health Expenditures, 1965–2000

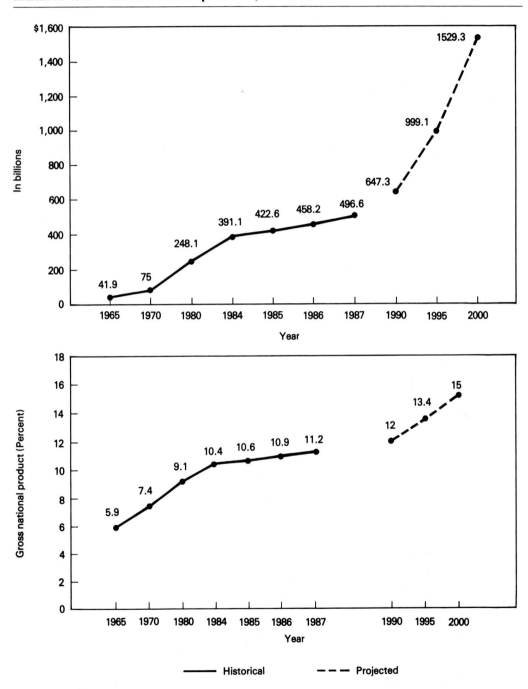

Source: Office of the Actuary, U.S. Health Care Financing Administration, "National Health Expenditures, 1986–2000," *Health Care Financing Review*, Vol. 8, No. 4 (Summer 1987), Table 12, p. 24.

ENVIRONMENTAL TRENDS FOR THE HEALTH CARE SECTOR

There are definite trends in the macroenvironment that will be influencing the health services environment over the next 10 years. Traditionally, the external macroenvironment is broken down into at least the following four segments: the technological environment, the social environment, the political/regulatory environment, and the economic environment.

The Environment for Health Care Technology

The rapid pace of technological and scientific advances will continue and possibly accelerate. From a marketing perspective, the increasing use and sophistication of medical technology and the assessment of medical practice variations are trends that will influence the ultimate diffusion of technologies and the long-term role of the technological imperative in medical care costs. In other words, we have better equipment to use for diagnosis (such as magnetic resonance imaging— MRI), but it is extremely expensive.

The Social Environment of Health Services

One of the singularly most important trends in the health services environment is the aging of the U.S. population. Although this trend has often been considered the consequence of the aging of the baby boom generation, such analysis overlooks another important factor that complicates our projections of the size of the elderly population in the future. The complicating factor concerns the assumptions made about mortality rates for our oldest citizens. For the first time, increases in life expectancy are occurring that are due to longevity rather than decreases in childhood deaths. In other words, we are adding significant years to life at the end of the life span.

The assumptions concerning the continued decline in mortality rates among the oldest old have significant implications. To illustrate, in one recent article, the population age 85 and older, currently numbering about 2.7 million, was projected by the Census Bureau to grow to 12.8 million by the year 2040. An alternative projection, with a reasonable assumption of a 2 percent mortality decline, increased the projected population 85 years and older to 23.5 million.[5] The implications of this trend for health services are enormous. In 1988, the per capita Medicare payments for the enrollees age 65 to 66 was $1,618. For enrollees age 85 and over, the per capita payment was $3,378. In 1985, 40 percent of all nursing home residents were 85 years of age and older.[6] The changing demographics of our oldest old will be one of the major trends in the 21st century.

[5] J. A. Guralnik, M. Yanagishita, and E. L. Schneider, "Projecting the Older Population of the United States: Lessons from the Past and Prospects for the Future," *Milbank Quarterly*, Vol. 66 No. 2 (1988), pp. 283–308.

[6] *Health United States 1990*, Tables 128 and 81, pp. 155, 212.

The Political/Regulatory Environment and Health Services

A significant trend in the political/regulatory environment that has implications for the health care sector is the increasing role of regulation in providing product information for the marketplace. Obvious examples of this trend exist in the regulations that require increased nutritional information on food products and health warning labels on tobacco and alcohol products. The influences of this trend on the health sector market are now beginning to emerge.

The Health Care Financing Administration publishes adjusted mortality rate information for nearly all hospitals in the United States. This is an example of an initial attempt to provide more quality- and outcome-oriented data on a provider-specific basis for use by health services consumers. The important characteristic of this regulatory trend is that the information is provider specific; results are presented for hospitals by name and location. It is one of the first examples of individual consumers having information with which to compare the success of various health care providers.

Health data/cost information programs have been initiated by legislation in at least 17 states. Although all of these programs do not currently address provider-specific outcome information, the political/regulatory trend appears to be following the greater trend in the macroenvironment to increase the information in the market for comparisons of products and services on the basis of price and quality.

The Economic Environment for the Health Services Sector

There are two economic trends that appear to be particularly cogent for the health services sector. These are the slowing of the U.S. economy after one of the longest sustained economic expansions in history and the continuing emergence of a worldwide marketplace for goods and services.

Although health care costs have increased significantly, during the past decade the entire U.S. economy has undergone a sustained expansion and hence the overall impact of the health care component has been somewhat muted. As stated in previous sections of this note, there are several reasons to believe that health care expenditures will continue to rise. However, the general economy may now be entering a period of zero or possibly very slow growth. Although it is normal for an economy to contract and hence adjust after an expansionary period, the most recent expansion has been uncommon. It had sustained growth for a much longer period of time than is typical. Some are now forecasting an atypical sustained period of contraction.[7]

A continuation of health care economic expansion during a sustained period of slow, zero, or negative growth for the general economy will heighten the frustrations and concerns of other components of our economy over health care

---

[7] K. Pennar, "This 'Dwarf Recession' Might Be—Giant," *Business Week*, October 15, 1990, p. 30.

EXHIBIT 13.6   Health Services Spending as a Percent of After-Tax Profit, 1965–1987

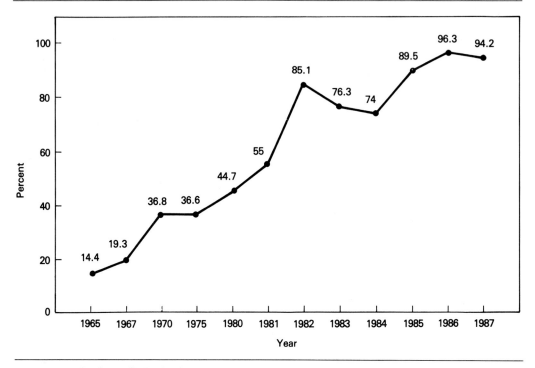

Source: K. R. Levit, M. S. Freeland, and D. R. Waldo, "Health Spending and Ability to Pay: Business, Individuals, and Government," *Health Care Financing Review*, Vol. 10, No. 3 (Spring 1989), Table 5, p. 9.

costs. Government and business, two of the most significant sponsors of health services, will be especially vulnerable. Economic contraction may mean decreased revenue for government and increased deficits. For the business sector, with health care costs now equal to after-tax profits, the bottom-line impact of health care will become a major strategic issue (Exhibit 13.6).

The continuing evolution of a global marketplace will further heighten the awareness of the impact of U.S. health care expenditures. The United States spends significantly more per capita for health care than any of its global-marketplace competitors. With health care for employees and beneficiaries becoming one of the most significant resource inputs for the production of many goods and services, the international competitiveness of U.S. producers may become an economic issue for the health services sector.

HEALTH SERVICES PRODUCTS

As the U.S. health care system attempts to deal with these environmental ,trends, the products of this sector of the economy will come under increased scrutiny and may have to change to reflect new marketplace realities.

Within those organizations that conduct health policy research, there continues to be a great deal of interest in better defining the products of the health services sector. This interest relates to concerns for improving the payment methods for health care and to the need for improving methods to judge the quality of health services. It is difficult to negotiate a price or judge the quality of a product you cannot define. If traditional marketplace methods based on competition are to allocate health care resources, then these are fundamental concerns for all participants in this market. The most well known outcome of this research is a patient categorization method known as diagnosis related groups (DRGs).[8] This method is currently used by the Health Care Financing Administration (Medicare) to define the products of the hospital sector so that a price for each product can be prospectively determined. Over the next decade, refinements for and alternatives to this type of product definition will undoubtedly surface.

For the purpose of this health services marketing note, the following very broad definitions for the products of this economic sector are provided. These definitions have been structured to provide an introduction to health services products in a manner that demonstrates the relationship between health care products and outcomes for individual health care consumers. The link between the structures and processes of medical care and the outcomes for individual patients is often very tenuous. Efforts to strengthen this linkage are an important research focus in the attempt to better define the health care product. Products of the health services industries are considered to be any good or service that is used to:

1. *Describe the current state of an individual's physiology.* X-ray machines, X-ray film, and the interpretation of an X-ray procedure are goods and services used to describe the current state of an individual's physiology. An X-ray of a hand may be used to determine whether or not a pain in that hand is due to a damaged bone. The X-ray procedure does not prevent, correct, or relieve the pain. It is used to help describe the physiological state that may be the underlying cause of the pain.

2. *Correct a deranged physiology.* Otitis media (an inflammation of the middle ear) is an example of deranged physiology that, if left untreated, can lead to serious complications. The derangement can generally be completely corrected through the use of medication. The medication and the services of a doctor to choose the most appropriate therapy are products that can correct a deranged physiology.

3. *Relieve pain, discomfort, or disability caused by deranged physiology.* Anti-inflammatory agents are often used to reduce the pain and discomfort associated with degenerative joint disease (osteoarthritis). The drugs do not correct or necessarily even slow the progression of the disease. They do, however, temporarily relieve the symptoms of the deranged physiology.

4. *Prevent or slow the derangement of human physiology.* Various vaccines, such as the oral polio vaccine, are produced and consumed because they are known to prevent infection in humans by agents that will derange an otherwise healthy physiology. Other products such as coronary artery bypass graft surgery, may slow the

[8] Robert B. Fetter, Y. Shin, J. L. Freeman, R. F. Averill, and J. D. Thompson, "Case Mix Definition by Diagnosis Related Groups," Working Paper no. 40, Yale School of Organization and Management, undated.

progression of a physiological derangement but do not correct the disease process. A bypass graft moves blood around a blocked coronary artery to provide oxygen to the heart muscle. It does not correct the disease process that led to the blockage of the artery.

HEALTH SERVICES PARTICIPANTS

The various products and services of the health services sector fall into the four broad categories as described. They are provided by a diverse group of professionals and organizations that represent one component of an even more diverse set of participants. The four major categories of participants in the health services sector are:

- Providers of health care goods and services
- Payers for health care goods and services
- Health sector regulators
- Health sector advocacy organizations

Due to the very dynamic and complex nature of the health services environment, these categories should not be considered as mutually exclusive or even as all-inclusive. For example, organizations that essentially provide services may in addition provide certain regulatory functions.

Providers of Health Care

Physicians. In terms of national expenditures for health services, physicians make up the largest single professional service component of the health services sector. Payments to physicians accounted for 19 percent of total health services expenditures in 1988. By contrast, dental services, the next largest professional service component, accounted for 5 percent of total expenditures. Physicians are the only professionals in the health services sector who are broadly licensed to perform any medical procedure. Thus, they have significant influence over the allocation of most health care resources. Physicians are generally considered to be either doctors of medicine or doctors of osteopathy. However, osteopaths represent only 5 percent of all active physicians in the United States. Currently, the number of physicians in active practice is approximately 600,000, or 2.4 per 1,000 population.[9]

Expenditures for physicians' services have grown at an average annual rate of 13.2 percent from 1986 to 1988. Such rapid growth in expenditures has led to increased emphasis on methods to slow this escalation. In 1989, Congress passed

[9] National Center for Health Statistics, *Health United States 1989* (Hyattsville, MD: Public Health Service, 1990), Table 85, p. 206.

physician payment reform legislation, which changed the way the federal government pays for physicians' services. As of 1992, physicians are paid on a resource-based relative-value-scale fee schedule. An example of how this may affect payments is presented in Exhibit 13.7.

Other Professionals.   As previously stated, the only other professional category that is individually significant in terms of health services expenditures is dentists (5 percent). In 1988, expenditures for dental services were $29.4 billion, an 8.5 percent increase from 1987. Private insurance coverage for dental services is rapidly expanding, while very little dental care is paid for from public sources.[10]

Other licensed professionals who often practice and bill independently include podiatrists, optometrists, private-duty nurses, chiropractors, and others (Exhibit 13.8). In 1988, $22.5 billion was spent for these services, or about 4 percent of health services expenditures.

EXHIBIT 13.7   Expected Change in Medicare Allowed Charges (By Specialty)

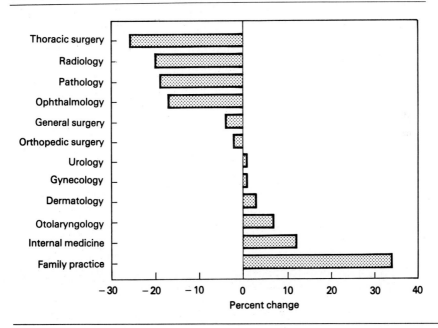

Source: J. M. Levy, M. J. Borowitz, S. F. Jenks, T. L. Kay, and D. K. Williams, "Impact of Medicare Fee Schedule on Payment to Physicians," *Journal of the American Medical Association*, August 1990, pp. 717–721.

[10] Office of National Cost Estimates, "National Health Expenditures, 1988," *Health Care Financing Review,* Vol. 11, No. (4) (Summer, 1990), p. 25.

EXHIBIT 13.8   Selected Health Professionals in Active Practice for 1970, 1980, and 1988

	1970	1980	1988
Physicians (Nonfederal)	290,862	409,480	517,482
Dentists	95,700	121,240	142,200
Optometrists	18,400	22,330	26,100
Podiatrists	7,110	8,880	11,500
Veterinarians	25,900	36,000	47,500

Source: National Center for Health Statistics, *Health United States 1990* (Hyattsville, MD: Public Health Service), Table 90, p. 165.

Hospitals.   The largest single component of the health services dollar pays for hospital care. Approximately 39 percent of all health care expenditures are for hospital services. The hospital industry is one of the most diverse components, a result of rapid growth and pronounced change. Hospitals use several different methods to categorize participants. For example, hospitals are classified by ownership, size in terms of beds, or type of services (e.g., long term vs. short term; children, mental, or burn care). Of the 6,243 hospitals in the United States in 1988, one commonly used categorization method based primarily on ownership indicates that nongovernment, not-for-profit hospitals are the largest segment.[11]

On a population basis, hospital beds are not evenly distributed throughout the United States. Also, the rate of beds to population has recently been decreasing (Exhibit 13.9).

Nursing Homes.   Nursing home services accounted for 8 percent of total health care expenditures in 1988. This is a significant increase over 1960, when nursing home care used 2 percent of the health care dollar. The 1970s experienced massive increases in average annual expenditures for these services. During that 10-year period, the average annual percentage increase in nursing home expenditures exceeded 15 percent. The rate of annual increase has decreased during the past five years to the 7 to 9 percent range.[12]

Between 1976 and 1986, the number of nursing homes increased from 14,133 to 16,033. In the same period, the inventory of nursing home beds grew from 1.292 million to 1.616 million. However, the availability of beds as measured by the ratio of nursing home beds to population aged 85 and over has decreased. In 1976, there were 681 beds per 1,000 residents 85 years of age and older. By 1986, that ratio had decreased to 582 per 1,000.[13]

---

[11] American Hospital Association, *Hospital Statistics*, 1989–1990 ed. (Chicago, AHA) Table 2A, pp. 8–9.

[12] Suzanne W. Letsch, K. R. Levit, and D. R. Waldo, "Health Care Financing Trends," *Health Care Financing Review*, Vol. 10, No. 2 (Winter 1988).

[13] *Health United States 1989*, Table 99, pp. 224–225.

EXHIBIT 13.9   Community Hospital Beds per 1,000 Population by Geographic Division

	1970	1980	1988
United States	**4.3**	**4.5**	**3.9**
New England	4.1	4.1	3.6
Middle Atlantic	4.4	4.6	4.1
East North Central	4.4	4.7	4.1
West North Central	5.7	5.8	5.1
South Atlantic	4.0	4.5	3.8
East South Central	4.4	5.1	4.7
West South Central	4.3	4.7	3.9
Mountain	4.3	3.8	3.3
Pacific	3.7	3.5	2.9

Source: National Center for Health Statistics, *Health United States 1990* (Hyattsville, MD: Public Health Service 1991), Table 99, pp. 176–177.

Other Facilities Providing Health Services.   Other types of facilities that provide a limited set of health services include:

Hospices—inpatient facilities for terminally ill patients.

Community Mental Health Centers—federally funded ambulatory mental health treatment.

Ambulatory Surgical Facilities—organizations that provide various types of surgical procedures that do not require an overnight hospital stay.

Ambulatory Diagnostic Facilities—organizations that provide only diagnostic services and no inpatient or other therapeutic services.

Urgent Care Facilities—essentially free-standing emergency rooms that provide primary care and limited emergency services. Commonly referred to as a "doc-in-the-box."

There are other examples of limited-service facilities in addition to those cited; however, this portion of the health services industry accounts for less than 2 percent of all expenditures.

Drugs and Other Medical Nondurables.   The drug and medical supply industry is represented by major international corporations such as Merck, Johnson & Johnson, and American Home Products. The portion of the domestic health care dollar devoted to products from these suppliers has declined. In 1960, drugs and medical nondurables accounted for 16 percent of health care expenditures. By 1988, the proportion had decreased to 8 percent. However, due to the rapid growth in total health care expenditures, the decrease still represented nearly a 10-fold increase in noninflation-adjusted dollars expended on these products from $4.34 billion to $43 billion in the same time period.[14]

[14] *Health United States 1990*, Table 105, p. 186.

The elderly consume the largest share of prescription drugs. By one estimate, people 65 and over use three times as many prescription drugs as all other
age groups. The Health Care Financing Administration estimates that the 12 percent of the population who are elderly account for 35 percent of expenditures on
prescription drugs.[15]

Vision Products and Other Durables.   Eyeglasses and other medical appliances
represent approximately 2 percent of the health services dollar. In 1988, over $10
billion was spent on products of this type.[16]

Government Public Health Activities.   Government public health activities do not
fit neatly into any individual category within the health services sector of the
economy. Public health is a provider of personal health services, a regulator of
service providers, a payer for services, and a major source of health-related research. Federal, state, and local governments all conduct public health activities
and expend resources on public health services. Services provided by this industry include maternal and child health care, health facility licensure, collection and
reporting of vital health statistics, environmental-health-related regulation, disease vector control, and others. These services amounted to 3 percent of total
health expenditures in 1988.[17] Public health is included in the provider category
because the largest component of this 3 percent share is used to deliver personal
health services, often to the medically indigent (Exhibit 13.10).[18]

Others.   Although the provider groups described account for the vast majority of
all health service expenditures (Exhibit 13.11), health research and medical education need to be addressed because of their impact on the future direction of
provider services.

Health Research is conducted by government organizations, nonprofit private organizations, and for-profit commercial companies. Total health research
expenditures in 1988 amounted to $18.85 billion. Federal government and industry
each contributed 45 percent of this total and the remaining 10 percent came from
state and local governments and not-for-profit private organizations.[19]

Medical education is conducted primarily through the 125 public and private
academic health sciences centers (AHSCs) in the United States. All AHSCs
contain a medical school, affiliated teaching hospital, and at least one other health
professional education program (i.e., nursing, dentistry, public health, and so on).
Between 1985 and 1989, total first-year enrollment in U.S. medical schools has
been between 16,500 and 17,000 students.

---

[15] "National Health Expenditures, 1988," p. 14.
[16] *Health United States 1990*, Table 105, p. 186.
[17] Ibid.
[18] Public Health Agencies, 1990, "Inventory of Programs and Block Grant Expenditures,"
Public Health Foundation, 1990, p. 3.
[19] *Health United States 1990*, Table 117, p. 198.

EXHIBIT 13.10   Public Health Expenditures: State Health Departments, Fiscal 1988

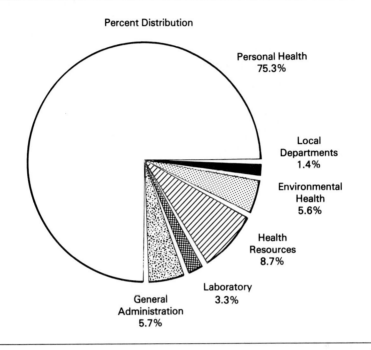

Percent Distribution

Personal Health
75.3%

Local
Departments
1.4%

Environmental
Health
5.6%

Health
Resources
8.7%

Laboratory
3.3%

General
Administration
5.7%

Source: Public Health Foundation, *Public Health Agencies 1990: An Inventory of Programs and Block Grant Expenditures* (Washington, D.C.: June 1990), Table 1, p. 3.

Payers for Health Care Goods and Services[20]

Another important component of the health services sector are those agencies, organizations, and individuals providing payment for health care goods and services. In general, health service payer organizations can be dichotomized into those in the private sector and those in the public sector.

Private Payers for Health Services.   Various categories of payment from individual households in the United States make up the largest single component. In 1987, individual households paid out slightly over $200 billion of the $483 billion expended on health services and supplies. There are four primary mechanisms by which households pay for health services: (1) direct out-of-pocket health spending

[20] Data on payers are excerpted from Katharine R. Levit, M. S. Freeland, and D. R. Waldo, "Health Spending and Ability to Pay: Business, Individuals and Government," *Health Care Financing Review*, Vol. 10, No. 3 (Spring 1989), pp. 1–11.

EXHIBIT 13.11   National Health Expenditures, Percent Distribution, 1987

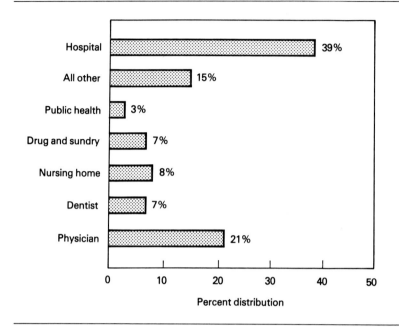

Source: National Center for Health Statistics, *Health United States 1989*
(Hyattsville, MD: United States Public Health Services, 1990), Table 102,
p. 228.

by individuals; (2) various premiums paid by employees and the self-employed into the Medicare hospital insurance trust fund; (3) premiums paid by individuals to the Medicare supplemental medical insurance trust fund; and (4) the employee paid share of private health insurance premiums and individual health insurance policy premiums (Exhibit 13.12).

Payments made by private businesses accounted for 28 percent of all expenditures for health services and supplies in 1987. Of this $135 billion, $97 billion was spent by employers for private health insurance premiums. These premiums were paid for both traditional indemnity types of insurance and, to an increasing degree, for employer self-insurance programs. Private employers also contributed nearly $25 billion into the Medicare hospital insurance trust fund and another $6.10 billion for workers' compensation and various forms of disability insurance. A small portion of the private expenditures ($2.6 billion) was made for in-company-provided health services (Exhibit 13.12).

The final category of private payments for health services and supplies is philanthropy. Although the dollar amount of philanthropy for health services has been steadily increasing, the role of philanthropy in terms of all payments for health services and supplies is becoming less significant. Philanthropy has increased from $500 million in 1965 to $3.3 billion in 1987. However, in terms of

EXHIBIT 13.12   Expenditures for Health Services and Supplies, 1970, 1980, and 1987 (In billions)

	1970	1980	1987
Individual Household Payers			
Individual Out-of-Pocket Spending	$26.5	$63.0	$123.0
Employee and Self-Employed Contributions and Voluntary Premiums Paid to Medicare Hospital Insurance Trust Fund	2.4	11.9	29.1
Premiums Paid by Individuals to Medicare Supplemental Medial Insurance Trust Fund	1.0	2.7	6.1
Employee Share of Private Health Insurance Premiums and Individual Policy Premiums	4.8	$13.0	42.5
Total	$34.7	$90.6	$200.7
Private Business Payers			
Private Employer Share of Private Health Insurance Premiums	$11.2	$51.1	$96.8
Private Employer Contribution to Medicare Hospital Insurance Trust Fund	2.1	10.5	24.5
Workers' Compensation and Temporary Disability Insurance Medical Benefits and Administration	1.4	5.1	10.6
Industrial In-Plant Health Services	0.6	1.4	2.6
Total	$15.3	$68.1	$134.6
Public Payers			
Federal Government Net Health Services and Supplies Spending	$10.3	$41.7	$78.5
Local and State Government Net Health Services and Supplies Spending	8.6	34.1	66.2
Total	$19.0	$75.8	$144.7

Source: R. R. Levit, M. S. Freeland, and A. R. Waldo, "Health Spending and Ability to Pay: Business, Individuals, and Government," *Health Care Financing Review,* Vol. 10, No. 3, (Spring 1989), p. 5.

percentage of total payments, philanthropy has decreased from a 1.3 percent share in 1985 to less than 0.7 percent in 1987.

Public Payers for Health Services.   Public expenditures from all levels of government accounted for nearly 30 percent of the payments for health services and supplies in 1987. The largest portion of these public payments, $78.5 billion, was from the federal government through its various health services programs. These programs include general revenue contributions, federal employer contributions, and interest income. The collected monies are allocated to Medicare that makes payments for the elderly and certain classes of disabled individuals, the federal portion of Medicaid payments that provide health services for some poor individuals, the health services system of the Veterans Administration that operates 171 VA medical centers throughout the United States with a budget in excess of $11 billion,[21] the Indian Health Service that provides health care services to Native Americans, and extensive military health service organizations operated by the various branches of the U.S. armed services. State and local governments contributed in excess of $66 billion to total payments for health services and supplies in 1987. In addition to health services programs provided directly by these governmental entities, this figure includes state and local government contributions to private health insurance programs for their employees as well as their contributions as an employer to the Medicare hospital insurance trust fund (Exhibit 13.12).

A review of the previous description of payers illustrates that, once again, there is no clear differentiation in the roles of various participants in the health services sector. Many of the categories of payers for health services and supplies are also providers of such services. The federal government is not only a payer to private providers through such programs as Medicare, but also operates federally owned service delivery mechanisms, such as the VA hospital system. Even private employers in non-health-related businesses often operate in-house employee health programs. Larger corporations such as the BellSouth Corporation headquartered in Atlanta, Georgia, have physicians, nurses, and other health professionals as full-time employees within the organization responsible for certain types of health care provisions for the employee population. As was described in the sector "Providers of Health Care," there are providers that also act as regulators. We now see payers that are also providers of health services.

Management Services to Payer Organizations.   There are organizations considered to be in the payer group that do not themselves pay for health services, but rather manage resources in some way for organizations that are payers. Many of these payment management firms market their services as a means to control the cost of health care for the client. Due to the very dynamic nature of the health services market, there are numerous variations on the cost-containment or cost-management theme.

Blue Cross and Blue Shield organizations in the various states are most often thought of as health insurance organizations. They do in fact sell traditional indemnity insurance plans; however, much of their business revolves around their role as an administrator for the self-insurance programs of large- and medium–sized corporations. In 1989, a majority of employer health plans were self-funded. Fully 84 percent of companies with 10,000 or more employees were self-insured.[22] The Blue Cross organization will act as a "third-party admin-

---

21 W. J. Hollingsworth and P. K. Bandy, "The Role of Veterans Affairs Hospitals in the Health Care System," *New England Journal of Medicine*, Vol. 322, No. 36 (June 28, 1990), pp. 1851–1857.
22 Blue Cross, Blue Shield Association, Environmental Analysis, 1990, p. 40.

istrator" and, for a fee, will adjudicate claims, disburse payments, account for funds, and provide other services for a self–insurance program of an employer. In this role, Blue Cross is not itself a payer, but is rather the manager of resources for a payer organization.

Another example in this category is an organization that provides such cost management services as "concurrent utilization review" and "preadmission certification." Such services are marketed to payers for health care to assure the appropriateness of services that are being provided. Preadmission certification attempts to evaluate the appropriateness of a hospital stay prior to the patient being admitted and hence to eliminate "inappropriate" services. Health services research studies have suggested that 20 to 40 percent of hospital admissions may be inappropriate.[23] Concurrent utilization review is a similar mechanism that attempts to evaluate the appropriateness of a patient's continuing stay in an inpatient facility. Again, these types of organizations do not actually pay for health services but assist in the management of the resources that payers provide.

There are many other examples and variations on this theme including preferred provider organizations (PPOs) and certain types of health maintenance organizations (HMOs). In many cases, these organizations are technically not providers of services in that they employ no providers, nor are they the actual payers for services. They are mechanisms between the providers and the payers that attempt to "manage the care" provided on behalf of the health service consumer and payer.

Health Sector Regulators

Regulation and its appropriate role in the health services sector continue to be among the most controversial issues in public policy debates. Regulation can provide for either the allocation of health services resources, the assurance of minimal quality standards, or the enhancement of marketplace competition for the allocation of health care resources. Although there is little debate that regulation can play a role in the assurance of minimal quality, the appropriate regulatory mechanisms for quality assurance are under intense debate. There is a more dramatic and long-standing debate concerning the role of regulation in the actual allocation of health services resources.

Resources can be allocated centrally through various regulatory mechanisms that would approximate a national health insurance or national health services program, or resources can be primarily allocated through marketplace mechanisms where regulation plays the role of ensuring and enhancing competition. At this time, regulators and regulations exist that are combinations of these varying philosophical positions.

The prospective payment system (PPS) used by Medicare to pay for hospital services is one of the most prominent examples of a resource-allocating regulatory

[23] A. L. Sui, F. A. Sonnenberg, W. G. Manning, G. A. Goldberg, E. S. Bloomfield, J. P. Newhouse, and R. H. Brook, "Inappropriate Use of Hospitals in a Randomized Trial of Health Insurance Plans," *New England Journal of Medicine*, Vol. 315, No. 20 (November 13, 1986), pp. 1259–1266.

approach. This system sets a fee in advance that the Health Care Financing Administration will pay for a particular patient in a given diagnostic category. There is no negotiation between the payer and the provider over price, nor is there any other market mechanism that determines price for the service. Effectively, this is a fixed price determined by the federal government. Price fixing by an organization with dominant market power can be viewed as a noncompetitive regulatory approach to allocating resources.

A second example of a regulatory approach to resource allocation is "certificate of need" programs. The majority of states have in place regulations that require prior approval by a state agency for certain capital expenditures proposed by health care providers. Such laws have been described as entry barriers to new participants in the marketplace. They effectively allocate resources by freezing the existing configuration of facility-based providers.[24]

In addition to regulatory structures that are command-and-control approaches to resource allocation, there have been attempts to reinvigorate market forces as the mechanism to allocate health care resources. For example, there has been an expanded use of antitrust laws in the health care arena. In a 1975 decision, the Supreme Court removed the "learned professions" exemption from antitrust. Professional practices are not immune from price-fixing restrictions and professional associations may not mandate bans on professional advertising.[25] In addition, there have been attempts to increase the information available to participants in the marketplace to further enhance competition. Such activities have included removing bans on advertising by professional organizations and the increased use of provider-specific comparative information. Approximately 17 states have laws in place that require individual providers to report utilization data to a state agency. To varying degrees, this information is then tabulated and made available to participants in the health services marketplace.[26] In addition, the Health Care Financing Administration began the publication of mortality statistics for hospitals throughout the United States. These statistics endeavor to identify excess mortality within individual institutions.[27] This is an early attempt to provide better information to the marketplace for assessing the comparative quality of provider organizations.

There are direct conflicts between regulatory approaches that attempt to allocate and regulatory approaches that attempt to enhance competition as the mechanism for allocating resources. The certificate of need laws impose entry barriers to new participants in a marketplace, yet antitrust laws attempt to ensure

[24] F. A. Sloan, "Containing Health Expenditures: Lessons Learned from Certificate of Need Programs," in F. A. Sloan, J. F. Blumstein, and J. M. Perrin, eds., *Cost, Quality and Access to Health Care* (San Francisco: Jossey-Bass, 1988), pp. 44–70.

[25] *Goldfarb v. Virginia State Bar*, 421 U.S. 773.

[26] National Conference of State Legislators, *What Legislators Need to Know about Health Data/Cost Information Programs* (Denver, CO: 1986), p. 2.

[27] Health Care Financing Administration, *Medicare Hospital Mortality Information*, Vol. 1 (Washington, D.C., undated), p. 111.

that entry barriers do not exist. In addition, there have been other conflicts between the philosophies of antitrust and various central allocation resource mechanisms. These conflicts have not been fully resolved. At this time, we have an ambiguous policy concerning the methods of choice for allocating health care resources in the United States.

There are other regulatory mechanisms that influence the provision of health care services that are fundamentally oriented toward ensuring a minimum level of quality or limiting the potential for adverse reactions from the use of medical services and products. For example, the Food and Drug Administration has regulatory procedures for approving the use of a new drug. The purpose is not only to assure that the drug is effective for its stated use, but also to assure that possible side effects are known and that the risks associated with such effects are reasonable. Another example is state licensure laws for health professionals that require minimum standards of education and training before an individual is sanctioned to provide health services.

There are also a number of voluntary regulatory mechanisms that attempt to assure minimum levels of quality. The Joint Commission on Accreditation of Health Care Organizations (JCAHO) is an industry-sponsored accrediting body that sets minimum structure and process standards in the delivery of hospital and other facility-based health services. In addition, there are numerous professional medical organizations, such as the American Board of Family Practice, the American Board of Pathology, and others, that provide certifications that attempt to assure minimum levels of quality in the delivery of specialized physician services. Although a state license to practice medicine is effectively an unlimited license to provide physician services, physicians may not claim certification in a particular specialty without advanced training and the successful completion of certifying exams provided by these national voluntary review boards.

There is an extensive role in quality assurance played by the judicial system in the United States. Tort actions in the form of malpractice cases against physicians or liability actions against health care facilities provide incentives to maintain standards of quality within various professional groups and provider organizations. Liability insurance now accounts for approximately 11 percent of the total operating expenses in a typical self–employed physician's office.[28] Finally a broad array of other state and local quality assurance functions, primarily through the public health mechanisms, provide inspections and licensure for health care providers.

Health Sector Advocacy Organizations

There is a fourth set of participants in the health services sector that is probably more diverse than any of the other participant groups. These are the

---

[28] American Medical Association Center for Health Policy Research, *Socioeconomic Characteristics of Medical Practice, 1989*, M. L. Gonzalez and D. W. Emmons, eds. (Chicago, 1989), pp. 106, 116.

organizations that represent the various health care special interests within the policy-setting arena in the United States. It is nearly impossible to identify and categorize all of the various advocacy groups that are active at any one time on issues related to the delivery of health care services. One proprietary listing of national and international associations identifies over 3,000 such organizations.[29] There are many thousands of additional state and regional associations. Some of these groups and organizations have categorical disease interests. For example, there are international, national, state, and regional associations that represent special interests in arthritis, blindness, cancer, cystic fibrosis, diabetes, heart disease, mental retardation, and numerous others. There are associations representing health-related interests of defined population subcategories. These include organizations such as the American Association for Retired Persons, the Children's Defense Fund, the National Rural Health Association, and others.

There are hundreds of organizations representing the interests of different professional groups. In addition to well-known groups, such as the American Medical Association and the American Hospital Association, there are groups representing every medical specialty and subspecialty, such as the American Academy of Family Physicians and the American College of Surgeons. Each of the numerous paraprofessional categories, such as laboratory technologists and medical record librarians, are represented by advocacy groups. There are associations that represent the interests of various types of nonhospital facility providers, including nursing homes, ambulatory surgical facilities, and home health agencies.

All of these advocacy organizations are concerned with the allocation of resources within the health services sector. They speak for the interests of their constituents primarily by providing information into the policymaking process. These organizations represent an important source of information, not only for policymakers but also for managers attempting to identify and monitor relevant trends in the rapidly changing health care market.

---

[29] K. Backus, ed., *Medical and Health Information Directory*, 5th ed., Vol. 1 (Detroit: Gale Research, 1989), p. ix.

CASE 14

Ito-Yokado Company

In mid-March 1991, Masanori Takahashi, a senior strategy analyst for Ito-Yokado Company, was preparing to depart for Dallas, Texas. Once there, he would be leading a team of Japanese and American managers responsible for establishing transitional and long-term strategies for the Southland Corporation. After nearly an entire year of intense bargaining and negotiation with Southland and its creditors, Ito-Yokado acquired Southland on March 5, 1991.

Takahashi began working with Ito-Yokado in 1972 as an assistant manager of one of the company's superstores. He had advanced to the position of regional manager by 1979. In early 1981, Ito-Yokado's Operation Reform Project was conceived and Takahashi was asked to be a member of the team leading the project.

During the first few months on the team, Takahashi quickly understood certain crucial aspects of the new project, most notably the use of point-of-sale (POS) systems. Since implementation of the project advanced most rapidly in Ito-Yokado's 7-Eleven Japan subsidiary, he also had become familiar with the operating environment of convenience stores in Japan.

As Takahashi left his Tokyo office, he could not help but feel both excitement and apprehension regarding his new position. He had gained confidence while involved with the successful Operation Reform Project at Ito-Yokado's superstores and 7-Eleven Japan convenience stores. But this experience might or might not prove to be useful in respect to Southland.

COMPANY BACKGROUND

Ito-Yokado's founder, Masatoshi Ito, was born in 1924 and graduated from a commercial high school in Yokohama. He worked briefly at Mitsubishi Heavy Industries before joining Japan's war effort in 1944. After World War II, he worked with his mother and elder brother at the family's 66-square-foot clothing

This case was written from public sources by M. Edgar Barrett and Christopher D. Buehler as a basis for class discussion rather than to illustrate either effective or ineffective handling of an administrative situation. Copyright © 1991 by M. Edgar Barrett. Used with permission from M. Edgar Barrett.

store in Tokyo.[1] The store was incorporated as Kabushiki Kaisha Yokado in 1958. By 1960, Ito was in sole control of the family business. During that same year he made his first visit to the United States.

In 1960, Ito visited National Cash Register (NCR) in Dayton, Ohio.[2] While in the United States, Ito was introduced to terms such as "supermarkets" and "chain stores" by NCR, which was interested in selling cash registers to Japanese retailers. In Japan, retailing was dominated by mom-and-pop stores and a handful of venerable department stores, with few types of retail outlets in between. At this time, Ito began to see the possible role of mass merchandisers in a society becoming "mass-oriented."

Ito soon opened a small chain of superstores in the Tokyo area. These stores carried a large selection of household goods, food, and clothing of generally lesser quality and lower price than either the mom-and-pop or department stores.[3] By 1965, Ito had opened eight superstores. In the same year, the name of the chain was changed to Ito-Yokado.

The Growth of Ito-Yokado as a Superstore

Ito's concept for the superstores was centered on having the rough equivalent of several types of retail stores contained within one multistory superstore. The initial stores were located near population centers and railroad stations in the Tokyo areas.[4] Often, several stores were located in close proximity in order to achieve "regional dominance."[5] The results were high name recognition, reduced distribution costs, and the effective squeezing out of competition.

Ito soon realized that social changes in Japan could create new opportunities for his retailing ideas. Younger and more mobile Japanese appeared to be less willing to spend a great deal of time shopping at numerous mom-and-pop stores. Also, the Japanese society was experiencing increased suburbanization. Ito decided to locate stores in suburban prefectures. There are 47 prefectures (provinces) in Japan.

One reason for locating stores in suburban areas was the lower cost of real estate. This allowed Ito-Yokado to open larger stores with more parking spaces than competitors located in congested urban areas. Ito continued to use a strategy of "regional dominance" with these new openings, most of which were concentrated in the greater Kanto district, which consists of the Tokyo metropolitan area and surrounding cities. By the early 1970s, Ito-Yokado stores were opening at the rate of four or five per year. By the late 1970s, 9 or 10 new stores were opened

[1] Andrew Tanzer, "A Form of Flattery," *Forbes*, June 2, 1986.

[2] Jim Mitchell, "Southland Suitor Ito Learned from the Best," *Dallas Morning News*, April 1, 1990.

[3] Ito was not the first to open this type of retail outlet. Isao Nakauchi opened the first Daiei superstore in the Osaka area a few years before the first Ito-Yokado store was opened. In 1990, Daiei was Japan's largest retailer in terms of gross sales.

[4] Mitchell, "Southland Suitor."

[5] Hiroshi Uchida, *First Boston/CSFB Report on Ito-Yokado, Ltd.*, April 20, 1988, p. 7.

annually.[6] In early 1987, 101 of 127 Ito-Yokado superstores were located in the greater Kanto district.

Ito also adopted a strategy of leasing some properties for new stores. As of the mid-1980s, over 87 percent of Ito-Yokado's aggregate sales floor space, 10 of the company's 11 distribution centers, and the company headquarters in Tokyo were all leased.[7] Often, property prices were astronomical, or the owners of well-located sites would not part with their property for any price.

Constraints on Growth

The initial success of Ito-Yokado and the other superstores soon resulted in retaliatory action by a powerful competitor: the mom-and-pop store owners. These small retailers were said to "pull the strings of Liberal Democratic Party politicians at the local level."[8] The action initiated by the small retailers resulted in the 1974 Large Store Restriction Act, which was subsequently strengthened in 1979. The original act restricted the opening of stores with sales areas of over 1,500 square meters (16,500 square feet). In addition, the act restricted the hours of operation of new and existing large stores. A series of changes in 1979 added restrictions on stores with sales areas greater than 500 square meters (5,500 square feet). A Commerce Coordination Committee was established in each area in order to set policy regarding large-store openings and hours of operation. The committees were effectively controlled by the small retailers. By the early 1980s, Ito-Yokado was opening only four or five new stores annually.[9]

Factors other than the Large Store Restriction Act adversely affected Ito-Yokado. Japanese consumers' real disposable income decreased by a little over 1 percent during 1980–1981.[10] Japan experienced a general economic downturn in the early 1980s, as did the rest of the world, again serving to limit consumer purchasing power. Net income for Ito-Yokado—which had grown almost 30 percent per year between 1976 and 1981—grew by 9.7 percent in 1982 and by 0.9 percent in 1983.[11] The legal restrictions imposed on large stores, when combined with the economic downturn, led to both lower current earnings and a projection of reduced rates of growth in future earnings.

Ito-Yokado as a Parent Company

During the early 1970s, Ito began pursuing new retailing interests. In 1972, he approached Dallas-based Southland Corporation in an attempt to secure a license to operate 7-Eleven stores in Japan. He was rebuffed.[12] He made a similar attempt in 1973 with the aid of a Japanese trading company, C. Itoh and Company,

[6] Ibid., p. 6.
[7] Ibid., p. 7.
[8] Tanzer, "A Form of Flattery."
[9] Uchida, *First Boston*, pp. 7–8.
[10] Ibid.
[11] Ibid., p. 8.
[12] Mitchell, "Southland Suitor."

and was successful in obtaining the license. Concurrently, Ito was pursuing another U.S. firm, Denny's Restaurants, in an attempt to obtain rights for opening Denny's Restaurants in Japan. Both subsidiaries, Denny's Japan and 7-Eleven Japan (originally called York Seven but renamed 7-Eleven Japan in 1978), were established in 1973. The first 7-Eleven and the initial Denny's in Japan were both opened in 1974. Stock for each of the two majority-owned subsidiaries was traded independently on the Tokyo Stock Exchange. Both subsidiaries became profitable around 1977.[13]

ITO-YOKADO IN THE 1980s

The Ito-Yokado group consisted of three business segments: Superstores and other Retail Operations, Restaurant Operations, and Convenience Store Operations. The Convenience Store Operations segment was made up of 7-Eleven Japan. The Restaurant Operations segment consisted of Denny's and Famil Restaurants. Ito-Yokado superstores, Daikuma discount stores, two supermarket chains (York Mart and York-Benimaru), Robinson's Department Stores, and Oshman's Sporting Goods Store made up the Superstores and other Retail Operations segment. Ito-Yokado's financial statements are shown in Exhibits 14.1 through 14.3.

SUPERSTORES AND OTHER RETAIL OPERATIONS

York Mart and York-Benimaru

York Mart was a 100 percent owned subsidiary established in 1975. In 1990, it operated 40 supermarkets located primarily in the Tokyo area.[14] These stores sold mainly fresh foods and packaged goods, and competition was high in this geographic and retail area. Ito-Yokado's Operation Reform Program was implemented by York Mart in 1986 as a means to boost efficiency and profits. By 1990 sales were increasing at 6 percent per year.[15]

York-Benimaru was a 29 percent owned affiliate of Ito-Yokado, and was an independently managed regional supermarket chain. York-Benimaru operated 51 stores as of 1988. The stores were located in the Fukushima prefecture of Koriyama-city in northern Japan.[16] Like York Mart, York-Benimaru operated with a higher profit margin than the supermarket industry as a whole. York-Benimaru's earnings growth rate of 13 percent per year was expected to last into the 1990s, and Ito-Yokado's share of this profit was the major contribution to the "equity in earnings of affiliates" portion of Ito-Yokado's income statement (see Exhibit 14.2).[17]

[13] Uchida, *First Boston*, p. 8.
[14] Ibid., p. 8; and *Moody's Industrial Manual*, 1990, Vol. 1, p. 1275.
[15] Ibid.
[16] Ibid.
[17] Ibid.

EXHIBIT 14.1   Ito-Yokado Company, Ltd., Consolidated Balance Sheet (In millions of yen)

	As of February 28				
	1986	1987	1988	1989	1990
Assets					
Cash	¥ 26,188	¥ 25,596	¥ 32,527	¥ 31,566	¥ 32,529
Time Deposits	32,708	64,894	55,631	125,809	163,524
Marketable Securities	33,882	33,635	75,924	63,938	60,905
Notes and Accounts Receivable	16,570	16,582	19,042	26,949	24,195
Inventories	48,813	48,163	49,372	56,519	56,168
Other Current Assets	13,014	13,951	13,655	15,156	17,892
Total Current Assets	171,175	202,821	246,151	319,937	355,213
Investments and Advertisement	18,097	21,642	24,352	25,589	33,779
Gross Property and Equipment	465,049	505,450	544,752	600,815	663,263
Less Accumulated Depreciation	160,409	183,185	207,561	237,079	262,958
Net Property and Equipment	304,640	322,265	337,191	363,736	400,305
Leasehold Deposits	81,500	88,386	93,358	98,639	114,678
Total Assets	¥575,394	¥635,114	¥701,052	¥807,901	¥903,975
Liabilities and Owners' Equity					
Short Term	¥23,577	¥22,425	¥17,815	¥20,090	¥20,140
Debt Due	13,450	8,396	5,689	3,964	6,815
Accounts and Notes Payable	105,790	103,519	119,982	135,516	153,551
Accrued Liability	40,892	45,217	53,654	61,077	65,941
Other Current Liability	12,777	13,523	17,297	20,458	25,404
Total Current Liabilities	196,486	193,080	214,437	241,305	271,851
Long-Term Debt	86,802	109,563	99,961	93,720	85,265
Accrued Sev. Indemnity	1,201	1,248	1,319	1,227	1,297
Deferred Income Taxes	1,912	2,036	969	0	2,150
Minority Interests	45,011	51,974	60,619	83,102	95,920
Owners' Equity					
Common Stock	17,364	18,184	22,462	28,913	33,328
Capital Surplus	78,202	82,070	88,139	95,817	100,230
Other Capital	9,292	9,292	9,292	16,210	16,210
Legal Reserve	4,029	4,837	5,715	6,741	7,858
Retained Earnings	135,307	163,042	198,351	241,078	290,078
Owners' Equity	244,194	277,425	304,725	388,759	447,704
Less Treasury Stock	(212)	(212)	(1,423)	(212)	(212)
Net Owners' Equity	¥575,394	277,213	303,302	388,547	447,492
Total Liabilities and Owners' Equity	¥243,982	¥635,114	¥701,052	¥807,901	¥903,975

Source: *Moody's Industrial Manual*, 1990, Vol. 1.

EXHIBIT 14.2   Ito-Yokado Company, Ltd., Consolidated Income Statement (In millions of yen)

	As of February 28				
	1986	1987	1988	1989	1990
Net Sales	¥1,201,347	¥1,281,203	¥1,371,960	¥1,524,947	¥1,664,390
Cost of Goods Sold	829,077	875,343	923,771	1,025,839	1,113,659
Gross Margin	372,270	405,860	448,189	499,108	550,731
Depreciation and Amortization	27,328	31,106	32,064	33,777	37,695
Selling, General, and Administrative Expense	252,355	271,204	294,208	324,295	354,321
Operating Income	92,587	103,550	121,917	141,036	158,715
Interest Income	6,585	5,827	7,173	8,662	12,838
Interest Expense	6,982	5,962	4,755	3,400	3,751
Foreign Currency Gains	2,089	488	74	—	—
Income Before Taxes	92,279	103,903	124,409	146,298	167,802
Income Taxes					
Current	5,449	61,005	72,191	84,930	91,561
Deferred	1,153	106	(1,400)	(2,498)	3,183
Total Income Taxes	55,605	61,111	70,791	82,432	94,744
Minority Interests	7,471	8,862	11,058	13,338	15,777
Equity in Affiliated Earnings	618	829	951	1,058	984
Net Income	¥ 31,824	¥ 34,759	¥ 43,511	¥ 51,586	¥ 58,465
Opening Retained Earnings	¥ 109,717	¥ 135,307	¥ 163,042	¥ 198,351	¥ 241,078
Cash Dividends	5,570	6,216	7,324	7,833	8,348
Transfer to Legal Reserves	664	808	878	1,026	1,117
Closing Retained Earnings	¥ 135,307	¥ 163,042	¥ 198,351	¥ 241,078	¥ 290,078
Per Common Share					
Net Income	¥ 81.44	¥ 88.05	¥ 108.40	¥ 127.35	¥ 143.71
Cash Dividends	¥ 15.70	¥ 18.18	¥ 19.55	¥ 20.00	¥ 23.00
Average Number of Shares	396,798	400,449	406,554	408,037	408,770

Source: *Moody's Industrial Manual,* 1990, Vol. 1.

Daikuma

Daikuma discount stores were consolidated into the Ito-Yokado group in 1986, when Ito-Yokado's ownership of Daikuma increased from 47.6 percent to 79.5 percent.[18] In 1990, Daikuma was one of the largest discount store chains in Japan with 14 stores. While Daikuma was popular among young Japanese consumers, the discount stores attracted the critical attention of competing small retailers. Because the discount stores were regulated by the Large Store Regulation Act, intensive effort was required to open new stores. Despite these circumstances, and increasing competition, Daikuma opened two discount stores in 1989.[19]

[18] Ibid.
[19] *Moody's Industrial Manual,* p. 1275.

EXHIBIT 14.3   Ito-Yokado Company, Ltd., Statement of Cash Flows (In millions of yen)

	As of February 28			
	1987	*1988*	*1989*	*1990*
Cash Flow from Operations				
Net Income	¥ 34,759	¥ 43,511	¥ 51,586	¥ 58,465
Adjustments				
Depreciation and Amortization	31,106	32,064	33,777	37,695
Minority Interest	8,862	11,058	13,338	15,577
Undistributed Earnings of Affiliates	(603)	(719)	(811)	(732)
Deferred Income Tax and Other	985	1,328	1,641	5,677
Increase in Accounts and Notes Receivable, Less Allowance	(12)	(2,140)	(10,675)	58
Decrease (Increase) in Inventory	650	(1,196)	(6,049)	740
Decrease (Increase) in Prepaid Expenses	(2,194)	734	(1,109)	(8,875)
Increase in Accounts and Notes Payable and Accrued Liability	2,054	24,740	22,296	22,388
Increase in Other Liability	718	3,744	2,945	4,815
Net Cash Provided by Operations	¥ 76,325	¥112,854	¥106,939	¥135,808
Cash Flow from Investing				
Increase in Property and Equipment	¥(50,832)	¥(50,075)	¥(55,802)	¥(72,927)
Increase in Investments and Advertising	(3,492)	(3,260)	(1,706)	(6,339)
Proceeds from Disposal of Property and Equipment	1,460	731	1,991	1,442
Other	(6,206)	(5,629)	(5,878)	(13,888)
Net Cash Used by Investing	¥(58,620)	¥(58,233)	¥(61,395)	¥(91,742)
Cash Flow from Financing				
Issue of Long-Term Debt	¥ 37,859	¥ 7,692	¥ 9,755	¥ 10,135
Repayment of Long-Term Debt	(15,331)	(9,321)	(6,472)	(7,112)
Proceeds from Issuance of Common Stock by Subs	0	0	18,554	0
Dividends Paid	(6,216)	(7,324)	(7,833)	(8,834)
Other	(2,670)	(5,711)	(2,317)	(3,096)
Net Cash Provided by Financing	¥ 13,642	¥(14,664)	¥ 11,687	¥ (8,421)
Net Change in Cash Equivalent	¥ 31,347	¥ 39,957	¥ 57,231	¥ 35,645
Cash Equivalent at Start of Year	92,778	124,125	164,082	221,313
Cash Equivalent at End of Year	¥124,125	¥164,082	¥221,313	¥256,958

Source: *Moody's Industrial Manual, 1990 and 1989,* Vol. 1.

Robinson's Department Stores

In 1984, the Robinson's Japan Company was established to open Robinson's Department Stores in Japan. The Robinson's name was used under the terms of a license granted by the U.S. store of the same name. The Japanese company was 100 percent owned by Ito-Yokado, and the first Robinson's Department Store in Japan was opened in November 1985 in Kasukabe City of Saitama Prefecture.[20]

[20] Uchida, *First Boston,* p. 10.

This was a residential community north of Tokyo and was a rapidly growing area. Although an Ito-Yokado superstore was located nearby, Ito-Yokado's management believed that a niche existed for a slightly more upscale retail store. Ito-Yokado had "shattered traditional wisdom by opening up a department store in the suburbs, not in the center of Tokyo."[21] The location was expected to serve a population area of over 600,000 residents and to offer a broad selection of consumer goods at prices higher than superstores yet lower than the downtown Tokyo department stores.

Many of the strategies employed by Ito-Yokado in opening its Robinson's Department Store followed similar strategies employed in its superstores. The land was leased (in a suburb). Instead of purchasing goods on a consignment basis as most other department stores did, Robinson's managers were made responsible for the outright purchase of goods from suppliers. This allowed Robinson's to purchase goods at a significantly reduced price. Robinson's reported its first profit in fiscal 1989, approximately four years after opening.[22] In contrast, most Japanese department stores operate approximately 10 years before reporting a profit.[23] The single Robinson's location grossed about ¥28 billion (US$220 million) in fiscal 1989.[24] The second Robinson's Department Store opened in late 1990 in Utsunomiya, about 100 kilometers (60 miles) north of Tokyo.

Oshman's Sporting Goods

Ito-Yokado licensed the Oshman's Sporting Goods name from the Houston, Texas, parent company in 1985. That year, two stores were opened. One of the stores was located inside the original Robinson's Department Store.

RESTAURANT OPERATIONS

Famil

The Famil Restaurant chain was started in 1979 as an in-store restaurant to serve customers at Ito-Yokado superstores. It had, however, expanded to 251 locations by 1988.[25] The Famil chain did not record its first positive earnings until 1986. In Famil's attempts to expand operations, the company had emphasized its catering business.[26] By 1990, the in-store operations (those located in Ito-Yokado superstores) accounted for 45 percent of Famil's sales, the catering business accounted for 32 percent of sales, and free-standing stores accounted for 23 percent of sales.[27]

[21] Ibid.
[22] *Moody's Industrial Manual*, p. 1275.
[23] Uchida, *First Boston*, p. 10.
[24] *Moody's Industrial Manual*, p. 1275.
[25] Uchida, *First Boston*, p. 12.
[26] Ibid.
[27] *Moody's Industrial Manual*, p. 1275.

Denny's Japan

Ito-Yokado opened the initial Denny's (Japan) Restaurant in 1974 with a license from Denny's of La Mirada, California. Ito-Yokado tailored the U.S. family restaurant to the Japanese market, and Denny's Japan became profitable around 1977. By 1981, 100 Denny's Japan restaurants had been established,[28] and in 1990 there were 320 such restaurants operated by Ito-Yokado.[29] In 1990, Ito-Yokado controlled 51 percent of Denny's Japan stock. In the early 1980s, Ito-Yokado decided that Denny's Japan should purchase all rights to the Denny's name in Japan. The purchase was made in 1984, and royalty payments to the U.S. parent were thereby discontinued.[30]

In fiscal year 1990 (March 1989, to February 1990), Denny's Japan reported a net annual sales increase of 10.9 percent, as compared to the 4.9 percent Japanese restaurant industry sales increase for the same period.[31] Exhibits 14.4 and 14.5 contain financial statements for Denny's Japan. In 1988, Denny's Japan began using an electronic order-entry system, which allowed managers of individual restaurants to quickly order food supplies based on trends in their own restaurant. It also allowed for the periodic updating of menus to reflect new food items.

CONVENIENCE STORE OPERATIONS

7-Eleven Japan

Since the opening of the first 7-Eleven store in 1974, the chain had grown to over 4,300 stores located in virtually all parts of Japan by February 1990.[32] At that time, about 300 new stores were being opened annually.[33] Ito-Yokado owned approximately 50.3 percent of 7-Eleven Japan in 1990.

Originally, young urban workers represented the primary customer base. As 7-Eleven penetrated the Japanese market, however, almost everyone became a potential customer. In Tokyo, for example, utility bills could be paid at the chain's stores.[34]

The 7-Eleven stores were small enough, with an average of only 1,000 square feet, to effectively avoid regulation under the Large Store Regulation Act. This allowed 7-Eleven to compete with the mom-and-pop retailers on the basis of longer hours of operation and lower prices. Faced with this competition, many of

[28] Ibid.
[29] Yumiko Ono, "Japanese Chain Stores Prosper by Milking American Concepts," *Asian Wall Street Journal*, April 2, 1990.
[30] Ibid.
[31] *Moody's Industrial Manual*, pp. 1275–1276.
[32] James Sterngold, "New Japanese Lesson: Running a 7-11," *New York Times*, May 9, 1991, p. C1.
[33] Ono, "Japanese Chain Stores Prosper."
[34] Ibid.

EXHIBIT 14.4   Denny's Japan Company, Ltd., Consolidated Balance Sheet (In millions of yen)

	As of February 28		
	1988	1989	1990
Assets			
Cash	¥ 1,436	¥ 1,686	¥ 1,516
Time Deposits	4,430	4,930	13,340
Marketable Securities	104	0	14
Notes and Accounts Receivable	76	87	111
Inventories	562	569	617
Prepaid Expenses	529	610	758
Short-Term Loans	4,527	6,241	5
Short-Term Leasehold Deposits	267	286	300
Other Current Assets	414	233	341
Total Current Assets	12,345	14,643	17,092
Investments and Advances	2,452	2,133	2,273
Gross Property and Equipment	18,894	21,291	23,739
Less: Accumulated Depreciation	9,108	10,397	11,937
Net Property and Equipment	9,786	10,894	11,802
Fixed Leasehold Deposits	5,177	5,334	5,496
Deferred Charges Other Assets	4,449	3,940	3,380
Total Assets	¥34,209	¥36,944	¥40,043
Liabilities and Owners' Equity			
Accounts Payable	¥ 3,728	¥ 3,865	¥ 3,932
Accrued Expenses	1,560	1,743	1,837
Income Tax	2,009	2,210	2,140
Consumption Tax Withheld	328	0	653
Other Current Liabilities	0	383	299
Total Current Liabilities	7,625	8,201	8,861
Common Stock	7,125	7,125	7,125
Additional Paid-In Capital	9,533	9,785	9,785
Legal Reserves	233	286	345
Closing Retained Earnings	9,724	11,547	13,927
Owners' Equity	26,584	28,743	31,182
Total Liabilities and Owners' Equity	¥34,209	¥36,944	¥40,043

Source: *Moody's International Manual,* 1989, 1990, Vol. 1.

the small retailers joined the ranks of 7-Eleven. By converting small retailers to 7-Eleven stores, Ito-Yokado was able to expand rapidly and blanket the country.[35]

7-Eleven Japan pursued a strategy of franchising stores instead of owning them. The franchise commission for 7-Eleven stores was approximately 45 per-

[35] Tanzer, "A Form of Flattery."

EXHIBIT 14.5 Denny's Japan Company, Ltd., Consolidated Income Statement
(In millions of yen)

	As of February 28		
	1988	1989	1990
Net Sales	¥58,241	¥64,604	¥70,454
Interest Income	317	434	650
Other Revenue, Net	223	236	290
Total Revenue	58,781	65,274	71,394
Cost of Sales	20,196	22,233	23,952
Gross Margin	38,585	43,041	47,442
Selling, Administrative, and General Expenses	32,444	35,990	40,177
Interest Expense	19	9	17
Loss on Sale of Property	73	153	119
Income before Taxes	6,049	6,889	7,129
Income Taxes	3,521	3,894	4,074
Net Income	¥ 2,528	¥ 2,995	¥ 3,055
Opening Retained Earnings	¥ 7,755	¥ 9,152	¥11,547
Cash Dividends	508	535	588
Transfers to Legal Reserves	51	53	59
Closing Retained Earnings	¥ 9,724	¥11,559	¥13,955
Earnings per Share (Based on 26,741,000 Weighted Average Shares)	¥ 94.50	¥112.40	¥114.20

Source: *Moody's International Manual*, 1989, 1990. Vol. 1. The data are presented here as shown in Moody's. Some minor math errors exist.

cent of the gross profit of the store (the commission was 43 percent for 24-hour stores). Ito-Yokado provided most of the ancillary functions for each store (e.g., administration, accounting, advertising, and 80 percent of utility costs). In 1987, 92 percent of all 7-Eleven stores in Japan were franchised,[36] and by 1990, only 2 percent of the 7-Elevens were corporate owned.[37]

Within the Ito-Yokado group, 7-Eleven contributed 6.8 percent of revenues in 1990. With this relatively small portion of overall corporate revenues, however, 7-Eleven Japan contributed over 35 percent of the group's profit. Under its licensing agreement, 7-Eleven Japan paid royalties of 0.6 percent of gross sales to the Southland Corporation. In 1989 and 1990, 7-Eleven Japan paid royalties of about $4.1 million and $4.7 million, respectively. The financial statements for 7-Eleven Japan for the years 1986 to 1990 are shown in Exhibits 14.6 and 14.7.

[36] Uchida, *First Boston*, p. 13.
[37] *Moody's Industrial Manual*, p. 1276.

EXHIBIT 14.6   7-Eleven Japan Consolidated Balance Sheet (In millions of yen)

	As of February 28		
	1988	*1989*	*1990*
Assets			
Cash	¥ 11,868	¥ 15,739	¥ 14,373
Time Deposits	23,440	31,090	65,510
Short-Term Loans	26,169	52,228	29,136
Notes and Accounts Receivable	2,343	2,517	2,582
Inventory	247	285	222
Prepaid Expenses	223	285	124
Less: Allowance for Other Debts	1,990	320	180
Other Current Assets	351	651	369
Total Current Assets	66,631	102,315	112,136
Investments and Advances	3,534	3,382	9,355
Gross Property and Equipment	94,703	108,319	123,871
Less: Accumulated Depreciation	25,665	30,316	35,010
Net Property and Equipment	69,038	78,003	88,861
Fixed Leasehold Deposits	4,351	6,501	7,725
Other Assets	1,460	2,213	8,248
Total Assets	¥145,014	¥192,417	¥226,325
Liabilities and Owners' Equity			
Accounts Payable	¥ 40,498	¥ 46,678	¥ 52,912
Accrued Expenses	1,427	1,487	1,738
Advances	685	778	718
Income Taxes	14,818	17,341	20,068
Other Current Liabilities	867	552	3,289
Total Current Liabilities	58,295	66,836	78,725
Long-Term Debt	1,612	1,781	1,933
Common Stock	5,902	17,145	17,145
Additional Paid-In Capital	13,073	24,619	24,589
Legal Reserves	1,142	1,491	1,919
Retained Earnings	65,233	80,545	101,984
Owners' Equity	85,107	123,800	145,667
Total Liabilities and Owners' Equity	¥145,014	¥192,417	¥226,325

Source: *Moody's International Manual,* 1989, 1990, Vol. 1.

OPERATION REFORM PROJECT

Ito-Yokado implemented the Operation Reform Project in late 1981 in a retail industry environment punctuated by reduced consumer spending and decreasing margins. The goals of the project were to increase efficiency and boost profitability by increasing the inventory turn while avoiding empty store shelves.

EXHIBIT 14.7   7-Eleven Japan Consolidated Income Statement (In millions of yen)

	As of February 28		
	1988	*1989*	*1990*
Revenue	¥96,236	¥102,314	¥118,490
Cost of Goods Sold	13,484	8,702	9,249
Gross Margin	82,752	93,612	109,241
Selling, Administrative, and General Expenses	39,672	42,491	49,185
Loss on Sale of Property	232	(66)	(230)
Income before Taxes	42,848	51,187	59,826
Tax Expenses	23,911	28,882	33,599
Net Income	¥18,937	¥ 22,305	¥ 26,227
Opening Retained Earnings	¥49,646	¥ 62,139	¥ 80,545
Dividends	3,054	3,495	4,280
Transfers to Legal Reserves	306	350	428
Officers' Bonus	0	54	80
Closing Retained Earnings	¥65,223	¥ 80,545	¥101,984
Earnings per Share (Based on 179,569,000 Weighted Average Shares)	¥ 129.1	¥ 126.7	¥ 146.1

Note: "Cost of Goods Sold" represents primarily the cost of merchandise sold in the 152 company-owned stores.
Source: *Moody's International Manual,* 1989, 1990, Vol. 1.

The plan was originally implemented in the Ito-Yokado Superstores and the 7-Eleven Japan convenience stores.

The implementation of the project involved a coordinated effort of catering to rapidly changing consumer preferences while, simultaneously, monitoring merchandise flow more closely. This coordination was accomplished by making individual store managers more responsible for such decisions as what merchandise was to be stocked on store shelves, thus allowing managers to tailor merchandise selection in their individual stores to local preferences. Top Ito-Yokado regional managers held weekly meetings with store managers to monitor the implementation of the project. As late as 1988, these meetings were still held on a weekly basis.[38]

In order to avoid depletion of store stocks, Ito-Yokado established an on-line ordering system with vendors. In 1982, the ordering system reached only 400 vendors. By 1988, however, the system linked Ito-Yokado with 1,860 vendors.[39]

[38] Hiroaki Komatsu, *Nomura Securities Report on Ito-Yokado Co., Ltd.*, June 7, 1988, p. 4.
[39] Ibid.

Point-of-Sale System[40]

As implementation of the Operation Reform Project began, Ito-Yokado paid increased attention to the importance of obtaining information regarding the flow of merchandise through individual stores. The tool chosen to accomplish this task was the point-of-sale system. POS system usage was increasing in the United States in the early 1980s, but the systems were used primarily to increase productivity at the cash register.[41] In contrast, Ito-Yokado used similar systems as a part of the project by monitoring specific merchandise flow. As of the late 1980s, many retailers in the United States had begun utilizing POS in similar capacities, and some had begun to use POS to track the purchases of individual consumers.[42]

The first use of POS systems in Japan came in 1982, when 7-Eleven Japan began installing them in its stores. By 1986, every 7-Eleven store in Japan was equipped with such a system.[43] The systems available were sophisticated enough to monitor the entire stock of merchandise in a typical convenience store having about 3,000 items.[44] The systems could monitor the flow of every item of merchandise through the purchase, inventory, sale, and restocking stages.

In late 1984, Ito-Yokado decided to install POS systems in the superstores. The sophistication of those systems installed in convenience stores, however, was not adequate to handle the merchandise flow of a superstore, which could stock up to 500,000 items.[45] New POS systems were developed in a coordinated effort by Ito-Yokado, Nippon Electric, and Nomura Computer Services.

The installation of POS systems in the existing superstores was completed in November 1985, with over 8,000 POS registers installed in 121 stores.[46] With 138 stores in 1990, Ito-Yokado had an estimated 9,000 POS registers in the

---

[40] POS systems are computer-based merchandise control systems. They can provide a variety of functions such as inventory monitoring, price identification and registering, and—in some circumstances—merchandise ordering.

The implementation of POS systems became a reality in the early 1970s, when IBM announced the creation of a merchandise system which later became the Universal Product Code (UPC). In 1974, Marsh Supermarkets became the first retail store to utilize UPC-based POS systems. Also in 1974, the European Article Number (EAN) system, which is virtually a superset of the UPC, was introduced in Europe. The EAN system was adopted by 12 European nations in 1977. In 1978, Japan joined the EAN association (EANA). By 1989, 40 countries were members of the EANA.

The Japanese domestic market utilizes the same bar-code system used in the United States and Europe for product marking under the EAN guidelines for product marking. The Japanese coding system for consumer goods is called Japanese Article Numbering (JAN). A similar system for product marking used by wholesalers and distributors in Japan is the value-added network (VAN). The first product utilizing the JAN code was introduced in Japan in 1978.

Source: Ryosuke Assano "Networks Raise Efficiency," *Business Japan,* October 1989, pp. 45–52; Radack et al., Automation in the Market-Place, March 1978; "Pointing Out Differences in Point-of-Sale," *Chain Store Age Executive,* October 1990, pp. 16B–17B.

[41] Tanzer, "A Form of Flattery."

[42] For an example of one such application, see Blake Ives et al., *The Tom Thumb Promise Club,* Edwin L. Cox School of Business, Southern Methodist University, 1989.

[43] Hiroaki Komatsu, *Nomura Securities Report on Seven-Eleven Japan,* March 15, 1988, p. 4.

[44] Uchida, *First Boston,* p. 13.

[45] Ibid.

[46] *Moody's Industrial Manual,* p. 1275.

superstores alone. In 1986, after the systems had been installed in all superstores and 7-Elevens, Ito-Yokado accounted for about 70 percent of the POS systems in use in Japan.[47] As of 1988, 7-Eleven Japan was the only major convenience store chain in Japan to have installed POS systems.[48] By August 31, 1989, Japan had 119,137 POS scanner-equipped registers in 42,880 stores, making it the country with the most POS systems in use.[49]

The POS systems used by 7-Eleven Japan and Ito-Yokado superstores were upgraded in 1986 to add a new dimension to Ito-Yokado's Operation Reform Project.[50] The upgraded systems allowed for bidirectional communication with the company headquarters. This feature essentially allowed information to flow not only from individual stores to a central location, but also from the central location back to individual stores. By linking the central system to other computer systems, more information than just sales of retail items could be transmitted. This capability allowed Ito-Yokado to increase the efficiency of deliveries by centralizing some orders. By increasing the total size of orders, Ito-Yokado increased its bargaining position with distributors. One result of this bargaining strength was more frequent deliveries of smaller volume. From 1987 to 1988, deliveries increased from one to three per week for stores in many regions of Japan, notably the Tokyo, Hokkaido, and Kyushu areas.

Using the POS systems, 7-Eleven began to offer customers door-to-door parcel delivery in conjunction with Nippon Express. In addition, some POS terminals were being used to issue prepaid telephone credit cards.[51] Since October 1987, Tokyo-area customers had been able to pay their electric bills at 7-Eleven; since March 1988, they had also been able to pay their gas bills.[52] Since women traditionally manage household finances in Japan, these services were designed to attract more women customers to the convenience stores.

Results

For the Ito-Yokado superstores alone, average days of inventory decreased from 25.8 in 1982 to 17.3 in 1987. By 1990, it was estimated to be 13 days.[53] The effect on operating margins and net income for the entire Ito-Yokado corporation was equally dramatic. In 1982, the company's operating margin stood at 5.1 percent. It had increased to 8.1 percent by 1987. By 1990, the operating margin had climbed to 10.5 percent. Net income for the corporation increased from ¥14,662 million in 1982 to ¥34,649 million in 1987, and ¥58,465 million in 1990.[54]

Seven-Eleven Japan recorded similar increases in operating margins and net income during the same period. In 1982, 7-Eleven Japan's operating margin

[47] Tanzer, "A Form of Flattery."
[48] Komatsu, *Nomura Securities Report*, p. 4.
[49] *Business Japan*, October 1989, p. 51.
[50] Komatsu, *Nomura Securities Report*, p. 5.
[51] Ibid.
[52] Ibid.
[53] Uchida, *First Boston*, pp. 12, 22; and *Moody's Industrial Manual*, p. 1276.
[54] Ibid.

EXHIBIT 14.8   Daiei, Inc. Consolidated Balance Sheet (In millions of yen)

	As of February 28		
	1988	1989	1990
Assets			
Cash	¥ 60,409	¥ 61,096	¥ 55,529
Time Deposits	89,090	61,866	85,713
Marketable Securities	18,919	18,762	20,022
Net Receivables	100,214	98,449	103,455
Inventories	95,924	90,203	108,241
Prepaid Expenses and Deferred Income Tax	7,784	11,149	15,338
Total Current Assets	372,340	341,525	388,298
Gross Property and Equipment	284,007	358,443	410,870
Less Accumulated Depreciation	108,540	120,955	141,172
Net Property and Equipment	175,467	237,488	269,698
Lease Depreciation and Loans to Lessors	231,996	245,139	266,474
Investment and Long-Term Receivables	118,009	170,676	164,853
Other Assets	13,689	16,540	21,306
Total Assets	¥911,501	¥1,011,368	¥1,110,629
Liabilities and Owners' Equity			
Short-Term Borrowings	¥256,539	¥338,188	¥350,274
Debt Due	51,488	47,816	34,667
Notes and Accounts Payable	176,450	186,390	221,815
Accruals	18,370	18,274	21,256
Income Taxes	7,872	7,284	8,445
Total Current Liabilities	510,719	597,952	636,457
Long-Term Debt	199,616	187,625	216,763
Lease Deposits	52,656	56,750	60,489
Estimated Retirement and Term Allowance	10,002	9,437	9,789
Reserve for Investment Losses	35,903	35,293	37,151
Deferred Income	7,423	7,343	7,425
Other Liabilities	1,636	4,604	7,314
Translation Adjustment	2,179	1,979	1,754
Minority Interests	663	692	2,794
Common Stock (¥50)	18,144	25,649	33,783
Additional Paid-In Capital	82,748	92,426	100,664
Legal Reserves	3,875	4,481	5,108
Deficit	(14,063)	(12,863)	(8,862)
Owners' Equity	90,704	109,693	130,693
Total Liabilities and Owners' Equity	¥911,501	¥1,011,368	¥1,110,629

Source: *Moody's International Manual,* 1990 and 1989, Vol. 1.

was 20.7 percent. It had increased to 34.6 percent by 1987. Net income from the
7-Eleven operations increased from ¥7,837 million in 1982 to ¥33,000 million in
1987.[55]

As of 1990, the Ito-Yokado corporation was the second largest retailer in
Japan, with ¥1,664,390 million of annual gross sales. The leading retailer was
Daiei, with ¥2,114,909 million of revenues. Ito-Yokado was, however, the most
profitable retailer in Japan, with net income of ¥58,465 million. In comparison,
Daiei recorded net income of only ¥9,457 million for 1990. Financial statements
for Daiei are shown as Exhibits 14.8 and 14.9.

**EXHIBIT 14.9   Daiei, Inc. Consolidated Income Statement (In millions of yen except
earnings per share)**

	As of February 28		
	1988	*1989*	*1990*
Net Sales	¥1,718,886	¥1,880,825	¥2,114,909
Real Estate Revenue	0	21,235	22,790
Other Revenue	45,588	37,623	55,171
Total Operating Revenue	1,764,474	1,939,683	2,192,870
Cost of Goods Sold	1,327,618	1,460,007	1,626,850
Gross Margin	436,856	479,676	566,020
Selling, General, and Administrative			
Expenses	392,914	432,269	510,469
Operating Income	43,942	47,407	55,551
Net Interest Expenditures	16,942	19,115	21,312
Other Expenses	1,760	1,283	3,401
Income before Taxes	25,240	27,009	30,838
Income Tax	13,405	14,868	17,101
Minority Interests	50	32	730
Equity Losses	7,204	4,229	3,504
Translation Adjustment	211	134	(46)
Net Income	¥ 4,792	¥ 8,104	¥ 9,457
Opening Retained Earnings	¥ (13,929)	¥ (14,063)	¥ (12,863)
Decrease Due to Merger of Chain Store			
Operations	0	0	1,497
Cash Dividends	5,083	6,059	6,269
Transfer to Legal Reserves	73	606	627
Bonuses	114	141	143
Translation Adjustment	(344)	8	(86)
Closing Retained Earnings	¥ (14,063)	¥ (12,863)	¥ (8,862)
Earnings per Share	¥ 14.27	¥ 21.67	¥ 24.72
Shares Outstanding	n/a	369,871,000	382,499,000

Source: *Moody's International Manual,* 1990 and 1989, Vol. 1.

[55] Ibid.

THE SOUTHLAND CORPORATION[56]

The Southland Corporation began in Dallas, Texas in 1927 when Claude S. Dawley consolidated several small Texas ice companies into the Southland Ice Company. This new company was under the direction of 26-year-old Joe C. Thompson, Sr. Under Thompson's guidance, Southland began to use its retail outlets (curb service docks) to sell products in addition to ice, such as watermelon, milk, bread, eggs, and cigarettes. With the addition of these products, the concept of the convenience store was born.

During the Great Depression and the 1940s, Southland's convenience store business added several more products, including gasoline, frozen foods, beauty products, fresh fruit and vegetables, and picnic supplies. Because the store opened at 7 AM and remained open till 11 PM, the store name 7-Eleven was adopted during this time.

The 1950s were a period of substantial growth in terms of the number of stores and of 7-Eleven's geographical coverage. The first stores located outside of Texas were opened in Florida in 1954. During the same year, 7-Eleven's operating profit surpassed the $1 million mark for the first time. By 1959, the entire 7-Eleven empire constituted 425 stores in Texas, Louisiana, Florida, and several other East Coast states.

John Thompson became president of Southland when his father, Jodie Thompson, died in 1961. During the 1960s, a population migration toward the suburbs and changing lifestyles presented Southland with new growth opportunities. John Thompson lead Southland on the path of expansion, and over 3,000 stores were opened in the decade. The product line of 7-Eleven also grew during this time, to include prepared foods, rental items, and some self-service gasoline pumps.

The 1970s were also a period of achievement for Southland. In 1971, the $1 billion sales mark was surpassed. Southland stock began trading on the New York Stock Exchange in 1972, and the 5,000th store was opened in 1974. It was at this time that Masatoshi Ito approached Southland with the prospect of franchising 7-Eleven stores in Japan.

During the 1970s and early 1980s, Southland's activities became more diversified. In 1986, the company had four operating groups: the Stores Group, the Dairies Group, the Special Operations Group, and the Gasoline Supply Division.

The Stores Group represented the largest of the operating groups in terms of sales through the 1980s. The Stores Group was responsible for the operating and franchising of convenience stores. At the end of 1985, there were 7,519 7-Eleven stores in most of the United States and five provinces of Canada. This group was also responsible for 84 Gristede's and Charles & Company food stores, 38 Super-7

---

[56] A more detailed history of Southland can be found in cases written by M. Edgar Barrett, of the American Graduate School of International Business: *The Southland Corporation (A)*, 1983, and *The Southland Corporation (B)*, 1990.

outlets, and 7-Eleven stores operated under area licensees in the United States, Canada, and several Pacific Rim countries, including Japan.

The Dairies Group was one of the nation's largest dairy processors in 1986, and served primarily the Stores Group, although aggressive marketing in the 1980s targeted service to institutional dairy needs. This group operated in all of the United States and parts of Canada. The Special Operations Group consisted of Chief Auto Parts (acquired in 1979); Pate Foods (a snack food company); Reddy Ice (the world's largest ice company); and Tidel Systems (a manufacturer of cash dispensing units and other retailer equipment). The Gasoline Supply Division was formed in 1981 to serve the gasoline requirements of the over 2,800 7-Eleven stores handling gasoline. This division's history was punctuated by the 1983 acquisition of Cities Service Refining, Marketing, and Transportation businesses (CITGO) from Occidental Petroleum.

Southland's Recent Activities[57]

Southland's dramatic growth and diversification during the 1970s and early 1980s resulted in 7-Eleven having a dominant position in the convenience store industry. Despite this position circumstances since the mid-1980s had greatly eroded 7-Eleven and Southland's strengths.

The oil price collapse of early 1986 was the sharpest drop of crude oil prices in history. The instability of crude oil and wholesale refined products, coupled with CITGO's inventory methods and various write-downs, resulted in only modest income for a previously very profitable company. The volatility of CITGO's financial position greatly affected Southland's earnings. Southland's equity interest in CITGO contributed to a $52 million loss for the entire corporation in 1986. In order to reduce the impact of an unstable crude oil market and the accompanying volatility of CITGO's earnings, Southland entered into a joint venture with Petroleos de Venezuela (PDVSA) in late 1986.

The joint venture with PDVSA had several components. Southland sold a half-interest in CITGO to a subsidiary of PDVSA for $290 million. In addition, PDVSA agreed to both supply CITGO with a minimum of 130,000 barrels of crude oil per day and provide its share of CITGO's working capital requirements.

A takeover attempt of Southland occurred in April 1987. Canadian financier Samuel Belzberg approached the Southland board of directors with an offer of $65 per share of common stock. Unwilling to relinquish control of Southland, the Thompson family tendered $77 per share for two-thirds of the outstanding shares in July 1987. The other third of the shares would be purchased at $61 per share (plus $16 per share of new preferred shares) by the would-be private Southland Corporation.

Financing for this acquisition came from $2 billion in loans from a group of banks and a $600 million bridge loan from Goldman, Sachs and Salomon Brothers. An additional $1.5 billion was generated by the issue of subordinated debentures

---

[57] Barrett, *The Southland Corporation (B)*, offers more detailed information.

(junk bonds) in November 1987. This occurred after the stock and junk bond markets crashed in October 1987. Southland's investment bankers had to sell the bonds at a blended rate of almost 17 percent, instead of the anticipated rate of 14.67 percent. The Thompson family emerged from the buyout owning 71 percent of Southland at a total cost of $4.9 billion.

Paying the High Costs of a Leveraged Buyout

After Southland had been taken private through the leveraged buyout (LBO), significant changes occurred in both Southland and 7-Eleven operations. Southland was restructured, with the elimination of two levels of middle managers. During this time, Southland began selling more 7-Eleven stores than it opened in the United States and Canada. Due to the increased number of licensees opening stores overseas, however, the total number of stores worldwide continued to increase. 7-Eleven Japan was primarily responsible for this increase, with the opening of 340 stores in 1988 and 349 stores in 1989. Southland also divested itself of many large assets in the 1988 to 1990 period (see Exhibit 14.10). Significant in this group of divestments were the entire Dairy Group, over 100 7-Eleven stores in

EXHIBIT 14.10   Asset Divestitures of Southland, 1988–1990

Date Announced	Asset	Buyer	Amount
January 1988	Tidel Systems	D.H. Monnick Corp.	Undisclosed
February 1988	Chief Auto Parts	Management & Shearson Lehman	$130 million
March 1988	Movie Quik	Cevax U.S. Corp.	$51 million
March 1988	Reddy Ice	Reddy Ice	$23 million
April 1988	402 Properties including 270 Houston area 7-Elevens	National Convenience Stores	$67 million plus $13 million for related inventories
April 1988	473 7-Eleven stores in 10 states	Circle-K	$147 million
April 1988	Southland Dairy Group	Morningstar Foods	$242.5 million
July 1988	Snack Food Division	Undisclosed	$15 million
November 1988	79 San Antonio area 7-Eleven	National Convenience Stores	Undisclosed
July 1989	184 7-Eleven in 3 states	Ashland Oil et al.	Undisclosed
October 1989	50% of CITGO	Petroleos de Venezuela S.A. (PDVSA)	$661.5 million
November 1989	58 7-Eleven in Hawaii, plus other properties	7-Eleven Japan	$75 million
April 1990	56 Memphis area 7-Eleven	Undisclosed	$12.9 million
August 1990	28 7-Eleven in Florida, plus other properties	Undisclosed	$7.5 million
December 1990	Cityplace in Dallas	Oak Creek Partners	$24 million

Source: *Dallas Morning News,* November 15, 1989, p. D-1; *Dallas Morning News,* October 10, 1988, p. D-1; *Automotive News,* February 8, 1988, p. 108; *Wall Street Journal,* February 19, 1988; *Wall Street Journal,* January 28, 1988; *Wall Street Journal,* March 4, 1988; *New York Times,* March 4, 1988; Southland Corporation, 1990 Form 10-K.

the continental United States, Southland's remaining interest in CITGO (sold to PDVSA), and 7-Eleven Hawaii, (purchased by 7-Eleven Japan).

In November 1989, 7-Eleven Japan purchased 58 stores and additional properties from Southland. These properties and stores, which were located in Hawaii, were exchanged for $75 million in cash. The 58 convenience stores were organized as 7-Eleven Hawaii, which was established as a subsidiary of 7-Eleven Japan.

As of December 31, 1990, Southland operated 6,455 7-Eleven convenience stores in the United States and Canada, 187 High's Dairy Stores, and 63 Quick Mart and Super-7 Stores. Southland owned 1,802 properties on which 7-Eleven stores were located. Another 4,643 7-Eleven stores in the United States and Canada were leased. In addition the company possessed 234 store properties held for sale, of which 109 were unimproved, 77 were closed stores, and 48 were excess properties adjoining store locations.[58]

Three of Southland's four food processing facilities were owned (the other was leased). The company owned six properties in the United States on which distribution centers were located. Five of the six distribution centers were company owned. The company also owned its corporate headquarters (called Cityplace) located near downtown Dallas.[59] Financial statements for Southland Corporation are shown in Exhibits 14.11 and 14.12.

THE PROPOSED PURCHASE OF SOUTHLAND BY ITO-YOKADO

The divestments of 1988, 1989, and 1990 constituted attempts by Southland to generate sufficient cash to service the massive debt incurred from the LBO of 1987. By early 1990, however, it was apparent that the cash generated from these divestments and Southland's operations was not sufficient to cover its interest expense. Some experts estimated that Southland's cash shortfalls would reach $89 million in 1990 and over $270 million in 1991.[60] Southland's long-term debt still totaled about $3.7 billion, and interest expense alone in the first three quarters of 1989 was almost $430 million.[61] In March of 1990, Southland announced that it was seeking "rescue" by Ito-Yokado.[62]

Proposed Acquisition of Southland by Ito-Yokado

Southland had "looked at possibilities of receiving assistance from other U.S. companies, but decided that . . . Ito-Yokado was the best potential partner."[63] The original proposal would have resulted in Ito-Yokado receiving 75 per-

[58] *Southland Corporation 1990 Form 10-K*, pp. 21–23.
[59] Ibid.
[60] Linda Sandler, "Southland's Junk Bonds Face Trouble," *Wall Street Journal*, September 7, 1989.
[61] Richard Alm, "Southland Seeks Rescue by Japanese Firm," *Dallas Morning News*, March 23, 1990.
[62] Ibid.
[63] Karen Blumenthal et al., "Japanese Group Agrees to Buy Southland Corporation," *Wall Street Journal*, March 23, 1990.

EXHIBIT 14.11   Southland Corporation Consolidated Balance Sheet
(In thousands of dollars)

	As of December 31			
	1988	*1989*	*1990*	*1990a*
Assets				
Cash and Short-Term Inventory	$ 21,783	$ 8,045	$ 108,294	$ 351,678
Accounts and Notes Receivable	208,686	188,251	161,778	161,778
Inventories	428,098	276,112	301,756	301,756
Deposits and Prepaid Expenditures	25,929	25,483	64,075	44,889
Investment in Citgo	—	469,687	—	—
Total Current Assets	684,496	958,578	635,903	860,101
Property, Plant, and Equipment	2,632,060	2,620,137	2,504,090	2,504,090
Less Depreciation	416,822	624,807	788,589	788,589
Net Property, Plant and Equipment	2,215,238	1,995,330	1,715,501	1,715,501
Investment in Citgo	440,777	—	—	—
Excess Acquisition Costs	986,356	—	—	—
Other Assets	534,644	484,847	447,638	397,349
Total Assets	$4,861,511	$3,438,755	$2,799,042	$2,972,951
Liabilities and Owners' Equity				
Debt Due	$ 527,174	$ 692,508	$3,522,647	$ 647,512
Accounts Payable	692,596	723,694	647,512	9,145
Income Taxes Payable	377	139	9,145	171,729
Total Current Liabilities	1,220,147	1,416,341	4,298,119	828,386
Deferred Credits	96,359	115,334	142,315	142,315
Long-Term Debt	3,787,578	3,457,015	182,536	3,118,797
Redeemable Preferred Stock	118,850	139,740	148,496	—
Redeemable Common Stock Purchase Warrants	26,136	26,136	26,136	26,136
Common Stock	2,050	2,050	2,050	41
Additional Paid-In Capital	18,318	18,318	20,364	594,146
Deficit	(407,927)	(1,736,179)	(2,018,926)	(1,736,870)
Total Owners' Equity	(387,559)	(1,715,811)	(1,998,560)	(1,142,683)
Total Liabilities and Owners' Equity	$4,861,511	$3,438,755	$2,799,042	$2,972,951

a This depicts the balance sheet for Southland on December 31, 1990, as if the later buyout by Ito-Yokado had been completed.
Source: Southland Corporation 1990 and 1989 Forms 10-K.

cent ownership of Southland for $400 million. This proportion of Southland would be split between Ito-Yokado and 7-Eleven Japan, with 7-Eleven Japan obtaining two-thirds of the 75 percent share.

The deal was contingent on Southland's ability to swap its outstanding publicly traded debt for stock and zero-coupon (non-interest-bearing) bonds. The publicly traded debt amounted to approximately $1.8 billion. There were five

**EXHIBIT 14.12   Southland Corporation Consolidated Income Statement
(In thousands of dollars)**

	As of December 31		
	1988	1989	1990
Net Sales	$7,950,284	$ 8,274,921	$ 8,347,681
Other Income	40,213	76,962	62,375
Total Revenues	7,990,497	8,351,883	8,410,056
Cost of Sales	6,268,854	6,544,237	6,661,273
Gross Margin	1,721,643	1,807,646	1,748,783
Selling, Administrative Expenses	1,543,090	1,607,312	1,664,586
Loss on Assets Sold	—	—	41,000
Write-Off, Acquired Assets	—	946,974	—
Interest Expense	560,268	572,248	459,500
Employee Benefits, Etc.	15,416	13,372	13,653
Net before Taxes	(397,132)	(1,332,260)	(429,956)
Income Taxes	(111,900)	(11,984)	(128,459)
Loss from Continuing Operations	(285,232)	(1,320,276)	(429,956)
Discontinued Operations			
Equity, CITGO	69,001	70,480	—
Loss, Equity Disposition	—	1,070	—
Loss before Extraordinary Charges	(216,231)	(1,250,866)	(301,497)
Extraordinary Charges	—	(56,047)	52,040
Effect of Account Change of Medical Benefits	(27,163)	—	(27,163)
Net Income	$ (216,231)	$(1,306,913)	$ (276,620)
Opening Retained Earnings	$ (166,998)	$ (407,927)	$(1,736,179)
Dividends Paid, Redeemable Preferred Stock	(20,856)	(12,634)	(1,011)
Accretion	(6,706)	(8,257)	(7,744)
Currency Translation Adjustment	2,864	(488)	2,628
Deficit	$ (407,927)	$(1,736,179)	$(2,018,926)
Earnings per Share Data			
Loss, before Extraordinary Charges	$ (15.63)	$ (62.02)	$ (15.14)
Effect of Extraordinary Charges	—	(2.74)	2.54
Net Loss	$ (12.19)	$ (64.76)	$ (13.93)
Year End Common Shares (000)	205,042	205,042	205,042

Source: Southland Corporation 1990 and 1989 Form 10-K.

classes of public debt, ranging in type and interest paid. The interest rate of the bonds varied from 13.5 percent to 18 percent. Ito-Yokado's offer was also contingent on 95 percent of all bondholders of each public debt issue accepting the swap. Under this original proposal, the Thompson family would retain a 15 percent stake in Southland, and the remaining 10 percent of the company would be held by bondholders.

The original proposal had a deadline of June 14, 1990, at which time either Ito-Yokado or Southland could cancel the agreement. Neither party indicated that such action would be taken, even though Southland's bondholders balked at the swap proposal. A bigger problem was facing the two companies: a rapidly approaching interest payment due on June 15, 1990. Southland's failure to pay the $69 million payment would result in Southland having a 30-day grace period in which to compensate bondholders. At the end of the 30-day period, unpaid bondholders could try to force Southland into bankruptcy court.[64]

Revisions to the Proposed Buyout

Southland did not make its scheduled interest payment that was due on June 15, 1990. Bondholders, meanwhile, had shown little regard for the original deal struck between Ito-Yokado and Southland.

Three more revisions of the proposed debt restructuring and terms for the buyout were submitted between mid-June and mid-July 1990. In each revision, either Ito-Yokado's or the Thompson family's stake in Southland was reduced and the share of Southland stock offered to bondholders increased. With each revision came increased bondholder support, yet this support was far short of either the two-thirds majority (as required in Chapter 11 restructuring cases) or the 95 percent acceptance rate dictated by Ito-Yokado. As revisions were submitted, the expiration dates of the debt restructuring and stock purchase by Ito-Yokado were extended.

On July 16, a bondholder filed suit against Southland for failure to pay interest on June 15, because on July 15 Southland's grace period had expired.[65] By September 12, a majority of bondholders had tendered their notes.[66] This majority was still far short, however, of the 95 percent swap requirement dictated by Ito-Yokado. The deadlines were extended to September 25 for both the debt swap offer by Southland and the stock purchase offer by Ito-Yokado.[67] As Southland was apparently headed for involuntary bankruptcy filing under Chapter 11, the proposal again seemed in jeopardy.

Acceptance of the Proposed Buyout

The deadline for Southland's debt swap offer was again extended. Bondholder approval was finally obtained in late October. Ito-Yokado's offer to buy out Southland was extended to March 15, 1991, pending court approval of the prepackaged bankruptcy deal.[68] The bankruptcy-court petition for approval of the prepackaged debt restructuring was filed on October 24, 1990.[69]

[64] Karen Blumenthal, "Southland Approaches 2 Crucial Dates in Plan to Rearrange $1.8 Billion in Debt," *Wall Street Journal*, April 12, 1990.

[65] Ibid.

[66] Kevin Helliker, "Southland May Be Considering Seeking Chapter 11 Status, Thus Risking Bailout," *Wall Street Journal*, September 14, 1990.

[67] Ibid.

[68] Kevin Helliker, "Southland Says Reorganization Clears Hurdle," *Wall Street Journal*, October 24, 1990.

[69] "Southland Chapter 11 Plan Needs Approval From SEC," *Wall Street Journal*, December 6, 1990.

EXHIBIT 14.13 Southland Corporation Debt Restructuring Terms for $1,000 Principal Debt of Various Classes as Accepted by Bondholders on February 21, 1991

	13.5% Senior Notes	15.75% Senior Notes	16.5% Senior Notes	16.75% Notes	18% Junior Notes
Principal Retained	$450	$300	$255	$200	$95
Interest Rate of New Debt Received	12%	5%	5%	4.5%	4%
Number of Shares of Common Stock Received	86.5	40.5	35	28	11
Number of Stock Warrants Received	1	7.5	6.5	6	6

Notes:
—"Principal retained" was in the form of newly issued bonds bearing interest as shown.
—Holders of 13.5% Senior Notes also received $57 cash per $1,000 principal of old debt.
—Holders of 16.5% Notes may have received $250 of 12% Notes with no stock warrants instead of $200 of 4.5% and 6 stock warrants (per $1,000 principal of old debt). In either case the holder would have been entitled to 28 shares of common stock.
—Stock warrants gave the holder the option to purchase one share of common stock per warrant for $1.75 per share from June 5, 1991, to February 23, 1996.
Source: Southland Corporation 1990 Form 10-K.

Although Southland did not have sufficient bondholder approval as dictated by Ito-Yokado, the bankruptcy court proceedings were swift. The last few bondholders who held out were placated in January when the Thompsons relinquished warrants for half of their 5 percent stake of Southland's stock.[70] On February 21, 1991, the U.S. bankruptcy court in Dallas approved the reorganization of Southland.[71] At that time, at least 93 percent of the holders of each class of debt issued by Southland had approved the reorganization.[72] On March 5, 1991, Ito-Yokado purchased 71 percent of Southland's stock for $430 million.[73] Two-thirds of this stock was purchased by 7-Eleven Japan, and the other third purchased directly by Ito-Yokado. The terms of the accepted debt-restructuring agreement between Southland and its bondholders are shown in Exhibit 14.13.

THE CONVENIENCE STORE INDUSTRY IN THE UNITED STATES

The convenience store industry in the United States changed dramatically during the decade of the 1980s. The number of convenience stores in the United States, the gross sales of these stores, and the gross margins all increased during this time period. The net income of convenience stores, however, decreased significantly. This outcome was largely the result of the rapid expansion of several

[70] David LaGeese, "Judge Approves Southland's Reorganization," *Dallas Morning News*, February 22, 1991, p. 1D.
[71] Ibid.
[72] Ibid.
[73] "Southland Sells 70 Percent Stake, Completing Reorganization, *Wall Street Journal*, March 6, 1991, p. A2.

chains of convenience stores and the increased number of convenience stores opened by oil companies.

Aggregate Measures of the Industry

The number of convenience stores grew from about 39,000 in 1982 to over 70,000 in 1989. From 1985 to 1989, industry sales increased from $51.4 billion to $67.7 billion, an increase of 6.3 percent per year. Gross margins increased from 22.8 percent in 1985 to 26.2 percent by 1988. Despite such growth, convenience store operations experienced a decrease in net profit in the late 1980s. The total industry pretax profit peaked in 1986 at $1.4 billion, fell to $1.16 billion in 1988, and plummeted to $271 million in 1989. Some trends are shown in Exhibit 14.14.[74]

The expansion of convenience stores in the 1980s was led by large convenience store chains and oil companies. In addition to the growth experienced by the Southland Corporation's 7-Eleven, Circle-K, a Phoenix-based convenience store chain, expanded from 1,200 stores in 1980 to 4,700 stores in 1990.

The Role of the Oil Companies

The impact of oil companies on the convenience store industry had been significant. Virtually all of the major U.S. oil companies began combining convenience store operations with gasoline stations in order to boost profits. In 1984, Exxon opened its first combination convenience store and gas station. By 1989, it had 500. Texaco operated 950 Food Marts in the same year. From 1984 to 1989, the number of convenience stores operated by oil companies increased from 16,000 to 30,000.[75]

Since gasoline sold at a lower margin (about 6 percent in 1984) than non-gasoline convenience store products (32 percent in the same year), the sale of convenience store items presented an opportunity for those gas stations with good locations (i.e., street corners) to increase profits. In order to capitalize on the potential for higher profits in retailing, the major oil companies boosted their

EXHIBIT 14.14   Industrywide Convenience Store Performance, 1985–1989

	1985	1986	1987	1988	1989
Number of Stores	61,000	64,000	67,500	69,200	70,200
Gross Revenue (In billions)	$51.4	$53.9	$59.6	$61.2	$67.7
Net Income (In billions)	$1.39	$1.40	$1.31	$1.16	$0.27
Average Per-Store Profit before Tax (In thousands)	$22.8	$21.9	$19.2	$16.8	$3.9

Source: National Association of Convenience Stores, *1990 State of the Convenience Store Industry*.

[74] This information is drawn largely from: National Association of Convenience Stores (NACS), *1990 State of the Convenience Store Industry*, 1990.

[75] Claudia H. Deutsch, "Rethinking the Convenience Store," *New York Times*, October 8, 1989.

marketing expenditures. In 1979, the petroleum industry spent about $2.2 billion for their marketing efforts. By 1988, these expenditures were almost $5 billion.[76]

The convenience stores operated by oil companies were growing in both number and size. In 1986, only about 20 percent of the oil company convenience stores were 1,800 or more square feet in size (the size of about 90 percent of traditional convenience stores). By 1990, however, over 50 percent of the oil company convenience stores were between 1,800 and 3,000 square feet in size.[77]

Merchandise Trends for Convenience Stores

Because of the intensified retailing efforts of oil companies and large convenience store chains, some trends (other than those mentioned above) evolved. In 1985, gasoline accounted for 35.4 percent of convenience store sales. By 1989, gasoline accounted for 40 percent of sales.[78] The gross profit margin for gasoline sales had increased from 7.3 percent to 11.7 percent over the same period.[79] Of the 61,000 convenience stores in the United States in 1985, 55 percent sold gasoline, and in 1989, 65 percent of 70,200 convenience stores sold gasoline. In 1989, 75 percent of the new convenience stores built were equipped to sell gasoline.[80]

Although gasoline sales and margins became an increasingly significant contributor to convenience store revenues, contributions of revenue from other merchandise stagnated. In 1985, merchandise (other than gasoline) sales for the convenience store industry amounted to $33.2 billion. In 1989, sales reached $40.6 billion.[81] This increase in merchandise sales, however, was offset by the large number of store openings. In 1985, the average yearly merchandise sales per store was $544,000. This number increased to only $578,000 in 1989.[82]

THE SETTING

While flying from Japan to the United States, Takahashi reflected on the success that both Ito-Yokado and 7-Eleven Japan had enjoyed over the course of many years. These achievements were the result of long-term strategies that were carefully tailored to the Japanese market. Could these same, or similar, strategies be the foundation for making Southland financially successful again? He realized that the convenience store industry in the United States was vastly different from that of Japan. Nevertheless, he was confident that, through careful and thorough planning, the goal of making Southland profitable could be achieved.

[76] National Association of Convenience Stores, Challenges for the Convenience Store Industry in the 1990s: A Future Study, p. 194.
[77] Ibid., p. 198.
[78] NACS, 1990 State of the Convenience Store Industry, p. 14.
[79] Ibid., p. 16.
[80] Ibid., pp. 25–26.
[81] Ibid., p. 14.
[82] Ibid., p. 16.

----------------------------------- CASE 15 -----------------------------------

AT&T
and the Residential Long-Distance Market (A)

Monica Barnes stood gazing out the window of her seventh-floor office in AT&T Communication's (AT&T-C) Atlanta regional office. Her attention was focused on the house that shared the block in downtown Atlanta with the AT&T-C building. When AT&T had decided to build on this location, the owners of the existing house had refused to sell, forcing AT&T-C to build on two sides of and close to the house. The contrast between the stately, traditional, old southern home and the tall, concrete and glass, modern office building was indicative of the transition period through which AT&T and the telecommunications industry were moving.

On January 8, 1982, AT&T and the Department of Justice had signed an accord that dropped the government's 1974 antitrust charges against AT&T, scrapped the 1956 antitrust settlement that had barred AT&T from engaging in unregulated businesses, and called for the spin-off of AT&T's 22 Bell operating companies (BOCs, or Baby Bells). Judge Harold Greene had formally approved the Modification of Final Judgement on August 24, 1982, giving AT&T until February 24, 1983, to submit a detailed divestiture plan, and until February 24, 1984, to execute the plan.

The two years since January 1982, had been extremely hectic for AT&T. The firm had been continually in courts or before Congress dealing with myriad suits and proposed bills that attempted to stop or alter the planned breakup. The plan had actually been implemented on January 1, 1984, with "old" AT&T being split into eight parts—seven new regional holding companies completely separate from AT&T and the "new" AT&T. (AT&T-C was a division of the new AT&T and was responsible for the provision of long-distance services.) However, the new AT&T still faced many changes and uncertainties as it pursued full implementation of the divestiture plan.

This case was prepared by Lew G. Brown under the supervision of Robert S. Harris with support of a grant from the AT&T Foundation. It is intended as a basis for class discussion rather than to illustrate either effective or ineffective handling of an administrative situation. Used with permission from Lew G. Brown and the North American Case Research Association.

Monica turned from the window and began reviewing her notes from the meeting she had just finished with her boss, David Lawrence, the district manager in charge of residential marketing for the 14 states in the southern region. Lawrence had asked Monica to prepare a regional marketing plan that was designed to get residential customers to select AT&T-C as their primary interexchange carrier (PIC, or Primary Carrier) as the "equal access" provisions of the judgment were implemented.

HOW LONG-DISTANCE WORKS

Exhibit 15.1 depicts the normal operation of long-distance service. A local subscriber wanting to place a long-distance call using AT&T-C would simply dial "1" plus, if necessary, the area code and then the seven-digit number of the subscriber being called. As depicted in the exhibit, AT&T-C had "trunk-side" access to the local telephone company's (LEC) switching office. However, if the customer wished to place a call using another common carrier (OCC), such as MCI or Sprint, the subscriber had to first dial a seven-digit number to gain access to the common carrier's switching office. Then the subscriber had to dial a 5- to 7-digit identification number; and then, the normal 7 to 10 digits. The customer had thus used the local telephone company's "line-side" connection to reach the common carrier's switching office.

The common carriers argued that because their customers had to dial additional digits that resulted in inferior technical quality and features due to the line-side access, the common carriers were at a disadvantage in competing with AT&T-C for long-distance customers.

EXHIBIT 15.1   Trunk-Side versus Line-Side Access for Long-Distance Calling

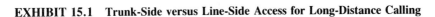

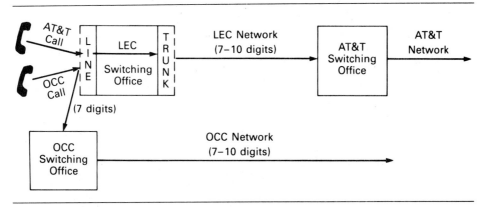

HOW EQUAL ACCESS WORKS

The judgment signed by Judge Greene in August 1982 had included the provision that local telephone companies must provide "to all long-distance carriers . . . exchange access . . . equal in type, quality, and price to that provided to AT&T and its affiliates." This stipulation had come to be known as "equal access." It had been included in the judgment as a result of Judge Greene's finding that the other common carriers were "disadvantaged" due to AT&T-C "superior" connections to the local distribution networks of the Baby Bells and the other independent telephone companies. Under the provision for equal access, common carriers would have the right to purchase trunk-side access, just as AT&T-C, so that their customers would dial the same number of digits and use similar local telephone company access lines as an AT&T-C customer.

The services offered by the local telephone companies were categorized into five groups called feature groups. These feature groups allowed long-distance carriers the option of offering different types and levels of service to their customers. The group of services involved in equal access was denoted as feature group D. In addition to the need to dial fewer digits, feature group D allowed rotary-dial telephones as well as touch-tone telephones to use the service (before equal access, only customers with touch-tone phones could use a common carrier) and provided answer supervision and automatic number identification services, which were important in accurate billing.

It is important to note that the judgment required only that equal access be made *available* to all long-distance carriers. It did not require any long-distance carrier to make any particular feature group available to its customers. A common carrier might decide not to offer feature group D to customers served by a particular exchange office (called end-office).

Customers served by an equal access end-office would access a long-distance carrier in one of four ways:

First, a customer would be able to designate a primary carrier. Once a primary carrier had been selected by the customer, any long-distance call dialed normally (1 + area code + number) would be automatically routed to that carrier. For example, if GTE Sprint had been selected by the customer as the primary carrier, all normal long-distance calls would be routed to the Sprint switch; and Sprint would bill the customer for those calls. It should be noted that the customer would have to establish an account with a common carrier in order to be able to use its services.

Second, although a customer had designated a primary carrier, the customer would still be able to place long-distance calls using another long-distance carrier. This nonprimary long-distance carrier must have subscribed to equal access in that exchange area and have decided to accept "access-code" traffic. The customer would dial 1 + 0 + a three-digit long-distance carrier code (1 + 0 + XXX) before dialing the normal area code and local number. The "XXXs" represent the vendor access code. For example, a customer who had designated MCI as his or her primary carrier would still be able to place calls using AT&T-C by following the above dialing procedure and using AT&T-C's access code. This procedure obviously allows customers the ability to "shop" for long-distance services and rates if they so desire and if common carriers have elected to provide equal access in the customer's area.

Third, operator-assisted calls would still be available by dialing 1 + 0 + XXX. AT&T-C was the only carrier offering operator assistance, although others might do so in the future. Local operators were available by dialing 0. They usually were AT&T-C employees under contract to the local telephone company.

Fourth, customers might continue to reach common carriers by dialing a seven-digit access code and a personal identification number if a common carrier chose to continue to provide feature group A or B service in an area (the same procedure as that in effect prior to equal access).

The judgment required equal access cutovers to begin by September 1, 1984. Cutover was defined as the date that long-distance calls begin to go, on a dial-1 basis, to the designated primary carrier. By the end of 1984, 134 exchange offices would be converted to equal access. An additional 1,900 would convert in 1985, and an additional 2,400 would convert in 1986. Beyond 1986, additional offices would convert at an estimated rate of 500 per year. Conversion would take place by end-office (denoted by the first three digits in the seven-digit telephone number). Since local telephone companies would convert office by office and some offices would take longer or be more complicated to convert, there would be no uniform pattern for cutover. Thus, a city served by nine exchange offices might have those offices converted at different times throughout the 1984 to 1986 period. Small end-offices (those serving less than 10,000 lines) and other offices that might be uneconomical to convert would not have to be modified, subject to court approval. Exhibit 15.2 shows the date and place where equal access first became available. As of these dates, in these places subscribers could designate the interexchange carrier that would carry all of their long-distance calls; subscribers were able to reach another interexchange carrier by dialing five digits (1 + 0 + XXX). As equal access became available, each interexchange carrier paid equal costs for access to local exchanges. With the phased implementation of the full schedule (July 1984 to September 1986), AT&T and its competitors competed for subscribers on an equal basis.

As noted above, local telephone customers would have the opportunity to select a primary carrier. The process for this selection prior to cutover was called presubscription. The specific steps to be followed in the presubscription process were to be established by each local telephone company. As of March 1984, those steps had not yet been finalized. However, there was a published general time frame that would be followed. An illustrative time frame is shown in Exhibit 15.3.

As noted in Exhibit 15.3, local customers were notified by the local telephone company 90 days prior to the cutover for their end-office of their right to choose a primary carrier. In addition, the customers had a 180-day period following cutover during which they could select a primary carrier or change their

EXHIBIT 15.2   Equal Access Schedule, 1984

Date	Place of First Equal Access (City End-Office)
July 15, 1984	West Virginia (Charleston, S. Charleston)
August 19, 1984	Minnesota (Minneapolis-Orchard)
August 24, 1984	California (San Francisco-Almeda)
	Nevada (Virginia City, Silver Spring, Carson City, Butte, Churchill)
August 25, 1984	Colorado (Denver)
August 27, 1984	Georgia (Atlanta-Toco Hills, Courtland St.)
	Alabama (Mobile-Springhill)
August 30, 1984	Indiana (Indianapolis-Trinity, Melrose)
August 31, 1984	Texas (Houston-W. Ellington)
	Illinois (Chicago-Wabash, Dearborn)
September 1, 1984	Massachusetts (Easter-Back Bay)
	New York (Metro New York City)
	New Jersey (Hackensack, Clifton)
	Pennsylvania (Philadelphia-Pennypacker, Locust)
	Delaware (Wilmington)
	Maryland (Baltimore-Liberty, Columbia)
	Washington, D.C. (Metro)
	Virginia (Norfolk)
	Ohio (Cleveland, Columbus)
	Michigan (Detroit)
	Wisconsin (Stevens Point, Milwaukee)
	Oregon (Portland)
October 1, 1984	Washington (Seattle)
October 22, 1984	Florida (Jacksonville)
October 28, 1984	Kentucky (Louisville-New Albany)
November 17, 1984	Utah (Salt Lake City)
November 26, 1984	Louisiana (Shreveport-Monroe)
	Tennessee (Memphis)
December 1, 1984	Rhode Island
December 16, 1984	Idaho (Roberts, Moore, Howe, McKay, Island Park, Arco, Idaho Falls)
December 29, 1984	Idaho (Boise)

Source: Federal Communications Commission.

original selection without any charge. Following the end of this 180-day period, customers were required to pay a minimal charge, perhaps $5, to choose a primary carrier. New customers entering the system during or after the cutover process were required to select a primary carrier as a part of opening their account.

Long-distance carriers could act as the customer's agent in the selection process. The customer could contract with the long-distance carrier for long-distance service. The long-distance carrier could then notify the local telephone company of the customer's selection.

One question that had not been resolved in the judgment dealt with how to handle those customers who, for whatever reason, failed to designate a primary carrier by the end of the 180-day period following cutover. This question was not

EXHIBIT 15.3   Example of Cutover Time Schedule

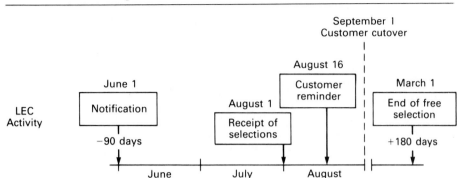

minor in that some estimates stated that up to 90 percent of customers might fail to make a choice.

In December 1983, Judge Greene had issued an opinion in response to a motion by Ameritech (a regional company) that it be allowed to route all "undesignated" traffic to AT&T-C by *default*. In that opinion, Judge Greene noted that the decree, subsequent opinions, and the Department of Justice supported the position that undesignated traffic should be routed to AT&T-C. The decree provided that customers were to be given the option of selecting an alternate carrier, but did not *require* them to make a selection. The judge noted the arguments of AT&T-C's competitors that such a situation would "perpetuate that company's [AT&T] dominant role in the interexchange market; and that Ameritech's proposal therefore conflicts with the bedrock principles underlying the decree." Judge Greene noted, however, that the alternatives to allocating undesignated traffic to AT&T-C by default had practical difficulties themselves.

A first alternative involved the *allocation* to all participating carriers of customers who had not actively chosen a long-distance company. The court argued that this alternative was entirely unsuitable, since the purpose of the antitrust laws was to protect the competitive process, "not to assure positive results for competitors." The opinion also noted that many of the long-distance carriers might not be prepared to serve all the customers who might be allocated to them either due to technological problems or to the inability of customers to meet the firms' service requirements. Further, the court noted the difficulty of carriers, which the customers had expressed no desire to use, sending bills to those customers. Even if these problems could be overcome, the court noted the problem of establishing a fair allocation formula. For these reasons, the court would not require allocation of undesignated traffic.

However, the court, while refusing to impose the allocation requirement on the operating companies, did not prohibit allocation if a local telephone company wished to use this method. In fact, Northwestern Bell had indicated it would randomly allocate undesignated customers to carriers in proportion to each carrier's share of those customers who did choose a primary carrier.

A second alternative known as *blocking* had been proposed. Advocates of this method had suggested that when a caller who had not presubscribed nor dialed a carrier-access code attempted to place a long-distance call, the caller would be referred to a recording. The recording would instruct the caller to dial the local telephone company's business office or an 800 number to obtain additional information. The caller would be given the access codes of several long-distance companies that would allow him or her to select a carrier. However, the caller still might not be able to complete the call if he or she did not have an account with the carrier. Attempts to complete a call in this way would also be complicated by holiday or emergency situations or by language or education problems.

The court noted that the blocking procedure could cause substantial inconvenience to customers and that, although the court wished to promote competition, it could not do so at the expense of the public interest. The court also noted that having AT&T-C as a carrier of last resort was in the public interest and should be encouraged. Judge Greene, therefore, refused to require blocking.

The court granted Ameritech's motion allowing the routing of undesignated traffic to AT&T-C with the requirements that the local telephone companies inform their customers of their options during the 90-day presubscription period and also provide the opportunity to designate a carrier, free of charge, during the 90-day period following cutover. Customers receiving new service who had previously failed to designate a primary carrier or who were new to the exchange area would not be assigned automatically to AT&T-C. They would be given the information on options and could be "blocked" until a primary carrier was chosen.

Judge Greene added:

> The court recognizes, of course, that this ruling may be of substantial assistance to AT&T. For the reasons stated, that is a result that cannot initially be avoided without exorbitant costs to the public. It does not follow, however, that the court, consistent with the promotion of competition, should not require the operating companies to make reasonable efforts to acquaint customers with their options with regard to interexchange service or that it should not take steps to preclude AT&T from receiving the calls of undesignated customers in perpetuity. Such measures are, indeed, entirely appropriate.

In a footnote, the court noted that some 20 percent of telephone customers receive new service annually. Therefore, any advantage accruing to AT&T-C from the court's action "should be largely dissipated in a relatively short period of time."

Thus, Judge Greene had approved the *default* procedure. Although the judge's ruling had supported AT&T-C's position on the handling of undesignated traffic, AT&T-C still found itself facing a situation in which almost all of its customer base would be "up for grabs" over the next two and a half years.

THE RESIDENTIAL LONG-DISTANCE MARKET

The U.S. residential long-distance market in 1984 included 80 million customers. Of these, some 60 million were connected to the Baby Bells, with the remainder connected to independent telephone companies.

AT&T-Communications

AT&T-C's total 1984 revenues from both business and residential long-distance markets were expected to total $36 billion. AT&T-C's residential revenue was, similar to its business revenue, highly concentrated in a small segment of large-volume users. Exhibit 15.4 presents information on this revenue distribution.

Total interstate and intrastate residential revenues for AT&T-C for 1984 were expected to total $13.8 billion, with the interstate portion of that market expected to grow at 8 percent per year over the next five years. (Intrastate calls refer to long-distance calls that begin and terminate within the same state. The equal access decisions applied only to interstate service. Therefore, theoretically, only interstate service revenues were at risk in the equal access process. However, the common carriers were beginning to offer intrastate service, thereby threatening those revenues as well.)

The interstate residential revenues at risk in the equal access process in 1984 totaled $327 million. This figure rose to $11.7 billion by 1989—two-thirds of the residence market revenue.

AT&T-C's southern region's 14 states included approximately 18 million of the 80 million residential long-distance customers. In 1984, residential long-distance billings in the region were estimated to total $2.6 billion. The 14 states in the region were North and South Carolina, Georgia, Florida, Louisiana, Alabama, Mississippi, Tennessee, Kentucky, Oklahoma, Missouri, Kansas, Arkansas, and Texas.

AT&T-C continued to be classified by the Federal Communications Commission (FCC) as the only "dominant" carrier. Thus, it was subject to more regulation than the common carriers. In addition to having its authorized rate of return capped at 12.75 percent, all capital construction plans, service offerings,

EXHIBIT 15.4   Residential Revenue Distribution

Monthly Expenditures on Interstate Long Distance	Percent of Households	Percent of Revenue	Interexchange Calls/Month
$ 0–10	74	20	0–3
10–25	17	29	4–10
25–50	7	26	11–20
50–100	2	16	21–40
100+	1	9	41+

Source: AT&T-C. Data based on market analysis using first-quarter 1983 average data.

and price changes had to be approved by the FCC. Further, AT&T-C had to have its intrastate services approved individually by the 50 state public utility commissions. In contrast, the common carriers were generally under no such requirements. Therefore, it took AT&T-C longer to implement changes, and those changes were "telegraphed" to the competition due to the regulatory processes.

Further, the common carriers were receiving a discount relative to AT&T-C for access to local telephone companies' networks. The access fees were levied to compensate the local telephone companies for nonusage-sensitive costs. However, the access fees were levied on a per-minute of usage basis. The base access charges for common carriers were 55 percent less than AT&T-C's; and in practice, the discount could even be greater. The common carriers used this cost differential to their advantage in pricing against AT&T-C.

However, the advent of equal access would put cost pressures on the common carriers. Carriers purchasing equal access would have to pay the same rates as AT&T-C. However, due to AT&T-C having to continue to serve less profitable customers, some analysts estimated that its rates would continue to be 10 percent higher than those of its competition. In addition, common carriers could continue to offer lower levels of service at reduced costs as they had done, even in equal access areas. To some extent, this capability would depend on the price differentials eventually offered by the local telephone companies for the various feature groups.

Competition

Although there were 400 common carriers serving the long-distance market, six (MCI, GTE Sprint, ALLNET, ITT, U.S. Telephone, and Satellite Business Systems) accounted for 88 percent of the $3.2 billion of common carrier's sales in 1983. The remaining companies were primarily resellers of AT&T-C WATS service. The common carriers served 3.8 million customers. (See Exhibit 15.5.)

EXHIBIT 15.5   Profile of Major Common Carriers, 1983

	Revenues[a] (In billions)	Percent	Subscribers (In thousands)	Percent
MCI[b]	$1.52	48	1,550	41
GTE Sprint	.75	23	920	24
ALLNET	.18	6	150	4
ITT	.17	5	95	3
U.S. Telephone	.14	4	80	2
SBS	.07	2	90	2
Other	.37	12	915	24
Totals	$3.20	100	3,800	100

[a] Includes both business and residence markets.
[b] MCI serves 85 percent of the country with its network; 30 percent of MCI's revenues comes from its residence long-distance voice service.
Source: AT&T-C Residence Market Management.

Both MCI and GTE Sprint appeared to be in the long-distance service market for the long run. Between them, they had announced plans to spend $2 billion on their networks in 1985. These expansion plans, however, at a time of rising access costs and price cutting to attract customers, would be predicted to bring on financial pressure in the short term.

Both firms also appeared to be adopting a strategy of offering the same services as AT&T-C. MCI had dropped its monthly premium fee and had introduced an initial-minute charge with a lower per-minute night rate for additional minutes (similar to AT&T-C's pricing). It had also contracted with the operating companies to offer immediate directory assistance at 45 cents per call (5 cents less than AT&T-C's charge) and, along with Sprint, was offering volume discounts on customers' monthly bills.

News reports on the equal access process indicated that the common carriers saw that process as a major opportunity to take market share from AT&T-C and would be aggressive in trying to do so. An article in the March 12, 1984, edition of the *Philadelphia Enquirer* quoted W. G. McGowan, chairman of MCI, as saying, "The most significant thing in our business is going to be that equal connection." M. J. Goodman, president of Allnet Communications, noted "It's going to be the best opportunity for market redistribution in over 100 years." The article also noted that some firms might pursue niche strategies. For example, some firms might provide service only between two particular cities, seeking to capture the profitable high-volume traffic.

THE ASSIGNMENT

David Lawrence had attended the first public relations strategy meeting on AT&T-C's presubscription marketing strategy on February 15, 1984. The meeting had involved all the district managers in charge of residential marketing from each of AT&T-C's regions and had dealt with development of marketing and public relations strategies for the first cutover that was scheduled for Charleston, West Virginia, with a tentative date of July 15, 1984. This date meant that customers in the affected area could begin to be notified as early as April 15, 1984, that they would be required to choose a long-distance carrier.

David Lawrence had returned from the meeting and scheduled a meeting with Monica Barnes. He had indicated to Monica that even though AT&T-C would receive undesignated traffic due to Judge Greene's ruling, the corporation's objective was to secure an *active* selection of AT&T-C as the primary carrier. Although no decision had yet been made as to whether the marketing strategy and implementation for the choice process would be carried out at the national or regional level, Lawrence wanted to be prepared with a regional strategy. The tight schedule involved left no time to wait until a final decision was made.

David had asked Monica to prepare the broad outlines of a marketing strategy for the 14 states in the southern region. He was not interested at this moment in end-office specific plans, but rather wanted a general plan on which end-office plans could be based. Specifically, he was interested in a recommended plan specifying which residential customers would be contacted, through which channels, when, with what messages, and how often during the 90-day pre-subscription process and, if necessary, the 180-day period following cutover. In addition, he was interested in cost estimates for any plan that might be proposed. Although Lawrence would not be responsible for overall media planning, he was interested in any suggestions or themes Monica might propose that he could refer to the AT&T- C offices responsible for media planning. He had asked to have the proposal by March 1.

Market Research

In anticipation of the upcoming equal access process, AT&T-C had conducted market research in 1983 to determine the important attributes of long-distance service from the customer's point of view. Five general attributes had been delineated: price, ubiquity, service quality, servicing, and innovation. Exhibit 15.6 presents a summary of the research findings.

In addition to the results presented in Exhibit 15.6, the research had found that 52 percent of those surveyed did not associate the name AT&T with long distance. Consumers also tended to overestimate both AT&T-C's and competitors' strengths. Differences in prices between AT&T-C and the competition were perceived to be larger than they actually were. Both MCI's prices and service quality were perceived as lower than they actually were.

The research allowed the identification of certain dominant market subsegments, as shown in Exhibit 15.7.

Market research studies had also been started in early 1984 in order to provide a bench mark for judging the results of marketing efforts. The research had focused on the 31 markets that would be subject to cutover in 1984. An independent company interviewed approximately 11,000 residence customers by telephone.

EXHIBIT 15.6   Residence Market Differentiation Research: Important Attributes of Long-Distance, 1983

Attribute	Residence Perception	Percent Ranking Attribute as Most Important
Price	Price performance	55
Service Quality	Lack of static, echo, disconnections	15
Ubiquity (Widely available)	Customer able to call anywhere, anytime	22
Servicing	Efficient, responsive customer representatives and operators	6
Innovation	New applications and services	2

Source: AT&T-C. Data based on market analysis using first-quarter 1983 average data.

EXHIBIT 15.7   Dominant Market Subsegments in AT&T-C Residence Market

Subsegment	Number of Customers (In millions)	Revenue (In billions)
Just Moved	15.0	$2.6
Working Women	43.0	3.4
Mature Adults (50+)	41.0	4.0
College	12.5	1.3
Hispanics	8.0	0.5
Military	3.5	0.3

Note: Segments are not mutually exclusive and cannot be added together.
Source: AT&T-C Residence Market Management.

Respondents were asked to rate long-distance companies they were aware of on a variety of attribute statements using a 1-to-5 scale with 1 meaning poor and 5 meaning excellent. The attribute statements had been grouped into four categories for analysis: price, quality, ubiquity, and servicing. Exhibit 15.8 presents a listing of the statements. Exhibit 15.9 presents some results of the bench mark studies.

EXHIBIT 15.8   Bench Mark Attribute Statements

Price

Having competitive prices.
Having discounted rates available during convenient time periods.

Quality

Having excellent sound quality.
Getting good quality for the price you pay.
Being an established and dependable company.

Ubiquity

The ability to call anytime, to or from anywhere.
Having the ability to make international calls.

Servicing

Having to pay no monthly service charge.
Providing accurate and reliable long-distance itemized billing.
Having a trained and knowledgeable customer service force.
Having long-distance directory assistance.
Providing accurate and reliable information about long-distance rates and services.
Having a long-distance operator available anytime you need one.
The ability to make person-to-person, collect or "bill to third-party" long-distance calls.

Innovation

Having the ability to make credit card calls.

**EXHIBIT 15.9   Respondents Giving "Excellent"
Rating to Selected Suppliers on Long-Distance
Attributes, 1984**

	Percent Giving Excellent Rating		
Attribute	AT&T-C	MCI	Sprint
Price	32	32	25
Quality	55	27	21
Ubiquity	72	31	25
Servicing	54	23	19

Source: AT&T Communications.

In the same survey, the mean rating for AT&T-C on the attribute, "Having Competitive Prices," was 3.35. For MCI, the mean rating was 4.25.

The bench mark survey asked respondents to name any suppliers of long-distance service. The percentage of respondents having *unaided* recall for AT&T-C was 57 percent; for MCI, 53 percent; and for Sprint, 40 percent. Interestingly, 31 percent listed the local Baby Bell as being the provider of long-distance service.

Respondents were asked how much they knew about the companies. The percentage of respondents who indicated they knew a lot about AT&T-C was 26 percent; about MCI, 8 percent; about Sprint, 6 percent.

Finally, respondents were asked to rate 20 characteristics of long-distance suppliers on the degree of importance of those characteristics to them. Top ratings were as follows:

- Getting good quality for the price you pay—80 percent
- Being able to call anytime, to anywhere—79 percent
- Being able to call anytime, from anywhere—78 percent
- Providing accurate and reliable itemized billing—77 percent
- Having excellent sound quality—75 percent
- Paying no monthly service charge—74 percent
- Being an established, dependable company—69 percent
- Having competitive prices—68 percent
- Having an operator available when you need one—67 percent
- Providing reliable information about rates and services—67 percent

The three lowest ratings were for:

- Having international calling capability—29 percent
- Being able to make time payments on bills—26 percent
- Having a telephone credit card—22 percent

With regard to contacting customers, Monica was aware of recent estimates that each direct mail piece cost between 60 cents and $1.20 and each telemarketing call cost between $4.50 and $5.00. She was aware of the on-going customer contact possibilities provided by the Residential Service Center (RSC) operation staffed by customer service representatives who handled in-coming calls from residential customers about bills or service.

Monica Barnes' Position

Monica realized the importance of the assignment she had been presented both in terms of AT&T-C and in terms of her own development. AT&T-C found itself in a very uncertain period. The firm had been required to act and react in very short time periods on matters involving millions and even billions of dollars in actual or potential revenues and costs. Employees at all levels had been required to stretch their efforts, often beyond their actual duties, in order to manage the workload.

Monica had joined AT&T-C five years earlier after completing her MBA at Rutgers. Although AT&T-C did not have what it formally called a management development program, Monica had participated in a series of assignments in the marketing area to familiarize her with the overall marketing function and thereby prepare her for a future management role. She had begun working at AT&T-C's headquarters in Basking Ridge, New Jersey, in a support role in marketing management. She had then designed sales strategies for the company's work with securities firms. Then she had worked in sales operations on sales force productivity issues. In early 1983, she had been assigned to the Atlanta office to help establish the residential marketing function in the southern region.

As she began outlining her work, she thought about the different points of view and expectations persons in other areas of AT&T-C would have relative to her proposal.

Network personnel were interested in maintaining network utilization and the network investment program. If utilization fell because of lost customers, Network's plans to invest in new facilities aimed at generating high value-added services targeted for the business community might have to be modified or postponed.

Finance personnel would be concerned about the cost of any program aimed at equal access marketing as well as AT&T-C's relative cost position with respect to other carriers. They would be concerned about a loss in volume and its effect on revenue (a 1 percent drop in volume nationwide would result in a 5 percent decrease in net income). See Exhibit 15.10 for overall financial information.

External affairs personnel would feel equal access was a success if the common carriers were moderately successful so as to supply the regulators with evidence that the market was truly competitive. This would help in their battle to end the unequal regulation of AT&T-C.

EXHIBIT 15.10   AT&T Pro Forma Income Statement for 1984a (In billions)

	MTSb Amount	WATSc Amount	PLSd Amount	Total Interstate
Total Revenues	$17.35	$ 6.25	$ 3.84	$27.44
Expense				
Maintenance	.59	.21	.48	1.28
Depreciation and Amortization	.58	.19	.22	.99
Commercial and Marketing	1.05	.37	.27	1.69
Traffic and Operation Rents	1.55	.31	.31	2.17
Relief and Pensions	.42	.13	.21	.76
Miscellaneous and Other Taxes	1.31	.46	.40	2.17
Access Charge	10.65	4.19	1.45	16.29
Federal Taxes	.43	.14	.18	.75
Total Expenses	$16.58	$ 6.00	$ 3.52	$26.10
Net Earnings	$ .77	$ .25	$ .32	$ 1.34
Average Net Investment	6.04	1.94	2.48	10.46
Earnings Ratios	12.72%	12.79%	12.78%	12.75%

a October 1983—With original access charge plan (including proposed rate change).
b MTS—Measured telecommunications service. This is the category that reflects typical long-distance service. Each call is billed on the basis of distance, duration, and time of day.
c WATS—Wide area telecommunication service. AT&T's bulk rate, public, switched long-distance telephone service. WATS users are billed partially on the basis of the number of hours of usage and partially on a per-call basis.
d PLS—A telecommunications channel or service that is leased in its entirety by AT&T for the sole use of one or more specific customers between two or more specific points.
Source: AT&T-C (FCC filing, October 3, 1983).

The legal staff would be concerned that common carriers, who were ordering private-line circuits from AT&T-C to serve their new customers, be treated in a nondiscriminatory manner.

Finally, marketing personnel would worry about any "victory" for a common carrier, even in an individual area, being seen as evidence that the common carriers were as good as AT&T-C. Such an event might give impetus to the common carriers' nationwide efforts.

Monica reflected that, for a company that did not even have a consumer marketing function 18 months ago, things had gotten awfully complicated. There were many factors to consider and many forces to balance in her plan.

——————————— CASE 16 ———————————

AT&T
and the Residential Long-Distance Market (B)

Monica Barnes sat in David Lawrence's office listening to the conference call coming over the speaker phone. They listened intently as their counterparts in AT&T-C headquarters in Basking Ridge, New Jersey, and at other locations around the country discussed the latest Federal Communications Commission (FCC) decision involving the equal access process.

The conference call was being held on June 15, 1985. Although the entire equal access process (see Case A) had been marked by uncertainty, confusion, and changes, this latest FCC decision seemed especially improbable. Monica glanced at David. She knew that neither of them was sure how much more of this they could take. The cliche "the straw that broke the camel's back" had suddenly taken on new meaning.

Monica rose from her chair and paced beside David's desk. "Well, now I have heard everything," she exclaimed, "not only does the future change in this business, but now the past even changes!"

THE END OF DEFAULT

This latest series of events in the two-and-a-half year cutover process had begun on May 31, 1985, with an order by the FCC that put an end to the default provision under which the equal access process had been operating generally for almost a year.

In the FCC order, issued on June 12, 1985, the commission began by reviewing the history of the default provision, noting the Modification of Final Judgment provisions, and summarizing Judge Greene's subsequent rulings on default. Since Judge Greene's 1983 ruling on default, the FCC had heard and considered the petitions of those who argued that the default provision gave an unfair competitive advantage to AT&T-C. The FCC subsequently had upheld the

This case was prepared by Lew G. Brown under the supervision of Robert S. Harris with support of a grant from the AT&T Foundation. It is intended as a basis for class discussion rather than to illustrate either effective or ineffective handling of an administrative situation. Used with permission from Lew G. Brown and the North American Case Research Association.

default process but had ordered that subscribers be allowed a six-month period following the cutover date to select a primary carrier without charge.

The equal access process continued in 1984 and early 1985 with all local telephone companies except Northwestern Bell (NWB) using the court-approved default process. However, parties continued to petition the FCC to reconsider its previous findings on the default process. On March 8, 1985, the FCC found that there was insufficient evidence to decide on the default question and had requested further comment and suggestions as to alternatives.

The May 1985 decision on which the June order was based resulted from the additional comments received. The FCC noted that the majority of the commenters favored a *pro rata* allocation plan. The commenters had argued that the default process preserved AT&T-C's monopoly power and that the NWB experience had demonstrated that allocation was workable and was stimulating a 20 percent increase in the number of customers choosing a long-distance company relative to local telephone companies that used default. Further, it was noted by the Department of Justice that the allocation process had proven to be cheaper than default to implement.

The NWB system called for two ballots. A customer was notified of the equal access conversion 90 days prior to cutover and given a ballot on which to indicate preference for a primary carrier. Customers who failed to return their ballots were sent a second ballot approximately 50 days before the cutover providing them another chance and indicating the primary carrier to which they would be assigned if they still made no selection. Undesignated customers were so assigned if they failed to return the second ballot and were given the 180-day period to change to another long-distance company without charge. The allocation of customers to primary carriers following the first ballot was a random process, with the percentage of unallocated customers being allocated to a primary carrier being based on the percentage of customers who selected it in the first round.

AT&T-C had argued that default was proper, cited the findings in the judgment, and stated, "As a matter of law and of fact, the customers involved here are already AT&T's customers, and were intended under the decree to remain so until they select another company as the primary carrier." AT&T-C had also submitted independent survey data of customer knowledge, attitudes, and actions to support its position.

In the May 1985 ruling, the commission found that the routing of all default traffic to AT&T could *not* be justified by a "strong showing of necessity." The FCC's prior concerns about customer burdens under allocation had been dispelled by NWB's experience. As a result, the FCC found the default procedure to be unreasonable and discriminatory and prescribed a *pro rata* allocation plan that was *required* of all local telephone companies.

The FCC's plan followed the NWB plan with one general exception. The commission had received requests that the time period allowed for selection be extended or altered. The FCC plan allowed flexibility in this aspect of the process. The local telephone companies would be allowed to send a second ballot with the allocated primary carrier designation to their customers as early as 40 days prior to but not later than 90 days after cutover.

No alternatives to the allocation process would be allowed. The FCC plan also suggested that local telephone companies and primary carriers develop clear and detailed information to be provided to customers on the selection process and required that local telephone companies provide information with the second ballot with respect to how the allocation process would work.

Carriers were required to implement the plan on a retroactive basis for all cutovers that took place on or after May 31, 1985. However, the FCC realized that it would take some time to implement the new plan and allowed local telephone companies to continue to default customers to AT&T during the transition period. The customer would then be subject to allocation once the local telephone company implemented its plan.

In addition to the basic NWB plan, the FCC also allowed customers to contact the primary carrier directly and make arrangements for service. The primary carrier could provide the local telephone company with a list of customers who had contacted it by the initial (first) ballot deadline. Any verbal commitments had to be followed up with a request for a statement signed by the customer to be sent to the local telephone company not later than the first bill.

Finally, the FCC required that nonpresubscribed customers in areas that had been converted prior to May 31, 1985, should receive from local telephone companies another ballot within 90 days of May 31. If the customers still did not return the ballot, they would be allowed to remain with their long-distance carrier.

Thus, AT&T-C not only found the default procedure terminated for all cutovers on or after May 31, 1985, it also found that customers with pre-May 31 cutovers, who had already been defaulted to it by not choosing a long-distance carrier and who it was serving, would now be asked to choose again.

BACK TO THE DRAWING BOARD

David turned to Monica. "Well, I'm sure there will be lots of questions and probably more interpretations of this order, but I guess you had better take a look at our marketing strategy in light of the allocation process to see what, if anything, we should change."

Despite the problems, Monica felt that she had some recent market research results that might help (see Exhibits 16.1 and 16.2).

The bench mark market research studies carried out in early 1984 had been followed by "selection" studies as the 31 cutover areas went through the equal access process later in 1984. Selection studies were carried out approximately 12 to 13 weeks after the equal access announcement in each specific market by an independent firm hired by AT&T-C.

Monica opened the research report and reread the executive summary.

EXHIBIT 16.1   Marketing Research "Selection Studies"

Executive Summary
Status of Choice and Notification

- Eighty-three percent of residential long-distance users in these 31 markets were aware of the announcement asking them to choose a main long-distance company. Respondents in heavy long-distance usage households, with higher incomes and in white-collar positions show higher levels of awareness.

- Of those aware of the election, 63 percent have made a decision on a main long-distance supplier. This translates into slightly over half, 52 percent of long-distance users interviewed. A higher portion of heavy users, upper-income and white-collar workers had made a choice.

- Of those making a decision, 64 percent chose AT&T and 36 percent decided on an OCC. This means out of the total interviewed, 33 percent selected AT&T and 18 percent chose an OCC. Nonchoosers and those not aware account for 48 percent of the total interviewed. A portion of nonchoosers, 5 percent of the total, did not make a decision as a way to stay with AT&T. Combined with those who actively decided on AT&T, brings the level of AT&T choice to 38 percent. MCI was the OCC most frequently chosen, selected by 13 percent.

- Compared to AT&T choosers, those selecting an OCC tended to be younger, better educated, more often employed full time and in white-collar jobs, have a higher average household income, and be heavier users of long-distance.

- Actual customer response to the equal access election somewhat reflects their behavior as predicted in the preannouncement research. At the bench mark study, conducted prior to the equal access announcement, 41 percent claimed they would definitely or probably not go with another carrier. This compared with the 33 percent who actively chose AT&T at selection (or the 38 percent choosing AT&T both actively or passively). In the preannouncement study, 21 percent were current subscribers or definite or probably adopters of an OCC. In the selection survey, 18 percent had chosen an OCC.

- In the earlier research, 37 percent were undecided as to whether or not they would subscribe to another carrier. This compares to 48 percent following the announcement who were either unaware or still undecided. It appears, then, that the predicted level of both AT&T retention and OCC adoption were only slightly overstated at the time of the bench mark research.

- Seventy-nine percent of respondents who had decided on a carrier notified their chosen supplier. This amounts to 41 percent of all respondents interviewed. In other words, nearly six out of ten long-distance users, at one week after cutover, had still not notified a carrier of their choice.

- Among AT&T choosers, 72 percent had notified. This represents 24 percent of all respondents choosing and notifying AT&T. The notification level is higher among OCC choosers: 91 percent who chose an OCC notified. Out of total respondents, this represents 17 percent. Twelve percent of all respondents chose and notified MCI.

EXHIBIT 16.1   (Cont.)

| | Percent of Total Respondents | | Percent of Choosers |
	Chose	Chose and Notified	Who Notified
AT&T	33	24	72
OCC	18	17	91
MCI	13	12	93

- Notifiers of any supplier, whether AT&T or an OCC, tended to be slightly older, better educated, more frequently in white-collar positions, have slightly higher incomes than defaulters, and be heavier users of long distance.
- Among all nonnotifiers, including "not aware" and "not chosen," in the nonallocation markets, 77 percent knew they would default to AT&T. This represents 31 percent of all respondents. In Minneapolis, 43 percent thought they would be assigned to AT&T.
- Combining respondents who would be likely to default to AT&T (not aware, not chosen, not notified) with those already choosing and notifying AT&T totals a maximum selection rate of about 82 percent for AT&T at the time of the survey one week after cutover.
- In the 31 markets studied, the level of notification ranged from 21 percent to 74 percent. The highest levels of notification occurred in Minneapolis (74 percent), the only allocation market in the study, and Charleston (60 percent), the first market to be subjected to the equal access election. Out of the 31 markets studied, 13 showed more than 20 percent choosing an OCC, 10 had an OCC penetration between 15 percent and 20 percent, and 8 markets had less than 15 percent selecting an OCC. In 8 markets AT&T choice exceeded 40 percent. In 10 markets AT&T choice was between 30 percent and 40 percent and in 12 markets, between 20 percent and 30 percent. Only one market, Baltimore: Liberty, showed an AT&T choice level under 20 percent. Markets showing a high OCC penetration level did not necessarily show a correspondingly low AT&T choice level.
- Aside from the 18 percent who had selected an OCC in response to the equal access notification, another 3 percent of total respondents predicted they would definitely subscribe to one. This could mean a likely penetration level of 20 percent or 21 percent. Another 8 percent of total respondents claimed probable intention to subscribe, indicating that the OCCs could possibly obtain an eventual 28 percent to 29 percent share of the market.

Factors Influencing the Selection Process

- The main reasons for choosing AT&T related to previous experience and satisfaction with the company. Cheaper pricing, including no minimum and discount rates, was the major reason for selecting an OCC. OCC choosers also mentioned the influence of advertising, company sales efforts, and friends' recommendations.
- OCC choosers tended to consult a greater variety of sources with greater frequency than did AT&T choosers in helping them choose a long-distance supplier, an average of 1.81

(Cont.)

EXHIBIT 16.1   (Cont.)

compared to 1.53. OCC choosers relied more heavily on various types of advertising, word of mouth, and contact with the company. Over a quarter of AT&T choosers (28 percent) consulted no sources in making their decision.

- Mail brochures were used considerably more often in making the decision of a long-distance supplier than had been anticipated in the bench market study. In the earlier study, 15 percent predicted they would consult a mail brochure. In making their selection, 47 percent said they consulted a mail brochure. Company representatives, referrals, and editorial sources were used less frequently than originally anticipated.

- Forty percent of OCC choosers claimed to have requested information from long-distance suppliers. This compares to only 19 percent of AT&T choosers who sought information. OCC choosers even sought information from AT&T with greater frequency than those who chose AT&T: 11 percent compared to 7 percent.

- Only 24 percent of AT&T choosers claimed to have been aware at the time they made their decision of at least one of the three promotional campaigns[1] intended to encourage AT&T selection. And only 6 percent reported that knowledge of the promotion had some influence in their decision of AT&T as main supplier.

- Among all respondents, AT&T "Opportunity Calling" was the most familiar of these programs, remembered by 44 percent. One-third recalled the "Reach Out America" promotion. Recall was lowest for the "Reach Out (State Name)" in those markets where it ran.

Awareness and Attitudinal Changes

- Seven out of ten respondents named AT&T as a supplier of long-distance on an unaided basis. Nearly as many, 67 percent claimed awareness for MCI. About half could name Sprint on a unaided basis. Awareness increased at about the same level for all three of the major long-distance suppliers.

Percent Unaided Recall For	Bench Mark	Selection	Change
AT&T	57%	70%	+13
MCI	53	67	+14
Sprint	40	54	+14

Aided awareness appeared nearly universal for both AT&T (98 percent) and MCI (93 percent). A large majority were also aware of Sprint on an aided basis: 88 percent.

The former confusion existing between AT&T and the local Bell Company appears to be largely resolved. In the bench mark survey, 31 percent named their local telephone company as a supplier of long distance. This decreased to only 2 percent in the selection study.

- While awareness increased about equally for all three major suppliers, the increase in the depth of this awareness was more dramatic for AT&T than for either MCI or Sprint.

EXHIBIT 16.1   (Cont.)

Percent Who Know a Lot About	Bench Mark	Selection	Change
AT&T	26%	37%	+11
MCI	15	18	+3
Sprint	11	12	+1

Choosers of MCI and Sprint claimed to know as much about AT&T as did those who chose AT&T.

• Slightly more respondents in the selection survey than in the bench mark study perceived AT&T as the "best provider" of long distance. There was virtually no change in perceptions of MCI and impressions of Sprint were slightly more negative.

Percent Who View as Best Provider	Bench Mark	Selection	Change
AT&T	35%	39%	+4
MCI	8	9	+1
Sprint	6	3	−3

• Respondents were asked to rate 20 characteristics of long-distance suppliers on their degree of importance. Over three-quarters of respondents gave the top importance rating to:

Getting good quality for the price you pay—80 percent
Ability to call anytime, to anywhere—79 percent
Ability to call anytime, from anywhere—78 percent
Providing accurate and reliable itemized billing—77 percent

Two-thirds or better gave a top-importance rating to:

Having excellent sound quality—75 percent
Paying no monthly service chage—74 percent
Being an established, dependable company—69 percent
Having competitive prices—68 percent
Having an operator available when you need one—67 percent
Providing reliable information about rates and services—67 percent

Perceived as least important are having a telephone credit card (22 percent), ability to make time payments on long-distance bills (26 percent), and international calling capability (29 percent). OCC choosers tended to rate price-related characteristics more highly, while AT&T choosers gave higher importance ratings to ubiquity and service attributes.

• There were no dramatic changes occurring between bench mark and selection in the percentage rating these characteristics as very important. The most substantial increases occurred on service and image attributes:

(Cont.)

EXHIBIT 16.1   (Cont.)

Ability to make person-to-person, collect calls— +7 percent

 Providing reliable information to make wisest selection— +5 percent

 Being an established, dependable company— +4 percent

 Providing reliable information about rates and services— + 4 percent

 Having directory assistance— +4 percent

 International calling capability— +4 percent

Importance ratings decreased on only one attribute: having discounted rates at convenient times (− 2 percent). The importance ratings on other pricing attributes remained relatively unchanged.

- Respondents were asked to rate the performance of the three major suppliers on their delivery of the same 20 long-distance supplier attributes. As it did in the bench mark study, AT&T continued in the selection survey to outperform both MCI and Sprint on all but price-related attributes.

Eight out of ten respondents rated AT&T as excellent on:

 Ability to call anytime, to anywhere—81 percent

 Ability to call anytime, from anywhere—79 percent

 Being an established, dependable company—79 percent

Two-thirds or better gave AT&T an excellent rating on ability to make person-to-person, collect calls (74 percent), directory assistance (71 percent), excellent sound quality (67 percent), and accurate, reliable billing (67 percent).

AT&T performed below both MCI and Sprint on having competitive pricing: 24 percent compared to 49 percent for MCI and 32 percent for Sprint. On quality for price and discounted rates, AT&T's ratings were below MCI's but superior to Sprint ratings.

No more than 50 percent gave MCI an excellent rating on any characteristic. The highest ratings for MCI were on price-related attributes. Sprint received excellent ratings from no more than a third of respondents.

- The percentage of respondents rating AT&T and MCI as excellent increased from the bench mark to the selection wave on all characteristics. The average overall increase in excellent ratings were about equal between these two carriers, about seven pecentage points. The most significant increases for AT&T occurred on sound quality (+13 percent), immediate credit for wrong numbers (+13 percent), ability to make person-to-person, collect calls (+11 percent), providing accurate information for wisest selection (+11 percent). The two latter attributes were the ones to see the most dramatic increases in importance ratings as well.

Excellent rating increases for MCI were most substantial on no monthly service charge (+18 percent), ability to call anytime from anywhere (+13 percent), providing accurate information to make wise selection (+10 percent), and having discounted rates (+9 percent).

Sprint showed fewer, and smaller, increases in excellent ratings and showed decreases in some areas.

---

[1] Campaigns were "Opportunity Calling," "Reach Out America," and "Reach Out (State Name)." The latter ran in all but three markets.

EXHIBIT 16.2   Status of Notification and Default

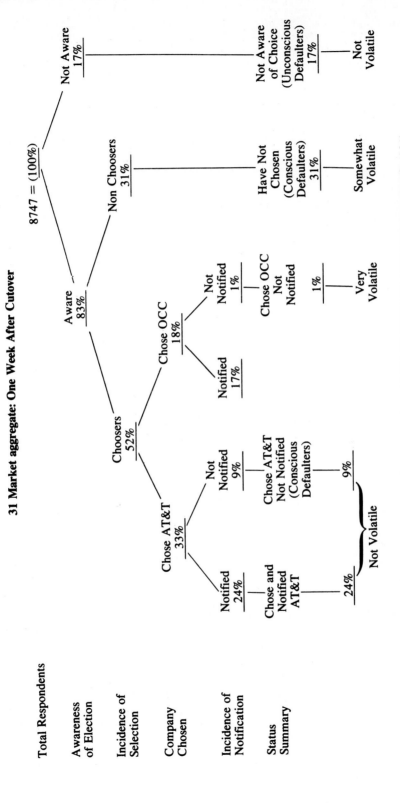

31 Market aggregate: One Week After Cutover

Total Respondents

Awareness of Election

Incidence of Selection

Company Chosen

Incidence of Notification

Status Summary

8747 = (100%)

Aware 83%

Not Aware 17%

Choosers 52%

Non Choosers 31%

Chose AT&T 33%

Chose OCC 18%

Notified 24%

Not Notified 9%

Notified 17%

Not Notified 1%

Have Not Chosen (Conscious Defaulters) 31%

Not Aware of Choice (Unconscious Defaulters) 17%

Chose and Notified AT&T 24%

Chose AT&T Not Notified (Conscious Defaulters) 9%

Chose OCC Not Notified 1%

Very Volatile 1%

Somewhat Volatile

Not Volatile

Not Volatile 9%

24%

Not Volatile

AT&T TOTAL AT WEEK ONE AFTER CUTOVER (NOTIFIERS AND DEFAULTERS): 82%

331

_____ CASE 17 _____

Apple Computer Targets
Desktop Engineering

Matthew Robertson was reviewing the first-quarter sales figures for the Macintosh II. It seemed amazing to him that the most challenging problem Apple faced at that point was how to keep up with the demand for Mac IIs. The corporate first-quarter results were impressive. Not only were sales up 35 percent compared to first-quarter results a year ago but net earnings increased more than 20 percent (Exhibit 17.1).

The phone rang suddenly and broke Matthew's concentration. "Hello Matthew, this is Jan." "Hi Jan, how's it going?" "Crazy, of course. Listen, I'm not going to be able to make this afternoon's meeting. Can we reschedule for tomorrow morning—first thing?" "Sure, no problem. I was just looking over the quarterly report. Have you seen it?" "I heard it was great, but did you hear that Sun is finally shipping their low-end workstation? And there's been a lot of press about our evolving the Mac as opposed to introducing new revolutionary machines." "Yeah, we've got a lot to talk about, don't we? Look, I'll call Tom and reschedule for tomorrow, okay? . . . All right, see you tomorrow."

Matthew looked around his office and saw the mountains of information he had been collecting and analyzing for the past three weeks. Tomorrow morning he would compare notes with his other team members, Janice Latham and Tom Kelly, and together they would come up with a program for Apple's formal entry into the engineering workstation market. Introducing the Mac II to Apple's new market would be a lot like his previous assignment as a member of the tremendously successful Desktop Publishing Market Development Team (MDT), but it would also be more challenging, Matthew thought. And Matthew realized *he* was now responsible for the success of this team—desktop publishing had been pioneered by Apple, but the engineering workstation market was already established. The competition would be ready.

This case was prepared by Robert O. Lewis, Linda E. Swayne, and Peter M. Ginter as a basis for class discussion rather than to illustrate either effective or ineffective handling of an administrative situation. Some facts have been altered to protect confidentiality of company information. Used with permission from Linda E. Swayne.

EXHIBIT 17.1   Apple Computer, First-Quarter Sales and Earnings

	1988	1989	Percent Change
Sales	$1.042 billion	$1.405 billion	+35%
Net Earnings	$121 million	$140 million	+20%

APPLE COMPUTER'S BACKGROUND

Apple manufactured and marketed two principal lines of personal computers, related software, and peripheral products. The first, which fueled the company's growth into 1986, was the Apple II product line. This line was geared to the educational (preschool through high school) and home computing markets. The second and the platform for the future growth of Apple was the Macintosh product line. Macintosh was developed for the business market (productivity and desktop publishing) and the higher education market. See Exhibit 17.2 for a chronological history of Apple. Apple had not escaped the industrywide computer

EXHIBIT 17.2   Chronological History of Apple Computer

March	1976	Apple Computer was founded by Steven Wozniak (26) and Steven Jobs (21). They produced a hobbyist computer that contained 16 times the memory of any other such computer. It was priced at $666.66. Officially formed on April Fools' Day.
January	1977	Jobs, Wozniak, and Mike Markkula incorporate Apple Computer and draft the first formal business plan.
April	1977	Apple II is introduced.
December	1977	First year sales are $774,000.
February	1980	Annual sales reach $100,000,000.
December	1980	Apple offers public stock.
August	1981	IBM introduces the PC.
January	1983	The Lisa is introduced (forerunner of the Macintosh).
April	1983	John Sculley becomes president and CEO.
December	1983	Apple annual sales reach $1 billion.
January	1984	Fully automated Macintosh factory begins operation. Less than 1 percent of the cost of a Macintosh unit can be attributed to labor.
March	1984	Apple ships the Macintosh.
June	1985	Steven Jobs is removed from operations at Apple.
December	1985	Annual sales reach $1.52 billion.
February	1986	Apple purchases a Cray supercomputer to assist in the design of new products.
April	1987	Apple announces a 2-for-1 stock split and a first-ever cash dividend.
May	1987	Apple introduces the Macintosh II. This machine is positioned for the power-user in markets such as corporate MIS departments and desktop publishing.
September	1987	U.S. sales organization splits into three regional divisions—Western, Central, and Eastern.
March	1988	Apple begins shipping A/US (UNIX software interface for engineering workstations).

slump of 1984 and 1985. However, through a well-organized restructuring, Apple emerged in 1986 as a leaner, more market-sensitive company and went on to record sales and profits.

When they founded Apple in 1976, Steven Wozniak and Steven Jobs had very specific ideas about what they wanted. The first business plan was written by retired Intel founder Mike Markkula. The original corporate objectives and key strategies are included in Exhibit 17.3.

In 1987, Apple's CEO, John Sculley, set corporate objectives that included achieving $4 billion in sales by 1990, spending $300 million on research and development by 1990, and maintaining the entrepreneurial spirit of a small company. He and the Apple employees were committed to the corporate mission: "To produce innovative products that place the individual, not the mainframe, at the center of the computing universe."

Organizational Structure

Apple's organizational structure was designed to meet the corporate objective of maintaining the entrepreneurial spirit of a small company. It could best be described as a hybrid design—neither centralized nor decentralized but actually a network. The network stemmed from the board and the single layer of upper management (six senior executives). It was given structure with functional areas like operations, marketing, finance, and so on. Senior members of the functional departments would recognize a problem or opportunity that needed to be ad-

---

EXHIBIT 17.3   Apple's Corporate Objectives and Strategies, 1976

Objectives

- Obtain a market share greater than or equal to two times that of the nearest competitor.
- Realize equal to or greater than 20 percent pretax profit.
- Grow to $500 million annual sales in 10 years.
- Establish and maintain an operating environment conducive to human growth and development.
- Continue to make significant technological contributions to the home computer industry.
- (Possible) Structure company for easy exit of founders within five years.

Key Strategies

- It is extremely important for Apple to be the first recognized leader in the home computer marketplace.
- Continually market peripheral products for the basic computer, thereby generating sales equal to or greater than the initial computer purchase.
- Allocate sufficient funds to R&D to guarantee technological leadership consistent with market demands.
- Attract and retain *absolutely* outstanding personnel.
- Rifle-shot the hobby market as the first stepping stone to the major market.
- Maintain significant effort in manufacturing to continually reduce cost of production.
- Grow at the same rate that the market grows.
- Design and market the computer to be more economical than a dedicated system in specific applications, even though all features of the Apple are not used.

Source: John Sculley, *Odyssey: Pepsi to Apple* (New York: Harper & Row, 1987).

dressed. Knowledge of the problem (or opportunity) came from either a member of a functional department or someone in the network. Then modular groups were set up to solve that specific problem or develop that opportunity and later disband when the task was completed and reform into other groups to take on new projects.

The marketing functional area stemmed from the corporate marketing and sales managers, to one of the three regional marketing managers, then to separate managers within the region for education, retail, and direct sales. Reporting to the sales managers were sales representatives of varying capacities as well as sales support people.

Apple believed that the network was a superior format because it was a natural way for communication to flow. Inside the network, idea exchange was not inhibited by functional boundaries or management levels. Creativeness, flexibility, innovation, and individuality were all fostered in the network schema. The high-technology industry is subject to rapid change; therefore, the company and its personnel had to be able to quickly share ideas about any change, develop alternatives, make a decision, and implement it. Another chief advantage of the network design was its efficiency. Apple's annual sales per employee was roughly $400,000—based on 1988 sales. Therefore, the network structure allowed Apple to operate leaner and achieve a corporate objective—to preserve its entrepreneurial spirit.

Through this network, Apple identified the engineering workstation market as a lucrative target for the future. A task group was formed to analyze the situation and develop strategies to be implemented through the marketing channels. They would recommend the direction for product development to meet the future needs of the identified target market.

Organizational Philosophy

Apple considered itself to be a "third wave" company (as opposed to a "second wave" company, that sees the future as an extension of the past and therefore focuses on ritual) and focused on the individual. Exhibit 17.4 illustrates the difference between a Third Wave and Second Wave company.

APPLE AND THE MICROCOMPUTER INDUSTRY

With a revenue increase of 53 percent in 1988, Apple Computer was in a strong position in the computer industry. Analysts projected 1989 revenues to approach $5.4 billion, a 30 percent increase (Exhibits 17.5 and 17.6).

The key to this success was the introduction of the Macintosh II, a machine that was equal to or better than (depending on the application) the high-performance machines offered by IBM, Compaq, and other similar microcomputer manufacturers. The Mac II featured superior color graphics, extremely fast processing speed, and an advanced 32-bit architecture with the ability to run multiple

EXHIBIT 17.4   Contrasted Management Paradigms

Characteristic	Second Wave	Third Wave
Organization	Hierarchy	Network
Output	Market share	Market creation
Focus	Institution	Individual
Style	Structured	Flexible
Source of Strength	Stability	Change
Structure	Self-sufficiency	Interdependencies
Culture	Tradition	Genetic code[a]
Mission	Goals/strategic plans	Identify directions/values
Leadership	Dogmatic	Inspirational
Quality	Affordable best	No compromise
Expectations	Security	Personal growth
Status	Title and rank	Making a difference
Resource	Cash	Information
Advantage	Better sameness	Meaningful difference
Motivation	To complete	To build

[a] Genetic coding is a term describing how a third-wave company refers to the past only for a sense of direction.

Source: John Sculley, *Odyssey: Pepsi to Apple* (New York: Harper & Row, 1987).

EXHIBIT 17.5   Apple Computer, Inc. Annual Sales

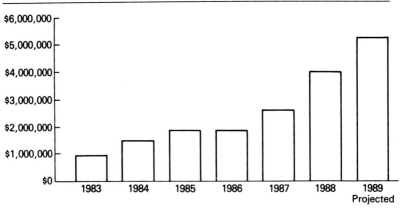

Source: Apple Computer, Inc.

operating systems. One operating system of importance to the engineering marketplace was UNIX. The Macintosh II would be configured to operate this complex system while maintaining its user-friendly interface.

The power of the Mac II gained the awareness of MIS professionals, many of whom had regarded the original Macintosh as a "toy." With the introduction of

EXHIBIT 17.6   Principal Sources of Revenue for Apple Computer, 1987

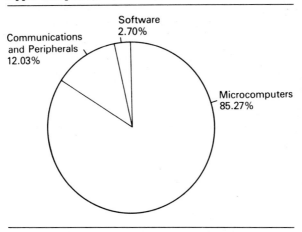

Source: "Inside Studies," *Datamation*, June 15, 1988, p. 52.

the Mac II, many business and MIS decision makers realized that Apple could compete with IBM and would remain a key player in the computer industry. The user interface Apple had touted was now on a powerful system and, to give Apple even more credibility, IBM copied it in the form of the OS/2 presentation manager (operating system).

On March 18, 1988, Apple filed suit against Microsoft Corporation and Hewlett-Packard for copyright violations concerning the Macintosh operating system. The suit directly charged that Microsoft's Windows 2.03 software copied the Macintosh interface.[1]

According to technical analysts, the Macintosh operating system was at least two years ahead of IBM's OS/2 in the evolutionary process (capabilities, upward expansion, and available software), and Apple's future depended on its ability to maintain that lead. IBM led the industry although its share eroded considerably between August 1987 and January 1988 (Exhibit 17.7).

Marketing research indicated that among potential buyers (those planning to buy within the next year), over the time periods shown in Exhibit 17.8, Apple's

EXHIBIT 17.7   Microcomputer Market Share

	August 1987	*January 1988*
IBM	66%	47%
Apple	8	17
Compaq	6	12
Compatibles	20	24

[1] Jim Forbes, Daniel Lyons, and Gregory Spector, *PcWeek*, March 22, 1988, p. 1.

EXHIBIT 17.8   Share of Year-Ahead Planned Purchases

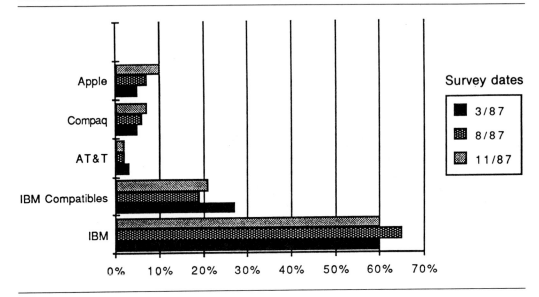

Source: Richard Stromer, *PcWeek*, January 12, 1988, p. 138.

"share of year-ahead planned purchases" has grown consistently while IBM's (though still large) had faltered. Among respondents who had considered purchasing a specific brand, some had not tried the brand (Exhibit 17.9). Of those respondents who had tried the brand they intended to buy, the percentage who actually bought that brand was somewhat less than the trial (Exhibit 17.10).

EXHIBIT 17.9   Percentage of Respondents Considering a Brand Who Have Tried the Brand

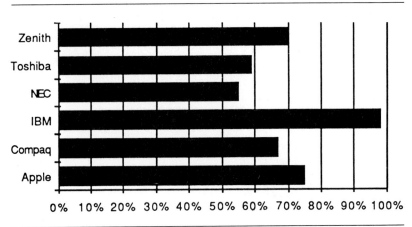

Source: Richard Stromer, *PcWeek*, March 22, 1988, p. 146.

EXHIBIT 17.10   Percentage of Respondents Who Have Tried a Brand and Have Purchased That Brand

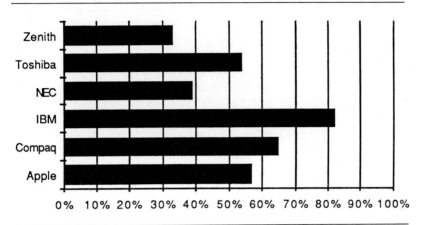

Source: Reprinted from *PcWeek*, January 12, 1988, and March 22, 1988. Copyright ©, Ziff Communications Company.

TARGET MARKET

Apple's primary markets were higher education, business, government, K-12 education, and international. International sales accounted for nearly 30 percent of the company's annualized revenue. Apple designated desktop engineering as the next target market.

The engineering workstation (desktop engineering) market consists of the various engineering fields—electrical, chemical, mechanical, civil, industrial, and architectural. Apple had segmented the market into two principal submarkets—the engineering workplace and engineering higher education. The UNIX workstation market was not limited to the United States, or engineers, and independent research projected the worldwide market potential to be more than $20 billion by 1990. Apple beefed up its international presence, implementing a strategy called *multilocal focusing* in recognition of this and other growing markets. Multilocal was Apple's term for regionalizing corporate communications as well as the ability to customize the product line for the end user.

Apple's objective was to secure a strong foundation within the two market segments in the more narrow scope of the engineering workstation market. Apple planned to leverage resources for long-term growth and development of the two targets. Once Apple established itself as a major workstation manufacturer, it would expand the objective to include all UNIX environments and applications.

Workstation Defined

In 1987, the U.S. engineering-specific workstation market, only eight years old, accounted for over $3 billion in sales. An engineering workstation is a microcomputer that is positioned in the market between a minicomputer and the traditional personal computer. A workstation has become a high-performance personal computer that typically uses a programming language called UNIX, which is a sophisticated operating system that controls the workstation and communicates with other computers of different manufacture.

UNIX became the preferred system because it supported networking (tying many different computers together through the use of electronic hardware and software), allowed the use of more than one application at a time, had full graphics support, and was not a proprietary system (meaning that with some adjustments most any computer can operate UNIX, allowing the use of any application software program written under UNIX). Engineers use this system to perform tasks that range from scientific analysis to product design simulation. With the decreased cost of computing, engineers and scientists are realizing the benefits that were once limited to the mainframe computer and the computers can now sit on their desks.

COMPETITION

Sun Microsystems, IBM, Digital Equipment, Apollo Computer, and NeXT made up the principal competitors in the engineering market. Hewlett-Packard was expected to bring its Spectrum computer to the UNIX marketplace. Apollo Computer pioneered the engineering workstation in 1980. In 1985, it had a 40 percent market share that has since eroded to around 18 percent. Revenues, market share, and profitability information for the major competitors are illustrated in Exhibit 17.11.

IBM

John F. Akers, chairman of IBM, instituted a complete reorganization to reestablish IBM as the most profitable company in the world. Analysts expected the changes to help IBM become more innovative and to move products out into the market more rapidly. "IBM has been taking too long bringing systems to the market," said Michael Geran, vice president for Nikko Securities International, a New York brokerage firm. "This is an evolutionary step by IBM to use an organizational change to speed up product releases and get closer to the marketplace."[2] The change was to be accomplished through decentralization. Mr. Akers planned to push decision-making power down to the younger managers, fostering an entrepreneurial spirit.[3]

The IBM strategy was a full product and service line offering approach. Faced with flat growth projections (revenues) for both mainframe and minicomputer products, IBM targeted personal computers, software, and services as the new and continued high-growth markets (Exhibit 17.12).

[2] Steven Burke, *PcWeek*, February 9, 1988, P. 127.
[3] *Business Week*, February 15, 1988; *Business Week*, July 18, 1988.

EXHIBIT 17.11   Major Competitor Revenue, Market Share and Profitability—Engineering Market

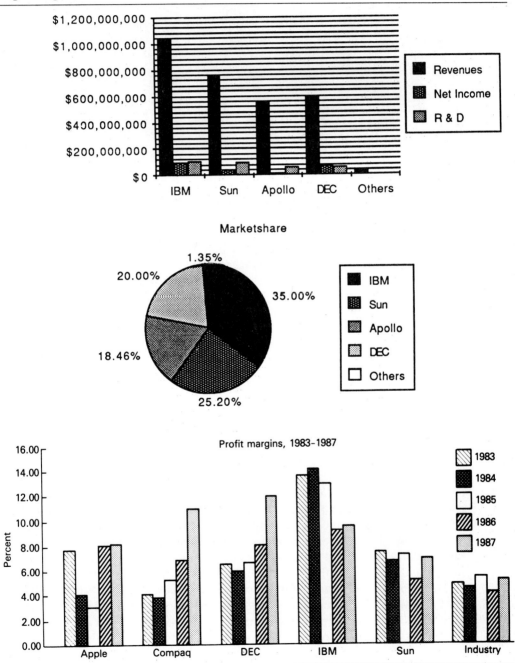

Marketshare

Profit margins, 1983-1987

Source: Compiled from *Business Week*, March 14, 1988, p. 134; *Datamation*, November 15, 1987, pp. 61–76.

EXHIBIT 17.12   IBM Principal Revenue Sources, 1987

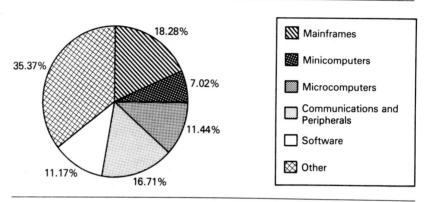

Source: "Inside Stories," *Datamation*, June 15, 1988, p. 42.

The machine IBM positioned for engineers was the Model 80. It was based on the 80386 Intel microprocessor with a speed of up to 20 MHz (a measure of raw processing speed). It operated with OS/2 and DOS system software, however, the computer had proprietary hardware set up to reduce the cloning potential (competitors who copied or purchased the same parts that IBM used).

The Model 80 could be categorized in IBM's new computer line as the Personal System 2 (PS/2). As of March 1988, IBM reported sales of 1.5 million PS/2 units and the Model 80 represented roughly 82,500 units sold. Due to the market's resistance to proprietary hardware, IBM instituted tough quotas for its dealer network (many of the same dealers carried the Apple line). This resulted in almost wholesale pricing—the Model 80 started out retailing for over $10,000 but then sold for approximately $7,000.[4]

Sun Microsystems

Sun manufactured a line of computers that ranged from desktop supercomputers to low-end workstations. These computers were positioned in the engineering market. Sun did not have the means to expand beyond that market. The company announced in February 1988 that their Triad Strategy would be comprised of three different computers all featuring the UNIX operating system and a user-friendly graphic interface similar to the Mac interface. Sun was well known for its marketing savvy (oriented toward personal selling) in the engineering market and was one of the fastest-growing computer manufacturers.

A principal component of Sun's success was the fact that its computers were built with widely accepted computing standards like Ethernet network protocols, Motorola's 68000 series processors, Intel's 80386 processor, and AT&T's UNIX operating system software. Another was Sun's ability to take off-the-shelf compo-

[4] *PcWeek*, March 29, 1988, pp. 10–11.

nents, like those mentioned above, to produce a high-performance machine at a lower price than other competitors.

This practice was a double edged sword for Sun. Using off-the-shelf components enabled them to take advantage of technological breakthroughs as they reached the market. On the other hand, this approach forced Sun to provide state-of-the-art machines constantly in order to keep margins up. As competitors continually matched Sun (or eventually outguessed the next off-the-shelf high-tech buy) customers could switch vendors for the very reasons they chose Sun—pricing and cutting-edge technology.[5]

With a UNIX operating system, Sun was seen as a "safe buy." But Sun was not without weaknesses; it was apparently vulnerable to manufacturing inefficiency (most of the system components were purchased) and had a lack of financial clout.[6] Sun recently announced the sale of a 20 percent block of stock to AT&T.[7] Analysts viewed this as a sign of the impact of larger companies entering and expanding the market. The smaller companies would have to rely on their responsiveness to changing technology and market needs in order to succeed or survive.

AT&T was not new to computers; they lost between $800 million and $1.2 billion in 1986 alone and laid off thousands of employees. AT&T was the original developer of the UNIX operating system and had seen many companies profit from it while they were regulated by the government and not permitted to sell computers until the early 1980s. Industry analysts expect several effects of the agreement between Sun and AT&T. Sun would gain the distribution channel AT&T was using (dealers), and Sun would receive financial resources to fuel its rapid growth. Analysts considered the price for Sun's 20 percent block of stock to be a bargain at $300 million, giving AT&T the opportunity to recoup previous losses.[8]

Sun's alliance with AT&T developed another problem. Customers and competitors suspected that UNIX would no longer be "open" to all computer systems as it had been. DEC, IBM, and others grouped together to develop an alternative to UNIX.[9]

Sun's newest computer, the Sun 386i, used a 80386 Intel microprocessor that was also purchased by IBM, Compaq, and others for use in their high-performance machines. The Sun 386i would be positioned against the IBM Model 80, Compaq 386, and the Macintosh II. Using a 386 processor would allow the Sun system to run DOS applications within the UNIX operating system software, giving the user access to all programs written for the IBM world. Jeff Elpern, manager of sales development for alternative distribution channels for Sun, was

5 Stuart Gannes, "America's Fastest-Growing Companies," *Fortune*, May 23, 1988, p. 30.
6 "Mid-Range Shootout: Mini/Micro Survey," *Datamation*, November 15, 1987, pp. 61–76.
7 *PcWeek*, January 12, 1988, p. 1.
8 Ibid.
9 Richard Brandt, Phane Peterson, and Geoff Lewis, "Getting Computers to Dance to the Same Music," *Business Week*, May 23, 1988, pp. 112–114.

quoted as saying that MicroAge, Entre Computer, and other independent dealers have been signed to distribution agreements. Mr. Elpern expected to have 100 dealers signed by the end of June 1988. Andrew Neff, an analyst with Bear, Stearns & Co., a New York investment company, said, "Last year, it was IBM who was getting eaten up by Compaq at the high end and by everyone else at the low end. Now it's Compaq's turn." (Note: reference to IBM's "high-end" is equivalent to the "low-end" Sun workstation.)[10]

William O'Shea, executive director of AT&T's Information Technology Division, stated, "It is key that we recognize the existence of DOS and OS/2 and that we operate effectively in environments that include those systems as well as UNIX."[11]

Apollo Computer

Although Apollo established the workstation market, recent competition with more financial resources and better marketing expertise contributed to Apollo's decline. Sales were increasing, but not at a rate in proportion to the growth of the market. Apollo's low-end workstation was the DN 3000. Their principal market for this system was the previous Apollo customer.

Digital Equipment Corporation (DEC)

Within 30 years, DEC was considered to be the world's second largest computer systems supplier. Exhibit 17.13 illustrates the principal revenue sources for DEC. As of 1987, no revenue was attributed to the sales of mainframe products.

EXHIBIT 17.13   Principal Revenue Sources for DEC, 1987

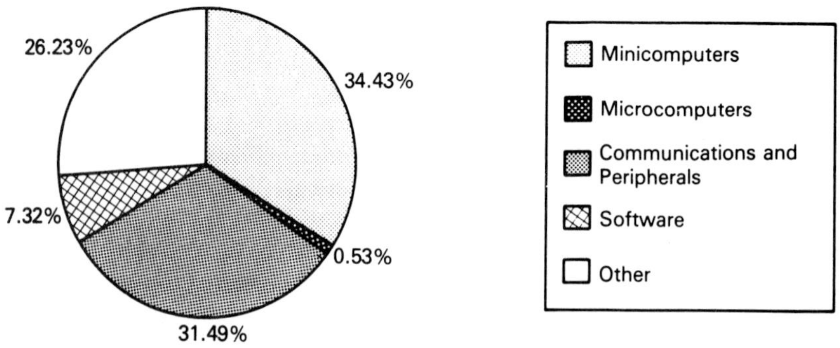

Source: "Inside Stories," *Datamation*, June 15, 1988, p. 42.

[10] Kenneth Siegmann, *PcWeek*, March 29, 1988, p. 139.
[11] Steven Burke, *PcWeek*, March 29, 1988, p. 139.

The DEC strategy was to move from the role of a microcomputer vendor to one of a full-line supplier. DEC embarked on a new product development campaign that included mainframes, communications, software, services, and individual workstations (high-performance PCs). DEC also developed relationships with Apple Computer, Compaq Computer, and Northern Telecom.

DEC made the most competitive progress against IBM in the minicomputer market. DEC successfully sold its VAX Cluster through the benefit of two main points. First, if a single VAX unit went down, service could continue without interruption. Second, additional VAX units could be added as more processing power was required. Under an IBM mainframe, service was lost when it broke down and if the IBM customer outgrew the system, management had to sell the old at market price and purchase a larger, more expensive system, often requiring software changes.

Some felt DEC's move into the mainframe product area was "antithema." Another problem facing DEC was the increasing power of personal computers, which were making inroads into individual workstation market share. The principal firms marketing such PCs were Apple, Compaq, IBM, and Sun Microsystems. Even more threatening to DEC was the fact that when better communications software was available from these competitors, PC customers would be able to connect their PCs together and form a system very comparable to the DEC VAX Cluster—at a substantial discount.[12]

Overall, analysts projected a conservative 15 percent revenue increase, but DEC will try to use its product expansion strategy to actualize a larger revenue gain.

In 1988, Apple Computer and Digital Equipment reached a marketing agreement for strategically aligning their products. Analysts expected DEC to concentrate on the high end of the engineering market and Apple to focus on the low to middle end. However, in late 1988, DEC announced it would market Tandy's PC clones and would manufacture a full line of workstation micros based on RISC (reduced instruction set computing) technology. It was unclear whether or not DEC would position these products directly against Apple.

Compaq

Compaq's strategy evolved into one similar to that of Sun Microsystems. In 1992, Compaq was introducing machines of greater performance and of at least equal quality to that of IBM machines. Compaq machines were priced consistently below comparable IBM models, but above competitors. The use of a high-quality image enabled Compaq to become a "next best alternative" to IBM and represented a "better value" to many computer customers.

The principal threat to Compaq was the "new standard" touted by IBM called the PS/2 or Personal System/2 computer line. If this would become the new

---

[12] Leslie Helm, John Verity, Geoff Lewis, Phane Peterson, and Jonathan Levine, "What Next for Digital?" *Business Week*, May 16, 1988, p. 91.

PC standard, Compaq might be forced into an adoptive strategy that could result in a margin decline. However, analysts felt that Compaq would have at least two years of healthy sales and income growth.

In 1992, Compaq was positioning its 386 machine as superior in performance, quality, and value compared to the IBM models. They were very successful. It is unknown what impact the Sun entry into the broad dealer channel will have upon Compaq's strategy.

Hewlett-Packard

The HP Vectra RS/20 computer was based on the 80386 microprocessor and operated on DOS similar to the IBM models.

The HP Spectrum was reported to use a RISC processor, a type of processor that executes 20 percent of all computer instructions in four-fifths the time of a normal processor. It is reported that the price will be near that of a low-end workstation, and that it will operate UNIX and run DOS similar to the Sun 386i. The graphic interface used on this computer is the subject of the Apple lawsuit.

NeXT

Founded by Steve Jobs after leaving Apple, NeXT introduced its first computer in late 1988. Although not scheduled to ship in quantity until late summer of 1989, and most application software not expected until early 1990, industry analysts viewed the NeXT machine as the "next" leap in technology.

The main processor was the 25 MHz Motorola (5 mips), which was somewhat faster than Apple's Mac IIx (based on the 16 MHz Motorola 68030 chip) and operated on a version of UNIX called Mach. The machine utilized separate microprocessors for operations such as video, sound, and input-output information processing. This enabled information to be handled much faster, from beginning to end, than any currently available micro using a comparable processor. Technical analysts considered this "mainframe on a desktop" approach to be the key advantage of the NeXT machine.

Mr. Jobs stated that the strategy of NeXT will focus on higher education, primarily to the engineering and computer science markets, and he did not rule out the possibility of entering the business market in the future. Mr. Jobs also announced IBM has entered into a license agreement with NeXT for the use of its graphic interface and programming environment to run on all IBM UNIX machines. Analysts considered this to be a hedge on the possible failure of IBM's OS/2.

THE MEETING

Tom Kelly, a software engineer and software market analyst, and Janice Latham, a hardware engineer and hardware analyst, were seated with Matthew as they began to discuss the decisions they would have to make.

Apple's marketing research team in conjunction with their product development team had determined than an unmet need existed in the engineering workstation market. Research indicated that engineers would request a computer that would do more than scientific applications especially if they were already using a high-end system or were seeking a system for subordinate engineers. Exhibit 17.14 illustrates engineer preferences when selecting a workstation.

Apple also recognized that MIS directors relied on input from engineers concerning workstation requirements, but MIS directors were still responsible for the results of the purchase decision. Exhibit 17.15 indicates the purchasing criteria used by MIS directors. Jan and Tom agreed that the surveys were fairly representative of customer attitudes.

Matthew reminded them that the market for engineering workstations was $3 billion in 1987. Projections for the low-end segment of the workstation market were $1.1 billion in sales for 1988, $1.15 billion in 1989, and $1.3 billion in 1990. Jan said, "Those projections seem conservative to me. Looking over this quarter's sales figures, we are selling all we can make, yet we don't know if we're meeting our potential." "You're right," Matthew responded. "We don't even know the real potential of this market. It might be just like desktop publishing where we found that any small business could benefit from using the product. Every engineering application could conceivably be performed on the Mac II and there are numerous types of engineers." (Exhibit 17.16).

Next Matthew brought up the point that support was ranked highly by engineers. Apple's primary salespeople would come from the dealer organization. Jan said, "There are different kinds of engineers, each with a certain need, and they're different primary markets. Yet electrical engineers are electrical engineers, although some are employed in business, some in government, and some

EXHIBIT 17.14   Ranked Criteria for Workstations by Engineers

Power, Benefits, Features	1
Support	2
Compatible/Networkable	3
Learning Curve	4
Cost Effectiveness	5

EXHIBIT 17.15   Ranked Criteria for Workstations by MIS Directors

System Quality/Reliability/Performance	1
Compatibility/Networkable	2
Vendor Reputation/Financial Strength	3
Application Software Availability	4
Price	5

EXHIBIT 17.16   Engineers by Discipline

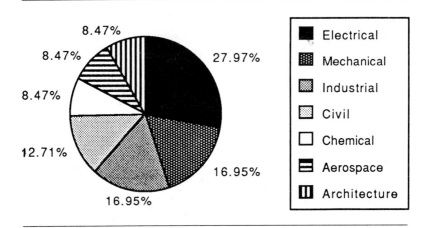

in higher education. I think we're kidding ourselves if we believe our dealer network can easily handle the more sophisticated installations."

"I can see that and yet we can't ignore the dealer network," commented Matthew. "I can't think of a way to reach as many engineering prospects as we did desktop publishing prospects."

Apple used a direct sales force primarily to sell to large corporations (approximately 100 accounts), all universities, and to the dealer network. The dealer network was divided into two types—retail accounts and independent resellers. The retail accounts were usually national chains like Computerland and Micro-Age. The independent resellers were individual stores that combined a retail plan with an outbound sales program.

Something else was bothering Tom. "Take a look at this computer comparison from *PcWeek* for low-end engineering workstations. Everybody's here except us."

"We should have been there! The Mac II has virtually the same performance as those in the article," said Jan. "We have the 68020 processor with a 2 mips rating and look at this price comparison." (See Exhibits 17.17 and 17.18.)

Matthew concentrated on another hurdle Apple would have to overcome. "Our image is very strong as a home computer marketer and the Macintosh seems to suffer from an image of being so easy to use it must lack power and sophistication." Jan jumped in, "Several participants in my hardware focus group study kept saying they didn't believe sophisticated software was available, even though

EXHIBIT 17.17   Computer Performance Comparison

IBM Model 80	Compaq 386	Sun 3/50	Sun 386i	Apollo DN 30
16 MHz 80386	20 MHz 80386	16 MHz 68020	25 MHz 80386	16 MHz 68020
1.5 mips[a]	2 mips	2 mips	3 mips	2 mips

[a]Mips (million instructions executed per second) is a benchmark used to compare processing power.
Source: *PcWeek,* March 29, 1988, p. 139.

EXHIBIT 17.18   Price Comparison

	IBM Model 80	Compaq 386	Sun 3/50	Sun 386i	Apollo DN 30	Mac II
Price	$7000	$7000	$7995	$8500	$8295	$6500
Price/Mips	$4500	$3500	$4000	$2800	$4000	$3250

Source: *PcWeek,* March 29, 1988, p. 139.

they knew the hardware was powerful." "Even Seymour Cray, the Cray super-computer designer, uses a Mac II to design his new systems. But it's expensive to change attitudes," exclaimed Tom.

"There's one more issue we've got to weigh," Matthew slowly leaned forward. "Jan mentioned to me yesterday the revolution versus evolution press we've been getting. I'm concerned about how this will affect our plans." Tom interrupted, "Matt, I was talking with Tim Morgan last night and he's involved with an assessment on that with public relations. I'm sure he's got some ideas and I'll talk with him as soon as we're finished."

"Okay, Tom, that sounds good. Our marketing budget for the engineering workstation segment has tentatively been set at $16 million. (Exhibits 17.19 and 17.20 present the financial statements.) That has to be allocated for the workstation in all our primary markets—engineers in business, government, and higher education," replied Matthew. He went on, "As I see it, we have three challenges: the image of the Macintosh being too easy to use, the perception that sophisticated software packages are not available, and the sales of engineering workstations through our current dealer network. Add to that the unknown effect of the press about how we're evolving the Mac rather than breaking new technological frontiers. Given these issues, Corporate still expects us to make the Mac II a major player in the workstation market."

EXHIBIT 17.19 Apple Computer, Inc., Balance Sheet, 1980–1988 (In thousands)

	1980	1981	1982	1983	1984	1985	1986	1987	1988
Assets									
Current Assets									
Cash & Short-term Investments	$363	$ 72,834	$153,056	$143,284	$114,888	$337,013	$ 576,215	$565,094	$545,717
Accounts Receivable	15,814	42,330	71,478	136,420	258,238	220,157	263,126	405,637	638,816
Inventories	34,191	103,873	81,229	142,457	264,619	166,951	108,680	225,753	461,470
Prepaid Expenses	NA	NA	NA	27,949	26,751	70,375	53,029	48,798	88,711
Other	3,738	8,067	11,312	18,883	23,055	27,569	39,884	62,143	48,280
Total Current Assets	54,106	227,104	317,075	468,993	687,551	822,065	1,040,934	1,307,425	1,782,994
Property, Plant, and Equipment	4,779	22,371	34,483	67,050	75,868	90,446	107,315	130,434	207,357
Other Assets	6,465	5,363	6,229	20,536	25,367	23,666	11,879	40,072	91,735
Total Assets	$65,350	$254,838	$357,787	$556,579	$788,786	$936,177	$1,160,128	$1,477,931	$2,082,086
Liabilities and Owners' Equity									
Current Liabilities									
Notes Payable	$ 7,850	$ 10,745	$ 4,185	$ 37,321	$ 71,094	$121,702	$ 124,550	$ 168,992	$ 127,871
Accounts Payable	14,495	26,613	25,125	52,701	109,038	74,744	118,053	205,929	510,475
Income Taxes Payable	8,135	8,621	15,307	0	11,268	27,800	14,652	20,242	62,465
Other Current Liabilities	24,301	24,301	41,139	38,764	63,784	71,179	71,280	83,585	126,282
Total Current Liabilities	37,780	70,280	85,756	128,786	255,184	295,425	328,535	478,678	827,093
Long-Term Debt	671	1,909	2,052	1,308	0	0	0	0	0
Deferred Income Taxes	951	5,262	12,887	48,584	69,037	90,265	137,506	162,765	251,568
Owners' Equity									
Par Value	0	0	0	0	0	0	0	0	0
Capital in Excess of Par Value	8,342	120,361	138,760	182,855	206,097	229,749	220,766	263,347	226,972
Retained Earnings	17,606	57,026	118,332	195,046	258,468	320,738	473,321	573,141	776,453
Total Equity	25,948	177,387	257,092	377,901	464,565	550,487	694,087	836,488	1,003,425
Total Liabilities and Equity	$65,350	$254,838	$357,787	$556,579	$788,786	$936,177	$1,160,128	$1,477,931	$2,082,086

EXHIBIT 17.20 Apple Computer, Consolidated Statement of Income, 1979–1988 (In thousands except per share data)

	1979	1980	1981	1982	1983	1984	1985	1986	1987	1988
Sales	$47,867	$117,126	$334,783	$583,061	$982,769	$1,515,280	$1,918,280	$1,901,898	$2,661,068	$4,071,373
Cost of Goods Sold	27,450	67,329	170,124	288,001	505,765	878,586	1,117,864	891,112	1,296,220	1,990,879
Gross Profit	20,417	49,797	164,659	295,060	477,004	637,290	800,416	1,010,786	1,364,848	2,080,494
Operating Expenses										
Research and Development	3,601	7,282	20,956	37,979	60,040	71,136	75,526	127,758	191,554	272,512
Marketing and Sales	4,079	12,110	55,369	119,945	229,961	392,866	478,079	476,685	655,219	952,577
General and Administrative	2,617	6,820	22,191	34,927	57,364	81,840	147,043	132,812	146,637	235,067
Total Expenses	10,315	26,212	98,516	192,851	347,365	545,842	690,157	737,255	993,410	1,460,156
Operating Income	10,102	23,585	66,143	102,209	129,639	91,448	102,768	273,531	371,438	620,338
Interest and Other Income, Net	3	567	10,400	14,563	16,483	17,737	17,277	36,187	38,930	35,823
Net Income before Taxes	10,105	24,152	76,543	116,772	146,122	109,185	120,045	309,718	410,368	656,161
Taxes	5,032	12,454	37,123	55,466	69,408	45,130	58,822	155,755	192,872	255,903
Net Income	$5,073	$11,698	$39,420	$61,306	$76,714	$64,055	$61,223	$153,963	$217,496	$400,258
Earnings per Share	$0.12	$0.24	$0.70	$1.06	$1.28	$1.05	$0.99	$1.20	$1.65	$3.08

CASE 18

Shades of Black

Alex Corbbrey cleared space on his desk to study the initial fiscal year financial results for Shades of Black. Alex founded the company to produce greeting cards and social expression items for black consumers in the United States. In 1987, operating as an unincorporated sole proprietorship, sales of 15,239 cards ($9,640) were achieved. In 1988, the first year of incorporation, 28,188 cards were sold, and revenues reached $42,396 for all product lines.

Alex had high expectations for his product line, and was somewhat disappointed in the 1988 results. The Shades of Black retail store was located in the Greenwood shopping area, a renovated and attractive predominantly black business district adjacent to the Tulsa, Oklahoma, downtown business zone. Although he personally, and Shades of Black as a business, had received good publicity in the local media, it just did not seem that the black population of Tulsa was large enough to support the retail store he envisioned. In particular, Alex contrasted the limited and somewhat depressed black community in Tulsa with the vibrant one he had recently visited in Atlanta, Georgia. This visit to Atlanta made him wonder if perhaps a location other than Tulsa would better fit with Shades of Black's needs. But his first concern was development of a product line strategy for his young company.

THE PRODUCT/MARKET DILEMMA

It was unseasonably warm in Tulsa for a February. Alex had to force himself to study the "financials" (see Exhibit 18.1); his mind was brimming with ways to expand the business. He and his small staff had discussed four options for the 1989 to 1991 period.

Option 1: Expand Retail Coverage. The greeting cards produced by Shades of Black were sold only in a limited number of black-owned shops in a few scattered cities in the United States. Chain drug, discount stores, and supermarkets com-

This case was prepared by Lester A. Neidell as a basis for class discussion rather than to illustrate either effective or ineffective handling of an administrative situation. Copyright © 1989 by Lester A. Neidell. Used with permission from Lester A. Neidell.

bined had the greatest market share and were also the most rapidly growing retail outlets in the United States for greeting cards. None of these retailers was carrying any Shades of Black product. Sales expansion could be achieved by expanding market coverage in the U.S. retail market.

Option 2: Military Market.   A possible untapped market was the U.S. military. An estimated 594,000 black Americans serve in the armed forces. Many were away from family and friends for extended periods, which would seem to auger well for a company whose principal products were designed to communicate with loved ones.

EXHIBIT 18.1   Shades of Black Financial Statements

	Year Ending December 31,	
	1987	*1988*
Income Statements		
Sales	$ 9,640	$ 42,396[a]
Cost of goods sold	8,337	20,224
Gross Margin	1,303	22,172
Expenses		
Rent and Utilities	4,258	5,696
Travel	2,682	4,863
Advertising	1,590	204
Auto Expenses	209	277
Taxes and License	2,155	20
Maintenance	701	109
Meetings	191	348
Professional Services	6,324	2,000
Office	655	1,235
Interest	426	2,232
Freight and Postage	546	0
Dues and Subscriptions	150	101
Depreciation	1,440	2,606
Insurance	306	692
Donations	0	115
Trade Shows	0	4,790
Wages	0	50
Telephone	0	2,453
Miscellaneous	421	294
Total Expenses	$22,054	$28,085
Net Income (Loss)	$(20,751)	$(5,913)

[a] Distribution of sales by product category:
Cards: Distributors	68.9%
Cards: Retail	7.1%
Art	3.3%
Clothing	20.8%

EXHIBIT 18.1   (continued)

	Year Ending December 31,	
	1987	*1988*
Balance Sheets		
Assets		
Current Assets		
Cash	$ 305	$ 145
Accounts Receivable	1,797	7,956
Accounts Receivable—Employees	0	14,029
Inventory	3,883	17,060
Total Current Assets	5,985	39,190
Fixed Assets		
Equipment	20,149	16,751
Furniture and Fixtures	0	3,477
Leasehold Improvements	0	754
Less: Accumulated Depreciation	(1,440)	(4,045)
Total Fixed Assets	18,709	16,937
Other Assets		
Deposits	610	660
Total Other Assets	610	660
Total Assets	$25,304	$56,787
Liabilities and Owner Equity		
Liabilities		
Accounts Payable	8,327	11,156
Sales Tax Payable	0	572
Notes Payable	16,190	0
Note Payable—TEDC	0	14,000
Note Payable—Phippe	0	10,000
Note Payable—Alex	0	4,692
Note Payable—Jackson	0	1,000
Total Liabilities	24,517	41,420
Equity		
Owner's Draws	− 5,043	0
Equity	24,543	0
Capital Stock	0	4,686
Paid-In Capital	0	16,595
Current Earnings	(18,713)	(5,914)
Total Equity	787	15,367
Total Liabilities and Equity	$25,304	$56,787

Option 3: Black Colleges.   Another market segment contained primarily black colleges and universities. Over 100 predominately black colleges and universities enroll over 173,000 students. Both campus bookstores and alumni could be reached. For example, it would be possible to "customize" greeting cards for

alumni associations to use as fund raisers. One such "package" was being designed for Morehouse College, in Atlanta, Georgia.

Option 4: Funeral Homes. Finally, the product line could be expanded even further in order to reach black-owned, or black community-serviced, funeral homes. A mailing list of 12,348 black-owned funeral homes was available. It did not include those funeral parlors that serviced the black community but were not black owned.

Alex knew he had to act quickly. The Christmas season, during which approximately 31 percent of all greeting cards were sold, had a design lead time of four to six months. And any market expansion would also require some new designs, although degree and type would vary according to which of the four markets he directed his company's efforts. Furthermore, there was increasing interest on the part of both major and minor competitors in segmenting the greeting card industry. At the moment, no strong national competition existed for black-oriented greeting cards, but a flurry of recent news articles about the segment seemed to indicate that this would not be true for very much longer.

THE GREETING CARD INDUSTRY IN THE UNITED STATES

Written greeting messages originated in ancient Egypt, following the discovery of papyrus, and the development of hieroglyphics and inks. "Standardized" greetings probably stem from the time of Christ, and the pen of Paul. Paul began his letters with "Grace to you and peace." During the Dark Ages of Europe, when chivalry reigned, letters and messages of good cheer were widely exchanged. Thoughts were conveyed not only by written expression but by symbols, such as a handkerchief or knot of ribbon. These more durable message forms were hurled over the walls of besieged castles or through windows to gain entrance.[1] Today, retail greeting card stores in the United States sell messages as well as more permanent remembrances.

Greeting cards are more than pretty designs, pictures, or messages of greeting. They mirror the expressions and personalities of their senders. About 7 billion greeting cards of all types were purchased in the United States in 1988, with retail sales exceeding $9 billion. Industry data at the manufacturers' level for the period 1984 to 1988 are contained in Exhibit 18.2. Real growth was expected to be approximately 3 to 4 percent through 1992, but it could increase dramatically as baby boomers age. Market studies have shown that the heavy purchaser of greeting cards and related products and services are women ages 35 to 54. Retail prices of greeting cards range from 36 cents to $7.50. The high price is for a sophisticated "musical" card; more typically, adult consumers pay between $1.00 and $1.25 per card purchase.

Greeting card sales have been highly seasonal. About 31 percent of all cards are sold in the Christmas season; Valentine's Day cards add 12 percent of sales.

[1] Earnest D. Chase, *The Romance of Greeting Cards* (Cambridge: University Press of Cambridge, 1956).

EXHIBIT 18.2   Greeting Card Publishing Industry Data (In millions)

	1984	1985	1986	1987	1988
Value of All Products and Services Sold by the Greeting Card Publishing Industry	$2,394	$2,588	$2,793	$3,022	$3,294
Value of Above in 1982 dollars	2,276	2,843	2,532	2,596	2,674
Value of Products Sold by the Greeting Card Publishing Industry	1,679	1,809	1,948	2,112	2,306
Value of Imports	14	15	19	23	27

Source: U.S. Department of Commerce, Bureau of the Census, Bureau of Economic Analysis.

Other seasonal "holidays" (Easter, Mother's Day, Halloween, and so on) each contribute less than 3 percent. Nonseasonal sales are primarily birthday cards, with almost a 23 percent market share. The distribution of 1987 sales by card category is shown in Exhibit 18.3.

Nonoccasion or "alternative" cards are becoming more popular.[2] These products often have blank interiors to allow the sender to write personal sentiments. Hallmark Cards, the overall market share leader, recently developed a product line targeted for parents to send to their children simply to express caring. Hallmark's advertisements for these particular alternative cards depict children discovering the cards in their lunch boxes and textbooks. This approach by Hallmark also bypasses one of the problems the industry has encountered. Postal rate increases negatively impact the sales of cards. Although actual cross-elasticity indices are not available, increases in postage have in the past most affected Christmas and other holiday cards. Alternative card sales however, seem to have been least affected by postage changes.

Although the possibility of more rapid sales growth exists as baby boomers age, the general consensus is that the greeting card industry is mature. Historically, major competitors created demand by capitalizing on "self-promoted" holidays, such as Bosses Day, Secretary's Day, and Grandparents' Day.

For these occasions, the suppliers, led by Hallmark, created designs and promotions as if everyone knew of the holiday, which were typically joint creations of the florists, the greeting card industry, and organizations such as the National Secretary's Association. However, the public seemed to have become satiated with these "events."

General consensus in the industry was that the cards themselves were the best promotional vehicle, and that advertising tended to stimulate industrywide sales rather than promote brand loyalty. Nevertheless, Hallmark and American Greetings each spent about $60 million annually on advertising.

[2] The term "alternative card" has had varied meanings in the greeting card industry. Originally this phrase was applied to cards that were not supplied by the three major competitors. These cards were often of an innovative design, although aimed at the standard seasons. When these nonstandard designs proved popular with consumers, Hallmark and the other national producers began to produce alternative designs for the standard seasons. Today, nontraditional seasonal cards are commonplace, with the result that the term "alternative" seems to be used principally as a synonym for nonoccasion cards.

EXHIBIT 18.3   Greeting Cards Sales by Card Category 1987

	Percent
Seasonal Sales	
Christmas	31.5
Valentine's Day	12.2
Easter	2.6
Mother's Day	2.1
Father's Day	1.3
Graduation	1.2
All Other Seasonal	1.8
(In decreasing sales order): Thanksgiving, Halloween, St. Patrick's Day, Jewish New Year, Hanukkah, New Year's, Grandparent's Day, Sweetest Day, Secretary's Day, National Boss' Day, Mother-in-Law Day, April Fool's Day	
Nonseasonal Sales	
Birthday	22.9
Alternative and/or Nonoccasion	24.3
(Not in sales order): Birth, Wedding, Sympathy, Retirement, Congratulations, New Home, Friendship, Love	

Source: Greeting Card Association, Washington, D.C.

The Black or Afro-American Segment

As competition increased and market growth slowed, product strategies of the "majors" began to emphasize segmentation. Social expression merchandise targeted at minorities was offered to those traditional outlets that had minority bases from which to draw. A black American, or other minority, has had a difficult time choosing a greeting card, or other social expression merchandise, suitable to his or her particular culture. The black population of the United States numbers about 12 percent of the total, and by the year 2080 is expected to account for almost one in five Americans. In 1986, blacks spent about $360 million for greeting cards. By 1988, Afro-Americans' expenditures on greeting cards and other social awareness merchandise approached $600 million.

In 1986, 64 percent of the black population was under the age of 35, and 27 percent of all blacks were under 15 years of age. Thus, a large number of blacks would shortly enter the prime card-buying years of 35 to 54. In general, black buying patterns differed somewhat from those of white Americans. Blacks tended to be more brand loyal, and often prefer to patronize black-owned businesses. Blacks tended to make less than whites in comparable jobs and have lower savings rates than whites. However, there were a growing number of "Buppies" (black urban professionals). Career patterns of Buppies mirrored those of Yuppies, with increased mobility and greater need to communicate with family and friends left behind.

Industry Competition

Exhibit 18.4 illustrates greeting card market shares. Three competitors, Hallmark Cards, American Greeting Cards, and Gibson Greetings, controlled 87 percent of the market. As many as 500 publishers vied for the remainder.

Hallmark Cards.   Privately owned, Hallmark distributed its products principally through 22,000 specialty retail outlets, most of which were privately owned. Hallmark also used selected department stores for distribution. Hallmark was a fully integrated producer, and was reputed to have the most efficient production facilities. Hallmark's advantages were its size and financial strength, its efficient distribution system, its quality image and "recognition" factor, and its licensed characters—Shirt Tale line, Rose Petal Place, Huge Bunch, and Rainbow Bright.

Hallmark's unique distribution could be a potential weakness. Recent studies showed that mass merchandisers and chain food and drug stores accounted for about 53 percent of retail greeting card sales. This trend was expected to continue, given the societal changes of single-parent families, dual-career families, and the popularity of one-stop shopping. Another potential weakness was the inability to produce in-house an authentic ethnic greeting card, although the company obviously had the financial resources to acquire this capability.

Hallmark's principal approach to serving the ethnic market segments was via a "minority vendor resource list," provided to their stores. These were vendors who had met certain minimum quality standards. Shades of Black submitted several designs to Hallmark for evaluation. Hallmark's reaction so far had been that Shades of Black's designs had a nice style; several had been picked for a test market that had not yet been completed. Two concerns were expressed by Hallmark. First, Hallmark was hesitant to include Shades of Black on the vendor list because of the uncertainty about Shades of Black's ability to service any quantity of orders. Second, although acknowledging that Shades of Black's designs were of high quality for a company of its size, they were not yet at a level which Hallmark sets for products included on their vendor lists.

EXHIBIT 18.4   Competitive Market Shares, 1987

Hallmark	40%
American Greetings	35
Gibson	12
All Others	13

American Greeting Cards.   American Greetings was the world's largest publicly owned manufacturer of greeting cards and social-expression merchandise. Since 1975, American Greetings was an aggressive competitor, with a marketing strategy designed to outflank Hallmark. Their primary weapon was inexpensive cards distributed through mass merchandise outlets. American Greetings cards were carried by more than 90,000 retailers worldwide. Thirty-five percent of their sales were through drug stores and, in decreasing order of importance, mass merchandisers, supermarkets, stationery and gift shops, military post exchanges, and department stores. American Greetings initiated the practice of developing licensed characters. Its characters included Holly Hobbie, Ziggy, Strawberry Shortcake, and Care Bears.

Gibson Greetings.   Gibson was the fastest growing of the three major competitors, although quite obviously the base was much smaller. Their principal distribution channels were (in decreasing order of importance) mass merchandisers, drug stores, and supermarkets. Gibson was very aggressive in licensing characters. The company had exclusive rights to the Walt Disney characters, and licensed Garfield,[3] the Sesame Street characters, and the Looney Tunes and D.C. Comics comic book creations. Gibson moved aggressively into the ethnic market with licensing arrangements. One result was a line of cards directed toward the black market. Licensed from Cousin Mattie's Daddy's Sister's People in Oakland, California, "Cousin Mattie's" cards featured "soft sculpture characters" of black folksy people set in humorous domestic scenes of yesteryear. Begun in 1984, Cousin Mattie's was distributed in about 350 retail outlets prior to its agreement with Gibson. Gibson was expected to distribute Cousin Mattie cards in more than 1,200 of its regular outlets.

Other Competitors   An important competitor in the black segment was L'Image Graphics of Culver City, California. This six-year-old, privately held company's investors included Sidney Poitier, and Don Clark and Barry Gordy of Motown Records. As of July 1988, L'Image cards were carried in 1,500 retail outlets in the United States, Canada, Puerto Rico, and England. About 50 sales representatives carried its line in the United States. L'Image had over 225 designs, generally of a "fantasy-oriented" contemporary image. Originally sold in exclusive, top-of-the-line department stores, which have a clientele that is over 90 percent white, L'Image created "cross-over" designs by using tan (rather than white or black) characters. This middle-of-the-road approach created a company whose sales doubled each of the past four years.

Over 20 black-owned and operated greeting card companies were reputed to exist in the United States. These were all small, regional in scope, and lacked financial and production resources to be major players in the market for black customers.

---

[3] Beginning January 1989 Hallmark became the Garfield licensee. Major in-store promotions were planned around the Garfield character.

SHADES OF BLACK HISTORY

In late 1986, Alex Corbbrey sketched a black Santa Claus and one other greeting card that he had printed and then sent to a few friends. Soon afterward, inquiries were received concerning the possibility of purchasing these cards. During the first Christmas season in operation, over 4,000 cards were sold. Alex Corbbrey had a varied and rich background, as his artist's vita (Exhibit 18.5) illustrates. Shades of Black was located in Tulsa, Oklahoma, with a small retail store and headquarters (total 718 square feet) in one building, and a moderate amount of warehouse space in another facility. In addition to the founder, Shades of Black employed two full-time and one part-time person. Important professional and managerial input was provided by the board of directors, including legal and accounting help.

MARKETING

Product

All designs produced were the inspiration of the founder, although several were "farmed out" to contract artists for completion after initial sketches were developed. In 1992, five contract artists were working on new designs. Shades of Black produced 27 copyrighted designs, equally divided between seasonal and alternative cards. Design examples are contained in Exhibit 18.6. One of its best-selling cards was one that celebrates "Kwanza," an African harvest festival that occurs near the Christmas season. Kwanza card sales were concentrated on the East Coast; the celebration is largely unknown in many other U.S. cities with large black populations.

Production was provided by four different printers in Oklahoma and Kansas. Only fine linen paper was used, and the print quality was excellent. As an artist, Alex Corbbrey prided himself on the quality of product produced by Shades of Black.

Other items sold by Shades of Black in 1988 included original art work, framed copies of the cards, and apparel.

Distribution

Shades of Black used independent distributors to service its markets. Distributorships were originally sold by Alex at the fall 1987 National Black Caucus, held in Washington, D.C. Despite having a display of only seven designs, three distributorships were sold at that time. Distributorships cost $125, which included up to $75 of product. Through fiscal 1988, 35 distributorships were sold. A list of distributors and their sales activity is shown in Exhibit 18.7. Distributorships were no longer being offered as Shades of Black reevaluated its distribution policies. However, all current distributorship agreements would be honored.

EXHIBIT 18.5   About Alex Corbbrey

Mr. Alex A. Corbbrey, founder of Shades of Black, took his formal training in art at Oklahoma State University at Stillwater and Chinourd Art Institute in Los Angeles, California.

Upon completing his academic training, Mr. Corbbrey, seeking employment as an Illustrator with I. Magnin's, an exclusive department store in the Los Angeles area, found himself instead working as a buyer trainee in retail. Having had virtually no college experience in marketing, Mr. Corbbrey returned to college, studying retail marketing, accounting, statistics, and business law.

During his five years with I. Magnin's, three years as assistant buyer and two years as buyer for the southern district which included seven stores throughout southern California, Mr. Corbbrey decided to apply his marketing experience to the business of art.

Realism, expressed through such media as oils, water-colors, acrylics, pastels, and pen and inks, was the focus of his creative interest during this period. His work drew wide attention from many people in the entertainment industry, some of whom had become his personal customers at I. Magnin. During the years 1966 to 1968, he was exhibited in private showings throughout southern California. In 1973, Mr. Corbbrey was commissioned to do several portraits of prominent citizens in the Los Angeles area, including Mayor Thomas Bradley.

After much success in the more traditional media, Mr. Corbbrey became fascinated with the possibilities of engraving. He experimented with many different types of materials, finally narrowing his efforts to wood and plexiglass. The detail expressed in his wood and drypoint engravings attracted the attention of collectors across the United States. One of his limited edition prints entitled "Call to Arms" hangs in the White House. He has displayed his work in such respected galleries as Jim Settle's Art Galleries in southern California and Scottsdale, Arizona; Variations of Palm Springs, L'Academie, Southern Cost Village, Costa Mesa, California; Old House Gallery, Orange, California; and several other galleries throughout the greater Southwest.

Since returning to Tulsa, Oklahoma, in 1978, Mr. Corbbrey has added to his fine list of credits such galleries as Fields Art Gallery, The Art Market, Up Against the Wall Graphics, and Accessory Street Gallery, Houston, Texas. His wild life studies won a first place Blue Ribbon in the 1978 Ducks Unlimited Art Show in Tulsa. However, his study of the late Mrs. Freddie Martin Rudisill on display at the Rudisill North Regional Library is one of his proudest achievements. An 8' x 10' sculpting by Mr. Corbbrey is also prominently displayed at Westview Medical Clinic of Tulsa, Oklahoma.

With such an impressive list of collectors as Dick van Dyke, actor and producer; H. B. "Toby" Haliciki, director, producer, and star of "Gone in Sixty Seconds"; Greg Morris of *Mission Impossible* and *Vegas* fame; Stevie Wonder, Diana Ross, and Nancy Laviska of Motown Recording Industries, Tulsa is proud to call Alex A. Corbbrey a native son.

EXHIBIT 18.6   Shades of Black Cards

The Kwanza Card

The Card That Started It All:
The Black Santa Claus

Kwanza Principles
There are Seven Principles (Nguzo Saba) that apply to the seven days of Kwanza. Each day one principle is observed. Drawn from the basic value system of African people, they are: Umoja (Unity), Kujichagulia (Self-determination), Ujima (Collective Work and Responsibility), Ujamaa (Cooperative Economics), Nia (Purpose), Kuumba (Creativity), and Imani (Faith).

*"Let us take time,
To reflect upon our growth,
Throughout the year."*

In Celebration of KWANZA

*May the
Christmas Spirit
remain
within your
Hearts
throughout
the
New Year*

Price

In 1992, the trade discount given by Shades of Black to its current distributors was two-thirds (66.7 percent). Thus, for a $1.25 retail card, Shades of Black receives 42 cents. Product was shipped UPS, cash on delivery. Sales to nonprofit organizations were conducted at a 50 percent discount from suggested retail price. The package of cards and stationery for Morehouse College were to

EXHIBIT 18.7   Unit Sales by Distributor

Name	Location	Date Registered	Sales 1987	Sales 1988
Ace	Missouri City, TX	11/87	$580	$1,480
Allen	Shawnee, OK	11/88	-	170
Atloms	Ferndale, MI	11/87	1,980	0
Burk	Broken Arrow, OK	02/88	-	430
Cassett	Somerset, NJ	09/88	-	0
Colbert	College Park, GA	10/87	970	0
Copeland	Hyattsville, MD	09/87	4,435	9,530
Curry	Tulsa, OK	12/87	0	525
Davis	Birmingham, AL	12/87	0	0
Evans	Tulsa, OK	02/88	-	320
Exciting Cards	Ft. Lauderdale, FL	10/87	500	0
Floral Crest	Omaha, NE	11/88	-	170
Ford	Tulsa, OK	11/87	1,800	200[a]
Francis	Jacksonville, FL	11/88	-	0
GSD Distributors	Cushing, OK	03/87	600	0
Hall	Morene Valley, CA	09/88	-	1,422[a]
Harriott	Huntsville, SC	08/87	300	0
Holman	Tulsa, OK	12/87	60	0
J & L Enterprise	Tulsa, OK	03/88	0	0[b]
Johnson, A.	E. Elmhurst, NY	12/87	664	2,470
Johnson, E.	Tulsa, OK	02/88	-	0
Joshua Enterprise	Nashville, TN	09/88	-	750[a]
LaCour	Tulsa, OK	03/87	260	0
Marshall	Austin, TX	09/87	300	0
Martin	Philadelphia, PA	09/88	-	4,960[a]
Mayo	Chicago, IL	10/87	360	0
Morans	Houston, TX	10/88	-	480[a]
Perkins	Baton Rouge, LA	10/87	300	0
RLWD Distributors	Dallas, TX	10/88	-	370
SB Marketing	Tulsa, OK	09/88	-	774
Simmons	Severna Park, MD	10/87	1,570	980
Smith	Chicago, IL	10/88	-	750
Unique Collect	Wheaton, IL	11/88	-	112[a]
Washington	Cushing, OK	11/87	560	1,115
Weathers	Kansas City, MO	10/88	-	1,180
Total Units Sold			$15,239	$28,188

[a]Purchased apparel
[b]Purchased letterhead

be sold for $4.20, and carried a "list price" of $20.00. The package price to funeral homes was $13.95 per unit. All prices to organizations were FOB Tulsa (the organization paid shipping). Shipments under 70 pounds went UPS unless the customer specified otherwise. Orders exceeding the UPS weight limit were shipped by truck.

In 1992, Shades of Black's average manufacturing cost of an existing black and white card was 7 cents. Economies of scale were important in the industry. Hallmark probably produced the typical $1.25 retail care for 3 cents. New designs were expensive. For Shades of Black, an initial production run of 5,000 units for a new design would cost 35 cents per unit, which included all initial set-up costs.

Promotion

Other than attendance at several trade shows, Shades of Black generated little in the way of paid promotional activities. Publicity was received in Tulsa and Oklahoma newspapers, and Sylvia Porter planned a feature in a forthcoming issue of her national publication, *Personal Finance*.

PRODUCT/MARKET EXPANSION OPPORTUNITIES

Enhanced Distribution

Primary targets were food and drug chains in the more heavily populated black cities and states. Contacts were made with the Food Lion chain (North and South Carolina and Virginia), Tom Thumb stores, Homeland supermarkets (Oklahoma), Giant Food Stores, Kroger, and Peoples' Drug Stores. As an example of requirements for these outlets, Food Lion required a one-time "slotting fee" of $240 per card rack, which would initially be stocked with 1,008 cards—84 seasonal and alternative designs. Smaller end aisle and counter display racks were possibilities. Production costs for the racks ranged from $20 to $300 apiece; slotting fees for end aisle and counter displays were negotiable. Based on talks with chain drug and supermarket executives, Alex believed that Shades of Black could have access to 325 stores by the 1989 Christmas season. The number of supermarkets and drugstores carrying Shades of Black cards would then be expected to double in 1990, and to increase another 10 percent in the third year of this market expansion strategy.

The Military Market

Black men and women comprised over 27 percent of the armed forces. Distribution by service is shown in Exhibit 18.8. Although blacks accounted for 12 percent of the U.S. population, only 8.8 percent of the American college population was black, and the number of black high school graduates continuing on to college was actually decreasing. Thus, black enlistment in the military was expected to continue to be high. If black military personnel would purchase cards at the national "average" rate of approximately 35 cards per year, military sales would exceed 40 million units. The Army and Air Force Exchange Service (AAFES) operated nearly 6,000 retail facilities on military installations worldwide, with annual sales in 1986 exceeding $6.2 billion. AAFES bought goods and

EXHIBIT 18.8   Blacks in the Armed Forces, 1987

Branch of Service	Total Active Duty	Number of Blacks
Army	781,000	305,698
Air Force	608,000	132,388
Navy	581,000	104,804
Marines	199,000	51,876

Source: *Statistical Abstract of the United States,* 1987

services from about 40,000 U.S. producers, 88 percent of which were classified as small businesses. Card racks available in AAFES facilities were identical to those in the U.S. chain stores; however, no slotting fees were charged. The three-year goal was to obtain distribution in 10 percent of the AAFES outlets.

Black Colleges

One hundred twenty-nine predominantly black colleges existed in the United States, with total enrollment approaching 175,000 students. A list of the 17 largest is contained in Exhibit 18.9. In 1992, Shades of Black had a contract with Morehouse College in Atlanta for its cards and was preparing a special "packet" for that school. Negotiations were under way for a similar display and material with Spelman College in Atlanta. Several other predominantly black colleges were located in Atlanta; black college and university population was about 17,000 in the city.

EXHIBIT 18.9   Largest Predominantly Black Colleges and Universities

School	Location	Enrollment
University of D.C.	Washington, D.C.	14,107
Howard University	Washington, D.C.	11,650
Southern University & A&M College	Baton Rouge, LA	9,177
Tennessee State University	Nashville, TN	8,556
Norfolk State University	Norfolk, VA	7,400
Jackson State University	Jackson, MS	6,900
North Carolina A&T State University	Greensboro, NC	5,200
North Carolina Central University	Durham, NC	5,000
Grambling State University	Grambling, LA	4,775
Alabama State University	Montgomery, AL	4,044
Fort Valley State College	Ft. Valley, GA	3,970
Tuskegee Institute	Tuskegee, AL	3,768
Hampton Institute	Hampton, VA	3,200
Virginia State University	Petersburg, VA	3,000
Spelman College	Atlanta, GA	3,000
Morehouse College	Atlanta, GA	3,000
University of Arkansas	Pine Bluff, AR	3,000

The Shades of Black product program for Morehouse was to develop a packet of cards and stationery displaying the college seal, a sketch of a campus landmark or of a famous alum, or a collage of unique school features. These items would be marketed not only to current students, but perhaps more importantly, would be targeted at graduates and for use by the alumni association, which could use the packets for fund raising. Similar materials could be developed for other predominantly black colleges. The sales goal was to place materials in 25 percent of these outlets by Spring 1990, and to achieve 75 percent penetration by the third year. In terms of the special college packets, designs would be prepared for a minimum order of 100 units.

The Funeral Home Program

As mentioned previously black-owned funeral homes existed in the United States. In 1992, there were no stationery-type products specifically tailored to the grieving black family. Shades of Black intended to fill this need by marketing via a direct mail campaign a package of products that the funeral homes would then resell to their customers. This package would contain a registration book, acknowledgment cards, things to remember booklets, and so on.

Initial informal reaction from the funeral home trade was very encouraging. Letters of endorsement were received from the National Funeral Directors and Morticians Association and from the State Embalmers and Funeral Directors of Oklahoma. Sales projections were to achieve distribution in 10 percent of this market by the end of the year, with a minimum order of 25 units per customer.

ADDITIONAL CONCERNS

Alex realized that these somewhat grandiose ambitions were dependent on raising additional capital. He received a $16,300 development loan from the Tulsa Economic Development Authority, and a private investor added $10,000. One of his pressing problems was to prepare a business plan that would be submitted to venture capitalists. Another problem he continually wrestled with was the hiring of competent people. It seemed that he personally was required to handle every problem whether it was in design, production, or sales. Finally, another matter that began to assume prominence was the possibility of moving the company headquarters to Atlanta. Retail sales in Tulsa had been much less than expected. On his visits to Atlanta he was very impressed with the vitality of Atlanta's black community and with the large number of black entrepreneurs, who were rare in Oklahoma. Alex had recently obtained a list of those areas in the United States with the largest number of black-owned businesses (Exhibit 18.10).

But the most immediate matter was to determine in what market segments his young company could most profitably compete.

EXHIBIT 18.10   Metropolitan Areas with the Largest Number of Black-Owned Businesses

Area	Number of Businesses
Los Angeles/Long Beach	23,520
New York	20,242
Washington	18,805
Chicago	13,660
Houston	12,206
San Francisco	9,388
Detroit	8,731
Philadelphia	8,581
Dallas	7,825
Atlanta	7,077

Source: *Statistical Abstract of the United States,* 1988.

—————————————— CASE 19 ——————————————

TenderCare Disposable Diapers

Tom Cagan watched as his secretary poured six ounces of water onto each of the two disposable diapers laying on his desk. The diaper on the left was a new, improved Pampers, introduced in the summer of 1985 by Procter & Gamble. The new, improved design was supposed to be drier than the preceding Pampers. It was the most recent development in a sequence of designs that traced back to the original Pampers, introduced to the market in 1965. The diaper on his right was a TenderCare diaper, manufactured by a potential supplier for testing and approval by Cagan's company, Rocky Mountain Medical Corporation (RMM). The outward appearance of both diapers was identical.

This case was prepared by James E. Nelson as a basis for class discussion rather than to illustrate either effective or ineffective handling of an administrative situation. Copyright © 1986 by the Business Research Division, College of Business and Administration and the Graduate School of Business Administration, University of Colorado, Boulder, Colorado. Used with permission from James E. Nelson.

Yet the TenderCare diaper was different. Just under its liner (the surface next to the baby's skin) was a wicking fabric that drew moisture from the surface around a soft, waterproof shield to an absorbent reservoir of filler. Pampers and all other disposable diapers on the market kept moisture nearer to the liner and, consequently, the baby's skin. A patent attorney had examined the TenderCare design, concluding that the wicking fabric and shield arrangement should be granted a patent. However, it would be many months before results of the patent application process would be known.

As soon as the empty beakers were placed back on the desk, Cagan and his secretary touched the liners of both diapers. They agreed that there was no noticeable difference, and Cagan noted the time. They repeated their touch test after one minute and again noted no difference. However, after two minutes, both thought the TenderCare diaper to be drier. At three minutes, they were certain. By five minutes, the TenderCare diaper surface seemed almost dry to the touch, even when a finger was pressed deep into the diaper. In contrast, the Pampers diaper showed little improvement in dryness from three to five minutes and tended to produce a puddle when pressed.

These results were not unexpected. Over the past three months, Cagan and other RMM executives had compared TenderCare's performance with 10 brands of disposable diapers available in the Denver market. TenderCare diapers had always felt drier within a two-to four-minute interval after wetting. However, these results were considered tentative because all tests had used TenderCare diapers, hand-made by RMM personnel. Today's test was the first made with diapers produced by a supplier under mass manufacturing conditions.

ROCKY MOUNTAIN MEDICAL CORPORATION

RMM was incorporated in Denver, Colorado, in late 1982 by Robert Morrison, a pediatrician. Sales had grown from about $400,000 in 1983 to $2.4 million in 1984 and were expected to reach $3.4 million in 1985. The firm would show a small profit for 1985, as it had each previous year.

Management personnel as of September 1985 included six executives. Cagan served as president and director, positions he had held since joining RMM in April 1984. Prior to that time he had worked for several high-technology companies in the areas of product design and development, production management, sales management, and general management. His undergraduate studies were in engineering and psychology; he earned an MBA in 1981. Dr. Morrison currently served as chairman of the board and vice president for research and development. He had completed his M.D. in 1976 and was board certified to practice pediatrics in the State of Colorado in 1978. John Bosch served as vice president of manufacturing, a position he held since joining the firm in late 1983. Lawrence Bennett, vice president of marketing, had primary responsibilities for marketing Tender-Care and RMM's two lines of phototherapy products since he joined the firm in

1984. Bennett's background included an MBA received in 1981 and three years' experience in grocery product management at General Mills. Two other executives, both of whom joined RMM in 1984, served as vice president of personnel and as controller.

Phototherapy Products

RMM's two lines of phototherapy products were used to treat infant jaundice, a condition experienced by some 5 to 10 percent of all newborn babies. One line was marketed to hospitals under the trademark Alpha-Lite. Bennett felt that the Alpha-Lite phototherapy unit was superior to competing products because it gave the baby 360-degree exposure to the therapeutic light. Competing products gave less than complete exposure, with the result that the Alpha-Lite unit treated more severe cases and produced quicker recoveries. Apart from the Alpha-Lite unit itself, the hospital line of phototherapy products included a light meter, a photo-mask that protected the baby's eyes while undergoing treatment, and a "baby bikini" that diapered the baby and yet facilitated exposure to the light.

The home phototherapy line of products was marketed under the trademark Baby-Lite.™ The phototherapy unit was portable, weighing about 40 pounds, and was foldable for easy transport. The assembled unit was 33 inches long, 20 inches wide, and 24 inches high (see Exhibit 19.1) The line also included photomasks, a thermometer, and a short booklet telling parents about home phototherapy. Parents could rent the unit and purchase related products from a local pharmacy or durable medical equipment dealer for about $75 per day. This was considerably less than the cost of hospital treatment. Another company, Acquitron, had entered the home phototherapy market in early 1985 and was expected to offer stiff competition. A third competitor was rumored to be entering the market in 1986.

Bennett's responsibilities for all phototherapy products included developing marketing plans and making final decisions about product design, promotion, pricing, and distribution. He directly supervised two product managers, one responsible for Alpha-Lite and the other for Baby-Lite. He occasionally made sales calls with the product managers, visiting hospitals, health maintenance organizations, and insurers.

TenderCare Marketing

Most of Bennett's time was spent on TenderCare. Bennett recognized that TenderCare would be marketed much differently from the phototherapy products. TenderCare would be sold to wholesalers, which in turn would sell to supermarkets, drugstores, and mass merchandisers. TenderCare would compete either directly or indirectly with two giant consumer goods manufacturers, Procter & Gamble and Kimberly-Clark. TenderCare represented considerable risk to RMM.

Because of the uncertainty surrounding the marketing of TenderCare, Bennett and Cagan had recently sought the advice of several marketing consultants. They reached formal agreement with one, a Los Angeles consultant named

EXHIBIT 19.1   Print Advertisement for Home Phototherapy Unit.

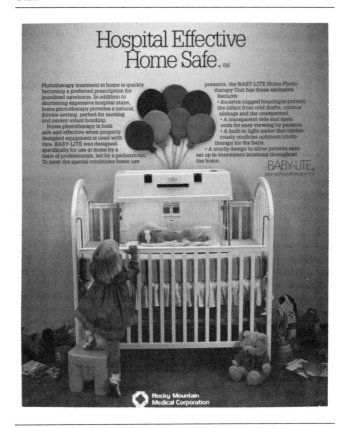

Alan Anderson. Anderson had extensive experience in advertising at J. Walter Thompson. In addition he had been responsible for marketing and sales at Mattel and Teledyne, specifically for the marketing of such products as IntelliVision,™ the Shower Massage,™ and the Water Pik.™ Anderson currently worked as an independent marketing consultant to several firms. His contract with RMM specified that he would devote 25 percent of his time to TenderCare the first year and about 12 percent the following two years. During this time, RMM would hire, train, and place its own marketing personnel. One of these people would be a product manager for TenderCare.

Bennett and Cagan could employ the services of a local marketing consultant who served on RMM's advisory board. The board consisted of 12 business and medical experts who were available to answer questions and provide direction. The consultant had spent over 25 years in marketing consumer products at several large corporations. His specialty was developing and launching new products, particularly health and beauty aids. He had worked closely with RMM in selecting the name TenderCare,™ and had done a great deal of work summarizing market characteristics and analyzing competitors.

MARKET CHARACTERISTICS

The market for babies' disposable diapers could be identified as children, primarily below age three, who use the diapers and their mothers, primarily between ages 18 and 49, who decide on the brand and usually make the purchase. Bennett estimated there were about 11 million such children in 1985, living in about 9 million households. The average number of disposable diapers consumed daily in these households was thought to range from 0 to 15 and to average about 5.

The consumption of disposable diapers is tied closely to birthrates and population. However, two prominent trends influence consumption. One is the disposable diaper's steadily increasing share of total diaper usage by babies. Bennett estimated that disposables would increase their share of total diaper usage from 75 percent currently to 90 percent by 1990. The other trend is toward the purchase of higher-quality disposable diapers. Bennett thought the average retail price of disposable diapers would rise about twice as fast as the price of materials used in their construction. Total dollar sales of disposable diapers at retail in 1985 were expected to be about $3 billion, or about 15 billion units. Growth rates were thought to be about 14 percent per year for dollar sales and about 8 percent for units.

Foreign markets for disposable diapers would add to these figures. Canada, for example, currently consumed about $250 million at retail, with an expected growth rate of 20 percent per year until 1990. The United Kingdom market was about twice the size and growing at the same rate.

The U.S. market for disposable diapers was clearly quite large and growing. However, Bennett felt that domestic growth rates could not be maintained much longer because fewer and fewer consumers were available to switch from cloth to disposable diapers. In fact, by 1995, growth rates for disposable diapers would begin to approach growth rates for births, and unit sales of disposable diapers would become directly proportional to numbers of infants using diapers. A consequence of this pronounced slowing of growth would be increased competition.

Competition

Competition between manufacturers of disposable diapers was already intense. Two well-managed giants—Procter & Gamble and Kimberley-Clark— accounted for about 80 percent of the market in 1984 and 1985. Bennett had estimated market shares at:

	1984	1985
Pampers	32%	28%
Huggies	24	28
Luvs	20	20
Other brands	24	24
	100%	100%

Procter & Gamble was clearly the dominant competitor with its Pampers and Luvs brands. However, Procter & Gamble's market share had been declining, from 70 percent in 1981 to about 50 percent. The company had introduced its thicker Blue Ribbon™ Pampers in an effort to halt the share decline. It had invested over $500 million in new equipment to produce the product. Procter & Gamble spent approximately $40 million to advertise its two brands in 1984. Kimberly-Clark spent about $19 million to advertise Huggies in 1984.

The 24 percent market share held by other brands was up by some 3 percentage points from 1983. Weyerhaeuser and Johnson & Johnson manufactured most of these diapers, supplying private-label brands for Wards, Penneys, Target, Kmart, and other retailers. Generic disposable diapers and private brands were also included here as well as a number of very small, specialized brands that distributed only to local markets. Some of these brands positioned themselves as low-cost alternatives to national brands; others occupied premium ("designer") niches with premium prices. As examples, Universal Converter entered the northern Wisconsin market in 1984 with two brands priced at 78 and 87 percent of Pampers' case price. Riegel Textile Corporation's Cabbage Patch™ diapers illustrated the premium end, with higher prices and attractive print designs. Riegel spent $1 million to introduce Cabbage Patch™ diapers to the market in late 1984.

Additional evidence of the intense competition in the disposable diaper industry was the major change of strategy by Johnson & Johnson in 1981. The company took its own brand off the U.S. market, opting instead to produce private-label diapers for major retailers. The company had held about 8 percent of the national market at the time and decided that this simply was not enough to compete effectively. Johnson & Johnson's disposable diaper was the first to be positioned in the industry as a premium product. Sales at one point totaled about 12 percent of the market but began to fall when Luvs and Huggies (with similar premium features) were introduced. Johnson & Johnson's advertising expenditures for disposable diapers in 1980 were about $8 million. The company still offered its own brand in the international market.

MARKETING STRATEGIES FOR TENDERCARE

Over the past month, Bennett and his consultants had spent considerable time formulating potential marketing strategies for TenderCare. One strategy that already had been discarded was simply licensing the design to another firm. Under a license arrangement, RMM would receive a negotiated royalty based on the licensee's sales of RMM's diaper. However, this strategy was unattractive on several grounds. RMM would have no control over resources devoted to the marketing of TenderCare; the licensee would decide on levels of sales and advertising support, prices, and distribution. The licensee would control advertising content, packaging, and even the choice of brand name. Licensing also meant that RMM would develop little marketing expertise, no image or even awareness among consumers, and no experience in dealing with packaged-goods channels of distribution. The net result would be that RMM would be hitching its future with respect to TenderCare (and any related products) to that of the licensee. Three other strategies seemed more appropriate.

The Diaper Rash Strategy

The first strategy involved positioning the product as an aid in the treatment of diaper rash. Diaper rash is a common ailment, thought to affect most infants at some point in their diapered lives. The affliction usually lasts two to three weeks before being cured. Some infants are more disposed to diaper rash than others; however, the ailment probably affects a majority of babies. The ailment is caused by "a reaction to prolonged contact with urine and feces, retained soaps and topical preparations, and friction and maceration" (Nelson's Text of Pediatrics, 1979, p. 1884). Recommended treatment includes careful washing of the infected area with plain warm water. Treatment also includes the application of protective ointments and powders (sold either by prescription or over the counter).

The diaper rash strategy would target physicians and nurses in either family or general practice and physicians and nurses specializing either in pediatrics or dermatology. Bennett's estimates of the numbers of general or family practitioners in 1985 was approximately 65,000. He thought that about 45,000 pediatricians and dermatologists were practicing in 1985. The numbers of nurses attending all these physicians was estimated at about 290,000. All 400,000 individuals would be the eventual focus of TenderCare marketing efforts. However, the diaper rash strategy would begin (like the other two strategies) where approximately 11 percent of the target market was located—California. Bennett and his consultants agreed that RMM lacked sufficient resources to begin in any larger market. California would provide a good test for TenderCare because the state often set consumption trends for the rest of the U.S. market. California also showed fairly typical levels of competitive activity.

Promotion activities would emphasize either direct mail and free samples or in-office demonstrations to the target market. Mailing lists of most physicians and some nurses in the target market could be purchased at a cost of about $60 per 1,000 names. The cost to print and mail a brochure, cover letter, and return postcard was about $250 per 1,000. To include a single TenderCare disposable diaper would add another $400 per thousand. In-office demonstrations would use registered nurses (employed on a part-time basis) to show TenderCare's superior dryness. The nurses could be quickly trained and compensated on a per-demonstration basis. The typical demonstration would be given to groups of two or three physicians and nurses and would cost RMM about $6. The California market could be used to investigate the relative performance of direct mail versus demonstrations. RMM would also advertise in trade journals such as the *Journal of Family Practice, Journal of Pediatrics, Pediatrics,* and *Pediatrics Digest.* However, a problem with such advertisements was waste coverage because none of the trade journals published regional editions. A half-page advertisement (one insertion) would cost about $1,000 for each journal. This cost would be reduced to about $700 if RMM placed several advertisements in the same journal during a one-year period. RMM would also promote TenderCare at local and state medical conventions in California. Costs per convention were thought to be about $3,000. The entire promotion budget as well as amounts allocated to direct mail, free samples, advertisements, and medical conventions had yet to be decided.

Prices were planned to produce a retail price per package of 12 TenderCare diapers at around $3.80. This was some 8 to 10 percent higher than the price for a package of 18 Huggies or Luvs. Bennett thought that consumers would pay the premium price because of TenderCare's position: the pennies-per-day differential simply would not matter if a physician prescribed or recommended TenderCare as part of a treatment for diaper rash. "Besides," he noted, "in-store shelf placement of TenderCare under this strategy would be among diaper rash products, not with standard diapers. This will make price comparisons by consumers even more unlikely." The $3.80 package price for 12 TenderCare diapers would produce a contribution margin for RMM of about 9 cents per diaper. It would give retailers a per-diaper margin some 30 percent higher than that for Huggies or Luvs.

The Special-Occasions Strategy

The second strategy centered on a "special-occasions" position that emphasized TenderCare's use in situations where changing the baby would be difficult. One such situation was whenever diapered infants traveled for any length of time. Another occurred daily at some 10,000 day-care centers that accepted infants wearing diapers. Yet another came every evening in each of the 9 million market households when babies were diapered at bedtime.

The special-occasions strategy would target mothers in these 9 million households. Initially, of course, the target would be only the estimated 1 million mothers living in California. Promotion would aim particularly at first-time mothers, using such magazines as *American Baby* and *Baby Talk.* Per-issue insertion costs for one full-color, half-page advertisement in such magazines would average about $20,000. However, most baby magazines published regional editions where single insertion costs averaged about half that amount. Black-and-white advertisements could also be considered; their costs would be about 75 percent of the full-color rates. Inserting several ads per year in the same magazine would allow quantity discounts and reduce the average insertion cost by about one-third.

Lately Bennett had begun to wonder if direct mail promotion could instead be used to reach mothers of recently born babies. Mailing lists of some 1 to 3 million names could be obtained at a cost of around $50 per 1,000. Other costs to produce and mail promotional material would be the same as those for physicians and nurses. ''I suppose the real issue is just how much more effective is direct mail over advertising. We'd spend at least $250,000 in baby magazines to cover California while the cost of direct mail would probably be between $300,000 and $700,000, depending on whether or not we gave away a diaper.'' Regardless of Bennett's decision on consumer promotion, he knew RMM would also direct some promotion activities toward physicians and nurses as part of the special-occasions strategy. Budget details were yet to be worked out.

Distribution under the special-occasions strategy would have TenderCare stocked on store shelves along with competing diapers. Still at issue was whether the package should contain 12 or 18 diapers (like Huggies and Luvs) and how much of a premium price TenderCare could command. Bennett considered the packaging and pricing decisions interrelated. A package of 12 TenderCare diapers with per-unit retail prices some 40 percent higher than Huggies or Luvs might work just fine. Such a packaging/pricing strategy would produce a contribution margin to RMM of about 6 cents per diaper. However, the same pricing strategy for a package of 18 diapers probably would not work. ''Still,'' he thought, ''good things often come in small packages, and most mothers probably associate higher quality with higher price. One thing is for sure—whichever way we go, we'll need a superior package.'' Physical dimensions for a TenderCare package of either 12 or 18 diapers could be made similar to the size of the Huggies or Luvs package of 18.

The Head-On Strategy

The third strategy under consideration met major competitors in a direct, frontal attack. The strategy would position TenderCare as a noticeably drier diaper that any mother would prefer to use anytime her baby needed changing. Promotion activities would stress mass advertising to mothers using television and magazines. At least two magazines would include a dollar-off coupon to stimulate trial of a package of TenderCare diapers during the product's first three months on the market. Some in-store demonstrations to mothers using touch tests might also be employed. Although no budget for California had yet been set, Bennett thought the allocation would be roughly 60 / 30 / 10 for television, magazines, and other promotion activities, respectively.

Pricing under this strategy would be competitive with Luvs and Huggies, with the per-diaper price for TenderCare expected to be some 9 percent higher at retail. This differential was needed to cover additional manufacturing costs associated with TenderCare's design. TenderCare's package could contain only 16 diapers and show a lower price than either Huggies or Luvs with their 18-count packages. Alternatively, the package could contain 18 diapers and carry the 9 percent higher price. Bennett wondered if he really wasn't putting too fine a point on the pricing/packaging relationship. "After all," he had said to Anderson, "we've no assurance that retailers or wholesalers would pass along *any* price advantage TenderCare might have due to a smaller package. Either one or both might instead price TenderCare near the package price for our competitors and simply pocket the increased margin!" The only thing that was reasonably certain was TenderCare's package price to the wholesaler. That price was planned to produce about a 3-cent contribution margin to RMM per diaper, regardless of package count.

Summary of the Three Strategies

When viewed together, the three strategies seemed so complex and so diverse as to defy analysis. The problem was partly one of developing criteria against which the strategies could be compared. Risk was obviously one such criterion, so were company fit and competitive reaction. However, Bennett felt that some additional thought on his part would produce more criteria against which the strategies could be compared. He hoped this effort would produce no more strategies; three were plenty.

The other part of the problem was simply uncertainty. Strengths, weaknesses, and implications of each strategy had yet to be given much thought. Moreover, each strategy seemed likely to have associated with it some surprises. An example illustrating the problem was the recent realization that the Food and Drug Administration (FDA) must approve any direct claims RMM might make about TenderCare's efficacy in treating diaper rash. The chance of receiving this federal agency's approval was thought to be reasonably high; yet it was unclear just what sort of testing and what results were needed. The worst-case scenario would have the FDA requiring lengthy customer tests that would eventually produce inconclusive results. The best case would have the FDA giving permission based on TenderCare's superior dryness and on results of a small-scale field test recently completed by Dr. Morrison. It would probably be a month before the FDA's position could be known.

"The delay was unfortunate—and unnecessary," Bennett thought, "especially if we eventually settle on either of the other two strategies." In fact, FDA approval was not even needed for the diaper rash strategy if RMM simply claimed that TenderCare diapers were drier than competing diapers and that dryness helps treat diaper rash. Still, a single-statement, direct-claim position was thought to be more effective with mothers and more difficult to copy by any other manufacturer. And yet Bennett did want to move quickly on TenderCare. Every month of delay meant deferred revenue and other postponed benefits that would derive from a successful introduction. Delay also meant the chance that an existing (or other) competitor might develop its own drier diaper and effectively block RMM from reaping the fruits of its development efforts. Speed was of the essence.

FINANCIAL IMPLICATIONS

Bennett recognized that each marketing strategy held immediate as well as long-term financial implications. He was particularly concerned with finance requirements for start-up costs associated with the California entry. Cagan and the other RMM executives had agreed that a stock issue represented the best option to meet these requirements. Accordingly, RMM had begun preparation for a sale of common stock through a brokerage firm that would underwrite and market the issue. Management at the firm felt that RMM could generate between $1 and $3 million, depending on the offering price per share and the number of shares issued.

Proceeds from the sale of stock had to be sufficient to fund the California entry and leave a comfortable margin remaining for contingencies. Proceeds would be used for marketing and other operating expenses as well as for investments in cash, inventory, and accounts receivable. It was hoped that TenderCare would generate a profit by the end of the fiscal year in the California market and show a strong contribution to the bottom line thereafter. California profits would contribute to expenses associated with entering additional markets and to the success of any additional stock offerings.

Operating profits and proceeds from the sale of equity would fund additional R&D activities that would extend RMM's diaper technology to other markets. Dr. Morrison and Bennett saw almost immediate application of the technology to the adult incontinent diaper market, currently estimated at about $300 million per year at retail. Underpads for beds constitute at least another $50 million annual market. However, both of these uses were greatly dwarfed by another application, the sanitary napkin market. Finally, the technology could almost certainly be applied to numerous industrial products and processes, many of which promised great potential. All these opportunities made the TenderCare situation that much more crucial to the company. Making a major mistake here would affect the firm for years.

_____ CASE 20 _____

Burroughs Wellcome and AZT

As the bell sounded to signify the opening of the New York Stock Exchange, it was soon drowned by another noise. Five men, chained to a balcony inside the Stock Exchange, were blowing a horn to draw attention to a banner that they held. The banner read: "Sell Wellcome."[1]

One April morning, four young men, nattily attired in business suits, audaciously walked into Burroughs Wellcome's headquarters in North Carolina. They ejected the occupant of an executive office, sealed the door tight, and chained themselves to a radiator. Meanwhile one of their cohorts called the press to describe the break-in.[2]

International terrorists attacking harmless establishments to seek release of their prisoner brothers? No, the above cases were incidents of AIDS activists protesting what they claimed were unfair pricing tactics employed by Burroughs Wellcome for its AIDS drug, azidothymidine (AZT). As charges flew back and forth between AIDS activist groups and the company, it is important to note the background to the events that led to the above-mentioned incidents.

The Pharmaceutical Industry

The major domestic players in the pharmaceutical industry (Standard Industrial Classification two-digit code 28) included Merck, Abbott Labs, American Home Products, Eli Lilly, Johnson & Johnson, Bristol-Myers Squibb, Schering-Plough, and Burroughs Wellcome. The primary competition from outside the United States came from Glaxo Holdings, Hoechst, and Ciba-Geigy. The industry was very competitive with no single company holding a dominant market share position. In 1989, the top four firms accounted for nearly 25 percent of industry sales.

[1] Marilyn Chase, "Burroughs Wellcome Reaps Profits, Outrage from Its AIDS Drug," *Wall Street Journal*, September 15, 1989, pp. A1–A5.

[2] Cynthia Crossen, "AIDS Activist Group Harasses and Provokes to Make Its Point," *Wall Street Journal*, December 7, 1989, pp. A1–A9.

This case was prepared by Ram Subramanian as a basis for class discussion rather than to illustrate either effective or ineffective handling of an administrative situation. The author wishes to thank Kathy Bartlett of Burroughs Wellcome Company. Research assistance was provided by Cindy Hietala and Ron Villenueva. Used with permission from Ram Subramanian.

After an unsuccessful attempt at unrelated diversification during the 1970s and early 1980s, pharmaceutical companies embarked on a strategy to build market share (within the industry) by investing heavily in research and development. The industry spends around 15 percent of sales on R&D, one of the highest among major U.S. industries. Experts believed that R&D spending was essential for effective product differentiation and consequently, for improved economic performance. Past history also indicated that being the first to introduce new drugs resulted in increased profits.

The industry's marketing expenses were around 20 percent of sales. The expenses were mainly for recruiting and training salespeople who visit physicians and hospitals providing information about their company's products. Other marketing expenses included advertising in scientific journals and direct mailing costs.

The industry exhibited annual revenue growth of around 8 percent from 1975 to 1985. Its return on equity (ROE) was consistently higher than other industries during the 1980s.

Several threats emerged for the pharmaceutical industry in recent times, however. Several foreign companies, apart from marketing their products with increased vigor in the United States, formed a large number of joint ventures with U.S. companies to strengthen their competitive position. In addition the government took several steps to reduce the time span of patent protection, presumably to open up the competition. Finally, the increasing popularity of generic drugs also posed a significant threat for the industry.

Historical Background to the Development of AZT

AIDS (acquired immune deficiency syndrome) is caused by a virus called human immunodeficiency virus (HIV). HIV is a retrovirus that has a unique capability that makes it very insidious. A retrovirus is a RNA virus that has a special enzyme. Ordinarily RNA viruses cannot replicate because they do not have DNA. But with the help of its special enzyme, a retrovirus is able to build DNA from its RNA. Sometimes these DNA copies become integrated into the host cells. Because they are similar, the host cell has no way of knowing that these are, in fact, "infected" DNAs manufactured by the retrovirus. Therefore, these foreign DNA also become part of the host cells and cause the disease when they multiply.

In 1964, a Michigan Cancer Foundation researcher first synthesized a compound called AZT as a possible cure for cancer. When tests showed that the compound was not effective as a cancer cure, the research was abandoned and the compound forgotten.

Burroughs Wellcome, a subsidiary of the British-based Wellcome PLC, always encouraged its scientists to find cures for obscure diseases. In 1981, the company resynthesized AZT in its quest for a compound that would be effective against bacterial infection.[3] Meanwhile, one of its chemists, Janet Rideout, was

---

[3] "The Development of Retrovir," Burroughs Wellcome Company Press Release, June 1990.

studying the chemical structure of the HIV virus. The intention was to find a cure for the disease by studying the chemical structure of the disease-causing agent. She found that AZT was similar in structure to the enzyme that the retrovirus needed to replicate inside the host cell. Because AZT was toxic, she felt that it would effectively neutralize the retrovirus and prevent it from multiplying inside the host cell. When Burroughs Wellcome was actively looking for a cure for AIDS, Ms. Rideout suggested AZT.

By late 1984, Burroughs had determined that AZT was effective against some cat-and-mouse retroviruses. Because the company then did not have the facilities for testing AZT on live HIV, it sought the help of the National Cancer Institute (NCI). Sam Broder, a senior researcher at the institute, took an active part in the testing process.

The tests conducted by the NCI and others proved that AZT was effective against HIV. Nineteen AIDS-affected patients were given the drug, and while two dropped out of the program, fifteen showed improvement in their immune system and also noticeably gained weight.[4] Public reports of the results of the early tests were enthusiastically received by the media and the medical community. In some ways, this enthusiasm sowed the seeds for Burroughs Wellcome's subsequent troubles with the drug.

Drug companies had to go through a lengthy period of field testing a drug before seeking approval from the Food and Drug Administration (FDA). After the initial tests by the NCI indicated the potency of the drug, the company established a program of wide-scale field testing. As the news of the drug's efficacy spread across the country, multitudes of AIDS patients begged the company to use them for the testing. The company then was faced with an ethical dilemma.

Drug companies tested drugs in one of two ways. One, called the "placebo trial," tested a drug by using two groups of people. The first group was given the experimental drug being studied, and the second group was given a placebo or a useless pill. The second method of testing was historical trials. In this type of test the drug was given to every patient and the health changes of these patients were compared with untreated patients.

Because of problems associated with intervening variables in historical trials, the scientific community generally preferred placebo trials. This and the fact that the compound tested may turn out to be harmful prompted Burroughs Wellcome to use placebo trials.[5] A great deal of negative publicity resulted from the company's decision. AIDS activists saw the decision as stemming from greed—because the company wanted to use the faster placebo trials instead of historical trials. Also, the company had to give placebos to half the group tested, knowing full well that these patients were likely to die, while those given AZT were likely to live.

[4] Brian O'Reilly, "The Inside Story of the AIDS Drug," *Fortune,* November 5, 1990, pp. 112–129.
[5] "Retrovir Milestones," Burroughs Wellcome Company Press Release, April 1991.

The company elected to proceed with large-scale testing using the placebo method. After testing almost the whole of 1986, the drug was approved by the FDA in March 1987. Before putting it on the market, the company thought long and hard about the drug's price. Finally, AZT was marketed under the brand name Retrovir in the middle of 1987 with a price that effectively cost an AIDS patient $10,000 for a year's supply of the drug.

The company had not bargained for the backlash on its pricing policy. Through various media, AIDS activists voiced their protests and sought the help of the federal government. The principal AIDS activists group was Act-Up (AIDS Coalition to Unleash Power), comprised largely of homosexual middle-class professionals.[6]

Using sophisticated confrontational techniques and a grass-roots approach to activism, Act-Up had considerable influence. In response to the strident protests of AIDS patients led by Act-Up, Burroughs Wellcome lowered the price of AZT in December 1987 by 20 percent so that the annual cost to a patient became $8,000. The company claimed that the price reduction was due to production efficiencies. The price was cut by an additional 20 percent ($6,400 per patient per year) in September 1989 because the drug was shown to benefit a substantially larger group of patients, thereby increasing its market.

Activists' Reasons for the Protests

AZT did not cure AIDS. It, however, prolonged the victim's life by slowing down the effect of the HIV virus.[7] Scientists calculated that with the help of AZT, an AIDS victim's life could be prolonged by as much as five years. When AZT was introduced commercially by Burroughs Wellcome in early 1987 at $10,000 for a year's supply, it was one of the most expensive drugs ever sold. Typically, consumers of pharmaceuticals are not price sensitive, because the cost of medication is covered by health insurance. However, in 1987, with Medicaid not yet authorized to cover the treatment of the disease, most AIDS patients did not have any insurance.

The company's pricing policy outraged AIDS activists, who banded together to voice their protests publicly. There was an underlying sense of urgency in the protesters' actions. The federal government had funded a $20 million program to provide AIDS patients with AZT. The program was due to expire in October 1989, leaving the 7,000 patients in the program to deal with the problem of raising funds in addition to dealing with their illness. Even the subsequent cuts that brought the price of the drug from $10,000 for a year's supply to $6,400 did not mollify AIDS activists. The activists based their protests on two factors that surrounded the introduction of AZT. One fact fueling the indignation of AIDS activists was that Burroughs Wellcome was reaping the profits of a drug that it did not develop. A

---

[6] Crossen, "AIDS Activist Group," p. A1.

[7] John Mills and Henry Masur, "AIDS-Related Infection," *Scientific American*, August 1990, pp. 50–57.

chemical that was originally developed as a cancer cure by a Michigan Cancer Foundation researcher was resurrected by the company based on published reports in 1974 by a West German scientist, W. Ostertag, who demonstrated that AZT was effective in blocking the reproduction of certain kinds of retroviruses.[8] Subsequent research by Burroughs Wellcome researchers confirmed Ostertag's findings, and AZT was developed as a drug that was effective against AIDS. Protesters claimed that the company saved millions of dollars because much of the basic research was already done for it by others. AIDS activists argued that since the drug did not cost nearly as much to develop as drugs normally do, the company's price for the drug indicated its greed and its propensity to exploit ill people. Burroughs Wellcome did not reveal details about costs and profit margins on AZT. However, analysts familiar with the drug industry believed that the company made a 70 to 80 percent gross profit on AZT, which though high, was in tune with average industry profit margins.[9] Drug industry people argued that these high margins were necessary to offset losses from hundreds of drugs that never saw the light of day.

The second reason for the protests was that much of the testing, a significant part of product development costs in the drug industry, was done by outside agencies such as the NCI. Normally, a drug company paid for the testing of its products and these costs were added to the drug's development cost. Protesters argued that the company saved millions of dollars because much of the expensive hospital testing was done by the NCI. These cost savings were not reflected in the drug's prices.

Company's Point of View

Burroughs Wellcome was owned by the London-based Wellcome PLC. Ironically, the company that caught a lot of negative publicity over its pricing policy for AZT was the largest charity in Great Britain, distributing $55 million in 1989 to fund medical libraries and research.[10]

Long known for concentrating its resources on finding cures for obscure diseases and providing an excellent atmosphere for scientific research, the company was totally unprepared for the wave of negative publicity that surrounded AZT. In recent interviews the company explained its rationale behind the pricing of AZT that was meant to pacify the protesters and diffuse the situation.

According to company officials, even though Burroughs Wellcome did not create the chemical AZT, it spent more than six years and a lot of money (the company did not reveal actual figures) taking an abandoned compound and making it a potent drug to treat AIDS. The company performed years of expensive animal testing and also gave away the drug free to 5,000 people at a cost of $10 million as part of an investigational new drug (IND) program prior to obtaining

[8] Chase, "Burroughs Wellcome Reaps Profits," p. A1.

[9] Ibid.

[10] "Retrovir Milestones."

FDA approval to market the drug.[11] To put the company involvement with the drug in perspective, a top executive of Burroughs Wellcome noted that although a project of this size would have taken up 20 percent of Merck's (the industry leader) time, it took 100 percent of Burroughs Wellcome's time.

Once the drug was approved by the FDA, the company had to spend more than $80 million in designing the production process for the compound. Because a drug normally takes a decade from conception to commercial development, a company has a lot of time to design the production process to make the drug at the lowest possible cost. But, in the case of AZT, since things began moving very quickly after the initial tests, the company had less than six months to perfect the production process. Supply of a key ingredient, thymidine, was hard to come by because worldwide demand for the compound, obtained as a side product from the DNA in salmon and herring sperm, was very low. Burroughs Wellcome had to locate companies with the appropriate technology to manufacture large quantities of both natural and synthetic thymidine. These sources, consequently, proved to be very expensive. The high price of AZT was justified, in part, by the expensive manufacturing costs incurred by the seven-month process of converting the raw material into the finished compound.[12] The company claimed that when the production process was streamlined in late 1987, the savings were passed on to the users.

The second reason for the high price of AZT, from the company's point of view, was the uncertainty about the market for the drug. When the drug was initially approved in 1987, the FDA permitted the use of the drug only for terminally ill patients—an estimated 50,000 people. This small market, coupled with the fear that a better drug to combat AIDS could come along anytime (as several companies were working on AIDS drugs) prompted the company to price AZT at $10,000 for a year's supply. The company pointed out that when the FDA subsequently approved the sale of the drug to all people who showed AIDS symptoms, the company cut prices in response to the expanded market. Also, recent medical evidence indicated AZT was effective even at half the normal dosage—effectively reducing the per-patient annual cost to around $3,000.

Did Burroughs Wellcome profit significantly from AZT? Estimated sales of AZT in 1989 were $200 million and $290 million in 1990—between 8 and 12 percent of Wellcome PLC's worldwide sales.[13] Its ROE, at 23.9 percent in 1990, was among the lowest in the drug industry (primarily because it generally chose to pursue the research and development of arcane, rather than, useful drugs). The industry leader in sales, Merck, earned 44 percent ROE and American Home Products (the maker of Anacin) earned 56 percent ROE.[14] To provide a financial

[11] "The Development of Retrovir."

[12] T. E. Haigler, "Testimony Before the House Committee on Energy and Commerce," March 10, 1987.

[13] Christine Gorman, "How Much a Reprieve from AIDS?" *Time*, October 2, 1989, pp. 81–82; "Retrovir Milestones."

[14] O'Reilly, "Inside Story of the AIDS Drug," p. 112.

EXHIBIT 20.1   Selected Financial Data for Firms in the Drug Industry, 1989–1990

Company	Sales (In billions)	Profits (In millions)	Return on Equity (%)
American Home Products	$6.75	1,102.2	55.9
Bristol-Myers Squibb	9.19	747.0	14.7
Burroughs Wellcome	2.40	332.8	23.9
Eli Lilly	4.18	939.5	25.0
Johnson & Johnson	9.76	1,082.0	27.5
Merck	6.55	1,495.4	44.8

Source: *Business Week*, April 13, 1990.

incentive to spur drug manufacturing, the federal government invoked the Orphan Drug Act in 1985, permitting Burroughs Wellcome to manufacture AZT on an exclusive basis for a period of seven years commencing from 1987. Exhibit 20.1 shows selected financial data for an illustrative list of companies.

Government's Role

As the protests against the pricing of AZT continued unabated, the federal government, at first highly supportive of the company, called company executives to Washington to respond to charges of gouging. A House Subcommittee on Health and the Environment conducted a hearing on the drug's pricing policy. Finally, Senator Edward Kennedy's office researched the possibility of nationalizing the drug in an effort to control its prices. Partly in response to these investigations, the company slashed the drug's prices on two occasions. But company officials maintained that changing market conditions, not governmental interference, led to a reduction in AZT's price.

CASE 21

Verbatim Challenges 3M for Market Leadership

A satisfied smile appeared on Bob Falco's face as he was reading the January 19, 1992, issue of *PcWeek*. As manager of branded marketing at Verbatim, he was pleased with the figures he saw in the computer publication. According to figures released by the Santa Clara Consulting Group, 3M had a 15.5 percent share of the floppy disk market, and Verbatim was right behind the market leader with a 15.2 percent share. "We *are* going to be the leader in this market," he though to himself. "But we're more than just a floppy disk manufacturer. With our excellent tape storage products and optical disk technology, we're going to be the leader in the overall computer media market."

COMPANY HISTORY

In 1969, Information Terminals Corporation was formed in Sunnyvale, California, to manufacture computer screens (terminals). In the early days, there was virtually no competition and profits for the company and its distributors were substantial. However, as personal computer use in business expanded rapidly, competitors entered the market and the high costs of producing screens persuaded the company managers to look to more profitable emerging markets and products. Recognizing that the sales potential for magnetic recording materials for personal computers was much larger than that of computer screens, the company began manufacturing 8" floppy disks and changed its name to Verbatim. Research and development concentrated on digital data cassettes and floppy disks. Having the new technology for data storage available during rapid market growth, management was in a position to choose a few key distributors; they refused other potential distributors in order to enhance the profit potential for both Verbatim and its selected distributors.

Attracted by the projected $4 billion market, a number of competitors entered the floppy disk field in the late 1970s and early 1980s and threatened

This case was prepared by Linda E. Swayne, Peter M. Ginter, and Chris M. Tucker as a basis for class discussion rather than to illustrate either effective or ineffective handling of an administrative situation. The authors wish to thank Bob Falco and Carol Hull, Verbatim Corporation, for their assistance. Used with permission from Linda E. Swayne.

Verbatim's dominant position.[1] Competitors such as 3M, Maxwell, Fuji, and Sony all looked for ways to differentiate their products. In the early 1980s, Verbatim was slow to adapt to the increasingly competitive market. "For a number of years Verbatim was making a lot of money and increasing its business—and that hid a lot of sins," said Bob Falco, Verbatim's manager of North American branded marketing. Several distributors began to carry the products of Verbatim's new competitors. These distributors were the very ones that Verbatim had previously refused to supply. When the marketplace continued expanding, many of these distributors in turn refused to deal with Verbatim.

Because of substantial reductions in profits, Verbatim cut 127 U.S. staff positions in November 1984 to reduce costs.[2] At the same time, the company invested more than $40 million in the development of 3.5" diskettes for personal computers under the DataLife label.[3] Leading the demand for higher disk capacities was the rapid expansion in user data bases. Software programs required more storage capacity. Generally, the easier new software programs were to use, the more sophisticated the set of instructions had to be between the software and the computer and the greater the disk capacity. Software programs were becoming available to the general consumer during this time and the popular IBM-PC required higher capacity disks.

The Kodak Era

In 1985, Eastman Kodak acquired Verbatim for $175 million and changed the company's marketing focus, manufacturing methods, and channels of distribution.[4] Kodak had been buying 8", 5.25", and 3.5" disks from Xidex (a competitor of Verbatim) for over a year before the purchase, and Kodak marketed a line of accessories including computer paper, printer stands, and surge suppressors. A new philosophy came to Verbatim with the transfer of ownership to Kodak: Product development was the key to increasing success. Both Kodak- and Verbatim-brand diskettes were available from Verbatim. Although Kodak-brand diskettes were a late entrant to the disk market, the high brand recognition for the Kodak name enabled the company to be a major competitor in the branded market. Mass merchandisers such as discount stores, warehouse clubs, and other retailers were particularly accepting of the Kodak name because of its recognition by consumers.

Sweeping changes occurred in 1987 with the hiring of Mark Welland as Verbatim vice president of North American marketing and sales. Welland, the former national sales and marketing manager for Maxell, recognized that prices for floppy disks were plummeting and concentrated on repositioning the majority of Verbatim's sales from low-priced, nonlabeled disks for the original equipment

[1] "Malcolm Northrup Needs a Flip-flop," *Industry Week*, January 7, 1985, p. 58.
[2] Ibid.
[3] Ibid.
[4] Sue Kapp, "Mechanic for Mending," *Business Marketing*, June 1988, p. 8.

manufacturer (OEM) market to a premium-priced floppy disk manufacturer for the branded market. Ironically, the fact that Verbatim already was a low-cost producer had allowed it to remain in business during the shake-out years in the mid-1980s. Welland wanted not only to be successful in the market, but to be first in the market with new products. Under Welland's direction, all efforts were put into branded items, especially the disks differentiated by a patented Teflon coating. The DataLifePlus brand name was superscripted by "Verbatim—A Kodak Company." The diskette line was extended with the addition of the Bonus brand for the price-sensitive market.

Mitsubishi Takes Over

Announced in March 1990 and completed in May 1990, Kodak sold Verbatim to Mitsubishi Kasei, the chemical division of the $9 billion Japanese conglomerate. Industry experts believed the undisclosed price to be $240 million, $65 million more than Eastman Kodak paid for Verbatim in 1985.[5]

A year before acquiring Verbatim, Mitsubishi had started manufacturing 3.5" disks under its own brand as well as other OEM diskettes in its Chesapeake, Virginia, facility. As a late entrant in the industry, Mitsubishi found it difficult to build brand awareness against 3M, Verbatim, Sony, and other well-established competitors. Therefore, Mitsubishi purchased Verbatim for its established brand name, distribution channels, and market share. Kodak agreed to allow Mitsubishi to continue using the Kodak name until May 1992, which provided Welland and Falco, who both continued with Verbatim after the sale, some time to formulate new marketing and promotional strategies.

The purchase of Verbatim by Mitsubishi offered a much-needed capital infusion that was limited under Kodak's ownership. Mitsubishi management subscribed to the belief inherent in many Japanese companies: Invest heavily in the present with an eye on long-term profitability. Mitsubishi provided more capital for Welland's ongoing advertising campaign. In contrast, Kodak had been lean in advertising dollars allotted directly to Verbatim and the DataLife brand. Instead, Kodak depended on increased sales through corporate advertising of its name, which capitalized on the fact that Kodak was the second most recognized name in the world (behind Coca-Cola).

THE INDUSTRY

The deluge of technology in the computer industry changed the way America did business. The introduction of the personal computer gave individual workers the power to write and edit documents, produce electronic spreadsheets, and compile large databases. Not only could businesspeople hook up to a company's mainframe, they could do it away from the office. The lap-top computer

[5] Clifford Glickman, "After Floppies, What?" *Charlotte Observer*, January 7, 1991, p. 7D.

meant that professionals could sit in a customer's office and work as easily as if they were sitting in their own office. Computer purchasers appeared to be interested in greater use of color and graphics, the ability to store more information on a single disk, and higher-quality printers.

In 1991, most Americans were concerned with the continuing weak economy. As a result of low consumer confidence and rising unemployment, Americans became extremely conscious of their spending behavior especially for big-ticket items such as personal computers. PCs at the office were considered a necessity. Although office managers were cutting operating costs, computer disks were not something that could be eliminated. In part because of the economy, more people were working at home. According to Falco, "The home office is driving the business now." Sales of diskettes to this market were up substantially. On the other hand, personal computers purchased for recreational use at home were considered to be a luxury, and disk expenditures by the recreational user were expected to decrease. The costs of manufacturing data storage products, such as rewritable optical disks and 8-mm and 4-mm tape products, were expected to rise as new technologies were researched and implemented. As a result, a highly competitive industry would have to be even more concerned with differentiating its products on something other than price.

The computer media market boasted $1.8 billion in total sales during 1990 as compared to $1.2 billion in 1989. Twenty-seven percent of the sales were attributed to 5.25" disks, while 3.5" disks made up over 30 percent of sales. Exhibit 21.1 outlines the market share for the various computer media. The overall growth of the 5.25" and the 3.5" segment of the media market averaged about 25 percent in the first three quarters of 1989. Sales of 5.25" diskettes did not decline as much as was forecasted but did decline about 3 percent because of the weakening demand for low-end machines for the home market. Sales of high-density (HD) 3.5" disks increased slightly, although they represented less than 20 percent of the total 3.5" units sold.[6]

EXHIBIT 21.1   Computer Media Market Shares

Medium	Percent Share
1/2" Reel-to-Reel Tape	16
1/2" Tape Cartridges	2
8" Disks	11
5.25" Disks	27
3.5" Disks	30
Data Cartridges	14

Source: "Floppy Disks," *Purchasing,* February 22, 1990, p. 76.

[6] "Say Good-bye to 3.5" Disk Shortage," *Purchasing,* February 20, 1990, p. 76.

EXHIBIT 21.2   Sales of Disks Worldwide, All Formats

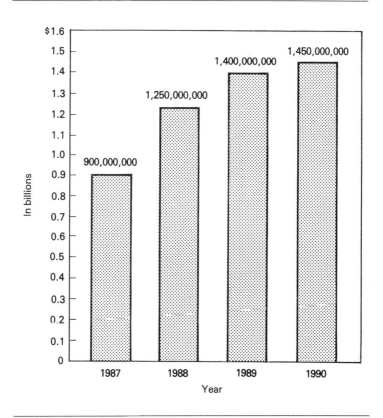

In billions

900,000,000
1,250,000,000
1,400,000,000
1,450,000,000

Year

Source: Santa Clara Consulting Group.

According to the Santa Clara Consulting Group, worldwide sales of floppy disks in 1990 increased slightly above 1989 sales (Exhibit 21.2). Computer Industry Forecasts, published by the Data Analysis Group, projected 1991 sales of floppy disks to be $2.7 billion.[7]

Magnetic floppy disks were viewed as commodities, and price competition was fierce. Welland stated, "We've experienced a price erosion of about 23 percent in 1990 and about the same the year before. It was probably the purest form of open market competition—but brutal competition." Exhibit 21.3 provides the average price of 5.25" floppy disks from 1985 to 1990. Although the price of branded double-density (DD) 5.25" disks and generic brands fell drastically (to as low as 17 cents each), the introduction of HD 5.25" disks kept the average higher.

---

[7] Computer Industry Forecast, Data Analysis Group, Georgetown, California, first quarter report, 1991.

EXHIBIT 21.3   Average Price for All 5.25" Floppy Disks, 1985–1990

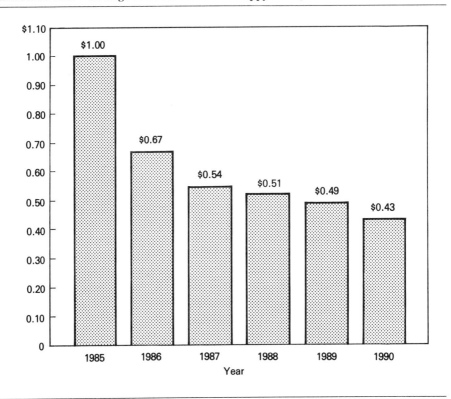

Source: Santa Clara Consulting Group.

Interestingly, worldwide sales of computers were expected to grow by only 6.5 percent in 1991, compared to the 8.4 percent growth in 1990. Personal computer sales were forecasted to drop from 13 percent of the market to 8 percent.[8] Slow sales growth could be partially attributed to fears of recession, office budget cutting, and a slowdown in the switching from large computer systems to less expensive desktop systems in business.[9] Price competition was expected to limit lap-top and microcomputer revenues in 1991.

COMPETITION

Verbatim was faced with a number of key competitors in a highly competitive industry. Several of the competitors such as 3M, Maxell, Sony, and

[8] John W. Verity, "Computers Will See Lots of Downtime," *Business Week,* January 14, 1991, p. 101.
[9] David P. Brousell, "Industry Outlook—1991," *Datamation,* January 1, 1991, p. 38.

BASF had highly recognized brand names that were used on a variety of products with synergistic effects.

"The market for data storage products contains three segments: premium, price, and economy," according to Falco. The premium market segment included 3M, Verbatim, Sony, and Maxell brands. Fuji, BASF, and Memorex competed in the price segment, which was typically 15 percent lower in price than the premium brands. The economy segment featured value through lower prices achieved by lower manufacturing costs and included the Bonus, TDK, and Highland (3M) brands. The premium category accounted for approximately 60 percent of the market. The remaining 40 percent of the market was divided between the price segment and the economy segment.

Verbatim operated primarily in the premium market. Although the majority of its products were targeted to the upper end of the mass market, Verbatim maintained its Bonus brand diskette at the lower end of the market. "This product is offered for people who want a quality brand name and are value conscious. They don't want the cheapest thing they can find, but a brand name they recognize and trust at a moderate price point," Falco stated.

Figures from a 1990 Magnetic Media Industry report for 1989 activity placed Verbatim as third in market share with 8.59 percent of the industry (Exhibit 21.4). The category leader, 3M, had 12.14 percent market share. Maxell (Hitachi) held the second position with 10.96 percent share. Falco commented that the January 1992 figures placed Verbatim second to 3M in market share worldwide. He felt that the market was so fiercely competitive that each quarter could register a different market share leader from among the top three. Companies have literally

EXHIBIT 21.4   Revenue and Unit Market Share Data for Floppy Disks

Company	Revenues (In millions)	Percent Total Industry Revenues	Percent Total Industry Units
3M	$205	12.14	12.13
Hitachi/Maxell	185	10.96	9.37
Verbatim	145	8.59	8.46
Sony	117	6.93	6.22
Xidex	99	5.86	9.62
BASF	93	5.51	5.59
Kao	92	5.45	3.87
Fuji	78	4.62	4.06
TDK	67	3.97	3.92
Nashua	35	2.07	2.66
Totals	$1,116	66.10	65.90

Source: Magnetic Media Information Services Floppy Disk Industry Report, February 15, 1990.

come and gone in the 1980s. Xidex, Elephant, and Syncom have all left the industry, although newcomers, primarily from Japan and Mexico, appeared occasionally.

A major factor affecting competition in the data storage industry was that the products (primarily diskettes) were relatively undifferentiated. The market was characterized by increasing technological advances by manufacturers that kept attempting to differentiate the products. Rumors were always circulating that some brands with low market share would be pulling out of the diskette market as competition heated up.

3M

Although the market share leader, 3M had only established disk production in the early 1980s and it represented only a small part of the multi-billion-dollar company. 3M was a strong global competitor in all areas of marketing, manufacturing, and distribution with worldwide visibility. In 1992, it was the only large U.S. manufacturer of diskettes that offered a complete line of media as well as many other well-known office products (Scotch tape, Post-It Notes, and so forth). The company had a strong reputation as a creative innovator of quality products. Considered the technology leader, 3M committed significant resources to R&D.

Maxell

Hitachi-Maxell was one division of Hitachi, Limited, Japan's largest electrical and electronics manufacturer. Maxell began disk production in the late 1970s; diskettes accounted for approximately 20 percent of the company's total business. The company has a reputation for high quality, especially in audio-visual products. Although it did not manufacture a full line of computer media, the company did produce diskettes and 4-mm and 8-mm tape, and purchased data cartridges with its brand name on them.

Sony

Sony Corporation was a leading manufacturer of electronic and entertainment products. In the United States, Sony's business activities shifted from electronics to entertainment with the purchase of CBS Records in 1988 and Columbia in 1989. Sony and the Japanese electronics conglomerate, Matsushita, developed a 2″ disk in 1988 and claimed that these would eventually be the industry standard. As of early 1992, this had not occurred.

Sony produced a full product line of computer media except for cassettes, 1/2″ reel-to-reel tape, and 1/2″ tape cartridges. Sony supplied many OEM customers with nonlabeled 3.5″ disks and both optical drives and optical disks.

Other Competitors

Fuji and BASF entered into a joint venture to produce 3.5″ disks in the late 1980s. Fuji had strength in the film market, and BASF had a strong brand image in the audio-visual market. Both competed in the lower-priced-value market for computer media. KAO manufactured for the OEM market and private-label customers. The company pursued bulk and bid business based on low prices. Through 1991, KAO had little success in the branded market.

Share of Mind

All of Verbatim's top competitors were manufacturers of a broad range of products that enhanced their ability to generate high levels of awareness through corporate advertising. In 1990 and 1991, 3M and BASF both used mass-media corporate advertising for all their products, which led to high levels of awareness. In 1991, BASF began an advertising campaign that emphasized its role in technological innovation and claimed, ''We don't make many of the products you buy—we make them better.'' In 1989, 3M spent almost three times the level of Verbatim (Exhibit 21.5). Such a large budget enhanced 3M's already high name recognition. 3M, in particular, received the fringe benefit of positive brand perceptions from its many other, quality products.

As indicated in Exhibit 21.6, there seemed to be a lack of consistency among competitors' advertising themes. Campaigns had no central focus or else they held the focus for a short period of time. Exhibit 21.6 summarizes the advertising campaigns of Verbatim's major competitors.

A top-of-mind awareness survey completed in 1991 by Verbatim found 3M leading, followed by Maxell, and then Verbatim (Exhibit 21.7). This corresponded to market-share sales figures (in Exhibit 21.5).

EXHIBIT 21.5   Competitive Advertising Expenditures, 1989

Company	1989 Total Diskette Advertising Budget	Percent of Total
3M	$2,705,716	40
Maxell	1,214,368	18
BASF	1,113,618	16
Verbatim	976,481	14
Sony	542,930	8
Mitsubishi	283,853	4
Totals	$6,836,966	100

Source: Kodak in-house study, 1989.

EXHIBIT 21.6   Advertising Campaigns of Major Competitors

3M

1988–89 Theme:	"Supporting the Dream."
Ad Message:	Teamwork that provides you with technological breakthroughs, superior quality and selection.
1990 Theme:	No consistent tag line, emphasis on reliability.
Ad Message:	"Wanted for breaking Murphy's Law" (3M diskettes); exclusive formulation and "Mark Q" manufacturing process. Secondary emphasis on convenience (preformatted diskettes).
Promotions:	11th disk free.

Maxell

1988–89 Theme:	"The Gold Standard."
Ad Message:	Maximum safety and reliability: "Ten times more reliable than conventional floppy disks, twice the durability, twice the resistance to dirt and dust."
1990 Theme:	"The Gold Standard."

BASF

1988–89 Theme:	"The Spirit of Innovation."
Ad Message:	100% error free, compatibility, data protection.
1990 Theme:	"Try it. Depend on it."
Promotions:	Cash sweepstakes.

Sony

1988–89 Theme:	"Sony. The One and Only" (corporatewide).
Ad Message:	World leader in high-densisty magnetic media.
1990 Theme:	No consistent tag line.
Ad Message:	Reliability.

EXHIBIT 21.7   Top-of-Mind Awareness for the Major Floppy Disk Competitors

Company	Percent Unaided Awareness*
3M	45
Maxell	24
Verbatim	23
Sony	16
BASF	7
Fuji	3

* Multiple responses

Source: Verbatim floppy disk tracking study, 1991.

VERBATIM CORPORATION MISSION

The mission of Verbatim was to be the recognized leader of the magnetic and optical media-data storage industry by being a profitable, worldwide quality manufacturer and marketer.

Verbatim Corporate Vision

Verbatim, on a worldwide basis, will:

- Be obsessed with customer satisfaction.
- Be known for product quality.
- Be dedicated to continuous quality improvement.
- Be a technology leader, positioned to provide new products to our customers when needed.
- Give people the information and resources necessary to continuously improve quality to their customers.
- Be #1 in revenue market share.
- Nurture partnerships with our suppliers to meet or exceed our quality goals.

Having purchased Verbatim, Mitsubishi planned to become the leader in diskette revenue market share with a continued emphasis on the most effective use of dollars for advertising, promotions, and new product introductions. CEO Nicky Hartery recently reminded employees of the importance of being "number one" in revenue market share as opposed to unit market share by saying, "You can't deposit units in the bank." Verbatim directed its advertising and promotions to attain market share equal to or greater than 3M, the industry leader.

PRODUCT STRATEGY

Product Line

Verbatim manufactured and marketed a wide variety of data storage media including magnetic storage media (floppy disks) and advanced mass storage devices (back-up tapes and optical disks). Exhibit 21.8 shows the Verbatim product line. Floppy disks were produced in 3.5", 5.25", and 8" sizes with varying features and were backed by Verbatim's lifetime guarantee. A new product for this market was the DataLife 3.5" extra-high-density (ED) microdisk that provided 4 MB of storage compared to 1 MB for DD and 2 MB for HD disks.

One segment of mass storage devices included 4-mm and 8-mm computer grade data cartridges, 1/4" data cartridges, high-density streamer cassettes, digital data cassettes, and 1/2" reel tape. These products were used for back-up and restoration of computer files, and archival purposes. As hard drives expanded in size, back-up media increased in importance, as it would take numerous floppy disks to back up a hard drive.

EXHIBIT 21.8   Verbatim's Product Line

OfferThe Best Storage Space InTown.

Offer your customers superior quality Verbatim disks. In addition to our regular line of data storage products, we now offer exciting value-added products like DataLifePlus disks with Teflon® coating, vivid DataLife Colors disks and DataLife factory formatted disks. Plus data cartridges, data cassettes and reel tapes. Which means now your customers can get any kind of data storage they need all from one source. **Verbatim**

The other segment of mass storage and the newest area for Verbatim was optical disk manufacturing. Within the industry, optical disks came in three formats: ROM (read-only memory), WORM (write once, read many), and rewritable disks. "We are on the threshold of optical being a very big product," Falco stated in 1991. Verbatim was one of the first companies to offer 5.25″ rewritable optical disks and the first with the 3.5″ rewritable optical disks.

Branded Products

Verbatim continued marketing the DataLife brand after being purchased by Kodak. Kodak wanted to use its name on disks that would be sold in mass merchant outlets because of the high recognition of the brand name. Verbatim and DataLife were better-recognized brand names in computer stores.

In the agreement with Mitsubishi, Kodak allowed Verbatim to use the Kodak name until May of 1992. The transition from Kodak to Verbatim brands progressed smoothly. The Kodak brand was sold primarily by the mass merchants such as Kmart and Target, where Verbatim did not have much brand recognition. While owned by Kodak, the box showed Verbatim in large letters with smaller letters underneath that stated, "A Kodak Company." Throughout 1991, as packages were redesigned, the Kodak brand was deleted. There was some resistance from the mass merchants to the conversion. The Verbatim product did not sell as well as the Kodak brand in the mass market, so at first, Verbatim sales reps had to convince the mass merchants to continue carrying the DataLife product, while advertising and promotion dollars were spent to reach the end user with information about Verbatim's brands. Sales of DataLife increased; most former purchasers of Kodak switched to Verbatim's DataLife.

During the time Kodak was being deleted from packages, there was a great deal of discussion concerning branding. Should Verbatim be the highlighted brand name with DataLife superscripted or subscripted, or should DataLife be highlighted with Verbatim superscripted or subscripted? Or should there be only one brand? If only one brand name was to be selected, should it be Verbatim or DataLife? Although "Verbatim" perfectly expressed the performance wanted from disks, it was difficult for many non-English speaking people to pronounce. As the company supplied media storage worldwide, careful study was required to make the decision.

Product Differentiation

Magnetic Floppy Disks. In 1986, Verbatim introduced an antistatic lining for diskettes called DataHold. It discharged static electricity, protecting disks from data loss. Every disk sold by Verbatim contained this protection.

Verbatim secured a patent on its Teflon coating process introduced in October 1987. DataLifePlus disks were protected from spills, fingerprints, and other office mishaps that might cause data loss. Many computer users were afraid of "mysterious data loss." The Teflon coating allowed the liner to wipe the disk clean inside the jacket as it was being used in the drive. Falco commented, "DataLifePlus is about 20 percent of our business. A lot of people don't worry about data loss until they have lost data." An agreement prohibited DuPont from selling Teflon to other disk manufacturers through 1991 and gave Verbatim a guaranteed, but short-lived competitive advantage in the marketplace. Although competitors could purchase Teflon from Dupont after 1991, they had to develop a process that did not infringe on the Verbatim coating patent. Apparently the competition did not judge the market to be of sufficient size to spend the R&D funds—especially when floppy disks became essentially a commodity product. As of the beginning of 1992, none of the competitors had challenged Verbatim for this segment.

Although Verbatim was the first in October 1987 to offer preformatted diskettes, 3M and others soon followed with this slightly more expensive, but more convenient product. Buyers could purchase diskettes preformatted for any number of machines from IBM and related machines, to Apple Macintosh.

In 1988, Verbatim introduced colored disk jackets for easier office organization. The new jackets tended to be more appealing to the consumer's eye. Branded under the DataLife Colors label, the colored diskettes encouraged brand loyalty by providing continuity to existing color filing systems. Other manufacturers developed their own versions of color disks since Verbatim's introduction.

In late 1990, Verbatim announced an additional enhancement for its 3.5" disks. Diskettes contained a metal shutter that is worn down by a computer's disk drive over time and could deposit potentially damaging shavings into the disk drive. Verbatim pioneered a flexible, nonmetallic DataSeal shutter that did not wear down and deposit shavings into the computer. Verbatim began shipping the product in March 1991; competitors quickly developed similar protection devices.

Magnetic Tape. In the spring of 1989, Kodak began to manufacture 1/2" reel-to-reel computer tape (with finish processing at Verbatim) under the DataLife brand name. However, other competitors, such as 3M, BASF, and Memorex were already established in this mature market. The tape was a late entrant to a mature market; data processing managers were not very interested in any new brands.

Expansion into highest density tape products occurred in 1991. DataLife high capacity tape in 8-mm and 4-mm widths competed against Sony, Maxell, and 3M.

Optical Disks. Although the technology had been available since 1985, it was not until August 1989 that 3M announced its entrance into the erasable (rewritable) optical disk market. Similar to popular compact disks, this product could be used repeatedly for media storage. One month after 3M, Verbatim announced that it would manufacture optical disks. This new product had required huge cash investments to develop a drastically different manufacturing process. Both Verbatim and 3M hoped that the cost of manufacturing and change in format to optical disks would prevent some competitors from entering the new market.

Unfortunately, purchases of the optical disk drives have not met expectations, thus the demand for optical disks has been disappointing as well. In early 1992, optical disk drives were too slow and expensive to replace magnetic media for most uses. Verbatim was still hoping to capitalize on the erasable optical disks. Unlike regular floppy disks, erasable optical disks were not yet considered commodities; therefore, there was little price erosion. In actuality, optical disks were not positioned to replace floppy disks. Optical disks had a huge storage capacity— 128 megabytes of storage on a 3.5″ disk compared to 1 or 2 megabytes for most 3.5″ floppies. The 5¼″ optical disks store up to 650 MB. The conversion to optical disk drives has been slow because of the high cost of the hardware, but optical drive prices have started to come down. In addition, the optical disks have declined in price. There has been a problem within the industry concerning standardization and compatibility.

The legality of supplying evidence on optical disks was another issue of critical importance. When WORM technology was the only form of optical disk available, legal concerns were not a problem. However, with the development of multifunction disk drives that can use WORM *and* rewritable disks, the courts were not certain how they could be sure that evidence had not been changed. Another unknown, because the product was so new, was the "life" of an optical disk. This was particularly important for hospitals, which required a guarantee that data would "stay" on a disk for a minimum of 25 years.

International Data Corporation expected customers to buy about $100 million worth of erasable optical disks in 1991.[10] Purchasers of optical disks tend to be involved with huge data storage needs such as libraries, government agencies, and large corporations. Some industry analysts expected optical disks to develop into an economical and popular product. Others felt that optical disks would never achieve more than a limited share of the market, and still others predicted that the 3.5″ optical disk would eventually replace the floppy disk. IBM introduced new personal computers that could use 3.5″ optical disks in June 1991.

Sony was expected to announce a 2.5″ optical disk drive in late 1992. It would combine video, audio, and data into a process called optical imaging. The new drive would require further miniaturization of optical disks.

THE FLOPPY DISK CUSTOMER

Verbatim's products were directed at two broad categories of users, the original equipment manufacturer market and the branded market. Exhibit 21.9 contains a summary of the computer media market. In the OEM market, manufacturers produced nonlabeled diskettes for companies that developed software packages or manufactured hardware that included operating system software. Lotus and Microsoft were two of Verbatim's OEM customers. Labels were added

---

[10] "Say Good-bye," p. 76.

EXHIBIT 21.9   Verbatim Market Opportunities

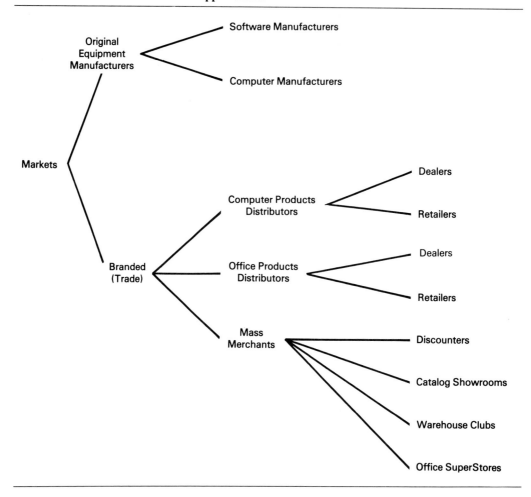

carrying the name of the purchaser rather than Verbatim's name. The branded market consisted of buyers who purchased Verbatim brands of unformatted or preformatted diskettes for personal or business use.

The OEM Market

Verbatim enjoyed a strong position in the OEM market. In fact, Verbatim was the largest nonlabeled supplier in the United States to OEMs and software publishers. The price competition in the OEM market forced Verbatim to search for economies in production and for product differentiation through quality and service. To speed delivery, Verbatim established East and West Coast distribution facilities. Although price remained an important factor, Verbatim differentiated its product through quality, durability, and meeting customers' specifications; these factors carried more weight with hardware and software producers when purchasing diskettes that would/bear their company's name. Quality was an extremely important factor in the OEM market, and Verbatim's reputation for quality products anchored its strong position in this area.

The Branded Market

The branded market was very price competitive at all levels. According to Falco, "Salespeople frequently come to me and say, 'I can sell 20,000 more diskettes to this account if we lower the price by 10 cents a diskette,' and I tell them that's not the type of business we're after. We could have made $40 million more in 1990 if we could have maintained the same price levels that existed in 1989." Despite the price decline, Verbatim continued to give attention to research and development of new products in addition to its enhancement of existing products. Falco characterized the market as a "pennies industry" alluding to the fact that margins are constantly squeezed by price competition on one side and R&D, production, and new technology costs on the other.

The branded market can be divided into home users or business users, buying from Verbatim's trade customers. Bob Falco commented, "Media Market Research profiled the end user, whether he or she is a home or office user, to be 35 years old; well educated; high income; married with children; a reader who is interested in new products, electronics, self-improvement and investments; and an active participant in individual sports activities."

Home Users.   In 1992, more than 26 million Americans performed job-related work at home. By 1993, that number was predicted to reach nearly 35 million. According to LINK Resources, a research and consulting firm, there were several different categories of homeworkers. These included salaried corporate employees, self-employed workers, contract workers, and freelancers. LINK profiled the average homeworker as 39 years old, part of a dual-career family with a family income of $42,000. This was and will be an important market for Verbatim as the numbers continue to grow. The phenomenal growth of homeworkers was credited for much of the growth in sales for office equipment, including copiers, fax units, calculators, and computers. The annual investment in home-office equipment including computers, copiers, fax units, calculators, and cellular phones in 1989 was $5.3 billion, and experts predicted 1993 sales to top $8.4 billion.[11]

Business Users.   The profile of users in a large business was similar to other end users, although their purchasing patterns were different. Large companies tended to have longer sales cycles, to buy in larger quantities, to buy in a highly organized

---

[11] "Working at Home: Growth Is Phenomenal," *The Office,* March 1991, p. 58.

fashion, and to look for value-added services. Seventy percent of large businesses purchased diskettes through a central purchasing agent primarily for efficiency and lower costs. Instead of multiple departments within a company each placing a single order, purchasing needs were pooled and one large order for one brand was placed, generally earning significant quantity discounts.

According to a 1987 in-house study by Kodak, business users had slightly larger diskette libraries than home users. Whether business or home user, the largest acquisition of disks occurred during the first year of computer usage. Hard disk drive owners purchased more disks in the first year, but that dropped off more in the second year than that of the nonowner of a hard disk drive. Both business and home users generally owned two brands of disks.

Trade Customers.   Verbatim sold branded products to various channel members (the trade) to resell to a variety of end users. The trade audience included computer distributors, computer dealers/retailers, software dealers/retailers, national/regional wholesalers, and office megastores such as Staples, Office Depot, and OW (Office Warehouse). Mass merchants could be divided into discount chains, catalog showrooms, warehouse clubs, hypermarkets, and drugstore chains.

A shift was under way in the branded market as sales of diskettes at computer specialty stores were leveling off but increasing in superstores such as Sam's Wholesale, Pace, Office Depot, and Office America. This was attributed to growing computer literacy among end users who once felt that a specialist was needed to aid in the selection of diskettes. Verbatim shifted much of its advertising and promotional attention to end users to correspond with this trend.

ADVERTISING AND OTHER PROMOTIONAL STRATEGIES AT VERBATIM

In 1991, Verbatim used its promotional budget to shift away from "push" advertising to the trade toward a focus on "pull" advertising to end users. Verbatim's advertising and promotion had become more dedicated to this facet of the business. Verbatim's branded advertising objectives included:

- Increasing brand name and advertising awareness levels of Verbatim above 3M,
- Establishing a preference for Verbatim,
- Establishing a specific position for Verbatim and its brands,
- Creating advertising that supports the chosen position and,
- Supporting the advertising program with sales promotions and public relations.

Verbatim used both vertical and horizontal trade publications. Full-page ads in the typical computer publications such as *Byte* and *PcWeek* were used to reach a variety of users. The vertical publications included magazines that specialized in the hospital, accounting, and legal professions. These publications targeted the corporate user and were a relatively inexpensive method of advertising. Ads would continue to be placed in trade journals. Verbatim hoped to increase advertising expenditures to match the spending of competitors resulting in increased visibility and name recognition.

Direct mail had been used occasionally to reach some specialized markets that would have a particular interest in a new product. It was used to introduce the Verbatim tape products to data processing managers in the New York City area and to introduce the worry-free DataLifePlus disks to CEOs.

Promotions

Promotions focused on each member in the channel of distribution. Rebates in the form of a credit on future Verbatim purchases to trade customers were based on volume and growth relative to history. Occasionally "spiffs" were offered to trade customers for each unit of Verbatim sold in a selected category. (Spiffs were cash payments by trade customers to their sales reps that were reimbursed by Verbatim.) End-user promotions included on-pack or in-pack (free 11th disk, rebates, coupons, free storage box, or cleaning kit).

Public Relations

Greater emphasis was sought in the public relations arena with attempts to place stories about Verbatim in various print media that would offer a form of "free" advertising. Case histories about the usage of Verbatim products were the best way to get placement in a publication.

Sales Force

The United States/Canada branded sales division consisted of five regional managers that each supervised up to eight sales representatives. The OEM sales group consisted of nine Verbatim sales representatives. Overall sales objectives for 1991 included increasing sales revenue by 19 percent and taking market share away from Verbatim's primary competitors. Verbatim had approximately 200 trade customers of which 35 contributed the majority of sales.

BACK TO THE BUSINESS OF CHALLENGING THE LEADER

As Bob Falco developed his plan to become the market share leader, he thought about the current situation in the industry. "In other recessions in the 1970s and 1980s floppy disks were not really affected. But the 1991–92 recession is a white collar recession and there has been a definite slowdown in the media business—particularly in the New England area. Fortunately, sales to the home office market are doing well. That market is really carrying the business right now. We're ready for the breakthrough in optical disks, but the way the life cycle for any new technology is compressed, that will probably become a commodity market, too, and in a very short period of time."

—————————————————— CASE 22 ——————————————————

Anheuser-Busch Dominates in the 1990s

On March 28, 1990, Patrick K. Stokes was appointed president of Anheuser-Busch, the beer subsidiary of Anheuser-Busch Companies (the holding company). He succeeded August A. Busch III, who had served as president of the subsidiary for the past three years. Mr. Busch, who maintained his position as chairman of the board, president, and chief executive officer of Anheuser-Busch Companies, said that "he will continue to participate in the management of the beer subsidiary, but will devote more time to corporate duties and working with other subsidiaries."[1] One analyst expressed his belief that Mr. Stokes' main challenge would be to reach the 50 percent market-share objective by or before the mid-1990s. The analyst went on to say, "Stokes will be under extra pressure since the achievement of this [50 percent market share] objective is a top priority of Mr. Busch."

Mr. Stokes had served as chairman and CEO of Campbell-Taggart and as chairman and president of Eagle Snacks, both food subsidiaries of Anheuser-Busch Companies. Also promoted was Michael J. Roarty, director of marketing for Anheuser-Busch, the beer subsidiary, to vice president of corporate marketing and communications for the company and chairman of Busch media group. During Roarty's 13-year tenure in the beer subsidiary, sales and market share had more than doubled—to 80.7 million barrels and 42.1 percent market share. Rather than appoint a new director of marketing, three veteran Anheuser-Busch managers shared the challenge of achieving 50 percent market share with Mr. Stokes.

COMPANY HISTORY—AN ENTREPRENEURIAL SPIRIT

In 1852, George Schneider founded the Bavarian Brewery in St. Louis, Missouri. Five years later, on the brink of bankruptcy, the brewery was sold to a competitor who renamed it Hammer and Urban. By 1860, the new company

This case was prepared by Thomas L. Wheelen, David B. Croll, and Moustafa H. Abdelsamad. Research assistance was performed by Paul Parker. The case is intended as a basis for class discussion rather than to illustrate either effective or ineffective handling of an administrative situation. Copyright © 1990 by Thomas L. Wheelen. Used with permission from Thomas L. Wheelen.

[1] "August Busch III Names Beer Successor," *Beverage World*, May 1990, p. 10.

defaulted on a loan to Eberhard Anheuser. Anheuser, a successful soap manufacturer, assumed control of Hammer and Urban and four years later asked his son-in-law, Adolphus Busch, to join the brewery as a salesman. Busch, who became the driving force behind the new venture, became a partner in 1873, and then president between 1880 and 1913. In 1879, the name of the brewery was changed to Anheuser-Busch Brewing Company.

Adolphus Busch was a pioneer in the development of a new pasteurization process for beer and became the first American brewer to pasteurize beer. In 1894, he and Carl Conrad developed a new beer that was lighter in color and body. This new beer, Budweiser, gave Busch a national beer, for which he developed many marketing techniques to increase sales. By 1901, the annual sales of Anheuser-Busch had surpassed the million-barrel mark.

In 1913, August A. Busch succeeded his father as president of the company, serving as president during the prohibition era between 1920 and 1933. He led the company in many new diversification endeavors such as truck bodies, baker's yeast, ice cream, corn products, commercial refrigeration units, and nonalcoholic beverages. With the passage of the 21st Amendment, which repealed Prohibition, Anheuser-Busch returned to the manufacturing and distribution of beer on a national basis, and in 1934 the company went public. August A. Busch's son, Adolphus Busch III, was president of the company from 1934 until his death in 1946.

August A. (Gussie) Busch, Jr., succeeded Adolphus Busch III as president and CEO in 1946. He was elected chairman of the board in 1956. During his tenure, eight new breweries were constructed and sales increased 11-fold, from 3 million barrels in 1946 to 34 million barrels in 1974. He guided the company as it continued its conglomerate diversification strategies into real estate, family entertainment parks, transportation, the St. Louis Cardinals baseball team, and can manufacturing. Busch was serving as honorary chairman of the board of Anheuser-Busch Companies, and chairman and president of the St. Louis National Baseball Club at his death on September 29, 1989. He was 90. Before his death, Mr. Busch had commented, "I've had a wonderful, competitive life filled with challenges and reward." He continued, "And I'm thankful for it all. Most of all, I'm thankful for my heritage, for my family, and for my children. I'm thankful for my life with my company, Anheuser-Busch." His death marked the last of the legendary "beer barons," and the end of an era.[2]

August A. Busch III, born on June 16, 1937, was the fifth generation of the Busch brewing dynasty. He started his career hauling beechwood chips out of 31,000-gallon aging tanks. In his youth "Little Augie" was a hell-raiser, but he changed to a conservative "workaholic" after attending the University of Arizona and the Siebel Institute of Technology, a Chicago school for brewers. He was elected president in 1974, and CEO in 1975. During his tenure, sales increased by more than two and a half times, or 264 percent, from 34 million barrels in 1974 to

[2] Anheuser-Busch Companies, *Annual Report 1989*, p. 1.

89.7 million barrels in 1989. The company maintained 12 breweries having a capacity of 85.1 million barrels, and Anheuser-Busch continued its successful conglomerate diversification efforts (Exhibit 22.1).

During his 15 years of managing the company, Busch transformed it from a large, loosely run company into a tightly run organization with an emphasis on the bottom line. Busch was known for his tough-mindedness and intensity, his highly competitive nature, and his attention to detail. As Mr. Dennis Long, former president of the company's brewing subsidiary, said, "There is little that goes on that he doesn't know something about." Busch, a brewmaster, was known for making unscheduled visits to the breweries at all hours of the day and night.

Mr. Busch would start his day at 5:30 A.M., then pilot his helicopter from his 1,000-acre farm in Saint Peters, Missouri, to the company's headquarters on the South Side of St. Louis—a 30-mile flight. He would hold his first meeting over breakfast, which would take place at 7:00 A.M., and would rarely leave the office before 6:00 P.M. One of his final rituals before retiring at 8:30 P.M. would be to taste-test daily samples of beer that are flown in from the company's breweries. Few batches of Budweiser, or any Anheuser-Busch beer, were shipped without his personal approval. Busch was described "as a man who absolutely never wastes time." "When you have a meeting with him, it is boom, boom, boom," stated Jerry Steinman, publisher of *Beer Marketer's Insights*, an industry newsletter. Professor Amand C. Stalnaker, on the board of directors of the company, put it another way. "He's not the guy who sits back, puts his feet up on the desk and says, 'Let's chat about this for an hour or two.' But I would call it intensity rather

EXHIBIT 22.1   Anheuser-Busch Subsidiaries

Anheuser-Busch
Anheuser-Busch Investment Capital Corporation
Anheuser-Busch International
Busch Agricultural Resources
Busch Creative Service Corporation
Busch Entertainment Corporation
Busch Media Group
Busch Properties
Campbell Taggart
Civic Center Corporation
Container Recovery Corporation
Eagle Snacks
International Label Company[a]
Manufacturers Railroad Company
Metal Container Corporation
Promotional Products Group
St. Louis National Baseball Club
St. Louis Refrigerator Car Company

[a] This is a joint venture company.
Source: Anheuser-Busch Companies, Inc., *Fact Book—1989/90*, pp. 6–26.

than abruptness."[3] Mr. Long added, "Let there be no doubt. He's at the helm and he sets the tone. For him, planning and management are one and the same, once a plan is drawn up, he tracks the follow-through to make sure that it is carried out."[4]

Encouraging openness and participation from his executives, Busch provided them with plenty of responsibility and freedom, and promoted group decision making. Henry King, former president of the United States Brewing Association, stated, ". . . the reason Anheuser-Busch leads the field is because it's got dynamic leadership. August Busch picks very talented people; he gives them enormous responsibilities, but he gives them the authority to execute those responsibilities and he holds people accountable."[5]

His policy committee was a 12-member forum in which each member must present an opinion on the current topic or issue and substantiate his position. Mr. Busch felt that "executives do not learn from success, they learn from their failures." What is his philosophy on success? As he stated, "The more successful that we become . . . the more humble we must be . . . because that breeds future success."[6]

Robert S. Weinberg, a brewing industry analyst and former consultant to the company, felt, "The thing that is extraordinary about A-B is their depth of management talent. . . . This is a very extraordinary team. They're not competing with each other; they're all working together for the common goal." However, a former employee warned, "The biggest mistake as an Anheuser executive is to wake up one morning and think you're a Busch," even though Mr. Busch speaks in endearing, almost emotional terms about the A-B family of employees.[7]

Mr. Busch's 26-year-old son, August A. Busch IV, has been learning the business over the past five years. He was the brand manager for Bud Dry. Commenting on the success of his four children, Mr. Busch said, "If they have the competency to do so, they'll be given the opportunity. You learn from the ground up. Those of us who are in this company started out scrubbing the tanks."[8] "The fact that he [August IV] is August III's son does not mean a free lunch," stated a friend of the immediate family. "It couldn't hurt, however."[9]

THE ORGANIZATION

On October 1, 1979, Anheuser-Busch Companies was formed as a new holding company. The company's new name and organization structure more

[3] Christy Marshall, "The Czar of Beers," *Business Month*, June 1988, p. 26.
[4] "How Anheuser Brews Its Winners," *New York Times*, August 4, 1985.
[5] Larry Jabbonsky, "What Keeps A-B Hot?" *Beverage World*, September 1988, p. 22.
[6] "How Anheuser Brews Its Winners," p. 28.
[7] Jabbonsky, "What Keeps A-B Hot?" p. 22.
[8] "How Anheuser Brews Its Winners," p. 18.
[9] Jabbonsky, "What Keeps A-B Hot?" p. 22.

clearly reflected Anheuser-Busch's mission and diversification endeavors of the past decades.

Reorganization of the Business Segments

As a result of the acquisition of Sea World in September 1989, Anheuser-Busch reorganized and redefined its principal business segments from prior years. For strategic planning purposes the company's three business segments became (1) beer and beer-related operations, which produced and sold the company's beer products; (2) food products, which consisted of the company's food and food-related operations (Campbell-Taggart and Eagle Snacks); and (3) entertainment, which consisted of the company's theme parks (Sea World, Cypress Gardens, Busch Gardens, Adventure Island, and Sesame Place), baseball team (St. Louis Cardinals), stadium (Busch Stadium and Civic Center), and real estate development and operations. Exhibit 22.2 is an outline of each of the 17 companies that comprise the three business segments.

Prior to the reorganization, the three principal business segments had been (1) beer and beer-related, (2) food products, and (3) diversified operations. The diversified operations segment included entertainment, real estate, transportation, and communications operations. In 1989, transportation and communications became part of the beer and beer-related segment.

In 1989, the beer and beer-related business segment contributed 78.1 percent of the corporation's net sales and 93.7 percent of the operating income. Financial information for each of these business segments is shown in Exhibit 22.3. Beer will remain the top priority according to Mr. Busch.

Because of the company's vertical integration strategy, knowledge concerning the economics of the various industries in which Anheuser-Busch competes increased, the quantity and quality of supply was better assured, and both packaging and raw materials were more strongly controlled. In cultivating internally developed businesses such as Eagle Snacks, Anheuser-Busch continued its philosophy of maintaining premium-quality and quantity of supply and control of both packaging and raw materials through self-manufacture. In 1985, Eagle Snacks added plant capacity through the acquisition of Cape Cod Chip Company and through plant expansion.

Company Philosophy

Anheuser-Busch's stated philosophy was "Anheuser-Busch's vision of greatness is today a reality. But the company isn't about to rest on its history of achievement. There are many new challenges to be met, and, as always, Anheuser-Busch will lead the way, because we believe that excellence is not just the act of achievement, but the process of constantly striving to achieve even more. We also believe that while a single achievement may signify luck, a history

EXHIBIT 22.2   Anheuser-Busch Companies—Business Segments

Beer and Beer-Related Companies

Company	Year Founded	Activities
Anheuser-Busch	1852	It ranked as the world's largest brewer, selling 80.7 million barrels of beer in 1989, and has been the industry leader since 1957. It distributed 14 naturally brewed products through 950 independent beer wholesalers and 10 company-owned wholesalers. Barrels sold have increased by 60.8 percent since 1980.
Busch Agricultural Resources	1962	It processed barley into malt. In 1989, it supplied 28 percent of the company's malt requirements. It grew and processed rice, and had the capacity to meet 50 percent of the company's rice needs.
Container Recovery Corporation	1979	It recycled more than 350 million pounds of aluminum, or more than 9 billion cans, and 29 million pounds of glass, or 58 million bottles, in 1989.
Metal Container Corporation	1974	It operated 10 can and lid manufacturing plants. In 1989, it produced nearly 10 billion cans and 12 billion lids. This represented 40 percent of the company's container requirements. This subsidiary was rapidly expanding into the soft drink container market.
Anheuser-Busch International	1981	It was the company's international licensing and marketing subsidiary. The world beer market was 3.5 times as large as the domestic market. Sales were up 20 percent in 1989. The company exported to 40 countries and license-brewed in six countries.
Busch Media Group	1985	It was the company's in-house agency to purchase national broadcast media time and to develop and place local advertising schedules.
Anheuser-Busch Investment Capital Corp	1984	It shared equity positions with qualified partners in A-B: distributorships. It had invested in 16 wholesale dealerships.
Promotional Products Group	n/a	It was responsible for licensing, development, sales, and warehousing of the company's promotional merchandise. In 1989, more than 1,500 new promotional items were created and approximately 5,000 different items were available at any one time.
Busch Creative Services	1980	It was a full-service business and marketing communications company, selling its services to Anheuser-Busch and other Fortune 500 companies. In 1986, it acquired Innervision Productions, which produced video programming and industrial films. In 1986, it acquired Optimus, which was a post-production facility.
St. Louis Refrigerator Car Company	1878	It was one of the company's transportation subsidiaries with three facilities. It provided commercial repair, rebuilding, maintenance, and inspection of railroad cars. The rail car division had record profits in 1989.

(Cont.)

EXHIBIT 22.2 (Cont.)

Beer and Beer-Related Companies

Company	Year Founded	Activities
Manufacturers Railway Company	1878	This was the other transportation subsidiary. It operated 42 miles of track in the St. Louis area, 247 insulated railroad cars used to ship beer, 48 hopper cars, and 77 boxcars. It included a fleet of 240 specially designed trailers. It also ran the warehousing for eight brewery locations.

Food Products Companies

Company	Year Founded	Activities
Campbell Taggart	1982	It had 75 plants and approximately 20,000 employees in the U.S., Spain, and France. It was a highly diversified food products company with operations in about 35 percent of this country. It consisted of the following divisions: bakery operations, refrigerated products, frozen food products (Eagle Crest Foods, Inc.), and international subsidiaries—Spain and France, and other interests—makes folding cartons.
Eagle Snacks	1978	It produced and distributed a premium line of snack foods and nuts. In 1984, it began self-manufacturing virtually all of its snack products, and in 1985 it purchased Cod Potato Chip Company. It continued to move toward its goal of gaining significant market share in the snack food industry (estimated sales in excess of $10 billion).

Entertainment

Company	Year Founded	Activities
Busch Entertainment	1959	It was the company's family entertainment subsidiary. It consisted of the Dark Continent (FL), The Old Country (VA), Adventure Island (FL), and Sesame Place (PA). These parks attracted 6.2 million people. In 1989, it acquired Sea World, Cypress Gardens, and Boardwalk and Baseball. The 1989 attendance at these parks was 14 million people.
Busch Properties	1970	It was the company's real estate development subsidiary with commercial properties in Virginia, Ohio, and California. It continued to develop a planned community, Kingsmill, in Williamsburg, VA.
St. Louis National Baseball Club	1953	St. Louis Cardinals.
Civic Center Corporation	1981	It owned Busch Stadium, the Civic Center, and two and three-fourths downtown city blocks currently used for parking.

n/a = not applicable.

of many achievements signifies great endeavor and the promise of more to come. Anheuser-Busch has lived that philosophy. And the result speaks for itself."[10]

Diversification Activities

The company acquired Sea World for $1.1 billion from Harcourt Brace Jovanovich in 1989. The acquisition consisted of three theme parks in central Florida: Boardwalk and Baseball (closed in January 1990 because it had never been profitable), Cypress Gardens (Winter Haven), and Sea World (Orlando). Harcourt Brace Jovanovich sold the parks because it had $2.9 billion of debt that occurred as it fought a 1987 hostile takeover bid from British publisher Robert Maxwell.

In 1989, Anheuser-Busch announced its plans to build a $300 million resort and theme park in Spain near Barcelona. The park would feature five theme villages—four of these would be China, Mexico, Polynesia, and old Western United States—to be opened in 1993. The resort would be modeled after the company's Kingsmill resort near Williamsburg, Virginia, and would feature a world-class hotel and conference center, 18-hole golf course, and swimming and tennis facilities.[11]

Because they did not meet objectives, a number of subsidiaries were sold in 1988 and 1989. Master Cellars Wines, Saratoga Spring Company, and Sante Mineral Water Company of the A-B Beverage Group were sold to Evian Waters of France. Busch Industrial Products Corporation (producer of yeast products) was sold to Gist-Brocades N.V. of the Netherlands. The majority interest in Exploration Cruise Lines was sold in 1988.

In 1985, the company became an investor in its first venture capital fund, Innoven, an established fund that has been very successful over the years. Anheuser-Busch gained exposure to new business areas being developed by the small start-up companies in which Innoven invested capital.

The company extended its research and development program with Interferon Sciences, which has been developing and clinically testing both material and recombinant forms of interferon, an antiviral agent found in the human body.

"Along with quality, Anheuser-Busch is committed to growth and innovation. That commitment has seen the company through rough times—two World Wars, prohibition, and the great depression. Although hundreds of breweries succumbed to difficult times like these and closed their doors, Anheuser-Busch survived and grew. During these trying periods, the company devised innovative ways to use its resources, its people, and its expertise. But in good times as well as bad, the company has always realized that while you have to do the best you can in the present, you must always keep your eyes turned toward the future."[12]

[10] Anheuser-Busch Companies, Inc., *Fact Book, 1989/90*, p. 3.
[11] "Busch Plans Theme Park in Spain," *Tampa Tribune*, May 25, 1989, pp. 1D, 8D; Anheuser-Busch, *Annual Report 1990*, p. 31.
[12] *Fact Book 1989/90*, p. 3.

EXHIBIT 22.3   Financial Information for Business Segments (In millions)

1989	Beer and Beer-Related[a]		Food Products		Entertainment[b]	
Net Sales	$7,405.7	78.1%	$1,803.0	19.0%	$ 286.3	3.0%
Operating Income	1,244.7	93.7	56.9	4.3	27.1	2.0
Depreciation and						
Amortization Expense	298.7	72.8	87.2	21.3	24.4	5.9
Capital Expenditures	846.6	78.6	120.2	11.2	109.9	10.2
Identifiable Assets	5,902.9	68.0	1,295.6	14.9	1,493.4	17.1
Corporate Assets						
Total Assets						
1988						
Net Sales	$6,902.0	77.3%	$1,680.9	18.8%		
Operating Income	1,168.2	92.4	55.0	4.4		
Depreciation and						
Amortization Expense	252.9	70.4	70.7	19.7		
Capital Expenditures	785.4	82.6	100.9	10.6		
Identifiable Assets	5,102.4	76.5	1,229.7	18.4		
Corporate Assets						
Total Assets						
1987						
Net Sales	$6,375.8	76.4%	$1,627.2	19.5%		
Operating Income	1,090.2	94.9	54.4	4.8		
Depreciation and						
Amortization Expense	215.4	67.3	70.4	22.0		
Capital Expenditures	630.4	74.9	149.1	17.7		
Identifiable Assets	4,580.5	74.7	1,230.1	20.0		
Corporate Assets						
Total Assets						
1986						
Net Sales	$5,892.0	76.0%	$1,552.7	20.0%		
Operating Income	945.2	92.9	56.6	5.6		
Depreciation and						
Amortization Expense	192.3	68.4	60.5	21.5		
Capital Expenditures	544.8	68.5	100.9	20.6		
Identifiable Assets	4,083.2	74.2	1,114.1	20.2		
Corporate Assets						
Total Assets						
1985						
Net Sales	$5,412.6	77.3%	$1,416.4	20.2%		
Operating Income	797.0	95.8	28.5	3.4		
Depreciation and						
Amortization Expense	161.7	68.5	53.2	22.5		
Capital Expenditures		76.7	103.7	17.3		
Identifiable Assets				20.2		
Corporate Assets						
Total Assets						

[a] In 1989, Communication and Transportation are included in this segment. It was part of Diversified Operations in previous years.

[b] In 1989, Entertainment became a principal business segment. It was part of diversified operations in previous years.

[c] Before 1989, Diversified Operations was a business segment. Notes a and b show how it was eliminated.

Source: Anheuser-Busch *Annual Report 1989, 1988, and 1985,* pp. 58–59; p. 46; and p. 50.

Diversified Operations[c]		Eliminations		Consolidated
		(13.7)	(0.1)%	$9,481.3
			0.0	1,328.7
			0.0	410.3
			0.0	1,076.7
			0.0	8,691.9
				343.8
				$9,025.7
$361.8	4.18%	($20.6)	(0.2)%	$8,924.1
40.9	3.2		0.9	1,264.1
35.4	9.9		0.0	359.0
64.2	6.8		0.0	950.5
340.0	5.1		0.0	6,673.0
				436.8
				$7,109.8
$366.1	4.3%	($19.4)	(0.2)%	$8,349.7
4.0	0.3		0.0	1,148.6
34.3	10.7		0.0	320.1
62.3	7.4		0.0	841.8
325.0	5.3		0.0	6,135.6
				412.3
				$6,547.9
$ 32.4	4.2%	($21.0)	(0.2)%	$7,754.3
15.6	1.5		0.0	1,018.0
28.4	10.1		0.0	281.2
87.1	10.9		0.0	796.2
307.0	5.6		0.0	5,504.9
				393.2
				$5,898.1
$189.6	2.7%	($13.9)	(0.2)%	$7,000.3
6.8	0.8		0.0	823.3
21.2	9.0		0.0	236.1
36.1	6.0		0.0	601.0
174.6	3.8		0.0	4,626.1
				495.3
				$5,121.4

In planning for the future, Anheuser-Busch would continue its long-term commitment to diversification. These efforts were to be maintained as long as they were consistent with meeting the company's objectives.

THE PRODUCT

Beer uniquely fits contemporary lifestyles. The five hallmarks of beer as a consumer beverage are convenience, moderation, health, value, and thirst-quenching properties. Each member of the Anheuser-Busch family of 14 beers was positioned to take advantage of this lifestyle. Exhibit 22.4 shows the target market for each of the company's beers.

Domestic consumption of alcoholic beverages continued to decline by about 2 percent annually.[13] Exhibit 22.5 provides information on the consumption of beer by segments (popular, premium, superpremium, light, low-alcohol, imported, malt liquor, and ale), and growth rates by segments and per capita consumption of beer, wine, distilled spirits, and coolers. The only projected growth segments for beer appeared to be light beer and imported beers; all other beer segments had a projected negative growth factor. Some of the reasons for the decline in alcohol consumption were the rising health consciousness among consumers and the focused attention on the dangers of drinking and driving. Also, the Census Bureau indicated a drop in the 20- to 39-year-old age group (see Exhibit 22.6).

EXHIBIT 22.4 Anheuser-Busch Beers

Beer	Class	Target Market
Budweiser	Premium	Any demographic or ethnic group and any region of the country
Bud Light	Light	Young to middle-age males
Bud Dry	Premium dry	New taste
Michelob	Superpremium	Contemporary adults
Michelob Light	Light	Young, active, upscale drinker with high-quality lifestyle
Michelob Dry	Dry	Yuppies
Busch	Popular	Consumers who prefer lighter-tasting beer at a value
Busch Light	Light	Popular-priced light beer
Natural Light	Light	Beverage to go with good food
LA	Low alcohol	Health-conscious consumers (ceased production May, 1990)
O'Doul's	Nonalcoholic	Great tasting beer without alcohol
King Cobra	Malt liquor	Contemporary male adults, aged 21–24
Carlsberg	Lager	Import market
Elephant Malt Liquor	Malt liquor	Consumers who enjoy imported beer

---

[13] "Beverage Industry," *Value Line*, November 23, 1990, p. 1533.

EXHIBIT 22.5   Apparent Beer Consumption by Segment (Barrels in millions)

	1970		1975		1980		1985		1990		1995		2000	
	Barrels	Share	Barrels	Share	Barrels	Share	Barrels	Share	Barrels	Share	Barrels	Share	Barrels	Share
Popular	71.6	58.3%	65.4	43.5%	30.0	16.9%	33.3	18.2%	30.5	16.5%	28.0	15.4%	26.0	14.4%
Premium	46.1	37.5	71.6	47.6	102.3	57.5	86.1	47.1	81.5	44.0	75.7	41.6	72.5	40.2
Super-premium	1.1	0.9	5.0	3.3	11.5	6.5	8.8	4.8	7.0	3.8	6.9	3.8	6.8	3.8
Light	—	—	2.8	1.9	22.1	12.4	39.4	21.6	49.0	26.4	52.0	28.6	54.0	30.0
Low Alcohol	—	—	—	—	—	—	0.4	0.2	0.1	0.1	0.1	0.1	0.1	0.1
Imported	0.9	0.7	1.7	1.1	4.6	2.6	7.9	4.3	11.0	5.9	13.5	7.4	16.0	8.9
Malt Liquor	3.1	2.5	3.8	2.5	5.5	3.1	5.5	3.0	5.2	2.8	4.7	2.6	4.2	2.3
Ale	—	—	—	—	1.9	1.1	1.3	0.7	1.0	0.5	0.9	0.5	0.7	0.4
Total	122.8	100.0	150.3	100.0	177.9	100.0	182.7	100.0	185.3	100.0	181.8	100.0	180.3	100.0

Source: *Impact Data Bank*, 1988 ed. Table 4–E, p. 30; Table 4–6, p. 31; Table 8–A, p. 75.

EXHIBIT 22.5   (cont.)

	Average Annual Compound Growth Rate					
Segment	1970–75	1975–80	1980–85	1985–90	1990–95	1995–2000
Popular	−1.8%	−14.4%	2.1%	−1.7%	−1.7%	−1.5%
Premium	9.2	7.4	−3.4	−1.1	−1.5	−0.9
Superpremium	35.4	18.1	−5.2	−4.5	−0.3	−0.3
Light	−	51.2	12.3	4.5	1.2	0.8
Low Alcohol	−	−	+	−24.2	−	−
Imported	13.5	22.2	11.6	6.8	4.2	3.5
Malt Liquor	4.2	7.7	−	−1.1	−2.0	−2.2
Ale	n/a	n/a	−7.3	−5.1	−2.1	−4.9
Total	4.1%	3.4%	0.5%	0.3%	−0.4%	−0.2%

Source: *Impact DataBank*, 1988 Ed., Table 8B, p. 76.

EXHIBIT 22.5   (cont.)

Per Capita Consumption
(Gallons per Adult)

	Year	
Category	1989E	2000E
Wine	2.54	2.12
Distilled Spirits	2.15	1.63
Beers	33.79	29.37
Coolers	0.62	0.37
Total Alcoholic Beverages	39.10	33.48

Source: *Market Watch*, April 1990, p. 24.

EXHIBIT 22.6 U.S. Population Projections[a]

	1990	1995	2000	2005	2010	2015	2020	2025
All Ages[a]	250,410,000	260,138,000	268,266,000	275,604,000	282,575,000	288,997,000	294,364,000	298,252,000
Under 5 years	18,408,000	17,799,000	16,898,000	16,611,000	16,899,000	17,213,000	17,095,000	16,664,000
5 to 9 years	18,378,000	18,759,000	18,126,000	17,228,000	16,940,000	17,225,000	17,542,000	17,428,000
10 to 14 years	17,284,000	18,847,000	19,208,000	18,575,000	17,670,000	17,380,000	17,674,000	18,000,000
15 to 19 years	17,418,000	17,567,000	19,112,000	19,477,000	18,839,000	17,930,000	17,642,000	17,940,000
20 to 24 years	18,698,000	17,482,000	17,600,000	19,109,000	19,453,000	18,818,000	17,931,000	17,657,000
25 to 29 years	21,511,000	18,966,000	17,736,000	17,822,000	19,310,000	19,642,000	19,020,000	18,144,000
30 to 34 years	22,414,000	21,996,000	19,413,000	18,175,000	18,262,000	19,750,000	20,080,000	19,457,000
35 to 39 years	20,220,000	22,244,000	21,820,000	19,274,000	18,041,000	18,115,000	19,576,000	19,906,000
40 to 44 years	17,677,000	20,092,000	22,091,000	21,678,000	19,161,000	17,931,000	18,015,000	19,463,000
45 to 49 years	13,947,000	17,489,000	19,885,000	21,892,000	21,482,000	18,980,000	17,769,000	17,855,000
50 to 54 years	11,540,000	13,808,000	17,338,000	19,736,000	21,725,000	21,328,000	18,866,000	17,679,000
55 to 59 years	10,623,000	11,229,000	13,459,000	16,917,000	19,259,000	21,195,000	20,811,000	18,422,000
60 to 64 years	10,741,000	10,096,000	10,699,000	12,846,000	16,171,000	18,420,000	20,276,000	19,925,000
65 to 69 years	10,251,000	10,056,000	9,491,000	10,106,000	12,163,000	15,319,000	17,467,000	19,257,000
70 to 74 years	8,122,000	8,874,000	8,752,000	8,304,000	8,876,000	10,705,000	13,506,000	15,420,000
75 to 79 years	6,105,000	6,607,000	7,282,000	7,246,000	6,913,000	7,419,000	8,981,000	11,378,000
80 to 84 years	3,828,000	4,315,000	4,735,000	5,287,000	5,295,000	5,068,000	5,462,000	6,647,000
85 to 89 years	2,065,000	2,433,000	2,803,000	3,141,000	3,554,000	3,587,000	3,459,000	3,769,000
90 to 94 years	873,000	1,074,000	1,302,000	1,539,000	1,759,000	2,017,000	2,061,000	2,014,000
95 to 99 years	260,000	330,000	417,000	520,000	631,000	738,000	864,000	903,000
100 years and over	56,000	76,000	100,000	131,000	171,000	217,000	266,000	325,000
Median age in years	33.0	34.7	36.4	37.8	39.0	39.5	40.2	41.0
Mean age in years	35.4	36.2	37.1	38.1	39.1	39.9	40.7	41.5

[a] Includes armed forces overseas.

Source: U.S. Department of Commerce, Bureau of the Census, Population Series, p. 14.

The perennial beer drinkers' preferences can and do change. Dry beer and nonalcoholic beer appeared to be successful in the test markets, but their true staying power remains unknown. For example, LA beer was dropped from the Anheuser-Busch line in 1990 because it lost its positioning when the company introduced O'Doul's brand of nonalcoholic beer.

Anheuser-Busch had 13 breweries located in 10 states, with an annual capacity of 85.1 million barrels of beer (see Exhibit 22.7). The 13th brewery at Centerville, Georgia, became operational in 1992 at a cost of approximately $300 million; its annual capacity was 6 million barrels. The expansion by Anheuser-Busch was the opposite of other brewers, which have been consolidating capacity. Mr. Busch sees ". . . expansion as necessary for 'market penetration and growth,' never blinking from Anheuser-Busch's projected 50-share by the mid-1990s."[14]

In order to meet the increasing demand for its beer, Anheuser-Busch developed an extensive expansion and modernization program. A 3.6-million barrel expansion at the Newark brewery was completed in 1990, and the capacity at the Tampa brewery was to be expanded by 800,000 barrels to 2.7 million. Mini-expansions were occurring at six other plants, and when completed would add approximately 2.5 million barrels of capacity.

Mr. Busch, talking about the cost of the ingredients (barley, rice, corn, hops, and others) to make beers, said, "We pay premium to the market because we demand the highest quality ingredients that money can buy. We have the highest cost of ingredients of anybody in the brewing industry. I can prove it to you. We

EXHIBIT 22.7   U.S. Production Facilities

Brewery	Year Opened	Capacity (In millions of barrels)
St. Louis	1880	12.6
Newark	1951	5.8
Los Angeles	1954	12.1
Tampa	1959	1.9
Houston	1966	9.7
Columbus	1968	6.4
Jacksonville	1969	6.7
Merrimack	1970	3.1
Williamsburg	1972	9.0
Fairfield	1976	3.7
Baldwinsville	1982	8.2
Fort Collins	1988	5.9
Total in 1990		85.1
Centerville	1992	6.0
Total in 1992		91.0

[14] Jabbonsky, "What Keeps A-B Hot?" p. 28.

must make sure that we are the lowest cost producer."[15] Mr. Busch went on to say, "Quality comes first." Mr. Busch's statements tied directly into the primary reason the company gives for Anheuser-Busch's outstanding record of achievement: "Quality—First and most importantly, Anheuser-Busch believes in quality. Quality is never sacrificed for economic reasons—or for any other reason. The company is firmly convinced that its belief in and strict adherence to quality is the fundamental, irreplaceable ingredient in its successful performance for more than 100 years. That quality is there for everybody to see, to taste, to experience, and to enjoy. 'Somebody still cares about quality' is more than a corporate slogan at Anheuser-Busch. It's a way of life."[16]

PROMOTION

Anheuser-Busch, probably the largest sponsor of sporting events, racing vehicles, and broadcasts, had its beers affiliated with sports for years (see Exhibit 22.8). In 1989, the company spent $32 million on advertising during the Olympic games.

The alcoholic beverage industry spent a total of $1,318,900,000 on advertising in 1988. The advertising mix by medium and by alcoholic beverage industry segment (beer, distilled spirts, wine, and coolers) is shown in Exhibit 22.9. The brewers spent nearly $900 million on advertising, or 68.3 percent of the total industry expenditures. The number one advertising medium for brewers continued to be television; magazines remained as the primary advertising medium for distilled spirits marketers.

Total media spending by the brewers for 1988 was over double the level for 1980. The per-case expenditure for beer has more than doubled during the same period, from 18 cents to 37 cents. Anheuser-Busch's advertising expenditures increased by 8 percent to $385 million, or 61.6 percent of the company's total for promotion. The company's total for 1988 increased 3.2 percent over 1987. Anheuser-Busch's advertising expenditures were 42.8 percent of total brewers' expenditures. Adolph Coors increased its advertising outlays by 30.7 percent to 126 million. Miller Brewing cut its media expenditures by $12.8 million, or 6.3 percent, from $202 million to $189 million or 21.0 percent of the total industry expenditures. G. Heileman Brewing (Bond Corporation) increased its expenditures by 41 percent to $42 million. Sam Frank, vice president of marketing for Heileman, said, "The way you try to build a regional brand is with regional affiliations to prevent more share erosion by national brands. You have to play on the big boy's turf, so to speak, if you want to prove to consumers that you're as good as national brands. You've got to advertise heavily."[17] G. Heileman sales declined by 10.4 percent despite the substantial increase in the marketing budget.

[15] Ibid.
[16] *Fact Book 1989/90*, p. 3.
[17] "Total Media Spending Drops 3.9% in '88 as Brewers Increase Outlays to $900 Million," *Impact*, Vol. 19, Nos. 16, 17, August 15 and September 1, 1989, p. 4.

EXHIBIT 22.8 Anheuser-Busch Companies, Sports Affiliation and Sponsorships

Budweiser

Horse Racing	Irish Derby
	Breeders' Cup
	Budweiser International
Hydroplane Racing	Miss Budweiser
CART/Indy Car	Truesports Indy Car
Drag Racing	King Funny Car
NASCAR	Junior Johnson Ford
CART/NASCAR	Budweiser International
	Race of Champions
Olympics	Corporate Sponsor
PGA Golf	Anheuser-Busch Golf Classic
Boxing	Golden Gloves
PBA Bowling	Budweiser Hall of Fame
Soccer	Major Indoor Soccer League
	U.S. Soccer Federation
	World Cup
	U.S. National Team
Shooting	Shooting Exhibitions by
	Willis Corbett
Surfing	Pro Surfing Tour

Bud Light

Powerboat Racing	Powerboat Racing Team
	ABC Masters
Bowling	
Triathlons	Ironman World
	Championship
	U.S. Triathlon Series

Busch

NASCAR	Official Beer of
	NASCAR
	Busch Pole Award
	Busch Clash
Pool	British Pool League

Michelob

Skiing	Team Michelob
Golf	Golf Advisory Staff

Source: Anheuser-Busch Companies, Inc., *Fact Book—1989/90*, p. 61

EXHIBIT 22.9   Alcoholic Beverage Advertising Expenditures by Medium[a] (In millions)

Medium	Beer	Distilled Spirits	Wine	Coolers	Total
Television	$679.7	$0.5	$64.2	$75.3	$819.7
Radio	144.8	1.0	11.6	3.9	161.3
Total Broadcast	824.5	1.5	75.8	79.2	981.0
Magazines	18.0	179.6	13.2	0.9	211.7
Outdoor	22.5	34.1	0.6	0.9	58.1
Newspapers	33.5	17.9	4.7	1.7	57.8
Newspaper Supplements	0.8	7.4	1.7	0.2	10.1
Total Print and Outdoor	74.8	239.0	20.3	3.7	337.8
	$899.3	$240.5	$96.2	$82.9	$1,318.9

[a] Columns may not add up because of rounding.
Source: *Impact DataBank*, Vol. 19, August 15 and September 15, 1989, p. 4.

Charles Fruit, vice president of corporate media for Anheuser-Busch said, "Our competitors continue to focus the majority of their television advertising in sports sponsorships and I would think that would continue to be a competitive area." In 1988, Anheuser-Busch allocated $11 million to introduce Michelob Dry on a national basis, while decreasing Michelob Light's expenditures from $33 million to $18 million. Mr. Fruit commented, "With the emergence of Michelob Dry, the whole Michelob family is registering positive trends again. Our regular Michelob brand had experienced the same softness. Dry invigorated the entire family."[18]

Anheuser-Busch Promotional Products Group had approximately 10,000 different items available at any one time. This included such items as caps, glassware, mugs, clothing, and key chains, all bearing the A & B eagle, Clydesdale, or beer-brand logos. Each year more than 1,500 new promotional items were created and authorized.

Anheuser-Busch acted as the Rolling Stones' primary U.S. sponsor for their 1989 27-city tour. A 30-second TV spot, "Honky Tonk Woman" featured the concert with a Bud bottle showing up every now and then.

In 1990, Anheuser-Busch announced its "market-share strategy," that was to pull millions of advertising dollars out of radio and television to spend more on "grass-roots" events and point-of-purchase promotions. This new strategy was announced to combat the price discounting in the industry (see Exhibit 22.10). According to Robert Weinberg, beer analyst, "Relative to competition, Anheuser-Busch was probably over advertising.[19]

[18] Ibid., pp. 3–4.
[19] Richard Gibson, "Bud Puts Stress on Promotions, Trims TV Ads," *Wall Street Journal*, February 21, 1990, p. B-5.

EXHIBIT 22.10   Anheuser-Busch Advertising Expenditures, 1989 and 1990

Media	1989	1990
Network Television	$181,467	$129,009
Spot Television	94,835	91,646
Syndicated Television	10,753	13,703
Cable Television	26,300	26,788
Network Radio	7,707	983
Spot Radio	42,073	21,147
Magazines	8,834	7,767
Newspapers	9,537	3,989
Newspaper Magazines	399	243
Outdoor	6,148	6,058
Total Measured Media	388,055	301,331
Total Unmeasured	203,400	157,900
Total	$591,455	$459,231

Source: *Advertising Age,* September 25, 1991, p. 4.

PRICING

The brewers were in the midst of a prolonged beer price war. During 1989, both Coors, the nation's fourth largest brewery, and Miller, number two, had been aggressively promoting and discounting their prices in order to boost volume for several of their key products, and in November, Anheuser-Busch joined the price war. Prices for Budweiser, the number one selling brand of beer, were discounted.

Value Line expected the price war "to lead to yet another industry shake-out. The playing field has narrowed considerably in recent years, but we think yet more changes are in the offing." They went on to say, "The most important questions are not who will be the winner and loser, but how long the price war will last and just what exactly do the victors win?" *Value Line* expected prices to continue on a downward trend and thought that the industry players recognized that there were significant long-term benefits at stake. One share point is approximately equal to 1 million barrels of beer.[20]

Most economists saw continuing recession at least through the first quarters of 1992. Historically, beer demand tended to hold up well during periods of downturns or recessions, but combined with the excise tax and inflation, brewers could experience a downturn as well. Anheuser-Busch's pricing strategy varied somewhat by market. Actually, by offering 14 different types of beer there was a product to satisfy each price point.

[20] "Beverage Industry," *Value Line*, November 1989, p. 1528.

DISTRIBUTION CHANNELS

The company distributed its beer in the United States and the Caribbean through a network of 10 company-owned wholesale operations employing approximately 1,600 people and about 950 independently owned wholesale companies (see Exhibit 22.11). The independent wholesalers employed approximately 30,000 people. Canadian and European distribution was achieved through special arrangements with foreign brewing companies.

The Anheuser-Busch Investment Capital Corporation, a subsidiary company, was formed in 1984 to share equity positions with qualified partners in Anheuser-Busch distributorships. This subsidiary provided operating general partners to function as independent wholesalers while increasing their equity and building toward total ownership. Anheuser-Busch Investment Capital Corporation played a key role in strengthening the brewer-wholesaler team.

EXHIBIT 22.11   Distribution Map

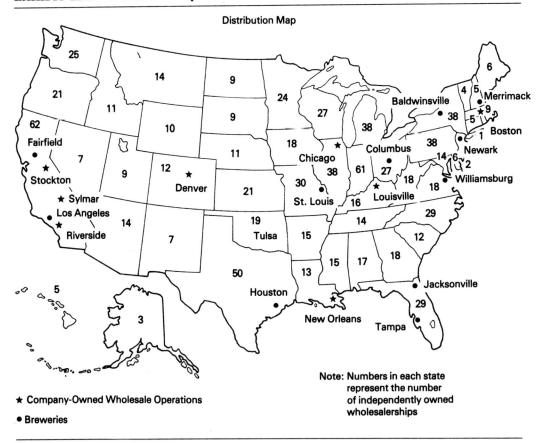

★ Company-Owned Wholesale Operations

● Breweries

Note: Numbers in each state represent the number of independently owned wholesalerships

When Mr. Busch was asked if "strong brewers and beer products make strong wholesalers or strong wholesalers make strong brewers, Busch lays the 'chicken-or-egg theory' to rest, noting succinctly, 'It takes both.'" Henry King, former president of the United States Brewing Association, said, "I've been with August when we've been driving along and he's spotted an A-B distributor's truck." Recalled King, "He pulled up behind it and spoke into his little cassette to dictate a memo to his secretary to send a letter of compliment to the wholesaler because his truck was beautifully cleaned and everything. Had that truck been dirty, there would have been a letter reprimanding him as well."[21]

Busch counts on the wholesalers as "one of our most important assets, who provide critical service to retailers. Personal service is key . . . they are the front-line merchandisers for the entire system and . . . indispensable to the system." "Together with our wholesalers," Busch stated, "we share a commitment to provide the consumer with the highest quality, best tasting, and freshest beer products through the three-tier system, in which the brewer, wholesaler, and retailer each play an important role." He went on to say, "Strong products, suppliers, wholesalers, and service equal retailer profitability. Quality to the consumer and product presentation equal sales success."[22]

THE EXTERNAL ENVIRONMENT

Competition

In 1970, the top five brewers in the United States comprised 33.3 percent of sales. In 1990, this had increased to 89.3 percent share of sales. During this same time period, Anheuser-Busch's market share increased from 18.1 percent to 43.4 percent. Miller Brewing, Stroh's Brewery, G. Heileman, and Adolph Coors increased their market share since 1970 as well. Exhibit 22.12 illustrates the market shares of the leading brewers in the United States.

The big market share shift in the decade of the 1980s was accomplished by Anheuser-Busch, as Miller Brewing remained at approximately the same level. A major part of Stroh Brewery's growth occurred with the acquisition of Joseph Schlitz Brewing Company in 1982, and F&M Schaefer in 1981.

The Market Share Leader.   Anheuser-Busch set a corporate objective of 50 percent market share by the mid-1990s. In 1990, the company's market share was 43.4 percent, compared with 37.1 percent share in 1985, and 28.2 percent a decade ago.

The Market Share Challenger.   Miller Brewing was Anheuser-Busch's prime competitor from the time Philip Morris Company acquired Miller in 1970. Its market

---

[21] Jabbonsky, "What Keeps A-B Hot?" p. 28.
[22] Ibid.

EXHIBIT 22.12   Sales of Leading U.S. Brewers (In thousands of barrels)

	1970		1980		1985		1990	
	Volume	Market Share	Volume	Market Share	Volume	Market Share	Volume	Market Share
Anheuser-Bush	22,202	18.1%	50,160	28.2%	68,000	37.1%	86,400	43.4%
Miller Brewing	5,150	4.2	37,300	21.0	37,100	20.3	43,550	21.9
Adolh Coors Company	7,277	5.9	13,779	7.7	14,738	8.1	19,250	9.7
Stroh Brewery	3,276	2.7	6,161	3.5	23,400	12.8	16,200	8.1
G. Heileman Brewing	3,000	2.4	13,270	7.4	16,200	8.8	12,250	6.2
Top 5 Total	40,905	33.3	120,670	67.8	159,438	87.1	177,650	89.3
Other Domestic	80,995	68.0	52,830	29.6	15,662	8.6	12,246	6.2
Total Domestic	121,900	99.3	173,500	97.4	175,100	95.7	189,896	95.5
Imports	900	0.7	4,600	2.8	7,900	4.3	9,000	4.5
Grand Total	122,800	100.0	177,900	100.0	183,000	100.0	198,896	100.0

Source: *Impact*, Vol. 19, Nos. 16 & 17, August 15 and September 1, 1990, p. 3, *Wall Street Journal*, January 15, 1991, p. B-1.

share in 1970 was 4.2 percent (5.1 million barrels), ranking it as seventh in the industry. The company experienced rapid growth in the 1970s due to the successful introduction of "Lite" beer. Although growth had been rapid during the 1970s, market share remained relatively flat through the 1980s. Offering eight different brands, Miller ranked second in the industry. Anheuser-Busch countered Miller with two separate strategies. First, the company increased its advertising budgets, taking on Miller in head-to-head competition. Second, Anheuser-Busch developed a strategy of flanking each of Miller's products in every beer category with two Anheuser-Busch beer products (e.g., premium beers—Budweiser and Busch flanked Miller High Life).

In December 1989, Miller Brewing introduced a new nonalcoholic beer called Sharp's. At about the same time, Anheuser-Busch delivered its planned O'Doul's brand. The two new brands challenged the industry leader in nonalcoholic beers, Kingsbury, brewed by G. Heileman Brewing, and a host of imported brands such as Cardinal Brewery's Moussy, Binding Brauerei's Clausthaler, and Guinness' Kaliber. Nonalcoholic beer represented less than one-half of 1 percent of domestic beer consumption, but it was growing at a 6 to 15 percent rate yearly.[23] Supposedly, Miller Brewing did not fully test market Sharp's in order to beat Anheuser-Busch into the market place.

Stroh Brewery.   In 1981, the Stroh Brewery purchased F&M Schaefer and closed its Detroit brewery (7.2 million barrel capacity). On April 27, 1982, the Joseph Schlitz Brewing Company was merged into Stroh Brewery, resulting in Stroh becoming the third largest brewer. The company shipped 16.2 million barrels of beer in 1990, representing an 8.1 percent market share, which was a decline from its peak of 12.8 percent share in 1985.

Adolph Coors Company.   The fourth largest brewer, Adolph Coors Company, had an 11.8 percent volume increase in sales in 1990. This increase was the largest of any of the major brewers in the United States. It was enough to move Coors from fifth place to fourth in market share.

In September 1989, Coors proposed the acquisition of Stroh Brewing Company for $425 million. The acquisition was opposed in the federal courts by S&P Company, a privately held company that owned Falstaff, Pabst, Pearl, and General Brewing Companies. S&P Co. alleged that the merger would violate the antitrust laws. In addition, G. Heileman Brewing was considering antitrust action against Coors as a purchaser. (Heileman also had considered making a bid for parts of the Stroh Company.) The merger had to be approved by the U.S. Department of Justice (DOJ). Peter H. Coors, president of Coors Brewery, had commented on why his company was interested in purchasing Stroh's, "You can't survive long term with a nine percent market share." The transaction was supposed to close in early 1990, but Coors eventually withdrew its offer.[24]

23 "This Safe Suds Is For You," *Newsweek*, March 5, 1990, p. 42.
24 "Insights," *Impact*, Vol. 19, No. 20, October 15, 1989, p. 12; "Coors May Take a Gulp of a Rival Brew," *Business Week*, October 21, 1989, p. 70.

G. Heileman Brewing. The United States' fifth largest brewer, Heileman had been very effective in competing against Anheuser-Busch in regional markets. It successfully developed and implemented a strategy of acquiring struggling local brewers at low cost. After acquiring the new brewery, Heileman reintroduced its brands with an aggressive marketing plan. Anheuser-Busch countered with a strategy focused on heavy price competition from its Busch brand. Although G. Heileman halted its planned expansion into the Southwest market, the company's market share grew from 2.4 percent (3.0 million barrels) in 1970 to 8.8 percent (16.2 million barrels) in 1985. The company's earnings from the brewing industry declined by 11 percent in 1985, and it closed its small Phoenix plant (500,000 barrels.)

In a hostile takeover in 1987, Bond Holding Corporation, an Australian conglomerate involved in the world beer market, acquired G. Heileman Brewing Company. Since the takeover, Heileman faced weakening sales and deteriorating finances. In 1989, Heileman suffered its third year of declining beer shipments. In Chicago, Heileman's largest market, "supermarket sales of Old Style last year slipped to 15 percent market share from 21 percent."[25] In April 1990, Bond announced that Heileman was close to restructuring its bank loans. The banks would write off the debt and take an equity investment in the company. Heileman management had previously announced plans to sell some unneeded breweries and, possibly, some minor brands. However, market share further deteriorated in 1990 to 6.2 percent, which caused Heileman to lose its fourth place position to Coors. A continuation of the price war would cause further deterioration of the weaker beer companies.

Niche Strategies. During the 1980s, many micro-breweries and boutique-type breweries were started. These breweries had a different target market from the national firms. The target market for these breweries was the connoisseur, the moderate beer drinker who is particular and seeks a certain taste. Actually, the select target market for the distinctive taste cuts across the traditional demographic lines and was not limited to any one class.

International Competition. Anheuser-Busch's world market share was approximately 9.5 percent. Miller Brewing, which was in second place, had approximately 5.0 percent of the world market. The top two brewers were American, and the next three (Heineken NV—4 percent, Kerin Brewery Co.—3.1 percent, and Bond Corporation—3.1 percent) were European. These top five brewers had approximately 30 percent of the world market. The annual growth rate for the entire world market was 3 to 4 percent a year.[26] The per capita consumption of beer for the top 20 countries ranged from 38.73 gallons in West Germany to

---

[25] Ira Teinowitz, "Heileman Close to Deal with Banks," *Advertising Age*, April 16, 1990, p. 66.
[26] Paul Heme, "King of Beers in Bitter Battle in Britain," *Wall Street Journal*, June 9, 1988, p. 26.

16.03 gallons in Venezuela. The United States was ranked in 12th place with 13.99 gallons. Eight nations exceeded the 30-gallon per capita figure.[27]

Leonard Goldstein, president of Miller Brewing Company, said, "I think U.S. brewers have a long way to go in the overseas markets . . . we're in more than 50 countries . . . they are all very small situations to get our foot in the door . . . [it allows] us [to] see what innovation is around the world."[28]

The international market was estimated to be three and one-half to four times the size of the U.S. market. In the Far East and Europe, the consumption of alcoholic beverages was on the rise. All the U.S. brewers, except Coors, were largely pursuing a share of these markets. *Value Line* "believes overseas sales will play an increasing larger role in the results of brewers . . . with 1990 easing of economic barriers in Europe."[29] The world market for beer, including the U.S. market, was approximately 700 million barrels.

Anheuser-Busch International, the company's international licensing and marketing subsidiary, was formed in 1981 to develop and explore markets outside the United States. Budweiser was introduced into England in 1984 and four years later had eked out only a 1 percent share of the market. It was the same Bud that was sold in the United States. By contrast, Australian Foster's, made by Elder IXL, modified its brew to appeal to British tastes. Foster's had a 6 percent market share after seven years. Norman Strauss, British marketing consultant, said, "Foster got into the British lager drinking culture with the humor of its ads [Paul Hogan of *Crocodile Dundee* is the Foster spokesperson] and an unerring eye for the pub lifestyle." Budweiser's first approach was to sell America without addressing British pub culture. Anheuser-Busch went through three advertising agencies in the past two years. John Dunsmore, a beer analyst, said, "The day Anheuser stops gaining share in the States' beer market, they'll go into overdrive in trying to develop their international business." He went on to say, "They could well be too late."[30]

Mr. Busch states, "As we go along, we are learning how to deal in these international markets from our partners."[31] Budweiser was licensed-brewed in 7 countries and exported to more than 30 others. Additional expansions were planned. Budweiser was marketed in Japan as a superpremium beer and led in the category. Bud had great success in Japan and Korea. Anheuser-Busch's prominent partners around the world included Carlsberg, Guinness, Suntory, and Oriental Brewery.

Robert S. Weinberg, beer analyst and consultant, said, "If you're talking about continuing to license and play the game as they are playing it . . . I think it is a very attractive and worthwhile game." He went on to say, "If you're talking

[27] *Impact Data Bank—1988 Edition*, Table 2-AA, p. 20.
[28] "Miller's Drive to Innovate," *Impact*, Vol. 20, No. 9, May 1, 1990, p. S.
[29] *Value Line*, November 23, 1990, p. 1533.
[30] *Impact Data Bank*, Table 4-AA, p. 43.
[31] Jabbonsky, "What Keeps A-B Hot?" p. 30.

about buying breweries and so forth, I don't think there are any great economies of scale in being an international brewing company."[32]

Social Values and Beer

Anheuser-Busch "is deeply concerned about the abuse of alcohol and the problem of driving while intoxicated. It supports the proposition that anything less than responsible consumption of alcoholic beverages is detrimental to the individual, society, and to the brewing industry."[33] The company was a leader in developing programs that support this position.

Anheuser-Busch designed programs to meet the needs of its employees, its wholesalers, its retailers, and its customers. The programs covered the following areas: (1) consumer education programs—Know When to Say When, The Buddy System, and Pit Stop; (2) training retailers—TIPS (Training for Intervention Procedures by Servers of Alcohol); (3) designated driver programs—Alert Cab and I'm Driving; (4) helping communities fight against alcohol abuse—Operation ALERT (Action and Leadership through Education Responsibility and Training) (5) helping employees deal with alcohol abuse—Employee Assistance Program; (6) company guidelines and policies—Industry Advertising Code and Young Adult Marketing Guidelines; (7) underage drinking—SADD (Students against Driving Drunk); and (8) Alcohol Research Center, UCLA.

Legislation and Litigation

In recent years, Anheuser-Busch became more active in monitoring and taking positions on issues that could have a major impact on the company. The Industry and Government Affairs Division expanded in order to identify and respond to such issues with specific programs.

Trademark Protection.   A lawsuit, filed by G. Heileman Brewing and joined by Miller Brewing Company against Anheuser-Busch's use of "LA" (low alcohol) as a brand name, was won by Anheuser-Busch with its claim that LA was a trademark and not a generic term. However, a short time later the company dropped LA from the product line when its O'Doul's brand was introduced.

Exclusive Distribution.   The Malt Beverage Interbrand Competition Act of 1985 dealt with the exclusive wholesale distribution rights for distributors within their territories. The state of Indiana was the only state to forbid exclusive distribution contracts, and 27 states required the contracts.

In 1977, a Supreme Court decision ruled such exclusive contracts could be legal if the contracts did not hamper competition, but that a decision would be made on a case-by-case basis. Distributors and brewers said that this court

---

[32] Ibid.
[33] *Fact Book 1989/90*, p. 33.

decision created lawsuits by inviting competitors, both wholesalers and retailers, to challenge the competitor's exclusive distribution contracts.

A new bill, which was cleared by the Senate Judiciary Committee, would preserve the right to sue for antitrust violations. The 140-member U.S. Brewers Association and the 2,000-member National Beer Wholesaler Association lobbied for the bill, because they felt it would clarify the existing antitrust law. Opponents to the bill, including the Federal Trade Commission, Senator Strom Thurmond, Senator Howard Metzenbaum, and numerous consumer groups, felt that exempting the beer industry from the antitrust laws would increase prices and reduce competition. In fact, the New York attorney-general filed a class action lawsuit against Miller, Stroh, Heileman, and Anheuser-Busch claiming that their exclusive agreements with distributors caused price increases and decreased competition.

Kickbacks.   Dennis P. Long, president of Anheuser-Busch, resigned in March 1988 when Joseph E. Martino, vice president of sales, and Michael A. Orloff, vice president for wholesaling, left the company after an internal investigation of kickbacks at Anheuser-Busch. Martino and Orloff were found guilty by a federal grand jury of fraud, conspiracy, and filing false tax returns. Mr. Long "was not accused of any wrongdoing, but stepped down because of what transpired under his nose."[34] With Mr. Long's departure, Mr. Busch became president of Anheuser-Busch, and kept this position until he appointed Mr. Stokes as president.

Minimum Drinking Age.   The National Minimum Drinking Age Act of 1984 granted the federal government the authority to withhold federal highway funds from states that failed to raise their legal drinking age to 21 by 1986. Currently, all 50 states have mandated a 21-year-old minimum drinking age.

Anheuser-Busch and Minorities.   In 1983, the Reverend Jesse Jackson's campaign PUSH was directed against Anheuser-Busch Companies. PUSH accused the company of discriminating against blacks and encouraged minorities to boycott Anheuser-Busch's products. Using the battle cry "Bud Is a Dud," Jackson claimed the company did not do business with enough minorities, did not hire and promote black employees, did not patronize black-oriented community organizations, and did not have enough black wholesalers in the distribution system. Eventually, Wayman Smith, vice president of corporate affairs, was able to make the Reverend Jackson aware of the company's minority hiring and promotion practices, its support to minorities throughout the country, and the role of minority suppliers.

[34] Jabbonsky, "What Keeps A-B Hot?" p. 26.

Excise Tax. In 1988, Anheuser-Busch paid $781 million in state and federal excise taxes. The company "believes that excise taxes discriminate against both the industries involved and consumers."[35]

Warning Labels. Congress passed legislation that went into effect in November 1989 requiring a warning statement to appear on all alcoholic beverage containers. The two-part statement read: "Government Warning: (1) According to the Surgeon General, women should not drink alcoholic beverages during pregnancy because of the risks of child defects. (2) "Consumption of alcoholic beverages impairs your ability to operate machinery and may cause serious health problems." The legislation required this two-part statement and restricted state governments from requiring any additional statements.

Advertising and Marketing Restrictions. There are proposals to ban beer and wine advertising from radio and television. In addition, some groups are calling for restriction of the brewing industry's ability to advertise or promote beer and wine at sporting events. Anheuser-Busch "strongly opposes such restrictions."[36]

Concentration and Possible Antitrust Review. A knowledgeable beer market analyst has wondered if the Department of Justice would take or propose antitrust action as Anheuser-Busch's market share approached 50 percent. This growth over the past decade from 28.2 percent in 1980 to 43.4 percent in 1990 was accomplished in a maturing industry through internal expansion. If Anheuser-Busch attempted to grow by merger to achieve 50 percent market share, the Justice Department would probably have rejected the mergers based on the Herfindahl Index. Named for Orris Herfindahl, an economist, the index is a calculation based on the premise that market leaders have even greater economic power in an industry than can be assumed by simply looking at market share. A possibility exists that one of the remaining small brewers will ask the Justice Department for protection or relief under the antitrust laws.

FINANCIAL CONDITION

In 1989 Anheuser-Busch completed the company's most successful decade in its 147-year history (see Exhibits 22.13 and 22.14). During the 1980s, net sales increased by 287.7 percent ($3,295,400,000 to $9,481,300,000); net income rose by 346.6 percent ($171,800,000 to $767,200,000); gross profits increased 332.3 percent

[35] *Fact Book 1989/90*, p. 54.
[36] Ibid., pp. 54, 59.

($741,500,800 to $3,205,500,000); and the total assets of the company increased 268.4 percent ($2,449,700,000 to $9,025,700,000). The company paid a stock dividend for 57 consecutive years (see Exhibit 22.15).

During 1989, the company established an employee stock ownership plan (ESOP) for its salaried and hourly employees. The plan borrowed $500 million to buy approximately 11.3 million shares of common stock from the company. The ESOP and other stock ownership plans would eventually lead to approximately 10 percent ownership by the company's employees.[37]

On November 26, 1989, Anheuser-Busch Companies registered more than 8 million shares of common stock with the Securities and Exchange Commission that may be sold periodically by the heirs of August Busch, Jr., who died in September 1989. This secondary share offering represented about 8.4 percent of the company's outstanding common stock. Before Mr. Busch's death, about 23 percent of the company was closely controlled—12 percent by Mr. Busch and 11 percent by Centerre Trust Company of St. Louis, and 1 percent by other directors.[38]

Over the next five years, the capital expenditures were expected to exceed $4.4 billion. The company was not opposed to long-term financing for some of its capital programs, but cash flow from operations would be the principal source of funds to support these programs. For short-term capital requirements, the company had access to a maximum of $500 million from a bank credit-line agreement. In 1992, the company had an AA bond rating. In 1989, the company's long-term debt almost doubled, from $1,615,300,000 in 1988 to $3,307,300,000 in 1989. (The acquisition of Sea World was for $1.1 billion.)

The beer and beer-related segment had sales of $7,405,700,000 (78.1 percent) and operating income of $1,244,700 (93.7 percent) in 1989. The food products segment had sales of $1,803,000,000 (19.0 percent) and operating income of $56,900,000 (4.3 percent), and the entertainment segment had sales of $286,300,000 (3.0 percent) and operating income of $27,100,000 (2.0 percent). The combined sales and operating income for the two nonbeer segments totaled 22.0 percent of sales and 6.3 percent of operating income. A former Anheuser-Busch executive would attribute the performance of the nonbeer segments to the fact that they were managed by "beer guys." He said, "They continue to use 'beer guys' on the diversifications. It's a big mistake."[39]

[37] "Directors Approve ESOP, Employees Could Own 10%," *Wall Street Journal*, April 27, 1989, p. C-17; "Heirs' Shares," *St. Petersburg Times*, November 27, 1989, B-1.
[38] "Anheuser-Busch," *Value Line*, August 25, 1989, p. 1531.
[39] Marshall, "The Czar of Beer," p. 30.

EXHIBIT 22.13   10 Year Financial Summary—Balance Sheet and Other Information
(In millions except per share and statistical data)

	1980	1981	1982	1983
Balance Sheet Information				
Working Capital	$ 26.3	$ 41.0	$ 60.2	$ 173.1
Current Ratio	1.1	1.1	1.1	1.2
Plant and Equipment, Net	1,947.4	1,324.5	3,579.8	3,269.8
Long-Term Debt	743.8	862.2	1,029.9	1,003.1
Total Debt to Total Debt Plus				
Equity (%)	43.4	42.5	36.8[a]	32.8[a]
Deferred Income Taxes	261.6	357.7	455.2	574.3
Shareholders' Equity	1,031.4	1,206.8	1,526.6	1,766.5
Return on Shareholders' Equity (%)	17.8	19.3	19.9[a]	18.0[a]
Book Value per Share	3.81	4.43	5.27	6.09
Total Assets	2,449.7	2,938.1	3,965.2	4,386.8
Other Information				
Capital Expenditures	$590.0	$441.5	$380.9	$441.3
Depreciation and Amortization	99.4	110.0	136.9	191.3
Total Payroll Cost	594.1	695.5	864.0	1,361.7
Effective Tax Rate (%)	35.7	33.2	40.0	43.7
Price/Earnings-Ratio	7.3	8.9	11.0	9.6
Percentage of Pretax Profit on				
Gross Sales (%)	7.1	7.3	9.1	9.2
Market Price Range of Common Stock				
High/	5 1/4	7 3/8	11 7/8	12 7/8
Low	3 1/2	4 1/2	6 1/2	9 3/4

Note: All per share information reflects the September 12, 1986 two-for-one stock split and the June 14, 1985, three-for-one stock split. All amounts reflect the acquisition of Campbell-Taggart, as of November 2, 1982, and the acquisitions of Sea World as of December 1, 1989. Financial information prior to 1988 has been restated to reflect the adoption in 1988 of Financial Accounting Standards No. 94, Consolidation of Majority-Owned Subsidiaries.

[a] This percentage has been calculated by including convertible redeemable preferred stock as part of equity because it was convertible into common stock and was trading primarily on its equity characteristics.

Source: *Annual Report 1989*, pp. 62–63.

	1984	1985	1986	1987	1988	1989
	$ 71.5	$ 116.0	$ (3.7)	$ 75.8	$ 15.2	$ (25.7)
	1.1	1.1	1.0	1.1	1.0	1.0
	3,579.5	4,494.9	4,994.8	4,994.8	5,467.7	6,671.3
	879.5	904.7	1,164.0	1,422.6	1,615.3	3,307.3
	28.2[a]	26.9[a]	31.6	33.0	34.2	52.4
	757.9	964.7	1,094.0	1,164.3	1,212.5	1,315.9
	1,951.0	2,173.0	2,313.7	2,892.2	3,102.9	3,099.9
	18.2[a]	18.9[a]	20.5[a]	22.4	23.9	24.7
	6.91	7.84	8.61	9.87	10.95	10.95
	4,592.5	5,192.9	5,898.1	6,547.9	7,109.8	9,025.7
	$532.3	$611.3	$796.2	$841.8	$950.5	$1,076.7
	207.9	240.0	281.2	320.1	359.0	410.3
	1,438.6	1,559.1	1,640.9	1,790.5	1,818.2	1,954.2
	43.5	43.4	45.3	42.2	38.3	37.5
	9.8	14.9	15.5	16.4	12.9	14.4
	9.6	10.1	11.2	11.7	12.0	11.9
	12 3/8	22 7/8	28 5/8	39 3/4	34 1/8	45 7/8
	8 7/8	8 7/8	20	26 3/8	29 1/8	30 5/8

EXHIBIT 22.14   **Consolidated Balance Sheet (In millions)**

	December 31	
	1988	*1989*
Current Assets		
Cash and Marketable Securities	$ 63.9	$ 36.4
Accounts and Notes Receivable, Less Allowance for		
Doubtful Accounts of $4.2 in 1989 and $4.1 in 1988	463.1	527.8
Inventories		
Raw Materials and Supplies	344.6	314.6
Work in Process	84.7	99.0
Finished Goods	82.9	118.1
Total Inventories	512.2	531.7
Other Current Assets	155.1	181.0
Total Current Assets	1,194.3	1,276.9
Investments and Other Assets		
Investments In and Advances to Affiliated Companies	82.3	87.4
Investment Properties	34.9	141.1
Deferred Charges and Other Non-current Assets	225.7	312.2
Excess of Cost Over Net Assets of Acquired Businesses,		
Net	104.9	536.8
	447.8	1,077.5
Plant and Equipment		
Land	126.6	289.6
Buildings	1,085.1	2,683.1
Machinery and Equipment	4,715.0	5,504.2
Construction in Progress	716.3	711.0
	7,643.0	9,187.9
Accumulated Depreciation	(2,175.3)	(2,516.6)
	5,467.7	6,671.3
Total Assets	$7,109.8	$9,025.7

EXHIBIT 22.14   (cont.)

	December 31	
	1988	*1989*
Liabilities and Shareholders Equity		
Current Liabilities		
Current Portion of Long-Term Debt	$ 0	$ 104.0
Accounts Payable	568.7	608.0
Accrued Salaries, Wages, and Benefits	229.4	212.0
Accrued Interest Payable	49.5	60.2
Due to Customers for Returnable Containers	40.7	42.2
Accrued Taxes, Other Than Income Taxes	60.1	65.4
Estimated Income Taxes	75.2	40.0
Other Current Liabilities	155.5	170.8
Total Current Liabilities	1,179.1	1,302.6
Long-Term Debt	1,615.3	3,307.3
Deferred Income Taxes	1,212.5	1,315.9
Common Stock and Other Shareholders' Equity		
Common Stock, $1.00 Par Value, Authorized 400 Shares	331.0	333.9
Capital in Excesss of Par Value	428.5	507.2
Retained Earnings	3,444.9	3,985.9
Foreign Currency Translation Adjustment	10.9	9.7
	4,215.3	4,836.7
Treasury Stock, at Cost	(1,112.4)	(1,236.8)
Employee Stock Ownership Plan Shares	0	(500.0)
	3,102.9	3,099.9
Total Liabilities and Shareholders' Equity	$7,109.8	$9,025.7

Source: *Anheuser-Busch Annual Report 1989*, pp. 44–45.

EXHIBIT 22.15   Financial Summary—Operations

	1975	1980	1981	1982
Barrels Sold	35.2	50.2	54.5	59.1
Sales	$1,036.7	$3,822.4	$4,435.9	$5,251.2
Federal and State Excise Taxes	391.7	527.0	562.4	609.1
Net Sales	1,645.0	3,295.4	3,873.5	4,642.1
Cost of Products and Services	1,343.8	2,553.9	3,001.9	3,384.3
Gross Profit	301.2	741.5	871.6	1,257.8
Marketing Distribution, and				
Administrative Expenses	126.1	428.6	518.6	758.8
Operating Income	175.1	312.9	353.0	499.0
Interest Expense	(22.6)	(75.6)	(90.7)	(93.2)
Interest Capitalized	0	41.7	64.1	41.2
Interest Income	10.9	2.4	6.2	17.0
Other Income (Expense), Net	1.9	(9.9)	(7.3)	(5.8)
Income before Income Taxes	165.3	271.5	325.3	478.6
Income Taxes	80.6	99.7	107.9	191.3
Net Income	84.7	171.8	217.4	287.3
Per Share—Primary Income				
before Cumulative Effect of				
Change in Accounting Method	.63	.64	.80	1.00
Cumulative Effect of Change in				
Accounting Method	—	—	—	—
Net Income	.63	.64	.80	1.00
Per Share—Fully Diluted	.63	.64	.77	.98
Cash Dividends Paid				
Common Stock	22.8	44.8	51.2	65.8
Per Share	.2133	.165	.188	.23
Average Number of Common				
Shares	135.3	271.2	272.4	288.6

1983	1984	1985	1986	1987	1988	1989
60.5	64.0	68.0	72.3	76.1	78.5	80.7
$6,714.7	$7,218.8	$7,756.7	$8,473.8	$9,110.4	$9,705.1	$10,283.6
624.3	657.0	683.0	724.5	760.7	781.0	802.3
6,090.4	6,561.8	7,073.7	7,754.3	8,349.7	8,924.1	9,481.3
4,161.0	4,464.6	4,729.8	5,026.5	5,374.3	5,825.5	6,275.8
1,929.4	2,097.2	2,343.9	2,727.8	2,975.4	3,098.6	3,205.5
1,226.4	1,338.5	1,498.2	1,709.8	1,826.8	1,834.5	1,876.8
703.0	758.7	845.7	1,018.0	1,148.6	1,264.1	1,328.7
(115.4)	(106.0)	(96.5)	(99.9)	(127.5)	(141.6)	(117.9)
32.9	46.8	37.2	33.2	40.3	44.2	51.5
12.5	22.8	21.8	9.6	12.8	9.8	12.6
(14.8)	(29.6)	(23.3)	(13.6)	(9.9)	(16.4)	11.8
618.2	692.7	784.4	947.3	1,064.3	1,160.1	1,226.7
270.2	301.2	340.7	429.3	449.6	444.2	459.5
348.0	391.5	443.7	518.0	614.7	715.9	767.2
1.08	1.23	1.42	1.69	2.04	2.45	2.68
—	—	—	—	—	—	—
1.08	1.23	1.42	1.69	2.04	2.45	2.68
1.08	1.23	1.42	1.69	2.04	2.45	2.68
78.3	89.7	102.7	120.2	148.4	188.6	226.2
.27	.3133	.3667	.44	.54	.66	.80
321.0	317.4	312.6	306.6	301.5	292.2	286.2

—————————————————— CASE 23 ——————————————————

HEALTHSOUTH Rehabilitation Corporation

———————————————————————————————————

HEALTHSOUTH Rehabilitation Corporation (HRC) was by all measures one of the most successful business ventures in modern health care. Its growth was nothing less than phenomenal. Yet growth involved its own challenge. As Richard M. Scrushy, chairman, chief executive officer, and president of HEALTHSOUTH Rehabilitation Corporation, read the first quarter 1991 earnings release (Exhibit 23.1) and reflected on the company's first seven years of growth he wondered about HRC's future.

With 19 consecutive quarters of earnings growth, HEALTHSOUTH had been the darling of Wall Street. The medical rehabilitation niche within the health care industry had been as successful as originally believed. The company had achieved and exceeded all of the objectives of its original business plan.

Scrushy realized that in order to sustain growth, continued hard work was even more necessary than during the start-up period. He also knew that some key strategic decisions would have to be made:

- Should the company continue to focus on the rehabilitation business?
- Should the company concentrate more on one business segment?
- Should the company diversify further into the acute-care hospital business?
- What pitfalls lie ahead?
- Can success continue?
- Where should we go from here?

BEGINNING OF SUCCESS

The company was organized in 1983 as AMCARE but in 1985 changed its name to HEALTHSOUTH Rehabilitation Corporation. HEALTHSOUTH was founded by a group of health care professionals, led by Scrushy, who were formerly with LifeMark Corporation, a large publicly held, for-profit health care

This case was prepared by W. Jack Duncan, Peter M. Ginter, and Michael D. Martin as a basis for class discussion rather than to illustrate either effective or ineffective handling of an administrative situation. Used with permission from W. Jack Duncan.

EXHIBIT 23.1   HEALTHSOUTH News Release

NEWS RELEASE

For Immediate Release
April 16, 1991

HEALTHSOUTH's Net Income for First Quarter Up 64 Percent

Birmingham, AL—HEALTHSOUTH Rehabilitation Corporation (NYSE:HRC) reported today that it generated a net income of $4,230,000 on net revenues of $50,574,000 for the quarter ended March 31, 1991. This represents a 64 percent increase as compared to the net income generated in the first quarter, 1990. Net revenues were 17 percent greater in this quarter than those experienced in the same period prior year. Primary earnings per share for the quarter were 31 cents, an increase of 29 percent as compared to last year. On a fully diluted basis, earnings per share for this quarter were 28 cents, a seven cent increase as compared to last year.

"During the first quarter," said Richard M. Scrushy, Chairman of the Board, President and CEO, "we opened four new outpatient centers, bringing the total number of operating locations to 55. The construction of our Kingsport, Tennessee, rehabiliation hospital is on schedule and is expected to contribute to our operating results in the third quarter."

HEALTHSOUTH Rehabilitation Corporation, a leading provider of comprehensive medical rehabilitation services in the United States, currently operates 55 locations in 22 states.

Summary of Operating Results
(unaudited, in thousands except per share data)

	Three Months Ended March 31,	
	1990	1991
Net Revenues	$43,308	$50,574
Net Income	2,573	4,230
Weighted Average Common and Common Equivalent Shares Outstanding	10,826	13,709
Earnings Per Share		
Primary	$.24	$.31
Fully Diluted	$.21	$.28

services chain that was acquired by American Medical International (AMI) in 1984.

In 1982, Richard Scrushy indicated how he first recognized the potential for rehabilitation services: "I saw the Tax Equity and Fiscal Responsibility Act (TEFRA) guidelines and the upcoming implementation of Medicare's prospective payment system (PPS) as creating a need for outpatient rehabilitation services. It was rather clear that lengths of stay in general hospitals would decrease and that patients would be discharged more quickly than in the past. It became obvious to me that these changes would create a need for a transition between the hospital and the patient's home." Medicare provided financial incentives for outpatient rehabilitation services by giving comprehensive outpatient rehabilitation facilities (CORFs) an exemption from prospective payment systems and allowed the services of these facilities to continue to be reimbursed on a retrospective, cost-based basis (reimbursement paid after patient care based on the cost of care).

Mr. Scrushy anticipated the impact of the upcoming reimbursement changes: "I also saw that LifeMark would suffer significant reductions in profitability as the use of the then lucrative ancillary inpatient services was discouraged under the new reimbursement guidelines. I discussed my concerns about the upcoming changes in Medicare with LifeMark management and proposed that we develop a chain of outpatient rehabilitation centers. I saw that the centers I proposed were LifeMark's chance to preserve its profitability under PPS, and when they rejected my proposal, I saw cutbacks and a low rate of advancement in the future."

Mr. Scrushy repeated his proposal for AMI's management when it acquired LifeMark, but AMI could not implement the program immediately after a major acquisition. Scrushy resigned his position to move to Birmingham, Alabama, a city with an international reputation in health care, and there founded HEALTH-SOUTH Rehabilitation Corporation in conjunction with three colleagues from LifeMark.

Early Development

Initially organized as an Alabama corporation and subsequently reorganized as a Delaware corporation, HRC began operations in January 1984. Its initial focus was on the establishment of a national network of outpatient rehabilitation facilities and a rehabilitation equipment business. In September 1984, HRC opened its first outpatient rehabilitation facility in Little Rock, Arkansas, followed by another one in Birmingham, Alabama in December 1984. Within five years, HRC was operating 29 outpatient facilities located in 17 states throughout the southeastern United States. In the first nine months of 1990, it opened eight more outpatient facilities and its growth was impressive as illustrated in Exhibit 23.2.

In June 1985, HRC started providing inpatient rehabilitation services with the acquisition of an 88-bed facility in Florence, South Carolina. During the next five years, the company established 11 more inpatient facilities in 9 states, with a 12th under development. Although the rehabilitation equipment business portion of the corporation had grown rapidly, in August 1989, most of it was sold to National Orthopedic and Rehabilitation Services in order to concentrate resources on HRC's core business. As of April 1991, HRC was a publicly traded for-profit health care services company that operated 43 outpatient and 11 inpatient facilities in 24 states. Its stock was listed on the New York Stock Exchange.

EXHIBIT 23.2 Quarterly Number of Outpatient Visits and Inpatient Days

		Outpatient			Inpatient[a]			
	Facilities	Visits (000s)	Visits/ Facility	Licensed Beds	Available Beds	Inpatient Days	Average Daily Census	Occupancy[b]
1986								
Q1	7	17.5	2,500	88	83	2,747	30	36.4%
Q2	8	27.5	3,438	88	83	3,164	35	41.9%
Q3	8	32.8	4,100	268	201	7,525	83	31.7%
Q4	9	35.0	3,889	358	351	17,129	188	53.6%
Total	8	112.8	14,100	358	351	30,565	84	23.9%
1987								
Q1	11	38.0	3,455	358	351	20,543	228	64.3%
Q2	12	48.0	4,000	358	351	19,334	212	60.5%
Q3	12	53.8	4,467	618	457	20,722	228	49.8%
Q4	13	60.0	4,615	618	457	23,201	255	55.8%
Total	12	199.8	16,633	488	404	83,800	230	57.0%
1988								
Q1	16	69.0	4,313	678	497	26,100	287	57.7%
Q2	17	78.0	4,588	830	597	28,578	314	52.6%
Q3	20	85.5	4,275	858	623	26,720	318	50.7%
Q4	21	88.7	4,129	858	623	30,511	335	53.5%
Total	19	319.2	17,254	805	585	113,909	313	53.5%
1989								
Q1	22	92.2	4,191	960	707	35,617	391	55.4%
Q2	23	104.2	4,530	960	707	38,533	423	59.9%
Q3	28	111.7	3,989	960	707	39,214	431	61.0%
Q4	30	123.0	4,100	960	727	49,928	472	64.9%
Total	26	431.1	16,742	960	712	158,292	429	60.3%
1990								
Q1	31	124.5	4,017	960	727	44,135	485	66.7%
Q2	33	140.7	4,265	1,020	787	45,500	500	63.5%
Q3	35	150.9	4,310	1,020	787	48,865	515	65.4%
Q4	37	166.1	4,490	1,020	787	48,230	530	67.3%
Total	34	600.0	17,647	1,005	772	184,730	508	65.7%
1991 Total	45	800.0	17,778	1,140	907	219,000	600	66.2%

[a]Does not include HEALTHSOUTH Medical Center.
[b]Calculated as average daily census divided by available beds. Available beds at some facilities differs from licensed beds.
Source: Company information and Alex. Brown & Sons estimates.

South Highlands Hospital Becomes HEALTHSOUTH Medical Center

A key development in HRC's growth strategy was the acquisition, in December 1989, of the 219-bed South Highlands Hospital in Birmingham, Alabama. Renamed HEALTHSOUTH Medical Center (HMC), this hospital developed into a flagship facility.

South Highlands was a marginally profitable facility but due to restricted financing capabilities, was unable to meet the needs of its physicians, particularly Drs. James Andrews and William Clancy, both world-renowned orthopedic surgeons. As Mr. Scrushy noted:

> My immediate concern was to maintain the referral base that Drs. Andrews and Clancy provided. HRC had benefitted from the rehabilitation referrals stemming from the extensive orthopedic surgery performed at South Highlands. The surgeons needed a major expansion at South Highlands to practice at maximum effectiveness and Drs. Andrews and Clancy would seek the facilities they needed elsewhere if something wasn't done. On the surface our acquisition of South Highlands was defensive.

The purchase of South Highlands Hospital for approximately $27 million was far from a defensive move. HRC immediately began construction of a $30 million addition to the hospital. Even during construction, referrals continued to flow from HMC to other HRC facilities. The construction created interest in the medical community, which in turn, created business. The emergency facility at HMC eliminated the necessity of delaying evaluation and treatment of athletic injuries that could be quickly transferred to the facility through HRC's extensive linkages with 396 high school and college athletic programs. A brief overview of selected events in HRC's history is summarized in Exhibit 23.3.

INDUSTRY OVERVIEW

Medical rehabilitation involves the treatment of physical limitations through which therapists seek to improve their patients' functional independence, relieve pain, and ameliorate any permanent disabilities. Patients using medical rehabilitation services include the handicapped and those recovering from automobile, sports, and other accidents; strokes; neurological injuries; surgery; fractures; disabilities associated with diseases; and conditions such as multiple sclerosis, cerebral palsy, arthritis, and heart disease.

Rehabilitation Services

Medical rehabilitation provider services include inpatient rehabilitation in dedicated free-standing hospitals and in distinct units of acute-care hospitals; comprehensive outpatient rehabilitation facilities, specialty rehabilitation pro-

EXHIBIT 23.3   Key Events in HEALTHSOUTH'S History

1984 • Company started by Richard Scrushy and others
      • Raised $1 million from CitiBank Venture Capital
      • Opened two outpatient centers

1985 • Acquired first inpatient facility
      • Opened four new outpatient facilities

1986 • Initial public offering raised $15 million
      • Acquired two inpatient facilities
      • Opened three outpatient centers

1987 • Secondary stock offering raised $24 million
      • Acquired two inpatient centers
      • Opened four outpatient centers

1988 • Developed and acquired three inpatient facilities
      • Opened eight outpatient centers

1989 • Issued $52 million of subordinated convertible debentures
      • Listed stock on New York Stock Exchange
      • Developed two inpatient facilities
      • Acquired South Highlands Hospital (HEALTHSOUTH Medical Center)
      • Opened eight outpatient facilities
      • Listed as the 11th fastest-growing company by *Inc.* magazine
      • Listed as the 41st largest percentage gainer on the New York Stock Exchange by
        Fortune magazine
      • Divested equipment businesses

1990 • Developed one inpatient facility
      • Opened 10 outpatient facilities
      • Listed as the 35th largest percentage gainer on the New York Stock Exchange by
        Fortune magazine
      • Secondary stock offering raised $49 million

grams, such as traumatic brain injury and spinal cord injury; pediatric; occupational and industrial rehabilitation; and rehabilitation agencies. For a summary of types of providers see Exhibit 23.4.

The availability of comprehensive rehabilitation services was limited in the United States. Provision of rehabilitation services by outpatient departments of acute-care hospitals was fragmented because services were provided through several departments, and private practice therapists rarely provided a full-range of comprehensive rehabilitation services. Often, patients requiring multidisciplinary services would be treated by different therapists in different locations, which would result in uncoordinated care.

Comprehensive inpatient rehabilitation services were provided by free-standing rehabilitation hospitals, distinct units in acute-care hospitals, and skilled nursing facilities. As of September 1990, there were 136 dedicated rehabilitation hospitals and 628 distinct inpatient rehabilitation units in acute-care hospitals as shown in Exhibit 23.5.

EXHIBIT 23.4 Rehabilitation Industry Segments, 1989 (Estimated)

Industry Segment	Capacity		Revenues		Payer Mix		
	Facilities	Beds	(In billions)	Per Day or Visit	Private[a]	Medicare	Medicaid and Other Government
Acute-Care Hospitals							
Inpatient Units	625	15,000	$2.4	$700–900	30%	55%	15%
Outpatient Departments	2,270	n/a	$1.1	$85–110	60	25	15
Free-Standing							
Rehabilitation Hospitals	120	13,200	$2.5	$550–750	45	45	10
Traumatic Brain Injury Programs[b]	450	12,000	$3.0	$115–1,300	40	n/a	60[c]
Outpatient Rehabilitation							
CORFs[d]	170	n/a	$0.2	$85–110	40	40	20
Other Facility-Based	200	n/a	$0.1	$85–110	40	40	20
Other[e]	1,000++	n/a	$0.5	$75–100	25	60	15
Total			$9.6				

[a]Includes workers' compensation, self-pay, Blue Cross/Blue Shield, commercial insurers, managed care.
[b]Includes acute and extended rehabilitation as well as transitional living programs.
[c]Contracted rates between provider and government programs, typically 10–15 percent discount from charges.
[d]Medicare-certified comprehensive outpatient rehabilitation facilities.
[e]Highly fragmented market including 1,000 Medicare certified agencies plus many private practitioners.
n/a = not applicable.

Source: American Hospital Association; National Association of Rehabilitation Facilities; National Head Injury Foundation.

Analysts with Goldman Sachs believed that the rehabilitation services segment of the health care industry in the United States would grow at a rate of 15 to 20 percent through 1993. A number of factors would influence this growth.

Increased Need for Services.   The incidence of major disability increases with age. Improvements in medical care enabled more people with severe disabilities to live longer. Data compiled by the National Center for Health Statistics showed that in 1989 there were 35 million people in the United States (one out of every seven people) with some form of disability. The National Association of Insurance Commissioners pointed out that 7 out of 10 workers will suffer a long-term disability between the ages of 35 and 65.

Economic Benefits of Services.   Purchasers and providers of health care services, such as insurance companies, health maintenance organizations (HMOs), businesses, and industry are seeking economical, high-quality alternatives to traditional health care services. Rehabilitation services, whether outpatient or inpatient, represent such an alternative. Often early participation in a disabled person's rehabilitation may prevent a short-term problem from becoming a long-term disability. Moreover, by returning the individual to the work force, the

EXHIBIT 23.5   HEALTHSOUTH's National Network

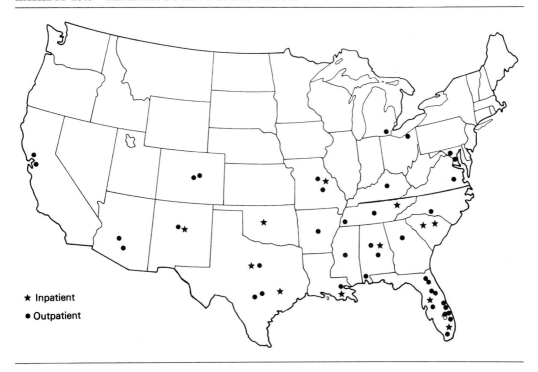

★ Inpatient

● Outpatient

number of disability benefit payments is reduced, thus decreasing long-term disability costs. Independent studies by companies such as Northwestern Life have shown that of every $1 spent on rehabilitation a savings of $30 occurs in disability payments.

Favorable Payment Policies for Services.   As noted previously, inpatient rehabilitation services, organized as either dedicated rehabilitation hospitals or distinct units, were eligible for exemptions from Medicare's prospective payment system. Outpatient rehabilitation services, which are organized as comprehensive outpatient rehabilitation facilities or rehabilitation agencies, were eligible to participate in the Medicare program under cost-based reimbursement programs. Inpatient and outpatient rehabilitation services were typically covered for payment by the major medical portion of commercial health insurance policies.

Competition

HRC's operating units were located in 36 primary markets in 24 states (refer to Exhibit 23.5). The competition faced in each of these markets was similar although unique based on the number of health care providers in a specific metropolitan area. The primary competitive factors in the rehabilitation services business were quality of services; projected patient outcomes; responsiveness to the needs of the patients, community, and physicians; ability to tailor programs and services to meet specific needs; and the charges for services.

Competition was faced every time HEALTHSOUTH initiated a certificate of need (CON) project or sought to acquire an existing facility or CON. This competition would arise from national or regional companies or from local hospitals filing competing applications or who opposed the proposed CON project. CONS were unique to the health care industry in that states having CON requirements demanded that hospitals, clinics, or other organizations wanting to open new facilities or purchase expensive and specialized equipment convince a regulatory or planning agency that such facilities or equipment were really needed and would not merely move patients from one provider to another. Although the number of states requiring CON or similar approval was decreasing, HRC continued to face this requirement in several states. The necessity for these approvals served as an important barrier to entry and potentially limited competition by creating a franchise to provide services to a given area. According to industry analysts with Donaldson, Lufin, and Jenrett, medical rehabilitation represented less than 2 percent of the health care industry. Relatively few providers of significant size existed; competition was fragmented. Major rehabilitation providers included four public companies (Continental Medical Systems, Greenery Rehabilitation Group, HEALTHSOUTH Rehabilitation Corporation, and Nova Care), National Medical Enterprises' Rehab Hospital Services Corporation, which is a subsidiary of NME, and MediCo, a new privately held trauma rehabilitation provider. Of a total of $8.2 billion in estimated 1988 revenues, the six largest providers represented less than 20 percent of total rehabilitation provider revenues. Consolidation was likely to occur because of the stronger entities' access to capital, strong clinical programs, and sophisticated management systems. However, major companies in this industry tended to compete only indirectly with one another because they targeted different market niches and/or different geographic markets.

Reimbursement

Reimbursement for services provided by HRC could be divided into two distinct categories: private pay and Medicare. The percentage of each varied by business segment and facility. Private pay represented 90 percent of all outpatient business and 50 percent of all inpatient business, or 62 percent of total revenues.

Private Pay.   Approximately 80 percent of the population under the age of 65 had medical insurance coverage. The extent of the coverage varied by location. Generally, charges for inpatient and outpatient rehabilitation were reimbursed 100 percent. Insurers preferred established programs that could demonstrate functional outcomes. The private-pay segment included general medical insurance, workers' compensation, health maintenance organizations, preferred provider organizations, and other managed-care plans.

Medicare.   Industry sources estimated that Medicare spent approximately $1.9 billion on inpatient medical rehabilitation during 1988. These sources also estimated that Medicare represented 45 percent of free-standing general rehabilitation inpatient stays and revenues, 55 percent of acute-care hospital rehabilitation unit stays and revenues, and 40 percent of CORF revenues.

Since 1983, the federal government employed a prospective payment system (PPS) as a means of controlling general acute-care hospital costs for the Medicare program. In the past, the Medicare program provided reimbursement for the reasonable direct and indirect costs of the services furnished by hospitals to beneficiaries, plus an allowed return on equity for proprietary hospitals. As a result of the Social Security Act Amendments of 1983, Congress adopted a prospective payment system to cover the routine and ancillary operating costs of most Medicare inpatient hospital services.

Under PPS, the secretary of Health and Human Services established fixed payment amounts per discharge based on diagnosis-related groups (DRGs). With limited exceptions, a hospital's payment for Medicare inpatients was limited to the DRG rate, regardless of the number of services provided to the patient or the length of the patient's hospital stay. Under PPS, a hospital could retain the difference, if any, between its DRG rate and the operating costs incurred in furnishing inpatient services, and was at risk for any operating costs that exceeded its DRG rate. HMC was generally subject to PPS with respect to Medicare inpatient services.

In 1992, Medicare paid certain distinct units, free-standing rehabilitation facilities, and certified outpatient units on the basis of "reasonable costs" incurred during a base year (the year prior to being excluded from Medicare's prospective payment system or the first year of operation) adjusted by a market basket index. However, many rehabilitation providers faced an increase in rates that was less than that of their actual costs. In addition, many Medicare intermediaries such as Blue Cross had an incomplete understanding of rehabilitation services and, therefore, might deny claims inappropriately.

Regulation

The health care industry was subject to regulation by federal, state, and local governments. The various levels of regulatory activity affected organizations by controlling growth, requiring licensure or certification of facilities, regulating the use of properties, and controlling the reimbursement for services provided. In some states, regulations controlled the growth of health care facilities.

Capital expenditures for the construction of new facilities, addition of beds, or acquisition of existing facilities could be reviewable by state regulators under a statutory scheme (usually referred to as a CON program). States with CON requirements placed limits on the construction and acquisition of health care facilities as well as the expansion of existing facilities and services.

Licensure and certification were separate, but related, regulatory activities. The former was usually a state or local requirement, and the latter was a federal requirement. In almost all instances, licensure and certification would follow specific standards and requirements set forth in readily available public documents. Compliance with the requirements was monitored by annual on-site inspections by representatives of various government agencies.

In order to receive Medicare reimbursement, each facility had to meet the applicable conditions of participation set forth by the U.S. Department of Health and Human Services relating to the type of facility, equipment, personnel and standards of medical care, as well as compliance with all state and local laws and regulations. In addition, Medicare regulations generally required entry into such facilities through physician referral.

HEALTHSOUTH TODAY

When patients were referred to one of HEALTHSOUTH's rehabilitation facilities, they underwent an initial evaluation and assessment process that resulted in the development of a rehabilitation care plan designed specifically for each patient. Depending upon the patient's disability, this evaluation process could involve the services of a single discipline (such as physical therapy for a knee injury) or of several disciplines (such as physical and speech therapy in the case of a complicated stroke patient). HRC developed numerous rehabilitation programs, including stroke, head injury, spinal cord injury, neuromuscular, sports, and work injury, that combined specific services to address the needs of patients with similar disabilities. When a patient entered one of these programs, the professional staff tailored the program to meet the needs of the patient. In this way, all of the facility's patients, regardless of the severity and complexity of their disabilities, could receive the level and intensity of those services necessary for them to be restored to as productive, active, and independent a lifestyle as possible.

The professional staff at each facility consisted of licensed or credentialed health care practitioners. The staff, together with the patient, his or her family, and the referring physician, formed the "team" that assisted the patient in attaining the rehabilitation goals. This interdisciplinary approach permitted the delivery of coordinated, integrated patient care.

Outpatient Rehabilitation Services

HEALTHSOUTH operated the largest group of affiliated proprietary CORFs in the United States. Comprehensive outpatient rehabilitation facilities played an important role in the health care industry by offering quality care at a reasonable price. The continuing emphasis on reducing health care costs, as evidenced by PPS, reduced the length of stay for patients in acute-care facilities. Some critics even suggested patients did not receive the intensity of services that may be necessary for them to achieve a full recovery from their diseases, disorders, or traumatic conditions. CORFs satisfied the increasing needs for outpatient services because of their ability to provide hospital-level services at the intensity and frequency needed.

HEALTHSOUTH had comparative advantages over most small therapy centers. HRC possessed state of the art equipment as well as experience in operations. HEALTHSOUTH's experience in operating its many outpatient centers offered:

- An efficient design that aided in the delivery of rehabilitation services in terms of quality and cost.
- Efficient management of the business office function—accounting, billing, managing, staffing, and so on.
- The ability to provide a full spectrum of comprehensive rehabilitation services.
- The ability to draw referrals from a large mass of sources due to its lack of affiliation with one specific group.

Inpatient Services

HEALTHSOUTH was one of the largest independent providers of inpatient rehabilitation services in the United States. HRC's inpatient rehabilitation facilities provided high-quality comprehensive services to patients who required intensive institutional rehabilitation care. These patients were typically experiencing physical disabilities due to various conditions such as head injury, spinal cord injury, stroke, certain orthopedic problems, or neuromuscular disease. Except for the St. Louis facility that exclusively provided head injury rehabilitation services, these inpatient facilities provided the same professional health care services as the company's outpatient facilities, but on a more intensive level. In addition, such facilities provided therapeutic recreation and 24-hour nursing care. An interdisciplinary team approach, similar to that used in the outpatient facilities, was employed with each patient to address rehabilitation needs.

HEALTHSOUTH MEDICAL CENTER

HMC was a world-class orthopedic surgery and sports medicine complex. It was an acute care hospital reimbursed under the prospective payment system. The key to the hospital's success was the affiliation with a group of renowned orthopedic surgeons. These surgeons treated famous patients such as Bo Jackson, the king and the prince of Saudi Arabia, Jane Fonda, golfers Jack Nicklaus and Greg Norman, Charles Barkley of the Philadelphia 76ers, and Troy Aikman of the Dallas Cowboys. The prestige and publicity of these patients enhanced the demand for local Birmingham services, HEALTHSOUTH's main business. One patient's father stated, "If HEALTHSOUTH was good enough for Charles Barkley, then it's good enough for my son" (a high school football player who suffered a knee injury). The group of surgeons had 8 to 10 "fellows" or physicians who spent a year studying under the group before returning to their practices. This provided a network for future business and additional outpatient and inpatient development for HEALTHSOUTH. Since acquiring HMC in 1989, the prominence of the affiliation with this network of physician "fellows" led to several new acquisitions and many more opportunities.

Rehabilitation Management

HEALTHSOUTH Rehabilitation Corporation provided, as an extension of its outpatient and inpatient rehabilitation services, one or more of its clinical services to outside client facilities on a contractual basis. These contract opportunities represented a limited investment and capital risk and were only a small portion of the company's total revenues.

FUNCTIONAL CONSIDERATIONS

HRC's management was comprised of a group of young energetic professionals. The average age was 38 years. See HRC's organization chart in Exhibit 23.6.

The corporate climate was characterized by a sense of urgency and was instilled in all of HEALTHSOUTH's employees directed by the chairman, chief executive officer, and president—Richard Scrushy. He founded HEALTH-

EXHIBIT 23.6 HEALTHSOUTH's Organization Chart

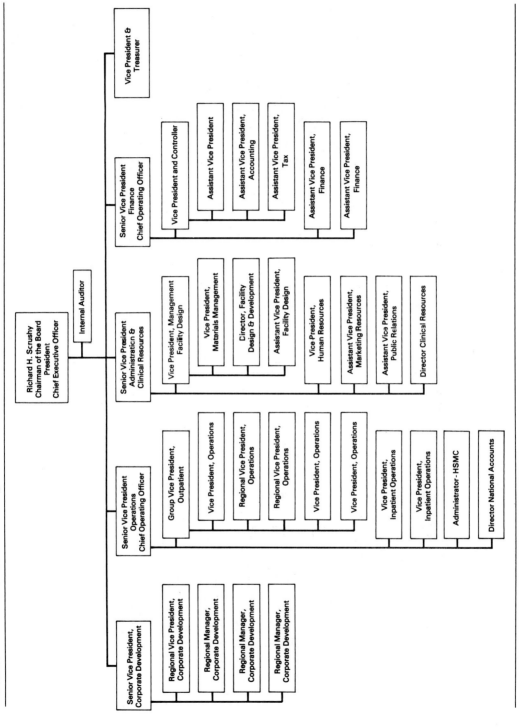

SOUTH at the age of 32. As with many entrepreneurs, he was a visionary and had the ability to make things happen. He worked virtually 365 days a year, 16 to 20 hours a day for the first five years, waiting until 1989 before taking his first vacation. His pace remained furious, working over 75 hours a week.

As a result of Scrushy's "hands-on" style, HRC was run; it did not drift. One of the company's most effective tools was a weekly statistical report, which was compiled every Thursday and distributed on Friday. The report included weekly statistics and trends such as payer mix, census, and revenue. It was reviewed over the weekend; if there was a negative trend, it was corrected. Thus, any problem was short-lived. In this manner the management team was focused on real and developing problems.

Another tool was effective communications. Every Monday morning at 7 A.M. there was a meeting of the company's officers, which included personnel from operations, development, finance, and administration. In this meeting each employee made a presentation detailing what he or she accomplished in the previous week and what was planned for the current week. Questions were answered and problems resolved. One additional benefit was that each employee was held accountable for his or her actions. While this could be perceived to be overkill, it was believed to be necessary and helpful to the participants. At one time the meetings were stopped for about six weeks. After the company experienced a slight dip in performances and coordination, the meetings were immediately reinstated.

Staffing and Compensation

Unlike many other health care companies, HEALTHSOUTH did not experience staffing shortages. Clinicians were in short supply, but HRC was able to recruit and maintain excellent personnel. The ability to offer a challenging environment was a key factor. A HEALTHSOUTH inpatient facility in a metropolitan location typically competed favorably against other hospitals and nursing homes for the skills of new therapists. HEALTHSOUTH's outpatient facilities offered an attractive alternative to the clinician by offering 8-hour workdays with weekends and holidays off.

All of the company's employees were competitively compensated. One compensation tool used was employee incentive stock options, which were granted to key corporate and clinical personnel. The options required a vesting period of four years with 25 percent of the amount being vested annually. If the employee left for another job, the options were lost. With the tremendous success of the company, the stock options created "golden handcuffs." Many employees had options that could be exercised at prices under $10 a share. In August 1991, the stock was trading for $30 per share. Additionally, during August the company created an employee stock ownership plan whereby eligible employees received HRC stock at a rate of about 100 shares per $20,000 of compensation.

Development

A key element of HEALTHSOUTH's growth was its ability to develop and acquire new facilities. The company had a development team led by three individuals who were with HRC from the beginning. Each was responsible for the development of facilities in a particular business segment. Before seeking to develop or acquire an inpatient or outpatient facility, a number of factors had to be considered, including population, number of orthopedic surgeons and physical therapists, industry concentrations, reimbursement, competition, and availability of staff.

HEALTHSOUTH had a stated goal to develop or acquire two new inpatient facilities and 8 to 10 outpatient centers per year. The acquisition of another acute-care hospital specializing in orthopedic surgery (to be patterned after HEALTHSOUTH Medical Center) was a possibility but was not a part of the stated plan.

Outpatient Development.   HEALTHSOUTH's outpatient units were usually acquired. The company targeted existing centers that were seeing 50 or more patients per day for purchase. New centers were set up as limited partnerships, typically with the former owners (physicians and therapists) maintaining a limited partnership interest. Ownership provided an incentive to continue referring patients to the center and the limited partners shared in the cash flow. Additionally, HEALTHSOUTH brought in other physicians and groups as partners and would give up 40 percent ownership in the facility. Interestingly, on the average, only 40 percent of the visits came from referrals of partners.

The cost of acquiring and opening a center ranged from $300,000 to $800,000. This included equipment and buildings of $200,000 to $350,000 and acquisition costs of $100,000 to $450,000. All centers were leased except one, allowing for lower capital requirements. The company was evaluating all of its leases and could possibly move toward acquiring buildings where existing facilities were proven and met financial requirements.

Inpatient Development.   Inpatient facilities were usually developed. They were customarily located in regulated environments requiring a CON. The company targeted a number of markets for rehabilitation hospitals; however, HEALTHSOUTH's competition was usually seeking the same markets. HEALTHSOUTH never lost a CON battle for two reasons. First, the quality of care provided by existing HEALTHSOUTH facilities was excellent. Second, the lower cost of the facility led to lower health care costs.

HEALTHSOUTH's inpatient facilities were typically located on or near the campus of an acute-care hospital that served as a trauma center. This provided a steady stream of patients when trauma victims were discharged from the hospital. Additionally, physical therapy could be conducted by HEALTHSOUTH for the hospital on an inpatient and outpatient basis. Typically, HEALTHSOUTH's inpatient facilities cost from $6 to $10 million compared to its competitors' costs of $10 to $12 million.

The development of additional acute-care hospitals stressing orthopedics similar to HMC was a future possibility. A potential acute-care hospital acquisition had to possess an orthopedic concentration. The cost of an acute-care hospital meeting HEALTHSOUTH's criteria ranged from $20 to $50 million depending on its size and types of equipment.

Marketing

The company's marketing efforts were similar for each business segment. The demand was controlled by physicians, workers' compensation managers, insurance companies, and other intermediaries. Administrators and clinicians were involved in the marketing effort. The company hired a number of individuals who were formerly case managers with local intermediaries, such as insurance companies and HMOs.

HRC recently entered into contracts to be the exclusive provider for rehabilitation services directly to industry. Firms such as General Motors were excellent targets, since they had many employees in various markets that HEALTHSOUTH served. In such cases, significant new business could be generated and in return HEALTHSOUTH could afford to discount its charges.

HEALTHSOUTH established a national marketing effort with training programs, national account managers, case managers, and a carefully developed plan. The objective was to put into place a consistent sales methodology throughout HEALTHSOUTH and take advantage of its national system of rehabilitation facilities. This national coverage enabled HEALTHSOUTH to provide services for national as well as regional companies.

HEALTHSOUTH's pricing was usually lower than that of competition. The company's daily inpatient charges were sometimes as much as $100 to $400 less per day than competition due to its lower cost of capital and facilities. However, pricing was not used as a major selling point but rather a bonus. HEALTHSOUTH focused mainly on quality of services and outcomes as the best marketing tool.

Financial Structure

HEALTHSOUTH's growth was funded through a mix of equity and debt. The company raised $13 million in venture capital before going public in 1986. Because of the company's start-up nature in its early years, commercial banks were reluctant to lend significant funds for development. After the company's initial public offering, commercial bankers were more responsive to financing growth plans. HRC continued to use a conservative mix of equity and debt and believed its cost of capital was the lowest in the health care industry. A decision to give up ownership was an easy one. The founders understood that a smaller percentage ownership of a larger company would be worth more and would not carry as much risk.

Earnings increases were significant, with compounded earnings growth of 416 percent from 1986 to 1990. About 75 percent of HRC's revenues were generated primarily through inpatient services. Typically, a mature inpatient facility generated $10 to $15 million annually in revenues, an outpatient center generated $2 to $3.5 million annually, and an acute-care facility generated $40 to $60 million. The operating margin on inpatient business ranged from 15 to 25 percent and outpatient margins were 20 to 30 percent. The return on assets of a given facility ranged from 10 to 30 percent with an average of 17 percent for all facilities. HRC financial statements are provided in Exhibits 23.7 through 23.11. Revenue summaries are shown in Exhibits 23.12 and 23.13.

EXHIBIT 23.7   Consolidated Balance Sheets (In thousands)

	December 31,	
	1989	*1990*
Assets		
Current Assets		
Cash and Marketable Securities	$ 31,830	$ 71,201
Accounts Receivable—Net of Allowances for Doubtful Accounts and Contractual Adjustments of $13,020,000 in 1989 and $20,093,000 in 1990	47,771	48,988
Inventories, Prepaid Expenses and Other Current Assets	7,213	7,626
Total Current Assets	86,814	127,815
Other Assets	8,613	9,848
Property, Plant and Equipment—Net	94,081	126,732
Intangible Assets—Net	29,622	36,785
Total Assets	$219,130	$301,180
Liabilities and Stockholders' Equity		
Current Liabilities		
Accounts Payable	$ 5,866	$ 7,342
Salaries and Wages Payable	3,414	3,972
Accrued Interest Payable and Other Liabilities	3,978	4,522
Current Portion of Long-Term Debt and Leases	1,637	1,394
Total Current Liabilities	14,895	17,230
Long-Term Debt and Leases	132,748	149,801
Other Long-Term Liabilities	3,870	5,172
Minority Interests—Limited Partnerships	1,742	1,076
Stockholders' Equity		
Preferred Stock, $.10 Par Value—1,500,000 Shares Authorized; Issued and Outstanding—None	--	--
Common Stock, $.01 Par Value—25,000,000 Shares Authorized; 10,290,000 and 12,713,000 Shares Issued at December 31, 1989, and 1990, Respectively	103	127
Additional Paid-in Capital	49,777	100,443
Retained Earnings	15,995	27,331
Total Stockholders' Equity	65,875	127,901
Total Liabilities and Stockholders' Equity	$219,130	$301,180

EXHIBIT 23.8   Consolidated Statements of Income (In thousands except per share data)

	Year Ended December 31,		
	1988	1989	1990
Net Revenues	$77,493	$118,862	$180,482
Operating Expenses	59,312	90,068	135,822
Provision for Doubtful Accounts	1,415	2,512	5,120
Depreciation and Amortization	4,088	7,110	11,056
Interest Expense	3,822	8,121	11,547
Interest Income	(942)	(1,954)	(4,136)
	67,695	105,857	159,409
Income before Minority Interests and Income Taxes	9,798	13,005	21,073
Minority Interests	857	495	924
	8,941	12,510	20,149
Provision for Income Taxes	3,208	4,363	7,226
Net Income	$ 5,733	$ 8,147	$ 12,923
Weighted Average Common and Common Equivalent Shares Outstanding	10,392	10,707	12,139
Net Income per Common and Common Equivalent Share	$ .55	$ .76	$ 1.06
Net Income per Common Share—Assuming Full Dilution	$ .55	$ .73	$ .96

WHERE DOES HEALTHSOUTH GO FROM HERE?

Richard Scrushy was reviewing company projections to plan for the continued success of HEALTHSOUTH Rehabilitation Corporation. Money managers continued to reward the company for its historical and expected performance with the stock trading at a price earnings ratio of 30 to 1.

Recently, Craig Dickson, an analyst with Rauscher, Pierce, Refsnes, had posed a question concerning HEALTHSOUTH's ability to continue the trend. Scrushy reflected on all the questions he had asked himself earlier and wondered if the rate of success could continue. "What will I need to do to make it happen? Are there things we should be doing differently? How can I ensure that HEALTHSOUTH does not outgrow its resources—either capital or management? Does the market provide sufficient opportunity to grow at 20 to 30 percent per year? What external factors do we face? What should we do to ensure that medical rehabilitation continues to be favorably reimbursed? What is the real number of facilities needed and how many acquisition targets are there?"

Scrushy focused on answering the questions. He knew that he could formulate a plan to ensure HEALTHSOUTH's success. In fact, in a probing interview in *Rehabilitation Today* (May 1991), Mr. Scrushy was careful to state that he would consider any acquisition where he believed "value could be added" and dismissed the possibility that the company's "regional name" implied that his aspirations were regional. Clearly, he was willing to go anywhere, anytime he believed opportunities existed.

EXHIBIT 23.9 Consolidated Statements of Stockholders' Equity (In thousands)

	Common Stock	Additional Paid-In Capital	Retained Earnings	Treasury Stock	Total Stockholders' Equity
			Years Ended December 31,		
Balance at January 1, 1988	$100.2	$48,400.0	$2,783.8	$ (.3)	$ 51,283.7
Proceeds from Issuance of 16,969 Common Shares	.2	279.8	—	—	280.0
Proceeds from Exercise of Options	.6	176.2	—	—	176.8
Purchase of Limited Partnership Units	—	—	(191.4)	—	(191.4)
Purchase of Treasury Stock (1,550 Shares)	—	—	—	(.1)	(.1)
Net Income	—	—	5,733.4	—	5,733.4
Balance at December 31, 1988	101.0	48,856.0	8,325.8	(.4)	57,282.4
Proceeds from Exercise of Options	2.0	953.1	—	—	955.1
Purchase of Treasury Stock (1,250 Shares)	—	(9.5)	—	(15.8)	(15.3)
Treasury Stock Used in the Exercise of Options	(.1)	—	—	9.6	—
Common Stock Exchanged in the Exercise of Options	—	(22.7)	—	—	(22.7)
Sale of Treasury Stock	—	—	—	6.1	6.1
Purchase of Limited Partnership Units	—	—	(477.8)	—	(477.8)
Net Income	—	—	8,147.3	—	8,147.3
Balance at December 31, 1989	102.9	49,776.9	15,995.3	0	65,875.1
Proceeds from Issuance of 48,196 Common Shares	.5	1,096.0	—	—	1,096.5
Proceeds from Issuance of 2,221,182 Common Shares	22.2	48,476.6	—	—	48,498.8
Proceeds from Exercise of Options	1.5	1,115.8	—	—	1,117.3
Common Shares Exchanged in the Exercise of Options	—	(22.6)	—	—	(22.6)
Purchase of Limited Partnership Units	—	—	(1,587.3)	—	(1,587.3)
Net Income	—	—	12,923.2	—	12,923.2
Balance at December 31, 1990	$127.1	$100,442.7	$27,331.2	0	$127,901.0

EXHIBIT 23.10   Consolidated Statements of Cash Flows (In thousands)

	Years Ended December 31,		
	1988	1989	1990
Operating Activities			
Net Income	$5,733	$8,147	$12,923
Adjustments to Reconcile Net Income to Net Cash (Used)			
Provided by Operating Activities			
Depreciation and Amortization	4,088	7,110	11,056
Income Applicable to Minority Interests of Limited			
Partnerships	857	495	924
Provision for Deferred Income Taxes	1,410	606	1,788
Provision for Deferred Revenue from Contractual Agencies	597	(101)	(230)
Changes in Operating Assets and Liabilities, Net of Effects of			
Acquisitions:			
Increase in Accounts Receivable	(11,906)	(15,806)	(183)
Increase in Inventories, Prepaid Expenses and Other			
Current Assets	(2,295)	(738)	(390)
Increase in Accounts Payable and Accrued Expenses	198	3,854	2,255
Net Cash (Used) Provided by Operating Activities	$(1,318)	$3,567	$28,143
Investing Activities			
Purchase of Property, Plant, and Equipment	$(16,934)	$(19,992)	$(37,548)
Additions to Intangible Assets, Net of Effects of			
Acquisitions	(7,323)	(8,908)	(9,051)
Assets Obtained through Acquisition, Net of Liabilities			
Assumed	(5,592)	(30,110)	(5,239)
Additions to Notes Receivable	(116)	(586)	(1,553)
Reduction in Notes Receivable	0	144	394
Proceeds Received on Maturity of Long-Term Marketable			
Securities	2,124	1,849	1,659
Investment in Long-Term Marketable Securities	(1,864)	(3,239)	(7,522)
Deposits Placed in Escrow Related to Acquisitions	(288)	288	0
Net Cash Used by Investing Activities	$(29,993)	$(60,554)	$(58,860)

EXHIBIT 23.10   (continued)

	1988	1989	1990
		(In thousands)	
Financing Activities			
Proceeds from Borrowings	$41,460	$104,246	$57,243
Principal Payments on Debt and Leases	(15,129)	(34,169)	(40,531)
Proceeds from Exercise of Options	177	923	1,095
Common Stock Issued on Acquisition	—	—	1,096
Proceeds from Issuance of Common Stock	—	—	48,499
Purchase of Treasury Stock	—	(15)	—
Sale or Transfer of Treasury Stock	—	16	—
Proceeds from Investment by Minority Interests	423	998	247
Purchase of Limited Partnership Interests	(365)	(733)	(1,460)
Payment of Cash Distributions to Limited Partners	(1,370)	(1,547)	(1,964)
Net Cash Provided by Financing Activities	25,196	69,719	64,225
(Decrease) Increase in Cash and Cash Equivalents	(6,115)	12,732	33,508
Cash and Cash Equivalents at Beginning of Year	21,959	15,844	28,576
Cash and Cash Equivalents at End of Year	$15,844	$28,576	$62,084
Supplemental Disclosures of Cash Flow Information			
Cash Paid During the Year for:			
Interest	$4,589	$7,657	$13,062
Income Taxes	2,375	3,617	5,008

Noncash Investing and Financing Activities:

Common stock was issued in 1988 for satisfaction of $280,000 due on a purchase agreement.

Assets related to three of the company's rehabilitation equipment businesses, having a net book value of $5,783,000, were sold during 1989. The consideration for the assets consisted of a note receivable, an interest in the purchaser's company, and the assumption of certain liabilities.

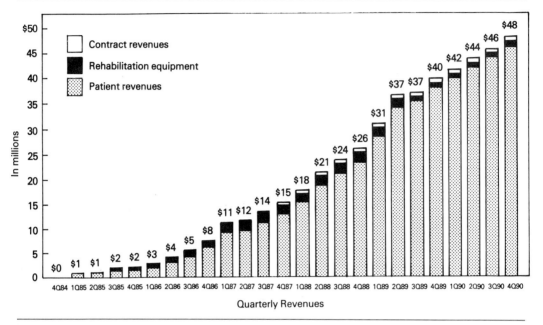

Source: HEALTHSOUTH Rehabilitation Corporation.

EXHIBIT 23.12   HEALTHSOUTH Rehabilitation Corporation Quarterly Gross Patient Revenues (In millions)

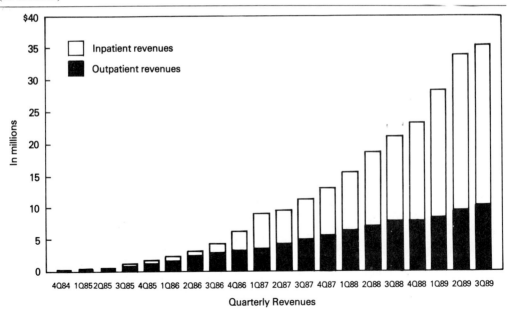

Source: HEALTHSOUTH Rehabilitation Corporation.

_____ CASE 24 _____

Circuit City Stores

Ed Kopf, director of planning for Circuit City Stores had just finished reviewing a consultant's report that concluded that Circuit City should once again offer products through mail order. More specifically the consultant recommended that Circuit City introduce a high-gloss mail-order catalog containing top-of-the-line, high-margin consumer electronic items.

The potential benefits of mail-order sales were attractive. Mail order seemed to offer a quick and inexpensive means of expanding geographically as well as increasing Circuit City's penetration in its existing markets. In addition, mail-order sales would allow Circuit City to extend its product lines to include high-margin but low-volume items that were not feasible to carry in all stores, and there would be promotional synergies between mail order and retail store operations.

The consultant believed that this was an opportune time for Circuit City to reintroduce mail-order selling. At the time there were no dominant mail-order catalogs specializing in Circuit City's merchandise lines. Furthermore, Circuit City had demonstrated an ability to satisfy diverse consumer markets. Circuit City's advanced point-of-sale (POS) system, which supplied on-line communications between all Circuit City operations and its corporate offices in Richmond, could give the company a competitive advantage in processing orders. Also, no existing consumer electronics mail-order firm could match Circuit City's buying power. Strategically, catalog sales would allow Circuit City to take advantage of growing consumer acceptance of in-home shopping. And it would put the company in a position to test new technologies in in-home shopping that many experts believed would significantly affect retailing in the near future.

Despite the consultant's enthusiasm, Ed had more than a few misgivings. If Circuit City were to offer a "high-end" catalog, as the consultant recommended, how would a high-price product offering affect Circuit City's "low-price" image and promotion strategy? How would a "skim" marketing strategy fit with one of Circuit City's greatest competitive strengths, its ability to underprice and out-

This case was prepared by James Olver under the supervision of Eleanor G. May, Professor of Business Administration, The Darden School of Business Administration. It is not intended to illustrate either effective or ineffective handling of an administrative situation. Copyright © 1985 by the Darden Graduate Business School Foundation, Charlottesville, Virginia. Used with permission from Eleanor G. May.

promote the competition by concentrating on volume? Circuit City had succeeded by mass marketing products with a broad-based appeal; would the company know how to promote more exclusive products to the electronics buff?

On the other hand, if Circuit City were to offer a catalog featuring items comparable to current in-store offerings, would it generate new business or would it cannibalize the existing customer base? Would the catalog prices have to match in-store prices? What would the catalog offer that other local retailers did not?

Regardless of the type of product offered, other issues would have to be resolved before deciding whether to enter the mail-order business. How would mail order fit into the volatile consumer electronics market? Today's prices and technology might be hopelessly outdated before the completion of the catalog's life. Would consumers buy high-ticket consumer electronics without having the opportunity to test the product or at least see it? Would they be confused by differences between the product and service offered in the retail stores and those available through the catalog? How would the product be serviced? An important question for Circuit City was whether there were better opportunities in areas other than mail order. Should the company get involved in what could be presumed to be a sideline, during a time of very rapid growth?

COMPANY BACKGROUND

Circuit City was the largest specialty retailer of name-brand consumer electronics and appliances in the United States. Through its outlets centered in the Southeast, Circuit City sold large and small appliances, audio and video equipment, and advanced consumer electronics (ACE). Circuit City sought to dominate the markets it entered and often achieved more than a 35 percent share of market in consumer electronics sales. Circuit City was the largest-volume member of the National Appliance and Television Merchants (NATM), the industry's largest buying group. Tremendous buying power, coupled with what the company's chairman, Alan Wurtzel, called a "critical mass" of convenient local outlets, allowed Circuit City to offer broad selections and low prices, as well as local repairs and optional extended warranties on most products.

Circuit City's promotional activities were well suited to its guaranteed-lowest-price strategy (within 30 days of purchase a customer received a refund of the difference if another retailer in the market area offered the identical merchandise for a lower price than that paid at Circuit City). Frequent storewide sales with names like "Midnight Madness," "Price Slasher," and "The Thing" contributed to Circuit City's tremendous sales volume, which averaged around $5.6 million per store—about 10 times that of the typical consumer electronics specialty store, by Circuit City estimates. Promotions were backed by full-page newspaper ads and inserts (freestanding inserts, FSIs) packed with sale-priced items, primarily at the lower price end of each product category (see Exhibit 24.1). In most markets, promotions were supported by television and radio advertising that the smaller

EXHIBIT 24.1   Example of Circuit City Newspaper Advertisement

local specialty stores typically could not afford to match. Circuit City's gross advertising expenditures in 1984 were 5.9 percent of sales.

Until 1979, Circuit City Stores then operating under the name Wards Company, had offered consumer electronics through mail order, first under the name Dixie Hi-Fi, which was the name used by Wards in its discount audio outlets located in southeastern states. Fair trade laws had allowed Dixie Hi-Fi to sell audio equipment through the mail at prices significantly lower than those at the retail stores in most areas, resulting in roughly $5 million in annual mail-order sales. The layout of the Dixie catalog emphasized a low-cost, "no nonsense" approach: black-and-white sketches of the items were accompanied by detailed descriptions of the product and its technical specifications.

In the early 1970s, Wards operated several retail consumer electronics and appliance chains of its own, plus the Dixie mail-order/discount outlet business, and leased departments in several discount department stores. During the recession of the mid-1970s, Wards suffered severe losses when several of the department store chains from which it leased went bankrupt. Between 1977 and 1981, the Dixie Hi-Fi discount audio stores, Custom Hi-Fi, and Sight and Sound consumer electronics stores were consolidated as Circuit City. The resulting entity offered consumer electronics at Dixie's low prices, with the superior service, selection, convenience, and aesthetic appeal of Custom Hi-Fi and Sight and Sound. In addition, the chain of discount appliance stores, Wards Loading Dock ("name-brand appliances at forklift prices"), was revamped, consumer electronics product lines available in the Circuit City stores were added, and the stores were renamed Circuit City Superstores. With the demise of the fair trade laws and the tremendous success of the Circuit City format, mail order was abandoned in favor of vigorous expansion through retail outlets. In 1984, the corporate name was changed from Wards to Circuit City to diminish confusion and to describe the firm more clearly.

The strategy paid off handsomely. Sales revenues had grown at a compound annual rate of 43 percent between 1982 and 1985; profits had increased almost sevenfold in the same period (see Exhibits 24.2 to 24.4). Circuit City's retail operations in 1985 included 35 Circuit City stores, 13 Circuit City Superstores, 12 Lafayette stores on the East Coast, and 33 leased departments in Zody's Department Stores on the West Coast (see Exhibit 24.5). The company had nearly 3,800 employees and 377,000 square feet of selling space (see Exhibit 24.6). In 1985, Circuit City was involved in a program of upgrading the Circuit City stores (to superstores if there was sufficient space, to "mini" supers if there was a space limitation) and opening free-standing superstores to replace the Zody's units.

CIRCUIT CITY STORES

Whether in superstore or regular format, the Circuit City store layout emphasized an expansion of "The Four S's" to five: The fifth "S" was for "Speed." As the 1985 annual report noted, "Circuit City has long recognized that retailing is

EXHIBIT 24.2   Balance Sheet (In thousands)

Years Ended February 28 or 29	1984	1985
Assets		
Cash	$ 21,761	$ 45,230
Accounts and Notes Receivable	8,318	10,544
Merchandise Inventory	47,346	73,688
Other Current Assets	1,642	1,749
Total Current Assets	79,067	131,211
Property and Equipment, net	21,566	43,984
Deferred Income Taxes	1,568	1,531
Other Assets	7,701	14,647
Total Assets	$109,902	$191,373
Liabilities and Stockholders' Equity		
Current Installments of Long-Term Debt	$ 277	$ 1,477
Accounts Payable	25,545	37,016
Accrued Expenses and Other Liabilities	6,550	8,160
Accrued Income Taxes	621	13,432
Total Current Liabilities	32,993	60,085
Long-Term Debt	15,187	27,885
Other Liabilities	1,297	1,652
Deferred Revenue	4,141	5,733
Excess of Value Received over Cost of Assets Acquired, Net	7,707	6,843
Total Liabilities	61,325	102,198
Stockholders' Equity		
Preferred Stock of $20 Par Value	591	590
Common Stock of $1 Par Value	9,882	10,861
Capital in Excess of Par Value	6,826	27,064
Retained Earnings	31,278	50,660
Total Stockholders' Equity	48,577	89,175
Total Liabilities and Stockholders' Equity	$109,902	$191,373

EXHIBIT 24.3   Statements of Earnings (In thousands)

Years Ended February 28 or 29	1983	1984	1985
Net Sales and Operating Revenue	$245,914	$356,708	$519,214
Cost of Sales, Buying, and Warehousing	176,755	253,887	370,765
Gross Profit	69,159	102,821	148,449
Selling, General, and Administrative Expenses	58,194	79,140	109,031
Interest Expense	1,758	1,372	1,409
Total Expense	59,952	80,512	110,440
Earnings before Income Taxes	9,207	22,309	38,009
Provision for Income Taxes	3,700	10,300	17,775
Net Earnings	$ 5,507	$ 12,000	$ 20,234
Earnings per Common Share (In dollars)	$.62	$1.23	$1.94

EXHIBIT 24.4   Sales and Earnings

Years Ending February 28 or 29	Net Sales	After-Tax Earnings
1985	$519,214,000	$20,234,000
1984	356,708,000	12,009,000
1983	245,914,000	5,507,000
1982	176,169,000	2,935,000
1981	131,881,000	2,701,000
1980	119,609,000	2,286,000
1979	111,534,000	2,570,000
1978	90,799,000	2,052,000
1977	72,360,000	1,250,000
1976	61,185,000	1,362,000

EXHIBIT 24.5   Number of Retail Units

Fiscal Year Ending February	Superstore	Circuit City	Lafayette	West Coast	Total
1985	13	35	12	33	93
1984	8	38	11	41	98
1983	7	36	8	50	101
1982	7	31	8	51	97
1981	4	37		41	82
1980	4	36		35	75
1979					70
1978					70
1977					61

EXHIBIT 24.6   Space and Employee Data

	Square Feet Selling Space	Sales per Square Foot	Number of Employees
1985	376,607	$1,371	3,796
1984	360,792	989	2,057
1983	349,389	704	1,664
1982	308,754	571	1,323
1981	230,936	571	1,052
1980	215,570	555	957
1979			943
1978			824
1977			610

part theater. The superstore has been carefully designed to dramatize and to deliver efficiently to the customer exceptional *Savings*, outstanding *Selections*, and high quality *Service* before and after the sale—all with *Speed* and guaranteed *Satisfaction*." The effect of this combination was particularly dramatic in the 30,000- to 40,000-square-foot superstores, which had up to 14,000 square feet of showroom space, 15,000 square feet of warehouse, plus space for service and sales support. (Other Circuit City stores and the Lafayette stores had a minimum of 4,000 square feet of selling space and 1,500 square feet of storage.)

Upon entering a typical superstore building, the customers walked by large picture windows behind which repairmen could be viewed working on Circuit City products. Adjacent was "Kiddie City," a playroom to occupy children while parents shopped. Inside the showroom, the customer was confronted by an impressive array of television and video equipment, appliances, and consumer electronics grouped by product category, each featuring a wide variety of price/ performance choices. The TV and appliance areas occupied 5,000 to 10,000 square feet. Appliances included washers and dryers, refrigerators, freezers, dishwashers, and microwave ovens. One wall in the television area was lined from floor to ceiling with sets of various sizes and descriptions. In front of these were aisles of shelves stocked with other television and video equipment and accessorics such as VCRs, cameras, and videodisc players. A vast assortment of tape decks, phonographs, receivers, tuners, amplifiers, and speakers, sorted by price and performance characteristics, were displayed. A listening room was available where the audiophile could test the stereo equipment; an adjacent, separate area contained car stereos. The advanced consumer electronics products and accessories included tape recorders, radios, handheld TVs, telephones and other communication devices, and portable stereo equipment. A limited line of home computer hardware and software had been carried, but by 1985 this merchandise had been discontinued.

All models of most products were set up for the shopper to try out. However, in contrast to most catalog showrooms, a knowledgeable and eager sales force was available to answer questions and offer advice both about the product and about the sales terms. Once a purchase decision was made, the salesperson entered the order on a POS computer terminal on the showroom floor, which simultaneously placed the order to the warehouse, updated the inventory, recorded the name and phone number of the customer, the size and type of the order, and the name of the salesperson, and computed the salesperson's commission.[1] Daily summary reports allowed store managers to evaluate sales and profit performance both of salespeople and of product categories (see Exhibit 24.7).

After the salesperson placed the order, the customer took the order slip to the cashier where payment was made or credit was arranged. Small accessories,

---

[1] According to *Mart* magazine (June 1985) the median salary for a floor salesperson selling this type of merchandise in appliance/TV stores, home electronics stores, specialty stores (i.e., telephone, computer, video, hi-fi), or department stores and mass merchandisers was $18,061 in 1984. Of the respondents that paid commissions, 40 percent paid between 1 percent and 3 percent, 13 percent between 4 percent and 9 percent, and 47 percent, 10 percent or over.

EXHIBIT 24.7   Example of "Daily Processed Sales Summary" for Store 0817

Salesperson	Number of Tickets	Merchandise (In dollars)	Gross Margin Percent	Extended Service Plans Dollars	Extended Service Plans Percent	SPIFF (In dollars)
A	15	$1,412.41	33.7%	$97.88	6.9%	$38.25
B	17	3,098.32	18.8	0	0	24.00
C	9	265.44	−10.6	−169.97	−64.0	8.50
D	11	2,377.64	22.1	0	0	44.00
E	1	−24.00	−100.0	0	0	.00
F	1	64.29	0	0	0	.00
G	2	357.00	11.5	0	0	1.00
H	14	1,044.75	27.3	88.94	20.0	38.25
I	16	1,490.54	32.5	83.26	6.1	60.25
J	2	118.88	0	0	0	6.00
K	1	599.00	28.9	0	0	20.00
L	7	141.16	20.2	0	0	.75
M	19	1,363.61	31.6	89.79	7.2	24.50
N	2	−140.65	−70.8	0	0	−2.00
O	13	3,452.89	21.0	229.91	6.7	47.00
P	1	0	0	69.97	0	.00
Q	2	298.00	23.2	0	0	2.50
R	8	95.33	27.9	0	0	1.50
S	9	125.72	18.6	0	0	1.25
T	16	172.83	10.3	2.50	1.5	1.00
U	13	3,823.67	21.4	0	0	27.00
V	7	218.07	31.1	1.00	0.5	4.50
W	10	135.92	15.4	17.66	13.0	2.50
X	18	4,302.56	19.4	225.88	5.3	34.75
Y	8	138.49	15.9	0	0	3.50
Z	2	−21.18	−100.0	29.97	−141.5	.00
AA	10	1,420.51	29.0	27.94	2.4	24.50
BB	15	3,124.98	21.7	129.88	4.2	36.50
CC	23	1,713.63	29.8	38.03	2.2	25.75
DD	13	29.31	14.4	0	0	5.25
EE	20	1,558.40	27.9	91.73	5.9	25.00
FF	21	2,388.33	19.8	0	0	10.25
Total	326	$35,145.85	22.7%	$1,054.37	3.0%	$516.25

such as tapes and batteries, were available next to the cashier. After the sale was consummated, the customer walked to the warehouse to pick up the order.

Although Circuit City often did not carry top-of-the-line models because of the company's reliance on volume, most departments had something for the vast majority of consumer electronics customers. Overall, Circuit City merchandise sales were about 50 percent video, 30 percent audio, 10 percent appliances, and 10 percent ACE. In addition to the merchandise sales, less than 10 percent of the revenues came from sales of services, including delivery, extended warranty, and repair services.

EXHIBIT 24.7   (cont.)

Category of Sales	Sales	Cost of Sales	Gross Margin Percent	Extended Service Plans	
				Dollars	Percent
Merchandise					
Video	$13,215.58	$10,602.86	19.8%	$413.55	3.1%
Major	8,765.57	7,209.69	17.7	204.73	2.3
Audio	8,236.33	5,594.88	32.1	121.22	1.5
ACE	5,088.34	3,879.57	23.8	211.26	4.2
Other	− 159.97	− 127.98	20.0	103.50	64.7
Subtotal	$35,145.85	$27,159.02	22.7%	$1,054.37	3.0%
Delivery	41.97				
Installation	.00				
Service Parts	.00				
Service Labor	.00				
VCR Membership	.00				
VCR Rental	56.50				
Service Charges	12.00				
Total	$35,256.32	$27,159.02		$1,054.37	

Offering a selection of ACE products, particularly home computers and accessories, was difficult, however. In prior years Circuit City stores and superstores had carried some of the more popular lines, such as Commodore, Texas Instruments, and Atari home computers and video systems. Rapid technological innovation in these products made demand and prices particularly unstable, and the wide range of options and accessories available (e.g., computer software) made it difficult to stock an adequate inventory. As a result, these ACE products had not been backed by Circuit City's 30-day lowest-price guarantee. One attempt by Circuit City to cope with product proliferation and obsolescence was an in-store "catalog" through which customers could order software and accessories that were not stocked in the stores. The catalog, actually a computer printout of product names and prices without any descriptive information, had to be updated weekly.

MAIL-ORDER FEASIBILITY STUDY

In the summer of 1984, Circuit City decided to reexamine the issue of mail-order catalog sales. A consulting firm was employed to examine trends in mail-order merchandising and in attitudes toward mail order of consumer electronics, and to recommend a course of action based on Circuit City's competitive strengths, broad strategic considerations, and a cost/benefit analysis. If mail order looked promising, the consultant would develop an implementation plan to include recommended product offerings, positioning of the catalog, development of a customer base, and the relationship between store and mail-order operations.

THE MAIL-ORDER MARKET

For purposes of the analysis, "mail order" was limited to mail, telephone, or catalog-desk orders of merchandise, and excluded telephone solicitation; it also excluded types of transactions in which the product ordered was immediately available to the customer. For example, store sales by catalog showrooms such as Best Products would not be included, although sales at Sears and Penney catalog order desks would be. By this definition, mail-order sales had been increasing nationally at an average annual rate of about 10 percent for the prior five years, roughly twice the growth rate of traditional retail outlets. The Direct Marketing Association estimated that Americans purchased about $40 billion worth of merchandise through the mail in 1983; other estimates ranged from $25 to $100 billion, depending on the definition of "mail order."

There were in 1983 between 4,000 and 5,000 mail-order catalogs for consumer goods; about 6.7 billion catalogs were mailed both by mail-order firms and by other retail firms. The market segments most relevant to Circuit City were classified as "audio-video" and "consumer electronics/scientific," with approximately 230 catalogs in audio-video and 190 in consumer electronics/science. Mail-order sales in 1982 for these two categories were estimated at $515 million, roughly 22 percent higher than in 1981.[2] The consultant's report noted that the largest competitors in these areas had roughly 10 percent of the sales share of their market segment, and no major U.S. retailer had entered either segment.

Marketing strategies in both of the segments relevant to Circuit City varied widely from firm to firm. Some firms, such as 47th Street Photo, were discount operations targeting a fairly broad-based audience (see Exhibit 24.8). Others, such as Sharper Image and Markline, featured list-price specialty products that would appeal to a select clientele (see Exhibit 24.9 and 24.10). Copy and layouts reflected the theme of the catalog and the characteristics of the target audience.

Mail-order merchandisers were able to target audiences with desired demographic, psychographic, and purchase-pattern profiles, through specialized mailing lists. As a result, some catalogs projected the image of an exclusive specialty shop yet generated large sales volumes. There was little evidence that a mass-appeal approach necessarily resulted in greater sales.

CONSUMER TRENDS

The consultant noted four broad consumer trends that had been credited with contributing significantly to the overall growth in mail order. These highlighted a growing demand for more specialized mail-order services:

[2] Total sales in 1984 of major appliances were reported by *Merchandising* magazine to be nearly $17 billion; for video equipment $12 billion; for audio, $7 billion; and for ACE (including personal computers), $5 billion.

EXHIBIT 24.8   Example of 47th Street Photo Catalog Page

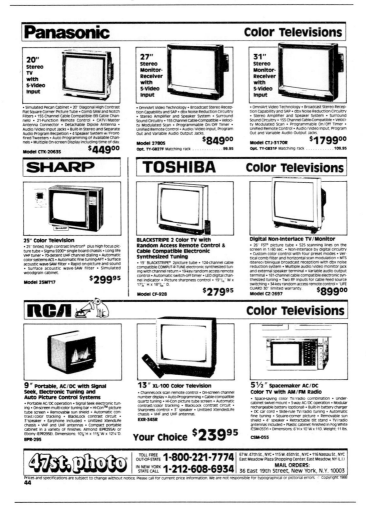

- As a result of increased emphasis on developing and maintaining personal individuality, consumers were demanding more choices than stores could display or stock.
- A higher proportion of women in the work force meant less time for shopping but increased household disposable income.
- Awareness of and demand for hard-to-find items had increased consumers' interest in alternatives to in-store retailing.
- Consumers' desire for more leisure time for self-development and creative expression was leaving less time to search for a particular item or service.

EXHIBIT 24.9   Example of Sharper Image Catalog Page

Aiwa improves the best $99 personal stereo.

Aiwa, Japan's most respected electronics innovator, is out to increase its market share. So they're building a high-performance AM/FM stereo cassette player, and offering it at a budget stereo price.

You enjoy outstanding AM/FM fidelity through the lightweight stereo headphones. The receiver is built into the compact case—no separate tuner pack is required. Now, a built-in three-band graphic equalizer lets you tailor the sound to your personal tastes over a broad ± 10db range.

Built-in Dolby™ noise reduction dramatically lowers tape hiss. You hear pure, clean highs and rich, satisfying bass—from both normal and metal tapes. And tape reversing is automatic—you never have to turn over the cassette to hear the other side. Anti-roll mechanism locks onto the tape for flutter-free music while you exercise.

Just slightly larger than a cassette tape: 4½H × 3½W × 1⅛D"; weighs 10 oz. Attaches to your belt with the included clip. Runs on 2 AA batteries (not included). Jack for AC adapter. Comes with headphones and 90-day labor, one-year parts warranty.

Order today, and enjoy your favorite music on the go.

■ Aiwa Personal Stereo #EAI925 $99 (4.00)

Super-charge your sit-ups.

Marcy's® Pro Abdominal Board turns ordinary sit-ups into powerful workouts. You shape up quickly because your muscles work harder. Perform abdominal roll-ups, leg lifts, twists—up to 20 exercises for a strong abdomen and trim, tight stomach. Five incline angles continue to challenge your muscles as your strength grows.

Premium vinyl covers the comfortably padded, extra-long board. Convenient carrying handles also provide balance for leg raises. Folds flat for easy storage. Measures 24H × 15W × 59D" (collapsed: 11H × 15W × 53D"); weighs 25 lbs. Assembly requires adjustable wrench. Six-month warranty.

Make every sit-up count. Order this rugged board and make your workouts more efficient and rewarding.

■ Marcy Pro Abdominal Board #EMP366 $79 (6.50)

The unfolding phone: Panasonic's futuristic cordless.

Space travellers in science fiction films communicate with small folding devices they carry in their pockets. Now, Panasonic makes this futuristic technology a reality.

Flip open the compact handset of this mini-cordless phone, and you can enjoy clear conversations up to a 700–1,000' range. Flip it closed, and it automatically switches from talk to the standby mode. Slip it in your pocket and always have your phone close at hand. Measures only 4¼L × 2¼W × 1¼D"; weighs just 8 oz.

The built-in conveniences are just as futuristic. The handset stores and auto dials 10 frequently called numbers (up to 16 digits each). It has one-touch redial, tone/pulse dialing with pause button and flash key, high/low volume, and a pull-out antenna to extend your range. Digital security coding protects the privacy of your calls.

There's a built-in speakerphone with mute button in the base. You can answer calls over the speakerphone, put them on hold, and communicate with the handset using the 2-way pager and full intercom. You can also switch on the speakerphone from the handset to monitor the room. Streamlined base measures 5H × 7½W × 5½D"; weighs 2 lbs. Can be wall-mounted (brackets included). Plugs into wall outlet and phone jacks. Comes with two battery packs, so you always have a freshly charged one to power the handset. Made in Japan. One-year warranty.

Order today and take your Panasonic communicator to regions of your house unexplored by conventional phones.

■ Panasonic Mini-cordless Phone #EPA210 $189 (4.50)

TECHNOLOGICAL DEVELOPMENTS AND FUTURE TRENDS

Technological developments had complemented, and perhaps accelerated, the movement toward greater acceptance of in-home shopping. For example, passive direct-response systems, such as toll-free 800 phone numbers, contributed to the growth in mail-order sales. An experimental cable TV channel offered "infomercials" 5- to 10-minute descriptions of particular products. Catalogia, Inc. consolidated a national network of 3,000 electronic multicatalog retail shopping systems into a central data base, through which consumers could obtain the

EXHIBIT 24.10   Example of Markline Catalog Page

A. Emerson's compact TV/video cassette player is a great Markline value at only $499!

This 10-inch color TV has a built-in video cassette player that's loaded with features. The AC/DC television has automatic fine tuning and color control. The video cassette player features 3-speed automatic playback, automatic rewind and replay, and speed search. It can even freeze a single frame for stop-action viewing. Unit measures 14x11.5x13.9".

EMVCT120 Emerson TV/Video cassette player
$499   (S&H $20)

SPECIAL VALUE!
"Big" screen TV/VCR in one unit!

At last, here's a VCR and 19" television you can tote around in one piece. The VCR is built right into the base of this 19", 105 channel, cable ready, high resolution monitor. Tote Vision (shown on p. 25) features TV/VCR wireless remote control of all functions. Allows up to 8 hours of record/playback time with auto playback speed selector. This direct-drive, front loading system has automatic rewind, 3 playback speeds, memory, LED indicators, visual cue/review search function and more. Ideal as a compact home entertainment center. Size is 62x22¾x22¼".

TOCB1900 Tote Vision
(was $799.00)   **NOW $699.00**
(S&H $25)

New
B. Go on tour with your favorite entertainer.

Bring the sound of live concerts inside your home or car with the Sony AC-DC Powered Digital Compact Disc Player. This remarkable Sony design combines state-of-the-art technology & quality in this miniaturized compact disc player. Features ultra-thin, three-spot laser pick-up system with a digital filter, minimizes noise and improves high frequency reproduction. Elastic damper arm with pick-up absorbs vibration and improves tracking. Features automatic music sensor for instant repeat or advance track selection up to 99 tracks forward or reverse. Auto off. Supplied with AC adaptor, DC adaptor, cassette adaptor, mounting plate and patch cords.

SXD160 Sony Portable CD Player
$279.95   (S&H $4.50)

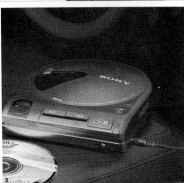

MARKLINE
Customer Service
1-800-225-8390

names of catalogs where a desired product was available. Sears and J.C. Penney had experimented with videodisc catalogs.

Teletext data transmission offered information varying from stock prices to weather reports; retailers could use teletext to present products to consumers. The Source, CompuServe, and Dow Jones Information/Retrieval were all examples of teletext services available in the United States. All three national television networks had competing teletext systems in test markets. Unlike other commercial teletext systems, which used computer terminals as vehicles, the network systems embedded a digital signal in the television vertical blanking interval (the technology used in captioning for the deaf). The signal could be read using a relatively inexpensive decoder, allowing the user to access, on the television, "pages" of information at will. When coupled with an 800 number, placing an order simply involved turning on the TV and dialing the phone.

One of the most promising and controversial technologies under development was videotex, a two-way interactive system that could operate through either home computers or cable TV. Unlike teletext, videotext subscribers could transmit as well as receive information. Videotex applications already included in-home financial transactions, electronic mail, reservation bookings, and retail sales transactions. Videotex, in use in Europe since 1976, was available commercially or publicly in several European countries and in Canada. In the United States, many of the largest communications, retailing, banking, and computer companies had been attempting to determine how to develop a dominant position in the business or consumer end of the videotex market. The list of firms involved in individual or joint ventures included CBS, Knight-Ridder, Times-Mirror, Time Inc., Cox Cable, Warner/AMEX, AT&T, Honeywell, Digital, IBM, and Chemical Bank, as well as Sears, Dayton Hudson, J.C. Penney, Melvin Simon, and Federated Department Stores.

Industry observers differed widely concerning time horizons for videotex development and adoption, as well as its eventual impact on retailing. There were several barriers to widespread consumer adoption, such as the cost of videotex terminals and user mistrust of the technology, as well as technological problems that needed to be resolved. Nonetheless, the consultant believed that videotex and related technologies had potentially significant ramifications for retailing, and it was important that Circuit City be prepared to adopt these technologies as they developed.

FURTHER CONSUMER RESEARCH

It was clear that some customers were willing to order some types of consumer electronics through the mail. In order to learn more about this market segment, the consultant had conducted a focus-group interview to determine the issues deemed important by mail-order customers.

These issues were then addressed in more detail in a survey of consumer electronics mail-order customers. A questionnaire (Exhibit 24.11) was mailed to 1,500 subjects chosen at random from the mailing list of a prominent consumer electronics mail-order firm. About a 30 percent response was received.

FOCUS GROUP FINDINGS

Most of the 10 focus group participants had some experience with mail order. Two of the attendees reported poor experiences—slow delivery or defective products—but this had not prejudiced them against using mail order.

There were three frequently cited advantages of store purchases over mail order:

- The opportunity to see, hear, and touch the merchandise
- The opportunity to take the purchase home immediately
- Greater confidence in warranty and repair availability

EXHIBIT 24.11   Survey Instrument Used for Mail-Order Survey

October, 1984

Dear Sir or Madam,

The enclosed survey is an important part of a project to analyze how people make choices when purchasing consumer electronics. I would appreciate it if you would take just a few minutes to complete and return this questionnaire. Your response is extremely important.

A postage-paid return envelope is enclosed. Please mail your responses as soon as possible.

Thank you for your help.

Sincerely,
Susan Quillen

Please note: For this survey, the terms "mail order" and "mail-order catalog" refer to the purchase of products from catalogs you have received through the mail (orders can be placed either by telephone or by mail).

1. For each of the products listed below, please check those which your household has purchased in the last three years, and indicate whether or not you purchased them through mail-order catalogs. (Check all that apply.)

	Bought in the last 3 Years	Bought through Mail Order
Computer peripherals	Yes____ No____	Yes____ No____
Computer software	Yes____ No____	Yes____ No____
Microwave oven	Yes____ No____	Yes____ No____
Portable stereo	Yes____ No____	Yes____ No____
Portable TV	Yes____ No____	Yes____ No____
Stereo system/components	Yes____ No____	Yes____ No____
Telephone	Yes____ No____	Yes____ No____
Video game systems	Yes____ No____	Yes____ No____
Video tape/disc player	Yes____ No____	Yes____ No____

2. If you have purchased any of the above products in the past three years, please circle the product you bought most recently (if you purchased more than one product at that time, circle the most expensive item). If you have not purchased any of the products in Question 1 in the last 3 years, please skip to Question 4.

3. Question 3 concerns the product you circled in Question 2.
   A) How much did you pay for the product?
      Under $20____ $20-$50____ $50-$200____ $200____ $500____ over $500____
   B) Which of the following sentences best describes your knowledge of this specific product before you purchased it?
      I had owned or tried the product before.   ____
      I had seen the product demonstrated but never tried it myself. ____
      I had seen the product myself but never saw it demonstrated.   ____
      I had seen only pictures of the product.   ____
      I had never seen the product or any picture of it.   ____

(Cont.)

EXHIBIT 24.11   (Cont.)

C) In deciding where to buy, did you compare prices or features . . .

. . . by speaking with store salespeople?	Yes____ No____
. . . by inspecting products in a store?	Yes____ No____
. . . by mail order catalogs?	Yes____ No____
. . . by telephone?	Yes____ No____
. . . by word-of-mouth?	Yes____ No____
. . . through advertising?	Yes____ No____
. . . by reading *Consumer Reports*?	Yes____ No____

D) Which of the following sentences best describes your use of mail-order catalogs in this purchase decision?

I never looked at this product in mail-order catalogs.   ____

I looked in mail-order catalogs but wouldn't consider buying
it through them.   ____

I considered buying it through a mail-order catalog, but chose
to buy it through a store instead.   ____

I bought the product through a mail-order catalog.   ____

E) Why did you choose the method of purchase indicated in Question D?

_____

F) If you purchased through a mail-order catalog (if not, proceed to Question H), how did you place your order?

Over the telephone_____   Through the mail_____

Why did you choose this method?_____

G) If you purchased through a mail-order catalog, did you seek additional information on the product over the telephone?

Yes____ No____

H) How important were each of the following considerations in your decision of where you bought the product? (Circle one in each row.)

	Extremely Important	Somewhat Important	Slightly Important	Not at all Important
low price	1	2	3	4
informative salespeople	1	2	3	4
convenient location	1	2	3	4
ease of purchase	1	2	3	4
past experience with the store/catalog	1	2	3	4
reputation of the store/catalog	1	2	3	4
availability of repairs	1	2	3	4
liberal return policy	1	2	3	4
sales people	1	2	3	4
credit availability	1	2	3	4
extensive product line	1	2	3	4

4. Question 4 concerns your use of mail-order catalogs for any type of product.

A) Approximately how many products have you purchased through mail-order catalogs in the past two years? (check only one)

None____ 1–2____ 3–5____ 6–10____ more than 10____

B) How many different mail-order catalogs have you ordered from in the past two years?

None____ 1–2____ 3–5____ 6–10____ more than 10____

EXHIBIT 24.11   (Cont.)

C) Please indicate your experience with the following mail-order catalogs:

	Have bought from	Have considered buying from	Have not considered buying from	Am not familiar with
Circuit City	——	——	——	——
Crutchfield	——	——	——	——
L.L. Bean	——	——	——	——
Land's End	——	——	——	——
Lubin & Sons	——	——	——	——
Radio Shack	——	——	——	——
Sears	——	——	——	——

5. Question 5 will only be used for statistical purposes and is completely confidential.
   A) Your current age:
      Under 18—— 18–24—— 25–34—— 35–54—— 55 and over——
   B) Your sex: Male—— Female——
   C) Your marital status: Single—— Married——
   D) Number of household members (including yourself) 18 years of age and over.
      None—— 1—— 2—— 3—— 4 or more——
   E) Number of household members (including yourself) under 18 years of age:
      None—— 1—— 2—— 3—— 4 or more——
   F) Your residence is located in which type of area:
      Urban—— Suburban—— Rural——
   G) Do you own your own home?
      Yes—— No, I am renting——
   H) Your highest level of education (check one only)
      Have not received high school diploma   ——
      High school graduate   ——
      Some post high school education   ——
      College graduate   ——
      University work beyond Bachelor's degree   ——
   I) What is the occupation of the head of your household (check one)
      Professional/Technical/Managerial   ——
      Sales/Clerical   ——
      Skilled Labor   ——
      Semi/Unskilled Labor   ——
      Retired   ——
      Student   ——
      Other, please specify _____
   J) Your total household income:
      Under $15,000   ——
      $15,000 to $25,000   ——
      $25,000 to $35,000   ——
      $35,000 to $50,000   ——
      $50,000 and above   ——

THANK YOU!

For the most part, participants saw little or no value in the information and recommendations provided by in-store salespeople. Salespeople were described variously as:

- Order-takers only
- Unpleasant to deal with
- Low paid and low skilled
- Not well versed in the characteristics of their own and their competitors' products
- Insensitive to the consumer's needs

Focus group participants seemed most likely to consider mail order if the following conditions were met:

- Merchandise could be returned unconditionally
- The company offering the catalog was known to the consumer
- The catalog offered brand-name products
- The desired product was unlikely to be damaged in shipping
- The product had a relatively low mark-up

Participants reported that generally they researched products prior to purchase, particularly in the case of expensive items. They were likely to seek recommendations from friends and family, *Consumer Reports*, and in-store demonstrations, and they were likely to compare prices among catalogs. Many indicated that they often visited specialty shops in the evaluation process but would purchase the item wherever they could secure the lowest price.

MAIL SURVEY FINDINGS

The demographic profile of the questionnaire respondents corresponded closely to that found among other consumers who used mail order. When compared with the general population, however, respondents tended to be:

- Concentrated between 25 and 54 years of age
- Largely male
- Suburban
- College graduates
- More likely to be employed in professional/managerial positions
- From households with incomes over $25,000

Demographics varied by product purchase category. Younger, less affluent subjects had bought proportionally more stereo components and portable stereos. ACE purchases, such as computer accessories, on the other hand, were concentrated among the more educated, affluent, professional respondents. Home-owners were more likely than nonhomeowners to have purchased appliances but were less likely to have purchased a home stereo.

Respondents who reported using mail order for their most recent consumer electronics purchase had also ordered proportionally more mail-order products in the prior two years and had ordered through more different catalogs than had other respondents. It appeared that consumers were most familiar with catalogs that had an image or product offering similar to that of catalogs they had purchased from in the past. For example, in general, respondents who were most familiar with Land's End (a catalog including a wide assortment of active sports-wear) were also familiar with L.L. Bean, and to a lesser extent with Sharper Image, but were less familiar with Circuit City. Circuit City customers, on the other hand, were generally quite familiar with Radio Shack, and somewhat with Sharper Image, but were less familiar with L.L. Bean. Reported familiarity with Lubin & Sons, a fictitious name included to check reliability of the answers, was very low.

The percentage of respondents who had used mail order was highest among the better-educated consumers, aged 35 to 54 years. This held across a variety of catalogs as well as for mail order in general, although Sears mail-orderers were more middle income, and Land's End and L.L. Bean had sales concentrated at both the high and low ends of the income scale. With the exception of Spencer Gifts, purchase experience increased with education.

Preferences for certain sources of product information varied according to respondents by age and education. Younger respondents relied more on friends, salespeople, and hands-on experience in purchase decisions. Those aged between 35 and 54 years were less inclined to shop around, either by visiting stores, checking ads, or asking advice. They were more likely to buy through catalogs, and more often sight unseen, than those either younger or older. Better-educated consumers were most likely to use catalogs as a means of comparison and were less concerned with helpful salespeople, familiarity with the store, or store reputation. They placed proportionally more orders by phone, and asked for additional information when placing orders.

In deciding where to purchase a product, in-store shoppers placed more importance on convenient location and availability of repairs than did mail-order shoppers. They also relied more on past experience with the retailer than did those who purchased through catalogs. Mail-order purchasers, on the other hand, were relatively more concerned than were in-store shoppers with the retailer's reputation, return policies, price, breadth of product line, and ease of purchase.

The consultant compared the relative importance of several purchase criteria across various types of consumer electronics and appliance purchases (see Exhibit 24.12, 24.13, and 24.14). It appeared that stereos and peripherals were deemed suitable for mail order, but only after first examining the product in a store. Telephones, portable stereos, and computer software seemed to be considered "safe" mail-order categories, even if the product had not been pretested in a

EXHIBIT 24.12   Consultant's Report—Most Recent Consumer Electronics/Appliance Purchase

Most Recent Purchase	Percent Who Bought It through Mail Order	Percent Who Had Considered Buying It through Mail Order	Percent Who Had Owned/Tried the Product before Buying	Percent Who Had Never Seen the Product before Buying
Stereo Component System	72	11	30	28
Computer Software	61	23	13	42
Telephone	46	23	32	39
Portable Stereo	38	23	38	29
VCR	37	26	29	25
Computer Peripherals	36	40	34	15
Television	9	44	36	26
Video Game System	9	46	64	0
Microwave Oven	6	38	41	0

EXHIBIT 24.13   Consultant's Report—Consumer Electronics/Appliance Purchases in the Past Three Years

Product Category	Percent Who Had Bought	
	Through Mail Order	Not Through Mail Order
Stereo Component System	34	32
Telephone	24	44
Computer Software	21	14
Computer Peripherals	15	36
Portable Stereo	9	27
VCR	6	18
Video Game System	5	21
Television	3	36
Microwave Oven	1	34

EXHIBIT 24.14   Consultant's Report—Purchase Decision Criteria by Product

Product Purchased	Decision Criteria			
	Informative Salesperson	Convenient Location	Outlet Reputation	Availability of Repairs
Microwave Oven	44[a]	31	44	69
Stereo Component System	31	10	58	32
VCR	31	24	31	23
Computer Peripherals	28	9	17	30
Television	21	37	37	33
Telephone	19	26	34	34
Video Game System	18	64	27	18
Computer Software	17	20	30	20
Portable Stereo	10	15	25	14

[a] To be read: "Of the respondents whose most recent consumer electronics/appliance purchase was a microwave oven, 44 percent rated 'informative salespeople' as 'extremely important' in their purchase decision."

store. Other products, such as televisions, video games, and microwave ovens, were not often purchased through the mail. The consultant believed the results indicated particular concern about dealer reliability and service when purchasing TVs and microwaves. Purchasers of video games, on the other hand, apparently were more interested in convenience, which was interpreted to mean getting the product quickly.

CONSULTANT RECOMMENDATIONS

The consultant saw a clear opportunity for Circuit City to build a prominent position in the consumer electronics segment of mail-order catalogs. There were, however, two basic strategies the Circuit City catalog could pursue.

First, Circuit City could develop a catalog with a similar format to its store operations; namely, guaranteed lowest price, low- to middle-line products across a wide spectrum of product categories, and high-volume sales with modest profit margins. The primary advantage to this approach would be that it matches the strengths that Circuit City had built and demonstrated successfully. However, the consultant believed that the following disadvantages made this strategy unattractive for implementation:

- This strategy had the greatest potential for cannibalizing current Circuit City sales, rather than adding incremental sales.
- The guaranteed lowest price would be extremely difficult to administer because the catalog would face price competition in virtually every part of the United States.
- There was a strong possibility that this strategy would fail to take full advantage of the higher margins mail order makes available through low overhead.
- If Circuit City wanted to modify the catalog's product mix in the future, it would be difficult to try to upgrade the quality and prices of a catalog that has already built a discount image and reputation.

Conversely, a catalog that carried a top-of-the-line group of products would not only avoid the disadvantages described above, but would also offer several advantages to Circuit City:

- Circuit City would be able to build purchasing power in top-end products by expanding its base of sales for those items (this would allow Circuit City to offer some of these items in their high-volume retail stores as well as in the catalog).
- Circuit City would have an opportunity to try new and different products on a limited basis without having to bump existing store products in favor of more uncertain items.
- This approach would place Circuit City in a market segment where the number one catalog (Sharper Image) had sales only a fraction of Circuit City's and where Circuit City could price lower than its major competitors without having to offer "rock-bottom" prices.

To pursue this aggressive strategy in the top-of-the-line catalog market, the consultant suggested that Circuit City develop its catalog along the following lines:

A. Products
   1. The catalog should contain a select number of consumer electronics products from the top end of Circuit City's current audio, video, telephonic, computer, and recording product categories. These products might not be available in Circuit City stores, and as such would supplement rather than compete with existing Circuit City sales. These products would represent approximately 90 percent of the catalog's contents.
   2. The catalog would also contain a few specialty, "one-of-a-kind" or "gadget" electronic items (e.g., video watches). These would be high-margin, gift/impulse items and would compose 10 percent of the catalog. However, at Christmas time, a larger proportion of such items should be included in the catalog.
   3. At least 20 percent of the products in each issue of the catalog should be new items. This approach assures that the catalog remains interesting to the consumer.

B. Prices
   1. Catalog prices should be slightly lower than competing specialty electronics/audio stores and catalogs. This should be feasible because of Circuit City's tremendous buying power. Although top-of-the-line products can command price premiums, if consumers find identical products in different catalogs, lowest price determines which catalog gets their order.
   2. The catalog should not pursue a lowest-price guarantee, thus allowing margins well above those in the Circuit City stores, and avoiding the disadvantage discussed above.
   3. Catalog prices should include shipping costs, to ensure that the face value of the Circuit City catalog price is the actual price paid by the consumer.

C. Layout
   1. The name of the catalog should suggest exclusivity and high technology, with only a small reference to its association with Circuit City. This approach takes advantage of potential Circuit City name recognition without confusing the catalog with Circuit City's discount image. Examples of appropriate types of names are as follows:
      a. THE CUTTING EDGE a division of Circuit City.
      b. UPTOWN ELECTRONICS a subdivision of Circuit City.
      c. SELECT CUSTOMER ELECTRONICS a subsidiary of Circuit City.
   2. The outside dimensions of the catalog should be somewhat smaller than most catalogs (approximately 7″ × 10″ overall) because when catalogs are stacked on the consumer's coffee table, this smaller catalog will be placed on top of the larger 8 1/2″ × 11″ catalogs published by Sharper Image, Markline, and others.
   3. The cover design should be uncluttered and clever. It should promote general interest rather than specific products. These covers will encourage the customer to open the catalog (clearly a critical step) and will help distinguish the catalog from other electronic catalogs that tend to print simply a barrage of products on their catalog covers.

4. The catalog should be relatively brief (between 24 and 48 pages), with four-color, high-gloss print, and with no more than two or three items per page. This format strongly supports an image of top quality and exclusivity.

5. The description of each item should be as brief as possible for easy browsing, but appropriate to the price and complexity of the specific item.

D. Distribution

1. The catalog should be mailed to a select number of Circuit City customers, based on their past history of buying top-end items or having spent a certain amount of money in the store, perhaps $500. This will limit the number of catalogs that will be sent, and more importantly, ensure that they are sent to segments of Circuit City customers that are most likely to purchase from the catalog.

2. The catalog should also be sent to people nationwide who have previous experience with consumer electronics through the mail, or who meet certain demographic characteristics as determined by the research. These people can be reached through one or more of the following methods:

   a. Renting mailing lists from companies such as American Express, Crutchfield, or Sharper Image.

   b. Placing advertisements with clip-out coupons for a free catalog in select national or regional magazines and newspapers.

   c. Producing television ads that promote one product, but that include an opportunity to call in for a free catalog.

3. The initial mailing should be at least 1 million pieces, sent in late September or early October on a staggered basis (200,000 each week for five weeks). One million catalogs must be printed to achieve economies of scale in printing costs. The staggered mailing will help Circuit City administer the flow of orders, since most of them will come soon after the catalog arrives in the customer's home.

4. The catalog should be updated on a quarterly basis, again with staggered mailings, to allow product-line changes and to replace catalogs that have been discarded or forgotten.

E. Services

1. Customers should be able to order items via mail, through a toll-free 800 number, or through a store. The first two are conveniences that catalog customers will expect. Use of the POS system would be an added convenience that Circuit City can provide as well, allowing store salespeople to sell catalog items not available in the stores.

2. Telephone salespeople should be trained to provide additional product information, encourage sale of related items, and promote extended warranty plans, in addition to taking orders. These talents will encourage consumers to purchase technical items that cannot be described fully in a few paragraphs; they will also allow Circuit City to achieve some of the trade-up and warranty sales often precluded by catalogs.

3. A 60-day, no-questions-asked return policy should be provided. A strong return policy is a major selling point for catalogs.

This strategy was highly aggressive and would entail significant start-up and operating costs. It would also provide significant returns to Circuit City. Based on only a 2 percent response rate on 1 million catalogs at an average of $120 per order (as seen in comparable catalogs), Circuit City would realize sales of $2.4 million.

The consultant felt that Circuit City was particularly well suited to succeed with this aggressive approach for the following reasons:

- Circuit City was substantially larger than the major players in the consumer electronics end of the mail-order industry (compare Circuit City's sales of $246 million to Sharper Image's sales of only $35 million).
- Circuit City had the buying power to allow higher margins than other competitors in this segment. Thus, even if pricing became the major form of competition, Circuit City should be able to win out.
- Circuit City already had some experience with catalogs and substantial experience in consumer electronics sales. Besides being a substantial plus in and of itself, its retail stores also gave Circuit City immediate access to a substantial list of potential catalog customers.

CONCLUSIONS

Ed Kopf, who had been director of marketing when the study of mail order was commissioned, realized that this subject was one of important concern for long-range planning. He saw the need to watch the developments of in-home shopping, but was unsure of their economic implications for Circuit City.

He knew that some firms whose business was primarily mail order reported significantly higher profit ratios than did the average retailers. Firms that distributed principally through stores and that had treated mail order as an add-on usually were not able to develop detailed cost data to determine the bottom line profitability of mail order. Indications were, however, that the profit results were not so successful for retail store firms that added mail-order operations as for the firms that had always concentrated on mail order.

The costs to develop and distribute a mail-order catalog were reported from one source to be 40 cents per copy, with 1.5 million mailed. The return (number of orders) ranged from below 2 percent to 5 percent of the mailings. A rule of thumb had been established in the business that a 2 percent return was needed to break even. To obtain a high number of returns when a firm began a catalog operation, it was necessary to "rent" names from other mail-order firms through list brokers. The cost of names printed on pressure-sensitive labels ranged from $2.50 to $10.00 per thousand, usually depending on the quality of the list.

Ed wondered whether the Circuit City warehouse system could handle the mail orders, or whether it would be necessary to set up a separate warehouse for fulfillment of mail orders. But his biggest concern was when the time would be right for Circuit City to enter the rapidly growing mail-order market. And, if the firm were to decide to embark on this venture, what should be the extent of the merchandise offered and where should responsibility for the project lie in the Circuit City organization?

_____ CASE 25 _____

Harley-Davidson

INTRODUCTION

The name's Johnny. You might've heard of me. I run a little business down off of 38th and Main. It's an investments business. You ain't heard of it? Oh, well. . . . Hey, you got a light? Thanks, man. Hey, while you're up, can you grab me a cold one? Thanks. Aaaah. That's more like it. Grab some wood, pal. I've got one helluva story to tell you.

It all started a few months ago. I had just stalled the landlady for another week. So I'm sitting in my office, sipping a Jack and Coke, minding my own business, when this incredible blonde walks in.

"Johnny," she says, "I need a loan."

"Well, beautiful, you came to the right guy."

So for the next few hours I listened to her story. Great girl. Really smart. Her name was Connie. Maybe you know her. But anyway, turns out she had this hot tip on Harley-Davidson. A sure thing, she said. But she needed my money to play the market. So we'd be partners, or something like that.

At first, I thought to myself, this can't miss. Harley's like apple pie. I used to ride around on my HOG back in the '60s. Damn, those were some good times. Then that little voice went off inside my head. Only this time my voice ain't whispering, he's shouting.

"Hey, yo, Johnny! You snapperhead! What're you thinking, huh? Look at the economy. We're heading for a friggin' recession and you want to put your wad in Harley? Geez. And what about Holiday Rambler? Yeah, you forgot about them, you dunce! They're the RV sub that keeps sucking all of Harley's profits! Come on Johnny, pull your head out before it's too late!"

Whew. My little voice never spouted off like that before. So I figured I'd better listen to him. So, I told the dame that before I shelled out my coin, I was gonna have to check out Harley for myself. She gave me a week. And here's what I found out. So light 'em if you've got 'em . . .

This case was prepared by Scott Draper, A. Scott Dundon, Allen North, and Ron Smith under the supervision of Sexton Adams and Adelaide Griffin as a basis for class discussion rather than to illustrate either effective or ineffective handling of an administrative situation. Copyright © 1990 by Sexton Adams and Adelaide Griffin. Used with permission from Sexton Adams.

COMPANY HISTORY

In the Beginning . . .

The year was 1903. Henry Ford introduced the first Model A, the Wright brothers flew over Kitty Hawk, and, in a shack near Milwaukee, Wisconsin, a machine called the Silent Gray Fellow was born. Three brothers—William, Walter, and Arthur Davidson had invented a machine that would exemplify "the American desire for power, speed, and personal freedom"—the Harley-Davidson motorcycle.[1]

The Davidson's first crude machines found a ready market among both individuals and law enforcement agencies,[2] and by 1907, production had reached 150 motorcycles per year.[3] Two years later, a new engine, the V-twin, was introduced and enabled motorcycles to attain top speeds of 60 mph.[4] Motorcycles were fast becoming the primary source of transportation in the United States.

The Harley-Davidson Motorcycle Company took pride in America, and when the United States joined Europe in World War I, Harley-Davidson motorcycles helped the U.S. Army chase the kaiser across Germany.[5] After World War I, however, it was the automobile, not the motorcycle, that gained popularity as the principal means of transportation in the United States. Harley's annual production plunged from 28,000 to 10,000 units immediately after the war. After a decade of struggle, Harley-Davidson again reached prewar production levels, only to be ravaged by the Great Depression. By 1933, only 3,700 motorcycles were produced by Harley-Davidson.[6]

The economic boost provided by World War II and the military's high demand for motorcycles enabled Harley-Davidson to again match its 1920 production level. But after World War II, the motorcycle industry crashed. As America's heroes returned, their focus was on housing and family necessities, not motorcycles.[7] At one time Harley-Davidson was one of 150 U.S. motorcycle manufacturers, but by 1953, the weak motorcycle market had eliminated its final U.S. competitor, Indian Motocycle Company. Harley-Davidson stood alone as the sole manufacturer of motorcycles in the United States.[8]

The AMF Reign

Harley-Davidson made its first public stock offering in 1965, and shortly thereafter, the struggle for control of Harley-Davidson began. In 1968, Bangor

[1] Mark Marvel, "The Gentrified HOG," *Esquire*, July 1989, pp. 25–26.
[2] Robert L. Rose, "Vrooming Back," *Wall Street Journal* (southwestern ed.), August 31, 1990, p. 1.
[3] Peter C. Reid, *Well Made in America—Lessons from Harley-Davidson on Being the Best*, (New York; McGraw-Hill, 1990), p. 9.
[4] Marvel, "Gentrified HOG," p. 25.
[5] Ibid.
[6] Reid, *Well Made*, p. 9.
[7] Ibid.
[8] Rose, "Vrooming Back," p. 1.

Punta, an Asian company with roots in the railroad industry, began acquiring large amounts of Harley-Davidson stock. At the same time, AMF, an international leader in the recreational goods market, announced its interest in Harley-Davidson, citing a strong fit between Harley-Davidson's product lines and AMF's leisure lines. Bangor Punta and AMF then entered a bidding war over Harley-Davidson. Harley's stockholders chose AMF's bid of $22 per share over Bangor Punta's bid of $23 per share because of Bangor Punta's reputation for acquiring a company, squeezing it dry, and then scrapping it for salvage. AMF's plans were initially perceived as being more favorable for Harley-Davidson's long-term existence by touting plans for expansion of Harley.[9]

AMF's plans did not, however, correspond with Harley-Davidson's ability to expand. Much of Harley-Davidson's equipment was antiquated and could not keep up with the increase in production. One company official noted that "quality was going down just as fast as production was going up."[10] These events occurred at a time when Japanese motorcycle manufacturers began flooding the U.S. market with high-quality motorcycles that offered many innovative features and cost less.

Many of Harley's employees felt that if AMF had worked *with* the experienced Harley personnel instead of dictating orders for production quotas, many of the problems could have been properly addressed. One Harley senior executive stated that "the bottom line was that quality went to hell because AMF expanded Harley production at the same time that Harleys were getting out of date, and the Japanese were coming to town with new designs and reliable products at a low price."[11] Unlike their Japanese competitors whose motorcycles failed to pass inspection an average of 5 percent of the time, Harley's motorcycles failed to pass the end-of-the-assembly-line inspection at an alarming 50 percent to 60 percent rate.

After a $4.8 million annual operating loss and 11 years under AMF control, Harley-Davidson was put up for sale in 1981. A management team, led by Vaughn Beals, vice president of motorcycle sales, used $81.5 million in financing from Citicorp to complete a leveraged buyout. All ties with AMF were severed and the "new" Harley-Davidson was created.[12]

The Tariff Barrier

Although Harley-Davidson had managed to obliterate its U.S. competition during the 1950s and 1960s, the company took a beating from the Japanese in the 1970s. Japanese competition, and the recession presiding over the nation's economy had taken nearly all of Harley-Davidson's business. The company's meager

[9] Reid, *Well Made in America*, p. 9.
[10] Ibid., p. 25.
[11] Ibid., p. 27.
[12] Rod Willis, "Harley-Davidson Comes Roaring Back," *Management Review*, March 1986, pp. 20–27.

3 percent share of total motorcycle sales led experts to speculate as to whether or not Harley-Davidson would be able to celebrate its 80th birthday. Tariff protection appeared to be Harley-Davidson's only hope. Fortunately, massive lobbying efforts finally paid off in 1983, when Congress passed a huge tariff increase on Japanese motorcycles. Instead of a 4 percent tariff, Japanese motorcycles would now be subject to a 45 percent tariff. The protection was to last for five years.[13]

Slowly, Harley-Davidson began to recover market share as the tariff impacted competitors. Management was able to relinquish their ownership with a public stock offering in 1986. Brimming with confidence, Harley-Davidson asked Congress to remove the tariff barrier in December 1986, more than a year earlier than originally planned. It was time to strap on the helmet and race with the Japanese head to head.[14]

Acquisition and Diversification

Holiday Rambler was purchased in 1986 by Harley-Davidson, a move that nearly doubled the size of the firm. As a wholly owned subsidiary, the manufacturer of recreational and commercial vehicles provided Harley-Davidson with another business unit that could diversify the risks associated with the seasonal motorcycle market. That move gave Harley-Davidson two distinct business segments, Holiday Rambler Corporation, and Harley-Davidson Motorcycle Division. In addition, during the late 1980s Harley-Davidson attempted to capitalize on its manufacturing expertise by competing for both government and contract manufacturing opportunities in an attempt to further increase the proportion of revenues derived from nonmotorcycle sources.

HOLIDAY RAMBLER CORPORATION

Harley-Davidson implemented many new management techniques at Holiday Rambler. The Yadiloh (Holiday spelled backward) program was created in 1989. Yadiloh was an acronym for "Yes Attitude, Deliver, Involvement, Leadership, Opportunity, Harmony." The goal of Yadiloh was to address cost and productivity problems facing Holiday Rambler. The employees of Holiday Rambler seemed to favor the program. "This program will help us solve a lot of problems in the long run. So I think it's a really big step, a positive step," said Raud Estep, a quality control inspector for Holiday Rambler. Another employee, Vickie Hutsell, agreed, "I think that most of the people who've gone through the Yadiloh training session are 'pumped up' about it."[15]

But Holiday Rambler did more than get employees excited. It built a new, centralized facility that was completed in late 1990 to handle all of the compa-

[13] Rose, "Vrooming Back," p. 1.
[14] "Harley Back in High Gear," *Forbes*, April 20, 1987, p. 8.
[15] Harley-Davidson Annual Report 1989, p. 13.

ny's manufacturing needs. They also installed more computer-aided design (CAD) equipment to support the research and development staff, which led to a $1.9 million increase in operating expenses.

Observers, however, felt that the success of Holiday Rambler had been mixed at best. Several strong competitors had entered the recreational vehicle (RV) market in 1988. Holiday Rambler responded by discontinuing its "Trail Seeker" line of recreational vehicles after the line experienced a $30 million sales decline in 1988. Holiday Rambler continued to trim poor performing areas. In October 1989, Parkway Distribution, an RV parts and accessories distributor was sold. A $2.8 million decline in revenues from the business units of Creative Dimensions, Nappanee Wood Products, and B & B Molders was recorded in that same year. Holiday Rambler enacted competitive pricing measures and a lower margin sales mix. The result was a decrease in gross margin percentage from 19.0 percent to 18.2 percent.

Some industry experts recognized a possible recovery for the sluggish RV market in 1990. However, the message of H. Wayne Dahl, Holiday Rambler president, was unclear. "Whether our business is RVs, commercial vehicles, or a related enterprise, we intend to keep it strong and growing by keeping in close touch with its customers."[16]

The Recreational Vehicle Market

In 1986, Harley executives claimed that the acquisition of Holiday Rambler would help to diversify the risks associated with the seasonal motorcycle market. However, some industry experts questioned whether such an acquisition was a wise move for Harley. They pointed out that although the acquisition smoothed seasonal fluctuations in demand, cyclical fluctuations caused by the economy were unaffected. One expert asserted, "Because both items (motorcycles and recreational vehicles) are luxury goods, they are dependent on such key economic factors as interest rates, disposable income, and gasoline prices."[17]

In addition to the economy, the demographics of the RV market presented a challenge to Harley. The main consumer of recreational vehicles in the 1970s was the blue-collar employee who worked a steady 40 hours per week. However, economic trends led to a switch from manufacturing to a more service-oriented economy. The trends left most consumers with little time on their hands for recreational activities. In 1989, statistics revealed that the typical owner of an RV was between 35 and 54 years old with an average income of $39,800. Census projections indicated that the U.S. population was growing older at the end of the 1980s. The high incomes and older ages gave RV manufacturers the opportunity to include extra features that allowed them to raise total vehicle cash prices by $20,000 and more.

[16] Ibid., p. 14.
[17] Raymond Serafin, "RV Market Puzzled," *Advertising Age*, July 1988, p. 52.

The RV industry had support from nonconsumer groups that existed specifically to accommodate the RV owner. The Escapees, for instance, offered insurance and cash-handling services to members driving RVs. The Good Sam's Club provided road service to RVs in need of repair. RV owners were even treated to their own television program to watch while on the road—"Wish You Were Here." The show, broadcast via satellite by the Nashville channel, highlighted RV lifestyles through interviews with owners across the country.[18]

MANAGEMENT

Vaughn Beals' outward appearance was far removed from the burly image that many might have expected of a "Harley" chief executive. The middle-aged Ivy Leaguer graduated from MIT's Aeronautical Engineering School and was known in manufacturing circles as a productivity guru.[19] But, on the inside, Vaughn Beals was a HOG (a member of the Harley owners group) in the truest sense of the word. He began working with Harley-Davidson as vice-president of motorcycle sales with AMF.[20] Disgruntled with AMF's declining attention to quality, Beals led a team of 12 others who successfully completed the leveraged buyout from AMF.

But Beals had a difficult mission ahead. Even after receiving protection, Harley-Davidson had to find a way to restore confidence in its products. So Beals decided to hit the road—literally. He drove Harley-Davidson motorcycles to rallies where he met Harley owners. In doing so, Beals was able to learn about product defects and needed improvements directly from the consumer. Industry experts believed that these efforts were vital to the resurgence of the company.

Willie G. Davidson, grandson of the company's founder, rode along with Vaughn Beals on Harley's road to recovery. "Willie G." provided a sharp contrast to Beals. If Vaughn Beals looked more at home in a courtroom, Willie G. might have looked more at home behind the bars of a jail cell. Davidson's appearance was that of a middle-aged man who was a remnant of the 1960s era. A Viking helmet covered his long, stringy hair, and his beard hid the hard features of a wind-parched face. He wore a leather jacket that, like his face, showed the cracks of wear and tear that the miles of passage over U.S. highways had caused. Nonetheless, Willie G. was named the new vice president of design for Harley in 1981. Industry observers believed that he had been instrumental in instigating much needed improvements in the Harley HOG.

Beals stepped down as CEO in 1989, passing the reins to Richard Teerlink, who was then serving as chief operating officer for Harley-Davidson Motorcycle Division. Beals, however, retained his position as chairman of the board. After the transition, Harley-Davidson retained a long list of experienced executives. The organizational chart (Exhibit 25.1) highlights the depth of the Harley-Davidson management team.

[18] Joe Schwartz, "No Fixed Address," *American Demographics*, August 1986, pp. 50–51.
[19] Willis, "Harley-Davidson," pp. 20–27.
[20] John Madock Roberts, "Harley's HOG's," *Forbes*, December 7, 1985, p. 14.

EXHIBIT 25.1   Harley-Davidson Organizational Chart

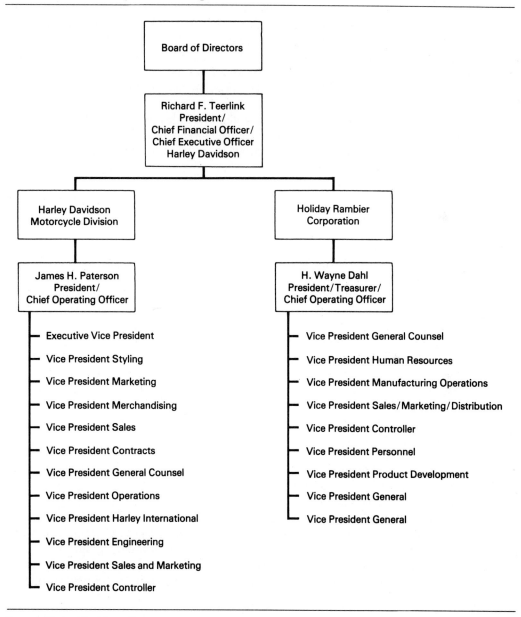

Source: Harley-Davidson, Inc.

In a somewhat ironic turn of events, Beals and other executives of Harley-Davidson had traveled to Japan in 1981 to visit the factories of their competition in an attempt to uncover any secrets. What they found was surprising. The Japanese did not run a low-cost production facility due to sophisticated machinery; instead, they simply used effective management techniques to maximize productivity. Armed with a new management perspective from the Japanese, Harley-Davidson began implementing quality circles (QCs), statistical operations controls, and just-in-time (JIT) inventory.[21]

The first dramatic change implemented by Harley management was to divide each plant into four to seven profit centers. The managers of each profit center were assigned total responsibility within their particular area. The increase in responsibility gave plant managers more authority and allowed Harley-Davidson to greatly reduce the staff functions previously needed to assist production. Harley-Davidson was able to reduce its employee work force by 40 percent after implementing these changes.[22] In 1982, the company adopted a JIT system for control of "in-plant" manufacturing and a materials-as-needed (MAN) system, which dealt with control of *all* inventories both inside and outside of the plants.

Next, Harley-Davidson attempted to increase employee involvement through the formation of quality circles. Thomas Gelb, Harley's executive vice president of operations, noted that even though QCs were only a small part of employee involvement programs, they played a significant role in helping to break down the communication barriers between line workers and supervisors. Line workers who were previously given quotas from high-level management became involved, through the use of QCs, in setting more realistic quotas based on actual production capacity and needs. Employee involvement gave workers a real sense of ownership in meeting these goals, according to Gelb.[23] Employees were viewed as links in a chain, and through employee involvement programs they could drive quality throughout the organization. Employees were involved, by direct participation, in discussions and decisions on changes that affected them in the performance of their own work. Also, management trained employees on ways to recognize and eliminate waste in the production process.[24] According to 1986 figures, Harley's tab for warranty repairs, scrap, and reworking of parts had decreased by 60 percent since 1981.[25]

Employee involvement was further increased through a program called statistical operator control (SOC). SOC gave employees the responsibility for checking the quality of their own work within a predetermined range. Employee quality checks took place on the production floor, and on many occasions, the workers themselves were given the responsibility to make the proper correcting

[21] Willis, "Harley-Davidson," pp. 22–23.

[22] Ibid., p. 26.

[23] Ibid., pp. 22–23.

[24] John A. Saathoff, "Workshop Report: Maintain Excellence through Change," *Target*, Spring 1989, p. 2.

[25] Dexter Hutchins, "Having a Hard Time with Just-in-Time," *Fortune*, June 19, 1986, p. 66.

adjustments. SOC helped to identify errors in the production process on a timely basis and gave line workers more responsibility through making quality checks and correcting adjustments in the production process.[26]

Although employees became more involved at Harley, labor relations remained strained. To correct the problem, management implemented an open-door policy to improve labor relations and increased stock options to include a broader base of employees. Management took a more sensitive stance toward the opinions of all employees. Union relations also improved when management voluntarily agreed to put the union label on all motorcycles produced and by sharing financial information with union leaders. Harley attempted to deal with all employees, even those affected by layoffs, in a humane way. Several employee assistance programs were put into place. Among these were outplacement assistance to cushion the blow of layoffs, early retirement (age 55) or voluntary layoffs, and drug abuse programs administered by the Milwaukee Council on Drug Abuse.[27]

In order for the above changes to work, Harley developed several overall goals. As stated in its annual report, Harley's 1989 management goals included improvement of quality, employee satisfaction, customer satisfaction, and shareholder return. Its long-term focus would address four major areas of concern for the 1990s: (1) quality, (2) productivity, (3) participation, and (4) flexibility.

1. Quality—Management efforts in the late 1980s attempted to overcome its reputation for poor quality. Because most of Harley's upper management believed that quality improvement was an ongoing process, they made a commitment to a long-term goal.
2. and 3. Participation and Productivity—These two areas led to overlapping objectives, according to Harley executives. Because of this, the company emphasized employee involvement programs throughout the firm.
4. Flexibility—The diminishing domestic marketplace and the slowing U.S. economy created the need for flexibility. Harley-Davidson management hoped to explore other options for the firm.

Management hoped to lead rather than follow the competition. In 1990, Harley cultivated the catch phrase "Do the right thing and do that thing right."

PRODUCTION AND OPERATIONS

After the leveraged buyout, manufacturing was still a major problem. According to one Harley executive, "Less than 70 percent of our motorcycles were complete when they reached the end of the assembly line."[28] Motorcycle production schedules were often based on the parts that were available instead of the

[26] Saathoff, "Workshop Report," p. 4.
[27] Willis, "Harley-Davidson," p. 27.
[28] Harley-Davidson Annual Report, 1989, p. 3.

planned master schedule. According to industry experts, "Japanese manufacturing techniques were yielding operating costs 30 percent lower than Harley's."[29] How did the Japanese do it? Though Beals and other managers had visited Japanese plants in 1981, it was not until they got a chance to tour Honda's assembly plant in Marysville, Ohio, after the buyout, that they began to understand Japanese competition. Beals said, "We were being wiped out by the Japanese because they were better *managers*. It wasn't robotics, or culture, or morning calisthenics and company songs—it was professional managers who understood their business and paid attention to detail."[30]

The Just-In-Time Inventory Method

A pilot JIT manufacturing program was quickly introduced in the Milwaukee engine plant. Tom Gelb, senior vice president of operations, called a series of meetings with employees, telling them bluntly, "We have to play the game the way the Japanese play or we're dead."[31]

Gelb was met with extreme skepticism. The York, Pennsylvania, plant, for instance, was already equipped with a computer-based control system that utilized overhead conveyors and high-rise parts storage. In a meeting with the work force of the York facility, Gelb announced that the JIT system would replace these overhead conveyors and storage with pushcarts. The production floor erupted with laughter. Surely, this was a joke. Plant managers mumbled that Harley-Davidson was returning to the 1930s.[32]

Observers noted that the overriding principle of the JIT method was that "parts and raw materials should arrive at the factory just as they are needed in the manufacturing process. This lets the manufacturer eliminate inventories and the costs of carrying them."[33] Anne Thundercloud, the York plant quality circle facilitator, stated, "It is the Harley employees who make JIT work, by having an investment in seeing it work." The same men and women who laughed out loud over the implementation of JIT began to believe in its "exacting discipline." Their belief was justified. Nearly 60,000 square feet of warehouse space was freed.[34] Costs of production plummeted. In 1986, Harley was able to lower its break-even point to 35,000 units—from 53,000 in 1981.[35]

Supplier cooperation was also critical to JIT success, but Harley-Davidson had a poor track record with its vendors. As one industry observer noted, "Harley was notorious for juggling production schedules and was one of the worst customers when it came to last-minute panic calls for parts." Furthermore, suppliers were wary of their role in the JIT picture. Edward J. Hay of Rath &

[29] Saathoff, "Workshop Report," p. 3.
[30] Hutchins, "Having a Hard Time," p. 65.
[31] Hutchins, "Having a Hard Time," p. 64.
[32] *Fortune*, September 25, 1989, p. 161.
[33] Ibid.
[34] Hutchins, "Having a Hard Time," p. 64.
[35] Willis, "Harley-Davidson," p. 14.

Strong, a Lexington, Massachusetts, management consulting firm, stated, "The big problem is that companies treat just-in-time as a way of getting the suppliers to hold the inventories."[36] One expert noted that Harley had to "abandon the security blanket that inventory often represented for them and learn to trust their suppliers."[37]

Critics believed that Harley erred initially by taking a legalistic approach in trying to sign up suppliers for a JIT system. The company insisted on contracts that were 35 pages long, devoted largely to spelling out suppliers' obligations to Harley. This strategy was ambitious and too pretentious. Early results did not meet management's expectations, and the animosity was growing between Harley and its suppliers. One supplier contended, "They're constantly renegotiating contracts, and tinkering with the layout of the plant."[38]

Finally, the company took positive steps to improve vendor relations. Contracts were reduced to two pages. According to one Harley executive, "We need to get out of the office and meet face-to-face." Experts noted, "Teams of buyers and engineers fanned out to visit suppliers: they began simplifying and improving designs and helping suppliers reduce setup time between jobs by modifying equipment to permit quick change of dies. To improve the quality of the parts, Harley gave suppliers courses in statistics to teach workers how to chart small changes in the performance of their equipment. The practice provides early tip-offs when machines are drifting out of tolerance."[39]

Materials-as-Needed

Harley's MAN system was tailored after that of Toyota's production system and was driven by "Kanban" technology—a control system that used circulating cards and standard containers for parts. The system provided real-time production needs information without the use of costly and complex resources which were typically needed for planning and support.[40] Tom Schwarz, general manager of Harley-Davidson Transportation Company, developed a strategically controlled inbound system for dealing with suppliers. As one executive noted, "Harley's ultimate goal is to control all inbound and outbound shipments themselves. They prefer to keep a minimum (number) of carriers involved. That reduces the chance of delays."[41] As an example, Harley-Davidson used its own leased fleet of 26 tractors and 46 trailers for the bulk of its road miles, using contract carriers only to supplement direct point service to its 700 dealers.

Harley-Davidson then began to evaluate its present suppliers based on manufacturing excellence and ability to provide small and frequent deliveries instead of evaluating suppliers strictly on price alone. Harley's trucks made daily,

[36] Roberts, "Harley's HOG's," p. 14.
[37] Hutchins, "Having a Hard Time," p. 64.
[38] Ibid.
[39] Ibid.
[40] Ibid., p. 65.
[41] Saathoff, "Workshop Report," pp. 3–4.

timed pickups from five to six suppliers on a predetermined route. Over the course of a week, the truck brought in all inbound shipments from 26 to 30 important vendors within a 200-mile radius of the plant.[42] This type of system also allowed for frequent, small deliveries while helping to reduce freight costs.[43] "From 1981–1986, MAN cut the York plant's inbound freight costs (mostly from vendor billing) by $50,000."[44]

An important element in keeping freight costs down was the elimination of nonproductive travel and Harley's new purchase order system. The company reported in 1986 that only 4 percent of the 2 million miles that the fleet traveled in the past year were empty. Harley changed its purchase order system in 1986 so that the only prices it would acknowledge were FOB vendors' shipping docks. This prevented suppliers from including freight in their prices and, in turn, discouraged them from using their own carriers for shipments to the motorcycle maker's plants.[45]

In 1986, Harley-Davidson began pressing some of its suppliers to start passing up the line more of the cost savings that JIT afforded. "It's time," said Patrick T. Keane, project engineer at Harley's York, Pennsylvania, plant, "to enter an era of negotiated price decreases. And right now we are holding meetings to accomplish that."[46]

After five years of using JIT, reviews poured in. Between 1981 and 1988, the following results were achieved:

1. Inventory had been reduced by 67 percent.
2. Productivity climbed by 50 percent.
3. Scrap and rework were down two-thirds.
4. Defects per unit were down 70 percent.[47]

Some industry experts believed that "the results for Harley and its suppliers have been good, although the company still has not achieved all its goals."[48] "We are very inefficient," said Keane, "but the comparison to where we were five years ago is phenomenal."[49]

Quality

In the 1970s, the running joke among industry experts was, "If you're buying a Harley, you'd better buy two—one for spare parts."[50] After the buyout from AMF, Harley-Davidson was determined to restore consumer confidence by

[42] "At Harley-Davidson JIT Is a Fine Tuned Cycle," *Purchasing*, April 24, 1986, pp. 46–48.
[43] Hutchins, "Having a Hard Time," p. 64.
[44] Saathoff, "Workshop Report," p. 5.
[45] "At Harley-Davidson," p. 48.
[46] Hutchins, "Having a Hard Time," p. 66.
[47] Ibid.
[48] Harley-Davidson News, 1988, p. 1.
[49] Huchins, "Having a Hard Time," p. 66.
[50] Ibid., p. 66.

raising the quality of its motorcycles. Harley-Davidson's quality improvements did not go unnoticed. John Davis, a Harley dealer mechanic, stated, "I've been wrenching on Harley-Davidson motorcycles for 26 years. I think the main key to their success is quality. And since '84 they have been very good."[51] Teerlink boasted in his 1990 letter to shareholders that Harley-Davidson would be competing for the Malcolm Baldridge National Quality Award in 1991. "We will follow the examples established by the 1990 winner (Cadillac)."[52]

Harley's commitment to quality may have led them to opt not to carry any product liability insurance after 1987. One Harley executive commented, "We do not believe that carrying product liability insurance is financially prudent."[53] Instead, Harley created a form of self-insurance through reserves to cover potential liabilities.

Other Production

In 1988, Teerlink proudly stated, "Capitalizing on its reputation as a world class manufacturer, Harley-Davidson is developing a strong contract manufacturing business. In April 1988, the company became the first Army Munitions and Chemical Command (AMCCOM) contractor to be certified under the U.S. Army's Contractor Performance Certification Program. The company achieved the certification for its application of advanced manufacturing techniques in the production of 500-pound casings for the U.S. Army. Additionally, the company is the sole supplier of high-altitude rocket motors for target drones built by Beech Aircraft."[54]

Harley-Davidson formed an agreement with Acustar, a subsidiary of Chrysler Corporation, in early 1988, to produce machined components for its Marine and Industrial Division. Harley also manufactured small engines for Briggs & Stratton. The company planned to further broaden its contract manufacturing business by aggressively marketing its proven and innovative manufacturing efficiencies to the industrial community. For 1990, management placed a goal of nonmotorcycle production to reach between 25 and 30 percent.[55] Teerlink felt strongly that "this goal is actually quite conservative and can be easily accomplished."[56]

International Operations

The international markets of Great Britain, Italy, and other European countries were hardly uncharted territory for Harley-Davidson. Since 1915, Harley-Davidson had been selling its products in these overseas markets. Harley-Davidson's international efforts increased significantly during the mid-1980s. In

[51] Marvel, "Gentrified HOGs," p. 25.
[52] Harley-Davidson Annual Report, 1989, p. 8.
[53] Ibid., p. 4.
[54] Ibid., p. 34.
[55] Harley-Davidson News, 1988, p. 2.
[56] Willis, "Harley-Davidson," p. 27.

1984, it produced 5,000 motorcycles for export; projections for 1990 called for production in the 20,000-unit range.[57]

Several international markets exploded for Harley-Davidson in the late 1980s. In 1989, it expanded its motorcycle sales in France by 92 percent, Great Britain by 91 percent, and Australia by 32 percent.[58] Europeans also bought other Harley products, such as T-shirts and leather jackets. Clyde Fessler, director of trademark licensing for Harley-Davidson, said, "In Europe we're considered Americana."[59]

MARKETING

> When it comes to pleasuring the major senses, no motorcycle on earth can compare to Harley. That's why I've tattooed my Harley's name on the inside of my mouth.
>
> Lou Reed[60]

Probably not every Harley-Davidson owner had Lou Reed's loyalty. Nonetheless, loyalty to Harley-Davidson had almost always been virtually unparalleled. According to the company's research, 92 percent of its customers remained with Harley.[61] Even with strong brand loyalty, however, Harley's marketing division had not reduced its advertising. Harley-Davidson limited its advertising focus to print media, opting not to explore a radio or television campaign. The company used print ads in a variety of magazines, including trade magazines and the company's own trade publication, the *Enthusiast*. The advertising department, headed by Carmichael Lynch, had the benefit of a very well known company name. Unfortunately, the company's name also carried serious image problems.

One major problem that plagued Harley's marketing efforts was that bootleggers were ruining the Harley-Davidson name by placing it on unlicensed, unauthorized goods. This condition might not have been a problem, except that the goods were of poor quality. Furthermore, society was turning away from the attitudes of the 1960s. With antidrug messages becoming a prevalent theme in American society, Harley-Davidson found itself linked to an image of the pot-smoking, beer-drinking, woman-chasing, tattoo-covered, leather-clad biker. One industry expert observed, "When your company's logo is the number one requested in tattoo parlors, it's time to get a licensing program that will return your reputation to the ranks of baseball, hot dogs, and apple pie."[62] This fact was not lost on management. Kathleen Demitros, who became director of marketing in

[57] Roberts, "Harley's HOG's," p. 14.
[58] Harley-Davidson Annual Report 1989, p. 9.
[59] "The Harley Priority," *Popular Mechanics*, June 9, 1989, p. 24.
[60] Robert Parola, "High on the HOG," *Daily News Record*, January 23, 1989, p. 74.
[61] Marvel, "Gentrified HOGs," p. 25.
[62] "Thunder Road," *Forbes*, July 18, 1983, p. 32.

1983, stated, "One of our problems was that we had such a hard-core image out there that it was basically turning off a lot of people."[63] Demitros was speaking from experience. The Milwaukee native had been with the company since 1971. Furthermore, like many of the company executives, she owned a Harley. By her own admission, Demitros chose not to ride her HOG to work. She saved it for the weekends.[64]

Harley-Davidson took a proactive approach to solving the image problem. It created a licensing division responsible for eliminating the bootlegged products. This new division was led by John Heiman, who was formerly a mechanical accessories products manager. Goods with the Harley-Davidson logo would have to be sold by licensed dealers to be legal. Using warrants and federal marshals, Heiman went to conventions of motorcycle enthusiasts and began to put an end to the bootleggers.[65]

After accomplishing this, Harley-Davidson was able to sell its own goods. It began to concentrate its efforts on a wide variety of products—ranging from leather jackets to cologne to jewelry—to supplement motorcycle sales.[66] The concept was not new to Harley-Davidson. As far back as the 1920s, Harley had designed and sold leather jackets. The hope was that consumers would buy the other products in order to get comfortable with the Harley name, and then consider purchasing Harley motorcycles. One company executive said, "It helped pull us through the lean years." He continued, "In 1988 we sold 35,000 bikes and over 3 million fashion tops."[67] For Harley-Davidson, these sales were crucial in offsetting the seasonal market of the motorcycle industry. Observers applauded Harley on this marketing strategy. "Historically, the winter months are tough on sales for the motorcycle industry. Harley-Davidson has been successful at selling fashion items." A Harley marketing executive went one step further. "If we can't sell someone a bike in the winter, we'll sell them a leather jacket instead."[68]

Essentially, the licensing division had become an extension of marketing. Heiman said, "If you've got a 6-year-old boy wearing Harley pajamas, sleeping on Harley sheets and bathing with Harley towels, the old man's not going to be bringing home a Suzuki."[69] Additionally, retailers found that the licensed goods were popular. Major retail chains began selling Harley-Davidson products. The logic behind the selection of Harley goods was simple. "Harley is the only motorcycle made in the United States today, and I thought with pride in America high, the time was right for the licensed goods," explained one major retailer.[70]

[63] Marie Spadoni, "Harley-Davidson Revs Up to Improve Image," *Advertising Age*, August 5, 1985, p. 30.
[64] "Thunder Road," p. 32.
[65] Spadoni, "Harley-Davidson Revs Up," p. 30.
[66] Ibid., p. 30.
[67] Parola, "High on the HOG," p. 24.
[68] Ibid.
[69] Marvel, "Gentrified HOGs," p. 25.
[70] Spandoni, "Harley-Davidson Revs Up," p. 30.

However, the hard-core biker image of Harley-Davidson was still a strong influence. For example, when Fifth Avenue Cards decided to sell Harley items, it did so in a satirical manner. According to Ethel Sloan, the card store chain's vice president of merchandising, "We were definitely shooting for tongue-in-cheek, selling this macho, all-black coloration merchandise to bankers in three-piece suits—it was a real hoot!"[71] It may have been this cynical and virtually unexpected market that Vaughn Beals hoped to exploit. Beals predicted the emergence of a new breed of Harley customer. "We're on the road to prosperity in this country, and we'll get there on a Harley."[72]

The customers he spoke of began to buy Harleys in record numbers. The new Harley consumers were a collection of bankers, doctors, lawyers, and entertainers who developed an affection for HOGs.[73] They became known as Rubbies—the rich urban bikers. The Rubbies were not frightened by the high price tags associated with the Harley-Davidson product line. The Sportster 883, which was Harley's trademark motorcycle, and the Nova, which was specifically designed to capture the college student market, sold in a price range of $4,000 to $15,000 in 1987.[74] Harley continued to expand its product line in 1988 with the addition of the Springer Softail, the Ultra Classic Electra Glide, and the Ultra Classic Tour Glide. James Paterson, president and chief operating officer of the motorcycle division, commented, "The Springer goes to the heart of Harley-Davidson, the custom-cruiser type of motorcycle. The Ultra Classics . . . are aimed at the touring market . . . a market we couldn't reach previously."[75] Product line expansion continued in 1989 with a move that several industry observers thought to be a questionable marketing decision. Harley-Davidson introduced the Fat Boy, its largest motorcycle with 80 cubic inches of V-twin engine.

The Rubbies had brought Harley back into the forefront. By 1989, Harley-Davidson was again the leader in the U.S. super heavyweight motorcycle market, with a nearly 60 percent market share (See Exhibit 25.2). One consequence of the Rubbie market was its impact on the demographics of the Harley-Davidson consumer. According to an August 1990 *Wall Street Journal* article, "One in three of today's Harley-Davidson buyers are professionals or managers. About 60 percent have attended college, up from only 45 percent in 1984. Their median age is 35, and their median household income has risen sharply to $45,000 from $36,000 five years earlier."

Even with the growth of the Rubbie market, Harley-Davidson was careful not to lose touch with its grass-roots customers. In 1990, roughly 110,000 members belonged to the HOG, Harley Owners Group.[76] The fact that upper management continued to ride along side of their loyal throng was an important marketing

---

[71] "Greeting Card Chain Scores Big with Macho 'Biker' Promotion," *Stores*, February 1986, p. 21.

[72] Ibid.

[73] Marvel, "Gentrified HOGs," p. 26.

[74] "Harley Priority," p. 24.

[75] Willis, "Harley-Davidson," p. 14.

[76] Rose, "Vrooming Back," p. 1.

EXHIBIT 25.2   U.S. Market Share of Super Heavyweight Motorcycles, 1989

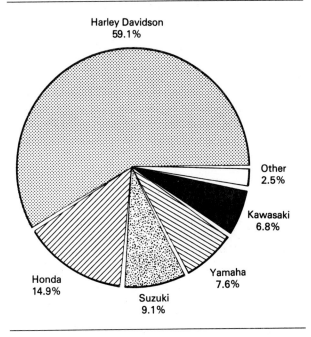

Harley Davidson 59.1%

Other 2.5%

Kawasaki 6.8%

Yamaha 7.6%

Suzuki 9.1%

Honda 14.9%

Source: R.L. Polk & Company.

tool. Paterson asserted, "Going to rallies and mixing with our customers has more value than you might initially expect. You begin to understand how important the motorcycle is and how important the Harley-Davidson way of life is to them. . . . At a motorcycle rally, everyone's part of the same family—sharing their love for motorcycling and life in general." Paterson's beliefs were shared by Harley owner Pat Soracino, "It's a family affair. My bike rides better with [wife] Vicki riding next to me. And our daughter has grown up with Harleys. It's more than a motorcycle to us. It's our lives."[77]

HOG and Harley-Davidson combined their efforts often in 1989. One such venture was a series of National Forest improvement projects. The First Annual National Poker Run motorcycle rally received the support of almost 160 Harley dealers nationwide. This rally and others raised about $1.7 million for the Muscular Dystrophy Association, a charity for which Harley-Davidson collected over $6.5 million in the decade of the 1980s.

Although high performance was not a strong selling point for Harley-Davidson motorcycles, the company did enhance its reputation on the racing circuit in 1988 and 1989. In both years, Harley's factory-sponsored rider, Scotty Parker,

[77] Harley-Davidson Annual Report 1989, pp. 5–10.

captured the Grand National and Manufacturer's Championship in the American Motorcyclist Association's Class C racing season.

COMPETITION

Motorcycle Competition

Harley faced stiff competition from Japan's big four motorcycle manufacturers—Honda, Yamaha, Suzuki, and Kawasaki (See Exhibit 25.3). Industry analysts claimed that the Japanese manufacturers held a commanding lead in the world market with 80 percent of total motorcycle production.

Honda. In 1990, Honda was the world's largest motorcycle manufacturer. The president of the company, Shoichiro Irimaziri, attributed Honda's success to the company's philosophy of producing products of the highest efficiency at a reasonable price. In every aspect of design for both cars and motorcycles, the company's engineers endeavored to achieve a reasonable level of efficiency and obtain the last increment of performance. The president also placed a high value on the early involvement of production and engineering. His vision was one where the marketing and production departments are part of engineering; production departments are part of a bigger unit aimed at achieving quality and efficiency.[78]

Yamaha. Yamaha grossed $3 billion in sales in 1989, as the second largest producer of motorcycles in the world. For decades, Yamaha remained extremely diversified as the leading producer of outboard motors, sailboats, snowmobiles, and golf carts. At Yamaha Motor, many of the products were developed almost exclusively for overseas markets. Why so much diversification? First, Yamaha executives believed that the motorcycle business in the late 1980s was a shrinking one. Second, as voiced by the president of the company, "Diversification is a hobby of my father's. He gets bored with old businesses."[79]

Suzuki. Suzuki made its name selling motorcycles, but in 1987 it almost doubled its sales with the introduction of a jeep, the Suzuki Samurai. When first introduced, critics thought it would be a modern-day Edsel. "When these oddball vehicles first came out nobody gave them a nickel's chance of success," said Maryann N. Keller, a vice president and automotive analyst with Furman, Seiz, Mager, Dietz & Birney.[80] But the critics were wrong. Suzuki had a record 48,000 sales in 1986—the best model launch in history of any Japanese auto manufacturer. Despite its success, however, the Samurai was hit with negative publicity in 1988. Specifically, the Consumer Union, a consumer protection organization,

---

[78] Andrew Tanzer, "Create or Die," *Forbes*, April 6, 1987, pp. 55–59.
[79] Shoichiro Irimaziri, "The Winning Difference," *Vital Speeches*, pp. 650–651.
[80] Tanzer, "Create or Die," pp. 55–59.

EXHIBIT 25.3   **Harley-Davidson's Share of the U.S. Super Heavyweight Motorcycle Market**

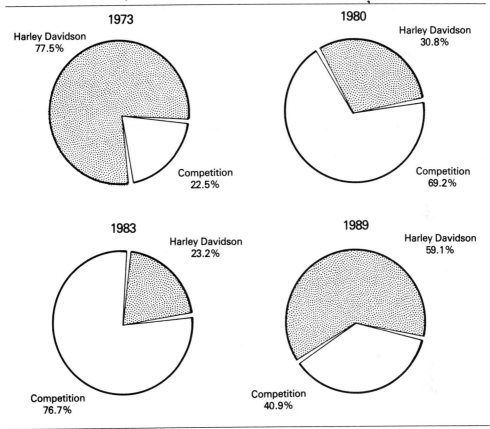

Source: R.L. Polk & Company.

gave the Samurai a "not acceptable" rating and pleaded for the recall of 150,000 Samurai and for full refunds to all owners. The union claimed that the vehicle was unsafe because it rolled over easily when turning corners. Although the negative publicity caused a temporary decline in sales, Suzuki rebounded in the second half of 1988 through utilization of dealer and customer incentives.[81]

Kawasaki.   In 1988, Kawasaki's motorcycle sales increased 5 percent, although the overall motorcycle market shrank 20 percent. Kawasaki's management attributed much of its success to a new service in which dealers could make sales with no-money-down financing. A computer network, Household Finance Corporation, allowed dealers to get nearly instantaneous responses on credit applications.

[81] Rebecca Fannin, "Against All Odds," *Marketing and Media*, March 1988, pp. 45–47.

Kawasaki focused efforts to accommodate its dealers. The K-share program was developed in 1986 to act as a sales support system for dealers. K-share allowed dealers to make payments electronically; as a result, interest expense was reduced and keying errors made by Kawasaki were virtually eliminated because the manual input of checks was no longer necessary.[82]

Recreational Vehicle Competition

With its acquisition of Holiday Rambler, Harley nearly doubled its revenues. However, experts indicated that it also bought into a very troubled industry with declining demand. They further claimed that greater competition in the industry would lead to increasing marketing costs and decreasing profit margins. Harley faced three top competitors in the RV industry—Fleetwood, Winnebago, and Airstream.

Fleetwood Enterprises was the nation's leading manufacturer of recreational vehicles in 1989. Its operations included 21 factories in 17 states and Canada. For 1989, its sales totaled approximately $719 million.[83]

Winnebago was number one in sales with $420 million in 1988. The company experienced financing problems in early 1990 when Norwest Bank canceled a $50 million revolving credit line. This situation caused Winnebago to fall to number two in industry sales in 1990.[84]

Airstream ranked third among the RV manufacturers with sales of approximately $389 million for 1989.[85] Thor Industries bought the failing RV manufacturer from Beatrice Foods in 1980. It made assembly-line improvements and upgraded components to cut warranty costs and help the RV's image. In 1990, thousands of Airstream owners were members of the Wally Bran Caravan Club International. The club was started by Airstream and held regional rallies and caravans throughout the year. This cultlike following provided a loyal customer base, accounting for 60 percent of all Airstreams sold.[86]

THE IMPACT OF THE ECONOMY

Historically, the success of Harley-Davidson hinged significantly on the performance of the U.S. economy. The company suffered along with everyone else during the Great Depression, while the boom periods of both world wars represented times of prosperity for Harley-Davidson. Changing demands of consumers during the postwar years in the 1940s and 1950s had an adverse effect on the motorcycle industry, and, just when Harley was on the road to recovery in the early 1980s, the economy fell into a recession.[87]

[82] Jack Bernstein, "Crisis Communications," *Advertising Age*, September 5, 1988, p. 29.
[83] Serafin, "RV Market Puzzled," p. 52.
[84] Fleetwood Annual Report 1989, p. 18.
[85] David Greising, "Unhappy Campers at Winnebago," *Business Week*, May 28, 1990, p. 28.
[86] Airstream Annual Report 1989, p. 17.
[87] David Carey, "Road Runner," *Financial World*, November 1986, pp. 16–17.

Harley-Davidson proved time and again that it was a survivor, having restored peak production levels after each economic downturn. The company had reached its highest levels of output in 1989. But, once again, the threat of recession was looming on the horizon. Standard & Poor's *Industry Surveys* warned that "leading indicators have been roughly flat and pointing to little growth . . . recent financial market activity alternates between fears of recession and inflation. Presently, inflation is a bigger worry for the markets, though recession is the larger worry for the moment."[88]

As the summer of 1990 was reaching its peak, a major international crisis unfolded. On August 2, Iraq invaded Kuwait, unleashing a series of events that seriously impacted the U.S. economy. In the August 16, 1990, *Trends & Projections*, Standard & Poor's discussed some of the effects of the anxiety in the Middle East: "The economy looks a lot more vulnerable than it did only a month ago. That was true before the Iraqi invasion; it is even truer with oil prices climbing. . . . A very slow, sluggish economy is predicted for the second half of 1990."[89]

Valueline offered some further insight into the risks of the Middle East situation to Harley-Davidson: "The chief cause for concern would be curtailment of fuel supply in case of a shooting war. In any event, higher oil prices mean more inflation, which increases the risk of recession and with that, a slump in spending for big-ticket recreational goods."[90] Harley-Davidson's products traditionally carried a reputation of producing less fuel efficient bikes than their Japanese counterparts. "This is no touring bike . . . that will take you nonstop from Tucson to Atlantic City."[91]

Other analysts predicted continued pessimism in the recovery of the RV market: "Consumers are getting nervous about the economy; recent consumer sentiment reports show deteriorating trends . . . . In the consumer durables category, weak auto sales are not likely to be reversed soon . . . the prospect of higher oil prices means more pressure on consumer spending. Because it is difficult to reduce energy consumption in the short run, many consumers react to higher oil prices by reducing their spending on other items."[92]

LEGAL AND SAFETY ISSUES

As of 1988, 21 states had laws that required motorcycles to operate with their headlights on during the daytime as well as nighttime hours. In addition, 20 states required motorcycle riders to wear helmets. Motorcyclists argued that such laws were a violation of their constitutional rights and that helmets actually prevented them from hearing sirens and other important road noises. But such

[88] Reid, *Well Made in America*, p. 9.
[89] Standard & Poor's *Trends & Projections*, August 16, 1990, p. 3.
[90] Ibid., pp. 1, 2.
[91] *Valueline*, p. 1751.
[92] Marvel, "Gentrified HOGs," p. 26.

legislation was not without justification. The number of deaths on motorcycles reached 4,500 in 1987—a rate approximately 16 times higher than that for automobiles. Cycle enthusiasts had a tendency to push the blame on unobservant car drivers. However, statistics from the Insurance Institute for Highway Safety (IIHS) showed that 45 percent of these accidents involved only one vehicle. Of particular concern to the IIHS were the high-speed superbikes that became available to the general public. These bikes accounted for almost twice the number of fatalities as other cycles. Moreover, the IIHS blamed the motorcycle industry for marketing these bikes for their high speed and power. It claimed that this encouraged the reckless use of an already dangerous product.[93] The president of IIHS stated, "The fact is motorcycles as a group have much higher death and injury rates than cars, so the last thing we need is this new breed of cycle with even higher injury rates."[94]

But what did all this mean to Harley? With the high revs of the traditional HOG and the production of lighter-weight race-style cycles like the Nova, industry experts claimed that they were sure to be hit with the same adverse publicity and criticisms as their Japanese counterparts.

The Rubbie Influence

> I love riding the motorcycle. What a shame it nearly throws you into the jaws of death.
>
> Blly Idol[95]

> Every motorcycle rider thinks about the possibility of an accident. But I figured I was sharp enough in my reactions not to have one. . . . But the fact is, on Sunday, December 4, 1988, there I was, sprawled at the feet of a policeman with paramedics on the way.
>
> Gary Busey[96]

Both Idol, the international rock star, and Busey, the Academy Award-nominated actor, suffered near-fatal accidents while riding Harley-Davidson motorcycles. Neither Idol nor Busey were wearing helmets at the time of their accidents. An apparent disdain for the safety of motorcycle riding was condoned by these role models. Busey, in fact, continued to be an opponent of helmet laws

---

[93] Standard & Poor's *Industry Surveys*, August 16, 1990, p. 4.
[94] Fannin, "Against All Odds," pp. 45–46.
[95] "Billy Idol," *Rolling Stone*, July 1990, p. 174.
[96] "Gary Busey: A Near-Fatal Motorcycle Crash Changes an Actor's Life, But Not His Refusal to Wear a Helmet," *People*, May 15, 1990, p. 65.

even after his ordeal. His stance remained among the throng of enthusiasts that felt "the decision to wear a helmet is a matter of personal freedom."[97]

The Rubbies that helped revive Harley-Davidson were a double-edged sword. Well-known personalities such as comedian Jay Leno, actors Sylvester Stallone, Mickey Rourke, Lorenzo Lamas, Kurt Russell, Daniel Day-Lewis, John Schneider, and Michael Hutchence of the rock group INXS were members of the Rubbie "fraternity." Their high-profile status drew attention to the helmet laws. Many of these celebrities were often seen in paparazzi, mounted on their Harleys, without wearing helmets. Peter DeLuise, star of television's *21 Jumpstreet*, explained, "Biking is like sliding through the air. When you put a helmet on, it takes away part of the feeling."[98] Ironically, DeLuise's show, which catered to an adolescent audience, often depicted teenagers cruising streets and highways without helmets.

Statistics showed that "142,000 Americans are injured in motorcycle accidents each year." In the early 1970s Congress used its power over the states to enact legislation that required all motorcycle riders to wear helmets. U.S. highway funds were cut in those states that did not pass the laws. Forty-seven states complied with the demand, but in the bicentennial year, aggressive lobbying efforts by biking groups succeeded in influencing Congress to revoke the sanctions. By 1980, 25 of the states had removed or weakened their helmet laws. Federal figures reported an increase in motorcycle fatalities of over 40 percent during this three-year period. General Motors did a study in 1986 that revealed that one-fourth of the 4,505 motorcyclists killed that year would have lived had they worn helmets.[99]

With models that can reach top speeds of 150 mph, Harley-Davidsons continued to satisfy the American desire for power, speed, and personal freedom. The company was never in the business of manufacturing helmets, nor did it take a stance on the helmet issue, but while the contention of pro-choice enthusiasts was that the decision was personal, statistics showed that society was absorbing the cost. According to *Time*, a 1985 survey in Seattle found that 105 motorcycle accident victims hospitalized incurred $2.7 million in medical bills, of which 63 percent was paid for from public funds.[100]

FINANCIAL HIGHLIGHTS

Harley-Davidson's financial position had improved greatly from 1986 to 1989 (see Exhibits 25.4 to 25.8). Even after the public stock offering in 1986,

[97] Ibid.
[98] Ibid., p. 66.
[99] Ibid., p. 65.
[100] Ibid.

EXHIBIT 25.4   Harley-Davidson Net Income Comparison

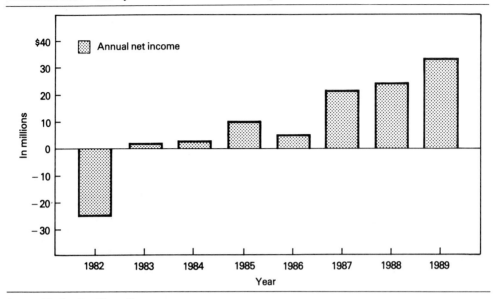

Source: Harley-Davidson, Inc.

insiders continued to maintain some ownership of the company. *Valueline* reported in September 1990 that insiders owned 11.6 percent of Harley-Davidson's stock. Other major shareholders included FMR Corporation (7.2 percent) and Harris Association (6.7 percent). In June 1990, Malcolm Glazer reduced his ownership in Harley-Davidson from 7.29 percent to less than 1 percent, earning a $10 million profit in the process.[101]

Management's concern for employee satisfaction impacted its financial statements, when in April 1989, Harley paid a $1.3 million signing bonus to the Wisconsin labor unions.[102] Harley lowered its debt-equity ratio considerably in 1989, with the repurchase of $37.1 million of debt during the year. This created a decrease in its debt-equity ratio from 55 percent to 40 percent. In 1990, Harley-Davidson's stock was pounded—from a high of $34, to a low of $13, before recovering to $18 as 1990 drew to a close.

[101] *Valueline*, p. 1761.
[102] Rose, "Vrooming Back," p. 6.

EXHIBIT 25.5   Consolidated Balance Sheets (In thousands except per share data)

	1988	1989
Assets		
Current Assets		
Cash and Cash Equivalents	$52,360	$39,076
Accounts Receivable, Net of Allowance for Doubtful Accounts	42,857	45,565
Inventories	89,947	87,540
Deferred Income Taxes	8,844	9,682
Prepaid Expenses	4,795	5,811
Assets of Discontinued Operation	12,488	—
Total Current Assets	211,291	187,674
Property, Plant, and Equipment, Net	107,838	115,700
Goodwill	68,782	66,190
Deferred Financing Costs	4,495	2,356
Other Assets	4,307	7,009
Noncurrent Assets of Discontinued Operation	4,401	—
Total Assets	$401,114	$378,929
Liabilities and Stockholders' Equity		
Current Liabilities		
Notes Payable	$21,041	$22,789
Current Maturities of Long-Term Debt	12,188	4,143
Accounts Payable	36,939	40,095
Accrued Expenses and Other Liabilities	63,047	69,334
Liabilities of Discontinued Operation	3,172	—
Total Current Liabilities	$136,387	$136,361
Long-Term Debt	$135,176	$74,795
Accrued Employee Benefits	3,309	5,273
Deferred Income Taxes	4,594	6,253
Commitments and Contingencies		
Stockholders Equity		
Series A Junior Participating Preferred Stock, 1,000,000 Shares Authorized, None Issued	—	—
Common Stock, 9,155,000 Shares Issued	92	92
Additional Paid-In Capital	76,902	79,681
Retained Earnings	44,410	77,352
Cumulative Foreign Currency Translation Adjustment	374	508
	121,778	157,633
Less		
Treasury Stock (447,091 and 520,000 Shares in 1989 and 1988, Respectively), at Cost	(130)	(112)
Unearned Compensation	—	(1,274)
Total Stockholders' Equity	121,648	156,247
Total Liabilities and Stockholders' Equity	$401,114	$378,929

Source: Harley-Davidson, Inc.

EXHIBIT 25.6 Consolidated Statements of Income (In thousands except per share data)

Years Ended December 31	1987	1988	1989
Net Sales	$645,966	$709,360	$790,967
Operating Costs and Expenses			
Cost of Goods Sold	487,205	533,448	596,940
Selling, Administrative, and Engineering	104,672	111,582	127,606
	591,877	645,030	724,546
Income from Operations	54,089	64,330	66,421
Interest Income	2,658	4,149	3,634
Interest Expense	(23,750)	(22,612)	(17,956)
Other—Net	(21,430)	165	910
Income from Continuing Operations Before Provision for Income Taxes and Extraordinary Items	30,854	46,032	53,009
Provision for Income Taxes	13,181	18,863	20,399
Income from Continuing Operations before Extraordinary Items	17,673	27,169	32,610
Discontinued Operation, Net of Tax			
Income (loss) from Discontinued Operation	—	(13)	154
Gain on Disposal of Discontinued Operation	—	—	3,436
Income before Extraordinary Items	17,673	27,156	36,200
Extraordinary Items			
Loss on Refinancing/Debt Repurchase, Net of Taxes	—	(1,468)	(1,434)
Additional Cost of 1983 AMF Settlement, Net of Taxes	—	(1,776)	(1,824)
Benefit from Utilization of Loss Carry Forward	—	—	—
Net Income	$21,215	$23,912	$32,942
Per Common Share			
Income from Continuing Operations	$2.72	$3.41	$3.78
Discontinued Operation	—	—	.41
Extraordinary Items	.55	(.41)	(.38)
Net Income	$3.27	$3.00	$3.81

Source: Harley-Davidson, Inc.

EXHIBIT 25.7   Consolidated Statements of Cash Flow (In thousands)

Years Ended December 31	1987	1988	1989
Cash Flows from Operating Activities			
Net Income	$21,215	$23,912	$32,942
Adjustments to Reconcile Net Income to Net Cash Provided by Operating Activities			
Depreciation and Amortization	15,643	17,958	20,007
Deferred Income Taxes	(2,875)	(1,375)	821
Long-Term Employee Benefits	(439)	1,037	2,741
Gain on Sale of Discontinued Operation	—	—	(5,513)
Loss on Disposal of Long-Term Assets	1,505	1,451	28
Net Changes in Current Assets and Current Liabilities	12,205	(30,346)	10,051
Total Adjustments	26,039	(11,275)	28,135
Net Cash Provided by Operating Activities	47,254	12,637	61,077
Cash Flows from Investing Activities			
Capital Expenditures	(17,027)	(23,786)	(24,438)
Less Amounts Capitalized under Financing Leases	—	2,877	809
Net Capital Expenditures	(17,027)	(20,909)	(23,619)
Proceeds on Sale of Discontinued Operations and Other Assets	—	—	19,475
Other—Net	901	(1,204)	(2,720)
Net Cash in Investing Activities	(16,126)	(22,113)	(6,864)
Cash Flows from Financing Activities			
Net Increase in Notes Payable	5,891	1,083	1,748
Reductions in Debt	(78,478)	(42,652)	(69,245)
Proceeds from Issuance of Common Stock	18,690	35,179	—
Proceeds from Additional Borrowings	70,000	—	—
Repurchase of Warrants	(3,594)	—	—
Deferred Financing Costs	(3,265)	—	—
Net Cash Provided by (Used in) Financing Activities	9,244	(6,390)	(67,497)
Net Increase (Decrease) in Cash and Cash Equivalents	40,372	(15,866)	(13,284)
Cash and Cash Equivalents:			
At Beginning of Year	$27,854	$68,226	$52,360
At End of Year	$68,226	$52,360	$39,076

Source: Harley-Davidson, Inc.

EXHIBIT 25.8   Consolidated Statements of Changes in Stockholders' Equity, 1987 to 1989 (In thousands except per share data)

	Common Stock		Additional Paid-In Capital	Retained Earnings (Deficit)	Cumulative Foreign Currency Translation Adjustment	Treasury Stock	Unearned Compensation
	Outstanding Shares	Balance					
Balance, December 31, 1986	6,200,000	$62	$26,657	$ (717)	$287	$(130)	$—
Net Income	—	—	—	21,215	—	—	—
Net Proceeds from Common Stock Offering	1,230,000	12	18,678	—	—	—	—
Repurchase of 230,000 Warrants in Connection With Public Debt and Common Stock Offering	—	—	(3,594)	—	—	—	—
Cumulative Foreign Currency Translation Adjustment	—	—	—	—	443	—	—
Balance, December 31, 1987	7,430,000	74	41,741	20,498	730	(130)	—
Net Income	—	—	—	23,912	—	—	—
Net Proceeds from Common Stock Offering	1,725,000	18	35,161	—	—	—	—
Cumulative Foreign Currency Translation Adjustment	—	—	—	—	(356)	—	—
Balance, December 31, 1988	9,155,000	92	76,902	44,410	374	(130)	—
Net Income	—	—	—	32,942	—	—	—
Issuance of 72,909 Treasury Shares of Restricted Stock	—	—	2,779	—	—	18	(1,274)
Cumulative Foreign Currency Translation Adjustment	—	—	—	—	134	—	—
Balance, December 31, 1989	$9,155,000	$92	$79,681	$77,352	$508	$(112)	$(1,274)

EPILOGUE

So at the end of the week I thought I'd go for it. I told Connie that I'd just need a few more days to raise some capital. So I'm hanging out at Bernie's Bank, flipping through a Wall Street Journal, *when I come across this ad* [Exhibit 25.9].

I couldn't believe it myself. Another American-made motorcycle. My little voice had some words of wisdom, but I already knew I was gonna have to break off the deal with Connie. It wasn't easy, but hey—that's why I'm Johnny Callatino. So there you have it. I don't know about you, but I could sure use another cold one.

EXHIBIT 25.9   *Wall Street Journal*, **Wednesday, November 7, 1990**

POSITIONS AVAILABLE   **POSITIONS AVAILABLE**

Indian Motocycle Co., Inc.

The Historic Indian Motocycle Company, Inc. of Springfield, MA is now accepting resumes for key executive positions in the manufacturing and marketing of the new Indian line of Motorcycles and accessories.

Please forward all resumes to:

Indian Motocycle Co., Inc.

86 Springfield Street
Springfield, MA 01107
Phone: 413-747-7233 Corporate Office
413-746-3766 Final Assembly
CEO. Philip S. Zanghi

CASE 26

Carolco Pictures

PROLOGUE

"Gentlemen, place your bets."

Mario F. Kassar, chairman of Carolco Pictures, pushed a stack of thousand-dollar chips forward. He turned toward a nearby waitress and ordered another bottle of Tattinger Compte de Champagne, 1981. He was in his element at the casino in Monte Carlo, and as usual the forthcoming bottle would be gratis. He was a favorite of the casino and would often vacation there to relax after the premiere of a Carolco production. The casino was expecting an active night, for, in recreational pursuits as in business, Mario Kassar spent freely. On this occasion Mario Kassar was celebrating the premiere of the most expensive movie ever made.

Terminator 2: Judgment Day had a production cost of $90 million. Did the movie's foreboding title allude to a coming apocalypse for Carolco? Indeed, the auditors had felt compelled to include a statement in the annual report addressing their concerns over the company's viability as an ongoing entity. The production had left Carolco in an ominous financial position. Cash strapped, the company had a negative cash flow from operations from 1988 to 1991. In addition to reporting a $6.3 million loss, the company had to seek concessions from its debt holders.[1]

None of that mattered to Kassar, for he was in the casino to unwind and escape such concerns. Here he could more easily control the outcome and receive instant gratification for his efforts. He motioned toward his evening companion to place all of his bet on one number. "Let her roll," he announced as the roulette wheel began to spin. "I need a winner."

This case was prepared by James Breshnahan, Karen Keniff, Mark Mitchell, and Dan Twing under the supervision of Sexton Adams and Adelaide Griffin as a basis for class discussion rather than to illustrate either effective or ineffective handling of an administrative situation. Copyright © 1991 by Sexton Adams and Adelaide Griffin. Used with permission from Sexton Adams.

[1] "Carolco Needs a Hero, and the Terminator May Prove to Be It," *Wall Street Journal* (southwest ed.) July 9, 1991, p. A1.

HISTORY

Mario F. Kassar first met Andrew Vajna at the Cannes Film Festival in 1975. Andrew Vajna was born in Hungary, raised in Los Angeles, and made his first fortune in Hong Kong manufacturing wigs and later blue jeans. In the early 1970s Vajna bought two Hong Kong movie theaters, which led him to become a film licensing agent in the Far East. Mario Kassar, born in Beirut and raised in Rome, became a sales agent for movies at age 18, specializing in the Middle East.[2] They formed a movie distribution company soon after meeting and ventured into film production in the early 1980s. The original purpose of the partnership was to obtain better terms by buying rights to movies for both the Far East and the Middle East.

Kassar and Vajna incorporated Carolco Pictures in Delaware in April 1986. They set up desks facing each other and together picked and produced most of Carolco's movies. They "hit the jackpot" quickly after making *First Blood* and later *First Blood II* starring Sylvester Stallone. The two movies took in $420.5 million at the box office domestically and in foreign distribution.[3] Soon after going public, Peter Hoffman, a top entertainment and tax lawyer, was recruited to be president and chief executive officer. One of his first duties was to establish a tax haven for Carolco in the Netherlands.[4] Hoffman also acquired operations in video and television distribution and production to help maximize revenues from Carolco movies.

Carolco pursued a strategic agenda dissimilar to other independent movie producers. Rather than limiting risks by making numerous small-budget productions, Carolco's main strategy had been to make four or five "event" pictures a year with budgets of $20 million and up while selling distribution in advance to help cover costs.[5] Because of the risk involved, Carolco had not engaged in the domestic theatrical distribution of its films. Instead, the company entered into a distribution agreement with Tri-Star Pictures. The company usually reserved all domestic pay and free television, domestic home video, and foreign rights to its films.[6]

In 1989, Carolco released three low-budget, nonaction films, all of which scored poorly at the box office. The same year cochairman Andrew Vajna decided to break up the 13-year partnership. "Colleagues say a clash in the style of the two co-founders contributed to the split, with Mr. Vajna opposing the high spending and rapid growth. At the time, a company official said Mr. Vajna 'would prefer to have a bag of cash instead of the pressure and stress in building a large public company.'" Mr. Vajna indeed received his "bag of cash." Mario Kassar bought

[2] Alex Ben Block, "Is There Life beyond Rambo?" *Forbes*, June 1, 1987, pp. 88–92.
[3] "Carolco Needs a Hero," p. A10.
[4] Block, "Is There Life Beyond Rambo?" p. 92.
[5] "Carolco Needs a Hero," p. A1.
[6] *Standard and Poor's Stock Reports*, New York Stock Exchange, February 1991, p. 448.

11.2 million shares from his partner for $108 million in December 1989.[7] This gave Kassar 63 percent controlling interest in the company. Mario Kassar had the reputation within the industry as a gambler. Said David Goldman, an agent at International Creative Management, "He's a movie mogul in the style of Samuel Goldwyn."[8]

MANAGEMENT

When he cofounded Carolco Pictures, Mario Kassar stated three basic principles to the stockholders. These guidelines included:

1. To produce and distribute a limited number of "event" motion pictures; that is, movies with cast and production values that would give them major box office appeal both within and beyond the borders of the United States.
2. To finance these often expensive productions through "presales" of exhibition rights in various media in countries around the world, with nearly all the marketing costs borne by our subdistributors, not by Carolco.
3. To maximize returns from such rapidly growing "ancillary" markets as video and television, both pay and free, via the establishment of a distribution capability for these markets, either within Carolco or in a separate publicly owned subsidiary.[9]

These three basic principles on which Carolco was founded were the same principles that guided operations in 1991. Carolco's mission was: "To develop an integrated worldwide independent motion picture, television, and video company with important strategic relationships. This would create a company equal to any major in the quality, if not quantity, of its film release schedule."[10]

Kassar endeavored to establish relationships with the most talented and sought-after creative individuals in the film industry. Both directors and stars of Carolco's films included the most consistently popular box office attractions. Carolco had produced such box office hits as *First Blood, Rambo: First Blood Part II, Red Heat,* and *Total Recall.* The company also produced other major event films such as *Rambo III, Basic Instinct, Extreme Prejudice, Johnny Handsome, Air America, Narrow Margin,* and *LA Story.*

In conjunction with Kassar's style of seeking out the most creative and talented individuals, he spared no expense. Industry analysts cited Kassar's management style as the leading cause of Carolco's soaring overhead. Kassar received a salary of $1.5 million in 1990, as well as the use of a Carolco jet. Carolco paid $410,000 to install security devices in Kassar's Beverly Hills mansion in 1988 and an additional $259,000 in security services in 1990.[11]

---

[7] "Carolco Needs a Hero," p. A10.
[8] Ibid., p. A1.
[9] Carolco Pictures, Inc. *Annual Report,* 1990, p. 2.
[10] Ibid., p. 4.
[11] "Carolco Needs a Hero," p. A1.

Directors and producers who contracted with Carolco enjoyed Kassar's liberal spending as well. "Mario Kassar does everything with a great deal of style, and he does it bigger and better than anyone else," according to David Goldman in a *Wall Street Journal* article. For example, in 1990, Carolco flew seventy of Hollywood's most famous to the Cannes Film Festival, transported them via a fleet of limousines accompanied by a police motorcade, to the Hotel du Cap, where they were lodged courtesy of Carolco. In addition, Kassar threw a gala aboard a yacht to promote Carolco's film. The party, complete with fireworks, was reported to be the most expensive in Cannes.[12]

Carolco was also setting spending precedents at home in Hollywood. In early 1990, Carolco paid scripter Joe Esterhas $3 million and producer Irwin Winkler $1 million for *Basic Instinct*. This was the highest amount ever paid for a spec script. Later that same year, Kassar set a new record by paying what was to be the highest amount ever to a writer on assignment. Kassar paid to Oscar-winning screen writer Barry Levinson of *Rain Man* fame $2 million to script an idea based on the supernatural thriller by T. M. Wright, *Manhattan Ghost Story*. One top agent remarked, "I've never heard of a deal where a writer is guaranteed $2 million for an idea."[13] In negotiations with Kassar, people rarely walked away feeling short-changed. When producer Brian Grazer's rights to *The Doors* were within hours of expiring, he contacted Kassar. After a 10-minute phone conversation, Kassar had agreed to do the movie and Grazer had a check within a few hours.[14]

Arnold Schwarzenegger, star of Carolco hit *Terminator 2: Judgment Day*, received approximately $15 million for the movie. According to *Entertainment Weekly*, Schwarzenegger spoke about 700 words. This cost Carolco approximately $21,429 per word. For example, Schwarzenegger's famous line from the movie, "Hasta la vista, baby," cost Carolco $85,716.[15]

Kassar's free spending did not set well with shareholders, however, and they complained that Kassar stacked the deck in his favor. In September 1990, Carolco agreed to purchase 3.4 million shares from Kassar at a price of $13 each when the market price was $7.25. In addition, during the 1988–1989 season, an $8 million loan was made to Kassar and Vajna with the stipulation that if Carolco's stock reached $11 per share before August 1989, the loan would be forgiven. The loan was forgiven when the stock reached the stipulated price in June 1989. A shareholders' suit was filed that charged Kassar with self-dealing. The suit stated that he used the company, which he controlled, to further his own interests. Further, the suit charged that the stipulated price of the stock was reached "due to the manipulative actions of Kassar and others." A judge froze 2.2 million shares of Carolco stock owned by Kassar and limited his ability to draw funds

12 Ibid.
13 Claudia Eller, "Scripter to Get $2 Million to Adapt 'Manhattan,'" *Variety*, October 8, 1990, p. 28.
14 "Carolco Needs a Hero," p. A1.
15 "News Summary—People," *Dallas Morning News*, July 15, 1991, p. A-2.

from the company pending further motions. Carolco has never paid dividends to its shareholders.[16]

OPERATIONS

Major Motion Picture Production

To produce its major event films, Carolco enlisted top producers, directors, writers, and stars. Some of Hollywood's most artistic, exciting, and commercially successful directors and producers worked on Carolco's films. These included Tim Burton, James Cameron, George Cosmatos, John Hughes, Robert Redford, Oliver Stone, and Paul Verhoeven. Big name stars were also part of Carolco productions including such names as Arnold Schwarzenegger, Sylvester Stallone, Michael Douglas, Lou Gosset Jr., Steve Martin, John Candy, Val Kilmer, and Jean-Claude Van Damme.

Carolco did not maintain a substantial staff of creative or technical personnel. Management believed that sufficient motion picture properties and creative and technical personnel (such as screenwriters, directors, and performers) were available in the market at acceptable prices, enabling the company to produce as many motion pictures as it planned or anticipated, at the level of commercial quality the company required. To ensure the availability of such personnel, Carolco had multiple-year production and development agreements with a number of prominent directors. Typically, under such agreements, the director submitted to Carolco on a "first-look" basis any project he or she wished to direct. In some cases, the director was obligated to direct one or two films for the company within a set period of time. Carolco provided office support and development funding for the director. In many cases, the director rendered services on outside projects controlled by other studios.[17]

As of April 1, 1991, Carolco employed approximately 295 people full time. Certain subsidiaries of Carolco were subject to the terms of collective bargaining agreements with the Writers Guild of America, Directors Guild of America, the Screen Actors Guild, and the International Alliance of Theatrical Stage Employees (concerning certain technical crafts such as director of photography, sound recording, and editing). A strike, job action, or labor disturbance by the members of any of these organizations could have had a tangible adverse effect on the production of a motion picture within the United States. Carolco believed its relationship with its employees was satisfactory.

Due to the level of talent and the grand scale of Carolco's major event productions, large budgets, usually over $25 million per film, were not uncommon. *Total Recall* cost $59 million to make.[18] *Terminator 2: Judgment Day* was

---

[16] "Carolco Needs a Hero," p. A1.

[17] Carolco Pictures, Inc., *Form 10-K*, 1990, pp. 1, 5.

[18] Claudia Eller and Don Groves, "Carolco Prexy Defends Its Talent Megadeals," *Variety*, October 29, 1990, p. 10.

rumored to cost $90 million.[19] Although some industry observers questioned the logic of such spending, Carolco continued to produce high-budget, high-tech action thrillers.

Besides making major event films, Carolco had several subsidiaries to perform such functions as production of moderate budget films, foreign leasing of theatrical productions, domestic and foreign distribution to television, merchandise licensing, operation of production studios, and home entertainment software distribution. These subsidiaries are shown in Exhibit 26.1.

EXHIBIT 26.1   Carolco Pictures Major Subsidiary Operations

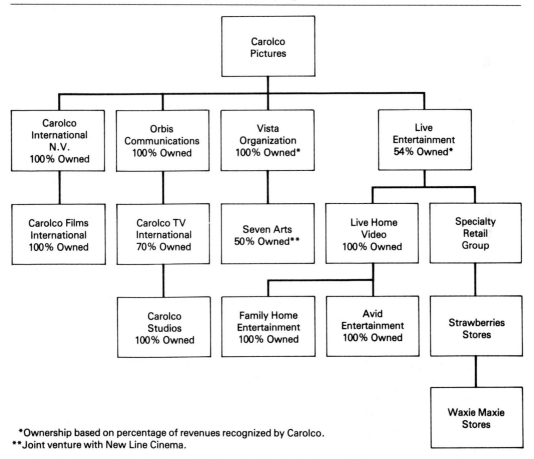

*Ownership based on percentage of revenues recognized by Carolco.
**Joint venture with New Line Cinema.

Source: Derived from Carolco Pictures *Annual Report* 1990 and *Form 10-K* 1990.

---

[19] "Carolco Needs a Hero," p. A1.

Moderate Budget Film Production

In 1989, Carolco purchased a one-third interest in the Vista Organization. Vista formed Seven Arts in 1990 as a joint venture with New Line Cinema. This venture was established to supplement the production of major event films. Seven Arts financed, produced, acquired, and distributed moderate budget motion pictures. This new division was formed to capitalize on Carolco's expertise in motion picture financing, strength in foreign distribution, and relationships with leading talent from around the world. Seven Arts' films were released theatrically in the United States through the joint venture with New Line Cinema. Seven Arts also made arrangements with LIVE Home Video (a partially owned subsidiary of Carolco) for domestic video release of its pictures, and with Carolco International for the foreign distribution of its pictures.

Foreign Leasing of Theatrical Productions

As the international appetite for American-made movies expanded into new markets, Carolco Pictures and its subsidiaries continued to be leading independent suppliers of major motion pictures throughout the world. At the international film festivals and markets held in Cannes, Milan, and Los Angeles, groups of Carolco's films were successfully sold to leading international distribution firms around the world. Carolco conducted foreign distribution through a wholly owned subsidiary, Carolco International N.V. (CINV), with offices and employees in Curacao, Zurich, and London. Although CINV's main activities involved the international leasing of Carolco-produced films, the division acquired foreign distribution rights for important films produced by other studios and producers.

Television Distribution

Although domestic theatrical distribution of Carolco major event films was accomplished through an agreement with Tri-Star Pictures, and Seven Arts films were distributed domestically through an arrangement with New Line Cinema, Carolco retained the rights to television distribution through its wholly owned subsidiary, Orbis Communications. Orbis Communications operated three main areas of business in 1990: domestic distribution of motion pictures for free and pay television; licensing of Carolco films and other programming in the international television market; and production and acquisition of television programming such as telefilms, miniseries, and game shows. Revenues from Orbis reached $42 million in 1990, almost double those of 1989.[20]

All foreign rights to Orbis' television products and television rights to Carolco's theatrical motion pictures were distributed to worldwide television outlets by Carolco Films International Ltd. (CFIL), a London-based wholly owned subsidiary of Carolco International N.V. During 1990, CFIL's priorities

---

[20] *Annual Report*, 1990, p. 5.

included licensing Carolco feature films in those territories where TV rights were available and marketing Orbis' catalog of television programming.

Although Orbis continued to make substantial progress in domestic syndication and international television licensing of Carolco's and others' films, Orbis' production activities consistently failed to reach management profit objectives. Television productions were not staying in syndication. For example, the game show *Joker's Wild* was not picked up for a second season. As a result, on April 11, 1991, Carolco signed an agreement with Multimedia to sell Orbis' production and development activities.

Merchandise Licensing

In operation since 1987, Carolco Licensing Division had evolved into a full-service licensing entity. In 1990, Carolco Licensing successfully exploited merchandising rights to *Total Recall* in a variety of categories. The *Total Recall* Nintendo game was a landmark for the video game industry, as the game was marketed in conjunction with the film's release. Carolco Licensing remained extremely active in publishing and 1990 saw the *Total Recall* novelization become a top seller. Through an expanding network of foreign licensing agents, Carolco Licensing coordinated the licensing of Carolco's properties worldwide, and was also responsible for the placement of products and corporate signage in Carolco films.

Production Studio Operations

In May 1990, a wholly owned subsidiary of Carolco merged with De Laurentiis Entertainment Group to form Carolco Television Inc. (CTI). CTI included a development library containing over 100 feature film projects and a full-service 32-acre production facility in Wilmington, North Carolina. The studio housed eight fully equipped sound stages with all necessary support facilities and services. The studio backlot had three blocks of city streets that were transformed to represent specific eras and locations. Carolco, as well as other companies, used these facilities for its productions.

Home Entertainment Software Distribution

Carolco distributed home entertainment software through its partially owned subsidiary, LIVE Entertainment. In 1990, Carolco recorded 54 percent of LIVE's net income in its earnings as a result of its ownership of approximately 47 percent of LIVE's outstanding common stock and 100 percent of its series A common stock. LIVE's operations were conducted through the following operating entities: video distribution through LIVE Home Video (LHV), rackjobbing through Lieberman Enterprises Incorporated (Lieberman), and entertainment software retailing through the Specialty Retail Group. As of July 22, 1991, Carolco's annual stockholders' meeting had been postponed to allow Carolco's board of directors to consider a proposal by LIVE to discuss a possible business combination of the two companies.[21]

LIVE Home Video

LIVE Home Video provided a broad selection of high-performance programming from Carolco Pictures, as well as such top film makers as IndieProd, Miramax Films, New Visions Pictures, Avenue Pictures, Gladden Entertainment, and Working Title Films, among others. Children's films were distributed through a division called Family Home Entertainment, and a newly formed division, Avid Entertainment, distributed midline home videos.

Lieberman Enterprises

Lieberman Enterprises was the nation's second largest supplier of prerecorded music, prerecorded videocassettes, and personal computer software (PCS) to mass merchandisers and specialty retailers in over 3,400 retail locations. Carolco was searching for sources of cash and, in an effort to allay its cash-poor standing, sold Lieberman Enterprises in 1991 for approximately $100 million.[22]

LIVE Specialty Retail Group

The LIVE Specialty Retail Group (LSRG) operated 144 retail stores in 11 states offering compact discs, audio cassettes, prerecorded videos, and accessories. The stores operated under the name of Strawberries in the Northeast, including New England, New York, Pennsylvania, and New Jersey, and under the name Waxie Maxie in the Mid-Atlantic area, including Maryland and Virginia.

MARKETING

Carolco's market niche was to produce big-star action films that had as much or more success abroad than in the United States. This meant it produced high-action movies starring popular actors with broad-based appeal to ensure that these films would perform very well both domestically and internationally. In fact, its high action films such as the *Rambo* series and *Total Recall* brought in more revenue abroad than domestically.

Once Carolco completed a motion picture, it would generally be distributed and made available for license in the steps illustrated in Exhibit 26.2.

During the late 1980s, revenues from licensing of rights to distribute motion pictures in ancillary (i.e., other than domestic theatrical) markets, particularly pay television and home video, had significantly increased. The company had obtained a substantial part of the advances and guarantees for its pictures from the license of distribution rights in these ancillary markets.

[21] Carolco Pictures Inc., *News Release*, June 10, 1991.
[22] "Carolco Needs a Hero," p. A1.

EXHIBIT 26.2   Timing of Carolco Distribution and License Procedures

Marketplace	Months after Initial Release	Approximate Period (Months)
Domestic Theatrical		6
Domestic Home Video	6	6
Domestic Pay Television	12–18	12–24
Domestic Network Television	30–36	30–36
Domestic Syndication Television	30–36	30–36
Foreign Theatrical		4–6
Foreign Video	6–12	6–18
Foreign Television	18–24	18–30

Source: Carolco Pictures Inc., *Form 10-K* 1990, p. 8.

Domestic Markets

Tri-Star handled domestic distribution of Carolco's feature products, which freed Carolco of the significant overhead and marketing costs that accompanied film distribution. Under the arrangement, Tri-Star paid the print and advertising costs, and after recouping those expenses, kept an average of 35 percent of Carolco's net profits.[23] Carolco did not want to distribute its own films domestically, since the demise of several other independent filmmakers was attributed to those costs.

Orbis Communication conducted Carolco's domestic distribution of motion pictures for free and pay television, production and acquisition of television programming, miniseries, and game shows. Orbis packaged and sold motion pictures to the U.S. broadcast market. In 1989, Carolco marketed its first motion picture package in domestic syndication under the "Carolco I" banner containing *First Blood, Angel Heart, The Terminator, Kiss of the Spider Woman*, and other motion pictures. In 1990, it sold "Carolco II," which included films such as *Rambo: First Blood Part II, Rambo III*, and *Hoosiers* to the USA Network for $25 million.[24] In December 1990, Carolco introduced "Carolco III," a package of 25 titles including such artistically successful pictures as *Platoon, The Last Emperor*, and *Red Heat*. As of April 15, 1990, this package had been sold to more than 60 percent of the U.S. broadcast markets, which resulted in over $21 million in revenue. Carolco continued to receive revenue from the earlier packages, and anticipated that an additional one or two motion picture packages would be marketed domestically in 1992 and 1993.

Also in 1990, under Carolco Television Productions (CTP), Orbis reintroduced the game show *Joker's Wild*, but it met with limited success. Orbis found greater success in the game show business with *The $100,000 Pyramid* before it sold CTP due to its inability to meet management's profit objectives.

[23] Geraldine Fabrikant, "Finding Success in Movie Niches," *New York Times*, April 4, 1990, p. C1(N).

[24] *Form 10-K*, 1990, p. 34.

Carolco distributed its own, as well as others', moderate-budget motion pictures domestically through its Seven Arts division. Seven Arts' films and videos were released domestically through a joint venture with New Line Cinema and LIVE Home Video, respectively. During 1990, Seven Arts released *Repossessed* and *King of New York*. In February 1991, Seven Arts released *Queens Logic*. Other films released later in 1991 included *Rambling Rose, The Dark Wind, Aces: Iron Eagle III*, and *Petleir*.

LIVE Entertainment (LIVE) was a leading distributor of home videos, which it marketed through LIVE Home Video and LIVE Specialty Retail Group. In 1990, LHV was the leading independent home video company and was fifth among all video software suppliers in the country. LHV had the second largest market share, falling just behind Disney in the sell-through video market. This market consisted of videos selling for less than $25, mainly from its Family Home Entertainment division sales. LHV's revenues from newly released rental titles rose by one-third in 1990 and sell-through revenues saw a fivefold increase, boosted in particular by two mega-hits: *Teenage Mutant Ninja Turtles: The Movie* and Carolco's *Total Recall*. LHV expanded in 1990 with Avid Entertainment, which offered titles generally priced under $15. Initial releases included such hits as *Eddie and the Cruisers II, Millennium,* and *Wired*. Strawberries and Waxie Maxie, LSRG's retail outlets, made them the leading music retailer in the greater Boston and Washington, D.C., areas and a strong retailer in Philadelphia, Baltimore, and upstate New York.

International Markets

In 1991, the international market for American-made movies had expanded and Carolco was a leading independent supplier of major motion pictures, videos, and related accessories throughout the world. In 1990, *Total Recall* met with great success overseas, bringing in $260 million as opposed to $118 million domestically.[25] The film's overseas success was mainly attributable to its star, Arnold Schwarzenegger, who was probably the biggest box office attraction of the world at the time.

Carolco's overseas marketing activities were conducted by Carolco International N.V. and included international leasing of Carolco produced action films, Seven Arts' films, and foreign distribution rights for important films produced by other studios. In 1990, foreign rights were acquired to three pictures from Universal Studios: *The Wizard, Opportunity Knocks,* and *Career Opportunities*. Carolco also acquired the foreign theatrical distribution rights to the 20th Century Fox production *Robin Hood*. Peter Hoffman speculated that Fox believed Carolco could generate more revenue through its distribution system than Fox could through its own channels.[26]

---

[25] Ibid., p. 25.
[26] Eller and Groves, "Carolco Prexy Defends Its Talent," p. 10.

During 1990, CINV signed distribution agreements with leading distributors including Guild Entertainment in the United Kingdom; Unirecord International S.A., in Spain; Pentafilm S.P.A., in Italy; and others in Europe, Japan, Australia, and Latin America. Foreign leasing amounted to 60 percent of Carolco's feature film revenues in 1990, and with the strong line up of releases scheduled for 1992, it was expected to continue to be a major profit center for the company.

To distribute Orbis' television products and Carolco's theatrical motion pictures worldwide, the firm used Carolco Films International. During 1990, CFIL sold $20 million in license fees through 150 licenses for Carolco feature films, telefilms and miniseries, and Orbis' catalog of television programming.[27]

Foreign sales were headed by Guy East, former international sales director for Goldcrest Film and Television. He commented on the prospects of Carolco in the foreign market: "There is every indication of huge growth in the foriegn area that Carolco wants to position itself to be part of."[28] East saw an expansion of the European market, with the advent of private television in France, Italy, and Spain, and from increased interest in construction of new screens. Additionally, the demise of several competitors, including PSO, Goldcrest, and Thorn EMI in Europe, gave Carolco opportunities to increase market share by capturing its competitors' lost distribution agreements. Executive vice president of foreign sales, Rocco Viglietta, stated, "The TV market overseas continues to grow particularly given the pending single Euro market in 1992 and the privatization of stations worldwide."[29]

As part of Carolco's international thrust, the company considered entering the home video market in the former Soviet Union through an arrangement with Sintez International in Moscow. Orbis' executive vice president, Ethan Podell, said, "We're very interested in exploiting opportunities in Eastern Europe and Russia." The Carolco exchange would have initially provided Sintez with TV documentaries, specials, and children's programming for the Russian market. Revenues were to be split between Sintez and Carolco and were required to remain in Russia where Orbis could use the rubles to finance productions in Russia.[30] A note of caution in this market was expressed by Viglietta, "People there are looking to be fed first . . . it will be sometime before the Eastern Bloc becomes capitalized and people get VCRs in their homes."[31]

Licensing

Many of Carolco's popular films created a great worldwide demand for action figures, books, games, and toys. Carolco's licensing division developed

[27] *Annual Report*, 1990, p. 27.

[28] James Greenberg, "Newly Formed Carolco Int'l Gets O'Seas Rights to Carpenter Pix," *Variety*, August 5, 1987, p. 28.

[29] "Carolco Presses on without Its Cofounder Vajna: Has 9-Title Package Ready," *Variety*, February 21, 1990, p. 88.

[30] "Carolco Says 'Da' to Pack," *Variety*, December 3, 1990, p. 19.

[31] Eller and Groves, "Carolco Prexy Defends Its Talent," p. 88.

into a full-service licensing entity. For example, *Total Recall* was a great success for Nintendo. Carolco also published the novel, which became a top seller. For *Terminator 2: Judgment Day*, Carolco licensing was also involved in heavy licensing activity of toys, Nintendo and computer software games, video and pinball arcade games, publishing, comic books, apparel, and collectible products. Also national promotions were planned during the release of the film including promotional tie-ins with Pepsi, Subway sandwich chain, and Hero Cologne by Faberge. Carolco Licensing was very successful in managing the licensing activities of Carolco's properties worldwide. For example, Rambo remained the number one action figure in Brazil and Argentina years after the series was released, and demand remained high for the toy in Europe and the South Pacific as well.

The licensing division was also responsible for product and corporate identity signage in Carolco films. The placement of products and logos in movies not only generated revenue for Carolco, but it also served as a base to build consumer promotion relationships with the client companies.

ECONOMIC ENVIRONMENT

In January 1991, reports from Washington regarding the nation's economic recession offered little encouragement. As real incomes were falling, consumer spending subsequently took a downturn. Consumer confidence fell approximately 12 percent in January to reach its lowest level in 10 years.[32] The nation fought a war with Iraq and consumer spending continued to decline. However, consumers were faced with rising inflation and increasing federal income and payroll taxes. This "double whammy" affected the typical family, consisting of two full-time wage earners with two dependent children, by lowering their real after tax net income.[33]

The movie business historically fared well in bad, even disastrous, economic times. Economist Albert Kapusinki's study of the years 1928–1975 showed that approximately 70 percent of the time the film industry thrived in economic troughs. In each of the three major recessions from 1971 to 1991, the strong countercyclical nature of the film industry triumphed.[34]

The recession of the early 1990s found the film industry competing in a diverse media spectrum. Viewers had the option to choose from a widening range of film entertainment as well as basic cable television to pay-per-view movies and events. Also in the arena was a fully matured home video business. "The argu-

[32] James C. Cooper and Kathleen Madigan, "The Consumer Is Blue, Broke, and Burdened with Debt," *Business Week*, February 11, 1991, p. 17.

[33] Gene Koretz, "A Double Whammy for Double-Income Families," *Business Week*, December 31, 1990, p. 32.

[34] Paul Nogolows, "Will B.O. Prove Recession-Proof This Time Out?" *Variety*, December 10, 1990, p. 1.

ment has been made that people are going to go out to the video store and rent a cassette and bring it home rather than going out to the movie theater and having a pizza and getting a babysitter, and I would agree with that,'' said analyst Chris Dixon of Kidder, Peabody & Co.[35] Dixon also noted that the film industry was driven by demand and revenues will continue to be at rates above normal in the consumer sector. Strength in the overseas theatrical market and increased penetration of television households in Europe were accredited for these revenues.[36]

COMPETITION

Carolco competed in the motion picture production and distribution industry. This industry was divided between two groups of competitors, major film production companies and independent film companies. Major film production companies included such common names as:

- Warner Brothers
- 20th Century Fox
- MGM/United Artists
- Orion
- Paramount
- Walt Disney-Buena Vista
- Others

Independent film companies included:

- Carolco
- Nelson Entertainment
- Samuel Goldwyn
- Miramax
- New Line/Seven Arts
- Castle Rock
- Cinergi Productions (formed by Carolco cofounder Vajna)

During the 1970s and 1980s, the number of films produced by independents increased from 133 in 1970[37] to a peak of 380 in 1987.[38] As shown in Exhibit 26.3, U.S. new film releases by independents increased between 1985 and 1987, while U.S. new film releases by majors decreased. During the period 1988 to 1990, the

[35] Ibid., p. 3.
[36] Ibid.
[37] Todd McCarthy, "Whopping Year For U.S. Independents," *Variety*, June 22, 1988, p. 22.
[38] Lawrence Cohn, "Fewer New Pix in '90, but More by Majors," *Variety*, December 24, 1990, p. 8.

EXHIBIT 26.3   New U.S. Feature Film Releases

	1985	1986	1987	1988	1989	1990
Film Source						
Majors	150	144	135	161	159	164
Independents	304	333	380	352	287	253

Source: Lawrence Cohn, "Fewer New Pix In '90, But More by Majors," *Variety,* December 24, 1990, p. 8.

majors released more films while independents released less, illustrating the direct competition for market share between the two groups.

Carolco's positioning between the two groups—by releasing major event films, distributing videos and television programming, and offering packages of movie titles, all worldwide—helped to hedge its position, protecting the organization from the cyclical swings in market share between the two segments.

Carolco's worldwide distribution network was beneficial as earnings from the domestic film market only covered the costs of making films. For example, the approximate aggregate investment by domestic producers in summer 1991 films, including ad costs, was $2 billion. However, the 1991 summer market size for the films was only approximately $2 billion. The summer season provided 40 percent of the total annual U.S. box office gross. Therefore, there were many pictures that did not receive a return on their investment from U.S. theatrical distribution and had to turn to ancillary markets around the world to make a profit. With so many pictures crammed into such a narrow corridor, it became intimidating for even the most stalwart veterans of the distribution wars. As one Hollywood CEO remarked, "No matter how you rationalize it, this exercise is basically suicidal. . . . By mid-summer you're going to see a succession of pictures yanked from the schedule."[39]

In 1991, industrywide domestic theatrical income accounted for only about 20 percent of the total revenue stream and rose to 35 percent including all foreign theatrical earnings. The rest of the pie consisted of worldwide video, television syndication, cable, satellites, and all other esoteric new markets. This meant that U.S. theatrical openings were helpful but not necessarily vital to a new film. If a movie did poorly in the United States, it could still be successful in foreign markets and from studio output deals with the Showtimes and the HBOs.

Since domestic markets failed to provide enough return on investment, offshore markets became vital to filmmakers. For many producers, foreign markets accounted for nearly half the gross of a hit film. Carolco claimed between 65 percent and 75 percent of its revenues from overseas. So vital were the foreign markets that independents were caught in a vice between major U.S. studios, which were intensifying their quest for a bigger share of the foreign market, and

[39] Peter Bart, "View from the War Room," *Variety*, May 27, 1991, p. 3.

the changing tastes of foreign viewers. Foreign audiences were becoming more sophisticated, switching from low-budget action, horror, and slam-bang adventures to movies with big budgets, big stars, and big production values. The independents were known for the low-budget films, but these movies were not selling overseas anymore. Sigrid Ann Davidson, a vice president at Skouras Pictures, said, "The most important thing is to acquire better-quality star vehicles, not necessarily stars of the quality of Meryl Streep, but actors who have value overseas. The days of selling a film with boobs, bullets, and happy endings are a fading memory."[40]

One problem facing all U.S. film companies was the development of quotas within the European Community. France, for example, set a local quota of 60 percent for all its filmed entertainment, and unless the independents associated with foreign firms in coproductions or had local offices, their opportunities in the expanding European market was limited. One independent, Nelson Entertainment, secured films from Columbia and Orion and was successful in distributing them in the foreign market. These types of arrangements allowed an independent to swing some heavy weight behind its name.[41]

Many independents accumulated catalogs of titles to sell to foreign operations. As Herb Fletcher, Crown International vice president for international sales, said, "We have the advantage of being able to sell groups of pictures to television," but even companies with large catalogs are discovering narrower buying patterns. For the independents operating on a shoe-string budget, the fear of being put out of business because they failed to keep up to date with changing global tastes became their number one concern.[42]

LITIGATION AND CONTINGENCIES

In September 1990, two similar lawsuits were initiated, one in a Delaware Court of Chancery, the other in a California Superior Court, by stockholders of Carolco. These suits were aimed at the directors of Carolco and specific lenders with whom the company had loans outstanding. The lawsuits, which sought unspecified compensatory damages, stemmed from alleged self-dealings and breach of various fiduciary duties in connection with an approval of a stock purchase by CINV (the company's wholly owned foreign affiliate) from New CINV (a Netherlands corporation that at that time owned 62 percent of Carolco's common stock). Under the terms of the previously negotiated agreement, CINV purchased 3,461,538 shares of Carolco's common stock from New CINV at a price of $13 per share. At the time the agreement was executed, the shares were trading at about $7.25 on the New York Stock Exchange.[43] Furthermore, New

[40] Elliot Tiegel, "Surviving as an Indie," *California Business*, August 1990, p. 18.
[41] Ibid., p. 19.
[42] Ibid., p. 67.
[43] Cohn, "Fewer New Pix in '90," p. 9.

CINV was deemed to be beneficially owned by Mario Kassar and certain trusts set up for the benefit of his family. CINV paid New CINV a total of $44,999,994 for the stock, which consisted of cash and the assumption of a significant amount of New CINV's liabilities. The breakdown of the $44,999,994 included (1) the assumption of obligations New CINV owed the company totalling $25,050,075, (2) the payment of a loan outstanding to Credit Lyannais Bank Nederland N.V. of $8,000,000, and (3) a promissory note payable to New CINV from CINV of $11,949,319.[44]

On December 24, 1990, a Los Angeles Superior Court judge imposed a freeze on 2.2 million shares of Carolco stock owned by Kassar. This freeze was made in lieu of the transaction between CINV and New CINV. Carolco claimed the transaction was approved by its board and that the transaction had received support from large stockholders that represented a majority of the shares now owned by Kassar and his family. The court, however, remained intent on imposing the order stating that, in its view, based on the evidence, there was a high probability that the plaintiffs would prevail in the litigation.[45]

Carolco and its predecessors paid little or no federal or state income taxes, as a significant amount of the company's total revenues were recognized from the foreign releases of its films through CINV, a Netherlands Antilles subsidiary of the company, which under the United States–Netherlands Antilles Tax Treaty was not subject to U.S. taxation (see explanation of CINV's tax situation under Financial Analysis below). Although the company anticipated that it would not pay substantial U.S. taxes in 1991, this tax position could have been adversely affected by the following:

1. The allocation of income and deductions between Carolco and CINV may have been subject to challenge by the Internal Revenue Service.
2. Carolco and its subsidiaries could have been deemed personal holding companies and the company's subsidiary could have been deemed a foreign personal holding company due to the substantial stock ownership potentially attributable to Kassar, thus requiring the company to pay dividends or a penalty tax on its income from motion pictures.
3. Even with the tax treaty in place, the Internal Revenue Service could have contended that some of CINV's income was directly subject to U.S. tax.

As of December 31, 1990, management stated that, in its opinion, none of the above-mentioned theories could have applied to Carolco's tax situation.[46]

---

[44] *Form 10-K*, 1990, p. 23.
[45] Cohn, "Fewer New Pix in '90," p. 9.
[46] *Form 10-K*, 1990, p. 33.

FINANCIAL ANALYSIS

The financial structure of Carolco included wholly owned and partly owned subsidiaries as well as wholly owned foreign affiliates. As previously mentioned, Carolco attempted to minimize the risks associated with the production and distribution of its major motion pictures through its distribution agreement with Tri-Star Pictures. Under this agreement Tri-Star was obligated to make certain advances to the company to cover Carolco's negative costs associated with the production of a motion picture, and to spend significant amounts on printing and advertising expenses associated with the marketing of the theatrical releases. For the year ending December 31, 1990, approximately one-fourth of the company's revenues were derived from the sale of both theatrical and nontheatrical rights of its major motion pictures to Tri-Star. The remaining three-fourths of Carolco's revenues were received through its affiliates and wholly owned subsidiaries.[47]

For the year ending December 31, 1990, approximately 15 percent of the company's revenues were derived from the domestic production and distribution of motion pictures to television through Orbis Communications. LIVE Entertainment was responsible for approximately 13 percent of Carolco's revenues for the year ending December 31, 1990.[48]

Carolco International N.V., a wholly owned foreign subsidiary, was responsible for the leasing of motion picture rights in foreign markets. CINV, as distinguished from other subsidiaries responsible for distribution, incurred only minimal distribution expenses and was responsible for only a small portion of general overhead expenses. However, because of the nature of the leasing transactions, CINV was responsible for a significant amount of Carolco's revenues (approximately 47 percent in 1990). Furthermore, under the United States–Netherlands Antilles Tax Treaty, none of the foreign source income from CINV was subject to U.S. taxation. Therefore, CINV's tax rates were significantly lower than U.S. statutory rates, resulting in substantial tax savings and deferrals for Carolco. As of December 31, 1990, CINV had accumulated approximately $153 million of earnings not subject to U.S. taxes.[49]

The breakdown of operating revenues by line of business for the year ending December 31, 1990, is included in Exhibit 26.4. Films released domestically contributed 23 percent of Carolco's revenue, while films released outside the United States contributed 35 percent. Video releases domestically represented 13 percent of revenue and TV releases domestically represented 15 percent. Revenues from distribution of TV and video releases outside the United States represented 10 percent. Other operating revenues from Canadian partnerships and unrelated foreign corporations, including interest from related parties, amounted to 4 percent.

[47] Ibid., p. 1.
[48] Ibid., p. 9.
[49] Ibid., p. 32.

EXHIBIT 26.4   Breakdown of 1990 Revenues

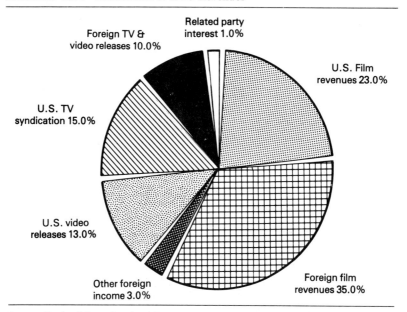

Source: Derived from Carolco Pictures, *Annual Report* 1990 and *Form 10-K* 1990.

The very nature of Carolco's business required huge amounts of working capital to fund the costs associated with the production of the films. A portion of these costs were borne by Tri-Star. However, in order to meet additional working capital requirements, the company and certain of its subsidiaries had to enter into agreements with two banks (BT/Chemical and CLBN) for revolving credit facilities. The amount of credit that both banks were committed to extend totaled $225 million. As of December 31, 1990, Carolco had a cumulative outstanding balance of approximately $156 million to BT/Chemical and CLBN. Substantially all of the company's assets were pledged under the credit agreements. Although the company was in compliance with its debt covenants at year end, the disclosures in the 1990 audit report indicated that the company might not be able to continue to conform to these covenants in 1991.[50] Therefore, the company submitted a Consent Solicitation Statement to the Securities and Exchange Commission, which sought to have the holders of the company's 14 percent senior notes approve a change in the financial covenants. On May 15, 1991, Carolco issued a press release stating that it had indeed received consent from the noteholders.[51] Among other things, the new amendments allowed the company to reduce its required cash flow coverage ratio from 1.5 to 1 to 1.2 to 1, and to restructure the

[50] Ibid., p. 14.
[51] Carolco Pictures Inc., *News Release*, June 5, 1991.

restrictions on liens which the company was permitted to incur. In return for these concessions, the company was required to make a one-time cash payment of $15 per $1,000 principal of notes, and to issue approximately 202,000 shares of its common stock to the noteholders.

In addition to the revolving line of credit with BT/Chemical and CLBN, the company had outstanding at December 31, 1990, approximately $76 million of 14 percent senior notes and $16 million in subordinated notes. Proceeds from the issuance of the senior notes were used to repay a large portion of the subordinated notes, as well as to fund additional working capital requirements.

Carolco also had an additional outstanding loan for $25 million from CLBN to finance the cash flow needs of Vista (the company's domestic group responsible for the Seven Arts joint venture). Vista was totally dependent on Carolco to finance its cash flow needs since its purchase on September 20, 1989. Although the company owned only one-third of the outstanding stock of Vista, it accounted for its investment as a purchase, since it funded all of Vista's cash needs and guaranteed Vista's loan from CLBN.

As shown in Exhibit 26.5, Carolco's debt load had increased significantly from 1988 to 1991. The majority of the debt was generated to provide the company with the needed capital to finance its major films as well as acquisitions. All costs associated with the production and filming of motion pictures were initially capitalized and subsequently written off as the films and made-for-television movies were released, based on management's expectations regarding the life of the films.

Operating revenues increased steadily from 1988 to 1991; however, operating and general and administrative expenses associated with these revenues rose sharply as well. Management attributed the large increases in general and administrative expenses in 1990 to an increase in the company's personnel in the legal and accounting areas, as well as increased distribution expenses. The company publicly stated that these increases would not continue.[52] However, the first-quarter results for the period ending March 31, 1991, showed a 46 percent increase in general and administrative costs over the first-quarter results for 1990.

Analysis of the company's cash flows from operations, shown in Exhibit 26.6, indicated large negative cash flows from 1988 to 1991. The negative cash flows forced the company to incur additional debt and issue equity capital in order to generate the cash needed to fund the company's on-going operations.[53] Management relied heavily on the success of its major motion picture releases in 1991 to provide the cash flow needed for operations.

Carolco's management stated that it was determined to build the equity base of the company during the 1990s through the formation of a series of strategic alliances with major worldwide entertainment and media companies. In 1990, three such alliances took place with the following companies: Canal +, an enter-

[52] Carolco Pictures Inc., *News Release*, May 16, 1991.
[53] "Carolco Needs a Hero," p. 1.

EXHIBIT 26.5   Selected Financial Information for Carolco Pictures, Inc. (In thousands)

	Year Ended December 31,			
	1987	*1988*	*1989*	*1990*
Operating Revenues				
Feature Films and Videocassettes	$ 54,477	$138,461	$115,113	$216,720
Television Syndication	42,790	19,597	21,552	42,130
Total Operating Revenues	97,267	158,058	136,665	258,850
Operating Expenses				
Film and TV Amortization	74,158	116,735	104,892	204,108
Total Operating Expenses	74,158	116,735	104,892	204,108
Gross Operating Profit	23,109	41,323	31,773	54,742
Gross Profit Percentage	24%	26%	23%	21%
Other Revenues				
Interest Income—Related Parties	2,452	1,696	858	2,148
Other Income—Foreign Affiliates	4,002	4,147	3,940	8,147
Other Expenses				
General and Administrative Expenses	12,907	14,122	19,879	32,942
Interest Expense	4,911	7,906	12,598	24,314
Income before Equity Income and Income Taxes	11,745	25,138	4,094	7,781
Equity in Income of Affiliates	2,682	11,197	10,862	13,340
Provisions for Income Taxes	95	831	920	3,823
Net Income Attributable to Common Stock	$ 14,332	$ 35,504	$ 14,036	$ 17,298
Balance Sheet Data				
Cash	$11,191	$8,094	$8,871	$12,552
Accounts Receivable	41,217	49,566	41,156	84,558
Film Costs, Net of Amortization	113,723	180,776	333,303	387,845
Total Assets	229,555	342,410	520,148	631,907
Long-Term Debt, Including Related Parties	80,582	136,788	274,368	294,934
Stockholders' Equity	$79,266	$118,894	$134,243	$191,077

Source: Carolco Pictures, Inc., *Form 10-K* 1990.

tainment company based in France; Technicolor, a U.S. film products company; and RCS Video, a media and publishing company in Italy. These companies purchased substantial amounts of Carolco stock during 1990, investing heavily in the long-term outlook of Carolco.[54]

Carolco had approximately 4,500 beneficial holders of common stock as of April 17, 1991. The amount of beneficial ownership that was attributable to officers and directors of the company constituted 79.2 percent of the common shares outstanding. Furthermore, Kassar was deemed to beneficially own up to

[54] *Annual Report*, 1990, p. 2.

EXHIBIT 26.6 Carolco Pictures Inc., and Subsidiaries Statements of Cash Flow (In thousands)

	Year Ended December 31,		
	1988	1989	1990
Net Cash Flow from Operating Activities			
Net Income	$35,504	$14,036	$17,298
Adjustment to Reconcile Net Income to Net Cash Provided (Used) by Operating Activities			
Amortization of Film Costs	96,287	80,091	175,601
Depreciation and Amortization	5,387	4,797	9,874
Equity in Income of Affiliates	(11,197)	(10,862)	(13,340)
Conversion of Video Guarantees to LIVE Series B Preferred Stock	(15,000)	(4,900)	—
(Increase) Decrease in Receivables	(8,949)	8,410	(35,753)
Increase (Decrease) in Payables, Accrued Liabilities, Accrued Residuals and Participations, Income Taxes Payable, and Other Assets	2,883	(24,418)	11,353
Increase in Film Costs and Rights	(163,340)	(232,618)	(224,540)
Payments on Contractual Obligations	(3,207)	(2,927)	(18,201)
Increase in Contractual Obligations	15,494	2,350	24,552
Increase (Decrease) in Advance Collections on Contracts	(8,214)	40,641)	4,225
Net Cash Used in Operating Activities	(54,352)	125,400	48,931
Cash Flow from Investing Activities			
Purchase of Property and Equipment	(11,746)	(3,065)	(2,420)
Sale of Marketable Securities	3,049	0	0
Investment in LIVE Entertainment, Inc.	(6,738)	805	(414)
Purchase of the Vista Organization, Ltd., the Vista Organization Partnership, L.P., and Carolco Television, Inc. Net of Cash Acquired	—	—	(21,003)
Net Cash Used in Investing Activities	(15,435)	(2,260)	(23,837)
Cash Flow from Financing Activities			
Proceeds from Debt	50,925	0	133,054
Payments on Debt	(71,913)	(1,077)	(106,166)
Increase in Borrowings from Banks	98,200	109,318	0
Borrowings from Vopic	0	30,000	0
Proceeds from Building Finance	12,900	0	0
Proceeds from Property and Equipment Financing	5,791	0	0
Decrease in Notes Payable to Related Parties	(4,000)	(941)	(17,003)
Increase in Receivables from Related Parties	(10,636)	(6,003)	(4,905)
Repurchase of Senior Subordinated Notes	(20,915)	(500)	(872)
Redemption of Warrants	—	—	(5,559)
Net Proceeds from Issuance of Preferred Stock—Series B	—	—	29,456
Net Proceeds from Issuance of Preferred Stock—Series C	—	—	56,559
Payment of Preferred Dividends	—	—	(971)
Proceeds from Sale of Stock	13,133	0	0
Repurchase of Common Stock	(1,379)	0	(45,385)
Increase in Debt Acquisition Costs	(3,089)	(4,037)	(2,221)
Exercise of Stock Options/Warrants	416	1,677	1,327

(Cont.)

EXHIBIT 26.6   (Cont.)

	Year Ended December 31,		
	1988	*1989*	*1990*
Issuance of Senior Notes and Common Stock in Connection with the Purchase of the Visa Organization, Ltd., and the Vista Organization, Partnership, L.P.	—	—	29,325
Net Cash Provided by Financing Activities	69,433	128,437	76,449
Increase (Decrease) in Cash	$ (354)	$ 777	$ 3,681
Supplemental Disclosure of Cash Flow Information			
Cash Paid During the Year for			
Interest (Net of Amount Capitalized)	$ 6,245	$ 23,167	$ 17,145
Income Taxes	$ 1,054	$ 637	$ 581

Source: Carolco Pictures Inc., *Annual Report,* 1990.

58.9 percent of the company, either directly or through entities that benefited Kassar or members of his family.[55]

Carolco's common stock traded on the New York Stock Exchange under the symbol CRS. Since January of 1989, the firm's stock had ranged from a high of $13.875 in the second quarter of 1990 to a low of $5.125 during the fourth quarter of 1990. Carolco's stock traded at $7.75 on July 23, 1991. Carolco never paid cash dividends on its common stock and intended to retain all future earnings to finance the expansion and development of its business. The consolidated balance sheet as of December 31, 1990, and the statement of operations for the year ending December 31, 1990, are included in Exhibits 26.7 and 26.8.

EPILOGUE

The champagne Mario Kassar ordered arrived perfectly chilled and in the hotel's signature crystal ice bucket. On the tray next to the bottle was an envelope bearing his name. Kassar ignored the envelope for the moment, as the roulette wheel began to slow and the ball began its descent. It bounced several times before settling to rest on black 2.

"Gentlemen, we have a winner."

Squarely positioned on the winning number was Kassar's stack of chips. With a sense of exhilaration, he reached for a flute from the tray at his side and, after inhaling the quintessential effervescence of its contents, emptied the flute in one celebratory flourish. As he set the stem back on the tray, his eyes fell upon the envelope. Kassar immediately knew its contents and ripped open the flap in

[55] *Form 10-K*, 1990, p. 42.

EXHIBIT 26.7   Carolco Pictures Inc. and Subsidiaries Consolidated Balance Sheets[a]
(In thousands)

	December 31, 1989	December 31, 1990
Assets		
Cash	$8,871	$12,552
Accounts Receivable, Net of Allowances of $2,545 (1989) and $5,821 (1990)	41,156	84,558
Accounts Receivable, Related Parties	10,839	5,933
Film Costs, Less Accumulated Amortization	333,303	387,845
Property and Equipment, at Cost, Less Accumulated Depreciation and Amortization	31,123	30,223
Investment in LIVE Entertainment Inc.	76,974	91,044
Other Assets	17,882	19,752
Total Assets	$520,148	$631,907
Liabilities and Stockholders' Equity		
Accounts Payable	$11,816	$16,775
Accrued Liabilities	26,717	26,159
Accrued Residuals and Participations	21,656	28,528
Income Taxes Current and Deferred	943	4,159
Debt	252,915	289,328
Advance Collections on Contracts	49,112	53,337
Contractual Obligations	1,293	7,644
Notes Payable, Related Parties	21,453	5,606
Total Liabilities	385,905	431,536
Commitments and Contingencies Due to Minority Shareholders	—	9,294
Stockholders' Equity		
Preferred Stock—$1.00 Par Value, 10,000,000 Shares Authorized: Series A Convertible Preferred Stock, 4,000,000 Shares Authorized, None Issued	—	—
Series B Convertible Preferred Stock, 30,000 Shares Authorized and Issued ($30,000,000 Aggregate Liquidation Preference)	—	30
Common Stock—$.01 Par Value, 100,000,000 Shares Authorized, 29,834,681 Shares Issued and Outstanding in 1989 and 30,281,075 Shares Issued and Outstanding, Including 3,475,538 Shares in Treasury in 1990	298	301
Additional Paid-In Capital	39,347	125,146
Treasury Stock	—	(45,385)
Retained Earnings	94,598	110,925
Total Stockholders' Equity	134,243	191,077
Total Liabilities and Stockholders' Equity	$520,148	$631,907

[a] A number of "Notes to Consolidated Financial Statements" have not been included in this exhibit. For a complete understanding of Carolco's financial situation refer to the *Annual Report*.

Source: Carolco Pictures Inc., *Annual Report* 1990.

EXHIBIT 26.8   Carolco Pictures Inc., and Subsidiaries Consolidated Statements of Operations[a] (In thousands except per share data)

	Year Ended December 31,		
	1988	*1989*	*1990*
Revenues			
Feature Films (Including $15,000 in 1988, $17,850 in 1989 and $27,625 in 1990 from a Related Party)	$138,461	$115,113	$216,720
Television Syndication	19,597	21,552	42,130
Interest Income from Related Parties	1,696	858	2,148
Other	4,147	3,940	8,147
Total Revenues	163,901	141,463	269,145
Cost and Expenses			
Amortization of Film and Television Costs, Residuals, and Profit Participation	116,735	104,892	204,108
Selling, General, and Administrative	14,122	19,879	32,942
Interest	7,906	12,598	24,314
Total Costs and Expenses	138,763	137,369	261,364
Income before Equity in Income of Affiliated Companies and Provision for Income Taxes	25,138	4,094	7,781
Equity in Income of Affiliated Companies	11,197	10,862	13,340
Income before Provisions for Income Taxes	36,335	14,956	21,121
Provision for Income Taxes	831	920	3,823
Net Income	$ 35,504	$ 14,036	$ 17,298
Preferred Dividends	0	0	971
Net Income Attributable to Common Stock	$ 35,504	$ 14,036	$ 16,327
Net Income per Share (Based on Weighted Average Shares and Common Share Equivalents Outstanding of 30,999,608 Shares (1988), 30,296,670 Shares (1989), and 30,015,720 Shares (1990))	$ 1.15	$ .46	$ .49

[a] A number of "Notes to Consolidated Financial Statements" have not been included in this exhibit. For a complete understanding of Carolco's financial situation refer to the *Annual Report*.
Source: Carolco Pictures Inc., *Annual Report* 1990.

anticipation. With a quick glance at the single sheet inside, he shouted, "Yes, indeed! We do have a winner."

The envelope contained the opening box office report for *Terminator 2*. The movie had opened to massive crowds, and the box office take had exceeded even Kassar's expectations. But as the euphoria of the moment subsided, Kassar reflected, "Would it be enough to save Carolco? Or, would it be 'Hasta la vista, Baby'?"

_____ CASE 27 _____

Baldor Electric Company:
Positioning for the Twenty-First Century

As Greg Kowert, vice president for strategic planning, looked at the quarterly report, a broad grin spread over his face. First-quarter sales were $55.1 million, an increase of 17 percent over the same period last year. The strategic initiatives were paying off. After several disappointing years, 1987 had been a record year for Baldor Electric with sales breaking the $200 million level for the first time. And the first-quarter results for 1988 were even better.

Kowert felt that previous strategies had enabled the company to maintain 21 straight years of growth at a rate about twice that of the gross national product (GNP). However, the environment changed in the 1980s. Baldor's customers were not growing, and they were inundated with foreign competition, resulting in declining sales. Therefore, Baldor sales declined as well.

In retrospect, the management team had identified the "strong dollar" as the major problem causing the decline in sales. A trade-weighted average indicated that 1985 was a peak year, which resulted in many industries suffering losses (Exhibit 27.1). Many of Baldor's customers were negatively impacted, as were machine tool sales.

Negative Impact of the "High" Dollar

Woodworking Machinery	−80%
Machine Tools	−55%
Textile Machinery	−54%
Semiconductor Equipment	−40%
Chemical-Processing Equipment	−40%
Packaging Machinery	−35%

Source: Adapted from U.S. Department of Commerce data.

Additionally, a correlation was identified between the strength of the dollar and the amount of exports although it was delayed (Exhibit 27.2). Fortunately, the

This case was prepared by Peter M. Ginter and Linda E. Swayne as a basis for class discussion rather than to illustrate either effective or ineffective handling of an administrative situation. Used with permission from Peter M. Ginter.

EXHIBIT 27.1   Exchange Rates

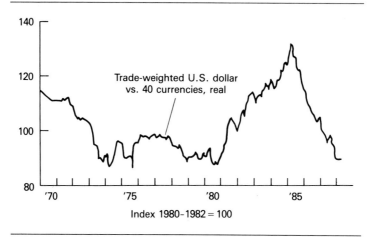

Source: Federal Reserve Bank and Morgan Guaranty Trust Company.

EXHIBIT 27.2   The Dollar's Delayed Impact on Exports

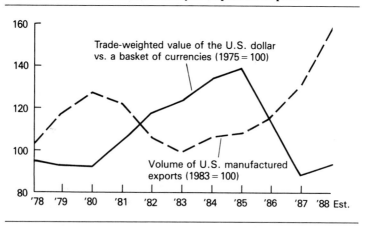

Source: *Business Week*, January 18, 1988.

environment was improved in 1987, and Baldor, as well as the company's customers, had improved results.

The following comparative advantages were considered by management to be responsible not only for Baldor's transition from a small to midsized company but also for Baldor's increased market share:

- Concentration on industrial electric motors—By manufacturing only electric motors for industrial markets, Baldor had been able to focus its resources on a highly specialized market.
- Most committed to the industry—Baldor had the largest percentage of its sales in electric motors. Many of the competitors were divisions of larger companies and had to compete with other divisions for allocations of resources.
- Energy-efficient motors—Through the years the company had followed the strategy of providing better products at competitive prices. For Baldor, this translated into better materials and superior engineering directed at durability and energy efficiency.
- Diversification into closely related products—By purchasing small companies that manufactured electric motor starters and adjustable-speed drives, Baldor enhanced its ability to sell its industrial motors.
- Independent representative sales organization—The company sold all of its products through independent representatives. Many reps derived most of their income from Baldor, and thus the selling task was accomplished by a group of semiautonomous entrepreneurs compensated by direct incentives.
- Availability—Baldor attempted to sell as many items as possible as stock products and carried heavy inventories positioned close to customers in 28 warehouses around the country. This inventory policy was unique in the industry.
- Backward integration—Baldor manufactured more of its component parts than the competition.
- Management team—Experienced managers from the field were brought in when several key managers retired.

BALDOR ELECTRIC COMPANY PROFILE

Edwin C. Ballman founded Baldor Electric Company in St. Louis, Missouri, in 1920 as a manufacturer of industrial electric motors. Baldor expanded primarily through internal growth. The company opened a plant in Fort Smith, Arkansas, in 1957, and subsequently moved the corporate headquarters there. In 1990, 16 plants employed more than 2,400 people.

From the very beginning, Baldor emphasized production of motors that delivered maximum output while consuming a minimum of energy. Management felt that the energy crisis in the early 1970s increased the interest in energy efficiency and led to rapid growth for the company.

Baldor was the fastest-growing company in the electric motor industry. During the period between 1971 and 1981, Baldor's growth was approximately 22 percent annually, almost 80 percent faster than the industry as a whole. As illustrated in Exhibit 27.3, Baldor's market share increased about 15 percent during the 1975 recession, by 20 percent during the 1982 business contraction, and doubled during the period between 1973 and 1982.

In 1978, Baldor was the 10th largest producer of industrial motors. By 1983, the company had moved to fifth largest and in 1987, Baldor became the third

EXHIBIT 27.3   Baldor's Market Share, 1973–1982[a]

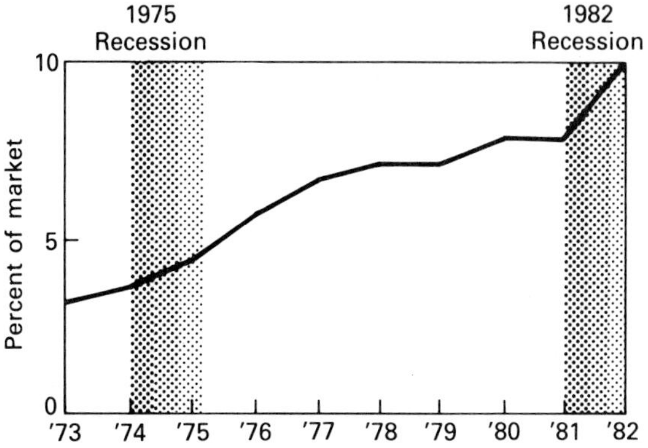

[a] Estimated share of Baldor product markets.

largest in the business. Craig W. Fanning of Dean Witter attributed the increased market share to "entering new, growing markets with innovative products, an outstanding record of product quality and efficiency, strong distribution, the industry's broadest product line in the 1/50 to 250 hp range, and responsiveness to customer needs."[1]

The period between 1983 and 1986 was particularly difficult for the industrial market, and Baldor was no exception. In 1983, the first-ever sales decline prompted the company to develop a strategic response. During this period, when customers in three key industries—agriculture, mining, and energy—stopped buying motors, and other traditional markets were negatively affected by the recession, Baldor was able to replace lost sales.

Rather than retreating as some companies (such as Westinghouse) did, or moving production to foreign or offshore facilities, Baldor maintained production in the United States, worked at developing new markets, and attacked costs. Capital investments were increased $89 million from 1977 to 1987 in order to improve production efficiencies (Exhibit 27.4).

New markets were developed in food processing, electronic manufacturing equipment, and electronics. The "wash down" motor was introduced in 1985 in response to customer needs in food processing for a motor that could withstand daily cleaning. Baldor purchased three small companies that "doubled its opportunity spectrum" by establishing the company in the electric motor starter, adjustable speed drive, and large DC motor businesses. The company made an increasing commitment to research and development (Exhibit 27.5).

---

[1] Craig W. Fanning, *Dean Witter Research Report on Baldor Electric*, September 1, 1987, p. 3.

EXHIBIT 27.4   Baldor's Capital Investments

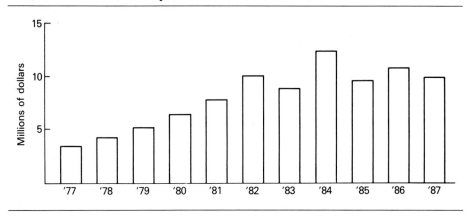

EXHIBIT 27.5   Research and Development Expenditures

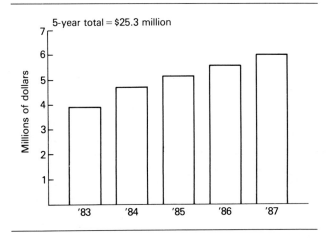

The Mission

The company's management was proud of the mission statement, which they considered to be the basis for their success: "BALDOR is to be the best (as determined by our customers) marketers, designers, and manufacturers of high-quality electric motors and related electronic products." According to Chief Executive Officer Roland S. Boreham, Jr., "We were one of the first to recognize that 'best' or 'quality' only has real meaning when it is defined as being determined by the customer. Other than the last four words which were added recently, this statement is many years old."

In 1985, Baldor started developing the superstructure on which to build the company into a world-class manufacturer. The first element was automated information flow, sometimes called computer-integrated manufacturing. The second was continuous-flow manufacturing as contrasted to batch manufacturing, and the third was a total quality system.

The company was a leader in automating information flow but was adding to that lead with a state-of-the-art material planning system and a new data processing operating system. A new data processing center, completed in 1989, allowed the company to improve information capabilities as well as substantially reduce the cost of processing information.

The changeover for the two largest plants from batch to flexible-flow manufacturing was completed late in 1987. The costs and time involved were greater than anticipated, but the benefits derived also were greater than anticipated— improved quality, more reliable delivery, lower costs, and less inventory.

The company hired Crosby Associates, a major consulting firm, to work with the total organization to achieve world-class quality. In independent surveys of customers, Baldor typically rated first or second in quality.

The Market

Baldor's products were sold to a variety of industries. Although agriculture, mining, and energy were major customers for the company, electric motors had applicability in most manufacturing situations. To meet company growth objectives, many industries were studied to see how Baldor could change and improve its product line to meet the needs of potential customers. Exhibit 27.6 lists the markets served by Baldor.

Product Line. Industrial electric motors, varying in size from 1/50 through 250 horsepower (hp), have been the principal product line, accounting for over

EXHIBIT 27.6   Markets Served by Baldor Electric

Packaging Equipment	Machine Tools
Motion Controls	Textile Machinery
Computer-Aided Design/Computer-Aided Manufacturing	Pollution Control
	Heating, Ventilation, Air Conditioning
Graphic Arts	Mining
Energy—Oil, Gas, Coal, etc.	Materials Handling
Distribution/replacement	Electric Vehicles
Agribusiness	Food Processing
Power Transmission	Medical Equipment
Chemical Processing	Woodworking
Design/Construct/Engineer	Pulp and Paper

90 percent of Baldor's sales. The company built motors to customer specification (custom) and for general purposes (stock) for the industrial rather than consumer (home appliance motors and others) market. About one-third of the business consisted of making motors to order, and the other two-thirds were stock products of which the company had over 2,000 items. Exhibit 27.7 identifies the major product lines produced by Baldor.

All Baldor's motors have been manufactured in accordance with industry standards supplied by the National Electrical Manufacturers Association (NEMA). The smallest, most precise motors were added in the late 1970s when a Connecticut company, Boehm, was purchased. In 1982, Baldor had vigorously expanded its new product development program, which increased both the depth and breadth of the company's line. In 1983, Baldor introduced a new superefficient line called the Baldor Super-E. As shown in Exhibit 27.8, the efficiency of the new Super-E line was considerably higher than the average "premium" motor.

EXHIBIT 27.7   Baldor Product Lines

Explosion-proof motors—The company supplies explosion-proof motors designed to operate in atmospheres containing combustible dust and vapors. Ranging to 100 hp, including models with all performance characteristics required for service on offshore drill rigs and crop drying.

Hostile environment motors—From 1 hp to 200 hp motors of cast iron frames to be used in chemical processing, dirty duty, and wash down duty (food service) applications.

Agribusiness—Baldor's line of agriduty motors has traditionally been considered one of the industry's broadest and most diversified. To further strengthen its position in this market, Baldor added a series of specialized models such as centrifuged fan motors, confinement house motors, vacuum pump motors, and grain stirring motors.

Fractional and subfractional horsepower motors—Baldor has been active in small motors as well. More than 70 models are offered in the subfractional (1/50 to 1/4 hp) motor category used in such applications as kidney dialysis and heart pumping.

Heavy-duty motors—The company also markets a variety of heavy-duty cast iron motors ranging in size from 1 1/2 hp to 15 hp in the 300 and corrosion-protected lines.

Super-E series—The Super-E line (super energy efficient) is designed primarily for applications where energy consumption is unusually high and motors are operated continuously for extended periods.

Custom motors—The company works with customers to design motors to fit unique applications.

Servomotors, servodrivers, and tachometers—Top-of-the-line technology in adjustable-speed drives has enabled Baldor to enter this market. The company's market share is small by design as only the high-end customers have been targeted.

Additional lines—Other product lines include close-coupled pump motors and motors specifically designed for use with six-step pulsewidth-modulated inverters.

EXHIBIT 27.8   Standard Motor Efficiencies

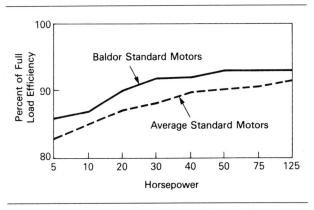

Source: U.S. Department of Energy, November 1980.

In 1986, two small firms that produced DC servomotors were purchased. Servomotors, and the servodrivers that control them, offered precise speed and motion control and complete programmability. Manufacturing robots, among other things, were driven by servomotors. The other acquisition in 1986 was a company that had developed a state-of-the-art solid-state motor starter—a device that turns motors on and off with less damage to the motor and the systems they power. Although Baldor had a very small share in each of these industries, servomotors and motor starters represented a $2 billion market.

Another new line introduced by Baldor in June 1987 was brushless DC motors. "Brushless DC motors have been used in aerospace, aircraft, and computers. They have not been used much in industry. But we intend to change that," stated Chairman Boreham.

The newest line consisted of "smart motors," those motors that will operate as directed. According to Boreham, "Not only will a 'smart motor' start when you tell it to, but will run at the speed you tell it to run at, it'll accelerate as you wish and decelerate as you wish, or even position where you wish it to. So it'll do a lot more for you than a standard motor, which enables the user of the motor to make his machine or the device that he is running more useful."

Sales and Marketing.   The products of the company were marketed in all 50 of the United States and in 40 foreign countries. Baldor's motors were sold through 27 district managers who were independent manufacturer's representatives. They had responsibility for 32 warehouses in the United States and Canada (Exhibit 27.9) and sold to over 2,000 distributors. A sophisticated computer network, capable of checking the status of customer orders and inventory counts, maintained communication among sales offices, plants, and corporate headquarters. Baldor did use a direct sales force for motor sales to some original equipment manufacturers.

EXHIBIT 27.9   Baldor's Sales Offices and Warehouses

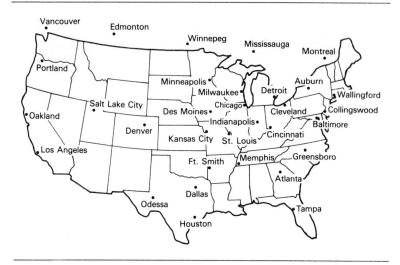

Because Baldor sold to such varied markets, the industrial distributor developed a more important role. Better design, increased applications, higher speeds, and greater reliability broadened the use of electric motors to various new industries. Distributors developed greater familiarity with their markets and, through constant contact with current and potential customers, were able to identify new opportunities.

The new acquisitions in servomotors and motor starters required Baldor to initiate a new channel of distribution. Because customers needed significantly more "help in buying" and service both before and after the sale, a new subsidiary was formed—the Motion Products Group. Baldor used direct selling for this technical and more sophisticated market.

Advertising and trade promotion traditionally were important elements in Baldor's marketing mix, serving as a direct line of communication to an extremely broad and growing audience of customer and sales prospects as the company expanded through market penetration. In addition, these efforts directly supported the selling activities of Baldor's representatives and distributors.

Advertising objectives were to develop brand recognition and brand preference. The investment in advertising and promotion continued to increase, in part due to the number of new products introduced to the various markets. The energy efficiency and savings and specific applications of Baldor motors were prominent in advertising to the trade (Exhibit 27.10).

After four extremely competitive years with no price increases, Baldor's selling prices for motors were raised 3.5 percent in the fall of 1987 followed by a

EXHIBIT 27.10   Baldor Advertisement

From BALDOR: a broad line of electric motors for a broad range of textile applications.

4 percent increase in April 1988. The 7 percent just covered the cost increases for raw materials, particularly copper, aluminum, and steel. Because all the domestic producers of motors generally priced their motors similarly, the other companies had price increases as well; however, Baldor's motors were more energy efficient.

Manufacturing.   Baldor had 16 manufacturing plants. All were located in the United States except for one plant in West Germany. Within the past two years, steps were taken to improve the production processes.

The conversion of the two largest plants to continuous-flow manufacturing resulted in direct cost savings, lower inventories, and a more productive work force. Each job was dated, which made it easy to determine if it was behind schedule. Quicker turnaround time was achieved as well as improved quality. Conversion of two more plants was in progress and scheduled for completion by 1989.

Management did not think they needed to open any more plants to fill the increased demand, as current plants converted to continuous-flow manufacturing had doubled capacity by freeing up floor space and using previously unavailable space.

Because the 32 warehouses had to maintain adequate motor inventories, careful production scheduling was critical. The inventory level and customer orders for each warehouse were on line to facilitate communication with all Baldor plants. Total inventory was monitored daily and used to develop the production schedule at the plants. The investment in computers had provided Baldor comparative advantages in avoiding stock-outs and reducing manufacturing lead time.

All labor was nonunion. "We don't even consider that we have labor relations; we have employee relations—without a third party," claimed Boreham. Plants were located in small towns (except for the St. Louis location). Although Baldor's wages and benefits were about half those of unionized industrial laborers, the wages were considered high when compared to other small-town employers. Even during the difficult years of 1983 to 1986, employees were maintained and large-scale layoffs were avoided. Baldor's stable work environment made it a highly desirable company to work for, and company turnover was low.

Financial Position.   The company was in a strong position as evidenced by the financial statements (Exhibits 27.11 and 27.12). According to R. L. Qualls, executive vice president of finance, "Over the past several years, we have been able to essentially finance all of our operating needs out of the cash flow of the company." (See Exhibit 27.13.)

Record sales were achieved in 1987 amounting to $200.1 million—an increase of 10.2 percent over 1986. "The 1987 increase in sales growth is about double the annual growth rate we experienced in the 1983 to 1986 period," stated Qualls.

The company maintained a conservative capital position. Long-term obligations were 15 percent of total capitalization on December 31, 1982—down from 18 percent in 1981. The ratio was reduced to 7.5 percent at the end of 1987. No new long-term financing was sought in 1987. Exhibit 27.14 presents a 10-year summary of important financial data for Baldor. Exhibit 27.15 shows the changes in Baldor's financial position, and Exhibit 27.16 provides a statement of stockholders' equity.

Penetration of International Markets.   For many years at Baldor, international sales were handled by an export management company. In 1982, when sales were dropping in the United States, Baldor completely changed its method of marketing to foreign countries. Each international market was studied individually, rather than collectively as in the past, to determine the best method of distribution. As a result, Baldor established representatives in many targeted countries and sought

EXHIBIT 27.11   Baldor Consolidated Balance Sheets (In thousands)

	December 31, 1986	January 2, 1988
Assets		
Current Assets		
Cash and Cash Equivalents	$ 15,787	$ 12,047
Receivables, Less Allowances of $700,000 and $640,000, Respectively	31,989	35,000
Inventories		
Finished Products	27,564	31,445
Work In-Process	7,015	7,522
Raw Material	16,577	17,129
	51,156	56,126
LIFO Valuation Adjustment (Deduction)	(15,762)	(18,051)
	35,394	38,075
Other Current Assets	3,543	89,315
Total Current Assets	86,713	89,315
Other Assets	3,682	3,004
Property, Plant, and Equipment		
Land and Improvements	1,907	1,922
Buildings and Improvements	12,575	13,070
Machinery and Equipment	63,740	70,932
Allowances for Depreciation and Amortization (Deduction)	(31,985)	(38,477)
	46,237	47,447
Total Assets	$136,632	$139,766
Liabilities and Stockholders' Equity		
Current Liabilities		
Accounts Payable	$ 6,724	$ 7,350
Employee Compensation	1,808	2,771
Profit Sharing	1,589	1,419
Anticipated Warranty Costs	2,300	2,250
Other Accrued Expenses	4,021	7,594
Income Taxes	2,906	
Current Maturities of Long-Term Obligation	1,030	1,050
Total Current Liabilities	20,378	22,434
Long-Term Obligations	8,808	7,743
Deferred Income Taxes	13,185	13,821
Total Liabilities	42,371	43,998
Stockholders' Equity		
Preferred Stock, $.10 Par Value		
Authorized Shares: 5,000,000		
Issued and Outstanding Shares: None		
Common Stock, $.10 par value		
Authorized Shares: 25,000,000		
Issued and Outstanding Shares 1987—6,302,725; 1986—6,249,664 (Less Shares Held in Treasury; 1987—308,776; 1986—142,993)	643	630
Additional Capital	11,314	8,825
Retained Earnings	82,304	86,313
Total Shareholders' Equity	94,261	95,768
Total Liabilities and Shareholders' Equity	$136,632	$139,766

	Year Ended		
	December 31, 1985	December 31, 1986	January 2, 1988
Net Sales	$174,710	$181,656	$200,099
Other Income—Net	987	1,172	1,086
	175,697	182,828	201,185
Cost and Expenses			
Cost of Goods Sold	124,831	131,568	148,240
Selling and Administrative	33,586	35,846	39,335
Profit Sharing	2,016	1,814	1,417
Interest	891	816	745
Restructuring	—	—	4,600
	161,306	170,044	194,337
Earnings before Income Taxes and Cumulative Effect of Accounting Change	14,391	12,784	6,848
Income Taxes	6,200	5,840	2,870
Earnings before Cumulative Effect of Accounting Change	8,191	6,944	3,978
Cumulative Effect of Accounting Change for Income Taxes	—	—	2,970
Net Earnings	$ 8,191	$ 6,944	$ 6,948
Earnings per Common Share			
Earnings before Cumulative Effect of Accounting Change	$1.26	$1.07	$.62
Cumulative Effect of Accounting Change for Income Taxes	—	—	.46
Net Earnings per Common Share	$1.26	$1.07	$1.08
Weighted Average Common Shares Outstanding	6,524,609	6,514,068	6,432,090

EXHIBIT 27.13   Baldor's Cash Flows, 1983–1987

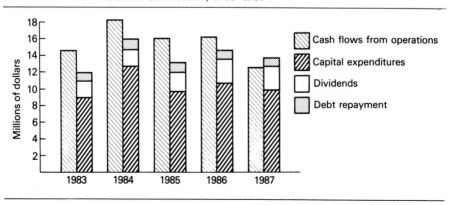

EXHIBIT 27.14 10-Year Summary of Baldor Financial Data (In thousands except per share data)

	Net Sales	Cost of Goods Sold	Net Earnings	Per Share Data		Stockholders' Equity	Total Assets	Long-Term Obligations	Working Capital
				Net Earnings	Dividends				
1987	$200,000	$148,240	$ 6,948	$1.08	$.46	$95,768	$139,766	$ 7,743	$66,881
1986	181,656	131,568	6,944	1.07	.41	94,261	136,632	8,808	66,335
1985	174,710	124,831	8,191	1.26	.37	91,677	136,650	9,834	66,170
1984	183,716	132,067	9,740	1.50	.33	85,887	128,670	10,833	59,706
1983	148,661	107,078	7,756	1.20	.32	77,364	114,742	11,805	54,885
1982	150,031	108,242	8,518	1.33	.32	70,844	106,065	12,610	53,639
1981	160,162	110,425	11,733	1.84	.29	63,470	102,276	13,497	52,217
1980	146,454	102,155	9,409	1.50	.24	52,448	81,973	10,318	43,733
1979	140,018	98,173	9,331	1.50	.19	42,985	74,112	11,210	36,310
1978	120,105	81,120	8,642	1.40	.14	33,929	60,466	7,427	28,462

EXHIBIT 27.15   Baldor Statement of Consolidated Cash Flows (In thousands)

	Year Ended		
	December 31, 1985	December 31, 1986	January 2, 1988
Cash Flows from Operations			
Net Income	$ 8,191	$ 6,944	$ 6,948
Depreciation and Amortization	7,115	8,314	8,890
Deferred Income Taxes	3,427	2,195	636
Cash Flows Provided by (used for) Changes in			
Current Assets and Liabilities (See table below)	(3,554)	(135)	(4,366)
Other—Net	$ 929	(982)	603
Net Cash Provided by Operating Activities	16,108	16,336	12,711
Cash Flows from Investments			
Additions to Property, Plant, Equipment	(9,758)	(10,920)	(9,965)
Cash Flows from Financing			
Reduction of Long-term Obligations	(972)	(995)	(1,045)
Repurchase of Company Stock		(1,785)	(3,119)
Dividends Paid	(2,411)	(2,664)	(2,939)
Stock Option Plans	10	89	617
Net Cash Used in Financing	(3,373)	(5,355)	(6,486)
Net Increase (Decrease) in Cash and Cash			
Equivalents	2,977	61	(3,740)
Cash and Cash Equivalents at the Beginning of the			
Year	12,749	15,726	15,787
Cash and Cash Equivalents at the End of the Year	$15,726	$15,787	$12,047
Cash Flows Provided by (used for) Changes in			
Current Assets and Liabilities			
Accounts Receivable	$ 1,813	$ (1,849)	$ (3,071)
Inventories	(1,937)	3,515	(2,681)
Other Current Assets	(3,165)	2,001	(650)
Accounts Payable	(2,792)	(351)	626
Accrued Expenses	930	(1,975)	4,316
Income Taxes Payable	1,597	(1,476)	(2,906)
	$ (3,554)	$ (135)	$ (4,366)

representation in others. In 1983, representatives were established in such markets as Latin America, Australia, the United Kingdom, West Germany, the Middle East, and Singapore. By 1987, additional offices were established in the Philippines, Thailand, South Korea, Taiwan, the Netherlands, Brazil, Spain, Austria, France, and Saudi Arabia.

Baldor increased its product capability in the international markets by introducing motors with standards that were interchangeable with those outside the United States. In addition, Baldor increased international advertising and participation in foreign trade shows.

EXHIBIT 27.16   Statements of Consolidated Stockholders' Equity (In thousands)

| | Common Stock | | Additional | Retained | |
	Shares	Amount	Capital	Earnings	Total
Balance January 1, 1985	6,516	$652	$12,991	$72,244	$85,887
Stock Option Plans	1		10		10
Net Earnings				8,191	8,191
Common Stock Dividends—$.37 per share				(2,411)	(2,411)
Balance December 31, 1985	6,517	652	13,001	78,024	91,677
Repurchase of Common Stock	(91)	(9)	(1,776)		(1,785)
Stock Option Plans	4		89		89
Net Earnings				6,944	6,944
Common Stock Dividends—$.41 per share				(2,664)	(2,664)
Balance December 31, 1986	6,430	643	11,314	82,304	94,261
Repurchase of Common Stock	(160)	(16)	(3,103)		(3,119)
Stock Option Plans (Net of Shares Exchanged)	33	3	614		617
Net Earnings				6,948	6,948
Common Stock Dividends—$.46 per share				(2,939)	(2,939)
Balance January 2, 1988	6,303	$630	$ 8,825	$86,313	$95,768

In 1987, international sales represented 10 percent of Baldor's sales (Exhibit 27.17). According to Boreham, "Our export business is now growing at about twice the rate of our domestic business and we believe that can continue. Our goal is to aim for 20 percent. We have sales offices pretty well around the world."

EXHIBIT 27.17   Baldor's International Sales

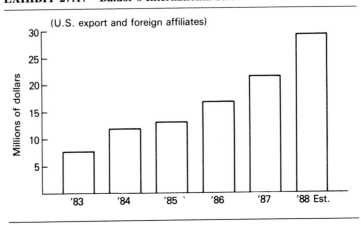

BALDOR LOOKS TO THE FUTURE

The company was extremely successful in differentiating its products from competitors by offering energy-efficient motors at competitive prices and diversifying its product line to include electronic servomotors and starters. Moving from the number five position to the number three position seemed to validate the company's commitment to satisfying customers with a quality product. "Is the number one position an unreasonable goal for Baldor?" questioned Greg. "What would it take to move to the number two position?"

Greg knew there were several options open to Baldor to aggressively pursue the leading position in the market. The electric motor market continued to offer opportunities because many small competitors had not been able to completely serve the market. A major competitor, Westinghouse, had dropped out of the market, and others were having difficulty competing. New products could be developed to meet the needs of new markets, which have been projected to grow rapidly, and international markets presented good opportunities. The lines between motors, controls, and the devices they control have blurred; thus, Baldor had the opportunity for further diversification into areas of computers or robotics.

Greg Kowert wondered which one or what combination of opportunities he should recommend for the continued growth of Baldor. He supposed he should start with a review of the electric motor industry.

_____ CASE 28 _____

The Electric Motor Industry

The U.S. electric motor industry was divided into two primary segments—industrial motors and consumer, or appliance, motors. A few of the big manufacturers, like General Electric (GE) and Westinghouse, supplied both markets. Some producers, such as Baldor, made only industrial motors. Still others specialized in consumer motors.

This industry note was prepared by Peter M. Ginter and Linda E. Swayne as a basis for class discussion rather than to illustrate either effective or ineffective handling of an administrative situation. Used with permission from Peter M. Ginter.

The industrial/consumer distinction was ordinarily used to identify the difference between motors made in extremely high volume (usually fractional hp consumer market motors) and those usually manufactured in lower volume (higher hp motors designed for special and heavy usage). Generally, consumer motors were made with less durable, lower-quality parts, while industrial motors were manufactured for greater durability and more rugged conditions.

KEY COMPETITORS

There were approximately 340 companies in the United States involved in the production of motors. In a 1981 company study, the top three companies in the industry accounted for over 50 percent of the industry's sales, while the top 11 companies accounted for approximately 80 percent of the industry's sales. Exhibit 28.1 illustrates electric motor sales comparisons for the top 11 companies.

The electric motor industry was a growing industry with strong competitors including many of the best-known companies in the United States (such as GE and Westinghouse). To a great degree, the relative strengths of competitors helped to maintain high-quality products. One measure of this quality was the industry's ability to export four times as many motors as was imported in the 1980s. The financial position and operating results of most of the top companies in the industry were very strong (Exhibit 28.2).

EXHIBIT 28.1   Estimated Electric Motor Sales for the Industry's Leading Firms

Company	1969		1981		
	Sales (Motor Only)	Rank	Sales (Motor Only)	Rank	Motor Percent of Total Sales
General Electric	519	1	1,200	1	4
Emerson (Including USEM)	285	3	700	2	20
Westinghouse	353	2	450	3	5
Exxon (Reliance)	122	4	290	4	n/a
W.W. Grainger	75	5	265	5	25
Baldor	18	11	151	6	94
Franklin Electric	30	9	150	7	94
Siemens-Allis (A-C)	70	6	125	8	n/a
Gould (Century)	60	7	120	9	7
Litton Industries (LA)	40	8	100	10	n/a
Marathon Electric	25	10	80	11	n/a

n/a = not available.
Source: Baldor Electric Company.

EXHIBIT 28.2 Operating Results for Selected Motor Firms, 1981

	Total Assets	Total Net Worth	Current Ratio	Long-Term Debt to Total Capital	Net Earnings to Total Sales	Return on Average Total Assets	Return on Average Equity
General Electric	$20,942	$ 9,128	1.2	.104	.061	.083	.190
Emerson	2,201	1,386	2.4	.106	.080	.130	.210
Westinghouse	8,316	2,837	1.03	.180	.047	.058	.163
Exxon	62,931	28,517	1.3	.153	.049	.093	.206
W.W. Grainger	472	335	2.2	.041	.065	.119	.180
Baldor Electric	103	63	3.3	.175	.073	.127	.202
Franklin Electric	98	53	2.3	.263	.041	.074	.141
Siemens-Allis (A-C)	1,594	656	1.5	.305	—	—	—
Gould (Century)	1,597	810	2.3	.299	.052	.061	.119

General Electric

General Electric was the industry leader and the only company manufacturing a full line of electric motors. The company was the single largest exporter of motors and generators, although its motor sales accounted for less than 10 percent of GE's total sales. General Electric was respected in the industry as a very well managed company producing quality products.

Emerson Electric

Emerson Electric was second in terms of motor sales and maintained a rapid growth rate over the past five years. Emerson's sales comprised approximately two-thirds of consumer motors distributed through Emerson Motor division and one-third of industrial motors sold through U.S. Electrical Motors.

Westinghouse

Westinghouse, third in sales among the motor manufacturers, had a broad line of electric motors. However, its growth rate was below the average of other leaders in the industry. Baldor's management speculated that the lack of growth was likely due to a number of other concerns that diverted management attention from motor sales in the past few years. (Westinghouse abandoned electric motor production in 1986.)

Reliance Electric

Reliance, a subsidiary of Exxon since 1979, maintained a good reputation regarding the quality of their electric motors, and continued to be a well-respected manufacturer of industrial motors and a tough competitor in the industry.

W.W. Grainger

Grainger's expertise was as a distributor of products to industry through its stores, its catalog (the "Blue Book"), and direct to original equipment manufacturers (OEMs). Motors represented about 25 percent of Grainger's sales.

Baldor Electric Company

Baldor focused on energy-efficient industrial electric motors sold to distributors and OEMs. Since 94 percent of its sales were electric motors, Baldor was committed to the electric motor industry.

ELECTRIC MOTORS

Rather than being used for one purpose by a single market, electric motors are used in many types of machinery and equipment by both consumers and industrial users throughout the world. The electric motor markets could be segmented into five major product categories:

- Fractional horsepower motors—motors under one horsepower
- Integral horsepower motors and generators
- Prime motor sets—internal combustion engine/generator combinations
- Motor generator sets—electric motor/generator combinations
- Other equipment (servos, synchros, resolvers, parts, and accessories)

The electric motor is a rotating machine used for the conversion of electrical energy to mechanical power. Motors can meet a variety of service requirements such as running, starting, holding, or stopping a load.

Electric motors were the sole method of converting electrical energy to mechanical power. No matter what the source of energy—coal, oil, gas, or nuclear—an electric motor was utilized for conversion of the electric energy to mechanical power. Advantages of electrical power were ease of transportation over great distances and ease of control compared to other forms of energy. In 1986, 30 percent of all energy was converted to electrical power and 64 percent of that generated electricity was used to power motor-driven equipment.

The basic science used in operation of the electric motor has remained the same since its invention early in the 19th century. There have, however, been substantial refinements in manufacturing processes and size of the components. Exhibit 28.3 summarizes the different types of AC- and DC-powered motors and indicates the many possible market-niche strategies available to manufacturers of electric motors.

Induction motors accounted for approximately 90 percent of the sales in the fractional and integral horsepower ratings. This type of motor was the simplest and most rugged. The stator "induced" an electric current in the rotor, which had no wiring, resulting in a motor that was less expensive and less subject to failure than other types of motors.

The major variations for induction motors related to the construction of the rotor (squirrel cage or wound rotor) and the operating current (single-phase or poly-phase). Most industrial systems were three-phase AC current while most consumer applications used single phase. However, the motor could be designed to run on either single- or poly-phase current.

Squirrel cage rotors utilized a laminated steel core fitted with slots into which conductors were placed as the rotor. Wound rotor units used a copper winding in the rotor assembly. Wound rotor units were more expensive and usually limited to variable-speed applications (electronic control devices).

Synchronous motors were used in applications where constant operating speed was required—the AC motor operated in perfect synchronization with the frequency of the line current. They could be constructed to run on single-phase or poly-phase current. Integral horsepower synchronous motors were constructed with a rotor that had to be supplied with DC current from an external source.

EXHIBIT 28.3 Summary of Motor Types

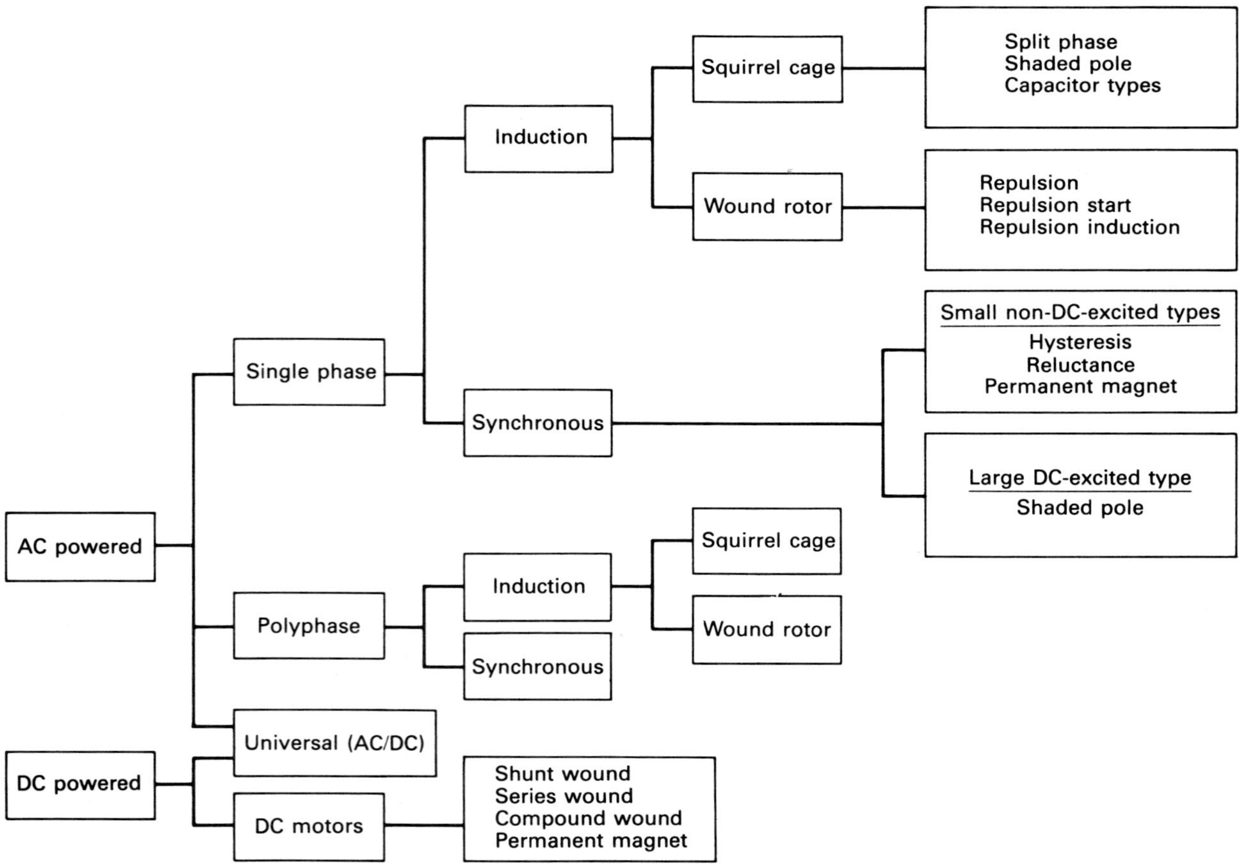

Split phase Shaded pole Capacitor types	— Squirrel cage — Induction ┐
Repulsion Repulsion start Repulsion induction	— Wound rotor ┘ Single phase — AC powered
Small non-DC-excited types Hysteresis Reluctance Permanent magnet	— Synchronous ┘
Large DC-excited type Shaded pole	

Squirrel cage — Induction ┐
Wound rotor ┘ Polyphase — AC powered
Synchronous ┘

Universal (AC/DC) ┐

Shunt wound
Series wound
Compound wound
Permanent magnet — DC motors — DC powered

Source: Research Group/Predicast, Inc.

560

Commutator motors produced rotary motion through the interaction of two stationary electromagnetic fields. The commutator functioned as a rotating switch that reversed the direction of current flow to the armature coil (or rotor) every half-revolution of the motor. Commutator motors could be run on either AC or DC current, although most were of the DC type.

DC motors had quick signal response, could be easily operated at different speeds, and could be given precise speed-torque relationships. Applications using DC motors included those that had precise control characteristics, such as instrumentation, material handling and automation equipment, computer output devices, and word processing equipment.

ELECTRIC MOTOR MARKET GROWTH

Electric motors are fundamental to a modern industrialized society. The 1980s held many changes for the United States as well as all the world economies. Specifically, emphasis was expected to increase on factory automation, electronics, and conservation of resources, which suggested greater demand for efficient electric motors. Thus, it appeared that the pace of change in the electric motor industry would accelerate.

Sales of motors increased from 107 million units in 1963 to over 300 million in 1978—an annual growth rate of over 7 percent. This growth exceeded the less than 5 percent growth in U.S. production of motors because of expanding mechanization and use of motorized equipment in all sectors of the economy. Although the prices of electric motors declined due to improved designs, materials, and manufacturing processes during this period, price increases were rapid since the mid-1970s primarily because of higher rates of inflation. Growth patterns by motor type and by selected industries for electric motors are summarized in Exhibits 28.4 and 28.5.

EXHIBIT 28.4   Market Growth by Motor Type (In percent)

Motor Type	Average Annual Growth 1970–1975	Average Annual Growth 1975–1980	Average Annual Growth 1970–1980
Fractional Horsepower Motors	5.7	16.1	10.8
Integral Horsepower Motors, Excluding Land Transportation	11.5	9.6	10.5
Land Transportation Motors	12.1	10.3	11.2
Prime Mover Generator Sets, except Steam or Hydraulic Turbine	16.3	12.2	14.2
Motor Generator Sets and Other Rotating Equipment	−0.4	12.5	5.9

Source: Business Trend Analysts.

EXHIBIT 28.5   Growth in the Purchase of Motors by Selected Industries (In millions)

Industry	1972	1977[a]
Refrigeration and Heating Equipment	$344.5	$593.9
Household Laundry Equipment	94.1	141.8
Household Refrigerators and Freezers	76.8	98.7
Construction Machinery	29.2	88.5
Electric Housewares and Fans	40.8	58.6
Electric Computing Equipment	34.1	55.2
Motor Vehicle Parts and Accessories	9.0	41.3
Blowers and Fans	23.4	37.9
Special Industry Machinery	25.1	37.4
Mining Machinery	12.4	35.4
Machine Tools, Metal Cutting Types	20.6	33.3
Household Appliances	20.5	31.0
Household Vacuum Cleaners	7.6	28.3
Office Machinery and Typewriters	6.0	28.2
Shipbuilding and Repair	9.8	26.0
General Industrial Machinery	12.5	23.5
Conveyors and Conveying Equipment	9.2	22.1
Industrial Trucks and Tractors	10.6	19.3
Printing Trades Machinery	8.0	16.5
Woodworking Machinery	8.6	16.1
Household Cooking Equipment	6.5	15.9
Machine Tools, Metal Forming Types	7.1	15.3
Measuring and Controlling Devices	2.2	14.6
Hoists, Cranes, and Monorails	8.4	13.6
Lawn and Garden Equipment	1.6	12.2
Elevators and Moving Stairways	11.7	12.0
Radio and TV Sets	13.0	11.7
Power-Driven Hand Tools	10.3	11.6
Engineering and Scientific Instruments	5.1	11.0
Food Products Machinery	11.2	10.6
Metal-Working Machinery	4.0	10.1

[a] Preliminary figures.
Source: Business Trend Analysts; Census of Manufacturers.

Projected growth by motor type indicated that projected real growth was largest for integral horsepower motors (approximately 10 percent annual growth), whereas growth for fractional horsepower motors was projected to be flat, and other motor type segments were expected to have moderate growth (Exhibit 28.6). Small motors, servo motors, and other motors used in factory automation were expected to grow to approximately $200 million to $400 million in the 1980s.

Demand for electric motors was projected to increase across all categories. Relative growth for selected electric motor markets is illustrated in Exhibit 28.7.

EXHIBIT 28.6 Projected Growth in Motor Sales by Motor Type, 1980–1990ᵃ (In percent)

Integral Horsepower Motors, Excluding Land Transportation	19.3
Land Transportation Motors	17.2
Prime-Mover Generator Sets, Except Steam or Hydraulic Turbine	15.0
Fractional Horsepower Motors	9.9
Motor Generator Sets and Other Rotating Equipment	7.8

[a] Includes estimated 10 percent annual inflation.
Source: Business Trend Analysts.

EXHIBIT 28.7 Relative Growth for Selected Motor Markets

Item	1978	1985	1990
Manufacturing Production Index	147	193	230
Million Motors/Index Point	1.82	1.99	2.12
Motor, Generator Sales (Million units)	267.2	383.5	488.0
Fabricated Metals	4.5	5.8	6.6
Machinery and Equipment	34.5	40.5	45.9
Electrical and Electronics	42.0	62.7	73.3
Transport Equipment	34.4	40.7	46.2
Instruments	5.6	8.1	10.1
Toys, Games, and Other Manufacturing	43.3	64.0	76.4
Interplant Transfers	102.8	161.7	229.5
Average Cost per Unit	16.5	26.5	42.6
Motor, Generator Sales (Million dollars)	$4,403.9	$10,170.0	$20,780.0
Fabricated Metals	101.9	203	290
Machinery and Equipment	1,823.1	3,854	5,856
Electrical and Electronics	620.5	1,427	2,250
Transport Equipment	455.7	1,266	6,772
Instruments	158.2	320	485
Toys, Games, and Other Manufacturing	145.6	270	392
Interplant Transfers	1,098.9	2,820	4,735

INDUSTRY DYNAMICS

The electric motor industry was capital intensive with substantial investments required in facilities, machinery, and tooling. The required high investments created formidable entry barriers. In addition, the industry was of a technical nature requiring sophisticated engineering skills. As a result, only one new company entered the top 11 competitors in the industry over the past 15 years. (This company was founded by a past owner of another one of the top companies.) Finally, the sunk costs of electric motor production also made it difficult for a company to exit the market.

Major factors affecting the electric motor industry included rising energy costs, electric vehicles, factory automation, and technological evolution. Rising energy costs resulted in an emphasis by customers for increased product quality and energy efficiency. Energy cost increases were projected by the federal government to continue for the foreseeable future. Many manufacturers were offering higher efficiency electric motors at premium prices to meet this demand. It is estimated that energy-efficient motors accounted for 11 percent of the 5 to 20 horsepower market, compared to 1 percent in 1977.

The difference of a few percentage points in energy efficiency can result in a complete payback of the motor's purchase cost within the first year for larger horsepower units. Exhibit 28.8 illustrates the possible savings with an energy-efficient 50-horsepower motor versus an average standard motor based on different hours of operation. Because of such cost savings, many users were considering replacing their less efficient motors with new, energy-efficient electric motors.

Forecasts were for electric vehicles to be used increasingly for consumer and industrial transportation. Increased usage would result from rising costs of fossil fuel, improved battery technology, and operating efficiencies of electric vehicles.

Factory automation was creating a whole new market for electric motors. This new field, electronic motors, included the servomotors and controls used for the movement and precise positioning of robots, machine tools, and factory vehicles. This particular portion of the industry was in its infancy and included many small companies. The most successful of these small electric motor companies would be subject to acquisition by the larger firms in the industry.

Technological evolution became important not only to the markets served but also to the individual companies within the motor industry. Automation of the electric motor manufacturer's factories, taking advantage of the new production technologies, would be critical to the companies' abilities to compete as low-cost producers.

EXHIBIT 28.8   Possible Savings through Energy-Efficient Motors

	Annual Savings 50-hp Motor		
Power Cost per KWH	40-Hour Week (1 Shift)	80-Hour Week (2 Shifts)	168-Hour Week (Continuous)
.02	$ 72.07	$144.15	$ 302.71
.04	144.15	288.30	605.42
.07	216.22	432.45	908.14
.08	288.30	576.60	1,210.85
.10	360.37	720.74	1,513.56
	50 Weeks per Year		

KEY FACTORS FOR SUCCESS IN THE ELECTRIC MOTOR INDUSTRY

Several factors were essential if a firm was to have long-term success in the electric motor industry. The key factors appeared to include:

- Market share
- Product differentiation
- Product quality and reliability
- Price/low-cost production
- Distribution
- Research and development
- Financial strength

Market Share

Market share was an important factor for success in the electric motor industry because the industry was maturing, and consolidation was quite likely. Firms that did not command significant share of the total market or were not firmly entrenched in a particular segment of the market would be subject to acquisition as competition became more intense.

Product Differentiation

Many of the larger firms attempted to compete in a number of distinct markets, whereas the smaller firms generally tended to concentrate on developing a special niche. Most of the highly successful firms in the industry segmented the market and developed different products to serve as many of the segments as possible. Examples of successful market segmentation included Franklin Electric—submersible pump motors; W.W. Grainger—unique distribution through catalog and company-owned stores; and Baldor—product availability and energy-efficient motors.

Although it was possible and perhaps even essential to be successful in the short run by serving specialized markets, broad market coverage would better assure long-term success, as the company was not dependent on the contingencies of a single market.

Product Quality and Reliability

Because much of the industry produced motors for the industrial market, durability and reliability were quite important. Quality issues included the mechanical and electrical functions, raw materials used, durability, efficiency, and care (maintenance) during manufacturing. Company image concerning quality was important in the consumer market as well.

Price/Low-Cost Production

In a mature industry, the low-cost producers are usually the most successful. As an industry matures, competition increases (the electric motor industry had 340 companies), and it becomes more difficult to provide a unique product. Therefore, as the technology of market segments stabilizes and products become relatively standardized, price becomes a major consideration. To offer low prices, manufacturers must be low-cost producers.

Distribution

The electric motor producer had to have well-established distribution systems in order to meet customer needs. Important factors in electric motor distribution were:

- Availability—the ability to deliver immediately from stock
- Delivery reliability—the ability to consistently meet delivery lead times
- Service—a close, friendly relationship with customers (primarily OEMs)

Research and Development

In this dynamic environment, modernized manufacturing methods and technical product developments were needed to remain competitive. Therefore, firms in the industry had to seriously engage in both process and product research and development.

Financial Strength

Adequate financial strength was required for companies in the industry to remain competitive and respond to possible strategic moves by other companies. Financial support was necessary for quality assurance programs, distribution system needs, and research and development requirements.

_____ CASE 29 _____

Rubbermaid

During 1990, we celebrated the 70th anniversary of the founding of the Company. It has progressed through seven decades of successful growth from the results of innovation, diversification, the company's emphasis on quality, and the contributions of extremely dedicated associates. Those same strengths position Rubbermaid to continue its success into the 1990s.

Today, Rubbermaid is a growing and vital enterprise. We have modern manufacturing facilities, aggressive plans for the future and, most importantly, experienced management with over 9,000 skilled and committed associates throughout the organization. We are confident that the Company will continue to perform vigorously and effectively and achieve another successful year in 1991.[1]

Stanley C. Gault

RUBBERMAID TODAY

Rubbermaid, under the highly respected leadership of chairman and chief executive officer Stanley Gault, enjoyed a banner year in 1990. In keeping with its corporate goals of increasing sales and earnings annually, the firm reported record net sales of $1.53 billion, a 6 percent increase over the $1.45 billion of 1989. Record net earnings were $143.5 million, or $1.80 per share, versus $125.0 million net earnings and $1.57 per share in 1989, an increase of 15 percent.

Sales for the fourth quarter of 1990 increased 13 percent to $382 million from the $337 million of 1989's comparable quarter. Earnings were $33.0 million, or 41 cents per share, a 15 percent increase over the $28.7 million, or 36 cents per share of last year. The fourth-quarter results represented the 40th consecutive quarter in which both sales and earnings increased over those of the prior year's period. Since 1980, Rubbermaid's sales quadrupled, and earnings rose sixfold.

This case was prepared by Bernard A. Deitzer, Alan G. Krigline, and Thomas C. Peterson as a basis for class discussion rather than to illustrate either effective or ineffective handling of an administrative situation. Copyright © 1991 by Bernard A. Deitzer. Used with permission from Bernard A. Deitzer.

[1] *Rubbermaid Annual Report*, Rubbermaid Incorporated, Wooster, Ohio, 1990, p. 5.

Consistent with its announced overall growth objectives, Rubbermaid acquired two companies in 1990, and entered into a joint venture with a European housewares company, confirming its plan to expand and diversify its rubber and plastic products in advance of the European Community (EC) markets of 1992.

COMPANY HISTORY

During 1990, Rubbermaid celebrated the 70th anniversary of the founding of the company. It was early May 1920 that the Wooster Rubber Company began manufacturing its first product—the Sunshine brand of toy balloons.

In the mid-1920s, Horatio B. Ebert and Errett M. Grable, executives of the Wear-Ever Division of the Aluminum Company of America, purchased Wooster Rubber as a personal investment. They then engaged Clyde C. Gault, Stanley Gault's father, who had been general manager of Wooster Rubber, to continue managing the business. By 1928, the company had prospered sufficiently to build a new factory and office building. However, the great depression of the 1930s caused sales to plummet.

First Housewares Product—The Rubber Dustpan

Meanwhile, James R. Caldwell of New England, who had developed a rubber dustpan, was forced into selling it door to door, because department store buyers refused to purchase because, they said, "We have no calls for a one dollar rubber dustpan. We can sell metal dustpans for 39 cents." Persistence paid off, and eventually Caldwell, the door-to-door entrepreneur, succeeded in convincing department store buyers to carry rubber dustpans. He adopted the brand name Rubbermaid and developed three other rubber items—a drainboard mat to protect countertops, a soap dish, and a sink stopper.

During this period, Ebert, while calling on New England department stores, saw and became interested in Caldwell's rubber housewares products. Subsequently the two combined businesses, and in July 1934 the manufacture of rubber housewares products began at the Wooster Rubber Company. The lowly dustpan had arrived.

The War Years

During World War II, civilian use of rubber was frozen by the government. The company's consumer business became in effect nonexistent. Survival came in the form of subcontracts to produce components for self-sealing fuel tanks for military aircraft in addition to life jackets and medical tourniquets.

The New Beginning

Following the war, Rubbermaid resumed the production and sale of rubber housewares products. Because coloring materials were not yet available, all products were produced in black. In 1950, the company established an operation in Canada and in 1955 issued its first public offering of stock, trading in the over-the-counter market.

The first plastic product, a dishpan, was introduced in 1956. In 1958, a salesman was assigned to call on hotels and motels to sell doormats and bathtub mats. Thus was the beginning of today's successful institutional business, established as Rubbermaid Commercial Products in 1967.

Wooster Rubber to Rubbermaid

In 1957, the firm officially changed its corporate name to Rubbermaid to capitalize on an already widely accepted brand name. When Caldwell retired as president in 1958, Donald E. Noble, who had joined Rubbermaid in 1941, was elected chief executive officer, serving first as president and later as chairman of the board. During Noble's 39 years of service, new businesses were entered, physical facilities were expanded, and an operation in West Germany was established. Rubbermaid's rite of passage from a small, rural Ohio company to a multinational firm with one of America's best-known brand names was under-way.[2]

THE BUSINESS

Rubbermaid operated in a single line of business: the manufacture and sale of plastic and rubber products for the consumer and institutional markets. It manufactured and marketed over 3,000 products worldwide, including kitchenware; laundry and bath accessories; microwave ovenware; toys; and home horticulture, office, foodservice, health care, and industrial maintenance products.

Rubbermaid owned one of the largest plastic and rubber housewares production facilities in the world: some 1.6 million square feet spread over a single floor. Half a million housewares products of all sizes, shapes, and colors were processed daily from plastic resin. With products as ordinary as Rubbermaid's, it was critical that the line always appeared up to date.

Corporate headquarters as well as the housewares products and specialty products divisions remained in Wooster, Ohio. Wooster's population was approximately 21,000 and it was located some 50 miles from downtown Cleveland.

Redesigned versions of the early and ordinary dustpan along with drain-board mats, sink mats, and soap dishes remained in the company's extended portfolio of rubber and plastic products. However, ordinary, colorless kitchen utensils were transformed into appealing, colorful, upscale housewares.

By 1990, with a brand name highly recognized and associated with quality household products, the maker of toy balloons, and later, dustpans had grown to over a billion-dollar firm with international ranking and acclaim for its spectacular

[2] *Rubbermaid Annual Report*, 1989, pp. 10–11.

successes by industry analysts. Stanley Gault was regularly hailed by the media for his stunningly superior leadership, as Rubbermaid was second only to Merck as one of *Fortune*'s most admired U.S. corporations.

RUBBERMAID'S MANAGEMENT

Stanley Carleton Gault, 65, chairman of the board, chief executive officer, and director, joined Rubbermaid in 1980. He had just ended an illustrious 31-year career at General Electric (GE), where he served as senior vice president and sector executive of the industrial products and components sector. He decided to leave GE when he realized that he was being passed over in the process of determining GE's next CEO.[3]

Walter W. Williams, 57, director, president, and chief operating officer, joined Rubbermaid in 1987. Similar to Gault, Williams left a 31-year career at General Electric, where he was senior vice president of corporate marketing. Williams' strong marketing skills were considered by Gault to be critical to Rubbermaid's future success.

Wolfgang R. Schmitt, 47, executive vice president, began his Rubbermaid career in 1966 as a management trainee after graduating from Otterbein College in Westerville, Ohio. He held numerous top marketing and management assignments before assuming his current position.

RUBBERMAID'S CORPORATE GOALS

Over the years Rubbermaid was widely recognized as an innovative company. The corporatewide drive for innovation apparently mirrored Gault's efforts to implement corporate growth objectives and to expand the corporation's markets. Rubbermaid's new product goal was to have 30 percent of sales each year come from products not in the line five years earlier. In confirmation of this, over 1,000 new products were introduced between 1985 and 1990.

Another Rubbermaid goal was to continue to be the lowest-cost, highest-quality producer in the household products industry. During the period from 1981–90, over $612 million was invested in the business' facilities to increase productivity, develop new products, and achieve world-class manufacturing status.

In 1989, Gault set a challenging goal of achieving $2 billion in annual sales by 1992, just five years after Rubbermaid had reached sales of $1 billion. Gault at that time predicted:

---

[3] Actually this was a return home for Gault, a graduate of the College of Wooster. His father Clyde was one of the founders of the Wooster Rubber Company. After six years, however, the elder Gault sold his ownership and remained until his retirement as general manager.

With a growth rate of 15 percent a year we can reach that goal. We have entered 1989 with existing product offerings supported by operating plans and merchandising programs designed to produce another record year. We expect to record favorable sales and earnings comparisons through 1989.[4]

Rubbermaid was expected to reach the $2 billion mark by the last quarter of 1992. Gault believed it could do so simply by following its present course. "We project our growth to come from a combination of areas. We'll see growth occur in the core product lines of Rubbermaid's domestic business, the effort under way to grow business internationally, from new product development in all our businesses, new product categories being added to existing businesses, and growth through a selective acquisitions program."[5]

Essentially Rubbermaid summarized its mission as an attempt to offer exceptional value to its customers with high-quality and cost-competitive products, excellent distribution, and a highly focused customer mentality. It was a business, according to management, whose fundamental corporate strengths served it effectively over the years with widely recognized and respected brand names, high-quality innovative products, strategic marketing direction, efficient modern manufacturing facilities, an enviable financial performance record, dedicated associates, and a focused direction for growth and profitability.[6]

RUBBERMAID'S OBJECTIVES FOR THE 1990s

1. The corporate objective was to increase sales, earnings, and earnings per share 15 percent per year, while achieving a 20 percent return on shareholders' equity.

2. It was also the company's objective to pay approximately 30 percent of current year's earnings as dividends to shareholders while using the remainder to fund future growth opportunities.

3. Each year, 30 percent of its sales was projected to come from new products introduced over the previous five years. It planned to enter an entirely new market every 12 to 18 months.

4. The objective for customers and consumers was to offer the best value possible. It intended to provide the highest-quality products that were reasonably priced, a continuous flow of new products, and exceptional service to its customers.

5. The company aimed to treat all constituents fairly and consider the interests of associates as individuals.

6. The company aimed to be an environmentally responsible corporate citizen.[7]

Rubbermaid had a number of fundamental strengths that would benefit the organization in achieving its objectives. Those strengths are outlined in Exhibit 29.1.

[4] *Rubbermaid Annual Report*, 1990, p. 9.
[5] *Rubbermaid Annual Report*, 1986, pp. 4–6.
[6] *Wall Street Transcript*, March 23, 1987, p. 84964.
[7] *Rubbermaid Annual Report*, 1990, p. 10.

EXHIBIT 29.1   Rubbermaid's Fundamental Strengths

Rubbermaid's growth is the result of seven fundamental strengths:

1. A focused direction to maximize the value of Rubbermaid for its shareholders. Each operating unit is well-positioned in attractive markets with quality products, has a strong organization and a well-defined mission for growth.
2. The strength of its franchise with customers and consumers. Its brand names are recognized and respected within each market segment it serves.
3. A reputation for quality products. All of its brand names connote quality and value within their respective markets.
4. An emphasis on new products. Its goal is to have 30 percent of sales each year come from products which were not in the line five years earlier.
5. Marketing, sales, and manufacturing capabilities. These organizations are among the strongest, best qualified in each of the industries it serves.
6. Financial performance and strength. Rubbermaid enjoys a strong financial position with very little debt. It has the capability to pursue its business objectives successfully.
7. Human resources. Capable and dedicated people throughout the organization have demonstrated their ability to perform impressively and consistently.

Source: Rubbermaid *Annual Report,* 1987, p. 9.

GAULT'S INITIAL STRATEGY

When Stanley C. Gault became CEO of Rubbermaid in 1980, revenues were climbing steadily, and, although sales totaled $341 million, earnings had dipped to $21 million. The company was facing the severe pressures and challenges of the 1980s.[8]

Prior to Gault's arrival, Rubbermaid employed a strategy of efficiency. The company was in a slow-growth business with increasing overhead and a declining rate of productivity and whose personnel, according to management, apparently had grown comfortable and unaccustomed to change. "Our product development lagged, our retail customers claimed we were arrogant, and our profit margins had fallen," summarized the new CEO.[9]

Accepting the challenge, Gault immediately restructured the firm and its in-place management. "You have to set the tone and pace, define objectives and strategies and demonstrate through personal example what you expect from others," advised Gault.[10] He reshuffled, hired, and fired. Ten percent of all salaried personnel were abruptly dismissed. Some two years later, only 2 of 172 Rubbermaid managers still held their original jobs.

[8] Kenneth Labich, "The Seven Keys to Business Leadership," *Fortune*, October 24, 1988, p. 60.
[9] Patricia Sellers, "Does the CEO Really Matter?" *Fortune*, April 22, 1991, p. 86.
[10] Labich, "Seven Keys to Business Leadership."

The housewares and commercial products divisions generated over 96 percent of total corporate income; the remaining units were "six weak soldiers." All operations were subsequently and rigorously evaluated to determine their strengths, weaknesses, and opportunities. Early on, Gault dramatically informed the organization that he was aiming for a 15 percent average annual growth in sales, profits, and earnings per share, plus $1 billion in sales revenues by 1990.[11]

Rubbermaid Restructured

The CEO's first strategic step in restructuring was to review Rubbermaid's eight lines of business and to excise half of them. One casualty was its in-home party plan company. Gault perceived that current demographics and the changing lifestyles of today's working women allowed little time for after-hours housewares parties. Furthermore, Rubbermaid did not have a presence commensurate with its competitive archrival, Tupperware.

In addition, Rubbermaid subsequently sold its domestic car mat and auto accessories business. Gault judged auto accessories to be a commodity business with stiff price and volume elastic competition where automakers tended to pressure suppliers.[12]

Rubbermaid's Acquisition Strategy

Gault's relentless and unyielding commitment to controlled growth earmarked the firm's approach to expansion. Rubbermaid consistently demonstrated an ability to expand its existing businesses. Both new product flow and new market entries thrived via opportunistic and related acquisitions. Gault deliberately looked for small companies that fit, that were number one or number two in their product category, and that could benefit from Rubbermaid's manufacturing and marketing expertise.

Acquisition-minded Gault's first target was Carlan, maker of Con-Tact Brand self-adhesive decorative shelf covering. Later came a vigorous expansion into entirely new markets. In 1982, Rubbermaid's commercial products company entered the burgeoning health care field. Next, Gault expanded into the horticulture and agriculture markets. In 1983, the firm entered the then $300 million microwave cookware business with an intense marketing drive.[13] In 1984, Gault acquired Little Tikes, which allowed the company to enter the preschool toy market. Rubbermaid entered the microcomputer accessories business by acquiring Micro-Computer Accessories Inc., and in 1990 entered the office molded products business by acquiring Elson Industries.

As Gault emphasized, "We are definitely receptive to good acquisition opportunities. We have made numerous acquisitions; they have all been top-notch

[11] Ibid.

[12] James Braham, "The Billion Dollar Dustpan," *Industry Week*, Penton Publishing Company, August 1, 1988, p. 47.

[13] "Special Citations," *Sales and Marketing Magazine*, January 16, 1984, p. 14.

EXHIBIT 29.2   Rubbermaid's Acquisitions and Joint Ventures

1981	Con-Tact Brand self-adhesive decorative coverings
1984	Little Tikes Company—leading quality manufacturer of preschool children's toys
1985	Gott Corporation—high-quality consumer recreational products
1986	SECO Industries—leading manufacturers of maintenance products
1986	MicroComputer Accessories—accessories for the microcomputer market
1987	Viking Brush Limited—household brushes
1987	Little Tikes Company (Ireland) Limited
1987	MicroComputer Accessories Europe S.A.—computer-related accessories
1987	Reynolds Compression—molding facilities of Polymer Engineering
1989	Rubbermaid Allibert (joint venture)—manufactures casual resin furniture for the North American market
1990	Curver Rubbermaid Group, Breda, the Netherlands—(joint venture) manufactures plastics and rubber housewares and resin furniture
1990	EWU AG, Switzerland—producer of floor care supplies and equipment
1990	Eldon Industries—distributor of molded plastic office products and equipment

companies. We want them to be companies that are well managed and where the management will want to stay and be part of the growing Rubbermaid family.''[14] Exhibit 29.2 summarizes Rubbermaid's acquisitions and joint-venture activities.

RUBBERMAID'S GROWTH STRATEGY

Gault strongly believed in developing strategies to control and direct new product activities to meet two types of ambitious growth objectives. The first was incremental growth, which concentrated on doing what Rubbermaid did best— only better. It focused on growth within the company's businesses that was responsive to customer's needs and in turn, provided value to Rubbermaid's customers.

Gault's second approach was leap growth, which involved a higher degree of risk because it created high visibility on the one hand yet high vulnerability on the other. The company won big or lost big. Within these two major classifications, there were eight strategic elements. Four of these applied to incremental growth and four were leap approaches.

Rubbermaid's Incremental Growth Strategies

- To increase the volume of Rubbermaid's existing products. The key to this growth area was in providing value to dealers, distributors, and consumers. The key to value is providing quality, low cost, and service.

[14] *Wall Street Transcript*, April 18, 1988, p. 9116.

- To upscale existing products to meet today's consumer and new design preferences. Upscaling includes introducing new colors to existing lines.
- To extend existing lines to capitalize on product successes, increase retail shelf space, and boost sales volume.
- To expand Rubbermaid's international business as a significant growth opportunity during the 1990s.[15]

Rubbermaid's Leap Growth Strategies

- To develop new products. Rubbermaid's goal is to have at least 30 percent of annual sales coming from new products introduced during the past five years.
- To hone product lines and optimize the number of stock units retained to keep the lines manageable and provide proper customer service levels.
- To enter entirely new markets. This is consistent with a corporate objective to enter a new market every 18 to 24 months.
- To engage in joint ventures or acquisitions to enter new markets by combining the capabilities of a strong outside partner with the many strengths of Rubbermaid.[16]

RUBBERMAID'S STRATEGIES FOR THE 1990s

1. The Company will continue its market-driven approach to product development and marketing, to listen to customers and consumers and effectively respond to the changes in needs, demographics, and lifestyles. This outside-in strategy will help develop new markets and create unique, proprietary products, and programs.

2. To continue to grow using both incremental and leap growth strategies. Incremental growth comes from continuous improvement in all aspects of the business such as line extensions, international expansion, and innovative marketing and sales programs. The leap approach involves new technologies, new market entries, acquisitions, and joint ventures.

3. To continue to invest for future growth and to keep facilities modern and efficient. It is the company's intention to continue to be the lowest cost, highest quality producer in its industry.

4. To continue to build partnerships with customers, suppliers, associates, and communities to enhance the value of Rubbermaid for shareholders and other constituencies.

5. To increase the use of technology in manufacturing and communications, both internally and externally.

6. To continue to pursue world-class status and compete on a global basis.[17]

---

[15] Adapted from remarks by Stanley C. Gault, chairman of the board and chief executive officer, Rubbermaid, before the Conference Board of Canada's 15th Annual Marketing Conference, Hilton International, Toronto, Canada, March 29, 1990.
[16] Ibid.
[17] Ibid., p. 10.

Focus on Quality

Rubbermaid was regularly honored as one of America's most admired corporations. Gault, recognized as among the nation's top 1,000 elite corporate executives, transformed Rubbermaid, a moderately successful firm, into a giant superstar using quality as its hallmark.[18]

The quality and consistency of Rubbermaid's products were aptly matched by the quality and consistency of its management. This could be seen from Rubbermaid's selection to the *Fortune* magazine's annual survey of "America's Most Admired Corporations." The poll, taken from more than 8,000 senior executives, outside directors, and financial analysts, placed Rubbermaid in the number two position. The year 1990 was the sixth consecutive year that the company was selected to be among the top 10, occupying second place in 1987, 1988, and 1990. Rubbermaid was the smallest company ever named to this list. The only other company to appear as consistently on the list was aforementioned Merck, the giant pharmaceutical company.

Indefatigable, Gault did not hesitate to personally phone and placate disgruntled dealers. He never stopped acting as Rubbermaid's top quality controller. Precise and methodical, the hands-on manager visited several stores a week to see how Rubbermaid products were displayed and to inspect the quality of workmanship. If he found an ill fitting lid or wrinkled label, Gault bought the offending goods and then later summoned his senior manager for a lecture. "He gets livid about defects," said Walter W. Williams, the chief operating officer.

When responding to the hint that plastic was once synonymous with junk, Gault launched into an energetic speech on the mixture of his polyethylene and the intricacies of his injection molding. Irrepressible Gault, when comparing his enormously popular garbage cans to flimsier competing versions remarked, "On quality I'm a sonofabitch. No one surpasses our quality." Gault declared of products that do not seem to ever break or wear out, "We use more and better resin. We don't buy any scrap resin. And we use a thicker gauge."[19]

Gault, viewed as a brilliant strategist, paid as much attention to how even simple products looked as he did to the ultraviolent inhibitors in their resins. Sales of big garbage cans jumped 20 percent when he suggested that his design engineer come up with a specific shade of blue instead of chocolate brown.[20]

Management Environment

Stanley Gault's leadership philosophy simply stated that a leader has to be a living example, has to inspire the organization, and has to be a part of the team yet

[18] Brian O'Reilly, "Leaders of the Most Admired Corporations," *Fortune*, January 29, 1990, p. 42.
[19] Ibid., p. 43.
[20] Ibid.

still be the manager. Gault judged that leaders must be supportive and, when sensing the need for change, must genuinely communicate the need for it. Highly interactive and strong on interpersonal communications, he regularly strolled through Rubbermaid factories to talk one on one with managers and workers alike. Looking to the future, Gault, who ran a lean and flat organization, believed, "Any incoming chief executive will need to be able to run a flatter organization. As companies continue to cut costs further, middle managers will be eliminated and the CEO will have more people reporting directly to him."[21]

Gault was recognized as a tireless, energetic leader who expected and rewarded hard work from his subordinates. He was a dynamic and affable person who was well liked by his staff even though he demanded a lot from them. His personal schedule often included 12- to 14-hour workdays six days a week. Furthermore, his relentless spirit was emulated at all levels of the firm. Hard driving, Gault was described by his associates as being a very involved manager who wanted to know everything that was going on in each of Rubbermaid's businesses.

Rubbermaid rigorously sought out managers with a strong work ethic who were entrepreneurial types, enthusiastic, competent, and ambitious. They were also good team players, hard-working managers, willing to enhance shareholder wealth, and whose bonuses were based on both increase in profit and increase in the firm's book value.

Gault believed successful CEO's should set strategic direction, align employees behind that strategy so they will carry it out, and groom a successor. "I am very demanding and I know it. But I'm demanding of myself, first. I set high standards and I expect people to meet them. I want all the business we can get, provided we get it fairly. If people can't meet my standards after training and counseling then a change has to be made. That's not saying they aren't good people but they are not cut out for the particular job."[22]

Hourly workers also generally reflected the feeling that the Rubbermaid family comes first and that there was no other way. Regularly enjoying profit sharing since 1944, workers offered over 12,000 cost-cutting suggestions in housewares alone. In 1987, the Housewares and Specialty Products Division saved $24.7 million and in late 1988, $30.8 million.

Although doubling sales, Rubbermaid increased its work force by only 50 percent and has halved its number of sales representatives. It held the line on prices, and all gains came from increased volume and productivity improvement. Relations with the United Rubber Workers were good. In 1987's negotiations, a new contract froze wages for three years in return for the company's pledge to maintain existing jobs.[23]

[21] Jennifer Reese, "CEO's: More Churn at the Top," *Fortune*, March 11, 1991, p. 13.
[22] Braham, "Billion Dollar Dustpan," p. 48.
[23] Ibid.

RUBBERMAID'S MARKETING STRATEGY

One of Gault's first moves upon assuming leadership in 1980 was to revamp Rubbermaid's sales and marketing strategy. The key, according to Gault, was strict adherence to fundamentals. At the time, Rubbermaid's sales force traditionally sold every product category such as sinkware, household containers, and space organizers to all customers.

Gault split off the field sales function from marketing and put sales strategies in place to cover each market segment. As Gault explained it, "A distribution channel that would serve supermarkets and drug stores would not necessarily work for mass merchants or hardware stores or catalog showrooms." Accordingly, he decentralized marketing into product categories and installed the product manager system. This allowed effective specialization and permitted a "more intense level of management involvement with customers."[24]

Consumer Research

Although the firm employed demographic and lifestyle analysis techniques to identify trends, the core of product development at Rubbermaid lay in the use of consumer research. Qualitative and quantitative research allowed by-passing of test marketing and still revealed shopper preferences.

Rubbermaid never test marketed its products. Instead, it tested color preferences year round through fact-finding consumer focus groups in five different cities, and it regularly quizzed people in shopping malls. To avoid tipping off competitors, it generated flows of consumer research through user panels, brand awareness studies, and diaries that consumers filled with notations about product use.[25]

Rubbermaid had some 150 competitors in home products alone but no one competed across its entire product line. Rubbermaid was regularly the only brand name with recognition, because competitor's products often carried no name. Frequently, with 95 percent brand recognition, the company received complaints about some other manufacturer's product. Gault took advantage of this. "We're the only name they can think of so they write us their complaint letters." Gault responded, "Please make certain that every time you buy a plastic product you look for our name. If we make it, our name is on it. But because you did mean to buy ours and made a mistake and will not do so in the future, here, have one on us."[26]

Rubbermaid's Promotion Strategy

Gault's meticulously honed growth strategy, a combination of market positioning, careful expansion, and emphasis on quality, achieved stunning sales and

[24] Christy Marshall, "Rubbermaid, Yes, Plastic," *Business Month*, December 1988, p. 38.
[25] Alex Taylor III, "Why the Bounce at Rubbermaid?" *Fortune*, April 13, 1987, p. 78.
[26] Ibid.

earnings growth and thoroughly dominated competition. Indeed, it was argued by analysts, Rubbermaid's proliferation of innovative, well-crafted, and colorful housewares virtually created a whole new market.[27]

The company, furthermore, supported its products with national television and radio commercials and magazine advertisements along with allowances for promotion and coop advertising. Such focus boosted Rubbermaid's outlets from 60,000 in 1980 to over 100,000 in 1988. Although Rubbermaid's prices might have been higher than those of competitors, it offered a wider range of promotable products that commanded more shelf space.[28] Industry analysts estimated that Rubbermaid's advertising and promotion budget for 1989 was about 3.6 percent of sales or about $5 million.[29]

New Product Development

Rubbermaid single-mindedly pursued its mission to introduce new products with almost fanatic fervor. It was adept at searching out ways to grow. Designers continually tweaked mature products to provide incremental sales.[30] Gault's recipe for success was simple and uncomplicated. "Our formula for success is very open. We absolutely watch the market and we work at it 24 hours a day."[31] Gault saw the business as being a disciple of demographics in lock step with current trends, forever listening to customers' stated and perceived needs.

Team Development at Rubbermaid

Rubbermaid practiced the team development approach, which it considered the productivity breakthrough of the 1990s. For example, in 1987 the firm considered developing the so-called auto office, a portable plastic device that straps onto a car seat. It holds files, pens, and other articles and provides a writing surface. Simultaneously, a cross-functional team composed of, among others, engineers, designers, and marketers was assembled. The team then entered the field to determine what features customers desired. With considerations from several different functions, Rubbermaid brought the new product to the market in 1990. Sales at last count were running 50 percent beyond projections.[32]

Keeping its many products flowing took a deep commitment to research and development. Each of Rubbermaid's operating divisions had its own R&D team, and some divisions were required to enter a new market segment every 18 to 24 months.[33] Rubbermaid's CEO oversaw the launch of more than 250 new products in each of the past two years.[34] The firm boasted a success rate, according to

[27] Marshall, "Rubbermaid, Yes, Plastic," p. 38.
[28] Ibid.
[29] Taylor, "Why the Bounce at Rubbermaid?", p. 78.
[30] Ibid.
[31] Ibid.
[32] Brian Dunmaine, "Who Needs a Boss?" *Fortune*, May 7, 1990, p. 53.
[33] Marshall, "Rubbermaid, Yes, Plastic," p. 38.
[34] Sellers, "Does the CEO Really Matter?" p. 86.

Gault, of 90 percent. The company's goal of 30 percent of sales each year coming from products less than five years old was consistently met and often exceeded.[35]

Rubbermaid looked for fresh design ideas anywhere: from trying to apply the Ford Taurus style soft look to garbage cans to successfully introducing stackable plastic chairs.[36] As Gault explained it, "We just keep bringing these new categories out while expanding categories we're already in, like bathware, sinkware, trash, and refuse collection, and gadgets."[37]

According to industry analysts, new product development appeared to be the single most important reason for Rubbermaid's rise to a billion-dollar multinational firm. Stanley Gault assigned top strategic importance to product development, and that was where he allocated capital. "I have this vision," he said, "that when you look down the aisle of a store you see nothing except Rubbermaid products."[38]

Rubbermaid was considered one of America's most innovative and fastest-growing companies. Since 1934, when Rubbermaid, then the Wooster Rubber Company, made the dust pan a radical addition to its line of balloons, product innovation has been the firm's signature. The humble dust pan spawned more than 2,000 mostly utilitarian products. Those new products kept both sales and earnings at Rubbermaid growing by at least 15 percent a year.[39]

In summarizing Rubbermaid's R&D strategy, Gault once disclosed, "The primary reason for developing so many new products is to identify and develop entirely new categories that permit us to enter new areas and new sections within a retail store. New lines keep the products fresh, up to date and highly salable."[40]

RUBBERMAID'S DIVISIONS

To stay close to its customers, Rubbermaid's eight businesses operated as autonomous companies. In addition to the Housewares Product Division, the firm had a Specialty Products Division, the Little Tikes Company, Rubbermaid Commercial Products, the Rubbermaid Office Products Group, Rubbermaid-Allibert, the international division, Rubbermaid Canada, and Curver Rubbermaid Group. All were expected to embrace the new product thrust of the core household business.

Rubbermaid's philosophy was that of a market-driven organization whose goal was to offer the best value by providing the highest-quality products plus a continuous flow of new products at reasonable prices with exceptional service to

---

[35] "Special Citations," *Sales and Marketing Management*, January 16, 1984, p. 14.

[36] "Masters of Innovation," *Business Week*, McGraw Hill, April 10, 1989, p. 10.

[37] Braham, "Billion-Dollar Dustpan," p. 46.

[38] Sellers, "Does the CEO Really Matter?" p. 86.

[39] Maria Mallory, "Profits on Everything but the Kitchen Sink," Innovations in America, *Business Week*, McGraw-Hill, 1989, p. 22.

[40] Marshall, "Rubbermaid, Yes, Plastic," p. 38.

all customers. Each operating company established and executed strategic plans to support this overarching corporate philosophy.

Housewares Products Division

Formerly the Home Product Division, the Housewares Product Division was renamed to define more clearly its mission of serving the housewares industry. It manufactured and marketed sinkware, space organizers, household and refuse containers, food preparation utensils and gadgets, microwave cookware, food storage products, bathware, rubber gloves, casual dinnerware and drinkware, workshop organizers, Con-Tact brand decorative coverings, shelf liners, and vacuum cleaner bags.

Rubbermaid entered the consumer recycling market with containers to separate and collect recyclable materials in the home. Containers themselves were manufactured using recycled post-consumer plastics such as milk and soft drink containers.

Specialty Products Division

This division was responsible for aggressively innovating, manufacturing, and marketing three major product categories having seasonality and outdoor leisure activity as common bonds. Categories included insulated products, home horticulture products, and outdoor casual resin furniture. Specialty Products made and marketed insulated chests, thermal jugs, water coolers, fuel containers, storage containers, Blue Ice refreezable ice substitute, planters, and bird feeders.

The Little Tikes Company

Many new products were introduced and added to the company's product lines in 1989, including three new categories—trucks, infant products, and a doll house. The doll house category included Little Tikes Place and miniature accessories of such highly popular items as the Cozy Coupe, Party Kitchen, and Play Slide. The infant product category offered 11 items including Stacking Clown, Baby Roller, Baby Mirror, and a variety of tub toys. The third new category, trucks, featured the Big Dump Truck and Big Loader.

The quality and integrity of Little Tikes products received favorable recognition as three products—Little Tikes Place, Little Tug, and Toddle Tots' child care center—were named first, second, and ninth among the top 10 nonvideo new toys for 1989 by the Consumer Affairs Committee of Americans for Democratic Action.[41]

Rubbermaid's market share in preschool and infant toys and furnishings gained steadily in the past three years.[42]

---

[41] *Rubbermaid Annual Report*, 1989, pp. 16–17.
[42] *Akron Beacon Journal*, March 15, 1989, p. 1.

	Market Share	
	1987	*1990*
Fisher Price	64%	44%
Rubbermaid (Little Tikes)	13%	22%
Hasbro (Playschool)	23%	22%
Mattel (Disney)	—	11%
Combined Sales	$1.2 billion	$1.4 billion

Little Tikes enjoyed a 40 percent annual growth and, since its founding in 1970, doubled sales every three years to about $300 million, although it spent less than $2 million for advertising. Little Tikes' fanatical attention to quality seemed to be gaining popularity with parents selecting larger toys such as plastic jungle gyms and slides.

Rubbermaid Commercial Products

Rubbermaid Commercial Products was established in 1967 to design and manufacture lines of products for the commercial, industrial, and institutional markets. It sold a wide variety of products to the sanitary maintenance, foodservice, industrial, and agricultural markets. In June 1990, Rubbermaid acquired EWU AG, a Swiss-based manufacturer of mopping equipment and cleaning tools, to gain increased commercial distribution throughout Europe.

The municipal recycling market offered many growth opportunities for Commercial Products. The operation pioneered the use of recycled plastics in many of its containers and participated in national efforts to help raise awareness that containers manufactured with post-consumer resin are used widely in municipal curbside recycling programs.

Office Products Group

Located in Inglewood, California, this business was established in January 1991 to focus on the office products industry, which was growing at a rate in excess of the gross national product. The acquisition of Eldon Industries enhanced Rubbermaid's position in the office products market as Eldon was the leading manufacturer of office accessories and offered a wide range of products for the desk. Rubbermaid was the leader in chair mats and MicroComputer Accessories led in computer-related accessories for personal computer, word processor, and data terminal users.

Davson produced communication boards, building directories, signage, and furniture such as lecterns and wall cabinets. Ungar served the electronics industry by supplying tools for the assembly and repair of electronic circuits.

Rubbermaid-Allibert

During 1989, this operation was established as a joint venture with Allibert S.A. of Paris, France, to manufacture and market resin casual furniture for the

North American market. Rubbermaid had 50 percent ownership and management control of the venture. Allibert was a leading European manufacturer of casual furniture and participated in international markets for years. It had extensive experience in materials technology, processing technologies, and furniture design.

Curver Rubbermaid

The Curver Rubbermaid Group became operational in January 1990 as a joint venture between Rubbermaid and the Dutch chemical conglomerate, DSM. The group manufactured and marketed plastic and rubber housewares and resin furniture for Europe, the Middle East, and North Africa.

As its venture share, Rubbermaid contributed its European housewares manufacturing facilities and distribution centers in Germany, France, Austria, the Netherlands, and Switzerland. DSM contributed its Curver Housewares Group, which included its manufacturing and marketing subsidiaries scattered throughout the European continent.

The integration of the two organizations, Rubbermaid and Curver, with their respective product lines, sales and marketing organizations, and manufacturing and distribution facilities, positioned Rubbermaid for a leadership role in the European Community of 1992 and the emerging Eastern Bloc markets.

International Operations

Rubbermaid's international businesses achieved record sales and earnings growth in 1990, particularly in Europe, Latin America, Mexico, the Far East, and Canada. With the exception of the Far East, the management of Rubbermaid businesses around the world plus the coordination of sales and marketing in foreign markets were the responsibility of the respective U.S. operating companies.

To maximize return on existing investments, Rubbermaid emphasized exporting from existing manufacturing facilities primarily in the United States and Europe. Where market size and economies justifed it, local manufacturing facilities were established. Licensing agreements were employed in those markets where the costs of importing were prohibitive and where local company-owned manufacturing was not economically justified.[43]

European Market.   The Curver Rubbermaid Group, the European joint venture, experienced exceptional growth in 1990. Little Tikes continued to enjoy substantial success in the European market. Its expanded facility in Dublin, Ireland, increased its product offering and established a more competitive cost base to serve the growing EC market.

Rubbermaid Commercial Products increased its presence with the acquisition of EWU AG, Switzerland. Eldon's presence in Europe expanded the opportunities for Rubbermaid Office Products Group.

[43] *Rubbermaid Annual Report*, 1990, p. 5.

Latin American Market. Rubbermaid's approach in Latin America was a mixture of exports from North America and licensing of local companies. In 1990, significant gains were achieved in all product lines in the Caribbean markets, and substantial growth was achieved in Mexico for consumer product lines.

Middle East Market. Middle East sales suffered a setback during the fourth quarter because of the Persian Gulf crisis, yet the Middle East remained an attractive market for exports from Europe and the United States, particularly for Specialty Products' insulated line and Little Tikes toys. Rubbermaid's position in the insulated product segment was strong, with insulated coolers holding a major market share in key markets.

Far East Market. All product categories registered gains in Asia during 1990. Far East activities were managed from Rubbermaid's Hong Kong office, which also served as a sourcing location. A sourcing office also opened in Taiwan. Substantial progress was made in broadening distribution for commercial products and Little Tikes toys.

   The Japanese housewares license, Iwasaki Kogyo, experienced continued growth of sales and products featuring the Rubbermaid name. An expanded line of Rubbermaid products was developed by Iwasaki to position the company in the upscale Japanese market.

PRODUCTION STRATEGY

   The skill of Rubbermaid's product planners was matched by the know-how of its production engineers. In 1990, the firm spent $104 million or 6.8 percent of net sales for capital expenditures (in an industry where the average was under 5 percent) in order to update and expand production equipment processes and facilities. By upgrading plants, worker productivity increased from 300 units per day in 1952 to 500 in 1980 and under Gault accelerated beyond 900 units.[44]

   During 1988, Rubbermaid witnessed the largest increase ever in material costs. Beginning in late 1987, volatile resin costs escalated at a double-digit rate, which required extremely fast response with cost-containment efforts and selling price increases to protect its required margin. Total resin costs increased over 50 percent from those of the prior year. Rubbermaid incurred some $100 million of increased expenses for resin in its 1988 product cost structure. Resin shortages, moreover, adversely affected production schedules, causing service and delivery problems during peak sales periods. Correspondingly, all operating companies moved aggressively and effectively. Expenditures were closely controlled, pro-

---

[44] Taylor, "Why the Bounce at Rubbermaid?" p. 78.

ductivity improvements were accelerated, and price increases were implemented.[45]

During 1986, Rubbermaid invested $68 million to expand manufacturing capacity, increase asset utilizations, improve productivity, and develop new products. In 1989, over $85 million was invested in capital expenditures, again to expand manufacturing and distribution facilities, to modernize equipment, to install process control systems and automatic packaging systems, to purchase new tooling for new products, and to increase capacity for existing ones. Overall, from 1981 to 1990, over $612 million was invested in the business's facilities to increase productivity, develop new products, and achieve world-class manufacturing status.[46]

FINANCIAL MANAGEMENT

Not only did Gault keep the firm's 9,000 plus employees informed through regular facility visits "to promote the genuine Rubbermaid family atmosphere," but he also made sure that the financial community knew the company's story as well. He personally made at least 20 to 25 formal presentations a year to financial analysts responsible for recommending Rubbermaid shares, all in the pursuit of satisfying the firm's overall financial objective of maximizing the shareholders' investment,[47] an objective realized in the firm's 32.5 percent increase in annual return to investors between 1980 and 1990.[48] Rubbermaid's financial statements are included in Exhibits 29.3 through 29.7.

Investment analysts saw Rubbermaid as a big-capitalization company whose very bigness should inspire investor confidence. Although rumored at times as a takeover candidate, Rubbermaid was considered a solid firm with an excellent long-term outlook, superior management, and sound position. Rubbermaid, said analysts, enjoyed little debt, and the company's many low-price "necessity products" made it relatively recession resistant. Its marketing and distribution system was enviable, and its product name was synonymous with quality, a value useful in horizontal integration.[49]

Gault, however, pointed out that a high price/earnings ratio not only gave shareholders a good return but also made the company less vulnerable to takeover attempts. Rubbermaid's daily stock price, posted prominently at corporate headquarters, rose about 900 percent during his tenure. According to company sources, had one invested $1,000 in Rubbermaid shares in 1980 and reinvested

[45] *Rubbermaid Annual Report*, 1988, p. 2.

[46] *Rubbermaid Annual Report*, 1990, pp. 9–10.

[47] Braham, "Billion-Dollar Dustpan," p. 48.

[48] Yalinda Rhoden, "Rubbermaid Profits up 10%," *Akron Beacon Journal*, April 11, 1990, p. B7.

[49] Ann C. Brown, "Big Plays," *Forbes*, January 23, 1989, p. 116.

EXHIBIT 29.3 Consolidated Statement of Earnings (In thousands except per share data)

| | Year Ended December 31, | | |
	1988	1989	1990
Net Sales	$1,291,584	$1,452,365	$1,534,013
Expenses			
Cost of Sales	886,850	967,563	1,014,526
Selling, General, and Administrative	221,497	268,148	286,647
	1,108,347	1,235,711	1,301,173
Operating Earnings	183,237	216,654	232,840
Other Charges (Credits), Net			
Interest Expense	7,987	8,810	8,627
Interest Income	(1,531)	(5,650)	(5,363)
Miscellaneous, Net	4,951	8,814	1,571
	11,407	11,974	1,693
Earnings before Income Taxes	171,830	204,680	231,269
Income Taxes	64,972	79,696	87,749
Net Earnings	$ 106,858	$ 124,984	$ 143,520
Net Earnings per Common Share	$1.34	$1.57	$1.80

Source: Rubbermaid Incorporated, *1990 Annual Report.*

dividends, the investment would be worth over $25,000 at the close of the first quarter 1991.

Rubbermaid was in an industry whose products were likely to be purchased during either good or bad economic times; therefore, a consistent and steady growth in sales was to be expected rather than not. In downturns consumers were likely to continue buying the relatively inexpensive and needed houseware-type products. However, in economic upturns consumers would not buy additional products simply because they had additional income. Accordingly, Rubbermaid's sales led market indexes in hard times and lagged behind them in good times. Thus, Rubbermaid was a nearly recession-proof company.

Although 1990 sales only increased by 6 percent over 1989 sales from $1,452,365 to $1,534,013, the annual growth of sales compounded from 1980 to 1990 was 15.1 percent for the 10-year period. Unit volume increased by 12 percent; prices were lower by 3 percentage points due to promotional discounts implemented to stimulate sales to overcome the sluggish economy in 1990. The improved sales performance for the year was due to increased sales of product and not price increases.

Similarly for net earnings, Rubbermaid's 10-year annually compounded growth rate was 20.2 percent; for earnings per share the annually compounded rate for the 10-year period was 19.6 percent. Return on average shareholders' equity increased from 15.0 percent in 1980 to a high of 20.8 percent in 1987, to 20.6

EXHIBIT 29.4   Consolidated Statement of Cash Flows (In thousands)

	Year Ended December 31,		
	1988	1989	1990
Cash Flows from Operating Activities			
Net Earnings	$106,858	$124,984	$ 143,520
Adjustments to Reconcile Net Earnings to Net Cash from Operating Activities			
Depreciation	46,134	57,341	55,346
Employee Benefits	7,411	12,409	16,484
Provision for Losses on Accounts Receivable	3,837	11,822	11,777
Other	4,933	8,556	515
Changes In			
Accounts Receivable	(37,794)	(41,084)	(64,292)
Inventories	(18,237)	(19,786)	(26,453)
Prepaid Expenses and Other Assets	3,443	(5,276)	(6,521)
Payables	(10,784)	17,864	10,926
Accrued Liabilities	(4,752)	4,166	20,904
Deferred Income Taxes and Credits	680	2,676	(5,153)
Net Cash from Operating Activities	$101,729	$173,672	$157,053
Cash Flow from Investing Activities			
Additions to Property, Plant and Equipment	$ (87,333)	$ (89,787)	$(103,720)
Other, Net	3,630	2,255	(32,199)
Net Cash from Investing Activities	$ (83,703)	$ (87,532)	$(135,949)
Cash Flows from Financing Activities			
Net Change in Short-Term Debt	$ (3,581)	$ (5,479)	$ 4,572
Proceeds from Long-Term Debt	9,003	16,870	—
Repayment of Long-Term Debt	(9,332)	(5,404)	(9,330)
Cash Dividends Paid	(29,520)	(35,975)	(42,621)
Other, Net	(21)	6,527	1,768
Net Cash from Financing Activities	$ (33,451)	$ (23,461)	$ (45,611)
Net Change in Cash and Cash Equivalents	(15,425)	62,679	(24,477)
Cash and Cash Equivalents			
At Beginning of Year	$ 54,721	$ 39,296	$ 101,975
At End of Year	$ 39,296	$101,975	$ 77,498
Supplemental Cash Flow Information			
Income Taxes Paid	$ 68,733	$ 94,791	$ 88,992
Interest Paid	$ 8,006	$ 8,507	$ 8,765

( ) Denotes decrease in cash and cash equivalents.
Source: Rubbermaid Incorporated, *1990 Annual Report.*

in 1988, 20.6 in 1989, and 20.2 in 1990. Return on average shareholders' equity was above 20 percent from 1983 to 1990. With the payment of $0.54 per share in 1990, dividends per share increased for the 36th consecutive year.

An important factor in the outstanding financial results achieved was Rubbermaid's handling of long-term debt. Although very low in comparison to its industry, the company used long-term debt and internal funding of acquisitions

EXHIBIT 29.5   Consolidated Balance Sheet (In thousands except per share data)

	Year Ended December 31,		
	1988	1989	1990
Assets			
Current Assets			
Cash and Cash Equivalents	$ 39,296	$ 101,975	$ 77,498
Receivables, Less Allowance for Doubtful Accounts of $15,426 in 1990, 9,629 in 1989	a	259,878	302,271
Inventories	a	199,525	216,808
Prepaid Expenses	a	5,929	6,120
Total Current Assets	452,639	567,307	602,697
Property, Plant, and Equipment, Net	347,677	3,797,107	405,520
Intangible and Other Assets, Net	42,389	38,591	106,033
Total Assets	$842,705	$ 985,005	$1,114,250
Liabilities and Shareholders' Equity			
Current Liabilities			
Notes Payable	a	$ 12,302	$ 16,866
Long-Term Debt, Current	a	3,376	1,908
Payables	a	96,696	101,089
Accrued Liabilities	a	102,747	115,437
Total Current Liabilities	197,431	215,121	235,300
Deferred Income Taxes and Credits	0	36,390	29,751
Other Deferred Liabilities	47,471	30,724	41,804
Long-Term Debt, Noncurrent	39,023	50,294	39,191
Shareholders' Equity			
Preferred Stock, No Par Value Authorized 20,000 Shares None Issued	—	—	—
Common Shares, $1 Par Value Authorized 200,000 Shares 79,992,610 Issued in 1990 79,556,748 Issued in 1989 and 79,381,000 Issued in 1988	79,381	79,557	79,993
Paid-In Capital	21,138	24,715	37,857
Retained Earnings	453,009	541,042	638,551
Foreign Currency Translation Adjustment	5,252	7,162	11,803
Total Shareholders' Equity	558,780	652,476	768,204
Total Liabilities and Shareholders' Equity	$842,705	$ 985,005	$1,114,250

a Figure does not appear in 1990 annual report.
Source: Rubbermaid Incorporated, *1990 Annual Report.*

with cash from operations that allowed great flexibility in timing. The company arranged for a line of credit that increased from $27 million in 1986 to $115 million in 1990, to compensate for fluctuations in working capital and operations that allowed for the selection of proper timing and negotiation for the best possible long-term financing. In 1990, long-term debt ($39,191,000) as a percentage of total capitalization fell from 15 percent to 5 percent.

EXHIBIT 29.6 Consolidated Financial Summary (In thousands except per share data)

	1986	1987	1988	1989	1990
Operating Results					
Net Sales	$864,721	$1,096,055	$1,291,584	$1,452,365	$1,534,013
Cost of Sales	554,421	727,927	886,850	967,563	1,014,526
Selling, General, and Administrative Expenses	166,954	199,145	221,497	268,148	286,647
Other Charges (Credits), Net	684	10,761	11,407	11,974	1,571
Earnings before Income Taxes	142,662	158,222	171,830	204,680	231,269
Income Taxes	67,658	67,499	64,972	79,696	87,749
Net Earnings	$ 75,004	$ 90,723	$ 106,858	$ 124,984	$ 143,520
Per Common Share	$ .95	$ 1.15	$ 1.34	$ 1.57	$ 1.80
Percentage of Sales	8.7%	8.3%	8.3%	8.6%	9.4%
Financial Position					
Current Assets	322,655	418,563	452,639	567,307	602,697
Property, Plant, and Equipment, Net	248,224	310,017	347,677	379,107	405,520
Intangible and Other Assets, Net	45,780	45,748	42,389	38,591	106,033
Total Assets	$626,659	$774,328	$842,705	$985,005	$1,114,250
Current Liabilities	$156,456	$209,771	$197,431	$215,121	$235,300
Deferred Taxes, Credits, and Other Liabilities	40,013	47,585	47,471	67,114	71,555
Long-Term Debt	35,668	40,042	39,023	50,294	39,191
Shareholders' Equity	394,522	476,930	558,780	652,476	768,204
Total Liabilities and Shareholders' Equity	$626,659	$774,328	$842,705	$985,005	$1,114,250
Long-Term Debt to Total Capitalization	9%	8%	7%	8%	5%
Working Capital	$176,199	$ 208,792	$ 255,208	$ 352,186	$ 367,397
Current Ratio	2.13	2.00	2.29	2.64	2.56
Other Data					
Average Common Shares Outstanding (000)	79,032	79,234	79,464	79,625	79,844
Return on Average Shareholders' Equity	20.5%	20.8%	20.6%	20.6%	20.2%
Cash Dividends Paid	$ 19,771	$ 24,581	$ 29,520	$ 35,975	$ 42,621
Cash Dividends Paid Per Common Share	.26	.32	.38	.46	.54
Shareholders' Equity Per Common Share	5.00	6.02	7.04	8.20	9.60
NYSE Stock Price Range, High-Low	29–17	35–19	27–21	38–25	45–31
Additions to Property, Plant, and Equipment	71,587	104,429	87,333	89,787	103,720
Depreciation Expense	34,135	44,155	46,134	57,341	55,346
Number of Shareholders' at Year End	8,379	10,104	10,482	11,225	13,305
Average Number of Associates	6,509	7,512	8,643	9,098	9,304

EXHIBIT 29.7 Statement of Shareholders' Equity (In thousands except per share data)

	Common Shares	Paid-In Capital	Retained Earnings	Foreign Currency Translation Adjustment	Total Shareholders' Equity
Balance at December 31, 1987	$79,249	$17,790	$376,307	$ 3,584	$476,930
Transactions for 1988					
Net Earnings	—	—	106,858	—	106,858
Cash Dividends, $.38 per Share	—	—	(29,520)	—	(29,520)
Employee Stock Plans	132	3,348	(497)	—	2,983
Foreign Currency Translation Adjustment	—	—	—	1,668	1,668
Other, Net	—	—	(139)	—	(139)
Balance at December 31, 1988	79,381	21,138	453,009	5,252	558,780
Transactions for 1989					
Net Earnings	—	—	124,984	—	124,984
Cash Dividends, $.46 per Share	—	—	(35,975)	—	(35,975)
Employee Stock Plans	176	3,577	(670)	—	3,083
Foreign Currency Translation Adjustment	—	—	—	1,910	1,910
Other, Net	—	—	(306)	—	(306)
Balance at December 31, 1989	79,557	24,715	541,042	7,162	652,476
Transactions for 1990					
Net Earnings	—	—	143,520	—	143,520
Cash Dividends, $.54 per Share	—	—	(42,621)	—	(42,621)
Employee Stock Plans	436	13,142	(3,313)	—	10,265
Foreign Currency Translation Adjustment	—	—	—	4,641	4,641
Other, Net	—	—	(77)	—	(77)
Balance at December 31, 1990	$79,993	$37,857	$638,551	$11,803	$768,204

Source: Rubbermaid Incorporated, *1990 Annual Report.*

Actually, long-term debt at Rubbermaid slowly increased from $25 million in 1980 to $39 million in 1990. The percentage of this debt to total capitalization fell due largely to the 489 percent increase in shareholders' equity over the years. The soundness of Rubbermaid's management was demonstrated not only by the low and falling percentage of long-term debt over the past 10 years, but also by rapid reduction of excess (by Rubbermaid's standards) long-term debt that appeared in 1989.

RUBBERMAID IN 1991

Assessing the impact of the Persian Gulf crisis on the company, Gault felt guardedly optimistic: "For the year ahead, we anticipate great uncertainty and slow economic growth. We have also experienced mounting apprehension and caution within the retail, institutional, and industrial sectors. However, each operating company has developed comprehensive contingency action plans for aggressive promotional programs and consumer advertising to assist our customers in selling Rubbermaid products. We have faced similar challenges in the past and are confident we can continue to produce record performances in the future."[50]

MANAGEMENT IN THE COMING DECADE

On May 1, 1991, Stanley Carleton Gault retired from Rubbermaid as chairman of the board and chief executive officer. The Board of Directors, meanwhile, confirmed a new management team to replace Gault. Walter W. Williams became chairman and chief executive officer, Wolfgang R. Schmitt became president and chief operating officer, and Charles A. Carroll became president and general manager of Rubbermaid's Housewares Products Division, the firm's oldest and largest consumer business. The company, in looking to the future, concluded that management transition as well as the entire management structure were well planned and successfully implemented over the past several years.[51]

Gault, who planned to maintain his association with Rubbermaid, promised, "I'm going to take some time and do some of the things I enjoy but just haven't had time to do."[52] "I certainly won't be running the company anymore, but I'll be around to talk about it."[53] Gault, who had a two-year consulting contract, was to maintain an office at Rubbermaid headquarters and be a member of the board of directors until he turned 70 years of age.[54]

[50] Yalinda Rhoden, "Gault Stepping Down as Rubbermaid Chief," *Akron Beacon Journal*, January 11, 1991, pp. B8, B12.
[51] Ibid., p. B8.
[52] Ibid.
[53] Alecia Swasy, *Wall Street Journal*, April 2, 1990, p. 26.
[54] Yalinda Rhoden, "Sans Gault," *Akron Beacon Journal*, April 22, 1991, p. D2.

_____ CASE 30 _____

Dakotah

In May 1987, Dakotah appeared to be on the brink of a new era of growth and profitability. The South Dakota-based manufacturer of bedcoverings and associated textile home furnishings had enjoyed record sales of over $13 million in 1986 and record after-tax profits of nearly $400,000. Its products, marketed from a posh showroom in New York City, were widely recognized by department store buyers and consumers alike as the top-of-the-line in textile home furnishings.

Dakotah was an employee-owned company headquartered in the small town of Webster, South Dakota (population 2,400). It had seven plants located in small towns in three counties in the northeastern corner of South Dakota that had a combined population of 24,448 (see Exhibit 30.1).

HISTORY OF DAKOTAH

In 1970, George Whyte was 21, an age when many of his peers were thinking about finishing college and finding a job, but Whyte was worried about pigs. As a VISTA (Volunteers in Service to America) volunteer, Whyte had encouraged the farm families of rural northeastern South Dakota to participate in an economic development program called "Pigs for Pork." Farmers were given bred sows by the federal government to raise and eventually sell at market. When the price of pork plummeted, the program failed. The pigs cost more to raise than their market value. The program had done nothing to improve the distressed economic condition of farmers in this depressed region.

Undaunted, Whyte hit upon another idea. He had noticed the farm wives making beautiful handcrafted quilts. His grandmother had made quilts and he knew something of their value. He turned his attention to the talent and skill of the women of the families who were participating in the Pigs for Pork program and realized this might be the opportunity he was looking for. Whyte convinced the wives and daughters of these farmers that they could successfully produce and sell

This case was prepared by Diane Hoadley and Philip C. Fisher as a basis for class discussion rather than to illustrate either effective or ineffective handling of an administrative situation. Used with permission from Philip C. Fisher. Presented at the 1987 Workshop of the Midwest Society for Case Research.

EXHIBIT 30.1 South Dakota Metropolitan Statistical Area, Counties, and Selected Places

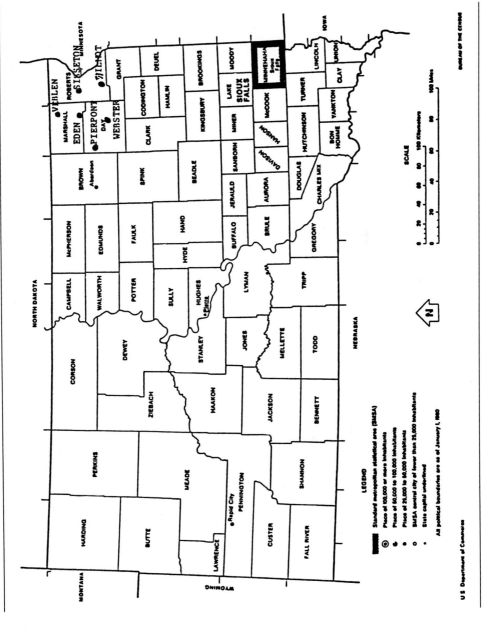

their handcrafted items. Whyte and Bob Pierce, who headed the Northeast South Dakota Community Action Program, collected hand-sewn quilts, afghans, pillows, shawls, and a variety of other items from the women in a three-county region of northeastern South Dakota. Armed with these samples, Whyte and Pierce flew to the East Coast in an attempt to market the products to department store buyers.

They failed miserably. They flew first to Washington, D.C., engaged a hotel suite, got out the telephone book, and contacted the department stores listed in the Yellow Pages. "Oh God, it was awful!" exclaimed Whyte recounting the events. No one even came to look at the products. Whyte and Pierce then flew to New York City and repeated the process with the same discouraging results. They knew the circumstances required more aggressive tactics, so they put their samples in a trunk and marched unannounced into the office of the quilt buyer for one of New York's leading department stores. They were promptly removed by the store's security guards.

On their way back to South Dakota, discouraged but still hopeful, they stopped at Dayton's, a department store chain based in Minneapolis. There they saw the assistant buyer for the drapery and bedspread department. He, too, was not interested in the handcrafted products being shown, but he put Whyte in contact with a leading independent manufacturers' representative in New York City, Park B. Smith.

Smith flew to South Dakota in September 1971, liked what he saw, made some suggestions for design changes, and negotiated a contract with Whyte to produce a line of samples to show in the November home furnishings market in New York. Twice a year, in November and May, buyers gathered on Fifth Avenue in New York City to preview new home furnishings merchandise and to place orders for the products that would appear in their stores.

The South Dakota farm women had from Labor Day to November 5 to style and produce their first product line. The women focused on quilts and pillow shams and succeeded in having a line of samples ready for the market. This time the products earned a better response from the department store buyers. *Home Furnishings Daily,* the home furnishings industry trade journal, ran a front-page article stating, "Dakotah has the freshest design ideas in the last 100 years in bed covers." Over $50,000 in orders were placed at that first show.

Back in South Dakota, a $54,000 Small Business Administration loan provided the capital to purchase sewing machines and enough fabric to fill the orders, but working capital was still inadequate. The Webster, South Dakota, Junior Chamber of Commerce raised $1,600 to buy fuel oil; the local Izaac Walton League donated the use of their building; and Whyte and the women worked for six months without pay until they delivered their first shipments to the buyers. They organized as the Tract Handicraft Industries Cooperative, and the firm was off and sewing.

In 1986, this employees' cooperative, reorganized as an employee-owned corporation in 1976, had sales of almost $14 million, had over 400 employees, and was considered to be the Mercedes-Benz of the bed-covering industry.

MARKETING

Dakotah manufactured and sold textile home furnishings products in four major categories, bed coverings (bedspreads, comforters, and so on), which accounted for 50 percent of sales; pillows (including decorator pillows), which made up 40 percent of sales; window treatments (curtains, draperies, valances), which were 5 percent of sales; and miscellaneous items (shower curtains, napkins, placemats, wall hangings, and others), which accounted for the remaining 5 percent of sales. Approximately 50 percent of these items were sold in department stores, 40 percent to mass and catalog merchants (Spiegel's was the largest single customer), 5 percent to bed and bath specialty stores, and 5 percent to the hotel and motel industry. Dakotah operated its own factory outlet store in Webster. Dakotah products were distributed in all 50 states and the company had a small amount of export sales.

Dakotah was a very small producer in a large industry. Manufacturer's sales in the textile home furnishings industry were estimated at $3.9 billion in 1985; of this amount, sales of bedspreads and bed sheets were $375.7 million (this did not include sheets and pillowcases, for which sales were estimated at $813.5 million). The largest competitor was Spring Mills with total sales of $1.5 billion, 64 percent of which was in textile home furnishings. Another major competitor was Fieldcrest Cannon with sales of $1.1 billion. The industry was becoming increasingly concentrated in the face of pressure from foreign competitors. Major developments had been the acquisition of Burlington Industry's sheet and towel division by J.P. Stevens, Fieldcrest's purchase of Cannon, and West Point Pepperell's purchase of Cluett Peabody. Firms chose acquisitions as a means of expanding product lines to avoid the risk and cost of establishing new brand names. Well-established brand names were considered important in succeeding against imports. Another industry response to foreign competition was the increased use of automated production techniques. All large producers used a relatively high degree of automation to produce both fabrics and finished goods. In spite of these developments, the textile industry averaged net profits of only 0.32 percent of sales in 1986.

In the face of such competitive pressures, Dakotah had succeeded in establishing strong brand identification. George Whyte explained how this was done: "Dakotah sells a lot of sizzle. Once you create the image, the product sells itself. So we have invested a great deal of time and money in creating the image." Dakotah's major thrust to create an image began in 1976 when the newly incorporated company contracted with a consulting firm that specialized in the development of corporate identities. The consulting firms's first recommendation was to change the name of the products from Dakotah Handcrafts by Tract, and the name of the organization from Tract Handcraft Industries Cooperative to just Dakotah. The company and its products were identified by the name, Dakotah, written in distinctive script (Exhibit 30.2 includes the company identification logo).

The next step in creating the Dakotah image was to develop a magnificent company showroom in the midst of the home furnishings market in New York

EXHIBIT 30.2   Bird of Paradise

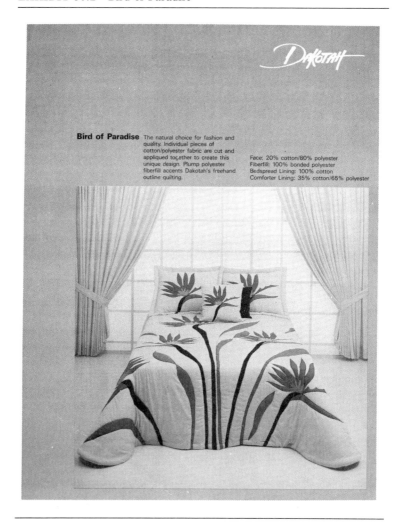

Bird of Paradise The natural choice for fashion and quality. Individual pieces of cotton/polyester fabric are cut and appliqued together to create this unique design. Plump polyester fiberfill accents Dakotah's freehand outline quilting.

Face: 20% cotton/80% polyester
Fiberfill: 100% bonded polyester
Bedspread Lining: 100% cotton
Comforter Lining: 35% cotton/65% polyester

City. Much time and money were spent in finding the right location and creating a suitable ambiance. Finally a space became available on the ground floor of the textile market building, located on Fifth Avenue between 30th and 31st Streets. The building houses offices for several textile and home furnishings manufacturers. Whyte created a spacious and dramatic office that rivaled the office of any chief executive officer for a *Fortune 500* company.

The New York showroom and offices were owned by a Dakotah subsidiary, Dakotah USA. Employees there were technically employees of the subsidiary. Sales were under the management of Neil Zuber, vice president of sales. Zuber ran the New York showroom and coordinated the selling activities of 11 independent sales representatives, each assigned an exclusive geographic area. John Panarello, the vice president of national accounts, sold to the large department stores and catalog merchants.

Great care was taken so that the Dakotah name written in its characteristic script was the only trademark to appear before the public. Whyte also insisted that the Dakotah name be featured in any catalog layout of the products, a practice ordinarily reserved for a few select designers such as Bill Blass and Ralph Lauren.

Whyte believed that Dakotah's principal strength was its ability to create high-fashion, uniquely designed items. Dakotah focused on designs that created an up-scale contemporary look. The first designs came from Whyte and other staff members. By 1982, Whyte recognized the need to hire a professional designer and asked one of Park Smith's former employees, Belinda Ballash, to join the Dakotah company. Ballash worked out of her office in Pacific Palisades, California, supplying Dakotah with designs reflecting the most up-to-date trends from the West Coast. In May 1987, Whyte hired another designer housed on the East Coast to provide designs reflecting East Coast trends. The designers were employees of Dakotah USA.

Although Dakotah products were styled to reflect current fashion taste, which, in 1987, was returning to a "country" look, Whyte believed that Dakotah's emphasis would remain on products with contemporary styling. Whyte's attention to creating a unique look for the Dakotah products had been successful. Dakotah had always had difficulty filling its orders, sometimes running months behind and occasionally not allowing its sales representatives to take new orders for periods of up to two months. In 1987, Whyte negotiated a licensing agreement with the Spring Mills Company, the leading manufacturer of sheets and pillowcases, for use of Dakotah designs for a new line that would feature the Dakotah name. Whyte believed that similar licensing agreements would be negotiated with manufacturers of other home furnishings products.

In 1986, Whyte decided to move Dakotah into the hospitality market. The company had previously sold furnishings to hotels and motels on a limited scale, decorating some suites for the Hyatt Corporation. Whyte was convinced that more appealing interior furnishings would improve occupancy rates. His first major deal was with the Super 8 Motel Company. The Super 8 Company, headquartered in Aberdeen, South Dakota, 50 miles from Webster, was a motel franchise chain with over 400 budget motels in the United States and Canada. After testing guest responses to some of the products, Super 8 agreed to purchase bedspreads, wall hangings, and pillow ensembles. Dakotah became the exclusive supplier of bed coverings to the corporate-owned motels, and a recommended supplier for the franchises.

With this success, Whyte planned to pursue the hospitality industry vigorously. In 1987, these sales were being handled by a two-person telemarketing effort located at the Webster headquarters. Initial results had been very encouraging. Company plans were for hospitality to be 15 percent of total sales by 1988, 30 percent in 1989, 40 percent in 1990, and 50 percent by 1991.

MANUFACTURING

Dakotah bed coverings were unique in that they were made with a technique called applique. In appliqueing, decorations are created by cutting pieces of one material and applying them to the surface of another. Manufacturing processes at Dakotah were a mixture of skilled handwork and highly automated processes. The decorative pieces of fabric were bound to the surface of the background material with adhesive then outlined with zigzag stitching, which was done by manually guiding the fabric through a sewing machine. This process was labor intensive and required considerable skill. Other manufacturing processes, such as the decorative stitching at the edges of the bed coverings, were performed by computer-controlled machines.

Dakotah operated seven plants in six small towns, all in northeastern South Dakota. Two plants were located in Webster—Webster 1 and Webster 2. Webster 1 employed 45 people who were engaged in the initial measurement and cutting of all fabric used in the other plants. In addition Webster 1 produced the batting or fiberfill used to give bulk to the bedspreads. Batting production was highly automated. It was made from bales of purchased fiber that were fed into hoppers. These fibers were then woven into rolls of batting 40 yards long in one continuous automated process that could be adjusted as to width and thickness of the batting.

Dakotah had recently acquired a computer-controlled laser fabric cutter that would be used to cut the pieces of cloth used in appliqueing. Patterns would be fed into the computer that would lay out the pieces on the fabric so as to minimize waste. Additional benefits from the laser cutter would be reduced labor and increased capacity. The laser cutting also would bind the edges to eliminate the raveling that sometimes occurred with the current method, which employed a hand-guided, power-driven, circular blade.

Webster 2 was located a block away from Webster 1 and included the company's administrative offices. This plant did the finishing and shipping for all products except pillows. In the final step of the manufacturing process, the decorated top of the bedspread and the underside fabric were placed on large frames with the batting in between. Large computer-controlled quilting machines sewed the three layers together. These machines also could be programmed to sew decorative designs on the bedspreads. Some bedspreads without applique were decorated entirely with the quilting machines. Appliqued coverings were then outlined and embellished with stitching, a process in which the coverings were again manually guided through a sewing machine. The operators of this process were the most highly skilled in the plant. The process not only required manual dexterity, but the operators sewed the designs from memory. Webster 2 employed 80 people in manufacturing.

Other Dakotah plants were located in Veblen, South Dakota (population 322), where 93 people produced and shipped pillows; Wilmot, South Dakota (population 492), which produced shams, or decorative pillow coverings, and employed 43 people; Eden, South Dakota (population 126), where draperies and bedskirts were made and 36 people were employed; Pierpont, South Dakota (population 165), where appliques were bound to the coverings and 30 people were employed; and Sisseton, South Dakota (population 2,717), where hanging samples used as point-of-purchase displays were made. Thirteen people were employed there. Several of these plants had the versatility to perform skilled hand-stitching operations used in making bedspreads and other products. Approximately 90 percent of the employees in manufacturing were women.

Company executives believed that Dakotah had an important competitive edge in manufacturing skills. Although design changes were important to retain the distinctive look of the Dakotah products, protection from copying came largely from the fact that the appliqued designs were difficult to manufacture and Dakotah had more expertise in the appliqueing processes than any one else. It was also a difficult process to automate or mechanize. Only one competitor made appliqued products. As one manager put it, ''We have an edge in marketing and design. Survival depends on success in manufacturing.''

Manufacturing operations were under the management of Ed Johnson. Company executives gave him credit for solving the production problems that had previously given the company a reputation for not being able to meet promised delivery dates. One company executive estimated that in 1986 the company had turned away from $2 million to $4 million in sales, and company sales representatives were quoting delivery dates of six months. He said, ''People can build a house faster than they can get the bedspreads.'' Continued automation was constrained by capital requirements. For example, the new laser cutter had cost $300,000. Dakotah had invested over $3 million in plant and equipment during the five years prior to 1987 and planned to invest well over $1 million in 1987.

Manufacturing workers at Dakotah were paid an average of $4.51 an hour. Skilled workers such as fabric cutters or applique stitchers could make as much as $4.92. The base wage was 20 to 30 percent below the manufacturing wages paid in larger eastern South Dakota cities such as Watertown or Sioux Falls, but well above the $1.50-an-hour labor costs of Korean and Taiwanese textile manufacturers. The clerical staff was paid at rates similar to those paid in Sioux Falls. Top managers at Dakota were paid salaries substantially below industry averages.

''The concept of this company is to make jobs,'' stated Richard Engel, the chief financial officer. ''So we try to control the cost of the product through mechanization, experimentation, and heavy investment.'' Engel saw the employee-ownership concept as being of mixed benefit. It gave employees a sense of commitment, but it severely limited its access to capital. Dakotah had $1.25 million in outstanding long-term notes. This included approximately $65,000 in a revolving working-capital loan financed at 1 percent above the prime rate and the rest in the form of a six-year loan secured by machinery and equipment at 1-1/2 percent above the prime rate. At one time the company had paid 4-1/2 to 5 points over prime. (For financial statements, see Exhibits 30.3 and 30.4.)

When asked about the company's improved performance in 1986, Engel attributed it to several factors. The recruitment of more experienced middle

EXHIBIT 30.3 Balance Sheets for Dakotah, Inc.

	1980	1981	1982	1983	1984	1985	1986
Assets							
Current Assets							
Cash	$ 12,162	$ 81,447	$ 81,629	$ 3,207	$ 25,558	$ 16,372	$ 18,171
Accounts Receivable Less Allowance for Doubtful Accounts	1,325,765	1,289,537	1,278,584	1,912,920	1,635,032	1,337,006	1,718,731
Merchandise Inventory	1,207,482	1,448,964	1,769,199	3,103,208	2,405,746	2,352,272	1,994,279
Prepaid Income Tax	35,915	29,398	12,880	115,392	80,114	66,441	16,094
Other Current Assets	19,413	3,831	17,587	25,142	7,239	12,686	
Total Current Assets	2,600,737	2,853,177	3,159,879	5,159,869	4,153,689	3,784,777	3,747,275
Property, Plant and Equipment—Less Accumulated Depreciation	775,438	904,634	1,325,579	1,780,827	1,640,582	1,415,983	1,732,239
Other Assets	19,240	19,420	22,700	11,830	11,101	9,190	9,270
Total Assets	$3,395,595	$3,777,231	$4,508,228	$6,952,526	$5,805,281	$5,209,950	$5,448,784
Liabilities and Stockholders' Equity							
Current Liabilities							
Notes Payable—Bank	$ 839,111	$ 927,856	$ 511,720	$1,849,604	$1,487,241	$1,124,104	$ 264,537
Capital Lease Obligations	21,700	21,700	14,868	16,336	17,718	19,140	20,886
Notes Payable—Other	101,385	92,654	49,593	31,153			
Accounts Payable	632,650	632,225	853,646	1,394,598	747,876	632,589	828,303
Income Tax Payable	8,891	16,607					
Other Current Liabilities	122,278	86,174	174,971	277,395	199,188	286,303	408,935
Total Current Liabilities	1,726,015	1,777,216	1,604,798	3,569,086	2,452,023	2,062,136	1,522,661
Long-Term Debt							
Notes Payable—Bank	496,347	475,398	880,000	1,210,000	1,140,000	870,000	1,250,000
Capital Lease Obligations	89,930	70,541	465,364	448,337	430,821	412,154	391,088
Notes Payable—Other							
Total Long-Term Debt	586,277	545,939	1,345,364	1,658,337	1,570,821	1,282,154	1,641,088
Stockholders' Equity							
Common Stock	679,448	928,999	927,948	927,435	926,434	936,382	1,159,383
Contributed Capital	13,207	13,207	13,207	13,207	13,207	13,207	13,207
Retained Earnings	390,648	511,870	616,911	784,461	842,796	916,071	1,152,445
Total Stockholders' Equity	1,083,303	1,454,076	1,558,066	1,725,103	1,782,437	1,865,660	2,325,035
Total Liabilities and Stockholders' Equity	$3,395,595	$3,777,231	$4,508,228	$6,952,526	$5,805,281	$5,209,950	$5,488,784

EXHIBIT 30.4 Income Statements for Dakotah, Inc.

	1980	1981	1982	1983	1984	1985	1986
Sales	$9,628,706	$10,721,784	$9,124,241	$12,300,726	$13,729,250	$11,708,748	$14,085,870
Less Returns and Allowances	487,616	462,897	344,014	479,567	605,621	645,166	410,329
Net Sales before Discounts	9,141,090	10,248,887	8,780,227	11,821,159	13,123,629	11,063,582	
Less Discounts	17,912	14,473	8,647	7,908	7,928	2,659	
Net Sales	9,123,178	10,234,414	8,771,580	11,813,251	13,115,701	11,060,923	13,675,541
Cost of Goods Sold							
Merchandise Inventory	1,251,533	1,207,482	1,448,964	1,769,199	3,103,208	2,405,746	2,352,272
Purchases	3,576,734	4,227,009	3,532,998	5,326,805	4,551,872	3,642,072	4,721,640
Freight In	195,760	191,943	207,934	238,175	164,711	123,026	141,341
Direct Labor	1,615,935	1,820,766	1,591,026	2,769,484	2,478,520	2,206,586	2,350,930
Employee Fringe Benefits	98,877						
Payroll Taxes	119,257	155,466	140,935	330,376	213,148	197,406	228,861
Cost of Goods Available for Sale	6,858,116	7,602,666	6,921,857	10,434,039	10,511,459	8,574,836	9,795,044
Less Merchandise Inventory —End of Year	1,207,482	1,448,964	1,769,199	3,103,208	2,405,746	2,352,272	1,994,279
Cost of Goods Sold	5,650,634	6,153,702	5,152,658	7,330,831	8,105,713	6,222,564	7,800,765
Gross Profit	3,472,544	4,080,712	3,618,922	4,482,420	5,009,988	4,838,359	5,874,776
Operating Expenses							
Manufacturing	462,506	601,535	729,888	1,023,828	1,276,410	1,349,893	1,574,785
Selling	1,254,170	1,772,059	1,393,449	1,788,532	1,831,548	1,656,810	1,844,953
Shipping	312,128	275,127	340,730	336,820	379,414	323,299	371,997
Financial	311,236	216,027	218,372	308,677	480,412	326,000	254,921
General/Administrative	617,110	722,736	758,941	920,559	937,439	1,060,443	1,148,188
Total Operating Expenses	2,957,150	3,587,484	3,441,380	4,378,416	4,905,223	4,716,445	5,194,844
Income from Operations	515,394	493,228	177,542	104,004	104,765	121,914	679,932
Royalty Income, Net	4,330						
Provision for Income Taxes	34,299	52,607	40,949	(83,951)	7,328	25,966	40,423
Contribution to Employee Stock Bonus Plan	371,213	250,000					250,000
Net Income	$ 114,212	$ 190,621	$ 136,593	$ 187,955	$ 97,437	$ 95,948	$ 389,509

managers, significant investments in machinery and equipment, better cost controls, and the development of new markets such as the hotel and motel industry were all judged to have been significant. Some of these initiatives began as early as 1983, and the results began showing up in the financial statements in 1986.

Dakotah had formal five-year goals for profit and growth. These included sales growth of 15 percent, net pretax earnings on sales of 4 percent in 1987 rising to 12 percent by 1991, and achievement of an average rate of return on stockholders' equity of 15 percent. "If we want to grow," Engel said, "we have to look to external equity. We can support 10 percent growth but 25 percent will require more. We have reached the limit of debt financing." Engel recognized that going outside the limits of employee ownership for equity capital was a departure from an important company policy. "One thing I have learned is that some things are sacred." Employee ownership was one of those things.

DAKOTAH'S FUTURE

Dakotah had begun as a manufacturing company established to create jobs in northeastern South Dakota. Over the years the focus of the company had shifted from manufacturing to marketing. "It is our forte," explained Whyte. He believed that marketing opportunities through licensing and franchising could allow Dakotah to grow to a $100 million company over the next 10 years.

Licensing possibilities included such products as wall and floor coverings, a more extensive line of window treatments, as well as other textile products. A franchised chain of Dakotah stores would allow the company greater access to a larger number of consumers. Both of these alternatives would allow the company to increase its revenues with a relatively small capital investment.

Dakotah was beginning to consider other markets. In 1986, Dakotah quietly began selling pillows to Wal-Mart, a large discount chain. Sales were $1.5 million with $2.5 million expected in 1987. The possibilities for increased sales through discount outlets raised the possibility that overseas manufacturing of Dakotah designs might be considered.

Finally, the capital limitation of confining equity ownership to employees was recognized as an obstacle to growth. Perhaps employee ownership was no longer "sacred." However, it was a decision with far-reaching consequences. "The intent is still to create jobs," Whyte said. "The concept of employee ownership has not changed yet."

_____ CASE 31 _____

Pirates Cove Inn

COROZAL TOWN, BELIZE, CENTRAL AMERICA

Holiday Crowds

The peace and quiet can't last long, thought Ramon as he sat in the shade of palm trees on the Caribbean beachfront of the Pirates Cove Inn. The 1989 Easter weekend crowds would soon find their way to this tranquil hideaway, although by that time Ramon along with the paratroopers would be back at camp. As a Belizean National Guardsman assigned to this British military unit as an "advisor," Ramon felt he had drawn a good assignment. The British were polite and easygoing and, after all, they were stationed in Belize to protect the nation from the claims made by neighboring Guatemala—claims that Ramon felt were unfair and a source of some anxiety. So he did not mind the duty at all.

As she watched the soldiers and other hotel guests from a corner table of the dining room just above the beach, Carole Hartman was amused at the variety of people who would make their way to her secluded resort. On this day, in addition to the soldiers, there were two Mexican families, an archeologist from Australia, a U.S. college professor and his family, a small tour group of middle-aged women from Texas, two football coaches from Florida, and a Canadian couple on their honeymoon. Added to these were a car full of local youths on holiday and, finally, two of Carole's relatives who had come from Great Britain for an extended visit.

Although the Easter weekend would bring a boost in income, Carole was not looking forward to the frantic pace of service that would be demanded of her staff. She felt that the intended attraction of the resort should be its gentle tempo of sailing and windsurfing and the sense of adventure that comes from exploring Mayan ruins and caves off the beaten path, the excitement of jungle river trips, and, for others, the relaxation of swimming or reading.

This case was prepared by Steven K. Paulson as a basis for class discussion rather than to illustrate either effective or ineffective handling of an administrative situation. This work was supported by a grant from the U.S. Department of Education—Business and International Education Program 1987–1990. Used with permission from Steven K. Paulson.

At times like this, Carole was not sure if the resort was a means to an end or if it had become an end in itself. Clearly, at the beginning, the idea of a resort was seen only as an intermediate step in the development of the business.

Real Estate Beginnings

Carole's dream from as early as she could remember was to be responsible for the development of the natural environment in a way that would preserve its original beauty yet allow people to feel secure and to be able to carry on their contemporary pursuits—be it business or holiday or retirement living. In the early 1970s, she had worked hard to sell small tracts of the family's holdings in the Corozal region of northeastern Belize, usually to British or Canadian nationals, with restrictions concerning the use of the land and surrounding wildlife.

As the most northerly port of the country, the village of Consejo experienced some variety, although for the most part its 50 or so inhabitants spent their lives in subsistence, living in thatched roof huts along a narrow road that led to a wooden pier on which a faded sign indicated that a Belizean customs official lived close by. The pier had a chain link gate across it to prevent immediate access to the country, although the shallow water would prohibit all but the smallest of boats from docking there. Consejo was located some seven miles northeast of Corozal Town, a center for government services and, in years past, the location of one of the two sugar refineries in the country. In the same vicinity a small Canadian and British community lived in fairly spacious, attractive block and wood frame houses.

Belize's main cash crop and leading export was raw ("brown") sugar. In 1985, the mill near Corozal closed, sending some 700 former employees looking for work; many left and for several years the area was economically devastated. But in the early 1970s, economic progress seemed inevitable with purchase guarantees from the United States and other nations. And that was the time when Belizeans were excited in anticipation of their independence from Great Britain, which occurred in 1981. Peace Corps volunteers from the United States and much economic aid became available during the early 1970s, and it seemed as if the future would be quite bright. For the Consejo land sales business, however, the combination of decreasing British influence with increasing U.S. influence had a stalling effect on business because of the uncertainty of future governmental policies concerning land ownership by foreigners.

An additional problem with attracting foreign buyers as well as Belizean buyers was that lodging was not located close to the tract and, further, the buyers were not clear as to the nature of development that the Hartmans had in mind. If these obstacles could be overcome, they felt that sales would pick up. Thus, in 1975 an attractive resort hotel, the Don Juan Hotel, was built on the property as a guest house for land sales prospects as well as a clear example of the standard that was to be met in developing the tracts. The hotel was pleasantly designed with breezy covered porches and high ceilings with a modest Spanish decor and, as originally designed, six very spacious rooms. All the rooms had, in one direction, a view of the Caribbean Sea beyond a field of coconut palms and, in the other direction, a view of the distant jungle.

Business Setbacks

For six years until 1981, the land sales company continued to operate but, even with an attractive promotional approach, sales did not keep up with expectations. A larger sales facility might have provided the volume necessary, but there was an economic problem as well. During this period the standard currency for international business transactions was the U.S. dollar; the United States was going through a severe recession, which made the acquisition of dollars extremely difficult.

This added a substantial burden to Carole's efforts in an already delicate business. The hotel in its own right was a success. It was considered by many to be the most elegant resort in the country; many of the country's most successful hoteliers, for example, got their start and initial training at the Don Juan. But the land sales part of the business suffered and dragged the rest of the operation into increasing financial difficulty.

In the end, the Hartmans decided to sell the Don Juan itself to a group of U.S. investors who promised to maintain the quality of the facility and keep it as a symbol of the type of structure that was appropriate for development. This 1981 sale turned out to be a large disappointment for Carole, however, as the U.S. investors let the hotel fall into disrepair; by the mid-1980s the structure was boarded up and had become an eyesore.

RETURN TO CANADA

Although British by birth, Carole was Canadian by marriage to Josh, an accomplished archaeologist and outdoorsman, and their next move was back to Canada. Through the early 1980s, Carole and Josh were involved in several ventures in Canada, but their hearts were in Belize, the Consejo village land, and the unspoiled jungles. From the day they departed for Canada, they began to plan how they would return.

To Carole, the idea of "exploiting" the natural environment by providing guided access to unusual sights and sounds while subtly demonstrating the need for protection of natural habitat had always seemed to be a sensible way to make a responsible economic return. Soon after their return to Canada, the Hartmans had created a tour company that provided exotic trips, jungle expeditions, caving trips, and similar adventures. This business was operating successfully out of Siesta Key near Sarasota, Florida.

BACK HOME IN BELIZE

In 1985, they moved their operations back to their land in Consejo where a large building and four thatched roof cottages were constructed in the local style at one end of the tract, two miles from the Don Juan, in a densely wooded area, to be a camp base. The new business would provide "hard adventures" in which the base would serve as a supply and training area for expeditions into the jungle to seek out Mayan ruins, and caves and to take river expeditions.

The cottages and dining facilities of the large building could be rented as a "motel," but Carole's desire was to avoid the traditional model and to provide an alternative retreat that would maximize the unique character of the natural environment as well as avoid some of the difficulties that were experienced with the earlier resort business. Inasmuch as the camp was located on an inlet of the Caribbean, and that there were stories that told that the region had once been a pirate hideaway, the name given to the new business was Pirates Cove Adventure Tours and Inn. The name was later shortened to Pirates Cove Inn.

Although the "hard" adventure tours were successful with those who sought them out, many more inquiries were received about the use of the cottages as a rustic resort—a modestly priced "motel" where people could get away from the rush of town life, away from the drudgery of meal preparation, and simply relax closer to nature than would be possible in a more conventional hotel with air conditioning and carpeted hallways. The staff was fluent in several languages, and the inn provided a wide array of "adventures" from windsurfing to jungle tours. Exhibit 31.1 shows the brochure used by Pirates Cove to send to prospective visitors.

Since 1986, this had seemed to be the market niche for Carole's business. Land sales were still being promoted and rugged expeditions were still being conducted, but for the most part the resort experiences and tours to nearby Lamanai were more of the "soft adventure" type. A secondary business also developed in conjunction with the dining hall, which had a reputation as one of the top restaurants in the area.

In 1988, the U.S. owners of the Don Juan leased the hotel to a group who refurbished the facility and reopened it as a more traditional resort. The businesses supported the development of each other by providing alternative accommodations and restaurants so that customers would not have to leave the immediate area. This combination of a traditional resort being located near a rustic alternative had been tried with success in several other areas of the Yucatan, especially on the Caribbean coast of Mexico and two other areas of Belize. Up until this point, direct service product competition had not been a concern for Carole. A concern that would continue to develop, ironically, was the question of possible saturation of the very thin market by international and national competitors.

EXHIBIT 31.1   Pirates Cove Inn Brochure

Pirates Cove Inn

...a refreshingly tropical relief from the hustle of the mainstream — friendly people, delicious food and comfortable thatch cottages overlooking the sparkling Caribbean Sea. Waters are excellent for windsurfing and sailing and there are exciting trips to MAYAN RUINS and jungle rivers. Tennis, nature trails, bicycle paths and lots of birds. Tiger Lilli's bar is a great place for swopping adventure stories. We will gladly help you plan your holiday and travel arrangements. RENTAL WINDSURFERS, SAILBOATS, BICYCLES, FISHING EQUIPMENT, GIFT SHOP.

Das Adventure Inn ist ein phantasticher ort mit freundlichen leuten, guter küche und gemuetlichen zimmern. Mit blick auf das Karibische meer. Belize hat viel zu bieten — es ist aufregend interessant und etwas besonderes. Subtropisches klima. Reisepass und visa (Britische botschaft) sind er forderlich.

C'est L' evasion et la différence dans un pays a découvrir : la Bélize! Allez-y pour la détente une cuisine authentique dans un décor unique et confortable, sur la mer des Caraïbes. Nouveau! Invitant! Chaleureux, en tout temps!
Passeport obligatoire.

Los invitamos a sentir una agradable experiencia. Venga a Adventure Inn a disfrutar de la vida. Comodas cabañas miran hacia el verde-azul mar Caribe, donde las aguas son ideales para nadar, para el sorfeo y paseos en veleros. La comida es deliciosa, la atmosfera maravillosmente tropical. La gente es amable y nuestro personal de habla hispana estan esperandolos para dar bienvenida.

RATES		$US	
DOUBLE EP	—	38	+5% GOV. TAX
SINGLE EP	—	32	
PICK UP			
BELIZE CITY		90	1-6 PERSONS
PLEASE REMIT 1 DAY'S RENTAL AS DEPOSIT.			
MAJOR CREDIT CARDS ACCEPTED.			

Reservations:

Travel to Belize

Belize, formerly British Honduras, is an easy-going friendly country with the atmosphere of a small town, which is not surprising as the population is a mere 160,000. The people are of various origin, ENGLISH SPEAKING, though spanish is widely used.

We have a wealth of natural sights, an abundance of birds, orchids, butterflies and wildlife, a barrier reef that is a paradise of multicoloured corals and tropical fish — the largest in the Western Hemisphere. We offer rustic hospitality, and for those looking for a commercialized destination this is not it. The small friendly and politically stable population together with its natural wonders make Belize a safe and exciting place to vacation.

US & commonwealth citizens require passports. 2 hour flight from Houston, New Orleans & Miami. Serviced by TACA, TAN/SAHSA, and EASTERN. For those coming through Mexico buses and flights are available to Chetumal Mexico (20 miles from Consejo).

THE INN

As of 1989, the Pirates Cove Inn had 12 cottages, all in the palapa style with thatched roofs, large screened windows, and heavy drapes to keep out strong winds and for privacy. Some cottages had a private bath inside and others shared an adjoining outside bath. Hot water was provided through gas heaters. The cottages ranged in size from a single cottage with twin beds to adjoining cottages with up to four double beds plus twin beds.

Although the new government was rapidly providing electrical service to all areas, the Consejo area was still without regular service; hence, the inn relied on its own generator for power in the early evening and rechargeable automobile batteries for other times. Telephone service was likewise an independent system using a citizens band radio to call, and to receive calls from, an operator in Corozal who would patch communications through to telephone lines that, in turn, could be connected to international communication systems. Bottled drinking water was provided by a maid who supplied fresh linen each day and washed the native mahogany floors.

The normal work day began at 6 A.M. when Raoul arrived in the company van with five or six female employees who lived in Corozal. One or two other women who lived within walking distance of the inn arrived at the same time. Carole, or her sister-in-law Rosa, who was the assistant manager of the inn, would discuss the day's work in terms of the cottages that would be occupied and the number of meals that would have to be served, special arrangements for tour groups, and so forth. Once the day's plan had been discussed, Raoul drove back into Corozal to purchase food and other items. At 3 P.M. he would return the women to their homes and pick up another group of five or six who would work until 11 P.M.

Having no continuous, specialized duties, the women were acquainted with all jobs and, depending on the number and nature of the guests, a worker might help to prepare meals, wait on tables, clean out cottages, or answer telephone calls. Occasionally, when the inn was very busy, a third shift of workers would be employed from among those women of the village of Consejo who were identified as being capable and willing to work on a part-time basis. Other men and women were employed on a daily or project basis especially during the months of May through December when the rainy season kept occupancy lower and there would be time to make repairs and add new items to the physical facilities.

Typically, the months of September and October were the very slowest; during one such period, more efficient lighting fixtures were added to the cottages and a row of lights was added to the main path that led along the front of the cottages to the lodge. The lodge was expanded to include dining seating for 30, and the bar was enlarged and a small souvenir shop was added. It was during one of these slow periods when a group of U.S. Peace Corps volunteer trainers visited the inn and expressed an interest in developing a training site on one of the adjacent parcels of undeveloped land. The most intense time for Peace Corps training occurred during the months after spring graduations at U.S. universities.

Carole's basic philosophy for customer service was to give as much personal, individualized attention as possible. People came to the inn expecting a unique experience, and personal attention served to reinforce this. Likewise, the employees were expected to do what ever was asked of them, and this would change daily or even more often. Under these conditions, Carole believed, a personal relationship with all staff members was crucial so that misunderstandings would not occur.

During the day, Rosa supervised workers in the lodge and cottage and did the bookkeeping but always had time to chat with a guest and to explain how things were done. At meal time she mingled with guests while tending to her baby, who often became a focus of conversation.

In the late afternoon after returning from business trips to Corozal or Belize City or perhaps from Chetumal, Mexico, looking for a hard-to-find item needed for a repair job, or meeting with prospective land buyers, Carole would join guests at the bar to listen to the stories of the day's adventures and to give tips for the next day's activities. She would soon be joined by her 10-year-old son, Zak, who had dinner with her in the lodge, which added to the informal, intimate atmosphere. About this time Josh would arrive with an exhausted but exhilarated small group that had been out on a jungle expedition; his competent and patient manner would add to the general feelings of camaraderie.

Business Prospects

With major tour agencies in U.S. cities such as Houston and Minneapolis promoting the inn and arranging for week-long stays, the question of immediate survival was no longer a daily concern. On occasion, these agencies stirred Carole's imagination with questions about developing other locations in the country. The central and southern part of Belize, they noted, had a different topography and mix of wildlife as well as cultural traditions. Such variety, they pointed out, could give them a greater range of options for their small but highly committed clientele. The commitment level, indeed, had never been a problem as evidenced by increasing numbers of return visits by people who found the mix of rugged resort living, with soft adventure opportunities, and personalized attention to be almost too good to be true.

Carole wondered what she should prepare for next. The inquiries by the U.S. Peace Corps training personnel were interesting. She could sell the adjacent land and use the capital to upgrade and expand the Pirates Cove Inn or perhaps establish another inn someplace else. She worried that an expanded Pirates Cove Inn might not be conducive to providing quality customer service in a quiet serene setting that the guests had come to expect.

Competition with the Don Juan was beneficial because it brought more visitors to the area and increased the dining room usage, but Carole wondered how many more competitors the area could support—economically and ecologically.

CASE 32

Lance Takes On New Challenges

In an article in 1982, *Forbes* observed, "The folks at Lance, Inc., the largest independent snack food manufacturer in the U.S., don't cotton much to management tools like debt financing, plant automation, or even advertising. But the company has a remarkable record of performance." The article quoted A. F. "Pete" Sloan, then president of Lance, "Hell, you don't need to go out and get yourself a computer and 14 MBAs to run a successful business." Performance spoke for itself: Over the five years through 1982, Lance had one of the best after-tax margins in the $11 billion snack food industry, averaging 8.1 percent versus an estimated 4 percent for Nabisco and 7 percent at PepsiCo's Frito-Lay division. Return on equity was above 19 percent and Lance had almost no debt. From sales of $291 million in 1982, the company has grown to $430 million in 1989. Return on equity was maintained at 20 percent, and the company had no long-term debt. Attempts had been made to grow through diversification, but results were disappointing. "Moving beyond our traditional markets is going to make continued growth more challenging," stated Bill Disher, newly appointed chief executive officer of Lance. "We may have to be more aggressive in the supermarket or maybe even consider advertising."

HISTORY

Lance began operations over 75 years ago by accident. Philip L. Lance, a coffee salesman and food broker from Charlotte, North Carolina, purchased 500 pounds of fine Virginia peanuts for a customer. After the customer decided that he could not use the peanuts, Mr. Lance took the peanuts home so as not to disappoint the Virginia peanut farmer. The peanuts were roasted in small quantities in Lance's kitchen and then were sold in brown paper bags for a nickel. The company was formed in 1913 when Philip Lance formed a partnership with S. A. Van Every, his son-in-law and an associate in the food brokerage business.

This case was prepared by Earl R. Sage and Linda E. Swayne as a basis for class discussion rather than to illustrate either effective or ineffective handling of an administrative situation. Used with permission from Earl R. Sage.

The business expanded, outgrowing the Lance home, and a mechanical roaster was added in the new space. The roaster purchase enabled the young company to manufacture peanut butter, which Mr. Lance spread on crackers for his customers to sample. This led to the first packaged peanut butter sandwich ever sold. Mr. Lance died in an automobile accident in late 1926, at which point Mr. Van Every took over operations and incorporated the company.

Lance added baking operations in 1938 in order to make its own crackers. In 1943, following the death of his father, Phil Van Every became president. Lance had become primarily a candy company prior to World War II but determined that the company could make more extensive use of its wartime sugar allowance by producing snack foods. Phil Van Every automated many operations and reorganized the sales and distribution network; his entrepreneurial and managerial skills helped the company build a recognized position in the snack food industry and paved the way for Lance to succeed even after his death in 1980. When Phil Van Every retired, he was succeeded by J. B. Meacham and then Glen G. Rhodes. When Mr. Rhodes retired in 1980, A. F. "Pete" Sloan was appointed as chairman. In 1992, the Van Every family, although no longer directly involved in management, was still represented on the board of directors and continued to control (either directly or in trust) over 44 percent of the outstanding shares of stock. Sloan stepped down as chief executive officer in April 1990 after 34 years with Lance (14 years as CEO), but retained the post of chairman of the board. He was succeeded as CEO by J. W. "Bill" Disher, a 25-year veteran of Lance who had been serving the company as president. A graduate of Wake Forest University, Bill Disher held finance positions prior to becoming president and CEO.

THE SNACK FOOD INDUSTRY

The lines between a snack food and traditional meal food have blurred and a significant portion of our population has adopted "grazing" or eating many small meals throughout the day. Because of busy American lifestyles, many consumers do not have the time nor the interest to prepare and sit down to eat three complete meals in a day. Instead, they eat portable snack foods while on the run. Others enjoy rewarding themselves for all their hard work with an expensive or highly caloric taste treat. Whether called fun foods, finger foods, portable foods, or fast foods, snacks are part of the American way of life and represent a $29 billion dollar industry.

The industry had at least 17 different categories of snack foods, but three major segments were dominant: candy, cookies and crackers, and salty snacks. The confectionery category (candy bars and candy morsels) had always accounted for the greatest percentage of snack food sales. The salted snack foods category, nearly half of which was potato chips, had traditionally accounted for the smallest share among the three.

The majority of snack food products appeared to have reached the maturity stage of the product life cycle; distribution was pervasive and per capita sales were stable. Growth in unit volume was not expected to exceed population growth, especially considering mounting consumer concerns about eating healthier foods. Snack foods were being increasingly scrutinized and avoided by health-conscious consumers.

New product development centered on line extensions of existing brands: new sizes (more small packages to meet the needs of busy consumers), new flavors of existing products, and new formulations (less salt, oil, or cholesterol). Many of the regional manufacturers followed the lead of the major competitors who spent huge sums on new product research and development as well as marketing research. Regional producers, such as Lance, faced strong competition, especially from the large marketing-knowledgeable companies such as Frito-Lay, Borden, and Eagle. Consolidation was expected to continue as the giants bought out regional producers to obtain better distribution. Distribution was critical in the industry because of the high cost of transportation for products that weighed very little but that were bulky and took up space. The price advantage of shorter distribution routes was a key factor in the success of regional snack manufacturers. All major competitors used a store-to-door delivery system where snack food company-owned trucks delivered and stocked product to individual stores rather than to a warehouse.

The bargaining power of raw material suppliers such as potato and corn farmers had become more influential; as weather and crop conditions boosted the costs for agricultural growers, snack food manufacturers found themselves incurring high prices for food ingredients. To some extent, large snack food manufacturers were in a stronger position to try to negotiate quantity discounts on raw material purchases than were small producers.

Another issue that had to be dealt with by snack food manufacturers was the bargaining power of their buyers, principally supermarkets. Concentration in the food retailing industry was high, and supermarket chains accounted for about 70 percent of total snack food sales. "It is risky to depend on a small number of large customers . . . diversification is important," according to Jack Moore, Lance executive vice president. He continued, "We have 300,000 customers which gives us the strength to stand up to any single customer. And we have to balance the various segments. The question is always, is it good for Lance?"

Jerry Swain, vice president of sales for Lance, observed, "Although snack sales have increased for retailers in recent years and are projected to continue growing in the near future, there is just not enough room on the shelf for the snack food category. The number of products and line extensions being introduced has caused a space crunch. This lack of shelf space has caused a problem with stock-outs and losses in sales and profits. Therefore retailers will use distribution channels, pricing, and manufacturer support programs as critical considerations in the choice between brands. Innovative advertising and couponing may direct the competitive forces of the market."

Another important influence was the differences that prevailed in regional taste preferences. Products such as pork skins, moon pies, and salt and vinegar potato chips were big sellers in some regions (Southeast) but generated very low sales volumes in others. In order to be competitive, one of the industry leaders, Frito-Lay, implemented a plan in 1987 to regionalize operations, sales, and marketing. The company defined eight regions and allowed managers to tailor product-line strategies to compete head-to-head with local and regional snack manufacturers.

Snack food consumption is related to population growth, the economy (during prosperous times a greater portion of disposable income is spent eating away from home and snack consumption decreases), and consumer concerns about health (use of salt in the diet, cholesterol, and weight concerns). Consumption patterns by age group were also changing as consumers were taking their snack habits with them as they grew older. Maturing baby boomers were bringing into their adult lives many of the snacks they ate as children. Although children were still the biggest group of snackers, adults were a growing portion of the market.

Another consumer trend affecting the industry was that of home entertainment. Whether due to the rise in VCR ownership or the increased concern about drunken driving, people were often entertaining their friends at home rather than meeting at a bar. The increasing desire to eat healthfully and conveniently created many opportunities for snack food makers to introduce low-salt, no-salt, low-fat, and no-cholesterol versions of their products. Additionally, companies introduced smaller sizes of their popular products as a way of helping consumers control the number of calories they consumed.

There was little concern in the industry concerning foreign entry into the market. "We're about to reach zero population growth and flour and snack foods are not high-tech," according to Bill Disher. He continued, "There are very low barriers to entry—most folks could make our products at home if they wanted to. . . . Demand is static. Most textbooks would say this is a poor industry, but we've been able to set net sales and earnings records for over a decade."

MAJOR COMPETITORS

Jack Moore stated, "Our competition is anything that doesn't have Lance's name on it. Anything that satisfies an appetite—a homemade sandwich, a piece of watermelon, peanuts, anybody else's potato chips, etc., is competition. If it doesn't have Lance on the label, we've lost an opportunity." Lance had a number of direct competitors in the mature snack food industry, however. Some, such as Frito-Lay, were national in scope but had developed regional strategies and product lines to enhance their competitive capabilities. Borden amassed a collection of 10 regional snack companies to achieve the advantages of regional customer satisfaction and the efficiencies from operating a larger company. Because of the significant freight charges previously mentioned, most of the competitors maintained regional manufacturing and distribution facilities. On the other hand, some of Lance's rivals were truly regional and operated only in a specific geographic area—Mike Sell's Chips sold only in Tennessee and Ohio, Coors Chips sold in seven western states, and Moore's Chips sold in eight mid-Atlantic states.

Frito-Lay: The Largest Producer of Snack Foods

Frito-Lay was the snack division of PepsiCo and its major profit center. Frito-Lay had 37 manufacturing and processing plants in the United States and 12 foreign countries. Its varied line of snack foods included Fritos brand corn chips, Lay's, Ruffles, and O'Grady's brand potato chips, Munchos brand potato crisps, Cheetos brand cheese-flavored snacks, Doritos and Tostitos brand tortilla chips, Funyun brand onion-flavored snacks, Baken-Ets brand fried pork rinds, Grandma's brand cookies, and Frito-Lay brand crackers, dips, and popcorn.

Over 1,600 distribution facilities and 10,000 route sales reps ensured that Frito-Lay products arrived fresh and were stocked daily onto supermarket shelves. This store-to-door delivery system allowed Frito-Lay to maintain close inventory control, reduced supermarket labor costs, and provided customers with fresh, uncrushed snack foods.

The company was building on its strength as the largest snack food producer in the United States. It had established brand strength and was seeking to further that strength through successful introduction of line extensions (e.g., Doritos Light) and reorganization of its marketing effort to create a stronger regional presence. Frito-Lay was rapidly expanding in existing markets as well as entering new markets both in the United States and abroad.

Borden: Snack Foods Division Targeted for Growth

Borden's snack division was one of six company divisions targeted for growth in the 1990s. Acquisitions in 1987 of the Snacktime Company and Laura Scudder's increased snack sales by about 40 percent and broadened the company's network of regional companies. Its principal national brands were Wise, La Famous, New York Deli, Borden, and Seyfert. In addition, the company had an assortment of purely regional brands such as Laura Scudder's, Geiser's Potato Chips, and Red Seal.

Borden intended to continue its profitable growth in the six designated divisions through carefully focused acquisitions and internal growth. Strong regional companies were prime targets for acquisition, as they offered established brands and provided synergy to an already strong regional network of snack companies.

Golden Enterprises: A Major Regional Competitor

The Golden Flake trademark is carried on a full line of snack foods that were distributed in 12 southeastern states. The snack products were manufactured by plants in Alabama, Tennessee, and Florida. Golden Flake's product line included potato chips, tortilla chips, corn chips, fried pork skins, baked and fried cheese curls, peanut butter crackers, cheese crackers, onion rings, and popcorn that were manufactured by the company. Also included in the product line were cakes and cookie items, canned dips, dried meat products, pretzels, and nuts that were manufactured by other companies but packaged under the Golden Flake label. The company's earnings were somewhat depressed for a period of time, primarily due to increased competition and because the level of sales had not been sufficient to offset the higher costs associated with increased production capacity, expanded reach, and higher advertising and promotional expenses.

Similar to Lance, Golden Flake used a "follow-the-leader" strategy. The company did not spend much on developing new products, but it did advertise and made profitable use of sales promotion. A tie-in with the Southeastern Conference (SEC) for football games, where a custom van in each SEC team's colors was given away, had been particularly effective.

Golden Flake dominated in Alabama and was usually second behind Frito-Lay in the other states where the brand was sold. Distribution was primarily through grocery stores, although the Golden Flake brands were sold in vending machines in the company's primary markets of Alabama, Mississippi, Georgia, and Tennessee. With new facilities recently completed and renovation to the Birmingham plant, Golden Flake could increase production 50 percent. Sales in 1990 surpassed $129 million.

CORPORATE CULTURE

Lance was founded as a family business and the company worked diligently to maintain that atmosphere despite its growth. Many of the employees spent their entire working careers dedicated to serving Lance and its customers. "Stay close to the customers and the customers are always right." Those company values, along with "quality and value in an honest product from a reputable company," form the core of the Lance culture. The company's business principles and philosophical values are set forth in Exhibit 32.1.

The family orientation at Lance was encouraged. Everyone at Lance was known on a first-name basis. All executives and employees ate together in a common cafeteria. At 9 A.M. each morning a bell rang for silent prayer; it happened again at 5:30 P.M. for the second shift. This custom started during World War II, with prayers for victory. After the war it continued, as a thanksgiving for peace. Jack Moore commented, "Lance believes in basic values of doing what's right . . . in family values. Employees of Lance are the salt of the earth."

Lance promoted from within; outsiders were brought in only when Lance people lacked the needed skills and knowledge. Every officer of Lance has worked on a route truck. Food science people with their specialized knowledge were hired early in their career so they could become enculturated with the Lance philosophy.

EXHIBIT 32.1   Lance Statement of Business Philosophy

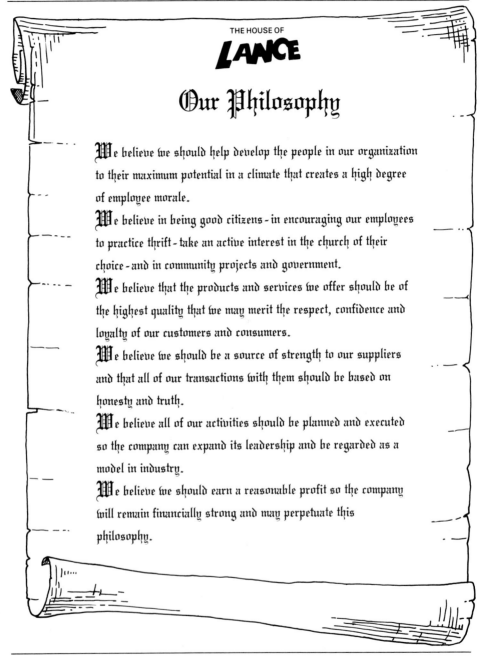

THE HOUSE OF

LANCE

Our Philosophy

We believe we should help develop the people in our organization to their maximum potential in a climate that creates a high degree of employee morale.

We believe in being good citizens - in encouraging our employees to practice thrift - take an active interest in the church of their choice - and in community projects and government.

We believe that the products and services we offer should be of the highest quality that we may merit the respect, confidence and loyalty of our customers and consumers.

We believe we should be a source of strength to our suppliers and that all of our transactions with them should be based on honesty and truth.

We believe all of our activities should be planned and executed so the company can expand its leadership and be regarded as a model in industry.

We believe we should earn a reasonable profit so the company will remain financially strong and may perpetuate this philosophy.

Source: Philip Lance Van Every, *The History of Lance* (New York: Newcomen Society in North America), 1974.

Lance operated by committees, a concept that was started in the early 1940s shortly after S. A. Van Every died. His son, Philip Van Every, observed multiple management in operation while visiting McCormick Spice Company in Philadelphia. Phil Van Every adopted and improved the concept. Although individuals had titles, Lance looked to its board of directors, executive committee, and administrative committee for leadership. The executive committee and the administrative committee were responsible for day-to-day operations. Important decisions with far-reaching implications were taken before the board of directors.

Other committees operated in the functional areas. For example, the products committee (comprised of company executives as well as sales, manufacturing, and technical representatives) approved a new product only when the sales department believed it could be sold, manufacturing believed it could be made, and purchasing believed it could obtain the ingredients. Various tests had to be passed, including the keeping test (length of time that the product could be maintained in inventory and through distribution while still keeping its freshness), profitability test, and the ingredients test (the ingredients have to be in keeping with the management philosophy of quality and good health with low cholesterol and low sodium).

In the spring, "P and R" (planning and review) meetings were held. P and R meetings included all branch managers who operated as route supervisors for up to nine reps. They were in constant contact with the customer, as they spent time with the route sales reps in the field. The P and R meetings were followed a few weeks later by a DSM (district sales manager) meeting, which included the corporate officers (in Lance's culture "the people from Charlotte"). Early in the summer, the Charlotte people reviewed and critiqued the minutes of the P and R meetings and the DSM meetings; those minutes became the worksheet for the summer. In the fall, the corporate personnel met with the district sales managers again to discuss how they resolved the problems or had taken advantage of the opportunities highlighted by the district sales managers. Then the district sales managers met with all the route supervisors in another round of P and R meetings, where the problems, solutions, and opportunities were reported to them.

PRODUCTION AND DISTRIBUTION

Lance manufactured, distributed, and sold a wide variety of packaged snack foods and bread basket items (products that would be placed in a basket at restaurants as an addition or alternative for bread). The principal snack items included cracker sandwiches filled with either peanut butter or cheese; cookie sandwiches; cheese bits and twists; peanuts; potato, tortilla, and corn chips; fried pork skins; popcorn; fig bars and cookies; and cakes, candies, and meat snacks. These products were sold under the Lance label to convenience stores, service stations, drug stores, supermarkets, schools, restaurants, hospitals, and other customers in 35 states and the District of Columbia. The majority of sales were from east of the Mississippi. Approximately 15 to 20 percent of the company's net sales volume was generated by products purchased from other manufacturers and distributed under the Lance label.

The company's principal bread basket items were wafers, crackers, bread sticks, and melba toast. These products were individually packaged and sold to restaurants, schools, and similar institutions, along with bulk-packaged croutons and cracker meal.

Thirty percent of the company's products were sold in company-owned vending machines that were made available to customers on a rental, sale, or commission basis. These machines were usually situated in noncompetitive locations where Lance did not have to fight for shelf space by offering deep discounts and promotions. Less than 5 percent of sales were made to outside vending distributors. Lance also packaged several of its most popular snack and bread basket items in convenient-sized "home-paks" sold in supermarkets and grocery stores. This product line, first introduced in limited markets in 1987, represented approximately 12 to 13 percent of snack sales. The bulk of Lance's market was the over-the-counter, single-serve pack sold in convenience stores, gas stations, and quick stops.

Through a program of continuous expansion, replacement, or renovation of facilities and equipment, and automation of processes, the company sought to utilize the most advanced technology available. This policy enabled the company to reduce operating costs and increase manufacturing efficiency, allowing Lance to maintain relatively consistent prices, an important advantage in vending sales where step pricing occurs. Lance and others who sold through vending machines had to increase prices in minimum 5-cent increments (steps) because the machines are not configured to accept pennies.

MARKETING

Lance's marketing strategy was anchored on a follow-the-leader strategy for new product development, devotion to a single-serving product size, and no advertising. By waiting for larger companies to develop and market new products and by maintaining its no advertising policy, Lance was able to incorporate new products into the line at about half the cost of the industry leaders. In the late 1970s, in an attempt to break out of its follower strategy, Lance introduced honey-coated peanuts. The product was unsuccessful in a small test area and was not introduced elsewhere. However, when Anheuser-Busch's Eagle Snacks Honey Roasted Peanuts caught on with consumers, Lance promptly reintroduced its honey-coated peanuts and at nearly half the price.

Product Development

Although Lance's main thrust was in the single-serve market, it had $65 million in supermarket sales in 1989. The company had resisted increasing its single-serving product size to capture more supermarket customers, although industry sources estimated that 70 percent of all snack foods were sold in the supermarket. The decision to enter the competition for shelf space was carefully considered. Pete Sloan had been reluctant to change the company's marketing mix to include larger-sized packages because "a supermarket sale takes away a vending machine sale." However, vending machines sales were growing at only about 3 percent a year. The company moved slowly into supermarket sales with its home-pak product line. Actually, the gas shortages between 1973 and 1975 caused Lance to begin thinking about supermarket sales. "Our drivers passed by the stores and we figured they might as well stop in and sell some products," Jack Moore remembered thinking. In addition, there were letters from Lance customers who wanted Captain's Wafers (crackers) in a convenient take-home size. Customers had enjoyed the good taste of Captain's Wafers in restaurants and wrote to Lance requesting that they be made available in local grocery stores. In 1982, Lance began supermarket sales with multipacks of Captain's Wafers. The home-pak consisted of eight of the individual packs combined in one package. This was a cost-effective way to enter the market without changing the product line.

Lance route sales reps knew how to sell the "racks" that were used for displaying single-serve products in over-the-counter sales. Because shelf space was always difficult to capture in supermarkets, Lance provided vertical, free-standing racks and a 5 percent discount to win the display space. The racks were totally maintained by Lance's sales force—another benefit to the store. It took Lance about four years to achieve distribution to supermarkets in all the company's territories.

Family-pack potato chips (large size containing six ounces as opposed to the one-ounce snack size) were introduced to the over-the-counter market on July 4, 1988. This expansion of the product mix to include a variety of family-size chip products was made possible by new computerized bagging machinery. Distribution was achieved in about 90 percent of the sales territories by September 1990.

Lance bought some food products from other manufacturers and planned to continue to do so. For example, only two or three companies produced melba toast because of the specialized manufacturing ovens required. Lance purchased the dried bread product from these companies because it was such a low-volume item. It was not economically feasible for Lance to manufacture melba toast, but it did fill out the line. Lance generated profits from manufacturing *and* distribution of its own products. For private-label items (such as melba toast) there was no manufacturing profit, but there was distribution profit achieved by the efficient store-to-door distribution. Companion products were added when the company felt that the items were necessary to be able to offer a full line to its customers. "We're slow to change," according to Jerry Swain.

Recently candy rolls were dropped from Lance's line. The product was private label (manufactured by someone else with Lance's name on it). Candy rolls competed head-to-head with Life Savers. Lance decided that the supplier's manufacturing quality was not up to Lance's standards. Lance always inspected a supplier's facilities, plants, sanitation methods, and quality control practices whenever the Lance name was going on a product. "Customers trust the quality of a product with the Lance label regardless of who makes it," Jerry stated.

New Products

Lance introduced a new product that combined popcorn with caramel coating and peanuts in a bar. Named Popscotch, it was being sold in vending machines and over the counter. However, Lance found it difficult to introduce a totally new product (such as Popscotch) without advertising. Lance generally used a copy-cat strategy (follow the leader) for new product development that was compatible with the company's no advertising philosophy.

Lance was adjusting to market forces by testing chocolate candy sales. Previously, it had not sold chocolate candy in vending machines because of the problems associated with chocolate melting while on the truck. In November 1990, Lance announced that it would offer four Mars Candy Company candies along with cookie and cracker snacks in about half of its 73,000 company-owned vending machines nationwide. The other half would be stocked with Lance brand chocolate candy made by a Georgia-based candy manufacturer. "We've had people tell us: 'We love your products, but one thing you're lacking is chocolate,'" said Bill Disher. "It's a test—to see if that, in fact, is correct." Disher said the goal was to determine whether Lance could increase the number of vending locations by adding candy to the mix in the machines. The Mars products included Snickers, Milky Way, and peanut and plain M&Ms. "We'll evaluate it in the spring and decide," Disher said.

Robinson Humphrey Company, an Atlanta-based regional brokerage firm that followed Lance, said the candy sold under Lance's label would carry a higher profit margin but probably would not have the sales volume of the popular Mars products. The test was scheduled to start in November so that no problems would be encountered with melting chocolate. If sales go well, a decision will be made about truck refrigeration—not a minor decision when the company had more than 2,000 trucks on the road.

New technology in packaging materials had been developed. What used to be a cellophane wrapper was now a layer of film that had a vapor barrier, a moisture barrier, and an odor barrier plus the logo within a layer of the film. Most of Lance's products had a six-week shelf life. Increased shelf life and fresher products would provide cost savings and consumer benefits. Lance was actively pursuing technological improvements in packaging and expected innovations to continue. Any packaging change was quickly copied by competitors, seldom offering a long-term competitive advantage.

Lance Leads with Healthier Snacks

In contrast to its traditional follow-the-leader strategy but in response to growing consumer preferences for health-conscious snacks, Lance gambled and reformulated its traditional recipes in 1988 to make them healthier. The company greatly reduced the saturated fats and cholesterol content for most of its snack foods in order to appeal to customers with health and nutrition concerns. Lance was the first in the snack food industry to respond to the changing emphasis on nutrition in the environment. Pete Sloan, the CEO at the time, was active in regulatory agencies in Washington. Noticing the trends in nutritional labeling and health concerns, Sloan became convinced that Lance should be the leader in providing nutritional snacks.

Lance decided early in the process that taste would have to drive the decision to switch to low-cholesterol ingredients. Taste tests were conducted within Lance until various groups of employees could not tell the difference between the old Lance products, which were higher in cholesterol, and the new Lance products. It took two years to develop the line of low cholesterol products. After limited market research but extensive taste testing, Lance instituted the changes, which resulted in 74 percent of its 69 snack food and bakery items being cholesterol-free and 97 percent being low in saturated fats. According to Jack Moore, "The company was particularly sensitive to taste because previously a granola cake tested awhile back was unsuccessful. For good health, it contained grains and was low in cholesterol, salt, and sugar. It was nutritious, but it didn't taste very good. Sales were disappointing and it was dropped. We concluded that while customers are interested in nutrition, they are more interested in good taste!"

The logistics of the changeover to the low cholesterol products were challenging. The packaging film for the new Lance products contained a low cholesterol "flag" on the label. Because each product had been changed, each required a new label. Logistically and economically, the old packaging film had to run out at the appropriate time. Lance set a date for every department to be ready to make the changeover. Additionally, all of the old products had to be off the shelf and out of the vending machines before Lance could publicize the new product line. Finally, management had to teach the sales force about saturated and unsaturated fats and cholesterol in order for the reps to be able to illustrate the "value-added" health benefit to the customer. Because the company did no advertising, it was up to the sales force, packaging, and trucks to build awareness.

Normally it took six weeks to move products through the channel of distribution, but Lance waited three months before announcing the low-cholesterol changeover. In December 1988, the facility was totally manufacturing the low-cholesterol products, but it was not until March 1989 that the announcement was made to the public to ensure that all the old products were out of vending machines and through distribution. The company planned for increased sales to offset the cost of using more expensive, healthier oils and did not increase the selling price. It was not until eight months later that there was a price increase and it was not solely because of increased ingredient prices but because of increased costs of other items such as employee health insurance.

The reformulation was considered a success by the company and thought to be one of the major contributors to increased revenues in 1989. The publicity following the formulation change was very favorable. Lance was one of a small number of companies that was recognized by the Washington-based Center for Science in the Public Interest for its move to lower the levels of fats and cholesterol in most of its snacks. Although Lance was the first cookie and cracker manufacturer to reformulate, other companies, notably Keebler, were quick to follow.

Lance's Strategy of No Advertising

As Pete Sloan said in an interview with *Forbes* magazine, "We have never advertised, and we don't plan to start . . . we get more for our money by putting it into manpower and improving the production line." Lance's policy of no advertising grew out of its experiences in the 1950s. In 1953, Lance had experienced sluggish sales; management felt that advertising might help. They engaged an advertising agency from Atlanta. The agency did away with the old logo—Lance in script letters with a charging knight holding a lance—and changed to the logo still used in 1992 (Exhibit 32.2). They developed television advertising (at a time when only 10 percent of the population had TVs), radio ads, billboards, and ads for Sunday supplements. In addition, the agency came up with the slogans "Don't Go around Hungry" and "Tasty Snacks in Cellophane Packs." The advertising was continued for four years through 1958.

The result was no change in sales. Management concluded, "Lance's products are small and unimportant to consumers. They won't cross the street to buy

EXHIBIT 32.2   Lance Logos

something to satisfy their appetite. Availability is much more important than the price or how the product is displayed or promoted. Substitutes are readily available to the customer." When the company saw no change in sales, it stopped advertising and emphasized what has become known as the "doctrine of availability," which states that "the best advertisement is a snack when you want it and where you least expect it."

During the time that Lance had been advertising, each sales branch had 18 sales reps. Redirecting efforts toward availability rather than advertising, the company cut all the sales branches in half so that there would be nine sales reps per territory and stipulated in the job description that the branch manager should spend 75 percent of the time working with the sales reps in the field. With greater emphasis on sales reps and with managers spending more time in the field, sales drastically increased.

Sales/Distribution Organization

Lance sold its products through a company-owned sales organization (Exhibit 32.3). Distribution operations were administered through 24 sales districts, which were divided into 291 sales areas, each under the direction of a branch manager and an assistant branch manager. There were 2,500 sales territories, each serviced by one sales representative who made every effort to visit customers at the same time each week. A new trainee spent up to six months learning the territory, the product, and the Lance sales techniques.

The company owned a fleet of trucks and trailers that were used to make weekly deliveries of product to the sales territories. The sales representatives were provided with stockroom space for their inventories, from which they loaded their trucks for delivery to customers. Because most on the sales force purchased their own delivery truck, Lance avoided high fleet-maintenance costs. Also, this direct store delivery system reduced or eliminated many excess retail costs such as warehousing, transportation, and maintenance.

An automated route accounting (ARA) system was in the process of being tested and implemented. Two markets were testing the ARA. At night the sales reps in the two test areas hooked up to a computer through a modem in the main terminal to report the day's activities. This in turn helped to set the baking schedule because it was known what was sold that particular day. Inventory and marketing knowledge were enhanced, and errors were eliminated. Because over 300,000 tickets were written per week, this system was expected to greatly improve communication with the route salespeople.

Local managers had the responsibility for recruiting, hiring, and training the route sales reps in their territory. Every Lance manager worked on a route at one time. Lance managers endeavored to hire only the best route reps because the performance of the branch affected the pay of the local manager. Because of Lance's reputation as a good company to work for, there were many applicants whenever a route sales rep position became available.

EXHIBIT 32.3   Lance Area of Distribution

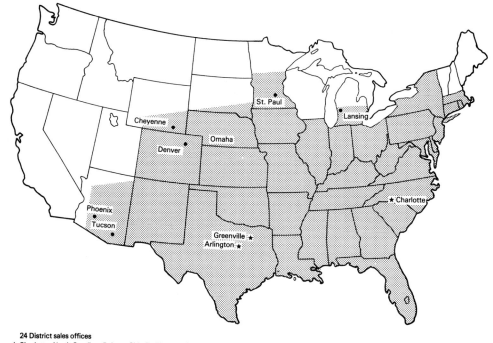

24 District sales offices
★ Charlotte, North Carolina, Bakery, Chip Facility, and General Office
★ Greenville, Texas, Bakery
★ Arlington, Texas, Chip Facility

DIVERSIFICATION

Lance had attempted to grow through diversification, but the results were generally "disappointing." The company sold its Hancock's Old Fashioned Hams division to Smithfield Packing Company in 1982. In 1986, the company sold its Tri-Plas division, a manufacturer of injection-molded plastic containers and Lance's only nonfood subsidiary. Both divestitures resulted in slight losses for Lance. Nutrition Pak Corporation, manufacturer of nutritional food products sold through contracts with distributors, was acquired in 1984. The subsidiary reported an increase in sales in 1987, but it was not enough to make it profitable, and operations ceased in January 1989.

On the other hand, Midwest Biscuit Company, a manufacturer of cookies and crackers acquired in 1979, had continued to grow and made a significant contribution to both sales and profits. Midwest's products were manufactured under both private label and its own "Vista" label. The subsidiary's sales were made through brokers and its own sales force to wholesale grocers, supermarket chains, and distributors throughout the United States, with the majority of its business in the Midwest. Bill Disher commented, "We're actively searching for acquisitions. We prefer companion items . . . especially those that fit our distribution system. It is our goal in 1991 to get proactive in acquisitions. We haven't been very successful in the past."

FINANCIAL POSITION

Although snack food sales generally had more than doubled in the past five years, Lance's unit volume was relatively flat with only moderate increases in revenues. Sales growth had averaged about 5 percent over the past five years with part of that growth being a result of price increases in 1983 and 1986. Earnings, on the other hand, had grown an average of 10 percent over the past decade.

Lance maintained a strong position of liquidity and had the financial strength to meet its regular operating needs, to fund its capital investment program, and to make cash dividend payments, all through funds provided by operations (Exhibits 32.4, 32.5, and 32.6). Lance had been consistently profitable with net income rising each year since 1973, dividends rising each year since 1974, and return on equity averaging more than 19 percent since 1974. Since the sale of Tri-Plas in May 1986, the company had maintained no long-term debt. From 1985 to 1987, new capital investment totaled $75.5 million, all of which was financed out of internal cash flows.

THE FUTURE

Lance tried to do a little "perimeter expansion" each year. Management looked to the boundary of current sales territories to see if there were any major markets that should be included. In 1990, Boston and Chicago became new markets for Lance. The company's strategic objective was consistent growth rather than peaks and valleys. In 1982, Pete Sloan said, "We have no plans to jump over 1,000 miles of jack rabbits to get to the people again." As succinctly stated by Jack Moore, "Lance believes sales without profit is swelling, not growth."

In actuality, the growth of the Sunbelt brought customers to Lance and made it less important for Lance to go seeking new markets. Sixty percent of the population of the United States is within 600 miles of Charlotte, where Lance's major manufacturing facility was located. A second plant was located in Greenville, Texas. Lance's expansion was restricted primarily by the development of personnel. The company wanted to maintain its policy of promotion from within. Therefore, it was growing only as much as its "good quality" and "doing things right" philosophy would allow.

EXHIBIT 32.4 Statements of Consolidated Income and Retained Earnings (In thousands except per share data)

	1984	1985	1986	1987	1988	1989
Net Sales and Other Operating Revenue	$337,420	$355,209	$366,912	$380,020	$407,683	$432,140
Cost of Sales and Operating Expenses						
Cost of Sales	157,340	160,388	157,938	168,585	182,727	188,691
Selling and Delivery	109,217	118,233	126,828	132,519	144,407	157,010
General and Administrative	11,153	12,714	13,414	12,789	14,117	15,399
Contributions to Employees' Profit-Sharing Retirement Fund	6,619	7,032	7,328	7,173	7,151	7,764
Total	284,329	298,367	305,508	321,066	348,402	368,864
Profit from Operations	53,091	56,842	61,404	58,954	59,281	63,276
Loss from Closing Subsidiary					(4,270)	
Other Income, Net	4,929	5,152	4,983	5,634	5,370	6,588
Income before Income Taxes	58,020	61,994	66,387	64,588	60,381	69,864
Income Taxes						
Current	24,522	26,213	30,661	26,376	21,992	22,245
Deferred (Benefit)	2,329	2,487	121	233	(754)	2,756
Total	26,851	28,700	30,782	26,609	21,238	25,001
Net Income	$ 31,169	$ 33,294	$ 35,605	$ 37,979	$ 39,143	$ 44,863
Retained Earnings at Beginning of Fiscal Year	129,422	146,239	163,975	167,669	186,221	204,048
Total Retained Earnings and Net Income	160,591	179,533	199,580	205,648	225,364	248,911
Less						
Cash Dividends	14,352	15,558	17,270	19,057	20,999	22,774
Stock Options Exercised			524	370	317	357
Retained Earnings at End of Fiscal Year	$146,239	$163,975	$181,786	$186,221	$204,048	$225,780
Per Share Amounts						
Net Income	$1.87	$2.00	$2.15	$1.17	$1.23	$1.42
Cash Dividends	.86	.93	1.04	.58	.66	.72

Source: Annual Report.

EXHIBIT 32.5   Consolidated Balance Sheets (In thousands)

	1985	1986	1987	1988	1989
Assets					
Current Assets					
Cash (including time deposits)	$ 19,102	$ 20,454	$ 17,382	$ 19,355	$ 27,191
Marketable Securities—at Amortized Cost which Approximates Market	57,407	66,296	51,628	33,864	37,182
Accounts and Notes Receivable (Less Allowance for Doubtful Accounts)	922	1,518	1,360	1,097	1,133
Refundable Income Taxes	—	—	2,280	—	—
Inventories—Finished Goods, Goods in Process, Materials, etc.	23,675	20,410	20,255	33,171	33,251
Deferred Income Tax Benefit	3,279	3,747	4,465	6,230	5,988
Total Current Assets	122,945	130,524	117,213	116,705	130,047
Property, Net	100,978	99,741	119,795	135,610	140,339
Other Assets					
Machinery Deposits	205	3,091	1,589	189	2,436
Notes Receivable, Prepayments, etc.	2,921	3,252	3,246	3,116	3,509
Total Other Assets	3,126	6,343	4,835	3,305	5,945
Total Assets	$227,049	$236,608	$241,843	$255,620	$276,331
Liabilities and Stockholders' Equity					
Current Liabilities					
Accounts Payable	$ 6,612	$ 5,694	$ 8,542	$ 7,795	$ 6,655
Accrued Compensation	8,938	9,615	9,499	10,306	8,452
Profit-Sharing Retirement Fund	4,623	4,316	3,662	3,643	4,955
Accrued Federal and State Income Taxes	2,177	3,966	1,804	1,573	1,628
Accrual for Self-Insurance	2,005	3,066	3,786	4,294	4,827
Other Payables and Accrued	2,798	3,050	3,446	4,345	2,225
Total Current Liabilities	27,153	29,707	30,739	31,956	28,742
Long-Term Debt	1,583				
Other Liabilities and Deferred Credits					
Deferred Income Taxes	13,822	15,208	17,164	18,982	22,185
Deferred Federal Income Tax Investment Credits	5,606	4,809	3,804	2,997	2,308
Supplemental Retirement Benefits	1,962	2,108	2,328	2,598	2,877
Total Other Liabilities and Deferred Credits	21,390	22,125	23,296	24,577	27,370
Stockholders' Equity					
Common Stock, $.83 1/3 Par Value (Authorized: 36,000,000 Shares; Issued: 16,940,279 Shares)	14,117	14,117	28,234	28,234	28,234
Additional Paid-In Capital	19				
Retained Earnings	163,975	181,786	186,221	204,048	225,780
Total	178,111	195,903	214,455	232,282	254,014
Less Treasury Stock at Cost	1,188	11,127	26,647	33,195	33,795
Stockholders' Equity	176,923	184,776	187,808	199,087	220,219
Total Liabilities and Stockholders' Equity	$227,049	$236,608	$241,843	$255,620	$276,331

EXHIBIT 32.6   Statements of Consolidated Cash Flows (In thousands)

	1987	1988	1989
Operating Activities			
Net Income	$ 37,979	$ 39,143	$ 44,863
Adjustments to Reconcile Net Income to Cash Provided by Operating Activities			
Depreciation	$ 16,011	$ 17,197	$ 18,607
Deferred Income Taxes	233	(754)	2,756
Other, Net	484	3,101	7
Changes in Operating Assets and Liabilities			
Decrease (Increase) in Accounts Receivable	(1,586)	(1,421)	(2,763)
Decrease (Increase) in Refundable Federal Income Taxes	(2,280)	819	413
Decrease (Increase) in Inventory	155	(12,916)	(80)
Increase (Decrease) in Accounts Payable	3,319	(357)	(1,140)
Increase (Decrease) in Accrued Income Taxes	(2,162)	(231)	55
Increase (Decrease) in Other Payables and Accrued Liabilities	365	2,196	(2,128)
Net Cash Flow from Operating Activities	$ 52,518	$ 46,777	$ 60,590
Investing Activities			
Purchases of Property			
Vending Machines	$ (8,574)	$(11,184)	$ (9,967)
Other Property	(21,290)	(20,542)	(12,217)
Deposits	(5,808)	(3,164)	(4,195)
Proceeds from Sale of Property	264	714	814
Net (Increase) Decrease in Marketable Securities with Maturities of 3 Months or Less	10,335	(1,149)	2,554
Purchases of Other Marketable Securities	(28,378)	(12,173)	(26,777)
Sales and Maturities of Other Marketable Securities	32,538	30,965	21,175
Other, Net	270	(407)	(410)
Net Cash Used in Investing Activities	$(20,643)	$(16,940)	$(29,023)
Financing Activities			
Dividends Paid	$(19,057)	$(20,999)	$(22,774)
Purchases of Treasury Stock, Net	(15,890)	(6,865)	(957)
Net Cash Used in Financing Activities	(34,947)	(27,864)	(23,731)
Increase (Decrease) in Cash	$ (3,072)	$ 1,973	$ 7,836
Cash at Beginning of Fiscal Year	$ 20,454	$ 17,382	$ 19,355
Cash at End of Fiscal Year	$ 17,382	$ 19,355	$ 27,191
Supplemental Information			
Cash Paid for Income Taxes	$30,818	$21,404	$21,777

Source: Annual Report.

Distribution costs represented an opportunity and a threat for Lance. The company's store-to-door delivery method was expensive in terms of people—labor costs and benefits—and trucks especially with unstable gasoline prices. If the company could efficiently continue its distribution, Lance could sustain its market position and even expand its customer base.

The company's acquisitions committee looked for and evaluated potential purchases. It was unlikely that Lance would be the target of a takeover attempt because the Van Every family owned approximately 44 percent of the shares of Lance (directly and in trust), and they were not interested in selling. Pete Sloan was quoted in *Forbes* as saying, "Sure, everything has a price—if you're a prostitute. But they can sell it once and they still got it. That ain't the way with companies." *Forbes* then went on to say, "Such conservatism, of course, is what had made Lance so successful. The danger is that changes in the snack food market could leave the company behind—one challenge that more of the same won't overcome."

The company expected to reach the $500 million mark in sales in the near future.

CASE 33

Sun Microsystems:
Competing in a High-Tech Industry

INTRODUCTION

In 1982, four individuals who were 27 years old combined forces to found Sun Microsystems, with the objective of producing and marketing computer workstations to scientists and engineers. Two of the four were Stanford MBA graduates—Michigan-born Scott McNealy and Vinod Khosla, a native of India. They were joined by Andreas Bechtolsheim, a Stanford engineering graduate who had constructed a computer workstation with spare parts in order to perform

This case was prepared by William C. House and Walter E. Greene as a basis for class discussion rather than to illustrate either effective or ineffective handling of an administrative situation. Used with permission from William C. House.

numerical analysis, and UNIX software expert William Joy from the Berkeley campus. Sun's founders believed there was demand for a desktop computer workstation costing between $10,000 and $20,000 in a market niche ignored by minicomputer makers IBM, Data General, DEC, and Hewlett-Packard.

Sun Microsystems was the market leader in the fast-growing workstation industry, expecting sales revenue growth of 90 percent annually during the next five years compared to the projected industry average of 5 to 10 percent for personal computers. Workstations can be used in stand-alone fashion or as part of networked configurations. The product lines produced range from low-priced diskless units to the top- of-the-line, higher-powered graphics-oriented stations.

In contrast to personal computers, workstations are characterized by 32-bit versus 16-bit microprocessors, a strong tendency to use the UNIX operating system instead of MS/DOS, more sophisticated software and graphics capabilities, large storage capacities, faster processing speeds, and the ability to function effectively in a networking environment. The principal users of workstations have been engineers and scientists. However, price reductions and technological improvements broadened the appeal of workstations so that they were being used in financial trading, desktop publishing, animation, mapping, and medical imaging applications.

Sun, the fastest-growing company in the computer hardware industry, had revenues that were increasing at a five-year compounded rate of 85 percent and income increasing at a 67 percent rate from 1985 to 1990.[1] For fiscal 1991, Sun's revenues were $3.2 billion and net income was $190 million.[2] The company's rapid growth rate severely drained its cash resources.

CHAIRMAN AND CEO OF SUN MICROSYSTEMS

In 1992, Scott McNealy was the chairman of Sun. He was a native of Detroit and grew up on the fringes of the U.S. automobile industry. Originally rejected by both Harvard and Stanford Business Schools, he graduated from Harvard with a major in economics. In between his Harvard and Stanford academic careers, he accepted a job as a foreman at Rockwell's International truck plant. After two months of hectic workplace activity, he was hospitalized with hepatitis. He entered Stanford University in 1978 on his third try.

In 1981, at the age of 26, McNealy became manufacturing director at Onyx Systems, a small microcomputer maker. The company was faced with serious quality problems. In two months, the operation showed drastic improvement as McNealy probed work rules and production bottlenecks, encouraging workers to identify problems and to overcome obstacles on the way toward improving workplace efficiency.

[1] John Markoff, "The Smart Alecs at Sun Are Regrouping," *New York Times*, April 28, 1991.
[2] G. Paschal Zachary, "Sun Challenges Microsoft's Hold Over Software," *Wall Street Journal*, September 4, 1991.

In 1982, former Stanford classmates Andy Bechtolsheim and Vinod Khosla asked him to join them as director of operations in a new company to be called Sun Microsystems. Two years later, McNealy was chosen by the board of directors to be CEO over Paul Ely, who became executive vice president of Unisys. During the first month after McNealy became CEO one of the three cofounders resigned, the company lost $500,000 on $2 million in sales, and two-thirds of its computers did not work.

McNealy was a workaholic, working from daylight to dark, seven days a week, rarely finding time for recreational activities. The frantic pace he brought to Sun was sometimes referred to as "sunburn." There was a tendency for Sun executives to take on too many projects at once, thereby creating tremendous internal pressure and organizational chaos.

McNealy's philosophy can be capsuled in these company sayings.[3]

1. On decision making—Consensus if possible, but participation for sure.
2. On management cooperation—Agree and commit, disagree and commit, or just get the hell out of the way.
3. On market response—The right answer is the best answer. The wrong answer is second best. No answer is worst.
4. On individual initiative—To ask permission is to seek denial.

He stated that the company was trying to achieve four goals—significant increases in revenue and book value, improved product acceptance, and higher profit margins.

CHIEF COMPUTER DESIGNER

Andreas Bechtolsheim, chief computer designer, was one of Sun's cofounders. At the age of 35, he had the title of vice president of technology. A native of West Germany, Bechtolsheim designed his first computer in 1980 while still a graduate student at Stanford University. It was a workstation designed for scientists and engineers. However, he was unable to sell the idea to any computer company at the time. Shortly thereafter, he joined Joy, Khosla, and McNealy in founding Sun Microsystems, and the company's first product was based on his machine.

Initially, Bechtolsheim persuaded Sun to use off-the-shelf products to develop its workstations instead of following the usual industry practice of utilizing proprietary components. This meant that company products would be easy for competitors to copy, but it also allowed quick entry into the marketplace. As nonproprietary open systems came to be more widely accepted, competitors such

---

[3] "Sun Microsystems Turns on the Afterburners," *Business Week*, July 18, 1988.

as Apollo, Digital Equipment Corporation (DEC), and IBM encountered problems in keeping pace with product lines that lacked the flexibility and performance of Sun's products. When Steve Jobs formed NeXT and announced the development of a desktop workstation, Bechtolsheim urged Sun officials to build a truly desktop computer. There was considerable resistance to the project, and he almost left the company at that point.

Almost at once, he began working on the new computer on his own. He spent $200,000 of his own funds on the project without official company backing. He also formed a small company called Unisun to provide the vehicle for marketing his new computer and persuaded Khosla, a member of Sun's board of directors to become president of Unisun. Khosla offered Sun the right to invest in or purchase the smaller company outright. Sun seriously considered both possibilities, but McNealy was fearful that the new venture might be considered a competitor of Sun.

In view of the possible negatives of a smaller company selling an identical clone of Sun, the larger company finally agreed to build the new computer and called it Sparcstation I. Initially, restrictions were placed on the project, and only engineers who had indicated they would resign to work on the new computer were allowed to join the team. Because the company had a culture based on building bigger boxes, the Sparcstation was widely criticized within the company as being too small. However, Bechtolsheim stubbornly refused to change the specifications and eventually prevailed.[4]

FIELD OPERATIONS DIRECTOR

Carol Bartz, national sales director and the number two executive at Sun Microsystems, had about half of the company's 12,000 employees reporting to her. Although many outsiders felt that she would soon be named chief operating officer, she abruptly dismissed the idea, observing that she did not believe the company needed a COO. At 42, the hard-driving and aggressive female seemed to be reaching new heights in her career.

Bartz attended the University of Wisconsin, receiving a Bachelor of Computer Science degree in 1971. After that, she spent seven years with DEC. Since joining Sun in 1983, she became intimately involved in marketing operations, including supervising field support activities and a subdivision that sold to federal government agencies. Bartz indicated that her relationship with McNealy permitted her to tell him what he was doing wrong as well as what he was doing right. According to Bob Herwick, an investment analyst, Bartz was a very effective problem solver, turning around a sluggish service organization and ensuring that the company fully exploited the market potential in the government market.[5]

[4] G. Paschal Zachary, "Sparc-Station's Success Is Doubly Sweet for Sun Microsystem's Bechtolsheim," *Wall Street Journal*, May 29, 1990.
[5] Andrew Ould, "Carol Bartz: Star Is Still Rising for Hard Driving Executive," *PC Week*, September 3, 1990.

TEAM AND CONSENSUS MANAGEMENT AT SUN

McNealy attended Cranbrook, a North Detroit prep school. While there, he excelled in a variety of activities including music, tennis, golf, and ice hockey. According to Alan De Clerk, a high school classmate, McNealy developed a strong self-image and competitive spirit as a result of participating in sports activities and competing with two brothers and a sister. Through the years he approached all activities as if they were team sports.

McNealy's father was the vice chairman of American Motors (AMC). Scott followed his dad on the golf course, listened to automobile industry discussions, and found himself pouring over internal company memos along with his father who was heavily involved in AMC's battle to stay alive. The elder McNealy ruled his household with an iron hand. Scott's strong commitment to consensus management may be a reaction to the type of environment in which they were raised, according to his brother who is an architect in St. Louis.[6]

McNealy's efforts to build consensus among executives before a decision was made became famous throughout the company. As he stated, "Give me a draw and I'll make the decision but I won't issue an edict if a large majority is in favor of an alternative proposal."[7] A frequently quoted example occurred in 1988 when he stubbornly resisted changing prices at a time when rapidly increasing memory costs were reducing profit margins. With a consensus arrayed against him, he finally agreed to some product price increases that were enacted without reducing sales. In fact, he had a hard time saying no to any project pushed by one or more company groups. He demanded loyalty within his concept of teamwork and became very angry if he believed that individuals or teams had let him down.[8]

PRODUCT LINE FOCUS

Sparcstation I was introduced in April 1989 at a stripped down price of $9,000. A lower-priced version was introduced in May 1990 at a price of $5,000. The machine processed data at 12 mips (about twice as fast as most personal computers). Sun expected the lower price to facilitate sales to large companies that often based computer purchases on quantity discounts. However, the low-end Sparcstation did not have disk drives, color monitors, or add-in slots. Therefore, it had to be networked and could not be used as a stand-alone unit.

An improved version of Sparc I was introduced in the summer of 1990 with a better graphics interface, a color monitor, and a sales price of $10,000. Sun asserted that a personal computer with the same characteristics as the Sparcstation I personal computer (IPC) would cost $15,000 to $20,000 and would have only about one-third the processing power of this workstation model. By 1991 Sparc-

---

[6] Jonathan B. Levine, "High Noon for Sun," *Business Week*, July 24, 1989, pp. 71, 74.

[7] "Sun Turns on the Afterburners," p. 32.

[8] Ibid.

EXHIBIT 33.1   A Comparison of Performance Measures for Major Workstation Makers

Manufacturer/Model	Price	Specmarks	Price per Specmark
Hewlett-Packard 9000	$11,990	55.5	$216.00
Sun Sparcstation ELC	4,995	20.1	248.50
IBM RS/6000	13,992	32.8	426.50
Sun Sparcstation IPX	13,495	24.2	557.60

Source: J. A. Savage, "Price Takes a Backseat with Users," *Computerworld,* September 2, 1991, p. 4.

station was Sun's top seller among all its product lines and Sparcstation products produced 80 to 90 percent of total company revenues.

Exhibit 33.1 illustrates prices and specmarks (a measure of processing power and speed) for two Sun models as well as for the latest Hewlett-Packard and IBM workstation models. The relative performance of Sun's products in terms of computing power per dollar compared favorably against the company's major competitors.

COMPANY STRATEGY

Early on, Sun executives believed that they only had a short time to focus on growing demand for computer workstations from scientists and engineers before large companies such as IBM, DEC, and Hewlett-Packard would aggressively move into that market niche. Therefore, company strategy was designed to emphasize gaining market share and concentrated on sales growth, no matter what the cost. At one point, the organization was adding more than 300 employees and a new sales office each month. Company engineers developed a steady stream of innovative but sometimes impractical prototypes. Products were sold largely by word of mouth with virtually no formal sales promotion programs.

In the mid-1980s, as part of the focus on market share, the company began creating autonomous divisions to develop and market its products. This policy allowed rapid movement into such market areas as sales to government agencies, universities, and financial institutions. A special team was created in 1986 to successfully counter the threat posed by Apollo. "Sun can win market share battles in such cases," noted F. H. Moss, formerly vice president for software development at Apollo, "because it has no strong preconceptions about what can or cannot be done."[9] The autonomous groups did create unnecessary duplication and contributed to developmental costs that were almost twice the industry average. When attempts were made to consolidate functions, fierce turf battles resulted and top executives were forced to step in and referee the conflicts.

[9] Michael Alexander, "PC Workstation Firms Prepare for Price War," *Computerworld*, September 20, 1989.

The market share/sales growth emphasis created many unexpected problems. Needed investments in customer service and data processing activities were postponed. The existence of independent, autonomous divisions caused numerous difficulties for both sales and manufacturing activities. At one point, the company had more than 10,000 computer and option combinations to track. Three different product lines based on three different microprocessors—Sparc, Motorola 68000, and Intel 386—required excessive investment and extensive coordination to ensure that they all operated on the same network. Overlaps and duplications in marketing and finance made forecasting all but impossible. At its increased size the company could no longer scramble madly to meet shipping deadlines at the last minute.

By summer 1989, the company was experiencing production bottlenecks as discounted sales of older products mushroomed. At the same time, demand for newer products increased faster than expected. Large backlogs of sales orders were not being entered into the inventory control system, preventing the company from knowing how many or what kinds of products it needed to produce.

In the last quarter of 1989, Sun experienced a $20 million loss due to misjudgments concerning consumer demand for its new Sparcstation as well as parts requirements. A new management information system produced inaccurate parts forecasts that contributed to order snafus and lower earnings. However, the company posted a $5 million profit in the first quarter of 1990. Sun produced revenues of $2.5 billion in fiscal 1990 and expected to achieve revenues of $3.3 billion in 1991.[10] Sun changed its approach to place more emphasis on profitability and less on growth, expanding its customer service and hiring fewer employees. McNealy tied executive pay to before-tax return on investment. In the 1989 annual report he stated that he desired performance to be judged on the basis of significant increases in revenues, acceptance of new products, improvements in profit margins, and increases in book value.

McNealy was one of the early pioneers pushing open systems that allowed computers of many different manufacturers to be linked together into networks. In fact, Sun actually encouraged competition through its focus on open systems development and invited the industry to build Sparc-based clones in order to expand the position of the workstation industry. As the percentage of totally Sparc-based computers sold by Sun began to decline, Sun changed its position on clones. Recently, it told its own dealers they would incur Sun's displeasure if they sold clones along with Sun workstations. Many of these dealers were angry at what they perceived to be Sun's arrogance.

Sun intentionally maintained a narrow product line. It gradually phased out all microprocessors except Sparc and concentrated on low-end workstations with the greatest market share growth possibilities. The company avoided entering markets for higher-priced lines and the personal computer segment with emphasis

---

[10] Kathy Rebello, "Sun Microsystems on the Rise Again," *USA Today*, April 20, 1990; "Workstations Makers Try to Reboot Sales," and "Sun to Market Workstation with PC Price," *USA Today*, May 14, 1990; "Sun Targets PCs with Workstation," *USA Today*, July 26, 1990; "H-P to Rattle Workstation Market," *USA Today*, March 18, 1991.

on low price and compactness. However, recently Sun announced plans to move into high-end workstation markets where processing speed and power requirements necessitated linking a series of microprocessors and using sophisticated software. Sun might encounter problems in this market, similar to those it experienced in product upgrades of its lower level models, because it did not have a good record in managing product introductions.

As workstations became more powerful and less expensive, manufacturers faced a serious challenge in maintaining profit margins. Newer models combined high functionality with high volume, in contrast to an earlier focus on producing highly functional units in small quantities. Extensive use of application-specific integrated circuits with fewer components reduced system sizes, increased reliability, and lowered product costs. Sun and other companies increasingly followed the practice of involving manufacturing representatives in the design process as early as possible in order to minimize manufacturing problems. Increased attention was also being paid to maintaining product quality and improved product testing before systems were shipped.

In past years, Sun's strategies included focusing on lower prices, well-developed marketing programs, and third-party software development. From 1,500 to 2,000 applications were available for the Sun Sparcstation compared to approximately 1,000 for Hewlett-Packard and DEC. The company was licensing its sparc chip to third-party clone companies with the intent of expanding the installed RISC computer base. The overall company goal was to deliver a complete processing solution, including graphics, input/output, software, and networking.

DISTRIBUTION CHANNELS AND CUSTOMER SERVICE

Workstation makers traditionally sold their units using manufacturers' sales representatives and specialized hardware resellers, who repackaged specialized software with other companies' workstations. Sun had about 300 value-added resellers (VARs) compared to more than 500 for Hewlett-Packard; DEC and IBM had between 300 and 500 each. Some experts thought the majority of VARs were not capable of selling workstations.[11] Sun then considered the possibility of selling some of its models through retailers such as MicroAge in a manner similar to personal computer distribution used by other manufacturers such as IBM, COMPAQ, and Apple. Management felt that the change would reduce selling and inventory costs but was having difficulty convincing dealers who were unaccustomed to handling complex workstation models.

Sun sold a large number of workstations through its 1,000-person sales force. In July 1990, Sun selected 200 dealers from three retail chains and provided

[11] Susan E. Fisher, "Vendors Court Resellers as Workstations Go Mainstream," *PC Week*, July 30, 1990.

them training for selling workstations. The company expected sales of workstations to reach $30 million through retail dealers in fiscal 1990, but it appeared that a full-fledged dealer network was going to require several years to develop. Because of the higher average selling prices and greater product differentiation of workstations compared to personal computers, many PC vendors have expressed interest in handling workstations despite the small volumes generated.

One area of concern was Sun's service organization which had not been very effective in supporting customer software. Bartz stated that the company wanted to improve customer service but without making large monetary expenditures or building a dinosaur service group.[12] In line with this, Sun announced plans to start using company-trained, third-party service personnel who could be dispatched to customer locations on demand.

CUSTOMER CATEGORIES

The workstation market for engineers and scientists rapidly became saturated. About one-third of Sun's customers came from the commercial side, up from only 10 percent several years ago. The company concentrated more of its efforts on airlines, banks, insurance and finance companies, trying to persuade them to utilize Sun workstations to solve new problems. Eric Schmidt, Sun vice president, said that Sun tended to get early adopters of new technology.[13] Often, by starting with a pilot program that proved to be successful, workstations could be expanded to other areas in a customer's operations. Eastman Kodak began using Sun workstations in engineering design and soon expanded their use to marketing data bases and mail room operations.

Sun machines were used by Wall Street firms such as Merrill Lynch, Shearson, Lehman, Hutton and Bear, Stearns on the trading floor. Northwest Airlines used 500 workstations in Minneapolis to monitor ticket usage, checking the correctness of airfare charges as well as the impact of flight delays or cancellations on revenues and profits. To increase customer satisfaction, Sun changed product designs to make its machines easier to install and improved understandability of product manuals. Sun discovered that commercial customers needed more help than engineers.

Dataquest predicted that by 1994, 29.1 percent of workstation sales would be made to commercial users as opposed to scientific or engineering users in a market expected to reach $22 billion.[14] Workstation manufacturers encroached into the personal computer market by offering UNIX versions that would run on both workstations and on personal computers. Workstations provided much greater computing power at a lower cost than would be available by upgrading a personal computer so that it possessed the equivalent capability of a typical

[12] "High Noon for Sun," p. 74.
[13] Julie Pitts, "The Trojan Horse Approach," *Forbes*, April 15, 1991.
[14] "Getting Down to Business," *Information Week*, January 14, 1991.

workstation. Workstations seemed to be making the biggest inroads into CPU-intensive applications previously performed on mainframes (e.g., stock transactions, airline reservations).

Sun's first major TV advertising effort occurred in April 1991 and took the form of a 30-second commercial seen on CNN, ESPN, and the three major TV networks. The commercial was not directed specifically at the consumer audience, but instead was an attempt to get broad exposure for a new message targeted to the business market. Sun expected the advertisement to reach 59 percent of U.S. households and 42 percent of the target market of senior-level corporate and computer executives. The campaign also included an eight-page insert in the *Wall Street Journal*.

Sun's advertising budget of approximately $4.6 million in 1990 was spent on computer and general interest business publications. Sun's advertising budget was only about 0.25 percent of sales revenues compared to 1.0 to 1.5 percent by its major competitors. Some observers questioned the cost-effectiveness of a high-priced TV advertisement by a company that sells high-priced computers to a limited group of customers.

SOFTWARE DEVELOPMENTS

Availability of software remained a major problem in expanding sales of workstations. Only about 5 to 10 percent of UNIX-based software was designed for business and commercial applications. Sun tried to sign up software developers to produce UNIX-based versions of many common personal computer products. UNIX-based versions of some popular PC software, including Lotus 1-2-3 and dBASE IV were available. The company expected that the increased availability of software plus the narrowing cost gap between low-end workstations and high-end personal computers would help it penetrate the personal computer market. However, it had to sell users on the benefit/cost performance of workstations compared to personal computers as well as expand its existing base of software developers.

The type of software to be run was often the determining factor in deciding between a personal computer or workstation. For productivity and business applications, PCs could be more cost-efficient. For technical and graphics applications, workstations were more appropriate. Price was no longer a major differentiating factor.

An entrenched personal computer MS/DOS-based operating system and lack of commercial workstation software hampered a switch from high-end personal computers to workstations. MS/DOS-based computers appeared adequate for a majority of user needs, especially with the advent of the Windows operating environment. PC users were more likely to change if complex applications such as multimedia, integrated data base, or windowing became desirable rather than on the basis of price alone. Workstations were likely to become less attractive if 80846-based personal computers with considerably more computing power than today's systems became more widely available.

Because product/price performance was no longer as important a differentiating factor as it once was, and software availability/usability had increased in importance, Sun formed two software subsidiaries—one for development of application software and one to concentrate on improvements in the UNIX operating system. The Open Look Graphical Interface had been added to make Sun Products more user friendly. The key to maintaining market position seemed to be improving software and convincing software developers and users on the benefits of workstations over other hardware options.

Sun announced that it would release a new version of its operating system designed to run on Intel-based personal computers. Some analysts said that Sun faced a stiff test in competing with Microsoft's DOS/Windows combination. They considered the introduction of the new operating system to be a defensive move, made because Sun could no longer generate enough revenue from its own machines to meet growth goals. McNealy denied that the Sun announcement was defensive, saying that high-powered PC owners would move to Sun's operating systems to take advantage of advanced capabilities (e.g., running multiple programs simultaneously), which was something that was only vaguely promised by Microsoft's new Windows NT version.[15] McNealy sharply criticized Windows NT, referring to it as illusionary or not there.

Sun's Solaris operating system was available in mid-1991 and worked on both Intel's X86 series and Sun's Sparc processors. The new operating system made it easier for Sun's customers to link Sun workstations with other computers in a network and increase the number of Sun users. Sun hoped that this would encourage independent software houses to write new programs for the Sun operating system. Thus far, approximately 3,500 application programs were available for Sun operating systems compared with more than 20,000 for IBM-compatible personal computers.[16]

COMPETITION IN THE WORKSTATION MARKET

Although still the workstation market leader, Sun faced increased competition from much larger computer companies. Sun shipped 146,000 workstations in 1990 out of a total of 376,000 (39 percent of the units sold). The company expected to ship 200,000 units in 1991.[17] Having fully absorbed Apollo into its

15 "Sun Challenges Microsoft," p. B1.
16 Robert D. Hof, "Why Sun Can't Afford to Shine Alone," *Business Week*, September 9, 1991.
17 Andrew Ould, "IBM Challenges Sun in Workstation Market," *PC Week*, February 28, 1991.

organization, Hewlett-Packard was selling about two-thirds as many workstations as Sun, with about 20 percent of the market; DEC, which completely reworked its product lines, had about 17 percent of the workstation market. Hewlett-Packard introduced a new workstation model, comparable in price to the Sparcstation, that ran about twice as fast as Sun's current model.[18] Exhibit 33.2 indicates the 1989 and 1990 market shares for the major firms in the workstation market.

IBM made a significant comeback in the workstation market with the RS/6000, after its workstation model proved to be a slow seller. In 1990, IBM shipped more than 25,000 workstations, producing revenue of $1 billion and attaining a market share of 6.6 percent, or more than double its 1989 market share.[19] In 1991, some analysts estimated that IBM would sell between $2 and $3 billion in workstations. IBM had a stated goal of overtaking Sun by 1993, achieving a 30 percent market share. Some experts predicted IBM was more likely to achieve a 15 percent market share by that date.[20] Its late entry, the entrenched positions of competitors in the market, lack of a low-priced entry-level model, and the use of nonstandard operating and graphics environments were likely to hamper IBM's efforts to achieve a market share much above 15 percent.[21] IBM's service and sales reputation, its large reseller base, and strong position in commercial markets should give the company leverage to enter the fast-growing markets for network servers and small or branch office multiuser

EXHIBIT 33.2   Computer Workstation Market Shares (In percent)

Company	1989	1990
Sun Microsystems	30.4	38.8
Hewlett-Packard	26.1	20.1
DEC	26.6	17.0
Intergraph	7.0	3.8
IBM	1.2	4.5
Silicon Graphics	5.1	2.6
SONY	—	3.3
NeXT	—	2.6
Other	3.6	7.0
Total	100.0	100.0

[18] Lawrence Curran, "HP Speeds Up Workstation Race," *Electronics*, April 1991.
[19] "IBM Challenges Sun," p. 134.
[20] Bob Francis, "Big Blue's Red Hot Workstation," *Datamation*, October 15, 1990.
[21] Andrew Ould, "What's Behind Lower Workstation Prices," *UNIX World*, July 1990.

systems. However, if IBM focused its efforts on penetrating these markets with its RS/6000, it ran a serious risk of undercutting sales of its AS/400.

FINANCIAL ANALYSIS

Exhibit 33.3 illustrates revenues, expenses, and income for the five-year period 1986 to 1990. Revenues increased at a more rapid rate than net income. Return on sales declined significantly to 4.5 percent from the peak of almost 7 percent in 1987. In addition, revenue per shipment declined in 1990 compared to the two previous years. Book value per share and unit shipments increased significantly during the five years.

Exhibit 33.4 indicates that Sun's sales, income, and asset growth were higher than the industry average in 1989 and 1990 with market value to equity above the industry average as well. However, the net income to sales figure was below the industry average in 1989 and slightly above the industry average in 1990. As Exhibit 33.5 indicates, Sun appeared to be very close to the industry average in terms of two common productivity measures, sales to assets and sales per employee. In reviewing the common leverage measures, Sun was well above the industry average for R&D expenses to revenues and R&D expenses per employee.

EXHIBIT 33.3   Revenues, Expenses, and Income for Five Years (In billions)

	1986	*1987*	*1988*	*1989*	*1990*
Net Revenues	$210	$538	$1,052	$1,765	$2,466
Cost of Sales	102	273	550	1,010	1,399
Gross Profit	108	265	502	755	1,067
R&D Outlays	31	70	140	234	302
Selling, Administrative, and General Expenses	57	127	250	433	588
Total	88	197	390	667	890
Operating Income	20	68	111	88	177
Interest Income	369	834	(302)	(10)	23)
Income Taxes	9	33	44	17	43
Net Income	$11	$36	$66	$61	$111
Net Income/Sales	5.3%	6.8%	6.3%	3.4%	4.5%
Net Income/Share	$0.21	$0.55	$0.89	$0.76	$1.21
Book Value/Share	$2.04	$3.57	$4.75	$7.77	$9.82
Unit Shipments (000s)	9.9	24.6	48.4	80.7	118.3
Revenue/Unit Shipped (000s)	$21.2	$21.8	$21.7	$21.9	$20.8

Source: Adapted from 1990 annual report.

EXHIBIT 33.4 Computer Industry Data, 1989 and 1990

Company	Sales Growth		Income Growth		Asset Growth		Net Income/ Sales		Market Value/Equity	
	1989	1990	1989	1990	1989	1990	1989	1990	1989	1990
Apple	1.21	1.07	1.05	1.14	1.24	1.12	8.2	8.7	3.21	4.81
COMPAQ	1.39	1.25	1.31	1.36	1.31	1.30	11.6	12.6	3.31	3.26
DEC	1.05	1.01	0.72	0.00	1.10	1.03	6.8	-.72	1.13	1.21
Hewlett-Packard	1.20	1.10	0.97	0.95	1.31	1.09	6.6	5.7	1.98	1.83
Intergraph	1.07	1.21	0.80	0.79	0.97	1.06	9.2	6.0	1.73	1.79
IBM	1.05	1.10	0.68	1.60	1.06	1.30	6.0	8.7	1.62	1.75
NCR	0.99	1.06	0.94	0.90	0.95	1.01	6.9	5.9	3.40	3.54
Silicon Graphics	1.73	1.41	1.94	1.97	0.94	1.37	5.9	8.3	4.30	3.57
Sun Microsystems	1.41	1.34	0.40	318.00	1.50	1.49	1.8	5.5	1.41	2.72
Wang	0.90	0.87	0.00	0.00	0.87	0.72	-13.9	-6.7	0.87	1.27
Average	1.20	1.14	0.88	32.7	1.12	1.15	4.9	5.4	2.37	2.58

Read as ''1989 sales growth was 1.21 times 1988 sales.''

Source: *Business Week 1000 Companies*, 1990, 1991.

EXHIBIT 33.5 Computer Industry Data, 1988 and 1989

	Sales/Assets[a]		Sales/Employee[b]		Advertising Expenses/Sales[c]		R&D Expenses/Sales[d]		R&D Expenses/Employee[e]	
	1988	1989	1988	1989	1988	1989	1988	1989	1988	1989
Apple	1.91	1.82	377	364	8.30	7.34	6.7	8.0	25,233	28,937
COMPAQ	1.38	1.32	289	303	2.87	1.75	3.6	4.6	10,849	13,945
DEC	1.15	1.13	94	101	1.01	1.38	11.4	12.0	10,753	12,123
Hewlett-Packard	1.21	1.22	113	125	2.35	2.69	10.4	10.7	11,713	13,358
Intergraph	1.07	1.20	110	105	1.00	1.00	11.1	10.6	12,216	11,157
IBM	0.81	0.79	154	164	0.44	1.17	7.4	8.3	11,415	13,572
NCR	1.32	1.38	100	106	0.53	1.06	7.0	7.5	6,940	7,964
Silicon Graphics	1.19	1.22	105	180	1.00	1.00	15.8	11.9	21,908	21,150
Sun Microsystems	1.41	1.27	148	172	0.74	1.00	13.3	13.3	19,733	22,934
Wang	1.12	1.35	97	109	1.02	1.00	8.7	9.8	8,510	10,543
Average	1.26	1.27	159	173	1.93	2.64	9.5	9.7	14,027	15,568

[a] Read as "$1.91 in sales for every $1 in assets for Apple in 1988."

[b] Read as "$3.77 in sales per Apple employee in 1988."

[c] Read as "advertising was 8.3 percent of sales in 1988 for Apple."

[d] Read as "R&D expense was 6.7 percent of sales in 1988 for Apple."

[e] Read as "$25,233 in R&D per Apple employee in 1988."

Source: *Business Week 1000–1991,* 1991; *Innovation in America,* Special Business Week Issues, 1990, 1989.

REFERENCES

ABBOTT, LAWRENCE. "Good Buys Abound in RISC Workstation." *Datamation*, April 15, 1991.

BRANDELL, WILLIAM. "Manager's Find RISC Not Worth Gamble." *Computerworld*, March 5, 1990.

BRENNAN, LAURA. "Resilient Sun Is on the Rise in PCs Turf." *PC Week*, September 3, 1990.

BULKELEY, WILLIAM L. "DEC's New Workstations May Shake Up Hot Market." *Wall Street Journal*, January 11, 1989.

BULKELEY, WILLIAM L. "Digital Unveils New Workstations: Cuts Some Prices." *Wall Street Journal*, April 4, 1990.

BUSH, PAUL. "Dangerous Liaisons." *Prepared Foods*, August 1990.

CARROLL, PETER B. "New Workstation Line Aims for Credibility." *Wall Street Journal*, February 12, 1990.

COFFEE, PETER. "Desktop Sizzlers." *Computerworld*, December 25–January 1, 1990.

COFFEE, PETER. "Japan Eyes Workstation Market." *Computerworld*, December 25–January 1, 1990.

COFFEE, PETER. "Price, Support, and Integration Are Key in Evaluating Software." *PC Week*, April 2, 1990, p. 25.

COFFEE, PETER. "RISC Software Has Turned the Corner." *PC Week*, April 16, 1990, pp. 18, 20.

DALEY, JAMES. "Can Sun Ride Out Stormy Weather." *Computerworld*, July 24, 1989.

DALEY, JAMES. "Sun Users Staying Loyal for Now." *Computerworld*, March 5, 1990.

DALEY, JAMES. "Workstation Market Leaving PC's Far Behind." *Computerworld*, February 5, 1990.

FISHER, SUSAN E. "Vendors Court Reseller Partners as Workstations Go Mainstream." *PC Week*, July 30, 1990.

FOLEY, MARY JO. "Microcomputers: High-End PC's vs. Workstations." *Systems Integration*, April 1990.

FRANCETT, BARBARA. "Workstations Dust Off after Rough Year's Ride." *Computerworld*, September 25, 1989.

FRANCIS, BOB. "Big Blue's Red Hot Workstation." *Datamation*, October 15, 1990.

FRANCIS, BOB. "Sun Compatibles: Who's Putting the Sizzle in Sparc." *Datamation*, May 1, 1991.

FREIBURN, RICHARD, and RONALD E. ROADES. "The Workstation Revolution," *Information Executive*, Winter 1991.

GANTZ, JOHN. "PC vs. Workstation Dominance Looms Near." *Infoworld*, May 14, 1990.

"Get It While It's Hot: Slicing Up the Worldwide Workstation Market." *PC Week*, January 29, 1990.

GROSS, NEAL. "Why Sun Is Losing Its Heat in the East." *Business Week*, September 10, 1989.

HILKIRK, JOHN. "Workstations, PCs Gain Popularity." *USA Today*, April 26, 1989.

HURLEY, KATHLEEN, and CARL FLOCK. "PCs vs. Workstations: The Battle Revisited." *Computer Graphics Review*, June 1990.

HOF, ROBERT D. "Where Sun Means to Be a Bigger Fireball." *Business Week*, April 15, 1991.

HOF, ROBERT D. "Will Sun Also Rise in the Office Market." *Business Week*, May 21, 1990.

KUCHARVY, THOMAS. "Can IBM Catch Up with the Workstation Market." *Computer Graphics Review*, June 1990.

LEIBOWITZ, MICHAEL R. "UNIX Workstations Arrive." *Datamation*, June 1, 1990.

LEWIS, PETER H. "Can Old Processing Technology Beat Back New Challenge." *New York Times*, February 25, 1990.

LEWIS, PETER H. "With Both Feet, IBM Jumps into Workstations." *New York Times*, February 18, 1990.

LEVINE, JONATHAN B. "Can Sun Stand the Heat in the PC Market." *Business Week*, April 24, 1989.

LEVINE, JONATHAN B. "Hewlett Packard's Screeching Turn toward Desktops." *Business Week*, September 11, 1989.

LEVINE, JONATHAN B. "High Noon for Sun." *Business Week*, July 24, 1989.

LUBERNOW, GERALD. "An Upstart's Rite of Passage." *Business Month*, May 1990.

MARKOFF, JOHN. "The Niche That IBM Can't Ignore." *New York Times*, April 25, 1989.

MARKOFF, JOHN. "A Prescription for Troubled IBM." *New York Times*, December 10, 1989.

MARKOFF, JOHN. "The Smart Alecs at Sun are Regrouping." *New York Times*, April 28, 1991.

McCROSSEN, MELANIE. "Workstations: A Market Niche Raises Eyebrows." *Standard and Poor's Industry Surveys*, April 1990, pp. 81–82.

OULD, ANDREW. "IBM Challenges Sun in Workstation Market." *PC Week*, February 28, 1991.

OULD, ANDREW. "Carol Bartz: Star Is Still Rising for Hard Driving Executive." *PC Week*, September 3, 1990.

OULD, ANDREW. "Sun's Color Workstation Bridges UNIX, High End PC's." *PC Week*, July 30, 1990.

McWILLIAMS, GARY. "DEC Is Changing with the Times—A Little Late." *Business Week*, April 9, 1990.

METHVIN, DAVE. "RISC-Based Systems Find Strength in Simplicity." *PC Week*, April 2, 1990.

SAVAGE, J. A. "HP/Apollo Duet Not Yet In Tune." *Computerworld*, September 2, 1991.

SEXTON, TARA. "IBM Raises the Ante in High Stakes RISC Arena." *PC Week*, April 2, 1990, pp. 8, 9.

SPIEGELMAN, LAURA. "RISC Buyers Turn Eyes toward IBM." *PC Week*, March 19, 1990.

SPIEGELMAN, LAURA. "Sun Focuses on SPARC to Fend Off Growing Competition." *PC Week*, March 19, 1990.

SCHNEIDAWAIND, JOHN. "DEC Launches Workstation Attack." *USA Today*, April 12, 1990.

SCHNEIDAWAIND, JOHN. "Sun Expected to Win Place in Fortune 1000." *PC Week*, October 8, 1990.

"Sun Microsystems Turn on the Afterburners." *Business Week*, July 18, 1988.

"Trends: Technical Workstations." *Computerworld*, February 26, 1990.

VERITY, JOHN W. "IBM Is Finally Saying in UNIX We Trust." *Business Week*, February 12, 1990.

"The Versatility of the New Workstations." *I/S Analyzer*, January 1989.

WELTON, THERESE R. "Workstations: Prophecies Coming to Pass." *Industry Week*, January 2, 1989.

WRIGHT, JETHRO. "What Is a Workstation?" *MIS Week*, February 15, 1990.

YODER, STEPHAN K., et al. "Rivals Take Aim at IBM's Workstations." *Wall Street Journal*, February 15, 1990.

YODER, STEPHAN K., et al., "Workstation Options Expanding." *Wall Street Journal*, May 9, 1990.

ZACHARY, G. PASCAL and STEPHAN K. YODER. "A Line Dividing Workstations and PC's Blurs." *Wall Street Journal*, March 20, 1990.

--------------- CASE 34 ---------------

American Greetings
Faces New Challenges in the 1990s

As CEO Morry Weiss looked at the corporate rose logo of the world's largest publicly owned manufacturer of greeting cards and related social-expression merchandise, American Greetings (AG), he reflected upon the decade of the 1980s. In 1981, he had announced the formulation of a corporate growth objective to achieve $1 billion in annual sales by 1985, which would represent a 60 percent increase over 1982 sales of $623.6 million.

It was 1986 before AG reached that goal with sales of $1.035 billion. The profit margin, however, was 5.75 percent, the lowest in five years and down from its high of 8.09 percent in 1984. In its fiscal year ending February 28, 1990, AG reported sales of $1.286 billion with a profit margin of 5.51 percent. Weiss looked at the 10-year sales, net income and selling, distribution, and marketing costs summary prepared by his corporate staff (Exhibit 34.1). He realized that AG's increase in sales had come at a high cost with an escalated and intensified battle

This case was prepared by Daniel C. Kopp and Lois Shufeldt as a basis for class discussion rather than to illustrate either effective or ineffective handling of an administrative situation. The authors would like to acknowledge the cooperation and assistance of American Greetings. Used with permission from Daniel C. Kopp. ʺ

EXHIBIT 34.1   Consolidated Statements of Financial Position, 1981–1990

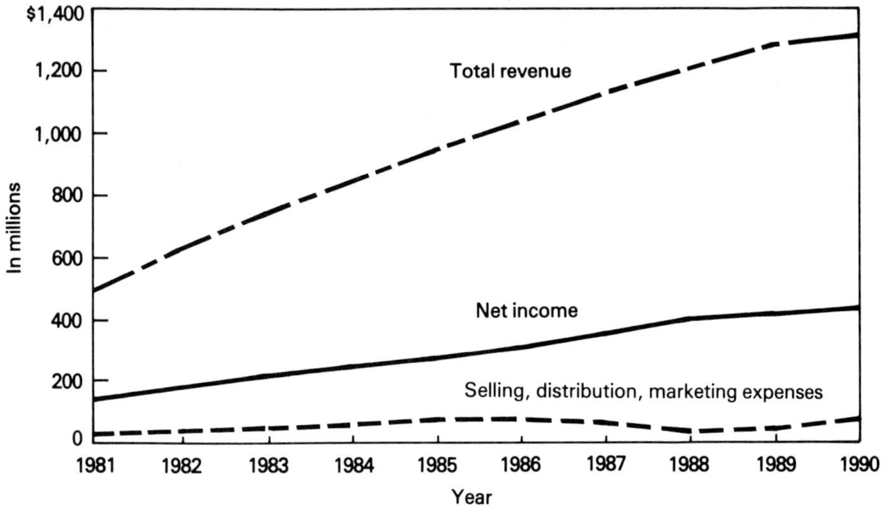

for market share dominance among the three industry leaders, Hallmark, Gibson, and AG. In the final analysis, market shares had not really changed that much among the big three. Each was determined to defend its respective market share, and the nature of the greeting card industry changed dramatically. Previously, the two leading firms, Hallmark and AG, peacefully coexisted by having mutually exclusive niches. Hallmark offered higher-priced, quality cards in department stores and card shops, and AG offered inexpensive cards in mass-merchandise outlets. However, AG's growth strategy to attack the industry leader and its niche, followed by Gibson's growth strategy and Hallmark's defensive moves, changed the industry. AG was now engaged in defending its competitive position.

HISTORY OF AMERICAN GREETINGS

The story of American Greetings is one of an American dream of a Polish immigrant who came to the land of promise and opportunity to seek his fortune. Jacob Sapirstein was born in 1884 in Wasosz, Poland, and because of the Russian-Japanese war of 1904, was sent by his widowed mother, along with his seven brothers and one sister, to live in America.

Jacob, also known as J. S., began his one-man business buying postcards made in Germany from wholesalers and selling them to candy, novelty, and drug stores in Cleveland in 1906. From a horse-drawn card wagon, the small venture steadily flourished.

J. S. and his wife Jennie, also a Polish immigrant, had three sons and a daughter; all three sons became active in their father's business. At the age of nine, Irving, the oldest, kept the family business afloat while J. S. was recovering from the flu during the epidemic of 1918. The business had outgrown the family living room and was moved to a garage at this time.

J. S. had a basic philosophy of service to the retailer and a quality product for the consumer. He developed the first wire rack as well as a rotating floor stand to make more attractive, convenient displays. In the 1930s the Sapirstein Card Company began to print its own cards to ensure the quality of its product. The name of the company was changed to American Greeting Publishers to reflect the national stature and functioning of the company. Its first published line of cards under the American Greetings name, the Forget Me Not line, went on sale in 1939 for a nickel. One card, which remains the company's all-time best seller, was designed by Irving.

The company saw great expansion throughout the 1940s, as loved ones found the need to communicate with World War II soldiers. The most significant effect of this was the widespread use of greeting cards by the soldiers. In the past, cards had been primarily a product utilized by women; thus, the expansion to the male market was a significant breakthrough for the card industry.

The 1950s marked the first public offering of stock, and the name change to American Greetings Corporation. Ground was broken for a new world headquarters, which led the way for expansion to world markets. The company made connections with several foreign markets and acquired a Canadian plant.

In 1960, J. S. stepped down at the age of 76. His son Irving succeeded him as president. Under Irving's leadership and with the assistance of his brothers, Morris and Harry Stone (all three brothers had changed their names from Sapirstein, meaning sapphire, to Stone in 1940 for business reasons), the company continued to expand into gift wrapping, party goods, calendars, stationery, candles, ceramics, and perhaps, most importantly, the creation of licensed characters.

Expansion into these related items somewhat diminished AG's recession-proof profits. Greeting card sales typically increase during recessions as people refrain from gift buying and instead remember others with a less expensive card. The supplemental items now constituted one-third of the company's sales, not enough to seriously jeopardize AG during down economies, yet greatly augmented the company's sales during good economic times.

AG's world expansion became a major pursuit throughout the 1960s and 1970s. Morry Weiss, a grandson-in-law of J. S., became the new president of AG in 1978; Irving continued as chairman of the board of directors.

THE GREETING CARD INDUSTRY

According to GM News, in 1988 Americans exchanged more than 7.1 billion cards—around 29 per person, which was down from the highest per capita card consumption of 30 per person in 1985.[1] And with the average retail price per card of $1.10, that made "social expression" nearly an $8 billion business. According to the Greeting Card Association, card buyers sent the following:

Holiday	Units Sold (In millions)	Percent
Christmas	2,200	30.99
Valentine's Day	850	11.97
Easter	180	2.54
Mother's Day	140	1.97
Father's Day	85	1.20
Graduation	80	1.13
Thanksgiving	40	0.56
Halloween	25	0.35
St. Patick's Day	16	—
Grandparent's Day	10	—
Chanukah	9	—
Other Seasons	5	—

Half of the total greeting cards purchased in 1988 were seasonal cards. The remainder were in the category of everyday cards. People living in the northeast and the northcentral parts of the country bought more cards than average, and southerners 30 percent fewer. People who bought the majority of them tended to be between 35 and 54 years of age, came from large families, lived in their own homes in the suburbs, and had an average household income of $30,000.

Women purchased over 90 percent of all greeting cards. Many women enjoyed browsing and shopping for cards, and tended to purchase a card only if it was appropriate—when the card's verse and design combined to convey the sentiment she wished to express. However, because an increasing number of women were working, they were shopping less frequently and buying less impulse merchandise.

Everyday cards, especially nonoccasion cards or alternative cards, were on the increase. According to *Forbes* and *American Demographics,* the alternative card market was the fastest-growing segment at 25 percent a year, and the card industry as a whole grew 5 percent a year.[2] Alternative cards were not geared to any holiday, but could be inspirational, satirical, or ethnic in nature. This segment was directed toward the estimated 76 million baby boomers. Changes in society—demographic and social—were fueling the growth of alternative cards. These changes included increases in the numbers of blended families, single-parent households, working women, divorcees and remarriages, and population seg-

[1] "Greeting Cards Departments . . . Mass Retail Outlets," *GM News,* October 1989, p. 10.
[2] "Flounder," *Forbes,* April 25, 1988, p. 352; "Funny Valentines," *American Demographics,* February 1989, p. 7.

ments that traditionally included the heaviest greeting card users—35- to 65-year-olds. Formerly, it was the focus strategy of the many small card makers who had 70 percent of the alternative card market. However, the big three captured 87 percent of this segment.

Most industry analysts considered the greeting card industry to be in or near the maturity stage. According to Prudential-Bache, the industry unit growth rate was 2 to 4 percent from 1946 to 1985. The greeting card industry was comprised of from 500 to 900 firms, which ranged from three major corporations to many small family organizations. The industry was dominated by the big three: Hallmark, American Greetings, and Gibson. The estimated market shares were:

Company	1977	1985	1989
Hallmark	50%	42%	40–42%
AG	24	33	32–33
Gibson	5	9	8–10

(Estimates vary according to the source.)

During the 1980s the big three engaged in market share battles through intense price, product, promotion, and place competition. The primary price competition (through discounts to retailers) was during the period 1985–1987, although it continued at a lesser rate. According to Value Line, the end result was the reduction of profits with little change in market shares.

Generally, there was a soft retailing environment. Overall slowdown in retail traffic resulted in reduced sales. The retailing industry was overstored and promotion oriented, which could result in retailers asking greeting card suppliers for lower prices to assist them in keeping their margins from shrinking. Retailers were losing their loyalty to manufacturers that supplied a full line of products—cards, gift wrap, and other items, and were looking instead for the lowest-cost supplier of each, according to Kidder, Peabody & Company.[3] Retailer concessions made to gain accounts were difficult to remove; retailers were reluctant to give them up. Competition in the industry was expected to intensify, especially in the areas of price, sales promotion, distribution, and selling.

Market niches were also attacked. According to the *Insider's Chronicle,* the biggest battlefields were the gift and specialy card shops, which once were the exclusive domain of Hallmark and alternative cards.[4] A 1989 comparison of the three firms reveals the following:

---

[3] E. Gray Glass III, Research Reports on American Greetings and Greeting Card Industry, Kidder, Peabody & Company, May 16, 1986; May 20, 1986; December 11, 1986; January 20, 1987.
[4] "American Greetings," *Insider's Chronicle,* February 8, 1988, p. 3.

Firm	Sales (In billions)	Net Income (In millions)	Number of Employees	Number of Products	Number of Outlets
Hallmark	$2.0	n/a	28,000	20,300	37,000
AG	$1.3	$44.2	29,000	20,000	90,000
Gibson	$0.4	$35.0	7,900	n/a	50,000

n/a = not available.

OBJECTIVES

When asked about AG's 1989 performance, Morry Weiss replied, "Our goal was to improve competitiveness and enhance future earnings prospects in order to maximize shareholder value. AG refocused its world wide business operating strategies. While we have not reached the upper levels of that goal, substantial progress was made in 1989. We are reducing seasonal product returns, accounts receivable, and inventories. These are indicators of how well a business is being operated, and the results show that our people have made substantial progress. We are committed to making even further improvement in these areas."[5]

Weiss further explained, "Sales in 1989 increased despite the loss of revenue caused by the divestiture during the year of the company's AmToy and Plymouth divisions and several foreign subsidiaries . . . net income was affected by restructuring costs which included the cost of relocating Carlton Cards/US to Cleveland, Ohio; consolidating certain manufacturing operations; and selling, consolidating or downsizing several unprofitable businesses." His assessment of AG's 1990 performance was: "It was the kind of year you have to feel good about. Our performance demonstrated our ability to produce outstanding earnings, even in a year when the revenue gain was modest. To accomplish this required enormous effort in every department. It required a diligent watch over expenses while increasing productivity."[6]

Morry Weiss also commented about AG's growth: "We are building a more synergistic relationship between our core business and our subsidiary operations in order to increase our value to our retailers. Our goal is to be a full-service provider to our retailer accounts. The more we represent a single source for a variety of consumer products, the more important a resource we become."[7]

To reach this aim of providing retailers not only greeting cards, but complementary products, AG made the following acquisitions:

[5] American Greetings *Annual Report*, 1989, p. 3.
[6] *Annual Report*, 1990. p. 2.
[7] *Annual Report, 1989, p. 3.*

Company	Products
Acme Frame Products	Picture Frames
Wilhold Hair Care Products	Hair Care Products
Plus Mark	Promotional Christmas Products
A.G. Industries	Greeting Card Cabinets/Displays

MARKETING STRATEGIES

Product

AG produced a wide product line, including greeting cards, gift wrap, party goods, toys, and gift items. Greeting cards accounted for 65 percent of the company's 1990 fiscal sales. The breakdown of sales by major product categories follows:

Category	1980	1984	1986	1990
Everyday Greeting Cards	34%	36%	37%	41%
Holiday Greeting Cards	27	27	29	24
Gift Wrap and Party Goods	21	21	18	17
Consumer Products (Toys, etc.)	9	7	7	9
Stationery	9	9	9	9

Source: AG's Annual Reports.

The essence of AG's product strategy was identifying consumer needs, creating responses that sold, and pretesting to determine the winners. AG believed in identifying consumer needs and responding to them with creative products. Research was a key ingredient. Over 12,000 North American households were surveyed annually to obtain information about every greeting card purchased and received. AG utilized focus group sessions, simulated shopping surveys, and shopping mall interviews. Especially important was ongoing lifestyle research to identify changing tastes and consumer needs for product development.

Research efforts resulted in new products. Couples, an everyday card line that answered the trend back to more sincere romantic relationships, and Kid Zone, which responded to the need for more effective communication with children, were introduced during fiscal 1990. Holly Hobbie designs, popular in the 1960s, were reintroduced when research indicated a trend toward more traditional values.

Morry Weiss commented on the Couples line: "We've proven our ability to meet the challenge of the marketplace. Couples takes its place alongside a pantheon of our major greeting card innovations."[8]

AG had one of the largest creative staffs in the world with over 550 artists, stylists, writers, designers, photographers, and planners who were guided by the latest research data available from computer analysis, consumer testing, and information from AG's sales and merchandising departments. Careful monitoring of societal changes, fashion and color trends, and consumer preferences provided further guidance to product development. They created more than 20,000 new greeting card designs each year. AG adhered to uncompromising quality—in papers, inks, and printing procedures.

AG also engaged in retail pretesting to determine which product ideas had the greatest chance of sales. This was extremely important because of the competitiveness of the market and retailers' needs for fast turnover. A network of retail test stores was used. New cards were rated based upon actual sales performance, and those with the best sales ratings were distributed worldwide.

AG was trying to take advantage of the alternative card segment. In 1992, alternative cards commanded 20 percent of the everyday greeting card market, and the double-digit annual growth rate was expected to continue. Carlton Cards was AG's speciality card subsidiary and recently moved from Dallas to AG's Cleveland headquarters. Carlton was to concentrate on "swiftly developing products unique to the more avant-garde tastes of the specialty store consumer."

AG pioneered licensing and was an industry leader in character licensing. Their strategy was to maximize the potential of their creative and marketing expertise. The following identifies some of AG's character licenses:

Character	Year
Holly Hobbie	1968/1989
Ziggy	1971
Strawberry Shortcake	1980
Care Bears	1983
Herself the Elf	1983
Popples	1983

Strawberry Shortcake was one of the most popular licensed characters. According to *Forbes,* however, all of AG licensed characters have not been successful.[9] One flop, Herself the Elf, was perceived by retailers as being too much like Strawberry Shortcake; it also missed the Christmas season because of

[8] "Flounder," p. 352.
[9] American Greetings *Form 10-K,* 1989, 1.

production problems. Another failure was Get Along Gang, which tried to appeal to both little girls and boys. Another licensing creation, Popples, added a new dimension to a field crowded with look-alikes. Poppies literally "popped out" from a plush ball to a lovable, furry, playmate. A plush toy that folded into its own pouch, Popples enabled children to make its arms, legs, and fluffy tail appear and disappear at will. AG's licensing income is shown below:

Year	Income (In millions)
1984	$17.5
1985	$20.9
1986	$17.6
1987	$17.0
1988	$16.5
1989	$13.3
1990	$11.8

Source: AG's Annual Reports.

Distribution

AG distributed its products in 90,000 retail outlets in 50 countries throughout the world and in 12 languages. AG's major channels of distribution, in order of importance, included drug stores, mass merchandisers, supermarkets, stationery, and gift shops, combo stores (stores combining food, general merchandise, and drug items), variety stores, military post exchanges, and department stores.[10]

AG's primary channels of distribution (which included supermarkets, chain drug stores, and mass retail merchandisers) experienced growth due to demographic and lifestyle changes. The increase of working women changed the location for many card purchases. In 1992, 55 percent of all everyday greeting cards were purchased in convenient locations.

AG's five largest customers accounted for about 17.4 percent of net sales. These customers included mass merchandisers, major drug stores, and military exchanges.

AG had 26 regional and 58 district sales offices in the United States, Canada, United Kingdom, France, and Mexico.

Promotion

Service was a key value to AG's marketing effort as reflected in the following statement by Morry Weiss: "One of our cornerstone values is service to the customer. Although we are a leader in marketing innovation, we earned our reputation for superior customer service by clinging to old-fashioned ideas. We

[10] *Annual Report,* 1990, p. 2.

get to know our customers—and their customers—and learn how their businesses operate."[11]

The services that AG provided its retailers were based upon three key ingredients: knowledgeable sales force, in-store service personnel, and quick response to needs. AG offered the following:

- Largest full-time sales force in the industry, which was composed of highly trained experts.
- National sales force of 12,000 part-time in-store merchandising representatives who visited mass retail stores to restock goods, realign products, set up new displays and point-of-purchase materials, generate reorders, and process returns.
- A computerized network that allowed AG to more quickly and consistently ship complete and accurate orders to retailers[12].

According to Weiss, "AG is focusing on building a strong partnership with retailers and consumers. We will expand distribution of our products in the global marketplace. We will 'partner' with retail accounts by making greeting card departments more profitable. And we will improve our response to consumers' needs for appropriate products and attractive, easy to shop departments."[13]

AG tried to achieve more sales and profits by making the space allocated by retailers more productive. This was accomplished by sophisticated merchandising that made greeting card displays more "consumer friendly." Since women purchased approximately 90 percent of all greeting cards, AG redesigned greeting card cabinets to respond to the fact that women spent less time in stores than previously. Redesigned greeting card cabinets displayed 40 percent more cards in the same amount of space. Point-of-purchase signs and new caption locators ("Mother," "Stepdaughter," and so forth) helped customers in a hurry find the right card.

Themes were becoming more important in merchandising. These were used for particular seasons or occasions that project a strong message to consumers and evoke an immediate awareness of the occasion. Related to this was a new concept called "occasion merchandising," which grouped various products for everyday occasions such as cards, gift wrap, candles, invitations, party goods, and so on.

AG tried to design its marketing programs to increase customer traffic and profitability of the greeting card department. Realizing the need for retailers to differentiate themselves and their products, AG attempted to work on an individual basis to customize the greeting card department for each retailer. This was accomplished via market research and technology. This was especially important to large chains that had to contend with regional differences. Greeting card

[11] Ibid.
[12] Ibid.
[13] Ibid., p. 5.

departments could be customized to reflect a specific area's demographics. If, for example, the demographic profile was comprised of a large number of elderly or "Yuppies," specific products would be featured to target that segment.

In 1982, AG became recognized nationwide, first through television commercials and then through a new corporate identity program. The updated corporate rose logo was featured prominently at retail outlets; the logo became a standard and highly recognizable feature on all product packaging, store signage, point-of-purchase displays, and even the truck fleet. The year-round advertising campaign in 1982 included the promotion of the major card-sending holidays and nonseasonal occasions during daytime and prime-time programming.

The aim of AG's national consumer advertising and public relations programs was to remind people to send cards, in that one of AG's chief competitors was consumer forgetfulness. AG was the only company in the industry to sponsor national consumer retail promotions. These consumer-directed programs served to establish brand identity and generate retail store traffic.

A summary of AG's selling, distribution, and marketing expenses as a percentage of sales is displayed below:

Year	Percent
1981	28.2
1982	28.7
1983	29.2
1984	29.3
1985	29.0
1986	29.9
1987	31.6
1988	33.4
1989	32.6
1990	32.9

PRODUCTION STRATEGIES

AG had 34 plants and facilities in the United States, Canada, the United Kingdom, France, and Mexico. This was down from the 49 plants and facilities in 1986. The company owned approximately 4.8 million square feet and leased 11.3 million square feet of plant, warehouse, store, and office space. It met its space needs in the United States through long-term leases of properties constructed and financed by community development corporations and municipalities.

AG had taken steps in 1987 to 1990 to decrease production costs. It tried to improve its production efficiency by cutting costs and reducing work-in-process inventories. AG also invested heavily in automated production equipment to cut labor costs in 1988. AG benefited from lower costs for raw materials and fewer product returns because of better inventory control. AG's material, labor, and other production costs are as follows:

Year	Percent of Sales
1981	44.7
1982	44.3
1983	41.3
1984	40.5
1985	39.9
1986	40.2
1987	42.3
1988	45.1
1989	42.8
1990	41.5

PERSONNEL STRATEGIES

In 1989, American Greetings employed over 15,000 full-time and 14,000 part-time people in the United States, Canada, Mexico, and Europe. This equated to approximately 20,500 full-time employees.

When asked about AG employees, Morry Weiss commented: "But perhaps our greatest strength is the men and women who create, manufacture, distribute, sell, and support our products. They are committed to knowing our customers, meeting their needs with quality products and providing service before and after the sale."[14]

AG had a noncontributing profit-sharing plan for most of its U.S. employees, as well as a retirement income guarantee plan. It also had several pension plans covering certain employees in foreign countries.

FINANCE STRATEGIES

Exhibits 34.2, 34.3, and 34.4 contain relevant financial information for American Greetings. The financial condition of AG has fluctuated over the years. In the early to mid-1980s, AG profit margins increased from 5.42 percent in 1981 to its high of 8.09 percent in 1984. However, AG's financial performance in the mid- to late 1980s was disappointing, with the profit margin falling to 2.84 percent in 1988 and a return on investment of 2.90 percent. In 1990, AG's profit margin had risen to 5.51 percent with a return on investment of 6.33.

[14] Ibid., p. 1.

EXHIBIT 34.2 Consolidated Statements of Financial Position (In thousands)

	1986	1987	1988	1989	1990
Assets					
Current Assets					
Cash and Equivalents	$ 26,853	$ 17,225	$ 36,534	$ 94,292	$ 122,669
Trade Accounts Receivable, Less Allowances for Sales Returns and Doubtful Accounts	240,471	284,135	278,559	242,582	254,285
Inventories					
Raw Material	59,343	56,057	56,122	48,478	51,075
Work in Process	60,179	69,668	61,406	51,625	42,139
Finished Products	181,237	202,412	245,801	197,618	208,918
	300,759	328,137	363,329	297,721	302,132
Less LIFO Reserve	76,552	75,392	77,274	83,017	85,226
	224,207	252,745	286,055	214,704	216,906
Display Material and Factory Supplies	26,826	29,770	30,299	25,192	25,408
Total Inventories	251,033	282,515	316,354	239,896	242,314
Deferred Income Taxes	36,669	26,593	39,935	49,542	51,315
Prepaid Expenses and Other	6,228	9,679	8,672	11,020	10,362
Total Current Assets	561,254	620,147	680,054	637,332	680,945
Other Assets	47,085	89,488	95,752	92,285	107,788
Property, Plant and Equipment					
Land	7,523	7,956	7,548	6,471	6,229
Buildings	165,241	183,481	223,491	216,545	215,458
Equipment and Fixtures	222,718	269,644	319,353	340,233	354,979
	395,482	461,081	550,392	563,249	576,666
Less Accumulated Depreciation and Amortization	130,519	148,097	175,917	205,246	224,383
Property, Plant, and Equipment—Net	264,963	312,984	374,475	358,003	352,283
Total Assets	$873,302	$1,022,619	$1,150,281	$1,087,620	$1,141,016

Liabilities and Shareholders' Equity

Current Liabilities

Notes Payable to Banks	$ 15,921	$ 25,092	$ 13,956	$ 17,201	$ 36,524
Accounts Payable	66,685	69,175	98,270	79,591	75,146
Payrolls and Payroll Taxes	28,675	31,230	33,759	38,839	10,878
Retirement Plans	11,697	10,966	4,148	8,573	10,878
State and Local Taxes	2,763	3,056	—	—	—
Dividends Payable	5,317	5,343	5,338	5,311	5,281
Income Taxes	18,988	—	13,782	6,693	6,430
Sales Returns	23,889	29,964	28,273	24,543	21,182
Current Maturities of Long-Term Debt	4,786	10,894	54,150	3,740	—
Total Current Liabilities	178,721	185,720	251,676	184,491	200,756
Long-Term Debt	147,592	235,005	273,492	246,732	235,497
Deferred Income Taxes	64,025	77,451	86,426	91,409	100,159
Shareholders' Equity					
Common Shares—Par Value $1:					
Class A	29,203	29,552	29,628	29,692	29,946
Class B	2,982	2,588	2,528	2,497	2,063
Capital in Excess of Par Value	94,744	102,718	104,209	105,245	110,234
Shares Held in Treasury	(1,689)	(15,409)	(14,199)	(14,767)	(26,692)
Cumulative Translation Adjustment	(16,801)	(11,604)	(7,564)	(4,790)	(8,186)
Retained Earnings	374,525	416,598	424,085	447,111	497,239
Total Shareholders' Equity	482,964	524,443	538,687	564,988	604,604
Total Liabilities and Shareholders' Equity	$873,302	$1,022,619	$1,150,281	$1,087,620	$1,141,016

Source: American Greetings.

EXHIBIT 34.3 Consolidated Statements of Income, Years Ending February 28 or 29 (In thousands except per share data)

	1986	1987	1988	1989	1990
Net Sales	$1,012,451	$1,102,532	$1,174,817	$1,252,793	$1,286,853
Other Income	23,200	23,463	24,155	22,566	22,131
Total Revenue	1,035,651	1,125,995	1,198,972	1,275,359	1,308,984
Cost and Expenses					
Material, Labor and Other Production Costs	416,322	476,725	540,143	546,214	543,602
Selling, Distribution, and Marketing	308,745	355,363	400,033	415,597	431,254
Administration and General	131,928	125,407	135,224	148,095	149,771
Depreciation and Amortization	23,471	29,059	34,191	39,527	40,251
Interest	19,125	24,875	32,787	33,479	27,691
Restructuring Charge	—	12,371	—	23,591	—
Total	899,591	1,023,800	1,142,378	1,206,503	1,192,569
Income before Income Taxes	136,060	102,195	56,594	68,856	116,415
Income Taxes	61,635	38,834	23,203	24,582	44,238
Net Income	$ 74,425	$ 63,361	$ 33,391	$ 44,274	$ 72,177
Net Income per Share	$2.32	$1.97	$1.04	$1.38	$2.25

Source: American Greetings.

EXHIBIT 34.4   Selected Financial Data, Years Ending February 28 or 29 (In thousands except per share data)

	1986	1987	1988	1989	1990
Summary of Operations					
Total Revenue	$1,035,651	$1,125,995	$1,198,972	$1,275,359	$1,308,984
Materials, Labor, and Other Products	420,747	476,725	540,143	546,214	543,602
Depreciation and Amortization	23,471	20,059	34,191	39,527	40,251
Interest Expense	19,125	24,875	32,787	33,479	27,691
Net Income	$ 74,425	$ 63,361	$ 33,391	$ 44,274	$ 72,177
Net Income per Share	$2.32	$1.97	$1.04	$1.38	$2.25
Cash Dividends per Share	.62	.66	.66	.66	.66
Fiscal Year End Market Price per Share	$35.62	$28,75	$17.63	$21.25	$31.25
Average Number Shares Outstanding	32,059,851	32,212,556	32,068,752	32,146,971	32,029,533
Financial Position					
Accounts Receivable	$ 240,471	$ 284,135	$ 278,559	$ 242,582	$ 254,285
Inventories	251,033	282,515	316,354	239,896	243,314
Working Capital	382,533	434,427	428,378	452,841	480,189
Total Assets	873,302	1,022,619	1,150,281	1,087,620	1,141,016
Capital Additions	61,799	68,740	96,682	41,938	42,869
Long-Term Debt	147,592	235,005	273,492	246,732	235,497
Shareholders' Equity	482,964	524,443	538,687	564,988	604,604
Shareholders' Equity per Share	$15.01	$16.32	$16.75	$17.55	$18.89
Net Return Average Shareholders' Equity	16.5%	12.7%	6.3%	8.0%	12.3%
Pretax Return on Total Revenue	13.1%	9.1%	4.7%	5.4%	8.9%
Summary of Operations					
Total Revenue	$ 498,272	$ 623,604	$ 742,683	$ 839,914	$ 945,658
Materials, Labor and Other Products	225,356	278,866	313,769	344,313	382,205
Depreciation and Amortization	10,863	12,752	13,890	15,507	18,799
Interest Expense	13,548	21,647	24,086	16,135	15,556
Net Income	$ 26,515	$ 32,843	$ 44,582	$ 59,658	$ 74,365
Net Income per Share	$.97	$1.20	$1.54	$1.91	$2.35
Cash Dividends per Share	.26	.27	.31	.40	.54
Fiscal Year End Market Price per Share	$5.50	$9.63	$18.69	$23.69	$33.06
Average Number Shares Outstanding	27,314,594	27,352,342	28,967,092	31,240,455	31,629,418
Financial Position					
Accounts Receivable	$ 114,051	$ 131,996	$ 148,018	$ 146,896	$ 173,637
Inventories	133,836	159,623	177,459	180,019	214,449
Working Capital	167,772	215,412	241,724	275,685	330,409
Total Assets	433,204	491,854	580,675	685,894	747,897
Capital Additions	22,768	26,720	33,967	46,418	43,575
Long-Term Debt	113,486	148,895	111,066	119,941	112,876
Shareholders' Equity	205,550	227,784	316,368	365,496	425,748
Shareholder Equity per Share	$7.52	$8.31	$10.18	$11.62	$13.35
Net Return Average Shareholders' Equity	13.7%	15.4%	17.1%	17.8%	19.2%
Pretax Return on Total Revenue	9.9%	9.2%	11.0%	13.0%	14.4%

Irving Stone commented about AG's 1990 performance: "Fiscal 1990 revenues were a record $1.31 billion. This marks the 84th consecutive year that revenues have increased since the Company's founding in 1906. And . . . revenue was driven by higher sales of everyday greeting cards, our low-cost high margin core products. Fourth quarter sales were particularly strong. We expect to continue reporting good sales results." He continued, "The market value of our common stock rose 47 percent, from $21.25 on February 28, 1989 to $31.25 at the fiscal year close on February 28, 1990. This compares favorably to 27 percent increases for both the Dow Jones Industrial Average and the Standard and Poor's 500 Stock Index. Total returns to stockholders—share price appreciation plus dividends—was 50 percent in fiscal 1990."[15]

AG's stock price ranged from a low of 9-1/2 in 1981 to a high of 37-1/8 in 1990.

MANAGEMENT

AG was organized via a divisional profit center basis. Each division had its own budget committee, although an executive management committee, comprised of five senior executives, approved the strategic plans for all the divisions. Strategic plans were established in 1-, 3-, 10-, and 20-year time frames. Corporate AG maintained strict budgetary and accounting controls.

The basic domestic greeting card business was placed under the U.S. Greeting Card Division. Domestic and international subsidiary operations, including the licensing division, were a second unit, with corporate management a third. AG decentralized its structure in 1983.

U.S. Greeting Card Division. This division emcompassed the core business of greeting cards and related products, including manufacturing, sales, merchandising, research, and administrative services. It produced and distributed greeting cards and related products domestically. The same products were distributed throughout the world by international subsidiaries and licensees.

Domestic and International Subsidiaries. AG's domestic and international subsidiary operations included the following:

Domestic

Acme Frame Products
A.G. Industries
Plus Mark
Summit Corporation/Summit Collection

---

[15] Ibid.

Those Characters from Cleveland
Wilhold Hair Care Products

International

Carlton Cards—Canada
Carlton Cards—England
Carlton Cards—France
Felicitaciones Nacionales S.A. de C.V.—Mexico
Rust Craft Canada

The number of domestic operations in 1990 included six versus seven in 1986. Firms divested included Amtoy, Drawing Board Greeting Cards, and Tower Products. The number of international operations in 1990 was 5 versus 13 in 1986. Among the international operations consolidated included one in Canada, four in Continental Europe, one in Monaco, and four in the United Kingdom.

AG's domestic and international sales are summarized below:

Sales Recap

Year	Domestic	Gross Profit Margin	Foreign	Gross Profit Margin	U.S. Percent	International Percent
1990	$1,088,438	11.86	$220,546	6.79	83.15	16.85
1989	1,039,464	7.75	235,895	9.22	81.50	18.50
1988	996,628	7.79	202,344	5.80	83.12	16.88
1987	940,565	13.28	185,430	1.19	83.53	16.47
1986	874,255	15.38	161,396	12.82	84.42	15.58
1985	799,805	16.51	145,853	13.18	84.58	15.42
1984	717,057	15.18	122,857	13.61	85.37	15.63
1983	631,143	14.29	111,549	13.94	85.00	15.00
1982	523,467	12.54	100,137	13.61	85.40	14.60
1981	440,516	12.27	57,756	14.87	88.41	11.59

Source: AG annual reports.

FUTURE OF AG

When asked about the future of AG, Morry Weiss responded, "We are poised for perhaps the most successful period in our history. We are prepared to strengthen our core business and improve our position in the greeting card industry; to provide a greater return to our shareholders; and to afford our employees even greater opportunities for growth and career advancement. The strategies we will employ to achieve our goals for the new year and beyond are clear. We have well defined corporate strengths which we will target to build even stronger partnerships with retailers and consumers.[16]

[16] *Annual Report*, 1989, p. 3.

Irving Stone's view of the future included the following: "We are optimistic about the future. We are confident that we can achieve even more exciting results . . . in the future. We face the future confident that our commitment to help people build and maintain relationships will produce even more innovative products like Couples."[17]

U.S. *Industrial Outlook* expected industry sales to grow between 3 to 4 percent annually through 1992. Moderate growth was predicted due to forecasted moderate growth in the gross national product, real disposable personal income, and personal consumption expenditures. For continued growth and profitability, U.S. *Industrial Outlook* recommended diversification into related product lines, institution of more cost-cutting strategies, monitoring of demand for current lines, divesting of unprofitable lines, and better matching of demand with supply to avoid after-holiday returns.[18]

The unit growth rate for the greeting card industry between 1987 and 2015 was estimated to be between 1 and 3 percent. Exhibit 34.5 provides the forecast according to Prudential-Bache Securities. The slowing of unit growth was primarily due to the postwar baby boomers who had already entered their high card-consumption years. With the declining birthrate of the 1970s and 1980s, consumption of cards was expected to decline.[19]

EXHIBIT 34.5   The Greeting Card Industry—Consumption Forecast

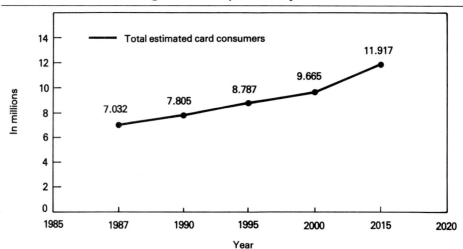

[17] *U.S. Industrial Outlook,* Department of Commerce, 1988, pp. 29–16, 29–17.
[18] "Greeting Cards Industry Update," Prudential-Bache Securities, December 30, 1988; August 9, 1989, September 27, 1989.
[19] Ibid.

However, greeting card officials optimistically projected that the rate of consumption would increase moderately from the current per-capita rate of 29 cards to 44 cards per-capita by 2015. Greeting card sources also reported that consumers were upgrading their purchases to higher priced cards, thus generating more profits per sale. The aging population, those over 55, also tended to send more cards than did younger persons.

Prudential-Bache's expectations for the future of the greeting card industry included the following:

Price competition would remain a concern because of the maturity of the industry and the limited number of large players.

At least 5 to 10 percent of the industry's current sales were to retail outlets that the industry leaders would never serve due to the small size of these outlets, which made it too expensive to reach.

The greeting card industry was an area ripe for potential acquisition.

AG was and would continue to experience increased competition in its promotional gift-wrap area.

The big three could be challenged by any small, well-run company.

It would be unlikely that the big three with combined market shares of 80 to 85 percent would continue to expand to "own the market." The dynamic competitive nature of the industry would prohibit this.

There was not much room for the big three to grow by capturing more of the remaining market they were not reaching.[20]

As CEO Morry Weiss thought about the future, he wondered what changes AG should make in its competitive strategies.

[20] Ibid.

_____ CASE 35 _____

Supportive Homecare: Positioning for the 1990s

The early 1980s was not the best time to start a new business. The economic climate was dismal, with the country going through a severe recession and interest rates hovering above 15 percent. Oshkosh, Wisconsin, was no different from the rest of the nation. Yet, in 1983, two people decided that it was a good time to start a business in the home health care industry.

Terri Hansen had worked for Upjohn Healthcare for 18 months as director of nurses. She thought that there was a definite need for home care in the Oshkosh area and that the time was right to start the new business. Her part-time partner, John Westphal, was employed full time in the insurance business.

THE HOME HEALTH CARE INDUSTRY

Home health care provided health care and social services in the patient's home rather than in a medical facility. Home health care was less expensive (see Exhibit 35.1 for home health care costs compared to institutional costs) and was considered to be less disruptive to patients.

Expenditures for home health care exceeded $9 billion in 1989. Although it was a small portion of the total $223.7 billion spent on health care, the amount and proportion for home care were expected to increase because of the growing number of people aged 65 and over, the generally lower cost of home care, support by insurers, and Medicare endorsement of home care as an alternative to institutionalization.

In 1990, the home health care market was divided into three basic services: home health care services, home medical equipment, and home infusion therapy. In 1989, home health services accounted for 68 percent, home medical equipment

This case was prepared by Jeffrey W. Totten and Linda E. Swayne as a basis for class discussion rather than to illustrate either effective or ineffective handling of an administrative situation. Used with permission from Jeffrey W. Totten.

EXHIBIT 35.1   Comparison of Various Home Health Care Costs with Institutional Costs

Average Cost per Day for Relatively Intensive Treatment	
Home Care	$25–200 per day
Hospital	$300–500 per day
Average Cost of Care for a Ventilator-Dependent Patient	
Home Care	$21,192 per year
Hospital	$270,830 per year
Average Cost of Care for an AIDS Patient	
Home Care	$94 per day
Hospital	$773 per day
Average Cost for a Quadriplegic Patient with a Spinal Cord Injury	
Home Care	$13,931 per month
Hospital	$23,862 per month
Average Cost of Care for Infant Born with Breathing and Feeding Problems	
Home Care	$20,200 per month
Hospital	$60,970 per month
Average Cost for Routine Skilled Nursing	
Home Care	$750 per month
Hospital	$2,000 per month

Source: Robin Richman, "High-Tech Home Care: What's in It for Hospitals?" *Health Care Strategic Management,* Vol. 8, No. 3 (March 1990), p. 21.

20 percent, and home infusion therapy 12 percent of this $16 billion industry.[1] The demand situation for home health care providers was relatively flat, home medical equipment declined slightly, and infusion therapy increased.

Home health care services were expected to grow to be $14.2 billion by the mid-1990s.[2] Medical equipment, because of changes in Medicare reimbursement, was a loss rather than a profit center for many in this saturated market. Home infusion therapies, such as intravenous (IV) antibiotic therapy and chemotherapy, allowed patients the flexibility of being treated at home instead of in the hospital. Because of cost-containment pressures and the changes in the composition of the patient population, home health care shifted from custodial to acute care. Thus, the home infusion therapy segment was predicted to grow and be more profitable than home health services (custodial care) or home medical equipment. Another growing home service was in the area of rehabilitation care. Because of advances in medical technology, many patients survived severe trauma. Home care could be a viable option.[3]

[1] Sandy Lutz, "Hospitals Reassess Home-Care Ventures," *Modern Healthcare*, Vol. 20, No. 37 (September 17, 1990), p. 26.
[2] Robin Richman, "High-Tech Home Care: What's in It for Hospitals?" *Health Care Strategic Management*, Vol. 8, No. 3 (March 1990), p. 19.
[3] Mary Wagner, "Despite Gains in Home Infusion Therapy, Home-Care Revenue Growth Remains Flat," *Modern Healthcare*, Vol. 20, No. 20 (May 21, 1990), p. 96.

In June 1988, there were about 11,000 home health care agencies, an increase over the 10,848 operating in 1987. About 50 percent were Medicare certified and about 25 percent were hospital based.[4] Since the implementation of the prospective payment system (PPS) in 1983, hospital-based home care agencies more than doubled in number, from 700 in 1983 to over 2,000 in 1989.[5] Hospitals actively sought additional revenues as third-party payer policies and practices resulted in shorter hospital stays. Home care seemed to offer an opportunity to add services, to remain visible in the community, and to obtain a competitive advantage. Since many hospitals provided referrals (98.4 percent of patients were referred by a hospital to a home health care agency), they had a decided advantage in developing home care services. They were motivated to enter the market because it helped to reduce a patient's hospital stay but still provided care for the patient. However, according to a study by SMG Marketing Group reported in the *Marion Long Term Care Digest, Home Health Care Edition for 1989*, long-term patients chose proprietary agencies over hospital-based home care (Exhibit 35.2).

As home care shifted from custodial to acute care, hospitals increased their diversification efforts into home infusion therapy, Medicare-certified home health agencies, hospices, home medical equipment companies, and private-duty nursing/supplemental staffing agencies. Home infusion gained favor over Medicare-certified home health agencies because agencies that relied on people as inventory were more difficult to operate.[6] Hospital-based home health care agencies experienced turnover rates of 18.7 percent for registered nurses and 47.8 percent for occupational therapists in 1989.

EXHIBIT 35.2   Home Health Care Choice

Type of Patient	Government	Hospital	Proprietary	Not-for-Profit Visiting Nurses Association	Average
Male	35.9%	39.0%	36.9%	35.2%	36.8%
Female	64.1	61.0	63.1	64.8	63.2
Adult	24.0	23.3	25.9	24.0	24.5
Pediatric	4.7	3.6	5.1	5.0	4.6
Senior Citizen	71.3	73.1	69.0	70.9	70.9
Patient <30 days	27.5	35.0	27.0	33.5	30.3
Patient >30 days	72.5	65.0	73.0	66.5	69.7
1 Visit/Week	44.5	36.6	18.2	24.9	29.8
2–3 Visits/Week	39.3	51.3	47.3	50.7	47.1
3+ Visits/Week	16.2	12.1	34.5	24.4	23.1
24-Hour Care Required	7.0	7.9	15.8	10.4	12.3

Source: "Planning Indicators," *Health Care Strategic Management*, Vol. 8, No. 4 (April 1990), p. 23.

[4] "Health Services," *U.S. Industrial Outlook 1990*, U.S. Department of Commerce, January 1990, p. 49–5.

[5] Lutz, "Hospitals Reassess Home-Care Ventures," p. 23.

[6] Richman, "High-Tech Home Care," p. 1.

Hospitals entered into the home infusion therapy business in various ways. In the past many hospitals developed arrangements with existing providers. They accomplished these arrangements through informal efforts, affiliations, contract services, fee-for-services, or joint ventures. For example, one hospital entered the home infusion therapy market through a joint venture with the local visiting nurses association (VNA). It was mutually beneficial for both parties because they expanded services without either having to invest full start-up costs.

Senior citizens represented 73.1 percent of the patients receiving IV therapies. AIDS patients were another growing segment of the patient mix that could benefit from home infusion therapy. There were 78,312 reported cases of AIDS in the United States in 1988. An estimated 1.5 million were infected by the HIV virus.[7]

Reimbursement for home infusion therapy was generally at a satisfactory level. Most private insurance carriers and health maintenance organizations provided sufficient reimbursement. Medicare covered some infusion therapies, but not all the available types. Case managers became common for in-home infusion therapy patients. Case managers were expected to scrutinize health care costs, bringing more checks and balances to the home infusion industry.[8]

Utilization of home health care agencies increased each year from 1980 to 1987 (Exhibit 35.3). Because home health care had been growing at a rate of 20 percent a year, the "dip" in 1987 was unusual, especially since there was an increasing proportion of people over 65. In 1987 the over-65 population accounted for 30 percent of total medical expenditures.[9]

EXHIBIT 35.3   Trends in Home Health Care Utilization

Year	Visits	Patients Served
1980	16,322	726
1981	22,688	948
1982	30,628	1,154
1983	36,898	1,318
1984	40,440	1,498
1985	39,462	1,549
1986	38,022	1,571
1987	35,676	1,295
1988	36,598	1,305

Source: "Health Services," *U.S. Industrial Outlook 1990*, U.S. Department of Commerce, January 1990, p. 49-5.

[7] "Health Services," p. 49-5.
[8] "Providers Eye Entry of Case Managers in Home Infusion," *Modern Healthcare*, Vol. 20, No. 37 (September 17, 1990), p. 30.
[9] Richman, "High-Tech Health Care," p. 19.

It appeared that the lessening of demand for home health care in 1987 may have been caused by a misunderstanding by the Health and Human Services Department concerning the number of days a week an eligible home care patient could receive care under full-time and part-time services. The misunderstanding was resolved by litigation in favor of the beneficiary (see *Duggan v. Bowen,* USDC(DC), No.87-0383, August 1, 1988).[10] Home care usage increased slightly in 1988.

Some for-profit home health care agencies started offering bonuses to hospital discharge planners as a method to increase business. Similar to the frequent-flyer programs implemented by airlines, the agencies provided free service to hospitals that referred private paying patients. Olsten Health Care Services returned to each participating institution (350 are enrolled) 10 percent of reimbursed service hours generated from a given institution's private pay referrals. The more hours referred, the more hours of free care accumulated. The institutions used the free hours for indigent patients. "What we're doing is giving something back to the community," commented Sal Morici, marketing manager in Olsten's health care division.[11] Not all hospitals were enthusiastic about the program. Public scrutiny of referrals (especially medicare referrals) made some hospitals reluctant to participate. Others were pleased to be able to offer the free home care to patients so that they could be discharged earlier.

HOME HEALTH CARE IN OSHKOSH

In 1983, before Terri Hansen started Supportive HealthCare, only Upjohn Health Care provided 24-hour home health care for the Oshkosh area. The Visiting Nurses Association and the Winnebago County nurses provided part-time, intermittent home care. Several hospitals in the Fox River Valley, including Mercy Medical Center (236 beds in Oshkosh), Theda Clark Regional Hospital (356 beds in Neenah), St. Elizabeth's Hospital (280 beds in Appleton), Appleton Medical Center (220 beds in Appleton), Kaukauna Community Hospital (52 beds in Kaukauna), and St. Agnes (62 beds in Fond Du Lac), provided acute (in-patient) care.

Oshkosh, a small urban community located on the western shore of Lake Winnebago in Winnebago County, Wisconsin had a population of approximately 54,000 people (Exhibit 35.4). The city, located on a major state highway, about 90 minutes from Madison, the state capital, had a strong Polish, German, and Scandinavian heritage, and was tied economically to the paper industry that is concentrated along the Fox River Valley. The city was also the home for Oshkosh Truck (heavy-duty vehicles), Leach (garbage trucks), Oshkosh B'Gosh (well-known children's clothing), the Experimental Aircraft Association, the University

---

[10] "Health Services," p. 49–4.
[11] Sandy Lutz, "Home-Care Agencies Offer Bonuses for Business," *Modern Healthcare,* August 20, 1990, pp. 73–74.

EXHIBIT 35.4   Map of Oshkosh and the Surrounding Counties

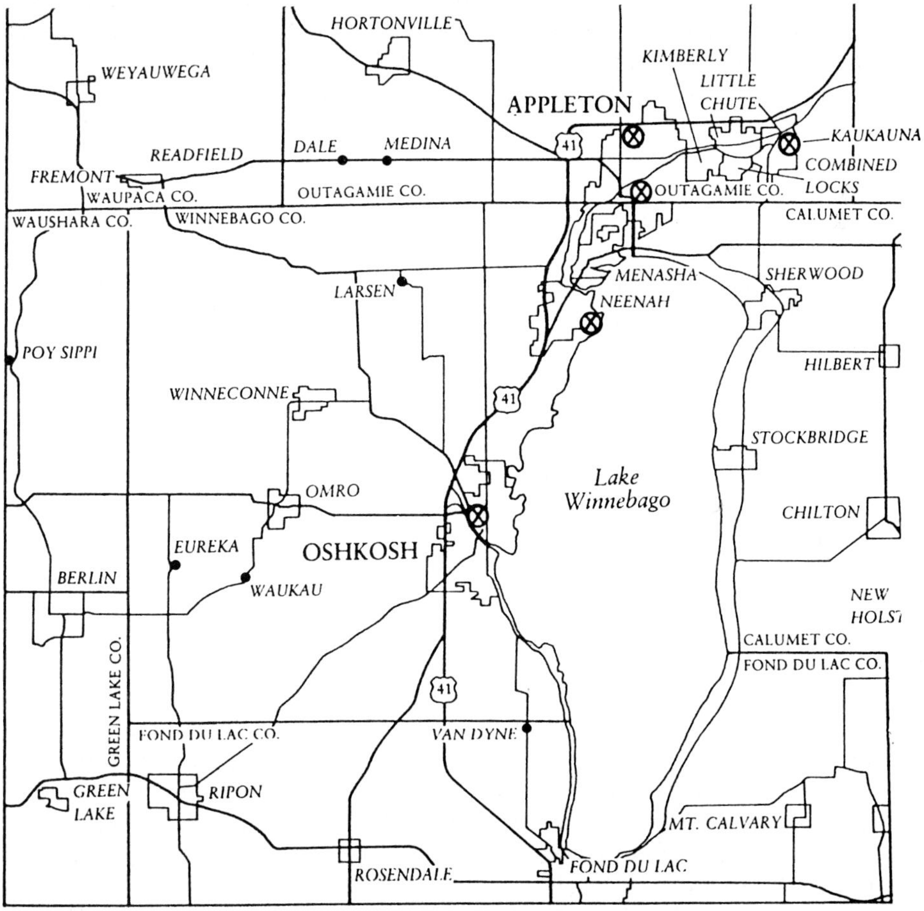

of Wisconsin–Oshkosh, Miles Kimball (catalog merchandise), Georgia Pacific (paper), and Mercury Marine (boat motors).

GETTING STARTED

Ms. Hansen started very small. "I did not want a lot of overhead, so I started the business in my home. I wanted to make sufficient income for myself and for my workers." She did not expect to generate any cash for at least six months. In fact, she had to borrow money from the bank to pay her own salary. Because she could afford so little help, she handled the nursing management, typing, telephone answering, and marketing herself. In the beginning, the company was a two-person office operation, with three part-timers providing care in the field.

Before she could actually get started, she had to apply for a license from the state. A lengthy proposal had to be written and submitted to the Wisconsin Department of Health and Social Services to show need for the service. Letters from physicians and social agencies indicating support for the idea had to be included. Three-year projections of operations were required to show that the business could be maintained for at least that period of time. The certificate of need (CON) was granted in January 1983; Supportive HomeCare became a privately owned, independent, state-licensed home care agency. It took the company until April to get certification for third-party billing by Medicare and Medicaid. During these four months, the company could only accept private-pay patients.

Ms. Hansen spent the first months talking about the company to agencies, churches, and doctors without generating any business. Finally in March, the company cared for its first patient, quickly followed by five more. "For that first year, I was on call twenty-four hours a day, seven days a week," remembered Ms. Hansen. The company grew to 2 full-time and 2 part-time office personnel and 30 employees in the field by the end of its first year of operation.

TARGET MARKET

Ms. Hansen targeted her services toward hospital discharge planners, doctors, county nurses, county social service agencies, and the Visiting Nurses Association. According to Terri Hansen, "We wanted to find a niche in the market where the company could fit in without rocking the boat, yet still provide a needed service. My goal was to provide a service with a positive image, one that works *with* other competitors, to be collaborative rather than competing against them." The population target was Winnebago County, where Ms. Hansen had her strongest contacts and greatest credibility as a health care professional. Potential consumers of home care included individuals recuperating from accidents and outpatient surgery, handicapped and disabled individuals, single and working parents, and private-duty individualized care for loved ones who were gravely ill. Exhibit 35.5 lists the client base for 1989.

CHOOSING HOME HEALTH CARE

In general, if the person who would be utilizing the home health care service were currently in the hospital, he or she would typically use the Yellow Pages to find the service providers and would rely on the advice of physicians, family,

EXHIBIT 35.5   Supportive HomeCare Client Base

	1986	*1989*
Primary Diagnosis of Clients Serviced		
Cardiovascular	29	53
Cancer	19	17
Arthritis	18	25
Cerebral Vascular Accident	17	24
Diabetes	11	21
Respiratory	10	22
Cerebral Palsy	7	5
Fractures	7	21
Paralysis	6	12
Mental Illness	2	13
Senile Dementia	1	19
Mental Retardation	1	8
Other Conditions	46	69
Total Clients	174	309
Referral Sources for Admissions		
Hospitals	27	36
Social Services	20	28
Supportive HomeCare Employees	6	12
Newspaper	6	10
Client/Former Client	5	26
Nursing Homes	5	2
Yellow Pages	5	4
Home Health Agency	3	19
Presentation	1	4
Other and Continuing Patients	11	168
Total Referrals	89	309
Number of Clients Discharged		
To Nursing Homes	13	33
By Death	29	26
To Self-Care	23	78
To Family	2	6
Other	20	32
Hospitalized	0	57
Total	87	232
Number of Clients Admitted by Age		
17 and Under		19
18–54		23
55–64		40
65–74		150
75–84		70
85–94		7
Total		309
Client Totals		
Number of Clients Carried Over from 1988		140
Number of New Admissions in 1989		169
Total Clients Served in 1989		309

Source: SHC State Annual Report, 1986 and 1989 (provided August 20, 1990).

EXHIBIT 35.6   Home Health Care Rate Comparisons

Type of Helper	Supportive HomeCare	Lakeshore Home Care	Mercy VNA[a]
Registered Nurse	$75/visit– $35 add. hr.	n/a	$79/2 hr. visit– $27 add. hr.
Licensed Practical Nurse	$55/2-hr. visit– $27 add. hr.	n/a	n/a
Home Health Aide	$36/2-hr. visit– $16.45 add. hr.	$12/hr. (1 hr. minimum)	$37/2-hr. visit– $18 add. hr.
Personal Care Worker/ Homemaker Companion	$11.50/hr.	$9.50/hr. (1 hr. minimum)	n/a
Live-in Companion	n/a	$110/24 hrs.[e]	n/a
Other			
Home Care Attendant	$16.45/hr.	n/a	n/a
Medical Social Worker	n/a	$100/2-hr. visit	$100/2-hr. visit
Speech Pathologist	n/a	n/a	$75/2-hr. visit
Occupational Therapy	n/a	n/a	$75/2-hr. visit
Physical Therapy	n/a	n/a	$75/2-hr. visit

[a] Sliding fee available.
[b] Fees for private pay only.
[c] Higher fees for specialized RN (e.g., pediatrics).
[d] Higher fees for "hi-tech" RNs, LPNs.
[e] State sees this as a babysitter, not personal care; switch to nurses' aide live-in at $154/24 hrs.
n/a = not available.
Source: Telephone interviews, October 4, 1990; Neenah-Menasha VNA Rate Sheet, October 8, 1990; Supportive HomeCare Rate Sheet, October 8, 1990.

friends, and "significant others" in choosing a home health care agency. Outside the hospital, prospective clients relied on their adult children and significant others for advice. The final decision is usually made by the client, the family, or close friends.

Supportive HomeCare found that clients or referral sources who made service inquiries were at one of four possible stages in their decision making: gathering information, semi-interested, desired home care services, or decided against using Supportive HomeCare. The personnel answering the telephone tried to respond promptly to all inquiries, assessing the level of decision making and determining what the client's needs were.

Fees for home health care varied considerably based on the type of care required as well as the company providing the care. Supportive HomeCare was competitively priced for the services offered (see Exhibit 35.6).

Preferred Health Care[b]	Upjohn Home Care	Neenah-Menasha VNA
$80 ($70) 2-hr. visit[c]	$32 ($27)/hr.[d]	$77/2-hr. visit–$29 add. hr.
$70/2-hr. visit–$22 add. hr.	$25 ($22)/hr.[d]	$77/2h. visit–$25 add. hr.
$41/2-hr. visit–$16.44 add. hr.	$18/hr.	$46/2-hr. visit–$16 add. hr.
$21/2-hr. visit–$9 add hr.	$11.05/hr.	$9.75/hr. (2-hr. minimum)–$45/overnight (8–10 hrs.)
$100/day	n/a	$110/day
n/a	$8/hr.	n/a
n/a	n/a	$95/visit
n/a	n/a	$77/visit
n/a	n/a	$77/visit
n/a	n/a	$77/visit

SERVICE GROWTH

Growth, measured in terms of hours of service provided, quadrupled every quarter during 1983 and 1984. By June 1984, Supportive HomeCare employed 40 people, including office personnel, nurses, and nurses' aides. Growth compelled the company to move out of Ms. Hansen's home. A vacant house on Mt. Vernon Street (two blocks east of Oshkosh's main street) became available, and the company moved during the summer of 1985.

Although Ms. Hansen had no formal business training, she developed and managed a very successful company. Her concern was that the health care industry was changing rapidly. There were more competitors entering the market, and the VNA was the acknowledged market leader in Winnebago County. In addition, she was concerned about the rumors warning that changes in private insurance and Medicaid would make home care less financially beneficial for patients.

Ms. Hansen decided to open an office in Appleton in January 1986. Outagamie was the largest of the three counties (Outagamie, Winnebago, and Calumet) that comprised the Appleton/Fox cities metropolitan statistical area (see Exhibit 35.7 for population statistics). She found that the Oshkosh market was a lot easier to break into than the Appleton market. The two major reasons for this more-difficult entry appeared to be the fact that she did not live in Appleton (though she had some connections there that have helped the company) and the strong visiting nurses programs in the area. The Appleton Visiting Nurses Association was well entrenched in that market, plus the Neenah-Menasha VNA was strong. Neenah and Menasha lay between Oshkosh and Appleton and were relatively closed communities (supportive of home-grown, lived-here-all-our-lives businesses).

The company continued strong growth through 1986 although not at the rapid pace of 1983 and 1984. By January 1987, Supportive HomeCare employed 30 full-time personnel in the office and 49 full-time and 150 part-time personnel in the field. It became evident that the company had to move again. Ms. Hansen investigated several options and chose a site on a corner of Main Street in Oshkosh. Supportive HomeCare wanted to stress being visible to potential customers. "The new office has 5,500 square feet of space and includes a computer department, billing and payroll, nursing department, marketing, personnel, financial services, and general administration." The location's high visibility did bring

EXHIBIT 35.7   Population Statistics for the Appleton/Fox Metropolitan Statistical Area

	1980	*1989*
Calumet County	30,867	34,729
Appleton	5,484	n/a
Outagamie County	128,730	139,769
Appleton	53,424	65,314
Winnebago County	131,772	140,781
Menasha	14,728	15,077
Neenah	22,432	24,180
Oshkosh	49,740	53,534
Town of Menasha	12,307	14,178

n/a = not available.

Source: Official population estimates for 1986, Madison: Demographic Services Center, Wisconsin Department of Administration, November 1986; Demographic Services Centers, Wisconsin Department of Administration, November 1989; Oshkosh, Wisconsin Community Profile, Wisconsin Public Service Corporation (Courtesy of Oshkosh Chamber of Commerce), October 8, 1990.

in additional growth in terms of walk-in business, which the company had never had before. Ms. Hansen anticipated that the new location would adequately serve the company for the next five years. At the end of December 1989, the staff was somewhat smaller reflecting the difficulty of recruiting employees. The office staff included 20 full-time and 3 part-time employees. In the field, there were 13 full-time and 121 part-time employees.

ENTREPRENEURIAL STYLE

Terri Hansen was an entrepreneur who learned how to manage an "overnight success." She developed a team concept in managing the company. She was grooming her team, which was comprised of the nurse manager, the personnel director, the financial director, and the marketing manager. Her partner, John Westphal, served as director of computer services until she bought his share of the partnership in late July 1987. Exhibit 35.8 is Ms. Hansen's organization chart. Her team was very strong, especially because of the different backgrounds of the members. Decisions were made as a team; Ms. Hansen seldom overrode them, but she would if she thought something else was best for the company.

Her nurses and office staff were involved in marketing. Each office employee was given certain marketing assignments to complete. The team was working on a companywide plan to keep Supportive HomeCare in the community's mind. Ms. Hansen acknowledged the market leadership of the local VNA in the area outside Oshkosh (see Exhibit 35.9 for market position). "We are aiming at being number two in the market outside of Oshkosh—a strong number two at that." Ms. Hansen summed up her style of management: "I believe in a strong management philosophy—I was never taught that; I just use common sense."

Ms. Hansen recognized the value of good community relations and was very active in the community. She took advantage of opportunities to speak to clubs in the area whenever possible and held an open house at Supportive HomeCare's offices.

A DIFFERENT INDUSTRY

The changes in the environment continued. More competitors entered the market and many private insurance companies decided to drop coverage of home health care programs. This really hurt the funding outlook for home care in general, and Supportive HomeCare was not immune to the problem. Within a span of 10 months, from September 1986 to July 1987, as shown in Exhibit 35.10, the funding mix changed for Supportive HomeCare, reflecting the problems created by insurance companies' modifications in the coverage granted for home care.

EXHIBIT 35.8   Table of Organization, Supportive HomeCare

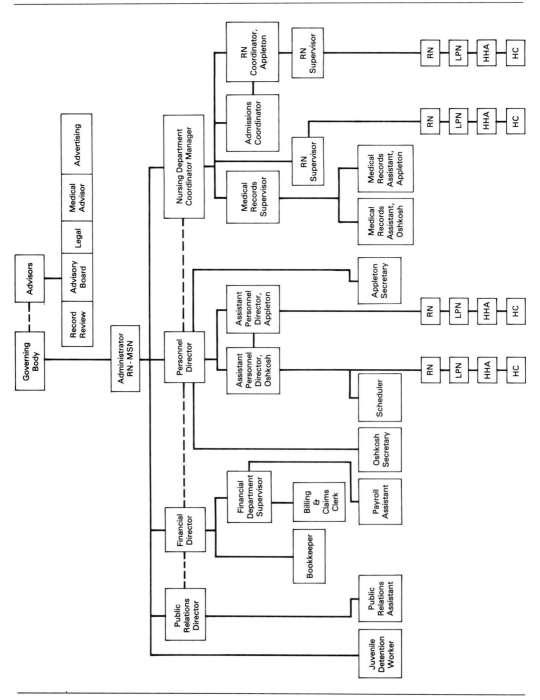

EXHIBIT 35.9   Market Positions for the Major Home Care Providers in the Oshkosh Area

Position	1987	1990
Oshkosh		
1	Supportive HomeCare	Supportive HomeCare
2	Mercy VNA	Mercy VNA
3	Upjohn	Upjohn
4	County Nurses	Lakeshore
5	Preferred Health	County Nurses
Appleton		
1	Appleton VNA	Appleton VNA
2	Supportive HomeCare	Supportive HomeCare
3	Upjohn	Upjohn
4	Preferred Health	Preferred Health
5	St. Elizabeth's	Lakeshore
Neenah/Menasha		
1	Neenah-Menasha VNA	Neenah-Menasha
2	Supportive HomeCare	Supportive HomeCare
3	Upjohn	Upjohn
4	Preferred Health	Preferred Health
5		Lakeshore

Source: Observations of Terri Hansen, August 1990.

EXHIBIT 35.10   Funding Mix

Sources	September 1986	1987–88	1988–89	1989–90
Private Pay	17%	39.8%	30.99%	22.33%
Medicaid	33	27.28	33.37	43.68
Private Insurance	40	13.85	11.00	10.10
Medicare	3	0.88	2.75	3.71
County Funds	7	7.70	10.11	13.80
Personnel Resource Network[a]		7.54	7.48	3.21
Lifestyle Connections[a]		0.23	0.81	0.66
Other	0	2.65	3.49	2.51

[a] New programs started in 1987.
Source: Supportive HomeCare company records.

In addition, Medicaid made changes that had a major impact on Supportive HomeCare. Similar to many others, the company had come to depend on third-party funding, but it appeared that third-party payments would continue to diminish. Ms. Hansen attempted to contract with other businesses, such as the city of Oshkosh, Georgia Pacific, or Mercury Marine, in order to move away from the dependency on third-party payments. She had contracts with the Appleton and Neenah-Menasha VNAs to provide extended care for hospice patients, and with nearly all nursing homes in the Fox River Valley to provide staffing when needed.

Supportive HomeCare provided a variety of services including registered nurses, licensed practical nurses, home health aides/nurses' aides, homemaker-companions, night service, insurance counseling, private duty, institutional staffing, and home care attendants.

Two new programs were introduced in 1987 when the use of home health care appeared to be declining. Personnel Resource Network (PRN) had two divisions: Home Management and Staffing. PRN Home Management was considered to be a burgeoning area primarily because of the increasing number of two-income families. Services offered included routine and extensive cleaning, laundry and ironing, grocery shopping and errands, meal preparation, and help with entertaining. Ms. Hansen admitted that she had not invested the money necessary to market this service. "It is a needed service, but health care is what we do best." PRN Staffing was successful because it provided temporary staff for hospitals, nursing homes, and other health care providers.

"LifeStyle Connections (LSC) was a concept before its time," according to Ms. Hansen. "In five years companies will be forced to provide this type of service to keep health insurance costs down." LSC provided custom services, including health assessment screenings, behavior-modification classes, fitness assessments, lifestyle assessments, and informational miniseminars. Only a few companies used the services of LSC.

SUPPORTIVE HOMECARE GOALS AND PHILOSOPHY

Ms. Hansen outlined the goals for Supportive HomeCare:

- To provide quality nursing and support services.
- To be a quality agency by providing superior services at a competitive cost; monitoring agency expansion to meet the needs of the community; functioning within local, state, and federal guidelines; and monitoring and evaluating agency operations continuously.
- To hire and retain qualified employees.
- To increase community and consumer awareness via marketing and community relations.
- To achieve maximum reimbursement from third-party payers.

Supportive HomeCare's unique selling proposition and philosophy are provided in Exhibit 35.11.

Staffing

"Staffing is our biggest problem," stated Ms. Hansen. "The nursing and other medical personnel shortage is real and it's everywhere. But we are not only competing with other health care organizations to get good people but with

EXHIBIT 35.11   Supportive HomeCare Positioning

Unique Selling Proposition

Supportive HomeCare provides skilled nursing, personal care, and homemaker/companion services up to twenty-four hours a day, seven days a week to clients in their homes. Initial contact, assessment of service needs, and exploration of payment options are at no charge to the client. Quality services are offered at a competitive price.

Supportive HomeCare maintains a reputation for being the quality service that truly cares about people and considers meeting its clients' needs as the number one goal. The agency acts as a client advocate. The staff have professional expertise in dealing with third-party payment sources and continually remain abreast of issues dealing with home care.

Supportive HomeCare maintains strict supervision policies, agency rules and regulations, service, and employment standards. Employees are thoroughly screened, trained, oriented, and inserviced on an ongoing basis.

Supportive HomeCare prides itself on case management. It maintains close communication with the client, family, physician, and significant others involved. The agency strives to develop a cooperative working relationship with other community agencies and facilities.

Philosophy of the Agency

It is the philosophy of the agency to provide quality and dependable nursing care, therapies, and homemaker/companion services, thus enabling individuals to remain as independent as possible in the least-restrictive environment. Services will be provided by employees who are qualified, experienced, and empathetic to the needs of home care clients. All aspects of the agency will be monitored to provide efficient and cost-effective quality care.

Supportive HomeCare will promote cooperative working relationships with other home health providers and community resources, to attain a comprehensive level of care.

Source: Supportive HomeCare brochure.

restaurants, factories, and so forth. Home health care has a problem with retaining people, too. It is difficult to predict or ensure working hours, the individual is isolated on the job because there are no other staff to talk to, the hours are often inconvenient, and travel—sometimes longer distances than I'd like—is often required."

Compounding the shortage of workers, the government instituted tougher regulations for training home health care "aides." However, a new category of health care providers was added that fit the old job description for "home health aid." A "personal care worker" could be paid about half of the wage given to a care giver ($9.00 per hour compared to $15.10 per hour).

Supportive HomeCare attempted to market itself to potential employees to entice them to come to work and developed retention strategies to keep the individuals once they were hired. On July 1, 1990, Supportive HomeCare instituted a number of changes for the field staff including increased employee benefits, higher wages to be more in line with competition, increased personal contact by Terri and the office staff, and development of a "retention budget."

Employees were rewarded with small gifts for beyond-the-call-of-duty service, flowers were sent for special occasions, and gift certificates were given for a holiday remembrance. Ms. Hansen met with the Personnel Department twice a month to actively work on problem solving for staffing. "We have the patients. We just don't have the staff," Terri lamented. She continued, "We stress the flexible hours we offer for part-time—and some full-time—staff. We are a compassionate employer. We know and understand the needs of working women. And we are a company that anyone can be proud to work for because we provide quality care and we have the reputation for providing quality care."

WHAT LIES AHEAD?

There were some challenges ahead for Ms. Hansen and her company. She predicted, "In the next six months, the home care industry will see a shake-out and some home care agencies will go out of business. Relying on third-party funding and problems in billing departments with uncollected payments are two key reasons home care agencies will go under or be sold." Competition was more intense and would be a factor. "Our competitors control discharges from the hospitals—Mercy Visiting Nurses for Mercy Hospital and the Appleton VNA does the discharge planning for Appleton Medical Center and St. Elizabeth's Hospital. It's tough to compete."

The environment changed. There was a shortage of qualified nurses not just in Oshkosh and Appleton, but all over the country. The federal, state, and local governments instituted tougher regulations for training and certifying home health aides. There were minimal increases in third-party reimbursements from Medicaid, Medicare, and county funds. Private insurance paid very few claims, and Ms. Hansen saw no turnaround in the future. Although there was an increased need for home care as the population aged, there was insufficient staff that was affordable. "People just can't afford personal home care. It is a real balancing act when the environment is hostile, there is a shortage of all health care providers, and demand exceeds supply."

According to Ms. Hansen, "Supportive HomeCare had its best year ever in 1989–90, but it was definitely the most stressful. I'd like to stop the world and get off—just for a few hours—and figure out exactly what I should do with Supportive HomeCare!"

_____ CASE 36 _____

Grasse Fragrances SA

Grasse Fragrances, headquartered in Lyon, France, was the world's fourth largest producer of fragrances. Established in 1885, the company grew from a small family-owned business, selling fragrances to local perfume manufacturers, to a multinational enterprise with subsidiaries and agents in over 100 countries.

For Marketing Director Jean-Pierre Volet, the past few years had been devoted to building a strong headquarters marketing organization. In February 1989, however, he returned to France after an extensive tour of Grasse sales offices and factories and a number of visits with key customers. As the Air France flight touched down in Lyon Airport, Jean-Pierre Volet was feeling very concerned about what he had learned on the trip. "Our sales force," he thought, "operates much as it did several years ago. If we're going to compete successfully in this new environment we have to completely rethink our sales strategy as it relates to our marketing strategy."

THE FLAVOR AND FRAGRANCE INDUSTRY

Worldwide sales of essential oils, aroma chemicals and fragrance and flavor compounds were estimated to be around $5.5 billion in 1988. Five major firms accounted for something like 50 percent of the industry's sales. The largest, International Flavors & Fragrances of New York, had 1988 sales of $839.5 million (up 76 percent from 1984), of which fragrances accounted for 62 percent. The company had plants in 21 countries and non-U.S. operations represented 70 percent of sales and 78 percent of operating profit.

Quest International, a wholly owned subsidiary of Unilever, was next in size, with sales estimated at $700 million, closely followed by the Givaudan Group, a wholly owned subsidiary of Hoffman-LaRoche, with sales of $536 million, and Grasse Fragrances with sales of $480 million. Firmenich, a closely held

This case was prepared by Michael H. Hayes as a basis for class discussion rather than to illustrate either effective or ineffective handling of an administrative situation. All names, including the company name, have been disguised. Copyright © 1989 by IMD (previously IMEDE), Lausanne, Switzerland. Used with permission from Michael H. Hayes and IMD.

Swiss family firm, did not disclose results, but 1987 sales were estimated at some $300 million.

Grasse produced only fragrances. Most major firms in the industry, however, produced both fragrances and flavors (i.e., flavor extracts and compounds mainly used in foods, beverages, and pharmaceutical products). Generally, the products were very similar. The major difference was that the flavorist had to match his or her creations with their natural counterparts, such as fruits, meats, or spices, as closely as possible. On the other hand, the perfumer had the flexibility to use his or her imagination to create new fragrances. Perfumery was closely associated with fashion, encompassed a wide variety of choice, and products had to be dermatologically safe. Development of flavors was more limited, and products were required to meet strict toxicological criteria because the products were ingested.

Markets for Fragrances

While the use of perfumes is as old as history, it was not until the 19th century, when major advances were made in organic chemistry, that the modern fragrance industry emerged. Focusing first on perfumes, use of fragrances expanded into other applications. In recent years manufacturers of soap, detergents, and other household products significantly increased their purchases of fragrances and represented the largest single consumption category. Depending on the application, the chemical complexity of a particular fragrance and the quantity produced, prices could range from less than FF40 per kilogram to over FF4,000.[1]

Despite its apparent maturity the world market for fragrances was estimated to have grown at an average of 5 to 6 percent during the early 1980s, and some estimates indicated that sales growth could increase even further during the last half of the decade. New applications supported these estimates. Microwave foods, for instance, needed additional flavorings to replicate familiar tastes that would take time to develop in a conventional oven. In laundry detergents, a significant fragrance market, the popularity of liquids provided a new stimulus to fragrance sales as liquid detergents needed more fragrance than did powders to achieve the desired aroma. Similarly, laundry detergents designed to remove odors as well as dirt also stimulated sales, as they used more fragrance by volume.

The New Buying Behavior

Over time, buying behavior for fragrances, as well as markets, had changed significantly. Responsibility for the selection and purchase of fragrances became complex, particularly in large firms. R&D groups were expected to ensure the compatibility of the fragrance with the product under consideration; marketing groups were responsible for choosing a fragrance that gave the product a competitive edge in the marketplace, and purchasing groups had to obtain competitive prices and provide timely deliveries.

[1] $1 = approximately FF6 in 1988.

Use of briefs (the industry term for a "fragrance specification and request for quotation") became common. Typically, a brief would identify the general characteristics of the fragrance, the required cost parameters, as well as an extensive description of the company's product and its intended strategy in the marketplace. Occasionally a fragrance producer would be sole sourced, generally for proprietary reasons. Usually, however, the customer would ask for at least two quotations, thus competitive quotes were the norm.

GRASSE FRAGRANCES SA BACKGROUND

The company was founded in 1885 by Louis Piccard, a chemist who had studied at the University of Lyon. He believed that progress in the field of organic chemistry could be used to develop a new industry—creating perfumes, as opposed to relying on nature. Using a small factory on the Siagne River near the city of Grasse, the company soon became a successful supplier of fragrances to the leading perfume houses of Paris. Despite the interruptions by World Wars I and II, the company followed an early policy of international growth and diversification. Production and sales units were established in Lyon, Paris, and Rome. In the 1920s, company headquarters were moved to Lyon. At that time the company entered the U.S. market, first establishing a sales office and then a small manufacturing facility. Acquisitions were made in Great Britain, and subsequently the company established subsidiaries in Switzerland, Brazil, Argentina, and Spain.

Faced with increased competition and large capital requirements for R&D, plant expansion, and new product launches, the Piccard family decided to become a public company in 1968. Jacques Piccard, oldest son of the founder, was elected president, and the family remained active in the management of the company. Assisted by the infusion of capital, Grasse was able to further expand its business activities in Europe, the United States, Latin America, and the Far East.

In 1988, total sales were $480 million, up some 60 percent from 1984; 40 percent of sales came from Europe, 30 percent from North America, 10 percent from Latin America, 5 percent from Africa/Middle East, and 15 percent from Asia/Pacific. In recent years, the company's position had strengthened somewhat in North America.

By the end of 1988, the company had sales organizations or agents in 100 countries, laboratories in 18 countries, compounding facilities in 18 countries, chemical production centers in 3 countries, and research centers in 3 countries. Employment was 2,500, of whom some 1,250 were employed outside France.

Products

In 1988, the company's main product lines were in two categories:

Perfumery products used for perfumes, eau de cologne, eau de toilette, hair lotion, cosmetics, soaps, detergents, and other household and industrial products.

Synthetics for perfume compounds, cosmetic specialties, sunscreening agents, and preservatives for various industrial applications.

According to Jacques Piccard:

> From the production side, flavors and fragrances are similar, although the creative and marketing approaches are quite different. So far we have elected to specialize in just fragrances, but I think it's just a matter of time before we decide to get into flavors.

Following industry practice, Grasse divided its fragrances into four categories:

Fine Fragrances
Toiletries and Cosmetics
Soaps and Detergents
Household and Industrial

Marketing at Grasse

In 1980, Jean-Pierre Volet was appointed marketing director after a successful stint as country manager for the Benelux countries. At the time, the headquarters marketing organization was relatively small. Its primary role was to make sure the sales force had information on the company's products, send out samples of new perfumes that were developed in the labs (usually with little customer input) and handle special price or delivery requests. As Volet recalled:

> In the 1940s, 1950s, and 1960s, most of our business was in fine fragrances, toiletries, and cosmetics. Our customers tended to be small and focused on local markets. Our fragrance salesman would carry a suitcase of 5 gram samples, call on the customer, get an idea of what kind of fragrance the customer wanted and either leave a few samples for evaluation or actually write an order on the spot. It was a very personal kind of business. Buying decisions tended to be based on subjective impressions and the nature of the customer's relation with the salesman. Our headquarters marketing organization was designed to support that kind of selling and buying.
>
> Today, however, we deal with large multinational companies that are standardizing their products across countries, and even regions, and using very sophisticated marketing techniques to guide their use of fragrances. Detergents and other household products represent an increasing share of the market. When I came to headquarters one of my important priorities was to structure a marketing organization which reflected this new environment.

In addition to the normal administrative activities such as field sales support, pricing, and budgeting, Volet built a fragrance creation group and a product management group. More recently he established an international client coordination group. The marketing organization in 1988 is shown in Exhibit 36.1.

EXHIBIT 36.1   Grasse Fragrances SA Partial Organization Chart

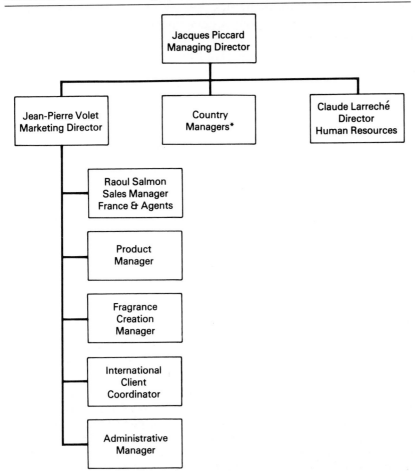

Note: In France, all major functions (e.g., marketing, manufacturing, R&D) reported
to Jacques Piccard. In most countries outside of France where the company did
business, a subsidiary company was established, headed by a country manager. All
company activities in each country reported to the country manager. In some
countries, generally small, the company did business through agents who reported
to Raoul Salmon.

The fragrance creation group served as a bridge between the basic lab work and customer requirements. It also ran the company's fragrance training center, used to train both its own sales force and customer personnel in the application of fragrances. The product management group was organized in the four product categories. Product managers were expected to be knowledgeable about everything that was going on in their product category—worldwide—and to use their specialized knowledge to support field sales efforts as well as guide the creative people. It was Volet's plan that international client coordinators (ICCs) would coordinate sales efforts.

Field sales in France reported to Piccard through Raoul Salmon, who was also responsible for the activities of the company's agents, used in countries where it did not have subsidiaries or branches. In recent years, use of agents had declined and it was the company's expectation that the decline would continue.

Outside France, field sales were the responsibility of Grasse country managers. In smaller countries country managers handled only sales, thus operating essentially as field sales managers. In other countries, where the company had manufacturing or other nonselling operations, the norm was to have a field sales manager reporting to the country manager. Although individual sales representatives reported to the field sales managers, it was understood that there was a dotted line relationship from the sales representatives to the ICCs and the product managers.

The company relied extensively on its field sales force for promotional efforts, customer relations, and order-getting activities. There were, however, two very different kinds of selling situations. As Salmon described them:

> There are still many customers, generally small-scale, who buy in the traditional way where the process is fairly simple. One salesperson is responsible for calling on all buying influences in the customer's organization. Decisions tend to be based on subjective factors and the sales representative's personal relations with the customer are critically important.
>
> The other situation, which is growing, involves large and increasingly international customers. Not only do we see that people in R&D and marketing, as well as those in purchasing, can influence the purchase decision but these influencers may be located in a number of different countries.

In either case, once the decision had been made to purchase a Grasse fragrance, the firm could generally count on repeat business, as long as the customer's product was successful in the marketplace. On occasion, however, purchase decisions were revised, particularly if Grasse raised prices or if the customer's product came under strong competitive price pressure, thus requiring that a less expensive fragrance be considered.

Grasse Fragrances used some advertising in publications to the trade and provided selling brochures for the sales reps. Its most successful promotion was at the "clinics" offered by the Fragrance Institute. At the clinic, the company could demonstrate its expertise in meeting customers' needs for fragrances.

The Quotation Procedure

For small orders the quotation procedure was relatively simple. Popular fragrances had established prices in every country and the sales force was expected to sell at these prices.[2] In some instances, price concessions were made but these required management approval and were discouraged.

For large orders it was the norm to develop a new fragrance. Increasingly, customers would provide Grasse with extensive information on their intended product and its marketing strategy, including the country, or countries, where the product would be sold. To make sure the fragrance fit the customer's intended marketing and product strategy, Grasse was expected to do market research in a designated pilot country on several fragrances, sometimes combined with samples of the customer's product.

According to Volet:

> Once we have found or developed what we think is the best fragrance, we submit our quotation. Then the customer will do his own market research, testing his product with our fragrance and with those of our competitors. Depending on the outcome of the market research, we may get the order at a price premium. Alternatively, we may lose it, even if we are low bidder. If, on the other hand, the results of the market research indicate that no fragrance supplier has an edge, then price, personal relationships, or other factors will influence the award.

Because of the extensive requirements for development and testing, headquarters in Grasse was always involved in putting a quotation together, and close coordination was vital between headquarters and the branch or subsidiary. When buying influences were located in more than one country, additional coordination of the sales effort was required to ensure that information obtained from the customer was shared and also to ensure a coherent account strategy.

Coordination of pricing was also growing in importance. Many large customers manufactured their products in more than one country and looked for a "world" price, rather than a country price. In these situations, country organizations were expected to take a corporate view of profits, sometimes at the expense of their own profit statements. The lead country (i.e., the country in which the purchasing decision would be made) had final responsibility for establishing the price. Increasingly, however, this price had to be approved in Lyon.

---

[2] Subject to approval by marketing headquarters, each Grasse producing unit established a transfer price for products sold outside the country. Country prices were established taking into account the country profit objectives and the local market conditions. Transfer prices were usually established for a year. Adjusting transfer prices for fluctuations in exchange rates was a matter of ongoing concern.

Submitting quotations in this environment was both complex and expensive. According to Volet:

> Receiving a brief from a customer starts a complex process. We immediately alert all our salespeople who call on various purchasing influences. Although the brief contains lots of information on what the customer wants, we expect our sales people to provide us with some additional information.
>
> The next step is for our creative people to develop one or more fragrances which we believe will meet the customer's requirements. They are aided in this effort by our product managers who know what is going on with their products worldwide. If additional information is needed from the customer, our international client people will contact the appropriate sales people.
>
> After creating what we think is the right product, or products, we may conduct our own market research, in a country designated by the customer. This is usually done under the direction of our product manager, working closely with our market research people. Throughout this process, our sales force is expected to stay in close touch with the customer to give us any changes in his thinking or any competitive feedback. Based on the results of this effort, we then submit our proposal which gives the customer the price, samples, and as much product information as possible.
>
> With some customers, there is little further sales effort after they receive our quotation, and the buying decision is made "behind closed doors." In other instances, we may be asked to explain the results of our research or to discuss possible modifications in our product and, sometimes, in our price. Frequently we find that the customer is more concerned with our price policy (i.e., how firm the price is and for how long) than with the price quoted at the time of the brief.
>
> When you make this kind of effort, you obviously hate to lose the order. On the other hand, even if we lose, the investment made in development work and market research is likely to pay off in winning another brief, either with the original customer or with another customer.

In 1988, about 50 percent of the firm's business came from some 40 international accounts. Looking to the future, it was expected that the number of international accounts would grow and some estimated that by 1994 as much as 80 percent of the firm's business would come from international accounts.

As of 1988, 18 to 20 international accounts were targeted for coordination by the ICCs in Lyon. The principal responsibility of each ICC was to really know assigned customers on a worldwide basis and put that knowledge to use in coordinating work on a brief. The rest were followed in Lyon, but coordination was a subsidiary responsibility. In either case, it was the view at headquarters that coordination was critical. As Volet described it:

> We rely extensively on account teams. European teams may meet as often as once a quarter. World-wide teams are more likely to meet annually. For designated accounts the ICC takes the lead role in organizing the meeting and, generally, coordinating sales efforts. For others the parent account executive (a PAE is the sales representative in the country selling the customer component with the greatest buying influence) plays the lead role. In these situations we hold the PAE responsible

for all the coordinating work. We also hold him responsible to be proactive and already working on the next brief long before we get a formal request.

Here in Lyon we prepare extensive world-wide "bibles" on international accounts which are made available to all the members of the team. We also prepare quarterly project reports for team members. Our next step will be to computerize as much of this as possible.

Sales Estimates

Sales estimates were developed from expectations of sales volume for fragrances currently being used by customers, in which case historical sales were the major basis for the estimate, and from estimates of sales of new fragrances. Although historical sales of currently used fragrances were useful in predicting future sales, variations could occur. Sales activity of the customer's product was not totally predictable. In some instances, customers reopened a brief to competition, particularly where the customer was experiencing competitive cost pressures. Predicting sales of new fragrances was even more difficult. Customers' plans were uncertain, and the nature of the buying process made it difficult to predict the odds of success on any given transaction.

Selling Worldwide

As Grasse Fragrances became more of a worldwide organization, national accounts influence selling increased in importance. According to Salmon:

> A number of our large accounts have their marketing groups located in Paris, and they have lots of influence on the buying decision. If we win the brief, however, purchasing is likely to take place in Germany or Spain or Holland, and the Paris office will not get any sales credit.

In a similar vein, Juan Rodriguez, sales manager for a group of countries in Latin America commented:

> We have a large account that does lots of manufacturing and purchasing in Latin America but does its R&D work in the United States. The customer's people in Latin America tell us that without strong support from R&D in the United States it is very difficult for them to buy our fragrances. The sales representative in New York is certainly aware of this but his boss is measured on profit, which can only come from direct sales in the United States, so he's not enthusiastic about his sales representative spending a lot of time on influence business.

In some instances, the nature of the buying process resulted in windfalls for some sales representatives. Commenting on this aspect Salmon observed:

> It can work the other way as well. Our Spanish subsidiary recently received an order for 40 tons of a fragrance but the customer's decision to buy was totally influenced by sales representatives in Germany and Lyon. Needless to say, our

Spanish subsidiary was delighted but the people in Germany and Lyon were concerned as to how their efforts would be recognized and rewarded.

Although there was general recognition that influence selling was vital, it was not clear how it could be adequately measured and rewarded. As Salmon pointed out:

> In some instances (e.g., the order in Spain) we're pretty sure about the amount of influence exerted by those calling on marketing and R&D. In other instances, it is not at all clear. We have some situations where the sales representative honestly believes that his calls on, say, R&D are important but, in fact, they are not. At least not in our opinion. If we come up with the wrong scheme to measure influence, we could end up with a lot of wasted time and effort.

Incentive Compensation

Compensation practices varied enormously from country to country and were a matter of some concern. The salary component was established at a level designed to be competitive with similar sales jobs in each country. Annual raises had become the norm, with amounts based on performance, longevity, and changes in responsibility. The bonus component was determined by the immediate manager, but there were concerns that bonuses had become automatic. Still further, some held the view that the difference between 1.5 and 2.5 times the monthly salary was not very motivating, even if bonus awards were more performance driven.

There was growing recognition of the increasing importance of team selling. Overall responsibility for compensation practices was assigned to Claude Larreche, director of human resources. According to Larreche:

> We're thinking about some kind of team incentive or bonus. But this raises questions about who should be considered part of the team and how a team bonus should be allocated. Should the team be just the sales representatives, or should we include the ICCs? And what about the customer service people, without whom we wouldn't have a base of good performance to build on?

In addition, when selling worldwide, variations in incentive compensation were needed because not every culture values incentive compensation. In fact, some sales reps considered incentive compensation to be inappropriate. Team incentives for these reps would be considered an insult.

Small Accounts

Despite the sales growth expected from international accounts, sales to smaller national accounts were expected to remain a significant part of the firm's revenues and, generally, had very attractive margins. According to one country sales manager:

With the emphasis on international accounts, I'm concerned about how we handle our smaller single country accounts. Many of them still buy the way they did 10 and 20 years ago, although today we can select from over 30,000 fragrances. Our international accounts will probably generate 80 percent of our business in the years to come but the 20 percent we get from our smaller accounts is important and produces excellent profits for the company. But I'm not sure that the kind of selling skills we need to handle international accounts are appropriate for the smaller accounts. Personal and long term relationships are tremendously important to these accounts.

Language

In the early 1980s, it had become apparent to Grasse management that French would not serve as the firm's common language. In most of its subsidiary countries, English was either the country language or the most likely second language. With considerable reluctance on the part of some French managers, it was decided that English would become the firm's official language. Personnel in the United States and Great Britain, few of whom spoke a second language, welcomed the change. There were, however, a number of problems. As the Italian sales manager said:

> We understand the need for a common language when we bring in sale representatives from all over Europe or the world. And we understand that English is the "most common" language in the countries where we do business. All of my people understand that they will have to speak English in international account sales meetings. What they don't like, however, is that the Brits and the Americans tend to assume that they are smarter than the rest of us, simply because we can't express ourselves as fluently in English as they can. It's totally different when my people talk to someone from Latin America, or some other country, where English is their second language, too.
>
> A related problem is the attitudes people from one country have toward those of another. This goes beyond language. Frequently our people from northern Europe or North America will stereotype those of us from southern Europe or Latin America as disorganized or not business-like. My people, on the other hand, see the northerners as inflexible and unimaginative. To some extent these views diminish after we get to know each other as individuals, but it takes time and there is always some underlying tension.

Language also influenced decisions on rotation of personnel. It was Volet's view that there should be movement between countries of sales managers and marketing personnel. Still further, he felt that sales representatives who aspired to promotion should also be willing to consider transfers to another country or to headquarters in Lyon. As he pointed out, however:

> Customer personnel in most of our international accounts speak English. Hence there is a temptation to feel that English language competency is the only

requirement when considering reassignment of sales personnel. In fact, if we were to transfer a sales representative who spoke only English to Germany, for instance, he would be received politely the first time, but from then on it would be difficult for him to get an appointment with the customer. It has been our experience that our customers want to do business in their own language, even if they speak English fluently.

An exception might be an international account where the parent company is British and it transfers a lot of British personnel to another country. Even here, however, there will be lots of people in the organization for whom English is not a native tongue. Therefore, we require that our sales people speak the language of the country and are comfortable with the country culture. Local people meet this requirement. The real issue is getting all, or most, of our people to be comfortable in more than one language and culture.

One of the most perplexing issues was what, if any, changes to make with regard to sales training. At headquarters there was considerable sentiment for standardization. As Volet put it:

I really don't see that much difference in selling from one country to another. Of course, personal relations may be more important in, say, Latin America or the Middle East than in Germany but I think that as much as 80 to 85 percent of the selling job can be harmonized. In addition, it's my view that our international accounts expect us to have a standardized sales approach. Sales training, therefore, should be something we can do centrally at Lyon.

This view was supported by those in human resources. According to Claude Larreche:

We no longer see ourselves as a collection of individual companies that remit profits to Lyon and engage in occasional technology transfer. Our view of the future is that we are a global company that must live in a world of global customers and markets. I think this means we must have a Grasse Fragrance culture that transcends national boundaries, including a common sales approach, i.e., this is the way Grasse approaches customers, regardless of where they are located. A key element in establishing such a culture is sales training here in Lyon.

Others disagreed with this point of view, however. Perhaps the most vociferous was the U.S. sales manager:

I understand what Jean-Pierre and Claude are saying and I support the notion of a common company culture. The fact is, however, that selling is different in the United States than in other parts of the world. Not long ago we transferred a promising sales representative from Sweden to our office in Chicago. His sales approach, which was right for Sweden, was very relaxed and he had to make some major adjustments to fit the more formal and fast paced approach in Chicago. I don't see how a sales training program in Lyon can be of much help. Plus, the cost of sending people to Lyon comes out of my budget, and this would really hit my country manager's profits. In fact, I think we ought to have more flexibility with regard to all our sales management practices.

As Jean-Pierre Volet waited for his bag at the Lyon Airport, he wondered how far he should go in making changes with regard to the company's marketing efforts. There were some limits on what he could do. He could not, for instance, change the basic structure of the company (i.e., the country manager form of organization), and he would have to get support from the country managers for his changes. Whatever he did would be controversial, but he was convinced some changes were necessary.

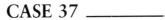

CASE 37

Lotus Development Corporation: Maintaining Leadership in the Competitive Electronic Spreadsheet Industry

With sales of microcomputers increasing faster than sales of minicomputers and mainframes, sales of microcomputer software were growing at a fairly rapid rate. The growth rate for microcomputer software was a respectable 24 percent in 1987 compared with 23 percent in 1986. Growth increased 27 percent in 1988 but fell slightly to 18 percent in 1989.[1] The United States software industry was expected to achieve its historical growth rate of approximately 20 percent per year during the first half of the 1990s.[2]

This case was prepared by William C. House, University of Arkansas, as a basis for class discussion rather than to illustrate either effective or ineffective handling of an administrative situation. Used with permission from William C. House.

[1] U.S. Industrial Outlook, Department of Commerce, January 1988, pp. 30-7, January 1990, pp. 30-12.
[2] "Software Plays Hardball," Time, May 11, 1987, p. 52.

According to Dataquest, worldwide shipments of personal computer units increased from 15.2 million units in 1986 to 17.4 million units in 1987.[3] Worldwide shipments of personal computers increased 9 percent in 1990, slightly less than the growth rate in 1989.[4] Although shipments of computers were not increasing at previous levels, revenues of the top 50 independent software companies continued to escalate. Revenues increased from $3.6 billion in 1986 to $5.2 billion in 1987, $6.7 billion in 1988, $8.3 billion in 1989, and $10.7 billion in 1990.[5] The top 50 company sales revenues increased 42 percent in 1988, 25 percent in 1989, and 29 percent in 1990, compared to the previous year.

The microcomputer software industry had thousands of small independent suppliers with less than $1 million in annual sales. The Big Three (LOTUS, Ashton Tate, and Microsoft) held about 50 percent of the market as represented by revenues of the top 100 vendors. The gap between these three companies and other companies seemed to be widening as a transition was made from a cottage industry to one dominated by a very few suppliers. The top 12 companies produced 77 percent of total industry revenues, a sizable increase from about two-thirds of total industry revenues in 1985.[6]

Barriers to entry increased as the industry experienced intense competition, a high degree of product similarity, and product changes geared to hardware innovations. Brand-name recognition and increased marketing and product development/implementation costs discouraged the entry of competitors. Small companies did not have the market position, sales forces, or financial resources for advertising and sales promotion necessary to compete successfully with the larger companies.

The Big Three possessed broad user bases, strong customer loyalty, and large, well-developed research and development programs. These companies had sufficient resources to acquire competitors, to expand product bases, and to diversify into application areas not previously covered. The acquisition of Ashton-Tate by Borland and Samma Corporation by LOTUS were examples of the trend. Ashton-Tate identified price/performance, marketing and sales expertise, ease of use, product support, product line integration, and vendor financial strength as key factors in product success.[7] Although price competition was not as important as brand-name recognition and product improvements in product sales growth, an industry trend toward site licensing and volume discounts could make price more important in future years.

---

[3] Peter C. Wood, "Computers Current Analysis," *Standard & Poor's Industry Surveys,* May 26, 1988, p. C61.

[4] U.S. Industrial Outlook, Department of Commerce, January 1991, pp. 28-8.

[5] *Software Magazine,* Special Report, June 1989, 1990, 1991.

[6] William M. Bulkeley, "Software Industry Loses Start-Up Zest as Big Firms Increase Their Dominance," *Wall Street Journal,* August 27, 1991, p. B1.

[7] *Standard and Poor's Industry Surveys,* p. C61.

LOTUS COMPANY HISTORY

Mitchell Kapor, a disc jockey with an interest in transcendental meditation, developed LOTUS 1-2-3 in 1981 along with associate Todd Agulnick. At the time, Kapor was president of Cambridge-based Micro Finance Systems, a small New England software company. Several years earlier, Dan Bricklin, a Harvard University dropout, had developed and introduced the first electronic spreadsheet, VisiCalc, which was designed for the Apple II computer.

LOTUS grew astronomically from the time of its inception in 1983. In that first year, LOTUS had sales of $53,000 and a staff of several dozen people. It increased in size to the point that by 1987, revenues were just under $400 million, and the number of employees had increased to 2,400. Jim Manzi, a former newspaper reporter and a scholar in Greek and Latin joined the firm in 1984 as sales and marketing manager. Kapor, an informal, undisciplined entrepreneur, came to rely increasingly on Manzi, who joined the company with a reputation as a hard-headed businessman.

Kapor left the company in 1986 and Manzi became president. The brash, aggressive, and competitive former newspaper reporter very quickly made it clear that he expected LOTUS to continue to be the number one microcomputer software company in terms of size, sales, profits, and image. He was one of the highest-paid executives in the industry, receiving more than $26 million in salary and stock options in 1987. Stock analysts pointed out that LOTUS' current president, unlike the chief executives of other major companies such as Microsoft, Ashton-Tate, and Borland, had no prior software company experience.

In 1987, as sales and growth began to level off, Manzi issued orders to staff members to exercise close control over costs. After a series of negative articles appeared in a New England newspaper in response to published reports of Manzi's salary and a series of insider stock sales shortly before announcement of further delays in introducing an updated version of LOTUS 1-2-3, Manzi ordered company employees not to talk with the reporters from that newspaper. The order was later rescinded. LOTUS claimed that officer salaries were not out of line with those of other industry leaders and justified the stock sales as necessary to cover income taxes on stock options granted to key executives. Concurrently with these developments, a number of key executives left the company, and the stock price declined sharply.

Frank King, a 17-year IBM veteran involved in the development of the PC/2, became senior vice president of software products in the spring of 1988. Because of his computer experience and engineering background he gained greater credibility with the LOTUS staff than his predecessor. Outsiders said the more highly organized work environment contrasted with the informal, individualistic environment fostered by Kapor. However, morale appeared to be better and annual turnover declined to 15 percent compared with an industry average of 20 percent.

In November 1991, LOTUS announced that Frank King was being replaced by John Landry, previously executive vice president and chief technology officer at Dun & Bradstreet Software. Some insiders said the move was an indirect result of the delayed introduction of 1-2-3 for Windows, a product plagued with slow operating speed and numerous bugs. During Chairman Manzi's tenure, at least a dozen senior executives left the company. These moves developed into a typical pattern—an initial announcement of the new executive as a company "savior" followed by a hasty exit as disappointment and disenchantment occurred when the company failed to meet expectations.

Landry had considerable experience with mainframe software products and client-server architecture, a concept involved with linking personal computers with mainframe data bases. The enticement of Landry to LOTUS was widely touted as a harbinger of the company's seriousness concerning delivery of its networked computing strategy. Manzi indicated that the company's focus would be to produce and market an integrated set of desktop products for work-group computing including cc:Mail, Notes, and Agenda. Industry observers said that Landry had both mainframe and personal computer experience as well as familiarity with expert systems and object-oriented technology that would be valuable in moving LOTUS away from its heavy dependence on spreadsheet software.

PRODUCT DEVELOPMENT

LOTUS' goal was to be number one in the microcomputer software industry in terms of sales, profits, size, and reputation. It relied heavily on one product, LOTUS 1-2-3, although a personal information manager, Agenda, and a word processing package, AMI, were added to its product lines in the late 1980s. Most of the new products introduced since 1984 were add-ons or add-ins designed to speed up worksheet operation or to enhance such functions as data base management, word processing, and graphics display. In recent years, its sales and profits lagged behind those of its number one competitor, Microsoft.

Spreadsheet

LOTUS desired to improve 1-2-3 while still retaining the familiar look of the present version. Competitors such as Borland, Microsoft, and Computer Associates, offered improved programs with added features at the same price as 1-2-3 or, in some cases, at even lower prices. LOTUS indicated its intention to develop versions of 1-2-3 that would run on all types of computer hardware, including mainframes, minicomputers, and microcomputers. If this goal were to be achieved, it would allow sharing of worksheets, files, and terminals and reduce training costs. However, achieving this objective was likely to be difficult. For example, writing one program that would work satisfactorily on the 8088, 80286, and 80386 microprocessor-based hardware presented formidable challenges.

From its introduction in 1983, LOTUS sold more than 5 million copies of its 1-2-3 program and at one time had 70 to 80 percent of the IBM PC-compatible spreadsheet market. In 1991, its market share ranged between 50 to 60 percent, based on estimates from several sources. In its early years, the only serious competitors were Microsoft's Multiplan and Sorcim's (now Computer Associates) SuperCalc. V-P Planner (later withdrawn) was introduced in 1986 followed by Microsoft's Excel and Borland's Quattro in 1987. LOTUS sold 100,000 copies of 1-2-3 in its first year of operation and by 1992 sold that many copies in one month.

LOTUS 1-2-3 was designed as a relatively easy-to-use product to appeal to a broad user base. It was a familiar, proven package with established compatibility across company lines and within company divisions. Added power and utility came from LOTUS add-ins such as HAL (natural language interface), Freelance Plus (graphics), and Manuscript (word processing). In comparison with the products of its competitors, LOTUS had limited functions, poorer graphics, and a higher price in many cases. It lost sales because of its restrictive site licensing and copy protection not attached to other spreadsheets. A lack of LAN (local area network) support caused some users to switch to other spreadsheets such as SuperCalc.

Spreadsheet linking for 1-2-3 was cumbersome, and multiple spreadsheets could not be displayed on the same screen. Graphics capabilities were limited, and printing was often unwieldy and time-consuming. LOTUS' macro capability permitted customization of the spreadsheet program to fit many different situations, and many users have invested a large amount of time, money, and effort in developing macros and templates for use with 1-2-3. Fortunately for LOTUS, the investment in time by users inhibited switching to other products unless they were vastly superior to 1-2-3 and could clearly demonstrate file and macro compatibility.

To overcome some of its inherent limitations, LOTUS developed several add-ins to perform functions not available on its 2.0 or 2.1 version. Speedup increased the effective operating speed of LOTUS by only recalculating cells affected by the previous command or command sequence. LEARN gave LOTUS the capability of memorizing keystrokes for macro generation without the need to use a complex series of commands. HAL, a natural language interface, provided an easier-to-use command structure and permitted easier linking of multiple spreadsheets than was possible with the original product.

LOTUS announced that after prolonged delay, version 3.0 of 1-2-3 would be made available during the fourth quarter of 1988. At that time a further postponement was announced, moving the target date for version 3.0 to the second quarter of 1989. Version 3.0 was expected to add a number of performance features not possible with earlier versions of 1-2-3 such as the ability to link several worksheets, display up to three worksheets on the same screen, and capability to merge text and graphics in the same worksheet. Layered worksheets could be stored in main memory, faster recalculation of spreadsheet changes was implemented, and the revised spreadsheet program could be automatically reconfigured to work with either DOS or OS/2 operating systems.

With all the new features and an easier-to-use interface the look and feel of version 3.0, while retaining many of the features of 2.0, *appeared* to be considerably different from previous versions. With the new version requiring some retraining, existing users of 1-2-3 were reluctant to switch to the newer version in some instances and a few even considered adopting a competitor's spreadsheet. Another problem was that version 3.0 would not run efficiently unless the user had a 286 or 386 microprocessor-based computer. LOTUS originally claimed that the new version of 1-2-3 would perform satisfactorily on an 8088-based system if users had 640K of internal memory and a hard drive.

LOTUS was striving to develop 1-2-3 versions that would run on both micros and mainframes, on minicomputers, and in distributed and nondistributed environments. New versions of 1-2-3 were being written in C language instead of assembler to ensure a high degree of portability, but these versions required more memory than those originally written in assembly language. As part of its plan to push 1-2-3 as an operating environment, LOTUS announced a high-level language for developing customized applications called "extended applications facility."

LOTUS' STRATEGIES IN A MORE COMPETITIVE ENVIRONMENT

LOTUS' early success with its spreadsheet allowed it to set the industry standard and made it time-consuming and difficult for users to change even if competing companies offered software products with superior performance. In addition, high product development costs and the willingness of software developers to create LOTUS-compatible products acted as a barrier to entry into the market. Despite these barriers, the success of two competitors motivated LOTUS to sue both Paperback Software, developer of V-P Planner, and Borland (Quattro) for alleged copyright infringement. As a result, V-P Planner was withdrawn from the market, but the suit against Borland was still in the appeals process.

Improvements in computer technology and changes in user expectations finally necessitated a change in the original 1-2-3 program. LOTUS reluctantly split its core product into two categories—one version for older PCs (version 2.0) and another for 286/386 machines (version 3.0). The 3.0 version offered improved graphics output and recalculation and allowed users to take advantage of the extended memory capacity of 286/386 machines to create multiple spreadsheets. The 3.0 consolidation, advanced file linking, and data base connectivity features required more memory than was available in older machines and publishing facilities were lacking in quality compared to competitors' software products. Version 3.1 was designed to correct many of these problems, but early indications were that not many users were upgrading to 3.1.

LOTUS 1-2-3 version 2.2, introduced after 3.0 sales lagged during the introductory period, was outselling version 3.0 by a margin of three to one. Many users were choosing not to upgrade, with current estimates indicating that only about 40 percent of existing 1-2-3 users upgraded to new versions. The current product line dilemma highlighted the difficulty that a dominant company could experience in defending its market position in a changing environment. LOTUS was in the position of a cash cow, milking existing products without good prospects for future growth in those products (Exhibit 37.1 provides details of the LOTUS product line). Some users felt that LOTUS made a mistake in concentrating too much on sales to large companies; some evidence existed that many customers in small businesses and users of home computers were switching to competitors' products.

LOTUS' goal was to have 1-2-3 installed on a wide variety of platforms including micros, minis, and mainframes. A decline in market share forced LOTUS to seek new markets and to diversify into new products. The company had two strategic alternatives. One was to engage in a price war with Excel and Quattro, defending its turf with drastic price reductions and cut-throat marketing practices. It would have had to sacrifice substantial profits with uncertain long-range returns, especially in the emerging Windows environment. A second approach was to diversify into other areas such as word processing, groupware, and text management, striving to obtain no more than 50 percent of its revenues from nonspreadsheet products. LOTUS followed the latter approach to some extent by acquiring the rights to the AMI Pro word processing package, and marketing Notes groupware and Agenda, a personal information manager. However, the returns from this strategy had been modest so far.

EXHIBIT 37.1   LOTUS' Breadwinners—Sales by Product (In millions)

	1990	1991[a]
1-2-3		
New Units Based on Intel Platforms	$442	$446
New Units Based on Other Platforms	22	45
Upgrades	40	65
AMI Word Processor	0	21
cc: Mail	0	20
Notes	4	25
I/S and Consulting Services	31	37
Freelance	62	70
Other Products	29	23
Symphony	53	57
Total	$683	$809

[a] estimated.

Source: Sanford C. Berbstein & Company, *Computerworld,* November 29, 1991, p. 8.

Stand-Alone Competitive Spreadsheet Products

Paperback Software introduced V-P Planner as a LOTUS clone for $99 during the mid-1980s and Borland introduced a lower-priced LOTUS compatible for $195 in 1988 that had more features than 1-2-3, could access all LOTUS files and performed most LOTUS functions. In addition, Borland acquired the rights to Surpass from Sergio Rubenstein, the developer of WordStar. Surpass was a higher-priced LOTUS-compatible spreadsheet that sold for $495 and offered many advanced features. In 1987, Microsoft introduced an IBM-compatible version of its popular Macintosh spreadsheet Excel for $495 that had a graphic interface characterized by ease of use. During 1988, LOTUS expected to sell 1.2 million copies of 1-2-3, Borland estimated sales of 150,000 copies of Quattro, and industry analysts expected Excel sales to be at least 120,000 units. Sales of V-P Planner and SuperCalc were forecasted to level off or even decline.

LOTUS competitors such as Microsoft, Borland, and Computer Associates offered additional features and ease of use along with function and file compatibility at the same price or a lower price than 1-2-3. However, other spreadsheets had two disadvantages: they required user retraining and had to demonstrate 1-2-3 file compatibility. Because of the use of 1-2-3 over the years, history files had been developed and maintained. These files had to be accessible, thus compatibility had to be demonstrated before the alternative products became viable contenders.

Microsoft

Microsoft had two spreadsheet products: Multiplan and Excel. Multiplan was a solid but not spectacular software product with a slightly different formula and command structure from 1-2-3. It had data base capability with mouse support, and ran under M/S Windows as well as on networks. Multiplan had 1-2-3 file read/write capability and could import files from dBase and R:Base. Although the worksheet had no graphics capability, it could import graphs from Microsoft's Chart program.

Excel, a Microsoft worksheet program that proved to be popular for the Apple Macintosh, had a graphics interface and was more powerful than 1-2-3. It could operate on arrays, handle trend projection and optimization calculations, and display multiple spreadsheets on the same screen, linking them through the use of a mouse or by keystroke commands. The maximum spreadsheet size was two times that of LOTUS, and graphs could be printed from within the spreadsheet. The user selected from 42 different graph formats and numerous font, boldface, and italic sizes. Variable character heights, borders, shaded areas, and underlying areas were easy to implement. It was not copy protected and offered flexible site-licensing provisions.

Excel was designed for 286 or 386 personal computers with high-resolution graphics, at least 640k of internal memory, and a hard drive. It was fully compatible with 1-2-3 files and contained a help facility that automatically gave the Excel equivalent when a 1-2-3 sequence was entered. However, Excel was not key-stroke compatible with 1-2-3 and was only 95 percent compatible with LOTUS macros. It had a macro translator that converted 1-2-3 macros into Excel macros. Some minimal recalculation was possible, and built-in auditing and data base capabilities were provided.

Microsoft emphasized high-resolution graphics interface, mouse applications, and an easy-to-use pull-down menu system in a package that could be run only on 286 and 386 machines. It expected Windows interface and OS/2 Presentation Manager with which its program was compatible to become an industry standard. Excel was written in C language, so portability was assured.

Borland—Quattro and Surpass

Quattro, at $195, was less expensive and offered more functions than 1-2-3. It provided selective recalculation, a greater variety of different types of graphs, and an impressive number of screen display and printing options. Graphs could be printed from within the spreadsheet, and the program took full advantage of EGA and VGA graphics adapters. Quattro offered full 1-2-3 file capability, improved macro development ability using a macro generator, and permitted extensive customization of applications. For debugging purposes, individual commands within a macro sequence could be executed one at a time. It required a minimum of 512k in internal memory and was not copy protected.

Surpass, at $495, appealed to users who had reached the limit of LOTUS 1-2-3 capabilities. A subset of Surpass could be used to implement all 1-2-3 key strokes, files, macros, and formulas, which made it unnecessary to completely retrain former 1-2-3 users. It handled multiple spreadsheets, aligned them in 3-D fashion, posted changes from one spreadsheet to others automatically, and referred to a spreadsheet without requiring that it be in main memory. Dynamic links between spreadsheets were provided, and a macro library contained command sequences that could be used on more than one spreadsheet. Multiple spreadsheets could be displayed on the screens, graphs could be displayed in 3-D format, and an undo command permitted easy correction of mistakes. A built-in file manager performed many common DOS functions.

Borland imitated LOTUS by writing Quattro in assembly language, making it as fast and as compact as possible. Unlike LOTUS, the company was opposed to using one product for multiple computer architectures. It preferred to develop a lower-priced package that would make the fullest possible use of a given type of machine. For users who wanted a higher- level LOTUS look-alike, the company offered Surpass with more features than 1-2-3 at a comparable price.

SuperCalc

SuperCalc, acquired by Computer Associates when it absorbed Sorcim in the mid-1980s, permitted use of larger spreadsheets than LOTUS (i.e., about 2,000 additional rows) and was not copy protected. The command structure differed somewhat from LOTUS, but a careful reading of menus allowed users to accomplish most of the functions possible with LOTUS. It could read and write 1-2-3 files and import or export VisiCalc, DIF, and ASCII files. Graphics and data base modules were included in the program, and as many as nine graphs per spreadsheet could be saved in memory. It permitted macro recording that offered more financial and logical functions than LOTUS. LAN support was also provided.

Version 5 of SuperCalc permitted faster retrieval of information from cells with similar names or codes than was previously possible. An optional 1-2-3 interface facilitated user transition from 1-2-3, and macros contained both 1-2-3 and SuperCalc commands. Enhanced presentation graphics, a toggle on and off minimum recalculation feature, and an undo command for ease of use in correcting errors were provided. In addition, macro debugging and built-in auditing capabilities were included. As a bonus feature with each SuperCalc purchase, a version of Sideways was provided at no additional cost. Computer Associates offered a volume discount and liberal site licensing for SuperCalc.

V-P Planner

V-P Planner, developed by Alex Osborne's Paperback Software, was a low-cost clone that cost $99 and used most LOTUS commands plus a few new ones. It would read and write dBase files, record macros, and open up to six windows. While work was being done on one spreadsheet, users could be printing another. V-P Planner could not run LOTUS add-ins, but some add-ons worked with this program (e.g., 1-2-3 Forecast, Ready-to-Run Accounting, Goal Seeker). V-P Planner had no built-in graphics capabilities but could develop graphs using the separate V-P Graph program. Another drawback was that unlike other spreadsheet companies, it charged users for technical support.

The notoriety from the LOTUS lawsuit charging copyright infringement based on the look-alike, feel-alike quality of V-P Planner hurt sales. However, it was obvious that V-P Planner was more than just a LOTUS clone. A new version, V-P Planner Plus carried a slightly higher price tag ($179.99) and provided twice as many financial and logical functions as LOTUS, permitted recalculation of selected calls, and was not copy protected. Graphics capabilities were only fair— definitely not in the same class as Quattro or Excel. An optional interface with pull-down menus made it easier to follow command sequences than what was possible with 1-2-3.

V-P Planner's data base capability permitted reading and writing dBase, V-P Info, and DIF files as well as viewing data in up to five dimensions. One obvious shortcoming of Paperback Software's marketing program was that it overstressed the value of V-P Planner as a low-cost LOTUS clone and did not emphasize its strong data base capability. In mid-1990, LOTUS won its copyright infringement suit against Paperback Software, forcing the company to withdraw V-P Planner from circulation. By the end of 1991, the LOTUS clone was no longer a significant factor in the spreadsheet market.

Ashton-Tate

Ashton-Tate, which obtained 60 percent of its sales from dBase, its data base manager, was not an active player in the spreadsheet market, although it did have an integrated package named Framework. The competitive position of Ashton-Tate had eroded because its basic dBase III program would not work on the 386 machines, and it was facing intense competition in the data base market from Oracle, Borland, and others. The merger with Borland in 1990 raised questions about Ashton-Tate's future role in both the data base and integrated software markets. However, both LOTUS and Microsoft were moving into the data base market with add-ins or built-in capabilities as part of their spreadsheet programs suggesting that Borland would do the same.

Integrated Software

Integrated software packages combined several functions such as word processing, spreadsheet, data base management, and communications all into one package. The major advantage was that a user performed a number of computer-based functions with one program using a common command structure. Not having to switch from one program to another each time a different function was performed saved time and effort. The disadvantage was that normally a given integrated package emphasized one or two functions such as spreadsheet or data base management and provided only minimum capabilities for others (e.g., word processing, graphics). Some users were reluctant to pay the extra price for a package containing four or five functions when only one or two would be used continually.

Many users desired a "core" product to be used for data base, spreadsheet, word processing, memo writing, desk calculating, scheduling, and so on. However, the market for individual applications grew faster than that for integrated software packages. It was estimated that integrated package sales increased 4 percent in 1986 over 1985, while sales of individual applications increased at a rate of 31 percent. Exhibit 37.2 shows actual and estimated individual application package revenues compared with those of integrated software packages for 1985–89.

EXHIBIT 37.2   **Revenues for Individual and Integrated Software Packages, 1985–1989 (In millions)**

Year	Individual Applications	Integrated Packages
1985	$ 625	103
1986	820	107
1987	967[a]	120
1988	1,150[a]	130[a]
1989	1,350[a]	140[a]

[a] Estimated.

Source: Compiled from various issues of *PC Week*.

The major integrated software packages included LOTUS Symphony, which had a strong spreadsheet and a fair data base, and Ashton-Tate's Framework, which had a strong data base, good word processor, and a fair spreadsheet. In 1986, revenues from Symphony were estimated to be $36 million (36 percent market share); Framework generated $26 million (26 percent share). The other major players were Innovative Software's Smartware, which produced $14 million in revenues for a 14 percent share of the market, and the Enable Group's Enable package, which captured 3 percent of the market with $4 million in sales. More than 40 other competitors divided the remaining 22 percent.

At the lower end of the scale, Software Publishing Company (SPC) introduced First Choice in August 1986 and sold 70,000 units during the first six months of product life. It sold 25,000 copies of its separate Professional Plan spreadsheet during 1986. It was estimated that SPC sold 200,000 copies of First Choice at a list price of $195 through mid-1988. Version 2 of First Choice added graphics capabilities to other functions. After introducing its Better Working Eight in One program at $59.95 (containing outlining, word processing, spell checking, spreadsheet, data base, graphics, communications, and desktop organizing capabilities with a memo pad, address book, and calendar), Spinnaker bought the rights to First Choice.

Microsoft converted its Macintosh integrated package Works for use on the IBM-PC and compatibles. With a price comparable to First Choice, it was proving to be a strong competitor at the low end of the market. The recent acquisition of Alpha Four by LOTUS gave the company an entry into the low end of data base management with a system that had many of the characteristics of an integrated package.

THE COMPETITIVE ENVIRONMENT IN PERSONAL COMPUTER SOFTWARE

The demand for electronic spreadsheet software grew less rapidly than other types of software. Sales increases in recent years did not match those of earlier years. Exhibit 37.3 shows the actual and expected unit sales of electronic spreadsheets from 1986 to 1990, according to one industry source. After leveling off in 1988, electronic spreadsheet sales were expected to grow at a slow but steady pace during the rest of the decade. The impact of PS/2-based hardware on spreadsheet demand was less than expected, but the popularity of the Windows-based environment fueled increased demand for Windows-based spreadsheets.

Spreadsheets and word processing programs were the most widely installed applications and represented slower growth and mature markets. Data base managers had somewhat more potential with modest growth possibilities. Graphics, CAD/CAM, project management, and desktop publishing applications represented the fastest-growing markets with considerable room to develop without saturation. A Sierra Group poll of over 1,500 users found that 60 percent of users

EXHIBIT 37.3   Sales of Electronic Spreadsheets (In millions of units)

Year	Number
1986	1.20
1987	1.40
1988	1.50
1989	1.80
1990	2.00

Source: IDC Corporation, *Computerworld*, December 21, 1987.

EXHIBIT 37.4   Shipments of Applications Software Packages (In millions of units)

	1987	1988[a]	1992[a]
Word Processing	3.2	3.5	4.9
Spreadsheets	2.2	2.5	3.4
Communications	2.1	2.5	3.8
Graphics	1.4	1.8	3.3
Data Base Management	1.0	1.4	5.0

[a] Estimated.
Source: Dataquest, *Personal Computing,* October 1988.

surveyed planned to buy word processing packages, 54 percent planned to buy data base managers, 51 percent planned spreadsheet purchases, and 35 percent expected to buy graphics presentation packages.[8]

Exhibit 37.4 contains actual and estimated shipments of word processing, spreadsheet, graphics, communications, and data base management systems. Only modest sales growth had been expected during 1987 and 1988. For the period 1988 to 1992, spreadsheet sales were expected to increase at an average annual rate of 33 percent compared to 35 percent for word processing packages, 45 percent for graphics systems, 38 percent for communication packages, and 89 percent for data base managers.

IMPACT OF COMPETITION ON MARKET SHARE IN THE SPREADSHEET INDUSTRY

Fierce competition in the personal computer spreadsheet industry resulted in lower prices, inexpensive upgrades, and free add-ins during the late 1980s.. Dataquest (1991) reported that LOTUS' market share declined from 54 percent in

[8] Stephen Jones, "Software Applications," *Computerworld*, May 9, 1988, p. 126.

1989 to 47 percent in 1990.[9] During the same period, Borland increased its market share from 3 percent to approximately 14 percent using aggressive marketing tactics and Excel increased its market share from 12 percent to 14 percent. Borland sold its Quattro spreadsheet for $99 to any user offering proof of LOTUS ownership, and Microsoft was selling Excel for $129 direct from the firm. A Vista Market Research survey found that 80 percent of Quattro users previously used 1-2-3.[10] Although it had not lowered its prices significantly, LOTUS countered by including AMI Pro word processing system for $20 in the LOTUS package and offered upgrades to existing LOTUS users for as little as $49.

Dataquest (1991) predicted that in the 1990s, Quattro and Excel would gain market share at the expense of LOTUS, SuperCalc 5, and Lucid 3-D.[11] The existing base of LOTUS users held firm, but many 1-2-3 users disregarded price discounts and giveaways. The biggest barrier to switching to 1-2-3 alternatives was the cost of retraining users and resistance to change by users who were familiar and comfortable with the existing program. However, this situation could change as users switch from DOS to Windows environments.

Market share figures in the spreadsheet industry were only estimates and varied widely depending on the source. However, there seemed to be general agreement that LOTUS' market share declined from about two-thirds of the total market in the middle 1980s to approximately 50 percent in 1990. Estimated market shares are given for major spreadsheet competitors for 1989 and 1990 in Exhibit 37.5. Both Borland and Microsoft experienced sizable gains in market share during this period, while LOTUS and Computer Associates suffered moderate declines.

Prolonged delays in offering a 1-2-3 version for Windows caused LOTUS to lose some customers, and LOTUS 1-2-3 Windows was likely to spark fierce reactions in that environment from its principal competitors. Some experts predicted that LOTUS would obtain only about one-third of the Windows spread-

EXHIBIT 37.5   Market Shares for Major Spreadsheet Competitors, 1989 and 1990

Company	1989	1990
LOTUS	51.2%	49.6%
Borland	4.3	20.3
Microsoft	7.2	11.7
Computer Associates	11.7	8.0
Other	25.6	10.3
Total	100.0%	100.0%

Source: IDC Corporation and Info Corporation.

[9] John Schneidawind, "1-2-3 Upgrade, New Software Boosts Software Firm," *USA Today*, March 1991, pp. B1, B2.

[10] Mark Hendricks, "Spreadsheet Clash Improves User Choices," *PC World*, May 1991, p. 59.

[11] Schneidawind, "1-2-3 Upgrade," p. B2.

**EXHIBIT 37.6   Estimated Worldwide
1990 Spreadsheet Shipments (In millions)**

Company	Shipments
LOTUS	$1,700
Borland	600
Microsoft	400
Computer Associates	275
Other	340
Total	$3,315

Source: IDC, *Computerworld,* January 7, 1991.

sheet market. Preliminary evaluations of 1-2-3 Windows indicated that LOTUS'
version was slower and less compatible with common Windows applications than
Excel. Borland and Microsoft had price advantages over LOTUS in the spreadsheet market, as both competitors derived 25 percent or less of their revenue from
spreadsheet programs and could afford to offer larger discounts than LOTUS,
which obtained about 70 percent of its revenues from 1-2-3.

1-2-3 Windows was selling at moderate but not spectacular levels. Some
corporate purchasers announced that they were delaying buying decisions. There
were some reports of 1-2-3 users switching to Excel, which was designed for
Windows and had superior graphics, consolidation functions, and embedded
objects as opposed to the more bland 1-2-3 Windows. The new version was
keystroke compatible with older 1-2-3 versions but was slower in performing
calculations, largely because it was designed to work in both DOS and Windows
environments. Exhibit 37.6 contains estimated 1990 shipments in dollars for the
major spreadsheet competitors.

REVENUE AND INCOME GROWTH

LOTUS had to lower its long-term growth goals to reflect a loss of market
share. Expected pretax profit margins were revised from 25 percent to 20 percent,
revenue growth was expected to stabilize at 20 to 25 percent annually, and return
on equity was forecasted to remain in the mid- to high 20s.[12] In 1989, revenue
increased 19 percent to $556 million, and actual profit margins were 15 percent in
1987 and 17 percent in 1988. LOTUS initiated a hiring freeze and announced
small-scale layoffs as Manzi maintained that slower growth in sales of personal
computers was the principal factor in slower revenue growth at LOTUS. Indicated cutbacks in advertising and marketing could result in further loss of market
share (Exhibit 37.7). The company work force of 3,100 was small by industry

[12] Patricia Keefe, "LOTUS Reshaping Long Term Goals," *Computerworld,* September 24,
1990, p. 96.

EXHIBIT 37.7   Advertising Expenditures for PC Software Companies, 1989 (In millions)

Company	Amount
Ashton-Tate	$ 6.10
Borland	4.56
Computer Associates	10.40
LOTUS	10.70
Microsoft	17.00
Novell	4.64
Oracle	9.80
Software Publishing Company	4.21

Source: *Computer Industry Almanac,* Brady, 1991.

standards with sales per employee of about $188,000 compared to an industry average of $175,000, but its operating costs were high compared to the industry average.[13]

LOTUS revenues increased 73 percent during the period from 1987 to 1990, but net income was down 26 percent during the same period. In contrast, Microsoft's revenues increased 342 percent and net income increased 571 percent during this period, while Computer Associates' revenues went up 436 percent and net income increased 725 percent. Exhibit 37.8 illustrates sales revenues for the years 1987 to 1990 for the eight major personal computer software companies. Exhibit 37.9 contains net income for the same companies during the 1987 to 1990 period.

EXHIBIT 37.8   Sales Revenues for Major PC Software Companies, 1987–1990 (In millions)

Company	1987	1988	1989	1990
Ashton-Tate	$ 211.0	$ 307.3	$ 265.3	$ 230.5
Borland	38.1	81.6	90.6	226.8
Computer Associates	309.0	709.1	1,030.0	1,348.2
LOTUS	396.0	468.5	556.7	684.5
Microsoft	346.0	590.8	830.5	1,183.4
Novell	—	—	421.9	497.6
Oracle	131.3	282.2	583.7	970.8
Software Publishing	38.6	73.1	103.5	140.6
Total	$1,470	$2,512.5	$3,854.5	$5,282.3
Industry Sales Growth	—	1.71	1.53	1.37

Source: *Business Week* R&D Scoreboard, 1990, 1991, 1992, and *Business Week* 1000 Companies, 1990, 1991, 1992.

[13] William Bulkeley, "LOTUS Replaces King as Head of Development," *Wall Street Journal,* November 22, 1991, p. C-15E.

EXHIBIT 37.9   Net Income for Major PC Software Companies, 1987–1990 (In millions)

Company	1987	1988	1989	1990
Ashton-Tate	$ 30.1	$ 73.5	$ (31.6)	$ (20.1)
Borland	1.3	3.8	(3.6)	41.9
Computer Associates	36.5	170.1	286.5	261.2
LOTUS	72.0	79.9	85.0	52.8
Microsoft	71.9	183.7	250.8	410.6
Novell	—	—	77.1	145.1
Oracle	15.6	65.0	120.2	172.7
Software Publishing	5.2	21.3	26.8	29.3
Total	$232.6	$1,182.3	$793.1	$1,093.5
Industry Income Growth	—	5.08	0.68	137.9

Source: *Business Week* R&D Scoreboard, 1988, 1989, and 1990, and *Business Week* 1000 Companies, 1988, 1989, and 1990.

Exhibit 37.10 shows total assets for the eight personal computer software companies for years 1987 to 1990. For the industry, assets increased from $1,556 million in 1987 to $5,459 million in 1990, or an increase of 351 percent compared to an increase of 359 percent in revenues and an increase of 470 percent in net income. LOTUS' assets increased 218 percent, revenues increased 173 percent, and net income declined to 73 percent of 1987 figures during the same period.

Exhibit 37.11 shows R&D outlays as a percentage of revenues and sales per employee for the eight personal computer software companies. R&D outlays compared to sales revenues for LOTUS declined during the period 1988 to 1990

EXHIBIT 37.10   Total Assets for Major PC Software Companies, for 1987 to 1990 (In millions)

Company	1987	1988	1989	1990
Ashton-Tate	$ 175	$ 293	$ 245	$ 246
Borland	28	54	53	87
Computer Associates	439	1,156	1,376	1,596
LOTUS	318	399	604	695
Microsoft	288	605	922	1,366
Novell	129	227	347	494
Oracle	144	321	584	855
Software Publishing	35	60	83	120
Total	$1,556	$3,115	$4,214	$5,459
Industry Growth	—	2.00	1.35	1.30

Source: *Business Week* 1000 Companies, 1988, 1989, and 1990; *Standard and Poor's Stock Reports,* Fall 1990.

EXHIBIT 37.11   R&D Outlays/Sales and Sales/Employee for PC Software Companies, 1988-1990

	R&D Investment/Sales			Sales/Employee		
Company	1988	1989	1990	1988	1989	1990
Ashton-Tate	17.2	25.9	17.2	$210.5	$185.5	$142.3
Borland	10.6	15.8	10.3	132.0	183.3	230.0
Computer Associates	11.5	13.0	13.2	158.7	164.2	201.2
LOTUS	17.9	17.0	16.1	187.4	198.6	195.6
Microsoft	11.8	13.7	15.3	211.5	199.0	210.0
Novell	—	10.1	11.9	—	199.5	205.7
Oracle	9.1	9.0	9.1	122.8	140.7	142.5
Software Publishing	16.1	15.7	16.1	188.5	217.4	214.0
Industry Average	13.5	15.0	13.6	$173.8	$186.0	$192.7

Source: *Business Week,* R&D Scoreboard 1989, 1990, and 1991.

while the industry average stabilized at around 13.5 percent. However, LOTUS' R&D ratio was still higher than the industry average. Industry average sales per employee steadily increased during this period; sales per employee for LOTUS also increased at about the same rate as the other companies in this industry segment.

REFERENCES

BULKELEY, WILLIAM. "After Years of Glory, LOTUS Is Stumbling in Software Market." *Wall Street Journal,* August 30, 1988, p. B1.

BULKELEY, WILLIAM. "LOTUS is Upgrading 1-2-3 Again; Move May Revive Sales, Earnings." *Wall Street Journal,* September 7, 1990, p. B2.

BULKELEY, WILLIAM. "LOTUS Effort to Please All with 1-2-3 Confuses Many." *Wall Street Journal,* July 20, 1990, p. B1.

BULKELEY, WILLIAM. "LOTUS Replaces King as Head of Development." *Wall Street Journal,* November 22, 1991, p. C-15E.

BRYAN, MARVIN. "How Spreadsheets Add Up." *Personal Computing,* September 1987, p. 202.

BURKE, STEVEN. "Borland's Attack on LOTUS Paid Off." *PC Week,* September 24, 1990, p. 160.

CURRAN, LAWRENCE. "Dueling Spreadsheets." *Electronics,* February 1991, p. 29.

DALY, JAMES. "Excel to Renew LOTUS Assault." *Computerworld,* January 7, 1991, pp. 1, 6.

DARROW, BARBARA, AND ED SCANNELL. "Manzi Admits That LOTUS Needs 1-2-3 for Windows." *Infoworld,* September 24, 1990, p. 51.

FERRANTI, MARC. "Version 2.2 Emerges as Sales Leader in LOTUS' 1-2-3 Family." *PC Week,* July 30, 1990, p. 5.

FERRANTI, MARC, AND BETH FREEDMAN. "At LOTUS, Landry Is In, King Is Out." *PC Week,* November 25, 1991, pp. 1, 6.

FISHER, SUSAN E. "1-2-3 for Windows Will Face Stiff Competition." *PC Week,* September 2, 1991, p. 99.

HAMMONS, KEITH. "Teaching Discipline to Six Year Old LOTUS." *Business Week,* July 4, 1988, p. 46.

HAMMONS, KEITH. "It's the Yawn of a New Age for LOTUS." *Business Week,* March 12, 1990, p. 42.

HENDRICKS, MARK. "Spreadsheet Clash Improves User Choices." *PC World,* May 1991, p. 59.

HOGAN, MIKE. "1-2-3 Opens Up Windows." *PC World,* July 1991, p. 15.

KEEFE, PATRICIA. "LOTUS Reshaping Long Term Goals." *Computerworld,* September 24, 1990, p. 96.

MARTIN, JAMES. "In Spreadsheet War, Excel Poses Serious Threat to 1-2-3." *PC Week,* November 27, 1989, p. 213.

MCWILLIAMS, GARY. "Another Year, Another Bitter Lesson for Jim Manzi." *Business Week,* December 9, 1991, p. 45.

RADDING, ALAN. "PC Spreadsheets." *Computerworld,* September 2, 1991, p. 59.

RADDING, ALAN. "Race of Power vs. Position." *Computerworld,* December 21, 1987, p. 117.

SCHNEIDAWIND, JOHN. "1-2-3 Upgrade, New Software Boosts Software Firm." *USA Today,* 1991, pp. B-1, B-2.

SCHWARTZ, JOHN. "LOTUS at War." *Personal Computing,* June 1989, p. 27.

WILKE, JOHN R. "LOTUS Fights to Regain Share with Discounts." *Wall Street Journal,* September 5, 1991, p. B1.

_____ CASE 38 _____

The Army and Air Force Exchange Service:
A New Era

In 1986, the Army and Air Force Exchange Service (AAFES) was one of the largest retailers in the United States with sales over $5.2 billion. However, the 1980s had brought increased competition in retailing both in the United States and worldwide. Additionally, there were pressures to increase AAFES' support of the military's Morale, Welfare, and Recreation (MWR) programs. Fifty percent of the AAFES proceeds were used to support MWR programs. General John Long, commander of AAFES, believed that some fundamental changes in the Exchange Service were required if it was to continue to be successful into the 1990s. With the widespread availability of low-priced merchandise across the United States, the competitive advantages of the Exchange Service had diminished.

The Army and Air Force Exchange Service—a worldwide retail, food, and service organization—was developed to benefit the men and women in the U.S. Armed Forces. The primary mission was to provide authorized patrons with merchandise and services of necessity and convenience at low prices. The secondary mission was to support the Morale, Welfare, and Recreation programs of the Army and Air Force. The stated objectives of AAFES that support the mission are presented in Exhibit 38.1.

EVOLUTION OF THE EXCHANGE SERVICE

Prior to 1880, traders literally followed the troops in order to sell goods to the soldiers. During the 1880s, the War Department contracted with specific traders to operate stores on the Army posts. Everything from clothing to kitchenware was sold. Because many Army posts were located far from major trading centers, traders often would sell low-quality goods at high prices. As a result, in 1889 the War Department authorized the establishment of Post Canteens, which were operated under the direction of each commander. These canteens were a

This case was prepared by Peter M. Ginter, Linda E. Swayne, and Tana J. Bisch as a basis for class discussion rather than to illustrate either effective or ineffective handling of an administrative situation. Used with permission from Peter M. Ginter.

EXHIBIT 38.1   Objectives of AAFES

1. To provide customers with more modern facilities comparable to what is now provided in the U.S. economy including building new facilities or renovation of existing facilities with the addition of more elaborate displays, lighting, and color schemes.
2. To develop a more clearly defined image to enhance customer and employee loyalty.
3. To provide higher quality and more specialized merchandise to meet customer demand.
4. To seek more aggressive marketing techniques.
5. To continue to generate sufficient earnings to support military MWR programs and activities.

Source: AAFES Strategic Plans & Policy Branch, AAFES Master Plan 1987, Dallas, Texas, March 26, 1986.

combination men's club and retail store. Canteens were self-supporting, with profits going into a general post welfare fund.

In 1895, General Order No. 46 established Post Exchanges—the beginning of the modern exchange service. The name change from "canteen" to "exchange" indicated the increasing retail emphasis of the system. Early exchanges operated independently. There were no standard policies or prices, and each funded its own activities. This arrangement worked well for a small domestic army but was inadequate for the 2.4 million troops that went overseas in 1918.

In 1919, a study of the exchange system indicated a lack of quality control and standard procedures. It suggested that exchanges were unprepared for modern war, but it was not until 1941 that the Army Exchange Service (the forerunner to AAFES), was established. It was placed within the War Department's Morale Branch, which provided broad policy guidance for operation of the exchanges.

AAFES was officially established in 1948. The Defense Department decreed that exchanges could make a small profit, a portion of which would be used to help support the military's MWR programs. In the 1950s and early 1960s, the Exchange Service was centralized and modernized. AAFES finances were consolidated enabling the profits of larger exchanges to be used to help support smaller exchanges. In addition, Congress allowed the Exchange Service to build new facilities with some of the profits instead of relying on military buildings. These new, more pleasant surroundings helped to stimulate business. In the 1960s, AAFES set up a centralized buying operation which helped not only to lower prices, but also to improve quality.

Operations in the 1980s

In the mid-1980s, AAFES operated in the United States and in more than 20 foreign countries as a military command under joint directives of the U.S. Army

EXHIBIT 38.2   AAFES Services

1. Retail—includes automotive equipment, jewelry, clothing, household goods, small appliances, toiletries, sporting goods, luggage, video, audio and photo equipment, computers, toys, and automobiles
2. Food and beverage establishments—includes snack bars, cafeterias, and ice cream parlors
3. Theaters
4. Military clothing
5. Vending centers
6. Personal services—includes photo developing, beauty/barber shops, optical, floral, laundry/dry cleaning, fuel stations, and bakeries

Source: HQ AAFES Public Affairs Division, AAFES-Overview Briefing, Dallas, Texas, 1986.

and Air Force. Modern military exchanges were similar to community shopping centers and normally included retail stores, cafeterias, snack bars, theaters, service stations, vending, personal service activities (such as laundry and dry cleaning, barber/beauty shops, photography services), concessions, and a wide variety of other activities (approximately 16,000 activities). Exhibit 38.2 provides a list of the service categories offered by AAFES.

Fifty percent of all AAFES proceeds (profits) were turned over to military MWR activities ($114.5 million in 1986, a 32 percent increase over 1985). These funds were used by the Army and Air Force for libraries, gyms, hobby shops, child development centers, and athletic equipment. Exhibit 38.3 presents a list of MWR activities funded by the exchanges. The remainder of the earnings were retained by AAFES to build new exchanges and renovate existing facilities.

EXHIBIT 38.3   Morale, Welfare, and Recreation (MWR) Programs

1. Retail—sporting goods, video, audio and photo equipment, and computers
2. Travel-related services (such as campgrounds, but not travel agencies)
3. Bowling centers
4. Child care centers, teen centers
5. Food and beverage establishments
6. Libraries
7. Recreation areas, gyms, tennis, golf
8. Hobby shops
9. Auditoriums

Source: HQ AAFES Public Affairs Division, AAFES-Overview Briefing, Dallas, Texas, 1986.

A NEW RETAILING ERA

As General Long pondered the past evolution of the Exchange Service, he realized that further changes, maybe dramatic, would be required if AAFES were to continue to successfully fulfill its mission. There were clear indications that a rethinking of the marketing strategy was required.

The AAFES commander was acutely aware that competition within the retail industry had become intense as more civilian stores offered discounted merchandise. These retail stores were direct competitors, resulting in leveling sales and reduced margins for AAFES.

In addition, Army and Air Force MWR programs and activities relied heavily on congressionally appropriated funds for their existence. For the past few years, these funds had been gradually reduced. The commander believed that further reductions were a strong possibility, at least through 1991. Moreover, Congress was interested in reorganizing MWR activities under the direct command of AAFES. If a decision were made to place all MWR activities under the AAFES command, there would be additional pressures for the Exchange Service to support all MWR activities.

Although past strategies were designed to meet the objective of providing the customers with more modern facilities (Exhibit 38.1), the commander wondered if AAFES should be placing greater emphasis on a different objective—to seek more aggressive marketing techniques. He wondered how AAFES could continue to aggressively renovate and build new facilities yet still provide sufficient support for MWR activities.

MARKETING

AAFES defined marketing as the process by which the demand for goods and services is anticipated and satisfied through the procurement, physical distribution, and sales of such goods and services. Marketing within AAFES consisted of the following programs:

1. *Sales Management Program.* This program developed the skills and resources to identify customer needs and planned the marketing of products and services to meet those needs.
2. *Merchandise Management Program.* This program provided information and policies that established the best merchandise mix to satisfy customer needs at the lowest possible price.
3. *Point-of-Sale Program.* This program used electronic cash registers to capture accurate, timely sales and markdown transactions for management analysis.[1]

[1] AAFES Strategic Plan & Policy Branch, AAFES Master Plan FY84-FY88, Dallas, Texas, December 23, 1982.

Product

A military exchange could be compared to a civilian hyperstore—a great variety of goods in one huge store. Merchandise consisted of items traditionally found in department stores (clothing, shoes, furniture), drug stores (over-the-counter drugs, prescriptions, cosmetics), food stores, hardware stores, and garden shops. AAFES also offered a complete line of personal services (i.e., fast food, film processing, beauty/barber shops, and others). The goal was to provide the convenience of one-stop shopping.

Service was one area of AAFES' marketing strategy that had received considerable emphasis. The AAFES' command believed that by enhancing services, customer loyalty would increase. As a result, AAFES maintained a mail-order catalog, check-cashing services, deferred payment plans, a liberal refund and adjustment policy, and major credit card purchase options (VISA, Master-Card, and Discover). In addition, all levels of management were encouraged to get personally involved in exchange operations. New items were introduced faster—from Reebok athletic shoes to Tandy (Radio Shack) computers. AAFES attempted to get new products on the shelves ahead of other retailers and prior to national advertising.

Some products, such as sporting goods, clothing, video, audio and photo equipment, and food and beverages, were sold within the MWR program. For these type of products, MWR was directly competing for the same customer, yet AAFES had to generate sufficient profit to support the MWR operations. Thus, AAFES often had to charge higher prices for the same products.

In order to ensure quality products, AAFES developed an excellent quality assurance program. Merchandise was subjected to stringent inspection and laboratory tests. Through this program, AAFES' customers received high-quality merchandise within the price lines. In addition, AAFES conducted a vigorous consumer product safety program to detect, prevent, and respond to potential product hazards.

One major difference between AAFES and other large retail operations was that AAFES had shorter operating hours. Most AAFES facilities closed at 6:00 P.M., whereas other large retail operations were typically open till 9:00 P.M. or longer, and some stores operated 24 hours per day.

Another profitable operation for AAFES was franchises (including 102 Burger Kings worldwide, one Pizza Inn, and one Popeye's Chicken franchise). The major benefits of the franchised operations were name recognition and standardized methods and procedures. AAFES would build the free-standing unit on the military installation and manage the outlet as if it were any other franchised Burger King. AAFES hired operating labor and received all income after expenses (including the Burger King franchise fee). Income from franchised operations had been increasing at a rate of 7 percent per year for the past five years. Many exchange managers believed that developing more franchised operations would be a way to offer AAFES customers additional products and services without incurring additional operating costs.

Price

The key marketing element within AAFES was price. AAFES' overall goal was to save customers 20 percent on comparable products sold in the civilian sector. The AAFES pricing policy was considered a form of compensation to military families. By providing savings to the customer, the military member's monthly pay was in effect increased.

Before a supplier could sell to the government (exchanges were included), the company had to be evaluated and earn a place on the "approved supplier" list. Only then could the company bid on government contracts. The bidding process assured lowest-cost contracts for exchange customers. Companies were willing to make low bids because AAFES represented a large piece of business. Thus, AAFES had the advantage of low costs, plus maintained low profitability margins in order to provide low prices on all products and services.

In order to monitor the goal of 20 percent average savings, AAFES contracted with the A.C. Nielsen Company to conduct annual price-comparison surveys. Prices of 300 brand-name products at the exchange were compared with the same items at stores in the local community. More than 25,000 price comparisons were made throughout the Exchange Service. The surveys were used for analysis by AAFES to review pricing for areas not reaching the 20 percent goal. In 1986, AAFES did not meet the overall goal of 20 percent savings because of increased competition from retail discounters. Exhibit 38.4 presents the results of the Nielsen savings survey for 1986. The survey showed that AAFES provided

EXHIBIT 38.4   AAFES Savings Survey, 1986

Department	Savings (In percent)
Automotive	13
Clothing	20
Food and beverage	2
Household	17
Jewelry	23
Stationery	27
Sundries	13
Tobacco	16
Toiletries	13

Source: HQ AAFES Public Affairs Division, AAFES-Overview Briefing, Dallas, Texas, 1986.

20 percent or more savings to the customer over other commercial retailers on many, but not all, of the items surveyed.

Promotion

Promotion within the retail industry often consisted of multipage advertisements in local newspapers, and television and radio commercials. However, AAFES, by regulation, was not allowed to use mass-media advertising. Instead, AAFES relied upon word-of-mouth, post (or base for the Air Force) circulars, and the post (or base) newsletter or newspaper.

In the mid-1980s, AAFES began a program to increase customer awareness among military personnel concerning the services available at the exchange by publicizing the AAFES story. This program consisted of seminars, briefings, and pamphlet distribution. Direct mail to military personnel was utilized in an attempt to expand the number of customers frequenting the exchange.

During this time, AAFES became more concerned about its image. New logos, colors, packaging, signage, and advertising were considered that would be more easily recognized and unique to AAFES (see Exhibit 38.5 for the current AAFES logo). It was hoped that changing merchandise displays, lighting, and the utilization of product demonstrations on a regular basis would create greater shopping interest. To increase customer shopping frequency, AAFES used market representatives, mall displays, and local sports and television personalities to assist in promoting its products and services. AAFES also promoted "Made in USA" merchandise and developed a direct-mail program targeted at retirees, reservists, and National Guardsmen.

Distribution

AAFES operated on a worldwide scale with command headquarters in Dallas, Texas (CONUS), and two overseas subordinate commands (AAFES-

EXHIBIT 38.5   AAFES Logo

Europe and AAFES-Pacific). Another major element of AAFES was catalog sales. In 1986, CONUS made up approximately 58 percent of total sales, while AAFES-Europe comprised about 28 percent, AAFES-Pacific about 13 percent, and catalog sales about 1 percent.

Within the United States, there were five exchange regions—the West, Southwest, Midwest, Northeast, and Southeast. Each region was divided into four to five areas headed by a general manager who directed operations. Each area was made up of four to nine military installations where the exchange manager was the senior official. The exchange manager was responsible for all exchange activities at the installation. A map of the Exchange Service in the United States is shown in Exhibit 38.6.

In the mid-1980s, AAFES began a $183 million program that was designed to provide an integrated, flexible, and centrally controlled distribution system. The development program was undertaken to consolidate and upgrade existing distribution facilities and create a major new centralized distribution facility on the East Coast. Interacting data systems were to be developed to maintain timely and comprehensive information to support merchandising, inventory control, physical distribution, accounting, and sales management. Information would be maintained that would allow for the identification of the most cost-effective combinations of freight and handling costs.

The distribution development program goal was to enable AAFES to maintain the proper level and mix of stock and ensure that merchandise was available to the customers when they needed it through the most cost-efficient channel. AAFES, in the past, had nagging problems with stock-outs, and distribution costs were high. The program was expected to be completely operational by 1990.

Exchanges operated only on military posts and bases in the United States and abroad. Within the military installation, the exchange could be a free-standing building centrally located or located "away from the congestion" or located in whatever makeshift space was available. In the 1980s, appropriated funds were no longer available to AAFES for construction of new exchanges. Thus, facility construction was limited to upgrading only those facilities badly needing improvements.

The AAFES Consumer Profile

In order to fulfill its mission, AAFES had to satisfy a broad range of customer interests. AAFES served approximately seven million customers per year. The composition of these customers is presented in Exhibit 38.7. Military dependents (family members) constituted the largest single customer group. The support of military dependents brought considerable change in merchandise and services offered by AAFES.

Rank and age were important demographic characteristics of AAFES customers. Over 80 percent of AAFES customers were enlisted personnel, earning

EXHIBIT 38.6   U.S. Exchange System

AAFES
ARMY & AIR FORCE EXCHANGE SERVICE

EXHIBIT 38.7   Composition of AAFES Customers

Customers	Number (In millions)
Active-Duty Military Personnel	1.4
Military Reservists	1.0
Military Retirees	0.9
Military Dependents (Family Members)	3.8
Total	7.1

Source: AAFES Commander, "AAFES & You," Pamphlet, Dallas, Texas, May 1982.

relatively low salaries. Basic pay and allowances by rank, as shown in Exhibit 38.8, indicated the wide variation in income for exchange customers.

The average age of AAFES customers is 26 years; 52 percent were married and had an average of two children. For the most part, these customers desired "value" items such as household goods, recreational merchandise, infant and children's clothing, adult fashions, and sportswear—all at low prices. At the same time, AAFES had to serve the needs of the officers and their families who might want higher-quality items.[2] AAFES' mission is to serve *all* its customers, which means that merchandise and service had to attempt to satisfy a broad range of interests.

The most recently available broad-based analysis of customer opinion was a 1979 AAFES survey of active-duty military personnel. The results of this survey are presented in Exhibit 38.9. The two main improvements customers recommended were lower prices and greater clothing selection, including more budget clothing. Surprisingly, larger stores and newer facilities were not recommended.

OPERATIONS

Fiscal 1985 was disappointing for AAFES. Although sales increased 1 percent over 1984, net earnings were down 28 percent from the prior year. Competition from civilian stores was keen, as there was aggressive expansion by many large retail chains. Exhibit 38.10 provides a list of the major U.S. retailers and the percentage change in sales from 1985 to 1986. These retailers represented the primary U.S. competition for AAFES.

Increased competition resulted in numerous discounts and early markdowns by military exchanges. As a result, AAFES exceeded its planned markdowns by $15 million in 1985. Sales and markdowns meant added savings for the AAFES customer but significantly reduced net earnings. In addition, the strong dollar

[2] HQ AAFES Public Affairs Division, AAFES-Overview Briefing, Dallas, Texas, 1986.

EXHIBIT 38.8 Air Force Monthly Pay and Allowances by Pay Grade and Years of Service, January 1, 1987

Years of Service

Pay Grade	Under 2	2	3	4	6	8	10	12	14	16	18	20	22	26
Commissioned Officers														
O-10	5378.10	5567.70	5567.70	5567.70	5567.70	5781.00	5781.10	5900.10	5900.10	5900.10	5900.10	5900.10	5900.10	5900.10
O-9	4766.70	4891.50	4995.60	4955.60	4995.60	5122.50	5122.50	5335.80	5335.80	5781.00	5900.10	5900.10	5900.10	5900.10
O-8	4317.30	4446.60	4552.20	4552.20	4552.20	4891.50	4891.50	5122.50	5122.50	5335.80	5567.70	5781.00	5900.10	5900.10
O-7	3587.40	3831.30	3831.30	3831.30	4002.90	4002.90	4235.10	4235.10	4446.60	4891.50	5227.80	5227.80	5227.80	5227.80
O-6	2658.90	2921.40	3112.50	3112.50	3112.50	3112.50	3112.50	3112.50	3218.10	3727.20	3917.70	4002.90	4235.10	4593.30
O-5	2126.40	2497.20	2669.70	2669.70	2669.70	2669.70	2750.70	2898.30	3092.70	3224.00	3514.80	3621.30	3747.60	3747.60
O-4	1792.50	2182.80	2328.30	2328.30	2371.50	2476.20	2645.10	2793.90	2921.40	3049.50	3133.80	3133.80	3133.80	3133.80
O-3	1665.90	1862.40	1990.80	2202.90	2308.20	2391.30	2520.60	2645.10	2710.20	2710.20	2710.20	2710.20	2710.20	2710.20
O-2	1452.60	1586.40	1905.60	1905.60	1969.80	2011.20	2011.20	2011.20	2011.20	2011.20	2011.20	2011.20	2011.20	2011.20
O-1	1260.90	1312.80	1586.40	1586.40	1586.40	1586.40	1586.40	1586.40	1506.40	1586.40	1586.40	1586.40	1586.40	1586.40
Commissioned Officers with more than 4 years active duty as Enlisted or Warrant Officer														
O-3E	0	0	0	202.90	2308.20	2391.30	2520.60	2645.10	2750.70	2750.70	2750.70	2750.70	2750.70	2750.70
O-2E	0	0	0	1969.80	2011.20	2074.80	2182.80	2266.20	2328.30	2328.30	2328.30	2328.30	2328.30	2328.30
O-1E	0	0	0	1586.40	1694.70	1757.10	1820.70	1884.00	1969.80	1969.80	1969.80	1969.80	1969.80	1969.80
Enlisted Members														
E-9	0	0	0	0	0	0	1974.00	2018.70	2064.30	2111.70	2158.80	2200.80	2316.60	2541.90
E-8	0	0	0	0	0	1655.70	1702.80	1747.50	1793.10	1840.20	1882.80	1929.00	2042.40	2270.10
E-7	1155.90	1247.70	1294.20	1339.20	1385.10	1429.20	1474.80	1520.70	1589.40	1634.70	1660.30	1702.20	1816.50	2042.40
E-6	994.50	1083.70	1129.20	1177.20	1221.00	1265.40	1311.90	1379.40	1422.60	1468.50	1491.00	1491.00	1491.40	1491.00
E-5	872.70	950.10	996.00	1039.50	1107.60	1152.60	1198.50	1242.60	1265.40	1265.40	1265.40	1265.40	1265.40	1265.40
E-4	814.20	859.50	909.90	980.70	1019.40	1019.40	1019.40	1019.40	1019.40	1019.40	1019.40	1019.40	1019.40	1019.40

Pay Grade														
E-3	766.80	808.80	841.50	874.80	874.80	874.80	874.80	874.80	874.80	874.80	874.80	874.80	874.80	874.80
E-2	738.00	738.00	738.00	738.00	738.00	738.00	738.00	738.00	738.00	738.00	738.00	738.00	738.00	738.00
E-1	658.20	658.20	658.20	658.20	658.20	658.20	658.20	658.20	658.20	658.20	658.20	658.20	658.20	658.20
E-1	608.40	608.40	608.40	608.40	608.40	608.40	608.40	608.40	608.40	608.40	608.40	608.40	608.40	608.40
E-1 with less than 4 months—590.70														

Note—Monthly pay limited to $5,900.10 by Level V of the Executive Schedule.

Basic Allowance for Subsistence

Officers (Including Commissioned Officers, Warrants and Aviation Cadets)		$112.65 per month

Enlisted	E-1 4 mos.	All Others
When Rations in Kind are Not Available	$5.61	$6.07
When on Leave or Granted Permission to Mess Separately	4.96	5.37
When Assigned under Emergency Conditions Where No Government Messing Is Available	7.43	8.03

Monthly Basic Allowance for Quarters without Dependents

Pay Grade	Full	Partial	With Dependents
O-10	$570.00	$50.70	$701.10
O-9	570.00	50.70	701.10
O-8	570.00	50.70	701.10
O-7	570.00	50.70	701.10
O-6	523.20	39.60	636.00
O-5	493.80	33.00	585.90
O-4	452.70	26.70	535.90
O-3	366.60	22.20	446.40
O-2	295.20	17.70	382.60
O-1	253.20	13.20	343.20
E-9	334.50	18.60	456.00
E-8	309.90	15.30	424.80
E-7	264.60	12.00	395.10
E-6	234.90	9.90	358.50
E-5	217.20	8.70	318.50
E-4	188.40	8.10	275.40
E-3	183.00	7.80	253.20
E-2	155.40	7.20	253.20
E-1	141.60	6.90	253.20

EXHIBIT 38.9   Survey of Customer Satisfaction

	Satisfied	Dissatisfied
Variety/Selection		X
Quality of Merchandise	X	
Prices		X
Up-To-Date Stock		X
Ease of Finding Items	X	
Meets Needs of Enlisted Personnel		X

Source: AAFES Strategic Plans & Policy Branch, AAFES Master Plan FY84-FY88, Dallas, Texas, December 23, 1982.

EXHIBIT 38.10   Major U.S. Retailing Companies by Sales

Company	1986 Sales (In millions)	Percent Change from 1985
Sears, Roebuck	$44,281	9
Kmart	23,812	8
Kroger	17,123	7
J.C. Penney	14,740	7
American Stores	14,021	1
Wal-Mart Stores	11,909	41
Federated Department Stores	10,512	5
May Department Stores	10,328	9
Dayton Hudson	9,259	12
Southland	8,620	0
Winn-Dixie Stores	8,580	7
A & P	7,072	10
F.W. Woolworth	6,501	9
Lucky Stores	6,441	3
Supermarkets General	5,508	11
Albertson's	5,380	6
Zayre	5,351	33
Melville	5,262	10
Wickes	4,770	70
Carter Hawley Hale Stores	4,090	3

Source: Business Week, April 17, 1987

overseas in early 1985 encouraged customers stationed at foreign posts to shop in the local community.[3]

AAFES sales increased over 5 percent to $5.2 billion in 1986, and net earnings increased about 34 percent to approximately $229 million. Retail sales (excluding gasoline) increased 7 percent, although gasoline sales were down

---

[3] Interview with Conners Alexander, exchange manager, AAFES-Weisbaden, Germany, September 15, 1988.

20 percent from the previous year. Food sales showed strong growth of 19 percent primarily due to the increase in the number of Burger King facilities. Service sales increased by 8 percent, although overall vending sales declined 2 percent. Reduced markdowns, 4 percent below 1985, and greater acceptance of AAFES-branded products impacted favorably on gross profit. Operating expenses increased 12 percent over the previous year due to the expansion of Burger King and implementation of credit. Although operating expenses overseas were hurt by the weaker dollar, the relatively weak dollar helped to bring customers back to the military exchanges and helped earnings. A five-year financial summary for AAFES is presented in Exhibit 38.11.

Financial Projections

AAFES financial projections for 1987–1991 were optimistic. Sales were forecasted to increase 4 percent per year, net earnings were forecasted to increase an average of 7 percent per year, and expenses to increase 3 percent per year. However, the AAFES cash position was projected to weaken through 1990 because of the costs of the distribution program. Exhibit 38.12 shows AAFES

EXHIBIT 38.11   AAFES Five-Year Financial Summary (In millions)

	FY 82	FY 83	FY 84	FY 85	FY 86
Direct Sales	$4,264.0	$4,386.0	$4,470.1	$4,484.8	$4,717.4
Concession Sales	354.7	383.9	411.0	433.2	469.4
Combined Sales	4,618.6	4,769.9	4,881.1	4,918.0	5,186.8
Gross Profit	1,010.6	1,050.1	1,047.9	1,080.4	1,254.0
Concession and Other Income	94.0	96.6	131.8[a]	118.3	
Selling, General, and Administrative Expense	901.7	925.8	934.4	1,027.6	1,152.4
Net Earnings	202.9	220.9	236.3[a]	171.1	228.9
Dividends	103.0	111.5	118.2	87.0	114.5
Dividends per Service Member (Dollar Amount)	78.28	84.59	87.71	64.49	84.38
Current Assets	990.0	1,057.2	1,121.1	1,163.5	1,228.7
Current Liabilities	461.5	485.1	493.4	494.4	599.8
Working Capital	528.6	572.1	627.7	669.0	$ 628.9
Fixed Assets (Net)	452.5	489.6	525.0	601.8	712.8
Total Assets	1,538.4	1,681.7	1,799.1	1,888.2	2,129.8
Total Liabilities	496.6	525.1	529.7	533.3	661.9
Net Assets[b]	$1,041.8	$1,156.6	$1,269.3	$1,354.8	$1,467.9
Ratio of Current Assets to Current Liabilities	2.1	2.2	2.3	2.4	2.0
Percent of Net Earnings to Average Net Assets	20.5	20.1	19.5	13.0	16.2

[a] Arithmetic differences are due to rounding.

[b] A significant amount of the assets of AAFES were originally donated by the U.S. Government. These assets were not placed on the balance sheet and have never been depreciated.

EXHIBIT 38.12   Financial Operating Projections FY 1985–1991 (In millions)

	Actual FY 1985		Estimated FY 1986		FY 1987	
Sales	$4,484,8	100.00%	$4,664.9	100.00%	$4.921.8	100.00%
Gross Profit	1,080.4	24.09	1,239.1	26.56	1,326.1	26.94
Concession Income	76.7	1.71	82.5	1.77	86.9	1.77
Other Income	41.6	0.93	41.8	0.90	40.0	0.81
Total Income	1,198.7	26.73	1,363.4	29.23	1,453.0	29.52
Personal Costs	755.9	16.86	833.7	17.87	889.8	18.08
Other Expenses	188.8	4.21	214.4	4.60	233.6	4.75
Depreciation	82.9	1.85	85.9	1.84	96.8	1.97
Total Expenses	1,027.6	22.91	1,133.9	24.31	1,220.2	24.79
Net Earnings	$ 171.1	3.81%	$ 229.5	4.92%	$ 232.8	4.73%
Return on Investment (Percent Earnings/ Net Assets)	13.04%		16.25%		15.23%	

Numbers may not add up due to rounding.

financial projections, which were based on corporate objectives, anticipated economic conditions, historical trends, inflation, the value of the U.S. dollar, and the financial benefits associated with implementation of the new distribution system. Exhibit 38.13 shows AAFES capital requirements projections.

MANAGEMENT

AAFES was operated as a military command with a functional organization structure. Exhibit 38.14 presents AAFES' organizational chart. The commander of AAFES was responsible to a Board of Directors established by the secretaries of the Army and Air Force through the respective chiefs of staff. The board consisted of seven Army and seven Air Force members plus the AAFES commander. The board met four times per year and the chairmanship of the board alternated, usually at three-year intervals, between the comptrollers of the Army and Air Force.

Functions of each organizational group are outlined in Exhibit 38.15. Within each sales region there were typically marketing, accounting and finance, human resources, general counsel, administrative, purchasing and distribution, engineering, and public affairs departments. Store managers retained responsibility for

| Long-Range Forecast | | | | | | | |
FY 1988		FY 1989		FY 1990		FY 1991	
$5,123.6	100.00%	$5,343.9	100.00%	$5,584.4	100.00%	$5,841.3	100.00%
1,396.2	27.25	1,464.2	27.40	$,532.9	27.45	1,603.4	27.45
90.8	1.77	94.7	1.77	98.8	1.77	103.0	1.76
41.2	0.80	42.5	0.79	43.8	0.78	45.1	0.77
1,528.2	29.83	1,601.4	29.97	1,675.4	30.00	1,751.5	29.98
927.9	18.11	967.2	18.10	1,008.1	18.05	1,049.6	17.97
242.2	4.73	251.7	4.71	262.0	4.69	273.3	4.68
101.5	1.98	105.2	1.97	109.3	1.96	114.0	1.95
1,271.7	24.82	1,324.1	24.78	1,379.4	24.70	1,436.9	24.60
$ 256.6	5.01%	$ 277.3	5.19%	$ 296.1	5.30%	$ 314.6	5.39%
15.54%		15.54%		15.36%		15.12%	

individual unit operations and were provided flexibility within broad sales policies. Management's primary concern was with providing service and convenience to the military community and sufficient earnings to support MWR programs.

POSITIONING STRATEGY

The AAFES commander believed that some fundamental decisions had to be made to better position AAFES in light of changes that have taken place in the retail industry. Historically, customers perceived AAFES as the most desirable place to shop, eat, and obtain various other services. Competition was limited and low prices compensated for any shortcomings.

Recently the situation changed dramatically. Large chains offering convenience, service, and low prices were readily accessible to the customer. Wal-Mart, Target, Kmart, hyperstores, warehouse clubs, fast food, and automotive parts discounters were in direct competition with AAFES. Many of the exchange customers no longer believed that AAFES was the only place to shop.

General Long advocated that AAFES was in direct competition with large retail discounters and would have to adopt marketing strategies that were suc-

EXHIBIT 38.13 Capital Requirements Projections FY 1985–1991 (In millions)

	Actual FY 85	EST FY 86	EST FY 87	EST FY 88	Long-Range Forecast		
					FY 89	FY 90	FY 91
Part 1: Sources and Applications							
Cash	$ (41)	$ (23)	$ (42)	$ (31)	$ (50)	$ (2)	$ 49
Inventory	895	890	956	978	1,004	1,034	1,068
Net Fixed Assets	602	724	867	993	1,139	1,218	1,307
Sinking Funds	174	189	142	146	151	156	161
DPP/Credit	109	111	118	123	129	135	141
Other Assets	110	135	141	150	160	170	181
Total Assets	1,849	2,026	2,182	2,359	2,533	2,711	2,907
Vendor Accounts Payable	301	294	306	319	327	336	347
Employee Benefits Payable	91	106	109	118	127	137	147
Other Liabilities	101	118	151	175	190	199	215
Dividends Payable	1	38	29	32	35	37	39
Total Liabilities	494	556	595	644	679	709	748
Capital Requirements	1,355	1,470	1,587	1,715	1,854	2,002	2,159
Part 2: Reconciliation of Capital Requirements							
Net Assets (Start of Year)	1,269	1,355	1,470	1,587	1,715	1,854	2,002
+ Earnings	171	230	233	257	277	296	315
− Dividends Declared/Estimated	85	115	116	128	139	148	157
Net Assets (Ending)	$1,355	$1,470	$1,587	$1,715	$1,854	$2,002	$2,159

Numbers may not add up due to rounding.

EXHIBIT 38.14 Army and Air Force Exchange Service Organization Chart

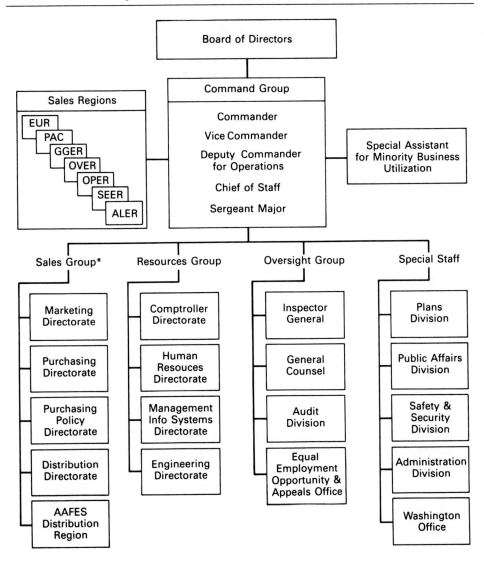

*Sales Group elements report directly to the Deputy Commander for Operations.

EXHIBIT 38.15   Organizational Responsibilities

Command Group	Directs AAFES organization within the guidelines established by Congress, Department of Defense, and the Army and Air Force. Establishes corporate policy and philosophy.
Special Staff	Responsible for representing the AAFES commander in the Washington, D.C., area with Congress, Department of Defense, and other governmental and commercial industry representatives. Provides administrative support, responsible for all planning aspects, public affairs programs, safety and security programs.
Oversight Group	Responsible for independent evaluations of the economy, effectiveness and efficiency with which management responsibilities are carried out, EOC program, morale and discipline matters affecting performance, and legal matters.
Resources Group	Responsible for financial management and accounting activities, engineering guidance, personnel, and management information systems.
Sales Group	Selecting, purchasing and controlling inventory, equipment, and supplies, distribution maintenance, purchasing policies, and marketing functions.

Source: HQ AAFES, AFESR 2.3: Organization & Functions, Dallas, Texas, October 1986.

cessful in that sector. The commander reviewed the differences and similarities of AAFES and civilian retail operations. He concluded that the primary difference between AAFES and other large retail operations was twofold. First, AAFES had a limited customer base. Second, AAFES operated under direct governmental supervision and had to support MWR programs. Most other aspects of the operation seemed very similar to civilian U.S. retail operations. As the commander pondered these similarities and differences, he thought about the strategies that would be appropriate for AAFES to fulfill its primary and secondary missions. Did AAFES no longer have a role in the compensation of military personnel? How could the exchange be positioned to compete against civilian retail stores? These and other questions needed to be carefully considered before recommendations were made to the AAFES board.

CASE 39

Schweppes Raspberry Ginger Ale

As Sam Johnson stood looking out from the window of his luxurious office, he wondered how he should go about evaluating the performance of his division's new product—Schweppes Raspberry Ginger Ale—during the first half of 1991, as compared to his expectations at the beginning of the year when the product was first introduced to the market. Further, he wondered if in fact, the product would take his division into the mainstream soft drink market as he had hoped.

COMPANY BACKGROUND

Cadbury Schweppes Public Limited Company was one of the largest British-owned confectionery and soft drinks companies with marketing operations in more than 100 countries around the world. In 1989, the company recorded total sales of £2,843.2 million and a before-tax profit of £251 million.[1] The company managed its beverage operations in North America through Cadbury Beverages North America (CBNA). CBNA was organized into several subdivisions each handling products under a specific brand, namely, Schweppes, Canada Dry, Sunkist, Crush, Hires, and Mott's. Although divisions of one company, they operated independently and competed freely in the market. A product director and an associate product manager, Sam Johnson, managed the Schweppes subdivision for the whole of North America. Exhibit 39.1 presents the organization structure of Cadbury Schweppes Public Limited Company.

THE ADULT SOFT DRINK BUSINESS

Of the several subdivisions of CBNA, both Schweppes and Canada Dry divisions marketed products that came under the broad category of adult soft

This case was prepared by Shreekant G. Joag as a basis for class discussion rather than to illustrate either effective or ineffective handling of an administrative situation. Used with permission from Shreekant G. Joag.

[1] £ 1 = U.S. $1.7.0.

EXHIBIT 39.1   Organization Structure of Cadbury Schweppes Public Limited Company

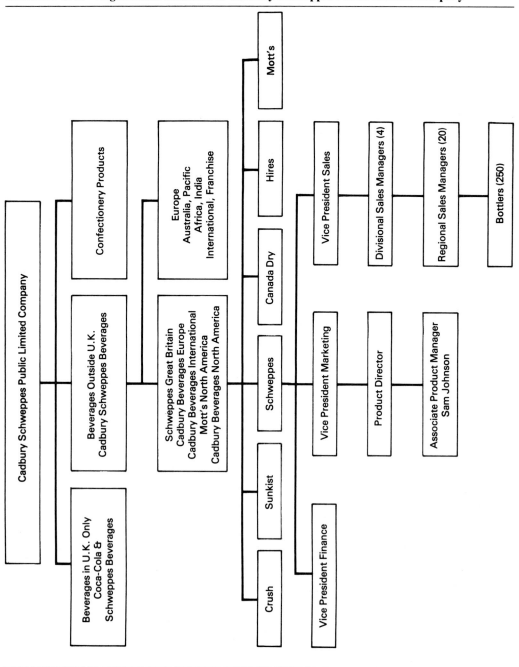

drinks. These included beverages that were used as mixers with alcoholic beverages as well as others that were consumed as general soft drinks. Adult soft drinks consisted primarily of ginger ale, club soda, tonic water, bitter lemon, unsweetened manufactured and natural sparkling waters, and sweetened sparkling waters. By composition, the sweetened sparkling waters were in fact identical to regular soft drinks even though they were marketed as waters. Exhibit 39.2 presents some basic information about adult soft drinks and the alcoholic beverages with which they are mixed. There were four leading brands in the adult soft drink market: Schweppes, Canada Dry, Seagrams, and Polar. Many brands sold flavored and unflavored versions of sparkling water. Exhibit 39.3 presents the adult soft drinks marketed by Schweppes and major competing brands.

EXHIBIT 39.2   Basic Information about Adult Soft Drinks

Soft Drink	Composition	Used as a Mixer With	Percent Consumed as a	
			Mixer	Soft Drink
Ginger Ale	Carbonated water, sugar syrup, ginger flavor	Bourbon, rye	5	95
Club Soda	Carbonated water, sodium carbonate (soda), common salt (sodium)	Whiskey	50	50
Tonic Water	Carbonated water, quinine, sugar	Gin, vodka, rum	85	15
Bitter Lemon	Carbonated water, quinine, sugar, lemon flavor	Gin, vodka	95	5
Unsweetened Sparkling Manufactured/Seltzer/ Seltzer Water	Purified water, carbonation	Used by itself for digestion	5	95
Natural	Carbonated water from natural springs	Used by itself for digestion	5	95
Sweetened Sparkling Waters	Soft drinks marketed as waters	Used by itself	5	95
Bottled Still Waters Manufactured	Purified natural lake or spring water	Used by itself for drinking	0	100
Natural	Lake or spring water as available in nature	Used by itself for drinking	0	100

Source: Schweppes, CBNA.

EXHIBIT 39.3   Competing Brands of Adult Soft Drinks

Adult Soft Drink	Schweppes (SP)	Canada Dry (CD)	Seagrams (SG)	Polar (PR)
Ginger Ale	SP ginger ale SP diet ginger ale	CD ginger ale CD diet ginger ale	SG ginger ale SG diet ginger	PR ginger ale PR diet ginger ale
Club Soda	SP club soda, SP sodium free club soda	CD club soda	SG club soda	PR club soda
Tonic Water	SP tonic water, SP diet tonic water	CD tonic water, CD diet tonic water	SG tonic water, SG diet tonic water	PR tonic water, PR diet tonic water
Bitter Lemon	SP bitter lemon	CD bitter lemon		
Unsweetened Sparkling Waters				
Manufactured- Unflavored	SP unsweetened unflavored sparkling water	CD unsweetened unflavored sparkling water	SG unsweetened unflavored sparkling water	PR unsweetened unflavored sparkling water
Manufactured- Flavored	SP unsweetened flavored sparkling water	CD unsweetened flavored sparkling water	SG unsweetened flavored sparkling water	PR unsweetened flavored sparkling water

Source: Schweppes, CBNA

Although these four brands dominated the adult soft drink market, numerous small local brands together contributed a large portion of sales. Exhibit 39.4 presents the sales of the leading brands, collective sales of all other small brands, and total industry sales of each type of adult soft drink in 1990. In the soft drink industry, general soft drinks constituted the bulk of the market. The share of adult drinks in the total soft drink market had increased modestly from 6 percent in 1980 to 7 percent in 1990. Exhibit 39.5 presents the trends in market shares of various soft drink flavors and the leading marketers within each flavor for the period 1980 to 1990.

The soft drink industry as a whole competed with all other hot and cold beverages and liquids for a share of the consumer's stomach. In the period between 1965 and 1990, the soft drink share of the average per capita consumption of all liquids increased from 17.8 gallons to 48.0 gallons per year. The total U.S. population increased from 194 million to 250 million in the same period resulting in the increase in total soft drink sales/consumption from 2,490 million cases per year to 7,940 per million cases per year. Exhibit 39.6 presents the market trends in terms of per capita consumption of various liquids in the United States from 1965 to 1990. The exhibit reports all liquid consumption figures based on the assumption that the consumer, on average, consumes 182.5 gallons of liquids in a year. The exhibit also presents the U.S. population figures and actual total sales of all soft drinks for comparison.

EXHIBIT 39.4 Sales and Market Shares of Major Brands of Adult Soft Drinks in 1990 (In thousands of cases)

Adult Soft Drink	Schweppes	Canada Dry	Seagrams	Polar	Others	Industry Total Cases	Percent of Industry
Ginger Ale	23,820	55,580	9,600	700	69,100	158,800	2.0
Club Soda	6,350	23,820	1,400	100	90	31,760	0.4
Tonic Water	19,850	15,880	2,500	450	8,960	47,640	0.6
Sparkling Waters	1,240	—	—	—	316,360	317,600	4.0
Others	—	17,845	2,980	—	177,675	198,500	2.5
Total Adult Soft Drinks	51,260	113,125	16,480	1,250	572,185	754,300	9.5
Other CBNA Products							
Sunkist		56,000					
Diet Sunkist		3,500					
Total Soft Drinks	51,260	172,625	16,480	1,250		7,940,000	100.0

Source: Estimates based on *Beverage Industry Annual Manual 90–91*, Edgell Communications Inc., New York, N.Y., 1990; Scanner Data, Schweppes, CBNA.

EXHIBIT 39.5   Soft Drink Market Trends in the United States by Flavor

	1980	1985	1990
Cola	63.0%	67.5%	70.0%
Coca-Cola Company	30.0	33.0	33.0
PepsiCo	25.0	25.0	26.0
Royal Crown Company	3.0	3.0	3.0
Others	5.0	6.5	8.0
Lemon-Lime	13.0	12.2	10.0
Coca-Cola Company	4.0	4.0	5.0
Seven-Up Company	5.0	5.0	4.0
Others	4.0	3.2	1.0
Pepper	6.0	4.9	5.0
Juice Added	—	3.9	—
Root Beer	3.0	2.7	3.0
Orange	6.0	4.7	2.5
Sunkist			0.8
Others			1.7
All Other Flavors[a]	9.0	8.0	9.5
Total All Flavors Together	100.0	100.0	100.0

All Other Flavors in 1990	9.5
Ginger Ale	2.0
Schweppes	0.3
Canada Dry	0.7
Other	1.0
Club Soda	0.4
Schweppes	0.08
Canada Dry	0.3
Other	0.02
Tonic Water	0.6
Schweppes	0.25
Canada Dry	0.20
Other	0.15
Sparkling Waters	4.0
All Remaining Flavors	2.5

[a] All figures are rounded up.

Source: Estimates based on *Beverage Industry Annual Manual 90–91,* Edgell Communications, Inc., New York, N.Y., 1990.

Because of their popular image and use as mixers, adult soft drinks were primarily sold in 1-liter polyethylene (PET) bottles rather than 12-ounce cans and 2-liter PET bottles, which were popular packages for all other soft drinks. Exhibit 39.7 presents U.S. market trends in packaging for the industry. Exhibit 39.8 presents similar market trends in the diet versus regular versions.

EXHIBIT 39.6   Liquid Market Trends in the United States

	U.S. per Capita Liquids Consumption in Gallons						
	1965	1970	1975	1980	1985	1989	1990
Soft Drinks	17.8	22.7	26.3	34.2	40.8	46.6	48.0
Coffee	37.8	35.7	33.0	27.4	25.8	24.7	23.6
Beer	15.9	18.5	21.6	24.3	23.8	23.3	23.0
Milk	24.0	23.1	22.5	20.8	20.2	20.9	20.5
Tea	3.8	5.2	7.3	7.3	7.3	7.3	7.3
Bottled Water	—	—	1.2	2.7	4.5	7.1	12.0
Juices	3.8	5.2	6.7	6.8	7.0	6.8	7.0
Powdered Drinks	—	—	4.8	6.0	6.2	4.8	5.0
Wine	1.0	1.9	1.7	2.1	2.4	2.2	2.4
Distilled Spirits	1.5	1.8	2.0	2.0	1.8	1.4	1.3
Subtotal	105.6	113.5	127.1	133.6	139.8	145.2	150.0
Imported Tap Water	76.9	69.0	55.4	48.9	42.7	37.3	32.5
Total	182.5	182.5	182.5	182.5	182.5	182.5	182.5
U.S. Population (In millions)	194.0	205.0	216.0	223.0	238.0	247.0	250.0
Soft Drink Consumption (192-oz cases in millions)	2,490	3,090	3,780	5,180	6,500	7,710	7,940

Source: *Beverage Industry Annual Manual 90–91,* Edgell Communications, Inc., New York, N.Y., 1990; figures estimated by extrapolation and *Current Population Reports: Population Estimates and Projections,* U.S. Bureau of the Census, Washington, D.C., various years.

EXHIBIT 39.7   Soft Drink Packaging Trends in the United States— Percent of Soft Drinks Using Each

Packaging	1980	1985	1990
Cans	40.0%	40.8%	50.0%
Polyethylene (PET) Bottles	30.0	30.6	30.0
Nonrecycled Glass	14.0	13.0	12.0
Recycled Glass	16.0	15.6	8.9
Total	100.0%	100.0%	100.0%

EXHIBIT 39.8   Soft Drink Market Trends in the United States— Diet versus Regular

		1980	1985	1990
Diet	M Cases	770.0	1,500.2	2,223.0
	%	15.0	23.1	28.0
Regular	M Cases	4,403.0	4,999.8	5,717.0
	%	85.0	76.9	72.0
Total	M Cases	5,180.0	6,500.0	7,940.0
	%	100.0	100.0	100.0

MANUFACTURING OF SCHWEPPES ADULT SOFT DRINKS

Both Schweppes and Canada Dry were primarily marketing companies. They imported the concentrate for tonic water from Great Britain. Concentrates for all other Schweppes soft drinks and most Canada Dry soft drinks were manufactured by the Dr. Pepper Company in the United States. Both Schweppes and Canada Dry sold the concentrate to their separate bottlers under a licensing agreement. Each bottler was assigned a territory on an exclusive basis.

Historically, colas dominated the U.S. soft drink market (70 percent market share in 1990) and to a much lesser extent by lemon-limes (10 percent market share in 1990). Further, the cola market was dominated by Coca-Cola or PepsiCo brands. Therefore, most major bottlers had exclusive agreements with either Coca-Cola or PepsiCo to market their colas as the primary product line.

Because of their heavy dependence on the cola giants, the bottlers were under great pressure to bottle and market the other soft drink products produced by the cola companies. Many medium-sized bottlers had exclusive agreements with the Seven-Up Company and depended on 7-UP as their principal product. The remaining bottlers were mostly small local companies dependent on other smaller soft drink brands. Once the principal product line was established by an exclusive agreement, the bottlers widened their product assortment by marketing other noncompeting adult soft drinks such as ginger ale, tonic water, sodas, and bottled waters and general soft drinks such as the peppers, oranges, and root beers. Thus a typical product line of a medium- to large-sized bottler would consist of one of the following three combinations:

1. Coca-Cola, Fanta, Sprite, and Schweppes or Canada Dry (but not both)
2. Pepsi Cola, Slice, Mountain Dew, and Schweppes or Canada Dry (but not both)
3. 7-Up, 7-Up Gold, a noncompeting cola, and Schweppes or Canada Dry (but not both)

Fortunately for Schweppes and Canada Dry, Coca-Cola, Pepsi, and Seven-Up did not have their own brands of adult soft drinks. Therefore, the products marketed by Schweppes and Canada Dry complemented the general soft drinks of the cola and the lemon-lime giants. This made it relatively easy for them to convince major bottlers to accept adult soft drinks as complementary to their main product lines. Thus, though rigidly defined by factors beyond their control, Schweppes and Canada Dry found the market structure to be excellent. In some territories Schweppes had exclusive agreements with Coca-Cola bottlers to market its adult soft drinks and Canada Dry had exclusive agreements with Pepsi bottlers. In some other territories, Schweppes went with Pepsi bottlers while Canada Dry went with Coca-Cola bottlers. Thus, Schweppes and Canada Dry both marketed their products through Coca-Cola as well as PepsiCo bottlers. However, in no territory did Schweppes and Canada Dry use a common bottler. The competition between Schweppes and Canada Dry was carried out in earnest in every aspect of the business.

In addition, historically, Canada Dry had developed a network of exclusive Canada Dry bottlers. Though totally committed to Canada Dry, their strength and importance in the market as well as to Canada Dry had gradually been reduced because of their limited product line. The total volume of soft drink business handled by each bottler ranged from 500 thousand cases to 50 million cases per year, with 3 million cases per year as the typical size.

DISTRIBUTION OF ADULT SOFT DRINKS

The exclusive agreements made the bottlers solely responsible for distributing the soft drinks of their principals in the assigned territories. Armed with the exclusive distributorship of a full range of products, each bottler competed with the others to market its products through the various channels available. Depending on its relative influence, each bottler obtained its share of the space in supermarkets, drug stores, retail chains, convenience stores, gas stations, vending machines, and other outlets for soft drinks.

Marketers commonly classified store space as shelf space or display space. Shelf space was the regular space allocated to a product on the shelves in the aisles. Display space was the space on the shelves located at the end of the aisles that faced outward toward the periphery of the store. Over half of all shoppers invariably circled the store to buy daily necessities such as meats, vegetables, dairy products, and bakery products which the stores positioned along the periphery. The customers entered the aisles only when they needed specific items located there. As such, the end-of-aisle displays received the maximum consumer exposure and served to remind consumers of the items they might need. Thus, the shelf space and the display space each had its unique role in generating sales. Both were very precious to retailers, bottlers, and the soft drink companies alike. Naturally, there was great competition to acquire an adequate share of the limited store space.

Once a bottler had negotiated the store space with the retailers, management had to determine how to allocate it optimally among the various soft drink brands so as to offer a complete assortment to the consumers and maximize sales and profits. Conventionally, the bottlers displayed the general soft drinks, adult soft drinks, and the bottled waters in separate groups, though in close proximity to one another. Typically the colas and the lemon-limes accounted for most of the business of a bottler with the adult soft drinks constituting an important but very small portion of the business. Invariably the cola and the lemon-lime companies were able to dictate their terms in deciding the allocation of the total store space available to a bottler. As such, the colas and the lemon-limes dominated all prime display space and a large portion of the shelf space as well. In comparison, adult soft drinks had to fight hard for adequate shelf space. Fortunately, the dominant position of Canada Dry and Schweppes in the adult soft drink group and the noncompeting nature of their product lines made the task of obtaining shelf space slightly less difficult. Adult soft drinks accounted for 1 to 15 percent of the total business of Schweppes' bottlers, with 3.3 percent as the typical proportion. Generally a store carried an average inventory of six cases of each soft drink product that turned over 25 times in a year. The relatively low bargaining power of even large bottlers of adult soft drinks made the marketing of adult soft drinks one of the toughest and most challenging tasks. Convincing the bottlers to allocate adequate space to adult soft drink brands became the primary focus of Schweppes' marketing efforts. Johnson described the task: "Our bottlers spill more Coke or Pepsi than the ginger ale they sell. We have no illusions here. Although we make an important contribution to their profits, it is only a small contribution. They do not really depend on us. We need them far more than they need us."

SCHWEPPES GINGER ALE PRODUCT LINE

Ginger ale consists of carbonated water, sugar syrup, and ginger flavor. Both Schweppes and Canada Dry marketed their own brands of ginger ale in regular and diet varieties. A much larger quantity of ginger ale was consumed when used as a soft drink than as a mixer. Therefore, in regions where both applications were popular, the consumption as a soft drink invariably generated the bulk of the sales volume. The relative consumption of the product for these two purposes varied in different regions of the United States. In the Northeast, ginger ale was equally popular as a soft drink or as a mixer. In the West, it was primarily consumed as a mixer with alcohol. Because the sales of both Schweppes and Canada Dry were heavily concentrated in the Northeast, a very large proportion of the total ginger ale marketed by the two divisions was consumed as a soft drink.

It was fair to assume that the various brands of ginger ale competed among themselves for the market segment preferring ginger ale flavor. However, in a general sense, they also competed with all other adult soft drinks as well as all general soft drinks, and even all hot and cold beverages. Canada Dry was the largest marketer of ginger ale in North America, controlling 33.5 percent of the U.S. ginger ale market. Schweppes was the second largest marketer with 16.6 percent share of the market. The third competitor, Seagrams, had only 3.1 percent of the market.

CONSUMER IMAGE OF GINGER ALE

Despite the predominant use of ginger ale as a soft drink, most consumers did not think of ginger ale as a soft drink. Several unaided recall tests among users and nonusers of ginger ale had shown that very few people remembered or considered ginger ale to be a general soft drink. Most people primarily considered it either as a mixer or as a soft drink for special occasions such as adult social gatherings when alcohol was being consumed. There were many possible explanations for this phenomenon.

As mentioned previously, a person tended to consume a much larger quantity of ginger ale as a soft drink as compared to the quantity consumed as a mixer. Although the bulk of the ginger ale was consumed as a soft drink, only a small number of consumers were involved in generating that volume with each person consuming a relatively large quantity. In contrast, a relatively larger number of consumers were involved in generating a relatively smaller sales volume of ginger ale as a mixer, with each person consuming a small quantity of the soft drink. Such consumption was often in an adult setting where at least some people were consuming alcohol. This further confirmed the association of ginger ale with alcohol in the consumers' perceptions.

In addition, the small market share of ginger ale compared to all soft drinks suggested that a large proportion of individuals were nonusers of the product. The image of ginger ale in the minds of such consumers was based on where they saw it being consumed and what they heard about it. On both these accounts, the probability was far greater that the nonusers encountered the ginger ale as a mixer rather than as a soft drink.

The bottlers also perceived ginger ale primarily as a mixer; therefore, they distributed it mainly in 1-liter PET bottles and promoted it as a mixer. This further confirmed and perpetuated the consumer image of ginger ale as a mixer. The only exception was in the Northeast, where the product was widely available in popular soft drink packaging of 12-ounce cans and 2-liter PET bottles.

Interestingly, surveys showed that even those who consumed ginger ale as a soft drink considered it primarily a mixer. Johnson was always puzzled by this apparent contradiction in the use of the product and its image. Further, he often felt that such a distorted image prevented ginger ale from exploiting its full potential as a tasty, refreshing general-purpose soft drink for all occasions. He wondered what he could possibly do to change the image of the product and reposition it in the consumer's mind as a mainstream general soft drink.

SCHWEPPES RASPBERRY GINGER ALE

In May 1988, one of the Schweppes' leading bottlers conceived the idea of marketing raspberry-flavored ginger ale as a general soft drink for all occasions. After obtaining initial clearance to explore the concept further, Johnson spent considerable time perfecting the product ingredients and conducting laboratory and field tests. The tests indicated that the product had a unique, appealing taste, and many of those who tried it felt that it was a fascinating new soft drink. By October 1990, the product was fully developed and Schweppes had to make the final decision about its commercial introduction. Johnson realized that product development was perhaps the easiest part of the whole process. The real challenge was to analyze the feasibility of the idea and prepare a new product proposal to convince top management to proceed with the product's introduction. Once that decision was made, Johnson would have to convince the bottlers to adopt the product and obtain their commitment to make it available in retail outlets by January 1991.

Johnson was really excited about Schweppes Raspberry Ginger Ale (SRGA). He had always felt that for some unknown reason all Schweppes adult soft drinks and especially ginger ale had been locked in the upscale mixer image that limited their growth potential and isolated them from the volume business of the mainstream general soft drinks. However, he was confident that the SRGA had a unique and distinct personality that was powerful enough to make a clear break from the ginger ale's traditional image and present itself as a legitimate general soft drink before the bottlers as well as the ultimate consumers. He felt that this product could launch the company on a totally new course to become a major player in the soft drink industry in time to come. This was an ideal way to bridge the gap between the company's image as a marketer of mixers and its desire to be a mainstream soft drink company.

In principle, the idea of creating new flavored versions of established soft drinks was not totally new. Other leading soft drink manufacturers had introduced different flavored soft drinks. Some of these products, such as Cherry Coke and Cherry 7-UP had achieved limited success in the market, whereas others such as 7-UP Gold had failed and had to be withdrawn. Although the moderately successful products had created small segments of loyal consumers, they had been tried and rejected by many others. These consumers may be less enthusiastic about trying such new product versions the next time. Thus, despite the support of a major bottler, the product's unique refreshing taste, and strong consumer appeal, the company feared that it might face strong consumer resistance or disinterest. Moreover, Schweppes had always taken pride in its upscale image, if not its snob appeal. The new product concept aimed at the mass market might not fit this image as well.

Another area of uncertainty was the effect SRGA would have on other Schweppes products, as well as on Canada Dry and other CBNA divisions. Johnson felt that his immediate concern was to estimate the extent to which SRGA would cannibalize Schweppes' own ginger ale business. As a conservative estimate, he felt that initially about 20 percent of all SRGA sales would come from ginger ale. The cannibalized volume of Schweppes ginger ale would peak at 2 million cases per year and level off. However, he had no idea how the new product would impact various other brands of CBNA and other competitors in the market.

Johnson realized that he would have to modify the strategy he developed to convince his top management for them to convince the bottlers. In turn, he would have to help the bottlers convince the retailers to adopt the product. His major thrust would have to be on the new business generated by SRGA and the increase in total profits earned by each channel member.

In order to analyze the feasibility of SRGA, Johnson had compiled all relevant information. He estimated that ginger ale sold at an average price of $10 per 192-ounce case to the ultimate consumer. SRGA would be sold at about the same price. The retailers expected a margin of 20 percent on their sales revenue. Similarly, bottlers expected a margin of 25 percent on their sales to the retailers. The cost of each case to the bottler was $1 for the ginger ale concentrate paid to Schweppes, $2 for other variable materials, and $3 for all other variable costs. In Johnson's opinion, the channel members earned similar margins on all other major competing brands. Schweppes would have to sell SRGA concentrate to the bottlers at the same price as that of ginger ale concentrate.

For Schweppes, the cost of buying the ginger ale concentrate from its supplier was 15 percent of its sales revenue. In addition, Schweppes spent 45 percent of its sales revenue for marketing expenses. The SRGA concentrate would cost Schweppes 20 percent of sales and its marketing costs would be 50 percent of sales. In addition, $990,000 would have to be spent on introductory promotions.

Johnson realized that his first task would be to analyze how consumers were likely to perceive the new product in comparison with Schweppes ginger ale. Such an analysis would help him to understand what efforts he had to make to successfully position SGRA as a main stream soft drink. On the basis of his previous experience with new products and considering the fact that SRGA was to be introduced as a main-stream soft drink, Johnson's conservative forecast of SRGA sales in the first five years was 2, 5, 8, 10, and 14 million cases. Using these figures as the basis, Johnson now had to establish SRGA's feasibility for Schweppes, its bottlers, and its retailers. He would also have to estimate the likely consumer response to the new product. He realized that he would have to prepare his new product proposal shortly so that there was sufficient time to approach the bottlers and actually introduce the product by January 1991.

MARKET INTRODUCTION OF SCHWEPPES RASPBERRY GINGER ALE

In January 1991, Schweppes Raspberry Ginger Ale was introduced nationally in the United States with full fanfare, spending a total of $1 million on introductory promotions. By the end of June, the company had surpassed all sales forecasts and sold 2 million cases of SRGA. When management compared the performance of various Schweppes product lines in the first six months of 1991 with the same period of 1990, they observed that Schweppes ginger ale sales had stayed at 15.6 million cases, although all other Schweppes products had recorded an increase of 4 percent, the same as the growth rate of the soft drink industry.

In an attempt to understand what impact SRGA had made on the other brands, the company conducted a consumer survey. Using a consumer panel the

EXHIBIT 39.9   Percent of SRGA Sales Sourced from Various Competing Brands

Soft Drink Types	Schweppes	Canada Dry	Other CBNA	Total CBNA	Other Competitors	Total
Colas					22	22
Lemon-Lime					10	10
Peppers					1	1
Root Beer					5	5
Orange			3	3	11	14
All Other Flavors[a]	4	23	—	27	21	48
Total	4	23	3	30	70	100
[a]All Other Flavors						
Ginger Ales	3	23		26	10	36
Club Soda +						
Tonic Water	1	0		1	0	1
Bottled Waters					1	1
Other					10	10

Source: Schweppes, CBNA Consumer Study, January–June 1991.

study compared actual purchases of various brands during the first six months of 1990 compared to the first six months of 1991. The data were analyzed to determine what percentage of total SRGA sales had been generated at the cost of various other brands. The results of the study are summarized in Exhibit 39.9. Johnson realized that he had only a few days to analyze the SRGA's sales performance and the results of the survey. By the following week, he would have to present his findings before CBNA's top management and recommend a future course of action.

--------------------- CASE 40 ---------------------

The *Dallas Morning News*

As they contemplated the situation facing the *Dallas Morning News* (MN), Burl Osborne (president and editor), Jeremy Halbreich (executive vice president and general manager), and other members of the MN's top management knew that they faced important and difficult decisions as they developed a strategic marketing plan into the 1990s. Further, these executives realized the necessity of their daily 10:00 A.M. meeting to review and adjust their strategic and tactical decisions.

The dynamics of the now-soft Dallas–Ft. Worth market plus the actions of the rival *Dallas Times Herald* (TH) and other media competitors for both readers' attention and advertisers' dollars, assured Osborne and Halbreich that developing a new five-year strategic marketing plan for the MN would be a challenging enterprise.

The trade press loved the continuing battle waged between the MN and the TH. For years the duel had been largely nip-and-tuck, but in the first half of 1985 the MN had gained a significant circulation advantage in the TH's long-term strength—Dallas County (see Exhibit 40.1). Some industry analysts suggested the battle in Dallas for newspaper supremacy was over—won by the MN.

In 1986, after 16 years in Dallas, the TH's corporate parent, Times-Mirror, sold the TH to the Media News Group for $110 million effective September 1, 1986. In announcing the sale, Robert Erburu, chairman and chief executive officer of Times-Mirror, commented, "Times-Mirror is very proud of the achievements of the *Dallas Times Herald*, but we believe that its sale at this time is consistent with our corporate strategy and is in the best interests of the long-term future of the *Times Herald*."

From the other side of the sale, Dean Singleton, president of Media News, boasted, "If I didn't think the *Times Herald* could beat the *Morning News*, I wouldn't have bought it."

Under Mr. Singleton's direction, the TH filed a circulation fraud suit in federal district court in Chicago against the MN, naming the Audit Bureau of Circulation as co-defendant. The MN promptly filed a countersuit against the TH

EXHIBIT 40.1   Circulation of Dallas Newspapers, 1978–1987 (In thousands)

		Daily			Sunday		
		City Zone[a]	MSA	Total	City Zone[a]	MSA	Total
1987[b]	MN	n/a	n/a	388	n/a	n/a	541
	TH	n/a	n/a	240	n/a	n/a	338
	Hhlds						
1986	MN	239	313[c]	390	320	425[c]	522
	TH	182	216[d]	245	254	305[d]	348
	Hhlds						
1985	MN	230	297[c]	369	295	384[c]	476
	TH	183	214[d]	241	257	303[d]	346
	Hhlds	679	1,290[c]		679	858[d]	
1984	MN	207	267[c]	331	258	339[c]	421
	TH	193	224[d]	252	259	304[d]	346
	Hhlds	656	1,239[c]		656	826[d]	
1983	MN	206	261	321	248	320	397
	TH	210	253	268	271	330	355
	Hhlds	647	n/a		647	n/a	
1982	MN	195	242	295	237	298	368
	TH	200	241	254	261	317	341
	Hhlds	628	n/a		628	n/a	
1981	MN	188	232	284	230	287	356
	TH	194	230	244	263	315	338
	Hhlds	607	1,138		607	1,138	
1980	MN	188	229	279	225	279	346
	TH	195	232	245	263	316	339
	Hhlds	592	1,105		592	1,105	
1979	MN	185	226	277	220	271	341
	TH	195	235	247	264	314	336
	Hhlds	538	989		538	989	
1978	MN	189	225	277	223	271	345
	TH	204	238	249	267	316	338
	Hhlds	522	954		522	954	

[a] City Zone is Dallas County. The MSA is an 11-county area made up of the following counties: Collin, Dallas, Denton, Ellis, Hood, Johnson, Kaufman, Parker, Rockwell, Tarrant, and Wise.

[b] 1987 figures are unaudited.

[c] In 1984, the MN switched from a MSA to a CSA, which consists of a nine-county area (the MSA less Hood and Wise.)

[d] In 1984, the TH switched from a MSA to a CSA, which consists of a six-county area (the MSA less Hood, Johnson, Parker, Tarrant, and Wise).

n/a = not available

Hhlds = households

Source: 1977–1986—ABC Audit Reports; 1987—*Adweek,* May 18, 1987, p. 3; *Sales & Marketing Management,* 1978–1986.

also claiming circulation fraud and suggested that the TH's legal action was designed primarily to cloud the circulation issue.

In November 1986, Texas Attorney-General Jim Mattox announced that he had begun investigating the circulation practices of both papers. Mr. Mattox quickly found no wrongdoing at the TH. On the other hand, in February 1987, Mr. Mattox formally notified the MN that he would continue his investigation of the MN to determine if the paper had violated the state's deceptive trade practices. MN officials contended that Mr. Mattox's actions were in retaliation for the MN's coverage of his conduct in office, questionable campaign contributions, and the MN's endorsement of his opponent in the fall 1986 election. The TH had endorsed Mr. Mattox.

More recently, the attorney-general indicated that he would examine the circulation practices of both newspapers. Further, his investigation would not begin until after new ABC circulation figures were available.

At the TH, Mr. Singleton, Art Wible (publisher), David Burgin (senior vice president and editor), John Wolf (senior vice president, marketing/advertising), and other members of the TH's top management team were experienced and aggressive competitors. They could be counted on to continue to generate aggressive marketing actions as they attempted to swing the tide to their advantage.

HISTORY OF THE *DALLAS MORNING NEWS*

Build the News upon
the rock of truth
and righteousness
Conduct it always
upon the lines of
fairness and integrity
Acknowledge the right
of the people to get
from the newspaper
both sides of every
important question
G. B. Dealey

The words above were inscribed on the facade of the present MN building. This admonition was an excerpt from a speech delivered in 1906 by G. B. Dealey, founder of the MN, at the dedication of an employees' library. This statement set forth the philosophy that has guided the newspaper since its inception.

Mr. Dealey began his newspaper career as an office boy with the *Galveston News* in 1874 at the age of 15. Because of his initiative and enthusiasm, he was asked to travel to north Texas in 1882 by Colonel A. H. Belo (owner of the *Galveston News*) to begin researching a plant site for a new newspaper.

Mr. Dealey recommended the growing railhead community of Dallas as the best location.

On October 1, 1885, the MN published its first edition as a subsidiary of the *Galveston News*. In 1894, Mr. Dealey was promoted from business manager to general manager of the MN and in 1920 he was elected president. In 1926, Mr. Dealey purchased the MN and a Dallas radio station from the Belo family. In addition, he reorganized the company and changed its name to the A.H. Belo Corporation. Mr. Dealey served as publisher of the MN from 1926 until his death in 1946 at the age of 86.

In 1981, the Belo Corporation sold shares of common stock in an initial offering on the American Stock Exchange (later the stock was moved to the New York Stock Exchange). Mr. Dealey's descendants remain the largest stockholders in Belo. The corporation was ranked as the 27th largest U.S. media company in 1986 by *Ad Age*. The principal business activities of Belo were newspaper publishing and network television broadcasting.

Belo's principal newspaper property was the MN. In addition, the company owned Dallas–Ft. Worth Suburban Newspapers, a group of seven community newspapers located in the suburbs of the Dallas–Ft. Worth metroplex. The corporation also owned five network affiliate television stations in Dallas, Houston, Sacramento, Tulsa, and Hampton-Norfolk, Virginia.

In 1984, newspaper publishing contributed 55 percent of Belo's revenues and 35 percent of profits. Broadcasting contributed roughly 45 percent of revenues and 65 percent of profits. In 1985, newspaper publishing contributed 57 percent of revenues and 39 percent of profits. Total operating revenues (in millions) were: 1982—$203.4; 1983—$242.6; 1984—$354.2; 1985—$385.1; and 1986—$397.2.

THE RIVAL: THE *DALLAS TIMES HERALD*

The TH is presently owned by the MediaNews Group Corporation, headquartered in Dallas. MediaNews was ranked as the 74th largest media company in 1986 by *Ad Age* before the company acquired the TH. MediaNews' principal business was newspaper publishing. The corporation owned 22 small- and medium-sized dailies plus the TH, which was the largest.

In 1985, the company reported revenues of $150 million. The privately held company was founded in 1983 by Dean Singleton and Richard Scudder when they jointly purchased the *Gloucester County Times* in Woodbury, New Jersey. Since the company's establishment, it followed an aggressive acquisition strategy.

Dallas Times Herald Strategy—1970s

In the mid-1970s, executives at the TH had become increasingly uneasy about growth trends in the Dallas market and the handicaps of an afternoon delivery. The population was growing at a very rapid rate and, at the same time, becoming more affluent demographically. TH executives worried that the MN's traditionally upscale appeal and positioning would allow the MN to dominate among the more affluent new residents who were arriving in large numbers. Further, the majority of the newcomers preferred a morning newspaper.

The trend in Dallas and across the country toward more white-collar, service-oriented jobs was running against the long-run viability of many afternoon dailies. Many considerations favored morning delivery—for example, morning newspapers enjoyed reduced competition with evening television, home delivery was cheaper, a larger geographic area could be served, classified advertising was more attractive, and morning papers had higher pass-along readership.

In developing a marketing strategy for long-term growth in this environment, TH management decided on two major actions. First, they targeted three reader groups—newcomers, females, and young adults. This strategy built on traditional TH strength among females and young adults. In addition, this strategy was seen as an investment in the future and one safe from MN retaliation. TH executives felt that the MN would be restricted by pressure from its establishment and rural base to maintain the status quo. Further, an assessment of the likely aggressiveness of the MN's top management suggested complacency. As one TH executive noted, "Times Mirror looked at the *Morning News* as some kind of country bumpkin who was fat and dumb."

Second, the TH became an all-day newspaper. On September 12, 1977, the TH published its first weekday morning edition. The MN no longer had a morning monopoly. This move by the TH sent a clear message to the MN that the level of competition was escalating.

The *Dallas Morning News* Responds

Early in 1979, in a move to add some research insights into their marketing strategy, the MN retained Yankelovich, Skelly, and White (a marketing research firm) to conduct a profile study of the Dallas market. The "All Market Study" sampled the entire Dallas–Ft. Worth area and was to be repeated every two years. Based on the findings, the MN would develop a plan to improve readership among the 25–34 and 35–44 age groups, gain the Sunday circulation lead in the metropolitan statistical area, publish the majority of all retail advertising linage, and strengthen its classified share. However, before priorities were set and a schedule for implementation was developed, MN management wanted to carefully study their options and find a replacement for their retiring editor.

Commenting on the "All Market Study," Jeremy Halbreich (at that time marketing director at the MN) stressed:

> The study tells us not only who is out there, more than just the demographics of the market. It tells us what the people in our market are interested in, what is important to them, what are their social, civic, economic, and education concerns, their likes, their dislikes and their lifestyles. And, of course, it tells us about their reading and other media habits.

Based on the Yankelovich study, management at the MN initially concluded that they should bolster coverage of the following areas: business, fashion, sports, arts and entertainment, plus local, state, national, and international news.

While the MN was studying the market and developing plans, the TH continued to press forward with changes designed to strengthen its product. (See Exhibit 40.2 for a summary of the MN–TH marketing battles.) On August 8, 1979, the TH introduced a redesigned format to project a more upscale image. The somewhat trendy and liberal design instituted in 1972 was replaced by a more classic and conservative look. TH management had hoped the new logo would create a sense of credibility and stability. Importantly, TH management sought to give the paper "the look of a morning newspaper."

In response to the TH's design changes, the MN reacted strongly through the vehicle of television commercials and print ads. For example, a 30-second television commercial portrayed the two newspapers as men buying clothing. The neat, slim, decisive man (MN) bought confidently and conservatively. On the other hand, the overweight, disheveled man (TH) was unable to choose between various styles and bought an unusual assortment. The voice-over sarcastically observed: "Some papers change their looks as often as some people change their clothes. At the *Dallas Morning News*, we know who we are."

The MN also began running a series of aggressive ads in the advertising trade press. These ads served to boost morale at the MN where management had been in a reacting posture for some time. The ads also served to irritate management at the TH.

In the fall of 1980, with time to analyze the results of the Yankelovich study and circulation trends, and with new leadership in place in the news department, senior executives of the MN consolidated their conclusions and set both short- and long-term objectives for their newspaper.

The overall objective was a significant increase in both the absolute and perceived margin of leadership in the market in terms of product quality, circulation, and advertising leadership.

Management at the MN decided that the pathway to dominance consisted of strong, broadly based product improvement accompanied by appropriate marketing and promotional activities, as the foundation for circulation growth. The executives felt that circulation growth obtained by following this strategy, although requiring more time, would be more enduring than growth obtained by heavy discounting, contests, or other short-term promotions. Further, it was agreed that a well-promoted high-quality product that could assist circulation growth also would help to achieve increased advertising market share.

Since initially the greatest need was seen to be in improving Sunday readership, much emphasis would be placed on product improvement that could be reflected in the Sunday package.

EXHIBIT 40.2   Marketing Battle Summary

Dallas Morning News	*Dallas Times Herald*
1978	
Launched "Fashion! Dallas" section for Wednesday paper.	Upcoming morning edition heavily advertised/promoted.
Established Ft. Worth News Bureau.	Expanded Sunday edition.
Introduced/expanded sports in "Sports Spectrum" (later discontinued).	Expanded coverage of Ft. Worth.
Expanded business coverage.	Added Saturday real estate section.
	Added Sunday travel section.
	Added Sunday fashion section "Style" (one week before MN's "Fashion! Dallas").
	Expanded business news coverage.
	Introduced/expanded sports in "Sportsweek" (later discontinued).
1979	
Promoted lead in circulation over TH in comparative ads.	Redesigned format—more upscale, classic, and conservative.
Radio advertising sarcastic and comparative.	Promoted redesigned format and expanded coverage begun in 1978.
Began expansion of investigative reporting staff and coverage.	Improved investigative reporting.
1980	
Expanded coverage throughout the state.	Distribution reorganized: morning distribution taken from independent distributors and brought in-house, afternoon distribution remained unchanged.
Expanded local news.	
Expanded sports.	
Added fashion to Sunday as well as Wednesday edition.	Morale among distributors plummets and many move to MN.
Added lifestyles/arts section to Sunday edition.	Sales promotions lower prices: newcomer discounts, complimentary copies distributed to hotels, etc.
Added television listing/events.	
Added "Business Tuesday" May 1, 1980.	
Increased price from 15 cents to 25 cents daily, June 1, 1980, no change in ad rates.	Dropped "Parade" magazine, replaced with TH's own "Westward." Increased price from 15 cents to 25 cents daily, classified ad rates raised as well.
1981	
Expanded national/international news coverage.	Sold weekend "package" for $3.50, same as MN price, but included Friday, as well as Saturday and Sunday.
50 percent discount to new subscribers for one month.	
Ad rates increased: daily rates same as TH, Sunday 50% less than TH, classified from $.35 to $.40 per line.	Expanded national/international news coverage.
	New subscribers promotion: for 3 months—7-day service for the price of 3-day service.
Redesigned graphics (masthead unchanged) to make paper "uncluttered and easy to read."	Returned distribution to independent distributors.
MN answers circulation fraud charges to ABC's satisfaction.	Ad rates increased: daily became same as MN, Sunday 50% more than MN, classified from $.40 to $.45.

EXHIBIT 40.2 (continued)

Dallas Morning News	*Dallas Times Herald*
Ann Landers column moves from TH to MN.	Requested investigation of ABC circulation figures for MN.
Weekend "package" expanded to include Friday.	After 23 years, Ann Landers column leaves TH.
Expanded sports coverage with "Sports Day" section.	Increased community involvement: programs honoring high school students, athletes, the arts (long considered a MN strength).
"Parade" magazine added to Sunday paper.	
Upgraded Sunday "Arts & Entertainment" section.	
Launched "La Vida American" series on Hispanic life in America.	
"Texas & Southwest" section introduced to expand coverage of state news.	

1982

Advertising rate increase (causes most advertisers to choose one newspaper).	Advertising rate increase, advertising market share decrease due to advertisers being able to afford only one paper—many chose MN.
Advertising market share increase (Exhibit 40.19).	Distribution brought back in-house and improved.
Heavily promoted sportswriter Skip Bayless moves to TH for big dollars, two new sports writers promoted—no apparent loss in circulation.	Expanded circulation discounts and sampling.
	Afternoon delivery outside Dallas county discontinued.
	7-11 promotion: cup of coffee and the TH for $.38.
	Sportswriter Skip Bayless hired away from MN (see Exhibit 40.17).
	Other "big names" added to editorial staff.
	"Mid-cities" section for local community coverage introduced (later dropped).
	Introduced Wednesday fashion section, "Unique."
	Discounted ad rates and offered selective rebates.
	Circulation and ad lineage are up (see Exhibit 40.18).

1983

Added special "Energy Report" to Wednesday business coverage.	Introduced Saturday Real Estate classified section.
Added economy emphasis to Thursday business coverage.	Emphasized promotions, especially games/contests.
Increased metro news coverage.	Distribution back to independent dealers because of low circulation for morning edition.
Expanded weather news coverage.	
Improved Sunday "TV Guide" quality.	
Expanded arts and entertainment coverage to seven days.	
Lured Blackie Sherrod, TH sportswriter, to MN, effective January 1, 1985.	
7-11 promotion: Free Sunday MN with coffee at 25 cents.	
Recognized "Sports Day" as one of the top 10 best sports sections in the United States.	

EXHIBIT 40.2   (continued)

Dallas Morning News	*Dallas Times Herald*
1984	
Requested investigation of ABC circulation figures for TH.	Major management changes occurred at all levels.
Increased price of weekend package (Friday, Saturday, Sunday) to $5, matching TH.	Sold half-price subscriptions by telephone.
Obtained exclusive rights to run Michael Jackson concert tickets.	Redesigned "living" section and arts/entertainment added.
Added extensive, extra coverage for the Republican convention held in Dallas.	"Community Close-Up" offered advertisers eight different geographic zones.
Upgraded MN "Sunday Magazine" to magazine-quality paper.	Moved "Unique" society section from Wednesday to Sunday, and "Style" from Sunday to Wednesday.
	Dropped "Perspectives" and "Living" as separate Sunday sections, "Arts & Leisure" added.
	Last day for acclaimed sportswriter Blackie Sherrod, December 31, 1984, who moved to the MN.
1985	
Blackie Sherrod joins the sports staff (see Exhibit 40.20).	50 percent discount offered for the second ad run in a one-week period.
Began offset printing in the new North Plant in Plano.	Subscription promotion: "3 months for the price of 2.
Added international component to the Monday business section.	Replaced Sunday magazine "Westward" with Dallas City.
National, retail, and classified ad rates increased 11 percent.	Promotions to increase single-copy sales.
	Cut classified ad rates 20 percent, offered 15 percent discount to agencies on classified linage.
1986	
Pulitzer prize awarded to two MN staff writers, finalist in three other categories; general news reporting, feature photography, spot news photography.	June: Times-Mirror announces sale of TH to MediaNews for $110 million (see Exhibit 40.21).
	Sale completed September 5:
	• 109 full-time employees removed
	• Four news bureaus closed
	• "Dallas City" magazine dropped
	• Section headings redesigned, more people-oriented information added, more/better color— TH became more "USA Todayish"
	• Focus on local news
	Dropped Friday "Entertainment," Sunday "Unique," Sunday "Arts & Entertainment," Wednesday "Fashion" sections.
	Added Sunday "Datebook" entertainment section, including gossip, events, movie reviews, etc.

Additionally, it was felt that greater margins of leadership in certain "franchise" areas of readership—business, sports, fashion, local, and lifestyle news—was essential. Because much planning for a special business section had already been done, it was decided that the first product change to be introduced would be in business.

On November 11, 1980, one of the priorities MN management identified through the Yankelovich research resulted in a new section—"Business Tuesday." Yankelovich data had clearly indicated that business news was critical to defending the MN's morning franchise. To produce the new section with greatly expanded local and regional coverage, the size of the business staff was doubled. A new design that included new headline faces, graphics, and indexes was added to give the section a crisp appearance.

The new expanded business coverage concentrating on Tuesday was part of the MN's overall strategy to substantially increase business coverage seven days a week. Growing financial linage prompted the MN to give its business section a high priority.

The MN launched "Business Tuesday" with major advertising support. Trade and consumer promotions began six weeks prior to the launch of the section. Radio and television spots plus outdoor were used extensively to promote the section. A four-week sampling program exposed thousands of nonsubscribers to the section.

Advertising had become a year-round, integral part of the MN's marketing strategy. In 1980, part of the MN's marketing strategy was to focus on building Sunday circulation. Sunday had long been the TH's strong suit, and management at the MN wanted to change the situation. To target its Sunday promotions, the MN selected radio as the most appropriate medium. A fixed jingle ("Sunday isn't Sunday without the *Dallas Morning News*) was created to build familiarity, and live feeds were inserted to provide specifics.

Other strategies were implemented to improve MN's market standing or negate gains of the TH. See Exhibit 40.2 for specific activities through the mid-1980s.

During 1983, independent research studies indicated that the MN was not only able to defend its leadership position with upscale readers but had made some progress with younger readers. The MN also performed well in retail, classified, and other advertising linage categories.

As a result of larger advertising volume and larger newshole, the MN consistently published a larger product. The MN ran more pages in classified, business, sports, local news, fashion, and the real estate sections.

In May 1985, the March ABC figures were released. These figures indicated a substantial circulation lead for the MN. The MN figures were up significantly over the previous period, while the TH figures dropped substantially. The MN featured this advantage in trade advertising (see Exhibit 40.3).

EXHIBIT 40.3   *Dallas Morning News* Advertisement

What's the real difference between the two Dallas dailies?

Over 125,000 papers. Every day.

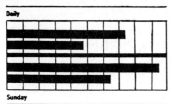

The latest circulation figures* are out. And the news is record-breaking!

As of March 31, 1985, the Audit Bureau of Circulations (ABC) shows The Dallas Morning News not only has the largest daily and Sunday circulation of any newspaper in Dallas history, but it also shows we lead the Times Herald by more than 125,000 papers every day of the week!

Over 125,000 more papers every single day. That's a stack of newspapers over a mile high!

Our readers have made The Morning News the biggest circulation winner in Dallas newspaper history.

So to reach more of Dallas, advertise with the overwhelming circulation winner, The Dallas Morning News. Call Harry M. Stanley, Jr., senior vice-president, at **(214) 977-8550.**

The Dallas Morning News

*Source: Audit Bureau of Circulations (ABC) FAS-FAX Report for the period ending March 31, 1985. Computations by The Dallas Morning News.

EXHIBIT 23.3 **Dallas Morning News** **advertisement**

THE EFFECTS OF A CONTINUING SOFT DALLAS ECONOMY
ARE FELT DURING 1987

In the first half of 1987, the effects of the sluggish economy were felt at both newspapers. Many advertisers reduced their budgets in response to the economic slowdown. To make matters worse, two major retail advertisers, Joske's and Safeway, closed their Dallas operations. Joske's was bought out by Dillard's and Safeway closed their north Texas division, which included Dallas. As a result, ad linage at both newspapers fell below 1986 volumes.

Operating expense increases also put pressure on management to take steps to maintain profitability. For example, average newsprint costs increased by 6 percent effective January 1 and were upped 7 percent effective July 1.

During March, the TH announced several advertising rate changes and deals designed to help reverse its declining share of newspaper advertising linage. To bolster classified, the TH introduced a guaranteed results program called "Super Seller Classified." The TH offered two lines for two weeks for $12 with an additional two weeks free if the merchandise advertised did not sell in the initial two weeks.

To build linage the TH offered single-location department store retailers a special concession. If the retailer would run the same dollar volume in the TH in 1987 as they had in 1986, they would receive a major reduction in their line rate. The net effect for the advertiser was a significant increase in linage at no cost increase over 1986.

The TH also offered a special pick-up advertising deal. If the advertiser ran four ads in a week, the second and third ads ran at a discount and the fourth ad was free. The first ad ran at the regular rate, the second at 50 percent, the third at 25 percent, and the fourth ad was free. On the other hand, in May, the MN offered pick-up discounts *only* on Sunday ads that were repeated during the next week in the business section. A second placement of a Sunday MN ad ran at 75 percent and a third ran at 55 percent.

In addition to their "Community Closeup" total market coverage product, the TH introduced a zoned advertising product "Community" in May. "Community" covered six zones with an editorial section designed to be attractive to small advertisers. Ads could be placed Wednesdays or Thursdays in any combination of the six zones.

In April, the MN received three Robert F. Kennedy Awards. These awards included the grand prize for a series on discrimination in Dallas County jury selection.

In May, both newspapers fired employees and announced cost-containment measures. The MN terminated 68 full-time and 27 part-time jobs, eliminated year-end bonuses, and placed strict reductions on controllable expenses such as travel. MN cuts affected all areas except circulation, advertising, and editorial. The TH laid off 47 workers for an indefinite period and froze the wages of the paper's 1,150 full-time employees. Further, the TH reduced some salaries. The TH staff reductions affected all areas except the newsroom.

THE DALLAS–FT. WORTH MARKET

Population and Employment

The North Central Texas Council of Governments estimated that the Dallas–Ft. Worth nine-county consolidated statistical area (CSA) population had increased 24.4 percent between April 1, 1980, and January 1, 1987. The population of the CSA on January 1, 1987, was estimated to be 3,649,887. The breakdown by counties in the CSA was as follows: Collin, 6.3 percent; Dallas, 48.7 percent; Denton, 6.5 percent; Ellis, 2.1 percent; Johnson, 2.5 percent; Kaufman, 1.4 percent; Parker, 1.6 percent; Rockwell, 0.6 percent; and Tarrant, 30.3 percent. (Exhibit 40.4 presents maps that indicate county locations.)

Although the rate of increase had slowed somewhat since the boom period of 1983–85, a relatively healthy increase was forecasted through 1988. Compounded annual growth rates between 1980 and 1987 by county were as follows: Collin, 7 percent; Dallas, 2 percent; Denton, 7.9 percent; Ellis, 3.5 percent; Johnson, 4.4 percent; Kaufman, 4.1 percent; Parker, 4.1 percent; Rockwell, 6.7 percent; and Tarrant, 3.9 percent.

Sales Management's projections through 1988 painted a continuation of earlier growth. By the end of 1988, the Dallas–Ft. Worth population was forecasted to increase 14 percent over 1983. Projected growth broken down by counties within the overall market indicated that the most rapid growth would occur in the suburban counties. Growth by county was estimated to occur as follows: Collin, +25.3 percent; Dallas, +11 percent; Denton, +24.9 percent; Ellis, +16.1 percent; Kaufman, +16.3 percent; and Rockwell, +24.1 percent. The Ft. Worth–Arlington portion of the Dallas–Ft. Worth market (Johnson, Parker, and Tarrant counties) was projected to grow at a 14.6 percent rate between 1983 and 1988.

Average household effective buying income was projected to grow by 69.2 percent to $44,618 by 1988. Again, the strongest Dallas market growth was forecasted to occur in outlying Denton, Rockwell, and Collin counties. Johnson, Parker, and Tarrant counties (the Ft. Worth portion of the market) were forecasted to grow at a slightly faster rate than the overall Dallas–Ft. Worth market.

The Dallas–Ft. Worth area of dominant influence (ADI) ranked as the eighth largest ADI in the United States in 1987. Arbitron estimated the TV household population distribution as follows: children aged 2–11, 15.2 percent; teens aged, 12–17, 9.2 percent; 18–34, 31.8 percent; 35–49, 20 percent; and 50+, 23.8 percent.

The Dallas–Ft. Worth economy was based on a diverse mix of employers and had shown resistance to economic downturns. A ranking of the largest revenue generators compiled by the MN revealed that the top five firms included a convenience store chain, a steel manufacturer, a semiconductor firm, an oil field services company, and an airline.

Top corporate employers included some of these same firms, plus a defense contractor, a telephone company, two department stores, and a grocery chain. In addition, federal, state, and local governments; schools and universities; and hospitals employed a large number of area residents. In 1986, J.C. Penney an-

EXHIBIT 40.4   Maps of Dallas–Ft. Worth

DALLAS MSA

DALLAS/FT. WORTH CSA

DALLAS/FT. WORTH ADI

nounced the relocation of its corporate headquarters to Dallas from New York. This move would bring 4,000 J.C. Penney employees into the Dallas area.

Media Competitors

In addition to the TH, the MN had to contend with a host of other media vehicles that sought to attract the attention of consumers and advertisers. These competitors applied constant pressure on the MN as they sought to expand their position in the market.

In Ft. Worth, the *Star-Telegram* was increasingly aggressive in competing with the two Dallas papers in the mid-cities area. The September 1986 ABC statement indicated that the daily circulation of the paper was 258,500 and 306,500 on Sundays. Compared to 1981, the *Star-Telegram* had grown 15.3 percent for daily and 21.0 percent for Sunday circulation.

The *Star-Telegram* had taken a number of steps to improve its product as well as to consolidate and expand its position in the Ft. Worth and Tarrant County market. Corporate ownership by Capital Cities Communications placed considerable resources and expertise at the disposal of the *Star-Telegram*.

The *Wall Street Journal* did well in the Dallas–Ft. Worth market. *USA Today* and the *New York Times* invested in significant marketing activities in attempts to wedge their way into the attractive Dallas–Ft. Worth market.

Three network affiliate television stations were important forces in the Dallas market. These stations were KXAS (NBC), KDFW (CBS), and WFAA (ABC). In addition, four Dallas independent stations held reasonably high shares of the viewing audience. These stations were KRLD, KTXA, KDFI, and KTVT. Average cost data for 30-second spots per household rating point during the second quarter of 1987 were $99 for daytime, $130 for early news, $288 for prime time, $213 for late news, and $137 for late evening. The average rating for the top three local stations in November 1894 was 6 for daytime, 11 for early news, 13 for prime time, 15 for late news, and 8 for late evening. Finally, cable television penetration stood at 38 percent of the ADI in July 1986.

The top five radio stations in Dallas based on average quarter-hour audiences were WBAP with 67,000; KVIL with 50,000; KRLD with 50,000; KKDA with 37,000; and KMEZ with 34,000. Second-quarter 1987 cost-per-rating-point estimates for 60-second spots in morning drive time were $134 for men aged 25–54 and $142 for women aged 25–54.

In addition to nationally distributed magazines (some with regional and single-market coverage capabilities), Dallas had five significant city magazines. These publications were *D Magazine*, *Dallas/Fort Worth Home & Garden*, *Dallas Business*, *Perspectives*, and *Texas Monthly*. *D Magazine*, for example, had a circulation of 81,000 and a one-time, four-color page cost of $4,590. A package buy of *Newsweek*, *Sports Illustrated*, *Time*, and *U.S. News & World Report* for coverage of the Dallas–Ft. Worth market cost $12,590 at the three-time rate for a four-color page. Circulation of the package was 165,200.

Outdoor and direct mail also provided competition for advertising dollars. The cost of a #50 showing of 30-sheet posters in Dallas through Foster & Kleiser (a major outdoor company) required 56 illuminated posters plus 8 nonilluminated and cost $18,176. (A #50 showing reaches 85 percent of the adult population with an average frequency of once every day for a 28-day period.)

Suburban newspapers in both the north and south areas of the Dallas market had become more aggressive in the past two years. To the north, Harte-Hanks owned a group with newspapers in Plano, Lewisville, Allen, and other communities. To the south, a group with weeklies and biweeklies in DeSoto, Cedar Hill, Lancaster, and other towns provided local coverage of these suburban communities.

CURRENT OPERATION OF THE *DALLAS MORNING NEWS*

Circulation Trends

Historically, the MN had been much stronger than the TH in total circulation. From the outset, the MN had viewed itself as more of a regional newspaper and bent its efforts toward that end. Partially as a result of these efforts, state circulation had always been a strength (the MN was the only paper distributed to all 254 counties in Texas). The MN also had significant circulation in the neighboring areas of Oklahoma and Louisiana.

The TH, on the other hand, had historically been stronger in Dallas county both daily and Sunday. Most of the circulation figures in Exhibit 40.1 reflect these historical strengths.

However, in 1984 the MN reversed the long-standing trend and took over the daily lead in Dallas county. In 1985 and 1986, the MN opened up a significant advantage in Dallas county daily and, for the first time, led the TH on Sunday in Dallas county. At the same time, the MN was extending its total circulation lead.

MN's penetration could be enhanced if newcomers and out-of-town visitors could be identified and introduced to the MN. Single-copy sales represented another opportunity, as did reaching and servicing apartment dwellers. Any new strategy undertaken had to balance resources required and likely benefits. Additionally, MN was looking for programs (1) that were insulated from competitive response and (2) that provided measurable results.

Pricing Trends

The MN has used its pricing policies for both advertising and circulation as a marketing weapon in the past to gain an advantage over its competition. Exhibit 40.5 presents data on single copy and subscription pricing of the two papers between 1978 and 1987.

EXHIBIT 40.5   Single-Copy and Home-Delivery Subscription Pricing for MN and TH, 1978–1987

	Single Copy Daily	Sunday
1981–1987	$.25	$.75
1980		
12/1 MN	.25	.75
11/1 TH	.25	.75
5/1 TH	.25	.50
5/1 MN	.25	.50
1979	.15	.35
1978	.15	.35

Monthly Home Delivery*

			Full Week	Sunday Only	Saturday, Sunday	Friday, Saturday, Sunday
1987	7/1	MN				$6.50
1986	10/1	TH				5.75
	6/1	MN				6.00
1985	12/1	MN	$9.00			
	10/1	MN				5.50
1984	10/1	MN	8.00			
	10/1	TH	8.00			
	6/1	MN				5.00
1983	12/1	MN	7.25			4.50
1982	1/1	TH	7.25			5.00
	6/1	MN				4.00
1981	9/1	MN		Drop	Drop	3.50
1980	12/1	TH	6.25		Drop	3.50
	12/1	MN	6.25	3.00	3.50	n/a
1979	11/1	MN	5.25	2.50	3.00	n/a
	12/1	TH	5.25		3.00	n/a
	7/1	TH	4.50			n/a
1978	4/1	MN	4.50			n/a
		MN	3.50	1.75	2.25	n/a
		TH	3.40	n/a	2.25	n/a

*Prices are entered only when there is a price change.

n/a = not available.

In terms of advertising space charges, the MN followed a strategy of pricing above the TH in absolute terms but below the TH on a cost per thousand (CPM) basis. This applied to all three categories of ad rates—general, classified, and retail. However, the recent TH advertising discount programs had brought the two papers much closer together on a CPM basis for many important advertisers.

Exhibits 40.6 and 40.7 present comparisons of retail rates of the two newspapers in 1985 and 1987, respectively.

Advertising Linage

Historically the MN had led the TH in total advertising linage based in part on the MN's considerably stronger classified performance. In 1986, the MN ranked second in the United States in full-run advertising linage

EXHIBIT 40.6   Retail Advertising Rates per Column Inch, 1985

				Contract Size				

Dallas Morning News

	Daily	Sunday		Daily	Sunday		Daily	Sunday
Open	$54.80	$63.65	1,200	$44.77	$50.97	14,300	$42.18	$48.38
50	47.61	54.08	2,400	44.24	50.45	19,000	41.66	47.35
100	47.09	53.18	3,600	43.99	49.94	23,800	41.14	47.09
150	46.58	53.30	4,800	43.47	49.16	28,600	40.63	46.83
200	45.28	52.27	7,100	43.21	48.91	33,300	40.36	46.58
500	45.02	51.49	9,500	42.95	48.64	38,100	39.85	46.31

Dallas Times Herald[a]

	Daily[b]	Weekend[b]	Sunday		Daily[b]	Weekend[b]	Sunday
Open	$50.00	$50.50	$56.00	5,500	$38.25	$38.75	$43.75
50	43.00	44.50	50.00	7,325	38.00	38.50	43.50
100	42.00	42.50	48.00	9,750	37.75	38.25	43.25
180	41.25	41.75	46.75	15,500	37.25	37.75	42.75
240	41.00	41.50	46.50	18,500	37.00	37.50	42.50
565	40.25	40.75	45.75	25,000	36.25	36.50	42.00
1,300	39.50	40.00	45.00	29,000	35.75	36.25	41.50
2,350	39.00	39.50	44.50	34,000	35.50	36.00	41.25
3,125	38.75	39.25	44.25	39,000	35.25	35.75	41.00

Frequency Contracts

Dallas Morning News			*Dallas Times Herald*			
	Daily	Sunday		Daily[b]	Weekend[b]	Sunday
7 Times	$47.09	$53.81	6 Times	$48.35	$49.55	$55.25
12 Times	45.28	52.27	12 Times	41.00	42.00	47.00
24 Times	45.02	51.49	24 Times	40.00	41.00	46.00
36 Times	44.24	50.45	36 Times	39.25	40.00	45.00
52 Times	43.99	49.94	52 Times	38.75	39.00	44.50

[a] TH rate card also included the following contract rates: 25, 75, 135, 320, 425, 750, 1,000, 1,750, 4,150, 13,000, and 22,000.

[b] Daily—Monday through Thursday; weekend—Friday and Saturday.

Source: Rate cards effective January 1, 1985, for TH; September 1, 1985, for MN.

EXHIBIT 40.7 Retail Advertising Rates per Column Inch, 1987

Bulk-Rate Contract Size

Dallas Morning News				Dallas Times Herald			
	Daily	Saturday	Sunday		Daily[a]	Weekend	Sunday
Open	$57.60	$59.90	$69.38	Open	$57.60	$58.10	$64.45
50	50.70	52.73	58.95	50	49.50	51.20	57.60
100	50.15	52.16	58.65	100	48.35	48.95	55.25
150	49.61	51.59	58.10	180	47.50	48.10	53.80
200	48.22	50.15	56.97	240	47.20	47.75	53.55
500	47.95	49.87	56.12	425	46.60	47.20	53.00
1,200	47.68	49.59	55.56	750	46.10	46.60	52.40
2,400	47.12	49.00	54.99	1,300	45.50	46.10	51.80
3,600	46.85	48.72	54.43	2,350	44.90	45.50	51.20
4,800	46.30	48.15	53.58	3,125	44.60	45.20	50.95
7,100	46.02	47.86	53.31	4,150	44.35	44.90	50.65
9,500	45.74	47.57	53.02	5,500	44.05	44.60	50.35
14,300	44.92	46.72	52.73	7,325	43.75	44.35	50.10
19,000	44.37	46.14	51.61	9,750	43.50	44.50	49.80
23,800	43.81	45.56	51.33	13,000	43.15	43.75	49.50
28,600	43.27	45.00	51.04	18,500	42.60	43.15	48.95
33,300	42.98	44.70	50.77	25,000	41.75	42.05	48.35
38,100	42.44	44.14	50.48	34,000	40.90	41.95	47.50
				39,000	40.60	41.15	47.20

Frequency Contracts

Dallas Morning News				Dallas Times Herald			
	Daily	Saturday	Sunday		Daily[a]	Weekend[a]	Sunday
7 Times	$50.15	$52.16	$58.65	6 Times	$48.35	$49.55	$55.25
12 Times	48.22	50.15	56.97	12 Times	47.20	48.35	54.10
24 Times	47.95	49.87	56.12	24 Times	46.10	47.20	52.95
36 Times	47.12	49.00	54.99	36 Times	45.20	46.10	51.80
52 Times	46.85	48.72	54.43	52 Times	44.60	44.90	51.20
				78 Times	43.10	43.70	50.55

[a] TH Daily—Monday through Thursday; weekend includes Friday and Saturday.
Source: Rate cards effective January 1, 1986, for TH; September 1, 1986 for MN.

(5,476,495 inches). In first place was the TH's former sister paper the *Los Angeles Times* with 5,637,854 inches. In terms of total 1986 classified linage, the MN led the nation by a substantial margin.

Exhibit 40.8 presents data on the top 10 retail accounts linage during 1984 and 1986. The two papers were relatively evenly split on most of the top retail accounts. In 1986, the MN did significantly better with Sanger Harris, Dillard's, and Joske's. The TH garnered a significantly larger share of Montgomery Ward and Kmart's ad budgets.

EXHIBIT 40.8   Newspaper Linage Data, Top 10 Retail Accounts, 1984 and 1986

	1984		1986
Account	MN Linage (Percent)[a]	Account	MN Linage (Percent)[a]
Sears	2,392,765 (50.4)	Sears	3,147,455 (50.3)
Sanger Harris	2,227,646 (54.8)	Sanger Harris	2,095,616 (61.1)
J.C. Penney	2,179,724 (50.6)	Mervyn's	1,952,393 (50.0)
Dillard's	1,921,227 (57.6)	Dillard's	1,910,888 (56.5)
Mervyn's	1,893,423 (50.0)	Theaters	1,714,549 (49.8)
Theaters	1,501,854 (48.9)	JC Penney	1,699,466 (51.5)
Montgomery Ward	1,271,890 (43.0)	Montgomery Ward	1,635,471 (46.1)
Tom Thumb/Page	1,259,003 (49.5)	Joske's	1,439,828 (56.1)
Skaggs Alpha Beta	1,224,172 (50.4)	Target	1,368,479 (50.0)
Kmart	814,701 (30.6)	Kmart	897,987 (34.0)

[a] Indicates percent of all linage placed in combined total of MN and TH that was placed in MN.
Source: *Media Records* 1984, 1986.

EXHIBIT 40.9   MN Percentage of Yearly Full-Run Advertising Linage by Categories, 1977–1987

	Total	Retail	Classified	General	Financial	Dept Store	Home	Food	General Merchandise	Apparel
1987[a]	58	55	60	56	62	56	59	50	47	74
1986[b]	57	55	60	54	62	54	62	47	45	70
1985[c]	55	53	59	55	61	53	57	46	46	65
1984	55	52	58	56	60	54	53	46	45	66
1983	55	53	57	54	60	54	55	49	45	66
1982	53	50	55	52	56	54	53	50	46	66
1981	53	50	57	51	56	51	52	48	38	66
1980	52	49	56	49	58	50	53	49	23	67
1979	52	49	55	50	55	50	53	50	35	65
1978	51	49	53	50	56	50	53	50	26	66
1977	51	49	55	49	59	47	52	49	30	60

[a] Partial year figures for four months January through April only. MN linage (inches): Total = 1,609,906; Daily = 1,019,640; Sunday = 590,266.
[b] 1986 MN linage (inches): Total = 5,476,495; Daily = 3,464,704; Sunday = 2,011,791.
[c] 1985 MN linage (inches): Total = 5,778,657; Daily = 3,631,492; Sunday = 2,147,165.
Source: *Media Records*, 1977–86.

The data in Exhibit 40.9 indicate the percentage of various categories of ad linage garnered by the MN. The MN strengthened its position in 1986 versus 1977 in eight categories out of nine.

Readership

The traditional readership strength of the MN had been among older adults with higher income and educational levels. The TH's strength had been among younger, middle and lower socioeconomic adults. These basic trends had accounted for the MN's stronger performance in the financial and apparel categories. At the same time, the TH had been stronger in the general merchandise category.

In terms of editorial philosophy, the TH had been characterized as more liberal in its political stands and aggressive in its investigative reporting on certain issues. The MN had traditionally been more conservative and establishment-oriented in its editorial views.

Exhibits 40.10 through 40.13 present 1986 data taken from research studies conducted by Scarborough for the MN and by Savitz for the TH. These data indicate some of the strengths and weaknesses of the newspapers.

EXHIBIT 40.10   Daily Readership of Dallas Newspapers by Adults in the Dallas/Ft. Worth ADI[a]

	Total Adults	Morning News	Times Herald
Total Adults	3,103,600	22.7%	19.7%
Age			
18–24	495,500	20.7	18.8
25–34	807,600	21.8	21.0
35–44	625,100	22.3	23.0
45–54	400,100	24.9	19.9
55–64	351,000	26.5	17.3
65+	424,300	21.9	15.0
Education			
College Graduate+	612,100	35.5	22.9
Some College	702,400	24.0	19.9
High School Graduate	1,046,200	21.1	20.1
Some High School	590,900	14.1	17.7
Grade School	152,000	8.5	9.5
Household Income			
$75K+	196,300	39.0	24.9
$50–74,999	353,700	30.2	23.3
$35–49,999	573,400	24.8	21.6
$30–34,999	354,500	22.7	21.5
$25–29,999	393,600	23.2	21.8
$20–24,999	409,600	19.5	22.8
$15–19,999	338,400	16.1	14.6
$10–14,999	242,400	16.7	11.1
Less than $10,000	241,700	12.9	9.9
Race			
White	2,649,400	22.0	18.7
Black	372,300	26.5	25.4
Other	81,900	25.3	24.3
Marital Status			
Married	1,998,700	23.0	19.5
Single	514,300	26.4	22.7
Divorced/Separated	357,300	19.5	20.5
Widowed	233,300	16.0	13.4

[a] Average weekday readers. The Dallas/Ft. Worth ADI is a 34-county area.
Source: Scarborough Research Corporation, 1986, Sample size—2,583.

EXHIBIT 40.11   Sunday Readership of Dallas Newspapers by Adults in the Dallas/Ft. Worth ADI[a]

	Total Adults	Morning News	Times Herald
Total Adults	3,103,600	28.6%	25.9%
Age			
18–24	495,500	27.6	28.4
25–34	807,600	28.9	27.1
35–44	625,100	27.7	29.8
45–54	400,100	30.2	27.2
55–64	351,000	34.0	19.3
65+	424,300	25.1	19.0
Education			
College Graduate+	612,100	44.1	27.1
Some College	702,400	34.2	24.8
High School Graduate	1,046,200	24.8	27.5
Some High School	590,900	15.8	24.0
Grade School	152,000	16.0	22.0
Household Income			
$75K+	196,300	40.3	28.5
$50–74,999	353,700	41.1	29.5
$35–49,999	573,400	31.4	29.0
$30–34,999	354,500	26.7	26.5
$25–29,999	393,600	26.9	26.3
$20–24,999	409,600	22.7	29.0
$15–19,999	338,400	24.2	23.5
$10–14,999	242,400	24.1	18.3
Less than $10,000	241,700	20.0	15.0
Race			
White	2,649,400	28.2	24.6
Black	372,300	30.7	33.9
Other	81,900	31.5	31.0
Marital Status			
Married	1,998,700	28.3	25.3
Single	514,300	32.9	30.9
Divorced/Separated	357,300	28.5	25.7
Widowed	233,300	21.5	20.2

[a] Average Sunday readers. The Dallas/Ft. Worth ADI is a 34-county area.

Source: Scarborough Research Corporation, 1986. Sample size—2,583.

Financial Data

Despite the heavy promotional, editorial, and other costs that resulted from the intense competition with the TH, the MN continued to be a very profitable operation. Exhibit 40.14 presents a five-year income statement for the MN. Total revenue had grown significantly over the five-year period, as had both advertising and circulation revenues.

EXHIBIT 40.12   *Times Herald* **Daily Reader Profile**

	Reader	Dallas Adult		Reader	Dallas Adult
Age			**Lived in Dallas**		
18–24	17.5%	16.0%	Less Than 2 Years	9.2%	13.6%
25–34	28.2	27.7	2–5 Years	8.1	6.0
35–49	27.9	26.1	5–10 Years	13.6	41.9
50–64	17.1	18.2	10+ Years	69.1	65.5
65+	9.3	12.0	**Occupation**		
18–49	73.6	69.8	Manager/Administrator	11.4	11.3
25–49	56.1	53.8	Professional/Technical	19.0	16.1
Median Age	37.3 yrs.	38.6 yrs.	Sales	10.7	11.3
Household Income[a]			Clerical	10.7	12.5
$25,000+	67.8%	68.1%	Craftsman/Service	21.3	19.0
$35,000+	49.2	48.3	Housewife	8.8	10.2
$50,000+	23.9	24.3	Other	2.9	1.2
$25–50,000	44.0	43.8	Unemployed/Retired	15.2	18.4
Median Income	$34,600	$34,100	**Residence**		
Marital Status			Rent	33.0	30.6
Married	59.1%	61.2%	Own	67.0	69.4
Single	40.9	38.8	**Presence of Children**		
Sex			Has Children	45.6	56.6
Male	51.0	47.6	No Children	54.4	43.4
Female	49.0	52.4	**Race**		
Women Who Work	62.7	61.5	White	78.3	82.0
			Black	15.5	11.7
			Hispanic	4.5	4.7
			Other	1.7	1.6

[a] Household income percentages do not reflect those respondents who refused to answer.

Source: 1986 *Dallas Times Herald* Continuing Market Survey, conducted by Savitz Research Center, Inc.

Marketing Budget

The 1987 marketing budget for the MN was forecasted to be approximately $4,810,000 (roughly a 9 percent increase over 1986). This budget did *not* include marketing personnel salaries or the expenses for public relations events. The overall budget was allocated by expense categories over 1986 and 1987 roughly as follows:

	1986	1987
Radio	40%	32%
Television	7	23
Media Production Services	20	14
Outdoor	18	11
In-Paper	7	11
Print	4	6
Office Supplies, Travel, Postage, Miscellaneous	4	3
Total	100%	100%

EXHIBIT 40.13   *Times Herald* **Sunday Reader Profile**

	Reader	Dallas Adult		Reader	Dallas Adult
Age			**Lived in Dallas**		
18–24	17.6%	16.0%	Less Than 2 Years	9.4%	13.6%
25–34	28.7	27.7	2–5 Years	8.8	6.0
35–49	26.9	26.1	5–10 Years	13.8	14.9
50–64	17.1	18.2	10+ Years	68.0	65.5
65+	9.7	12.0	**Occupation**		
18–49	73.2	69.8	Manager/Administrator	10.9	11.3
25–49	55.6	53.8	Professional/Technical	16.6	16.1
Median Age	37.1 yrs.	38.6 yrs.	Sales	11.9	11.3
Household Income[a]			Clerical	11.5	12.5
$25,000+	69.2%	68.1%	Craftsman/Service	21.7	19.9
$35,000+	48.1	48.3	Housewife	10.0	10.2
$50,000+	24.0	24.3	Other	2.3	1.2
$25–50,000	45.2	43.8	Unemployed/Retired	15.1	18.4
Median Income	$34,100	$34,100	**Residence**		
Marital Status			Rent	31.8	30.6
Married	60.3%	61.2%	Own	68.2	69.4
Single	39.7	38.8	**Presence of Children**		
Sex			Has Children	46.1	56.6
Male	49.2	47.6	No Children	53.9	43.4
Female	50.8	52.4	**Race**		
Women Who Work	62.8	61.5	White	80.9	82.0
			Black	13.3	11.7
			Hispanic	4.1	4.7
			Other	1.7	1.6

[a] Household income percentages do not reflect those respondents who refused to answer.
Source: 1986 *Dallas Times Herald* Continuing Market Survey, conducted by Savitz Research Center, Inc.

The bulk of the MN's media advertising was directed to potential readers, subscribers, and users of classifieds. In addition, the MN utilized the trade press (e.g., *Advertising Age, AdWeek, Editor & Publisher*) to reach potential advertisers. Roughly 65 percent of the MN's media advertising was aimed at increasing the paper's circulation, 10 percent focused on promoting the use of display advertising, and 25 percent promoted classified usage.

Exhibit 40.15 presents a representative advertisement directed at advertisers. Exhibit 40.16 presents a 30-second radio commercial promoting the MN's sports coverage.

The MN's public relations department's nonsalary budget for 1987 was approximately $1 million (roughly a 4 percent increase over 1986). Examples of significant line items in the MN's public relations budget included the G.B. Dealy Awards, the MN's Tennis Classic, the MN's Basketball Classic, and the Newspapers in Education program.

EXHIBIT 40.14   Income Statement, *Dallas Morning News*, January 1–December 31, 1982–1986 (In thousands)[a]

	1982	1983	1984	1985	1986
Revenue					
Advertising Revenue	$113,409	$139,233	$164,574	$186,133	$186,599
Circulation Revenue	11,542	14,427	20,563	23,331	23,876
Other Revenue	447	608	784	1,441	738
Total Revenue	$125,397	$154,268	$185,921	$209,905	$211,213
Expense					
Editorial					
Payroll	$4,117	$6,256	$8,568	$9,725	$10,634
Expense	3,258	3,756	4,647	4,979	5,487
Production					
Payroll	12,475	13,661	15,743	20,750	23,337
Expense	3,097	3,270	3,331	4,120	4,697
Newsprint, Ink, Supplies	43,627	49,496	61,074	69,900	66,116
Transportation					
Payroll	1,169	1,513	1,755	2,010	2,264
Expense	454	473	504	539	547
Circulation					
Payroll	2,921	4,121	6,789	7,807	7,994
Expense	5,586	5,878	7,133	7,989	8,020
Advertising					
Payroll	5,398	6,270	8,245	9,070	9,657
Expense	1,611	2,027	2,047	2,211	2,336
Administrative					
Payroll	3,026	3,648	4,621	4,991	4,521
Depreciation	7,232	8,243	9,034	11,473	12,827
Expense	15,358	16,512	18,995	20,515	23,234
Total Expenses	$109,329	$125,124	$152,486	$176,079	$181,716
Operating Income	$16,068	$29,144	$33,435	$33,826	$29,497
Operating Ratio	12.81%	18.89%	17.98%	16.11%	13.97%
Other Income	88	221	408	412	398
Other Expenses	(137)	(245)	(281)	(521)	(540)
Income Before Taxes	$16,019	$29,120	$33,562	$33,717	$29,355
Income Tax (current + deferred)	8,155	12,530	13,637	15,857	15,429
Net Income	$7,864	$16,590	$19,925	$17,860	$13,926

[a] The data presented in this table have been disguised.

STRATEGIC PLAN FOR THE 1990s

At the next day's 10 A.M. meeting, specific objectives, strategies, and anticipated competitive responses were to be discussed. Mr. Osborne, Mr. Halbreich, and others in MN's top-management group understood that the battle for Dallas newspaper supremacy was still being waged.

EXHIBIT 40.15 *Dallas Morning News* **Advertisement**

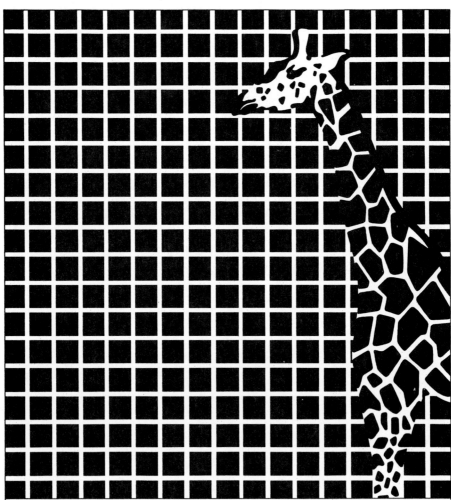

Often, with circulation numbers, a pattern begins to emerge.

If you've kept an eye on the two Dallas newspapers, you've seen one consistently rise head and shoulders above the other. And the most recent numbers show The Dallas Morning News outselling the competition again.

In total daily circulation, The Morning News has more than a 50% edge on the Dallas Times Herald. With 368,683 copies

sold every day. On Sunday, the lead is 37% when 476,004 copies are sold.

That means The Dallas Morning News has the highest one-time penetration by any advertising medium in Dallas.

Including radio.

Including television.

And your advertising also benefits from the quality editorial environment for which

The Dallas Morning News is recognized.

All of which means you'll see another pattern emerge. Results. That's why you advertise in the first place.

And that's why The Dallas Morning News should be the first place you advertise in Dallas.

The Dallas Morning News. The nation's leader in full-run ad linage.

The Dallas Morning News

Nobody beats The Dallas Morning News in the morning.

*Source: ABC Publisher's Statement for the period ending March 31, 1985. Calculations by The Dallas Morning News Media Records year end 1984
Represented by Cresmer, Woodward, O'Mara & Ormsbee, Inc.; The Leonard Co.: Florida, Mexico, Caribbean; Lenha Hawaii: Hawaii

EXHIBIT 40.16 *Dallas Morning News* **Sports 30-Second Radio Commercial**

	[Up-tempo music]
[Singers]	To follow the action . . . on the field . . . on the court . . .
[Umpire]	"Let's play ball!"
[Singers]	For the latest report
[SFX]	(Crack of bat hitting baseball and roar of crowd.)
[Singers]	On your favorite sports.
[Fan]	"Knock the ball out!"
[Singers]	Hey Dallas! You've got all the moves! 'cause Dallas reads the *Dallas Morning News!*
[Announcer 1]	For Ringolsby's baseball column.
	For late breaking scores.
	For digging into the dugout.
	For Rangers' action.
	I read the *Morning News!*
[Announcer 2]	Nobody beats the *Dallas Morning News* in the morning!

EXHIBIT 40.17   Skip and Blackie *Dallas Times Herald* Advertisement

SKIP & BLACKIE

TWO GREAT WRITERS IN ONE GREAT PAPER.

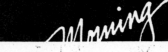

Dallas Times Herald.

SKIP BAYLESS

Thumbs up for Cowboys

The thumb, of course, is the runt finger. Short, stubby, always getting in the way of hammers and kitchen knives and your right guard's helmet. Thumbs aren't fit for Super Bowl rings, as Pittsburgh found out, but the metacarpal, phalangeal joint is a necessary evil. One can't throw a football or give a thumbs-up without one. Which brings us to

BLACKIE SHERROD

Shake, rattle and bankroll

Even before the shake had hit the fan. Rafael Septien ran his bill up to $200.
    While the Dallas and Buffalo stalwarts were loosening up, Septien and Isiah Robertson crossed paths near the Cowboy bench area, shook hands and stopped to exchange pleasantries. When the Dallas kicker and the Buffalo linebacker finished their chat, they shook hands

EXHIBIT 40.18   *Dallas Times Herald* Advertisement

EXHIBIT 40.19   *Dallas Morning News* **Advertisement**

The next time a Times Herald ad rep calls on you, ask him to fill in the blanks.

1. _____	14. _____		
2. _____	15. _____		
3. _____	16. _____		
4. _____	17. _____		
5. _____	18. _____		
6. _____	19. _____		
7. _____	20. _____		
8. _____	21. _____		
9. _____	22. _____		
10. _____	23. _____		
11. _____	24. _____		
12. _____	25. _____		
13. _____			

• **1.** SANGER HARRIS	**14.** PFAU TIRE CO.	
2. SEARS	**15.** HAVERTY'S	
3. MONTGOMERY WARD	• **16.** WEIR'S	
• **4.** J.C. PENNEY	• **17.** NEIMAN MARCUS	
• **5.** DILLARD'S	• **18.** PAGE SUPER DRUG	
• **6.** JOSKE'S	• **19.** ECKERD'S	
7. WOOLCO	**20.** WINN DIXIE	
8. TARGET	**21.** KROGER	
• **9.** SAFEWAY	**22.** AMERICAN AIRLINES	
• **10.** TOM THUMB	• **23.** LIGHTS FANTASTIC	
11. K-MART	• **24.** SKAGGS DRUGS	
12. MINYARDS	**25.** RICK FURNITURE	
• **13.** SKAGGS ALPHA BETA		

The 25 top Dallas advertisers according to the Times Herald.

The 25 top Dallas advertisers according to Media Records.

Very recently, the Times Herald ran an ad claiming that "22 of the top 25 Dallas newspaper advertisers place more ad dollars in the Times Herald than in the #2 paper."

Yet, somehow, they failed to list them.

Because the only way their claim could be construed to be true is that the number 22 represents *their own* top 22 advertisers. Media Records, an independent auditing firm that measures advertising in *both* Dallas papers, presents us with quite a different list.

Asterisks indicate advertisers who run a majority of their advertising with The Dallas Morning News. Through October. The Dallas Morning News leads in total full run advertising linage among these top 25 advertisers by 1,255,488 lines.

Source: Media Records. October, 1982.

In black and white, it shows that The Dallas Morning News carries the majority of advertising linage in 13 of the 25 top advertisers in this market. More than half place more advertising with us than with them. And we're not counting just our own advertisers, we're counting everyone who advertises in a newspaper in Dallas.

An important difference that shows up rather clearly in round numbers. Through October of this year, The Dallas Morning News has run over 10.3 million *more* lines of total full-run advertising than the evening paper. Over 3,500 more pages of advertising. And in the critical full-run

retail advertising category, we lead by over 3.2 million lines.

Those are the facts. Now if a Herald ad rep wants to explain their ad to you, we've given the rep the space.

Just one more reason why nobody beats The Dallas Morning News in the morning.

EXHIBIT 40.20   *Dallas Morning News* **Advertisement**

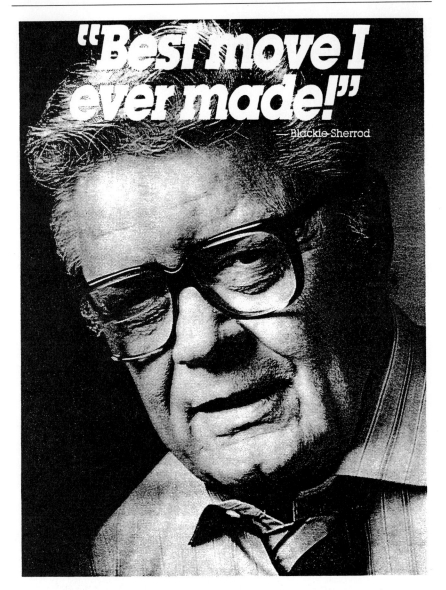

Blackie Sherrod, the dean of Texas sports writers, has made his move to the
pages of SPORTS DAY. Now you've got Galloway, Casstevens *and* Sherrod.
Read them today.
To subscribe call 745-8383 or toll-free 1-800-442-7044.

𝕿𝖍𝖊 𝕯𝖆𝖑𝖑𝖆𝖘 𝕸𝖔𝖗𝖓𝖎𝖓𝖌 𝕹𝖊𝖜𝖘

EXHIBIT 40.21 *Dallas Times Herald* **Advertisement**

APPENDIX A

Analyzing Strategic Marketing Cases
by W. Jack Duncan, Peter M. Ginter, and Linda E. Swayne

How does a manager learn to make strategic marketing decisions? The most obvious way, and perhaps the most valuable if you were to have the opportunity, is to work your way up the organization and observe how senior executives deal with strategic issues. Then, when the opportunity presents itself, combine what you have learned with your own marketing philosophy to do the best you can. In this ideal world, there would never be "negative consequences" for mistakes, because the fear of losing our job or looking stupid restricts our willingness to try creative or unusual solutions that might not work. We learn best from our mistakes. Unfortunately, such opportunities are not practical in most organizations.

Even if this approach were feasible, it is very risky; and business firms, hospitals, educational institutions, and other organizations trust important strategic decision making only to the most "seasoned managers." For this reason, the case method has been successfully used to give aspiring managers opportunities to make strategic decisions without "betting the organization" on the outcome. In other words, cases offer an opportunity to deal with real decisions in a low-risk environment—an opportunity to try creative and unusual solutions.

LEARNING THROUGH CASE ANALYSIS

Cases contain situations actually faced by managers documented in a way that makes them useful in training decision makers. The decisions required to solve cases represent a wide range of complexity so that no two are addressed in exactly the same manner.

CASES: REAL AND IMAGINED

Many different types of cases are used in strategic marketing texts. Sometimes the cases are invented to illustrate a specific point. Usually these appear as "Ajax Corporation" or some similar name. Other cases are real but disguised. A writer may, for example, have information from an organization such as IBM or Maytag Corporation, but the company, for some reason, has requested that the case author not use its name. The information and the situation are real. Only a few cases in this book are disguised. If a case has been disguised, there is a statement in the footnote at the bottom of the first page of the case.

The best cases are real and undisguised. Cases like Gatorade, Humana, Verbatim, Lance, Harley-Davidson, and most others in this book are real, on-going organizations dealing with today's problems and opportunities. In addition, there are less well known cases that have been selected because of the important issues they present to prospective managers. Sometimes the issues presented are not "problems" in the negative sense of something being wrong or impending doom for the company. Often the greatest challenge facing an organization is recognizing and acting on an opportunity rather than solving a problem.

Cases that have obvious solutions upon which everyone agrees are not good aids to learning decision-making skills. Managers rarely face decisions where the solution is self-evident to everyone. This does not mean that there are no good and bad answers or solutions in case analysis. However, the evaluation of a case analysis as good, better, or best is more often based on the approach and logic employed rather than on the precise recommendation offered.

CASES AND STRATEGIC MARKETING

Cases add realism that is impossible to achieve in traditional lecture classes, a realism that comes from the essential nature of cases. We may justifiably complain that cases fail to provide all the information necessary for decision making, but the fact is that decision makers never have all the information they want or need when they face strategic decisions. Risks must be taken in case analysis just as in any other decision-making activity.

Risk Taking in Case Analysis

Decisions about the future involve uncertainty. Strategic decision making, because it is futuristic and involves judgment, is particularly risky. Decision making under conditions of uncertainty requires that we devise some means of dealing with the risks faced by managers. Cases are valuable aids in this area, since they allow us to practice making decisions in low-risk environments. A poor case analysis may be embarrassing, but at least it will not result in the bankruptcy of a company. At the same time, the lessons learned by solving cases and participating in discussions will begin to build problem-solving skills.

Unfortunately, many future decision makers are not familiar with how to analyze cases. Customarily, prospective managers learn how to succeed as students by taking objective examinations, writing occasional term papers, and crunching numbers on a computer, but they seldom solve real case problems. For this reason this appendix may be helpful—not to prescribe how all cases should be solved but to offer some initial direction on how to "surface" the real issues presented in the cases.

Solving Case Problems

Solving a case is much like solving any problem. First, the issues are defined, information is gathered, and alternatives are generated, evaluated, selected, and implemented. Although the person solving the case seldom has the opportunity to implement a decision, he or she should always keep in mind that recommendations must be tempered by the limitations imposed on the organization in terms of its human and nonhuman resources. As the strengths and weaknesses of the recommendations are analyzed, lessons are learned that can be applied to future decision making.

ALTERNATIVE PERSPECTIVES: PASSION OR OBJECTIVITY

Different hypothetical roles can be assumed when analyzing cases. Some students prefer to think of themselves as the chief executive or key administrator in order to impose a perspective on the problems presented in the case. This allows us the liberty to become a passionate advocate of a particular course of action. Others like to observe the case from the detached objectivity of a consultant who has been employed by the organization to solve a problem.

Either perspective can be assumed, but we believe the first offers some unique advantages. Since there are no absolutely correct or incorrect answers to complex cases, the most important lesson to learn is why managers behave as they do, why they select one alternative over all others, and why they pursue specific strategies under the conditions presented in the case. Becoming the manager, at least mentally, helps us learn the lessons case histories have to teach. On the other hand, a consultant may be able to look at a situation more objectively. If you are having difficulty developing a solution for a particularly challenging case, try assuming a different perspective.

Looking at a case from different perspectives assists in moving beyond strategy to implementation and includes political issues within the organization, including the importance of interpersonal preferences in decision making.

Although the approach outlined here is logical, it is important to remember that each case should be approached and appreciated as a unique opportunity for problem solving. The unlimited combinations of organization, industry, and environment make every case different.

DOING YOUR HOMEWORK

Effective case analysis begins with data collection. This means carefully reading the case, rereading it, and sometimes reading it again. Rarely can we absorb enough information from the first reading of a comprehensive case to adequately solve it. Therefore, collect information and make notes about details as the case unfolds. We have found that if the case is read *several* days ahead of the due date, the student has the opportunity for "free" thinking time—when you stand in line for tickets, in traffic, in the shower, and so on. Although some people are creative under pressure, too much pressure leads to poor case analysis.

Getting Information

The information required to successfully solve a case comes in two forms. The first type of information is given as part of the case and customarily includes things such as the history of the organization, its form of organization and management, its financial condition, and its current marketing strategy. Frequently a case will include information about the industry and maybe even some problems shared by competing firms. This is the easy part, since the author of the case has done the work.

A second type of information is "obtainable." This information is not given in the case or by the instructor but is available from secondary sources in the library in familiar magazines and related publications. Obtainable secondary information helps us understand the nature of the industry, the competition, and other important environmental factors *at the time of the case*. Unless your instructor indicates otherwise, you should not investigate beyond the time of the case. It is natural, once you may have discovered what the company actually did in a given situation, to think that its response was the "correct" one. Often other solutions would have been better.

If the case does not include industry information, your instructor may expect you to do some detective work before proceeding. Find out what is happening in the industry and learn enough about trends to position the problems discussed in the case in a broader industry context. The culture of the organization or the style of the chief executive officer may also constitute relevant information.

CASE ANALYSIS

In the following discussion, one method of case analysis is presented. This approach, illustrated in Exhibit A.1, offers a process or way of thinking about cases rather than prescribing the only way to approach the task of case analysis. Exhibit A.1 is a model or outline that may be used to direct your thinking about solving problems and developing strategic marketing plans. This general framework for thinking through problems or opportunities can be applied to a variety of organizations. We believe this approach to case analysis is useful because it is a logical method of decision making.

First, it is important that we learn about the economic, social, technological, and political environments facing the organization. We begin with economic,

EXHIBIT A.1   An Outline for Case Analysis

I. Situational Analysis
   A. External Environmental Analysis
      1. General Environmental Analysis—Economic, Social, Political, Technological
      2. Industry Analysis—Economic, Social, Political, Technological
      3. Market Analysis
   B. Internal Environmental Analysis
      1. Evaluation of the Mission
      2. Evaluation of the Objectives
      3. Evaluation of the Functional Areas
         a. Marketing
         b. Finance
         c. Production
         d. Human Resources
      4. Evaluation of Marketing Strategies
         a. Target Market
         b. Product Strategies
         c. Pricing Strategies
         d. Distribution Strategies
         e. Promotional Strategies
            (1). Advertising Strategies
            (2). Selling Strategies
            (3). Public Relations/Publicity Strategies
            (4). Sales Promotion Strategies
   C. Strengths, Weaknesses, Opportunities, and Threats (SWOT) Analysis
II. Identification of the Problem (Opportunity)
III. Development of Strategic Alternatives
IV. Evaluation of the Strategic Alternatives
V. Recommendations
VI. Implementation
VII. Finalizing the Report

social, political, and technological aspects of the general environment and then progress to the specifics of the industry in which the firm competes.

Next we gather as many facts as we can about the environment of the organization under examination. This may be a consumer durable goods manufacturer, hospital, retail operation, or industrial goods marketer. We then relate the strategic capabilities of the organization to the external environment. A thorough and objective analysis of the organization's internal strengths and weaknesses is required. It is also necessary to understand the unique culture of the organization including its mission and strategic objectives.

Next the capabilities and interactions of the various subsystems—marketing, finance, operations, personnel—must be evaluated. These subsystems will determine, to a great extent, the likelihood that a particular strategy will be implemented. Although marketing strategy might dictate introduction of a new product line, financing may be too limited or the plant already may be operating at full capacity.

Once the situational analysis is complete, strategic alternatives can be generated as possible solutions to the problems identified in the case. This is the strategy formulation stage and is an important part of solving strategic marketing cases. The strategic direction is determined on the basis of the unique "fit" between the organization's internal strengths and weaknesses and the external opportunities and threats. Companies should attempt to take advantage of the opportunities in the environment and avoid the threats—based on organizational strengths. Organizational weaknesses may suggest areas that management needs to investigate and change, especially if a weakness is related to a threat.

The problem is identified, strategic alternatives generated, and a course of action is recommended. Finally, the effectiveness of the chosen strategic alternative must be evaluated. Because of the nature of case analysis, this aspect of strategic control is not always possible. However, at least some thought must be given to the likely outcomes resulting from different strategic choices.

SITUATION ANALYSIS—A CLOSER LOOK

The first step in case analysis is to understand the environment, the organization, the industry, and the decision makers at the time a strategic decision is needed. This is called "situation analysis" because we must understand the circumstances and the environment facing the organization if good decisions are to result from our analysis. Situation analysis is one of the most important steps in analyzing a case. The list below highlights some of the important areas that might be included in this stage of case analysis.

A. External Environmental Analysis
   1. The General Environment.
      What are the macroenvironmental factors that will affect the organization? What are the prevailing economic conditions affecting the nation or world? What regulatory philosophies and trends, and legislation, will affect citizens and organizations within the society? What lifestyle and demographic factors are changing and how rapidly? What technological forces are likely to influence strategic decison making?
   2. The Environment within the Industry.
      What is the size of industry? Growth trends?
      What is the nature of the competition? How many direct competitors are there, and is the competition increasing or decreasing? What are the relative market shares of the different competitors? Which organizations are indirect competitors?
      What are the macroenvironmental factors that will affect the industry? What are the prevailing economic conditions? What regulatory philosophies, trends, and

legislation will affect the industry? What lifestyle and demographic factors are changing and how rapidly? What technological forces are likely to influence strategic decision making within the industry?

3. The Market.

Who are the organization's primary customers—baby boomers, the elderly, working mothers? To what extent are the customers loyal to the organization's products and services? Is price the only major determinant in the purchasing decision? Will customers travel and otherwise be inconvenienced to obtain the organization's products and services?

How sophisticated are the organization's customers in terms of their buying habits and processes? What does this tell management about advertising and promotion?

Is the market for the organization's products geographically concentrated? Located in the top 100 ADIs (areas of dominant influence)?

Are market segments easily identified? Are different strategies for each feasible or advisable?

B. Internal Environmental Analysis

1. Mission. Does the organization have a clear sense of mission? Is there a mission statement and is it communicated to those responsible for accomplishing it? Does the organization have the human and nonhuman resources necessary to accomplish its mission?

2. Objectives. Are there well-developed and communicated long- and short-range objectives? Are they shared with those responsible for achieving them?

3. Functional Area Analysis. Are the functional areas working synergistically to achieve the organization's objectives?

Are the financial resources needed to compete available, or is the organization undercapitalized, too highly leveraged, or not leveraged enough? How do the key financial ratios of this organization compare with others in the industry and region?

Is the organization operating at capacity? Are equipment, facilities, and so forth new and up to date? Are the company's products labor intensive? Is quality at a desirable level?

Are the organization's managers and employees skilled in their work? Is turnover a factor? Is there a shortage of trained personnel to fill jobs?

4. Marketing Strategies. Are the organization's marketing strategies appropriate to achieve the organization's objectives?

How sophisticated is the organization in terms of its marketing activities? How flexible are the organization's marketing policies? When was the last time management tried something new and innovative in the area of marketing? More important perhaps, has the organization ever done any serious marketing of its services?

What about products and services? Does the organization offer a full range of products? Is the present product mix complementary, or does the organization compete with itself in some areas? Could the overall level of business be significantly increased if selected new products and services were added? Should any products or services be discontinued?

Are the company's prices acceptable to customers? Are the prices above, at, or below competition? What image is price meant to convey?

Has the appropriate channel(s) of distribution been identified and utilized? Is distribution national or regional? Is company ownership of the channel appropriate? Would intensive, selective, or exclusive distribution be most appropriate? Is location an important factor?

Has serious thought been given to a promotion strategy? What is the proper blend of the promotional elements—advertising, personal selling, publicity, sales promotion?

If you are not comfortable with your answers to this list of questions, read the case for a second or third time.

Purpose or Mission of the Organization

Peter Drucker says that anyone who wants to "know" a business must start with understanding its purpose or mission.[1] If a mission statement is included in the case, does it serve the purpose of communicating to the public why the organization exists? Mission statements provide valuable information, but they also leave much to be inferred and even imagined. Missions are broad, general statements outlining what makes the organization unique.

A good mission should answer a series of questions. When you read the assigned case, ask if you know enough about the organization's mission to confidently speculate about the following:

1. Who are the customers? The customers may be children, older adults, women, or patients in a hospital. This group or these groups must be identified before any serious strategic analysis of the organization can be initiated.
2. What are the organization's principal services? Does the organization have unique experience and expertise in some areas of specialization?
3. Where does the organization intend to compete? Is the case about a small retail outlet that competes only in one local market, or is it a regional or national force in the delivery of consumer goods?
4. Who are the competitors? Is the case about an industrial product with a few well-known competitors, or does it operate in a market along with many other similar competitors? In other words, how much competition is actually present in the market(s) where the organization competes or intends to compete?
5. What is the preference of the organization with regard to its public image? If a large clothing manufacturer wants to be perceived in certain ways, it may have to limit its options when defining and solving strategic issues. Is it, for example, important to the leadership of the clothes manufacturer that it be regarded as a producer of designer clothing or a good value for the money?
6. What does the organization want to be like in the future? Does the information in the case indicate the organization wants to continue to operate as it does at the present time, or does it wish to expand its markets and services offered or even change its own basic operating philosophy?[2]

[1] Peter F. Drucker, *Management: Tasks, Responsibilities, and Practices* (New York: Harper & Row, 1974).
[2] John Pearce II and Fred David, "Corporate Mission Statements: The Bottom Line," *Academy of Management Executive*, May, 1987, pp. 109–116.

If a formal mission statement is not presented in a case, it may be important to attempt to construct one based on the information provided.

Objectives: More Specific Directions

Mission statements are broad and provide general direction. Objectives should be specific and explicitly point to where the organization is expected to be at a particular time in the future. Sometimes the case will indicate what the organization plans to achieve in the next year, where it hopes to be in three years, or even its five-year objectives. As with mission statements, if the objectives are not explicitly stated, there is a need to speculate about them, as they will be the standards against which the success or failure of a particular strategy will be evaluated.

When constructing or modifying organization objectives, be sure they are as measurable as possible. This is important so that decision makers can use them as a reflection of organizational priorities and as a way of determining how to set their own personal and professional priorities. Make sure that the objectives are motivational and inspirational, yet feasible and attainable. Moreover, because strategic marketing is futuristic and no one can predict the future with complete accuracy, objectives should always be adaptable to the changing conditions taking place in the organization and in the industry. Sometimes an organization will have to face a major strategic problem simply because it was unwilling to alter its objectives in light of changing conditions in the industry.

As a test of your own understanding of the organization under examination, before attacking problems, reflect on what your reading of the case told you about the mission and objectives of the organization. Are the objectives being pursued consistent with what you understand to be the mission of the organization? Are the aspirations of the organization's managers realistic in view of the competition and the organization's strengths and weaknesses?

Strategic Marketing Issues

Once the corporate mission and objectives have been reviewed, the current marketing strategies should be evaluated. A good starting point for this analysis is to consider the company's stated target market in relation to what you have discovered concerning the external environment. Proper identification of the target market is a key decision in strategic marketing. In most cases you should consider such questions as:

1. Has the market been segmented by competitors? What is the basis for segmentation? Which segments are the largest? Which have the most potential? How well are the segments being served?
2. Is the total market growing? Is the company's segment growing? Is the company's segment of the market large enough to support the product or service?
3. Are there segments that are not currently being served? Could the company successfully serve these markets?

4. Are the company's products and services matched well with the specified target market?
5. Are there any economic, social, political, regulatory, technological, or competitive changes anticipated that will change the dynamics of the industry?

In addition to these important questions, you should do a complete analysis of the marketing mix developed to meet the needs of the target market. This analysis will require you to perform a comparative analysis of industry pricing practices, promotional approaches, distribution methods, and product attributes. As the marketing mix for direct and indirect competitors is linked with their segmentation strategies, you will gain new insights as to the dynamics of the industry. If you are to develop an effective marketing strategy, you need to understand the key "players" in the industry.

Strengths, Weaknesses, Opportunities, and Threats

Once we have reviewed our situation, a better evaluation of the opportunities and threats facing the organization can be made. Moreover, we must be able to look objectively at our own organization and ask: "Given the organization's apparent strengths and weaknesses how do we take advantage of our opportunities and avoid the dangers in the environment?" An effective way of asking these questions is with the use of SWOT (strengths, weaknesses, opportunities, and threats) analysis. Exhibit A.2 presents an example of how SWOT analysis is organized.

EXHIBIT A.2   Strengths, Weaknesses, Opportunities, and Threats (SWOT) Analysis

Internal Strengths	Internal Weaknesses
1. The ability to deliver a quality product at a reasonable price.	1. Limited menu.
2. Strong consumer franchise in the southeastern region of the United States.	2. Limited geographic area.
3. Operating at near capacity with current menu.	3. Limited number of qualified restaurant managers.
4. Strong in current market niche.	4. Aging restaurants.

External Opportunities	External Threats
1. Eating out is increasing in the United States.	1. Health trends in the consumption of red meat.
2. Dining out market is extremely large.	2. Aggressive competition.
	3. Decline in the steak segment of the eating-away-from-home market.

An illustration may help you to understand how SWOT analysis relates strengths, weaknesses, opportunities, and threats. Suppose in the case that you are studying, the chief executive officer of a regional restaurant chain, specializing in steaks, is considering expansion into a new geographic region (market development). An environmental analysis confirms that people are increasingly eating out because of more disposable income, more two-income families, and less time available for meal preparation. In addition, the analysis has revealed that the market is extremely large and well segmented. Also, it has been determined that interest rates are at a 20-year low and expansion could be financed through debt. Research reveals that the consumption of red meat is on the decline and there is a trend toward declining market share for steak menu restaurants. In addition, there is increasing competition in the non-red meat segment.

The CEO believes that the restaurant chain has a number of internal strengths. It has, for example, a reputation for delivering a quality product at a reasonable price. It has developed a strong image and loyalty in the southeastern region of the United States. In addition, the chain is operating at near-full capacity with their steak menu. There are few strong competitors in its niche of the market. A review of the restaurant chain's financial statements indicated that it could easily absorb additional debt financing that would be necessary for aggressive expansion.

The CEO does worry about the chain's limited menu. In addition, many of the company's restaurants are aging and will need to be remodeled in the coming years. Although management is currently strong, finding well-qualified restaurant managers is becoming increasingly difficult. The CEO also worries that because of his current level of penetration in the southeastern market, further growth will be limited without expansion into a new geographic market.

Through the use of SWOT analysis, the CEO can systematically look at the opportunities, threats, strengths, and weaknesses and make a more informed decision.

FINDING PROBLEMS

From your very first reading, start to list the strategic marketing problems and opportunities facing the organization. When a problem is discovered, mark it for more detailed examination. Situation analysis is designed to surface present and potential problems. Perhaps there are few, if any, apparent problems. In case analysis, problems include not only the usual idea of a "problem" but also situations where things may be working well but improvements are possible. As noted previously, the "problem" may actually be an opportunity that can be capitalized on by the organization if it acts consciously and decisively.

When we analyze things carefully, patterns can be detected, and discrepancies between what actually is and what ought to be become more apparent. In other words, fundamental issues, not mere symptoms, begin to emerge.

Looking for Real Causes Not Symptoms

It is important to realize that the things observed in an organization and reported in a case may not be the "real" or essential problems and opportunities. Often what we observe are the symptoms of more serious core problems. For example, declining sales appears to be a problem in many case analyses. In reality, the problem may be poor training of the sales force, inferior product quality, distribution problems causing out of stocks, incorrect positioning, prices that are too high (or too low), and so forth. The fundamental problem, however, might be changes in the demographics of the market. Problems may have more than a single cause, so do not be overly confident when a single, simple reason is isolated. In fact, the suggestion of a simple solution should increase rather than decrease our skepticism.

Getting to core problems requires that information be carefully examined and analyzed, and quantitative tools can often help. Financial ratio analysis of the exhibits included in the case will sometimes be helpful in identifying the real problems. Appendix B illustrates how financial analysis and information can be used to identify core problems in an organization.

In arriving at the ultimate determination of core problems, case analysis should never be "paralyzed by analysis" and waste more time than is necessary on identifying problems. At the same time, premature judgments about problem areas should not be made because of the risk of missing the "real" issues.

Always review the obtainable sources of data before moving to the next step. One general guideline is that when research and analysis cease to generate surprises (when we can confidently say, "I have seen that before") we can feel relatively, but not absolutely, sure that adequate research has been conducted and the core problems have been identified.

Identifying Important Issues

Once the problems are identified, they must be precisely stated and the selection defended. The best defense for the selection of the core problem is the data set used to guide the problem discovery process. The reasons for selection of the problems and issues should be briefly and specifically summarized along with the supportive information upon which judgments have been based.

The problem statement stage is not the time for solutions. Focusing on solutions at this point will reduce the impact of the problem statement. If the role of consultant has been assumed, the problem statement must be convincing, precise, and logical to the client organization or credibility will be reduced. If the role of the strategic decision maker has been selected, you must be equally convincing and precise. The strategic decision maker should be as confident as possible that the correct problems have been identified in order to pursue the appropriate opportunities. After all, the manager will be the one responsible for ensuring things actually happen and strategies are actually implemented.

The statement of the problem should relate only to those areas of strategy and operations where actions have a chance of producing results. The results may be either increasing gains or cutting potential losses. Long- and short-range aspects of problems should also be identified and stated. In strategic analysis the emphasis is on long-range problems rather than merely patching up emergencies and holding things together.

It is important to keep in mind that most strategic decision makers can deal with only a limited number of issues at a single time. Therefore, identify key result areas that will have the greatest positive impact on organizational performance.

ANALYSIS

When the problems in the case are satisfactorily defined, they must be analyzed. This involves generating alternative solutions and evaluating the alternatives. This should not be done without thinking about and using the concepts that you have previously learned in marketing and other courses that you have taken.

Developing a Theoretical Perspective

One of the most serious mistakes made in case analysis is to attempt analysis inside a "theoretical vacuum." It is important that the problems be defined and opportunities be evaluated according to some consistent theoretical perspective. Do not be afraid to use the concepts and terms that you have learned from various marketing classes. At the same time, do not "load" your analysis with explanations and definitions of those concepts and terms. Your professor has taught those ideas, and fellow students are supposed to know them.

It might be that problems concerning lack of revenue growth are really problems of not responding adequately to customer needs—the lack of a marketing orientation. In the past, some organizations have tended to disregard the importance of the "strategic decision" to focus on the customer. Many revenue shortfalls could be resolved with the use of the relatively simple marketing philosophy. A proper theoretical perspective, for example, might suggest that consumers are less concerned with the location than they are with how they are treated when they arrive.

Diffusion of innovation is a concept that could be used to explain why a product in the introductory stage of the product life cycle is not increasing in sales as rapidly as the company had hoped. Suggesting that a dominant firm in an industry buy out competition to increase market share illustrates that you do not understand the forms of business competition and the constraints facing each form. Do not become so focused on the case that you forget the realities of the marketplace.

Alternative Actions and Solutions

If the job of obtaining and organizing information has been done well, the generation of alternatives will be a challenging yet attainable task. Good alternatives possess specific characteristics. They should be *practical,* or no one will seriously consider them. Alternative courses of action that are too theoretical or abstract to be understood by those who have to accomplish them are not useful. Alternatives should be *carefully stated* with a brief justification of why they are useful ways of solving at least one of the core problems in the case. Alternatives should be *specific.* Relate each alternative to the core problem it is intended to address. This is a good check on your work. If the alternatives generated do not directly address core problems, ask yourself if they are important to the case analysis or whether they should be eliminated from consideration.

Finally, alternatives should be *usable.* A usable alternative is one that can be reasonably accomplished within the constraints of the financial and human resources available to the organization. Alternatives should be ones that can be *placed into action* in a relatively short period of time. If it takes too long to implement a proposed solution, it is likely that the momentum of the recommended action will be lost. Of course, implementation should always take place in light of potential long-range effects of shorter-term decisions.

After the alternatives have been generated and listed, each one must be (1) evaluated in terms of the core problems and key result areas isolated in the prior analysis, (2) evaluated in terms of its relative advantage or disadvantage compared to other possible solutions to core problems, and (3) justified as a potentially valuable way of addressing the strategic issues found in the case.

Evaluating Alternatives

Alternatives should be evaluated according to both quantitative and qualitative criteria. Break-even analysis provides one basis for examining the impact of different courses of action. However, a good alternative course of action is more than merely the one with the lowest break-even. A poorer-quality product, offered at a low price, would achieve a low break-even, but would it diminish the prestige of the company's other brands? What other long-term effects might occur?

Carefully think through the advantages and disadvantages of each alternative. All alternatives have disadvantages; you cannot ignore an evaluation/ assessment of the risks associated with an alternative. Sometimes information in the case will provide the basis for evaluating the alternatives. The company states that it is intent on growth but refuses to borrow money. Which alternatives can offer growth at a very low cost?

Once the alternatives have been evaluated, one must be selected. At this point it is *absolutely essential* to completely understand the criteria upon which the selection is being made and the justification for the criteria. Sometimes the key to identifying the criteria is in the case itself. At other times it is necessary to look outside to what is going on in the industry. Is competition for services so fierce that capital investment decisions are likely to radically affect the organization's ability to compete? If so, should the organization intentionally postpone short-term actions to ensure sufficient resources are dedicated to modernization of facilities and the purchase of up-to-date technologies in order to improve the chances of long-range growth and development?

MAKING RECOMMENDATIONS

Making good recommendations is a critical aspect of successful case analysis. If recommendations are theoretically sound and justifiable, people will pay attention to them. If they are not, little is likely to result from all the work done to this point.

One effective method for presenting recommendations is to relate each one to organizational strengths. Or, if necessary, a recommendation can illustrate how it assists in avoiding known weaknesses. For example, if the marketing resources are limited, it will be important to avoid recommendations that rely on resources that are not available. Beware of recommending marketing research. In most instances the decision maker does not have six months or a year that it would take to perform the research. If you see no other alternative, specify concisely the type of research you would do, what results you expect, what decision you would make based on the results expected, and your prediction as to the likelihood of the results you expect. In case analysis, further research is a difficult recommendation to support.

IMPLEMENTATION

Once the strategic alternative(s) has been selected to recommend, implementation has to be considered. Implementation moves the decision maker from the realm of strategic marketing to marketing management. The question becomes, "How do we get all this done in the most effective and efficient way possible?"

The task of case analysis cannot require that the student implement a decision in a real firm. However, since alternatives must be "implementable," it is necessary that thought be given to how each alternative would actually be put into action. Implementation requires two important steps for each recommended alternative. First, the decision maker must decide what activities are needed to accomplish the alternative action. This involves thinking through the process and outlining all the steps that will be required. Next the list of required activities should be carefully reviewed to determine who in the organization will be assigned the responsibility for accomplishing the different tasks.

Although implementation is not generally possible in case analysis, it is important that consideration be given to how, in a real organization, the recommendations would be accomplished. If, in the process of thinking about completing the different activities it becomes apparent that the organization does not have the resources nor the structure to accomplish the recommendations, other approaches should be proposed.

FINALIZING THE REPORT

The preparation and presentation of the case report are the end result of case analysis. The report can be either written or oral, depending on the preference of the instructor, but the goal is the same—to summarize and communicate in an effective manner what the analysis has uncovered. In view of the strategic problems and the operational condition of the organization the *alternative* courses of action can now be generated and listed. Each of the alternatives can then be *evaluated*. When the evaluation is complete, the *recommendations* should be presented in considerable detail and particular attention given to the problem of *implementation*.

CONCLUSIONS

Case analysis is an art, and there is no one precise way of accomplishing the task. Adapt the analysis to the case problem under review. The thing to keep in mind is that case analysis is a logical process that involves (1) understanding the organization, industry, and environment; (2) clear definition of strategic problems and opportunities; (3) generation of alternative courses of action; (4) analysis, evaluation, and recommendation of the most promising courses of action; (5) and at least some consideration of implementation.

The work of case analysis is not over until all these stages are completed. Often a formal written report or oral presentation of the recommendations is required (see Appendix C). Case analysis and presentation should always be approached and accomplished in a professional manner. Case problems provide a unique opportunity to integrate all you have learned about decision making and direct it toward specific problems and opportunities faced by real organizations. It is an exciting way to gain experience and decision-making skills. Take it seriously and develop your own systematic and defensible way of solving strategic marketing problems.

REFERENCES

EDGE, ALFRED G., AND DENIS R. COLEMAN. *The Guide to Case Analysis and Reporting,* 3rd ed. Honolulu: System Logic, 1986.
RONSTADT, ROBERT. *The Art of Case Analysis.* Dover, MA: Lord, 1980.

—————————— APPENDIX B ——————————

Financial Analysis for Marketing Strategists
by Bennie H. Nunnally, Jr.

INTRODUCTION

Marketers cannot make decisions without considering the financial implications of those decisions. It requires capital to pursue growth opportunities, to battle for market share as a challenger against a strong market leader, to introduce new products, and to try a multitude of other alternatives that a marketing manager may consider. But does the firm have sufficient flexibility, in a financial sense, to pursue one or more alternatives? An investigation of the firm's financial condition can lead to better decision making.

Financial condition is represented by the firm's profitability, liquidity, asset management, and financing pattern. Although profitability is probably self-explanatory, the other concepts, which may be observed and analyzed from the firm's financial statements, will briefly be explained. Liquidity represents the firm's ability to pay its current liabilities (e.g., accounts payable, wages/taxes payable) out of its current assets (e.g., cash and accounts receivable). Asset management information reveals the firm's ability to make use of its cash, land and buildings, and equipment in order to increase the value of the firm. The firm's financing pattern refers to the amount of debt used by the firm to finance its assets, and how, if at all, that pattern compares to similar firms or to the firm's own operating history.

Once specific alternatives have been determined and marketing managers are assessing the costs and benefits of each alternative, break-even analysis can provide additional useful information. Break-even analysis has as its foundation those factors that affect profit: sales volume, variable costs, and fixed costs. Break-even volume is that level of sales wherein profit is zero, or revenue equals fixed plus variable (total) costs.

Financial planners, marketers, and others involved in planning are interested in the break-even concept because it highlights the sales volume of the firm's products. The level of sales affects profitability, production, purchasing, personnel, and more, and bears directly on the need for funds, either short term or long term.

THE BASIC FINANCIAL STATEMENTS

The financial statements issued by for-profit firms are found in their annual reports. The annual report is both an official (audited financial statement) and unofficial (management assessments and projections of a relatively nonquantitative nature) record of the company's position at that point in time. An annual report is issued by all firms whose stock is publicly traded. The financial statements found in the annual report are the balance sheet, income statement, statement of changes in financial position, and the statement of retained earnings.

To analyze financial statements it is necessary to understand the relationship among the statements. In order to understand such an interrelationship it is important to become familiar with each individual statement. A first step in becoming skillful in statement analysis is to learn the general format. If the format is familiar, it becomes much easier to learn the techniques of analysis.

For example, there is a pattern to the structure or format of the balance sheet. Simply, the balance sheet items are arranged in descending order of liquidity. Familiarity with the statements will greatly contribute to the interesting, useful, and, yes, marketable things that will be learned in this note.

Exhibits B.1, B.2, B.3, and B.4 illustrate the financial statements of the Wick Manufacturing Company. The format of each statement is typical of those released by most firms. Wick manufactures various paper and cardboard containers, and most sales are to the grocery industry.

The Income Statement

The firm's income statement, sometimes called a profit and loss statement, reflects the sales less the expenses related to making those sales for a specific period of time. Taxes are also shown on the income statement, with a final figure being net income. In Exhibit B.1 the net income after-tax is divided by the number of common shares outstanding to reflect the earnings as it applies to each share of outstanding common stock (earnings per share, or EPS). In addition, the amount of net income actually paid out as dividends is shown on Wick's income statement. The dividends paid are based on a predetermined and relatively stable company policy but are declared by the board of directors in each dividend period.

The Balance Sheet

A balance sheet (Exhibit B.2) shows the financial condition of the firm at a particular point in time. In the case of Wick Manufacturing Company, the balance sheets are provided for the end of the calendar years 1992 and 1993. The calendar year and the firm's fiscal year (the accounting period that begins and ends at a

EXHIBIT B.1   Wick Manufacturing Company Income Statement for Years Ended 1992 and 1993

	1992	1993
Sales	$109,848	$126,540
Cost of Goods Sold[a]	68,065	72,834
Gross Profit	41,783	53,706
Expenses (Selling, Administrative, Interest, Depreciation)	27,462	31,044
Profit before Tax	14,321	22,662
Taxes (45%)	6,444	10,198
Net Income	$ 7,877	$ 12,464
Earnings per Share (EPS)	7.88	12.46
Dividends per Share (DPS 49% of EPS)	3.86	6.11
[a] Determined as follows:		
Beginning Inventory	$ 28,663	$ 27,462
Purchases	66,864	76,953
Goods Available for Sale	95,527	104,415
Ending Inventory	27,462	31,581
Costs of Goods Sold	$ 68,065	$ 72,834

EXHIBIT B.2   Wick Manufacturing Company Balance Sheet, December 31, 1992, and December 31, 1993

	1992	1993
Assets		
Cash	$ 6,925	$ 8,185
Account Receivable	418	481
Inventory	27,462	31,581
Total Current Assets	34,805	40,247
Property, Plant, Equipment	14,328	16,477
Accumulated Depreciation	1,194	1,374
Net Property, Plant, Equipment	13,134	15,104
Total Assets	$47,939	$55,351
Liabilities and Stockholders' Equity		
Accounts Payable	4,537	5,218
Accrued Wages and Taxes	2,448	2,815
Total Current Liabilities	6,985	8,033
Long-Term Debt (12%)	5,134	5,134
Common Stock (1,000 Shares)	11,940	11,940
Paid-In Capital	5,970	5,970
Retained Earnings	17,910	24,274
Total Liabilities and Stockholders' Equity	$47,939	$55,351

particular time during the year, as determined by company management and at the end of which the annual reports are issued) may not coincide. The assets shown in Exhibit B.2 represent the means of production that are owned by the firm. The liabilities and equity represent the claims on these assets. That section shows all current liabilities and other debt items and the owner-supplied capital such as stockholders' equity. (The sum of common stock, retained earnings, and paid-in capital, which is dollars received for common stock in excess of par value, equals stockholders' equity.) The assets must equal the liabilities plus capital of the firm.

Statement of Retained Earnings

A firm has two uses for its profit (Exhibit B.3). A portion is paid to the owners (equity holders) as dividends. The remaining profit is retained in the firm, thereby becoming a part, or perhaps all, of the financing for the assets of the firm. That part retained in the firm is added to the balance sheet item "retained earnings" at the end of each accounting period. This is an important way in which the income statement and balance sheet are interrelated.

Statement of Changes in Financial Position

A company's managers, its creditors, and other individuals or organizations will at some point be interested in a firm's liquidity. Liquidity refers to the ease with which an asset can be converted to cash. This would be most important to creditors, say, if the firm were to become bankrupt. The change in financial position, as well as the current financial position, relates directly to the question of liquidity. Exhibit B.4 illustrates the uses of funds by Wick Manufacturing Company, and the sources of funds between 1992 and 1993. The statement of changes in financial position is often referred to as a "source and use of funds" statements because it illustrates the origin or source of money used by the firm in a given time period. The following definitions may help to clarify the nature of sources and uses of funds.

A *source of funds* is an increase in the liability or capital account or a decrease in an asset account. A *use of funds* is a decrease in a liability or capital account or increase in an asset account. For example, in Exhibit B.2 Wick Manufacturing had an increase in accounts receivable of $63 ($481 − $418) between year-end 1992 and year end 1993. That was a use of funds of $63 for that period because Wick committed $63 in additional funds for that period to an asset.

EXHIBIT B.3   Wick Manufacturing Company Statement of Retained Earnings

Retained Earnings Balance, December 31, 1992	$17,910
Plus Net Income, 1993	12,464
Less Dividends Paid, 1993	(6,100)
Retained Earnings Balance, December 31, 1993	$24,274

EXHIBIT B.4   Wick Manufacturing Company Statement of Changes in Financial Position, December 31, 1993

Sources

Profit after Tax	$12,464
Depreciation	180
Total Sources	$12,644

Uses

Dividends	$ 6,101
Fixed Assets	2,149
Net Change in Working Capital	4,394
	$12,644

Analysis of Working Capital Changes

Increase (Decrease) in Current Assets		Increase (Decrease) in Current Liabilities	
Cash	$1,260		
Accounts Receivable	63	Accounts Payable	$ 681
Inventory	4,119	Accruals	367
Total	$5,442	Total	$1,048

Increase in Current Assets	$5,442
Increase in Current Liabilities	1,048
Net Change in Working Capital	$4,394

By contrast, the $681 increase in accounts payable for the same period represents a source of funds for the firm because Wick's suppliers financed Wick's increased payables for that period.

The preparation of the sources and uses of funds statement begins with the selection of an interval of time, one fiscal year to the next, for example. Then the items that provided cash or require cash, for that time period, are compared. The result will be the effect of the "cash movement" upon working capital. *Working capital* is current assets and current liabilities collectively; *net working capital* is current assets minus current liabilities.

A sources and uses of funds statement also permits the maturity of the sources and uses to be compared. It is necessary, in general, that the maturity of the source (short term, such as an increase in accounts payable) be matched with the maturity of the use (short term, such as an increase in inventory). Such maturity matching will likely lead to improved control over the firm's working capital. That improved control will likely reduce the level or frequency of borrowed funds.

SELECTED FINANCIAL RATIOS

The analysis of financial statements involves recognizing the information conveyed by each statement and the interrelationships among the statements. In addition, the time for which the statement is analyzed should be consistent if more than one type of statement is being reviewed. The information content of the financial statements can best be illustrated in terms of financial ratio analysis.

Financial ratio analysis is a means of reviewing financial data relative to some standard. That standard may be trend (activity over time) or industry comparison or both. The ratios may be divided into five categories: (1) current ratios, (2) debt ratios, (3) asset managment ratios, (4) profitability ratios, and (5) market value ratios. The financial data presented for Wick Manufacturing Company will be used to illustrate the ratios used most by marketers: the liquidity ratios, the asset management ratios, and the profit to sales ratio.

Liquidity Ratios

As noted previously, a firm's liquidity is a major concern for anyone who has dollars invested in that firm or anticipates investment in the firm. Liquidity ratios indicate whether a firm has enough cash or other liquid assets to meet its short-term obligations.

Current Ratio. The current ratio is equal to current assets divided by the current liabilities. Current assets are those assets that will be converted to cash within the near future, usually a year or less. Current liabilities are those liabilities that will likely be paid within a year's time. The current assets and liabilities are liquidated as a normal part of the firm's business activities. The current ratio is a direct measure of the firm's liquidity. For Wick Manufacturing the current ratios for 1992 and 1993 are as follows:

$$\text{Current ratio} = \frac{\text{Current assets}}{\text{Current liabilities}}$$

$$\text{Current ratio}_{1992} = \frac{\$34,805}{\$6,985} = 4.98 \times$$

$$\text{Current ratio}_{1993} = \frac{\$40,247}{\$8,033} = 5.0 \times$$

An interested party can immediately draw the following information from the company's current ratio: (1) if the firm had to liquidate (pay its creditors and cease operation), it would be able to cover each dollar owed in current liabilities with approximately $5 of current assets. (2) Assuming an industry average of 4 times, then Wick is 25 percent more liquid than the average firm in the industry. Therefore, Wick's current ratio is favorable.

Quick Ratio. Again, the items on the balance sheet are arranged in descending order of liquidity—if inventory (often the least liquid of the current assets) is not a part of the firm's liquidity then we may calculate a "quick" ratio for Wick. The quick ratio is equal to the current assets, minus inventory, divided by total current liabilities. Thus, if Wick had to liquidate quickly it could still cover its current liabilities even if inventory were not readily convertible to cash. As with the current ratio, the quick ratio (sometimes called the acid-test ratio) can be compared to an industry average or to the firm's own performance during some prior period.

$$\text{Quick ratio} = \frac{\text{Current assets } - \text{ inventory}}{\text{Current liabilities}}$$

$$\text{Quick ratio}_{1993} = \frac{\$40,247 - \$31,581}{\$8,033}$$

$$= 1.08 \times$$

Asset Management Ratios

The asset management ratios illustrate the firm's effectiveness (relative to an industry or trend comparison) in managing its assets. In order for a firm's performance to be at maximum, the assets should be neither too high nor too low in terms of their dollar value as shown on the balance sheet. Excessive asset levels (e.g., inventory) will generally reduce the return on total assets, and inadequate asset levels may cause missed sales opportunities.

Average Collection Period (ACP).   The ACP provides a view of the firm's management of its accounts receivable. Specifically, the ratio answers the question "How long have the receivables, on average, been outstanding?" Thus, the ratio provides an answer in number of days:

$$\text{ACP} = \frac{\text{Accounts receivable}}{\text{Average sales per day}}$$

$$\text{ACP}_{1993} = \frac{\$481}{(\$126,540/360 \text{ days})} = 1.37 \text{ days}$$

The foregoing ACP implies that Wick does virtually a "cash" business, meaning it has very little (1.37 days) lag time between the time a sale is made and the time of collection for that sale. If Wick's terms of sale are cash, then its ACP corresponds very closely to those terms. A very high number of days may indicate the firm is too liberal in its credit policies.

Inventory Utilization.   The inventory utilization ratio (sometimes called stock turnover) is sales divided by inventories:

$$\text{Inventory utilization} = \frac{\text{Sales}}{\text{Inventories}}$$

$$\text{Inventory utilization}_{1993} = \frac{\$126,540}{\$31,581} = 4.01 \times$$

Again, the ratio of slightly over four times for Wick's inventory utilization may be compared to the industry average or to the company's trend data. It would be more representative of the month-by-month sales of the company's goods if the average inventory were used as the denominator in the foregoing ratio. Average inventory may be thought of as the addition of the beginning of the year inventory plus the end of year inventory divided by 2. Other averaging techniques should be used if sales follow a seasonal pattern or a pattern that is other than evenly spread throughout the year.

Fixed Asset Utilization.   Many of the funds obtained by a firm to produce continued growth in sales and earnings are invested in fixed assets. The fixed asset utilization ratio tells us in very specific, comparative terms how well the fixed assets are being used as a means of generating sales. We see those assets shown as "property, plant, and equipment" on Wick's balance sheet:

$$\text{Fixed asset utilization} = \frac{\text{Sales}}{\text{Net fixed assets}}$$

$$\text{Fixed asset utilization}_{1993} = \frac{\$126,540}{\$15,104} = 8.38 \times$$

Profitability Ratios

The firm's profitability is important to every individual or organization connected in any way to the success of that firm. In the business media we hear or read about "profits," return on equity, and other references to a company's profitability. There are several ways to measure profitability.

Profit Margin.   One of the most commonly used measures is the profit margin on sales or the relationship of dollars of profit to dollars of sales:

$$\text{Profit margin on sales} = \frac{\text{Net income}}{\text{Sales}}$$

$$\text{Profit margin on sales}_{1993} = \frac{\$12,464}{\$126,540}$$

$$= 9.8\%$$

Thus, for each dollar of sales made by Wick in 1993, 9.8 cents was profit after all expenses have been paid. The dividends to the firm's owners (stockholders) are paid from the 9.8 percent of profit, and the remainder becomes a part of the balance sheet item identified as "retained earnings." Retained earnings represent the accumulation of the dollars reinvested in the business over the entire life of the firm.

Return on Assets (ROA).   This ratio measures company profitability as it relates to the total assets of the firm. It answers the question "How much profit is earned on each dollar of assets?"

$$ROA = \frac{\text{Net income}}{\text{Total assets}}$$

$$ROA_{1993} = \frac{\$12,464}{\$55,351}$$

$$= 22.5\%$$

Each dollar of assets earned Wick 22.5 cents in after-tax profit in 1993. That level of return may be assessed against an industry average or Wick's previous years.

Return on Equity (ROE).   Those who invest equity funds in the firm, the common stockholders, will obviously be interested in the profitability of their investment. If we are able to determine the profitability of assets (ROA) or of sales (profit margin), then it is also useful to compute the return on the equity portion of the firm's financing:

$$ROE = \frac{\text{Net income}}{\text{Common equity}}$$

$$ROE_{1993} = \frac{\$12,464}{\$42,184} = 29.5\%$$

From the profitability ratios, then, we may view profitability in terms of sales, assets, or equity. As before, industry and trend comparisons allow an evaluation to be made about the firm's effectiveness in any of these areas.

LIMITATIONS OF RATIO ANALYSIS

The financial ratios that have been discussed in the preceding sections provide valuable, easily interpreted information concerning a firm and the industry in which it operates. We see that much of what is illustrated by the ratios—profitability, asset management, and so on—depend upon certain reasonable similarities between the firm's financial condition and the industry in which it operates, or between the firm's present and past operating environments, or both.

If inflation were severe in the early or later years of a trend analysis, the trend comparison would be less meaningful. For example, abnormally higher inventory prices in a period may distort resulting inventory values and corresponding ratios. Another example would be more or less cash on hand based on the prevailing economic conditions or the expected economic conditions.

If the age of the assets owned by the company is less than is typical in the industry, certain ratios may also be affected. For example, if old assets, fully depreciated, are held by the industry, and the firm's assets are new, the firm's asset management ratios (e.g., fixed asset utilization) cannot be meaningfully compared to industry ratios.

Therefore, when conducting a trend or industry comparison using financial ratios, the foregoing precautions must be taken into consideration. How to take such factors into consideration and to what extent require judgment relative to each situation. Such judgment is developed by the "learning-by-doing" method based on the techniques presented in this note.

THE BREAK-EVEN POINT

The steps involved in assessing the break-even point (BEP) of a firm require the following: (1) Costs must be separated into one of two categories—fixed costs or variable costs. (2) The firm's production capacity must be known. (3) Equally important is a clear knowledge of the demand level for the product.

Once the foregoing factors are well understood, work can focus upon the break-even analysis. The break-even analysis is merely a tool. It has relevance for the following functions:

a. Marketing

b. Capital acquisitions (property, plant, and equipment)

c. Production

Marketing personnel are interested in break-even analysis because it provides the very valuable information necessary for comparing break-even volume to demand. If break-even volume is 100,000 units for a product and the demand forecast is for 80,000 units, the product under most circumstances will be omitted from the firm's product line.

Much the same could be said for the capital budgeting analysts' use of break-even analysis. A combination of demand and break-even volume information will assist in the decision concerning whether new machinery or plant space should be acquired. Production personnel would use similar information as gathered by the other two functions for use in the production planning process.

The components of break-even analysis are fixed costs (FC), variable costs (VC), and selling price per unit (SP). The formula for determining break-even is:

$$BEP = \frac{FC}{SP - VC}$$

Data for the Garrison Engineering Company, a maker of precision metal stress measuring devices, is provided in Exhibit B.5 to illustrate the break-even concept.

The company developed a new metal X-ray device called product G-3. G-3 will sell for $300 per unit. The variable cost per unit to produce G-3 is $150. The company's cost accountants have, in addition to estimating variable costs, determined total fixed costs of production to be $1,200,000. What is the break-even point for G-3? That is, what number of units of the product must be produced and sold to just cover total costs?

$$BEP_{G3} = \frac{\$1,200,000}{\$300 - \$150}$$

$$= 8,000 \text{ units}$$

Eight thousand units of the G-3 device must be sold in order for the firm to break even on the product. Put differently, if 8,000 units are produced and sold, revenue will just cover total cost. Profit at 8,000 units will be zero. Exhibit B.5, which illustrates costs and volume at various levels of production, further highlights the concept of the break-even point.

The information in Exhibit B.5 permits an inspection of the interrelatedness of the sales and costs as they directly affect the profit or loss of the product. It may be equally useful to depict that interaction using a graphical representation as shown in Exhibit B.6. The intersection of the sales revenue and total cost lines is the product's break-even point. Again, at the break-even sales level of 8,000 units of the G-3 device, total costs and total revenue are equal at $2,400,000. Profit is zero at the break-even point. As usual, the graph permits a more visual interpretation of the idea. A graph often facilitates a more immediate and clear understanding of the facts or assumptions at hand.

Break-Even Analysis and Risk

The concept of the break-even point is a risk assessment concept. Break-even analysis permits the firm's management to more clearly answer the following questions: (1) What quantity of a product must be sold in order to begin to earn a profit? (2) How likely is it that such a sales level will be reached? The break-even point permits a straightforward answer to the first question.

The second question can be answered with greater assurance if the weighted average probabilistic concepts are put to use. Sources from inside or outside the firm familiar with the sales prospects of the product can provide data and information on the likely sales level. Such information can easily be transformed into a weighted average level of sales. That sales level, along with pessimistic and optimistic sales levels, is then compared to the break-even volume. A decision is then possible as to whether to proceed with production.

EXHIBIT B.5   Garrison Engineering Corporation—Sales Level, Cost, and Profit

1 Units Sold	2 Variable Cost	3 Fixed Cost	4 Total Cost	5 Total Revenue	6 Profit (Loss)
0	0	$1,200,000	$1,200,000	0	$(1,200,000)
4,000	600,000	1,200,000	1,800,000	$1,200,000	(600,000)
8,000	1,200,000	1,200,000	2,400,000	2,400,000	0
12,000	$1,800,000	$1,200,000	$3,000,000	$3,600,000	$ 600,000

EXHIBIT B.6   Garrison Engineering Corporation Break-Even Chart

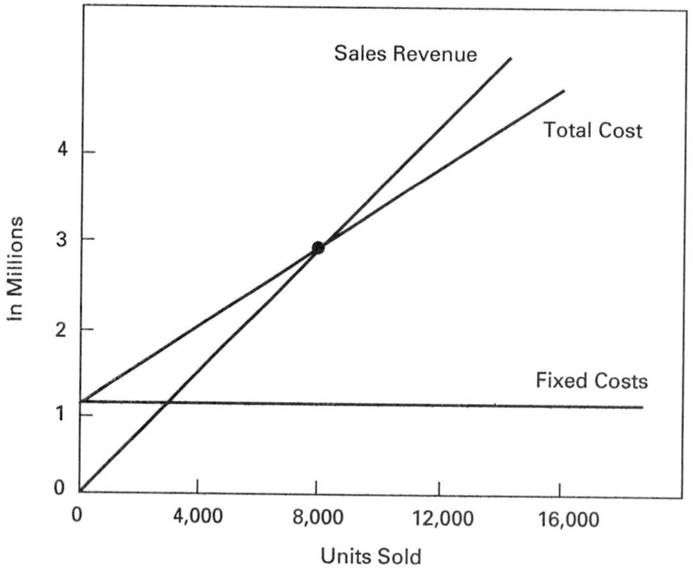

For example, if the most likely (weighted average) sales level is 12,000 units as in the case of Garrison, then the firm can see that reaching the break-even sales level is likely. If the weighted average demand for the product were 8,500 units, or even 9,000 units, then the chance of reaching the BEP would seem less likely. Such judgments, however, depend upon the probability distribution of the sales projections.

Contribution to Fixed Costs and Profit

To return to the actual dollar values in the break-even concept, the concept of contribution margin is important. When variable costs are covered by the selling price of an item, as in the case of product G-3, for example, the difference between the variable cost per unit and the selling price per unit is called the contribution margin—the amount above the variable cost that contributes to the coverage of fixed costs and profit.

If we consider Exhibits B.5 and B.6, sales of 8,000 units (the break-even point) allows coverage of the fixed costs. When the sales level goes beyond the break-even point, the $150 contribution margin contributes entirely to profits. Exhibit B.6 illustrates an increasing profit level (the distance between the total cost and total revenue lines) as the sales level exceeds the break-even point.

Cash Break-Even Analysis

The discussion of break-even analysis to this point has focused upon variable and fixed costs without considering the composition of these costs. Not all the fixed costs call for an outlay of cash. Consider depreciation, a common element of the firm's total fixed costs. Since depreciation is not a cash item, the break-even concept developed so far may represent an overstatement of the true break-even concept in terms of cash. If we again consider Exhibit B.5, the fixed costs amount to $1,200,000. If we assume that 10 percent of the fixed costs is depreciation, then what is the break-even point on a cash basis? That is, what sales level must be achieved in order to cover the firm's cash needs? The answer would appear as follows:

$$\text{Cash break-even} = \frac{\text{Fixed costs} - \text{noncash portion}}{\text{selling price} - \text{variable cost per unit}}$$

$$= \frac{\$1,200,000 - (\$1,200,000 \times .10)}{\$300 - \$150}$$

$$= \frac{\$1,080,000}{\$150}$$

$$= 7,200 \text{ units}$$

Thus, the break-even sales level necessary to cover the cash needs of production is 7,200 units, fewer than the 8,000 units needed to break even relative to total fixed costs.

What does it mean for the firm if it operates at say, 7,500 units of production—above cash break-even but below the "total cost" break-even? The 7,500-unit operation level will sufficiently cover the firm's cash needs. The significance of the firm's operations being below total cost coverage depends upon the level of noncash charges in the total cost amount. If depreciation is greater than the total of any negative profits after tax, the firm is in no danger in the short run. Over the longer term, however, the cash benefit of the depreciation charge (i.e., depreciation is charged against revenue but is not actually paid out, thus reducing the firm's tax liability) will be offset by fixed assets that need to be replaced or expanded. Therefore, the continued health of the firm depends upon pricing policies and cost control that will ensure operations above the BEP. Generally, firms are concerned with the coverage of total fixed costs, since that approach conforms to reported income.

Before leaving the specific idea of break-even, it is important to note that the BEP formula will accommodate a desired profit level. For example, following the earlier illustration of a break-even point of 8,000 units for product G-3, suppose Garrison Engineering Company desired a 15 percent pretax profit on the item. The BEP formula would be adjusted as follows:

$$\text{Break-even point, with 15\% profit requirement} = \frac{FC + 15\% \text{ of } FC}{SP - VC}$$

$$= \frac{\$1{,}200{,}000(1.15)}{\$300 - \$150}$$

$$= \frac{\$1{,}380{,}000}{\$150}$$

$$= 9{,}200 \text{ units}$$

Thus, to generate a 15 percent pretax profit, in addition to achieving the break-even sales level, the company must achieve a sales level of 9,200 units.

The concept of a break-even level of sales is important for many decision makers in the firm. Marketing will be interested in the concept of break-even when the question of new-product introduction arises. Marketing personnel are usually the first to know what the likely demand for a product will be, based upon the general economic and industry analysis that is a part of market research. Such information will be shared and coordinated with production personnel. Also, it is often necessary that those responsible for "capital budgeting" be brought into the planning process as new depreciable assets are needed for production.

The advantages of the break-even concept are many and varied. Once the idea of break-even is clearly understood (i.e., its components defined and measured and properly assembled), it can be used in many situations within the firm. It must be remembered, however, that it is only a tool and as such is subject to revision as the items included in the calculation change based upon the experiences of the firm. The break-even concept refers to a relationship among costs, fixed and variable, and production level. In general, added fixed costs will increase the break-even point. Beyond the break-even point, however, the sales-to-profit relationship is magnified.

APPENDIX C

Presenting Marketing Cases Orally
by Gary F. Kohut and Carol M. Baxter

The methods for communicating information orally are similar whether you are presenting to a large or a small group, to your classroom peers, or to a business audience. Regardless of the audience or the type of presentation, effective oral presentations involve three major steps: planning, organizing, and delivering the information.

PLANNING THE PRESENTATION

Before you can plan your presentation effectively, you must determine the type of presentation you are making, analyze your audience, conduct your research, and consider the logistics of the speaking site.

Types of Presentations

Generally, oral presentations are divided into two broad categories: informative and persuasive. Informative presentations convey information or ideas, while persuasive presentations sell an idea or a product to an audience. Informative presentations include progress reports, instructions, and explanations. For example, you may need to convey the status of a new product that is being developed; you might discuss past progress, current developments, and work yet to be done. At other times, you may need to train employees on techniques for conducting telephone surveys or leading focus groups.

Many presentations in marketing are persuasive. For example, you may need to convince individuals to contribute to a charitable organization's fund drive. On other occasions, you may need to sell a promotional campaign to a client, persuade a customer to purchase a product or to frequent a particular place of business, or you may need to influence the buying decisions of your organization. In case analysis, you are attempting to persuade your audience to understand the logic of your arguments and accept your recommendations.

Types of Appeal

Three appeals are used in persuasion: the ethical, the emotional, and the logical. The **ethical appeal** addresses an individual's or an organization's credibility. It is impossible to separate the speaker's effect on an audience from the content of a message. If listeners regard the speaker highly, they will adopt a more favorable attitude toward the product or service than if they have a negative impression of the person. Consequently, a speaker must bring to the platform a strong, positive, personal style. Credibility hinges on believability; you may have a high ethical appeal with members of an audience if they perceive you to have acted with integrity in the past. If you have acted rudely, unethically, or unprofessionally toward the audience, your ethical appeal will be very low. Many characteristics such as honesty, dependability, and expertise help to develop credibility. Although it takes some time to establish credibility, it takes only an instant to lose it.

The **emotional appeal** uses the audience's motivations to change their thinking or behavior. Because emotion provokes action, speakers often seek to arouse the feelings of their listeners. The emotional appeal is characterized by the use of fear, sympathy, love, jealousy, desire for attention, or a host of other emotions to persuade the audience. To use the emotional appeal, first analyze the specific emotions to which the audience will respond. Then determine which words, pictures, or actions will best evoke the desired emotion. Once members of the audience are drawn into the persuasion by the emotional "hook," it is easy to ask them to take action to meet the need or to satisfy the emotion that was touched. Speakers should be aware, however, that attempts to arouse emotions excessively can lead to a rejection of their arguments by an audience. The emotions should not be aroused beyond believable or common-sense levels.

The **logical appeal** draws on a person's ability to think and reason. This appeal uses good reasons to show members of an audience why they should change their opinions or actions. The reasoning process and the supporting materials used to give credence to an argument comprise the elements of the logical appeal. For example, if you needed to persuade an audience to buy a compact auto, you might stress fuel efficiency, style, and dependability. Another example is in industrial advertising. Such ads show purchasing agents how products work and how they can benefit the purchasing company. Since the purchasers are not buying the product for their own use, the emotional appeal would not work as it does in consumer advertising.

Audience Analysis

Since you will give your presentation to a specific audience, you need to analyze that audience carefully. Audience analysis is a method of examining the knowledge, interests, and attitudes of the people who will hear your presentation. Your analysis will help you determine how to organize your material, select supporting information, choose the appropriate wording, and select or produce appropriate visual aids.

Some considerations in analyzing your audience include the size of the group, their knowledge about the subject, their interest in the material, their predisposition toward the information, and their relationship to you. Every audience is unique. The differences among people cause every presentation to be different. Individuals have different perceptions based on personal experiences that influence their attitudes about any subject. Understanding these predispositions will prevent your making assumptions that may offend the audience.

For example, if your audience is made up of individuals aged 60–70, don't *automatically* assume that they would be interested in denture adhesives, laxatives, and Big Band music. On the other hand, if your audience is made up of people aged 20–30, don't assume, by virtue of their age, that they would be interested in rock music, fashion, and alcoholic beverages.

We may look at individuals as members of a group and categorize them accordingly, but we should also look for those things that make each individual member unique. For example, if we know an audience appreciates details, we may include more than the usual details in our message.

The more you know about the members of an audience, the better you can predict what will appeal to them. For instance, avoid using examples that audience members cannot understand because they have not experienced them. Since experience is such an important factor in understanding an audience, you would not use the same explanations and examples with an audience who had children as with an audience made up entirely of childless people. When analyzing an audience, ask yourself, What does this group want, need, or expect from me?

Gather Information

Your effectiveness as a speaker depends on what you say about the topic you have selected. For case analysis presentations, a thorough understanding of the case is crucial. Knowing where to look is a starting point for finding the best possible information on your topic. Sometimes the information will come from your own knowledge, experience, or research. At other times you may use information collected by others such as census data, sales records, inventory records, or pricing information. Furthermore, information from electronic data bases provides current data that may enhance the quality of your presentation.

Your credibility as a speaker will be largely determined by the quality of the information you present. For example, if you are talking about recent trends, data from the 1980 census would damage your credibility. Conversely, year-to-date sales records would be beneficial to an audience that needs to establish sales goals for the forthcoming year.

Logistics of the Speaking Site

Before you can organize your presentation, you must consider some logistical concerns. First, you need to know where you will make the presentation. Will it be made in a conference room, in a traditional classroom, a large auditorium, an office, or a dining hall? The location of your presentation will determine the kind of delivery and the types of visual aids you will use as well as how you set up the room. Some guidelines for setting up the speaking site are:

1. Arrange seating so that every member of the audience can see and hear you. The horseshoe arrangement is preferred if the room and the size of the audience will allow for it.
2. Check the lighting, temperature, and noise level of the site to ensure that your audience will be comfortable. Avoid high traffic areas, such as a room next to a kitchen, which may distract your audience.
3. Check any equipment you intend to use to be sure that it can be easily viewed or heard by your audience. Remember, if anything can go wrong, it generally will. Therefore, try to anticipate any problems before they occur. For example, when using any kind of projected visual aids, you should carry an extra bulb or have alternate visual aids in case the equipment breaks down. If you are speaking at a site that you have not visited previously, you may even want to bring an extension cord and an adaptor plug, tape, push pins, or other supplies that may not be available at the site.

ORGANIZING THE PRESENTATION

In an oral presentation, your audience may not have the opportunity to refer to written material; therefore, you must structure the information so that it is very easy to understand the first time it is heard. Every effective presentation has an introduction, body, and conclusion. We suggest that you prepare a written outline of the information you want to include in these three parts.

Introduction

Since people tend to remember the beginning and the end of presentations, a strong introduction is necessary. An introduction should fulfill three purposes: (1) gain the audience's attention, (2) establish rapport or goodwill with the audience, and (3) introduce the audience to the topic. Introductions may include the following:

1. A reference to the event or the occasion
2. A brief story that relates to the topic
3. A quotation by a recognized authority on the subject
4. A thought-provoking question that requires the audience members to participate by answering the question or to get involved by raising their hands
5. A startling statement; it may or may not be a statistic
6. A personal story or reference about the topic
7. A joke

Remember, your introduction should relate to the topic and set the stage for the next part of the introduction. Once you have successfully chosen an attention-getting statement, tell the audience the *purpose* of your presentation by stating the thesis. The **thesis** is a statement that tells what you want to accomplish in the presentation. While the introduction is designed to get the audience members to think about the topic, you must be sure that they understand what you intend to do with the topic. The thesis statement helps focus the entire presentation. Below are examples of thesis statements from two team members making a case analysis presentation to the class:

Speaker One: Our team believes that consumer tastes are changing and the steak-only menu restaurants' share of the dining out market will continue to decline.

Speaker Two: Our team proposes an alternative marketing strategy for the regional steak-only menu restaurant chain that will better position it with respect to the changing tastes of the dining-out market.

The attention span of an audience varies from one occasion to the next. Therefore, keep your audience attuned to what you are saying by **previewing** the main points of your presentation. Below are two examples of previews that come after the thesis statements of the case analysis team members:

Speaker One: Steak-only restaurants' share of the dining out market will continue to decline because (1) consumers have become more health conscious, (2) there is a decline in the consumption of red meat because of concerns over cholesterol, (3) people are eating "lighter," and (4) there is an increasing number of alternative restaurants.

Speaker Two: The regional steak-only menu restaurant chain should change its marketing strategy by redefining its target market, expanding its menu options, and engaging in a promotional campaign to inform customers of the new positioning.

Later, during the body of the presentation, you will develop in more detail each point mentioned in the preview.

Body

Various methods are available to develop the body of each of the presentations used in the examples above. Below are some common ones:

1. Use statistics or other facts
2. Cite quotations or expert testimony
3. Employ examples, real or hypothetical
4. Refer to personal experiences
5. Use comparisons, contrasts, or analogies to experiences the audience has had

Conclusion

A presentation can have an excellent introduction and body but still not be effective. Good speakers must leave a favorable impression in the minds of members of the audience. An effective conclusion can accomplish this objective. Conclusions can be developed in a number of ways:

1. Summarize your main points
2. Ask the audience to take some action such as buying your product or service or contributing to a particular cause
3. Recall the story, joke, or anecdote in the introduction and elaborate on it or draw a "lesson" from it

Now that you have structured your presentation, you must find ways to enhance it further. Visual aids are the tools to accentuate the information you want to share.

Visual Aids

Because we live in a visually oriented society, we expect to see as well as hear information. Therefore, effective speakers show as well as tell their points. Two broad categories of visual aids are available to enhance presentations. One category, **direct viewing visuals,** includes such things as real objects, models, flip charts, diagrams and drawings, photographs, and handouts. The second category, **projected visuals,** includes transparencies, slides, and videotapes.

Visual aids attract and hold attention, clarify the meaning of your points, emphasize ideas, or prove a point. Several factors must be considered in selecting the appropriate visual aid:

1. *The constraints of the topic.* Some topics will limit your choice of visual aids. For example, if you were explaining how a large robot operates, you would probably use a videotape of the robot in operation. A scaled-down model of the robot may not be as effective, since the scope and movement of the machinery may be a persuasive point. Similarly, a drawing or photograph of the robot would be the least effective visual aid.
2. *The availability of the equipment.* If the speaking site does not have an overhead projector, you could not use transparencies. Similarly, if the site does not have an electrical outlet near the podium, you would not be able to use a projected visual. Always check to see what equipment is available or bring your own.
3. *The cost of the visual.* If your budget is very small, a transparency, flip chart, or a handout may be preferable to the more elaborate types of visual aids such as slides or videotapes.
4. *The difficulty of producing the visual.* If you have only two days to prepare for your presentation, it may be impossible to assemble a scale model of a home interior or process slides of a manufacturing operation.

5. *The appropriateness of the visual to the audience.* The type of audience and the nature of the presentation affect the choice of visual aids. Some charts, graphs, and diagrams may be too technical for anyone but specialists to grasp. Detailed and complicated tables and charts that require considerable time to digest should be avoided. When in doubt, keep your visuals short and simple.

6. *The appropriateness of the visual to the speaker.* Visual aids require skill for their effective presentation. A person must be able to write legibly and draw well-proportioned diagrams to use a flip chart. Projected visuals require skill in handling slides, videotape, or film. If you do not feel comfortable with a particular visual medium, do not use it.

7. *The appropriateness of the visual to the time limit.* The speaker should carefully check the time required to display and explain a visual aid to make sure the main ideas of the presentation will not be neglected. Any visual aid that needs too much explanation should be avoided. An appropriate visual aid should be simple, clear, and brief.

Once you have planned and organized the content of your presentation and prepared your visual aids, you are ready to deliver your presentation.

DELIVERING THE PRESENTATION

The delivery of a presentation is mainly determined by the situation, the audience, and the speaker. The formality or informality of the situation greatly affects delivery. The more formal it is, the fewer gestures and movements speakers make. They limit themselves more to their position behind the lectern and use a more emphatic speaking style. In very informal situations, speakers are free to move away from the podium.

The available equipment will also determine delivery. For instance, if the size of the audience necessitates a microphone, speakers should not move away from the microphone. They may also need to adapt themselves to various tables or other unusual speaking platforms that will hold their notes, visuals, or other forms of support.

The larger the audience, the louder speakers must talk unless there is a microphone. Likewise, eye contact is more challenging with large groups. Generally, delivery to small groups can be more informal and conversational.

Types of Delivery

There are several methods for delivering material to an audience and each has its unique advantages. The four methods of delivery are (1) impromptu, (2) manuscript, (3) memorized, and (4) extemporaneous.

Impromptu delivery requires speaking spontaneously on a topic. This type of delivery is generally inappropriate for technical or complex material because you may forget crucial information if the presentation has not been carefully planned. Impromptu delivery is often used at social occasions such as introductions at an after-dinner speaking engagement or at a professional meeting.

Manuscript delivery requires that the speaker read from a prepared text. This type of delivery is ineffective in most presentations because audiences generally prefer more eye contact (they also dislike having material read to them). However, manuscript delivery is a must in one particular situation: when a crisis has occurred. For example, if someone dies as a result of a tampered product, the media will immediately "look for the story." The spokesperson for the organization should never deliver the information in an impromptu manner. Rather, the response should be carefully prepared and read to the media because any misstatement in such a situation could result in litigation against the organization.

Memorized delivery is self-explanatory. In most cases it should be discouraged because memorized presentations usually sound "canned" rather than natural. However, this type of delivery might be appropriate in situations where the presentation will be only a few minutes long, such as a short advertisement.

Extemporaneous delivery is the preferred approach for most presentations. This type of delivery involves using notes or an outline to deliver your information. The speaker should talk in a conversational tone but refer periodically to notes to be sure that all the information is covered.

Practicing the Delivery

Preparation influences a speaker's delivery. A speaker who is well prepared and has something valuable to communicate will be more comfortable physically and vocally. If speakers are unsure of themselves and the material, they may be tempted to read word for word from their outline. Being too self-conscious or nervous can cause physical and vocal qualities and mannerisms that detract from the message. Too much concern with the ideas and too little with the audience will also hinder a speaker's delivery. Practicing aloud what you want to say will give you confidence.

Delivery is not something added to a speech but a part of it. Consider the following when delivering a presentation:

1. *Focus on the specific purpose.* Effective speakers know what they want from an audience and therefore should avoid such distractions as fiddling with a pen or pencil, scratching the nose, playing with hair, and jingling coins.
2. *Work toward being heard and understood.* A speaker's voice must be loud enough to be heard in the very last row. Pronunciation and articulation must be distinct.
3. *Convey enthusiasm.* An essential part of delivery is to keep the audience listening. One way of conveying enthusiasm is to vary the qualities of the voice such as volume, rate, and pitch. Movements and gestures should also be varied.
4. *Stress the main points.* Some points in a speech are more important than others. If all ideas are spoken in exactly the same way, the importance of your key points will suffer. A slower speaking rate, a pause before and after an idea, a shift in body

position, an increase or decrease in volume are only a few of the many ways to emphasize points through delivery.

5. *Involve your audience.* Each member of the audience should feel that the speaker is imparting information to her/him personally. Consequently, eye contact is a critical part of effective delivery. The speaker should look at all audience members, talking to each one from time to time but no particular person or segment of the audience for a prolonged time.

Establishing Credibility

Credibility is crucial to effective presentations. As mentioned earlier, credibility refers to the confidence an audience has in a speaker. Several factors work together to determine credibility, including the speaker's enthusiasm, expertise, and trustworthiness.

Enthusiasm is projected through tone of voice, eye contact, and energy. Obviously, the major ways speakers can display these characteristics are by believing in the subject and acting as if they enjoy conveying the information. For example, a sincere smile at the beginning of a presentation sets the tone for both the speaker and the audience.

Expertise is conveyed through the accuracy of your information, the amount of experience you have had with the subject, and the confidence with which you speak. Make sure you check your facts before you communicate them to the audience.

Trustworthiness refers to whether the speaker is perceived as biased. Consistency in conveying information over a period of time is important to establishing trust with an audience.

Controlling Speech Anxiety

One factor that detracts from credibility is excessive nervousness. Most speakers are nervous, but they have learned techniques for handling the condition so that there are few outward signs of anxiety. Several techniques are recommended for managing speech anxiety:

1. Avoid taking medications that will dry your mouth and produce more anxiety
2. Practice deep breathing exercises just before speaking to reduce your anxiety
3. Reduce tension by squeezing your hand into a fist and releasing it, tensing your leg muscles and releasing them, or stretching your facial muscles with exaggerated expressions

Using Your Visuals Effectively

Although visual aids enhance presentations, poor use of them can actually hurt your credibility. Some guidelines for using visual aids are as follows:

1. Avoid turning your back on the audience while you look at a visual aid; talk to the audience, not to the visual aid.

2. Show the visual aid only when you are using it; otherwise, the audience may be distracted from what you are saying. For example, if you are using transparencies, cover everything except the information you are talking about at the moment.

3. Refrain from removing the visual before the audience members have had an opportunity to look at the information for themselves. Also, avoid talking about something on a visual aid after you have put it aside.

4. Organize the visuals in the order in which you will use them so you will appear prepared and confident when using them.

Managing Nonverbal Communication

Nonverbal communication enhances or detracts from the credibility you have worked to establish. Several dimensions of nonverbal communication include (1) **kinesics,** the way people use their bodies to communicate; (2) **proxemics,** the way people use space to communicate; and (3) **paralanguage,** the way people use their voice to enhance the verbal message.

When making presentations, two of the most important types of kinesic behavior are gestures and eye contact. Speakers are rarely credible when they stand rigidly behind a podium, grasp it as if it were a crutch, and seldom glance from their notes to look at the audience. Similarly, poor posture, hands in pockets, and playing with objects such as chalk or pointers lessen a speaker's impact.

Speakers who recognize that "space communicates" will use it wisely. For example, if an audience is very small, it may be better to sit at the head of the group rather than standing to deliver your information. Also, if you are conveying unfavorable information, it may be better to stand close to the audience as if to appear sincere and understanding.

Aspects of the voice that affect credibility include volume, rate, pitch, tone, and voice quality. The "sound" of the voice (voice quality) such as raspiness or a nasal whine evokes images in the mind of listeners; however, it is very difficult to change the voice quality you have. On the other hand, tone, pitch, rate, and volume are easily controlled. For example, a person who has a monotone can make the voice *seem* less monotonous by saying some words softly and others quite loudly. Even though the speaker's tone has not changed, the audience perceives that the tone is varied. Pitch is often associated with nervousness. Speakers should start speaking at the lowest pitch they can achieve, since a lower pitch is generally viewed as more credible in our culture.

Handling Questions from the Audience

Some speaking situations require that the speaker give the audience an opportunity to ask questions. At other times, the speaker may simply want to involve the audience by following a presentation with a question-and-answer session. Whether or not you use this procedure depends on the occasion, the audience, and the amount of time available. You can use this procedure to reinforce key points and gain acceptance of your ideas. Any question-and-answer period should be well organized and brief. To make the most of the available time, follow these guidelines:

1. Ask for questions in a positive way. For instance, you could say, "Who has the first question?" If no one asks a question, you may say, "You may be wondering . . . " or "I am often asked . . . " After supplying an answer to the question you have asked, you may ask, "Are there any other questions?

2. Look at the entire audience when answering a question. You are addressing everyone, not just the person asking the question.

3. Keep your answers concise and to the point; do not give another speech. You risk losing the audience's attention as well as discouraging further questions.

4. Cut off a rambling questioner politely. If the person starts to make a speech without getting to the question, wait until he or she takes a breath and then interrupt with, "Thanks for your comment. Next question." Then look to the other side of the room.

5. Remain in control of the situation. Establish a time limit for questions and answers and announce it to the audience before the questions begin. Anticipate the types of questions your audience may ask and think how you will answer. Never lose your temper as you respond to someone who is trying to make you look bad. You may respond with something like, "I respect your opinion even though I don't agree with it." Then restate your response to the issue.

Since your presentation does not end when you finish your speech, your credibility can be enhanced or lost in the question-and-answer period. Prepare intelligently and establish strategies for handling difficult situations.

CLOSING COMMENTS

Developing the skills needed to present your point of view in a convincing manner is essential to reaching your personal and career goals. Presenting information orally is a challenging task. However, if you follow the guidelines we have suggested, your presentation will be rewarding to both you and your audience.